1991-92
WHO'S WHO
IN CANADIAN FILM AND TELEVISION

QUI EST QUI
AU CINÉMA ET À LA TÉLÉVISION AU CANADA

Published for the
Academy of Canadian Cinema and Television
Académie canadienne du cinéma et de la télévision
by Wilfrid Laurier University Press

Published for the Academy of Canadian Cinema and Television by Wilfrid Laurier University Press, Waterloo, Ontario.

Copyright © 1991 Academy of Canadian Cinema and Television

All rights reserved
No part of this book may be reproduced or transmitted in any form or by any means, electronic or mechanical, including photography, recording, or any information storage of retrieval system, without permission in writing from the publisher.

First published in 1986 by the Academy of Canadian Cinema and Television
653 Yonge St., 2nd Floor
Toronto, Ontario M4Y 1Z9

This book has been published with the financial assistance of Telefilm Canada and the Ontario Film Development Corporation.

Canadian Cataloguing in Publication Data
The National Library of Canada has catalogued this serial as follows:
Main entry under title:
Who's Who in Canadian Film and Television = Qui est qui au cinéma et à la télévision au Canada

1986-
Annual.
Text in English and French.
ISSN 0831-6309
ISBN 0-88920-210-9 (1991-1992)

1. Motion picture producers and directors - Canada - Directories. 2. Television producers and directors - Canada - Directories. 3. Motion picture editors - Canada - Directories. I. Academy of Canadian Cinema & Television.

PN1998.A2W48   791.43'025'71   C86-030678-XE rev

Reasonable effort has been made in the accurate compilation of information contained in this publication; the publisher, however, assumes no liability for errors or omissions, but would appreciate being notified of any that are found.

Cover design by Scott Gibbs

Printed in Canada by John Deyell Company

Publié pour l'Académie canadienne du cinéma et de la télévision par Wilfrid Laurier University Press, Waterloo, Ontario.

© 1991 Académie canadienne du cinéma et de la télévision

Tous droits réservés
Toute reproduction pour fins commerciales, par procédé mécanique ou électronique y compris la microreproduction, est interdite sans permission de l'éditeur.

Première édition en 1986, Académie canadienne du cinéma et de la télévision
653, rue Yonge, deuxième étage
Toronto, Ontario M4Y 1Z9

Le présent ouvrage est publié avec le concours financier de Téléfilm Canada et de la Société de développement de l'industrie cinématographique ontarienne.

Données de catalogage avant publication (Canada)
La Bibliothèque nationale du Canada a catalogué cette publication en série de la façon suivante:
Vedette principale au titre:
Who's Who in Canadian Film and Television = Qui est qui au cinéma et à la télévision au Canada

1986-
Annuel.
Textes en anglais et en français.
ISSN 0831-6309
ISBN 0-88920-210-9 (1991-1992)

1. Producteurs et réalisateurs de cinéma - Canada - Répertoires. 2. Producteurs et réalisateurs de télévision - Canada - Répertoires. 3. Monteurs (Cinéma) - Canada - Répertoires. I. Académie canadienne du cinéma et de la télévision.

PN1998.A2W48   791.43'025'71   C86-030678-XF

Les renseignements contenus dans la présente publication sont exacts à notre connaissance: l'éditeur se dégage donc de toute responsabilité concernant les erreurs ou omissions, mais serait reconnaissant au lecteur de lui faire part de ces dernières le cas échéant.

Couverture par Scott Gibbs

Imprimé au Canada par John Deyell Company

Who's Who in Canadian Film and Television

Qui est Qui au cinéma et à la television au Canada

Contents
Table des matières

Contents/Table des matières

Foreword/Préface x

Abbreviations/Abréviations
Types of Production/Types de production xvii
Credits xvii
Mentions au générique xxiii
Countries/Pays xxvi
Unions, Guilds and Associations/
    Syndicats et associations xxviii
Awards/Prix xxx
Index Codes/Codes d'index xxx
Explanatory Notes/Notes explicatives xxxi

Professional Categories/Catégories professionnelles
ArtDirectors/Directeurs artistiques 2
Cinematographers/Directeurs-photo 24
Composers/Compositeurs 68
Costume Designers/Costumes 94
Directors/Réalisateurs 104
Editors/Monteurs 236
Music Editors/Monteurs musique 272
Postproduction Sound Mixers/
    Mixeurs son postproduction 276
Producers/Producteurs 288
Production Managers/Régisseurs 454
Production Sound Mixers/
    Mixeurs son production 472
Publicists/Publicistes 484
Sound Editors/Monteurs son 494
Writers/Scénaristes 504

Index 588

Advertisers/Commanditaires 618

Foreword
Préface
Prefacio
Premessa
Ergänzung

Foreword

The Academy of Canadian Cinema and Television is proud to make available this revised and expanded fourth edition of **Who's Who in Canadian Film and Television** – the most comprehensive and accurate reference guide to the Canadian production community to date.

We began publication in 1986 with the goal that Who's Who should serve as the one and only authoritative guide to behind-the-camera talent in Canadian film and television. Our first edition of the directory contained information on 400 Canadian film and television directors and picture editors.

In 1987 the Academy produced a revised second edition, expanded to include writers, producers, cinematographers, art directors, composers and production managers. The response to the publication was so great that we were able to provide listings on 1400 industry members.

Coinciding with the Academy's tenth anniversary in 1989, we published our third edition of Who's Who – updated and again expanded to include the categories of costume designers and sound personnel. Over 2000 entries were contained in this largest directory to date.

The response from over 2500 industry members, to be included in our fourth 1991-92 edition was overwhelming. Significantly, it represents to us the value that this guide holds to the production community at large. The **Who's Who** is recognised as **the authoritative guide** when consulting production personnel. As well, this edition marks two exciting developments:

the book has been expanded to include the category of publicists; and, for the first time, we are pleased to announce that the **Who's Who** will receive worldwide distribution through the assistance of Wilfrid Laurier University Press.

Through the financial assistance of Employment and Immigration Canada, Telefilm Canada, and the Ontario Film Development Corporation, the Academy is pleased that this revised and enlarged fourth edition continues to support the policy of providing Canadian production personnel with the first opportunity to fill positions in the film and television industries.* The **Who's Who** serves as an invaluable reference source, an employment resource, and an effective means of promoting Canadian talent within our own country and abroad.

* For your convenience, a copy of Canada's "Canadians First" employment policy is included as an appendix on page *611* of this book

Préface

L'Académie canadienne du cinéma et de la télévision est heureuse de diffuser la quatrième édition révisée et élargie du **Qui est qui au cinéma et à la télévision au Canada**, le guide de référence du monde de la production le plus complet et le plus exact qui soit.

En lançant cet ouvrage en 1986, nous avions un but: produire le seul et unique guide crédible des artisans de l'industrie du film et de la télévision au Canada. La première édition répertoriait 400 réalisateurs et monteurs.

Dans la deuxième édition révisée, parue en 1987, l'Académie a ajouté les catégories suivantes: scénaristes, producteurs, caméramen, directeurs artistiques, compositeurs, et directeurs de production. L'enthousiasme suscité par cet élargissement nous a permis de porter à 1400 le nombre des membres de l'industrie figurant dans cet ouvrage.

L'année du dixième anniversaire de l'Académie, soit 1989, nous avons publié la troisième édition du **Qui est qui**, enrichie cette fois-ci des catégories costumiers et personnel du son. Le répertoire comptait alors plus de 2000 entrées.

L'annonce de la quatrième édition, 1991-92, a été très bien accueillie, puisque plus de 2500 membres de l'industrie ont envoyé leur demande d'inscription. Cela témoigne de la valeur que l'ensemble du monde de la production accorde à ce guide. Le **Qui est qui** est assurément une source de référence qui fait autorité dans cette industrie. Qui plus est, cette édition innove encore en accueillant une autre catégorie, soit les publicistes. Autre grande nouvelle: pour la première fois, le **Qui est qui** sera distribué à l'échelle internationale par Wilfrid Laurier University Press.

L'Académie est fière de constater que cette quatrième édition révisée et élargie, appuyée financièrement par Emploi et Immigration Canada, Téléfilm Canada, et la Société de développement de l'industrie cinématographique ontarienne, s'inscrit dans la ligne de conduite qu'elle a toujours soutenue et qui prévoit de donner priorité d'embauche aux canadiens dans l'industrie du film et de la télévision au pays.* Le **Qui est qui** est une précieuse source de référence et d'emploi et un moyen efficace de promouvoir le talent canadien au pays et à l'étranger.

* Pour votre information, la politique du gouvernement canadien favorisant l'emploi des travailleurs canadiens est reproduite en page *611* du guide.

Prefacio

La "Academy of Canadian Cinema and Television" tiene el orgullo de presentar esta cuarta edición revisada y agrandada del **Who's Who in Canadian Film and Television** – la guía de referencia más completa y exacta de la comunidad de producciones canadienses hasta esta fecha.

Nosotros comenzamos nuestra publicación en 1986 con el objetivo de que **Who's Who** sirva de guía única de autoridad para el talento del cine y la televisión canadienses, que se encuentra detrás-de-la-cámara. Nuestra primera edición del directorio contenía información sobre 400 directores de cine y televisión y editores de películas del Canadá.

En 1987, la Academia produjo una segunda edición revisada, agrandada para incluir escritores, productores, camarógrafos, directores artísticos, compositores, y directores de producción. La respuesta a la publicación fue tan grande que nos permitió proporcionar información sobre 1400 miembros de la industria.

Coincidiendo con el décimo aniversario de la Academia en 1989, hemos publicado nuestra tercera edición de **Who's Who** - puesta al día y nuevamente agrandada para incluir categorías de diseñadores de vestuario y personal de sonido. Esta guía, que es la más grande hasta el presente, contiene más de 2000 entradas.

La respuesta de más de 2500 miembros de la industria, para que se los incluya en nuestra cuarta edición de 1991-92, fue arrolladora. Significativamente, representa para nosotros el valor que esta guía tiene en la comunidad general de producción. El **Who's Who** se reconoce como **la guía de autoridad** cuando se quiere consultar el personal de producción. Al mismo tiempo, esta edición marca dos desarrollos excitantes: el libro se ha agrandado para que incluya la categoría de publicistas; y, por primera vez, tenemos el placer de anunciar que el **Who's Who** recibirá una distribución internacional con la asistencia de Wilfrid Laurier University Press.

A través de un apoyo financiero del Employment and Immigration Canada, Telefilm Canada, y la Ontario Film Development Corporation, la Academia tiene el placer de saber que esta cuarta edición revisada y agrandada continúa apoyando la política de proporcionar al personal de producción canadiense una primera oportunidad de ocupar puestos en las industrias del cine y la televisión.* El **Who's Who** sirve de incomparable fuente de referencia, fuente de empleo y un medio eficaz de promover talento canadiense dentro de nuestro país y en el exterior.

* Para su conveniencia, incluimos una copia de la política de empleo del Gobierno de Canada llamada "Canadians First" como apéndice en la página *611* de este libro.

Premessa

La "Academy of Canadian Cinema and Television" è fiera di mettere a disposizione questa quarta edizione riveduta e ampliata di **Who's Who in Canadian Film and Television**, la guida più completa e accurata al mondo della produzione cinetelevisiva canadese mai edita.

La nostra pubblicazione iniziò nel 1986 con l'obiettivo di fare di **Who's Who** l'unica e sola guida di sicuro riferimento ai talenti del cinema e della televisione canadesi che operano dietro l'obiettivo. La nostra prima edizione della guida conteneva dati su 400 registi, sia cinematografici che televisivi, nonché artisti del montaggio canadesi.

Nel 1987 l'Accademia produsse una seconda edizione riveduta e ampliata e tale da includere scrittori, produttori, cineasti, direttori artistici, compositori, e direttori di produzione. Il responso dato alla pubbli-cazione fu tale che fummo in grado di pubblicare resoconti su 1400 membri operanti nel settore.

Nel 1989, in concomitanza con il decimo anniversario dell'Accademia, pubblicammo la nostra terzo edizione di **Who's Who**, aggiornata e ulteriormente ampliata in modo tale da includere le categorie dei disegnatori dei costumi e dei tecnici del suono. In tale guida, la più ampia mai pubblicata fino ad allora, erano contenute oltre 2000 voci.

La risposta dataci da oltre 2500 membri del settore da includere nella nostra quarta edizione 1991-92 è stata superiore ad ogni aspettativa. Ciò rappresenta per noi, in modo significativo,

il valore che questa guida riveste nell'ambito dell'intera comunità del campo della produzione. **Who's Who** è riconosciuta come **la guida di sicuro affidamento** quando il personale addetto alla produzione viene consultato. Nello stesso tempo la presente edizione contrassegna due emozionanti sviluppi: il libro è stato ampliato in modo tale da includere la categoria dei pubblicisti. E per la prima volta siamo lieti di annunciare che **Who's Who** verrà distribuita in tutto il mondo grazie all'assistenza della Wilfrid Laurier University Press.

Grazie all'assistenza finanziaria di Employment and Immigration Canada, di Telefilm Canada, e della Ontario Film Development Corporation, l'Accademia è lieta di poter constatare che questa quarta edizione riveduta e ampliata rappresenta la continuazione dell'opera intesa a mettere a disposizione degli operatori canadesi del settore della produzione la prima opportunità in assoluto per operare assunzioni nel cinema e nella televisione.* **Who's Who** svolge una funzione di fonte di riferimento di valore incalcolabile, di risorsa per le assunzioni e di mezzo efficace di promozione del talento canadese sia nel nostro paese che all'estero.

* Per vostro opportuno riferimento, a pagina *611* del libro è allegata, quale appendice, una copia delle norme seguite in tema di assunzioni dall'ente del governo canadese "Canadians First".

Ergänzung

Die "Academy of Canadian Cinema and Television" freut sich, daß diese überarbeitete und erweiterte vierte Auflage des **Who's Who in Canadian Film and Television** – das derzeit umfangreichste und genaueste Nach-schlagewerk der kanadischen Filmindustrie – jetzt erhältlich ist.

1986 haben wir mit der Veröffentlichung begonnen. Dabei war es unser Ziel, **Who's Who** zum einzigen maßgebenden Nachschlagewerk in Bezug auf die Fachleute des kanadischen Films und Fernsehens hinter der Kamera zu machen. Unsere erste Auflage des Werks enthielt Informationen über 400 kanadische Film und Fernsehregisseure und Cutter.

1987 veröffentlichte die Akademie eine überarbeitete zweite Auflage, die um Autoren, Produzenten, Kameraleute, Art-Direktoren, Komponisten, und Produktionsmanager erweitert wurde. Das Werk wurde so begeistert aufgenommen, daß wir 1.400 Mitglieder der Filmindustrie neu auflisten konnten.

Zum zehnten Jubiläum der Akademie 1989 veröffentlichten wir unsere dritte Auflage des **Who's Who** – aktualisiert und wieder erweitert um die Kategorien Kostümdesigner und Tontechniker. Dieser bis jetzt umfangreichste Führer enthielt über 2.000 Eintragungen.

Die Anfrage von über 2.500 Mitgliedern der Filmindustrie, in unserer vierten Auflage für 1991-92 ebenfalls aufzuscheinen, war überwältigend. Für uns ist es bezeichnend für den Wert, den dieses Nachschlagewerk für die Filmindustrie im allgemeinen hat. **Who's Who ist das maßgebende Nachschlagewerk für Fachleute in der Filmproduktion.** Außerdem gibt es bei dieser Auflage zwei neue, wichtige Weiterentwicklungen: das Buch wurde um die Kategorie Publicitymanager erweitert, und wir freuen uns, daß **Who's Who** heuer zum ersten Mal mit Unterstützung der Wilfrid Laurier University Press weltweit vertrieben wird.

Mit der finanzieller Unterstützung von Employment and Immigration Canada, Telefilm Canada, und der Ontario Film Development Corporation kann die Akademie ihre Politik, nämlich kanadischen Produktionsfachleuten die erste Chance bei der Besetzung von Posten in der Film- und Fernsehindustrie zu geben, auch mit dieser überarbeiteten und erweiterten vierten Auflage weiterverfolgen.* **Who's Who** ist eine unschätzbare Nachschlagequelle, Personalquelle und ein wirksames Medium, um kanadische Fachleute im eigenen Land und außerhalb zu fördern.

* Praktischerweise finden Sie eine Kopie der "Canadians First" - Beschäftigungspolitik der kanadischen Regierung im Anhang auf Seite *611* dieses Buchs.

Abbreviations
Abréviations

Types of Production/Types de production
C	Cinéma (longs et courts métrages)
Cm	Commercial/Annonce
ED	Educational/Education
In	Industrial/Industriel
MV	Music Video/Vidéo-clips
Th	Theatrical (features and shorts)
TV	Television/Télévision

Credits
1st AD	1st Assistant Director
1st Assist Cam	1st Assistant Cameraman
1st Assist DOP	1st Assistant Director of Photography
1st Assist Ed	1st Assistant Editor
1st Assist Snd Ed	1st Assistant Sound Editor
2nd AD	2nd Assistant Director
2nd Assist Art Dir	2nd Assistant Art Director
2nd Assist Cam	2nd Assistant Cameraman
2nd Assist Ed	2nd Assistant Editor
2nd Cam	2nd Cameraman
2nd Cam Op	2nd Camera Operator
2nd Op	2nd Operator
2nd U AD	2nd Unit Assistant Director
2nd U Cam	2nd Unit Cameraman
2nd U Dir	2nd Unit Director
2nd U DOP	2nd Unit Director of Photography
2nd U PM	2nd Unit Production Manager
3D	3D
3rd AD	3rd Assistant Director

A
Act	Actor
Adapt	Adaptation
Add'l Dial	Additional Dialogue
Add'l Ed	Additional Editing
Add'l Phot	Additional Photography
ADR Ed	ADR Editor
ADR Record	ADR Recordist
An	Animation

An Co-Des	Animation Co-Design
An Des	Animation Design
An Dir	Animation Director
An Svp	Animation Supervisor
Area Head Prod	Area Head Producer
Arr	Arranger
Art Dept Coord	Art Department Coordinator
Art Dir	Art Director
Assemb Ed	Assembly Editor
Assist ADR Ed	Assistant ADR Editor
Assist Art Dir	Assistant Art Director
Assist Cam	Assistant Cameraman
Assist Comp	Assistant Composer
Assist Cos	Assistant Costume Designer
Assist Des	Assistant Designer
Assist Dial Ed	Assistant Dialogue Editor
Assist Dir	Assistant Director
Assist Ed	Assistant Editor
Assist Loc M	Assistant Location Manager
Assist Mus Dir	Assistant Music Director
Assist Mus Ed	Assistant Music Editor
Assist PM	Assistant Production Manager
Assist Pro Acc't	Assistant Production Accountant
Assist Prod	Assistant Producer
Assist Prod Des	Assistant Production Designer
Assist Set Des	Assistant Set Designer
Assist SFX	Assistant Special Effects
Assist SFX Ed	Assistant Special Effects Editor
Assist Snd Ed	Assistant Sound Editor
Assist Snd FX ED	Assistant Sound Effects Editor
Assist Story Ed	Assistant Story Editor
Assist to Dir	Assistant to Director
Assist to Prod	Assistant to Producer
Assist to Prod Des	Assistant to Production Designer
Assist Unit M	Assistant Unit Manager
Assoc Dir	Associate Director
Assoc Ed	Associate Editor
Assoc PM	Associate Production Manager
Assoc Prod	Associate Producer
Assoc Prod Des	Associate Production Designer
Audio Dir	Audio Director
Audio Prod	Audio Producer

B

Boom	Boom Operator
Broad	Broadcaster

C

Cam	Cameraman
Cam Assist	Camera Assistant
Cam Op	Camera Operator
Cast	Casting
Casting Dir	Casting Director
Ch	Choreographer
Chief Dec	Chief Decorator
Cin	Cinematographer
Comm	Commentator
Comp	Composer
Cond	Conductor
Cons Dir	Consulting Director
Cons Prod	Consulting Producer

ABBREVIATIONS / ABREVIATIONS

Consult	Consultant
Cont	Continuity
Cont Wr	Continuity Writer
Contr Dir	Contributing Director
Contr Wr	Contributing Writer
Coord	Coordinator
Coord Prod	Coordinating Producer
Cos	Costume Designer
Cos Spv	Costume Supervisor
Cr Dir	Creative Director
Creat Cons	Creative Consultant

D

Des	Designer
Design Coord	Design Coordinator
Dial	Dialogue
Dial Dir	Dialogue Director
Dial Ed	Dialogue Editor
Dial Engin	Dialogue Engineer
Dir	Director
Dir of Dev	Director of Development
Dir Mus	Director of Music
Dir of Postprod	Director of Postproduction
Dir Postsynchro	Director of Post-Synchronization
Dir SFX	Director of Special Effects
Dist	Distributor
DOP	Director of Photography
DOP Consult	Director of Photography Consultant

E

Ed	Editor
Ed Consult	Editing Consultant
Entertain Ed	Entertainment Editor
Exec Prod	Executive Producer
Exec Script Cons	Executive Script Consultant
Exec Story Ed	Executive Story Editor

F

Fest Pub	Festival Publicist
Field Dir	Field Director
Field Prod	Field Producer
Film-Tape Coord	Film to Tape Coordinator
Fl Dir	Floor Director
Focus Pull	Focus Puller
Foley Rec	Foley Recordist
FX An	Effects Animator
FX Des	Effects Designer
FX Ed	Effects Editor

G

Gaf	Gaffer

H

Head Cos	Head Costume Designer
Head Wr	Head Writer

I

Illustr	Illustrator
Interv	Interviewer
Isolation Dir	Isolation Director

J
Jr ADR Ed	Junior ADR Editor

L
Lay Art	Layout Artist
Lay Seq Dir	Layout Sequence Director
Light Cam	Lighting Cameraman
Light Dir	Lighting Director
Light Tech	Lighting Technician
Line Prod	Line Producer
Loc Dir	Location Director
Loc M	Location Manager
Loc Snd Mix	Location Sound Mixer
Loc Snd Rec	Location Sound Recordist
Looping Dir	Looping Director

M
MIDI Sys Prog	MIDI Systems Programmer
Mus	Music
Mus Cons	Music Consultant
Mus Dir	Music Director
Mus Ed	Music Editor
Mus Engin	Music Engineer
Mus Prod	Music Producer
Mus Spv	Music Supervisor

N
Narr	Narrator
Narr Wr	Narration Writer
News Ed	News Editor

O
Off-Line Video Ed	Off-Line Video Editor
Op	Operator
Orch	Orchestrator

P
P Audio	Post Audio
P Pro Cons	Postproduction Consultant
P Pro Spv	Postproduction Supervisor
P Prod	Post Producer
P Prod Snd Mix	Postproduction Sound Mixer
PA	Production Assistant
Perf	Performer
Pict Ed	Picture Editor
PM	Production Manager
Post Audio Exec	Post Audio Executive
Post Audio Spv	Post Audio Supervisor
Post Mix	Postproduction Mixer
Post PM	Postproduction Manager
Post Pro Dir	Postproduction Director
Postprod Coord	Postproduction Coordinator
Pro Acc't	Production Accountant
Pro Assoc	Production Associate
Pro Coord	Production Coordinator
Pro Des	Production Designer
Pro Exec	Executive in Charge of Production
Pro Spv	Production Supervisor
Prod	Producer
Prod Cons	Production Consultant
Prod Coord	Production Coordinator

Prod Snd	Production Sound
Prod Snd Mix	Production Sound Mixer
Props	Property Master
Pub	Publicist

R

Re-record Mix	Re-recording Mixer
Rel Pub	Release Publicist
Report	Reporter
Res	Researcher

S

Sc Dir	Scene Director
Score Comp	Score Composer
Score Mix	Score Mixer
Scr	Screenplay
Scr Adapt	Screen Adaptation
Script Cons	Script Consultant
Script Ed	Script Editor
Script Rewr	Script Rewriter
Script Spv	Script Supervisor
Seg An Dir	Segment Animation Director
Seg Dir	Segment Director
Seg Prod	Segment Producer
Series Consult	Series Consultant
Series Prod	Series Producer
Serv Prod	Service Producer
Set Dec	Set Decorator
Set Des	Set Designer
Set Dr	Set Dresser
SFX	Special Effects
SFX Des	Special Effects Designer
SFX Ed	Special Effects Editor
SFX Make-up	Special Effects Make-up
SFX Mix	Special Effects Mixer
SFX Spv	Special Effects Supervisor
Sing	Singer
Snd Des	Sound Designer
Snd Ed	Sound Editor
Snd FX Ed	Sound Effects Editor
Snd Mix	Sound Mixer
Snd Rec	Sound Recordist
Snd Spv	Sound Supervisor
Spv	Supervisor
Spv ADR Ed	Supervising ADR Editor
Spv Art Dir	Supervising Art Director
Spv Assist Ed	Supervising Assistant Editor
Spv Dial Ed	Supervising Dialogue Editor
Spv Ed	Supervising Editor
Spv Lay	Supervisor of Layout
Spv Pro Acc't	Supervising Production Accountant
Spv Prod	Supervising Producer
Spv Set Dec	Supervising Set Decorator
Spv Snd Ed	Supervising Sound Editor
Spv St'board	Supervisor of Storyboards
Spv Wr	Supervising Writer
Sr Ed	Senior Editor
Sr Prod	Senior Producer
Sr Spv Lay	Senior Supervisor of Layout
Sr Spv St'board	Senior Supervisor of Storyboards
Sr Wr	Senior Writer

St'board	Storyboard
St'cam	Steadicam Operator
Staff Ed	Staff Editor
Staff Wr	Staff Writer
Stills	Stills Photographer
Story Cons	Story Consultant
Story Ed	Story Editor
Story Prod	Story Producer
Studio Dir	Studio Director
Sw	Switcher

T

T'play	Teleplay
Tech Dir	Technical Director
Tech Prod	Technical Producer
Theme Comp	Theme Composer
Titles Des	Titles Designer
Track Brkdwn	Track Breakdown
Trainee Art Dir	Trainee Art Director
Trans	Translation

U

U Loc M	Unit Location Manager
Uncr Rewr	Uncredited Rewrite
Unit M	Unit Manager
Unit PM	Unit Production Manager
Unit Pub	Unit Publicist

V

VFX 2nd Spv	Visual Effects 2nd Supervisor
VFX Co-Spv	Visual Effects Co-Supervisor
VFX Des	Visual Effects Designer
VFX Spv	Visual Effects Supervisor
Vid Paint	Video Paintbox Artist
Video Ed	Video Editor
Visual Consult	Visual Consultant
VO	Voice Over

W

Ward	Wardrobe Mistress
Ward Assist	Wardrobe Assistant
Ward Buy	Wardrobe Buyer
Wr	Writer
Wr Cons	Writing Consultant
Wran	Wrangler

Mentions au générique

1er ass cam	1er assistant caméraman
1er ass dir phot	1er assistant directeur-photo
1er ass mont	1er assistant monteur
1er ass mont son	1er assistant monteur son
1er ass réal	1er assistant réalisateur
2e ass cam	2e assistant caméraman
2e ass mont	2e assistant monteur
2e ass réal	2e assistant réalisateur
2e cam	2e caméraman
2e mont	2e monteur
3e ass réal	3e assistant réalisateur

A

Acc plateau	Accessoiriste de plateau
Acces	Accessoiriste
Adapt	Adaptation
Aide Tech	Aide technique
An	Animation
Anim	Animateur
Ann	Annonceur
Arr	Arrangeur
Ass cam	Assistant caméraman
Ass décor	Assistant décorateur
Ass dir art	Assistant directeur artistique
Ass dir mus	Assistant directeur musical
Ass eff sp	Assistant effets spéciaux
Ass mont	Assistant monteur
Ass mont son	Assistant monteur son
Ass pro	Assistant à la production
Ass prod	Assistant producteur
Ass réal	Assistant réalisateur
Ass rég	Assistant régisseur
Assist cos	Assistant costumier
Assist des	Assistant designer
Assist mont dial	Assistant monteur dialogue
Aut	Auteur
Aut comp	Auteur-compositeur
Aut cons	Auteur conseil

B

Bruit	Bruitage

C

Cadr	Cadreur
Cadr 2e éq	Cadreur deuxième équipe
Cam	Caméraman
Cam 2e éq	Caméraman deuxième équipe
Cast	Casting
Ch	Chorégraphe
Chant	Chanteur
Chef cos	Chef costumier
Chef d'orch	Chef d'orchestre
Chef déc	Chef décorateur
Chef mont	Chef monteur
Chef rég	Chef régisseur
Com	Comédien
Comp	Compositeur
Comp thème	Compositeur thème
Conc	Concepteur
Conc gén	Concepteur du générique

Conc son	Concepteur son
Conc vis	Concepteur visuel
Cons D phot	Conseiller direction-photo
Cons scén	Conseiller scénario
Cons vis	Conseiller visuel
Coord pro	Coordonateur de production
Cos	Costumes
Cost	Costumier

D
D phot	Directeur-photo
D photo 2e éq	Directeur-photo deuxième équipe
Décor	Décorateur
Des	Designer
Des eff sp	Designer effets spéciaux
Dess	Dessins
Dial	Dialogue
Dir art	Directeur artistique
Dir éclairages	Directeur éclairages
Dir eff sp	Directeur effets spéciaux
Dir mus	Directeur musical
Dir p pro	Directeur postproduction
Dir post-synchro	Directeur post-synchro
Dir pro	Directeur de production
Dir tech	Directeur technique

E
Eff sp	Effets spéciaux

G
Gén an	Générique animé

I
Ing son	Ingénieur de son
Inter	Interviewer

J
Journ	Journaliste

M
Mach	Machiniste
Maq	Maquillage
Mix mus	Mixeur musique
Mixeur son post	Mixeur son postproduction
Mont	Monteur
Mont 2e éq	Monteur deuxième équipe
Mont ADR	Monteur ADR
Mont dial	Monteur dialogue
Mont eff sp	Monteur effets spéciaux
Mont mus	Monteur musique
Mont son	Monteur son
Mont son eff sp	Monteur son effets spéciaux
Mont vidéo off-line	Monteur vidéo off-line
Mus	Musique

N
Narr	Narrateur

O
Op	Opérateur
Op son	Opérateur son

ABBREVIATIONS / ABREVIATIONS **xxv**

Orch	Orchestration

P

Parol	Parolier
Partic sc	Participation au scénario
Phot	Photographie
Phot plat	Photographie de plateau
Pren son	Preneur de son
Prod	Producteur
Prod assoc	Producteur associé
Prod coord	Producteur coordonnateur
Prod dél	Producteur délégué
Prod exéc	Producteur exécutif
Prod tech	Producteur technique

R

Réal	Réalisateur
Réal an	Réalisateur d'animation
Réal dél	Réalisateur délégué
Rech	Recherche
Rég	Régisseur
Rég ext	Régisseur aux extérieurs
Rég gén	Régisseur général
Rel	Relationniste
Rep	Reportage

S

Sc	Scénariste
Script éd	Scripte éditeur
Séq an	Séquence d'animation
Sup	Superviseur
Sup ADR	Superviseur ADR
Sup mont	Superviseur montage
Sup mont son	Superviseur montage son
Sup p pro	Superviseur postproduction
Sup pro	Superviseur production
Sup son	

T

Trad	Traduction

Countries/Pays

A	Austria/Autriche
AN	Antigua
AS	South America/Amérique du Sud
AUS	Australia/Australie
B	Belgium/Belgique
BAH	Bahamas
BER	Bermuda
BL	Belize
BR	Brazil/Brésil
BUR	Burundi
BVI	British Virgin Islands/Iles Vièrges Britannique
CDN	Canada
CH	Switzerland/Suisse
CHI	Chile/Chili
COL	Colombia/Colombie
CS	Czechoslovakia/Tchécoslovaquie
CY	Cayman Islands/Iles Cayman
D	Germany/Allemagne
DK	Denmark/Danemark
EEC	European Economic Community/Communauté Economique Européenn
ETH	Ethiopa/Éthiopie
EUR	Europe
E	Spain/Espagne
F	France
GB	Great Britain/Grande-Bretagne
GH	Ghana
GM	Gambia/Gambie
H	Hungary/Hongrie
HK	Hong Kong
I	Italy/Italie
IND	India/Inde
IL	Israel
IRL	Ireland/Irlande
IRN	Iran
IV	Ivory Coast
J	Japan/Japon
K	Korea/Corée
L	Luxembourg
LAO	Laos
MEX	Mexico/Mexique
MZ	Mozambique
N	Nepal/Népal
NC	Nicaragua
NL	Netherlands/Pays-Bas
NOR	Norway/Norvège
NZ	New Zealand/Nouvelle-Zélande
PE	Peru/Pérou
PH	Philippines
PL	Poland/Pologne
R	Romania/Roumanie
RA	Argentina/Argentine
RC	China/Chine
RFC	Cameroon/Cameroun
RWA	Rwanda
S	Sweden/Suède
SA	Saudi Arabia/Arabie Séoudite
SF	Finland/Finlande
SKO	South Korea/Corée du Sud
SN	Senegal/Sénégal

T	Thailand/Thailande
TT	Trinidad-Tobago/Iles de la Trinité-Tobago
TZ	Tanzania/Tanzanie
UAE	United Arab Emirates/Emirats arabes unis
USA	United States/Etats-Unis
USR	Soviet Union/Union soviétique
YU	Yugoslavia/Yougoslavie
ZA	South Africa/Afrique du Sud
Z	Zambia/Zambie
ZB	Zimbabwe

Unions, Guilds and Associations/Syndicats et Associations

ABS	Association of Broadcasting Staff (Great Britain)
ACCT	Academy of Canadian Cinema and Television/Académie canadienne du cinéma et de la télévision
ACFA	Association of Canadian Film Craftspeople
ACFTP	Association of Canadian Film and Television Producers
ACTRA	Alliance of Canadian Cinema, Television and Radio Artists
ACTT	Association of Cinematograph, Television and Allied Technicians (Great Britain)
ADC	Associated Designers of Canada
ADISQ	Association du disque et de l'industrie de spectacle du Québec
AES	Audio Engineering Society
AFN	American Federation of Musicians of the United States and Canada
AFTRA	American Federation of Television and Radio Artists
AGVA	American Guild of Variety Artists
AMPAC	American Motion Picture Association of Composers
AMPAS	Academy of Motion Picture Arts and Sciences (US)
APFVQ	Association des producteurs de film et de vidéo du Québec
AR	Association des réalisateurs (Radio-Canada)
ARRFQ	Association des réalisateurs et réalisatrices de films du Québec
ARRQ	Association des réalisateurs de Radio-Québec
ASC	American Society of Cinematographers
ASIFA	Association internationale du film d'animation
ASWA	Aviation Space Writers Association
ATPD	Association of Television Producers and Directors (CBC)
BAE	British Actors Equity
BFF	Black Filmmakers Foundation (US)
BFVN	Black Film and Video Network
BKSTS	British Kinematograph, Sound and Television Society
BUPD	Broadcast Union of Producers and Directors
CAMERA	Canadian Association of Motion Picture and Electronic Recording Artists
CAPAC	Composers, Authors and Publishers Association of Canada
CAS	Canadian Audio Society
CDG	Costume Designers Guild (Los Angeles)
CFEG	Canadian Film Editors Guild
CFSS	Canadian Film Sound Society
CFTA	Canadian Film and Television Association
CIFC	Canadian Independent Film Caucus
CIPC	Canadian Independent Producers Caucus
CLC	Canadian League of Composers
CSC	Canadian Society of Cinematographers
CST	Commission supérieure technique (France)
CTPDA	Canadian Television Producers and Directors Association (CBC)
CULR	Canadian Union of Labour Representatives
CUPE	Canadian Union of Public Employees
DGA	Directors Guild of America
DGC	Directors Guild of Canada
FPRRTC	Fédération professionnelle des réalisateurs et réalisatrices de télévision et de cinéma
GCFC	Guild of Canadian Film Composers
GdMQ	Guilde des musiciens du Québec
IATSE 873	International Alliance of Theatrical and Stage Employees and MovingPicture Machine Operators of the United States and Canada
IATSE 210	(Edmonton)
IATSE 644	International Photographers of the Motion Picture and Television Industries (New York)
IATSE 659	International Photographers of the Motion Picture and Television Industries (Los Angeles)
IATSE 667	International Photographers of the Motion Picture and Television Industries (Toronto and Vancouver)

IATSE 771	Motion Picture and Videotape Editors (New York)
IATSE 776	Motion Picture and Videotape Editors (Los Angeles)
IATSE 928	Art Directors (Canada)
IATSE 891	Motion Picture (Film and Video) Studio Production Technicians
MPEG	Motion Picture Editors Guild (US)
MPSE	Motion Picture Sound Editors (US)
NABET	National Association of Broadcast Employees and Technicians
NARAS	National Association of Recording Arts and Sciences (US)
NATAS	National Association of Television Arts and Sciences (US)
NATPE	National Association of TV Program Executives (US)
OACETT	Ontario Association of Certified EngineeringTechnicians and Technologists
PGA	Producers Guild of America
RRPFQ	Regroupement régional des producteurs de films du Québec
SACD	Société des auteurs et compositeurs dramatiques (France et Canada)
SAG	Screen Actors Guild (US)
SARDEC	Société des auteurs, recherchistes, documentalistes et compositeurs
SCL(LA)	Society of Composers and Lyricists (Los Angeles)
SGCT	Syndicat général du cinéma et de la télévision (ONF)
SMPTE	Society of Motion Picture and Television Engineers
SOGIC	Société générale des industries culturelles
STCQ	Syndicat des techniciennes et techniciens du cinéma du Québec
STLD	Society of Television Lighting Directors
SWG	Saskatchewan Writers Guild
TMA	Toronto Musicians Association
TRACS	Toronto Recording Association of Commercial Studios
TWIFT	Toronto Women in Film and Television
TWIFV	Toronto Women in Film and Video
UBCP	Union of B.C. Performers
UdA	Union des artistes
USA	United Scenic Artists (New York)
WGAe/w	Writers Guild of America (East or/ou West)
WGC (ACTRA)	Writers Guild of Canada
WGGB	Writers Guild of Great Britain

Awards

The following awards appear in the **Selected Filmography** when the person, and not the production, receives the award/Les prix suivants apparaissent dans la **Filmographie sélective** lorsque la personne au lieu de la production en est la récipiendaire:

ACTRA	BFA
ANIK	EMMY
BIJOU	GENIE
CFA	GEMINI
CFTA	GEMEAUX
CLIO	CSC
CESAR	BSC
CFEG	OSCAR

Well-known festivals referred to, usually by city, in the **Biography** section are/Les festivals dont on fait référence par ville dans la **Curriculum vitae** sonts les suivants:

Alberta Motion Picture Industry Association Awards (AMPIA)
American Film Festival (New York)
Banff Festival of Mountain Films
Banff Television Festival
Biennale de Venezia
CanPro Awards
Chicago International Film Festival
Columbus International Film Festival (Ohio)
New York International Film and Television Festival
Oberhausen International Short Film Festival
San Francisco International Film Festival
Yorkton Short Film and Video Festival

The Data Bank

Information in this publication is stored in the Academy's *Who's Who/Qui est qui* data bank. The computer program has extensive crossindexing possibilities, which enables the Academy to respond to requests for various kinds of lists of people in film and television.

La Banque de donnés

Les renseignements donnés dans la présente publication font partie de la banque de données *Qui est qui/Who's Who* de l'Académie. Il existe de nombreuses possibilités de contre-indexation en vue de la compilation de listes spécialisées en cinéma et en télévision.

Index Codes / Codes d'index

Writer WR	Scénariste SC
Producer PR	Producteur PD
Director DR	Réalisateur RE
Production Manager PM	Directeur de production RG
Art Director AD	Directeur artistique DA
Costume Designer CD	Costumes CT
Cinematographer CI	Directeur photo DP
Production Sound Mixer PS	Mixeur son production SP
Composer CO	Compositeur CM
Editor ED	Monteur MO
Sound Editor SE	Monteur son MS
Music Editor ME	Monteur musique MM
Postprod'n Snd Editor PE	Mixeur son postprod. MP
Publicist PB	Publiciste PL

Explanatory Notes

Our data base contains several thousand names of people working in Canadian film and television. We mailed each one a *Who's Who* data form and followed up by phone in order to make this directory as comprehensive as possible; thus, if a familiar name does not appear, we did not receive a response from that person. Should you be aware that someone you know is not included and should be, please encourage him or her to get in touch with us in order to be in the next edition.

Accordingly, all information in this directory has been obtained from the people listed. Although we have tried to verify and have crosschecked the data to ensure accuracy, we would appreciate being notified of mistakes so they may be corrected for the next edition.

Entries appear in English or French, whichever was used by the person supplying information on his or her data form.

The ◇ symbol appearing after a person's name indicates that we did not receive an update and that the entry remains the same as in the 1989 edition.

The first line of each entry contains union, guild or association membership(s), home address and/or business and/or agent addresses and phone numbers. The section called **Types of Production and Credits** includes the medium the person usually works in and in what professional capacity. **Genre** refers to the kind of material (drama, documentary, variety and so on) specialized in. We have usually permitted a maximum of four main genres for each person; this may not necessarily cover all the genres in which he or she has experience. The **Selected Filmography** section lists individual productions (series titles appear in quotations and single titles in italics) and credits and also indicates production year, producing country and various major national and international awards won. Other important awards are mentioned in the **Biography** section, usually by city (see Awards key for list). Whenever two or more people share a credit on the same film or television program, each person's credit is preceded by *Co-* (e.g., Co-Prod, Co-Wr). We realise that this causes problems in the case of producers because the term has a different meaning when applied to official co-productions and in certain other cases, but we have not yet been able to devise a more workable system.

We have used the date of completion of principal photography as the production date, especially for feature films.

A list of the credits mentioned in each **Selected Filmography** begins on page *xvii*.

The key to the category codes used in the index appears on the preceding page.

Notes explicatives

Notre banque de données contient des milliers de noms de professionels du cinéma et de la télévision au Canada. Nous avons fait parvenir à ceux-ci une formule de demande d'inclusion au *Qui est qui*, puis nous les avons appelés pour les inviter à s'inscrire: tous ne l'ont pas fait, et nous le regrettons. Les lecteurs connaissent des professionels du cinéma et de la télévision qui devraient être mentionnés au *Qui est qui* nous obligeraient grandement en attirant leur attention sur notre répertoire. Nous pourrons ainsi en tenir compte dans la prochaine édition.

Tous les renseignements fournis dans le présent ouvrage nous ont été fournis par les sujets de nos articles. Nous avons vérifié les renseignements dans la mesure du possible, mais il s'est sans doute glissé des erreurs ou des omissions. Nos lecteurs, encore une fois, pourraient nous assister en nous faisant part de toute imprécision.

Les notices des professionels qui ont répondu à notre questionnaire en français sont données en français; même chose pour l'anglais.

Sont marquées d'un ◇ suivant le nom de la personne les entrées pour lesquelles nous n'avons pas reçu de mise à jour.

Chaque notice donne d'abord le nom des unions, syndicats, guildes ou associations professionnelles auxquelles appartiennent les sujets ainsi que leur coordonnées à domicile ou au travail. La section intitulée **Types de production et générique** donne des renseignements généraux sur le médium et l'activité professionnelle. On explique sous **Types d'oeuvres** le genre de matérial (dramatique, documentaire, variété, etc.); comme on ne mentionne que quatre genres au maximum, il arrivera que certains professionels travaillent aussi dans des domaines dont on ne fait pas état dans nos pages. La section intitulée **Filmographie sélective** donne le titre des productions auxquelles le sujet a participé (les séries sont entre guillemets, les réalisations simples en italique), son rôle particulier, l'année de réalisation, le pays producteur et les prix qui ont pu être gagnés au Canada ou à l'étranger. D'autres prix sont mentionnés dans le **Curriculum vitae** (voir la section Prix pour une liste des prix qui paraissent dans le répertoire).

Dans le cas des collaborations, le préfix *co* est ajouté: e.g., co prod, co sc. Nous reconnaissons que cela crée certains problèmes dans le cas des productions étant donné le sens que prend le mot coproducteur dans certaines productions officielles ou autres, mais c'est le meilleur système que nous ayions trouvé jusqu'ici.

Dans le cas des longs métrages en particulier, la fin de la photographie principale est considerée comme la date officielle de réalisation de l'oeuvre.

On donne à la page *xvii* la liste des abréviations utilisées dans la section **Filmographie sélective**.

A la page précédent, on donne la liste des codes des catégories utilsées dans l'index.

Who's Who in Canadian Film and Television

Published bi-annually by the Academy of Canadian Cinema and Television

For their support and assistance, the Academy wishes to thank Telefilm Canada, Employment and Immigration Canada, the Ontario Film Development Corporation, Trans-Canada Press and the following individuals: Paul Audley, Kimberley Biggar, Bob Brooks, Raynald Desmeules, Louisa Dupré, Eric Ferguson, Willy Fizet, Scott Gibbs, Nancy Green, Marcia Hackborn, Gillian Holmes, Kerry Holmes, Chapelle Jaffe, Allison Kendal, Jessica London, Vee MacLaren, Peter Mortimer, Alison Reid, Andra Sheffer, Marilyn Sing, Mary Stevenson Rourke, Doug Stewart, Heather Thibault, Sandra Woolfrey, June Yee and Matthew Ying.

Qui est Qui au cinéma et à la télévision au Canada

Publié tous les deux ans par l'Académie canadienne du cinéma et de la télévision

L'Académie remercie de leur appui et de leur aide Téléfilm Canada, Emploi et Immigration Canada, la Société de développement de l'industrie cinématographique ontarienne, Trans-Canada Press et les personnes suivantes: Paul Audley, Kimberley Biggar, Bob Brooks, Raynald Desmeules, Louisa Dupré, Eric Ferguson, Willy Fizet, Scott Gibbs, Nancy Green, Marcia Hackborn, Gillian Holmes, Kerry Holmes, Chapelle Jaffe, Allison Kendal, Jessica London, Vee MacLaren, Peter Mortimer, Alison Reid, Andra Sheffer, Marilyn Sing, Mary Stevenson Rourke, Doug Stewart, Heather Thibault, Sandra Woolfrey, June Yee et Matthew Ying.

BETACAM SP

TAKE ONE

If television is your medium, video production is the medium you should be using.

Sony Betacam is the television production system that will give you the superior quality camera realism you want with the film-style handling you're accustomed to, through every step of your production while the actors and sets are all in place.

Speed efficiency and reliability unrivalled in the production world. Superior picture and sound quality. Deceptively simple, worry-free operation that won't interfere with your creativity.

Take one … with Sony Betacam SP.

SONY
Communication Products Group

Art Directors
Directeurs artistiques

AMES, Paul
ABS, CUPE. 951 Logan Ave., Toronto, ON M4K 3E3 (416)463-3878. CBC, Box 500, Stn. A, Toronto, ON M5W 1E6 (416)975-7009.
Type of Production and Credits: TV Film-Art Dir; TV Video-Art Dir; Th Film-Art Dir.
Genres: Drama-Th&TV; Variety-TV; News-TV; Current Affairs-TV.
Biography: Born 1949, London, England; British and Canadian citizenship. Diploma, Film and TV Design, Medway College of Design, England. Awarded the MSIAD in film and TV art direction by the Society of Artists & Industrial Designers, 74; IOS Diploma, Film and TV Art Direction, 84, Toronto. Has been employed by London Weekend TV, BBC, Thames, ETV (London), TVOntario and CBC. 2 Gemini nominations for art direction.
Selected Filmography: *Grand Larceny*, TV, 91, CDN, Pro Des; *Love & Hate*, TV, 89, CDN, Pro Des; "Material World" (6 eps), TV, 89-90, CDN, Pro Des; *Getting Married in Buffalo Jump*, TV, 88, CDN, Pro Des; "Market Place" (36 eps), TV, 88, CDN, Pro Des; *A Nest of Shining Birds*, TV, 87, CDN, Pro Des; "Video Hits" (48 eps), TV, 87, CDN, Art Dir; *The Last Season*, TV, 86, CDN, Pro Des; *Murder Sees the Light*, TV, 86, CDN, Pro Des; *And Miles to Go*, TV, 85, CDN, Pro Des; *Moving Targets*, TV, 82, CDN, Pro Des; "For the Record" (5 eps), TV, 81-84, CDN, Pro Des; "Backstretch" (8 eps), TV, 82, CDN, Pro Des; *You've Come a Long Way, Katie*, TV, 81, CDN, Pro Des; *Actra*

Command Performance, TV, 81, CDN, Pro Des.

BAILIE, Philip
- see COSTUME DESIGNERS

BASARABA, Catherine
DGC. 550 Ontario St., #513, Toronto, ON M4X 1X3 (416)923-8442. CBC, Set Design Dept., (416)975-7060.
Type of Production and Credits: Th Film-Asst Loc M; TV Film-Art Dir/Loc M; TV Video-Art/Loc M; Comm-Art Dir/Asst Loc M.
Genres: Drama-TV; Variety-TV; Children's-TV; Industrial-TV; Com-mercials-TV.
Biography: Born 1954, Montreal, Quebec. Studied Fine Art, Ontario College of Art,Toronto, 72-74; B.A.A., Interior Design, Ryerson Polytechnical Institute, Toronto, Ontario, 79. Worked as restaurant designer, 79-80; began work in TV, 80; Assistant Art Director for *Tour of the Universe, Space Port 2019,* CN Tower, Toronto, Ontario. Studied in Florence, Italy, and Banff, 87.
Selected Filmography: *Grand Larceny,* TV, 91, CDN, Art Dir; *Conspiracy of Silence* (mini-series), TV, 90, CDN, Art Dir; "Scales of Justice" (1 eps), TV, 90, CDN, Assist Art Dir; *George Fox Special,* TV, 90, CDN, Assist Art Dir; *Sanity Clause,* TV, 89, CDN, Assist Art Dir; *Mad Avenue,* TV, 88, USA, Assist Loc M; *Dream Team,* Th, 88, USA, Assist Loc M; "My Secret Identity", TV, 87, CDN/USA, Assist Art Dir; "Mariah State" (6 eps), TV, 87, USA, Assist Art Dir; "Street Legal" (6 eps), TV, 86, CDN, Assist Art Dir; "OWL-TV" (12 eps), TV, 85, CDN, Assist Art Dir; *Blindside,* TV, 85, CDN, Assist Art Dir; *Nowhere to Hide,* Th, 85, CDN/USA, Assist Art Dir; "Today's Special" (20 eps), TV, 84, CDN, Art Dir; *Gentle Sinners,* TV, 83, CDN, Assist Dir.

BEAUCHEMIN, Guy
SPEQ, APASQ. 330 chemin des Patriotes sud, Mont St-Hilaire, PQ J3H 3G8 (514)467-9854. La Boîte du Pinceau D'Arlequin, 1919 William, Montreal, PQ H3J 1R7 (514)939-1919.
Types de production et générique: TV Film-Dir art; TV Video-Dir art.
Types d'oeuvres: Drame-TV; Variété-TV; Annonces-TV; Video-Clips-TV.
Curriculum vitae: Née au Québec en 1953. Langues: français et anglais. Education: Scénographie. Design d'Environnement, Direction Artistique, Muséographe, Design.
Filmographie sélective: *Poulet Frit Kentucky,* TV, 90, CDN, Dir Art, Prix Gemeaux; *Jeunesse "AD Lib",* TV, 85, CDN, Décor.

BEETON, William ◇
(416)531-3271.
Type of Production and Credits: Th Film-Pro Des; TV Film-Art Dir; TV Video-Art Dir/Pro Des.
Genres: Drama-Th&TV; Comedy-TV; Variety-TV; Horror-Th.
Biography: Born 1935, Toronto, Ontario. Educated at various art schools. Employed at CBC, 58, first in special effects, then design department; established freelance production design/art direction company, 79.
Selected Filmography: *April Morning,* TV, 87, USA, Pro Des; "My Secret Identity" (pilot), TV, 87, CDN/USA, Pro Des; *Ford: The Man and the Machine* (mini-series), TV, 87, CDN, Pro Des, (GEMINI 87); *The Gate,* Th, 86, CDN, Pro Des; *Barnum,* TV, 86, USA, Pro Des; *The Execution of Raymond Graham,* TV, 85, CDN, Pro Des; *Grown Ups,* TV, 85, USA, Art Dir; "Check It Out!", TV, 85, CDN/USA, Pro Des; *The Boy in Blue,* Th, 84, USA/CDN, Pro Des; *Pygmalion,* TV, 83, CDN, Art Dir; "Fraggle Rock", TV, 82, CDN, Art Dir; *Best Revenge,* Th, 80, CDN, Pro Des; *Blind Faith,* "For the Record", TV, 80, CDN, Art Dir; *Riel,* TV, 79, CDN, Pro Des, (ANIK); "A Gift to Last", TV, 76, CDN, Pro Des, (ANIK).

BLACKIE, John S.
IATSE 210, DGC. 11 Dayton Cresc., St. Albert, AB T8N 4Y1 (403) 459-4083.
Type of Production and Credits: Th Film-Pro Des; TV Film-Pro Des; TV Video-Pro Des.
Genres: Drama-Th&TV; Comedy-Th&TV; Science Fiction-Th&TV; Commercials-TV.
Biography: Born 1950, Lethbridge, Alberta; Canadian citizenship. Studied Art at the Alberta College of Art. Worked as Graphic Artist (Animation) in the advertising industry; Set Decorator, Props Master, Art Director, Production Designer. 3 Alberta Motion Picture Industry Awards (83, 89, 90); 3 Honourable Mentions (82 - Music, 89 - 2 Art Direction). 1989 Ace Award for Art Direction, American Cable Excellence.
Selected Filmography: *Solitaire,* Th, 91, CDN, Pro Des; *Bordertown Cafe,* Th, 90, CDN, Pro Des; *Angle Square,* Th, 90, CDN, Pro Des; "Ray Bradbury Theatre", TV, 89, CDN/USA, Pro Des, (ACE); *Bye Bye Blues,* Th, 88-89, CDN, Pro Des, (AMPIA); *Cowboys Don't Cry,* Th, 87, CDN, Pro Des.

BOLTON, Michael ◊
(604)261-6732.
Type of Production and Credits: Th Film-Art Dir; Th Short-Art Dir; TV Film-Art Dir; TV Video-Art Dir.
Genres: Drama-Th&TV; Comedy-Th&TV; Action-Th&TV; Science Fiction-Th&TV.
Biography: Born 1945; Canadian citizen. Started in television at CBC Vancouver, 68; Art Director, drama and variety series including "The Irish Rovers," "The Beachcombers," "For the Record"; freelance since 80.
Selected Filmography: *Astro & Son*, TV, 86, USA, Pro Des; *Stranger in My Bed*, TV, 86, USA, Pro Des; *Tripwire*, Th, 86, USA, Art Dir; *I-Man*, TV, 85, USA, Pro Des; *Fire with Fire*, Th, 85, USA, Art Dir; *Love Mary*, TV, 85, USA, Art Dir; *Rainbow War*, Expo 86, ED, 85, USA, Art Dir; *The Journey of Natty Gann*, Th, 84, USA, Art Dir; *Runaway*, Th, 84, USA, Art Dir; *The Glitter Dome*, TV, 83, CDN/USA, Art Dir; *Draw!*, TV, 83, CDN/USA, Art Dir; *Iceman*, Th, 83, USA, Art Dir; *The Golden Seal*, Th, 82, USA, Set Dec; *Star 80*, Th, 82, USA, Art Dir; *Eureka*, Th, 82, GB, Props.

BONNIERE, Claude ◊
(416)922-6463.
Type of Production and Credits: Th Film-Art Dir/Pro Des; TV Film-Art Dir/Pro Des.
Genres: Drama-Th&TV; Comedy-Th; Children's-Th&TV.
Biography: Born 1932, Paris, France; French and Canadian citizenship. Languages: English, French and Spanish. Educated at Ecole des Arts Appliqués, Paris; Ecole du Musée du Louvre. Has travelled extensively; Art Director since 1962.
Selected Filmography: "OWL-TV", TV, 84-86, CDN, Pro Des; *Mafia Princess*, TV, 85, USA, Pro Des; *Labour of Love*, TV, 84, CDN, Pro Des; *My Mother Was Never a Kid*, TV, 82, CDN/USA, Pro Des, (EMMY); *Paradise*, Th, 81, CDN, Pro Des; *Love*, Th, 80, CDN, Pro Des; *Your Ticket Is No Longer Valid*, Th, 79, CDN, Pro Des; *Crunch*, Th, 79, CDN/USA, Pro Des; *Circle of Two*, Th, 79, CDN, Pro Des.

BRODIE, Bill
ACTT, DGC, ACCT. 18 Nursewood Rd., Toronto, ON M4E 3R8 (416)699-3016. Lynn Kinney, Credentials, 1235 Bay St., Suite 501, Toronto, ON M5R 3K4 (416)967-1179.
Type of Production and Credits: Th Film-Art Dir/Pro Des; TV Film-Art Dir/Pro Des.
Genres: Drama-Th&TV; Comedy-Th&TV; Action-Th; Science Fiction-Th.
Biography: Born 1931, Ottawa, Ontario; Canadian and British citizenship. Directed/co-produced *Terry Whitmore for Example*, which was invited to Directors' Fortnight, Cannes, 69; received Quality Award, Swedish Film Institute, 69.
Selected Filmography: *Body Parts*, Th, 91, USA, Pro Des; *The Little Kidnappers*, TV, 90, CDN/USA, Pro Des; *Short Circuit II*, Th, 87, USA, Pro Des; *Dead of Winter*, Th, 86, USA, Pro Des; *One Magic Christmas*, Th, 85, CDN/USA, Pro Des; *Beer*, Th, 84, USA, Pro Des; *The Undergrads*, TV, 84, USA, Pro Des; *Draw!*, TV, 83, CDN/USA, Pro Des; *The Grey Fox*, Th, 80, CDN, Pro Des, (GENIE); *Silence of the North*, Th, 79, CDN, Pro Des; *Superman*, Th, 78, USA/GB, Spv Art Dir; *Barry Lyndon*, Th, 74, GB, Art Dir; *Terry Whitmore for Example*, Th, 69, GB/S, Dir/Co-Prod; *Peace Game*, Th, 68, S, Art Dir; *Privilege*, Th, 66, GB, Art Dir/Pro Des.

BROMLEY, Karen
DGC, ACCT. 385 Carlton St., Toronto, ON M5A 2M3 (416)960-4962.
Type of Production and Credits: Th Film-Art Dir/Pro Des; TV Film-Art Dir/Pro Des; TV Video-Art Dir/Pro Des.
Genres: Drama-Th&TV; Action-Th&TV; Science Fiction-Th&TV; Horror-Th&TV.
Biography: Born in Brandon, Manitoba. Has worked in professional theatre in Ontario and the United States; extensive video work including CTV Public Affairs. Experienced in electronic effects, models, projection systems as well as mattes and film effects.
Selected Filmography: *Special People*, TV, 83, CDN/USA, Pro Des; *A Matter of Sex*, TV, 83, CDN/USA, Pro Des; *Something's Afoot*, TV, 82, USA, Pro Des; *Will There Really Be a Morning?*, TV, 82, USA, Pro Des; "Romance" (30 eps), TV, 82, CDN, Pro Des; *The Sins of Dorian Gray*, TV, 81, USA, Pro Des; *Harry Tracy*, Th, 80, CDN, Pro Des; *Mom, the Wolfman and Me*, TV, 80, USA, Pro Des; *Title Shot*, Th, 79, CDN, Pro Des; *Middle Age Crazy*, Th, 79, CDN/USA, Pro Des; *Circle of Children*, TV, 78, USA, Pro Des; *Separation*, TV, 77, CDN, Art Dir; *Power Play*, Th, 77, CDN/GB, Art Dir; *Outrageous!*, Th, 77, CDN, Art Dir; *Wedding in White*, Th, 72, CDN, Art Dir, (CFA).

CHARLES, David Orin ◇
(416)761-9073.
Type of Production and Credits: Th Film-Art Dir; TV Film-Art Dir; TV Video-Art Dir.
Genres: Drama-TV; Comedy-Th&TV; Educational-TV; Commercials-TV.
Biography: Born 1944, Toronto, Ontario. Architecture degree, Univ. of Hawaii and New Mexico State Univ., 66; taught Theatre Arts, Connecticut and Penn State Univ; B.Ed., M.A., Univ. of Toronto. In professional theatre since age 12; worked on over 30 films and 700 commercials; early experi-ence in acting, radio and newspaper journalism. Working towards Ph.D. in Dramatic Literature, U. of T.
Selected Filmography: *Case of Libel*, TV, 83, USA, Assist Art Dir; *I Am A Hotel*, TV, 83, CDN, Assist Art Dir; "Gilbert" (4 eps), TV, 79, CDN/USA, Pro Des; *Meatballs*, Th, 78, CDN, Pro Des.

CHICK, Russell David
CUPE. 73 Courcelette Rd., Scarborough, ON M1N 2S9 (416)699-3437. CBC, Box 500, Stn. A, Toronto, ON M5W 1E6 (416)975-7029. FAX: 975-7081.
Type of Production and Credits: TV Film-Pro Des; TV Video-Art Dir.
Genres: Drama-TV; Variety-TV; Children's-TV; News-TV.
Biography: Born 1948, London, England; immigrated to Canada, 72. Studied Theatre Design at Camberwell Art College and Wimbledon Art College. Resident designer for London Theatre Company. Graduate, London School of TV/Stage Make-up Design and CBC Institute of Scenography. Emmy award nomination for Boston TV News Design. Gemini Award winner, 90, Best Production Design for *The Private Capital*.
Selected Filmography: "CBC News Magazine", TV, 91, CDN, Pro Des; *Brian Orser Special - "Night Moves"*, TV, 91, CDN, Pro Des; "Son of Jack and the Beanstalk", TV, 90, CDN, Art Dir; "The Journal"/"Midday"/"The National", TV, 81-84, 90-91, CDN, Prod Des/Art Dir; "the fifth estate", TV, 89-90, CDN, Art Dir; "The Story Teller, The Henson Hour", TV, 88-89, CDN, Art Dir; "The Jim Henson Muppet Hour", TV, 88-89, CDN/USA, Pro Des/Art Dir; *The Private Capital* (mini-series), TV, 87-88, CDN Pro Des; *Family Reunion*, TV, 87, CDN, Art Dir; *Spoof*, TV, 87, CDN/USA, Art Dir; *Skate*, TV, 87, CDN, Art Dir; "Sesame Street" (sev seg), TV, 84-86, USA, Art Dir; "Fraggle Rock", TV, 84-86, USA/CDN/GB, Art Dir; "Home Fires" (31 eps), TV, 80-83, CDN, Art Dir; *Turning to Stone*, TV, 86, CDN, Pro Des.

CHRISTIE, Keith
- see DIRECTORS

CSABA, Kertész A.
DGC. 365 Clinton St. #2, Toronto, ON M6G 2Z1 (416)538-1614.
Type of Production and Credits: Th Film-Art Dir; Th Short-Pro Des; TV Film-Art Dir; TV Video-Art Dir.
Genres: Drama-Th&TV; Comedy-Th&TV; Science Fiction-Th&TV; Children's-Th&TV.
Biography: Born in 1943 in Hungary. Came to Canada as a political refugee after the 1956 revolt in Budapest. Educated in Toronto. Background as a commercial artist and in fine art. Began film work in 1977 in Montreal. Decorated *In Praise of Older Women* which won the Canadian Academy Award for Art. Also worked as Art Director under the Production Designer on *Atlantic City*, an Oscar nominee.
Selected Filmography: *Drop Dead Gorgeous*, TV, 91, CDN/USA, Set Dec; "Power Pack" (pilot), TV, 90, CDN/USA, Art Dir; *White Light*, Th, 90, CDN, Set Dec; *Nowhere To Hide*, Th, 86, CDN/USA, Prod Des; *Separate Vacations*, Th, 85, CDN/USA, Prod Des; *For One Night Only*, TV, 84, CDN/USA, Art Dir; *Perfect Timing*, TV, 84, CDN/USA, Art Dir; *New Orleans*, TV, 83, CDN/USA, Art Dir; *Joy*, Th, 82, CDN/F, Art Dir; *Scandal*, Th, 82, CDN, Prod Des; *Till Death Do Us Part*, TV, 81, CDN, Prod Des; *Vibrations*, Th, 80, CDN, Prod Des; *Pick Up Summer*, Th, 79, CDN, Art Dir; *Atlantic City*, Th, 79, CDN, Art Dir; *In Praise of Older Women*, Th, 77, CDN, Set Dec.

DALTON, Ninkey
920 Iliff St., Pacific Palisades, CA 90272 (213)469-7001.
Type of Production and Credits: Th Film-Pro Des; TV Film-Pro Des.
Genres: Drama-Th&TV; Comedy-Th&TV.
Biography: Born in 1951 in Toronto, Ontario. Bachelor of Fine Arts from the University of Guelph. Lives in Los Angeles and is a production designer for film and television. Nominated for a Genie Award in 1982 and won an Emmy for Best Special Effects, "Hugga Bunch", 1985.
Selected Filmography: *Strange Voices*, TV, 89, USA, Pro Des; *Jessee*, TV, 89, USA, Pro Des; *Poker Alice*, TV, 88, USA, Pro Des; *The Champions*, Th, 87, USA, USA Pro Des; *Deadly Eyes*, Th, 85, CDN, Pro Des.

DAVIS, David

DGC. 281 Booth Ave., Toronto, ON M4M 2M7 (416)466-2703. Gerald K. Smith, P.O. Box 7430, Burbank, CA 91501 USA. (213)849-5388.

Type of Production and Credits: Th Film-Art Dir; Th Short-Art Dir; TV Film-Art Dir.

Genres: Drama-Th&TV; Action-Th&TV; Children's-TV.

Biography: Born 1945, Wales; landed immigrant Canada. M.A., Fine Arts, Chelsea School of the Arts; graduate scholarship, Yale University. Ten years experience in all aspects of theatre art direction.

Selected Filmography: *Courage*, TV, 86, USA, Art Dir; *Act of Vengeance*, Th, 85, USA, Art Dir; *Separate Vacations*, Th, 85, CDN, Assist Art Dir; *Evergreen* (miniseries), TV, 84, USA, Art Dir, (EMMY); *Heavenly Bodies*, Th, 83, CDN, Assist Art Dir; *Bedroom Eyes*, Th, 83, CDN, Assist Art Dir; *Draw!*, TV, 83, CDN/USA, Assist Art Dir; *Special People*, TV, 83, CDN/USA, Assist Art Dir; *A Matter of Sex*, TV, 83, CDN/USA, Assist Art Dir; *Falcon's Gold/Robbers of the Sacred Mountain*, Th, 82, CDN, Pro Des; *Will There Really Be a Morning?*, TV, 82, USA, Assist Art Dir; *The Sins of Dorian Gray*, TV, 81, USA, Assist Art Dir; *Koza Dereza*, Th, 80, CDN, Art Dir; *Harry Tracy*, Th, 80, CDN, Assist Art Dir.

de COTIIS, Franco

DGC. 662 Huron St., #2, Toronto, ON M5R 2R9 (416)921-9547.

Type of Production and Credits: Th Short-Art Dir; TV Film-Art Dir.

Genres: Drama-Th&TV; Action-TV; Science Fiction-TV; Commercials-Th&TV.

Biography: Born 1942, Rome, Italy; Canadian citizenship. Languages: English and Italian. Studied Architecture, Academy of Fine Arts, Rome; obtained teaching fine art certificate, Institute of Scenography, CBC. Nominated for Bessie and Gemini awards. Works as freelance Art Director for commercials, film and TV. Participated as Production Designer on projects with the Canadian Centre for Advanced Film Studies, 88.

Selected Filmography: *Someone Like You*, ED, 88, CDN, Art Dir; *A Date*, ED, 88, CDN, Pro Des; Pepsi-Cola Canada Inc., Cm, 88, CDN, Pro Des; Diet Pepsi, Cm, 88, CDN, Art Dir; GM Pontiac/Speedy Muffler/Seagram Inc./Clairol Canada Inc., Cm, 87, CDN, Art Dir; *A Moving Picture*, TV, 87, CDN, Art Dir; *Christmas Special*, TV, 85, CDN, Art Dir; *Stuart Burrow in Canada*, TV, 85, CDN, Art Dir; *We're Really Moving*, CN for Expo 86, ED, 85, CDN, Art Dir; *10th Annual Juno Awards*, TV, 84, CDN, Art Dir; *Chemical People*, TV, 83, USA, Assoc Prod Des; *Waiting for the Parade*, TV, 83, CDN, Art Dir; *Parade Quebec Canada, 1995*, TV, 83, CDN, Art Dir; "Rear View Mirror" (12 eps), TV, 81, CDN, Art Dir; *Coming Out Alive*, TV, 80, CDN, Assist Art Dir.

de LUCY, François ◆

(514)271-9761.

Types de production et générique: l métrage-Dir art; c métrage-Dir art; TV film-Dir art.

Types d'oeuvres: Drame-C&TV; Action-C&TV; Annonces-TV.

Curriculum vitae: Né en 1916, Bordeaux, France; citoyenneté canadienne depuis 77; réside au Canada depuis 61. Langues: français et anglais. Partage son temps entre la peinture, la décoration et le cinéma; nombreuses expositions de groupe et solo.

Filmographie sélective: *Fate of a Hunter*, C, 86, CDN, Des; *La Manette, la cassette*, Cm, 86, CDN, Dir art; *The Park Is Mine*, C, 84, CDN, Dir art; *Au nom de tous les miens*, C, 83, CDN/F, Dir art; *Black Mirror*, C, 80, CDN/F, Dir art; *Your Ticket Is No Longer Valid*, C, 79, CDN, Dir art; *Keep It in the Family*, C, 70, CDN, Dir art; "L'Homme devant la science" (26 eps), TV, 62, CDN, Chef déc; "Aux frontières de la science" (26 eps), TV, 61, CDN, Chef déc; *L'Arbre*, TV, 61, CDN, Chef déc; "Les Histoires extraordinaires" (13 eps), TV, 61, CDN, Chef déc.

DEL ROSARIO, Linda

DGC. 39 Allen Ave., Toronto, ON M4M 1T5 (416)462-9252.

Type of Production and Credits: Th Film-Pro Des; Th Short-Pro Des.

Genres: Drama-Th; Commercials-TV.

Biography: Born in Sarnia, Ontario. Canadian citizen. B.F.A. (specialization in theatre) from the University of Victoria, 1981. Co-founder of Paris Del Rosario Productions, 1990. Designed/co-designed 3 Cannes Film Festival Selections: *Speaking Parts*, Directors' Fortnight 1989; *Sam and Me*, Critics' Week 1991; *The Adjuster*, Directors' Fortnight 1991.

Selected Filmography: *Vue D'Ailleurs-Montreal Vue Par*, Th, 91, CDN, Co Prod Des/Co Set Dec; *Les Nuits d'Etés*, Th, 91, CDN, Prod Des; *The Adjuster*, Th, 90, CDN, Co Prod Des/Co Set Dec; *Sam and Me*, Th, 90, CDN, Co Prod Des/Co Set Dec; *When Gravity Fails*, Th, 89, CDN, Art Dir; *The High Flying Mermaid*, Th, 89,

CDN/DK, Art Dir/Set Dec; *Unnatural Causes*, Th, 89, CDN, Art Dir; *Cold Comfort*, Th, 89, CDN, Set Dec; *Speaking Parts*, Th, 88, CDN, Art Dir; *Odyssey In August*, Th, 88, CDN, Art Dir; *Family Viewing*, Th, 86, CDN, Art Dir.

DESKIN, Andrew
DGC, ACCT. Sundance Film Services, 600 Wardlaw Ave., Winnipeg, MB R3L 0MZ (204)453-5151.
Type of Production and Credits: Th Film-Art Dir; Th Short-Art Dir; TV Film-Art Dir; TV Video-Art Dir.
Genres: Drama-Th&TV; Comedy-Th& TV; Action-Th&TV; Horror-Th&TV.
Biography: Born 1951. B.F.A., Concordia University, 76.
Selected Filmography: *The Curse of the Viking Grave*, TV, 91, CDN, Pro Des; *Lost in the Barrens*, TV, 90, CDN, Pro Des; *The Mayor of Odessa*, "Inside Stories", TV, 90, CDN, Pro Des; *A Dance to Remember*, "Inside Stories", TV, 90, CDN, Pro Des; *Mob Story*, Th, 89, CDN, Pro Des; *Freak Show*, Th, 88, CDN, Pro Des; "Detectives in the House" (pilot), TV, 87, USA, Art Dir; *Oklahoma Smugglers*, Th, 86, USA, Art Dir; *Higher Education*, Th, 86, CDN, Art Dir; *Overnight*, Th, 85, CDN, Art Dir; *Flying*, Th, 84, CDN, Art Dir; *Heartsounds*, TV, 84, USA, Props; *The Killing Fields*, Th, 84, GB, Props, (in Canada); *Thrillkill*, Th, 83, CDN, Art Dir; *Between Friends*, TV, 83, CDN, Props.

DOBBIE, Scott
IATSE 210. Site 3, Box 4, RR #2, Millet, AB T0C 1Z0 (403)387-4356. Westcom Productions, 5325 - 104 St., Edmonton, AB T6H 5B8 (403)436-1250.
Type of Production and Credits: Th Film-Art Dir; TV Film-Pro Des/Art Dir.
Genres: Drama-Th&TV; Comedy-TV; Variety-TV; Science Fiction-TV; Horror-Th; Children's-TV; Commercials-TV; Industrial-TV; Music Video-TV; Current Affairs-TV.
Biography: Born in 1953 in Edmonton, Alberta. Special skills include training in wilderness travel, navigation, mountaineering, off-piste skiing, white water open canoeing; also extensive experience in wilderness first aid. Fully fluent in both MS-Dos and MacIntosh computer systems. Trained at the Univ. of Alberta, B.F.A., (Drama), Theatre Design.
Selected Filmography: "Ray Bradbury Theatre" (4 eps), TV, 90, USA/CDN/NZ, Pro Des; "Ray Bradbury Theatre" (4 eps), TV, 89, USA/CDN/NZ, Art Dir; *Bye Bye Blues*, Th, 88, CDN, Art Dir; *Stone Fox*, Th, 87, USA/CDN, Pro Des; *Hello Mary Lou - Prom Night II*, Th, 86, CDN, Assist Art Dir; "The Little Vampire", TV, 85, CDN/GB/D, Art Dir; "Mania" (4 eps), TV, 85, CDN, Pro Des; *A House, A Mystery and Me*, TV, 87, CDN/USA, Art Dir; *Bridge to Terabithia*, TV, 84, CDN/USA, Art Dir; "SCTV" (26 eps), TV, 81-82, CDN/USA, Pro Des.

DOHERTY, Tom
DGC, ACCT. 6 Woodgreen Place, Toronto, ON M4M 2J2 (416)461-5118.
Type of Production and Credits: Th Film-Art Dir; TV Film-Art Dir.
Genres: Drama-Th&TV.
Biography: Born 1933, Boston, Massachusetts; landed immigrant Canada. B.Architecture, Massachusetts Institute of Technology, 58. Worked as an architect with The Architects' Collaborative, Boston, 59-61, and with Arthur Erickson, Toronto, 74-76; theatrical set design for 90 productions, 52-83, including Shaw Festival, Theatre Calgary, Theatre New Brunswick.
Selected Filmography: *Leona, Queen of Mean*, TV, 90, USA, Art Dir; *Conspiracy of Silence*, TV, 90, CDN, Set Des; *Sea of Love*, Th, 88, USA, Art Dir; *The Emissary*, "Ray Bradbury Theatre", TV, 88, CDN, Art Dir; *Martha, Ruth & Edie*, Th, 87, CDN, Art Dir; *Echoes in the Darkness* (mini-series), TV, 87, USA, Art Dir; *Concrete Angels*, Th, 86, CDN, Art Dir; *Christmas Eve*, TV, 86, USA Art Dir; "Philip Marlowe Private Eye" (3 eps), TV, 85, CDN, Art Dir; *Children of a Lesser God*, Th, 85, USA, Assist Art Dir; *One Magic Christmas*, Th, 85, CDN/USA, Assist Art Dir; *Beer*, Th, 84, USA, Assist Art Dir; *Class of 1984*, Th, 81, CDN, Assist Art Dir; *Incubus*, Th, 81, CDN, Assist Art Dir; *Death Hunt*, Th, 80, USA, Assist Art Dir.

DORN, Rudi
DGA. 31 Ashgrove Place, Don Mills, ON M3B 2Y9 (416)444-1974.
Type of Production and Credits: Th Film-Art Dir/Dir/Wr; Th Short-Art Dir/Dir/Wr; TV Video-Art Dir/Dir/Wr.
Genres: Drama-Th&TV; Variety-Th&TV.
Biography: Born 1926, Vienna, Austria. Degrees in Engineering and diploma in Architecture from Vienna Academy of Fine Arts. Began working in CBC design department, 1952; writing and directing, 1967; has worked on approximately 47 productions to date.
Selected Filmography: *Gemini Awards, 1991*, TV, 91, CDN, Pro Des; *SkyDome Opening Ceremony*, TV, 90, CDN, Pro

Des; *Olympic Winter Games*, Calgary 88, TV, 88, CDN, Pro Des.

DUNPHY, Barbara
DGC. 50 Leopold St., Toronto, ON M6J 1J9 (416)536-8427. 4025 Oakfield Dr., Sherman Oaks, CA 91423 USA (818)990-6975. The Gersh Agency, P.O. Box 5617, Beverly Hills, CA 90210 USA (213)274-6611.
Type of Production and Credits: Th Film-Pro Des; Th Short-Dir; TV Film-Pro Des.
Genres: Drama-Th&TV; Comedy-Th&TV; Musical-Th&TV.
Biography: Born Saskatoon, Saskatchewan. Canadian citizen. Speaks English; has worked in French. Lived and worked in Ottawa, Toronto, Montreal and Los Angeles. Associate of the Ontario College of Art. Producer and Director of TV shorts for CBC and Radio Canada; has worked as a film editor at Citytv. Experienced with stunts, ultimatte, intravision, various SPFX and prosthetics. Has worked in all periods from 1900 to present. Has also worked in Mexico, New York, Jamaica and various states and provinces. Certified SCUBA diver and rock climber.
Selected Filmography: "Sweating Bullets", TV, 91, CDN/MEX/USA, Pro Des; *Good Cops, Bad Cops*, TV, 90, USA, Pro Des; *Children of the Bride*, TV, 90, USA, Pro Des; *Best Intentions*, TV, 90, USA, Pro Des; *Summer Dreams: The Story of the Beach Boys*, TV, 89, USA, Pro Des; *Cross of Fire*, TV, 89, USA, Pro Des; *A New Life*, Th, 88, USA, Pro Des; "Men" (7 eps), TV, 88, USA/CDN, Pro Des; *Tidy Endings*, TV, 87, GB/CDN/USA, Pro Des; *Adventures in Babysitting*, Th, 86, USA, Art Dir; *Hearts of Fire*, Th, 86, GB/USA, Art Dir; "Airwaves" (13 eps), TV, 85, CDN, Pro Des; *House of Dies Drear*, TV, 84, USA, Pro Des; *King of Friday Night*, TV, 84, CDN, Pro Des; *Dead Zone*, Th, 82, CDN, Art Dir.

DUNLOP, Charles L.
DGC. 3630 Henri-Julien, #2, Montreal, PQ H2X 3H5 (514)499-0883. See Dunlop Designs Inc., 34 Aberdeen Ave., Toronto, ON M4X 1A2 (416)964-8973.
Type of Production and Credits: Th Film-Art Dir/Pro Des/Set Des; TV Film-Art Dir/Pro Des/Set Des; TV Video-Art Dir/Pro Des/Set Des.
Genres: Drama-Th&TV; Comedy-Th&TV; Horror-Th&TV; Commercials-TV.
Biography: Born in Edinburgh, Scotland; Canadian and E.E.C. passports. Professional theatre, sets and costume designer.
Selected Filmography: *The First Circle/Le premier cercle* (mini-series), TV, 90, CDN/F, Pro Des; *Whispers*, Th, 89, CDN/USA, Pro Des; *Princes in Exile*, Th, 89, CDN, Pro Des; *Millenium*, Th, 88, CDN, Art Dir; "T and T" (24 eps), TV, 87-88, CDN, Art Dir; *Switching Channels*, Th, 87, USA/CDN, Assist Pro Des; *Fight for Life*, TV, 87, USA/CDN, Pro Des; *The Case of the Shooting Star*, "Perry Mason", TV, 86, USA, Pro Des; *Popeye Doyle*, TV, 85, USA/CDN, Art Dir; *Half a Lifetime*, TV, 85, USA/CDN, Art Dir; *In Like Flynn*, TV, 85, USA/CDN, Pro Des; *Meatballs III*, Th, 84, CDN, Pro Des; *Heartsounds*, TV, 84, USA/CDN, Art Dir; *The Surrogate*, Th, 83, CDN, Pro Des; *The Tin Flute*, Th, 82, CDN, Pro Des.

DUPUIS, Raymond ◆
(514)288-7480.
Types de production et générique: l métrage-Dir art; TV film-Dir art/Prod /Réal; TV vidéo-Dir art/Mont.
Types d'oeuvres: Drame-C; Comédie-C; Documentaire-TV; Enfants-TV.
Curriculum vitae: Né en 1953, Québec. Langues: français et anglais. Un an d'étude en communications, Université Concordia, 77-78. A travaillé à titre d'accessoiriste, assistant décorateur, décorateur, adjoint au directeur artistique et directeur artistique depuis 78.
Filmographie sélective: "Lance et Compte", TV, 87-88, CDN/F/CH, Dir art; *Hennessy/Where the Dark Streets Go*, TV, 86, CDN/USA, Assist des; *La Ligne de chaleur*, C, 86, CDN, Ass dir art; *Wild Thing*, C, 86, CDN/USA, Assist des; *Garnet Princess*, TV, 86, CDN, Dir art; *Echoes in Crimson*, TV, 86, CDN/USA, Dir art; *La Guêpe*, C, 85, CDN, Ass dir art; *Toby McTeague/Toby*, C, 85, CDN, Ass dir art; *Apocalypse Carle - le tournage de Maria Chapdelaine* (versions fr et angl), TV, 84, CDN, Prod/Réal; "The Hitchhiker" (10 eps), TV, 84, USA, Assist pro des; *Le Crime d'Ovide Plouffe* (aussi 6 eps TV), C, 83, CDN/F, Ass dir art; "Les Fils de la liberté" (5 eps), TV, 80, CDN, Ass dir art; *Final Assignment*, C, 79, CDN, Ass dir art; *Fantastica*, C, 79, CDN/F, Ass dir art; "Bonjour, comment mangez-vous?" (12 eps), TV, 78, CDN, Acces/Ass pro.

FIRUS, Karen
- see DIRECTORS

FISCHER, David
IATSE 891, ADC. David Fischer Design Inc., 6044 Gleneagles Dr., West Vancouver, BC V7W 1W2 (604)921-7653.

Type of Production and Credits: Th Film-Pro Des/Art Dir; TV Film-Pro Des/Art Dir; TV Video-Pro Des/Art Dir.
Genres: Drama-Th&TV; Comedy-Th&TV; Action-Th&TV; Science Fiction-Th; Commercials-TV.
Biography: Born 1950, Hamilton, Ontario. B.A., University of Western Ontario, 73; M.F.A., University of British Columbia, 78; Diploma, Television Design, CBC Institute of Scenography. Freelance stage designer; Jesse award for set design for *Amadeus*, Vancouver, 84; co-designer, Ramses Pavillion, Expo 86, Vancouver.
Selected Filmography: *A Mother's Justice*, TV, 91, USA, Pro Des; *Pure Luck*, Th, 91, USA, Art Dir; *The Sea Will Tell*, TV, 90, USA, Pro Des; *Deadly Intentions*, TV, 90, USA, Pro Des; "Booker" (22 eps), TV, 89, USA, Pro Des; *The First Season*, Th, 88, CDN, Pro Des; *The People Across the Lake*, TV, 88, USA, Pro Des; *The Experts*, Th, 87, USA, Pro Des; "The New Adventures of Beans Baxter" (7 eps), TV, 87, USA, Pro Des; *A Stranger Waits*, TV, 86, USA, Pro Des; *Roxanne*, Th, 86, USA, Art Dir; "The Hitchhiker" (13 eps), TV, 85, USA, Art Dir; *Rocky IV*, Th, 85, USA, Art Dir; *The Vindicator*, Th, 83, CDN, Art Dir; "The Beachcombers" (29 eps), TV, 82-83, CDN, Art Dir.

FLANNERY, Seamus
ACTT, DGC. 550 Jarvis St., #113, Toronto, ON M4Y 1N6 (416)921-7639.
Type of Production and Credits: Th Film-Pro Des; Th Short-Pro Des; TV Film-Pro Des; TV Video-Pro Des.
Genres: Drama-Th&TV; Musical-Th&TV; Action-Th&TV; Science Fiction-Th&TV.
Biography: Born in Eire; Canadian citizenship. Educated at St. Paul's, London, England, and Ontario College of Art. Was manager of design department for BBC 1, BBC 2. Has won awards from BISFA, US Industrial, San Francisco and Cannes film festivals; Kraft Best Art Director, Berlin; 2 Genie nominations, Palme d'Or.
Selected Filmography: "My Secret Identity", TV, CDN/USA, Pro Des; "The Campbells" (98 eps), TV, 85-88, CDN/USA/GB, Pro Des; "Night Heat" (24 eps), TV, 84-85, CDN/USA, Pro Des; *Beautiful Dreamers*, Th, CDN, 89, CDN, Pro Des; *Bells*, Th, 80, CDN, Pro Des; *High Point*, Th, 79, CDN, Pro Des; *Klondike Fever*, Th, 79, CDN, Pro Des; *Angela*, Th, 76, CDN, Pro Des; *Wicker Man*, Th, 73, GB, Pro Des; *Up Pompeii*, Th, 71, GB, Pro Des; *Whatever Happened to What's 'is Name*, Th, 68, GB, Pro Des; *Drop Dead Darling*, Th, 66, GB/USA, Pro Des; *He Who Rides the Tiger*, Th, 65, GB, Pro Des; *Inadmissable Evidence*, Th, 65, GB, Pro Des; *Repulsion*, Th, 65, GB, Pro Des.

FRASER, Eric
IATSE 891, DGC. 100 Circle Ave., Mill Valley, CA 94941 (415)389-0410. (818) 765-6507.
Type of Production and Credits: Th Film-Art Dir; TV Film-Art Dir.
Genres: Drama-Th; Comedy-Th; Action-Th; Science Fiction-Th.
Biography: Born in Oshawa, Ontario. Canadian citizen, U.S. resident alien. Speaks reasonable French and survival Spanish. Art school background; theatre experience in set and lighting design, performing and touring.
Selected Filmography: *The Vagrant*, Th, 91, USA, Art Dir; *The Hitmen*, Th, 91, USA, Art Dir; *Pay Off*, TV, 90, USA, Art Dir; *It*, TV, 90, USA, Art Dir; *Shortime*, Th, 89, USA, Art Dir; *The Death of the Incredible Hulk*, TV, 89, USA, Art Dir; *The Trial of the Incredible Hulk*, TV, 89, USA, Art Dir; "Bordertown", TV, 88, CDN/F, Art Dir; *Bridge To Silence*, TV, 88, USA, Art Dir; *Hands of a Stranger*, TV, 87, USA, Art Dir; *A Christmas Star*, TV, 86, USA, Art Dir.

FREED, Reuben
12 Swanwick Ave., Toronto, ON M4E 1Z1 (416)690-2028. The Gersh Agency, 222 N. Canon Dr., Beverly Hills, CA 90210 USA (213)274-6611.
Type of Production and Credits: Th Film-Art Dir/Pro Des; Th Short-Art Dir/Pro Des; TV Film-Art Dir/Pro Des; TV Video-Art Dir/Pro Des.
Genres: Drama-Th&TV; Comedy-Th&TV; Action-Th&TV; Horror-Th&TV.
Biography: Born 1949, Johannesburg, South Africa; Canadian and US citizenship. Languages: English and French. Graduate architect. Extensive travel in Southern Africa, Europe, USA and Canada; has had photographs published in South Africa and UK; set up and taught course for black architectural draughtsmen in South Africa.
Selected Filmography: *And The Dance Goes On*, Th, 90, CDN, Pro Des; *Look Who's Talking Too*, Th, 90, USA, Pro Des; *Prom Night III*, Th, 89, CDN, Pro Des; *Murder by Night*, TV, 89, USA, Pro Des; *Cold Dog Soup*, Th, 88, USA, Pro Des; *Look Who's Talking*, Th, 88, USA, Pro

Des; *Whattley-by-the-Bay*, TV, 88, USA, Pro Des; *Palais Royale*, Th, 87, CDN, Pro Des; *Sticky Fingers*, Th, 87, USA, Pro Des; "Kay O'Brien, Surgeon" (13 eps), TV, 86, USA, Pro Des; *Spearfield's Daughter* (mini-series), TV, 85, US/CDN/AUS, Pro Des; *A Christmas Story*, Th, 83, CDN, Pro Des; *Porky's I, Porky's II*, Th, 81/82, CDN, Pro Des; *By Design*, Th, 80, CDN, Pro Des; "Tales of the Klondike" (6 eps), TV, 80, CDN, Pro Des.

GALLO, Carmi
USA. Smith, Gosnell & Nicholson Associates, PO Box 1166, Pacific Palisades, CA 90272 USA (213)459-0307.
Type of Production and Credits: Th Film-Pro Des; Th Short-Pro Des; TV Film-Pro Des; TV Video-Art Dir.
Genres: Drama-Th&TV; Variety-Th&TV; Musical-Th&TV; Music Video-Th&TV.
Biography: Born in Toronto, Ontario. Canadian citizen, resident of the United States. Nominated for an ACE Award, 1990 for *Looking For Miracles*. Has a background in advertising, marketing and fine arts.
Selected Filmography: *Pretty Hattie's Baby*, Th, 90, USA, Pro Des; *I'll Take Romance*, TV, 90, USA, Pro Des; "The Hitchhiker" (11 eps), TV, 89, CDN/F, Pro Des; *Foreign Nights*, Th, 89, CDN, Pro Des; *Age Old Friends*, TV, 88, CDN, Pro Des; *Looking For Miracles*, Th, 88, CDN, Pro Des; *The Ann Jillian Story*, TV, 87, USA, Pro Des; "T and T" (pilot, 26 eps), TV, 87, USA/CDN, Pro Des; *Sadie & Son*, TV, 87, USA, Pro Des; "Stingray" (9 eps), TV, 86, USA, Pro Des; "The Edison Twins" (78 eps), TV, 83-86, CDN/USA, Art Dir.

GAUTHIER, Vianney
STCQ. 1280 est, St-Zotique, Montréal, PQ H2S 1N7 (514)272-2923.
Types de production et générique: l métrage-Dir art; c métrage-Dir art; TV film-Dir art; TV vidéo-Dir art.
Types d'oeuvres: Drame-C; Comédie-C; Enfants-C&TV; Animation-C.
Curriculum vitae: Né en 1944, Montréal, Québec. Langues: français et anglais. Diplôme en esthétique, option décoration intérieure, Institut des Arts Appliqués de Montréal, 66; boursier du Québec pour une année de perfectionnement en France, 68-69. *J. A. Martin photographe* remporte Meilleure Direction Artistique, Festival du Film de Cork. *A corps perdu*, nomination, Meilleure Direction Artistique, 90; *No Blame*, nomination aux Geminis, 89.
Filmographie sélective: *Il etait une fois dans un piano*, TV, 90, CDN, Dir art; *La Demoiselle Sauvage*, C, 90, CDN/CH, Dir art; *Simon les nuages*, C, 89, CDN, Dir art; *Une portion d'éternité*, C, 89, CDN, Dir art; *No Blame*, TV, 89, CDN/F, Dir art; *Bino Fabule*, C, 88, CDN/B/F, Dir art; *A corps perdu*, C, 87, CDN/CH, Dir art; *Tommy Tricker and the Stamp Traveller*, C, 87, CDN/RC/AUS, Dir art; "Les Enfants de la rue" (2 eps), TV, 87, CDN, Dir art; *Juke-Bar*, C, 87, CDN, Dir art; *Image par image*, C, 85-86, CDN, Dir art; *Qui a tiré sur nos histoires d'amour?*, C, 85, CDN, Dir art; *The Peanut Butter Solution*, C, 85, CDN, Dir art; *Anne Trister*, C, 855, CDN, Dir art; "Un amour de quartier" (13 eps), TV, 84, CDN, Décor.

GOODWIN, Michael ◇
(416)533-9263
Type of Production and Credits: TV Video-Art Dir.
Genres: Drama-Th&TV; Commercials-TV; Industrial-Th&TV.
Biography: Born 1953, Vancouver Island. Languages: English and some French, German and Italian. B.Mus., University of Victoria, 76; studied in Paris (was design assistant at Paris Opéra), 83-84. Also fine artist with considerable experience in production design for theatre and opera; has worked on art direction for a variety of commercials.
Selected Filmography: *Fidelio*, TV, 88, CDN/USA, Pro Des.

GORRARA, Perri
DGC, ACCT. 35 Langley Ave., Toronto, ON M4K 1B4 (416)469-8154. Lynn Kinney, Credentials, (416)926-1507.
Type of Production and Credits: Th Film-Pro Des; TV Film-Pro Des.
Genres: Drama-Th&TV; Variety-TV; Children's-TV; Science Fiction-Th.
Biography: Born 1951, London, England. Graduate of Ontario College of Art, 80. Nominated for Genie, 80, for *The Brothers' Keeper*. Specializes in designing for futuristic and period films and TV productions. Production Designer for CBC feature, *I'll Never Get to Heaven*, currently in production.
Selected Filmography: *Psychic*, Th, 90, USA/CDN, Pro Des; *Clearcut*, Th, 90, CDN, Pro Des; "Avonlea", TV, 89-90, CDN/USA, Art Dir; *The Last Winter*, Th, 89, CDN, Pro Des; *Millennium*, Th, 88, CDN, Assist Art Dir; "Sharon, Lois and Bram's Elephant Show" (39 eps), TV, 85-88, CDN, Art Dir; *Here Comes the Bride*, TV, 87, USA, Art Dir; *Glory Enough for All* (mini-series), TV, 87, CDN/GB, Art Dir, (GEMINI); *Arrest the Book*, TV, 86,

USA, Art Dir; "The Prodigious Hickey" (1 eps), TV, 86, CDN/USA, Art Dir; *Try, Try Again*, TV, 86, CDN, Art Dir; "Rockit Records" (pilot), TV, 86, CDN, Art Dir; *Miles to Go*, TV, 86, CDN, Assist Art Dir; *Tour of the Universe* (installation/environment and film), Th, 85, CDN, Art Dir; "Backstretch" (12 eps), TV, 85, CDN, Assist Art Dir.

HACKBORN, Robert
CUPE, DGC, TMA, ACCT. 219 Lord Seaton Rd., Willowdale, ON M2P 1L2 (416)225-2145. CBC, Box 500, Stn. A, Toronto, ON M5W 1E6 (416)975-7008.
Type of Production and Credits: TV Film-Art Dir; TV Video-Art Dir.
Genres: Drama-TV; Variety-TV; Musical-TV; Children's-TV.
Biography: Born 1928; Canadian citizen. Graduate of Ontario College of Art, Toronto. Has developed and used in-camera (film) glass matte shots and other special visual effects. Lectures at York University and Ryerson Polytechnical Institute, Toronto, Ontario.
Selected Filmography: "The Valour and the Horror" (3 eps), TV, 90, CDN, Art Dir; *The Killing Grounds*, TV, 88, CDN, Art Dir; "Inside Stories" (6 eps), TV, 88, CDN, Art Dir; "The King Chronicle" (3 eps), TV, 88, CDN, Pro Des; *Canadian Brass*, TV, 86, CDN, Art Dir/VFX Des; *Twelfth Night*, TV, 85, CDN, Art Dir; *Canada's Sweetheart: The Saga of Hal C. Banks*, TV, 85, CDN, Art Dir; "Fraggle Rock" (31 eps), TV, 84-85, CDN, Art Dir; *Rich Little's Robin Hood*, TV, 82, CDN, Art Dir; "I Married the Klondike" (6 eps), TV, 81, CDN, VFX Des; "Royal Canadian Air Farce" (8 eps), TV, 80, CDN, Art Dir; "Music of Man" (1 eps), TV, 78, CDN, Art Dir; "The Great Detective" (1 eps), TV, 77, CDN, Art Dir; *The Dumbells*, TV, 76, CDN, Art Dir; *Paradise Lost*, TV, 75, CDN, Art Dir.

HALINSKI, Andrzej
DGC, USA 829, SFP. 614 Indian Rd., Toronto, ON M6P 2C6 (416)604-8592. Lynn Kinney/Credentials, 386 Bloor St. E., Ste. 500, Toronto, ON M4W 1H7 (416)926-1507.
Type of Production and Credits: Th Film-Pro Des/Art Dir; Th Short-Pro Des/Art Dir; TV Film-Pro Des/Art Dir.
Genres: Drama-Th&TV; Comedy-Th&TV; Action-Th&TV; Science Fiction-Th.
Biography: Born in 1945 in Poland. Permanent resident of Canada. Languages: English, German, Polish, Russian. Education: Master of Architecture. Several awards including international film festivals in Cannes (1973), San Sebastian (1980), Locarno (1984). Other skills: architectural interior design and photography.
Selected Filmography: *Three Believers*, Th, 89, USA, Pro Des; *Pay Off*, Th, 87, USA/S, Pro Des; *The Young Magician*, Th, 86, CDN/PL, Art Dir; *The Deserters*, Th, 85, PL/H, Pro Des; *The Ninja Mission*, Th, 84, GB/S, Art Dir; *The Scribe*, Th, 84, PL, Pro Des; *Thais*, Th, 83, PL, Pro Des; *An Uninteresting Story*, Th, 82, PL, Pro Des; *The War of the Worlds*, Th, 81, PL, Pro Des; *The Salt Rose*, Th, 80, PL, CS, Pro Des; "Queen Bona" (12 eps), TV, 79, PL, Pro Des; "The Career of Nikodem Dyzma" (7 eps), TV, 78, PL, Pro Des; "Sherlock Holmes & Dr. Watson" (2 eps), TV, 78, USA/PL, Art Dir; "The Doll" (13 eps), TV, 77, PL, Art Dir; *The Hourglass*, Th, 73, PL, Art Dir.

HARVEY, Rolf
DGC. 23 Kenway Rd., Toronto, ON M8Z 4W7 (416)239-1747.
Type of Production and Credits: Th Film-Art Dir; TV Film-Art Dir; TV Video-Art Dir.
Genres: Drama-Th; Comedy-TV; Science Fiction-Th&TV; Horror-Th; Children's-Th.
Biography: Born 1947, St. Thomas, Ontario. Honours B.A., York University; B.Ed., Ontario Teacher Education College. Has published 5 books.
Selected Filmography: *Hidden Room*, TV, 91, USA, Art Dir; *A Fist, A Nail and Two Windows*, Th, 90, CDN, Pro Des; "War of the Worlds" (44 eps & pilot), Th, 88-90, CDN, Pro Des; "Adderly" (44 eps), TV, 86-88, CDN, Art Dir; *The Fly*, Th, 86, USA, Art Dir; *Agnes of God*, Th, 85, CDN, Assist Art Dir; "SCTV", TV, 84, CDN, Art Dir; *Follow That Bird*, Th, 84, USA, Assist Art Dir; *The Terry Fox Story*, TV, 82, CDN, Assist Art Dir; *If You Could See What I Hear*, Th, 82, CDN, Assist Art Dir; *Spasms*, Th, 81, CDN, Assist Art Dir; *Off Your Rocker*, Th, 79, CDN, Assist Art Dir.

HESLIP, Dale
- see DIRECTORS

HOLMES, Gerald
DGC. 46 Chine Dr., Scarborough, ON M1M 2K7 (416)264-4081.
Type of Production and Credits: Th Film-Art Dir; TV Film-Art Dir; TV Video-Art Dir.
Genres: Drama-Th&TV; Action-Th&TV; Science Fiction-Th.
Biography: Born 1935, London, England; Canadian citizenship. Graduate of

Campbell School of Art, London. Has worked as theatre stage manager in West End; entered Art Dept, Thames TV; also did set dressing and special effects for Hammer Films and Associated British Pathé. *The Fighter,* ("Night Heat") was nominated for Best Production Design, Geminis 87; "Counterstrike" was nominated for Outstanding Art Direction for a Series, Emmy 91.
Selected Filmography: "Top Cops" (26 eps), TV, 90-91, CDN/USA, Art Dir; "Counterstrike" (20 eps), TV, 90, CDN/USA/F, Pro Des; *Divided Loyalties,* TV, 89, CDN, Pro Des; "E.N.G." (pilot), TV, 89, CDN, Pro Des; *Passion and Paradise,* TV, 85-89, USA/CDN, Pro Des; "Night Heat" (90 eps), TV, 85-89, USA/CDN, Pro Des; "Diamonds" (22 eps), TV, 87-89, CDN, Pro Des; *Letting Go,* TV, 85, USA, Art Dir; *Starcrossed,* TV, 84, USA, Art Dir; *Reckless Disregard,* TV, 84, USA, Art Dir; "The Littlest Hobo" (72 eps), TV, 81-84, CDN, Art Dir; "Matt and Jennie" (26 eps), TV, 79, CDN, Art Dir; *The Shape of Things to Come,* Th, 78, CDN, Pro Des; *Shoot,* Th, 77, USA, Art Dir; *Goldenrod,* Th, 76, CDN, Art Dir.

HUDOLIN, Richard
DGC, IATSE 210, IATSE 891. 2220 Nelson Ave., West Vancouver, BC V7V 2P8 (604)925-3773.
Type of Production and Credits: Th Film-Art Dir/Prod Des; TV Film-Prod Des/Art Dir; TV Video-Prod Des/Art Dir.
Genres: Drama-Th&TV; Action-Th&TV; Variety-TV; Comedy-Th&TV.
Biography: Born Thunder Bay, Ontario. Attended Ontario College of Art. Ampia Award for art direction for *The Hounds of Notre Dame*; Honourable Mention for *Loyalties*; Genie nomination for *Latitude 55*.
Selected Filmography: *Yes, Virginia, There is a Santa Claus,* TV, 91, USA, Pro Des; "Scene of the Crime" (11 eps), TV, 90-91, USA/F, Pro Des; *K-2,* Th, 90, USA/GB, Art Dir; *Bird on a Wire,* Th, 90, USA, Art Dir; "Dracula: The Series" (pilot), TV, 90, CDN/L, Art Dir; *Speed Zone,* Th, 88, USA /CDN, Pro Des; *Dead Bang,* Th, 88, USA, Art Dir; *Christmas Comes to Willow Creek,* TV, 87, USA, Pro Des; *Stakeout,* Th, 87, USA, Art Dir; *I'll Take Manhattan* (mini-series), TV, 86, USA, Art Dir; *Vanishing Act,* TV, 86, USA, Art Dir; *Hyper-Sapien,* Th, 85, USA, Art Dir; *Loyalties,* Th, 85, CDN/GB, Pro Des; *Latitude 55,* Th, 80, CDN, Pro Des; *Superman III,* Th, 83, USA/GB, Assist Art Dir.

JOBIN, Louise
- voir COSTUMES

JOLY, Jocelyn
ACCT. 4287, Esplanade, Montréal, PQ H2W 1T1 (514)845-2617.
Types de production et générique: l métrage-Dir art/Pro Des; c métrage-Dir art; TV film-Dir art/Pro Des.
Types d'oeuvres: Drame-C&TV; Comédie musicale-C; Science-fiction-C&TV; Enfants-C.
Curriculum vitae: Née en 1940, Sorel, Québec. Langues: français et anglais. Education: Beaux arts, 3 ans. Genie, *Maria Chapdelaine,* 84; CFA, *L'Age de la Machine,* 78.
Filmographie sélective: "Les Filles de Caleb" (20 eps), TV, 90-91, CDN, Décor; *La peau et les os,* C, 87, CDN, Dir art; *Vive Québec,* C, 87, CDN, Dir art; *The Broken Vow,* C, 86, USA, Pro des; *La Ligne de chaleur,* C, 86, CDN, Dir art; *Toby McTeague,* C, 85, CDN, Pro des; *La Guêpe,* C, 85, CDN, Dir art; *Secret Weapons,* TV, 84, USA, Pro des; "The Hitchhiker" (10 eps), TV, 84, USA, Pro des; *Le Crime d'Ovide Plouffe* (aussi 6 ém-TV), C, 83, CDN/F, Dir art; *Maria Chapdelaine,* C, 82, CDN/F, Dir art, (GENIE); "Les Fils de la liberté" (5 eps), TV, 80-81, CDN/F, Dir art; *Fantastica,* C, 79, CDN/F, Dir art; *Final Assignment,* C, 79, CDN, Pro des; *L'Age de la machine,* C, 78, CDN, Dir art, (CFA).

JOY, Michael
DGC, ADC, ACCT. 3997 St. Dominique, Montreal, PQ H2W 2A4 (514)288-7648. 2439-9719 Que Inc., 3955 St. Laurent Blvd., Montreal, PQ H2W 1Y4 (514)844-4856.
Type of Production and Credits: Th Film-Art Dir; Th Short-Art Dir; TV Film-Pro Des; TV Video-Art Dir.
Genres: Drama-Th&TV; Comedy-Th&TV.
Biography: Born 1955, Montreal, Quebec. Languages: English and French. Attended National Theatre School; received Koerner Foundation Grant for studies at NTS; widely travelled; former executive, Associated Designers of Canada; former Assist Head of Design, National Theatre School with extensive theatre design career; Designer, Exhibit "Transports Burlesques", Cités-Cinés, Montreal, 90. Has worked on commercials and rock videos. Award at Yorkton and Hugo award.
Selected Filmography: *Scanners III,* Th, 90, CDN, Pro Des; *The Quarrel,* Th, 90, CDN/USA, Pro Des; *Here Comes the*

Groom, "Inside Story", TV, 90, CDN, Art Dir; *Oui, Allo...Estelle?*, TV, 88, CDN, Art Dir; *Liberace: Behind the Music*, TV, 88, USA/CDN, Art Dir; "Shades of Love" (14 eps), TV, 86-87, CDN, Pro Des; *First Offender*, TV, 86, USA, Art Dir; "Northern Lights" (6 eps), TV, 85, CDN, Art Dir; *Earthwatch*, Th, 85, CDN, Art Dir.

KEYWAN, Alicia
DGC. 13 Castle View Ave., Toronto, ON M5R 1Z1 (416)324-9730.
Type of Production and Credits: Th Film-Art Dir; Th Short-Prod Des; TV Film-Prod Des; TV Video-Prod Des.
Genres: Drama-Th&TV; Comedy-Th&TV; Musical-Th; Action-Th.
Biography: Born 1950. Graduated with B.E.S., B.Arch., University of Waterloo, Ontario and University of Illinois, Chicago. Arthur Erickson Architects, 1981-83. Received Canada Council Award for the Arts, 1984.
Selected Filmography: "Scales of Justice" (3 eps), TV, 91, CDN, Prod Des; *Unknown Parts*, Th, 91, USA, Art Dir; *Stepping Out*, Th, 90, USA, Art Dir; *The Freshman*, Th, 89, USA, Art Dir; *Stanley and Iris*, Th, 88, USA, Art Dir; *Dead Ringers*, Th, 88, CDN, Spv Art Dir; *Short Circuit II*, Th, 87, USA, Art Dir; *Conspiracy of Love*, TV, 87, USA, Prod Des; *Dead of Winter*, Th, 86, USA, Art Dir; *Bradbury Theatre II*, Th, 85, USA/CDN, Prod Des; *Le Premier Choix*, ED, 85, CDN, Des; *Youngblood*, Th, 84, USA, Art Dir; *Silence of the North*, Th, 80, CDN, Art Dir.

KROEGER, Wolf ◊
David Gersh, The Gersh Agency, 232 N. Canon Dr., Suite 201, Beverly Hills, CA 90210 USA. (213)274-6611.
Type of Production and Credits: Th Film-Art Dir/Pro Des; TV Film-Pro Des.
Genres: Drama-Th&TV; Comedy-Th; Action-Th.
Selected Filmography: *The Sicilian*, Th, 86, USA, Pro Des; *Ladyhawke*, Th, 85, USA, Pro Des; *Year of the Dragon*, Th, 84, USA, Co-Prod Des; *Streamers*, Th, 83, USA, Pro Des; *The Bay Boy*, Th, 83, CDN/F, Art Dir; *First Blood*, Th, 82, USA, Pro Des; *Split Image*, Th, 82, USA, Pro Des; *Popeye*, Th, 80, USA, Pro Des; *Health*, Th, 80, USA, Pro Des; *Quintet*, Th, 79, USA, Pro Des; *The Execution of Private Slovik*, TV, 74, USA, Pro Des.

KUPER, Jack
- see DIRECTORS

LEBRUN, Luc
(613)832-2439
Type of Production and Credits: TV Video-Art Dir.
Genres: Drama-TV; Variety-TV; Musical-TV; Current Affairs-TV.
Biography: Born 1953, Ottawa, Ontario. Languages: English and French. Studied Visual Arts, Sheridan College, Toronto. Production designer for television since 70s.
Selected Filmography: *National Access Awareness Week Gala*, TV, 88, CDN, Des; *Handel's Messiah*, TV, 87, CDN, Pro Des; *Children's Miracle Network Telethon*, TV, 87, CDN, Des; *Master Peter's Puppet Show*, TV, 86, CDN/GB, Pro Des; *Inter-parliamentary Union Gala*, TV, 85, CDN, Pro Des; *Grand Pianos*, TV, 85, CDN, Pro Des; *HDTV Colloquium*, In, 85, CDN/USA/J/GB, Art Dir; "Rock Wars" (3 eps), TV, 85, CDN, Pro Des; *Jon Vickers*, TV, 84, CDN, Pro Des; "Fame Game" (3 eps), TV, 84, CDN, Pro Des; "Lawyers" (5 eps), TV, 84, CDN, Pro Des; *Symphony of a Thousand*, TV, 83, CDN, Pro Des; "Pulsion" (25 eps), TV, 76-80, CDN, Pro Des; "Café Hibou" (15 eps), TV, 78-80, CDN, Pro Des; "Today from Ontario" (30 eps), TV, 79-80, CDN, Pro Des.

LECLERC, Catherine
ACCT. 2715 Pl. des Sarcelles, Laval, PQ H7L 3R2 (514)622-0037. Télé-Metropole Inc., 1600 est boul. de Maisonneuve, Montréal, PQ (514)526-9251.
Types de production et générique: TV vidéo-Dir art.
Types d'oeuvres: Drame-TV; Comédie-TV; Variété-TV; Affaires Publiques-TV.
Curriculum vitae: Née en 1944 à Shawinigan. Langues: français, anglais et espagnol. Diplômée en 1964 de l'Institut des Arts Appliqués, option décoration d'intérieur. Au service de Télé-Métropole depuis 1969.
Filmographie sélective: *Dans Le Décor*, TV, 91, CDN, Décor; *Le Gala Métrostar*, TV, 91, CDN, Décor; "D'Amour & D'Amitié" (30 eps), TV, 90, CDN, Décor; *Gala Métrostar*, TV, 90, CDN, Décor; *Bien Dans Sa Peau*, TV, 89, CDN, Décor; "Chop Suey" (60 eps), TV, 87, CDN, Décor; *Casse-Tête*, TV, 86, CDN, Décor; "R.S.V.P." (66 eps), TV, 85, CDN, Décor; *Gala Des 10 Femmes De L'Année*, TV, 85, CDN, Décor; "L'Ame Soeur" (33 eps), TV, 85, CDN, Décor; "Belle-Rive" (33 eps), TV, 83, CDN, Décor; *La Printanous*, TV, 82, CDN, Décor; "Toulouse-Extra" (8 eps), TV, 80, CDN, Décor; "Marisol" (60 eps), TV, 79, CDN, Décor; *Spécial Gilles Villeneuve*, TV, 79, CDN, Décor.

LEE, Judith
ADC, ACCT. Straight Lines Designs, 851 Richmond St. W., Toronto, ON M6J 1E2 (416)368-0851. FAX: 368-1839.
Type of Production and Credits: Th Film-Art Dir; TV Video-Pro Des/Art Dir.
Genres: Variety-TV; Musical-TV; Children's-TV; Commercials-TV.
Biography: Born 1952, Montreal, Quebec. Languages: English and working knowledge of French. B.A., Drama, University of Guelph; Special Studies in Theatre and Television Design, Wimbledon School of Art, London. Designed sets and costumes for more than 40 theatre, dance and opera productions at major theatres across Canada. Received Tyrone Guthrie Award and Dora Mavor Moore Award, Best Set Design, for *Pumpboys & Dinettes*.
Selected Filmography: *Anne Murray in Disney World*, TV, 91, CDN/USA, Pro Des; *George Fox's New Country*, TV, 90, CDN, Pro Des; *Anne Murray's Greatest Hits Vol. II*, TV, 89, CDN, Pro Des; *k.d. lang's Buffalo Café*, TV, 89, CDN, Pro Des; *Anne Murray's Family Christmas*, TV, 88, CDN, Pro Des; *Casby Rock Show*, TV, 87, CDN, Pro Des; *Toronto Arts Awards*, TV, 86, CDN, Art Dir; *Ian & Sylvia Reunion*, TV, 86, CDN, Art Dir; *Casby Music Awards*, TV, 86, CDN, Art Dir; "Vid Kids II" (13 eps), TV, 86, CDN, Art Dir; *Casby Music Awards*, TV, 85, CDN, Art Dir; "Let's Make a Deal" (96 eps), TV, 81, CDN/USA, Art Dir; "Tom Jones Show" (12 eps), TV, 81, CDN/USA, Assist Art Dir; *Loose Screws*, Th, 84, CDN, Art Dir.

LONGMIRE, Susan
DGC, ACCT. 66 Hampton Ave., Toronto, ON M4K 2Y6 (416)465-2619.
Type of Production and Credits: Th Film-Art Dir/Pro Des; TV Film-Art Dir/Pro Des; TV Video-Art Dir.
Genres: Drama-Th&TV; Comedy-Th; Horror-Th; Children's-TV; Commercials-TV.
Biography: Born 1943, Kingston, Ontario. B.A., Fine Art (art history), University of Toronto. Former scenic artist; film and theatre set designer in England and Canada; 15 years experience in most art department categories for film and TV.
Selected Filmography: "The Hitchhiker" (9 eps), TV, 90, CDN/USA, Art Dir; "The Magic Hour" (4 eps), TV, 89, CDN, Art Dir; *Firing Squad*, TV, 89, CDN/F, Art Dir; "The Twilight Zone" (30 eps), TV, 88, CDN/USA, Art Dir; *Captain Power and the Soldiers of the Future*, TV, 87, CDN, Art Dir; *Anne of Green Gables - The Sequel* (mini-series), TV, 86, CDN, Art Dir, (GEMINI 88); *Hugga Mugga Max*, Cm, 86, CDN, Set Des; *Pippi Longstocking* (2 parts), TV, 85, USA, Pro Des; "Sharon, Lois and Bram's Elephant Show" (13 eps), TV, 85, CDN, Art Dir; "SCTV" (8 eps), TV, 85, CDN, Set Des; *Incubus*, Th, 81, CDN, Art Dir; *Ticket to Heaven*, Th, 80, CDN, Pro Des; *Cries in the Night*, Th, 80, CDN, Art Dir; *Silence of the North*, Th, 79, CDN, Co-Art Dir; *Running*, Th, 78, CDN, Art Dir.

MACKAY, David
- see PRODUCERS

MAJOR, Pierre
ACCT. 3105, Somerset, St-Laurent, PQ H4K 1R7 (514)332-1707. FAX: 332-2169.
Types de production et générique: TV film-Dir art/Décor; TV vidéo-Dir art/Décor.
Types d'oeuvres: Drame-TV; Comédie-TV; Variété-TV.
Curriculum vitae: Né en 1942, Montréal, Québec. Langues: français et anglais. Diplôme en design, l'Institut des arts appliqués, 64. 25 ans au service de la Scénographide Radio-Canada, Montréal. A remporté plusieurs prix pour les décors.
Filmographie sélective: *Bye Bye 90*, TV, 90, CDN, Des/Décor, (ANIK); *Gala des Prix Gémeaux 90*, TV, 90, CDN, Décor; *Gala de la Presse 90*, TV, 90, CDN, Décor; *Bye Bye 89*, TV, 89, CDN, Des; *La Vie d'Artiste/Gala de l'Union des Artistes*, TV, 88, CDN, Décor; "L'Autobus du Show Business" (35 eps), TV, 88, CDN, Décor; *Top Secret*, "Les Beaux Dimanches", TV, 87, CDN, Décor, (FELIX); *Genie en Herbe*, TV, 87, CDN, Décor; *Follement Vôtre*, "Les Beaux Dimanches", TV, 86, CDN, Décor, (GEMEAUX); *Bye Bye 86*, TV, 86, CDN, Décor, (GEMEAUX); *Silence en Chante*, TV, 86, CDN, Décor; *La Celeste Bicyclette*, TV, 83, CDN, Décor.

MANDALIAN, Joseph
ACCT. 205 Brookfield, V. Mont-Royal, PQ H3P 2A5 (514)731-2309. Société Radio-Canada, 1400 est, boul. René-Lévesque, Montréal, PQ H2L 2M2 (514)597-6215.
Types de production et générique: l métrage-Dir art; TV film-Dir art.
Types d'oeuvres: Drame-C&TV; Comédie-C&TV; Science-fiction-C&TV; Annonces-C&TV.
Curriculum vitae: Né en 1936. Langues: français et anglais. Diplôme, Décors, Théâtre, Ecole des Beaux-Arts de Rome,

62; Décors, Cinéma, Centro Sperimentale di Cinematografia, Cinecittà, Rome. A travaillé comme designer à l'Expo 67 pour le Pavillon canadien; en 66, entré à Radio-Canada ou il travaille depuis lors; a travaillé au cinéma italien et comme peintre à une douzaine d'expositions de peinture à son actif.
Filmographie sélective: "Cormoran" (78 eps), TV, 90-91, CDN, Décor; "Le Par des braves" (145 eps), TV, 84-88, CDN, Des; *Comment acheter son patron*, TV, 85, CDN, Des; *La Pépinière*, TV, 83, CDN, Des; *Les Grandes Marées*, TV, 81, CDN, Des; *Referendum 80*, TV, 80, CDN, Des; *Les Jeunes Délinquants*, TV, 79, CDN, Des; "Grand Papa" (116 eps), TV, 76-79, CDN, Des; *Fermer l'oeil de la nuit*, TV, 79, CDN, Des; *L'Autonomie*, TV, 78, CDN, Des; "La Petite Semaine" (36 eps), TV, 74-75, CDN, Des; "Quelle Famille" (36 eps), TV, 74-75, CDN, Des.

MARSOLAIS, Michel
STCQ, ACCT. 3535, Papineau, #911, Montréal, PQ H2K 4J9 (514)525-8957. Spectel-Vidéo, 355 ouest, Ste. Catherine, Suite 305, Montréal, PQ H3B 1A5 (514)288-5363.
Types de production et générique: l métrage-Décor; c métrage-Dir art; TV film-Dir art; TV vidéo-Dir art.
Types d'oeuvres: Drame-C&TV; Comédie-C&TV; Action-TV; Enfants-C&TV.
Curriculum vitae: Né en 1949, Montréal, Québec. Langues: français et anglais. Baccalauréat en art plastique; 2 ans d'études, architecture et architecture scénique, Université McGill et l'Université de Montréal; 3 ans, base scénique en théâtre et spectacles musicales, Place des Arts, Montréal. Président du Studio 703 inc.

MATIS, Barbra
DGC, USA 829. 80 Quebec Ave., #207, Toronto, ON M6P 4B7 (416) 762-0148. Designers Touch Inc., 222 Riverside Dr., 2D, New York, NY 10025 USA (212) 865-0239.
Types of Production and Credits: Th Film-Pro Des/Art Dir.
Genres: Drama-Th&TV; Comedy-Th&TV; Commercials-TV.
Biography: Born 1952, Montreal, Quebec. Canadian citizenship; US resident. Languages: English and French. Design graduate, National Theatre School, 73. Has designed sets and costumes for over 100 shows for various theatres across Canada since 72. Experience includes several years as scenic artist and costume cutter. Recipient of 1981 Dora Mavor Moore Award for stage production of *Balconville*.
Selected Filmography: *This Is My Life*, Th, 91, USA, Art Dir; *New Jack City*, Th, 90, USA, Art Dir; "Road to Avonlea," TV, 89, CDN, Set Des; *Shadow Dancing*, Th, 88, CDN, Pro Des' "The Lawrenceville Stories" (2 eps), TV, 87, CDN/USA, Art Dir; *Moonstruck*, Th, 86, USA, Art Dir; *Children of a Lesser God*, Th, 85, USA, Art Dir; "Max Haines' Crime Flashback" (1 eps), TV, 86, CDN, Cos; *Balconville*, TV, 86, CDN, Pro Des.

McCROW, William ◊
(715) 369-1565
Type of Production and Credits: Th Film-Art Dir/Pro Des; Th Short-Art Dir; TV Film-Art Dir/Pro Des; TV Video-Art Dir.
Genres: Drama-Th&TV; Comedy-Th&TV; Musical-Th&TV; Science Fiction-Th&TV.
Biography: Born 1912, Princeton, Ontario. Languages: English, French, German. Associate, Ontario College of Art, Painting and Design; won the Lieutenant Governor's Medal at graduation. His architectural credits include Windrush Project, Kleinberg; Graphic Associates' Studio; many private residences. First Director of Design, CBC TV, Toronto, 51-54; Art Director, Production Designer, CBC, 55-61; Telefis, Eireann, Dublin, Eire (also Theatre Designer), 61-64; BBC 1, BBC 2, ABC TV, Associated Rediffusion (now London Weekend), London, 64-68. Has worked on features in Canada and Europe.
Selected Filmography: *Les Plouffe*, Th, 80, CDN, Pro Des, (GENIE); *Kings and Desperate Men*, Th, 79, CDN, Pro Des; *City on Fire*, Th, 78, CDN/USA, Pro Des; "The Newcomers" (3 eps), TV, 77, CDN, Pro Des; *The Third Walker*, Th, 77, CDN/USA, Pro Des; *The Squeeze*, Th, 76, CDN, Pro Des; *Operation Daybreak*, Th, 74-75, GB/CS, Pro Des; *Legend of the Christmas Messenger*, TV, 74, CDN, Pro Des; *Dracula*, Th, 74, GB, Art Dir; *Home*, TV, 73, GB, Art Dir; *Family Life*, Th, 71, GB, Art Dir; *Running Scared*, Th, 71, GB, Art Dir; *Unman, Wittering and Zigo*, Th, 70, GB, Art Dir; *The Body*, Th, 69, GB, Art Dir; *Kes*, Th, 68, GB, Art Dir.

MITCHELL, Gavin
DGC, ACCT. 224 Crawford St., Toronto, ON M6J 2V6 (416)536-1550.
Type of Production and Credits: TV Film-Pro Des; Th Film-Pro Des; TV Video-Pro Des.

Genres: Drama-Th&TV; Comedy-Th&TV; Commercials-TV.
Biography: Born in Perth, Scotland; Canadian citizenship. Member, Canadian Owners and Pilots Association, Seaplane Pilots Association, Aerobatics Canada; PADI dive certified. More than 20 years experience in film and television.
Selected Filmography: "The Hidden Room", TV, 91, CDN/USA, Pro Des; *Black Robe*, Th, 90, CDN/USA, Art Dir; "War of the Worlds" (44 eps), TV, 88, USA, Pro Des; "Adderly" (44 eps), TV, 86-88, CDN, Pro Des.

NOONAN, Donna
DGC, STCQ. 155 - 52nd Ave., Lachine, PQ H8T 2X1 (514)639-1079.
Type of Production and Credits: Th Film-Art Dir; TV Film-Art Dir.
Genres: Drama-Th&TV; Action-Th; Horror-Th; Commercials-TV; Industrial-TV; Music Video-Th&TV.
Biography: Born of Cree, Ojibway, Irish descent in Northern Ontario, 1955. Received B.F.A. (cum laude) from Concordia University, 79, majoring in Theatre Scenography. Since 1979, has worked professionally in film starting as a prop maker; became an art director in 1989. Active with native organizations; served three years as President of the Native Friendship Centre of Montreal and currently serves as a Director of the Society of Canadian Artists of Native Ancestry. Consultant on native art for *Black Robe*.
Selected Filmography: *King's Ransom*, Th, 91, CDN/F, Chief Dec; *Whispers*, Th, 89, CDN, Art Dir; *Princes in Exile*, TV, 89, CDN, Art Dir; *Ghost Town*, Cheap Trick, MV, 89, GB, Art Dir; "Shades of Love" (8 eps), TV, 87-88, CDN/US, Art Dept Coord/Props; *Choices*, TV, 86, CDN/US, Props; *Domino Tags*, CN, In, 90, CDN, Art Dir; *Handling Dangerous Commodities*, CN, In, 89, CDN, Art Dir; *Cool Customer*, CN, In, 88, CDN, Art Dir; *Expo '86*, CN, In, 86, CDN, Art Dir.

O'DELL, Dean A.
DGC, CSC, ACCT. 42 Hudson Cres., Bradford, ON L3Z 2J6 (416)775-9455. (416)775-9449.
Type of Production and Credits: Th Film-Prod/Art Dir; Th Short-Prod/Art Dir; TV Film-Prod/Art Dir; TV Video-Prod/Art Dir.
Genres: Drama-Th&TV; Comedy-Th&TV; Variety-TV; Commercials-TV.
Biography: Born 1955, St. Thomas, Ontario. Studied Graphics/Illustration, Sheridan College; University of Western Ontario, Applied Arts Program; B.A.A., Motion Picture Studies, Ryerson Polytechnical Institute. Cinematographer/DOP/Operator. Has worked on many commercials. Winner of Bessie Award.
Selected Filmography: *The Roman Line*, Th, 91, CDN, Prod/Wr/Dir; *Married to It*, Th, 90, USA, Assist Art Dir; "Kids in the Hall" (20 eps), TV, 89, CDN, Art Dir; "Jim Henson Hour" (9 eps), TV, 88, CDN, Art Dir; *Genie Awards*, TV, 88, CDN, Assist Set Des; *Horse Racing Series* (8 eps), TV, 88, CDN, Art Dir; *Gemini Awards*, TV, 87, CDN, Assist Set Des; *Canadian Masters' Snooker*, TV, 87, CDN, Art Dir; "Marketplace", TV, 87, CDN, Assist Set Des; *Canadian Snooker Championships*, TV, 87, CDN, Art Dir; *The Light Keeper*, Th, 87, CDN, Prod/Wr/Dir; *The Road Not Taken*, Th, 86, CDN, Prod/Wr/Dir; *The Trainer*, Th, 86, CDN, Prod/Wr/Dir; television commercials (over 30), TV, 85, CDN, Art Dir.

OUELLETTE, Réal
STCQ. 4130, Drolet, Montréal, PQ H2W 2L4 (514)843-8291.
Types de production et générique: l métrage-Dir art; c métrage-Dir art; TV film-Dir art.
Types d'oeuvres: Drame-C&TV; Comédie-C&TV; Comédie musicale-C; Action-C.
Curriculum vitae: Né en 1943, Trois-Rivières, Québec. Langues: français et anglais. Education: Ecole Nationale de Théâtre. A fait les décors et les costumes d'une quarantaine de pièces de théâtre; enseigne décors et costumes de théâtre au niveau de Cégep et à l'Ecole Nationale de Théâtre.
Filmographie sélective: *Une Histoire Inventée*, C, 89, CDN, Dir art; "Day One" (6 eps), TV, 88, CDN, Décor; *Les Tisserands du pouvoir* (2 films/6 ém TV), C, 87, CDN/F, Dir art; *The Great Land of Small*, Th, 86, CDN, Décor; *Le Matou* (aussi 6 ém TV), C, 85, CDN/F/I, Décor; *Breaking All the Rules*, C, 84, CDN, Décor; *Caravane*, C, 82, CDN, Décor; *Massabielle*, C, 81, CDN, Dir art; *Les Plouffe* (aussi 6 ém TV), C, 80, CDN, Chef décor; *Hey Babe!*, C, 79, CDN, Dir art; *Final Assignment*, C, 79, CDN, Décor; *La Cuisine rouge*, C, 79, CDN, Dir art; *Night Flight*, C, 78, CDN, Décor; *L'Eau chaude l'eau frette*, C, 75, CDN, Décor; *The Apprenticeship of Duddy Kravitz*, C, 73, CDN, Décor.

PARCHER, Milton
Production Design, 419 St. Clair Ave. E.,

Toronto, ON M4T 1P6 (416)482-1994.
Type of Production and Credits: Th Film-Art Dir; TV Film-Art Dir; TV Video-Art Dir.
Genres: Drama-Th&TV; Variety-TV; Action-TV; Children's-TV.
Biography: Born 1940, Canada. Has worked in TV since 63 as Graphics and Set Designer, Art Director and Production Designer; comprehensive knowledge of Ultimatte and Glass shots.
Selected Filmography: "Seeing Things" (15 eps), TV, 85-86, CDN, Art Dir; Doritos/Arctic Power, Cm, 86, CDN, Set Des; Blue Cross/Eastern Airlines, Cm, 85-86, USA, Set Des; *Love and Larceny*, TV, 84, CDN, Art Dir; "Venture", TV, 84, CDN, Des; *L.A. Olympics*, TV, 84, CDN, Set Des; *Gentle Sinners*, TV, 83, CDN, Art Dir; *Magic Planet*, TV, 83, CDN, Set Des; *Juno Awards*, TV, 83, CDN, Art Dir; *Meeting Place*, TV, 83, CDN, Set Des; *A Far Cry from Home/By Reason of Insanity/P-1*, "For the Record", TV, 80-82, CDN, Art Dir; "Canada Confidential" (2 eps), TV, 81, CDN, Art Dir; "The Great Detective" (2 eps), TV, 81, CDN, Art Dir; *Strawberry Ice*, TV, 81, CDN, Pro Des, (ANIK); *The Wordsmith*, TV, 78, CDN, Art Dir, (GENIE).

PARIS, Richard
DGC. 39 Allen Ave., Toronto, ON M4M 1T5 (416)462-9252.
Genres: Drama-Th&TV; Comedy-Th& TV; Commercials-TV.
Biography: Born in Kitchener, Ontario. Canadian citizen. Attended the Ontario College of Art, continuing education at UCLA (Los Angeles) Filmmaking & Screenwriting. Began career as Illustrator/ Creative Director and with still shoots. Published author, screenwriter. Co-founder of Paris Del Rosario Productions, 1990. Co-Production Designer of two official selections at the Cannes Film Festival 1991, *The Adjuster* and *Sam and Me*.
Selected Filmography: *Vue D'Ailleurs, Montreal Vue Par*, Th, 91, CDN, Co Prod Des/Set Dec; *The Adjuster*, Th, 90, CDN, Co Prod Des/Set Dec; *Sam and Me*, Th, 90, CDN, Co Prod Des/Set Dec; *Lady In a Corner*, TV, 89, USA, Assist Set Dec; *Beautiful Dreamers*, Th, 89, CDN, Assist Set Dec; *Brown Bread Sandwiches*, Th, 89, CDN/I, Assist Set Dec; *When Gravity Fails*, CDN, Des Cnslt/Set Dec; *Speaking Parts*, Th, 88, CDN, 1st Art Set/Props Coord.

PHILLIPS, Jim
2241 Pasqua St., Regina, SK S4T 4M5 (306)525-8297. Ideo Forma Design, PO Box 463, Regina, SK S4P 3A2 (306)525-1432.
Type of Production and Credits: TV Film-Art Dir/PM; TV Video-Art Dir/PM.
Genres: Drama-TV; Educational-TV; Commercials-TV.
Biography: Born 1952, Medicine Hat, Alberta; grew up in Regina, Saskatchewan. Studied Fine Arts at the University of Regina. 2 years travel in Europe, Asia and Africa. Became a journeyman carpenter and ran a construction business. Studied furniture design at Sheridan College in Toronto and industrial design and photo-electric arts at the Ontario College of Art. Was a production manager and designer for a Regina furniture manufacturer before working in film and video.
Selected Filmography: *Healthy Living Goals*, Cm, 91, CDN, Art Dir; *Buy Saskatchewan*, ED, 91, CDN, Art Dir; *Max Smart*, Saskatchewan Tourism (5 spots), Cm, 91, CDN, Art Dir; *Home on the Range*, "Inside Stories", TV, 90, CDN, Art Dir; *The Garden*, TV, 90, CDN, Set Dec; *Reflections in a Prairie Slough*, ED, 90, CDN, Set Dec; *Community Bonds*, ED, 90, CDN, PM; *The Heart of Christmas*, TV, 90, CDN, Set Dec/2nd Unit PM.

PRESTON, Earl
DGC. P.O. Box 450, Mont Tremblant, PQ J0T 1Z0 (819)425-7458.
Type of Production and Credits: Th Film-Art Dir/Pro Des; TV Film-Art Dir/Pro Des.
Genres: Drama-Th&TV.
Biography: Born 1926, Buffalo, New York; Canadian citizenship. Attended University of Toronto and Ontario College of Art. Theatre Set Designer in London (England), Toronto, Montreal. Set Designer, Variety/Drama, CBC TV, Toronto, 55-56; Art Director, Studio Manager, NFB, 56-58; freelance since 69. Artist (serigraph, lithography, painting, drawing); has taken part in many group exhibitions; member, Print and Drawing Council of Canada, Conseil Québécois de l'Estampe.
Selected Filmography: *The Jeweller's Shop*, Th, 87, I/CDN, Pro Des; *John and the Missus*, Th, 86, CDN, Pro Des/Art Dir; *Alex, the Life of a Child*, TV, 85, USA, Art Dir; *Happy Birthday to Me*, Th, 80, CDN, Pro Des; *Dirty Tricks*, Th, 79, CDN, Art Dir; *L'Homme en colère*, Th, 78, CDN/F, Art Dir; *Revolution's Orphan*, TV, 78, CDN, Pro Des; *The Black Stallion*, Th, 78, USA, Co-Art Dir; *The War Is Over*, Th, 77, CDN, Pro Des; *War Between the Tates*,

TV, 76, USA, Pro Des; *Shoot*, Th, 75, CDN, Art Dir; *Why Rock the Boat?*, Th, 74, CDN, Pro Des; *The Pyx*, Th, 72, CDN, Art Dir; *Fortune and Men's Eyes*, Th, 71, USA, Art Dir.

PRITCHARD, Anne
DGC, ACCT. 3629 ave. Laval, Montreal, PQ H2X 3E1 (514)288-3999.
Type of Production and Credits: Th Film-Pro Des/Cos.
Genres: Drama-Th.
Selected Filmography: *L'Emprise*, TV, CDN, Pro Des; "L'Or et le Papier" (13 eps), TV, CDN/F, Pro Des; *Dead Man*, TV, USA, Pro Des; *Descending Angel*, TV, USA, Pro Des; *Nénette*, TV, CDN, Pro Des; *Perfectly Normal*, Th, CDN, Pro Des; *Switching Channels*, Th, 87, USA, Pro Des; *Les Portes tournantes*, Th, 87, CDN/F, Pro Des; *Unnatural Causes*, TV, 86, USA, Pro Des; *Miles to Go*, TV, 86, USA, Pro Des; *Time to Live*, TV, 85, USA, Pro Des; *Joshua Then and Now*, Th, 84, CDN, Pro Des, (GENIE 86); *Atlantic City*, Th, 79, CDN/F, Pro Des, (GENIE); *Fantastica*, Th, 79, CDN/F, Cos, (GENIE); *The Far Shore*, Th, 75, CDN, Pro Des, (CFA); *The Act of the Heart*, Th, 69, CDN, Pro Des/Cos, (CFA).

RIDOLFI, Paola
STCVG, IATSE, DGC. P.O. Box 66, Westmount, PQ H3Z 2T1 (514)937-8788. P.O. Box 356, Prince Street Station, New York, NY 10012 (212)840-1234. Jennifer Lyne/The Gersh Agency, 130 W. 42nd St., New York, NY (212)997-1818.
Type of Production and Credits: Th Film-Pro Des/Art Dir; Th Short-Pro Des; TV Film-Pro Des/Art Dir; TV Video-Pro Des.
Genres: Drama-Th&TV; Action-Th&TV; Children's-Th&TV; Commercials-Th& TV; Music Video-Th&TV.
Biography: Born in 1953 in the US; Canadian and US citizenship. Languages: English, French and Japanese.
Selected Filmography: "The Babysitters Club" (7 eps), Th/TV, 90-91, USA, Pro Des; *Life in the Food Chain*, Th, 90, USA, Pro Des; *Whispers of White*, Th, 90, USA, Pro Des; *Getting Ready For Later*, Th, 90, USA, Pro Des; *The Jack Archer Story*, AT&T/Universal, In, 90, USA, Pro Des; *Seriously*, Phil Collins, MV, 90, USA, Art Dir; *Out of the Rain*, Th, 89, USA, Pro Des; "La misère des riches" (9 eps), TV, 89, CDN, Art Dir; *Religion Inc.*, Th, 88, USA, Pro Des; *Mortal Sins*, Th, 88, USA, Art Dir; *Python Wolf*, Th/TV, 87, USA/CDN, Art Dir; "Ben Casey", TV, 87, USA/CDN, Art Dir; *God Bless The Child*, TV, 86, CDN/USA, Art Dir.

ROBERTS, Rick
IATSE 212, IATSE 928. P.O. Box 4354, Stn. C, Calgary, AB T2T 5N2 (403)269-4041. 2R Design & Production, P.O. Box 4354, Stn. C, Calgary, AB T2T 5N2 (403)269-4041.
Type of Production and Credits: Th Film-Art Dir; TV Film-Art Dir; TV Video-Art Dir.
Genres: Drama-Th&TV; Action-Th&TV; Science Fiction-TV; Music Video-TV.
Biography: Born in 1949 in Saskatchewan. B.F.A, Drama, Univ. of Alberta, 73. Former theatrical designer, 15 years.
Selected Filmography: *Blood River*, TV, 90, USA, Art Dir; *Blood Clan*, Th, 90, CDN, Prod Des; *The Day It Rained*, "Ray Bradbury Theatre" (1 eps), TV, 90, CDN/USA, Art Dir; *The Reflecting Skin*, Th, 89, CDN/GB, Prod Des; *Trail of Broken Hearts*, k.d. lang, MV, 89, USA, Art Dir; *The Fourth War*, Th, 89, USA, Art Dir; *Primo Baby*, Th, 88, CDN, Prod Des; *Cops I & II*, "Knightwatch" (2 eps), TV, 88, USA, Art Dir; *Blindside*, Th, 86, CDN, Art Dir.

ROLOFF, Stephen
DGC, ACCT. 36 Lakeview Ave., Toronto, ON M6J 3B3 (416)536-1031.
Type of Production and Credits: TV Film-Prod Des.
Genres: Drama-TV; Comedy-TV; Horror-TV; Children's-TV.
Biography: Born in 1958, Montreal, Quebec. Languages: English, rusty French and erratic German. Education: Institute of Scenography, Certificate in Production Design & Art Direction; Queen's University, Hons B.Sc. Civil Engineering. Has travelled globally. Gemini award nominee for "Friday The 13th: The Series" and *A Child's Christmas in Wales*.
Selected Filmography: "Maniac Mansion", TV, 90, USA/CDN, Pro Des; "Friday The 13th: The Series" (72 eps), TV, 87-89, USA/CDN, Pro Des; *A Child's Christmas in Wales*, TV, 86, USA/CDN, Art Dir; "Vulcan" (pilot), TV, 86, CDN, Art Dir; *Walking On Air*, TV, 86, USA/CDN, Pro Des; *Heaven on Earth*, TV, 86, CDN, Art Dir; "Frontier/Company of Adventurers", TV, 85, CDN/GB/F, Art Dir.

ROSEMARIN, Hilton
IATSE 873, DGC, ACCT. Nuance Inc., 277 Crawford St., Toronto, ON M6J 2V7 (416)534-2548.

Type of Production and Credits: Th Film-Art Dir; Th Short-Art Dir; TV Film-Art Dir.
Genres: Drama-Th&TV; Comedy-Th&TV; Action-Th&TV; Commercials-Th&TV.
Biography: Born 1952, Montreal, Quebec. Languages: English and French. Diploma, Theatre, Cégep, Montreal; 2 years of Technical/Production, Ryerson Poly-technical Institute. Numerous theatre tours across Canada and US.
Selected Filmography: *Billy Bathgate*, Th, 90, USA, Dec; *Mermaids*, Th, 89, USA, Dec; *Everybody Wins*, Th, 89, USA, Dec; *The Good Mother*, Th, 88, USA, Art Dir; *Three Men and a Baby*, Th, 87, USA, Dec; *Cocktails*, Th, 87, USA, Dec; *Jimmy Reardon*, Th, 86, USA, Dec; *The Bedroom Window*, Th, 86, USA, Dec; *Raw Deal*, Th, 85, USA, Dec; *Maximum Overdrive*, Th, 85, USA, Dec; *Eleni*, Th, 85, USA/GB(Dec buyer, Cdn seg); *Silver Bullet*, Th, 84, USA, Assist Art Dir; *Joshua Then and Now*, Th, 84, CDN, Dec; *Mrs. Soffel*, Th, 84, USA (Dec Buyer); *Glitterdome*, TV, 83, CDN/USA, Dec.

ROTSTEIN CHEIKES, Sarina
On Set Film Promotions Inc., 4497 Marine Dr., West Vancouver, BC V7W 2N8 (604)925-3354. Creative Technique, P.O. Box 311, Stn. F, Toronto, ON M4Y 2L7 (416)466-4173.
Type of Production and Credits: Th Film-Art Dir/Pro Des; TV Film-Art Dir/Pro Des; TV Video-Art Dir.
Genres: Drama-Th&TV; Comedy-TV; Action-Th&TV; Horror-Th&TV; Commercials-TV.
Biography: Born in Toronto, Ontario. Languages: English and German. Studied Interior and Environmental Design, Fashion Institute of Design and Merchandising. Six years as art director; teaches Art Direction at Vancouver Film School; Vice-President of On Set Film Promotions Inc., a product-placement company for film and TV.
Selected Filmography: *Cold Front*, Th, 88, CDN, Art Dir; *Dead of Night*, Th, 88, CDN, Art Dir; "Wiseguy" (8 eps), TV, 87, CDN, Art Dir; *Nice Girls Don't Explode*, Th, 87, USA, Pro Des; *Jenny's Story*, TV, 86, USA, Art Dir; *The Kindred*, Th, 86, USA, Art Dir; "Scary Tales", TV, 86, USA, Art Dir; "Tales from the Dark Side" (12 eps), TV, 86, USA, Art Dir; "Faces in Time" (4 eps), TV, 85, USA, Art Dir.

ROWAN, Patrick
22 Allen Ave., Toronto, ON M4M 1T4 (416)463-7567.
Type of Production and Credits: TV Film-Art Dir/Snd Rec; TV Video-Art Dir/Snd Rec.
Genres: Documentary-TV; Children's-TV; Industrial-TV; Current Affairs-TV.
Biography: Born 1959, Toronto, Ontario. Graduate of Ontario College of Art. Has worked as curatorial assistant, Art Gallery of Ontario; graphic designer, McClelland & Stewart; Associate Art Director, Ray Cattell Ltd.; freelance graphic designer and illustrator, packaging film projects, books.
Selected Filmography: "The Canadians" (2 eps), TV, 87, CDN, Snd Rec; *Royal Trust: Positioning*, In, 88, CDN, Co-Prod/Art Dir; "Live It Up" (110 eps), TV, 81-87, CDN, Snd Rec; "Going Great" (65 eps), TV, 82-85, CDN, Snd Rec; *A Million to One*, TV, 85, CDN, Co-Prod/Art Dir/Snd Rec; *Zam Bam Bony Moroni*, MV, 85, CDN, Art Dir/ADR Ed; *Hello Margaret, Goodbye Marguerite*, TV, 84, CDN, Snd Rec; *The Villa Experience*, Cm, 83, CDN, Co-Prod/Art Dir; "American Caesar" (13 eps), TV, 82, CDN, Snd Rec; *National Safety Drill*, TV, 82, CDN, ADR Ed; *Kids' Case against Vandalism*, ED, 81, CDN, Snd Rec; TV, 81, CDN, Snd Rec; *Never Too Young*, TV, 81, CDN, Snd Rec.

ROZON, Gilbert
ACCT. 87, McCulloch, Outremont, PQ H2V 3L8 Les Films Rozon Inc., 63 est, rue Prince-Arthur, Montréal, PQ H2X 1B4 (514)845-3155.
Types de production et générique: TV vidéo-Dir art.
Types d'oeuvres: Comédie-TV; Variété-TV.
Curriculum vitae: Né en 1954, Québec. Langues: français et anglais. Avocat, membre du Barreau.
Filmographie sélective: "Juste pour rire" (22 eps), TV, 83-85, CDN, Dir art.

SARAFINCHAN, Lillian
DGC, IATSE 873, ACCT, TWIFT. 7 Astley Ave., Toronto, ON M4W 3B3 (416)923-4939.
Type of Production and Credits: Th Film-Pro Des; TV Film-Art Dir; Th Film-Loc M; TV Film-Loc M.
Genres: Drama-Th&TV; Comedy-Th; Variety-TV; Action-Th&TV.
Biography: Born 1935, Vegreville, Alberta. Studied at Banff School of Fine Arts; Ontario College of Art. Associate Fellow, Stong College, York University, 69-77. As an artist, has had many solo exhibitions in Canada, USA; group exhibitions in Kiev, Lvov, Uzhgorod, Ukraine. Has designed for the Royal

Ontario Museum as well as various theatres, schools.
Selected Filmography: "Hitchhiker", TV, 89, USA, Loc M; *Termini Station*, Th, 88, CDN, Pro Des; *Dead Ringers*, Th, 88, CDN, Loc M; *Just U.N. Me, Babe*, TV, 88, USA, Loc M; *Lakota*, Th, 88, USA, Loc M; "Mariah State" (7 eps), TV, 87, USA, Loc M; *Bay Coven*, Th, 87, USA, Loc M; *The Ann Jillian Story*, TV, 87, USA, Loc M; *Amerika*, TV, 86, USA, Loc M; *Many Happy Returns*, TV, 86, USA, Loc M; *Dancing in the Dark*, Th, 85, CDN, Pro Des, (GENIE 87); "Philip Marlowe Private Eye" (2 eps), TV, 85, CDN, Loc M; *Head Office*, Th, 84, USA, Loc M; *Charlie Grant's War*, TV, 83, CDN, Assist Des, (ANIK); *Sunday in the Country*, Th, 73, CDN/GB, Assist Art Dir.

SAURIOL, Gaudeline
STCQ. 362, Labadie, #1, Montreal, PQ H2V 2J8 (514)273-6081.
Types de production et générique: l métrage-Dir art; TV film-Dir art.
Types d'oeuvres: Drame-C&TV.
Curriculum vitae: Née à Montréal, Québec. Langues: français et anglais. Assiste l'Ecole des Métiers Commerciaux, Montréal. Aussi directeur artistique sur des douzaines d'annonces.
Filmographie sélective: *Transit*, TV, 86, CDN, Dir art; *Le Sourd dans la ville*, C, 86, CDN, Dir art; *Le Déclin de l'Empire américain*, C, 85, CDN, Dir art; *Anne Trister*, C, 85, CDN, Dir art; *Caffè Italia Montréal*, C, 84, CDN, Dir art; *La Femme de l'hôtel*, C, 83, CDN, Dir art; *Rien qu'un jeu*, C, 82, CDN, Dir art.

SCHMIDT, Phil
IATSE 891. 2221 Gordon Ave., West Vancouver, BC V7V 1W2 (604)922-7082.
Type of Production and Credits: Th Film-Pro Des/Art Dir; TV Film-Pro Des/Art Dir.
Genres: Drama-Th&TV; Comedy-Th&TV; Action-Th&TV; Science Fiction-Th&TV; Horror-Th&TV.
Biography: Born 1947, Wadena, Saskatchewan. *My American Cousin* was nominated for Best Art Direction and won Best Picture, Genies 86.
Selected Filmography: "Neon Rider" (40 eps), TV, 89-91, CDN, Art Dir; *The Girl from Mars*, Th/TV, 90, CDN/USA/NZ, Art Dir; *Chaindance*, Th, 90, CDN, Pro Des; *American Boyfriends*, Th, 88, CDN, Pro Des; *Snakeeater*, Th, 88, CDN, Cons; *The Outside Chance of Maximilian Glick*, Th, 87, CDN, Art Dir; *My Ameri-can Cousin*, Th, 85, CDN, Art Dir/Assoc Prod.

SEGUIN, François
DGC. 1033, St-Hubert, Montréal, PQ H2L 3Y3 (514)287-1125.
Type of production and Credits: Th Film-Art Dir/Pro Des; TV Film-Art Dir/Pro Des.
Genres: Drama-Th&TV; Comedy-Th&TV; Action-Th&TV; Documentary-Th&TV.
Biography: Born 1951, Montreal, Quebec. Languages: French and English. Diploma, specializing in theatre production, Cégep de Lionel Groulx. Production Designer on over 12 features.
Filmographie sélective: *Lapse of Memory*, Th, 90, F/CDN, Pro Des; *Moody Beach*, Th, 89, CDN, Pro Des; *Un Autre Homme*, TV, 89, CDN, Pro Des; *Blanche est la nuit*, TV, 89, CDN, Pro Des; *Jésus de Montréal*, Th, 88, CDN, Pro Des, (GENIE); *Milk and Honey*, Th, 87, CDN, Pro Des; *Exit*, Th, 86, CDN, Des; *Night Magic*, Th, 84, CDN/F, Pro Des.

SHINER, Judy
30 Beaconsfield Ave., #3, Toronto, ON M6J 3H9 (416)538-2944.
Type of Production and Credits: Th Short-Art Dir; TV Film-Art Dir; TV Video-Art Dir.
Genres: Drama-Th&TV; Educational-TV; Commercials-TV; Industrial-Th&TV.
Biography: Born in 1961 in Toronto, Ontario. Educated at the University of Toronto, York University, Interlochen, Michigan. 5 years workshop leader with Kit Hood for all levels of acting for Degrassi Repertory Company. 5 years teaching gifted program with the Toronto Board of Education, drama and art. Background as graphic artist. Extensive travel in Europe, Asia, South America, USA, Mexico and the Middle East.
Selected Filmography: *Norha & the Microbabe*, Th, 91, CDN, Art Dir; Clear Tech (2 spots), Cm, 91, CDN/USA, Stylist; *School's Out*, TV, 91, CDN, Art Dir; "Degrassi High" (28 eps), TV, 89-90, CDN/USA, Art Dir; *Tip - ASAP*, ED, 90, CDN/USA, Art Dir; "Degrassi Jr. High" (42 eps), TV, 86-89, CDN/USA, Art Dir; *Target*, ED, 89, CDN, Art Dir; *Rap On Rights*, MV, 89, CDN, Art Dir; *Connections*, In, 89, CDN, Art Dir.

SPIER, Carol
DGC, ACCT. R.R. #1, Campbellcroft, ON L0A 1B0 (416) 797-2264. Sandra Marsh Management Inc., 9150 Wilshire Blvd., Suite 220, Beverly Hills, CA 90210 USA. (213) 285-0303.
Type of Production and Credits: Th

Film-Art Dir/Pro Des; TV Film-Art Dir/Pro Des; TV Video-Pro Des.
Genres: Drama-Th&TV; Comedy-Th&TV; Science Fiction-Th&TV; Horror-Th&TV.
Biography: Born 1948, Daysland, Alberta. Studied Interior Design, Faculty of Architecture, University of Manitoba.
Selected Filmography: *Naked Lunch,* Th, 91, CDN/GB, Pro Des; "Scales of Justice" (2 eps), TV, 90, CDN, Pro Des; *Where the Heart Is,* Th, 89, USA, Pro Des; *Sing,* TV, 88, USA, Pro Des; *Dead Ringers,* Th, 88, CDN, Pro Des, (GENIE); *Gotham,* TV, 87, USA, Pro Des; "Friday the 13th: The Series" (main sets), TV, 87, CDN/USA, Pro Des; *The Believers,* Th, 86, USA, Art Dir; *The Fly,* Th, 86, USA, Pro Des; *Anne of Green Gables,* TV, 85, CDN, Pro Des, (GEMINI 86); *Agnes of God,* Th, 85, CDN, Art Dir; *Follow That Bird,* Th, 85, USA, Pro Des; *Overdrawn at the Memory Bank,* TV, 83, CDN/USA, Pro Des; *The Dead Zone,* Th, 83, USA, Pro Des; *Running Brave,* Th, 83, CDN/USA, Pro Des; *Videodrome,* Th, 81, CDN/USA, Pro Des; *Escape from Iran: The Canadian Caper,* TV, 80, CDN, Pro Des.

STEER, Kim
- see PRODUCERS

TASSÉ, Richard
STCVQ, DGC. 1193 Croissant du Collège, #6, Lasalle, PQ H8N 2Y4 (514)368-1345.
Types de production et générique: l métrage-Pro Des.
Types d'oeuvres: Drame-C; Action-C; Science-Fiction-C; Horreur-C.
Curriculum vitae: Né en 1954 à Montréal, Québec. Citoyenneté canadienne. Langues: français et anglais. Université Concordia, Film, Publicité, Relation-Publique et Journalisme. Designer depuis plus de 15 ans dont 5 dans le milieu cinéma-tographique.
Filmographie sélective: *Scanners II - The New Order,* C, 90, USA/CDN, Pro Des; *Back Stab,* C, 90, USA/CDN, Pro Des; *The Amityville Curse,* C, 89, USA/CDN, Pro Des; *Blind Fear,* C, 89, USA/CDN, Pro Des.

THRASHER, Harold E.
DGC. T.H.E. Production Co. Inc., R.R. #1, Harrow, ON N0R 1G0 (519)738-4187. FAX: 738-3673.
Type of Production and Credits: Th Film-Art Dir; TV Film-Art Dir.
Genres: Drama-Th&TV; Comedy-Th&TV; Action-Th&TV; TV Film-Art Dir.
Biography: Born 1945, Windsor, Ontario; US resident alien. Languages: English and French, B.A., M.A., Communications, University of Detroit; also studied at National Theatre School. Taught university-level Design/Theatrical and Technical Theatre for 6 years; designed more than 150 theatrical plays; designed and renovated a variety of stage formats.
Selected Filmography: *Young Catherine* (mini-series), TV, 90, USA/CDN/GB/USR, Pro Des; "African Journey" (3 eps), TV, 89, USA/CDN, Art Dir/Des; *When Harry Met Sally,* Th, 88, USA, Art Dir; *Young Guns,* Th, 88, USA, Art Dir; *Patti* (Patti Hearst story), Th, 87, USA, Art Dir; *Illegally Yours,* Th, 87, USA, Art Dir; *Rolling Vengeance,* Th, 86, USA, Des; *Raising Arizona,* Th, 86, USA, Art Dir; *L.B.J.,* TV, 85, USA, Art Dir/Set Dr; *Rockabye,* TV, 85, USA/CDN, Art Dir; *In Like Flynn,* TV, 85, USA, Art Dir; *Joshua Then and Now,* Th, 84, CDN, Art Dir; *Of Unknown Origin,* Th, 82, CDN/USA.

TRANTER, Barbara
- see PRODUCERS

VON HELMOLT, Vonnie
- see PRODUCTION MANAGERS

WHITE, Nicholas
149 Hillingdon Ave., Toronto, ON M4C 3J1 (416)694-8064.
Type of Production and Credits: Th Film-Art Dir; TV Film-Art Dir; TV Video-Art Dir.
Genres: Drama-Th&TV; Comedy-Th&TV; Action-Th&TV; Science Fiction-Th&TV.
Biography: Born England, 1962; came to Canada in 1974 and now a Canadian citizen. Works primarily in the English language. Graduated from the Ontario College of Art, 85; specialized in Film Studies, Animation and Commercial Design. Solid background in design as well as extensive drawing capabilities, both in drafting and illustration.
Selected Filmography: *New Souls/Murder Blues,* Th, 90, CDN/GB, Art Dir; *My Happy Days in Hell,* Th, 90, CDN, Art Dir; "T and T" (21 eps), TV, 89, CDN/USA, Assist Art Dir; *The Gate II,* Th, 88, CDN, Set Dec; *A Whisper to a Scream,* Th, 88, CDN, Art Dir; *Graveyard Shift II - The Understudy,* Th, 88, CDN/USA, Art Dir; *The Brain,* Th, 87, CDN, Set Dec; *Black Roses,* Th, 87, CDN, Art Dir; *Night of Retribution,* Th, 87, CDN, Art Dir; *Architects of Fear,* Th, 86, CDN, Art Dir.

WILCOX, Richard
IATSE 891, IATSE 928, USA 829, DGC. 3615 Marine Dr., West Vancouver, BC V7V 1N3 (604)922-6109. Jay Gilbert,

8400 Sunset Blvd., Los Angeles, CA 90069 USA (213)656-5906.
Type of Production and Credits: Th Film-Pro Des; TV Film-Pro Des.
Genres: Drama-Th&TV; Comedy-Th&TV.
Biography: Born 1933, San Luis Opisbo, California; Canadian citizenship. B.A., University of California; M.F.A., Yale Drama School. Scene and costume designer, Goodman Theatre, Chicago; Front Street Theatre, Memphis; Tulane University, New Orleans; Frederic Wood Theatre, Vancouver; Citadel Theatre, Edmonton; Associate Professor, University of British Columbia; taught Design at Art Institute of Chicago and Tulane University.
Selected Filmography: *Nightmare Café*, TV, 91, USA, Pro Des; *Omen IV*, TV, 91, USA, Pro Des; *Last Flight Out*, TV, 90, USA, Pro Des; *Perfect Witness*, TV, 90, USA, Pro Des; *The Accused*, Th, 87, USA, Pro Des; *Privileged Information*, TV, 87, USA, Pro Des; "The Hitchhiker" (26 eps), TV, 85-86, USA, Pro Des, (ACE); *A Letter to Three Wives*, TV, 85, USA, Pro Des.

Cinematographers
Directeurs-photo

ALLEN-WOOLFE, Nicholas
CSC, IATSE, ACCT. Nikko Productions, 146 Sherwood Ave., Toronto, ON M4P 2A8 (416)485-3447. The Gersh Agency, 130 W. 42nd St., 24th Flr., New York, NY 10036 USA. (212)997-1818.
Type of Production and Credits: Th Film-DOP; Th Short-DOP; TV Film-DOP; TV Video-DOP.
Genres: Drama-Th&TV; Documentary-Th&TV; Commercials-Th&TV.
Biography: Born 1944, Wiltshire, England. Thirty years professional experience in the camera department in all aspects of film/video production. Winner of 4 Bessies and 6 CSC awards for Best Cinematography.

ALPERT, Herbert
ASC, CSC, IATSE 644. 150 Heath St. W., #503, Toronto, ON M4V 2Y4 (416)484-4335.
Type of Production and Credits: Th Film-Dir/DOP/Prod.
Genres: Drama-Th; Horror-Th; Documentary-Th&TV.
Biography: Born 1918, New Haven, Connecticut; landed immigrant Canada. Served in US Air Force, HQ 4th Fighter Group, World War II. Filmmaker since 36; first President, 2 terms, Canadian Society of Cinematographers; member by invitation, American Society of Cinematographers, 25 years; President, Ultimus Films Limited; Secretary, board member, FCMI Financial Corporation, Chairman of the Board, First Mercantile Currency Fund; President, Hilary-Hollis Corp.

AQUILA, James
CSC. Aquila Film & Video Inc., 48

Proctor Blvd., Hamilton, ON L8M 2M4 (416)545-4773.
Type of Production and Credits: Th Short-DOP; TV Film-DOP; TV Video-DOP.
Genres: Drama-TV; Documentary-Th&TV; Educational-TV; Industrial-TV.
Biography: Born 1948, Italy; Canadian citizenship. Languages: English, Italian, some French and Spanish. Full member, CSC. Many industrial awards. Works with film or tape; has 16mm film and Betacam equipment packages.
Selected Filmography: "Earth Journal", TV, 91, CDN, DOP; *First Hand Science*, ED, 90, CDN, DOP; *Friends for Life*, In, 89, CDN, DOP; *One Warm Line: Stan Rogers*, TV, CDN, 88, DOP; *To Hurt and to Heal*, ED, 87, CDN, Cin; *Cantel: Corporate Profile*, In, 87, CDN, DOP; "A.I. Fulfilling the Dream" (4 eps), TV, 86, CDN, DOP; *Artie Shaw: Time Is All You've Got*, Th, 85, CDN, Co-DOP; *Spadina*, TV, 84, CDN, DOP; *The Music Inside*, TV, 84, CDN, DOP; "Home Fires" (pilot), TV, 79, CDN, DOP; *Franco: The Story of an Immigrant*, Th, 75, CDN, DOP/Wr.

AZIZ, Stewart
IATSE 667. Shoreline Pictures Inc.,527 Mary St. N., Oshawa, ON L1G 5E6 (416)728-0684.
Type of Production and Credits: Th Film-Cam.
Genres: Drama-Th&TV; Documentary-TV; Educational-TV; Industrial-TV.
Biography: Born in 1958. Operates Shoreline Pictures Inc. Sony Beta SP Camera Package.
Selected Filmography: *The Mrs.*, Th, 91, USA, Assist Cam; *Stepping Out*, Th, 90, USA, Assist Cam; *White Light*, Th, 90, CDN, Assist Cam; *End Run*, TV, 90, USA, Assist Cam; *In the Frame*, TV, 90, CDN/GB, Assist Cam; *Blood Sport*, TV, 90, CDN/GB, Assist Cam; *Stella*, Th, 90, USA, Assist Cam; *Wilderness*, ED, 90, CDN, Cam; *Hubble/Scope*, ED, 90, CDN, Cam.

BAIRD, Douglas
1187 Wellington Dr., North Vancouver, BC V7K 1L3 (604)980-8378. (604)643-8811. PAGER: 643-8811.
Type of Production and Credits: TV Video-Cam; TV Film-Cam.
Genres: Documentary-TV; Current Affairs-TV.
Biography: Born 1952, Calgary, Alberta. Honours B.Sc., Kinesiology, University of Waterloo. Betacam specialist in TV current affairs and documentary production for CBC, CTV, ABC, CBS, BBC and NFB. Part of Host Broadcaster crew at Expo 86. Worked for TVO Brisbane, Film Australia, BBC, TF-1 France, TV-2 Finland, Televisa-Mexico, TVB-Hong Kong, RAI-Italy, and NRK-Norway. Certified diver and underwater photographer. Canadian Society of Cinematographers (CSC) - Roy Tash Award, 87; National Association of Press Photographers (NPPA), USA & Canada, Spot News award, 87. Also camera on CBC documentary, *The Making of Kootenai Brown*, 90-91.
Selected Filmography: "the fifth estate", TV, 89-91, CDN, Cam; "The National", TV, 85-91, CDN, Cam; "The Journal", TV, 85-91, CDN, Cam; "Midday", TV, 85-91, CDN, Cam; "Man Alive", TV, 91, CDN, Cam; "Marketplace", TV, 89-91, CDN, Cam; "Venture", TV, 86-91, CDN, Cam; "Canadian Gardener", TV, 88-91, CDN, Cam; "Sportsweekend", TV, 85-91, CDN, Cam; "Sesame Street", TV, 88-90, CDN, Cam; "Pacific Report", TV, 86-90, CDN, Cam; "Wide World of Sports", TV, 74-79, CDN, Cam; "BCTV Newshour", TV, 79-84, CDN, Cam.

BALL, Christopher
- see DIRECTORS

BEAUCHEMIN, François ◇
ONF, 3155 Côte de Liesse, Montréal, PQ H3C 3H5 (514)283-9364.
Types de production et générique: l métrage-D photo; c métrage-Cam; TV film-D photo; TV vidéo-D photo.
Types d'oeuvres: Drame-C&TV; Comédie-C&TV; Action-C&TV; Documentaire-C&TV.
Curriculum vitae: Né en 1943, Noranda, Québec. Langues: français et anglais. Etudes à l'Ecole de Cinéma, Institut National des Arts du Spectacle, Bruxelles (3 ans). Caméraman vidéo, Radio-Québec, 68-71; pigiste, caméraman et directeur-photo, 71-82; à l'ONF depuis 82. *Ti-Cul Tougas* gagne le Prix de la critique Québécoise.
Filmographie sélective: *Sommet de la Francophonie*, TV, 87, CDN, Ass cam; *Image par image*, C, 86, CDN, D phot; *Prodigal*, TV, 85, CDN, D phot; *Place aux jeunes*, TV, 85, CDN, D phot; *L'Inconduite*, "Prendre la route", TV, 85, CDN, D phot; *Le Drame d'Isidore Tremblay/Piekouagami*, TV, 84, CDN, D phot; *L'Hiver, les blés*, TV, 84, CDN, D phot' *L'Emotion dissonante*, C, 84, CDN, D phot; *De mains et d'espoir*, TV, 82, CDN, D phot; *Quitte ou double*, C, 81, CDN, D phot; *En plein coeur*, C, 81,

CDN, D phot; "Vivre ici... maintenant" (13 eps), TV, 81, CDN, D phot; *Une vie en prison* (3 parties), TV, 80, CDN, D phot; *Contrecoeur*, C, 79, CDN, D phot; *Le Château de cartes*, Cm 79, CDN, D phot.

BELLEMARE, Rénald ◊
(514)849-5816.
Types de production et générique: TV film-Comp/Aut comp; TV Vidéo-Cam/Mont.
Types d'oeuvres: Documentaire-C&TV; Education-C&TV; Expérimental-C&TV.
Curriculum vitae: Né en 1954, Montréal, Québec. Langues: français, anglais, espagnol. Baccalauréat spécialisé en communications. Directeur-photo et caméraman, film et vidéo; conception visuelle de spectacles de scène; producteur de film et vidéo, Imagidé inc. Plusieurs tournages et voyages à l'étranger: Afrique, Amérique centrale et du sud, Asie, Europe.
Filmographie sélective: *Faveladas*, TV, 86, CDN, Cam; *Ethiopia: Canadian Aid*, TV, 86, CDN, Cam; *Les Contes des mille et un nez*, TV, 85, CDN, Cam; *Femme sans frontières*, TV, 85, CDN, Cam; "Cousin Cuisine" (13 eps), TV, 85, CDN, D phot/Cam; *Le Rêve éveillé*, MV, 85, CDN, Prod/Réal/Cam/Mont; *Petite Fille*, Belgazou, MV, 85, CDN, D phot; *C'est comme une peine d'amour*, TV, 84-85, CDN, Cam; *Rock at Chouka 4*, TV, 84, CDN, Réal/Cam/Mont; *Michel Lemieux, l'oeil rechargeable*, TV, 84, CDN, Réal/Cam/Mont; "Le Choc des Amériques" (6 eps), TV, 83-84, CDN, Cam/Mont; *Margie Gillis: New Dreams*, TV, 84, CDN, Cam; *El Salvador: la guerre civile et les élections 82*, TV, 82, CDN, Mont; *Les Bleus...la nuit...*, TV, 81, CDN, Prod/Cam; *Charlevoix, pays du huitième jour*, TV, 80, CDN, Prod/Cam.

BELZILE, Jocelyn ◊
(514)598-7256.
Types de production et générique: TV film-D photo.
Types d'oeuvres: Drame-TV; Variété-TV; Documentaire-TV; Vidéo clips-TV.
Curriculum vitae: Né en 1927, Trois-Pistoles, Québec. Langues: français et anglais. Education: humanités, latin, grec, Collège de l'Assomption.
Filmographie sélective: *Henryk Szering/Maria Pellegrini/Kenneth Gilbert*, "Les Beaux Dimanches", TV, 85-86, CDN, D phot; "Steppin' Out" (120 eps), TV, 82-86, CDN, D phot, (ANIK); *Charles Dutoit/Gerald Godin*, "Gzowski & Co.", TV, 85, CDN, D phot; *Gaspé - 3 families*, TV, 84, CDN, D phot.

BENISON, Peter ◊
(416)698-4482.
Type of Production and Credits: Th Film-DOP; Th Short-DOP; TV Film-DOP; TV Video-DOP.
Genres: Drama-Th&TV; Comedy-Th&TV; Action-Th&TV; Science Fiction-Th&TV.
Biography: Born 1950. B.Sc., McGill University, 71. Certified scuba diver. Received CSC Award for best Television Drama for "Captain Power and the Soldiers of the Future," 88.
Selected Filmography: "Diamonds" (4 eps), TV, 87-88, CDN, DOP; "The Twilight Zone" (3 eps), TV, 88, CDN/USA, DOP; "Captain Power and the Soldiers of the Future" (22 eps), TV, 87, CDN, DOP; *Oklahoma Smugglers*, Th, 86, USA, DOP; "Women of the World" (7 eps), TV, 85-86, CDN/USA, DOP; "Night Heat" (4 eps), TV, 85-86, CDN, DOP; Brador/Panasonic/Irving Oil/American Dream, Cm, 83-86, CDN, DOP; Air Canada/CN/Alcan/General Electric/IBM/Avon/VIA/Bell Canada, In, 72-86, CDN, DOP; "Hot Shots" (11 eps), TV, 86, CDN, DOP; "National Geographic" (2 eps), TV, 85, CDN, DOP; Wayne Biscayne/Beau Geste, MV, 84-85, CDN, DOP; *Meatballs III*, Th, 84, CDN, DOP; *Joshua Then and Now*, Th, 84, CDN, 2nd U DOP; *The Juggler*, TV, 83, CDN, DOP; *The Hotel New Hampshire*, Th, 83, USA, 2nd U DOP.

BINNINGTON, Andrew
CSC, STLD. 1495 Parkridge Rd., Mississauga, ON L5E 3A1 (416)278-1878. CBC Film Services, 790 Bay St., Toronto, ON M5G 1N8 (416)975-7602.
Type of Production and Credits: TV Film-DOP; TV Video-DOP.
Genres: Drama-TV; Comedy-TV; Documentary-TV; Commercials-TV.
Biography: Born 1953, Toronto, Ontario. Languages: English and some French. B.A., York University; Arts diploma, McGill University. Gemini Award, Best Photography in a Comedy, Variety or Performing Arts Program or Series for *In Rehearsal: Mozart's Don Giovanni*, 89; CSC nominee for Cinematography on a Documentary, *A Radical Romantic*, 90.
Selected Filmography: *CBC and You*, Cm, 91, CDN, DOP; *James Bay*, Cm, 91, CDN, DOP; *Northwood*, Cm, 91, CDN, DOP; *Lasers*, "The Nature of Things", TV, 91, CDN, DOP; *Animals in Research*, "The Nature of Things", TV, 91, CDN, DOP; *CBC at Six*, Cm, 90, CDN, DOP; *Monitor*, Cm, 90, CDN, DOP; *Degrassi*

High, Cm, 90, CDN, DOP; *Revolution Down on the Farm*, "The Nature of Things", TV, 90, CDN, DOP; *Chris Giannou: A Profile*, "Man Alive", TV, 90, CDN, DOP; *The Valor and the Horror*, TV, 90, CDN, DOP; "The Kids in the Hall" (10 eps), TV, 90, CDN, DOP; *Turning to Dust*, "The Nature of Things", TV, 89, CDN, DOP; *A Sky Full of Planes*, "The Nature of Things", TV, 89, CDN, DOP; "Inside Stories" (13 eps), TV, 88, CDN, DOP.

BOCKING, Robert V.
CSC, SMPTE, ACCT. 75 Hucknall Rd., Downsview, ON M3J 1W1 (416)631-9845.
Type of Production and Credits: Th Film-Ed/Snd Ed; Th Short-Ed/Snd Ed; TV Film-Dir/Prod/Ed/Snd Ed; TV Video-Dir/Prod/Ed/Snd Ed.
Genres: Documentary-Th&TV; Educational-Th&TV; Children's-Th&TV.
Biography: Born 1936, Thunder Bay, Ontario. Specializes in nature subjects; digital audio editing for film/video in any format. *The Great Cover-up* awarded Special Citation for Nature Cinematography, Award for Creative Excellence, US Industrial Film & Video Festival, and Silver Lone Star Award, 88; *Spirit of the Wilderness* won Silver Lone Star, 89; *The Northlands* and *Backyard Birds* were nominated for Best Cinematography, CSC 89; *Farming* won award of Creative Excellence, US Industrial Film & Video Festival; *The Four Seasons* nominated for Golden Sheaf, Yorkton 83 and "Summer" won Best Cinematography, CSC 84; *Solitudes* won Silver, 84 and *Images of Galapagos* won Bronze, 83 at the NY International Film/TV Festival. 1979 Bill Hilson Award (CSC) for outstanding service, contributing to the motion picture industry in Canada; 1981, Special Award, Conestoga College, in recognition of dedication and creativity as coordinator of Film Program, 76-81; 1990 New Century Award, presented by Kodak Canada, in recognition of outstanding contributions to the art of cinematography, service to the CSC and education of young people pursuing this field.
Selected Filmography: *Spirit of the Wilderness*, ED, 91, CDN, Prod/Dir/DOP/Ed/Snd Ed; *The Northlands*, "National Geographic," ED, 89, CDN, Prod/Dir/DOP/Ed/Snd Ed; *Backyard Birds*, ED, 87, CDN/USA, Prod/Dir/Cam/Ed; *The Great Cover-up: Animal Camouflage*, "National Geogra-phic," ED,

AGFA

MOTION PICTURE FILM STOCKS
For the Professional 16mm and 35mm filmmaker

For more information on these films please contact:

AGFA CANADA INC.

MONTREAL
889 Montee de Liesse, St-Laurent, Quebec H4T 1P5
Tel: 514-738-3300 Fax: 514-738-8998

TORONTO
77 Belfield Road, Etobicoke, Ontario M9W 1G6
Tel: 416-241-1110 FAX: 416-241-5409

87, CDN, Prod/Dir/Cam/Ed; *Farming, In*, 85, CDN, Prod/Dir/Cam/ Dir/Ed; *The Four Seasons* (4 parts), ED, 84, CDN, Prod/Dir/Cam/Ed; *Solitudes*, "Profiles of Nature", TV, 84, CDN, Ed/Snd Ed; *Images of Galapagos*, TV, 83, CDN, Pro Spv; *North to the Top of the World*, "Wild Canada", TV, 81, CDN, Prod/Dir/DOP/ Ed/Snd Ed.

BOISVERT, Paul Camille
NABET 72, CSC, NACFO. 53 Maughan Cres., Toronto, ON M4L 3E6 (416)691-5583. TVOntario, 2180 Yonge St., Toronto, ON M4S 2B9
Type of Production and Credits: Th Film-DOP; TV Film-DOP; TV Video-DOP.
Genres: Drama-Th&TV; Documentary-Th&TV; Educational-TV; Experimental-TV; Current Affairs-TV.
Selected Filmography: "Work Week" (5 eps), ED, 91, CDN, Cam; "Speaking Out" (12 eps), ED, 90, CDN, Cam; "Polka Dot Door" (10 eps), ED, 90, CDN, Cam; "Book Mice" (10 eps), ED, CDN, Cam; "Femme et santé" (13 eps), ED, 91, CDN, Cam; "Report Canada" (30 eps), ED, 90-91, CDN, Cam; "Lys & Trillium" (7 eps), ED, 91, CDN, Cam; "Imprint" (8 eps), ED, 91, CDN, Cam; *Paraitre*, ED, 89, CDN, 2nd Unit DOP; *Don't Be Long*, Th, 88, CDN, DOP; *Father John*, Th, 88, CDN, DOP; *Donato*, Th, 88, CDN, DOP.

BONNER, Michael
- see DIRECTORS

BONNIERE, Christophe
CSC, CGC. 441 Bathurst St., Toronto, ON M5T 2S9 (416)368-2024.
Type of Production and Credits: Th Film-DOP; TV Film-DOP; Th Short-DOP.
Genres: Drama-Th&TV; Action-Th&TV; Documentary-TV; Commercials-TV.
Biography: Born 1956, Ottawa, Ontario; French and Canadian citizenship. Languages: French and English. Received Casby award for Best Rock Video, *I am an Adult Now*.
Selected Filmography: "Sweating Bullets" (2 eps), TV, 91, CDN/USA/MEX, DOP; "Top Cops" (22 eps), TV, 90-91, CDN/USA, DOP; "War of the Worlds" (20 eps), TV, 89-90, CDN/USA, DOP; "Alfred Hitchcock Presents" (1 eps), TV, 87, CDN/USA, Cam; "Captain Power" (20 eps), TV, 87, CDN, Cam; "Mariah State" (6 eps), TV, 87, USA, Cam; *Drop-Out Mother*, TV, 87, USA, Cam.

BORREMANS, Guy
STCQ. 5899, Hutchison, Montréal, PQ H2V 4B7 (514)495-2367.
Types de production et générique: l métrage-D photo; c métrage-D photo/ Réal.
Types d'oeuvres: Drame-C; Documentaire-C&TV.
Curriculum vitae: Né en 1934, Dinant, Belgique; citoyenneté canadienne, 60. A vécu et travaillé à New York, San Francisco, Paris, Londres, Amsterdam, Mexico; photographe de presse et photo-journaliste, 53; ex-correspondant pour *Paris-Match*; débute dans le cinéma en 56; participe au mouvement cinéma-vérité, ONF, 61. Constructeur et navigateur de voilier. Connaissance particulière de l'Afrique. A remporté plusieurs prix dont le Prix de la Critique québécoise pour *Le Journal inachevé* et *24 heures ou plus*. Spécialiste du noir et blanc; portraitiste renomé; scénariste-fiction et documentaire; journaliste/essayiste; direction photo en vidéo.
Filmographie sélective: *Maria Chapdelaine*, C, 82, CDN/F, Cam 2e éq; *Le Journal inachvé*, C, 80, CDN, D phot; *Les Plouffes*, C, 80, CDN, Cam 2e éq; *Le Soulier*, C, 79, CDN, D phot; *Le Revenant* (unfinished), C, 79, CDN/SN, D phot; *Pakuashipu/Mistashipu* "Carcajou et le péril blanc", TV, 72-79, CDN, D phot; *La Barrière/Le Passage des tentes aux maisons*, TV, 72-79, CDN, D phot; *24 heures ou plus...*, C, 78, CDN, D phot; *Kouchibouguac*, C, 77, CDN, Réal; *Chissibi/Job's Garden*, TV, 71, CDN, D phot; *Le mépris n'aura qu'un temps*, C, 69, CDN, D phot; *No Harvest for the Reaper*, TV, 68, USA, D phot; *Dimanche d'Amérique*, C, 65, CDN, D phot; *Percé on the Rocks*, C, 64, CDN, D phot; *L'Homme vite*, C, 63, CDN, Réal.

BRAULT, Michel
- voir REALISATEURS

BROOKS, Nicholas ◊
(416)346-4226.
Type of Production and Credits: Th Short-DOP; TV Film-DOP.
Genres: Drama-Th&TV; Musical-Th&TV; Documentary-Th&TV; Commercials-Th&TV.
Biography: Born 1948, London, England; British and Canadian citizenship. Founder and Chairman, Film and TV Health and Safety Committee; DOP, Director and Producer of numerous commercials, 85-88. Toronto Art Directors' Gold award, Japan Art Directors' Gold award and Clio, 85, for Panasonic shaver commercial; Emmy nomination for *The Medium*; winner, Montreux, for *Chris de Burgh Live*.

Specialist in blue matte process.
Selected Filmography: *Ontario Department of Communications*, In, 88, CDN, DOP; *Diamond in the Rough*, TV, 87, CDN, DOP.

BROOKS, Robert
CSC, CFTAP, NABET, SMPTE, ACCT. 34 Cheval Dr., Don Mills, ON M3B 1R6 (416)445-5334. Robert Brooks Associates Ltd., 49-6A The Donway W., Suite 501, Don Mills, ON M3C 2E8 (416)445-5334.
Type of Production and Credits: Th Film-DOP; Th Short-DOP; TV Film-DOP; TV Video-DOP.
Genres: Drama-Th&TV; Documentary-Th&TV; Educational-Th&TV; Industrial-Th&TV.
Biography: Born 1929, Regina, Saskatchewan; Candian citizenship. Entered film industry with Associated Screen News, 47; joined Chetwynd Films Ltd, as DOP and Head of Camera Dept., 56; began freelance work and established Robert Brooks Associates Ltd., 69. Shot the first 35 mm Eastman colour negative in Canada, 55. Has worked on many award-winning films; active in industry-related organizations; received Kodak New Century Award, 89 "In Recognition of Personal Contribution to the Art of Cinematography"; CSC, "Best Cinematographer Award" for Documentaries, 82; Bill Hilson Award, 76, for "Outstanding Service Contributing to the Development of the Canadian Motion Picture Industry"; appointed DOP, *Share the Flame*, official film of the XV Olympic Winter Games, Calgary, Alberta, 88.
Selected Filmography: "Hands over Time" (48 eps), TV, 88-90, CDN, DOP; "Caring for Young Children" (6 eps), TV, 90, CDN, DOP; *Bodyguard*, TV, 89, CDN, DOP; *Share the Flame*, TV, 88, CDN/USA, DOP; *Seoul 88 - 16 Days of Glory*, TV, 88, USA, DOP; *Skin*, TV, 88, CDN, DOP; "Family Matters" (8 eps), TV, 86-87, CDN, DOP; "People Patterns" (28 eps), TV, 83-87, CDN, DOP; "Hooked on Reading" (6 eps), TV, 84-85, CDN, DOP; *The Making of the Terry Fox Story*, TV, 82, CDN, DOP; *Variations of a Theme*, In, 80, CDN, DOP; *Deadly Harvest*, Th, 76, CDN, DOP; *A Sweeter Song*, Th, 75, CDN, DOP; *Lions for Breakfast*, Th, 74, CDN, DOP; *Trooping the Color P.P.C.L.I.*, Th, 55, CDN, DOP.

BURSTYN, Thomas
CSC, IATSE 669, ACCT. 175 Isleview Place, P.O. Box 463, Lions Bay, BC V0N 2E0. Creative Technique Inc., P.O. Box 311, Stn. F, Toronto, ON M4Y 2L7 (416) 466-4173.
Type of Production and Credits: Th Film-DOP; TV Film-DOP.
Genres: Drama-Th&TV; Comedy-Th&TV; Action-Th&TV.
Biography: Born 1954, Montreal, Quebec. Languages: French and English. Silver Plaque, Chicago; ACE Awards, Best Cinematography - 85, 86, 87; CSC Award, Best Cinematography - 86; *The Tadpole & the Whale* was nominated for Best Cinematography, Academy of Canadian Film and Television; *Homebodies*, *True Believer* and *Murderous Feelings* (episodes of "The Hitchhiker") each won ACE Award for Best Direction of Photography for Comedy or Dramatic Series; *True Believer* also won CSC Award for Best Cinematography.
Selected Filmography: "Empire City" (pilot), TV, 91, USA, DOP; *A Mighty Fortress*, TV, 90, USA, DOP; *Toy Soldiers*, Th, 90, USA, DOP; "Tales from the Monkey House" (3 eps, pilot), TV, 90, CDN, DOP; *Perfect Tribute*, TV, 90, USA, DOP; *Cold Front*, Th, 89, CDN, DOP; *Dreamer of Oz*, TV, 89, USA, DOP; *Liberace*, TV, 89, USA, DOP; *Cheetah*, Th, 88, USA, DOP; *Leap of Faith*, TV, 88, USA, DOP; *The Tadpole & the Whale*, Th, 87, CDN, DOP; *Promised a Miracle*, TV, 87, USA, DOP; *Native Son*, Th, 86, USA, DOP; "The Hitchhiker", TV, 84-86, CDN/USA, DOP; *Dark of Night*, Th, 85, NZ, DOP; *The Lost Tribe*, Th, 81, NZ, DOP.

CAMPANELLI, Stephen
IATSE 667 & 669. 824 East 21st St., North Vancouver, BC V7J 1N9 (604) 644-1102.
Type of Production and Credits: Th Film-Cam Op/St'cam; Th Short-Cam Op/St'cam; TV Film-Cam Op/St'cam.
Biography: Born in 1959 in Montreal, Quebec. Canadian citizen. Languages: English, French, Italian. University (B.F.A.). Steadicam operator and "A" camera operator. Worked on numerous features such as *The Freshman* and *Stella*. Director, *From a Whisper...To a Scream*, Best Student Film (1st Prize), Canadian Student Film Festival.
Selected Filmography: *Lovebirds*, TV, 91, USA, Cam Op/St'cam; *A Mother's Justice*, TV, 91, USA, Cam Op/St'cam; "Scene of the Crime" (11 eps), TV, 91, CDN/USA/F, Cam Op/St'cam; *And the Sea Will Tell*, TV, 90, USA, Cam Op/St'cam; *Enemies: A Love Story*, Th, 89, USA, St'cam; *Stella*,

Th, 89, USA, St'cam; *Stanley and Iris*, Th, 89, USA, St'cam; *The Freshman*, Th, 89, USA, St'cam.

CASEY, Bill
CSC, ACCT. Bill Casey Productions Inc., 4256 Westhill, Montreal, PQ H4B 2S7 (514)489-8167.
Type of Production and Credits: TV Film-Cam; TV Video-Cam.
Genres: Documentary-TV; Children's-TV; Commercials-TV; Industrial-TV.
Biography: Born 1947, Montreal, Quebec. Languages: English and French. B.A., Communication Arts, Loyola University, 68. Cameraman/photographer for CN Railways (15 films), 68-72; freelance cameraman since 72. Formed Bill Casey Productions Inc., 76. *CN - 50 Years Later* won a Gold Camera Award, Chicago.
Selected Filmography: *Sing! - Canadian Children's Choirs in Concert*, TV, 89-90, CDN, Prod/DOP; *The Last Train Across Canada* (2 parts), TV, 89-90, USA/GB, DOP; *Ida Haendel - A Voyage in Music*, Th, 88, CDN, DOP; *Festival de Lanaudière*, Th, 88, CDN, DOP; *Elections in Haiti*, "CBC National News", TV, 88, CDN, DOP; *Cop*, "the fifth estate" (1 eps), TV, 87, CDN, DOP; *Runaways: 24 Hours on the Street*, TV, 87, CDN, DOP; "National News", TV, 76-86, CDN, Cam; *Road to Patriation*, TV, 84, CDN, Co-Cam; *I Like to See the Wheels Turn*, TV, 82, CDN, Cam; "the fifth estate" (6 eps), TV, 81, CDN, Cam; *Coaches*, TV, 75, CDN, Cam; *CN - 50 Years Later*, In, 72, CDN, Cam.

CASSAR, Jon
IATSE 667, CSC, ACCT. 98 Des Bosquets, Aylmer, PQ J9J 1Y9 (819)682-4412. Jon Cassar Steadicam Photography Inc., PO Box 3010, Stn. C, Ottawa, ON K1Y 4J3 (613)238-8644.
Type of Production and Credits: Th Film-Cam/St'cam; TV Film-Cam/St'cam; TV Video-Cam/St'cam.
Genres: Drama-Th&TV; Comedy-Th&TV; Variety-TV; Science Fiction-Th&TV.
Biography: Born 1958, Malta. Canadian citizenship. Languages: English and Maltese. Graduate, TV Program, Algonquin College; various workshops for Steadicam, film production and camera operation, Maine. Regular teaching assistant for Garrett Brown at Steadicam workshops. Winner of CSC award, , Best Cinematography, Corporate Video (Director of Photography); Best Cinematography, Television Drama, (Camera Operator). Was a film critic for 5 years.
Selected Filmography: *The Cutting Edge*, Th, 91, USA, Cam Op; "Sweating Bullets" (10 eps), TV, 90-91, CDN/USA/MEX, Cam/St'cam Op; *Enchantment: Mark Twain & Me*, TV, 90, USA, Cam/St'cam Op; *Clearcut/Dream Like Mine*, Th, 90, CDN, Cam/St'cam Op; *Car 54*, Th, 90, USA, "B" Cam; "Road To Avonlea" (1 eps), TV, 90, CDN, St'cam; "E.N.G." (1 eps), TV, 90, CDN, St'cam; *Queen of Mean*, TV, 90, USA, St'cam; *Sam and Me/New Man In*, Th, 90, CDN, St'cam; *Rick Emmett*, MV, 90, CDN, St'cam; *New Souls/Murder Blues*, Th, 90, EUR, St'cam; *Last Winter*, Th, 90, CDN, St'cam; "War of the Worlds" (20 eps), TV, 89-90, USA, Cam op; *Millennium*, Th, 88, USA, St'cam; *Dream Team*, Th, 88 USA, St'cam/"B" Cam.

CHAMMAS, Robert
- see PRODUCERS

CHAMPION, Marc
CSC, CST, SMPTE. Integra Film Inc., 95 Heath St. E., Toronto, ON M4S 1S5 (416)484-0236.
Type of Production and Credits: Th Film-DOP; TV Film-DOP; TV Video-DOP.
Genres: Drama-Th&TV; Action-Th; Commercials-TV; Music Video-TV.
Biography: Born in France; Canadian citizenship. Languages: English and French. Graduated from Ecole Nationale de Cinématographie and the Institut des Hautes Etudes Cinématographiques (IDHEC), Paris. Worked in France, 46-67; in Canada since 67. DOP on numerous features and award-winning commercials shot around the world. Has won 2 Craft awards for Cinematography for commercials for Canada Dry (81) and Cadbury's (84); *Slipstream* won Best Canadian Cinematography, L.A. Film Festival.
Selected Filmography: "Bordertown" (16 eps), TV, 90, CDN/F, DOP; "My Secret Identity" (23 eps), TV, 88, CDN/USA, DOP; "Mr. T" (pilot), TV, 87, CDN, DOP; *Anne of Green Gables: The Sequel* (mini-series), TV, 86, CDN, DOP, (GEMINI 88); "Frontier" (6 eps), TV, 85, CDN/GB/F/D, DOP; *The House of Dies Drear*, TV, 84, USA, DOP; *Helix/Triumph/Gowan*, MV, 84, CDN, DOP; *Samuel Lount*, Th, 84, CDN, DOP; *Out of the Blue*, Th, 80, CDN, DOP; *Why Shoot the Teacher*, Th, 76, CDN, DOP; *Partners*, Th, 75, CDN, DOP; *Sunday in the Country*, Th, 73, CDN/GB, DOP;

Slipstream, Th, 72, CDN, DOP; *The Heart Farm*, Th, 70, CDN, DOP.

CHAPMAN, Christopher
- see DIRECTORS

CHENTRIER, Bernard
121 Rang Ste-Julie, St-Guillaume, Cté Yamaska, PQ J0C 1L0 (819)396-3063.
Types de production et générique: l métrage-D phot; TV film-D phot; TV vidéo-D phot.
Types d'oeuvres: Drame-C&TV; Comédie-C&TV; Annonces-TV.
Curriculum vitae: Directeur de photographie en long métrage, film pour télévision, séries télévisées, documentaires, films industriels, et messages publicitaires. Prix Gémeaux pour meilleure photographie, série "Lance et Compte", 87, 88, 89. Etrog Palmarès du Film Canadien pour meilleur prise du vue, film *Red*, 70.
Filmographie sélective: *Les naufragés du Labrador*, C/TV, 90-91, CDN, D phot; "Lance et Compte" (53 eps), TV, 85-90, CDN, D phot, (GEMEAUX); *Mindfield*, C, 88-89, CDN, D phot; "Les misère des Riches" (8 eps), TV, 88-89, CDN, D phot; *Clémence Aletti*, C/TV, 83-84, CDN, D phot; campagne publicitaire Métro Richelieu, Cm, 83-84, CDN, D phot; *Le dossier noir*, C/TV, 82, F, D phot; *Two Solitudes*, C, 78-79, CDN, D phot; *Black Out*, C, 78-79, CDN, D phot.

CHICOINE, Nicole
- voir REALISATEURS

CHOJNACKI, Julian
IATSE 667, ACFC, CSC, STLD. 2009 Granby Dr., Oakville, ON (416)845-4270.
Type of Production and Credits: Th Film-Cam Op/St'cam Op; TV Film-Cam Op/St'cam Op; TV Video-DOP/St'cam.
Genres: Drama-Th&TV; Comedy-Th&TV; Musical-Th&TV; Action-Th&TV.
Biography: Born 1953, Bradford, England; came to Canada, 57. Extensive back-ground in electronics. Various film festival showings of Super 8 films before becoming a professional cameraman; Steadicam operator since 82.
Selected Filmography: "The Hidden Room" (13 eps), TV, 91, USA, Cam Op; *Agaguk*, Th, 91, CDN/F, Cam Op; *If Looks Could Kill*, Th, 90, USA, Cam Op; "Sweating Bullets" (3 eps), TV, 90, CDN/USA/MEX, Cam Op; "The Hitchhiker" (21 eps), TV, 89-90, USA, Cam Op; *Looking for Miracles*, TV, 89, CDN, Cam Op; *Lantern Hill*, TV, 89, CDN, Cam Op; *Betrayed*, Th, 89, USA, St'cam Op; *Dead Bang*, Th, 89, USA, St'cam Op; *Cocktail*, Th, 88, USA, Cam Op; *Sing*, Th, 88, USA, Cam Op; *Short Circuit II*, Th, 88, USA, St'cam Op; *The Kiss*, Th, 88, USA, St'cam Op; *Three Men and a Baby*, Th, 87, USA, St'cam Op; "Kay O'Brien" (13 eps), TV, 86, USA, Cam Op.

CHOW, Wang ◊
(416)762-5448.
Type of Production and Credits: TV Film-DOP; TV Video-DOP.
Genres: Documentary-TV; Educational-TV; Industrial-TV; News-TV.
Biography: Born 1953, China; Canadian citizenship. Languages: Chinese and English. B.A.A., Ryerson Polytechnical Institute. DOP, specializes in lighting and camera operating on industrial, documentary and educational subjects.
Selected Filmography: *Chinese Cafés in Rural Saskatchewan*, TV, 85, CDN, DOP.

CIUPKA, Richard
- see DIRECTORS

COUTURE, Bernard
327 Logan, St-Lambert, PQ J4P 1H9 (514)466-9451. PAGER: (514)843-9441, #40061.
Type of Production and Credits: Th Short-DOP; TV Film-DOP; TV Video-DOP.
Genres: Drama-TV; Documentary-TV; Industrial-TV; Music Video-TV.
Biography: Born in 1956 in Trois Rivières, Quebec. Canadian citizen. Speaks English and French.
Selected Filmography: *Les Oreilles ont des Murs*, Vivianne Mongeau, MV, 91, CDN, DOP; *Graffiti*, Mario Chenart, MV, 91, CDN, DOP; *Jour Apres Jour*, Francis Martin, MV, 90, CDN, DOP; *C'est L'été*, Ralph et Barouix, MV, 90, CDN, DOP; *Balcon Perce*, Nanette Workman, MV, 90, CDN, DOP; *A la Belle Vie*, Th/TV, 90, CDN, DOP.

CRESSEY, John
STCQ. 105 rue Lauriston, Paris, 47271890, France
Type of Production and Credits: Th Film-DOP/Dir; Th Short-DOP; TV Film-DOP; TV Video-DOP.
Genres: Drama-Th&TV; Action-Th&TV; Documentary-Th&TV; Educational-Th&TV.
Biography: Born 1950, Canada. Languages: English and French. B.A., Communication Arts; M.F.A. Prix Jean Louis Bory, 82; 1st Prize, La Rochelle Film Festival, 85, and Mannheim, 85, for *The Last Sailors*; Label de la Qualité, France, 83-85, for short theatricals.
Selected Filmography: *Les Allumés*, TV, 91, F, Dir/DOP; "Les accords du Diable" (2 eps), TV, 90, F, Dir; *Nomads*, TV, 90,

F, Dir/DOP; "Reporters" (2 eps), TV, 90, F, Dir/DOP; *Riding the Rails*, Th, 88, USA, Co-Prod/DOP; *Legends of the World*, TV, 86, CDN/GM, DOP; "Great Ports of the World" (6 eps), TV, 86, USA/GB/F, Co-Prod/DOP; *Gold Lust*, TV, 85, CDN, DOP; "Lifestyles of the Rich and Famous" (4 eps), TV, 83-85, USA, DOP; "The Last Sailors" (3 eps), TV, 84, CDN/GB/F, DOP; *Health Focus*, TV, 82-84, GM, DOP; "Entertainment Tonight", TV, 84, USA, DOP; *Lettres d'amour en Somalie*, Th, 82, F, DOP; *Chassé croisé*, Th, 82, F, DOP; *Justocoeur*, Th, 80, CDN/F, Prod/DOP.

CRONE, David
CSC, IATSE. 23 Leacrest Rd., Toronto, ON M4G 1E4 (416)421-3388.
Type of Production and Credits: Th Film-Cam; TV Film-Cam.
Genres: Drama-Th&TV; Action-Th&TV; Commercials-Th&TV; Sports-Th&TV.
Biography: Born 1954, Buffalo, NY; US and Canadian citizenship. B.A., University of Western Ontario. Steadicam specialist; operator on numerous feature films. Member of Steadicam Association of America.
Selected Filmography: *Year of the Gun*, Th, 90, USA/I, St'cam Op/Op; *Kaleidoscope*, TV, 90, USA, St'cam Op/Op; *Stepping Out*, Th, 90, USA, St'cam Op/Op; "Wiseguy" (2 eps), TV, 90, USA, St'cam Op/Op; *4th War*, Th, USA, Op/St'cam Op; *The Lady Forgets*, TV, 89, USA, Op/St'cam Op; AT&T (Superbowl Cm), Cm, 89, F/USA, St'cam Op; *The Freshman*, Th, 89, USA, St'cam Op; *Stella*, Th, 89, USA, St'cam Op; *Paul McCartney Tour*, TV, 89, GB, Op; *Knight Watch*, TV, 88, USA, DOP/Op; *Welcome Home*, Th, 88, USA, Op/St'cam Cam; *Short Circuit II*, Th, 87, USA, 2nd U DOP/St'cam Op; *Adventures In Babysitting*, Th, 87, USA, St'cam Op/2nd U Cam; "Kay O'Brien - Surgeon" (pilot), TV, 86, USA, Op/St'cam Op.

CRONE, Robert C.
CSC, DGC, IATSE 669. 8175 Pasco Rd., West Vancouver, BC V7W 2T5 (604)921-6500.
Type of Production and Credits: Th Film-DOP; TV Film-Dir/Prod; TV Video-Dir/Prod.
Genres: Drama-Th; Documentary-TV; Educational-Th&TV.
Biography: Born 1932, Toronto, Ontario. Educated at Bob Jones University, South Carolina; Television Workshop of New York (Gold Camera Award). Lighting cameraman, operator, Steadicam/Panaglide specialist with 28 years of experience, gathered all over the world shooting for major TV networks and theatrical releases. Life member: CSC, DGC, Film Editors' Guild. Has won numerous awards for his work, including: 4 Genies, Air Canada Award for Outstanding Contribution to the Growth of The Canadian Film Industry, Ohio State University, The Television Workshop of New York, US Commercial Festival of Chicago, International Film and TV Festival of New York and Anik Awards. Founder and President, Film House Ltd., 63-73; former President, Association of Motion Picture Producers and Laboratories of Canada; past Chairman of the Canadian Film Awards; President, IATSE 667, 87-88. Provided Steadicam and operated live on-air via satellite for Host Broadcaster: Economic Summit Conference, Commonwealth Conference of Prime Ministers, Pope's Visit in Canada, Opening and Closing TV specials, Expo 86, Canada Day Celebrations, CBC-TV; also credits on series: "Black Stallion," "Bordertown," "Miami Vice," "Mom P.I.," and "The Hitchhiker.".
Selected Filmography: *The Hitman*, Th, 91, USA, St'cam/Cam Op/2nd U DOP; *Omen IV - The Awakening*, Th, 91, USA, St'cam/Cam Op/2nd U DOP; *The Taking of Beverly Hills*, Th, 90, USA, St'cam/Cam Op/2nd U DOP; *Look Who's Talking/Look Who's Talking Too*, Th, 89-90, USA, St'cam/Cam Op/2nd U DOP; *Run*, Th, 90, USA, St'cam/Cam Op/2nd U DOP; *Neon Rider*, Th, 90, USA, St'cam/Cam Op/2nd U DOP; *209 Hamilton Drive*, Th, 90, USA, St'cam/Cam Op/2nd U DOP; *Trial of the Incredible Hulk*, TV, 90, USA, St'cam/Cam Op/2nd U DOP; *The Kids Are All Right*, Th, 89, USA, St'cam/Cam Op/2nd U DOP; *Ashes to Ashes*, "Friday the 13th", TV, 89, CDN/USA, St'cam/Cam Op/2nd U DOP; "21 Jump Street", TV, 88-90, CDN, St'cam/Cam Op/2nd U DOP; "Wiseguy", TV, 88-90, USA, St'cam/Cam Op/2nd U DOP; *Stakeout*, Th, 88, USA, St'cam/Cam Op/2nd U DOP; *Anne of Green Gables - The Sequel*, TV, 87, CDN/USA, St'cam/Cam Op/2nd U DOP.

DE CARUFEL, René ◊
(514)273-6689.
Types de production et générique: c métrage-D photo/Prod/Réal/Cam.
Types d'oeuvres: Drame-C; Documentaire-C.
Curriculum vitae: Né en 1954, Montréal,

Québec. Langues: français, anglais et connaissance de l'espagnol. Baccalauréat en production-cinéma, Université Concordia, 83; Certificat en photographie, Cecil Community College, Maryland, EU, 75. Fonde son propre studio de photographie commerciale, 77.

Filmographie sélective: "Malle et Fils" (6 eps), C, 88, CDN, D phot; "Bread and Puppet Theatre: A Song for Nicaragua" (8 eps), C, 86, CDN, Réal/Prod/Cam; *It Is Not the Same in English*, C, 84, CDN, D phot; *Grayhound Fauna*, C, 83, CDN, D phot; *Daughter in My Shadow*, C, 83, CDN, D phot; *La Crevaison*, C, 82, CDN, D phot.

DE VOLPI, David
47 Dobie Ave., Mount Royal, PQ H3P 1R9 (514)738-4409. NFB, 3155 Cote de Liesse, Montreal, PQ H3C 3H5 (514) 283-9000.
Type of Production and Credits: Th Film-DOP; Th Short-DOP; TV Film-DOP.
Genres: Drama-Th&TV; Documentary-TV; Children's-Th&TV; Experimental-Th&TV.
Biography: Born 1942, Montreal, Quebec. Attended Loyola College. Began at the NFB, 64, as Assistant Cameraman. Apart from dramas, main skill lies in special effects work, especially the blue screen.
Selected Filmography: *Chandlers Mill*, TV, 91, CDN, DOP; *Justice Denied*, Th, 89, CDN, DOP; *Company of Strangers*, Th, 88, CDN, DOP; *The Bus*, Th, 88, CDN, Cin; *Welcome to Canada*, Th, 88, CDN, Cin; *Other Tongues*, Th, 85, CDN, DOP; *Running Scared*, TV, 85, CDN, DOP; *To Set Our House in Order/A Good Tree*, "Bell Canada Playhouse," TV, 84-85, CDN, DOP; *Out of a Job*, TV, 85, CDN, DOP; *Starbreaker*, Th, 83, CDN, DOP; *The First Winter*, TV, 82, CDN, DOP; *Revolution's Orphan*, Th, 78, CDN, DOP; *The Red Dress*, TV, 78, CDN, DOP; *Breakdown*, TV, 77, CDN, DOP; *Happiness Is Loving Your Teacher*, TV, 77, CDN, DOP.

DELACROIX, Yves
STCQ. 4591, des Erables, Montréal, PQ H2H 2E1 (514)524-7627.
Types de production et générique: c métrage-D photo; TV film-D photo; TV vidéo-D photo.
Types d'oeuvres: Documentaire-C&TV; Education-C&TV; Enfants-C&TV; Industriel-C&TV.
Curriculum vitae: Né en 1936; citoyenneté canadienne. Langues: français et anglais. Baccalauréat, Sciences humaines, Louvain, Belgique. Radio-Canada, 60-64; réalisateur de films industriels et annonces; assistant caméraman sur des annonces et documentaires depuis 66; écrit présentement des scénarios de courts métrages.

DELOREY, Walter J
- see PRODUCERS

DESHARNAIS, Jacques
CSC, SMPTE. 3414 rue Dorion, Montréal, PQ H2K 4B6 (514)598-5870. PAGETTE: 739-7923, #61079.
Types de production et générique: TV vidéo-D phot.
Types d'oeuvres: Documentaire-C&TV; Education-TV; Industriel-TV; Affaires Publiques-TV.
Curriculum vitae: Né en 1959. Langues: français et anglais avec connaissance de l'espagnol. Etudes en techiques photographiques et cinématographiques. Oeuvrant dans le milieu depuis 1980 et depuis 1985 comme directeur photo accréditation de la "Canadian Society of Cinematographers" en 1990.
Filmographie sélective: "Comment ça va?" (86 eps), TV, 88-90, CDN, D phot, (GEMEAUX).

DIBAI, Nastaran ◊
(514)486-4020.
Type of Production and Credits: TV Film-DOP/Prod; Th Film-DOP/Prod.
Genres: Drama-TV; Documentary-Th&TV; Educational-Th&TV; Commercials-TV.
Biography: Born 1960, Tehran, Iran; Canadian citizenship. Languages: English, French and Persian. Diploma (DEC), Cinema and Photography major, Vanier College; B.A., Communication Studies, Concordia University; Fellowship in Cinematography, American Film Institute, Los Angeles.
Selected Filmography: *The Feud*, Th, 87-88, USA, DOP; *World Vision*, PSA, ED, 86-87, USA, DOP; *Speaking of Nairobi*, ED, 85-86, CDN, Prod/DOP; "Q.S.A." (3 eps), ED, 85, CDN, Prod/DOP.

DION, Jean-Yves
CSC, DSC. Badomanstraade 20, 2, 1407 Copenhagen K, Denmark, (031)544-626.
Type of Production and Credits: Th Film-DOP; Th Short-DOP; TV Film-DOP; TV Video-DOP/Prod/Dir.
Genres: Drama-Th&TV; Documentary-TV; Educational-TV; Industrial-TV.
Biography: Born in 1962. Algonquin College Film School, Ottawa, Ontario, 1982, major in Camera and Editing. Certified Steadicam Operator, 1983

(Rockport, Maine, USA). Certified CSC Assistant Cameraman, 1982. Presently living in Denmark and working freelance as DOP/Director/Producer.
Selected Filmography: *Denmark*, TV, 91, DK/EEC, DOP/Dir; AF, (4 spots), Cm, 91, DK, DOP; "While the Island is Resting" (7 eps), TV, 91, DK, DOP/Dir/Ed/Prod; *The Baltic Pearl*, TV, 91, EEC, DOP/Ed; "4 Episoder" (4 eps), ED, 90, DK, DOP; *Samspil i Spanien*, TV, 90, DK, DOP; "Bornholmske Billeder" (7 eps), TV, 90, DK, DOP/Dir/Prod/Ed; "Afseatnings Okonomi" (3 eps), ED, 89, DK, DOP; *Street Tough/Heavy Beat*, ED, 89, DK, DOP; VO5, Cm, 89, DK, DOP; *Pa Monday*, Th, 89, DK, DOP; *A Life*, Th, 88, CDN, DOP; *Radio Meter Oxi*, In/Cm, 87, DK, DOP; *Blues pour une PME*, In/ED, 87, CDN, DOP.

DOSTIE, Alain
STCQ. 1903, Lionel-Groulx, Montréal, PQ H3J 1J2 (514)932-4159.
Types de production et générique: l métrage-D photo; c métrage-D photo; TV film-D photo; TV vidéo-D photo.
Types d'oeuvres: Drame-C&TV; Comédie-C; Documentaire-C.
Curriculum vitae: Né en 1943, Québec. Baccalauréat en Pédagogie, Université de Montréal, 63. Assistant caméra à partir de 63; caméraman, ONF, 67-74; pigiste depuis 74.
Filmographie sélective: *Le Dortoir*, TV, 91, CDN, D phot; *Perfectly Normal*, C, 90, CDN, D phot; *Le Party*, C, 89, CDN, D phot; *Dans le Ventre du Dragon*, C, 89, CDN, D phot; *Iron Eagle II*, C, 88, CDN/IL, D phot; *Les Fous de Bassan*, C, 86, CDN, D phot; *Kalamazoo*, C, 86, CDN, D phot; *Elvis Gratton*, C, 85, CDN, D phot; *Les Amées de rêves*, C, 83, CDN, D phot; "Empire Inc." (6 eps), TV, 82, CDN, D phot; *Au pays du Zom*, C, 80, CDN, D phot; *Le soleil se lève en retard*, C, 75, CDN, D phot; *Gina*, C, 74, CDN, D phot; *Pour le meilleur et pour le pire*, C, 74, CDN, D phot; *Les Vautours*, C, 74, CDN, D phot.

DUCKWORTH, Martin
- see DIRECTORS

DUFAUX, Georges
4653 Christophe-Colombe, Montréal, PQ H2J 3G7 (514)597-1767.
Types de production et générique: l métrage-D photo/Réal/Mont; c métrage-D photo/Réal/Mont; TV film-D photo/Réal/Mont.
Types d'oeuvres: Drame-C; Documentaire-C&TV; Expérimental-C; Sports-C.
Curriculum vitae: Né en 1927, Lille, France; citoyenneté canadienne. Langues: français et anglais. Diplômé de l'Ecole nationale de cinématographie, Vaugirard, Louis Lumière, Paris, 47. Technicien de laboratoire de cinéma, Brésil, 53-56. Office national du film du Canada, 56-89; caméraman depuis, 57, réalisateur et directeur photo depuis 63. Directeur général du programme français de l'ONF 86-89. Pigiste depuis 89. Récipiendaire de plusieurs prix internationaux.
Filmographie sélective: *La Demoiselle sauvage*, C, 91, CDN/CH, D phot/Co prod; *Une Histoire inventée*, C, 90, CDN, D phot; *Hotel Chronicles*, TV, 89, CDN, D phot; *10 Days, 48 Hours*, TV, 85, CDN, Réal/Cam/Mont; *Bayo*, C, 84, CDN, D phot; *La Femme de l'hôtel*, C, 83, CDN, D phot; *Les Enfants des normes post scriptum*, TV, 83, CDN, Réal/Cam/Mont; "Gui Daò" (3 eps), TV, 80, CDN, Réal/Cam; *Les Beaux Souvenirs*, C, 80, CDN, D phot; "Les Enfants des normes" (8 eps), TV, 78, CDN, Réal/Cam; *Au bout de mon âge*, TV, 75, CDN, Réal/Cam/Mont; *Partis pour la gloire*, C, 74, CDN, D phot; *A votre santé*, TV, 73, CDN, Réal/Cam/Mont; *Fortune and Men's Eyes*, C, 71, CDN, D phot/Mont; *L'Homme multiplié*, C, 69, CDN, Réal/Cam/Mont.

DUFAUX, Guy ◆
(514) 523-0558.
Types de production et générique: l métrage-D photo; c métrage-D photo/Réal; TV film-D photo.
Types d'oeuvres: Drame-C&TV; Comédie-C&TV; Action-C&TV; Documentaire-C&TV.
Curriculum vitae: Né en 1943, Lille, France; citoyenneté canadienne. Etudes aux Beaux-Arts à Marseille, France. Monteur et caméraman aux Cinéastes Associés; ONF, 66-70; directeur fondateur des Productions Prisma, 70-77; Président du Syndicat National du Cinéma, 69-70; Président de l'ARRFQ, 75-76; Directeur du Conseil d'Administration de l'Institut Québécois du Cinéma.
Filmographie sélective: *Un Zoo la Nuit*, Th, 86, CDN, D phot, (GENIE 88); *Scalp*, C, 85, CDN, D phot; *Le Déclin de l'Empire américain*, C, 85, CDN, D phot; *Equinoxe*, C, 85, CDN, D phot; *Pouvoir intime*, C, 85, CDN, D phot; "Un amour de quartier" (13 eps), TV, 84, CDN, D phot; *Le Jour "S..."*, C, 83, CDN, D phot; *De l'autre côté de la glace*, C, 83, CDN, Co réal; *Sonatine*, C, 82, CDN, D phot; "Zigzag" (5 eps), TV, 82, CDN, D phot;

Le Futur intérieur, C, 81, CDN, D phot' *La Mer de Beaufort*, TV, 81, CDN, Réal/Cam; *Les Fleurs sauvages*, C, 81, CDN, D phot; *L'Equipe des Grands défis*, In, 81, CDN, Phot/Réal; *Les Pièges de la mer*, C, 81, CDN, Cam; "L'Age de l'énergie" (13 eps), TV, 79, CDN, Cam.

DUNBAR, George
George Dunbar Photography, 39 Tralee Avenue, Scarborough, ON M1G 3E3 (416)439-2361.
Type of Production and Credits: TV Film-DOP.
Genres: Documentary-TV; Industrial-TV.
Biography: Born 1934, Toronto, Ontario. Has received awards from the Professional Photographers of Canada, Toronto Art Directors' Club, Chicago Industrial Film Festival, *Communication Arts* magazine, *Studio* magazine, International Association of Business Communicators.
Selected Filmography: *IBM Annual Corporate Report*, In, 85, CDN, DOP.

DUNK, Albert ✧
(416)961-6857.
Type of Production and Credits: Th Film-DOP; TV Film-DOP.
Genres: Drama-Th&TV; Comedy-Th&TV; Action-Th&TV; Music Video-TV.
Biography: Born 1944, Regina, Saskatchewan. Studied Photography, Germaine School of Photography, New York. Started career as Assistant Cameraman in New York; Operator, then freelance DOP; DOP on numerous commercials and music videos.
Selected Filmography: "Murphy's Law" (pilot), TV, 88, USA, DOP; "Passion and Paradise", TV, 88, CDN/USA/GB, DOP; *Fight For Life*, TV, 87, USA, DOP; *Haunted by Her Past*, TV, 87, USA, DOP; *Child Saver*, TV, 87, USA, DOP; *The Ruling Passion*, TV, 86, USA, DOP; *Perry Mason Returns*, TV, 85, USA, DOP; *Illusions*, TV, 85, USA, DOP, (CSC); *If You Could See What I Hear*, Th, 82, CDN, 2nd U Cam; "Cagney and Lacey" (pilot), TV, 81, USA, DOP, (CSC); *Incubus*, Th, 81, CDN, DOP; *Hank Williams: "The Show He Never Gave"*, Th, 81, CDN, DOP; *Class of 1984*, Th, 81, CDN, DOP; *Escape from Iran: The Canadian Caper*, TV, 80, CDN, DOP; *Murder by Phone/Bells*, Th, 80, CDN, 2nd U Cam.

EARNSHAW, Philip
CSC. 177 Geoffrey St., Toronto, ON M5R 1P6 (416)536-5241.
Type of Production and Credits: TV Film-DOP/Dir; TV Video-DOP/Dir.
Genres: Drama-TV; Documentary-TV; Educational-TV; Children's-TV; Commercials-TV.
Biography: Born 1951, Hamilton, Ontario. Honours B.A., Fine Arts, York University, 75. Worked for 3 years as a photojournalist and news cameraman; Staff Cameraman, Global TV News, 75-78; freelance DOP/Director 78 to present.
Selected Filmography: "Degrassi Talks" (6 eps), TV, 91, CDN, Dir/Cam; "Degrassi High" (28 eps), TV, 89-90, CDN, DOP; "Degrassi High" (2 eps), TV, 90, CDN, Dir; "Degrassi Junior High", TV, 86-88, CDN, DOP; "Owl TV" (20 eps), TV, 85-86, CDN, DOP; "Kids of Degrassi Street" (26 eps), TV, 79-85, CDN, DOP; *The Passion*, TV, 82, CDN, Dir.

ENNIS, Bob
3924 Blantyre Place, North Vancouver, BC V7G 2G4 (604)929-5355. Argus Productions, 1040 - 475 West Georgia St., Vancouver, BC V6B 4M9 (604)687-4707. FAX: 682-4800.
Type of Production and Credits: Th Film-DOP; Th Short-DOP; Th Short-DOP; TV Film-DOP.
Genres: Drama-Th&TV; Comedy-TV; Action-TV; Documentary-TV.
Biography: Born 1943, Calgary, Alberta. Director, Producer of commercials and short documentaries. Has won the Governor General's Award and Gold Camera Award, Chicago.
Selected Filmography: "Nancy Drew" (pilot), TV, 90, CDN, DOP; "The Black Stallion" (8 eps), TV, 90, CDN, DOP; *In Perfect Harmony*, TV, 90, CDN, DOP; "Danger Bay" (88 eps), TV, 86-89, CDN/USA, DOP; *Home Is Where The Hart Is*, Th, CDN, 88, CDN, DOP; *Stone Fox*, TV, CDN/USA, 88, DOP.

ETHIER, Martial
- voir MONTEURS

EVDEMON, Nikos
CSC, ACCT. 72 Southwood Dr., Toronto, ON M4E 2T9 (416)690-6644.
Type of Production and Credits: Th Film-DOP; TV Film-DOP.
Genres: Drama-Th&TV; Comedy-TV; Action-TV; Documentary-TV; Commercials-TV.
Biography: Born in 1949 in Salonika, Greece; Greek and Canadian citizenship. Languages: English, German and Greek. Attended Academy for Film and TV, Berlin, Germany. Has won 5 Anik and 3 Gemini awards; also received nominations for Canadian Film Award, Bijou (for *Final Edition*), and Anik.
Selected Filmography: "Material World"

(6 eps), TV, CDN, DOP; *Getting Married in Buffalo Jump*, TV, CDN, DOP; *Millennium in Russia*, TV, CDN, DOP, (ANIK); *The Private Capital*, TV, CDN, DOP; *Glory Enough for All* (mini-series), TV, CDN/GB, DOP, (GEMINI 89, ANIK); *Nest of Singing Birds*, TV, CDN, DOP; "Seeing Things" (42 eps), TV, CDN, DOP, (GEMINI 86, GEMINI 87); *Breaking All The Rules*, TV, CDN, DOP; *The Marriage Bed*, TV, CDN, DOP; *One Foot In Heaven*, "Man Alive", TV, CDN, DOP, (ANIK); *May's Miracle*, "Man Alive", TV, CDN, DOP, (ANIK); "For the Record" (3 eps), TV, CDN, DOP; *Final Edition*, TV, CDN, DOP; "Sidestreet" (8 eps), TV, CDN, DOP; *Lost Battle*, "News Magazine", TV, CDN, DOP, (ANIK).

FERGUSON, Graeme
- see DIRECTORS

FIKS, Henri
CSC, IATSE 667, STCQ. 66 Hampton Ave., Toronto, ON M4K 2Y6 (416)466-8739. True Greed Inc. (416)466-8739.
Type of Production and Credits: Th Film-DOP; Th Short-DOP; TV Film-DOP.
Genres: Drama-Th&TV; Comedy-Th&TV; Documentary-Th&TV; Educational-Th&TV.
Biography: Born 1938, Paris, France; Canadian and French citizenship. Languages: English, French and Spanish. Specialized in 2nd unit cinematography. *A Fine Line* won Silver Hugo, Chicago; *Life Machine* won Gold Medal, NY; *Whistling Smith* received an Oscar nomination.
Selected Filmography: *Rolling Stones: Steel Wheels* (Imax), Th, 90, CDN, Cam Op; *Clearcut*, Th, 90, CDN, 2nd U DOP; *The Dream Team*, Th, 88, USA, Cam Op; *Three Men and a Baby*, Th, 87, USA, Cam Op; *Martin's Day*, Th, 83, CDN/GB, 2nd U DOP; *A Fine Line*, ED, 81, CDN, DOP; *Life Machine*, "Camera and Song", ED, 76, GB, DOP; *Whistling Smith*, TV, 76, CDN, DOP.

FILLINGHAM, Tom ✧
(604)736-9601.
Type of Production and Credits: Th Film-Prod/1st AD; TV Film-DOP.
Genres: Drama-Th&TV; Documentary-TV; Educational-TV.
Biography: Born 1949, Noranda, Quebec. Languages: English and French. B.A., major in Sociology.
Selected Filmography: "21 Jump Street" (28 eps), TV, 86-87, CDN, Op/2nd U DOP; *The Outside Chance of Maximilian Glick*, Th, 87, CDN, Op; "His Highness the Aga Khan" (5 eps), In, 85, CDN/F, DOP; *Focus on Korea*, In, 85, CDN/USA/SKO, DOP; "Stir Crazy" (6 eps), TV, 85, USA, 2nd U DOP/Op; "Danger Bay" (1 eps), TV, 85, CDN, 2nd U DOP; *Samuel Lount*, Th, 84, CDN, Op.

FOX, Lloyd M
IATSE, NABET. 701 - 29 Roslyn Rd., Winnipeg, MB R3L 0G1 (204)452-9181. CBC, 541 Portage Ave., Winnipeg MB R3C 2H1 (204)788-3222.
Type of Production and Credits: Th Film-Light Dir; TV Video-Light Dir.
Genres: Variety-Th&TV; Musical-Th&TV; News-Th&TV; Sports-Th&TV.
Biography: Born 1953, Winnipeg, Manitoba; Canadian citizenship. Languages: English, some French and Portuguese. B.A., B.Comm., Certificate in Labour Relations, University of Manitoba. Production/Technical Co-ordinator at the Winnipeg Convention Centre for 16 years. Freelance Production/Lighting Designer for CBC, CTV, TSN, CKND (Global) and WDAY (ABC affiliate). Background in stage, theatre, dance (ballet), jazz, rock & roll. Production design awards for various commercials and productions (Houston, San Francisco and New York).
Selected Filmography: *Kastin*, "Adrienne Clarkson Presents", TV, 91, CDN, Light Dir; "Hymn Sing" (24 eps), TV, 91, CDN, Co Light Dir; "Penner's Place" (24 eps), TV, 91, CDN, Assist Light Dir; "Meeting Place" (3 eps), TV, 91, CDN, Light Dir; *Budweiser Pro Rodeo*, "CBC Sports Weekend", TV, 91, CDN, Assist Light Dir; *Fina Cup Diving* (2 seg), "CBC Sports Weekend", TV, 91, CDN, Assist Light Dir; "CBC Newsworld" (4 eps), TV, 91, CDN, Light Dir; "Festival du voyage" (5 eps), TV, 91, CDN, Assist Light Dir; "Hockey Night in Canada", (5 eps), TV, 90, CDN, Light Dir; *NDP National Convention*, "CBC News", TV, 89, Tech-Light Dir; "CTV National News" (5 eps), TV, 89, CDN, Light Dir; "Canada A.M.", (5 eps), TV, 89, CDN, Light Dir; *Indian Time* (pilot), TV, 88, CDN, Assist Light Dir; *Welcome Home* (pilot), TV, 87, CDN, Light Assist; *Geography Club Presents ...Brazil*, Th/TV, 85, CDN/ USA/BR, Assist Cam.

GANDER, Mogens
- see PRODUCERS

GAUVREAU, Gil
- see DIRECTORS

GEDDES, David ✧
(604)929-4760.
Type of Production and Credits: Th Film-Cam; Th Short-DOP; TV Film-

DOP/Cam.
Genres: Drama-Th&TV; Comedy-Th&TV; Action-TV; Documentary-Th&TV.
Biography: Born 1949, Vancouver, BC. Honours Diploma, Photographic Technology, Northern Alberta Institute of Technology; Film Studies, Banff School of Fine Arts; Photography, Simon Fraser University. Freelance cinematographer since 74; extensive experience in TV series, features, theatrical shorts, documentaries, educational films and commercials; familiarity with Showscan and Omnimax formats. Films he has shot have received nominations for Genie, Gemini and other awards.
Selected Filmography: "21 Jump Street" (49 eps), TV, 87-89, CDN, DOP; *Dead Bang*, Th, 88, USA, Cam; *Experts*, Th, 88, USA, 2nd U DOP; *People Across the Lake*, TV, 88, USA, Cam; "The Beachcombers" (2 eps), TV, 88, CDN, DOP; *Moving Day*, "Lies from Lotusland", TV, 87, CDN/USA, DOP; *Little Match Girl*, TV, 87, USA, Cam; *Whalesong*, TV, 86, CDN, Cin; *World Drums*, TV, 86, CDN, DOP; *Home Is Where the Hart Is*, Th, 86, CDN, Cam; *The Climb*, Th, 85, CDN/GB, Cam; *Rad*, Th, 85, USA, Cam; *My Kind of Town*, Th, 84, CDN, DOP; *No Vacancy*, Th, 83, CDN, Dir/DOP; *Spartree*, Th, 77, CDN, Cam.

GÉLINAS, Michel
- voir PRODUCTEURS

GEORGE, Laszlo
IATSE 644, 667, 659. 80 Greenbrook Dr., Toronto, ON M6M 2J9 (416)656-8586. 8616 East Worthington Dr., Los Angeles, CA 91775 USA (213)271-1686. 3341 Pt. Grey Rd., Vancouver, BC V6R 1A4 (604)731-2322.
Type of Production and Credits: Th Film-DOP; TV Film-DOP.
Genres: Drama-Th&TV; Action-TV; Commercials-Th&TV.
Biography: Born in Budapest, Hungary; Canadian citizenship; US resident alien. Languages: English and Hungarian. Diploma, Academy of Film and Dramatic Arts, Budapest. Has won Best Cinematography Award (CFA) and Achievement Award (CSC).
Selected Filmography: *Christmas on Division Street*, TV, 91, CDN/USA, DOP; *Danielle Steele's Daddy*, TV, 91, USA, DOP; *Seduction in Tarvis County*, TV, 91, USA, DOP; *Mimi and Me*, TV, 91, USA, DOP; *Hamilton Drive*, TV, 90, CDN/USA, DOP; *Always Remember That I Love You*, TV, 90, CDN/USA, DOP; *Kaleidoscope*, TV, 90, CDN/USA, DOP; *Last Flight Out*, TV, 89, USA, DOP; "Hardball" (13 eps), TV, 89, USA, DOP; *Turn Back the Clock*, TV, 89, USA, DOP; *The Prize Pulitzer*, TV, 89, USA, DOP; *Tarzan in Manhattan*, TV, 89, USA, DOP; *Swimsuit*, TV, 89, USA, DOP; *Kennedys of Massachusetts* (mini-series), TV, 88, USA, DOP.

GILDAY, Leonard
ACFC, CSC, CIFC. 13 Browning Ave., Toronto, ON M4K 1V8 (416)489-0545.
Type of Production and Credits: TV Film-DOP/Prod/Dir.
Genres: Documentary-TV.
Biography: Has twenty years experience in documentaries with a special interest in international development and natural history subjects.
Selected Filmography: *Oil*, "The Nature of Things", TV, 91, CDN, DOP/Prod/Dir; *Urban Watershed*, "The Nature of Things", TV, 91, CDN, DOP/Prod/Dir; *Northern Development*, "The Nature of Things"/ "National Geographic," TV, 90, CDN/USA, DOP/Assoc Prod/Co Dir; *Temagami*, "The Nature of Things", TV, 90, CDN, DOP/Prod/Dir; *Herschel Island*, "The Nature of Things", TV, 90, CDN, DOP/Prod/Dir.

GRAVELLE, Raymond
- voir PRODUCTEURS

GREGG, Kenneth W.
CSC. 3650 Kaneff Crescent, #908, Misscentissauga, ON L5A 4A1 (416)848-2029.
Type of Production and Credits: TV Film-DOP; TV Video-DOP; Th Film-DOP.
Genres: Drama-Th&TV; Musical-TV; Documentary-TV; Educational-TV.
Biography: Born 1928, Winnipeg, Manitoba. Graduated with top marks from the Royal Canadian Air Force School of Photography, 49; served as photographer for 5 years. Joined CBC, Winnipeg, 54; stills photographer, film editor and cinematographer, 13 years; transferred to CBC Toronto. Awarded CBC President's Award, 82.
Selected Filmography: *The Magic Season of Robertson Davies*, TV, 90, CDN, DOP; *The Great Teacher: Northrop Frye*, TV, 89, CDN, DOP; "The Campbells" (4 eps), TV, 88, CDN/USA/GB, DOP; *2 Men*, TV, 88, CDN, DOP; "The Beachcombers" (9 eps), TV, 87, CDN, DOP, (ANIK); *Momma's Going to Buy You a Mockingbird*, TV, 87, CDN, DOP; *Karsh: The Searching Eye*, TV, 86, CDN, DOP; *Oakmount High*, TV, 85, CDN, DOP;

The Mystery of Henry Moore, TV, 84, CDN, DOP; *Gentle Sinners*, TV, 83, CDN, DOP; *Raymond Massey: Actor of the Century*, TV, 82, CDN, DOP; "The Music of Man" (8 eps), TV, 78, CDN, DOP; *One Night Stand*, TV, 77, CDN, DOP; *Homage to Chagall*, Th, 75, CDN, DOP; *A Bird in the House*, TV, 73, CDN, DOP, (CFA).

GREGORY, Colin Hugh
IATSE 669, CSC. 202 - 9133 Capella Dr., Burnaby, BC V3J 7K3 (604) 421-6119. Procam Camera Services Inc., 202 - 9133 Capella Dr., Burnaby, BC, V3J 7K3 (604) 650-2931. Dot Bristow Management, 1006 - 1166 Alberni St., Vancouver, BC V6E 3Z3 (604) 681-7666.
Type of Production and Credits: TV Video-DOP.
Genres: Drama-TV; Documentary-TV; Commercials-TV; Industrial-TV.
Biography: Born 1951, Christchurch, New Zealand; Canadian and New Zealand citizenship. B.A., Photography and Theatre Arts, University of Saskatchewan. 20 years industry experience; owner/ operator Betacam SP. Specialties: video drama, electronic press packaging, documentaries "film-look" camera and lighting. *A Duck in the Wilderness* won Award of Merit, Intercom; *Distant Battles* won Certificate of Creative Excellence: US Industrial Film Festival.
Selected Filmography: *The Journey Home*, TV, 91, CDN, DOP; *Let's Eat - with Burt Wolf*, TV, 91, USA, DOP; *TWU: Basic Grievance Procedures*, In, 90, CDN, DOP; *Cold Water Wash*, BC Hydro, Cm, 90, CDN, DOP; *Billy Jacob's Story*, TV, 90, CDN, DOP; "Vancouver '86" (13 eps), TV, 86, CDN, DOP; *Distant Battles*, TV, 85, CDN, DOP; *The Last Time*, MV, 84, CDN, DOP; *A Duck in the Wilderness*, "The Achievers", ED, 82, CDN, Dir.

GRIPPO, Michael
NABET. 39 Northgate Dr., Downsview, ON M3K 1R3 (416)630-6766. The Journal, CBC, 100 Carlton St., Toronto, ON (416)975-7800.
Type of Production and Credits: TV Video-Cam.
Genres: Documentary-TV; Current Affairs-TV; News-TV; Sports-TV.
Biography: Born in 1960 in Toulon, France. Canadian citizen. Languages: English, French, Italian. Seneca College of Applied Arts and Technology. News and current affairs cameraman, Global Television News, 1981-88; Cameraman, "Le Tele Journal", 1988-89. Documentary cameraman, "The Journal", CBC, 1989 to date. Special interests: film, sports, travel.

HALLIS, Ron
- see DIRECTORS

HARTMANN, Peter
176 Hammersmith Ave., Toronto, ON M4E 2W8 (416)693-5648. Cinemarine Inc., 176 Hammersmith Ave., Toronto, ON M4E 2W8 (416)464-4364.
Type of Production and Credits: Th Film-DOP; Th Short-DOP.
Genres: Commercials-Th&TV; Drama-Th&TV; Documentary-Th&TV; Music Video-Th&TV.
Biography: Born in 1937 in Esslingen, Germany. Canadian citizen. Special skills in underwater and aerial cinematography. DOP on many award-winning commercials. Winner of the Best Cinematography Award, Canadian Society of Cinematographers for the commercial *Classics Parking Lot*, 1990. *Cat & Mouse* won First Place, U.S. Mobius Award in category and was short-listed for first overall. It was also awarded the Canadian Gold Bessie for first overall and Gold for first in category. *Artist* was awarded the Silver Bessie in category. *Point of No Returns* won the Bronze Bessie in category. *Water Babies* was awarded a Certificate of Merit Bessie and Unique Cinematography from the CSC. *Sad Clown* was also awarded a Certificate of Merit Bessie.
Selected Filmography: *Cat & Mouse*, Cm, 90, CDN, DOP; *Artist*, Cm, 90, CDN, DOP; *Point of No Returns*, Cm, 90, CDN, DOP; *Water Babies*, Cm, 90, CDN, DOP; *Sad Clown*, Cm, 90, CDN, DOP; *Classics Parking Lot*, Cm, 89, CDN, DOP.

HASSEN, Christopher
IATSE 667. Appaloosa Media Prod. Ltd., 168 Beedfield Cl. N.E., Calgary, AB T3K 3K8 (403)275-0210.
Type of Production and Credits: TV Film-DOP; Th Film-Cam; Th Short-Cam.
Genres: Drama-Th&TV; Documentary-TV; Commercials-TV; Music Video-TV.
Biography: Born 1955, New Westminster, BC. Graduate of Film program, Southern Alberta Institute of Technology. Photographed several commercials, 88.

HEATON, Pauline
IATSE 667, IATSE 669. Watervisions Underwater Camera Systems, 479 Shannon Way, Delta (Vancouver), BC V4M 2W6 (604)943-2332. FAX: 943-3608.
Type of Production and Credits: Th Film-DOP; Th Short-DOP; TV Film-DOP.

Genres: Drama-Th&TV; Action-Th&TV; Documentary-Th&TV; Commercials-TV.
Biography: Born 1959, Glenwilliams, Ontario. B.A.A., Motion Picture, Ryerson Polytechnical Institute. Professional scuba diver; specializes in underwater cinematography; designed and developed underwater lighting and camera systems, including state-of-the-art Aqualight underwater lighting system. Aqualights sold and rented internationally; feature rentals include Ridley Scott's *Thelma & Louise* and Industrial *Light and Magic*. Extensive consulting services on various productions including work on the completion of *Children of a Lesser God*. Credits listed refer to underwater projects.
Selected Filmography: "Scene of the Crime", TV, 91, USA, Cam; *And the Sea Will Tell*, Th, 90, CDN, DOP; Bob's Your Uncle, MV, 90, CDN, DOP; *Submarine Toy*, Irwin Toys, Cm, 90, CDN, Prod Cons/Tech Dir; *Clearcut*, Th, 90, CDN, DOP; *Grey Whales*, "Sesame Street", TV, 90, CDN, DOP/Pro Coord; *Cocos Islands*, TV, 90, USA, DOP/Prod Cons; "21 Jumpstreet", TV, 90, USA, DOP; *Octopus*, TV, 90, USA, DOP/Prod Cons/PM; *Booker*, TV, 90, USA, DOP; Red Cross Commercials, Cm, 89, CDN, Cam; *Belize*, TV, 89, Cam/Light Tech; "Danger Bay", TV, 89, CDN, DOP/Pro Coord; *Arctic*, TV, 89, I, Cin/Tech Dir; *Salt Water People*, Th, 89, CDN, Cam/Tech Dir.

HEBB, Brian R.R.
CSC, ACCT. 34 Brunswick Ave., Toronto, ON M5S 2L7 (416)923-7102.
Type of Production and Credits: Th Film-DOP; TV Film-DOP.
Genres: Drama-Th&TV; Documentary-TV.
Biography: Born 1949, Nova Scotia; grew up in England, 55-68. Canadian and British citizenship. Attended Photographic Art College England. Life-long study of drama. Commercial photographer since 66; employed at CBC, 69-85; DOP since 77; freelance DOP since 85. Has phototgraphed over 120 dramatic productions for theatre and TV, many of which have won awards and for which he has had numerous personal nominations. Writer, director and producer of 5 short films; writer of short stories and essays.
Selected Filmography: *On Thin Ice*, TV, 90, USA, DOP; *Running Against Time*, TV, 90, USA, DOP; *The Challengers*, TV, 89, CDN, DOP; *Murder by Night*, TV, 89, USA, DOP; *Termini Station*, Th, 88, CDN, DOP; "The Twilight Zone", Th, 88, CDN, DOP; "Ray Bradbury Theatre" (4 eps), TV, 87, CDN/USA/GB/F, DOP; *Cowboys Don't Cry*, Th/TV, 87, CDN, DOP; *Sadie and Son*, TV, 87, USA, DOP; "Alfred Hitchcock Presents" (13 eps), TV, 86-87, CDN/USA, DOP; "Street Legal" (9 eps), TV, 86-87, CDN, DOP; *The Shell Game*, TV, 85, CDN, DOP; "For the Record" (8 eps), TV, 82-84, CDN, DOP; *Humongous*, Th, 82, CDN, DOP; *Something's Rotten*, Th, 78, CDN, DOP.

HENDERSON, Clark
- see DIRECTORS

HERRINGTON, David C.
IATSE 667, ACCT, CSC. Kandan Productions Inc., 22424 De Grasse Dr., Woodland Hills, CA 91364 (818)591-9754. Stacy Cheriff, 650 North Bronson Ave., Ste. 148, Los Angeles, CA 90004 (213)962-9030.
Type of Production and Credits: Th Film-DOP; TV Film-DOP.
Genres: Drama-Th&TV; Comedy-TV; Commercials-Th&TV; Music Video-TV.
Biography: Born 1948, London, England; Canadian and British citizenship. Worked at Film House as Chief Timer, 72-74; Technical Director, 75-78; Camera Assistant, Focus Puller on various features, 78-84; DOP on 100 commercials since 84, winning 10 awards including Bronze Lion at Cannes, Bessie. Nominated for an Emmy for *Pippi Longstocking*. Was invited to become a full member of CSC in January 1988 because of the outstanding body of work that he has produced in such a short time. Nominated for a Gemini for *Hoover vs. The Kennedys*.
Selected Filmography: *Pleasant Little Murder*, TV, 90, USA, DOP; *Common Crowd*, TV, 90, USA, DOP; Canada Tourism, Cm, 1987/90, CDN, DOP; *Primo Baby*, Th, 88, CDN, DOP; *Love and Murder*, Th, 88, CDN, DOP; "War of the Worlds" (5 eps), TV, 88, CDN, DOP; *Ciao Romeo*, Cm, 88, CDN, DOP; *Ghost of a Chance*, Th, 87, USA, DOP; *Hoover vs. The Kennedys*, TV, 87, CDN, DOP; *Judgement in Stone*, Th, 86, CDN, DOP; *Deadly Business*, TV, 86, USA, DOP; Chanel Promo, Cm, 86, CDN, DOP; *Pippi Longstocking*, TV, 85, USA, DOP; Black Diamond Cheese, Cm, 85, CDN, DOP; Q-Tips, Cm, 84, CDN, DOP.

HERRON, J. Barry ✧
(619)471-7857.
Type of Production and Credits: Th Film-DOP; Th Short-DOP/Dir; TV Film-DOP/Dir.
Genres: Drama-Th&TV; Action-Th&TV; Documentary-Th&TV.

Biography: Born 1935, Vancouver, BC. Trained as junior newspaper photographer on the *Daily Province*; joined RCAF and served as public relations photographer for 5 years; emigrated to US, 58; began to work with film industry in Hollywood, 62; freelance DOP and director since; specializes in aerial and underwater cinematography and familiar with Circlevision, Showscan, Imax and Omnimax formats.
Selected Filmography: *The Young Graduates*, Th, USA, DOP; "Air Wolf" (22 eps)(DOP 20 eps/Dir 2 eps), TV, 86-87, CDN, DOP; "Watch Dog" (pilot), TV, 87, USA, DOP; "Love Boat" (5 eps), TV, 85-86, USA, 2nd U Dir/DOP; *New Magic* (Showscan/partial Cin), Th, 85-86, USA, DOP; *Oh Canada* (Epcot/Circlevision), Th, 85, USA, DOP; "Fall Guy" (2 eps), TV, 84, USA, 2nd U DOP; "Magnum P.I." (5 eps), TV, 81, USA, 2nd U DOP; *A Whale for the Killing*, TV 78, USA, 2nd U Dir/DOP; *Orca the Killer Whale*, Th, 75, USA/I, 2nd U Dir/DOP; *Mustang Country*, Th, 72, USA, DOP; "The Challenging Sea" (4 eps), TV, 70s, USA, Dir/DOP; "National Geographic Specials" (4 eps), TV, 60s, USA, DOP; "Animal World" (9 eps), TV, 60s, USA, DIr/DOP.

HOFFMAN, Philip
- see DIRECTORS

HOLMES, Robert
ACFC. (416) 461-9589.
Type of Production and Credits: TV Film-DOP; TV Video-DOP.
Genres: Drama-Th&TV; Documentary-Th&TV; Industrial-TV; Current Affairs-TV.
Biography: Born 1947.
Selected Filmography: "W5" (22 eps/yr), TV, 84-91, CDN, DOP.

HOLOSKO, John
IATSE, SMPTE, CSC. 78 Tunney Cr., Markham, ON L3P 4L3 (416)471-4401.
Type of Production and Credits: Th Film-DOP; Th Short-DOP; TV Film-DOP; TV Video-DOP.
Genres: Drama-Th&TV; Comedy-Th&TV; Documentary-Th&TV; Commercials-Th&TV; Music Video-Th&TV.
Biography: Specials skills: helicopter systems - Tyler, Westcam; remote camera systems - Cam-Remote, Power Pod, Hot Head; Anamorphic Format; snorkel systems; underwater cinematography. Testing film for Kodak.
Selected Filmography: *Cap'n Crunch*, Cm, 91, CDN, DOP; *The Cutting Edge*, Th, 91, USA, 2nd Unit DOP; *Homework Bureau*, Th, 91, CDN, DOP; *Wintario*, Cm, 91, CDN, DOP; *Air Canada*, In, 91, CDN, DOP; *Headache Clinic*, In, 91, CDN, DOP; *Molson Indy*, Cm, 90, CDN, DOP; *CFNY/Howard & Fred*, Cm, 90, CDN, DOP; *Molson Grand Prix*, Cm, 90, CDN, DOP; *Tre-Stella Cheese*, Cm, 90, CDN, DOP; *I Used To Cry*, MV, 88, CDN, DOP.

HORNBECK, Gordon
Cine Services, 227 Haddon Rd. S.W., Calgary, AB T2V 2Y8 (403)253-0281.
Type of Production and Credits: Th Film-Cam; Th Short-DOP; TV Film-DOP/Dir; TV Video-DOP/Dir.
Genres: Drama-Th&TV; Documentary-Th&TV; Commercials-TV; Industrial-Th&TV.
Biography: Born in 1948 in Winnipeg, Manitoba. B.A., B.Ed., University of Brandon. Film cameraman for 17 years; scuba instructor; equipment includes complete Arri 16SR and Betacam packages.
Selected Filmography: "Olympic Winter Games - Calgary 88" (5 eps), TV, 88, CDN, Cam; "Olympic Volunteer Training" (10 eps), TV, 87, CDN, DOP; *Daughters of the Country* (underwater seq), Th, 86, CDN, DOP; *Ghostkeeper*, Th, 81, CDN, 2nd U Cam; "Canadian Crimes" (15 eps), TV, 75, CDN, DOP.

HORVATH, Stefan
IATSE 667, SMPTE. 325 Bogert Ave., #1108-C, Toronto, ON M2N 1L8 (416)733-9287.
Type of Production and Credits: Th Film-DOP/Cam; Th Short-DOP/Cam; TV Film-DOP/Cam.
Genres: Drama-Th; Comedy-Th; Musical-Th; Documentary-Th; Industrial-Th&TV; Dance-Th&TV; Children's-Th; Educa-tional-Th; Science Fiction-Th.
Biography: Born 1929, Timisoara, Romania; Canadian citizenship. Languages: Hungarian, Romanian, Russian, English, German and French. Attended VGIK Unional State Film Art Institute, Moscow, 49-54. Professor for 13 years, Institute for Film and Theatrical Arts (I.L. Caragiale), Bucharest, Romania. Has won awards for science fiction films at Edinburgh, Trieste, Mamaia, Paris; for TV ballet at Adelaide. Co-creator of Transcolor, a special colour effect invention (Romania).
Selected Filmography: *Running Brave*, Th, 83, CDN/USA, 2nd U DOP/2nd U Cam; *Manor Gardens/Year of the Child and Family in B.C.*, Cm, 79, CDN, Dir/Cam /Ed; *The Story of Love*, Th, 77, R, DOP; *The Fantastic Comedy*, Th, 75, R,

DOP; *The Desperates/An August in Flames*, Th, 74, R, DOP; *Captain John's Arrow*, Th, 73, R, DOP; *On a Certain Happiness*, Th, 73, R, Cam; *Bihor Under the Sun*, TV, 72, R, DOP; *Take-Off*, Th, 72, R, DOP; *The Happy Prince*, TV, 70, R, DOP; *The Girl with the Matches*, TV, 69, R, DOP; *The Silent Friends/Dogs to the Rescue*, TV, 69, CDN/R, DOP; *In Romania*, ED, 68, CDN/R, DOP; *The Cyclists Are Coming*, Th, 67, R, DOP; *The Legend of Skylark*, TV, 66, R, DOP.

HOSEK, George
1229 Marlborough Court, #1005, Oakville, ON L6H 3B6 (416)338-6422.
Type of Production and Credits: Th Film-DOP; TV Film-DOP; TV Video-DOP.
Genres: Drama-Th; Variety-Th&TV; Documentary-Th; Music Video-Th&TV.
Biography: Born in 1951 in Prague, Czechoslovakia. Landed immigrant. Speaks English, Czech, Russian, Serbo-Croatian and Bulgarian. Received diploma and technical certificate, Department of Film and TV Pictures, Academy of Arts, Prague, 1970-75.
Selected Filmography: *Graveyard Story*, Th, 90, CDN, DOP; HDV, MV, 90, CDN, DOP; GE, Cm, 1990, CDN, DOP; *Songs Don't Have To Die*, Th, 83, CS, DOP; *Where The Courier Disappeared*, Th, 81, CS, DOP.

HUCULAK, William
- see EDITORS

HUTTON, Joan
CSC, IATSE 667, ACCT. High Road Productions, 52-R Badgerow Ave., Toronto, ON M4M 1V4 (416)461-3089. FAX: 466-8423.
Type of Production and Credits: TV Film-DOP; TV Video-DOP.
Genres: Documentary-TV; Educational-Th&TV; Children's-TV.
Biography: Born 1947, Toronto, Ontario. B.A.A., Ryerson Polytechnical Institute. *Here's to the Cowboy* won an award at Chicago; *To a Safer Place* was nominated for a Gemini and a CSC award; *Doctor, Lawyer, Indian Chief* also nominated for CSC award.
Selected Filmography: *The Famine Within*, TV, 90, CDN, DOP; *Playing for Keeps*, TV, 89, CDN, DOP; *For Richer, For Poorer*, TV, 88, CDN, DOP; *Albania*, TV, 88, CDN, DOP; *No Way, Not Me*, ED, 87, CDN, DOP; *North Buxton*, TV, 87, CDN, DOP; *The Birth of Language*, ED, 86, CDN, DOP; *Yukon Story Teller*, TV, 86, CDN, DOP; *To a Safer Place*, TV, 86, CDN, DOP; *Doctor, Lawyer, Indian Chief*, "Prime Time", ED, 85, CDN, DOP; *Olympic Profiles*, TV, 84, CDN, DOP; *Going Great*, TV, 84, CDN, DOP; *Do It Or Die!*, TV, 83, CDN, DOP; *Here's to the Cowboy*, TV, 82, CDN, DOP; *The Spring and Fall of Nina Polanski*, Th, 75, CDN, Dir.

IANZELO, Tony
- see DIRECTORS

IRVING, Todd
Cine Design Camera Services, 217 - 3410 Park St., Regina, SK S4V 2M8 (306)789-7527.
Type of Production and Credits: Th Short-DOP; TV Video-DOP.
Genres: Drama-Th; Documentary-Th; Experimental-Th&TV; Music Video-TV.
Biography: Born 1962 in Regina, Saskatchewan. B.F.A., Film and Video, University of Regina. Now working as a camera assistant/DOP. Also designs camera mounts.
Selected Filmography: *Saskatchewan River*, Th, 90, CDN, Cin; *Final Acts*, Th, 90, CDN, Cam Assist; *Roots and Wings*, ED, 90, CDN, DOP; *Last Days of Contrition*, Th, 89, CDN, Cam Assist; *All in Passing*, Th, 88, CDN, DOP.

IRWIN, Mark
IATSE 659, IATSE 644, ACFC. 4055 Tujunga Ave., #305, Studio City, CA USA (818)752-8243. Spiro Skouras, 305 Gayley Ave., Westwood, Los Angeles, CA USA (213)208-2100.
Type of Production and Credits: Th Film-DOP; TV Film-DOP.
Genres: Drama-Th&TV; Action-Th&TV; Science Fiction-Th; Horror-Th&TV; Documentary-TV.
Biography: Born 1950, Toronto, Ontario. Canadian citizenship; US resident alien; British working papers. Graduate of York University, Film, 73. Nominated for 2 Genies, 2 CSC awards, 2 ACE awards; winner of 4 CSC awards.
Selected Filmography: *Showdown in Little Tokyo*, TV, 91, USA, DOP; *Heatwave*, TV, 90, USA, DOP; *Robocop II*, Th, 90, USA, DOP; *I Come in Peace*, Th, 89, USA, DOP; *Class of 1999*, Th, 88, USA, DOP; *Paint It Black*, Th, 88, USA, DOP; *The Blob*, Th, 88, USA, DOP; *Fright Night II*, Th, 87, USA, DOP; *Bat 21*, Th, 87, USA, DOP; *Hanoi Hilton*, Th, 86, USA, DOP; *The Fly*, Th, 85, CDN/USA, DOP; *Youngblood*, Th, 84, CDN/USA, DOP; *Dead Zone*, Th, 83, CDN/USA, DOP; *Videodrome*, Th, 81, CDN, DOP; *Scanners*, Th, 79, CDN, DOP.

JACOBS, Ronald
416 18th Ave., Regina, SK S4N 1G1

(306)359-7236.
Type of Production and Credits: Th Short-DOP; TV Video-DOP.
Genres: Drama-Th; Experimental-Th; Music Video-TV.
Biography: Born and raised on the Saskatchewan prairie in the rural small town of Esterhazy. Now in Regina working freelance. B.F.A ., Film and Video, University of Regina. Has worked since 1989 at Saskatchewan Filmpool Co-op as part-time equipment manager. Keen interest in environmental issues and scuba diving. Currently producing a short theatrical release experimental film.
Selected Filmography: *Crooked Hand Jack*, The Stoaters, MV, 91, CDN, Cin; *Theological Reflections*, "Spirit Connection", TV, 91, CDN, Cin; *Don Quinn*, Th, 90-91, CDN, Cin.

JANSONS, Maris H.
ACFC, CSC. 3 Riverstone Dr., Etobicoke, ON M9P 3P3 (416)246-1840. Lightsource Inc., 258 Wallace Ave., Toronto, ON M6P 3M9 (800)461-1278.
Type of Production and Credits: Th Film-DOP; TV Film-DOP; TV Video-Light Dir.
Genres: Drama-Th&TV; Action-Th&TV; Science Fiction-Th&TV; Commercials-TV.
Biography: Born 1950, Winnipeg, Manitoba; Canadian citizen. Languages: English and Latvian. Grew up in Toronto, Ontario. Graduated from Humberside Collegiate; University of Western Ontario (B.A.); Columbia University, N.Y.C. (M.F.A. in film). Owns his own lighting company and 35mm motion picture cameras. Has worked on 35 feature films as grip or gaffer. Has shot 150 hours of TV dramas as Director of Photography. Has shot in Africa, Luxembourg, Scotland, Caribbean, Italy, USA and British Columbia, Alberta and Prince Edward Island. "War of the Worlds" awarded a CSC Award for Best TV Drama, 1990.
Selected Filmography: *Certs Minis*, Cm, 91, CDN, DOP; *Kurt Browning: Tall in the Saddle*, TV, 90, CDN, DOP; "Kids in the Hall" (8 eps), TV, 90, CDN/USA, DOP; "Dracula - The Series" (21 eps), TV, 90, CDN/USA/L, DOP; "War of the Worlds" (20 eps), TV, 89-90, DOP; *Bionic Showdown*, Th/TV, 89, USA, DOP; "Alfred Hitchcock Presents" (37 eps), TV, 88, CDN/USA, DOP; "Alfred Hitchcock Presents" (4 eps), TV, 87, CDN/USA, 2nd Unit DOP; "Captain Power" (18 eps), TV, 87, 2nd Unit DOP/Gaffer; *Almost Grown*, TV, 87, 2nd Unit DOP, Gaffer; *Blindside*, Th, 86, 2nd Unit DOP; *Hearts of Fire*, Th, 86, USA/GB, 2nd Unit; *Niagara Falls: Myths, Miracles and Magic*, Imax, 86, CDN, Light Dir; *King of Friday Night*, TV, 84, CDN, Light Dir; *Quest For Fire*, Th, CDN/F, 80, Gaffer.

JOBIN, Daniel
STCQ. 4136, St-Christophe, Montréal, PQ H2L 3Y2 (514)527-2884.
Types de production et générique: l métrage-D photo; c métrage-D photo; TV film-D photo; TV vidéo-D photo.
Types d'oeuvres: Drame-C&TV; Action-C&TV; Science-fiction-C&TV; Annonces -TV.
Curriculum vitae: Né en 1949, Québec. Langues: français et anglais. Etudes à l'INSAS, Bruxelles, 70-73. Douze ans assistant caméraman; 4 ans directeur-photo et cadreur. Inventeur du Panaflasher acheté par Panavision (disponible début 87); consultant au développement des projets pour Panavision, 86-91. Directeur de photographie pour de nombreux commerciaux: Coke diète, Labatt 50, Vin Si Si Si, Vin Maison, Peinture Dulux, campagne "Oeufs," campagne "Ultramar," Cité-Ciné 5 minutes.
Filmographie sélective: *Enfant sur le lac*, TV, 91, CDN, D phot; *L'Automne Sauvage*, C, 91, CDN, D phot; *Cargo*, C, 89, CDN, D phot; *Malarek*, C, 88, CDN, Cadr; *Thank You, Satan*, C, 88, CDN, D phot; *Georgia I et II*, MV, 88, CDN, D phot; *Room*, C, 88, CDN, D phot; "Shades of Love", TV, 87, CDN, Cadr; *Lalala Human Sex Duo No. 1*, MV, 87, CDN, D phot; *Au Milieu du spectacle*, C, 87, CDN, D phot; *Les Fous de Bassan*, C, 86, CDN/F, D phot 2e éq; *Transit*, TV, 86, CDN, D phot; *Marie s'en va t'en ville*, C, 86, CDN, D phot; *La Nuit avec Hortense*, C, 86, CDN, D phot; *Montréal Dance* (I-II-III), MV, 86, CDN, D phot.

KENDALL, Nicholas
- see DIRECTORS

KIEFER, Douglas
CSC, ACCT, ACFC. DWK Film Productions Ltd., 83 Greensides Ave., Toronto, ON M6G 3P8 (416)656-6774.
Type of Production and Credits: Th Film-DOP; Th Short-DOP; TV Film-DOP/Dir.
Genres: Drama-Th&TV; Documentary-Th&TV; Educational-TV; Children's-TV.
Biography: Born 1938, Dundas, Ontario. Attended Ryerson Polytechnical Institute. Worked in NFB camera department, 65-85; currently freelance DOP.
Selected Filmography: *Transplant*, TV,

90, CDN, DOP; "Question of Justice" (4 eps), TV, 90, CDN, DOP; *Between Two Worlds*, TV, 90, CDN, DOP; "Street Legal" (8 eps), TV, 89, CDN, DOP; "T and T" (44 eps), TV, 87-88, CDN/USA, DOP; "Ramona" (10 eps), TV, 87, CDN, DOP; "Vulcan E.F.T.S." (pilot), TV, 86, CDN, DOP; "The Edison Twins" (39 eps), TV, 85, CDN, DOP; *Tucker and the Horse Thief/Working for Peanuts/My Father, My Rival*, "Family Playhouse", TV, 84, CDN, DOP; *Unfinishing Business*, Th, 83, CDN, DOP; "War" (7 eps), TV, 80-83, CDN, DOP/Dir; *One Man*, Th, 76, CDN, DOP; *Volcano: An Inquiry into the Life and Death of Malcolm Lowry*, Th, 75, CDN, DOP; *Waiting for Fidel*, TV, 73, CDN, DOP; *Prologue*, Th, 68, CDN, DOP.

KINSEY, Nicholas
- voir REALISATEURS

KONOWAL, Charles
CSC, ACFC, ACCT. 218 Enfield Cres., Winnipeg, MB R2H 1B4 (204)237-5649. FAX: 237-1563.
Type of Production and Credits: Th Short-DOP; TV Film-DOP/Prod.
Genres: Drama-Th&TV; Documentary-Th&TV; Educational-TV; Commercials-TV.
Biography: Born 1948 in Melfort, Saskatchewan. Began to work in film industry in 71.
Selected Filmography: *Kind of Family*, TV, 91, CDN, DOP; *Flower in the Sky* (Imax Magic Carpet, Jap. Expo 90), Th, 90, CDN, DOP; *Mozambique: Build a Future*, ED, 88, CDN, DOP; *House Divided*, ED, 88, CDN, DOP; *Kamik*, ED, 88, CDN, DOP; *Swift Fox*, TV, 88, CDN, DOP; *Crown Prince*, ED, 88, CDN, Op; *Punchline*, TV, 88, CDN, Op; *Einstein Tonight* (special), TV, 88, CDN, 2nd U Cam; *SaskFirst: Excellence*, In, 87, CDN, DOP; *Not Another Hero*, In, 86, CDN, DOP; *T.C. Douglas: Keeper of the Flame*, TV, 85, CDN, DOP; *Shipbuilder*, TV, 84, CDN, Prod/DOP; *At First Sight*, TV, 83, CDN, DOP; *Everyone's Business*, TV, 81, CDN, DOP.

KRIZSAN, Les
Krizsan Film Productions, 23 Fairbanks St., Dartmouth, NS B3A 1B9 (902)425-6939.
Type of Production and Credits: Th Film-DOP; TV Film-DOP/Dir.
Genres: Drama-Th; Documentary-TV; Industrial-TV.
Biography: Born 1941, Budapest, Hungary; Canadian citizenship, 62. Languages: English and Hungarian. Has worked in radio and TV since 59; started shooting film, 65; freelance with networks and production houses for many years; has own production company; experience in all phases of production. *A Day in the Life of N.S.* won Best Industrial Film, Calgary; *The Gray Seals* won Best Cinematography, World Wildlife Fund; *George's Island* won Best Children's Film, Chicago International Film Festival, 90.
Selected Filmography: *George's Island*, Th, 89, CDN, DOP; *Little Kidnappers*, TV, 89, CDN, 2nd U DOP; *Journey Into Darkness: The Bruce Curtis Story*, TV, 90, CDN, 2nd U DOP; *A Switch in Time*, Th, 87, CDN, 2nd U DOP; *A Good Place to Live*, In, 87, CDN, Dir/Cam; *Business Profiles*, In, 87, CDN, Dir/Cam; *A Day in the Life of N.S.*, In, 86, CDN, Dir/Cam; *The Gray Seals*, "Profiles of Nature" (1 eps), TV, 86, CDN, Dir/Cam; *Design by Carpet*, In, 85, CDN, Dir/Cam; *Siege*, Th, 84, CDN, DOP; *Defcon-4*, Th, 84, CDN, DOP; *South Pacific 1942*, Th, 79, CDN, DOP.

LABREQUE, Jean-Claude
- voir REALISATEURS

LABROSSE, Sylvain
3261, boul. Ste-Rose, Fabreville, PQ H7P 4L7 (514)625-1837. Les Productions Rive Nord inc., 31, Chemin Notre-Dame, Blainville, PQ J7C 2L8 (514)437-3366.
Types de production et générique: l métrage-D photo; c métrage-D photo; TV vidéo-Prod/Mont.
Types d'oeuvres: Action-C; Education-TV; Animation-C&TV; Industriel-TV.
Curriculum vitae: Né en 1962, Laval, Québec. Langues: français et anlgais. Etudes en cinéma, Collège St-Jérome. Fonde Les Productions Rive Nord, 88. Meilleure Production, Festival Super 8, Caracas, *Moonlight*; Mention spéciale, Bruxelles, *Le Meilleur Ami*.
Filmographie sélective: *Animation Marionnettes, Quelle expérience*, TV, 89, CDN, D phot; *Infographie*, TV, 89, CDN, D phot; *Pen Pals*, Cm, 89, CDN, Cam; "Sesame Street" (1 eps), ED, 88, CDN, D phot; *Bino Fabule*, C, 88, CDN/B/F, D phot; *La vie est belle*, C, 87, CDN, D phot; *G.A.B.A., C'est quoi?*, ED, 86, CDN, Prod/Cam/Co mont; *Une Pof?...Bof!*, ED, 85, CDN, D phot/Dir art; *Le Champion*, C, 84, CDN, D phot/Co mont; *Moonlight*, C, 82, CDN, D phot/Co mont; *Le Meilleur Ami*, C, 82, CDN, Prod/An; *Humanoide d'un temps*, C, 81, CDN, Dir art/D phot.

LADOUCEUR, Serge
STCVQ. 409 Ave du Mont-Royal ouest,

#1, Montréal, PQ H2V 2S6 (514)271-2700.
Types de production et générique: l métrage-D photo; c métrage-D photo; TV film-D photo; TV vidéo-D photo.
Types d'oeuvres: Drame-C&TV; Variété-TV; Action-C; Documentaire-C&TV.
Curriculum vitae: Né en 1952. Langues: français et anglais. Etudes: Université Loyola et London International Film School. Prix Gémeaux 89, Meilleure Direction photo, toutes catégories d'émissions de variétés, des arts de la scène ou d'humour - *Rock et Belles Oreilles* - grande liquidation des fêtes, 88.
Filmographie sélective: "Montréal ville ouverte" (13 eps), TV, 91, CDN, D phot; "La misère des riches" (30 eps), TV, 90-91, CDN/CH/F/D, D phot; *Nikon*, Cm, 90, CDN, D phot; *Bonjour la police*, MV, 89, CDN, D phot/Cadr; *Grande Liquidations des Fêtes*, "Rock et Belles Oreilles", TV, 88, CDN, D phot (GEMEAU); "Rock et Belles Oreilles" (35 eps), TV, 87-89, CDN, D phot; *The Kiss*, Cm, 87, CDN/USA, D phot 2e éq; *Paroles d'échanges* (8), Cm, 89-90, CDN, D phot/Cadr; *Le Gros de la classe*, Cm, 86, CDN, D phot/Cadr; *Logan Road Renewal*, Cm, 79, USA, D phot/Cadr; *Visage Pâle*, C, 84-85, CDN/J, D phot; *Of Unknown Origin*, C, 83, CDN, D phot 2e éq.

LANGEVIN, Andrew A. G.
IATSE 667 & 873. The Langevin Group, 1065 Deta Rd., Mississauga, ON L5E 2R6 (416)274-3696.
Type of Production and Credits: TV Film-Dir/Cam
Genres: Action-Th&TV; Commercials-TV; Industrial-TV; Music Video-TV.
Biography: Born 1954, Toronto, Ontario. Canadian citizen. College graduate, trade courses, 1974. Started in film, 1978. Film background includes work as Producer, Director, DOP, Lighting Director, Gaffer. Has worked on many commercials including Labatt's, Whiskas Cat Food, A & P, Pepsi etc.
Selected Filmography: *James Cavendish*, Th, 91, CDN, DOP.

LANK, Barry
- see DIRECTORS

LARUE, Claude
CSC, STCQ. 5, rue Faucher, #6, St-Roch-de-l'Achigan, PQ J0K 3H0 (514)588-5116.
Types de production et générique: l métrage-D photo; c métrage-D photo; TV film-D photo/Réal/Prod; TV vidéo-D photo.
Types d'oeuvres: Drame-C; Documentaire-C&TV; Education-C; Enfants-C&TV.
Curriculum vitae: Né en 1940, Montréal, Québec. Caméraman, directeur-photo pigiste depuis 71.

LAVALETTE, Philippe
STCQ. 760, avenue Champagneur, Outremont, PQ H2V 3P8 (514)276-5728.
Types de production et générique: l métrage-D photo; c métrage-D photo/Réal; TV film-D photo/Réal; TV vidéo-D photo/Réal.
Types d'oeuvres: Drame-C&TV; Comédie musicale-C&TV; Documentaire-C&TV; Industriel-C&TV.
Curriculum vitae: Né en 1949, Paris, France; citoyenneté canadienne. Licencié en Biologie. *Les Colères de l'Hidalgo* remporte le Grand Prix, Festival du Film d'Auteur, Belfort, France; *La Syntaxe du regard*, Grand Prix de l'URTI, Bruxelles; *Lola Zipper*, Grand Prix Chamrousse; *Comment ça va?*, Prix Gémeaux, meilleure direction photo, 90; *Les îles ont une âme*, nomination meilleure photo, 90.
Filmographie sélective: *Lola Zipper*, C, 91, CDN/F, DOP; *La fille du Maquignon*, C, 90, CDN, DOP; "Comment ça va?", TV, 90, CDN, DOP; *Le marché du couple*, C, 89, CDN, DOP; *Les îles ont une âme*, C, 89, CDN, DOP; *Plein feux sur la ronde*, In, 86, CDN, Réal; "Les Chasseur de pôle" (2 eps), TV, 86, CDN/F, Réal/Cam; *Robert Bardston*, TV, 86, CDN, D phot; *Juste une image*, C, 86, CDN, D phot; *Nous près, nous loin*, C, 86, CDN, D phot; *Laval: tout un potentiel*, Ep 86, In, 85, CDN, Réal/Cam; *Beaujolais nouveau*, TV, 85, CDN, Réal/Cam; *Justice blanche*, TV, 85, CDN, D phot; *Zone de turbulence*, TV, 85, CDN, D phot; *La Grande Traversée*, C, 84, CDN/F, D phot.

LAVERDIERE, Jim
CSC. 32 Killarney Gardens, Pointe-Claire, PQ H9S 4X8 (514)695-4781. Le Groupe Syne, Linie Lussier, 465 rue St-Jean, #302A, Montreal, PQ H2Y 2R6 (514)849-7962. FAX: 849-6371.
Type of Production and Credits: TV Video-Cam.
Genres: Documentary-TV; Commercials-TV; Industrial-Th&TV; Educational-TV; Corporate-Th.
Biography: Born 1954, Quebec City, Quebec. Languages: English and French. Studied Motion Picture Production, Algonquin College. Public affairs (Radio-Canada, CBC), documentaries, industrial and educational films; has done work for "The Journal," M&M Productions,

Toronto, Montreal; Elie Goron Productions, Vancouver.
Selected Filmography: *Aerosport*, TV, 91, CDN, DOP; "Info Jeunes" (26 eps), TV, 90, CDN, DOP; *Sécurité*, In, 90, CDN, DOP; "Nature en jeu" (13 eps), TV, 90, CDN, Cam.

LeBLANC, Lloyd ◊
(506)548-9401.
Type of Production and Credits: TV Film-Cam/Prod; Th Short-Cam/Prod; TV Video-Cam.
Genres: Documentary-TV; Industrial-TV; Current Affairs-TV; News-TV.
Biography: Born 1954, Saulnierville, Nova Scotia. Languages: English and French. B.A.A., Ryerson Polytechnical Institute; studied Cinematography, International Film and TV Workshops, Rockport, US; film and TV workshops, CBC; Technical Training Centre, Montreal. Twelve years experience as a cameraman.
Selected Filmography: *L'Original de Nouveau Brunswick*, ED, 87, CDN, Cam; "Les Maritimes aujourd'hui", TV, 77-85, CDN, Cam; *La musique nous explique*, Th, 80, CDN, Prod/Cam; "Land and Sea" (6 eps), TV, 76-77, CDN, Cam.

LECLERC, Martin ◊
(514)455-2328.
Types de production et générique: l métrage-Cam; c métrage-D photo; TV film-Cam.
Types d'oeuvres: Drame-C&TV; Documentaire-C; Education-C.
Curriculum vitae: Né en 1945, Montréal, Québec. Etudes collégiales à Montréal et en France; études en photographie, Famous Photographers School, EU. Formation d'assistant caméraman, ONF, Montréal, 71; assistant permanent, 75; caméraman officiel, 79.
Filmographie sélective: *L'Homme à la traine*, "Bioéthique", TV, 86, CDN, Cadr; *Jeunesse en direct*, TV, 85, CDN, Cam; *Pays de sable*, TV, 85, CDN, Cam; *La Famille latino*, TV, 85, CDN, Cam; *Famille en délire*, TV, 85, CDN, Cam; *Une guerre dans mon jardin*, C, 85, CDN, 2e cam; *La Grande Allure*, C, 84, CDN, Cam; *Anticostie*, TV, 84, CDN, Co cam; *Les Traces du rêve*, TV, 84, CDN/F, Cam; *Zarico*, TV, 83, CDN, Cam; *La Couleur encerclée*, C, 83, CDN, Cam; *Garde Pinet*, TV, 82-83, CDN, Cam; *Les Voiles bas et en travers*, TV, 83, CDN/F, Cam; *La Bête lumineuse*, TV, 82-83, CDN, Cam; *De l'autre côté de la glace*, TV, 83, CDN, Cam.

LEHMAN, Douglas E.
CSC. 27 Breckenridge Ave., Dollard des Ormeaux, PQ H9G 1E9 (514)626-0036. Viewpoint Productions, 260 Mansion St., Kitchener, ON N2H 2K7 (519)745-8373.
Type of Production and Credits: TV Film-DOP; TV Video-DOP.
Genres: Drama-TV; Comedy-TV; Documentary-TV; Commercials-TV.
Biography: Born 1936, Kitchener, Ontario. 13 years experience, CKCP-TV, CFCF-TV, film and tape cinematographer; 17 years as partner in production house in Montreal as DOP; 5 years experience editing, mostly off-line VCR; experience with Arrivision 3-D system.

LEITERMAN, Richard
IATSE 667, IATSE 659, ACTT, CSC, DGC, RCAA. 15 - 1019 Gilford St., Vancouver, BC V6G 2P1 (604)688-4955. Creative Techniques, 483 Euclid St., Toronto, ON M6G 2T1 (416)466-4173.
Type of Production and Credits: Th Film-DOP; Th Short-Dir/DOP; TV Film-DOP; TV Video-Dir.
Genres: Drama-Th&TV; Comedy-Th&TV; Action-Th&TV; Documentary-Th&TV; Educational-Th&TV; Commercials-Th&TV; Industrial-Th&TV; Music Video-Th&TV.
Biography: Born 1935, Dome Mines, Ontario. Languages: English and working knowledge of French and Spanish. Worked as a cameraman, London, England, 61-69; returned to Toronto, 69; filmed documentaries for CBC, ABC, CBS, BBC, NET; filmed commercials in Canada. Nominated twice for an Emmy; Best Cinematography awards, Yorkton, Chicago, CSC, as well as Genie, 82, CFA, 76.
Selected Filmography: *Lovebirds*, TV, 91, USA, DOP; *A Mother's Justice*, TV, 91, USA, DOP; "Scene of the Crime" (11 eps), TV, 90-91, USA, DOP; *And the Sea Will Tell*, TV, 90, USA, DOP; *It* (Stephen King), TV, 90, USA, DOP; *Passing Thru Veils*, TV, 90, USA, DOP; *Dead Reckoning*, TV, 90, USA, DOP; *Cadence*, Th, 89, CDN, DOP; *The People Across the Lake*, TV, 88, USA, DOP; *Watchers*, Th, 88, CDN/USA, DOP; *Higher Ground*, TV, 88, USA, DOP; *The First Season*, Th, 88, CDN, DOP; *Squamish Five*, Th, 87, CDN, DOP; "Sea Hunt" (21 eps), TV, 87, CDN/USA, DOP/Dir; *Silence of the North*, Th, 79, CDN, DOP, (GENIE).

LENTE, Miklos
DGC, ACCT. 79 Laurentide Dr., Don Mills, ON M3A 3E2 (416)445-2442.
Type of Production and Credits: Th Film-DOP/Dir; TV Film-DOP/Dir; TV

Video-DOP/Dir.
Genres: Drama-Th&TV; Comedy-Th&TV; Action-Th&TV.
Biography: Born 1930, Hungary; Canadian citizenship. Thirty years experience in film production; DOP on numerous commercials in Canada, US. Won a Certificate of Merit for *Scribe*; Genie and CSC awards for *In Praise of Older Women*. Nominations include: Gemini, 1987, for "Night Heat"; CSC, 1982, for *Finishing Touch*; Genie, 1981, for *Suzanne*; Genie, 1980, for *Agency*; CSC, 1976, for *Ontario/Summertime*, Imax; CSC, 1966, for *Each Day That Comes*.
Selected Filmography: "Counterstrike", TV, 90-91, CDN/USA/F, DOP/Dir; "Diamonds", TV, 88-89, CDN/USA/F, DOP/Dir; *The Little Kidnappers*, TV, 89, USA/CDN, DOP; "Night Heat", TV, 84-88, USA/CDN, DOP/Dir; *Gunfighters*, TV, 87, USA, DOP; *Daring Life*, TV, 86, USA, DOP; *Bedroom Eyes*, Th, 89, CDN, DOP; *Happy Birthday To Me*, Th, 80, CDN, DOP; *Finishing Touch*, Th, 79, CDN, DOP; *Suzanne*, Th, 79, CDN, DOP; *Agency*, Th, 78, CDN, DOP; *In Praise of Older Women*, Th, 77, CDN, DOP, (CSC).

LHOTSKY, Antonin
CSC. 4 Nina St., Toronto, ON M5R 1Z3
Type of Production and Credits: TV Film-DOP; TV Video-DOP.
Genres: Drama-Th&TV; Documentary-Th&TV; Commercials-TV.
Biography: Born 1942, Prague, Czechoslovakia; Canadian citizenship. Languages: English, Czech and French. Graduated from Film Academy, Prague, 65. Worked in Paris for ORTF (service de la recherche); came to Canada, 67, worked for SPEAC (special effects), Montreal; set up film and TV unit for the National Museum of Man; cinematographer on over 50 commercials, 80-85; teaches film/video production, York University.
Selected Filmography: *The Secret*, TV, 85, CDN, Cin; *Taming of the Demons* (Expo 86), Th, 85, CDN, Cin; *Act of God*, TV, 84, CDN, Cin; *Year of the Tall Ships*, In, 84, CDN, Cin; *Marrakech*, ED, 83, CDN, Cin; *The Right Time, the Right Place*, In, 82, CDN, Cin; *Energy PI*, ED, 82, CDN, Cin; *A Visit to the Bank of Canada*, In, 81, CDN, Cin.

LIVINGSTON, Neal
- see DIRECTORS

LLOYD-DAVIES, Scott R. ◇
(416)362-3155.
Type of Production and Credits: TV Film-Dir/Cam.
Genres: Commercials-TV; Industrial-TV.
Biography: Born 1944, Deadwood, South Dakota; landed immigrant Canada. Attended Chouinard Art Institute, Los Angeles. Has worked in the film business since 64, primarily as DOP for the past 12 years. Has won awards for TV commercials including Clios, Cannes and New York Festival Awards.
Selected Filmography: American Airlines/Mitsubishi/Reebok, Cm, 86, USA, Cam/Dir; *Porsche 9285*, In, 86, USA, Cam/Dir; *Twining's Tea*, Cm, 86, GB, Cam/Dir; *Molson 200th/CN Railways*, Cm, 85, CDN, Cam/Dir.

LOMAGA, Ihor George ◇
(416)769-4597.
Type of Production and Credits: Th Film-DOP/Prod/PM; TV Film-DOP/Prod/PM.
Genres: Drama-Th&TV.
Biography: Born 1952, Toronto, Ontario. M.A., Film Production, York University, 83. Member of board of directors, Toronto Feature Film Workshop.
Selected Filmography: *Brooklyn Nights*, TV, 88, CDN, DOP; *Ghost of a Chance*, TV, 87, USA (Cam Trainee); *Cocktail*, Th, 87, USA (Cam Trainee); *Family Viewing*, Th, 86, CDN (add'l stills photo); *Chambers of Terror*, TV, 86, CDN, PM.

LUCA, Claudio
- voir PRODUCTEURS

LUPTON, Doug ◇
(604)437-8887.
Type of Production and Credits: TV Film-Cam; TV Video-Cam.
Genres: Documentary-TV; Educational-TV; Industrial-TV; Sports-TV.
Biography: Born 1951, Vancouver, BC. College Diploma, Arts.
Selected Filmography: *Room With A View*, TV, 86, CDN, DOP; *Looking for Our Past*, "Discovering B.C.", ED, 85, CDN, Cam; *Ski Kimberly/Kwik Hole - A Revolution in Drilling*, In, 85, CDN, Cam; *The Swiftsure Yacht Race*, TV, 85, CDN, Cam.

MacDONALD, Robert
142 Rushton Rd., Toronto, ON M6G 3J1
(416)658-0345.
Type of Production and Credits: Th Film-DOP; Th Short-DOP; TV Film-DOP.
Genres: Drama-Th&TV; Documentary-TV; Commercials-TV; Music Video-TV.
Biography: Canadian citizenship. Languages: English, Spanish and French. *Family Viewing* won Citytv Award, Best Canadian Feature and was selected for Festival of Festivals, 87; *Peggy* won Best

Short Television Film, Calgary Canadian Celebration Festival, 91.
Selected Filmography: *Peggy*, TV, 90, CDN, DOP; *Family Viewing*, Th, 87, CDN, DOP; *Jive After Five*, Th, 87, CDN/GB, DOP.

MacFARLANE, Duncan
CSC, SMPTE. 27 Stonehedge Hollow, Unionville, ON L3R 3Y9 (416)477-8798. CTV, Box 565, Stn. F, Toronto, ON M4Y 2L8 (416)609-6314.
Type of Production and Credits: TV Film-DOP/Cam; TV Video-DOP/Cam; Video-DOP/Cam.
Genres: Documentary-TV; Industrial-TV; Current Affairs-TV; Sports-TV.
Biography: Born in Wallingford in England; British and Canadian citizenship. Started in film editing with Associated Rediffusion, London, England, 59; joined CFTO/CTV, 66, editing "W5." Freelanced, 71, including "Rogers Report," "the fifth estate," "Market Place," "TGIF," "CBC Sports," "News Magazine," CBC "National," "CTV News," CBS, NBC, ABC, UPITN, CBLFT and CBET. Industrial, PR and sports films for independent companies.
Selected Filmography: "W5", TV, 76-91, CDN, Cam, (GEMINI 87); "Live It Up", TV, 76-88, CDN, Cam; *1988 Winter Olympics*, TV, 88, CDN/USA, Cam; Air Canada Cargo, In, 87, USA, DOP; Delta II, In, 86, CDN, DOP; Excel Winter Performance, In, 85, CDN, DOP; Metro Mail, In, 85, USA, DOP; *The New Voyageur*, In, 82, CDN, DOP.

MacPHERSON, Glen
ACFC, STCVQ. 203 Hanson St., Toronto, ON M4C 1A7 (416)694-9616. Suzanne Depoe/Creative Technique Inc., 483 Euclid Ave., Toronto, ON M6G 2T1 (416)466-4173.
Type of Production and Credits: Th Film-DOP; Th Short-DOP; TV Film-DOP.
Genres: Drama-Th&TV; Comedy-Th&TV; Action-Th&TV; Commercials-TV.
Biography: Born in 1957 in Montreal, Quebec. Speaks English and French. Based equally in Toronto and Montreal. ACE award nominee, Best Cinematography for "The Hitchhiker".
Selected Filmography: *Conspiracy of Silence*, TV, 90, CDN, DOP; *Journey Into Darkness: The Bruce Curtis Story*, TV, 90, CDN, DOP; *Clarence*, TV, 90, CDN/USA, DOP; *Rookies*, TV, 90, CDN, DOP; "The Hitchhiker" (6 eps), TV, 89, CDN/USA, DOP; *Snakeeater*, Th, 89, USA, DOP.

MAGDER, Zale
CSC, IATSE 667. Magder Entertainment Corp., 189 Church St., Toronto, ON M5B 1Y7 (416)866-2121.
Type of Production and Credits: Th Film-DOP/Prod; TV Film-DOP.
Genres: Drama-Th&TV.
Biography: Born 1930, Toronto, Ontario. Studied at Ontario College of Art. DOP and President, Magder Studios, Magder Entertainment Corporation of America.
Selected Filmography: *Shocktrauma*, TV, 83, CDN, DOP; *Frank and Fearless*, TV, 83, CDN, DOP; *Terminal Choice*, Th, 82, CDN, DOP/Prod; *The Sins of Dorian Grey*, TV, 81, USA, DOP; *Time to Quit*, TV, 81, CDN, DOP; *Mom, the Wolfman and Me*, TV, 80, USA, DOP; *The Family Man*, TV, 79, USA, DOP; *The War Between the Tates*, TV, 77, USA, DOP; *Tell Me My Name*, TV, 77, USA, DOP; *Shoot*, Th, 75, CDN, DOP.

MAGUIRE, Rick
IATSE. R.R. #1, Ashburn, ON (416)655-8007.
Type of Production and Credits: Th Film-DOP/Cam; TV Film-DOP/Cam.
Genres: Drama-Th&TV; Action-Th&TV; Commercials-Th&TV.
Biography: Born 1947, Toronto, Ontario. Qualified to work in US (green card). Started as a PA, 69. DOP for the past 10 years; has worked on more than 300 commercials, 78-85; commercials exclusively in the US, 90-91.
Selected Filmography: "The Black Stallion", TV, 91, CDN/F, 2nd U Cam/Dir; "Street Legal" (29 eps), TV, 87-88, CDN, DOP; *Too Outrageous!*, Th, 87, CDN, Cam; *Police Academy IV*, Th, 86, USA, Cam; *I'll Take Manhattan*, TV, 86, Dir/2nd U Cam; "Rockit Records" (pilot), TV, 86, CDN, DOP; *National Ballet*, TV, 86, CDN, DOP; *State Park*, Th, 86, CDN, 2nd U DOP.

MARKWART, Glenn
SMPIA. Box 245, Blaine Lake, SK S0J 0J0 (306) 497-3545. Cinepost Productions, 1937 Ontario Ave., Saskatoon, SK S7K 1T5 (306) 244-7788.
Type of Production and Credits: Th Short-DOP; TV Film-DOP; TV Video-DOP.
Genres: Drama-TV; Documentary-TV.
Biography: Born 1957, Saskatchewan; Canadian citizenship. Member of CPPA, SPPA. Seven years of experience working in the film and television industry. Videographer and DOP for over 100 television commercials and corporate

videos; has worked on several half-hours for television - including both documentary and drama.
Selected Filmography: *Winter Seasoned,* TV, 90-91, CDN, DOP; *Knowing Each Other,* TV, 90-91, CDN, DOP; "Take a Vacation in Your Own Backyard" (11 eps), TV, 90-91, CDN, DOP; *Lightbridge,* In, 91, CDN, DOP; *New Kids on the Farm,* In, 91, CDN, DOP; *Community Bonds* (12), Cm, 91, CDN, DOP; United Way (3), TV, 90, CDN, DOP, (BESSIE); *Lloyd Mall,* Cm, 88, CDN, DOP.

MATTER, Armin
IATSE 669. P.O. Box 3794, High River, AB T0L 1B0 (403)652-4866. (604)984-4342.
Type of Production and Credits: TV Film-DOP/Cam.
Genres: Drama-TV; Action-Th&TV; Documentary-TV; Commercials-TV.
Biography: Born 1944, Bern, Switzerland; Canadian citizenship. Languages: English, French and German. B.A.A., Motion Picture, Ryerson Polytechnical Institute. DOP on several commercials, dramas and documentaries.
Selected Filmography: *Welcome to the Monkey House,* "Kurt Vonnegut Theatre", TV, 90, CDN, Cam Op; "Mom P.I." (10 eps), TV, 90, CDN, Cam Op; *Crooked Hearts,* Th, 90, USA, Cam Op; *Fourth War,* Th, 89, USA, 2nd Cam Op; *Calgary Winter Olympics,* Th, 88, CDN, Cam Op; "Danger Bay", TV, 88, CDN, Cam Op; "Airwolf", TV, 87, CDN, Cam Op; *Gunsmoke,* TV, 87, CDN, Cam Op; *Betrayed,* Th, 87, USA, Cam Op; *Hamilton's Quest,* TV, 86, CDN, Cam Op; *Golden Harvest,* TV, 86, CDN, Cam Op; *Rad,* Th, 85, USA, Cam Op; *Thirteen Minutes to Wait,* TV, 81, CDN, DOP; *The Dream Never Dies,* Th, 80, CDN, DOP.

McGLYNN, Gordon Paul
- see DIRECTORS

McLACHLAN, Robert B.
CSC, ACCT. 4331 Lions Ave., North Vancouver, BC (604)980-9025. Key Light Images Inc., Shapiro-Lichtman, 8827 Beverly Blvd., Los Angeles, CA 90048 USA (213)859-8877.
Type of Production and Credits: Th Film-DOP; Th Short-DOP; TV Film-DOP; TV Video-DOP/Dir.
Genres: Drama-Th&TV; Action-Th&TV; Horror-Th&TV; Documentary-Th&TV; Commercials-TV.
Biography: Born 1956, San Francisco, California; Canadian and US citizenship. Studied Film and Fine Art at U.B.C. and Simon Fraser University, BC. Founded Omni Film Productions, 79; shot and directed over 300 commercials and several industrial and international documentary films prior to leaving Omni in 88. Now concentrates on shooting TV and theatrical drama in US and Canada. Has received numerous awards for documentary and commercial cinematography.
Selected Filmography: "MacGyver" (20 eps), TV, 90-91, USA, 2nd U DOP; "MacGyver" (2 eps), TV, 90, USA, DOP; "The Beachcombers" (30 eps), TV, 88-90, CDN, DOP; *Run,* Th, 90, USA, Cam Op; *Comic Book Chase,* "Inside Stories", TV, 90, CDN, DOP; *Heartbreak Hotel,* "Inside Stories", TV, 90, CDN, DOP; "Bordertown" (16 eps), TV, 89, CDN/F, Cam Op; *What's Wrong With Neil?,* "Family Portraits", TV, 88, CDN, DOP; *The Wish,* "Family Portraits", TV, 88, CDN, DOP; *Watchers,* Th, 88, CDN/USA, Cam Op; *Give'm Enough Rope,* "Family Pictures", TV, 88, CDN, DOP; *The Anniversary,* "Family Pictures", TV, 88, CDN, DOP; "Sea Hunt" (2 eps), TV, 87, CDN/USA, DOP; "Sea Hunt" (20 eps), TV, 87, CDN/USA, Cam Op; *Abducted,* Th, 86, CDN, DOP.

McLELLAN, Doug
225 Lake Shore Dr., Toronto, ON M8V 2A7 (416)503-2164. McLellan Productions Inc., 119 Spadina Ave., The Balfour Bldg, Suite 1105, Toronto, ON M5V 2L1 (416)597-2020. FAX: 597-9444.
Type of Production and Credits: TV Film-DOP; TV Video-DOP; Video-DOP/Dir.
Genres: Documentary-TV; Animation-TV; Industrial-TV; Current Affairs-TV.
Biography: Born 1950, Sudbury, Ontario. Studied Chemistry, Physics, University of Waterloo, University of Toronto. Did camera work on a variety of network shows, including "W5," "The Journal," "Live It Up" before establishing own production company.
Selected Filmography: *The Canadians,* TV, 88, CDN, DOP; *Small Miracles,* TV, 88, CDN, DOP; *Positioning,* Royal Trust, In, 88, CDN, Dir/Prod/DOP; *Canada Post Today,* In, 88, CDN, Dir/Prod/DOP; Weall & Cullen (series), Cm, 87-88, CDN, DOP; "The Explorer Series" (1 eps), TV, 87, USA, Cam.

McLENNAN, Peter ✧
(604)689-7969.
Type of Production and Credits: Th Film-DOP/Cam; TV Film-DOP/Cam; TV Video-DOP/Cam; Video-DOP/Cam.

Genres: Drama-Th&TV; Documentary-Th&TV; Commercials-Th&TV; Industrial-TV.
Biography: Born 1946, England; Canadian citizenship. Degree in Instrumentation and Control Systems, BC Institute of Technology. Extensive aerial experience; snorkel camera experience; director/cameraman 2nd unit on features, TV movies, series, commercials, documentaries.
Selected Filmography: *Dead Bang*, Th, 88, USA, 2nd U DOP/Cam; "Danger Bay" (parts), TV, 83-88, CDN, 2nd U DOP; *The Experts*, Th, 87, USA, Cam; *Bitter Creek*, TV, 87, USA, 2nd U DOP/Cam; "MacGyver" (2 eps), TV, 87, USA, Cam; *Shoot to Kill/Mountain King*, Th, 87, USA, Cam; *Stakeout*, Th, 87, USA, 2nd U DOP/Cam; "Stingray" (part), TV, 87, USA, 2nd U DOP; "Airwolf II" (parts), TV, 86-87, CDN/USA, 2nd U DOP; *The Christmas Story*, TV, 86, USA, Op; *Astronaut and Son/A Hero in the Family*, TV, 86, USA, 2nd U DOP/Op; "Power's Play" (pilot), TV, 86, USA, 2nd U DOP/Cam; *The Indestructible Man*, TV, 86, USA, 2nd U DOP/Cam; *Love Is Never Silent*, TV, 86, USA, Cam; *Just Another Missing Kid*, TV, 86, USA, Cam.

MEARS, Graeme
Tecnifoto, P.O. Box 33, Woodbridge, ON L4L 1A9 (416)851-5053. FAX: 851-8789.
Type of Production and Credits: Th Film-DOP; TV Film-DOP; TV Video-DOP.
Genres: Documentary-TV; Commercials-Th&TV; Industrial-TV.
Biography: Born 1940, New Zealand; landed immigrant Canada. New Zealand National Film Unit, 64-69; Film Technique Ltd., Toronto, 69-71; Film Effects, Toronto, 71-84; Mae Studios, Toronto, 84-88; freelance director/cameraman, 88 to present. Area of specialty: Special Effects, mechanical & photographic.
Selected Filmography: *Time Magazine*, Corp, 91, CDN, DOP; *Be There To Cheer*, Visa, Cm, 91, CDN, DOP; *Macleans Magazine*, Corp, 90, CDN, DOP; *Super Mario*, McDonalds, Cm, 90, CDN, Dir/Cam; Canon, Cm, 88, CDN, Dir/Cam; Air Thief, Cm, 88, CDN, DOP; Leon's, Cm, 88, CDN, DOP; *Millenium*, Th, 88, CDN; Xerox, Cm, 88, CDN, Dir; Visa, Cm, 88, CDN, Dir; *A New Life*, Th, 87, CDN, 2nd U Dir; Cineplex Odeon, Cm, 87, CDN, Dir/ Cam; Simmons, Cm, 87, CDN, Dir/Cam; All, Cm, 87, CDN, Dir/Cam; Rolaids, Cm, 87, CDN, Dir/Cam.

MERCER, Jim
CSC. 6 Tarlton Rd., Toronto, ON M5P 2M4 (416)489-2271.
Type of Production and Credits: TV Video-DOP.
Genres: Documentary-TV; Industrial-TV; Current Affairs-TV; News-TV.
Biography: Born 1939, St. John's, Newfoundland. Specializes in documentary, public affairs and industrial film and video productions requiring extensive travel and light-weight equipment packages.
Selected Filmography: "W5" (20 eps), TV, CDN, DOP; *The Dolphin Breed*, ED, E, DOP.

MESTEL, Stanley
IATSE, ACTT, CSC. 16 Teagarden Crt., Willowdale, ON M2N 5Z9 (416)226-5423. The Partners Film Co., 508 Church St., Toronto, ON M4Y 2C8 (416)966-3500.
Type of Production and Credits: Th Film-DOP; TV Film-DOP.
Genres: Commercials-Th&TV.
Biography: Born 1937, London, England; Canadian and British citizenship. For past 12 years has worked exclusively on TV commercials; shot features before coming to Canada and joining The Partners Film Company, 77.

METCALFE, Bill
- see DIRECTORS

METTLER, Peter
- see DIRECTORS

MIGNOT, Pierre
STCQ. 4735, Meridian, Montréal, PQ H3W 2C2 (514)482-1616.
Types de production et générique: l métrage-D photo; c métrage-D photo; TV film-D photo.
Types d'oeuvres: Drame-C&TV; Comédie-C; Action-C; Documentaire-C.
Curriculum vitae: Né en 1944, Montréal, Québec. Langues: français et anglais. Assistant caméraman, caméraman, ONF, 67-79; directeur de la photographie, pigiste depuis 79. Honoré Grand Montréalais en cinéma, 83.

MONTESI, Jorge
- see DIRECTORS

MORIDE, Roger
NABET 700, CSC. 4138, Marcil, Montréal, PQ H4A 2Z6 (514)486-9370.
Types de production et générique: l métrage-D photo; c métrage-D photo; TV film-D photo.
Types d'oeuvres: Drame-C&TV; Variété-C&TV; Comédie-C&TV; Documentaire-

C&TV.
Curriculum vitae: Né en 1927, France; citoyenneté canadienne. Langues: français, anglais, portugais et breton. Baccalauréat, Philosophie, Université de Rennes, France; diplôme de l'Ecole technique de Photographie et Cinématographie (Paris), et de l'Institut des Hautes Etudes Cinématographiques (IDHEC, Paris). Expérience dans l'élaboration des budgets, le recrutement du personnel technique, le contrôle de la qualité, la post-production, l'éclairage et la production en vidéo. Chef caméraman et directeur technique, Cinetel inc., 71-73, et Onyx Films, 66-69; chef caméraman, Niagara Films, 56-61.
Filmographie sélective: *Montréal Interdit*, C, 91, CDN, D photo; *Vent de Folie*, C, 90, CDN, D phot; *Ernest Livernois*, C, 88, CDN, D phot; "Rhyme On" (6 eps), TV, 86, CDN, Dir phot; "Mosaïc" (39 eps), TV, 83-86, CDN, D phot; *Jim Valentine*, C/TV, 84, CDN/USA, D phot; "Modern Country" (3 eps), TV, 83, CDN, D phot; "Les fils de la Liberté" (6 eps), TV, 81, CDN, D phot; "Cities" (6 eps), TV, 80, CDN, D phot.

MORITA, George
IATSE 667, IATSE 6444, CSC, DGC. The Partners Film Company Ltd., 508 Church St., Toronto, ON M4Y 2C8 (416)966-3500.
Type of Production and Credits: TV Film-DOP/Dir; TV Video-DOP/Dir.
Genres: Commercials-TV.
Biography: Born in Chemainus, BC. Attended Ryerson Polytechnical Institute. Has worked for Batten Films, Clenman Davidson Productions, The Guest Group, Rabko TV; now at The Partners Film Company Ltd. DOP on numerous documentaries and music specials, CBC; DOP/director on commercials (since 65), which have won Bessies, Clios and awards at Cannes.

MORRIS, Reginald H.
CSC, IATSE 644, IATSE 667, ACTT. 255 Bamburgh Circle, #308, Scarborough, ON M1W 3T6 (416)497-9266. Miller Agency, 23560 Lyons Ave., #209, Santa Clarita, CA 91321 USA (213)849-2363.
Type of Production and Credits: Th Film-DOP; Th Short-DOP; TV Film-DOP; TV Video-DOP.
Genres: Drama-Th&TV; Comedy-Th&TV; Action-Th&TV; Science Fiction-Th&TV.
Biography: Born in Ruislip, Middlesex, England; Canadian citizenship. Combat cameraman during WWII, being twice mentioned in despatches. Immigrated to Canada, 55, after 20 years in British film industry. Has won 2 Bronze Awards at the International Film and TV Festival, New York, and Mulholland Award for *Essay on Science*; 3 Genie nominations; 2 CSC awards.
Selected Filmography: *Lady In A Corner*, TV, 89, USA, DOP; *Loose Cannons*, Th, 88, USA, DOP; *Sing*, Th, 88, USA, Co-Cin; *Christmas Eve*, TV, 88, USA, DOP; *The Ann Jillian Story*, TV, 87, USA, DOP; "The Fortunate Pilgrim" (5 eps), TV, 87, USA, DOP; "Popeye Doyle" (pilot), TV, 86, CDN/USA, DOP; *Barnum*, TV, 86, USA, DOP; *Easy Prey*, TV, 86, USA, DOP; "The Hitchhiker" (6 eps), TV, 85, USA, DOP; *Turk 182!*, Th, 85, USA, DOP; *Yes Concert*, TV, 84, USA, DOP; *A Christmas Story*, Th, 83, CDN, DOP; *Porky's II*, Th, 82, CDN, DOP; *Porky's*, Th, 81, CDN, DOP.

MORRONE, Tony
- see PRODUCERS

MULLER, Helmfried
CSC. 21 Coleridge Ave., Toronto, ON M4C 4H4 (416)423-2871.
Type of Production and Credits: Th Film-Cin; Th Short-Cin; TV Film-Cin; TV Video-Cin.
Genres: Drama-Th&TV; Variety-Th&TV; Action-Th&TV; Documentary-Th&TV; Educational-Th&TV; Children's-Th&TV; Commercials-Th&TV; Industrial-Th&TV; Music Video-Th&TV; Current Affairs-Th&TV.
Biography: Has international experience. Works in television programs, documentaries, corporate, commercials and music videos.
Selected Filmography: "Sketches of our Town" (42 eps), TV, 86-91, CDN, Cin; *Dream Warriors*, MV, 91, CDN, Cin; "Streetnoise" (13 seg), TV, 90, CDN, Cin; "Really Me" (72 vig), TV, 90, CDN, Cin; "Rock 'N' Talk" (13 seg), TV, 90, CDN, Cin; *...and Then There Were Seven*, "Adrienne Clarkson Presents", TV, 89, CDN, Cin; *The Shantymen*, "Canada In View", TV, 89, CDN, Cin; *And Softly Falls the Winter*, TV, 88-89, CDN, Cin; "Second Chance" (2 eps), TV, 88, CDN, Cin; "Automotive Awareness" (13 eps), TV, 88, CDN, Cin; *Honda Motorcycle Engines*, In, 86, CDN, Cin; *The Construction of the John B. Aird*, In, 85, CDN, Cin; *American Express*, Th, 85, CDN, Cin; *Letter to Vietnam*, TV, 85, CDN, Cin; *National Sea Corporation*, In, 85, CDN, Cin.

MUNRO, Douglas ✧

(403)246-0328.
Type of Production and Credits: Th Film-Cam; TV Film-DOP/Cam; TV Video-DOP.
Genres: Drama-TV; Science Fiction-TV; Documentary-Th&TV; Industrial-TV.
Biography: Born 1957, Edmonton, Alberta. B.F.A., York University; Panavision courses. Winner of award for best student cinematography, 80. Specializes in electronic cinematography.
Selected Filmography: *Official Olympics Film* (Calgary), TV, 88, CDN, Cam; *Satan's House*, Th, 88, CDN, DOP/Op; *Little Girls Don't Kill*, TV, 88, CDN, DOP/Op; *Chrysalis*, TV, 88, CDN, DOP/Op.

NASON, Kent ✧
(902)857-3848.
Type of Production and Credits: Th Film-DOP/Cam; Th Short-DOP/Dir; TV Film-DOP/Dir; TV Video-DOP.
Genres: Drama-Th&TV; Documentary-Th&TV.
Biography: Born 1949, New Brunswick. Received art scholarship, 68. Originally still photographer; moved to Montreal, freelanced at NFB, etc.; worked as assistant cameraman with Crawley Films, Ottawa; joined NFB, 73; has worked on many documentaries, some dramas; has done some directing and producing.
Selected Filmography: "Canada: True North" (1 eps), TV, 78-88, CDN/USA, Cin; "Reckoning: The Political Economy of Canada" (1 eps), TV, 88, CDN, Cin; "The Nature of Things" (1 eps), TV, 87-88, CDN, Prod; *Something About Love*, Th, 87, CDN, Cam; *Holding Our Ground*, TV, 86-87, CDN, Cin; "Planet I", TV, 86, CDN/GB, Cin; *The Lonely Passion of Brian Moore*, TV, 85, CDN, Cin; *First Stop China*, TV, 85, CDN, Cin; "War" (4 eps), TV, 83, CDN, Cin; *Putting Our House in Order*, TV, 83, CDN, Op; "The Nature of Things" (1 eps), TV, 83, CDN, Cin; *Singlehanded*, TV, 80, CDN, Dir/Cin.

NEUBACHER, Roman M
- see PRODUCERS

NICOLLE, Victor W. ✧
(604)266-9224.
Type of Production and Credits: Th Short-DOP; TV Video-DOP/Wr.
Genres: Documentary-Th&TV; Educational-TV.
Biography: Born 1955, Vancouver, BC. B.A., Psychology, Simon Fraser University. Attended SFU Film Workshop for 2 years. Worked as cinematographer in Vancouver for approximately 5 years (documentaries, commercials, educationals, feature films, television). Began writing feature film scripts several years ago.
Selected Filmography: *Ladies of the Lotus*, Th, 86, CDN, DOP; *Weight Training: Your Key to Fitness/See How We Run*, ED, 84-85, CDN, DOP/Wr; *Vancouver: A Portrait by Arthur Erickson*, TV, 84, CDN, DOP/Wr; *Hypothermia: Nature's Cold Killer/Ski Cross Country*, ED, 82-83, CDN, DOP/Wr.

NOWAK, Danny
CSC. #103 - 857 Beatty St., Vancouver, BC V6B 2M6 (604)669-3456.
Type of Production and Credits: Th Film-DOP; Th Short-DOP; TV Film-DOP; TV Video-DOP.
Genres: Drama-Th&TV; Action-Th; Science Fiction-Th; Music Video-Th&TV.
Biography: Born 1959, British Columbia. Fully equipped with Arriflex 16SR package.
Selected Filmography: *Silhouette*, Th, 91, CDN, DOP; *In Exile*, Th, 91, CDN, DOP; *Flash Gordon II*, Th, 90, CDN, DOP; *Chance for Change*, TV, 90, CDN, DOP; *Drug Awareness* (3 cm), Cm, 90, CDN, DOP; *Spirit of the Mask*, TV, 90, CDN, DOP; *Funky Music*, Vanilla Ice, MV, 90, USA, DOP; Skinny Puppy, MV, 90, CDN, DOP; *Baby Blues*, ED, 90, CDN, DOP; *Empire of Ash III*, Th, 88, CDN, DOP.

OHASHI, Rene
CSC, CAMERA, ACCT. 564 Palmerston Ave., Toronto, ON M6G 2P7 (416)536-4680. (416)587-7975.
Type of Production and Credits: TV Film-DOP; TV Video-DOP; Th Film-DOP.
Genres: Drama-Th&TV; Documentary-Th&TV; Commercials-TV.
Biography: Born 1952, Toronto, Ontario. Honours B.F.A., Film Production. Winner of Juno award, 84, Best Music Video for *Sunglasses at Night* and CSC award, 86, Best Music Video for *We Run*. Gemini awards for Best Photography in Dramatic Program/Series, 86 and 87; Best Photography in Comedy, Variety or Performing Arts Program, 87 and 88. CSC Awards for Feature Film Cinematography, 89 and 90.
Selected Filmography: *Sound and Silence* (mini-series), TV, 91, CDN/NZ/USA/GB, DOP; *To Catch a Killer* (mini-series), TV, 91, CDN, DOP; "The Wonder Years" (14 eps), TV, 90-91, USA, DOP; *Deep Sleep*, Th, 89, CDN, DOP; "Men" (5 eps), TV, 88-89, USA, DOP;

Where the Spirit Lives, Th, 88, CDN, DOP; *Millennium*, Th, 88, USA, DOP, (CSC); *Shadow Dancing*, Th, 87-88, CDN, DOP, (CSC); *Master Class with Menuhin*, TV, 87, CDN, DOP, (GEMINI); *Almost Grown*, TV, 87, USA, DOP; *Blindside*, Th, 86, CDN, DOP; *A Moving Picture*, TV, 86, CDN, DOP, (GEMINI); *The Truth About Alex*, TV, 86, CDN, DOP, (GEMINI); *Sweet Lorraine*, Th, 86, USA, DOP; *Anne of Green Gables* (mini-series), TV, 85, CDN, DOP, (GEMINI).

ORIEUX, Ron
CSC, IATSE 669. 3050 S.W. Marine Dr., Vancouver, BC V6N 3Y3 (604)266-9368. Suzanne Depoe, Creative Technique Inc., 483 Euclid Ave., Toronto, ON M6G 2T1 (416)924-0936.
Type of Production and Credits: Th Film-DOP; Th Short-DOP; TV Film-DOP.
Genres: Drama-Th&TV; Comedy-TV; Action-Th&TV; Commercials-TV.
Biography: Born 1942, Winnipeg, Manitoba; raised in Vancouver. B.A., English, Sociology, University of British Columbia; B.Ap.Sc., Civil Engineering.
Selected Filmography: *Not Quite Human*, TV, 91, USA, DOP; *My Son Johnny*, TV, 91, USA, DOP; *Night of the Hunter*, TV, 91, USA, DOP; *Kootenai Brown*, Th, 90, CDN, DOP; *The First Circle* (mini-series), TV, 90, CDN/F, DOP; *Deadly Intentions*, TV, 90, USA, DOP; *Burning Bridges*, TV, 90, USA, DOP; *Anything to Survive*, TV, 89, USA/CDN, DOP; *Small Sacrifices* (mini-series), TV, 89, USA, DOP; *The Lady Forgets*, TV, 89, USA, DOP; "Murphy's Law" (13 eps), TV, 88-89, USA, DOP; "The Twilight Zone" (3 eps), TV, 88, CDN, DOP; "J.J. Starbuck" (11 eps), TV, 87-88, USA, DOP; "Beans Baxter" (16 eps), TV, 87, USA, DOP; "The Hitchhiker" (13 eps), TV, 86, USA, DOP.

OSTRIKER, David M
- see PRODUCERS

OUELLETTE, Michel L.
5224 - 185 St., Edmonton, AB T6M 2G1 (403)444-4141. Vastra Productions Ltd., 5224 - 185 St., Edmonton, AB T6M 2G1 (403)444-4148.
Type of Production and Credits: TV Film-DOP/Prod; TV Video-DOP/Prod.
Genres: Documentary-TV; Industrial-TV; Music Video-TV; Sports-TV.
Biography: Born in 1955 in Montreal, Quebec. Canadian citizen. Fluent in English and French. Education: Media Arts, Sheridan College, Oakville, 1974-77; Electronic and Film Media, Banff Centre, Banff, 1982; Electronic Cinematography and Feature Film Lighting, International Film and Television Workshop, Maine, 1989. Freelance cameraman since 1988. Owner of Vastra Productions Ltd. which won a 1990 A.M.P.I.A. Award for "Best Music Video". Very well equipped (BVW300 +). Associate member of CSC.
Selected Filmography: *Jari Kurri - At The Crossroads*, TV, 91, CDN, DOP; *Albertville 92 - A Year Ahead*, TV, 91, CDN, DOP/Co Prod; *Barcelona 92*, TV, 91, CDN, DOP/Co Prod; *One River*, MV, 91, CDN, DOP/Prod; *Shall Not Want*, MV, 90, CDN, DOP/Co Prod; *Jamais Vu*, MV, 89, CDN, Co DOP.

PARRELL, Barry
CSC. 2834 Rae St., Regina, SK S4S 1R3 (306)585-1421.
Type of Production and Credits: Th Film-DOP; TV Film-DOP.
Genres: Drama-TV; Documentary-TV; Commercials-TV; Music Video-TV.
Biography: Born in 1961. Educated in film at Ryerson Polytechnical Institute, Toronto, 1981-85. Has travelled extensively throughout Asia, Europe and the Americas. Two best cinematography awards in 91, for *The Heart of Christmas* from SMPIA and for *The Spirit of Success* from the CSC.
Selected Filmography: *Get Smart*, Cm, 91, CDN, DOP; *The Spirit of Success*, In, 90, CDN, DOP; *The Heart of Christmas*, TV, 90, CDN, DOP; *The Garden*, TV, 90, CDN, DOP; *Home of the Range*, "Inside Stories", TV, 90, CDN, DOP.

PATTERSON, Carol
CFTA, CSC. 387 Roehampton Ave., Toronto, ON M4P 1S3 (416)484-6648. Patterson-Partington International Television Productions, 206 Laird Dr., Suite 200, Toronto, ON M4G 3W4 (416) 696-9633. FAX: 696-9640. Skytech Satellite Services, 206 Laird Dr., Suite 200, Toronto, ON M4G 3W4 (416) 696-9626. FAX: 696-9640.
Type of Production and Credits: TV Film-DOP/Dir/Prod; TV Video-DOP/Dir/Prod.
Genres: Documentary-TV; Commercials-TV; Industrial-TV.
Biography: Canadian citizen. Languages: English and French. B.A., English, University of Toronto; B.Ed., OISE.
Selected Filmography: "Players' GM and Formula Atlantic Car Racing Series" (41 eps), TV, 90-91, CDN, Prod; "World Cup Skiing" (4 eps), 90-91, CDN, Prod; "Canadian Ski Champs" (9 eps), TV, 90-

91, CDN, Co-Prod/Dir; *Moscow McDonald's*, TV, 90, CDN/USR, Prod/Dir/Wr; *The Green Plan* (2 parts), ED, 90, CDN, Prod/Dir; *National Pagette* (2 parts), ED, 90, CDN, Prod; *Bell Cellular* (2 parts), ED, 90, CDN, Prod.

PAYRASTRE, Georges
3657 W. 1 Ave., Vancouver, BC V6Z 1H1. Okexnon Films Inc., Box 33961, Station D, Vancouver, BC V6J 4L7 (604)733-6101.
Type of Production and Credits: Th Short-Dir/Cam/Prod; TV Film-Dir/Cam/Prod.
Genres: Drama-Th; Documentary-TV; Educational-TV; Children's-TV.
Biography: Born 1944, Paris, France; Canadian and French citizenship. Languages: English, French and Spanish. Studied Film, Simon Fraser University; B.Mathematics, France. Numerous credits as cameraman on TV productions (film and tape).

PENDRY, Phillip C. ✧
(416)488-0689.
Type of Production and Credits: Th Film-DOP; TV Film-DOP; Th Short-DOP; TV Video-DOP.
Genres: Documentary-TV; Educational-TV; Commercials-TV; Industrial-TV.
Biography: Born 1927, London, England; Canadian and British citizenship. Languages: English and some French, German and Italian. Has pilot's licence, aqualung and diving certificates. Extensive personal photography and sound recording equipment. International experience as cameraman and director, e.g., Pinewood, Rank, Pathé, NFB, CBC, CTV, etc. Winner of 2 NPPA awards and Cameraman of the Year Award, CSC, 71.
Selected Filmography: "Fire Prevention" (13 eps), TV, 88, CDN, DOP; "L'Auto" (96 eps), TV, 83-87, CDN, DOP; "The American Century" (6 eps), TV, 86, CDN, DOP.

PERAK, Branko
Arts Creation Inc., 45 Myrtle Ave., Toronto, ON M4M 2A4 (416)461-2500. FAX: 461-2500.
Type of Production and Credits: Th Film-DOP; TV Film-Cam; TV Video-Cam.
Genres: Drama-Th&TV; Comedy-Th&TV; Action-Th&TV; Documentary-Th&TV.
Biography: Born 1933, Mrkonjic, Yugoslavia; Canadian and Yugoslav citizenship. Studied Film, Architecture and Music. "Artist of the Republic of Serbia," 70; 1st Special Prize , Best Photography, Film Festival in Pula, *The Girl*, 65; 2nd Special Prize, *The Great Day*, 60.
Selected Filmography: *The Spy on Spike Heels*, Th, 88, YU, DOP; "The Fortunate Pilgrim" (3 eps), TV, 87, USA/I, 2nd U Cam; *Marineland and Game Farms*, Cm, 75, CDN, DOP; *They're Alive, You Know*, TV, 75, CDN, Cam; *Marko Perov*, Th, 74, YU, DOP; *The Music Box*, Th, 72, YU, DOP; *The Social Game*, Th, 72, YU, DOP; *England Made Me*, Th, 71, GB, 2nd U Cam; *Plastic Jesus*, Th, 71, YU, DOP; *Romance of the Horse Thief*, Th, 70, USA/I/YU, 2nd U Cam; *Gifts of My Cousin Mary*, Th, 69, YU, DOP; *Girl in the Park*, Th, 68, YU, DOP; *Innocence Without Protection*, Th, 68, YU, DOP; *Restless*, Th, 66, YU, DOP; *Time for Love*, Th, 66, YU, DOP.

PERZEL, Anthony
- see PRODUCERS

PETERSEN, Curtis
DGC, IATSE 669, BCMPA, MPPA, CSC. 305 - 1360 Hornby St., Vancouver, BC V6Z 1W5 (604)685-2106. PPI Camera Corp./Petersen Productions, 314 West Pender St., Vancouver, BC V6B 1T3 (604)669-8890.
Type of Production and Credits: Th Film-Prod/DOP/Dir; TV Film-DOP.
Genres: Action-Th&TV; Commercials-Th&TV; Sports-Th&TV.
Biography: Attended the University of British Columbia and majored in Film Production, Commerce and Business Administration. Worked as a freelance producer and DOP. Has worked on locations worldwide; Has produced award-winning television commercials, documentaries, television specials and feature films for the last thirteen years. Formed Petersen Productions Inc. in 1978, and is sole owner and President; also President and owner of PPI Camera Corp., a full-service film and video equipment rental facility , co-owner of Petersen-Robison Productions, a Vancouver-based full-service production house, and Vice-President of Production for Rose and Ruby Entertainment of Toronto, Hollywood and Zurich. Professional skier, Naui certified scuba diver, professional horseman and trainer; extensive mountaineering and whitewater experience. Has been nominated for CSC and Genie awards and has won many awards for cinematography.
Selected Filmography: *Bloodrush/Happy Hell Night*, Th, 91, CDN/YU, Prod/DOP; *Ski Doo '92*, In/Cm, 91, CDN, Dir/DOP; *Crooked Hearts*, TV, 90, USA, 2nd Unit DOP; *Ski School*, Th, 90, USA/CDN,

DOP; *Dragonfight*, Th, 90, USA/CDN, DOP; *Abraxas - Guardian of the Universe*, Th, 90, CDN, Prod/DOP; *Ski Doo '91*, In/Cm, 90, CDN, Dir/DOP; *Thunderground*, Th, 89, CDN, DOP; *Time In Your Hands*, Cm, 89, CDN, Dir/DOP; *Watchers*, Th, 89-90, CDN, Co DOP; *Short Time*, Th, 89, USA, 2nd Unit DOP; *Shoot To Kill*, Th, 89, USA, 2nd Unit DOP; *The Climb*, Th, 86, CDN, 2nd Unit DOP..

PETRIE, Robert J
- see PRODUCERS

PIRKER, Roland K. ✧
(613)521-3603.
Type of Production and Credits: TV Film-DOP/Ed/Prod/Dir; TV Video-DOP/Ed/Prod/Dir.
Genres: Documentary-TV; Educational-TV; Industrial-TV; Sports-TV.
Biography: Born 1940, Klagenfurt, Austria; Canadian citizenship. Languages: German and English. Graduate of Film Studies, Conestoga College, 72. Worked for 7 years in visual anthropology; shot in Asia, Africa and Europe; interest in Third World country development films. Winner of several international awards including Vienna, New York, Velden and Lausanne.
Selected Filmography: *Pompe Ko'om, le goût de participer*, ED, 88, CDN/GH, Prod/Cam/Ed; *Getting Serious*, ED, 87, CDN, DOP; *Les Habitats de la montagne*, Cm, 87, CDN, Prod/Cam/Ed; *Canada's Gold Maple Leaf*, In, 86, CDN, DOP; *African Famine*, ED, 86, USA/IV; Cam; *Costain, the Movie*, In, 86, CDN, Cam; *World Health Organization Conference*, ED, 86, CDN, Cam/Ed; *Ottawa-Hull: Canada's Meeting Place*, Cm, 86, CDN, Cam; *Gearing Up*, ED, 86, CDN, Cam; *City of Ottawa*, In, 85, CDN, Cam; *Oh Canada* (TV sign-off), Cm, 85, CDN, DOP; *City of Nepean*, In, 85, CDN, Cam; *Pompe Ko'om: A Sense of Commitment*, ED, 84, CDN/GH, Prod/Cam/Ed; *20th Anniversary-African Development Bank*, ED, 84, USA/IV, Cam; *Bob Kelly in Asia*, ED, 83, CDN, Cam.

POSTER, Steven
IATSE 667, 659 & 666, ASC, CSC, AMPAS. 5757 Wilshire Blvd., Ste. 660, Los Angeles, CA 90036 (213)656-1045. Kendall Giler Management, 224 S. Detroit, Los Angeles, CA 90036 USA (213)936-6013.
Type of Production and Credits: Th Film-DOP.
Genres: Drama-Th&TV; Comedy-Th&TV; Action-Th&TV; Commercials-Th&TV.
Selected Filmography: *Life Stinks*, Th, 91, USA, DOP; *Rocky V*, Th, 90, USA, DOP; *Opportunity Knocks*, Th, 89, USA, DOP; *Next of Kin*, Th, 88, USA, DOP; *Big Top Pee-Wee*, Th, 87, USA, DOP; *Someone To Watch Over Me*, Th, 86, USA/GB, DOP; *The Boy Who Could Fly*, Th, 86, USA/CDN, DOP; *Blue City*, Th, 86, USA, DOP; *Heavenly Kid*, Th, 85, USA, DOP; *Aloha Summer*, Th, 85, USA, DOP; *Testament*, Th, 84, USA, DOP; *Strange Brew*, Th, 83, CDN/USA, DOP; *Dead and Buried*, Th, 81, USA, DOP; *Blood Beach*, Th, 80, USA, DOP.

POULSSON, Andreas
CSC, IATSE 669. A. Poulsson Films Inc., #25 - 4957 Marine Drive, West Vancouver, BC V7W 2P5 (604)926-0416.
Type of Production and Credits: Th Film-DOP; Th Short-DOP; TV Film-DOP.
Genres: Drama-Th&TV; Documentary-Th&TV; Educational-Th&TV.
Biography: Born 1944, Oslo, Norway; Canadian citizenship. Languages: English, Danish, some French and German. Has worked as a documentary cinematographer and director of photography for 18 years; 67-86 at the NFB; freelance since 86.
Selected Filmography: "Mom P.I." (26 eps), TV, 90-91, CDN, DOP; "Max Glick" (13 eps), TV, 90, CDN, DOP; *Vincent and Me*, Th, 89, CDN/F, DOP; "Twilight Zone - The Series" (11 eps), TV, 88, CDN/USA, DOP; *Tommy Tricker and the Stamp Traveller*, Th, 87, CDN/AUS/RC, DOP; "Airwaves" (13 eps), TV, 86-87, CDN, DOP; "Bell Canada Playhouse" (14 eps), TV, 84-85, CDN, DOP; *Canada's Sweetheart - The Saga of Hal C. Banks*, TV, 85, CDN, DOP; *Sitting in Limbo*, Th, 84, CDN, DOP; *After the Axe*, TV, 80, CDN, DOP; *Henry Ford's America*, TV, 76, CDN, DOP.

PROTAT, François ✧
(514)273-9552.
Types de production et générique: l métrage-D photo.
Types d'oeuvres: Drame-C; Comédie musicale-C; Documentaire-C.
Curriculum vitae: Né à Paris, France; citoyenneté française et canadienne. Baccalauréat en Sciences; cours en cinéma, Ecole National du Cinéma, Paris. Directeur de la photographie sur 500 annonces et 35 longs métrages. *Les Ordres* remporte le prix de la mise en scène, Cannes.

Filmographie sélective: *Joshua Then and Now,* C, 84, CDN, D phot, (GENIE 86); *Le Crime d'Ovide Plouffe,* C, 83, CDN/F, D phot; *Running Brave,* C, 83, CDN/USA, D phot; *Between Friends,* C, 83, CDN, D phot; *Les Plouffe,* C, 80, CDN, D phot; *Au revoir...à lundi,* C, 79, CDN/F, D phot; *Fantastica,* C, 79, CDN/F, D phot; *La Tête de Normande St-Onge,* C, 75, CDN, D phot; *Les Ordres,* C, 73, CDN, D phot.

RACINE, Pierre
STCQ. Les Promotions Multivisions, 492 ouest, rue Arago, Québec, PQ G1K 2J8 (418)683-5481.
Types de production et générique: c métrage-Mont/Ass réal; TV film-Mont/Réal; TV vidéo-Mont/Prod/Réal.
Types d'oeuvres: Documentaire-C&TV; Education-C&TV; Industriel-C&TV.
Curriculum vitae: Né à Québec. Langues: français et anglais. Etudes faites dans les arts oeuvre dans le domaine du cinéma depuis 71.
Filmographie sélective: *La femme miroir,* C, 91, CDN, Dir tech; *Clippe mais clippe égal,* TV, 90, CDN, Prod/D photo; *Stowaway,* C, 90, CDN, Dir tech; *Réveille ton rêve,* TV, 89, CDN, Dir photo; *Manu Manu,* MV, 89, CDN, Dir tech; *Ballade urbaine,* In, 89, CDN, Dir photo; *Short Change,* C, 89, CDN, Dir tech; *Le contrôleur des finances,* TV, 89, CDN, Dir photo; *Un complément essential,* ED, 88, CDN, Dir phot/Réal; *Le système redère,* ED, 88, Dir photo/Réal; *Granicor,* In, 88, CDN, Prod/Réal/Dir photo.

REUSCH, Peter
- see DIRECTORS

ROWAN, Monty
IATSE, CSC. 37 Horizon Ave., Venice, CA 90291 USA (213)396-4799. (213)304-1795.
Type of Production and Credits: Th Film-DOP/Cam Op.
Genres: Drama-Th; Comedy-Th; Action-Th; Children's-Th.
Biography: Born 1952, Toronto, Ontario; US resident alien. Spent 7 years as 1st assist cameraman on feature films for TV and theatrical release, as well as extensive commercial work;. works as a camera operator and cinematographer and DOP.
Selected Filmography: *Where Sleeping Dogs Lie,* Th, 90, USA, Cam Op; *Blood Ties,* TV, 90, USA, Cam Op/2nd U DOP; *The Big One* (mini-series), TV, 90, USA, 2nd U DOP; *Robocop II,* TV, 90, USA, Cam Op; *Enid Is Sleeping,* Th, 89, USA, Cam Op; *Family of Spies* (7 eps), TV, 89, USA, Cam Op; *Breaking In,* Th, 88, USA, Cam Op; *Heartbreak Hotel,* Th, 88, USA, Cam Op; *Two Floor Junction,* Th, 87, USA, Cam Op/2nd U DOP; *To Heal A Nation,* TV, 87, USA, Cam Op; *Foxfire,* TV, 87, USA, Cam Op; *Native Son,* Th, 86, USA, Cam Op.

ROY, Maurice ◆
(514)849-4942.
Types de production et générique: TV film-D photo; TV vidéo-D photo.
Types d'oeuvres: Variété-TV; Documentaire-C&TV; Education-C&TV; Annonces-TV.
Curriculum vitae: Né en 1947. Premier prix, National Computer Graphics Association, USA,, la Clip Cup Trophée, Meilleur Clip canadien au MIDEM 88, et le Prix Monitor, New York, 88.
Filmographie sélective: *Uniprix* (Noël), Cm, CDN, D phot/Cadr; *Mon royaume pour un bleuet,* TV, 87-88, CDN, D phot/Cadr; *Le Chant des étoiles,* MV, 87, CDN, D phot/Cadr; *Remixez-moi,* MV, 87, CDN, D phot/Cadr; *Escale à Memphis,* TV, 87, CDN, D phot/Cadr; "Gamelle et Sac à dos" (13 eps), TV, 87, CDN, D phot/Cadr; *Le Centenaire de l'ingéniérie,* TV, 87, CDN, D phot/Cadr; *La Ronde/T-Fal/Coke/TV Hebdo,* Cm 87, CDN, D phot/Cadr; *Romantic Complica-tion,* 86, CDN, D phot/Cadr; *Celle qui va,* MV, 86, CDN, D phot/Cadr; "Rock et Belles Oreilles" (8 eps), TV, 86, CDN, D phot/Cadr; *Tapis rouge à Paris,* MV, 85, CDN/F, D phot/Cadr; *Tapis rouge - Concerto pour Picasso,* TV, 85, CDN/F, Cadr; *Cirque du Soleil,* TV, 85, CDN, D phot/Cadr; *Manipule/Les Jeux vidéo,* TV, 85, CDN, D phot/Cadr.

RUCK, Wolf
Wolf Ruck Productions, 1720 Lincolnshire Blvd., Mississauga, ON L5E 2S7 (416)278-0296.
Type of Production and Credits: Th Short-Prod/Dir/DOP; TV Film-DOP/Snd Rec.
Genres: Drama-TV; Action-Th&TV; Documentary-TV; Educational-Th&TV.
Biography: Born 1946, Augsburg, West Germany; Canadian citizen. Languages: English, German, working knowledge of French, Spanish and Italian. B.P.H.E., University of Toronto. Independent filmmaker, freelance cinema-tographer and sound recordist since 76; translator, author, photographer, illustrator of 3 books on sports (McGraw-Hill). Member of Canadian Olympic Canoeing Team, Mexico, 68. *Paddles Up!* won 1991 Waterwalker Film Festival Competition/Technique Award.

Selected Filmography: *Burden on the Land*, TV, 91, CDN, Cin; *AIDS in Africa*, TV, 90, CDN, Cin; *1-2-3 Zoom*, TV, 87, CDN, Prod/Dir/DOP/Ed; "Chasing Rainbows" (2 eps), TV, 86-87, CDN, 1st Assist Cam/Op; *Freewheelin'*, TV, 85, CDN, Prod/Dir/Cin/Ed; *Lost!*, Th, 85, CDN, 1st Assist Cam/2nd U Cam; *Turning to Stone*, TV, 85, CDN, Assist Cam/2nd U Cam; *Final Offer*, TV, 84, CDN, Snd Rec; *Heart/Water Weeds/Cyclosporin-A*, "The Nature of Things", TV, 82-84, CDN, Snd Rec; *This Is Cross Country*, TV, 83, CDN, Prod/Dir/Snd Rec/Cin; *Orchids*, "The Nature of Things", TV, 82, CDN, Cin; *Telidon*, "The Nature of Things", TV, 82, CDN, Add'l Phot; *Medicare*, "Quarterly Report", TV, 82, CDN, Snd Rec; *World Cup Soccer/Maturity/Queen's Plate/Mennen Cup Squash*, "Sportsweekend", TV, 82, CDN, Cin; *Paddles Up!*, TV, 78, Prod/Dir/Cam.

SAAD, Robert ◊
(416)481-5429.
Type of Production and Credits: Th Film-DOP; TV Film-DOP; TV Video-DOP.
Genres: Comedy-Th&TV; Action-Th&TV; Horror-Th&TV; Documentary-Th&TV.
Biography: Born 1936, Haifa, Israel; came to Canada, 67. Languages: English, French, Arabic and Italian. Spent most of childhood in Lebanon and Egypt; attended Jesuit school and worked his way up from apprentice to camera operator at Studio Nahas in Cairo.
Selected Filmography: *Mad Avenue*, TV, 88, USA, Op; "War of the Worlds" (4 eps), TV, 88, USA, DOP; *Millennium*, Th, 88, CDN, 2nd U DOP; *Bluffing It*, TV, 87, USA, Op; "Wiseguy", TV, 87, CDN, Op; *Short Circuit II*, Th, 87, USA, Op; *Police Academy IV*, Th, 86, USA, DOP; *The Return of Billy Jack*, Th, 86, USA, DOP; *Police Academy III*, Th, 85, USA, DOP; *One Magic Christmas*, Th, 85, CDN/USA, Op; *Beer*, Th, 84, USA, Op/2nd U DOP; *Evergreen* (mini-series), TV, 84, USA, Op; *He's Fired, She's Hired*, TV, 84, USA, Op; *Martin's Day*, Th, 83, CDN/GB, Op; *Police Academy*, Th, 83, USA, 2nd U DOP.

SARIN, Victor
- see DIRECTORS

SAROSSY, Ivan
CSC, NABET. 28 Albert St., Barrie, ON L4M 3S6 (705)721-4385. Citytv, 299 Queen St. W., Toronto, ON M5V 2Z5 (416)591-5757.
Type of Production and Credits: TV Video-DOP/Prod.
Genres: Documentary-TV; Educational-TV; Commercials-TV.
Biography: Born in 1926 in Hungary; Canadian citizenship. Studied at Ontario College of Art, 52. DOP, CKVR TV (Barrie) for 15 years; producer/DOP, Citytv Commercials Dept., Toronto, 86 with numerous commercials to his credit.
Selected Filmography: *I Am a Hotel*, TV, 84, CDN, 2nd U DOP; "Showbiz" (200 eps), TV, 72-80, CDN, Prod; "Faces of Small Places" (100 eps), TV, 74-78, CDN, Prod.

SAROSSY, Paul
CSC. 1183 Islington Ave., Toronto, ON M8Z 4S8 (416)233-9928.
Type of Production and Credits: Th Film-DOP; Th Short-Dir/DOP; TV Film-DOP.
Genres: Drama-Th&TV; Comedy-Th; Musical-Th; Action-Th; Commercials-Th&TV; Music Video-TV.
Biography: Born 1963, Barrie, Ontario. Honours B.F.A., Film, York University. *Speaking Parts* and *The Adjuster* were selected for Directors' Fortnight at Cannes; *Revenge of the Radioactive Reporter*, Best Independent Feature at Houston; *Let Your Backbone Slide*, Most Popular Music Video, Much Music Awards, 89; *Drop the Needle* won Juno, 90 for Best Music Video.
Selected Filmography: *Grand Larceny*, TV, 91, CDN, DOP; *Petrograd*, Th, 91, CDN, Dir/DOP; *Vue d'Ailleurs/Montreal Stories*, Th, 91, CDN, Dir/DOP; *Masala*, Th, 90, CDN, DOP; *The Adjuster*, Th, 90, CDN, DOP; *Drop the Needle*, Maestro Fresh Wes, MV, 90, CDN, DOP; *Ludi*, Dream Warriors, MV, 90, CDN, DOP; *Terminal City Ricochet*, Th, 89, CDN, DOP; *White Room*, Th, 89, CDN, DOP; *Let Your Backbone Slide*, Maestro Fresh Wes, MV, 89, CDN, DOP; *Revenge of the Radioactive Reporter*, Th, 88, CDN, DOP; *Speaking Parts*, Th, 88, CDN, DOP; *Black and White*, Th, 88, CDN, Dir/DOP.

SAVOIE, Michael Patrick
NABET. 190 Bayview Heights Dr., Toronto, ON M4G 2Z2 (416)696-7939.
Type of Production and Credits: TV Film-DOP; TV Video-DOP.
Genres: Documentary-TV; Current Affairs-TV.
Biography: Born in 1949 in St. Catharines, Ontario. Canadian citizen. 15 years experience as film/video cameraman/DOP.
Selected Filmography: "Brain Sex" (3 eps), TV, 91, CDN/USA/GB, Cam; *Gospel Music*, "Man Alive", TV, 91, CDN,

Cam; "the fifth estate" (20 eps), TV, 90-91, CDN, Cam; *Born in Africa*, TV, 89, CDN/USA, DOP; *India*, "The Journal", TV, 89, CDN, Cam; *Agony of Bophal*, "The Journal", TV, 88, CDN, Cam; *Black Market Babies*, "The Journal", TV, 87, CDN, Cam; *Blue City Slammers*, Th, 87, CDN, 2nd Unit Cam; *Heart Frontier*, "The Journal", TV, 86, CDN, Cam; *Peter Ustinov's China*, TV, 86, CDN, Cam; *Black Ice*, Th, 80, CDN, DOP.

SCHERER, Karl
IATSE 667, IATSE 873. 45 Norden Crescent, Don Mills, ON M3B 1B7 (416)445-1106.
Type of Production and Credits: Th Short-DOP/Snd Rec; TV Film-DOP; Video-DOP/Prod/Dir.
Genres: Drama-Th&TV; Action-Th&TV; Educational-Th&TV; Industrial-Th&TV.
Biography: Born 1941, Leoben, Austria; Canadian citizenship. Languages: English, French and German. DOP for past 5 years; works in various capacities for The Partners Film Company in commercial production. Won Genie for Best Overall Sound for *The Changeling*, 80.
Selected Filmography: *Marineland*, In, 89, CDN, Cam; "Value Showcase" (pilot), TV, 88, CDN, DOP; *The Trojan Horse*, In, 88, CDN, DOP; *Toys R Us*, Cm, 86-87, CDN, Prod/DOP; *The Red Dog*, Th, 87, CDN, DOP; *Brenda*, Th, 86, CDN, DOP; *The Sheraton*, In, 85, CDN, DOP; Black Sabbath, MV, 85, CDN, DOP; *The Sodaman*, MV, 85, CDN, DOP.

SCHUURMAN, Hubert
- see DIRECTORS

SEALE, Neil
IATSE 667, 669. 502 - 1920 Alberni St., Vancouver, BC V6G 1B5 (604)688-4411. (416) 759-4108.
Type of Production and Credits: Th Film-Cam/DOP; Th Short-Cam/DOP; TV Film-Cam/DOP; TV Video-Cam/DOP.
Genres: Drama-Th&TV; Comedy-Th&TV; Documentary-TV; Music Video-TV.
Biography: Born 1951, Barbados, West Indies; Canadian citizenship. Studied Electrical Eng., McMaster University, 70-72. Lighting designer, occasional set designer for theatre productions. Won a CSC Award for Outstanding Service, 86.
Selected Filmography: *Bingo*, Th, 90, USA, 2nd Unit DOP; "MacGyver" (11 eps), TV, 90, USA, 2nd Unit DOP; *Kootenai Brown*, Th, 90, CDN, 2nd Unit DOP; *Burning Bridges*, TV, 90, USA, 2nd Unit DOP; *Small Sacrifices*, TV, 89, USA, 2nd Cam Op; "21 Jump Street" (24 eps), TV, 88-89, USA, Cam Op; *Discover the Sea*, ED, 88, CDN, DOP; *Cousins*, Th, 88, USA, 2nd Cam Op; "Danger Bay" (19 eps), TV, 87, CDN, Cam Op; *Suspect*, Th, 87, USA, 2nd Cam Op; *After Midnight*, TV, 87, USA, Cam Op; *The Liberators*, TV, 86, USA, Cam Op; *Amerika*, TV, 86, USA, Cam Op; *Police Academy III*, Th, 86, USA, Cam Op; *Teri-Ann*, MV, 86, CDN, DOP.

SECRETAN-COX, Michael
- see DIRECTORS

SIRETEANU, Ion-Dragos
- see PRODUCERS

SMOFSKY, Lenny
- see DIRECTORS

SPIESS, Fritz
CSC, IATSE 644, IATSE 667, SMPTE. 168 Church Ave., Willowdale, ON M2N 4G5 (416)225-5970.
Type of Production and Credits: TV Film-DOP/Dir; TV Video-DOP/Dir; Video-DOP/Dir.
Genres: Commercials-TV.
Biography: Born 1925, Germany; Canadian citizenship. Languages: English and German. Apprenticeship in photography, Germany, 43-48; Master of Photography, Munich Photoschool, 49. Own photo studio in Heidelberg, 49-51. Came to Canada, 51. Commercial photography with Panda Photography, 51-54; DOP At S.W. Caldwell Ltd, 54-58; DOP at Robert Lawrence Productions, 58-67; DOP at TDF Film Productions, 67-76; DOP at Schulz Productions, 76-87; DOP at Rawi-Sherman Films Inc., 87-91. Was DOP for the 9-camera Disney Circlevision film for the Telephone Pavilion, Expo 67. Has won numerous national and international awards, including Bessies, Clios, Bronze, Silver and Gold Lions in Cannes. In 79, the TV Bureau of Canada created an annual award, the Fritz Spiess Award, for "continuing consistent dedication to excellence in the art of the television commercial." First recipient of the Kodak Award, 87. More than 3,000 commercials to his credit.

SPRINGGAY, Barry E.
239 Bedford Pk. Ave., Toronto, ON M5M 1J4 (416)483-1387.
Type of Production and Credits: TV Film-DOP; TV Video-DOP.
Genres: Documentary-TV; Industrial-TV; Music Video-TV; Current Affairs-TV; Corporate-Th.
Biography: Born Sault Ste. Marie,

Ontario. Honours B.F.A., York University. World location shooting (Hong Kong, China, Australia, Thailand, Middle East, North America, etc). Specializes in corporate and industrial video; enjoys live-action, "cinéma verité" style.
Selected Filmography: *Darlington Nuclear Plant Constructibility* (6 parts), Corp, 89-91, CDN, Cam/DOP; *We Stand Together*, "Kapuskasing Survives", TV, 91, CDN, Cam/DOP; *Australian Report*, "Northern Telecom Presents", Corp, 90, AUS/CDN, Cam/DOP; "Get Away" (pilot), TV, 89, CDN, Cam/DOP; *Keevil: Man with the Golden Touch*, TV, 88, CDN, Cam/DOP; *Isabel Bassett Special*, TV, 85, CDN, Cam; *From China with Love*, TV, 85, CDN, Cam; "Paradox" (4 eps), TV, 84, CDN, Cam.

STANNETT, Ronald Edward
CSC, IATSE, APCQ, CAMERA. 140 Spruce St., Toronto, ON M5A 2J5 (416)964-7394.
Type of Production and Credits: Th Film-DOP; TV Film-DOP; TV Video-DOP.
Genres: Drama-Th&TV; Documentary-TV; Commercials-TV; Music Video-TV.
Biography: Born 1944, Townsville, Australia; landed immigrant, Canada. CSC award for Best Documentary cameraman in Canada, 76; nominated for Best Photography, 1988 Gemini Awards for *Making Opera*; winner for Best Photography, 1990 Gemini Awards, *Rita MacNeil - Flying on Her Own*.
Selected Filmography: "Top Cops", TV, 91, USA/CDN, DOP; "The Hitchhiker", TV, 90, USA/CDN, DOP; "War of the Worlds", TV, 89, USA/CDN, DOP; *Flying on Her Own*, TV, 89, CDN, Dir/DOP; *Rita MacNeil's Christmas Special*, TV, 90, CDN, Dir/DOP; *Keeping Track*, Th, 85, CDN, DOP; *Obsessed/Hitting Home*, Th, 88, CDN, DOP; *The Originals*, TV, 88, CDN, DOP; *Connect Me*, Platinum Blonde, MV, 88, CDN/USA, DOP; *The Brain*, TV, 88, CDN/USA, Dir/DOP; *Making Opera*, TV, 87, CDN, DOP.

STANTON, Greg
CSC. 2607 Edgar St., Regina, SK S4N 3L8 (306)757-7978. CKCK-TV, Box 2000, Regina, SK S4P 3E6 (306)569-2000.
Type of Production and Credits: TV Video-DOP.
Genres: Drama-TV; Documentary-TV; Current Affairs-TV; News-TV.
Biography: Born in 1960 in Winnipeg, Manitoba. Canadian citizen. Languages: English and some French. Studied film production at Confederation College specializing in cinematography and lighting. Employed as E.N.G./Production Cameraman for CKCK-TV since 1982. DOP and Lighting Director for 6-part series called "John Archer's Saskatchewan" which called for some elements to be shot in Southern England. Cinematography/lighting for numerous CanPro-winning programs through CKCK-TV. Darkroom work with own facilities since 1974.
Selected Filmography: "John Archer's Saskatchewan" (6 eps), TV, 89-91, CDN, DOP/Light Dir.

STEWART, Barney
Komart Productions Inc., 32 Saybrook Ave., Toronto, ON M8Z 2V4 (416)233-7804.
Type of Production and Credits: Th Film-DOP; TV Film-DOP; TV Video-Light Dir/Des.
Genres: Drama-TV; Comedy-Th&TV; Variety-TV; Industrial-Th&TV,
Biography: Born 1941, Toronto, Ontario; Canadian citizen. Has worked on projects in the Middle East, Latin America, Hong Kong and the Caribbean. ANIK and Montreux Golden Rose award for *I Am A Hotel*. Emmy nomination for *Execution of Raymond Graham*, 1985.
Selected Filmography: "The Super Dave Osborne Show" (117 eps), TV, 87-91, CDN/USA, Light Dir; *Raffi in Concert*, TV, 88, USA/CDN, Light Dir; *Pope John XXIII*, TV, 86, USA, Light Dir; *LBJ*, TV, 86, USA, Light Dir; *Goofballs*, Th, 85, CDN, DOP; *Execution of Ramond Graham*, TV, 85, USA/CDN, 2nd Unit Light Dir; *Schmenge Brothers: The Last Polka*, TV, 84, USA/CDN, Light Dir; "SCTV" (48 eps), TV, 81-84; USA/CDN, Light Dir; *I Am A Hotel*, TV, 83, CDN, Light Dir, (ANIK); *George Washington at Valley Forge*, "Hallmark Hall of Fame", TV, 75, USA, Light Dir; *Harvey*, "Hallmark Hall of Fame", TV, 75, USA, Light Dir; *The Borrowers*, "Hallmark Hall of Fame", TV, 73, USA, Light Dir; *The Country Girl*, "Hallmark Hall of Fame", TV, 73, USA, Light Dir; *Look Homeward Angel*, "CBS Playhouse", TV, 72, USA, Light Dir; *All The Way Home*, "Hallmark Hall of Fame", TV, 71, USA, Light Dir.

STONE, Barry
44 Pembroke St., Toronto, ON M5A 1S6 (416) 361-0714. 197 Queen St. E., Toronto, ON M5A 2N7 (416) 860-1265. FAX: 860-1293.
Type of Production and Credits: TV Film-DOP.

Genres: Drama-TV; Industrial-Th&TV; Music Video-TV.
Biography: Born 1945, England; Canadian and British citizenship. Languages: English, French and Spanish. President, Camera Guild of Canada. *Always Welcome* won Certificate of Merit at Yorkton and O.P.S. Forum Award.
Selected Filmography: "Counterstrike" (3 eps), TV, 91, F/CDN, DOP; *Always Welcome*, ED, 90, CDN, Dir/Prod; "T and T" (13 eps), TV, 89, CDN/USA, DOP; *Graveyard Shift/The Understudy*, Th, 88, CDN/USA, DOP; *Party Girl*, Patti Jenatta, MV, 88, CDN, Dir/Ed; *Everyday*, Frank De Carlo, MV, 88, CDN, DOP/Ed; "Chestnut Avenue" (pilot), TV, 88, CDN, Dir/Ed; *Open Up the Door*, Junior Barnes and the Cadillacs, MV, 87, CDN, DOP; *Sammy*, Norm Hacking, MV, 87, CDN, DOP/Ed; *Congo Toronto*, Robert Priest, MV, 87, CDN, DOP/Dir/Ed, *Hello Mary Lou*, Ronnie Hawkins, MV, 87, CDN, DOP; "Mariah State", TV, 87, USA, 2nd U DOP; *Street Justice*, Th, 87, USA, 2nd U DOP; "Max Haines' Crime Flashback" (pilot), TV, 86, CDN, DOP; *Me and Joey*, Murray McLauchlan, MV, 84-86, CDN, DOP

STONEMAN, John
CFTA, IATSE 667, ACTRA, CSC. 219 Strathearn Ave., Richmond Hill, ON L4B 3C3 (416)770-1164. Mako Films Ltd., 70 East Beaver Creek, Unit #19, Richmond Hill, ON L4B 3B2 (416)882-9600. FAX: 882-9605.
Type of Production and Credits: Th Film-DOP/2nd U Dir/Wr; Th Short-Prod/Dir/Cin/Wr; TV Film-Prod/Dir/Cin/Wr.
Genres: Drama-Th&TV; Action-Th&TV; Documentary-Th&TV; Commercials-Th&TV; Sports-TV.
Biography: Born in England; Canadian citizenship. Languages: English and Swahili. M.Sc., Zoology. Underwater cinematographer, expert in sharks; race driver. Over 100 international film awards including Lifetime of Excellence in Cinematography; other awards include Best TV Series, CFTA, Golden Sheaf Award nomination and Silver Medal for "The Last Frontier"; Gold Medal (Festival of the Americas), Chris Plaque (Columbus) and Gold Medal (New York) for *The Last Giants*; awards also at Houston and US Industrial Film Festivals; numerous environmental awards. Awarded Plaque of Dedication in Marine Conservation (U.C.O.N.N. Scuba Club, Connecticut); Distinguished Service Award (Ontario Underwater Council); Lifetime Award of Excellence in Cinematography (Antibes Juan Les Pins Festival Mondial de l'Image Sous-Marine). Currently President of Mako Films Ltd. and Director of the Foundation for Ocean Research.
Selected Filmography: "The Last Frontier" (100 eps), TV, 83-90, CDN, Exec Prod/Dir/Cin/Wr; *Dead Zone*, Th, 83, Cin; *The Last Giants*, TV, 83, CDN, Prod/Dir/Wr/Cin; *Shark*, TV, 82, CDN/GB, Prod/Dir/Wr/Cin; *Mythical Monsters of the Deep*, TV, 82, CDN, Prod/Dir/Wr/Cin; *Sentinel of the Sea*, TV, 81, CDN, Prod/Dir/Wr/Cin; *Lord of the Sea*, TV, 81, CDN, Prod/Dir/Wr/Cin; *Defenders of the Sea*, TV, 81, CDN, Prod/Dir/Wr/Cin; *Sanctuary of the Sea*, TV/Th, 80, CDN/USA, Prod/Dir/Wr/Cin; *Coral Reef*, "The Nature of Things", TV, 80, CDN, Cin; *Ghost Ships*, TV, 80, CDN, Prod/Dir/Cin/Wr; *Nomads of the Deep*, Th, 79, CDN, Prod/Dir/Cin; *The Fragile Sea*, TV, 79, CDN, Prod/Dir/Wr/Cin; *Sea Nymph*, TV, 78, CDN, Prod/Dir/Wr/Cin; *Cries in the Night*, Th, 78, USA, Cin.

STOREY, Michael
356 Beresford Ave., Toronto, ON M6S 3B5 (416)769-3867.
Type of Production and Credits: Th Film-DOP; TV Film-DOP; TV Video-DOP.
Genres: Drama-TV; Musical-Th&TV; Documentary-TV; Music Video-TV.
Biography: Born 1955, Toronto, Ontario. DOP for 5 years. Certified ski instructor and scuba diver; has done films on the slopes and under water.
Selected Filmography: "E.N.G." (22 eps), TV, 90-91, CDN, DOP; *Wojeck*, TV, 90, CDN, DOP; *Romeos & Juliets*, TV, 90, CDN, DOP; *When the Fire Burns*, TV, 90, CDN, DOP; *Don Giovanni in Rehearsal*, TV, 90, CDN, DOP; *Behind the Mask*, TV, 89, CDN, DOP; "9B" (6 eps), TV, 88, CDN, DOP; Richard Citroien, MV, 88, CDN, DOP; Con Can, MV, 88, CDN, DOP; "Man Alive" (2 eps), TV, 88, CDN, DOP; "Not My Department" (12 eps), TV, 87, CDN, DOP; *Skate*, TV, 87, CDN, DOP; *Dance*, TV, 87, CDN, DOP; *The Philippines*, TV, 84, CDN/USA, DOP.

STRATYCHUK, Perry Mark
- see DIRECTORS

STRINGER, Richard A.
CSC, ACFC. 196 Hallam St., Toronto, ON M6H 1X7 (416)533-6085.
Type of Production and Credits: Th Film-DOP; TV Film-DOP/Prod; TV

Video-DOP/Prod.
Genres: Drama-Th&TV; Commercials-TV; Documentary-TV; Educational-TV.
Biography: Born 1944; Canadian citizen. B.A.A., Ryerson Polytechnical Institute, 67. 25 years experience in many genres of cinematography and video tape; many award-winning film credits. Now specializing in dramatic films. Works in Toronto and is an active member of the Winnipeg film community; has worked in many locations across Canada and in the Far North; extensive international travel. Specializes in hand-held operation; extensive aerial experience and innovative lighting and camera rigs; owns 16mm and 35mm equipment. Has recently worked on commercials for Discount Car Rental, Mikita Tools, Pizza Pizza, General Motors, McDonalds and Fairweather; latest work, *Entry in a Diary*, is now in production.
Selected Filmography: *The Reckoning*, TV, 91, CDN, DOP; *Dance to Remember*, "Inside Stories", TV, 91, CDN, DOP; *Uncut Gem*, TV, 89, CDN, DOP; *Lonely Knights*, TV, 89, CDN, DOP; *Rescue Me*, TV, 89, CDN, DOP; *Now And Then*, "Family Pictures", TV, 89, CDN, DOP; *Canada - Another Government Movie* (Expo 88), Th, 88, CDN, DOP; "Space Experiment" (6 eps), TV, 87, CDN, DOP; *Papermaking*, "The Nature of Things", TV, 86, CDN, DOP; *Let's Dance*, TV, 83, CDN, DOP; "The World's Children" (4 eps), ED, 80, CDN, DOP; *Bush Pilot*, ED, 78, CDN, DOP; *The Country Is Alive*, "Man Alive", TV, 76, CDN, DOP; *Recess 10:15-10:30*, TV, 72, CDN, Prod.

STUNDEN, William J.
CSC. Film Quest Productions Inc., 98 Bowman Way, Thornhill, ON L3T 4Z8 (416)731-2659.
Type of Production and Credits: TV Film-DOP/Cam Op.
Genres: Drama-TV; Documentary-TV; Commercials-TV; Music Video-TV.
Biography: Born in 1950. B.A., major in film, University of Manitoba, Winnipeg. 17 years of professional film-making experience with CBC. Has worked up from stagehand, dolly grip, key grip, camera assistant to camera operator and 2nd unit DOP. Has worked on numerous dramas and documentaries such as "The Nature of Things", "Man Alive", arts & science specials, "Sidestreet", "For The Record" and various drama specials.
Selected Filmography: "Street Legal" (50 eps), TV, 88-90, CDN, 2nd Unit DOP/Cam Op; *Asylum*, TV, 88, CDN, Cam.

SWICA, Adam
ACFC. 40 River St., Toronto, ON M5A 3N9 (416)360-5250.
Type of Production and Credits: Th Short-DOP; TV Film-DOP; TV Video-DOP.
Genres: Drama-Th&TV; Musical-Th&TV; Experimental-Th&TV; Commercials-Th&TV; Music Video-TV.
Selected Filmography: *Over The Edge*, Th, 91, CDN, 2nd Unit DOP; *Prom Night IV*, Th, 91, CDN, B Cam Op; *Ofra Harnoy*, MV, 91, USA, DOP; *Toronto Arts Awards - Recipient Profiles*, In, 90-91, CDN, DOP; *Deadline*, Th, 90, CDN, DOP; *Kumar & Jones*, Th, 90, CDN, DOP; *General Motors Atlantic Canada*, Cm, 90, CDN, DOP; *Why*, Manteye, MV, 90, CDN, DOP; *No Tattoos*, Andy Curran, MV, 90, CDN, DOP; "The Hitchhiker", TV, 90, CDN/F, B Cam Op; *Answering Your Call*, Bell Canada, In, 90, CDN, DOP; *Cowboy Junkies*, ED, 90, USA, DOP; *Dupont Videos*, In, 90, CDN, DOP/Dir; *You Are My Sunshine*, Sunshine Dairies, Cm, 90, CDN, DOP; *4th Corner of the World*, TV, 90, CDN, DOP.

SZALAY, Attila
IATSE 669, CSC. 402, 1176 West 6th Ave., Vancouver, BC V6H 1A4 (604)736-7567. Hun Productions Ltd., 402, 1176 West 6th Ave., Vancouver, BC V6H 1A4.
Type of Production and Credits: Th Film-Cam; TV Film-2nd Unit DOP/Cam.
Genres: Drama-Th&TV; Action-Th&TV; Documentary-TV; Commercials-TV.
Biography: Born in 1961 in Budapest, Hungary. Canadian citizen. Languages: English and Hungarian. Graduate degree in Applied Art, Sheridan College. 10 years experience.
Selected Filmography: *Home Movie*, Th, 91, CDN, Cam; *Christmas on Division St.*, TV, 91, USA, Cam; *K2*, Th, 90, USA/GB, Cam; *Always Remember I Love You*, TV, 90, USA, Cam; "The Black Stallion" (5 eps), TV, 90, CDN/F, 2nd Unit DOP; *A Winter to Remember*, TV, 88, CDN, Cin.

TAMMARO, Christopher ◊
(416)485-6542.
Type of Production and Credits: TV Film-DOP.
Genres: Commercials-TV.
Biography: Born 1950, Toronto, Ontario.

TARKO, Mihai Gabor ◊
(416) 593-5969.
Type of Production and Credits: Th

Film-DOP; TV Film-DOP/Dir.
Genres: Drama-Th; Musical-TV; Documentary-TV; Commercials-TV.
Biography: Born 1952, Arad, Romania; Canadian citizenship. Languages: English, Italian, Hungarian, Romanian and French. Education: Faculty of Dramatic Arts, Cinematography and Television, I.L., Caragiale, Bucharest; Faculty of Physics, University of Bucharest. Cinematographer on over 400 comm-ercials in Canada and US. Winner of 2 Silver Medals, Houston.
Selected Filmography: *Roger Edwards/Roger Edwards Convertibles II*, Cm, 85-86, CDN, Dir/Cin; *Ford/Eaton's/Sea Queen*, Cm, 85-86, CDN, Cin; *Cruise*, Th, 80, R, DOP; *Winter Stars*, Th, 80, R, DOP; *The Pale Light of Sorrow*, Th, 79, CDN, DOP; *Death Arrives on Tape*, Th, 78, R, DOP.

TERRY, Christopher
- see DIRECTORS

TETRAULT, Cameron
Cam's Video Camera, 924 - 9 Ave. N., Saskatoon, SK S7K 2Z4 (306)242-8792.
Type of Production and Credits: Th Short-Cam; TV Video-DOP.
Genres: Documentary-TV; Educational-TV; Commercials-TV; Industrial-TV.
Biography: Born 1957, Middleton, Nova Scotia. Bachelor of Arts, Bachelor of Ed., University of Saskatchewan. Freelance videographer, 84 to date; owns 3CCD ENG video camera. Awards for scale-model work (con-struction, painting, etc); 6 Best of Show awards; several awards for Radio Control Aircraft Flying. Constructed travelling diorama for Monsanto Canada at proposed research station, and railroad shipping display for Monsanto Canada as well as privately commissioned model projects.
Selected Filmography: *U.F.O.s: Facing the Contradiction*, TV, 91, CDN, Asst Cam/Grip; *Snooze News*, Th, 91, CDN, Cam; *Absence of Love*, ED, 91, CDN, Ed; *Frontier Mike's Boomtown Country Christmas*, Th/TV, 90, CDN, Asst Cam/ Light; *S.T.O.P.*, Pokebusters, Cm, 90, CDN, Cam/VO; *Drinking and Driving* (for Hearing Impaired), TV, 90, CDN, Cam/Light/Grip; *Westside Medical Clinic*, Doc, 90, CDN, Cam/Grip; *Putt 'n' Bounce*, Cm, 90, CDN, Cam/Grip; Northern Telecom, In, 90, CDN, Cam/ Ed; Cdn Corps of Commissionaires, In, 90, CDN, Cam/Ed/VO; Paradise Manu-facturing, In, 90, CDN, Cam/Ed/VO; *My City*, Th, 89, CDN, Cam; *89 Canada Games*, Cm, 89, CDN, Cam; *AIDS: It's Your Choice*, TV, 88, CDN, Cam; *Sask Resources: Oil*, ED, 88, CDN, Grip.

THOMAS-d'HOSTE, Michel
4850, Côte des Neiges, #106, Montréal, PQ H3V 1G5 (514)735-3994.
Types de production et générique: l métrage-D phot; c métrage-D phot; TV film-D phot.
Types d'oeuvres: Documentaire-C; Experimental-C; Drame-C; Variété-C&TV.
Curriculum vitae: Né en 1927, Paris, France. Au service cinéma des Armées françaises, 47-48; photographe et caméraman de reportage, Société familiale Thomas-d'Hoste et Cie, 49-53; assistant caméraman, Oméga Productions, Montréal, 54-57; caméraman, TV, 57-62; ONF, 62-79; caméraman pigiste, séries film et vidéo pour TV depuis 80.
Filmographie sélective: *Palme d'Or*, TV, 85, CDN, Cam; *Et du fils*, C, 71, CDN, Cam; *L'Exil*, C, 70, CDN, Cam; *Labyrinth* (Expo 67), C, 67, CDN, Cam; *Le Grand Rock*, C, 67, CDN, Cam; "Au pays de la Neuve-France" (13 eps), TV, 58, CDN, Cam.

THOMSON, Brian
CSC, IATSE. 6 Prust Ave., Toronto, ON M4L 2M8 (416)461-5933.
Type of Production and Credits: TV Film-DOP/Dir; TV Video-DOP.
Genres: Commercials-TV; Music Video-TV.
Biography: Canadian citizen. DOP/Director for 10 years on many award-winning commercials and music videos. Won the CSC Award for Canada Tourism commercial; nominated for an Emmy for *Enigma of Bobby Bittman*; Genie nomination, Best Photography for *Looking for Miracles*; *The Meeting Place* was awarded Best in Show, Multi Media International Competition.
Selected Filmography: *The Meeting Place*, Th, 89, CDN, DOP; *Second City 15th Anniversary Show*, TV, 88, CDN/USA, DOP; *Lantern Hill*, TV, 88, CDN/USA, DOP; *Looking for Miracles*, Th/TV, 88, CDN/USA, DOP; *Enigma of Bobby Bittman*, TV, 87, CDN/USA, DOP.

TOUGAS, Kirk
1818 Grant St., Vancouver, BC V5L 2Y8 (604)253-0047.
Type of Production and Credits: Th Film-DOP; TV Film-DOP.
Genres: Drama-Th; Documentary-Th&TV; Educational-Th&TV; Experimental-Th.
Biography: Born 1949. His films and photographs have been exhibited at the Vancouver Art Gallery and the Grierson

Seminars, Canada; Cinémathèque Française, Musée d'Art Moderne, Centre George Pampidou and the Centre National de la Photographie in Paris. Has had his one-man show, *Issue des Récits*, exhibited in Paris, Nice and Avignon. As DOP, specializes in documentaries with cultural, social or political focus and in low-budget experimental features. Worked on *My American Cousin*, *Kootenai Brown* and *Map of the Human Heart* as stills photographer. Won Best Documentary Cinematographer for *A Rustling of Leaves*.
Selected Filmography: *Time Immemorial*, "As Long as the Rivers Flow", TV, 91, CDN, Cin; *The Learning World*, "As Long as the Rivers Flow", TV, 91, CDN, Cin; *Father and Son*, Th, 91, CDN, Cin; *R.D. Laing at Sixty*, Th, 88, CDN, Prod/Dir/Cin; *Says*, Th, 88, CDN, DOP; *A Rustling of Leaves*, Th, 87, CDN, Cin; *Winners and Losers*, TV, 85, CDN, Cin; *The Three Watchmen*, Th, 84, CDN, Cin; *Single Fathers*, ED, 84, CDN, Cin; *Low Visibility*, Th, 84, CDN, Co-Cin; *Bitter Medicine, Part II: Medicare in Crisis*, Th, 82, CDN, Co-Cin; *Buy Buy Vancouver*, TV, 81, CDN, Cin; *A Time to Rise*, Th, 80, CDN, Co-Cin; *Return to Departure*, Th, 79, CDN, Prod/Cin; *Letter from Vancouver*, Th, 73, CDN, Prod.

TROW, Susan
895 rue Cardinal, Ville St-Laurent, PQ (514)747-7316. NFB, P.O. Box 6100, Stn. A, Montreal, PQ H3C 3H5 (514) 283-9000. FAX: 283-5487.
Type of Production and Credits: Th Film-Cin; Th Short-Cin; TV Film-Cin.
Genres: Drama-Th&TV; Documentary-Th&TV; Educational-Th&TV.
Biography: Born 1948, Toronto, Ontario. B.A., Fine Art, University of Guelph; studied Photographic Arts, Ryerson Polytechnical Institute. Worked as photographer; several exhibits of work at NFB and Art Gallery of Ontario. Head of English Camera Department, NFB, June 87-May 90.
Selected Filmography: *The Greenpeace Years - "Bearing Witness" & "The Next Generation"*, TV, 90, CDN, Cin; *Towards Intimacy*, Th, 90, CDN, Cin; *Repatriation - Oka*, Th, 90, CDN, Cin; *Full Circle*, Th, 90, CDN, Cin; *L'Audition*, Th, 89, CDN, Cin; *The First Emperor*, Th, 88, CDN, Cin; *The Drive Away*, Th, 88, CDN, Cin; *Life of Riley*, Th, 88, CDN, Cin; *The King Chronicles*, TV, 87, CDN, Cam Op; *The Burning Times*, Th, 86, CDN, Assoc Dir/Cin; *Goddess Remembered*, Th, 86, CDN, Assoc Dir/Cin; *Crazy Moon*, Th, 85, CDN, Cam Op; *A Critical Choice*, Th, 85, CDN, Cin; *Donald Sutherland*, Th, 85, CDN, Cin; *Family Tree*, Th, 85, CDN, Cin.

TUSTIAN, Jim
- see PRODUCERS

VALLÉE, Jean-Marc
- voir REALISATEURS

VAMOS, Thomas ✧
(514)274-1564.
Types de production et générique: l métrage-D photo/Réal; c métrage-D photo/Réal; TV film-D photo.
Types d'oeuvres: Drame-C&TV; Action-C; Documentaire-C.
Curriculum vitae: Né en 1938, Hongrie; citoyenneté canadienne. Quatre ans d'études cinématographiques, Ecole Supérieure de Cinéma et Théâtre, Budapest. Travaille en Hongrie comme directeur-photo sur de nombreux courts et longs métrages, en particulier avec Istvan Szabo. Au Canada depuis 65; travaille à l'ONF comme directeur-photo et réalisateur, 65-81; pigiste depuis 81 (longs métrages et annonces).
Filmographie sélective: *Le Chaperon rouge, an 2000*, C, 88, CDN/H, D phot; *Les Portes Tournantes*, C, 87, CND/F, D phot; *Captive Hearts*, C, 87, USA, D phot; "Les Enfants de la rue", TV, 87, CDN, D phot; *The Gate*, C, 86, CDN, D phot; *Operation Ypsilon*, TV, 86, CDN/F, D phot; *The Peanut Butter Solution*, C, 85, CDN, D phot; *La Dame en couleurs*, C, 83, CDN, D phot; *La Plante*, C, 82, CDN, Réal; *Le Jongleur*, C, 81, CDN, Réal; *L'Enfant fragile*, C, 79, CDN, Réal; *Les Héritiers de la violence*, C, 77, CDN, Réal; *His Mother*, C, 76, CDN, D phot; *La Fleur aux dents*, C, 74, CDN, Réal; *O.K....Laliberté*, C, 72, CDN, D phot.

VAN DER LINDEN, Paul
IATSE 667. 264B Hastings Ave., Toronto, ON M4L 2M1 (416)778-1163.
Type of Production and Credits: Th Film-DOP; Th Short-DOP; TV Video-DOP.
Genres: Drama-Th&TV; Comedy-Th; Action-Th; Documentary-Th.
Biography: Born in 1941 in Amsterdam, The Netherlands; landed immigrant Canada, 66. Languages: English, French and Dutch. Attended Latin School, Amsterdam (Barlevs Gymnasium). Operator for Wesscam Camera systems (helicopter).
Selected Filmography: *Céline Dion* (2), MV, 90, CDN, DOP; *Brown Bread Sandwiches*, Th, 89, CDN, DOP; "The Campbells" (22 eps), TV, 87-88, CDN/

USA/GB, DOP; *The Blue Man*, Th, 85, CDN, DOP; *Deep Sea Conspiracy*, Th, 85, CDN, DOP; *Circokraft*, In, 85, CDN, DOP; *Rien qu'un jeu*, Th, 82, CDN, DOP; *The River to China*, Th, 81, CDN, DOP; *La Guerre du feu*, Th, 81, CDN/F, 2nd U DOP; "Littlest Hobo" (12 eps), TV, 80, CDN, DOP; *Kelly*, Th, 80, CDN, DOP; *Willie Heaps*, Th, 79, CDN, DOP; *Winston Churchill*, Th, 79, CDN, DOP; *Kings and Desperate Men*, Th, 79, CDN, DOP; *The Last Chase*, Th, 79, CDN/USA, DOP.

VANHERWEGHEM, Robert
STCQ. 2518, Route 202, Franklin Centre, PQ J0S 1E0 (514)827-2483.
Types de production et générique: l métrage-D photo; c métrage-D photo; TV film-D photo.
Types d'oeuvres: Drame-C; Comédie-C; Action-C; Documentaire-C.
Curriculum vitae: Né en 1948, Belgique. Ecole Technique de Photographie, Diplôme A2, 64-67; Etudes Techniques supérieures de cinéma, Diplôme A1; 3 ans d'étude à temps plein en direction photo cinéma, 67-71. A donné des cours à l'Université de Montréal, 83-85. Gagne le Prix Alberta/Québec pour *Mémoire d'une guerre oubliée*, 88.
Filmographie sélective: *Montreal Off*, C/TV, 91, CDN, D Phot; "L'écran" (13 eps), TV, 91, CDN, D Phot; *Le fabuleux voyage de l'ange*, C, 90, CDN, D Phot; *Spasme de vie*, C/TV, 90, CDN, D Phot; *L'amour volé*, C, 90, CDN, D Phot; *Mémoire d'une guerre oubliée*, C, 87, CDN, D phot; *Le Dernier Havre*, C, 85, CDN, D phot/Co réal; *La Fuite*, C, 83, CDN, D phot; *L'Objet*, C, 83, CDN, D phot; *La Turlute des années dures*, C, 81, CDN, D phot; *Ça peut pas être l'hiver; on a même pas eu d'été*, C, 79, CDN, D phot; *L'Amiante ça tue*, C, 79, CDN, D phot; *La Belle Apparence*, C, 78, CDN, D phot/Co réal; *La Cure*, C, 76, CDN, Co réal/Co sc; *Deux Contes de la rue Berri*, C, 75, CDN, D phot.

VOLKMER, Werner
- voir SCENARISTES

WALKER, John
- see DIRECTORS

WALTON, Lloyd A.
- see PRODUCERS

WANNAMAKER, Tony
NABET, CSC. 66 Emily St., Belleville, ON K8N 2R2 (613)968-8744. (416)447-4066.
Type of Production and Credits: Th Film-DOP; Th Short-DOP; TV Film-DOP; TV Video-DOP.
Genres: Drama-Th&TV; Documentary-Th&TV; Industrial-TV; Music Video-Th&TV.
Biography: Born in 1958; Canadian citizenship. Graduated with High Honours, Radio and TV Broadcasting, Seneca College, 81; undergraduate, Film, York University, 90; International Film and Television Workshops, Rockport, Maine: camera 35mm courses 85, 87; Steadicam course, 86; DOP Lighting Workshop, 89. Steadicam operator; advanced open water diver specializing in night diving and underwater photography; student pilot. Shared CSC nomination for Best Cinematography in music video, 89; CSC Provincial Government Information Officer Forum Gold Award, 90; nomination for Best Cinematography in a Unique Production, CSC, 91.
Selected Filmography: "Much Music Big Ticket Simulcast" (sev eps), TV, 84-91, CDN, Cam Op; *Mondo Moscow*, TV, 90, CDN/I, DOP; *Eyes Like Fire*, Leroy Sibbles, MV, 90, CDN, DOP; *Nicaraguan Wheelchair Repair Workshop*, ED, 89, CDN/NC, DOP; *At the Scene*, In, 89, CDN, DOP; U4EA, MV, 89, CDN, DOP; *Theresa*, In, 88, CDN, DOP; *Triumph*, MV, 88, CDN, St'cam; Downchild Blues Band, MV, 88, CDN, Op; *No-Contest, The Cathy Evelyn Smith Story*, TV, 86, CDN, Op; "CityPulse News" (sev eps), TV, 81-84, CDN, Op.

WEBB, Dan ✧
(818)843-4361.
Type of Production and Credits: TV Film-DOP; TV Video-DOP; Th Short-DOP.
Genres: Comedy-TV; Variety-TV; Musical-TV; Documentary-Th&TV; Commercials-TV; Music Video-TV.
Biography: Born 1952, North Grimsby, Ontario; US resident alien. Languages: English and Spanish. Has photographed numerous music videos, concerts and road tours for artists such as Donna Summer, Kiss, Oingo Boingo, Duran Duran, Rush, The Rolling Stones, Frank Zappa, Led Zeppelin, Leon Russell, Lionel Richie, Heart, Dweezil Zappa, Randy Newman, ZZ Top, The Who; has also photographed a variety of material for TV, documentaries as well as sitcoms, soap operas and specials; owner and operator of complete Sony Betacam package; experience with ENG and EFP; also does underwater and aerial cinematography. Winner of 2 Emmys and several other awards.
Selected Filmography: "20/20" (sev seg), TV, USA, Cam; "60 Minutes" (sev seg),

TV, USA, Cam; "Barney Miller" (6 eps), TV, 85, USA, Cam; "Laughing Matters", TV, 85, CDN, Cam; "Shelley Duvall's Faerie Tale Theater" (6 eps), TV, 83, USA, Cam; *Working*, TV, 81, USA, Cam; *La Gioconda*, TV, 80, USA, DOP.

WEGODA, Ron
CSC, IATSE. Apex Films Ltd., 1260 Dr. Penfield Ave., #1102, Montreal, PQ H3G 1B6 (514)845-6731.
Type of Production and Credits: TV Film-Cam; TV Video-Cam.
Genres: Drama-Th&TV; Action-Th&TV; Documentary-Th&TV; News-TV.
Biography: Born 1929, England; Canadian citizenship. Wide experience working for all major TV networks as cameraman; currently on staff at CFCF-TV, Channel 12, Montreal.
Selected Filmography: *The Only Way to Fly*, TV, 87, CDN, Cam; *3 Blue Panthers*, Th, 67, D/I, 2nd U Op; *Wait Until Dark*, Th, 66, USA, 2nd U Op; "Radisson"/"Tomahawk" (20 eps), TV, 56-58, CDN, Op; "La vie qui bat" (9 eps), TV, 56, CDN, Op.

WILLIAMS, Roger
IATSE 669. 4431 Cove Cliff Rd., North Vancouver, BC V7G 1H7 (604)929-9625. Ramblin Productions Ltd., 101 - 1626 West 2nd Ave., Vancouver, BC V6J 1H4 (604)732-4524.
Type of Production and Credits: TV Video-Prod/Dir/DOP.
Genres: Documentary-TV; Industrial-TV; Current Affairs-TV; Sports-TV.
Biography: Born in 1960 in Edmonton, Alberta. Canadian citizen. Education: Business Administration; TV Production. West coast prod. bureau for The Sports Network, 1991. Camera operator for CBC, CTV, MuchMusic & the Disney Channel. Professional Ski Patrol. (Skiing cameraman).
Selected Filmography: "9 O'Clock Pacific" (3 eps), TV, 91, CDN, Prod/Dir; *Balance Master*, Cm, 91, CDN, Prod/Dir; *Canadian Football League Players' Association*, ED, 91, CDN, Prod; "Much Music Big Ticket Specials" (5), TV, 90-91, CDN, Cam; *For the Love of the Game*, The Sports Network, (2), TV, 90-91, CDN, DOP/Cam; *C.D. Howe: Minister of Everything*, TV, 90, CDN, DOP/Cam; "Passport to Skiing", TSN (4 eps), TV, 89-90, USA/CDN, DOP/Cam; "B.C. At Work" (13 eps), TV, 89-90, CDN, DOP/Cam.

WILTSHIRE, Peter Wayne
Magic Images Film & Video, 239 Helena Ave., Winona, ON L0R 2L0 (416)643-3475.
Type of Production and Credits: TV Video-Cam.
Genres: Commercials-TV; Industrial-TV; Sports-TV; Corporate-TV.
Biography: Born in 1967 in Hamilton, Ontario. Studied broadcasting at Niagara College with a major in film. Student film *From Here to Micronesia* won second place at the 1990 CBC Telefest awards in the Film Short (now Documentary) category. After graduating, completed the course for camera assistants of the Canadian Society of Cinematographers. Affiliate member, #715, CSC. For "Raceline," the crew won Best Broadcast Coverage of 1990 Molson Export 400 by the Eastern Motorsport Press Association.
Selected Filmography: "Raceline" (13 eps), TV, 90, CDN, Cam; "Ontario Fisherman" (13 eps), TV, 90, CDN, Cam; *Parkinsons*, ED, 90, CDN, Cam Assist; *Emergency Services*, Cm, 90, CDN, Cam Assist.

WINCENTY, Richard
CAMERA 81. 158 Jones Ave., Toronto, ON M4M 3A3 (416)462-0175. Suzanne Depoe, Creative Technique Inc., P.O. Box 311, Stn. F, Toronto, ON M4Y 2L7 (416)466-4173.
Type of Production and Credits: Th Film-Cam; TV Film-DOP; TV Video-DOP.
Genres: Drama-Th&TV; Documentary-TV; Industrial-TV.
Biography: Born 1949, London, England; Canadian citizenship. Is also wrangler for exotic animals and does special effects cinematography.
Selected Filmography: "Hidden Room" (13 eps), TV, 91, USA, DOP; *Prom Night IV*, TV, 91, CDN, DOP; "The Hitchhiker" (9 eps), TV, 90, CDN/F, DOP; "Friday the 13th: The Series" (3 eps), TV, 87-88, CDN/USA, DOP; "Friday the 13th: The Series" (26 eps), TV, 87-88, CDN/USA, 2nd U DOP/SFX.

WOESTE, Peter F
IATSE 669, CSC. 1862 Mathers Ct., West Vancouver, BC V7V 2L2 (604)925-3529.
Type of Production and Credits: Th Film-Op; Th Short-DOP; TV Film-Op/DOP.
Genres: Drama-Th&TV; Comedy-Th&TV; Action-Th&TV; Documentary-TV.
Biography: Born in 1950 in Unna, Germany. Fluent in English and German. Canadian and German citizen. Education:

Television, Radio and Screen Arts, S.A.I.T., Calgary, 1983. IATSE 659 Assistants Course, Hollywood, 1980. Awards: Roy Tash News, 1977; AMPA, Cinematography, 1977; Emmy and ASC awards, Cinematography for *Christmas Snow*, as Operator with Phil Lathrop, ASC.
Selected Filmography: *Not Quite Human*, TV, 91, USA, Op; *Leaving Normal*, Th, 91, USA, Op; *Bingo*, Th, 90, USA, Op; *It*, TV, 90, USA, Op; *Passing Through Veils*, TV, 90, USA, Op; *Burning Bridges*, TV, 90, USA, Op; *Dead Reckoning*, TV, 89, USA, Op; *Cadende*, Th, 89, USA, Op; *We're No Angels*, Th, 89, USA, Op/DOP/2nd Unit; "The Kids are Alright" (pilot), TV, 89, Op; *Immediate Family*, Th, 89, USA, Op/2nd Unit DOP; "MacGyver" (3 eps), TV, 88, USA, DOP/2nd Unit; *Cousins*, Th, 88, USA, Op; *Distant Thunder*, Th, 87, USA, Op.

WOLSZTEJN, Jean-Victor
- see PRODUCERS

WUNSTORF, Peter
IATSE 669. 12124 - 93 St., Edmonton, AB T5G 1E8 (403)474-3802. (604)731-3372.
Type of Production and Credits: Th Film-DOP; TV Film-DOP.
Genres: Drama-Th&TV; Documentary-Th&TV; Commercials-Th&TV; Music Video-TV.
Biography: Born in 1959 in Edmonton, Alberta. Languages: English and some French and German. AMPIA award, Best Cinematography for *Bordertown Cafe*. Certified scuba diver.
Selected Filmography: *Solitaire*, Th/TV, 91, CDN, DOP/Op; *7 Bullets*, Th, 90, CDN, DOP/Op; "MacGyver", TV, 90, USA, "B" Op; *The Grocer's Wife*, Th, 89, CDN, DOP; *City of Champions*, Th, 89, CDN, DOP; *Bordertown Cafe*, "Family Pictures", TV, 88, CDN, DOP/Op, (AMPIA); *U of Agers*, TV, 88, CDN, DOP/Op; *Just My Luck*, TV, 87, CDN, DOP/Op; *The Edmonton Fringe*, TV, 87, CDN, DOP/Op; 7 music videos, MV, 86/87, CDN, DOP/Op.

YOUNG, James B.
NABET. 251A Smithfield Ave., Winnipeg, MB R2V 0C6 (204)338-3924. Polo Park, Winnipeg, MB R3G 0L7 (204)775-0371.
Type of Production and Credits: TV Video-DOP.
Genres: Documentary-TV; Drama-TV; Musical-TV; Commercials-TV.
Biography: Born in 1962 in Winnipeg, Manitoba. Canadian citizen. English. 3 year television course, Winnipeg Technical School. Certified scuba diver (underwater photography).
Selected Filmography: *Cayman Christmas*, TV, 91, CY, Dir/DOP; *Pirates Week*, TV, 90, CY, Dir/DOP; *Gathering of Geese*, TV, 89, CDN, DOP; *Festival du voyageur*, TV, 89, CDN, DOP; *Special Request*, TV, 89, CDN, DOP; Motley Crue, MV, 87, CDN/J, Op.

YOUNG, Perci
IATSE, ACFC. 45 Don Valley Drive, Toronto, ON M4K 2J1 (416)467-5654.
Type of Production and Credits: Th-DOP; TV Film-DOP.
Genres: Drama-Th; Documentary-TV; Commercials-TV; Music Video-Th.
Biography: Born in 1946 in Cape Town. Canadian citizen.
Selected Filmography: *The Plant Shop*, Th, 79, ZA, DOP; *Black Mirror*, Th, 81, CDN/F, DOP; *Flying*, Th, 85, CDN, DOP; *Sunbeam*, Cm, 86, CDN, Cam, (CLIO).

Composers
Compositeurs

AIREY, Paul
4018 W. 37th Ave., Vancouver, BC V6N 2W7 (604)266-7266. Avenue Music Productions, 202 - 1334 W. 6th Ave., Vancouver, BC V6H 1A7 (604)737-0112. FAX: 737-0196.
Type of Production and Credits: Th Film-Comp; Th Short-Comp; TV Film-Comp; TV Video-Comp.
Genres: Drama-TV; Documentary-TV; Educational-TV; Commercials-TV; Industrial-TV; News-TV.
Biography: Born 1957, Vancouver, BC. B.A., University of British Columbia; A.R.C.T., University of Toronto. Studied composition under Stephen Chatman at UBC; has composed for radio and television commercials, numerous themes resulting in album releases, *The Mystery of SS433* and *Horizons* from the H.R. MacMillan Planetarium. Awards won include: National Gold ITVA Canada, 3 First Place Awards, A.P.T.A. Adwheel Awards and Golden Reel Award, ITVA North America.
Selected Filmography: *Guarding*, Workers' Compensation Board, In, 91, CDN, Comp; *Don't Take the Keys* BC Transit, Cm, 91, CDN, Comp; *Ray of Hope*, TV, 91, CDN, Comp; *Ethiopia/Seeds of Hope*, ED, 91, CDN, Comp; *Voices on the Wire*, BC Telephone (4 seg), ED, 91, CDN, Comp; "Driver's Seat" (26 eps), TV, 90, CDN, Comp; *News Hour Theme*, BCTV News Hour, TV, 90, CDN, Comp; *BC - Handle with Care*, World Energy Conference, In, 90, CDN, Comp; *Enemy*, "Best of the Best", Th, 89, CDN, Comp; *Gradpass*, BC

Transit, ED, 89, CDN, Comp; *Forests Are Our Future,* Fletcher Challenge, In, 89, CDN, Comp; *Asian Pacific Initiative,* Tourism BC, In, 89, CDN, Comp; *People Helping People,* Employment/Immigration Canada, In, 89, CDN, Comp; *C.P.R.,* BC Tel, In, 88, CDN, Comp; *Nimmo Bay,* Visa, Cm, 88, CDN, Comp.

ALEXANDRA, Christopher P.
470 Westmount Ave., Toronto, ON M6E 3N5 (416)654-7314.
Type of Production and Credits: Th Film-Comp; Th Short-Comp; TV Film-Comp.
Genres: Drama-Th&TV; Action-Th&TV; Science Fiction-Th&TV; Animation-Th&TV.
Biography: Born 1951, Los Angeles, California; landed immigrant Canada. B.A., Goddard College, Vermont; M.F.A., Mills College, California. Has recorded own compositions, composed for radio and participated in multimedia performances internationally. Teacher at Ryerson Polytechnical Institute, summer 88.
Selected Filmography: *A Brighter Moon,* Th, 86, CDN, Comp.

APPLEBAUM, Louis
OC, OO, AFM, SOCAN, GCF, ACCT. Affiliated Arts Co. Ltd., 1210 Don Mills Rd., #214, Don Mills, ON M3B 3N9 (416)444-0034.
Type of Production and Credits: Th Film-Comp; Th Short-Comp; TV Film-Comp; TV Video-Comp.
Genres: Drama-Th&TV; Comedy-Th&TV; Action-Th&TV; Documentary-Th&TV.
Biography: Born 1918, Toronto, Ontario. Attended University of Toronto; New York University. Music direction, NFB, 41-46; composed more than 200 scores, 41-53; worked in New York for all radio and TV networks and United Nations Radio, 46-50; feature and avant-garde films, Hollywood, 45-46; back to Canada, 50; first music director, Stratford Festival, 53; composed and conducted on 10 Harry Rasky documentaries, 72-87. Has composed scores for theatre in Canada, US, England; conductor, music director as well as composer. Executive Director, Ontario Arts Council, 71-79; Chairman, Federal Cultural Policy Review Committee, 79-82; President, SOCAN, 89 to present. Won the Canadian Music Council Award for *The Masseys*; Oscar nomination, 46, for *The Story of G.I. Joe*; Wilderness Award, *Folly on the Hill.* Became Officer of the Order of Canada, 76; LL.D., York University, 79; Hon. A.R.C.T., 82; Hon. Fellow, OISE, 88; Order of Ontario, 90; Arts Person of the Year, 91.
Selected Filmography: *Glory Enough for All,* TV, 87, CDN/GB, Comp; *The Masseys* (2 parts), TV, 78, CDN, Co-Comp/Cond; *Journey without Arrival,* TV, 76, CDN, Comp/Cond, (ANIK); *Homage to Chagall,* Th, 75, CDN, Comp/Cond; "The National Dream" (8 eps), TV, 74, CDN, Comp/Cond; *Folly on the Hill,* TV, 73, CDN, Comp/Cond; *Athabasca,* TV, 68, CDN, Comp, (CFA); "Seaway" (26 eps), TV, 65, CDN, Comp; "Graphic" (54 eps), TV, 56-58, CDN, Comp; *Whistle at Eton Falls,* Th, 51, USA, Comp/Cond; *Teresa,* Th, 51, USA, Comp/Cond; *Dreams That Money Can Buy,* Th, 48, USA, Comp/Cond; *Lost Boundaries,* Th, 48, USA, Comp/Cond; *The Story of G.I. Joe,* Th, 45, USA, Comp/Cond; *Tomorrow the World,* Th, 44, USA, Comp/Cond.

ARCAND, Michel
- voir MONTEURS

BAKER, Michael Conway
CLC, GCFC, ACCT. 2440 Treetop Lane, North Vancouver, BC V7H 2K5 (604)929-8732. FAX: 929-0164.
Type of Production and Credits: Th Film-Comp; Th Short-Comp; TV Film-Comp; TV Video-Comp.
Genres: Drama-Th&TV; Action-Th&TV; Documentary-Th&TV; Educational-Th&TV.
Biography: Born 1937, West Palm Beach, Florida; Canadian citizenship, 70. B.Mus., University of British Columbia, 65; Associate, London College of Music (A.L.C.M.); M.A., University of Western Washington, 71. Currently teaches film scoring at UBC. Nominated for awards nine times for film music; received 5 awards: 3 Genies, 1 ACTRA,(Ben McPeek Award), Golden Sheaf. Has written more than 95 concert works.
Selected Filmography: *Kootenai Brown,* Th, 91, CDN, Comp; *A Chance for Change,* ED, 91, CDN, Comp; *Sea of Slaughter,* TV, 90, CDN, Comp; *Anything to Survive,* TV, 90, USA/CDN, Comp; *A Gift of Sight,* Cm, 90, CDN, Comp; *What's Wrong with Neil,* "Family Pictures", TV, 89, CDN, Comp; *The Last Season,* TV, 87, CDN, Comp; *John & The Missus,* Th, 86-87, CDN, Comp, (GENIE); *Loyalties,* Th, 86-87, CDN, Comp; "A Planet for the Taking" (6 eps), TV, 86, CDN, Comp, (ACTRA); *The Emerging North,* In, 86, CDN, Comp; *One Magic Christmas,* Th, 85, USA/CDN, Comp; *Deserters,* Th, 84, CDN, Comp; *The Grey*

Fox, Th, 83, CDN, Comp, (GENIE); *Nails*, In, 80, CDN, Comp, (GENIE).
BARNES, Milton
GCFC. Ari-Mic-Dan Music, 192A Lowther Ave., Toronto, ON M5R 1E8 (416)961-9925.
Type of Production and Credits: Th Film-Comp; TV Film-Comp; TV Video-Comp.
Genres: Drama-Th&TV; Documentary-Th&TV; Children's-Th&TV; Animation-Th&TV.
Biography: Born 1931, Toronto, Ontario. Languages: English, French and German. Studied at Royal Conservatory of Music; Vienna Academy of Music, Austria; Berkshire Music Centre, Tanglewood, USA; Chigiana Music School, Italy. Full-time composer, orchestrator, conductor for concert hall, theatre, dance and film.
Selected Filmography: *A Mystery, a Mouse and Me*, TV, 87, USA, Orch/Cond; *The Care Bears Adventure in Wonderland*, Th, 87, CDN, Orch/Cond; *The Care Bears Movie II*, Th, 86, CDN, Orch/Arr/Cond; "The Edison Twins" (sev eps), TV, 84-86, CDN, Orch/Cond; *The Care Bears Movie*, Th, 85, CDN, Orch/Arr/Cond; *The Great Heep*, TV, 85, CDN, Orch; "Sharon, Lois and Bram's Elephant Show", TV, 85, CDN, Orch/Arr; *Ready for Slaughter*, "For the Record", TV, 83, CDN, Comp/Cond; *Strawberry Ice*, TV, 82, CDN, Orch; *Spirit of the Hunt*, TV, 82, CDN, Comp/Cond; "Portraits of Power" (sev eps), TV, 79-80, CDN, Cond; *Blood & Guts*, Th, 77, CDN/USA, Comp/Cond; *The Betrayal*, TV, 76, CDN, Comp/Cond.
BARRA, Gemma
- voir SCENARISTES
BEKKER, Hennie
TMA 149. 94 Abbeywood Trail, Don Mills, ON M3B 3B5 (416)391-0215. Bekker Kavanagh Productions/Hennie Bekker Music, 94 Abbeywood Trail, Don Mills, ON M3B 3B5 (416)391-0215. FAX: 391-2646.
Type of Production and Credits: Th Film-Comp; TV Film-Comp; Th Short-Comp; TV Video-Comp.
Genres: Drama-TV; Action-TV; Commercials-TV; Industrial-Th&TV.
Biography: Born 1934, Zambia. Educated in Zimbabwe. Arranged and conducted London Symphony Orchestra for Stanley Black album; produced and arranged albums for Freddie Cole, Magna Carta, etc.; composed and arranged music for many TV series and industrials; composed and produced music for over 1,000 TV and radio commercials internationally; uses Synclavier digital recording and sampling systems.
Selected Filmography: Canon, Cm, 91, CDN, Comp/Arr; Toshiba, Cm, 90, CDN, Comp/Arr; Burger King, Cm, 90, CDN, Comp/Arr; Stelco Steel, Cm, 90, CDN, Comp/Arr; Mutual Group, Cm, 90, CDN, Comp/Arr; Fit for Life, TV, 90, CDN, Comp/Arr; Loon on Echo Lake, TV, 90, CDN, Comp/Arr; Recycling, Cm, 89, CDN, Comp/Arr; *Northern Telecom*, In, 88, CDN, Comp/Arr/Mus Prod; "Mannheim Saga" (15 eps), TV, 87, ZA, Comp/Arr/Mus Prod; Colgate, Cm, 87, ZA, Comp/Arr/Mus Prod; "Children's Island", TV, 86, IL/D, Comp/Arr/Mus Prod; *Tigers Don't Cry*, Th, 80, GB, Comp/Arr/Mus Prod; *Beautiful People*, Th, 75, ZA, Comp/Arr/Mus Prod.
BELL, Allan Gordon
AFM, GCFC. Synergy Music Productions Ltd., 222 Ranchlands Court N.W., Calgary, AB T3E 1N9 (403)239-8068.
Type of Production and Credits: Th Short-Comp; TV Film-Comp; TV Video-Comp.
Genres: Drama-TV; Action-Th&TV; Documentary-Th&TV; Educational-Th&TV.
Biography: Born 1953, Calgary, Alberta. B.A., M.Music (composition), University of Alberta; film music synchronization with Earl Hagen. Commissions: Canada Council, CBC, Alberta Culture. Created works for soloists, chamber ensembles, orchestra, electronic media; arranger for numerous recording projects and commercials.
Selected Filmography: *Gaea*, Th, 90, CDN, Comp; *Junior High Ethics*, TV, 89, CDN, Comp; *Walk Before You Run*, TV, 89, CDN, Comp; *Technology*, "Breaking the Unseen Barrier", TV, 89, CDN, Comp; *Oral Language/Social Skills/Self-Esteem*, "Breaking the Unseen Barrier", TV, 88, CDN, Comp; *Programme Planning/Reading/Mathematics*, "Breaking the Unseen Barrier", TV, 87, CDN, Comp; *Flip A Switch*, Th, 87, CDN, Comp; "Connecting" (13 eps), TV, 85, CDN, Comp; *Loram '85*, In, 85, CDN, Comp; Leon's, Cm, 85, CDN, Comp; *Alberta Agriculture*, In, 84, CDN, Comp; *Catherine Burgess: Sculptor in Steel*, Th, 83, CDN, Comp; *Freedom of Choice*, Th, 83, CDN, Comp; *A Film About Justice*, ED, 82, CDN, Comp; "Stony Plain" (13 eps), TV, 81, CDN, Comp.
BENOIT, Jean-Marie
ACTRA, UDA, GDM. 216 Côte Ste-

Catherine, Outremont, PQ H2V 2A8 (514)271-7565. (514)937-9571.
Types de production et générique: long métrage-Comp; TV Film-Comp; TV Video-Comp.
Types d'oeuvres: Drame-C&TV; Comédie-C&TV; Action-C&TV; Annonces-C&TV.
Curriculum vitae: Né au Guigues en 1954. Citoyenneté canadienne. Université McGill. Collaboré aux disques et aux spectacles de nos plus grands artistes tels que: Félix Leclerc, Gilles Vigneault, Ginette Reno, Robert Charlebois, Diane Dufresne, Michel Rivard. Pour une deuxième année d'affilée, l'Académie Canadienne du Cinéma et de la Télévision l'honorait dans la catégorie "Meilleure musique originale" pour la mini-série dramatique "La Fin des Jeux" et le téléfilm "Un autre homme".
Filmographie sélective: *Ding et Dong le Film*, C, 90, CDN, Comp; *Un Autre Homme*, C, 89-90, CDN, Comp,; *Jésus de Montréal*, C, 89, CDN, Comp; "La Fin Des Jeux" (3 d'ep.), TV, 88, CDN, Comp; *Le Temps d'Une Paix*, TV, 87-91, CDN, Comp; *Entre le Ciel et l'Eau*, TV, 86, CDN, Comp.

BHATIA, Amin
AFM, BMI, SCL(LA). 3955 Graveley St., Burnaby, BC V5C 3T4 (604)291-0978. FAX: 291-6909. Shopan Entesari, 4760 Brewster Dr., Tarzana, CA 91356 USA (818)344-0400.
Type of Production and Credits: Th Film-Comp; TV Film-Comp; TV Video-Comp TV Comm-Comp.
Genres: Drama-Th; Science Fiction-TV; Horror-Th; Commercials-TV; Comedy-Th&TV.
Biography: Born 1961. Twice won the Roland International Synthesizer Tape Competition; 6 Clio Awards for work in commercials; 5 Ampia awards for music composition in film and television. Consultant to Roland Synthesizers, Canada, US, Europe and Japan. Before film music, was involved in broadcasting and has extensive experience in sound design from radio to theatre to planetarium presentations. Works out of Vancouver, Calgary, Toronto and Los Angeles. Music clients include: CBC Radio and Television, Calgary 1988 Olympic Games, Steve Porcaro (Toto), David Foster, Tommy Banks, Gus Dudgeon (producer for Elton John), Vancouver Planetarium. Solo album on Capitol Records, "Interstellar Suite."
Selected Filmography: *Café Romeo*, Th, 91, CDN/USA, Comp; "Ray Bradbury Theatre" (2 eps), TV, 90, CDN/USA, Comp, (AMPIA); *Primo Baby*, Th, 90, CDN, Comp; *Iron Eagle II*, Th, 88, CDN/IL, Comp; *Storm*, Th, 87, CDN/USA, Comp, (AMPIA); *Satan's Room*, Th, 83, CDN, Comp; "Vanishing Point", TV, 87-92, CDN, Comp; Calgary Cannons, Cm, 91, CDN, Mus Prod; A.G.T., Cm, 90, CDN, Mus Prod; Leon's Furniture, Cm, 89, CDN, Mus Prod; Calgary Herald, Cm, 88, CDN, Mus Prod; *Wismag*, ED, 90, CDN, Comp; *Ice Time*, ED, 90, CDN, Comp; *Calgary Stampede*, In, 90, CDN, Comp; *3 Minutes to Live*, ED, 86, CDN, Comp.

BLUE, Julie ◇
(604)876-3254.
Type of Production and Credits: Th Short-Comp; TV Film-Comp.
Genres: Musical-Th; Documentary-TV; Children's-Th; Commercials-TV; Industrial-Th.
Biography: Born 1961, Calgary, Alberta. Languages: English, Spanish and some Japanese. Studied Composition and Arranging, Capilano College of Music; extensive private study in jazz and classical music. Has been involved in theatrical as well as television productions. Nominated for Best Musical Score, AMPIA, 86.
Selected Filmography: *Closing the Gap*, ED, 87, CDN, Comp; *Close to the Heart*, TV, 86, CDN, Comp.

BRADSTREET, David
ACTRA, AFM. Bradstreet Music, 6 Oaklands Ave., Toronto, ON M4V 2E5 (416)926-7530. FAX: 963-5156.
Type of Production and Credits: Th Short-Comp; TV Film-Comp; TV Video-Comp.
Genres: Documentary-TV; Commercials-TV; Industrial-Th&TV.
Biography: Born 1947, London, England; Canadian citizenship. Songwriter and vocalist, creator of Bradstreet Music; has produced several albums of his own work and that of other artists, including Jane Siberry and Bill Hughes; has written music for numerous commercials for TV and radio as well as film scores. Has won awards including Juno for Best New Male Vocalist, 77.
Selected Filmography: *Doll House*, Black Flag, Cm, 91, CDN, Comp/Mus Prod; "For the Love of the Game", TV, 91, CDN, Comp/Mus Prod; Young Drivers of Canada/USA, Cm, 90, CDN, Comp/Mus Prod; *Great Waters of France*, Perrier, Cm, 90, CDN, Comp/Mus Prod; Drink Sells the Dream, In, 90, USA, Comp/Mus

Prod; "N.E.W.S." ("Not Exactly What It Seems"), TV, 90, CDN, Comp/Mus Prod; Globe & Mail, Cm, 89, CDN, Comp/Mus Prod; Revenge of the Radio-Active Reporter, Th, 1989, CDN/USA, Comp/Mus Prod; M.I.L.E., ED, CDN, Comp; Honda Prelude, In, 83, CDN, Comp.

BRONSKILL, Richard
ACTRA, AFM, ACCT, BMI. 828 N. Sweetzer Ave., Los Angeles, CA 90069 USA (213)653-3986. FAX: 653-3986.
Type of Production and Credits: Th Film-Comp; Th Short-Comp; TV Film-Comp; TV Video-Comp.
Genres: Drama-Th&TV; Comedy-Th&TV; Action-Th&TV; Science Fiction-Th&TV.
Biography: Born 1951, Ottawa, Ontario. B.Mus., University of Toronto, 73; M.Mus, 77. Secretary-Treasurer, Guild of Canadian Film Composers, 84-86; composer, record producer, conductor, orchestrator, arranger, editor. *Over the Edge* won Best Music Score, Torelli Film Festival, Spain; awarded Emmy for "contributions to the Emmy-winning achievement for Best Music Score for mini-series or special" for *The Shell Seekers*.
Selected Filmography: *The Village of the Darned*, Th, 91, USA, Comp; *Beastmaster 2*, Th, 91, USA, Orch/Arr; *The Perfect Bride*, Th, 90, USA, Comp; *Lucky* (mini-series), TV, 90, USA, Orch/Arr; *The Josephine Baker Story* (mini-series), TV, 90, USA, Orch/Arr; *Over the Edge*, Th, 89, USA, Comp; *All Dogs Go to Heaven*, Th, 89, USA, Orch/Arr; *Around the World in Eighty Days* (mini-series), TV, 89, USA, Orch/Arr; "The Shell Seekers", TV, 89, USA, Orch/Arr; *9B*, TV, 86, CDN, Comp; *And Miles to Go*, TV, 85, CDN, Comp; "Some Honourable Gentlemen" (5 eps), TV, 82-85, CDN, Comp; *Once*, TV, 80, CDN, Comp.

BURKE, Dennis ✧
(604)734-8001.
Type of Production and Credits: Th Film-Comp/Snd Rec/Snd Mix.
Genres: Documentary-Th&TV; Educational-Th&TV; Experimental-Th.
Biography: Born 1954, Edmonton, Alberta. Professional musician; composer for concert stage and dance as well as film; composes integrated soundtracks, including SFX and ambience.
Selected Filmography: *Determinations*, Th, 87, CDN, Comp/Snd Des/Snd Rec; *Centre for the Arts*, ED, 87, CDN, Comp/Snd Rec; *Lenz*, Th, 85, CDN, Comp; *Reconnasonce*, Th, 84, CDN, Comp; *George Norris in Depth*, TV, 83, CDN, Comp.

COHEN, Leonard
OC. Kelley Lynch, Stranger Music, 419 North Larchmont Blvd., Los Angeles, CA 90004 USA (213) 935-9939.
Type of Production and Credits: Th Film-Comp; TV Video-Comp.
Genres: Musical-Th&TV; Documentary-Th.
Biography: Born 1934, Montreal, Quebec. Languages: English and French. B.A., McGill University. Composer, lyricist, novelist, poet.
Selected Filmography: *First We Take Manhattan*, MV, 89, USA, Comp; *Dance Me to the End of Love*, MV, 84, USA, Comp; *I Am A Hotel*, TV, 84, CDN, Comp; *Night Magic*, Th, 84, CDN/F, Lyrics, (GENIE 86); *Bird on the Wire*, Th, 78, GB, Comp.

COLLIER, Ron
CLC, GCFC. 28 Confederation Way, Thornhill, ON L3T 5R5 (416)731-7276. Humber College - Music Dept., Humber College Blvd., Rexdale, ON (416)657-3111.
Type of Production and Credits: Th Film-Comp; Th Short-Comp; TV Film-Comp; TV Video-Comp.
Genres: Drama-Th&TV; Musical-Th; Documentary-Th&TV; Educational-Th&TV.
Biography: Born 1930, Coleman, Alberta; moved to Vancouver, 43; to Toronto, 51. Studied with Gordon Delamont; formed the Ron Collier Quintet; concerts at Stratford, Massey Hall, etc.; trombonist, CBC TV, radio; recorded album with Duke Ellington, *Collages*, 69; stopped playing in 70 to do more composing and conducting; resident composer at Humber College since 72. Won the Big Band Open Class in the Canadian Stage Band Festival 3 times (75, 82, 86).
Selected Filmography: *Indonesia Opening Ceremonies*, In, 77, CDN, Comp; *Back to Beulah*, TV, 74, CDN, Comp; *Follow the North Star*, TV, 72, CDN, Comp; *Paperback Hero*, Th, 72, CDN, Comp; *Face-Off*, Th, 71, CDN, Comp; "Talking to a Stranger" (4 eps), TV, 71, CDN, Comp; *A Way Out/A Place to ...?/You Take the Credit*, ED, 69-71, CDN, Comp; *The Shield Project/Growing Downstream*, In, 68-71, CDN, Comp; *Life Lines/Rye on the Rocks*, In, 68-71, CDN, Comp; *Planed, Dipped or Fancy/Shebandowan - A Summer Place*, In, 71, CDN, Comp; *A Fan's Notes*, Th, 70, CDN, Comp; *Seven Critieria/Call Me*, In, 67, CDN, Comp; *Silent*

Night/Lonely Night, TV, 65, CDN, Comp; *Hear Me Talkin' to Ya*, TV, 64, CDN, Comp.

CONSTANTINEAU, Daniel
SOCAM, SODRAC, GDM, ACO. 5000 Grosvenor, Montréal, PQ H3W 2M1 (514)737-9950.
Types de production et générique: TV Video-Comp/Arr/Chef d'orch.
Types d'oeuvres: Drame-C&TV; Comédie-C&TV; Affairs Publiques-C; Nouvelles-C.
Curriculum vitae: né au Québec en 1955. 76-85, Formation au Conservatoire de musique de Montréal; études complétées auprès de Serge Garant et Charles Dutoit; travaille activement pour TV du Québec(Société Radio-Canada, Télé-Métropole et Radio-Québec); direction de musique instrumentale et vocale: contemporain, classique, pop-rock.
Filmographie sélective: "Jamais deux sans toi" (54 eps), TV, 90-91, CDN, Comp/Arr/Chef d'orch; *L 'Or du temps*, TV, 89-91, CDN, Comp/Arr; *Magazine Montréal*, TV, 89-91, CDN, Comp/Arr; *Question de sport*, TV, 89-90, CDN, Comp/Arr; *Les Nouvelles TVA*, TV, 89-90, CDN, Comp/Arr; *Mon argent*, TV, 88-89, CDN, Comp/Arr; *Nord-Sud*, TV, 88-91, CDN, Comp/Arr; *Auto-promos Fêtes 1987, Radio-Qué*, TV, 87, CDN, Comp/Arr; *Tourtière de mon coeur*, TV, 87, CDN, Comp/Arr.

COOPER, Richard
- see WRITERS

CORRIVEAU, Jean
ACCT, CAPAC, GDM. Corrivo Productions, 457, rue Lasalle, Longueuil, ON J4K 3G4 (514)442-4286. Diane Jutras, 457, rue Lasalle, Longueuil, PQ J4K 3G4 (514)674-0396.
Types de production et générique: l métrage-Comp/Mix son; c métrage-Comp; TV film-Comp; TV vidéo-Comp.
Types d'oeuvres: Drame-C; Documentaire-C&TV; Education-TV; Annonces-TV.
Curriculum vitae: Né en 1954, Laval, Québec. Langues: français et anglais. Etudes au Conservatoire de Musique à Montréal (classe de composition avec Gilles Tremblay, 75-78). Depuis 81, enseigne à l'Université du Québec à Montréal l'audiographie numérique et la création sonore et dirige séminaires d'audiographie à l'intention des professeurs de musique (2e niveau), Université McGill, Ecole Ste-Croix. Pionnier dans les domaines de l'électroacoustique, synthétiseurs, studios numériques. A inventé un des premiers synthétiseurs québécois, baptisé "la machine à Corriveau."
Filmographie sélective: *Bonjour! Shalom!*, TV, 91, CDN, Mus/Conc son; *La Demoiselle Sauvage*, C, 91, CDN, Comp; *La Complainte du Beluga*, TV, 90, CDN, Mus/Conc son, (GEMEAUX 90); *Violence conjugale*, Cm, 88, CDN, Mus; *Centrale des enseignants du Québec*, Cm, 88, CDN, Mus; *Le Monde selon Elie Wiesel*, In, 88, CDN/USA, Mus; *Ouverture* (spectacle Michel Lemieux), C, 88, CDN, Mus; *Tristesse modèle réduit*, C, 88, CDN, Mus; *Des amis pour la vie*, TV, 87, CDN, Mus; *Un zoo la nuit*, C, 86, CDN, Mus, (2 GENIES 88); "Erithrea" (3 eps), C, 86, CDN, Mus; *La Guerre sale*, C, 85, CDN, Mus; *Bad News*, C, 85, CDN, Mus/Conc son; *Les Fleurs sauvages*, C, 82, CDN, Mus; *Les Bons Débarras*, C, 79, CDN, Chef d'orch.

CROSLEY, Lawrence (Larry)
ACCT, AFM, SOCAN, CLC. 8 King George St., Ottawa, ON K1K 1V8 (613)741-2364.
Type of Production and Credits: Th Film-Comp/Dir Mus; Th Short-Comp; TV Film-Comp/Prod; TV Video-Comp/Prod.
Genres: Drama-Th&TV; Documentary-Th&TV; Animation-Th&TV; Music Video-TV.
Biography: Born in 1932 in Oaklandon, Indiana. Canadian citizen. B.M. and M.M. from Eastman School of Music. Came to Canada in 1959 as staff composer for Crawley Films. Freelance since 1966. Head of Music and Postproduction Sound at NFB, 1978-80. Composed, conducted and produced music for more than 200 films, including Oscar winners, *The Man Who Skied Down Everest* and *I'll Find a Way*. Nominated for a 1990 Gemini for Best Original Music Score for *Teddy Bears' Picnic*. Won the Bijou Trophy, Canadian Short Film & TV Awards, 1981 for *The Lost Pharaoh*; Music Category Award, CFTA Awards, 1977 for *The Narwhals Came*; Best Music Score, Canadian Film Awards, 1972 for *Journey to Power* and the Etrog Trophy for Best Original Music, Canadian Film Awards, 1971, for *Seasons in the Mind*.
Selected Filmography: *Searching*, MV, 91, CDN, Prod; *Family Treasures*, ED, 90, CDN, Comp; *Teddy Bears' Picnic*, TV, 89, CDN, Comp/Cond; *The Relationship*, "Canada:True North", TV, 88, CDN/USA, Comp/Cond; *The Knife Edge of Deterrence*, TV, 85, USA, Comp; *The Land That Devours Ships*, TV, 84, CDN,

Comp/Cond; "War" (7 eps), TV, 83, CDN, Comp/Cond; *I Know a Secret*, TV, 82, CDN, Comp/Cond; *The Lost Pharaoh*, TV, 80, CDN, Comp/Cond, (BIJOU); *Atmos*, Th, 80, USA/CDN, Comp/Cond; *The Narwhals Came*, TV, 76, CDN, Comp/Cond, (CFTA); "Path of the Paddle" (4 eps), ED, 76, CDN, Comp/Cond; *The Man Who Skied Down Everest*, Th, 74, J/USA/CDN, Dir Mus; *Journey to Power*, Th, 72, CDN, Comp/Cond, (CFA); *Seasons in the Mind*, Th, 71, CDN, Comp/Cond, (CFA).

CULLEN, Patricia ✧
(416)862-7579.
Type of Production and Credits: Th Film-Comp; TV Film-Comp; TV Video-Comp.
Genres: Drama-Th; Documentary-TV; Children's-Th&TV; Animation-Th&TV.
Biography: Born 1951.
Selected Filmography: "The Originals" (13 eps), TV, 88, CDN, Comp; *The Care Bears Adventure in Wonderland*, Th, 87, CDN, Comp; *A Mystery, a Mouse and Me*, TV, 87, USA, Comp; *Can't Happen to Me*, Th, 87, CDN, Comp; *The Care Bears Movie II*, Th, 86, CDN, Comp; *The Care Bears Movie*, Th, 85, CDN, Comp; "Ewoks" (13 eps), TV, 85, CDN, Comp; "The Edison Twins" (26 eps), TV, 83-85, CDN, Comp; *The Great Heep*, TV, 85, CDN, Comp; *Strawberry Shortcake Meets the Berrykins*, TV, 84, CDN, Comp; "Mr. Microchip" (13 eps), TV, 83, CDN, Comp; *Strawberry Shortcake and the Baby Without a Name*, TV, 83, CDN, Comp; *Unfinished Business*, Th, 83, CDN, Co-Comp; *Strawberry Shortcake: A Housewarming Surprise*, TV, 82, CDN, Comp; *Rock & Rule/Ring of Power*, Th, 82, CDN, Comp.

DALE, James ✧
(416)927-8661.
Type of Production and Credits: Th Film-Comp; Th Short-Comp; TV Film-Comp; TV Video-Comp.
Genres: Drama-Th&TV; Comedy-Th&TV; Variety-Th&TV; Musical-Th&TV.
Biography: Born 1935, London, England; to Canada, 47. Trained with Gordon Delamont in composition and orchestration. Has worked in television and film since 63; Los Angeles, 69-75; currently works out of Toronto. Has composed for many TV series including David Steinberg, Ken Berry, Ray Stevens; pianist/com-poser/arranger with Rob McConnell's Boss Brass, winning Grammy and Juno Awards; accompanist and/or writer for Peggy Lee, Nancy Wilson and many others.
Selected Filmography: *Olympic Theme* (for CTV), TV, 88, CDN, Comp; "Super Dave", TV, 87-88, CDN, Comp; *Ticker Test*, TV, 87, CDN, Comp; *The Execution of Raymond Graham*, TV, 85, CDN, Comp/Cond; *Timing*, Th, 85, CDN, Co-Comp/Cond; *Markham*, In, 85, CDN, Comp; *Actra Awards*, TV, 85, CDN, Comp/Cond; *Genie Awards*, TV, 85, CDN, Comp/Cond; NHL Awards, TV, 85, CDN, Comp/Cond; *Best of Both Worlds*, Th, 84, USA, Comp; "Bizarre" (167 eps), TV, 78-84, CDN/USA, Comp; "Sonny and Cher" (100 eps), TV, 71-75, USA, Comp/Cond; *Wacky World*, TV, 74, USA, Comp; "Andy Williams" (50 eps), TV, 69-71, USA, Comp/Cond.

DANNA, Mychael
ACCT. McLaughlin Planetarium, 100 Queen's Park Cres., Toronto, ON M5S 2C6 (416)586-5746.
Type of Production and Credits: Th Film-Comp; TV Film-Comp; Th Short-Comp; TV Video-Comp.
Genres: Drama-Th; Action-Th; Science Fiction-Th; Documentary-Th&TV.
Biography: Born 1958, Winnipeg, Manitoba. B.Mus., Composition and Conducting, University of Toronto. Twice winner of CAPAC Hugh LeCaine Composition Award; Glenn Gould Composition Scholarship, U. of T. Piano music published by the Royal Conservatory of Music, 78-present; resident music producer/composer, McLaughlin Planetarium, Toronto, 87-present. Genie nominations for: *Family Viewing*, *Cold Comfort* (Co-composer with Jeff Danna), and *Speaking Parts*. Nomination for Best International Score, Film Festival of Flanders for *Speaking Parts*. Also known for his New Age genre albums.
Selected Filmography: *The Adjuster*, Th, 91, CDN, Comp; *Johann's Gift to Christmas*, TV, 91, CDN, Comp/Arr; *Genie Awards 1990*, promotional trailer, In, 90, CDN, Comp; *Foster Parents Plan PSAs*, In, 90, CDN, Comp; *Cold Comfort*, Th, 89, CDN, Comp; *Speaking Parts*, Th, 89, CDN, Comp; *Termini Station*, Th, 89, CDN, Comp; *Not by Choice*, ED, 89, CDN, Comp; *Blood Relations*, Th, 88, CDN, Comp; *Murder One*, Th, 88, CDN, Comp; *One Man Out*, Th, 88, CDN, Comp; *Walking After Midnight*, Th, 87, CDN, Comp; *Caribe*, Th, 87, CDN, Comp; *Family Viewing*, Th, 87, CDN, Comp.

DAVIES, Victor
AFM, DGC, GCFC, SOCAN. Lily Pad Productions, 102 Lyall Ave., Toronto, ON M4E 1W5 (416)698-5995.
Type of Production and Credits: Th Film-Comp; TV Film-Comp.
Genres: Drama-Th&TV; Musical-Th&TV; Children's-Th&TV.
Biography: Born 1939, Winnipeg, Manitoba. B.Mus. in Composition, Indiana University, 64. Freelance composer, pianist, conductor, musical director; has composed scores for film, TV, radio, theatre.
Selected Filmography: "The Rockets" (68 eps), TV, 87-91, CDN, Comp/Lyrics; *The Nutcracker Prince*, Th, 90, CDN, Comp; *The Last Winter*, Th, 89, CDN, Comp; "Let's Go" (200 eps), TV, 77-85, CDN, Comp; *The Journey of Lan Tran*, TV, 84, CDN, Comp; *Possession*, Th, 83, CDN, Comp; *And When They Shall Ask*, Th, 83, CDN, Comp; "American Caesar", TV, 83, CDN, Comp; *The Pedlar*, TV, 82, CDN, Comp; *The Catch*, TV, 81, CDN, Comp; *Latitude 55*, Th, 80, CDN, Comp; *The Curse of Ponsonby Hall*, TV, 79, CDN, Comp; *The Pit*, Th, 79, CDN, Comp; "Man and Nature" (13 eps), TV, 78, CDN, Comp; *Wilderness Trails*, Th, 75, CDN, Comp.

DOLGAY, Marvin Ian
AFM, ACCT, SOCAN, CARAS. 51 Kingswood Rd., Toronto, ON M4E 3N4 (416)699-5815. Tambre Productions Inc., 250 The Esplanade, Suite 100, "The Mill", Toronto, ON M5A 1J2 (416)367-9797. FAX: 367-9803.
Type of Production and Credits: Th Film-Comp; Th Short-Comp/Mus Prod; TV Film-Comp/Mus Prod; TV Video-Comp/Mus Prod; TV Comm-Comp/Audio Prod.
Genres: Drama-Th&TV; Comedy-Th&TV; Variety-Th&TV; Action-Th &TV; Commercials-TV.
Biography: Born 1955, Toronto, Ontario. President and Creative Director of Tambre Productions Inc. Music and audio productions for radio and TV. Has had Genie and Gemini nominations and has won numerous national and international awards for his advertising music and sound design work.
Selected Filmography: *Skating II*, TV, 91, CDN, Comp/Mus Dir; "Little Rosie" (13 eps), TV, 90, USA/CDN, Comp; "Inside Stories" (13 eps), TV, 90, CDN, Prod (series theme); *Divided Loyalties*, TV, 90, CDN, Mus Prod; *Whales/Wolves/Loons*, "The Natural Campaign", Bell Canada, Cm, 90, CDN, Comp/Prod, (BESSIE); "Katts and Dog" (4 eps), TV, 89, CDN/F, Mus Prod; *Straightline*, Th, 89, USA/CDN, Co-Comp; "T and T" (65 eps), TV, 87-89, CDN/USA, Co-Comp; *Gemini Awards* (2 shows), TV, 88/89, CDN, Comp/Mus Dir; *Babar, the Movie*, Th, 89, CDN, Song Comp; "My Pet Monster" (13 eps), TV, 87, USA/CDN, Theme Comp; *Blue Man*, Th, 85, USA/CDN, Comp; "4 on the Floor" (13 eps), TV, 85, CDN, Comp/Mus Dir; *The Gift of Christmas*, TV, 85, CDN, Comp.

DUGUAY, Raôul ✧
(514)248-3536.
Types de production et générique: l métrage-Comp.
Types d'oeuvres: Drame-C; Science-fiction-C; Expérimental-C.
Curriculum vitae: Né en 1939, Val d'Or, Abitibi, Québec. Docteur en philosophie (esthétique phonétique); chercheur en holisme (physique, chimie, biologie); spécialiste des harmoniques (sons diphoniques); aussi réalisateur et directeur artistique.
Filmographie sélective: *Avoir des ailes*, ED, 86, CDN, Comp; *Les Fleurs sauvages*, C, 80, CDN, Comp; *O ou l'invisible enfant*, C, 73, CDN, Réal/Sc/Comp.

ELLIOTT, Keith
- see POSTPRODUCTION SOUND MIXERS

ERBE, Micky
ACTRA, AFM 149, ACCT. Mickymar Productions Ltd., 86 McGill, Toronto, ON M5B 1H2 (416)581-1400.
Type of Production and Credits: Th Film-Comp; Th Short-Comp; TV Film-Comp; TV Video-Comp.
Genres: Drama-Th&TV; Comedy-Th&TV; Musical-Th&TV; Documentary-Th&TV.
Biography: Born 1948, Paterson, New Jersey; landed immigrant Canada. Studied at Manhattan Academy; studied composition/arranging with Torrie Zito and Charlie Callello; trumpet with John Ware. Produces, arranges records and commercials; Clio and Craft Award winner, 4-time Juno Award nominee for The Spitfire Band; 2-time Genie nominee. Has written for Canadian Brass, Maureen Forrester, The Nylons; a specially commissioned viola concerto for Rivka Golani.
Selected Filmography: *Blue Planet*, Imax, Th, 91, CDN/USA, Co comp; "E.N.G." (44 eps), TV, 90-91, CDN, Co comp; "Street Legal" (36 eps), TV, 89-91, CDN, Co comp; *True Confections*, Th, 91, CDN,

Co comp; *African Journey*, Th/TV, 90, CDN, Co comp; *Blood Sport*, TV, 90, CDN/IR, Co comp; "Struggle for Democracy" (10 eps), TV, 89, CDN/USA/GB, Co comp, (GEMINI); "The Twilight Zone" (2 eps), TV, 89, CDN/USA, Co comp; "Adderly", TV, 88-89, USA/CDN, Co comp, (GEMINI); "Alfred Hitchcock Presents" (11 eps), TV, 88-89, CDN/USA, Co comp; *The Dream is Alive*, Imax, Th, 86, USA/CDN, Co comp; *Hail Columbia*, Imax, Th, 84, USA/CDN, Co comp; *Threshold*, Th, 80, CDN, Co comp; *Ticket To Heaven*, Th, 80, CDN, Co comp; *North of Superior*, Imax, Th, 71, CDN, Co comp.

ESSIAMBRE, Gaetan
GDM, UDA, ACTRA. 6865, 29th Avenue, Montréal, PQ H1T 3H5 (514)374-6724. Suzann Methot, 6865, 29th Avenue, Montréal, PQ H1T 3H5 (514)374-6724.
Types de production et générique: l métrage-Arr; TV Film-Arr; TV Vidéo-Comp.
Types d'oeuvres: Variété-TV; Comédie-TV; Enfants-C&TV; Annonces-TV.
Curriculum vitae: Né en 1956. Langues: français et anglais. Compositeur interprète-musicien musiques publicité.
Filmographie sélective: "Rock et Belles Oreilles" (28 eps), TV, 87-89, CDN, Comp; *La Grenouille et La Baleine*, C, 87, CDN, Arr; *C'est Pas Parce Qu'On Est Petit Qu'On Peut Pas Etre Grand*, C, 86, CDN, Arr.

FEINGOLD, Stan
- see WRITERS

FORMAN, Howard
AFM. Visual Music International, 5241 Trans Island Ave., Montreal, PQ H3W 2Z9 (514)481-0051. (514)481-0042.
Type of Production and Credits: Th Film-Comp; Th Short-Comp; TV Film-Comp.
Genres: Drama-Th; Musical-TV; Educational-TV; Children's-Th.
Biography: Born 1957, Montreal, Quebec; Canadian and US citizenship. Attended university in Canada. Session guitarist, Muscle Schoals Sound Studio, Alabama; national commercials in Canada and US; solo albums in Canada and Europe; music videos; produces radio spots, jingles, records and film soundtracks; adapts lyrics for film; tour guitarist for international acts; English production on Michel Lemieux's "Mutations." Nominated for Genie, Best Original Song, 86 and 88, for *The Peanut Butter Solution* and *The Young Magician/Le Jeune Magicien* respectively.

Selected Filmography: *Bantu!*, TV, 91, CDN/AFRICA, Comp/Prod; "Visual Music CD Library", Th, 91, CDN, Comp/Prod; *Fumbles*, Cm, 91, GB, Comp; *The Sequin Mines*, MV, 90, B, Comp; "In Flight" (4 eps), In, 90, CDN, Comp/Prod; *Shades of Love*, TV, 89, CDN, Perf; *One Step Away*, Th/TV, 88, CDN, Comp; *The Young Magician/Le Jeune Magicien*, Th, 86, CDN, Theme Comp/Prod; *N.G.T.*, Quebec Govt, In, 85-86, CDN, Comp; *Bach et Bottine*, Th, 86, CDN, Theme Comp; *The Peanut Butter Solution*, Th, 85, CDN, Comp/Lyrics; *Here's the Last Time*, MV, 85, CDN, Act; *The Prodigal*, TV, 84, CDN, Comp; *Running Scared*, TV, 84, CDN, Comp; *Music ETV*, TV, 84, USA, Act.

FORTIN, Richard
York Music Production, 93 Victoria Park Ave., Toronto, ON M4E 3S2 (416)690-5965.
Type of Production and Credits: TV Film-Comp.
Genres: Drama-TV; Documentary-TV; Educational-TV.
Biography: Born 1956, Lévis, Québec. Languages: French and English. M.Mus., Composition, University of Montreal. Arranger/composer for various artists including Marilyn Lightstone and Liona Boyd; 2-guitar concerto for Liona Boyd; producer for RCA and local artists; composer for Lee Dyment, Detroit; 2 original pieces recorded in Los Angeles with Gene Page as producer; original material in 4 music books distributed in Canada and US; manager of York Music Production, original music for film.
Selected Filmography: *The Guitar*, TV, 87, CDN, Comp; *Forêts du Québec*, TV, 81, CDN, Comp; *La Trappe*, TV, 81, CDN, Comp; *La Passion*, TV, 80, CDN, Comp.

FREEDMAN, Harry
OC, CLC, ACMC. 35 St. Andrew's Garden, Toronto, ON M4W 2C9 (416)921-5530.
Type of Production and Credits: Th Film-Comp; Th Short-Comp; TV Film-Comp; TV Video-Comp.
Genres: Drama-Th&TV; Musical-Th&TV; Documentary-TV; Children's-TV.
Biography: Born 1922, Poland; Canadian citizenship, 31. Languages: English and French. Senior matriculation (Honours), Winnipeg School of Art, Royal Conservatory of Music; Tanglewood Scholarship, R.C.M. Scholarship. Has

written music in all forms including 3 symphonies, 9 ballets, a one-act opera, chamber music, choral music and scores for film, TV and theatre. Founding member of Canadian League of Composers; Guild of Canadian Film Composers. Part-time film animator and painter (Japanese sumi-e). *All That Glistens* won Gold Award, NY Int'l Film and TV Festival; *Against Oblivion* won Bronze Chris Plaque, Columbus. *The Act of the Heart* won Etrog (now Genie), Best Musical Score, Feature Film, 70, Canadian Film Awards. He was named Canadian Music Council Composer of the Year, 79; Officer, Order of Canada, 84.
Selected Filmography: *Connections*, TV, 85, CDN, Comp; *Against Oblivion/All That Glistens*, "Hand and Eye", TV, 83, CDN, Comp; *Something Hidden: A Portrait of Wilder Penfield*, TV, 81, CDN, Comp; *Pyramid of Roses*, Th, 80, CDN, Comp; *The Courage of Kavik the Wolf Dog*, TV, 78, CDN, Comp; *1847*, "The Newcomers", TV, 77, CDN, Comp; *The Bells of Hell*, TV, 73, CDN, Comp; *Tilt*, Th, 72, CDN, Comp; *The Pyx*, Th, 72, CDN, Comp; *November*, Th, 70, CDN, Comp; *The Act of the Heart*, Th, 69, CDN, Comp, (CFA); *Isabel*, Th, 67, CDN, Comp; *The Mills of the Gods: Viet Nam*, "This Hour Has Seven Days", TV, 66, CDN, Comp; *The Roots of Madness*, TV, 66, USA, Comp; *Let Me Count The Ways*, TV, 65, CDN, Comp.

FREWER, Terry
ACTRA, AFM. 1444 Argyle Ave., West Vancouver, BC V7T 1C2 (604)926-6288. S.L. Feldman, 1534 W. 2nd Ave., Vancouver, BC V6H 3Y4 (604)734-5945.
Type of Production and Credits: Th Short-Comp; TV Film-Comp; TV Video-Comp.
Genres: Musical-Th&TV; Documentary-TV; Commercials-TV; Industrial-Th&TV.
Biography: Born 1946; Canadian. B.Mus., University of British Columbia, 69. Vocalist, musician, composer, producer; orchestral works performed by major Canadian symphony orchestras. Musical director and arranger for many rock acts; production and arrangement for: Tom Jones, Isaac Hayes, Martin Mull, Carroll Baker, Ann Mortifee, The Temptations, Lou Rawls, Phoebe Snow, Terry Jacks, Jerry Lee Lewis, Paul Horn, Paul Hyde, Sass Jordon.
Selected Filmography: "Scene of the Crime" (22 eps), TV, 91, F/USA, Comp; "Adventures of the Black Stallion" (26 eps), TV, 90-91, CDN, Comp; "Neon Rider" (39 eps), TV, 89-91, CDN, Comp; *The Dig*, ED/TV, 90, CDN, Comp; *American Boyfriends*, Th, 89, CDN, Comp; *Cleo Rocks*, "MacGyver", TV, 88, US/CDN, Comp; *Bathysphere*, Th, 86, CDN, Comp; *Vertical Desert*, TV, 71, CDN, Comp; *Life & Times of Chester-Angus Ramsgood*, Th, 70, CDN, Comp; *Summer Centre*, ED/TV, 69, CDN, Comp; "Story Theatre" (40 eps), TV, 68, CDN, Comp; *Seraphine*, TV, 68, CDN, Comp; *Desert Ranch*, TV, 68, CDN, Comp; *The Plastic Mile*, Th, 68, CDN, Comp.

FRICKER, Brock
- see PRODUCTION SOUND MIXERS

FRITZ, Sherilyn
AFM. 172 Cornell Way, Port Moody, BC V3H 3W2 (604)939-8521.
Type of Production and Credits: Th Short-Comp/Mus Prod; TV Video-Comp/Mus Prod.
Genres: Musical-Th; Industrial-Th; Commercials-TV.
Biography: Born 1957, Princeton, BC. B.Mus., University of British Columbia; M.Mus., Composition, University of Alberta. Has won many awards including the William Rea Award. Has been involved with studio and stage productions, Vancouver, taught at UBC, Vancouver Community College, University of Alberta, Vancouver Youth Theatre.
Selected Filmography: *The Great Escape*, In, 91, CDN, Comp/Mus Prod; *Family Counsellors*, In, 91, CDN, Comp/Mus Prod; *Ears*, Cm, 90, CDN, Comp/Mus Prod; *Still Life*, Th, 90, CDN, Comp/Mus Prod; *When to Call Ident*, "Roll Call Series", In, 90, CDN, Comp/Mus Prod; *Emily Carr Outreach*, Cm, 88, CDN, Comp/Mus Prod; *Audition*, Th, 80, CDN, Comp/Mus Prod; *Observances*, Th, 79, CDN, Comp/Mus Prod; *Eleventh Hour*, Th, 79, CDN, Comp/Mus Prod.

FUREY, Lewis
Ralph Zimmerman, Great North Artists Mgmt., 350 Dupont St., Toronto, ON M5R 1V9 (416)925-2051.
Type of Production and Credits: Th Film-Comp; TV Film-Comp; Th Film-Dir; TV Film-Dir.
Genres: Drama-Th; Musical-Th; Children's-Th.
Biography: Born 1949, Montreal, Quebec. Educated at McGill University and Julliard, NY. Began career at age 11 as violin soloist with Montreal Symphony Orchestra. Began making albums, 75;

recorded 10. Director/actor/composer of various TV variety specials and musical stage shows; feature film director, 85. *Night Magic* was the official Canadian selection, Cannes, 85.
Selected Filmography: "Mount Royal", TV, 88, CDN/F, Comp; *Shadow Dancing*, Th, 88, CDN, Dir; *Too Outrageous!*, Th, 87, CDN, Comp; "Shades of Love" (Dir 1 eps), TV, 87, CDN, Comp; *Sauve-toi, Lola*, Th, 86, F, Comp; *The Peanut Butter Solution*, Th, 85, CDN, Comp; *American Dreamer*, Th, 84, USA, Comp; *Night Magic*, Th, 84, CDN/F, Dir/Co-Scr/Comp, (GENIE); *Maria Chapdelaine*, Th, 82, CDN/F, Comp, (GENIE); *Au revoir...à lundi*, Th, 79, CDN/F, Comp; *Fantastica*, Th, 79, CDN/F, Comp/Act; *The Rubber Gun*, Th, 77, CDN, Comp; *L'Ange et la femme*, Th, 77, CDN, Comp/Act; La Tête de Normande St-Onge, Th, 75, CDN, Comp, (CFA); *Jacob Two Two Meets the Hooded Fang*, Th, 75, CDN, Comp.

GAGNON, André
a/s Guy Latraverse, 3962, av. Laval, Montréal, PQ H2W 2J2 (514)526-7090. FAX: 526-7873.
Types de production et générique: l métrage-Comp; TV film-Comp.
Types d'oeuvres: Drame-C&TV; Documentaire-C.
Curriculum vitae: Formation en musique classique. Jusqu'en 67, fut le pianiste accompagnateur et l'arrangeur pour plusieurs artistes dont Claude Léveillée, Monique Leyrac, Renée Claude. Depuis, il a présenté des spectacles à la Place des Arts et dans des salles à travers le monde; a représenté le Québec à l'Exposition Universelle d'Osaka, 70. A enregistré 13 microsillons dont *Les Turluteries, neiges, Mouvements* et *Virage à gauche* (tous des disques d'Or). Récipiendiaire du prix Gémeaux, "Musique originale" (*Des Dames de Coeur*), 88. Compositeur de la musique du ballet *Mad Shadows* (Ballet national du Canada); a joué plusieurs fois avec l'Orchestre symphonique de Montréal.
Filmographie sélective: "Des dames de coeur" (26 eps), TV, 86, CDN, Comp/Arr, (GEMEAUX 88); *Cyrano*, TV, 85, CDN, Comp/Arr; *Le Film d'Ariane*, C, 85, CDN, Comp/Arr; *La Céleste Bicyclette*, TV, 83, CDN, Comp/Arr; *Tell Me That You Love Me*, C, 82, CDN/IL, Comp/Arr; *Hot Touch*, C, 80, CDN/USA, Comp/Arr; *Phobia*, C, 79, CDN, Comp/Arr; *Running*, C, 78, CDN, Comp/Arr; *Jeux de la XXIe Olympiade*, C, 76, CDN, Comp/Arr; *Les Forges de St-Maurice*, TV, 70-73, CDN, Comp/Arr; *Kamouraska*, C, 72, CDN/F, Comp/Arr.

GELINAS, Marc
CAPAC, SARDEC, UDA. 495, de la Colline, C.P. 1757, Ste-Adèle, PQ V0R 1L0 (514)229-6707.
Types de production et générique: l métrage-Comp; TV vidéo-Comp/Sc.
Types d'oeuvres: Comédie-C&TV; Variété-C&TV; Enfants-TV.
Curriculum vitae: Né en 1937, Montréal, Québec. Langues: français et anglais. Trente ans de carrière comme auteur compositeur, chanteur, comédien. Plus gros vendeur de disques canadien français. Auteur-compositeur pour plusieurs annonces publicitaires. A publié le roman *Je voudrais être 'put' mais j'ai pas de clients*.

GILLIS, Kevin
- see PRODUCERS

GRAY, John H
- see WRITERS

GREGOIRE, Richard
GDM, ACCT. 3000, rue Paradis, Montréal, PQ H1Y 1C3 (514)376-8030. FAX: 376-7936.
Types de production et générique: l métrage-Comp; c métrage-Comp; TV film-Comp.
Types d'oeuvres: Drame-C&TV; Variété-TV; Documentaire-C&TV; Annonces-C&TV.
Curriculum vitae: Né en 1944, Montréal, Québec. Licence en musique, Université de Montréal, 68; Stage à l'ORTF et au Conservatoire de Paris, 69-70. Compositeur, arrangeur, producteur de musique: disque, cinéma, TV, publicité. Récipiendaire du prix Félix arrangeur de l'année, 83; nomination aux Génie pour *Exit*, 86; Trophée SDE, Musique de film, 86.
Filmographie sélective: *L'homme de rêve*, TV, 91, CDN, Mus; *Perfectly Normal*, C, 90, CDN/GB, Mus; "Les Filles de Caleb", TV, 90-91, CDN, Mus; *Cruising Bar/Meet Market*, C, 89, CDN, Mus; *Richard coeur de nylon*, TV, 89, CDN, Mus; "Blue" la Magnifique, TV, 89, CDN, Mus; *Bonjour Monsieur Gauguin*, TV, 88, CDN, Mus; *Dans le Ventre du Dragon*, C, 88, CDN, Mus; *T'es Belle Jeanne*, TV, 88, CDN, Mus; *La Ligne de Chaleur*, C, 87, CDN, Mus; *Les Bottes*, TV, 87, CDN, Mus; *Les fous de Bassan*, C, 86, CDN, Mus; *Exit*, C, 86, CDN, Mus; *Pouvoir intime/Blind Trust*, C, 85, CDN, Mus.

HARDY, Hagood
ACTRA, AFM. Hagood Hardy Productions Ltd., 277 Lakeshore Rd. E. Oakville, ON L6J 1H9 (416) 338-0723.

Spotlite Enterprises, 8865 Wilshire Blvd., Beverly Hills, CA, USA (213) 657-8004.
Type of Production and Credits: Th Film-Comp; TV Film-Comp.
Genres: Drama-Th&TV; Documentary-Th&TV; Animation-Th&TV; Commercials-TV.
Biography: Born 1937; Canadian and US citizenship. Composer/arranger for over 50 features and TV films; commercial jingles. Selected *Billboard* magazine's recipient for the award of American Instrumentalist of the Year; received the William Harold Moon Award; 3-time Juno Award winner; Gemini, 86, and CanPro award, 85.
Selected Filmography: "Road to Avonlea" (9 eps), TV, 89-91, CDN/USA, Comp/Cond; *Liberace*, TV, 88, USA, Comp/Cond; "Wonderful Wizard of Oz" (52 eps), TV, 87, USA, Comp/Cond; *Anne of Green Gables: The Sequel*, TV, 87, USA/CDN, Comp/Cond; "Lawrenceville Stories" (3 eps), TV, 87, CDN/USA, Comp/Cond; *Frontier*, "Aventuriers de la Baie Hudson" (6 eps), TV, 86, GB/F/CDN, Comp/Cond; *This Child Is Mine*, TV, 85, USA, Comp/Cond, (GEMINI); *Anne of Green Gables*, TV, 85, CDN/USA, Comp/Cond; "Amateur Naturalist" (13 eps), TV, 83, GB/CDN, Comp/Cond; *Care Bears Special #1*, TV, 83, CDN/USA, Comp/Cond; *Mazes and Monsters*, TV, 82, USA, Comp/Cond; *Forbidden Love*, TV, 82, USA, Comp/Cond; *Portrait of Escort*, TV, 81, USA, Comp/Cond; *An American Christmas Carol*, TV, 79, CDN/USA, Comp/Cond.

HASIAK, Steve S. ✧
(306)757-5628.
Type of Production and Credits: Th Short-Comp; TV Film-Comp; TV Video-Comp.
Genres: Musical-TV; Documentary-TV; Educational-TV; Industrial-Th&TV.
Biography: Born 1955, Wolseley, Saskatchewan. Extensive musical education since age 9. Familiar with SMPTE/EBV time code and synchronization processes. Produced album and individual cuts on several albums as well as radio commercials and industrial shorts.
Selected Filmography: *One Night Stand*, MV, 86-87, CDN, Comp/Sing/Mus Prod; *Story of George*, ED, 86, CDN, Comp; Renaissance Regina, Cm, 86, CDN, Comp/Sing; *Jimmy's Game*, Th, 85, CDN, Songwriter/Act; City of Melville Theme, Cm, 85, CDN, Comp/Sing; *Fame Game*, MV, 83, CDN, Comp/Sing.

HENDERSON, Judy
ACTRA, AFM, UDA. Air Tango, 2359 Duvernay, Suite 200, Montreal, PQ H3J 2X1 (514)933-0232.
Type of Production and Credits: Th Film-Comp; Th Short-Comp; TV Film-Comp; TV Video-Comp.
Genres: Drama-Th&TV; Documentary-Th&TV; Animation-Th&TV; Commercials-Th&TV.
Biography: Born 1950, Montreal, Quebec. Languages: English and French. B.A., Communications, Loyola University. Music Director of Red Plum Productions Inc. Award-winning composer (IBAs, Clios) for TV and radio commercials; nominated for Gemini for *George and the Star*.
Selected Filmography: *The Rise and Fall of Humpty Dumpty*, TV, 90, CDN, Comp; "Smoggies!", TV, 88, CDN/F, Comp; *Ghost Ship*, Th, 87, CDN, Comp; *George and the Star*, Th, 86, CDN, Comp; *Native Women*, Th, 86, CDN, Comp; *Speaking Our Peace*, Th, 86, CDN, Comp.

HILLOCK, Graydon
AFM. 11122 Morrison St., #209, North Hollywood, CA 91601 (818)761-9188.
Type of Production and Credits: Th Film-Comp; TV Video-Comp.
Genres: Drama-Th&TV; Horror-Th&TV; Animation-TV; Commercials-TV.
Biography: Born in 1953 in Guelph, Ontario. Hometown is Georgetown, Ontario. Canadian citizen, English speaking. Bachelor of Music, Major in Composition, Dean's List, Magna Cum Laude, Berklee School of Music, Boston, Ma. Studied harmony, counterpoint, arranging and composition with Neil Pooley and Gordon Delamont, Toronto, Ontario. Performances with Anne Murray, Gordon Lightfoot, André Gagnon, jazz-guitar virtuoso Pat Martino (New York and Philadelphia), Jack Jones and The Good Brothers. Composed and produced commercials in Canada and the U.S. including Pizza Pizza, Suzuki Motorcycles, Heinz Ketchup, Budweiser Beer, Shell Gasoline, and Levi 501 Blues. Canada Council Arts Grant "B" awarded twice. Special skills: composer, arranger, orchestrator, music producer, programmer, engineer, songwriter and lyricist.
Selected Filmography: *Blood Relatives*, Th, 91, USA, Comp/Mus Prod; *Fighting Back*, ED/In, 91, USA, Comp/Mus Prod; *Double Trouble Championship Wrestling 1 & 2*, Cm/In/TV, 91, USA, Comp/Songwriter; "Starstreet" (6 eps), TV, 88-

89, USA/BVI/NL, Comp/Mus Prod; Budweiser Beer (32 spots), Cm, 89, USA, Mus Prod; *Top of the Rock* (2 spots), Cm, 88, USA, Comp/Mus Prod; Pizza Pizza (14 spots), Cm, 85-87, CDN, Mus Prod; "Strange But True" (26 eps), TV, 85, CDN/GB, Comp/Mus Prod; "Champions ...The World's Greatest Athletes" (8 eps), TV, 85, CDN, Comp/Mus Prod.

HOFFERT, Brenda
ACTRA, ACCT. Hoffert Communications Corp., 73 Brookview Dr., Toronto, ON M6A 2K5 (416)781-4191. Gorfaine/Schwartz, 3301 Barham Blvd., Suite 201, Los Angeles, CA 90068 USA (213)969-1011.
Type of Production and Credits: Th Film-Mus Spv/Mus Coord/Wr/Lyr; TV Film-Mus Spv/Mus Coord/Wr/Lyr; TV Video-Mus Spv/Mus Coord/Wr/Lyr/Prod.
Genres: Drama-Th&TV; Variety-Th&TV; Musical-Th&TV; Commercials-Th&TV.
Biography: Born 1944, Toronto, Ontario. Studied 8 years, Toronto School of Drama; grade XIII piano; studied voice, Royal Conservatory and with Aura Rully; co-leader of The Lizard People (children's performing ensemble), 79-81; writer/director/producer of numerous commercials; creative director of Morgan Earl Sounds, 79-83; regular in continuing series, "Children's Theatre of the Air." Has received numerous Clios and other advertising awards. Lyricist for more than twenty television and theatrical films including the Genie award-winning *Outrageous*.
Selected Filmography: *Eddie and the Cruisers II - Eddie Lives*, Th, 89, CDN, Mus Coord; *Speed Zone*, Th, 89, CDN, Mus Coord; *Genie Awards*, TV, 88, CDN, Exec Prod; *Monkeyshines*, Th, 88, USA, Mus Spv; *Jesse*, TV, 88, USA, Mus Spv; *Defense Play*, TV, 87, USA, Mus Spv; *Genie Awards*, TV, 87, CDN, Exec Prod; *One Fine Weekend - Lighthouse Reunion*, TV, 82, CDN, Prod/Wr; *Mr. Nice Guy*, Th, 86, CDN, Lyr; *Special Delivery*, TV, 86, CDN, Lyr; *The Exile*, TV, 85, CDN, Lyr; *Circle of Two*, Th, 80, CDN/USA, Lyr; *Wild Horse Hank*, Th, 79, CDN, Lyr; *Outrageous*, Th, 77, CDN, Lyr; *Seemed Like a Good Idea*, Th, 74, CDN, Lyr.

HOFFERT, Paul
ACCT, GCFC, CSA, SOCAN. 73 Brookview Dr., Toronto, ON M6A 2K5 (416)787-7728. (416)781-4191. Gorfaine/Schwartz, 3301 Barham Vlvd., Suite 201, Los Angeles, CA 90068 USA (213)969-1011.
Type of Production and Credits: Th Film-Comp/Mus Spv; TV Film-Comp/Mus Spv; TV Video-Comp/Mus Spv.
Genres: Drama-Th&TV; Musical-Th&TV; Action-Th&TV; Horror-Th&TV.
Biography: Born in 1943. Canadian and U.S. citizen. Winner of 4 Juno awards; 7 Gold records and 1 Platinum record for Lighthouse. 1980, Film Composer of the Year. Experienced orchestrator and conductor for large orchestras. Has worked with Placido Domingo, Dionne Warwick, etc. Extensive music studio with complete synthesis and digital recording. Author of *Understanding Music in Media*. Has been a part-time faculty member of York University since 1983. Executive Producer of the Gemini Awards 1985/86. Former Chairman of the Academy of Canadian Cinema and Television (1981-82).
Selected Filmography: "Canada A.M." (daily), TV, 90, CDN, Comp; *Eddie and the Cruisers II - Eddie Lives*, Th, 89, CDN, Mus Spv; *Monkeyshines*, Th, 88, USA, Mus Spv; *Hoover vs. the Kennedys* (miniseries), TV, 87, USA/CDN, Comp; "The Hitchhiker", TV, 85, CDN/F, Comp Theme; *Strawberry Ice*, TV, 83, USA/CDN, Comp; *Fanny Hill*, Th, 84, GB, Comp; *Paradise*, Th, 81, IL/CDN, Comp; *Circle of Two*, Th, 80, CDN, Comp; *Double Negative*, Th, 80, CDN, Comp; *Shape of Things to Come*, Th, 79, CDN, Comp; *Highballin'*, Th, 78, CDN, Comp; *Outrageous*, Th, 77, CDN, Comp; *The Groundstar Conspiracy*, Th, 72, USA, Comp.

JONES, Cliff
- see PRODUCERS

KAVANAGH, Gregory
TMA 149. Bekker/Kavanagh Productions/Greg Kavanagh Music, 94 Abbeywood Trail, Don Mills, ON M3B 3B5 (416)391-0215. FAX: 391-2646.
Type of Production and Credits: TV Film-Comp; TV Video-Comp; Th Short-Comp.
Genres: Drama-TV; Action-TV; Documentary-TV; Commercials-TV; Industrial-TV.
Biography: Born 1956, Halifax, Nova Scotia. Studied music production for film and record in Toronto and Los Angeles.
Selected Filmography: *Eye on Toronto*, TV, 90-91, CDN, Comp; Canon, Cm, 91, CDN, Comp/Prod; Toshiba, Cm, 90, CDN, Comp/Prod; Burger King, Cm, 90, CDN, Comp/Prod; *Fit for Life*, TV, 90, CDN, Comp/Arr; *Northern Telecom*, In,

88, CDN, Comp; *Quebec Today*, TV, 87, CDN, Comp/Arr; "The War Years" (2 eps)(background music), TV, 87, CDN, Comp; "Lifetime" (5 eps)(background music), TV, 86, CDN, Comp.

KEYES, Sonny
ACTRA, AFM. 66 Arundel Ave., Toronto, ON M4K 3A4 (416)463-1309.
Type of Production and Credits: TV Film-Comp/Mus Prod; TV Video-Wr/Comp.
Genres: Commercials-TV; Industrial-TV.
Biography: Born in 1955 in Winnipeg, Manitoba. Canadian citizen. Songwriter, vocalist and keyboardist for rock group "The Kings"; has composed and produced music for short films as well as industrial and pop videos; has been involved in post-production of numerous TV commercials as keyboardist, MIDI programmer and arranger, and has on-set experience both acting and assisting production sound teams.
Selected Filmography: *Fishing/Golf/Dive*, Bud Light, Cm, 91, CDN, MIDI Sys Prog; *UFO's*, Heinz, Cm, 90, CDN, MIDI Sys Prog; *Spin/Pour*, Labatt's Blue, Cm, 90, CDN, MIDI Sys Prog; *The Boxer/The Jockey*, BC Tel, Cm, 90, CDN, MIDI Sys Prog; *Out on a Limb*, "My Secret Identity", TV, 89, CDN, Comp; *Antigua: Share the Memory*, In, 88, CDN/AN, Comp/Mus Prod.

KOBYLANSKY, Karl ✧
(604)980-0053.
Type of Production and Credits: Th Film-Comp; TV Video-Comp.
Genres: Drama-Th&TV.
Biography: Born 1932, Winnipeg, Manitoba. Languages: English, Russian and Ukrainian. Conductor, Vancouver Pro Musica Art Ensemble; Capilano Symphony Orchestra; recording sessions for NFB films. Teaches music composition, counterpoint, harmony, Capilano College, 86; has scored many college and community TV productions.
Selected Filmography: *Dead Wrong*, Th, 81, CDN, Comp.

LAING, Alan R.
GCFC. P.O. Box 1772, St. Mary's, ON N0M 2V0 (519)284-1942.
Type of Production and Credits: TV Film-Comp; TV Video-Comp.
Genres: Drama-Th&TV.
Biography: Born 1937. Languages: English and working knowledge of French. Has composed scores for dramatic production (theatre, TV) in Canada and USA. Former actor, director, conductor, concert recitalist; plays 10 instruments professionally; has had a long association with the Stratford Festival.
Selected Filmography: *Cat's Play*, TV, 77, CDN, Comp; "A Gift to Last", TV, 76, CDN, Comp.

LANCETT, Anthony J.
- see SOUND EDITORS

LANCTOT, François
GDMQ. 508, rue Pine, Saint-Lambert, PQ J4P 2P3 (514) 923-2326.
Types de production et générique: l métrage-Comp; c métrage-Comp; TV film-Comp; TV vidéo-Comp.
Types d'oeuvres: Drame-C; Variété-TV; Documentaire-TV; Industriel-TV.
Curriculum vitae: Né en 1954, Montréal, Québec. Carrière depuis 75; 3 longs métrages, multitude de vidéos industriels, arrangements pour spectacles de variétés de travail pour scène.
Filmographie sélective: *La Poursuite du bonheur*, C, 87, CDN, Comp; *Playback*, TV, 86, CDN, Comp; *Sonatine*, C, 82, CDN, Comp; *L'Homme à tout faire*, C, 79, CDN, Comp.

LANGLOIS, Jérôme
CAPAC. 5316, rue Fabre, Montréal, PQ H2J 3W5 (514)527-6905. Les Productions Molignar inc., 1599A, rue Panet, Montréal, PQ H2L 2Z4 (514)522-2339.
Types de production et générique: l métrage-Comp; c métrage-Comp; TV film-Comp; TV vidéo-Comp.
Types d'oeuvres: Drame-C&TV; Comédie musicale-C&TV; Documentaire-C&TV; Animation-TV.
Curriculum vitae: Né en 1952, Providence, Rhode Island; citoyenneté canadienne. Langues: français et anglais. Cours classique, Conservatoire de musique, Montréal; cours privés de composition avec André Prévost; contrepoint, harmonie avec Jacques Faubert. Fondateur, compositeur principal du groupe Lasting Weep, 68-72, et de Maneige, 72-76; a enregistré 2 microsillons. Depuis 76, a joué ses compositions en concert à plusieurs reprises; écrit pour la danse, le théâtre et la chanson. 1984, *Thèmes*, album de piano solo.
Filmographie sélective: "G. Tout vu Reporter" (26 eps), TV, 91, CDN, Mus orig; *20 décembre*, C, 89-90, CDN, Mus orig; *Le Grand Remous*, TV, 88, CDN, Comp; *C'est pas toujours du cinéma*, ED, 87, CDN, Comp; "The Adventures of Albert and Sidney" (150 eps), TV, 86, CDN/USA, Comp; "Les Gnomes" (24 eps), TV, 86, USA, Arr; *Visage pâle*, C, 85, CDN/J, Comp; *Le Film d'Ariane/Petites*

Cruantes/La Terapene, "Petits Contes cruels", TV, 84, CDN, Comp; "Les Arts: Clarence Gagnon" (3 eps), TV, 84, CDN, Comp; *Les Enfants des normes post scriptum*, TV, 83, CDN, Comp.

LAUBER, Anne
GDMQ, LCC. 372A ouest, Fairmount, Montréal, PQ H2V 2G4 (514)279-7992.
Types de production et générique: l métrage-Comp; c métrage-Comp.
Types d'oeuvres: Drame-C&TV; Comedy-C&TV; Documentaire-C&TV; Enfants-C&TV.
Curriculum vitae: Née en 1943, Zurich, Suisse; citoyenneté canadienne depuis 72. Doctorat en Musique, Faculté de Mus. de l'Université de Montréal. Plus de 35 oeuvres créées pour tous genres d'instruments d'orchestre, solistes et orchestres, musique de chambre, musique de film. Subventions reçues: Ministère des Affaires Culturelles du Québec, Conseil des Arts du Canada.
Filmographie sélective: *Les Terribles Vivantes*, TV, 89, CDN, Comp; *Marie Uguay*, TV, 86, CDN, Comp; *Louky Bersianick*, TV, 86, CDN, Comp; *Nicole Brassard*, TV, 86, CDN, Comp; *Jovette Marchessault*, TV, 86, CDN, Comp; *L'Affaire Coffin*, C, 79-80, CDN, Comp/Chef d'orch.

LEGRADY, Thomas ✧
(416)494-9306.
Type of Production and Credits: TV Film-Comp; TV Video-Comp.
Genres: Comedy-TV; Variety-TV; Musical-Th&TV; Documentary-Th&TV.
Biography: Born 1920, Budapest, Hungary; Canadian citizenship. Languages: English, French, German and Hungarian. Ph.D., Political Science; Master's, Music Composition and Orchestra Direction. First Prize in Canadian Composition Competition, 64; OMTA Award as Music Director, 85. Four band compositions published in Canada by Gordon Thompson, one by Chappell; five in The Netherlands by Molinara.
Selected Filmography: "Frontrunners" (1 eps), TV, 85, CDN, Comp/Cond; *Charlie Grant's War*, TV, 84, CDN, Comp/Cond; "A la romance" (39 eps), TV, 56-59, CDN, Arr; *Sunshine and Eclipse*, Th, 56, CDN, Comp; *They Saw London*, ED, 56, H, Comp; *Aggtelek*, ED, 55, H, Comp; *The Blood*, ED, 54, H, Comp; *Agrolszakadt Urilany*, Th, 46, H, Arr.

MacDONALD, Brad
25 Janellan Ter., West Hill, ON M1E 3M8 (416)282-0170. Brad MacDonald Music, 151 John St., #505, Toronto, ON M5V 2T2 (416)348-8901.
Type of Production and Credits: TV Film-Comp; TV Video-Comp.
Genres: Documentary-TV; Commercials-TV; News-TV; Sports-TV.
Biography: Born 1950. Professional composer/musician with classical and pop experience.
Selected Filmography: "My Secret Identity" (24 eps), TV, 90-91, CDN/USA, Comp; *It's Everywhere You Want to Be*, Visa (6 cm), Cm, 90, CDN, Comp/Prod; "Man Alive" (26 eps), TV, 89, CDN, Comp; "the fifth estate" (26 eps), TV, 89, CDN, Comp; "CBC News Saturday Report" (26 eps), TV, 88, CDN, Comp; "Commander Crumbcake" (13 eps), TV, 87, CDN, Comp; "Peter Ustinov's Russia" (6 eps), TV, 86, CDN, Comp; "CBC News Sunday Report", TV, 86, CDN, Comp; "Wonderstruck" (26 eps), TV, 85, CDN, Comp; "Hockey Night in Canada", TV, 84, CDN, Comp.

MANNE, Lewis
ACCT. Zap Productions Limited, 118 Granby St., Toronto, ON M5B 1J1 (416)598-3103.
Type of Production and Credits: TV Film-Comp; TV Video-Comp.
Genres: Drama-Th&TV; Documentary-Th&TV; Educational-Th&TV; Children's-Th&TV.
Selected Filmography: "Degrassi High" (28 eps), TV, 89-91, CDN, Comp; "Home Studies" (140 eps), TV, 90-91, CDN, Comp; "Speaking Out" (weekly), TV, 90-91, CDN, Comp; Toys 'R' Us, Cm, 91, CDN, Comp; Youthline (4 cm), Cm, 91, CDN, Comp; Terry Fox Run (2 cm), CM, 89-90, CDN, Comp; "School Works" (6 eps), TV, 90, CDN, Comp; TVO Promo, Cm, 90, CDN, Comp; *Canadian Science Fair*, In, 90, CDN, Comp; "Degrassi Junior High" (26 eps), TV, 86-88, CDN, Comp; "The Kids of Degrassi Street" (26 eps), TV, 83-85, CDN, Comp.

McCARTHY, John
AFM. 594 Queen St. W., Ste. 1, Toronto, ON M6J 1E3 (416)369-0684.
Type of Production and Credits: Th Short-Comp; TV Film-Comp/Lyr; TV Video-Comp/Lyr.
Genres: Drama-TV; Documentary-Th&TV; Industrial-Th&TV; Commercials-TV.
Biography: Born 1961, Toronto, Ontario. Attended Humber College (composition and performance); Royal Conservatory of Music. Studied flute with Anthony

Antonacci, Sam Baron (Julliard School of Music). Performer, composer, producer. Toured and recorded with numerous acts which include: Frozen Ghost, Ian Hunter, Wild T Springer and But I'm Just a Kid. "Born Talking" received a Bronze award for Best Documentary at the Houston International Film & TV Festival, 1991.
Selected Filmography: *R.S.V.P.*, Th, 91, CDN, Comp; "Born Talking" (4 eps), TV, 90, CDN/GB/AUS, Comp; "Vision of Victory" (7 eps), In, 90, CDN, Comp/Lyr; *A Coca-Cola Day*, In, 90, Cdn, Comp; *On Our Own*, TV, 90, CDN, Comp/Lyr; *Lifestyles of the 90's*, Cm, 91, USA, Comp.

McKEOWN, Terence
AFM. Insert Music Ltd., 811 Duplex Ave., Apt. B, Toronto, ON M4R 1W6 (416)487-3521.
Type of Production and Credits: Th Film-Comp/Snd Rec; TV Film-Comp/Snd Rec; TV Video-Comp/Snd Rec.
Genres: Documentary-Th&TV; Educational-Th&TV; Current Affairs-TV; Sports-TV.
Biography: Born in 1952 in Ottawa, Ontario. Canadian citizen. 12 years as a performing musician playing guitar, bass, keyboards and saxophone. 7 years as a record producer, arranger, songwriter, studio musician and engineer. Working in film and television since 1985 as a composer, music supervisor and sound recordist. Two Gemini nominations in 1990. Extensive experience in negotiating, publishing and composer agreements and all aspects of music rights acquisitions.
Selected Filmography: "Millennium: Tribal Wisdom and the Modern World" (10 eps), TV, 91, CDN/GB/USA, Mus Spv/Snd Rec; *Hockey Night in Hollywood*, TV, 91, CDN, Comp Theme; "the fifth estate" (weekly), TV, 90, CDN, Comp Theme; *Strangers in a Strange Land*, TV, 90, CDN, Comp/Snd Rec; "Ken Dryden's Home Game" (5 eps), TV, 90, CDN, Snd Rec; "Medical Video Library" (120 eps), TV, 89, CDN, Comp/Snd Rec; *The Boys on the Bus*, TV, 88, CDN, Comp/Snd Rec; *Les Canadiens*, TV, 86, CDN, Comp.

MILLS-COCKELL, John ✦
(416)762-1360.
Type of Production and Credits: Th Film-Comp; Th Short-Comp; TV Film-Comp; TV Video-Comp.
Genres: Drama-Th&TV; Action-Th; Horror-Th&TV.
Biography: Born 1943, Toronto, Ontario. Attended Royal Conservatory, Faculty of Music, University of Toronto; won the BMI student composer award. Fifty percent of his work has been in conventional media; also specialist in electronic music with an interest in science fiction; has recorded often in Europe and the US.
Selected Filmography: "The Little Vampire" (13 eps), TV, 85, CDN/GB/D, Comp/Cond; *Half a Lifetime*, TV, 85, CDN, Comp; *Striker's Mountain*, TV, 85, CDN, Comp/Cond; *Labour of Love*, TV, 84, CDN, Comp/Cond; *Maggie and Pierre*, TV, 84, CDN, Comp; *Moving Targets*, "For the Record", TV, 83, CDN, Comp; *Snow*, Th, 83, CDN, Comp; *Gongga Shan: White Peak Beyond the Clouds*, TV, 82, CDN, Comp; *Challenge: The Canadian Rockies*, TV, 82, CDN, Comp/Cond; "Ark on the Move" (13 eps), TV, 81, CDN/GB, Comp/Cond; *Humongous*, Th, 81, CDN, Comp; *The Italians*, "The Newcomers", TV, 81, CDN, Comp, (CFTA); "Cities" (4 eps), TV, 80, CDN, Comp/Cond; *Terror Train*, Th, 79, CDN/USA, Comp/Cond; *Deadly Harvest*, Th, 76, CDN, Comp.

MOLLIN, Fred
ACTRA, AFM, ACCT. c/o It's Been Real Inc., 3876 Chesswood Dr., Downsview, ON M3J 2W6 (416)630-7150. FAX: 630-7157.
Type of Production and Credits: Th Film-Comp; Th Short-Comp; TV Film-Comp; TV Video-Comp.
Genres: Drama-Th&TV; Comedy-Th&TV; Musical-Th&TV; Children's-Th&TV.
Biography: Born 1953, New York; landed immigrant Canada. Has composed music for numerous films and TV series and has produced albums and individual recordings. Three Juno awards, a Genie nomination, 83, for *Spring Fever* and more than 25 gold and platinum albums.
Selected Filmography: "Sweating Bullets", TV, 91, CDN/USA, Comp/Perf; *Whispers*, Th, 90, CDN/USA, Comp/Perf; "My Secret Identity" (48 eps), TV, 88-90, CDN/USA, Comp; "Friday the 13th, The Series" (72 eps), TV, 87-90, CDN/USA, Comp; *Friday the 13th, Part VIII*, Th, 89, USA, Comp/Perf; *Friday the 13th, Part VII*, Th, 88, USA, Comp/Perf; *Skeleton*, "Ray Bradbury Theatre" (1 eps), TV, 88, CDN/USA/GB/F, Comp/Perf; "The New Gidget" (40 eps-2 seasons), TV, 86-88, USA, Comp; *Hanoi Hilton*,Th, 87, USA, (title song and score producer), "Ramona" (10 eps), TV, 87, CDN/USA, Comp; *The Incredible Ida Early*, TV, 87, USA, Comp/Perf; "It's Only Rock 'n' Roll" (14

eps), TV, 87, CDN, Mus Dir/Co-Host; *Read Between the Lines*, TV, 87, USA, Comp/Perf; "Airwaves" (13 eps), TV, 86-87, CDN, Comp; *Family Reunion*, TV, 87, CDN, Comp/Perf.

MOORE, James
- see EDITORS

MORLEY, Glenn
AFM, GCFC, ACCT. 100 Manor Rd. E., Toronto, ON M4S 1P8 (416)929-9324. Tambre Productions, 250 The Esplanade, 100 The Mill, Toronto, ON M5A 1J2 (416)367-9797. FAX: 367-9803.
Type of Production and Credits: Th Film-Comp; TV Film-Comp; TV Video-Comp.
Genres: Drama-Th&TV; Comedy-Th&TV; Documentary-TV; Educational-TV.
Biography: Born Toronto, Ontario. Languages: English, French and Spanish. B.F.A., York University. Partner in Morley/Shragge Multi Media Music; extensive theatrical work as composer and musical director; approximately 85 productions in Canada and internationally; musical and technical director for York's graduate program in Theatre, 75-76; lecturer in Musical Theatre, George Brown College, 79-81; numerous concert works performed by Toronto Symphony, National Arts Centre Orchestra, and other major orchestras; composer, orchestrator, arranger for numerous jingles and record projects; music director on live extravaganzas: Bicentennial Showcase, Mitchener Gala and various industrial showcases.
Selected Filmography: *Farther West*, "Stage on Screen", TV, 91, CDN, Comp; "Little Rosey" (13 eps), TV, 90, CDN/USA, Comp; "Road to Avonlea" (13 eps), TV, 89-90, CDN/USA, Cond/Orch; *Looking for Miracles*, TV, 89, CDN, Cond/Orch; "The Nature of Things", TV, 79-89, CDN, Theme Comp; "Inside Stories" (7 eps), TV, 88, CDN, Comp; *Without a Clue/Sherlock and Me*, Th, 88, USA, Mus Prod; "The Campbells" (100 eps), TV, 85-88, CDN/USA/GB, Comp,(GEMINI 87, GEMINI 86); *Hooked on Reading*, "Parents and Reading" (6 eps), TV, 86, CDN, Co-Comp; *The Exile*, TV, 85, CDN, Co-Comp; *One Magic Christmas*, Th, 85, CDN, Co-Comp; "Spirit Bay" (7 eps), TV, 84-85, CDN, Co-Comp; "Home Fires" (31 eps), TV, 80-83, CDN, Co-Comp; *Coming Out Alive*, TV, 81, CDN, Co-Comp; *The KGB Connections*, TV, 81, CDN, Co-Comp.

NATALE, Louis
ACTRA, AFM, ACCT. 111 Pine Glen Rd., Toronto, ON M4E 1K8 (416)698-4409. Natale Music Inc., 400 King St. E., Toronto, ON M5A 1L4 (416) 867-8888. FAX: 867-9040.
Type of Production and Credits: Th Film-Comp; Th Short-Comp; TV Film-Comp; TV Video-Comp.
Genres: Drama-Th&TV; Comedy-Th&TV; Science Fiction-TV; Commercials-TV.
Biography: Born 1950, Rochester, New York; landed immigrant Canada. B.A., English and Philosophy, Univ. of Toronto, 72. Composer, arranger, songwriter, music producer. 10 years as a jingle writer on a wide variety of national accounts, including Pepsi, Coke, IBM, Chrysler, Xerox, 3M, GM, Bell, Procter & Gamble, and Neilson's. Has won 72 national and international awards, including 9 Clios, 3 Andies, 8 at the International Radio Festival of New York, and 3 at the London International Advertising Awards; Genie, Best Original Song, for [Cowboys Don't Cry].
Selected Filmography: *The Girl from Mars* (movie & 5 eps), TV, 91, CDN, Comp; *Murmurs*, TV, 91, CDN, Comp; "Maniac Mansion" (22 eps), TV, 90-91, CDN, Comp; *Journey into Darkness: The Bruce Curtis Story*, TV, 90, CDN, Comp; *Clarence* (movie & 4 eps), TV, 90, CDN, Comp; "Ray Bradbury Theatre" (8 eps), TV, 90, CDN/USA, Mus Dir; *Christmas in America*, TV, 89, USA, Comp; *Tom Alone*, "Magic Hour", TV, 89, CDN, Comp; *The Long Road Home*, Th, 89, CDN, Comp; "The Twilight Zone" (10 eps), TV, 88-89, CDN/USA, Comp; "Alfred Hitchcock Presents" (1 eps), TV, 88, CDN/USA, Comp; *Cowboys Don't Cry*, Th, 88, CDN, Comp, (GENIE); *The Emissary*, "Ray Bradbury Theatre", TV, 87, CDN/USA, Comp; *A Child's Christmas in Wales*, TV, 87, CDN, Comp; "Vulcan" (pilot), TV, 86, CDN, Comp.

NAYLOR, Steven J.
GCFC. P.O. Box 3731, Halifax S., NS B3J 3K6 (902)826-1435. FAX: 826-1435.
Type of Production and Credits: TV Film-Comp; TV Video-Comp; Th Film-Comp; Th Short-Comp.
Genres: Drama-TV; Documentary-Th&TV; Children's-TV; Educational-Th&TV.
Biography: Born 1949, Woodstock, Ontario. B.A., English, Waterloo Lutheran University, 69; B.Independent Studies, Music, University of Waterloo, 73; studies in composition, film

composition, electronic music; various grants and scholarships. Active in concert and theatre music, music production; special interest in folklore and world music. Film/TV credits since 74. Recent awards include: Association for MultiImage, Canada - Gold Award, *Kouchibouguac*, 86; Silver Award, *When Continents Collide*, 91; Bronze Award, *A Wonderful Fine Coast*, 91.
Selected Filmography: "Sesame Street" (sev segs), TV, 85-91, CDN, Comp/Mus Prod; *A Wonderful Fine Coast*, ED, 90, CDN, Comp/Mus Prod; *Who's Lookin After My Forests?*, ED, 89, CDN, Comp/Mus Prod; *When Continents Collide*, ED, 89, CDN, Comp/Mus Prod; *Rivers to the Sea*, "The Nature of Things", TV, 88, CDN, Comp/Mus Prod; *Smokedown/Hero of the Family/The Oatman*, "The Way We Are", TV, 86-88, CDN, Comp/Mus Prod; *Ballad of South Mountain*, TV, 86, CDN, Comp/Mus Prod; *A New World Below*, TV, 86, CDN, Comp/Mus Prod; *The Lamplighter*, TV, 86, CDN, Comp/Mus Prod; *The Last Log Drive*, TV, 85, CDN, Comp/Mus Prod; *Kouchibouguac*, ED, 85, CDN, Comp/Mus Prod; *The Job*, TV, 85, CDN, Comp/Mus Prod; *Don Connolly's Halifax*, "Cityscapes", TV, 84, CDN, Comp/Mus Prod.

NIMMONS, Phil ✧
(416)889-9980.
Type of Production and Credits: Th Film-Comp; Th Short-Comp; TV Film-Comp.
Genres: Drama-Th&TV; Variety-TV; Musical-Th&TV; Documentary-Th&TV.
Biography: Born 1923, Kamloops, BC. B.A., University of British Columbia; Julliard School of Music, NY; Composition, Royal Conservatory of Music, U. of T. Co-founder, teacher, Advanced School of Contemporary Music, Toronto, 60-63. Composer of contemporary classical works for piano, strings; over 400 original jazz compositions; radio and stage plays; has recorded 10 albums; band leader, Nimmons 'n' Nine; composer for numerous TV series and specials, 69-70. Has won many awards including BMI, 68, Juno, 76, PRO Canada, 80; received Toronto Arts Award, 86.
Selected Filmography: *The Trojan Women*, Th, 78, CDN, Comp/Arr; *Power by Proxy*, TV, 60, CDN, Comp/Arr; *A Cool Sound from Hell*, Th, 59, CDN, Comp/Arr; *A Dangerous Age*, Th, 56, CDN, Comp/Arr.

O'FARRELL, Marc ✧
(514)670-9870.
Types de production et générique: l métrage-Comp; TV film-Comp.
Types d'oeuvres: Drame-C; Comédie-C; Documentaire-C; Annonces-C&TV.
Curriculum vitae: Né en 1943. Quinze ans d'expérience comme musicien (guitariste) de studio. Diverses tournées au Canada, en Europe, aux Antilles avec chanteurs, chanteuses, groupes folkloriques.
Filmographie sélective: *Qui a tiré sur nos histoires d'amour?*, C, 85, CDN, Comp; *Le Choix d'un peuple*, C, 80, CDN, Comp/Arr; *Ça peut pas être l'hiver, on n'a même pas eu d'été*, C, 79, CDN, Comp.

OUELLET, Gilles
AFM. 3525 Chemin Royal, Ile d'Orléans, Ste-Famille, PQ G0A 3P0 (418)829-3564.
Types de production et générique: c métrage-Comp; TV vidéo-Comp.
Types d'oeuvres: Drame-TV; Variété-TV; Affaires Publiques-TV; Nouvelles-TV.
Curriculum vitae: Naissance: Amos, Québec. Citoyenneté canadienne. Langues: anglais, français. Expériences: Depuis 1976, directeur musical (à la pige) à la télévision (Radio Canada, TM, TQS). Expérience en orchestrations symphoniques (directeur du Pop Philharmonique de la Capitale).
Filmographie sélective: *Sur la rue Tabaga*, TV, 90, CDN, Arr; *Fierro/L'été des secrets*, C, 90, CDN, Orch; *Symphonique and Roll/Diane Dufresne*, TV, 90, J/NHK, Orch/Dir mus; *Le P'tit Champlain*, TV, 90, CDN, Dir mus; *C'est à ton tour*, TV, 90, CDN, Dir mus; *Johanne Blouin/Festival d'été*, TV, 90, CDN, Orch; *Première Ligne*, TV, 89, CDN, Comp; *Céline Dion*, TV, 89, CDN, Orch; *Symphonique and Roll/Diane Dufresne*, TV, 88, CDN, Orch/Dir mus; *Cap espoir*, C, 86, CDN, Comp; *Le Monde (Pathonic)/Nouvelles*, TV, 86, CDN, Comp; *Vivre A*, TV, 85, CDN, Comp; *Action Débat*, TV, 84, CDN, Comp.

PAABO, Iris
- see DIRECTORS

POLGAR, Tibor
GCFC. 21 Vaughan Rd., #1903, Toronto, ON M6G 2N2 (416)654-7835.
Type of Production and Credits: Th Film-Comp; Th Short-Comp; TV Film-Comp; TV Video-Comp.
Genres: Drama-Th&TV; Musical-Th&TV; Documentary-Th&TV; Educational-Th&TV.
Biography: Born Budapest, Hungary; Canadian citizenship. Languages: English,

German and Hungarian. Attended Humanistic Gymnasium; studied Philosophy at university. Head of the Music Department and conductor of the Hungarian Radio Symphony Orchestra for 25 years; has composed music for stage and scores for 200 Hungarian films (features, documentaries, cartoons); in Canada, has worked for CBC Radio and TV; has also written music for films and commercials. Awarded Senior Arts Fellowships by the Canada Council, 66 and 67.
Selected Filmography: *In Praise of Older Women,* Th, 77, CDN, Comp; *The House on Front Street,* Th, 77, CDN, Comp; *Energy,* ED, 76, CDN, Comp; *The Cutty Stool,* TV, 76, CDN, Comp; *The Glove,* TV, 75, CDN, Comp; *Dracula,* TV, 75, CDN, Comp.

QUAN, Donald
AFM 149, ACCT. Q Music Productions, 104 Greenwood Ave., Toronto, ON M4L 2P6 (416)462-0400.
Type of Production and Credits: Th Film-Mus Ed; Th Short-Comp/Mus Ed; TV Film-Comp/Mus Ed; TV Video-Comp/Mus Ed.
Genres: Drama-Th&TV; Children's-TV; Animation-TV; Sports-TV.
Biography: Born 1962, Toronto, Ontario. Canadian and U.S. citizenship. Bachelor of Music degree from Berklee College of Music, Boston. Specialist in ethnic/world musics. Also a studio synthesist for film scores, commercials etc. Released a Canadian Top 10 New Age/World CD, "Tear of the Sun" on Oasis Records. Member of the rock group, Eye Eye (Duke Street Records).
Selected Filmography: "Children's Animation Workshop" (3 eps), TV, 89-91, CDN, Comp; "Street Legal" (32 eps), TV, 89-91, CDN, Mus Ed; "E.N.G." (44 eps), TV, 89-91, CDN, Mus Ed; *The People's Accord,* "W5", TV, 91, CDN, Comp; "Road to Avonlea", TV, 89-91, CDN, Mus Ed; "Ray Bradbury Theatre" (3 eps), TV, 90, CDN/USA/NZ, Co Comp; *Clearcut,* Th, 90, CDN, Mus Ed/Orch; *True Confections,* Th, 90, CDN, Mus Ed; *Arctic Quest Video,* In, 90, CDN, Comp; "Canadian Football Network" (120 eps), TV, 86-90, CDN, Comp; "My Secret Identity" (24 eps), TV, 90, CDN/USA, Mus Ed; *Imax Promo Video,* In, 89, CDN, Mus Ed/Comp.

RAINE-REUSCH, Randy
AFM. Box 1119, Stn. A, Vancouver, BC V6C 2T1 (604)255-2506.
Type of Production and Credits: Th Short-Comp.
Genres: Documentary-Th; Educational-Th; Experimental-Th.
Biography: Born 1952, Halifax, Nova Scotia. Composes and performs on over 500 traditional instruments; specialist in ethnic and world music. *Solus* won an award at the New York Dance and Film Festival; Best Film in its class, Chicago Film Festival.
Selected Filmography: *Building the Mosaic,* TV, 88, CDN, Comp; *Salt Water City,* TV, 87, CDN, Co-Comp; *Kangaroos Under Fire,* Th, 85, CDN, Comp; *Solus,* Th, 84, CDN, Co-Comp; *River of Ice,* Th, 82, CDN, Co-Comp; *The Long Fist,* Th, 81, CDN, Comp.

RATHBURN, Eldon
545 St. Laurent Blvd., #305, Ottawa, ON (613)745-9340. 545 St. Laurent Blvd., #2006, Ottawa, ON (613)744-3729.
Type of Production and Credits: Th Film-Comp; Th Short-Comp; TV Film-Comp.
Genres: Drama-Th&TV; Documentary-Th&TV; Animation-Th&TV.
Biography: Born 1916, Queenstown, New Brunswick. Staff composer, NFB, 47-76. Studied with Healey Willan at the Royal Conservatory. Recordings: *Labyrinthe* (Expo 67), *The Metamorphic Ten - Canadian Brass Rag;* composed *Rise and Fall of the Steam Railroad - Turbo-Junction; Six Railroad Preludes; Apparition* and *The Iron Horses of Delson.* Won the Los Angeles Young Artist Award, 44, New concert work: *Trio* ("Dorion Crossing").
Selected Filmography: *The Creative Process,* ED, 90, CDN, Comp; *The First Emperor* (Imax), Th, 89, CDN/RC, Comp; *The Last Buffalo* (Imax), Th, 89, CDN/J, Comp; *Beavers* (Imax), Th, 88, CDN, Comp; *The Defender,* TV, 88, CDN, Comp; "The King Chronicle" (3 eps), TV, 88, CDN, Comp; *Final Chapter,* "The Champions", TV, 86, CDN, Comp; *Transitions,* Th, 85-86, CDN, Comp; *Canada's Sweetheart: The Saga of Hal C. Banks,* TV, 85, CDN, Comp; *J.W. Morrice,* Th, 85, CDN, Comp; *Skyward,* Th, 84, CDN, Comp; *I Like to See the Wheels Turn,* TV, 81, CDN, Comp; *Who Has Seen the Wind,* Th, 76, CDN, Comp; *For Gentlemen Only,* TV, 76, CDN, Comp; *The Hecklers,* TV, 76, CDN, Comp.

ROBERTSON, Eric N.
AFM. 34 Westmount Park Rd., Weston, ON M9P 1R6 (416)245-3151.
Type of Production and Credits: Th Film-comp; TV Film-Comp; TV Video-Comp.

Genres: Drama-Th&TV; Science Fiction-Th; Horror-Th; Documentary-Th&TV.
Biography: Born 1948; British citizenship, landed immigrant status in Canada. Has scored numerous theatrical and TV films and written hundreds of TV and radio jingles; record producer and keyboardist. Recipient of many awards including BMI Harold Moon Film Award, Juno award, several Gemini nominations, a triple platinum record and over two dozen gold and platinum records for work as a solo artist or producer.
Selected Filmography: *Tall in the Saddle*, TV, 91, CDN, Comp/Mus; "OWL Television", ED, 91, CDN/UK, Comp/Mus; "Sweating Bullets", TV, 91, CDN/USA, Comp/Mus; "Tommy Hunter Show", TV, 90-91, CDN, Arr/Mus Dir; "Street Legal" (38 eps), TV, 86-91, CDN, Comp/Mus; "Ken Dryden's Home Game" (6 eps), TV, 90, CDN, Comp/Mus; *Ice Princess*, TV, 90, USA/CDN, Comp/Mus; *Love and Hate*, TV, 89, CDN, Comp/Mus; *The Challengers*, TV, 89, CDN, Comp/Mus; *Getting Married in Buffalo Jump*, TV, 89, CDN, Comp/Mus; *The Greening of Ian Elliot*, TV, 89, CDN, Comp/Mus; *Muppet Christmas Specials*, TV, 88/89, CDN/USA, Comp/Mus; *Millenium*, Th, 88, CDN/USA, Comp/Mus; *Lighthouse Island*, TV, 88, USA, Comp/Mus; *If You Could See What I Hear*, Th, 82, CDN, Comp.

SEREDA, John
1763 E. Pender, Suite 202, Vancouver, BC V5L 1W5 (604)253-3998.
Type of Production and Credits: Th Film-Comp; TV Film-Comp; TV Video-Comp.
Genres: Drama-Th&TV; Musical-TV; Documentary-Th&TV; Animation-Th&TV.
Biography: Born 1953, Alberta. Performer/composer/producer. Active in film, TV, theatre, recordings, concerts. Music and lyrics for award-winning *Sex Tips for Modern Girls*; Jesse award for Outstanding Original Score, *The Mystery of Irma Vep*.
Selected Filmography: *In Search of the Dragon*, TV, 91, CDN, Comp; *Bicycle Ladies*, TV, 90, CDN, Comp; *Attack of the Grizzly*, Th, 90, CDN, Comp; *Abbott*, TV, 89, CDN, Comp; *Down to Earth*, TV, 89, CDN, Comp; *Dinosaur*, TV, 89, CDN, Comp; *Empire of Ash III*, Th, 88, CDN, Comp; *Land of Fire & Ice*, TV, 88, CDN, Comp; *Empire of Ash II*, Th, 87, CDN, Comp; *Conveyor Madness*, TV, 85, CDN, Comp.

SHORE, Howard
AFM, ACCT. 1619 Broadway, 9th Flr., New York, NY 10019 (212)265-7621. Brian Gersh, Triad Artists, (213)556-2727.
Type of Production and Credits: Th Film-Comp.
Genres: Drama-Th.
Biography: Born 1946, Toronto, Ontario. Attended Berklee College of Music, Boston.
Selected Filmography: *A Kiss Before Dying*, Th, 91, USA/GB, Comp; *The Silence of the Lambs*, Th, 90, USA, Comp; *Postcards From the Edge*, Th, 90, USA, Mus Spv; *An Innocent Man*, Th, 90, USA, Comp; *She-Devil*, Th, 89, USA, Comp; *Dead Ringers*, Th, 88, CDN, Comp; *Big*, Th, 88, USA, Comp; *Nadine*, Th, 87, USA, Comp; *The Fly*, Th, 86, USA, Comp; *Places in the Heart*, Th, 85, USA, Mus Prod; *After Hours*, Th, 85, USA, Comp; *Videodrome*, Th, 81, CDN, Comp; "Saturday Night Live" (121 eps), TV, 75-80, USA, Comp; *Scanners*, Th, 79, CDN, Comp; *The Brood*, Th, 78, CDN, Comp.

SHRAGGE, Lawrence
925 - 14th St., #28, Santa Monica, CA 90403 (213)393-7831.
Type of Production and Credits: Th Film-Comp/Mus Spv; Th Short-Comp/Mus Spv; TV Film-Comp/Mus Spv; TV Video-Comp/Mus Spv.
Genres: Drama-Th&TV; Comedy-Th&TV; Musical-Th&TV; Action-Th&TV; Science Fiction-Th&TV; Horror-Th&TV; Documentary-Th&TV; Educational-Th&TV; Children's-Th&TV; Animation-Th&TV.
Biography: Born 1954, Montreal, Quebec. Attended Berklee College of Music, Eastman School of Music. "The Campbells" won Gemini, 86 and Gemini, 87; "Inside Stories" won Golden Sheaf award, 89.
Selected Filmography: "Street Justice" (22 eps), TV, 91, CDN, Comp; "Parker Lewis Can't Lose" (3 eps), TV, 90, USA, Comp; "Generations" (200 eps), TV, 90, USA, Comp; *Beautiful Dreamers*, Th, 89, CDN, Comp; *Palais Royale*, Th, 89, CDN, Comp; *Brown Bread Sandwiches*, Th, 89, CDN, Co-Comp; "Inside Stories" (7 eps), TV, 88-89, CDN, Co-Comp; "The Campbells" (100 eps), TV, 85-88, CDN/USA/GB, Co-Comp, (GEMINI 87, 86); *Dance for Modern Times*, Th, 88, CDN, Co-Comp; *One Night Only*, Th, 87, CDN, Comp; "Spirit Bay" (13 eps), TV, 85-86, CDN, Co-Comp; *A Case of Libel*, TV, 84, CDN, Co-Comp; "Home Fires" (31 eps), TV, 83-88, CDN, Co-Comp; *KGB Connections*, TV, 81, CDN,

Co-Comp; *Firebird 2015 AD*, Th, 80, CDN, Comp.

SIMON, Marty
AFM, ACTRA, CARAS, SCL(L.A.). Mars Music Corp., 111 Chatillon Dr., Dollard des Ormeaux, PQ H9B 1B4 (514)685-1717. Seth Caplan, Derek Power/The Derek Power Co., 127 Broadway, Santa Monica, CA 90401 (213)395-1077, 394-1221.
Type of Production and Credits: Th Film-Comp; TV Film-Comp; TV Video-Comp.
Genres: Drama-Th&TV; Action-Th&TV; Science Fiction-Th&TV; Children's-Th&TV.
Biography: Born in 1950 in Montreal, Quebec. Attended McGill Faculty of Music, majoring in piano and drums. As keyboardist, drummer and arranger, worked in New York, Atlanta, London and Paris on sessions with Jimmy Page, Donovan, Mick Jagger, Wilson Pickett and Brian Eno among others during the 70s. In the 80s, became record producer and Music Director for Quebec superstars Diane Dufresne and Robert Charlebois. Won 2 Anik Awards for 'Follement Votre' L.P. (Diane Dufresne) and 4 Felix awards as Music Director for Live Show of the Year in 1983, 84, 85 and 87. In 1987, began current career as composer, arranger and performer of film and TV scores. Composed the original song for *Lionheart*. *George's Island* won (General) First Prize, 1990, Chicago Children's Feature Film Festival.
Selected Filmography: *Scanners III*, Th, 92, CDN, Comp; "Urban Angel" (9 eps), TV, 91-92, CDN, Comp; *Scanners II - The New Order*, Th, 91, CDN, Comp; *Lionheart*, Th, 91, USA, Comp; "Urban Angel" (6 eps), TV, 91, CDN, Comp; *Deadly Surveillance*, Th, 91, CDN, Comp; *George's Island*, Th, 91, CDN, Comp; *Backstab*, Th, 90, CDN/USA, Comp; *The Ticket Back*, TV, 90, CDN, Comp; *Eddie and the Cruisers II - Eddie Lives*, Th, 89, USA, Comp; *The Wolf*, "The Predators" (1 eps), TV, 88, CDN, Comp; *The Squamish Five*, TV, 88, CDN, Comp; *And Then You Die*, TV, 87, CDN, Comp.

SKOLNIK, Bill ◊
(416)828-9594.
Type of Production and Credits: Th Film-Comp; Th Short-Comp; TV Film-Comp; TV Video-Comp.
Genres: Drama-Th&TV; Documentary-Th&TV; Educational-TV; Animation-TV.
Biography: Born 1950, Montreal, Quebec. Languages: English and French. B.A., Political Science, University of Toronto. Has worked for CBC, CTV, TVO, Global and PBS; has written more than 20 scores for radio drama; 3 published stage musicals; produced 2 recordings. Productions he has worked on have won several awards.
Selected Filmography: *You're No Bunny Till Some Bunny Loves You*, TV, 88, CDN, Comp/Arr; *Dead Ringers*, Th, 88, CDN, Mus Cons; "Sesame Street", TV, 86-87, CDN, Comp/Arr/Lyrics; *It Can't Be Done*, Th, 86, CDN, Comp/Arr; *Tales of the Mouse Hockey League*, TV, 86, CDN, Comp/Arr; *Industry in B.C./The Salmon Fishery*, ED, 86, CDN, Comp/Arr; *John and the Missus*, Th, 86, CDN, Mus Cons; *Canada Export Award Ceremony*, In, 86, CDN, Comp/Arr; "Sesame Street" (56 seg/lyrics-26 seg), TV, 83-85, USA, Comp/Arr; "Chalk Talk" (15 eps), TV, 84, CDN, Comp/Arr; *To Annedale and Back*, Th, 84, CDN, Comp/Arr; *Cowboys Don't Cry*, Th, 84, CDN, Comp/Arr; *My American Cousin*, Th, 84, CDN, Arr; *Seasons of the Mind*, Th, 82, CDN, Comp/Arr; *Petrocan*, In, 82, CDN, Comp/Arr.

SOLOMON, Maribeth
AFM 149, ACTRA, ACCT. Mickymar Productions Ltd., 86 McGill St., Toronto, ON M5B 1H2 (416)581-1400.
Type of Production and Credits: Th Film-Comp; Th Short-Comp; TV Film-Comp; TV Video-Comp.
Genres: Drama-Th&TV; Comedy-Th&TV; Musical-Th&TV; Documentary-Th&TV.
Biography: Born 1951, Toronto, Ontario. Attended York University, Royal Conservatory of Music for piano theory harmony; studied flute with Robert Aitken; harmony and composition with Gordon Delamont. Toured US and Canada extensively; wrote songs recorded by Anne Murray and others; has won Clios, radio and TV awards for commercials; 3 Genie nominations; produced for Juno award-winning recording artists; plays piano, synthesizers and flute.
Selected Filmography: *Blue Planet*, Imax, Th, 91, USA/CDN, Co Comp; "E.N.G." (44 eps), TV, 89-91, CDN, Co Comp; "Street Legal" (38 eps), TV, 89-91, CDN, Co Comp; *True Confections*, Th, 91, CDN, Co Comp; *African Journey*, Th/TV, 90, CDN/USA, Co Comp; *Babar The Movie*, Th, 90, CDN/USA, Comp (3 songs); *Bloodsport*, TV, 90, CDN/IR, Co Comp; "Struggle for Democracy" (10 eps),

TV, 89, USA/CDN/GB, Co Comp, (GEMINI); "The Twilight Zone" (2 eps), TV, 89, CDN/USA, Co Comp; "Adderly" (44 eps), TV, 88-89, USA/CDN, Co Comp, (GEMINI); "Alfred Hitchcock Presents" (11 eps), TV, 88-89, USA/CDN, Co Comp; *The Dream Is Alive*, Imax, Th, 86, CDN/USA, Co Comp; *Threshold*, Th, 80, CDN, Co Comp; *Ticket To Heaven*, Th, 80, CDN, Co Comp; *North of Superior*, Imax, Th, 71, CDN, Co Comp.

STRAUGHAN, Brent
GCFC, NABET. R.R. #1, Ashburn, ON L0B 1A0 (416)655-4867.
Type of Production and Credits: Th Short-Dir/Comp; TV Video-Ed.
Genres: Musical-Th; Current Affairs-TV; News-TV.
Biography: Born 1946, Edmonton, Alberta. B.Sc., Zoology, University of Washington, Seattle, 68; M.A., Communications, Simon Fraser University, 73. Entertainment editor (tape), CTV's "National News" and "Canada AM," 82-88. Has 2 albums, *Mama Plays the Golden Oldies* and *Enfilony*.
Selected Filmography: *Light's Edge*, National Ballet of Canada, TV, 90, CDN, Comp/Prod/Ed/Cam; "Canada AM" (daily), TV, 82-88, CDN, Ed; *Enfilony*, Th, 78, CDN, Comp/Dir/DOP.

STRONG, Philip ✧
(416)534-7464.
Type of Production and Credits: Th Film-Comp; TV Film-Comp; TV Video-Comp.
Genres: Drama-Th&TV; Action-Th&TV; Science Fiction-Th&TV; Horror-Th&TV.
Biography: Born 1963, England; Canadian citizenship.
Selected Filmography: *Chambers of Terror*, Th, 87, CDN, Comp; *Fight Back*, TV, 87, CDN, Comp; *Don't Turn Out the Light*, Th, 87, CDN, Comp.

TATE, Brian ✧
(604)228-1696.
Type of Production and Credits: TV Film-Comp/Prod; TV Video-Comp/Prod.
Genres: Variety-TV; Educational-TV; Industrial-TV.
Biography: Born 1954, Vancouver, BC. Studied Composition with Elliot Weisgarber, University of British Columbia; B.Mus., 76; with Sir Lennox Berkeley, London, 77. Assistant conductor, Hammersmith Symphony, Ariann Chamber Orchestra, Toronto, 79-81. Received several commissions for new works, including Toronto Symphony Brass Ensemble; conductor with Royal Conservatory's Training Program, Vancouver, 81. Music director/composer for musical theatre, film, radio drama, a/v, concert stage.
Selected Filmography: *The Legend of Sinter Klaas*, TV, 86, CDN, Comp/Mus Prod; "Take Part" (65 eps), TV, 86, CDN, Comp/Mus Prod; *The Great Divide*, "Landscape as History", ED, 85, CDN, Comp/Mus Prod; *Explorations in Mass Communications/Control Technologies*, In, 85, CDN, Comp/Mus Prod; "Mixed Company" (daily), TV, 85, CDN, Comp/Mus Prod; *Growing Up with Logo/Order from Chaos/Out of Harm's Way*, ED, 85, CDN, Comp/Mus Prod; "Hollywood Showcase" (pilot), TV, 84, USA, Comp/Mus Prod; "Venture Capital" (13 eps), TV, 84, CDN, Comp/Mus Prod; "Gerol" (pilot), TV, 84, CDN, Comp/Mus Prod; *Play, Gypsies*, TV, 83, CDN, Assist Mus Dir/Arr.

TROIANO, Domenic
AFM, ACCT. 48 Johnson St., Thornhill, ON L3T 2N7 (416)886-7489.
Type of Production and Credits: TV Film-Comp.
Genres: Drama-TV.
Biography: Born in Modugno, Italy; Canadian citizenship. Began career playing in bands including, Bush, Mandala, The James Gang, The Guess Who); work with bands included making albums and song-writing; released 5 solo albums; played guitar on records by Diana Ross, Joe Cocker, Donald Fagen, David Clayton Thomas, Etta James, Jean-Michel Jarré, Ronnie Hawkins, Three Dog Night, James Cotton and others; started doing film and TV work in 1984. Produced records for Shawne Jackson, Moe Koffman, David Gibson and Johnny Rutledge. Nominated for Geminis for his work on "Diamonds", "Night Heat" and "Hot Shots"
Selected Filmography: "Top Cops" (57 eps), TV, 90-91, CDN/USA, Comp; "Counterstrike" (44 eps), TV, 90-91, USA/CDN, Comp; "True Blue" (13 eps), TV, 89-90, USA, Comp; "Diamonds" (44 eps), TV, 87-90, USA/CDN/F, Comp; "Cop Talk" (13 eps), TV, 89, CDN, Comp; "Night Heat" (96 eps), TV, 84-88, USA/CDN, Comp; "Lifetime" (200 eps), TV, 86-88, CDN, Comp; *Juno Awards*, TV, 88, CDN, Mus Dir; *Gunfighters*, TV, 87, USA, Comp; "Airwaves" (26 eps), TV, 85-87, CDN, Comp; *Gemini Awards*, TV, 87, CDN, Mus Dir; "Hot Shots (13 eps), TV, 86, USA/CDN, Comp; *The*

Playground, "Ray Bradbury Theatre", TV, 85, CDN/USA/NZ, Comp.

URSELL, Geoffrey
- see WRITERS

VANDERBURGH, Clive
- see PRODUCERS

WALKER, Russell
AFM. 52 R. Bedgerow Ave., Toronto, ON M4M 1V4 (416)462-1312.
Type of Production and Credits: TV Film-Comp; TV Video-Comp.
Genres: Drama-TV; Documentary-TV; Commercials-TV; Industrial-TV.
Biography: Born 1954, Toronto, Ontario. Educated extensively in both classical and electronic music; travelled all over the world studying local music in different countries. Has released 3 records with WEA and RCA Records; worked for 9 years as a recording engineer/producer; began composing for film, 79.
Selected Filmography: *The Famine Within*, Th/TV, 90, CDN, Comp; "Chestnut Avenue" (pilot), TV, 90, CDN, Comp; "Reading Rap" (8 eps), ED/90, CDN, Comp; *Albanian Journey*, TV, 90, CDN, Comp; "The Riddle of Wizards Oak" (8 eps), TV, 89, CDN, Comp; "The Last Frontier" (2 eps), TV, 89, CDN, Comp; *The Birth of Language*, TV, 86, CDN, Comp; *Keys to the Office*, TV, 86, CDN, Comp; *The Joy of Stress/Tiem/The Future's Past/We are Motion/Idea Corp.*, In, 85-86, CDN, Comp; *The Other Face of Leprosy*, "The Nature of Things", TV, 86, CDN, Comp; "Speaking Out", TV, 85, CDN, Arr; Sutton Place, Cm, 85, CDN, Arr; *The No Name Show*, TV, 84, CDN, Comp; *From Grape to Glass*, TV, 82, CDN, Comp; Cida/Motorola/Algoma Steel/Inter Metco, In, 79-82, CDN, Comp.

WATSON, Wendy
ACCT. Zap Productions Limited, 118 Granby St., Toronto, ON M5B 1J1 (416)598-3103.
Type of Production and Credits: TV Film-Comp; TV Video-Comp.
Genres: Drama-Th&TV; Documentary-Th&TV; Educational-Th&TV; Children's-Th&TV.
Selected Filmography: "Degrassi High" (28 eps), TV, 89-91, CDN, Comp; "Home Studies" (140 eps), TV, 90-91, CDN, Comp; "Speaking Out" (weekly), TV, 90-91, CDN, Comp; Toys 'R' Us, Cm, 91, CDN, Comp; Youthline, Cm, 91, CDN, Comp; "School Works" (6 eps), TV, 90, CDN, Comp; Terry Fox Run, Cm, 89/90, CDN, Comp; TVO Promo, Cm, 90, CDN, Comp; *Canadian Science Fair* (4), In, 90, CDN, Comp; "Degrassi Junior High" (26 eps), TV, 86-88, CDN, Comp; "The Kids of Degrassi Street" (26 eps), TV, 83-85, CDN, Comp.

WELSMAN, John J.
ACCT, AFM, GCFC. The Welsman Company, 74 Fern Ave., Toronto, ON M6R 1K3 (416)533-1765.
Type of Production and Credits: Th Film-Comp; Th Short-Comp; TV Film-Comp; TV Video-Comp.
Genres: Drama-Th&TV; Variety-TV; Documentary-TV; Animation-TV.
Biography: Born in 1955 and living in Toronto, Ontario. Piano and theory study at the Royal Conservatory of Music in Toronto. Studied at the Faculty of Music, University of Western Ontario, 1974-75. Two years of voice study with Gloria Ferrer. Study of orchestration and composition through the Gordon Delamont Course with Todd Booth. Study of orchestration and composition with Dr. Samuel Dolin, also with Milan Kymlicka. *Looking for Miracles, Turning to Stone, Replanting the Tree of Life, Megan Carey*, and *Krieghoff* have each earned numerous awards at film and television festivals in Canada, the United States and Europe. Awarded the Gemini for Best Original Music Score for a Series for "Road to Avonlea".
Selected Filmography: "Road to Avonlea" (16 eps), TV, 89-91, CDN, Comp, (GEMINI); *Jane of Lantern Hill*, TV, 89, CDN, Comp; "The Twilight Zone" (7 eps), TV, 89, CDN/USA, Comp; *Looking for Miracles*, Th/TV, 89, CDN, Comp; *Replanting the Tree of Life*, TV, 87, CDN, Comp; "My Pet Monster" (13 eps), TV, 87, CDN/USA, Comp; *Turning to Stone*, TV, 85-86, CDN, Comp; *Stop the World*, TV, 85, CDN, Comp; "The Edison Twins", TV, 85-87, CDN, Comp; *The Juggler*, TV, 82, CDN, Comp; *The Back Attack*, "Vista", TV, 83, CDN, Comp; *Corletto and Son*, TV, 81, CDN, Comp; *Krieghoff*, Th/TV, 80, CDN, Comp; *Megan Carey*, Th/TV, 79, CDN, Comp; *The Fir Tree*, Th/TV, 79, CDN, Comp.

XALIMAN, Don
- see DIRECTORS

ZAZA, Paul ✧
Zaza Sound Productions Ltd., 322 Dufferin St., Toronto, ON M6K 1Z6. (416)534-4211.
Type of Production and Credits: Th Film-Comp; TV Film-Comp; TV Video-Comp.
Genres: Drama-Th&TV; Horror-Th&TV.

Biography: Born 1952. President, owner of Zaza Sound; has composed scores for over 30 feature films and has numerous credits in the recording and television industries.
Selected Filmography: Bullies, Th, 85, CDN, Comp; "Kids of Degrassi Street", TV, 84-85, CDN, Orch; *The Pink Chiquitas*, Th, 85, CDN, Comp; *High Stakes*, Th, 85, CDN, Comp; "Mania" (4 eps), TV, 85, CDN, Comp; *Turk 182!*, Th, 85, USA, Comp; "Just Jazz" (52 eps), TV, 84-85, CDN, Mus Dir; *Breaking All the Rules*, Th, 84, CDN, Comp; *Meatballs III*, Th, 84, CDN, Comp; *The Vindicator*, Th, 84, CDN, Comp; *Isaac Littlefeathers*, Th, 84, CDN, Comp; *Size Small*, TV, 83-84, CDN, Comp; *Birds of Prey*, Th, 84, CDN, Comp; "Modesty Blaise" (pilot), TV, 83, USA, Comp; *A Christmas Story*, Th, 83, CDN, Comp.

ZERAFA, Guy
AFM, ACCT, CARAS. Airborne Productions, 28 Livingston Rd., #47, Scarborough, ON M1E 4S5 (416)266-6492.
Type of Production and Credits: Th Film-Comp; Th Short-Comp; TV Film-Comp; TV Video-Comp.
Genres: Drama-Th&TV; Action-Th&TV; Documentary-TV; Commercials-TV.
Selected Filmography: *Dead Time*, TV, 91, CDN, Comp; *Silent Conversations*, Th, 91, CDN, Comp; "Imprint" (26 eps), TV, 91, CDN, Comp; "Ontario Lottery Live" (52 eps), TV, 91, CDN, Comp; "Eye on Toronto", TV, 91, CDN, Seg Contr; "The Dini Petty Show", TV, 91, CDN, Seg Contr; "The Shirley Show", TV, 91, CDN, Seg Contr; *With or Without Quebec*, TV, 91, CDN, Comp; *Telefest Awards Show*, TV, 91, CDN, Comp; "Canada In View/The Tour", TV, 90, CDN, Seg Contr; *Nightmare in the Neighbourhood*, TV, 90, CDN, Comp; *Teen Gangs*, TV, 89, CDN, Comp; "Left, Right & Centre" (6 eps), TV, 89, CDN, Comp.

Costume Designers
Costumes

ALEXANDER, Alisa
ACFC. 9 Deer Park, #1705, Toronto, ON M4V 2C4 (416)923-2727.
Type of Production and Credits: Th Film-Cos; TV Film-Cos.
Genres: Drama-Th; Comedy-Th; Variety-TV; Commercials-TV.
Biography: Born in Chicago in the United States. Worked in Los Angeles before moving to Canada in 1986. Experienced in costume design, pattern-making and construction.
Selected Filmography: *True Confections*, Th, 90, Cos; *African Chronicle*, Th, 88, Cos; *Too Outrageous*, Th, 86, Cos; *We're All Crazy*, Th, 82, Cos; *Seven Graves for Rogan*, Th, 80, Cos.

AUDY, Michel
- voir REALISATEURS

BAILIE, Philip ◊
(604)683-6625.
Type of Production and Credits: TV Film-Cos/Art Dir/Pro Des; TV Video-Cos/Art Dir/Pro Des.
Genres: Drama-TV; Comedy-TV; Variety-TV; Musical-TV.
Biography: Born 1950, Northern Ireland; Canadian citizenship. Honours B.A., Wimbledon School of Art. Twenty years experience in theatre and television; thirteen years with CBC. Nominated for Gemini Award for Best Costume Design, 1987.
Selected Filmography: *A Different Dance*, TV, 88, CDN, Cos; "The Beachcombers" (20 eps), TV, 87, CDN, Cos; "Red Serge" (12 eps), TV, 86-87, CDN, Cos; *Driving School*, TV, 87, USA, Cos; *Finding a Job*, TV, 87, USA, Cos.

CAINES-FLOYD, Eydi
ACFC, NABET. 123A Davenport Rd., Toronto, ON M5R 1H8 (416)972-6465.
Type of Production and Credits: Th Film-Cos; TV Film-Ward; TV Video-Cos.
Biography: Born in Newfoundland, Canada. Studied Fine Arts for 5 years. Studied costume in England for 1 year. Travelled throughout Europe and Asia, studying painting and designing. Fashion designer in Europe and Canada before entering the film and televison world 10 years ago. Paints in watercolour and acrylic as well as designing and mistressing for TV and film. Speaks English and "Newfounese".
Selected Filmography: "Counterstrike" (5 eps), TV, 90-91, CDN/USA/F, Ward; "Top Cops" (20 eps), TV, 90-91, CDN/USA, Ward Buy; *Thin Ice*, Th, 90, CDN/USA, Assist Cos; "T and T" (22 eps), TV, 89-90, CDN/USA, Cos; "Friday's Curse", TV, 89, USA/CDN, Ward; "Learning the Ropes" (24 eps), TV, 88, USA/CDN, Cos; "Check It Out" (66 eps), TV, 85-88, USA, Cos; *True Confessions*, TV, 87, CDN, Ward; "The Elephant Show" (13 eps), TV, 85, CDN, Ward.

CRONENBERG, Denise ◊
(818)848-0808.
Type of Production and Credits: Th Film-Cos; TV Film-Cos; TV Video-Cos.
Genres: Drama-Th&TV; Comedy-Th&TV; Musical-Th&TV; Horror-Th&TV.
Biography: Born in Toronto, Ontario; US and Canadian citizenship. B.A.A., Radio and TV Arts, Ryerson Polytechnical Institute; Banff School of Fine Arts. Was a member of the Royal Winnipeg Ballet; was a performer/dancer on CBC-TV variety shows for 15 years; designed and sold children's and adults' clothes for York County Dressworks Inc.
Selected Filmography: *Dead Ringers*, Th, 88, CDN, Cos; *Shoot Me*, Th, 87, CDN, Cos; *Hot Paint*, Th, 87, USA, Ward Assist; *The Fly*, Th, 86, USA, Cos; "Murder Ordained" (2 eps), TV, 86, CDN, Cos; *Knightflyers*, Th, 86, USA, Ward Assist; *Killer Party*, Th, 84, USA, Ward Assist; "The Edison Twins" (2 eps), TV, 84, CDN, Wardrobe; *The Dead Zone*, Th, 83, USA, Assist Des; *Videodrome*, Th, 81, CDN/USA, Ward Assist.

DAFOE, Francis ◊
(416)923-2716.
Type of Production and Credits: Th Film-Cos; TV Film-Cos; TV Video-Cos.
Genres: Drama-Th&TV; Comedy-Th&TV; Variety-Th&TV; Industrial-Th&TV.
Biography: Born in Toronto, Ontario. Attended Parsons School of Design, New York City. Former world figure skating champion, 54 and 55. Listed in world *Who's Who of Women*. Prix Anik Award, Outstanding Costume Design for Television, "Strawberry Ice"; winner of several other awards for costume design, including San Francisco.
Selected Filmography: "Air Farce" (6 eps), TV, CDN, Cos; *The Choice*, TV, CDN, Cos; *Les Feux follets*, TV, CDN, Cos; *Movie Magic*, Th, CDN, Cos; *Tommy Hunter* (5 years), TV, CDN, Cos; "Wojeck" (5 eps), TV, CDN, Cos; *Tom Jones*, TV, CDN, Cos; *Multicultural*, TV, CDN, Cos; *Genie Awards*, TV, CDN, Cos; *Hockey Awards*, TV, CDN, Cos; *ACTRA Awards*, TV, CDN, Cos; *Calgary Winter Olympics*, TV, 88, CDN, Cos; "Wayne & Shuster" (72 eps), TV, 70-88, CDN, Cos; "Seeing Things" (2 eps), TV, 86, CDN, Cos; "True Gift of Christmas" (1 eps), TV, 85, CDN, Cos.

DEVEAU, Marie-Sylvie
NABET, ACFC. 737 Euclid Ave., Toronto, ON M6G 2V1 (416)535-4486. Les Productions M.S. Deveau Inc., 737 Euclid Ave., Toronto, ON M6G 2V1 (416)535-4486.
Type of Production and Credits: TV Film-Cos.
Genres: Drama-TV; Documentary-TV.
Biography: Born in 1962 in Montreal, Quebec. Graduated from the National Theatre School, Montreal, 1987. Speaks fluent French and English.
Selected Filmography: "Top Cops", TV, 90-91, CDN/USA, Cos; "Moment of Truth" (pilot), TV, 91, CDN/USA, Cos; "Friday The 13th - The Series", TV, 89-90, CDN/USA, Cos.

DIMITROV, Olga
RCA, IATSE 873, ACCT. 132 Indian Rd., Toronto, ON M6R 2V6 (416)532-6187. Dimitrov Design Services Ltd., 132 Indian Rd., Toronto, ON M6R 2V6 (416)532-6187.
Type of Production and Credits: Th Film-Cos.
Genres: Drama-Th&TV; Comedy-Th&TV; Musical-Th&TV; Science Fiction-Th&TV; Children's-Th&TV.
Biography: Born Czechoslovakia. Canadian citizen. Fluent in English, Czech and Slovak. Attended the College of Applied Arts in Prague. Studied costume design, graphic illustration. Has designed for theatres, operas, ballets, film and TV.

Worked on the Oscar-winning Best Foreign Film, 1967, *Closely Watched Trains* and *End of August in Hotel Ozon* which won the Vatican Peace Prize in 1967. Was nominated for a Genie Award for Best Costume Design for *Silence of the North*, 1981; *One Magic Christmas* and *Samuel Lount*, 1986; *Millennium*, 1990. Nominated for a Dora Mavor Moore Award for the theatrical production of *The Boyfriend*, 1981 and won a Dora Mavor Moore Award for Best Costume Design for the theatrical production of *Man of La Mancha*, 1982.
Selected Filmography: *Agaguk*, Th, 90-91, CDN/F, Cos; *Millennium*, Th, 88, US, Cos; *Bethune: The Making of a Hero*, Th, 87-88, CDN, Cos; *John & The Missus*, Th, 86, CDN, Cos; *One Magic Christmas*, Th, 85, USA, Cos; *Samuel Lount*, Th, 84, CDN, Cos; *Dead Zone*, Th, 83, CDN, Cos; *Harry Tracey*, Th, 80, USA, Cos; *Death Hunt*, Th, 80, CDN, Cos; *Silence of the North*, Th, 79, USA, Cos; *In Praise of Older Women*, Th, 77, USA, Cos.

DRAKE, Christopher
CUPE, ACCT. 4 Sherbourne St. N., #307, Toronto, ON M4W 2T1 (416)929-0980. CBC Costume Department, 90 Sumach St., Toronto, ON (416)975-7095.
Type of Production and Credits: TV Film-Cos; TV Video-Cos.
Genres: Drama-TV; Comedy-TV.
Biography: Born 1952, Montreal, Quebec. B.F.A., Concordia University, 74; graduate, Design, National Theatre School, 76.
Selected Filmography: *Brian Orser - Night Moves*, TV, 91, CDN, Cos; "Street Legal" (55 eps), TV, 88-91, CDN, Cos; "Material World" (pilot-6 eps), TV, 89, CDN, Cos; *And Then You Die*, TV, 86, CDN, Cos; "Welcome to Ottawa" (pilot), TV, 86, CDN, Cos.

GELLMAN-FRIEDMAN, Judith R.
57 Sandringham Dr., Toronto, ON M5M 3G4 (416)486-7775.
Type of Production and Credits: Th Film-Cos; TV Film-Cos; TV Video-Cos/Prod.
Biography: American citizen, landed-immigrant Canada. Educated at the University of Wisconsin (Bachelor of Science, 1972); the Fashion Institute of Technology, New York (Associate in Applied Arts & Sciences, High Honours, 1971)
Selected Filmography: "The Rob Cormier Show", TV, 90, CDN, Assoc Prod; *Hyundai*, Cm, 89, CDN, Des; *Hostage*, TV, 89, USA, Cos; *Echoes in the Darkness*, TV, 87, USA, Cos; *Adventures in Babysitting*, Th, 87, USA, Cos; *Head Office*, Th, 84, USA, Cos; *Heartsounds*, TV, 84, USA, Cos; *Cougar*, TV, 83, USA, Cos; *Frank & Feerless*, TV, 79, USA, Cos; *Nobody Makes Me Cry/Between Friends*, TV, 83, USA, Cos; *The Plutonium Incident*, TV, 79, USA, Cos; *The Family Man*, TV, 79, USA, Cos; *Torn Between Two Lovers*, TV, 79, USA, Cos; *Meatballs*, Th, 78, USA/CDN, Cos; *Circle of Children Part II*, TV, 78, USA, Cos.

GORD, Eva
5 Relmar Gardens, Toronto, ON M5P 1S1 (416)484-4496.
Type of Production and Credits: Th Film-Cos; TV Film-Cos.
Genres: Drama-Th; Comedy-Th&TV; Action-Th&TV; Horror-Th&TV.
Biography: Born in Budapest, Hungary. Canadian citizen. Languages: English, French and Hungarian.
Selected Filmography: "Sweating Bullets" (pilot), TV, 91, CDN/MEX/USA, Cos; "Dog House" (Pilot, 4 eps), TV, 90, CDN, Cos; *Daughter of Darkness*, TV, 89, USA, Cos; *Night Sticks*, Th, 89, CDN, Cos; *The Brain*, Th, 87, CDN, Cos; *Recruits*, Th, 85, CDN, Cos.

HAALMEYER, Juul
NABET, ACFC, ACTRA. 6 Glen Edyth Dr., Toronto, ON M4V 2V7 (416)924-1936. Homemade Tarts, 9 Walker Ave., Toronto, ON (416)923-8078. Fred Levy, 26 Soho St., Suite 310, Toronto, ON M5T 1Z7 (416)597-2185.
Type of Production and Credits: Th Film-Cos; Th Short-Cos; TV Film-Cos; TV Video-Cos.
Genres: Drama-Th&TV; Comedy-Th&TV; Variety-Th&TV; Musical-Th&TV.
Biography: Born 1949, Amsterdam, The Netherlands; Canadian citizenship. Languages: English and Dutch.
Selected Filmography: "Codco" (32 eps), TV, 89-91, CDN, Cos; *Skating I & II*, TV, 90, USA, Cos; "Diamonds" (22 eps), TV, 88, CDN, Cos; *The Enigma of Bobby Bittman*, TV, 87, CDN/USA, Cos; *All My Sons*, TV, 86, CDN/USA, Cos; *The Incredible Time Travels of Henry Osgood*, TV, 85, CDN/USA, Cos; "SCTV" (74 eps), TV, 81-84, CDN/USA, Cos; *The Borrowers*, TV, 73, CDN/USA, Co-Wr.

HAY, John M.
IATSE 873. 254 Pine Island Turnpike, Warwick, NY 10990 (914)986-5811. (212)661-1940.
Type of Production and Credits: Th

Film-Cos; Th Short-Cos; TV Film-Cos; TV Video-Cos.
Genres: Drama-Th; Comedy-Th&TV; Variety-Th&TV; Children's-TV.
Biography: Born in Canada in 1954; Canadian citizen, US resident. Languages: English, French and Italian. Nominated for ACE award for Costume Design on *The 3 Little Pigs* episode of "Shelley Duvall's Faerie Tale Theatre"; Genie for Costume Design on *Quest for Fire*.
Selected Filmography: *Black Robe*, Th, 90, CDN/AUS, Cos; *Teenage Mutant Ninja Turtles*, Th, 89, USA, Cos; *Babycakes*, TV, 88, USA, Cos; *Sing*, Th, 88, USA, Cos; *Beyond Therapy*, Th, 86, USA/F, Cos; *Boy in Blue*, Th, 84, USA/CDN, Cos; *The 3 Little Pigs* "Shelley Duvall's Faerie Tale Theatre", TV, 84, USA, Cos; *The Pied Piper* "Shelley Duvall's Faerie Tale Theatre", TV, 84, USA, Cos; *Quest For Fire*, Th, 81, CDN/F, Cos, (GENIE); *Popeye*, Th, 80, USA, Cos.

JOBIN, Louise
STCQ, ACCT. 1598 est, Mont-royal, Montréal, PQ H2J 1Z2 (514)523-5621. Atelier de Costumes B.J.L. inc., 5669, Casgrain, Suite 214, Montréal, PQ H2T 1Y3 (514)272-7422. FAX: 274-0875.
Types de production et générique: l métrage-Cos/Dir art; TV film-Cos/Dir art.
Types d'oeuvres: Drame-C&TV; Expérimental-C&TV; Documentaire-C&TV; Expérimental-C&TV.
Curriculum vitae: Née en 1944, Montréal, Québec. Langues: français et anglais. Cours classique. A dessiné les costumes d'environ 35 pièces de théâtre; co-fondatrice et directrice de l'Atelier B.J.L. inc. avec François Barbeau et François Laplante. Membre, Cinémathèque Québécoise I.N.I.S.
Filmographie sélective: *Being at Home with Claude*, C, 91, CDN, Cos; *Montréal vu par: J. Leduc*, C, 91, CDN, Dir art/Décor/Cos; *Une nuit à l'école*, TV, 91, CDN, Dir art; *L'Ange Noir/Nelligan*, C, 90, CDN, Dir art; *On a marché sur la lune*, TV, 90, CDN, Dir art/Décor/Cos; *Ding et Dong, le film*, C, 90, CDN, CDN, Dir art; "Super sans plomb" (26 eps), TV, 89, CDN, Dir art; *Jésus de Montréal*, C, 88, CDN/F, Cos, (GENIE); *Ford: The Man and the Machine*, TV, 87, CDN, Cos, (GEMINI); *Joshua Then and Now*, C, 84, CDN, Cos; *Suzanne*, C, 79, CDN, Cos; *Cordélia*, C, 78, CDN, Cos, (GENIE); *Les Ordres*, C, 73, CDN, Cos; *La course du lièvre à travers les champs*, C, 71, F, Cos; "D'Iberville" (36 eps), TV, 66-68, CDN, Chef cos.

JOY, Michael
- see ART DIRECTORS

KEMP, Lynda
IATSE 873. 66 Brooklyn Ave., Toronto, ON M4M 2X5 (416)462-0506. Thunder Thighs Costumes Ltd., 16 Busy St., Toronto, ON M4M 1N8 (416)462-0621.
Type of Production and Credits: Th Film-Cos; TV Film-Cos.
Genres: Drama-Th; Comedy-TV; Action-Th&TV; Horror-Th&TV.
Biography: Born in 1953 in Hamilton, Ontario. Canadian citizen. Educated at the theatre department of Ryerson, Toronto. Studied music at the Royal Conservatory of Music, Toronto.
Selected Filmography: *Body Parts*, Th, 91, USA/CDN, Cos; *Mark Twain & Me*, TV, 90, USA/CDN, Cos; *Kaleidoscope*, TV, 90, USA/CDN, Cdn Cos; *Defense of a Married Man*, TV, 90, USA/CDN, Cos; *Maggie's Secret*, TV, 90, USA/CDN, Cos; *Personals*, TV, 89, USA/CDN, Cdn Cos; *In The Frame*, TV, 89, USA/CDN, Cdn Cos; *Blood Sport*, Th, 89, USA/CDN, Cos; *Final Notice*, TV, 89, USA/CDN, Cos; *Love & Murder*, Th, 88, CDN, Cos; *Ghost of a Chance*, TV, 87, USA/CDN, Cos; *Bluffing It*, TV, 87, USA/CDN, Cos; *The Liberators*, TV, 86, USA/CDN, Cos; *High Price of Passion*, TV, 86, USA/CDN, Cos; *Young Again*, TV, 86, USA/CDN, Cos.

KIELLERMAN, Gina
ACFC, NABET 700. Yaya's Ltd., 658 Queen St. W., Top Floor, Toronto, ON M6J 1E5 (415)361-1952.
Type of Production and Credits: Th Film-Cos; TV Film-Cos; TV Video-Cos.
Genres: Drama-Th&TV; Horror-Th&TV; Children's-Th&TV; Commercials-TV.
Biography: Born 1955, Toronto, Ontario. Languages: English, Polish and Italian. Studied costume design at the Instituto Artistico dell'Abbligliamento, Milan. Fine arts and theatrical background has led to designing feature films since 80. Specializations include contemporary haute couture, fantasy high style, urban park and ethnic, rural, surreal costuming.
Selected Filmography: "Sweating Bullets" (5 eps), TV, 91, CDN/USA/MEX, Cos; *Bonaparte*, "OWL-TV" (20 eps), TV, 89-91, CDN/GB, Cos; *Sun Up It's Tuesday Morning*, Cowboy Junkies, MV, 90, USA, Art Dir; "Eric's World" (13 eps), TV, 90, CDN, Cos; *Renegades*, Th, 89, USA, Cos; *The Reckoning*, Th, 89, CDN, Cos; "My Secret Identity" (5 eps), TV, 88, CDN/USA, Cos; *Criminal Law*, Th, 87, USA, Cos; *Sadie and Son*, TV, 87,

CDN/USA, Cos; *The Truth About Alex*, TV, 86, CDN, Cos; "Airwaves" (13 eps), TV, 85-86, CDN, Cos; *The Playground*, "Ray Bradbury Theatre", TV, 85, CDN, Cos; "The Littlest Hobo" (26 eps), TV, 83-84, CDN, Cos; *Baker County U.S.A./The Killer Instinct*, Th, 80, CDN/USA, Cos.

LÉPORÉ, Marcella
6278 De Chateaubriand, Montréal, PQ H2S 2N4 (615)277-4016, 272-0295.
Types de production et générique: l métrage-Cos; TV film-Cos; TV vidéo-Cos.
Types d'oeuvres: Drame-C&TV; Comédie-C&TV; Science-Fiction-C&TV; Vidéo-Clips-C&TV.
Curriculum vitae: Née en 1962 à Montréal. Citoyenneté canadienne. Langues: français, anglais, italien. D.E.C. en lettres (1982) Formation Techniques du Vêtements au Collège Marie-Victorin de 1982-88. Habilleuse de 1984 à 1986. Devenue Assistant Conceptrice Costumes puis Conceptrice Costumes. Ai touché au théâtre avec le Spectacle des 100 Watts en Tournée, 1991, ainsi que d'autres productions des Trouble. Scène (troupe théâtre amateur).
Filmographie sélective: "Le Club des 100 Watts" (565 eps), TV, 88-91, CDN, Cos; "S.O.S.-Télé" (pilote), TV, 88, CDN, Assist Cos; *MacKenzie King*, TV, 87, CDN, Assist Cos; "Station-Soleil" (150 eps), TV, 85-87, CDN, Cos.

LEVESQUE, Gaétanne
STCQ. 4421A Brébeuf, Montréal, PQ H2J 3K8 (514)522-5843.
Types de production et générique: l métrage-Cos; c métrage-Cos; l métrage-Cos; TV vidéo-Cos.
Types d'oeuvres: Drame-C&TV; Comédie-C&TV; Variété-TV; Education-TV.
Curriculum vitae: Née en 1956, Murdochville, Gaspésie. Option théâtre - production, Cégep Bourg Chemin de St-Hyacinthe, 76-78. Expérience aux décors, au son, à l'éclairage; costumière à la TV et au Théâtre depuis 78; costumière, Radio-Québec, 80-87; travaille au cinéma depuis 86; est présentement pigiste.
Filmographie sélective: *Un Léger Vertige*, TV, 90, CDN, Cos; *Les Amazones*, C, 90, CDN, Cos; *Love-Moi*, C, 90, CDN, Cos; *Terre à Taire*, TV, 89, CDN, Cos; *Les Matins infidèles*, C, 87-88, CDN, Cos; "The King Chronicle", TV, 88, CDN, Assist cos; "Traquenards" (1 eps), TV, 87, CDN, Assist cos; *Les Voisins*, TV, 86, CDN, Assist cos; *La Nuit de Bonzai*, TV,

**Costume Rentals for Feature Film, Television and Commercials.
Period, Contemporary and Uniforms**

Lynda G. Kemp
Costume Designer

Vicki Gliserman
Manager

Thunder Thighs Costumes Ltd.
16 Busy Street, Toronto, Ontario M4M 1N8
(416) 462-0621

86, CDN, Assist cos; *Les Reporters masqués*, TV, 85, CDN, Assist cos; *Victor le vampire*, TV, 85, CDN, Assist cos; *Les Somnambules*, TV, 85, CDN, Assist cos; "La Soirée de l'impro" (1 eps), TV, 85, CDN, Cos; La Chambre de notaires (3 cm), TV, 85, CDN, Cos; *Le Matou*, C, 85, CDN/F/I, Assist cos.

MACDONALD, Aleida
CDG, USA. 180 Frederick St., #804, Toronto, ON M5A 4H9 (416)862-2892.
Type of Production and Credits: Th Film-Cos; Th Short-Cos; TV Film-Cos; TV Video-Cos.
Genres: Drama-Th&TV; Science Fiction-Th&TV; Commercials-TV; Music Video-Th&TV.
Biography: Born in Dutch West Indies; Canadian citizenship; US "Green Card." Languages: Dutch, English, Spanish and good knowledge of German. Educated in Holland, New York City (Fashion Institute), Toronto (Ontario College of Art). Special skills in cutting and building costumes.
Selected Filmography: *The Freshman*, Th, 89, USA, Cos Spv; *Looking for Miracles*, TV, 88, CDN, Cos Spv; *The Child Saver/Jackie Watson*, TV, 87, USA, Cos; *Hoover vs the Kennedys* (mini-series), TV, 86, USA, Cos Spv; *Police Academy IV*, Th, 86, USA, Cos; *Police Academy III*, Th, 85, USA, Cos; *Falcon's Gold*, Th, 82, USA/CDN, Cos; Holland Cheese, Cm, 80, CDN, Cos; *Phobia*, Th, 79, CDN, Cos; *Never Trust a Thief*, Th, 79, CDN, Cos; *Second Wind*, Th, 75, CDN, Cos; *Quiet Day in Belfast*, Th, 74, CDN, Cos; *Girl Cried Murder*, TV, 73, CDN, Cos; *Tom Sawyer*, TV, 72, USA, Cos; *Rollin' on the River*, "Kenny Rogers & the 1st Edition", TV, 69-70, USA, Cos.

MacKAY, Lynne
IATSE 873. 64 Wroxeter Ave., Toronto, ON M4J 1E6 (416)466-5220.
Type of Production and Credits: Th Film-Cos; TV Film-Cos.
Genres: Drama-Th&TV; Comedy-Th&TV; Action-Th&TV; Commercials-TV.
Biography: Born in 1952 in Windsor, Nova Scotia. Canadian citizen. Graduated from the Ontario College of Art. Studied fine art, photography and textile design. Studied pattern drafting and cutting at George Brown Community College, Toronto.
Selected Filmography: *Honor Bright*, TV, 91, USA, Cos; *Last Wish*, TV, 91, USA, Cos; *Queen of Mean: The Leona Helmsley Story*, TV, 90, USA, Cos; *Hitler's Daughter/The Phoenix*, TV, 90, USA, Cos; *Alex, Life of a Child*, TV, 86, USA, Cos; *Willmar 8/A Matter of Sex*, TV, 84, USA, Cos; "Cagney & Lacey" (pilot), TV, 83, USA, Cos; *Martin's Day*, Th, 83, USA/CDN, Cos; *Tulips*, Th, 81, CDN, Cos; *Will There Really Be a Morning?*, TV, 82, USA, Cos; *Class of '84*, Th, 80, USA/CDN, Cos; *Happy Birthday, Gemini*, Th, 79, USA/CDN, Cos; *Bear Island*, Th, 78, GB/USA/CDN, Cos; *Outrageous*, Th, 77, CDN, Cos; *Love at First Sight*, Th, 77, CDN, Cos.

MATHESON, Linda F.
4100 Whitsett Ave., #107, Studio City, CA 91604 (818)769-7604. Sandra Marsh Management, 14930 Venture Blvd., Ste. 200, Sherman Oaks, CA 91403 USA (818)905-6961.
Type of Production and Credits: Th Film-Cos Des; Th Short-Cos Des; TV Film-Cos Des; TV Video-Cos Des.
Genres: Drama-Th&TV; Comedy-Th&TV; Musical-Th&TV; Action-Th&TV.
Biography: Born in Charlottetown, Prince Edward Island. Canadian citizen with the right to work in the United States. Spoken language is English. University degree with extras at OECA and three schools of art; Canada Council Grant. Genie nominations for *Middle Age Crazy* and *Fish Hawk*. Emmy citation for *Pippi Longstocking*.
Selected Filmography: *The Mrs*, Th, 91, USA, Cos Des; *FX-2*, Th, 90, USA, Cos Des; *Where The Heart Is*, Th, 89, USA, Cos Des; *Gotham*, Th/TV, 88, USA, Cos Des; *Secret Passions/Haunted By Her Past*, TV, 87, USA, Cos Des; *After Midnight*, TV, 87, USA, Cos Des; *Burning Love/Love At Stake*, Th, 86, USA, Cos Des; *Judgement in Stone/The Housekeeper*, Th, 85, CDN, Cos Des; *Strange Invaders*, Th, 83, USA, Cos; *Humongous*, Th, 81, CDN, Cos Des; *Love*, Th, 80, CDN, Cos Des; *Misdeal*, Th, 80, CDN, Cos Des; *Middle Age Crazy*, Th, 79, USA, Cos Des; *Title Shot*, Th, 79, USA, Cos Des; "SCTV" (52 eps), TV, 77-78, CDN/USA, Cos Des.

McCARTY, Mary Jane ◊
(212)807-1550.
Type of Production and Credits: Th Film-Cos; TV Film-Cos.
Genres: Drama-Th&TV; Horror-Th; Children's-Th&TV; Commercials-TV.
Biography: Born 1956, Washington, D.C.; landed immigrant, Canada. Studied Fashion Design, George Brown College.
Selected Filmography: "After School Special" (4 eps), TV, 87-88, USA, Cos; *Empire of Reason*, TV, 87, USA, Cos; *Super*

Mom's Daughter, TV, 86, USA, Cos; *Doing Life*, TV, 86, USA, Cos; *Execution of Raymond Graham*, TV, 85, USA, Cos; *High School Narc*, TV, 85, USA, Cos; *Hockey Night*, TV, 84, CDN, Cos; *Maggie and Pierre*, TV, 83, CDN, Cos; *Skullduggery*, Th, 82, CDN/USA, Cos; *Paradise*, Th, 81, CDN, Cos; *A Choice of Two*, TV, 81, CDN, Cos; *Curtains*, Th, 80, CDN, Cos; *Clown White*, TV, 80, CDN, Cos; *The Last Chase*, Th, 79, CDN/USA, Cos; *Cries in the Night*, Th, 79, CDN, Cos.

McLEOD, Mary E. ◆
(416)462-0411.
Type of Production and Credits: Th Film-Cos; Th Short-Cos; TV Film-Cos; TV Video-Cos.
Genres: Drama-Th&TV; Comedy-Th&TV; Musical-Th&TV; Commercials-Th&TV.
Biography: Born 1951, Toronto, Ontario. B.A., History and Communications, University of Waterloo. Has worked on hundreds of TV commercials in Canada and US; also designed contemporary clothing for retail trade. Genie nomination for costume design for *Christmas Story*.
Selected Filmography: *A New Life*, Th, 87, USA, Cos; *Switching Channels*, Th, 87, USA, Cos; *Christmas Eve*, Th, 87, USA, Co-Cos; *Deadly Business*, TV, 85, USA, Cos; *He's Fired, She's Hired*, TV, 84, USA, Cos; *Christmas Story*, Th, 83, USA, Cos; *Porky's II*, Th, 82, CDN, Cos; *Running Out*, TV, 82, USA, Cos; *Porky's*, Th, 81, CDN, Cos.

MOHR, Margaret M.
IATSE 873 & 764. 308 Westwood Ave., Toronto, ON M4J 2H7 (416)462-9255. 69 Lynhurst Ave., Staten Island, NY 10305 USA (718)727-1114.
Type of Production and Credits: Th Film-Cos; Th Short-Cos; TV Film-Cos; TV Video-Cos.
Genres: Drama-Th&TV; Comedy-Th&TV; Musical-Th&TV; Commercials-Th&TV.
Biography: Born in New York City. Attended New York University and Shakespeare Institute in Stratford, England. Designed for theatre and television in New York and England before moving to Canada. Designed at the CBC in Toronto from 1975-83. Has designed feature films and television series since 83. Worked on over 100 commercials for the Partners' Film Company, 1982-90. Works both in New York and Toronto. Has won 2 Prix Anik Awards (CBC).
Selected Filmography: *Car 54, Where Are You?*, Th, 90, USA/CDN, Cos; *Perfectly Normal*, Th, 89, CDN, Cos; *Sorry, Wrong Number*, TV, 89, USA, Assist Cos; "Knightwatch" (11 eps), TV, 88, USA/CDN, Cos.

MUIR, Linda
ACFC. 163 Strachan Ave., Toronto, ON M6J 2T1 (416)864-0256.
Type of Production and Credits: Th Film-Cos; TV Film-Cos.
Genres: Drama-Th&TV; Comedy-TV; Action-TV; Children's-TV.
Biography: Born Toronto, Ontario. Designed for theatre since 75; designed Toronto production of *Tamara* for which she was awarded Dora Mavor Moore Award for Outstanding Costume Design; designed environments for Toronto Festival of Festivals, 79-82 and 84-85.
Selected Filmography: *Johann's Gift to Christmas*, TV, 91, CDN, Cos; "My Secret Identity" (26 eps), TV, 89, CDN, Cos; *Cold Comfort*, Th, 88, CDN, Cos; ABC Sports Promo, Cm, 88, CDN, Cos; *Eric Nagler: A Special for All Seasons*, TV, 88, CDN, Cos; "Sharon, Lois and Bram's Elephant Show" (26 eps), TV, 86-87, CDN, Cos; "Men", TV, 89, CDN, Cos; *Almost Grown*, TV, 87, USA/CDN, Assist Cos; *The Canadian Conspiracy*, TV, 85, CDN, Assist Cos; *Mafia Princess*, TV, 85, USA, Assist Cos; *A Private World*, Th, 81, CDN, Art Dir.

PARTRIDGE, Wendy ◆
(403)453-2929.
Type of Production and Credits: Th Film-Cos; Th Short-Cos; TV Film-Cos; TV Video-Cos.
Genres: Drama-Th&TV; Musical-Th&TV; Action-Th&TV; Science Fiction-Th&TV.
Biography: Born 1953, Colchester, England; Canadian and British citizenship. Two Genie nominations and one award.
Selected Filmography: *Opening Ceremonies - 1988 Winter Olympics*, TV, 88, CDN, Cos; *Loyalties*, Th, 85, CDN/GB, Cos, (GENIE 87); *Isaac Littlefeathers*, TV, 84, CDN, Cos; *Draw!*, TV, 83, CDN/USA, Cos; *Running Brave*, Th, 83, CDN/USA, Co-Wr; *Latitude 55*, Th, 80, CDN, Cos; *Firebird 2051 AD*, Th, 80, CDN, Cos; *The Hounds of Notre Dame*, Th, 80, CDN, Cos.

PRITCHARD, Anne
- see ART DIRECTORS

RATE, Michèle ◆
(514)651-7599.
Types de production et générique: TV film-Cos; TV vidéo-Cos.

Types d'oeuvres: Drame-TV; Comédie-TV; Variété-TV; Enfants-TV.
Curriculum vitae: Née en 1952, Alma, Lac St-Jean. Deux ans d'études en haute couture chez Mme Dibelo, 74.

SCHILT, Sara
ACFC. 513 Queen St. W., #5, Toronto, ON M5V 2B4 (416)362-2990. Mustard & Relish Designs Inc., 513 Queen St. W., #5, Toronto, ON M5V 2B4 (416)362-2990.
Type of Production and Credits: Th Film-Cos; Th Short-Cos Buyer; TV Film-Ward Assist.
Genres: Drama-TV; Comedy-Th&TV; Action-Th&TV; Horror-Th.
Biography: Born in 1959 in Seattle, Washington. An American citizen living in Canada for the past 12 years. Trained at the National Theatre School of Canada in Montreal, in set and costume design. Worked professionally in theatre for several years before branching out into film and television. Also designs dance costumes. Special skills include furniture design, fabric/fibre art and creation of artificial food.
Selected Filmography: "Katts & Dog" (26 eps), TV, 90-91, CDN/USA/F, Cos; *Over the Edge/Intimate Delusions*, Th, 91, CDN, Cos; *Prom Night IV*, Th, 91, CDN, Cos; "Katts & Dog" (12 eps), TV, 90, CDN/USA/F, Ward; *World's Oldest Living Bridesmaid*, Th, 90, USA/CDN, Ward Assist; *New Souls*, Th, 90, USA/CDN, Cos Buyer; *Happy Days In Hell*, Th, 90, CDN, Cos Buyer; "T and T" (18 eps), TV, 89, USA/CDN, Assist Cos; "War of the Worlds" (4 eps), TV, 89, USA/CDN, Assist Ward; *Where The Heart Is*, Th, 89, CDN, Ward Assist; "Friday's Curse" (3 eps), TV, 89, USA/CDN, Ward Assist; "T and T" (22 eps), TV, 88, USA/CDN, Ward Assist; *Sister Ruth*, Th, 88, USA/CDN, Ward Assist; *The Brain*, Th, 87-88, CDN, Assist Ward.

SECORD, Ruth
IATSE 873. 17 Wayland Ave., Toronto, ON M4E 3C6 (416)698-3567. 676989 Ont. Inc., 17 Wayland Ave., Toronto, ON M4E 3C6 (416)698-3567.
Type of Production and Credits: Th Film-Cos; TV Film-Cos.
Genres: Drama-Th&TV; Comedy-Th&TV; Children's-TV; Commercials-TV.
Biography: Born 1953, Edmonton, Alberta; Canadian citizen. English speaking. Graduate in Fashion Design, Ryerson Polytechnical Institute and National Theatre School, design division. Has been a costume designer in theatre and TV for 15 years; prefers period pieces of any era.
Selected Filmography: "Two for Joy" (1 eps), TV, 91, CDN, Cos; *Toyota Canada*, Cm, 90, CDN, Cos; *The Little Kidnappers*, TV, 89, CDN/USA, Cos; *Beautiful Dreamers*, Th, 89, CDN, Cos; *Brown Bread Sandwiches*, Th, 89, CDN/I, Cos; "The Campbells" (100 eps), TV, 84-88, CDN/GB, Cos; "Mr Dress-Up" (100 eps), TV, 83, CDN, Cos.

SNETSINGER, Martha
402 - 1176 West 6th Ave., Vancouver, BC V6H 1A4 (604)736-7567. 1 Killdeer Cres., Toronto, ON M4G 1M4 (416) 425-3606.
Type of Production and Credits: Th Film-Cos; TV Film-Cos.
Genres: Drama-Th&TV; Comedy-Th&TV; Action-Th&TV.
Biography: Born in 1958 in Toronto, Ontario. Studied art history, Queen's University, Kingston, 1977-79. Certificate and diploma, costume studies, Dalhousie University, Halifax, 1982-85. Designed sets and costumes for theatre before working in film. Genie nomination for Costume Design for *The Last Winter*, 1990.
Selected Filmography: *Silent Motive*, TV, 91, CDN/USA, Cos; *Mario & the Mob*, TV, 91, USA, Cos; "The Hitchhiker" (22 eps), TV, 89-90, CDN/USA/F, Cos; *Highway 61*, Th, 90, CDN, Cos; *Lost in the Barrens*, TV, 89, CDN, Cos; *The Last Winter*, Th, 89, CDN, Cos; *Age Old Friends*, TV, 88, USA/CDN, Cos; *Act of God*, Th, 88, CDN, Cos; *Tidy Endings*, TV, 88, USA/CDN, Cos; *Higher Education*, Th, 86, CDN, Cos; *Oklahoma Smugglers*, Th, 86, USA/CDN, Cos.

VIEIRA, Kathy ✧
(416)971-6373.
Type of Production and Credits: Th Film-Cos; Th Short-Cos; TV Film-Cos; TV Video-Cos.
Genres: Drama-Th&TV; Comedy-Th&TV; Children's-Th&TV; Commercials-Th&TV.
Biography: Born 1950, Antigua; Canadian citizenship. Studied at Ontario College of Art and George Brown College; apprenticed in theatre. Has worked in costume for film and theatre since 72. Has taught and organized costume seminars for the ACFC in Toronto. Has designed costumes for film productions in Toronto, England, Los Angeles and New York.
Selected Filmography: "Family Man" (1 eps), TV, 88, CDN/USA, Cos; *Palais*

Royal, Th, 87, CDN, Cos; *Drop Out Mother*, TV, 87, CDN/USA, Cos; *Heaven on Earth*, TV, 86, CDN/GB, Cos; "Frontiers" (5 eps), TV, 85, CDN/GB/F, Cos; *Reckless Disregard*, TV, 84, CDN, Cos; *Crisis*, TV, 84, CDN, Cos; "Edison Twins" (13 eps), TV, 83, CDN/USA, Cos; "Hyannis Affair" (5 eps), TV, 82, CDN/USA, Cos; *Frank Mills Christmas Special*, TV, 82, CDN, Cos; *Deadline*, Th, 79, CDN, Cos; *Off Your Rocker*, Th, 79, CDN, Cos; *Title Shot*, Th, 79, CDN, Cos; *Stone Cold Dead*, Th, 78, CDN, Cos; *Just Jesse*, Th, 77, CDN, Cos.

WELLS, Larry S.
IATSE 873 & 891. RR #1, Box W6, Bowen Island, BC V0N 1G0 (604)947-0383. Leonard Bonnell, 1505 West 2nd Ave., Ste. 200, Vancouver, BC V6H 3Y4 (604)733-9800.
Type of Production and Credits: Th Film-Cos; TV Film-Cos.
Genres: Drama-Th&TV; Comedy-Th&TV; Variety-TV; Commercials-TV.
Biography: Completed his Fine Arts education at the University of Arizona. While on holiday in Toronto from his native America, he landed a costume designing assignment on the series "Police Surgeon", then decided to stay in Toronto and work at his craft.
Selected Filmography: "Scene of the Crime" (9 eps), TV, 90-91, CDN/F, Cos; *Bingo*, Th, 90, USA, Cos; *Kootenai Brown*, Th, 90, CDN, Cos; *Small Sacrifices*, TV, 89, USA, Cos; *The Dream Team*, Th, 88, USA, Assoc Cos; *Short Circuit II*, Th, 87, USA, Cos; *Three Men and a Baby*, Th, 87, USA, Cos; *I'll Take Manhattan*, TV, 86, USA, Cos; *The Right of the People*, TV, 85, CDN, Cos; *Porky's*, Th, CDN, Cos; *The Black Stallion*, Th, USA, Cos.

WENAUS, Lee ◊
(306)352-0697.
Type of Production and Credits: Th Short-Cos; TV Film-Cos; TV Video-Cos.
Genres: Drama-Th&TV; Variety-Th&TV; Musical-Th&TV.
Biography: Born 1959, Saskatchewan. B.A., B.Ed., Visual Arts and Music, University of Regina. Produced multimedia visual arts show and conceptual art in body masks. Visual display work, set dressing, props, wardrobe.
Selected Filmography: *Vaudeville Inside Out*, TV, 88, CDN, Wardrobe; "Switchback" (13 eps), TV, 88, CDN, Res; *Across the Medicine Line*, Th, 87, CDN, Cos; *The Bottom Line*, In, 87, CDN, Cos; Saskatchewan Drug and Alcohol Commission, Cm, 87, CDN, Cos; City of Saskatoon, Cm, 87, CDN, Cont; *Expo 86: Saskatchewan*, Th, 86, CDN, Props; *Mistress Madeline/Daughters of the Country*, Th, 86, CDN, Props.

WOODWARD, Pamela ◊
(416)651-2922.
Type of Production and Credits: TV Film-Cos; TV Video-Cos.
Genres: Drama-Th&TV; Comedy-Th&TV; Variety-Th&TV; Children's-Th&TV.
Biography: Born 1945, Kansas City, Missouri; Canadian citizenship. Studied Painting and Drawing, University of Iowa. Began working in theatre: Toronto Workshop Productions, Young People's Theatre, St. Lawrence Centre, Canadian Opera Company, National Ballet of Canada, 68-73; assistant to costuming instructor, York University, 73-75; joined CBC, 76. Specialized in fabric dyeing and artistic fabric treatment.
Selected Filmography: *Squamish Five*, Th, 87, CDN, Cos; *Family Reunion*, TV, 87, CDN, Cos; *Dancemakers*, TV, 87, CDN, Cos; "Seeing Things" (10 eps), TV, 86-87, CDN, Assist Cos.

Directors
Réalisateurs

ADAIR, Trayton
Trayton Adair Productions, 103 Charles St. E., Toronto, ON M4Y 1V2 (416)922-2930.
Type of Production and Credits: TV Film-Dir; TV Video-Dir.
Genres: Commercials-TV.
Biography: Born in Saskatoon, Saskatchewan. B.A., University of Saskatoon. Director of 800 commercials since 74; has won awards including Toronto Art Directors' Association, Broadcasting Executive Society Award, Clio and US Commercials Festival awards.

ADETUYI, Alfons
- see WRITERS

AIKENHEAD, Chris
- see PRODUCTION SOUND MIXERS

ALEXANDRA, Christopher P.
- see COMPOSERS

ALIANAK, Hrant
ACTRA. 629 Broadview Ave., Toronto, ON M4K 2N3 (416)463-1552. Oscars & Abrams Associates Inc., 59 Berkeley St., Toronto, ON M5A 2W5 (416)860-1790. FAX: 860-0236.
Type of Production and Credits: Th Short-Dir/Wr; TV Film-Dir; TV Video-Dir/Wr.
Genres: Drama-TV; Comedy-TV; Action-Th; Experimental-Th&TV.
Biography: Born 1950; Canadian citizenship. Languages: English, French and Armenian. Attended McGill University and York University. Writer, director in theatre since 72; has worked in Canada, US, UK; actor in TV and films since 80; plays written and directed include *Lucky Strike, Night Passion and Sin* and *The Blues*.

Selected Filmography: *A Problem*, Th, 90, CDN, Wr/Dr/Prod; *Michael and Kitty*, TV, 85, CDN, Dir; *The Sacrifice*, Th, 78, CDN, Dir/Wr; *Paranoid Fractions*, "Microdramas", TV, 75, CDN, Dir/Wr.

ALLAN, Don
ACCT. Revolver Film Company, 217 Richmond St. W., 2nd Floor, Toronto, ON M5V 1WZ (416)979-7777. FAX: 971-6188.
Type of Production and Credits: TV Film-Prod/Dir; TV Video-Prod/Dir.
Genres: Variety-TV; Musical-TV; Commercials-TV; Music Video-TV.
Biography: Born 1958, Toronto, Ontario. Graduate of Ontario College of Art. Founded own video and film production company, D'Allan Film and Video Productions, 84. Has won many awards for films and music videos including Golden Rose, Best Variety and Critics' Choice, Montreux for *I Am A Hotel*; Silver Medal, Best Variety, Critics' Choice, NY; Golden Sheaf, Yorkton; Special Jury Award, CFTA; Best Foreign Variety Program, Iris Award; Golden Gate, San Francisco; ANIK and 2 CanPros. *In Fashion* won Media Award; Genie nomination, Best Editing; Best Fashion Video, Video Culture. *Tears Are Not Enough* earned Genie nomination for Best Documentary. *One More Colour* won Gold Medal, NY and Best Music Video, Houston. *I Muse Aloud* won Silver Medal, NY and earned a Gemini nomination. *What You Do to My Body* earned a Juno nomination, Canadian Music Video Awards, Best Metal Video. Won Best Director, Canadian Music Video Awards and Juno nomina-tion, Best Music Video for *I Wanna Know*. *Listen Up* won Broadcast Award, NCGA; First Place-Commercial Art, CCGA; Best Animated Commercial, Mobius Award. *A Vision for the Future* won Best Corporate Production, Quasar Award. *Between the Earth and Sky* won Best Music Program, Houston.
Selected Filmography: *INXS Down Under*, Labatt's, Cm, 91, CDN, Dir; *Sharon, Lois and Bram - Sing A to Z*, TV, 91, CDN, Dir; *What You Do To My Body*, Lee Aaron, MV, 90, CDN, Dir; *I Wanna Know*, John James, MV, 90, CDN, Dir; *I Am A Wild Party*, Kim Mitchell, MV, 90, CDN, Dir; *Listen Up*, McDonalds, Cm, 90, CDN, Dir; *A Vision for the Future*, Rogers Communications, Corp, 90, CDN, Dir; *Between the Earth and Sky*, Luba, TV, 89, CDN, Dir; *One More Colour*, Jane Siberry, TV, 88, CDN, Dir; *I Muse Aloud*, Jane Siberry, TV, 88, CDN, Dir; *Tears Are Not Enough*, TV, 87, CDN, 2nd U Dir; *In Fashion*, TV, 86, CDN, Dir/Prod/P Pro Dir; *I Am A Hotel*, Leonard Cohen, TV, 83, CDN, Dir.

ALMOND, Paul
DGA, DGC, ACTT. 1272 Redpath Cres., Montreal, PQ H3G 2K1 (514)849-7921.
Type of Production and Credits: Th Film-Dir/Prod; TV Film-Dir; TV Video-Dir/Prod.
Genres: Drama-Th&TV; Comedy-TV; Action-Th&TV; Horror-TV.
Biography: Born 1931, Montreal, Quebec. Attended Bishop's College School, Lennoxville; McGill University; B.A., M.A., Balliol College, Oxford. Directed and produced more than 100 TV dramas in Toronto, London, NY, LA, 54-67. *Ups & Downs* won the Bronze Prize, Houston; won 3 Ohio State Awards for TV Dramas; won CFA for Best Director of TV Drama for *Every Person is Guilty*.
Selected Filmography: *Captive Hearts*, Th, 87, USA, Dir; *Ups & Downs*, Th, 81, CDN, Wr/Prod/Dir; *Every Person is Guilty*, TV, 80, CDN, Dir, (CFA); *Final Assignment*, Th, 79, CDN, Dir; *Journey*, Th, 71, CDN, Wr/Prod/Dir; *The Act of the Heart*, Th, 69, CDN, Wr/Prod/Dir, (CFA); *Isabel*, Th, 67, CDN, Wr/Prod/Dir.

AMINI, Stephen
DGA, IATSE. Champagne Pictures, 437 Sherbourne St., Toronto, ON M4X 1K5 (416)928-3001.
Type of Production and Credits: TV Film-Dir/Cam.
Genres: Commercials-TV.
Biography: Born 1949. Director/cameraman on numerous US and Canadian television commercials. Awards include Bessies, Clios and Gold Camera (US Industrial Film Festival); Finalist, NY Film Festival.

AMITAY, Jonathan
- see PRODUCERS

ANDERSON, Jon C.
- see PRODUCERS

ANDERSON, Michael
ACTT, DGA, DGC, ACCT. c/o DGC, 3 Church St., Suite 202, Toronto, ON M5E 1M2 (416)364-0122.
Type of Production and Credits: Th Film-Dir; TV Film-Dir.
Genres: Drama-Th&TV; Comedy-Th; Action-Th; Science Fiction-Th&TV.
Biography: Born in London, England; British and Canadian citizenship. Languages: English, French, German and Italian. Attended Lycée Corneille, France;

Treitschke Schule, Berlin; London Polytechnic. *Around the World in 80 Days* nominated for 10 Oscars, won 5 including Best Picture, and 52 international awards. *The Shoes of the Fisherman*, won Best Picture, National Board of Review. *Conduct Unbecoming* tied for Best Picture, National Board of Review.
Selected Filmography: *Young Catherine* (mini-series), TV, 90, USA/CDN/GB/D/I, Dir; *Millennium*, Th, 88, USA/CDN, Dir; *The Jeweller's Shop*, Th, 87, CDN/I/F, Dir; *The Sword of Gideon* (mini-series), TV, 86, CDN, Dir; *Separate Vacations*, Th, 85, CDN, Dir; *The Martian Chronicles*, TV, 79, USA, Dir; *Orca*, Th, 77, USA, Dir; *Logan's Run*, Th, 75, USA, Dir; *Conduct Unbecoming*, Th, 74, GB, Dir; *Doc Savage*, Th, 73, USA, Dir; *The Shoes of the Fisherman*, Th, 68, USA, Dir; *The Quiller Memorandum*, Th, 66, GB, Dir; *Operation Crossbow*, Th, 65, GB, Dir; *The Naked Edge*, Th, 61, USA, Dir; *The Wreck of the Mary Deare*, Th, 60, USA, Dir.

ANDREWS, Neil
- see PRODUCERS
ANGELOVICI, Gaston André
- voir PRODUCTEURS
APOR, Gabor
- see PRODUCERS
ARCAND, Denys
ACTRA, ARRFQ, SARDEC, ACCT.
3365 Ridgewood, #1, Montréal, PQ H3V 1B4 (514)341-6139.
Types de production et générique: l métrage-Réal/Sc; c métrage-Réal/Sc; TV film-Réal/Sc; TV vidéo-Réal/Sc.
Types d'oeuvres: Drame-C&TV; Documentaire-C&TV.
Curriculum vitae: Né en 1941, Québec. Maîtrise en histoire, Université de Montréal. *Le Confort et l'indifférence* a gagné le Prix Ouimet-Molson. *Le Déclin de l'empire américain* a remporté le Prix de la Fédération Internationale de la Press Cinématographique, Cannes (Quinzaine des Réalisateurs), le Prix John Labatt Classic pour le film le plus populaire et le Prix CITY, Meilleur Film Canadien, Festival du Film de Toronto, 86.
Filmographie sélective: *Jésus de Montréal*, C, 88, CDN, Sc/Réal; *Le Déclin de l'empire américain*, C, 85, CDN, Réal/Sc, (2 GENIE 87); *Le Crime d'Ovide Plouffe* (réal, sc-2 ém TV), C, 83, CDN/F, Réal/Co sc; "Empire Inc." (3 eps), TV, 83, CDN, Réal; *Le Confort et l'Indifférence*, C, 81, CDN, Réal; *Duplessis*, TV, 76, CDN, Sc; *Gina*, C, 74, CDN, Réal/Mont/Sc; *Réjeanne Padovani*, C, 72, CDN, Réal/Sc; *La Maudite Galette*, C, 71, CDN, Réal/Sc; *Québec: Duplessis et après...*, C, 70, CDN, Réal/Mont; *On est au coton*, C, 70, CDN, Réal.

ARCHIBALD, Nancy
- see PRODUCERS
ARMATAGE, Kay
53 Brunswick Ave., Toronto, ON M5S 2L8 (416)968-3224. University of Toronto, Innis College, 2 Sussex Ave., Toronto, ON (416)978-4671.
Type of Production and Credits: Th Short-Dir.
Genres: Drama-Th; Documentary-Th; Experimental-Th.
Biography: Born 1943, Lanigan, Saskatchewan. B.A., Queen's University; Ph.D., University of Toronto. Has written extensively in Canadian publications, including *Take One* and *Canadian Forum*. Film Reviewer, CBC Radio, CTV; programmer, Festival of Festivals; teaches Cinema and Women's Studies, University of Toronto. *Striptease* won the Silver Hugo, and *Storytelling* won the Bronze Hugo, Chicago Film Festival; *Artist on Fire* earned Honourable Mention, San Francisco Golden Gate awards and Award of Excellence in Documentaries, Toronto Festival of Festivals, 87. Has been awarded YWCA's Woman of Distinction, 88; Toronto Women in Film Award of Merit, 88. Has written for the *Canadian Journal of Social and Political Theory*.
Selected Filmography: *Artist on Fire: The Work of Joyce Wieland*, Th, 87, CDN, Dir; *Storytelling*, Th, 83, CDN, Dir; *Striptease*, Th, 80, CDN, Dir; *Speak Body*, Th, 79, CDN, Dir; *Bed And Sofa*, Th, 79, CDN, Dir; *Gertrude and Alice in Passing*, Th, 78, CDN, Dir; *Jill Johnston*, Th, 77, CDN, Dir.

ARMSTRONG, Antony
- see PRODUCERS
ARMSTRONG, Mary
- see PRODUCERS
ARSENAULT, Ray
236 Balliol St., Toronto, ON M4S 1C5 (416)489-4783. (416)485-3141. FAX: 485-3141.
Type of Production and Credits: TV Film-Dir; TV Video-Dir.
Genres: Drama-TV; Comedy-TV; Documentary-TV; Industrial-TV.
Biography: Born in US; landed immigrant, Canada. Attended Wayne State University. Served in the United States Marines. Extensive TV production since 51; staff director, 54-68: live television, stage, film videotape, multi-camera, single-camera, drama, comedy,

documentaries, commercials, corporate, training, education, etc.
Selected Filmography: "Pet Peeves", TV, CDN, Dir; "Lifetime", TV, CDN, Dir; "Imprint", TV, CDN, Dir; *Come Sail A Legend*, TV, CDN, Dir; *Bio-Technology: Blessing or Curse?*, TV, CDN, Dir; *Commander Crumbcake*, TV, CDN, Dir; *EMU-TV*, TV, CDN, Dir; *Dilemma of the Modern Man*, TV, CDN, Dir; *Mary & Michael*, TV, CDN, Dir; *Menachem Begin*, TV, CDN, Dir; "Tracy", TV, CDN, Dir; *Mixed Doubles*, TV, CDN, Dir; *Challenge*, TV, CDN, Dir; *High Hopes*, TV, CDN, Dir; "King of Kensington", TV, CDN, Dir.

ARSENAULT, Yvon
629 Querbes, Outremont, PQ H2W 3W7 (514)495-9529.
Types de production et générique: l métrage-Réal/Prod/Sc; c métrage-Réal/Prod/Sc; TV film-Réal/Prod/Sc; TV vidéo-Réal/Prod/Sc.
Types d'oeuvres: Drame-C&TV; Education-C&TV; Annonces-C&TV; Industriel-C&TV.
Curriculum vitae: Né en 1950, Shawinigan. Etudes classiques. Etudes en communications à L'UQUAM. Stage de mise en scène en France avec Claude Chabrol. Gémeau, meilleure émission inf. pour "Comment ça va?".
Filmographie sélective: "Comment ça va?" (26 eps), TV, 89, CDN, Réal; "Des Puces pour écrire" (2 eps), TV, 89, CDN, Réal; *Modudent*, In, 89, CDN, Réal; "L'Or et le Papier" (26 eps), TV, 88, CDN/F, 1er ass réal; "Formule 1" (26 eps), TV, 87, CDN/F, 1er ass réal; *Babe*, C, 82, CDN/ USA, 1er ass réal; "Neuf et Demi" (7 eps), TV, 82, CDN, 1er ass réal; *Suzanne*, C, 82, CDN, 2e ass réal; *Au revoir... à lundi*, C, 81, CDN/F, 2e ass réal; *Yesterday*, C, 81, CDN, 2e ass réal; *Violette Nozière*, C, 79, CDN/F, 2e ass réal; *L'Homme en Colère*, C, 79, CDN/F, 2e ass réal; *La Nuit de la Poésie*, C, 78, CDN, 1er ass réal; "Les anglais sont arrivés" (10 eps), TV, 78, CDN, 1er ass réal; *Pris au Collet*, C, 73, CDN, 1er ass réal.

AUDY, Michel
ARRFQ. 193, boul. Bécancour, St-Grégoire de Nicolet, PQ G0X 2T0 (819)233-2585.
Types de production et générique: l métrage-Réal/Sc/Mont/D photo; c métrage-Prod/Réal/Sc/Mont; TV film-Prod/Réal; TV vidéo-Prod/Réal.
Types d'oeuvres: Drame-C&TV; Documentaire-C&TV; Education-C&TV; Industriel-C&TV.
Curriculum vitae: Né en 1947, Grandmère, Québec. Langues: français et anglais. Equivalent d'une maîtrise en cinéma, Ministère de l'Education du Québec. Producteur/réalisateur de 25 courts métrages et d'une série pour télévision. Spécialiste en télévision éducative et en moyens techniques d'enseignement; chargé de cours (Université Laval, Cégeps de Victoriaville et Trois-Rivières); réalisateur/concepteur au Service Audio-Visuel, Cégep de Trois-Rivières, depuis 70; Directeur du Service, 85-86; a fondé Les Films Michel Audy Ltée, 73. A gagné le Prix du Ministère de l'Education du Québec, 80 et 83.
Filmographie sélective: *Crever à 20 ans*, C, 84, CDN, Prod; *Luc ou la part des choses*, C, 82, CDN, Prod; *La Comptabilité II*, C, 80, CDN, Prod; *La Comptabilité I*, C, 79, CDN, Prod; *Ma soeur, ma soeur...*, ED, 76, CDN, Sc/Réal/Mont/D phot; *Bécancour-Québec*, C, 74, CDN, Réal/Mont; *La maison qui empêche de voir la ville*, C, 74, CDN, Sc/Prod/Mont/Réal; *Toccate et fugue*, C, 73, CDN, Sc/Réal/Prod/Mont; *Corps et Ame*, C, 72, CDN, Réal/Sc/ Mont; *Jean-François-Xavier de...*, C, 69, CDN, Réal/Sc/Mont; *A force d'homme*, C, 68, CDN, Réal/D phot/Mont.

AYLWARD, Alan W.
ACCT. 287 Jackson St. W., Hamilton, ON L8P 1M6 (416)529-0294.
Type of Production and Credits: Th Film-Wr/Dir; TV Film-Prod/Wr.
Genres: Drama-Th; Documentary-TV; Educational-TV; Industrial-Th&TV.
Biography: Born 1949, Toronto, Ontario. Studied Business and Marketing, Seneca College. Trained and worked in theatre as actor and puppeteer in Canada, US, Europe; acted on stage, in TV and film. Postproduction and production training in 16 mm and 35 mm with several Canadian film companies; wrote educational films and radio commercials; taught disabled children film and TV (video) production techniques, 75-80. Winner, Gold, American Film Festival, New York; *Flight for Freedom* won Gold at Houston, 91. *Guilt By Omission* and *Twice Upon a Time* are in development.
Selected Filmography: *Chaindance*, Th, 90, CDN, Wr; *Flight for Freedom*, TV, 90, CDN, Prod/Dir; *Work & Family*, In, 90, CDN, Exec Prod; *Freedom Flight*, Cm, 90, CDN, Prod/Wr; *All in the Same Boat/A Sea of Dreams*, TV, 89, CDN, Prod/Dir/Wr; *Disability Myth* (3 parts), TV, 81-84, CDN, Prod/Dir/Wr.

AZZOPARDI, Anthony
ACCT. 345 Bain Ave., Toronto, ON M4J 1B9 (416)466-7379.
Type of Production and Credits: Th Film-Dir/Prod/Wr; TV Film-Dir/Prod/Wr.
Genres: Drama-TV; Documentary-Th&TV.
Biography: Born 1950, Malta; Canadian citizenship. Languages: English, Maltese and Italian. B.F.A.(Honours), Film and Theatre Directing, York University. As a theatre director/actor worked in Canada, US and Poland. Films shown at various national and international festivals.
Selected Filmography: *Latin Sounds*, TV, 91, CDN, Dir/Prod/Wr; *Making Opera*, TV, 87-88, CDN, Wr/Prod/Dir; *Motherlove*, TV, 87, CDN, Dir/Prod; *The Pelican*, TV, 87, CDN, Dir/Prod; *John Kim Bell*, TV, 83-84, CDN, Dir/Prod; *The Stronger*, TV, 82, CDN, Dir/Prod; *The World of Ahmed Fez Ben-Zine*, TV, 82, CDN, Dir/Prod/Wr; *Surfacing*, Th, 79, CDN, Assoc Prod; *Toronto - The People City*, TV, 79, CDN, Dir/Prod.

AZZOPARDI, Mario
DGC. 2395 Carrington Place, Oakville, ON L6J 5P5 (416)844-6645. FAX: 8447022. Don Kopaloff (213) 203-8430.
Type of Production and Credits: Th Film-Dir; TV Film-Dir.
Genres: Action-Th&TV; Documentary-TV; Children's-TV.
Biography: Born 1950, Malta; Canadian citizenship. B.A., Royal University of Malta.
Selected Filmography: "In the Heat fo the Night" (3 eps), TV, 90-91, USA, Dir; "The Flash" (4 eps), TV, 90-91, USA, Dir; "E.N.G." (pilot), TV, 89, CDN, Dir; "Night Heat" (24 eps), TV, 85-86, CDN, Dir; *Nowhere to Hide*, Th, 86, CDN, Dir; *Neighbours/Street-Wise/Golden Promise*, "Toronto Trilogy", TV, 84, CDN, Dir/Prod; *Deadline*, Th, 80, CDN, Dir.

BACKUS, Barry
- see POSTPRODUCTION SOUND MIXERS

BAILEY, Norma
ACCT. Flat City Films, 336 Queenston St., Winnipeg, MB R3N 0W8 (204)489-6181.
Type of Production and Credits: Th Film-Prod/Dir; TV Film-Prod/Dir.
Genres: Drama-Th&TV; Documentary-Th&TV.
Biography: Born 1949, Winnipeg, Manitoba. Graduate of Architecture, University of Manitoba. Many awards including New York, Yorkton, Geminis.
Selected Filmography: *Bordertown Café*, Th, 91, CDN, Prod/Dir; *Martha, Ruth & Edie*, Th, 87, CDN, Co-Dir; *Heartland* (Imax), Th, 87, CDN, Dir; "Daughters of the Country" (4 eps), TV, 86, CDN, Prod/Dir, (GEMINI 87); *It's Hard to Get It Here*, Th, 85, CDN, Prod/Dir; *Nose and Tina*, Th, 80, CDN, Dir, (2 BIJOU); *Performer*, Th, 79, CDN, Dir.

BAKER, Bob
NABET, CULR. 1168 Ste. Therese Lane, Orleans, ON K1C 2A6 (613)837-1286. Canadian Labour Congress, 2841 Riverside Dr., Ottawa, ON K1V 8X7 (613)521-3400 EXT: 206.
Type of Production and Credits: TV Film-Dir/Prod/Ed; TV Video-Dir/Prod/Ed.
Genres: Documentary-TV; Educational-TV; Children's-TV; Industrial-TV.
Biography: Born in 1947 in Toronto, Ontario. Worked at CFTO-TV, ABC, NBC, TVOntario and CLC Educational Services, audio/visual. Has won numerous awards (CALM and ILPA) for labour-produced documentary productions and commercials. Active in golf, bowling and baseball.
Selected Filmography: *A Day in the Life of a Racist*, TV, 91, CDN, Coord/Ed; *When Enough is Enough*, TV, 90, CDN, Coord/Ed; *The Waterdrop Torture*, TV, 89, CDN, Coord/Ed; *AIDS: The Workplace Facts*, TV, 87, CDN, Dir/Ed; *The Microelectronics Revolution*, TV, 83, Dir/Ed.

BALL, Christopher
DGC. R.R. #1, King City, ON L0G 1K0 (416)833-6645. (416)720-7996.
Type of Production and Credits: Th Film-Assist Dir; Th Short Film-Dir/Prod/Wr/DOP; TV Film-Dir/Prod/DOP; TV Video-Dir.
Genres: Drama-Th&TV; Comedy-Th&TV; Industrial-Th; Music Video-Th.
Biography: Born 1962, Toronto, Ontario. Canadian citizenship; EEC passport holder. B.A.A., Motion Picture, Ryerson Polytechnical Institute; workshop for actors, directors and writers, NFB. Winner of Norman Jewison Filmmaker Award and CBC Telefest Short Drama award for *After the Argument*. Areas of special skill include whitewater canoeing, skiing and wilderness tripping. Currently involved with Tapelock Sound Studio as sound editor.
Selected Filmography: *Betrayal*, TV, 90, CDN, Prod/DOP; "Dracula: The Series", TV, 90, CDN/L, 2nd AD; *Foreign Nights*, Th, 89, CDN, 2nd AD; *The Greening of*

Ian Elliot, TV, 88, CDN, 2nd AD; *Discovering King Township's Heritage*, ED, 87, CDN, Dir/DOP/Ed; *Western Canoeing "Clipper"*, ED, 87, CDN, Dir/DOP/Ed; *It Was A Dark and Stormy Night*, Th, 86, CDN, Dir/Prod/Wr; *Hold On*, MV, 86, CDN, DOP; *After the Argument*, Th, 84, CDN, Dir/Prod; *Escape*, TV, 84, CDN, Dir/Prod.

BARCLAY, John
ACCT. 680 Queen's Quay West, Toronto, ON M5V 2Y9 (416)260-0428. Triune Productions Inc., 24 Ryerson Ave., Suite 304, Toronto, ON M5T 2P3 (416)362-9120.
Type of Production and Credits: Th Short-Prod/Dir; TV Film-Prod/Dir; TV Video-Dir/Ed.
Genres: Drama-Th&TV; Comedy-TV; Educational-TV; Commercials-TV.
Biography: Born 1956, Pembroke, Ontario. Honours B.F.A., Film Production, York University, 80. *Bay Street Tap*, winner, Canadian Independent Short Film Showcase, 83; Canada Council film production grant, 84; *A Laughing Matter* won Silver Apple at National Educational Film and Video Festival, 91.
Selected Filmography: *A Laughing Matter*, TV, 90, CDN, Dir/Ed; *Dialogue on Development*, Th, 88, CDN, Prod/Dir; *Key to Freedom*, Cm, 87, CDN, Prod/Dir; *The Diplomat*, "Money Tales", TV, 86, CDN, Ed; *Little People*, Cm, 85, CDN, Ed; *Technology Today/A Better Way*, In, 85, CDN, Ed; "Earth Odyssey" (13 eps), TV, 83, CDN, Ed; *Dancing Feet*, TV, 83, CDN, Assoc Prod; *Bay Street Tap*, Th, 82, CDN, Co-Prod/Co-Dir; *Jack Has It Made*, "Motley Tales", TV, 82, CDN, Dir; "There's No Place Like Home" (12 eps), ED, 78, CDN, Assist Dir.

BARCLAY, Robert
DGC. 129 Walmer Rd., Toronto, ON M5R 2X8 (416)964-1547.
Type of Production and Credits: Th Short-Dir; TV Film-Dir/Prod/Wr/Ed; TV Video-Dir/Prod/Wr/Ed.
Genres: Drama-Th&TV; Variety-Th&TV; Documentary-Th&TV.
Biography: Born 1930, Calgary, Alberta. Educated at Carleton University, Ottawa. Has made over 200 films and television programs, which have won 25 Canadian Film Awards, AMPIA, CanPro, Chris and Teddy Awards. President, DGC, 78-80.
Selected Filmography: *Mission to Moscow*, TV, 90, CDN, Wr/Prod/Dir; *Evelyn Hart's Moscow Gala*, TV, 87, CDN, Dir/Prod; *k.d. lang's Odyssey in Japan*, TV, 85, CDN, Dir/Prod; *Ian and Sylvia on the Trail of '98*, TV, 74, CDN, Dir; *Stampede in Scarlett*, Th, 73, CDN, Dir/Wr/Ed; *Walt Disney's Magic Carpet Tour 'round the World*, Th, 71, USA, Dir; *Manitoba Festival Country*, TV, 71, CDN, Dir/Ed; *Helicopter Holyland*, TV, 70, CDN, Dir; *Virginquest*, TV, 70, CDN, Dir; *One Canada/Two Nations*, TV, 68, CDN, Dir; *Badmen of BC*, "Telescope", TV, 67, CDN, Dir/Ed; *Canada '67*, Th, 66, USA, Dir; *The Dumbells*, TV, 65, CDN, Dir; *Children of Peace*, TV, 62, CDN, Dir; *Light for the Mind*, Th, 61, CDN, Dir.

BARDE, Barbara
- see PRODUCERS

BARLOW, David
- see PRODUCERS

BARRIE, Scott
- see WRITERS

BARTON, Natalie
- voir PRODUCTEURS

BATTISON, Jill
- see PRODUCERS

BATTLE, Murray
369 Sunnyside Ave., Toronto, ON M6R 2R9 (416)531-2519.
Type of Production and Credits: Th Short-Dir; TV Film-Dir/Wr; Interact V-Dir/Wr.
Genres: Drama-Th; Documentary-Th&TV; Educational-TV.
Biography: Born 1951, Calgary, Alberta. Attended York University (Film Production).
Selected Filmography: "The Spacewatch Club", TV, 91, CDN/USA, Wr/Dir; *Kolyma*, "The Hand of Stalin", TV, 90, UK/CDN, Dir; *Alan Bean*, TV, 89, CDN/USA, Co-Wr; *The Bartletts*, ED, 86, CDN, Wr/Dir; *The Hospital*, TV, 85, CDN, Dir.

BAUMAN, Larry ◊
(306)352-4569
Type of Production and Credits: Th Short-Prod/Dir/Ed; TV Film-Dir/Wr/Ed; TV Video-Prod/Dir; Video-Dir/Ed.
Genres: Drama-TV; Documentary-TV; Educational-TV; Commercials-TV.
Biography: Born 1954, Regina, Saskatchewan. Honours B.A., Psychology, University of Regina, 77; studied film under Jean Oser, University of Regina, 73-77. Producer, director, editor with Camera West Film Associates Ltd. since 78; 38 independent and sponsored documentary, educational and promotional films and audio visual productions; 36 institutional/government commercial campaigns. Winner of awards at Yorkton and Saskatchewan Showcase.
Selected Filmography: *The Human*

Eclipse, TV, 88, CDN, Dir/Wr/Ed; *Excellence*, Th, 87, CDN, Dir/Wr/Ed; *Concept Based Teaching*, ED, 87, CDN, Dir/Prod; *Heart and Soul*, TV, 86, CDN, Prod/Dir/Wr/Ed; *Expo 86 - Welcome*, In, 86, CDN, Prod/ Dir/Ed; *Trust Initiatives Program*, ED, 86, CDN, Prod/Dir; *The Individual and Society*, ED, 86, CDN, Prod/Dir; *The Move*, TV, 85, CDN, Dir/Wr/Ed; *Dreams...*, Th, 85, CDN, Prod/Ed; *At First Sight*, TV, 85, CDN, Ed; *Saskatchewan Past and Present*, ED, 85, CDN, Dir; *Passing Shadows*, Th, 84, CDN, Ed; *Don't Blame It on the kids*, ED, 84, CDN, Dir/Wr; *Energy Efficient Homes*, In, 83, CDN, Dir/Ed; *Potash*, In, 83, CDN, Dir/Ed.

BEAIRSTO, Ric ✧
(604)261-6956.
Type of Production and Credits: TV Film-Dir/Wr; TV Video-Dir/Wr.
Genres: Drama-TV.
Biography: Born 1953.
Selected Filmography: "The Beachcombers" (1 eps), TV, 86, CDN, Dir; *A Life of Independence*, TV, 86, CDN, Wr; *Close to Home*, Th, 85, CDN, Dir/Co-Wr.

BEAUBIEN, Conrad
- see PRODUCERS

BEAUDET, Michel
APFVQ. Les Productions Mag 2+, 400, rue McGill, #400, Montréal, PQ H2Y 2G1 (514)393-1843.
Types de production et générique: c métrage-Réal/Prod; TV film-Réal/Prod; TV vidéo-Réal/Prod.
Types d'oeuvres: Documentaire-TV; Annonces-TV; Industriel-TV; Vidéo clips-TV.
Curriculum vitae: Né en 1949 à Québec. Langues: français et anglais. Deux ans d'études en électronique, l'Institut Tech Art, 67-69. Monteur à Radio-Québec, 69-72; Directeur technique, monteur, réalisateur et producteur, Inter Vidéo, 72-80; depuis 80, Président, fondateur, réalisateur, producteur, Les Productions Mag 2+; a réalisé et produit plus de 600 messages publicitaires et plusieurs documents corporatifs.
Filmographie sélective: Campagne de publicité Ro-Na: Ro-Na Info, Cm, 91, CDN, Réal/Prod; *Un moteur en vacances*, In, 90, CDN, Réal/Prod; *Le hockey: notre passion* (6 eps), TV, 90, CDN, Réal/Prod; *Une affaire de succès*, In, 90, CDN, Réal/Prod; *Tradition et Innovation*, In, 90, CDN, Réal/Prod; *Protection*, Cm, 90, CDN, Réal/Prod; *Le nouveau visage de Steinberg*, Cm, 89, CDN, Réal/Prod; *It's Time To Look Into It*, In, 89, CDN, Réal/Prod; *Au delà de la carte*, In, 89, CDN, Réal/Prod; *The Symphony Answering Machine*, In, 89, CDN, Réal/Prod; *Service Plus*, In, 89, CDN, Réal/Prod; *La commande*, In, 89, CDN, Réal/Prod; *Captation FONDIA*, In, 88, CDN, Réal/Prod; *Superquiz-la rénovation*, In, 88, CDN, Réal/Prod; *Sept bannières*, In, 88, CDN, Réal/Prod.

BEAUDOIN, Jean
- voir MONTEURS

BEAUDRY, Jean
AQRRCT, UDA. 5037, Marquette, Montréal, PQ H2J 3Z1 (514)521-0544. Les Prod. du Lundi Matin, 7770, Casgrain, Montréal, PQ H2R 1Z2 (514)274-5743.
Types de production et générique: l métrage-Réal/Sc/Com/Mont; c métrage-Réal/Mont.
Types d'oeuvres: Documentaire-C; Drame-C.
Curriculum vitae: Né en 1947, Trois-Rivières, Québec. Baccalauréat ès Arts, 67; cours de scénarisation, ACPAV, 83. Metteur en scène et comédien, 65-75. *Jacques et novembre* a remporté le Prix Spécial du Jury, Festival international de Tokyo; Prix du Jury Catholique, Mannheim, Allemagne; Meilleur Film étranger (ex aequo), Festival de Belfort, France; primé à la qualité par la Société générale du cinéma du Québec. *Les Matins Infidèles*, Prime à la Qualité de la SOGIC (ex aequo avec *Jésus de Montréal*).
Filmographie sélective: *Pas de répit pour Mélanie*, "Contes pour tous", C, 90, CDN, Réal; *Les Matins Infidèles/Duluth et St-Urbain*, C, 89, CDN, Co-Réal/Co sc/Com/Mont; *MoMo*, C, 88, CDN, Co sc; *Marie s'en va t'en ville*, C, 86, CDN, Réal; *Jacques et novembre*, C, 84, CDN, Réal/Mont/Sc/Com; *Une Classe Sans Ecole*, C, 80, CDN, Réal; *Mission Réadaptation*, C, 80, CDN, Mont; *J'sors avec lui pis je l'aime*, C, 77, CDN, Réal/Mont/Rech; *La maison qui empêche de voir la ville*, C, 74, CDN, Com.

BEAUDRY, Michel ✧
ARRFQ. 6, Henderson, Chambly, PQ J3J 3G5 (514)658-2568.
Types de production et générique: TV Vidéo-Réal/Prod/Sc/Mont; c métrage-Réal/Prod/Sc/Mont; TV film-Réal/Prod/Sc/Mont.
Types d'oeuvres: Drame-C&TV; Documentaire-C&TV; Education-C&TV; Enfants-C&TV.
Curriculum vitae: Né en 1945, Montréal, Québec. Langues: français et anglais. Baccalauréat, Université de Montréal.

Journaliste; a été à l'emploi de plusieurs compagnies de film dont Delta, Cinéfilms, Onyx Film; pigiste depuis 74. "Herzberg" a remporté la 1er prix, Festival de Yougoslavie, 80.

BECKMAN, Henry
- see WRITERS

BEDARD, Jean-Thomas ◆
(514)598-8862.
Types de production et générique: c métrage-Réal; TV film-Réal/Sc.
Types d'oeuvres: Documentaire-C&TV; Animation-C.
Curriculum vitae: Né en 1947, Chicoutimi, Québec. Diplôme d'études générales en Histoire de l'Art, Université de Montréal; cours de peinture et de gravure, Ecole des Beaux-Arts de Montréal. Diverses expositions collectives et particulières en peinture, dessin, sérigraphie, photo. Voyage autour du monde, 79-80. Coordonnateur d'un stage de 10 mois au Brésil où 9 courts métrages ont été réalisés par de jeunes cinéastes brésiliens. Prix du Jury, Festival d'Annecy, France, 80; 1er Prix, Festival de Chicago et Main Award, Festival d'Oberhausen, 80, pour *L'Age de chaise.*
Filmographie sélective: *A force de bras,* ED, 88, CDN, Sc/Réal; *Le Combat d'Onésime Tremblay,* TV, 85, Rech/Sc/Réal; *L'Age de chaise,* C, 79, CDN, Sc/Réal; *Ceci est un message enregistré,* C, 73, CDN, Sc/Réal; *La Ville,* C, 70, CDN, Réal.

BEDEL, Jean-Pierre ◆
(604)922-9272.
Type of Production and Credits: Th Short-Dir/Prod; TV Film-Dir/Prod; TV Video-Dir/Prod.
Genres: Variety-TV; Documentary-TV.
Biography: Born 1944, Dammartin En Serve, Yvelines, France; Canadian and French citizenship. Raised in France, England, Germany, Spain. B.Sc., Telecommunications, Kent State University, Ohio, 74. French Army, 64-66.
Selected Filmography: *Something About Peace,* TV, 84, CDN, Dir/Prod; "CBC News" (300 eps), TV, 84, CDN, Dir; "The Vancouver Show" (150 eps), TV, 83-84, CDN, Dir/Prod; "Laurier's People" (30 eps), TV, 83-84, CDN, Dir; "CBC Midday News" (200 eps), TV, 82-83, CDN, Dir; "Pile ou face" (28 eps), TV, 81-82, CDN, Dir/Prod; "Vendredi vingt heures" (18 eps), TV, 81-82, CDN, Dir/Prod; *Le Pissenlit par la racine,* TV, 82, CDN, Dir/Prod; *Le Salon du livre,* TV, 81, CDN, Dir/Prod; "Ce Soir" (200 eps), TV, 81, CDN, Dir; "A contrepoids" (12 eps), TV, 80, CDN, Dir/Prod; *Le Jour du Seigneur,* TV, 80, CDN, Dir/Prod; "Ile-de-France actualité" (150 eps), TV, 77-78, F, Dir; "Ce Soir" (Manitoba), TV, 76, CDN, Dir; *The Champ,* TV, 74, USA, Dir/Prod; *L'Eau,* Th, 68, LAO, Dir/Prod.

BELANGER, André A. ◆
5245, av. Durocher, Outremont, PQ H2V 3X9 (514)270-1496. Ciné Groupe J.P. inc., 1151, Alexandre-de-Sève, Montréal, PQ H2L 2T7 (514)524-7567.
Types de production et générique: l métrage-Réal; c métrage-Réal; TV film-Réal/Prod; TV vidéo-Réal/Prod.
Types d'oeuvres: Documentaire-C&TV; Education-C&TV; Enfants-C&TV; Animation-C&TV.
Curriculum vitae: Né en 1942, Montréal, Québec. Langues: français et anglais. Diplôme en Communication graphique, Ecole des Beaux-Arts de Montréal, 67. Environ 75 films comme réalisateur et 30 comme producteur; producteur, Ciné Groupe J.P. inc.; co-fondateur, Productions Prisma inc., 70; développe présentement des connaissances en animation traditionelle, infographie et animation de marionnettes comme producteur.

BELANGER, Fernand
ARRFQ, 2429, Route 348, Canton de Rawdon, PQ J0K 1S0 (514)834-4508. ONF, 3155, Côte de Liesse, Montréal, PQ (514)283-9366. Louise Dugal, 4080, Chateaubuan, Montréal, PQ (514)525-9988.
Types de production et générique: l métrage-Réal/Mont; c métrage-Réal/Mont; TV film-Mont.
Types d'oeuvres: Documentaire-C&TV; Education-C; Experimental-C; Enfants-C&TV.
Curriculum vitae: Né en 1943, Rivière-du-Loup, Québec. Langues: français, anglais et espagnol. Baccalauréat ès Arts. Vingt ans de métier.
Filmographie sélective: *La musique de la langue,* C, 91, CDN, Sc/Réal; *Passiflora,* C, 85, CDN, Co réal/Mont/Sc; *L'Emotion dissonante,* C, 84, CDN, Réal/Mont/Sc; *L'Après cours,* TV, 84, CDN, Réal/Mont; *Debout sur leur terre,* C, 80, CDN, Mont; *De la tourbe et du restant,* C, 79, CDN, Sc/Réal/Mont; *Contebleu,* C, 76, CDN, Sc/Réal/Mont; *Chronique de la vie quotidienne,* C, 75, CDN, Mont; *Débarque-moué au Lac-des-Vents,* C, 75, CDN, Mont; *Où est-ce que tu vas de même?,* C, 74, CDN, Mont; *Le Pois fou,* TV, 72, CDN, Sc/Réal/Mont; *Ty-Peupe,* C, 70, CDN, Sc/Réal/Mont; *Ti-Coeur,* C,

69, CDN, Sc/Réal/Mont; *Via Borduas,* C, 68, CDN, Sc/Réal/Mont; *Initiation,* C, 67, CDN, Sc/Réal/Mont.

BELANGER, Raymond ◊
(416)463-3629.
Type of Production and Credits: TV Film-Dir/Prod.
Genres: Drama-TV; Documentary-Th&TV; Comedy-TV; Educational-TV.
Biography: Born 1950. B.A., University of Western Ontario, 72. Film editor for 12 years prior to producing/directing. Awards include Best Theatrical Documentary, 82.
Selected Filmography: *Inside Split,* TV, 87, CDN, Dir; *Streetgames,* TV, 87, CDN, Dir/Wr; *Cowboy,* TV, 87, CDN, Wr; "American Century" (2 eps), TV, 86, CN, Dir; "Frontrunners" (5 eps), TV, 85, CDN, Dir/Wr; "Energy: Search for an Answer" (4 eps), TV, 84, CDN, Ed; "Vista" (2 eps), TV, 83, CDN, Ed; "Going Great" (13 eps), TV, 83, CDN, Ed; "American Caesar" (2 eps), TV, 83, CDN, Ed; "Worldwide" (13 eps), TV, 82, CDN, Ed; The Soldiers Story, Th, 81, CDN, Ed; "The Ten Thousand Day War" (8 eps), TV, 80, CDN, Ed; "Headstart" (13 eps), TV, 79, CDN, Ed.

BELEC, Marilyn A.
NFB, 1571 Argyle St., Halifax, NS B3J 2B2 (902)426-6010.
Type of Production and Credits: TV Film-Dir/Prod; TV Video-Dir/Prod.
Genres: Drama-TV; Documentary-TV; Educational-Th&TV; Children's-Th&TV.
Biography: Chief, English Program, Atlantic Centre, National Film Board. President & Chief Operating Officer, Mobius Media Corporation, 79-91. During her 12-year tenure at Mobius, she produced, wrote and/or directed films and videos ranging from drama to documentary to animation, and garnered over 20 Canadian and international awards. As a distributor, has expertise in the health and educational markets. Has been a member of the Board of Directors of the Canadian Film and Television Association (now CFTPA), the Rules and Regulations Committee of the Gemini Awards for the Academy of Canadian Film and Television, the Advisory Board to the Department of Communications Non-theatrical Fund, and was Co-Vice-President of Toronto Women in Film and Television. Part of previous work with the NFB included preparing a major study on the Canadian film industry which included extensive research in Atlantic Canada.
Selected Filmography: *Anglosea* (3 films), Th, 87-88, CDN, Prod; *Sexual Harassment/Le Harcèlement sexuel au travail,* ED, 88, CDN, Prod/Dir; *Life after Eight/Après la huitème,* In, 88, CDN, Prod/Dir; *Smoke Rings/Rondes de fumée,* ED, 86, CDN, Prod; *Here Today...Where Tomorrow?,* ED, 85, CDN, Prod/Dir; *Safe Passage,* In, 85, CDN, Prod; *Theophylline Therapy Update,* In, 83, CDN, Prod; *Tom Magee - Man of Iron,* TV, 83, CND, Prod, (CFTA); *The Menopause Story,* ED, 82, CDN, Prod/Dir; *Teen Mother: A Story of Coping,* ED, 81, CDN, Prod; *The Investment Picture,* In, 80, CDN, Co-Prod; *Taking Chances,* ED, 79, CDN, Prod/Dir.

BELEC, Philip
Innovision Inc., 4935 Queen Mary Rd., Suite 204, Montreal, PQ H3W 1X4 (514)591-7660. FAX: 739-9798.
Type of Production and Credits: TV Film-Dir/Prod; TV Video-Dir/Prod.
Genres: Commercials-TV; Industrial-TV; Music Video-TV.
Biography: Born Montreal, Quebec. Languages: English and French. Studied Communications and Market Research, Concordia University. M.B.A., now partially completed. Background as lighting cameraman; has custom-built rigs for skiing and windsurfing shoots.
Selected Filmography: *Provi-Soir,* In, 89-91, CDN, Prod/Dir; Shari Claskin, MV, 90, CDN, Dir; Saular Plus, Cm, 90, CDN, Prod/Dir; Convectair, Cm, 90, CDN, Dir; Nautilus Plus, Cm, 90, CDN, Dir; Request Jeans, Cm, 90, CDN, Prod/Dir; Place Bonaventure, Cm, 90, CDN, Dir; Lise Watier, Cm, 90, CDN, Dir; Gorski Furs, Cm, 89, CDN, Prod/Dir; *Standard Life,* In, 89, CDN, Prod/Dir; *Belcourt,* In, 89, CDN, Dir; *Northern Telecom,* In, 89, CDN, Prod/Dir; *JOFF,* In, 89, CDN, Prod/Dir.

BELISLE, Pierre ◊
(514)688-4120.
Types de production et générique: TV film-Réal/Prod; TV vidéo-Réal/Prod.
Types d'oeuvres: Drame-TV; Comédie-TV; Documentaire-TV; Education-TV.
Curriculum vitae: Né en 1935, Ottawa, Ontario. A occupé les postes de technicien à l'éclairage, technicien de son et, ensuite, réalisateur, 55-68, Radio-Canada, Ottawa; depuis 68, réalisateur/producteur pigiste.
Fimographie sélective: "Entrepreneur incorporé" (39 eps)(hebdo), TV, 88-89, CDN, Réal; "Téléservice" (39 eps) (quot), TV, 85-87, CDN, Réal; "Vision francophone" (5 eps), TV, 87, CDN, Réal; *Les Bourgaults de Saint-Jean-Port-Joli,* "Visages", TV, 82, CDN, Réal/Prod;

"Viewpoint" (3 eps), ED, 82, CDN, Réal/Prod; *Spécial André Perry*, "Visages", TV, 81, CDN, Réal/Prod; "Télé-Ressources" (30 eps), TV, 71, CDN, Réal.

BELL, John G.
DGC, DGA. Bell Films Inc., 5 Edgemore Dr., Toronto, ON M8Y 2M6 (416)239-1883. Jerry Adler, 12725 Ventura Blvd., Unit B, Studio City, CA 91604 USA (818)761-9850.
Type of Production and Credits: TV Film-Dir/Prod; TV Video-Dir.
Genres: Drama-TV; Comedy-TV.
Biography: Canadian citizen; US "Green Card."

BENEDIKT, Bozidar
- see WRITERS

BENOIT, Denyse
ARRFQ, SARDEC. 2518, Route 202, Franklin Centre, PQ J0S 1E0 (514)827-2483.
Types de production et générique: c métrage-Réal/Sc.
Types d'oeuvres: Documentaire-C&TV.
Curriculum vitae: Née en 1949, Québec. Langues: français et anglais. Etudes à l'Ecole des Beaux-Arts, Montréal, 66; diplômée de l'Institut des Arts de Diffusion, Bruxelles, 71. Mise en scène de théâtre, comédienne.
Filmographie sélective: *Liliana, baby et moi*, C, 91, CDN, Réal/Sc/Prod; *Le Dernier Havre*, C, 85, CDN, Réal/Sc; *L'Etiquette*, TV, 81, B, Sc/Rech; *La Belle Apparence*, C, 78, CDN, Réal/Sc/Prod; *La Crue*, C, 76, CDN, Réal/Sc/Co prod; *Les Enfants d'abord*, C, 76, CDN, Cast; *Les maladies c'est les compagnies*, C, 75, CDN, Rech; *L'Amiante ça tue*, C, 75, CDN, Rech; *Un instant près d'elle*, C, 74, CDN, Réal/Sc/Prod; *Denyse Benoît, comédienne*, C, 74, CDN, Anim/Comp; *Coup d'oeil blanc*, C, 73, CDN, Réal/Sc/Prod.

BENOIT, Ted
- see PRODUCERS

BENSIMON, Jacques
ACCT. 297 Cleveland, Toronto, ON (416)485-3401. TVOntario, C.P. 200, Succ. Q, Toronto, ON M4T 2T1 (416)484-2636.
Types de production et générique: TV film-Réal; TV vidéo-Réal.
Types d'oeuvres: Documentaire-TV; Affaires publiques-TV.
Curriculum vitae: Né en 1943, Agadir, Maroc; citoyenneté canadienne. Langues: français et anglais. Etudes cinématographiques, New York College. Expérience comme monteur, caméraman, producteur; Directeur du Comité du programme français, ONF, 81-82; Directeur du marketing international, ONF, 81-82; ONF, 83-85; Directeur du secteur grand public, TVO, 86; Directeur secteur adulte - La chaîne française TVOntario; depuis 88, Directeur en chef de la chaîne française de TVOntario. Spécialiste en cinéma du Tiers Monde, télévision éducative, documentaires et le multiculturalisme.
Filmographie sélective: "Carnets de Maroc" (3 eps), TV, 84-88, CDN, Réal; *De mains et d'espoir*, TV, 82, CDN, Réal/Mont; *20 ans après*, TV, 76, CDN, Réal/Mont; *Rock A Bye*, TV, 74, CDN, Réal/Mont; *Aqua Rondo*, TV, 70, CDN, Réal/Mont; *Le Défi du devenir*, TV, 69, CDN, Mont; *Once Agadir*, TV, 69, CDN, Réal/Mont; *The World of Me in Fire*, TV, 68, CDN, Mont; *Volleyball*, TV, 68, CDN, Conc/Mont; *We Are Going to Have Recess*, TV, 67, CDN, Mont.

BERGERON, Guy
- voir PRODUCTEURS

BERGMAN, Robert
322 Clinton St., Toronto, ON M6J 2Y8 (416)535-5393.
Type of Production and Credits: Th Film-Prod/Dir/Wr.
Genres: Drama-Th; Comedy-Th; Action-Th.
Selected Filmography: *Hurt Penguins*, Th, 91, CDN, Dir/Prod; *A Whisper to a Scream*, Th, 89, CDN, Dir/Prod/Co-Wr; *Skull-A Night of Terror/Don't Turn Out The Light*, Th, 88, CDN, Dir/Prod/Co-Wr.

BERMAN, Brigitte ◊
(416)927-0663.
Type of Production and Credits: Th Film-Dir/Prod/Wr; TV Film-Dir/Prod.
Genres: Documentary-Th&TV.
Biography: Born in Frankfurt am Main, Germany; German and Canadian citizenship. Languages: English, German, French. B.A., Queen's University; B.Ed., MacArthur College. *Bix: Ain't None of Them Play Like Him Yet* won a Bronze Hugo, Chicago, and a Merit Award, Athens. *Artie Shaw: Time Is All You've Got* won an Oscar, 87, and First Prize in World History Section, Valladolid, Spain. Director/Resident at the Canadian Centre for Advanced Film Studies, 88. Director/Observer on David Cronenberg's "Dead Ringers," 88.
Selected Filmography: *A Date*, Th, 88, CDN, Dir; *The Making of Castaway*, TV, 86, GB, Dir; *Artie Shaw: Time Is All You've Got*, Th, 85, CDN, Dir/Prod/Wr/Co-Ed, (OSCAR); "Take 30" (90 eps), TV, 81-84, CDN, Dir/Prod; "Quarterly Report", TV, 77-81, CDN, Co-Dir; *Bix*, Th, 79, CDN,

Dir/Prod/Co-Wr/Ed; *How Music Came to the Garden City/The Many Faces of Black*, "This Monday", TV, 76-77, CDN, Dir/Prod; "In Good Company" (sev seg), TV, 75-76, CDN, Dir.

BERRY, Michael J.
DGC, CPDA. 6455 Argyle Ave., West Vancouver, BC V7W 2E8 (604)921-3300. FAX: 921-8303. Contemporary Artists Ltd., 132 Lasky Dr., Beverly Hills, CA 90212 USA (213)278-8250.
Type of Production and Credits: TV Film-Dir/Prod; TV Video-Dir/Prod.
Genres: Drama-TV; Comedy-TV; Children's-TV; Current Affairs-TV.
Biography: Born 1939, Harrow, England; Canadian citizenship, 75. Graduate of Royal Academy of Dramatic Art, London. Clifford Bax prize for student production; considerable acting experience in UK (over 70 plays); company and stage manager for London West End productions. Assistant Director with BBC Drama Department (2 yrs); senior instructor British Drama League; TV/radio newscaster with Capital Broadcasting, Bermuda; drama instructor, Contact Seminars, Vancouver; works with multicam.
Selected Filmography: "Neon Rider" (1 eps), TV, 90, CDN, Dir; "Hillside"/ "Fifteen" (26 eps), TV, 90-91, USA, Dir; "Sea Hunt" (2 eps), TV, 87, CDN/USA, Dir; "The Botts" (17 eps), TV, 86, CDN/F, Dir; "Danger Bay" (11 eps), TV, 84-85, CDN, Dir; "Constable, Constable" (pilot), TV, 85, CDN, Dir; "The Beachcombers" (64 eps), TV, 72-82, CDN, Dir; "Huckleberry Finn" (6 eps), TV, 80-81, CDN/USA/D, Dir; "Minikins" (7 eps), TV, 81, CDN/USA, Dir; "Stony Plain" (6 eps), TV, 79-80, CDN, Dir; "Any Number Can Win" (2 eps), TV, 77-80, CDN, Prod/Dir; *Remembrance Day*, TV, 79, CDN, Dir; "The Irish Rovers", TV, 78, CDN, Dir; *Special*, TV, 78, CDN, Dir; "Leo and Me" (4 eps), TV, 78, CDN, Dir.

BERTOLINO, Daniel
- voir PRODUCTEURS

BESEN, Ellen
Zayer-Shane, 135 Aldwych Ave., Toronto, ON M4J 1X8 (416)463-9705.
Type of Production and Credits: Th Film-Dir(An); Th-Short-Prod/Dir.
Genres: Educational-Th; Children's-Th&TV; Animation-Th&TV.
Biography: Born in 1953 in Chicago, Illinois. Citizenship: Canadian and US.. Studied animation at Sheridan College, Oakville, Ontario. Moved to Montreal to make *Sea Dream* for the NFB; completed in 1978 and screened at numerous festivals including Ottawa '80 and the American Film Festival, where it won second and first prizes respectively. Has recently acted as a co-producer and animation co-ordinator, taught at Sheridan College, and lectured at other institutions such as York University. Founded the Toronto Animated Image Society, has programmed screenings, organized art shows.
Selected Filmography: *Illuminated Lives*, ED, 89, CDN, Dir/Assoc Prod; *Comic Book Confidential*, Th, 88, CDN, An Coord; *The Crow & The Canary*, ED/Th, 88, CDN, Assoc Prod; *Slow Dance World*, ED/Th, 86, CDN, Co Prod/Co Dir; *Sea Dream*, ED/Th, 79, CDN, Dir; *Metric - Metrique*, ED, 76, CDN, Prod/Dir; *To Spring*, ED/Th, 73, CDN, Dir.

BESSADA, Milad
- see PRODUCERS

BISSONNETTE, Sophie
ARRFQ. 5350, rue Waverly, Montréal, PQ H2T 2X9 (514)948-0657. Les Productions Contre-Jour, 5352, rue Waverly, Montréal, PQ H2T 2X9 (514)271-6180. FAX: 271-6450.
Types de production et générique: l métrage-Réal/Prod/Mont; c métrage-Réal/Prod/Mont; TV vidéo-Réal/Prod.
Types d'oeuvres: Documentaire-C; Education-C.
Curriculum vitae: Née en 1956. Langues: français et anglais. Baccalauréat en Cinéma/Sociologie, Université Queen's. A été professeur de cinéma. *Une histoire de femmes* a gagné le Prix de la Critique québécoise.
Filmographie sélective: *Des lumières dans la grande noirceur*, C, 91, CDN, Prod/Réal/Sc; *L'Amour...a quel prix?*, C, 88, CDN, Réal/Rech; *Ne ratons pas le train vers l'accès à l'égalité* (vidéo), C, 87, CDN, Prod/Réal/Rech/Mont; *Quel numéro?/What Number?/The Electronic Sweatshop*, C, 84, CDN, Réal/Rech/Co prod; *Luttes d'ici, luttes d'ailleurs*, C, 80, CDN, Réal/Rech/Mont; *Une histoire de femmes/A Wives' Tale*, C, 79, CDN, Co réal/Co mont.

BITTMAN, Roman
- see PRODUCERS

BJORNSON, Michelle
- see WRITERS

BLAIS, Micheline
- voir PRODUCTEURS

BLAIS, Pascal ◊
ASIFA. (514)866-7272.
Types de production et générique: TV film-Réal/An.
Types d'oeuvres: Animation-TV; Annonces-TV.

Curriculum vitae: Né en 1959, Montréal, Québec. Langues: français et anglais. Réalisateur et animateur de nombreuses annonces depuis 5 ans; animation et effets spéciaux pour les longs métrages "The Peanut Butter Solution," "Great Land of Small," "Tommy Tricker and the Stamp Traveller."

BLANCHARD, André
- voir SCENARISTES

BLOOMFIELD, George
DGA, DGC, WGA, ACTRA. 50 Admiral Rd., Toronto, ON M5R 2L5 (416)967-0826. FAX: 967-0242. Debbi Peck, ACI, (416)363-7414.
Biography: Contact agent for information.

BLOUIN, Paul ◊
(514)931-4986.
Types de production et générique: TV film-Réal/Prod; TV vidéo-Réal/Prod.
Types d'oeuvres: Drame-C&TV.
Curriculum vitae: Né en 1925, Dauphin, Manitoba. Langues: français et anglais. Comédien au théâtre anglais et français, et à la radio anglaise au Québec, 45-53; récipiendaire de la bourse, "Imperial Relations Trust," de Radio-Canada pour un stage de 6 mois en théâtre et à la BBC en Angleterre. Récipiendaire d'une bourse du Conseil des Arts pour un stage de 6 mois en théâtre, cinéma et télévision en Europe; régisseur de plateau, TV Radio-Canada, Montréal, 54; réalisateur, TV réseau français, Radio-Canada, 55-86; depuis 86, réalisateur pigiste. Récipiendaire de nombreux prix pour la réalisation dont le Prix Victor Morin pour *Des souris et des hommes* et l'ensemble de son travail, 71.
Filmographie sélective: *Un parc en automne*, TV, 85, CDN, Réal; *Le Fauteuil à bascule*, TV, 85, CDN, Réal; *Bonne Fête, Maman*, TV, 84, CDN, Réal; *Le Malentendu*, TV, 83, CDN, Réal, (ANIK); *Gapi*, C, 81, CDN, Réal; *Le Bateau pour Lipaï*, TV, 80, CDN, Réal, (ANIK); *Ces dames de l'Estuaire*, TV, 78, CDN, Réal; *Britannicus*, TV, 78, CDN, Réal; *The Zoo Staory*, TV, 75, CDN, Réal; *Hedda Gabler*, TV, 73, CDN, Réal; *Des souris et des hommes*, TV, 70, CDN, Réal; *La Collection*, TV, 69, CDN, Réal; *Le Gardien*, TV, 69, CDN, Réal/Adapt; En pièces détachées, TV, 69, CDN, Réal; *L'Amant*, TV, 68, CDN, Réal.

BLOW, Peter
- see WRITERS

BOCKING, Richard C.
- see PRODUCERS

BODOLAI, Joe
- see WRITERS

BOND, Timothy
ACTRA, DGC, WGAe. 44 Palmerston Gardens, Toronto, ON M6G 1V9 (416)535-3870. 1954 Hillcrest Rd., #2, Hollywood, CA 90068 USA (213)851-6840. Scott Yoselow, Gersh Agency, 130 West 42nd St., 4th Flr., New York, NY 10036 USA (212)997-1818.
Type of Production and Credits: Th Film-Dir/Wr; TV Film-Dir/Wr; TV Video-Dir.
Genres: Drama-Th&TV; Comedy-Th&TV; Horror-Th; Educational-TV.
Biography: Born 1942, Ottawa, Ontario; B.A., English Drama, and B.Sc., Chemistry and Physics, Carleton University, 65. Twenty years of extensive stage directing credits in Canada and abroad.
Selected Filmography: *The Lost World* (mini-series), TV, 91, USA, Dir; "Top Cops" (6 eps), TV, 90-91, CDN/USA, Dir; "Sweating Bullets" (3 eps), TV, 91, CDN/USA/MEX, Dir; "One Life to Live", TV, 90, USA, Dir; "Nancy Drew and Daughter" (pilot), TV, 90, CDN, Dir; "Over My Dead Body" (1 eps), TV, 90, USA, Dir; "Star Trek - The Next Generation" (2 eps), TV, 90, USA, Dir; *Hard Time on Planet Earth*, TV, 90, USA, Dir; "The Campbells" (12 eps)(3 eps Co-Wr), TV, 85-88, CDN/USA/GB, Dir/Co-Wr; "Night Heat" (2 eps), TV, 87-88, CDN, Dir/Co-Wr; "Friday the 13th: The Series" (12 eps), TV, 87-88, CDN/USA, Dir; "Alfred Hitchcock Presents" (5 eps), TV, 87-88, CDN/USA, Dir; "Adderly" (5 eps), TV, 86-87, CDN, Dir; *First Offender*, TV, 86, CDN, Dir; *Oakmount High*, TV, 85, CDN, Dir/Co-Wr.

BONENFANT, Mario
AQRRCT. 5691, Waverly, Montréal, PQ H2T 2Y2 (514)273-6689.
Types de production et générique: c métrage-Réal; TV film-Réal; TV vidéo-Réal.
Types d'oeuvres: Drame-C&TV; Documentaire-C&TV; Expérimental-C; Affaires publiques-TV.
Curriculum vitae: Né en 1962, Trois-Rivières, Québec. Langues: français et anglais. Baccalauréat en Cinéma, Université Concordia; formation musicale à l'école des petits chanteurs de Trois-Rivières; formation en sciences pures, Cégep de Trois-Rivières.
Filmographie sélective: *Sadick/L'Afrique de Charlie*, "Latitude Sud" (2 eps), TV, 91, CDN, Réal; *Le Grand Age*, "Regards de Jeune"*, TV, 90, CDN, Réal; *Malle et Fils*, C, 88, CDN, Réal; "Le Sens d'affaires" (16 eps), TV, 87-88, CDN, Réal/Rep; *Une*

journée dans la vie du Canada, TV, 85, CDN, Ass réal; *Ouverture*, C, 83, CDN, Réal; "La Course autour du monde" (21 eps), TV, 82-83, CDN, Réal/Rep; *Derrière une photo*, C, 81, CDN, Réal; *Europe 80*, ED, 80, CDN, Réal.

BONNER, Michael
CSC. 1398 Montreal St., Kingston, ON K7K 3L6 (613)542-9600. GT Video & Film Productions, 180 Kirkpatrick St., Kingston, ON K7L 2P5 (613)544-0942.
Type of Production and Credits: Th Short-Dir; TV Video-Wr.
Genres: Documentary-Th&TV; Educational-Th&TV; Industrial-Th&TV.
Biography: Born in 1953 in Kingston, Ontario. B.A.(Hons), Film Studies, Queen's University; Major student project was *Katie Short*, a short 16mm documentary about a young handicapped woman. Joined GT Video & Film Productions in 1987. Has since worked on all aspects of production from conception to completion in the industrial/promotional market and has given seminars in media studies. Grade VI Conservatory piano certificate.
Selected Filmography: *Dave Broadfoot's Comedy Crusade*, In, 91, CDN, Cam Assist; *Correction Services Security Seminar*, In, 90, CDN, Dir/Ed; *1000 Island Tours: Your Vacation Destination*, In, 90, CDN, Script; *Canadian Tenpin Federation 1990 Youth Championship*, In, 90, CDN, Cam; *Watch Us Grow In Frontenac County*, In, 90, CDN, Cam/Script; *It's All Here In Frontenac County*, In, 90, CDN, Cam; *The Next Move*, In, 89, CDN, Cam/Co-Ed; *Room To Grow*, In, 89, CDN, Cam/Ed; *Queen's Electrical Engineering*, In, 89, CDN, Ed; *The Island Queen*, In, 88, Cam Op/Mus/Script; *A Place To Go*, In, 87, CDN, Cam Op/Co-Ed; *Preparation and Delivery of ALRV*, In, 87, CDN, Cam Assist; *Katie Short*, Th, 85, CDN, Dir.

BONNIERE, René
DGC, ACCT. 100 Hazleton Ave., Toronto, ON M5R 2E2 (416)922-6463.
Type of Production and Credits: Th Film-Dir; Th Short-Dir; TV Film-Dir; TV Video-Dir.
Genres: Drama-Th&TV; Comedy-Th&TV; Action-TV; Documentary-TV.
Biography: Born 1928, Lyon, France; Canadian citizenship. *Fertility Rites* won Gold Medal, New York.
Selected Filmography: "Counterstrike" (2 eps), TV, 90-91, CDN/F, Dir; "E.N.G." (6 eps), TV, 89-91, CDN, Dir; "Bordertown" (10 eps), TV, 89-90, CDN/F, Dir; "Road to Avonlea" (4 eps), TV, 89-90, CDN/USA, Dir; "Dracula - The Series" (5 eps), TV, 90, CDN/USA, Dir; "Alfred Hitchcock Presents" (10 eps), TV, 89, CDN/USA, Dir; "Diamonds" (6 eps), TV, 88-89, CDN, Dir; "Night Heat" (12 eps), TV, 84-86, CDN, Dir; "The Little Vampire" (13 eps), TV, 85, CDN/GB/D, Dir; *Islands*, TV, 84, CDN/USA, Dir; *Labour of Love*, TV, 84, CDN, Dir; *Hide and Seek*, "For the Record", TV, 83, CDN, Dir; *S.P.A.*, "The Nature of Things", TV, 83, CDN, Prod/Dir; *Guido/Lypa*, "The Newcomers", TV, 78, CDN, Dir; *Fertility Rites*, TV, 76, CDN, Prod/Dir.

BOOTH, Alan
17 Trail's End, Yellowknife, NT (403) 873-5911. Yellowknife Films, P.O. Box 2562, Yellowknife, NT X1A 2P9 (403)873-8610.
Type of Production and Credits: Th Short-Prod/Dir/Cin; TV Film-Prod/Dir/Cin; TV Video-Prod/Dir, Cin.
Genres: Documentary-Th&TV; Educational-TV; Animation-Th&TV.
Biography: Born in 1951 in Sudbury, Ontario. Canadian citizen. Educated at Loyola in filmmaking; received diploma in filmmaking from Algonquin College, Ottawa. Has lived in the Northwest Territories since 1974. Began producing films about the NWT in 1981; wrote, shot, edited and directed first 3 films. President of Yellowknife Films. Has directed and shot four award-winning films, *Ice Roads*, *The Emerging North* for Expo 86, *Whole Language: A Northern Experience* and *A Fishing Tale*.
Selected Filmography: *The Northern Lights*, TV, 91, CDN, Prod/Dir/Cin; *Whole Language: A Northern Experience*, ED, 90, CDN, Dir/Cin; Literacy spots (2), Cm, 90, CDN, Dir/Cin; *Nursing North of 60* (2), In, 90, CDN, Dir/Cin; Education spots (7), Cm, 88, CDN, Dir/Cin; *The Emerging North*, Th, 86, CDN, Prod/Dir/Cin; *Ice Roads*, TV, 85, CDN, Prod/Dir/Cin; *A Fishing Tale*, TV, 85, CDN, Dir/Cin.

BORRIS, Clay
DGC. 14 Wembley Dr., Toronto, ON M4L 3E1 (416)465-8388. Ralph Zimmerman, Great North Artists Mgmt., 350 Dupont St., Toronto, ON M5R 1V9 (416)925-2051.
Type of Production and Credits: Th Film-Dir/Wr; TV Film-Dir/Wr; TV Video-Dir/Wr.
Genres: Drama-Th&TV; Action-Th&TV; Documentary-Th&TV.
Biography: Born 1950, New Brunswick.

Languages: French and English. Won Golden Ducat, Best Director, Mannheim Film Festival, for first feature, *Alligator Shoes*; also shown in Directors' Fortnight, Cannes and won Silver Hugo, Chicago.
Selected Filmography: *Prom Night IV*, Th, 91, CDN, Dir; "Top Cops" (5 eps), TV, 90, CDN/USA, Dir; "Katts & Dog" (23 eps), TV, 89-90, CDN/USA, Dir; "T and T" (1 eps), TV, 90, CDN/USA, Dir; *The Gunfighter*, TV, 88, USA, Dir; "Night Heat" (1 eps), TV, 88, CDN/USA, Dir; *Quiet Cool*, Th, 87, USA, Wr/Dir; *Alligator Shoes*, Th, 81, CDN, Prod/Wr/Dir; *Rose's House*, Th, 77, CDN, Wr/Dir; *One Hand Clapping*, "Of All People", TV, 74, CDN, Wr/Dir; *Sheila's X-mas*, "Browndale", ED, 74, CDN, Wr/Dir; *Mistawasis*, "Browndale", ED, 74, CDN, Wr/Dir; *Paperboy*, Th, 71, CDN, Wr/Dir; *Parliament St.*, Th, 69, CDN, Wr/Dir.

BORSOS, Phillip
DGA, DGC, ACCT. The Radio-Telegraphic Company, 240 Indian Rd., Toronto, ON M6R 2W9 (416)769-7508. Bauer-Benedek, 9255 Sunset Blvd., Ste. 716, Los Angeles, CA 90069 USA (213)275-2421.
Type of Production and Credits: Th Film-Dir; Th Short-Dir.
Genres: Drama-Th; Documentary-Th.
Selected Filmography: *Bethune*, Th, 88, CDN/RC/F, Dir; *One Magic Christmas*, Th, 85, CDN/USA, Dir/Exec Prod/Co-Story; *The Mean Season*, Th, 84, USA, Dir; *The Grey Fox*, Th, 80, CDN, Dir/Co-Prod, (GENIE); *Nails*, Th, 79, CDN, Dir/Prod, (GENIE); *Spartree*, Th, 77, CDN, Dir/Prod, (CFA); *Cooperage*, Th, 76, CDN, Dir/Prod, (CFA).

BOUCHARD, Louise
ARRQ, ARRFQ. 2237, Melrose, Montréal, PQ H4A 2R7 (514)481-0015. Radio-Québec, 800, rue Fullum, Montréal, PQ H2K 3L7.
Types de production et générique: TV film-Réal; TV vidéo-Réal.
Types d'oeuvres: Documentaire-C&TV; Affaires publiques-C&TV.
Curriculum vitae: Née en 1943, La Tuque, Québec. Langues: français et anglais. Etudes en anthropologie et histoire de l'art. "La Conquête de l'espace," sélectionné au Festival Palizeau, France, 87, et mis en nomination pour le Grand Prix Magnolia, Festival Shanghai, 88.
Filmographie sélective: "Nord-Sud", TV, 89-91, CDN, Réal; "Première ligne", TV, 88-89, CDN, Réal; "La Conquête de l'espace" (21 eps), TV, 85-87, CDN, Réal; *Une planète jamais visitée*, TV, 84, CDN, Réal; "Nord-Sud", TV, 83, CDN, Réal; "Les Grandes Maladies" (2 eps), TV, 82-83, CDN, Réal; "Planète" (2 eps), TV, 82, CDN, Réal; "L'Objectif", TV, 81-82, CDN, Réal; *La Vie: un mystère à décoder*, TV, 81, CDN/CH, Co réal.

BOUCHARD, Michel
AQRRCT. 6670, av. de Gaspé, Montréal, PQ H2S 2Y2 (514)277-5667.
Types de production et générique: l métrage-Réal/Sc; c métrage-Réal/Prod/Sc.
Types d'oeuvres: Drame-C&TV; Comédie-C; Documentaire-TV.
Curriculum vitae: Né en 1949, Montréal, Québec. Langues: français et anglais. Etudes: Langues (allemand, espagnol, italien), Institut des Arts Appliqués, 67-68.
Filmographie sélective: *Doubles Jeux*, "Haute Tension", TV, 89, CDN/F, Sc; *La Terrapène*, TV, 84, CDN, Réal/Prod/Sc; *Les Petites Cruautés*, TV, 84, CDN, Réal/Prod/Sc; *Le Toaster*, TV, 82, CDN, Réal/Prod/Sc; *La Bien-Aimée*, C, 80, CDN, Réal/Prod/Sc; *La Loi de la ville*, C, 77, CDN, Réal/Rech/Narr; *Noël et Juliette*, C, 73, CDN, Réal/Sc.

BOURASSA-DUTTON, John
4830 Côte Ste-Catherine, #18, Montreal, PQ H3W 1M3 (514)345-8344.
Type of Production and Credits: TV Video-Dir/Ed.
Genres: Drama-TV; Documentary-TV; Commercials-TV; Music Video-TV.
Biography: Born 1966, Warrington, England; Canadian citizenship. Languages: English, French and German. Honours B.A., Film, Video and Photographic Arts, Polytechnic of Central London. Director for Musique Plus, 88.
Selected Filmography: "He Shoots, He Scores" (2 eps), TV, 87-88, CDN/F/CH, Ed; "Hohokam" - "Point of View", MV, 87, GB, Dir/Ed; *Linzi Breaks the Fashion Barrier*, Cm, 87, GB, Dir/Ed; *Age-Old Myths*, ED, 87, GB, Dir/Ed/Co-Wr; *Healthy? Wealthy? And Wise!*, TV, 87, GB, Ed; *Family Conflicts*, TV, 86, GB, PM/Ed; *Gethsemene*, TV, 85, GB, Dir/Ed.

BOYDEN, Barbara
- see PRODUCERS

BRADSHAW, John R.
WGC (ACTRA), ACCT. 134 Balmoral Ave., Toronto, ON M4V 1J4 (416)922-3801. Charles Northcote, The Core Group, 489 College St., #501, Toronto, ON M6G 1A5 (416)944-0193.
Type of Production and Credits: Th Film-Dir/Wr/PM/1st AD; Th Short-1st AD.

Genres: Drama-Th; Comedy-TV; Action-Th; Horror-Th.
Biography: Born 1952, Stratford, Ontario; B.A.A., Photographic Arts, Motion Picture, Ryerson Polytechnical Institute, 78. Most recent theatrical feature, *The Undertaker* is currently in development.
Selected Filmography: *Les Nuits d'été*, TV, 91, CDN, 1st AD; *The Big Slice*, Th, 90, CDN, Dir/Wr; *Red Blooded American Girl*, Th, 90, CDN, 1st AD; *Still Life*, Th, 89, CDN, 1st AD; *One Man Out*, Th, 88, CDN, 1st AD; *Office Party*, Th, 88, CDN, 1st AD; *Blood Relations*, Th, 88, CDN, 1st AD; *Murder One*, Th, 87, CDN, 1st AD; *Caribe*, Th, 86, CDN, 2nd AD; *Treble Rebels/Rebels With a Cause*, Th, 85, CDN, PM/1st AD; *That's My Baby*, Th, 82, CDN, Co-Dir/Co-Wr.

BRANDT, C.V. (Caryl)
- see PRODUCERS

BRASSARD, André ✧
(613)996-5051.
Types de production et générique: l métrage-Réal; TV film-Réal.
Types d'oeuvres: Drame-C&TV.
Curriculum vitae: Né en 1947, Montréal, Québec. Langues: français et anglais. Metteur en scène de théâtre depuis 68; a réalisé la première pièce de théâtre au Centre National des Arts, Ottawa, 69, où il est Directeur Artistique (et metteur en scène) depuis 82. A aussi réalisé des pièces pour la télévision, don *Les Belles Soeurs* et *Sainte Carmen de la main*.
Filmographie sélective: *Le soleil se lève en retard*, C, 75, CDN, Réal/Co aut; *Il était une fois dans l'Est*, C, 74, CDN, Réal/Co sc; *Françoise Durocher waitress*, TV, 72, CDN, Réal, (2 CFA).

BRAULT, Michel
ARRFQ, APFVQ. 1168, Richelieu, Beloeil, PQ J3G 4R3 (514)467-0317. Nanouk Films Ltée, 1600, av. de Lorimier, Montréal, PQ H2K 3W5 (514)521-1984.
Types de production et générique: l métrage-D photo/Réal; c métrage-D photo/Réal/Prod.
Types d'oeuvres: Drame-C&TV; Documentaire-C&TV.
Curriculum vitae: Né en 1928, Montréal, Québec. Récipiendaire de plusieurs prix dont le Prix de la mise en scène, Cannes, Prix de la Critique québécoise pour *Les Ordres*; *Les Raquetteurs*, Plaque d'Argent, Dei Popoli, Florence; Prix Alberta-Québec, 85; Prix Albert Tessier, 86. *Les Noces de Papier* a gagné Gémeaux et Prix Québec-Alberta.
Filmographie sélective: *Les Noces de Papier/Paper Wedding*, Th, 89, CDN, Réal; *L'Emprise*, TV, 88, CDN, Réal; *L'Ami disparu*, TV, 87, CDN, Phot; *No Mercy*, C, 86, USA, Phot; *The Great Land of Small*, C, 86, CDN, Phot; *A Freedom to Move*, C, 85, CDN, Prod/Réal; *Half a Lifetime*, TV, 85, CDN, D phot; *Louisiana*, C, 83, CDN/F, D phot; *M.A. Fortin*, TV, 82, CDN, D phot/Prod; *Elia Kazan: An Outsider*, C, 81, F, D phot; *La Quarantaine*, C, 81, CDN, D phot; *Threshold*, C, 80, CDN, D phot, (GENIE); *Le Son des Français en Amérique*, TV, 74-80, CDN, Prod/Réal; *Les Bons Débarras*, C, 78, CDN, D phot, (GENIE); *Mourir à tue-tête*, C, 78, CDN, D phot.

BROCHU, Pierre
- voir SCENARISTES

BROMFIELD, Rex
- see WRITERS

BRONSARD, Louis
1010 Cherrier St., Apt. 1702, Montreal, PQ H2L 1H8 (514)525-1002.
Type of Production and Credits: Th Film-1st AD/Ed/Dir; Th Short-Dir; TV Video-Dir.
Genres: Drama-Th&TV; Documentary-Th&TV; Industrial-TV.
Biography: Born 1958, Montreal, Quebec. Languages: French, English, Spanish. B.A., Anthropology, McGill University, 86; B.A., Art History, University of Montreal, 81; 1 year, Film, Concordia University, 80. *Ne retenez pas votre souffle* was invited to Montreal International Film Festival of New Cinema and Video, Rendez-vous du Cinéma québécois and Madrid Film Festival.
Selected Filmography: *Ne retenez pas votre souffle*, Th, 87, CDN, Dir/Ed; *Mindbenders*, Th, 87, USA, 1st AD; *Clair Obscur*, Th, 87, CDN, Dir; *The Carpenter*, Th, 87, CDN, Set Des; *Seeing for Ourselves*, TV, 83, CDN, Narr; *Blue Whale*, Th, 83, CDN, Wr/1st AD; *Musique*, Th, 81, CDN, Dir.

BROWN, Alastair
ACTRA. 68 Robert St., Toronto, ON M5S 2K3 (416)922-7451.
Type of Production and Credits: Th Film-Dir; TV Film-Dir/Prod; TV Video-Dir/Wr.
Genres: Drama-Th&TV; Action-Th&TV; Documentary-Th&TV; Educational-TV.
Biography: Born 1944, Peterborough, England; Canadian citizenship. B.A., English, Trinity College, Dublin. Trained at BBC London; worked as film director in London, New York and Los Angeles; over 80 televised documentaries to his credit.

Selected Filmography: *Last Chance*, Th, 86, CDN/AUS, Dir/Wr; *The Price of Vengeance*, TV, 85, CDN, Dir/Co-Wr; "The Amateur Naturalist" (6 eps), TV, 83-84, CDN/GB, Dir; "Ark on the Move" (13 eps), TV, 81, CDN/GB, Dir.

BROWNE, Christene
- see PRODUCERS

BROWNE, Colin
2032 West Third Ave., Vancouver, BC V6J 1L5 (604)739-4359, (604) 738-2032.
Type of Production and Credits: Th Film-Dir/Wr/Prod/Ed; Th Short-Dir/Wr/Ed; TV Film-Dir/Wr/Ed.
Genres: Documentary-Th&TV; Educational-Th&TV; Experimental-Th.
Biography: Born in 1946 in Victoria, British Columbia. Canadian citizen. Languages: English and French. Filmmaker who has also worked as a poet, fiction writer, editor, publisher and teacher. *White Lake* nominated for Canadian Film Award, Best Feature-Length Documentary. Special Jury Award, Yorkton, for *Hoppy: Portrait of Elisabeth Hopkins*.
Selected Filmography: *White Lake*, Th, 89, CDN, Prod/Dir/Wr/Ed; *The Image Before Us*, ED/Th, 87, CDN, Dir/Wr; *Hoppy: A Portrait of Elisabeth Hopkins*, ED/Th, 85, CDN, Dir/Wr.

BRUNELLE, Wendy A.
- see WRITERS

BRUYERE, Christian
- see WRITERS

BRYDON, Loyd
- see PRODUCERS

BUDGELL, Jack
- see PRODUCERS

BUGAJSKI, Richard
41 Lavinia Ave., Toronto, ON M6S 3H9 (416)763-4560. Lynn Kinney, Credentials, 387 Bloor St. E., Toronto, ON M4W 2H7 (416)926-1507. Peter Rawley, ICM, 8899 Beverly Blvd., Los Angeles, CA 90048 USA (213)550-4165.
Type of Production and Credits: Th Film-Dir/Prod/Wr; TV Film-Dir/Wr; TV Video-Dir/Wr.
Genres: Drama-Th&TV; Action-Th&TV.
Biography: Born 1943, Warsaw, Poland; Canadian citizenship. Studied Philosophy, Warsaw University; Directing, Film and Theatre Academy, Lodz. Warsaw National TV, 74-79; also directed theatre. Worked at Studio X, Poland (headed by Andrzej Wajda), 73-83. Published 2 novels, *Interrogation* and *I Confess My Guilt*. Has won several awards including Best Director, Polish TV Festival, 78; *Interrogation* won Palme d'Or for Best Actress, Cannes 90, Silver Hugo, Chicago, 90, and Best Picture, Rotterdam, 87.
Selected Filmography: *Clearcut*, Th, 90, CDN, Dir; "Saying Goodbye" (1 eps), TV, 90, CDN, Dir; "The Hitchhiker" (1 eps), TV, 89, CDN/USA, Dir; "E.N.G." (1 eps), TV, 89, CDN, Dir; "The Twilight Zone" (4 eps), TV, 88, CDN/USA, Dir; "Alfred Hitchcock Presents" (2 eps), TV, 86, CDN/USA, Dir; *Interrogation*, Th, 82, PL, Dir/Prod/Wr; *A Woman and a Woman*, Th, 80, PL, Co-Dir/Co-Prod/Co-Wr; *Classes*, TV, 79, PL, Dir/Wr; *Spanish Blood*, TV, 78, PL, Dir; *Trismus*, TV, 78, PL, Dir; *Don Carlos*, TV, 77, PL, Dir; *The Other Side of the Flame*, TV, 76, PL, Dir.

BURKE, Martyn
DGC, WGAw. 1007 Ocean Ave., #304, Santa Monica, CA 90403 (213)458-3211. 175 Howland Ave., Toronto, ON M5R 3B7. David Wirtschafter, c/o I.C.M., 8899 Beverly Blvd, Los Angeles, CA 90046 (213) 550-4000.
Type of Production and Credits: Th Film-Dir/Wr; TV Film-Dir/Wr; TV Video-Dir/Wr.
Genres: Drama-Th&TV; Comedy-Th&TV; Action-Th&TV; Documentary-TV.
Biography: Born in Canada. Attended McMaster University. Member of Author's Guild. Author of three novels, *Laughing War*, *The Commissar's Report*, and *Ivory Joe*; currently adapting *Ivory Joe* for MGB; co-writer on *Top Secret* with Zucker Brothers. Extensive documentary experience; *Connections* won ANIK for Best CBC Documentary, 77, and ACTRA for Best Documentary, 79. *Power Play* won Genie for Best Screenplay. *Cinq Défis* won Gemini for Best Directing, 89.
Selected Filmography: *Witnesses: What Really Happened in Afghanistan*, TV, 88-90, CDN, Dir; *Cinq Défis pour le Président*, TV, 89, CDN/F, Co-Dir; *The KGB Connections*, TV, CDN, 81, Dir; *Connections: An Investigation into Organized Crime in Canada*, TV, 77-79, CDN, Dir/Co-Prod, (ACTRA/ANIK); *Idi Amin: My People Love Me*, TV, 75, CDN, Dir; *The Last Chase*, 80, CDN, Dir/Co-Scr; *Power Play*, TV, 78, CDN/GB, Dir/Co-Scr; *The Clown Murders*, Th, 75, CDN, Dir/Scr.

BURTON, Robert H.
- see PRODUCERS

BUTTIGNOL, Rudy
- see PRODUCERS

CACOPARDO, Max
AR, ACCT. 149, ave. Balfour, Montréal,

PQ H3P 1L8 (514)737-2405. Radio-Canada, 1400 est, boul. René-Lévesque, Montréal, PQ H2L 2M2 (514)597-5339.
Types de production et générique: TV film-Réal/Sc; TV vidéo-Réal/Sc.
Types d'oeuvres: Documentaire-TV; Education-TV; Enfants-TV; Affaires publiques-TV.
Curriculum vitae: Né en 1932, Palerme, Italie; citoyenneté canadienne. Langues: italien, français, anglais. B.Sc., Rome; Maîtrise en Sciences économiques, Université de Montréal. Annonceur-réalisateur Service International, Radio-Canada, 53-55; réalisateur TV, Radio-Canada, 58-63; Directeur-adjoint des programmes TV, Radio-Canada, 65-66; réalisateur TV, Radio-Canada, 67-73; réalisateur pigiste, 74-86; réalisateur TV, Radio-Canada depuis 87; scénariste, auteur et traducteur. Prix Communauté des télévisions francophones CTF, Actualités nationales, pour "Télé-dollars," 87.
Filmographie sélective: "Découverte" (7 eps), TV, 91, CDN, Réal; "Palme d'Or" (6 eps), TV, 90, CDN, Réal/Aut/Sc; *Idées et révolutions*, "Democraties", TV, 88, CDN, Réal/Co-Sc, (GEMEAUX 89); "Les Sens des Affaires" (32 eps), TV, 87-88, CDN, Réal/Prod coord; "Télé-dollars" (2 eps), TV, 87, CDN, Réal/Sc/Dial, (3 GEMEAUX, 87); "Ecran-Témoin" (20 eps), TV, 86, CDN, Réal; "Les Surtaxes" (4 eps), TV, 85, CDN, Réal; "Palme d'Or" (39 eps), TV, 85, CDN, Réal/Sc; "Les Grands du cinéma" (13 eps), TV, 85, CDN, Prod dél; "Le Prix du spectacle" (4 eps), TV, 84, CDN, Réal; "Dossier de presse" (13 eps), TV, 84, CDN, Réal; "Le Point", TV, 83, CDN, Réal; *Science-Réalité*, TV, 82, CDN, Réal; "Salut santé" (26 eps), TV, 78-82, CDN, Conc/Sc; "Téléjeans" (75 eps), TV, 78-81, CDN, Réal.

CAHILL, T.J.
- see WRITERS

CAMPBELL, Graeme N.
DGC. 155-1/2 Euclid Ave., Toronto, ON M6J 2J8 (416)368-2627. Stone Manners Agency, 9113 Sunset Blvd., Los Angeles, CA 90069 USA (213)275-9599.
Type of Production and Credits: Th Film-Dir; Th Short-Dir; TV Film-Dir.
Genres: Drama-Th&TV; Comedy-Th&TV; Horror-Th&TV; Documentary-Th&TV; Educational-Th&TV.
Biography: Born in 1954 in Montreal, Quebec. Canadian citizen. Languages: English and French
Selected Filmography: *Let Death Do Us Part*, "Hidden Room", TV, 91, CDN/USA, Dir; *Journey Into Darkness:The Bruce Curtis Story*, TV, 90, CDN, Dir; *Still Life*, Th, 90, CDN/US, Dir; *Blood Relations*, Th, 89, CDN, Dir; *Murder One*, Th, 88, CDN/USA, Dir; *Into The Fire*, Th, 87, CDN, Dir.

CAMPBELL, Norman
OC, ATPD, DGC, DGA, ACCT 20 George Henry Blvd, Willowdale, ON M2J 1E2. (416)494-8576. CBC, Box 500, Station A, Toronto, ON M5W 1E6 (416)975-6877.
Type of Production and Credits: Th Film-Dir; TV Film-Dir/Prod; TV Video-Dir/Prod.
Genres: Drama-TV; Comedy-TV; Variety-Th&TV; Documentary-TV.
Biography: Born 1924, Los Angeles, California; Canadian citizenship. B.A., Mathematics and Physics, University of British Columbia, 44. Joined CBC, 52; directed specials in England and the US including for the series "All in the Family," "The Mary Tyler Moore Show," and "One Day at a Time." Composer of the score for the musical, *Anne of Green Gables*. Awarded Order of Canada, 79; member, Royal Canadian Academy. Has won many awards including: the Celia Award from the National Ballet of Canada; Prix René Barthelemy, Monte Carlo; Chris Statuette, Columbus; John Drainie Award.
Selected Filmography: *Alice*, TV, 89, CDN, Dir/Prod; *La Ronde*, TV, 89, CDN, Dir/Prod; *Comedy of Errors*, TV, 89, CDN, Dir/Prod; *Tosca*, TV, 89, CDN, Dir/Prod; *La Bohème*, TV, 89, CDN, Dir/Prod; *The Makropoulos Case*, TV, 89, CDN, Dir/Prod; *Karen Kain: Prima Ballerina*, TV, 89, CDN, Dir/Prod; *The Taming of the Shrew*, TV, 88, CDN, Dir/Prod; *The Big Top* (circus ballet), TV, 88, CDN, Dir/Prod; *Don Giovanni*, TV, 88, CDN, Dir/Prod; *La Forza des Destino*, TV, 87, CDN, Dir/Prod; *The Merry Widow*, TV, 87, CDN, Dir/Prod; *The Boys from Syracuse*, TV, 86, CDN, Dir/Prod; *The Opera Dialogues of the Carmelites*, TV, 86, CDN, Dir/Prod; *Onegin*, TV, 85, CDN, Dir/Prod.

CAMPBELL, Peg
(604)669-3253.
Type of Production and Credits: Th Short-Dir/Prod/Wr.
Genres: Comedy-Th&TV; Educational-Th&TV; Children's-TV.
Biography: Born 1954, Port Arthur (Thunder Bay), Ontario. B.A., Communications, Simon Fraser University. In her work, prefers to combine experimental form with social-issue

content. Winner of several awards, including Yorkton, Gold Cindy, Northwest Film and Video festival, BC Student Film Festival.
Selected Filmography: *In Search of the Last Good Man*, Th, 88, CDN, Dir/Co-Prod/Co-Wr; *Bombs Away!*, ED, 88, CDN, Dir; *It's a Party!*, TV, 86, CDN, Dir/Co-Prod/Co-Wr; *Wife Assault*, ED, 85, CDN, Dir/Wr; *Inside/Outside*, TV, 85, CDN, Dir/Prod; *Street Kids*, ED, 85, CDN, Dir; *New Canadian Kid*, ED, 82, CDN, Dir; *A Sign of Affection*, ED, 77, CDN, Dir/Prod; *A Rule of Thumb*, ED, 76, CDN, Dir/Prod; *Pause*, ED, 76, CDN, Dir.

CAMPBELL, Robin
1002 Coxwell Ave., #7, Toronto, ON M4C 3G5 (416)423-6296. Triune Productions Inc., 24 Ryerson Ave., Suite 304, Toronto, ON M5T 2P3 (416)362-9120.
Type of Production and Credits: Th Short-Wr/Dir; Video-Wr/Dir.
Genres: Drama-Th&TV; Comedy-Th&TV; Corporate-TV.
Biography: Born 1956, Toronto, Ontario. Honours B.F.A., Film Production, York University, 80. Sterling Campbell Award, 80; *Performances* won Norman Jewison Award, 80. *A Laughing Matter* won Silver Apple at National Educational Film & Video Festival, Oakland. Founding member, Triune Arts.
Selected Filmography: *A Laughing Matter*, TV, 90, CDN, Prod; *Part of Life*, TV, 90, CDN, Wr/Dir; *The Promotion*, Foster Parents Plan, Cm, 90, CDN, Dir; *Respect*, MV, 90, CDN, Wr/Dir; *Our Power is in Our Potential*, Corp, 90, CDN, Wr/Dir; *Alternative Blowing Agents*, Corp, 90, CDN, Wr/Dir; *Inspiration*, Corp, 89, CDN, Wr/Dir; *Customer Service*, Corp, 89, CDN, Wr/Dir; *Nissan 240 SX*, Corp, 89, CDN, Wr/Prod; *TRSI*, In, 89, CDN, Wr/Dir; *Spies*, In, 88, CDN, Wr; *Tear into the Weekend*, In, 88, CDN, Dir; *The Pepsi Gang*, In, 88, CDN, Dir; *Dew 'n' Pepper*, In, 87, CDN, Dir; *Diet Pepsi Taste Drive*, In, 87, CDN, Dir.

CANELL, Marrin
- see PRODUCERS

CANNING, Bob
IATSE, DGC. 667 Anchor Dr., Sanibel, FL 33957 (813)472-8667. Prairie Flower Productions, 544 Richmond St. W., Toronto, ON M5V 1Y4 (416)362-4848.
Type of Production and Credits: TV Video-Dir.
Genres: Commercials-Th&TV.
Biography: Born in 1940. Director of over 1500 commercials. Has won 2 Gold Lions/Silver/Bronze at Cannes; 18 Gold Clios; numerous Bessie awards. Canadian citizen, U.S. resident.
Selected Filmography: Florida Lottery, Cm, 91, USA, Dir; Pontiac, Cm, 90/91, CDN/USA, Dir; B & G Wine, Cm, 91, CDN, Dir; Michelob, Cm, 90, USA, Dir; American Express, Cm, 90, USA, Dir.

CAPISTRAN, France
ACCT. 4398, boul. St-Laurent, bureau 103, Montréal, PQ H2W 1Z5 (514)288-1400.
Types de production et générique: l métrage-Ass réal; c métrage-Réal/Ass réal.
Types d'oeuvres: Drame-C&TV; Documentaire-C&TV; Education-C&TV.
Curriculum vitae: Née à Montréal, Québec. Langues: français et anglais. Université Laval en psycho-pédagogie; Universite de Montréal en relations public; Université Laval en télévision et audio visuel. Directrice générale d'un centre de formation. Formatrice en Techniques d'animation par l'audiovisuel et en faire face au public et aux médias, Participation à plus de 80 tables de travail en scénarisation et tests en cours de montage et en prédistribution Prix du leadership québécois de la Chambre de commerce du Montréal métropolitain.
Filmographie sélective: *Signe ça*, In, CDN, Réal; *Les Jeunes et la cybernétique*, TV, CDN, Sc; *Corridors*, C, 78, CDN, Rech/ Ass réal; *Le soleil a pas d'chance*, C, 75, CDN, Rech; *L'amour blessé*, C, 75, CDN, Rech/Sc (aide); *Pris au piège*, C, 78, CDN, Rech; *Claude Gauvreau, poète*, C, 77, CDN, Rech;

CARDINAL, Roger
DGC, ARRFQ, ACCT. 799, Jean-Bois, Boucherville, PQ J4B 3G2 (514)641-2118.
Types de production et générique: l métrage-Réal; c métrage-Réal; TV film-Réal.
Types d'oeuvres: Drame-C; Comédie-C; Documentaire-C&TV; Annonces-TV.
Curriculum vitae: *Malarek* a été mis en nomination pour "Best Director", Genies, 89; *Alcan: Hommage au Québec Créateur* gagne Coq d'Or et Mondial d'Or, 87; *Enfants Battus* et *La Voiturettes rouges* gagnant Mondial d'Argent; *You've Come a Long Way, Ladies* a été mis en nomination pour meilleur film, Geminis, 85.
Filmographie sélective: *Postcards from the Past*, "Urban Angel", TV, 91, CDN, Réal; *Lost and Found*, TV, 90, CDN, Réal; *Dracula-Live from Transylvania*, TV, 90, CDN, Réal; *Malarek*, C, 89, CDN, Réal; Alcan, Hommage au Québec Createur,

Cm, 87, CDN, Réal; *You've Come A Long Way Ladies*, TV, 85, CDN, Réal; *Etre informé c'est être libre*, TV, 84, CDN, Réal; *Dis le Canada, c'est loins de l'Amérique*, TV, 84, CDN, Réal; *Civvy Street*, TV, 82, CDN, Réal; *Life-Part Two*, TV, 81, CDN, Réal; *Second Debut*, TV, 81, CDN, Réal; *Les Plus Grandes Neiges du Monde*, TV, 81, CDN, Réal; *Montreal: An Olympic City*, TV, 75, CDN, Réal; *L'Apparition*, C, 71, CDN, Réal; *The Storm*, C, 70, CDN, Réal.

CARLE, Gilles ◊
ARRFQ, ACCT. (514)282-1326.
Types de production et générique: l métrage-Réal/Sc; c métrage-Réal/Sc; TV film-Réal/Sc; TV vidéo-Réal/Sc.
Types d'oeuvres: Drame-C; Comédie-C; Variété-C&TV; Documentaire-C&TV.
Curriculum vitae: Né en 1929, Maniwaki, Québec. Langues: français et anglais. Etudes: Belles-Lettres et Beaux-Arts. Plus de 300 films dont 20 longs métrages. *La Vraie Nature de Bernadette, La Mort d'un bucheron* et *Fantastica*, sélections officielles à Cannes; *La Tête de Normande St-Onge, Les Plouffe* et *L'Ange et la femme* furent présentés à la Quinzaine des Réalisateurs, Cannes; ses films ont aussi remporté plusieurs prix à des festivals de films internationaux.
Filmographie sélective: *Vive Québec*, C, 87, CDN, Réal/Sc; *La Guêpe*, C, 85-86, CDN, Réal/Sc; *O Picasso*, C, 85, CDN, Réal/Sc; *Cinéma, Cinéma*, TV, 84, CDN, Réal/Scl "Le Crime d'Ovide Plouffe" (4 eps), TV, 83, CDN/F, Réal/Sc; *Jouer sa vie*, TV, 82, CDN, Réal; *Maria Chapdelaine*, C, 82, CDN/F, Réal/Sc; *Les Plouffes*, C, 80, CDN, Réal/Co sc, (2 GENIE/BIJOU), *Fantastica*, C, 79, CDN, Réal/Sc; *L'Age de la Machine*, C, 78, CDN, Réal/Sc, (2 CFA); *L'Ange et la femme*, C, 77, CDN, Réal/Sc; *La Tête de Normande St-Onge*, C, 75, CDN, Réal/Sc; *A Thousand Moons*, "For the Record", TV, 75, CDN, Réal/Sc; *Les Corps célestes*, C, 73, CDN, Réal/Sc.

CARTMER, Debbie
Esprit Films Limited, P.O. Box 1683, St. Catharines, ON L2R 7K1 (416)685-8336.
Type of Production and Credits: TV Video-Prod/Dir; Video-Prod/Dir.
Genres: Documentary-TV; Educational-TV; Children's-TV; Industrial-TV.
Biography: Born 1961, Fredericton, New Brunswick. Graduated with Honours, Broadcasting Radio and Televison, Film Studies, Niagara College, 81. Film House Group Award; Radio and Television Faculty Award. Seven years of broadcasting experience as an on-air personality. *Break the Cycle* was nominated for Best Instructional/ Educational Film, Yorkton Short Film and Video Festival. Participant, Electronic & Film Media Program, Banff Centre School, 90. Instructor, Film Department, Niagara College of Applied Arts & Technology, 85-87 and 91 - present.
Selected Filmography: *Invictus*, Th, 90, CDN, Dir/Prod/Wr; *Break the Cycle*, ED, 87, CDN, Prod/Dir; *Growing Together*, In, 87, CDN, Prod/Dir; *Ms. Math*, TV, 86, CDN, Prod/Dir; *Up Front*, ED, 85, CDN, Script; "Child Abuse: Definitions and Causes" (3 eps), In, 84, CDN, Prod/Ed; *Being There*, In, 83, CDN, Prod/Dir/ Script; *Heart Catheterization*, In, 82, CDN, Snd Rec; *Alligator Shoes*, Th, 80, CDN, Cos/Make up.

CASTRAVELLI, Claudio
DGC. 3453 Peel St., Montreal, PQ H3A 1W7 (514)282-1993. Taurus 7 Film Corp., 999 de Maisonneuve W., Suite 1725, Montreal, PQ H3A 3L4 (514)848-9068. Taurus 7 Films (USA), 6570 Santa Monica Blvd., Hollywood, CA 90038 (213)462-3529.
Type of Production and Credits: Th, Film-Prod/Dir/Wr; Th Short-Prod/Dir; TV Video-Prod/Dir.
Genres: Drama-Th&TV; Comedy-Th&TV; Action-Th; Music Video-TV.
Biography: Born 1950; Canadian citizenship. Languages: English, French and Itlaian.
Selected Filmography: *Dark Eden*, Th, 91, USA, Prod/Dir/Wr; *In the Blood*, Th, 91, USA, Assoc Prod; *Dangerous Dreams*, TV, 90, CDN, Prod/Wr; *Touch of Murder*, TV, 90, CDN, Prod; *Friends Like These*, TV, 90, CDN, Prod; *Scorpio Factor*, Th, 89, CDN/F, Prod; *Heat Waves*, Th, 88, CDN, Prod; *Remembering Mel*, Th, 85, CDN, Prod; *Evil Judgment*, Th, 84, CDN, Prod/Dir/Wr; "Les Transistors" (6 eps), TV, 81, CDN/F, Prod/Dir.

CAULFIELD, Paul
- see PRODUCERS
CHAMMAS, Robert
- see PRODUCERS
CHAPDELAINE, Gérard ◊
AR. (514)849-2615.
Types de production et générique: TV film-Réal; TV vidéo-Réal.
Types d'oeuvres: Documentaire-TV; Education-TV; Enfants-TV.
Curriculum vitae: Né en 1927, St-Hyacinthe, Québec. Etudes: Philosophie, Université d'Ottawa; Relations inter-

nationales, Université Laval, Québec. Réalisateur à Radio Canada depuis 55.
Filmographie sélective: "Parcelles de soleil" (30 eps), TV, 88-89, CDN, Réal; "Nicole et Pierre" (57 eps), TV, 86-87, CDN, Réal; "Quatre voix...une parole" (26 eps), TV, 85-86, CDN, Réal; "Micro-Monde" (13 eps), TV, 85, CDN, Réal; *Sur les lieux de la passion*, TV, 84, CDN, Réal; "Ma Soeur, la Terre" (36 eps), TV, 82, CDN, Réal; "En terre sainte" (13 eps), TV, 79, CDN, Réal; "Les Pèlerins" (36 eps), TV, 78, CDN, Réal; "L'Eglise en papier" (36 eps), TV, 77, CDN, Réal; "La Bible en papier" (36 eps), TV, 76, CDN, Réal; "L'Evangile en papier" (36 eps), TV, 77, CDN, Réal; "Format 60" (40 eps), TV, 65-67, CDN, Réal; "Aujourd'hui" (80 eps), TV, 65-67, CDN, Réal.

CHAPMAN, Christopher
OC, CSC, DGC. R.R. #4, Sunderland, ON L0C 1H0 (705)357-2213. Christopher Chapman Ltd., 415 Merton St., Toronto, ON M4S 1B4 (416)487-3005.
Type of Production and Credits: Th Film-Dir; Th Short-Dir/Prod/Ed; TV Film-Dir/Ed/DOP.
Genres: Documentary-Th.
Biography: Born 1927, Toronto, Ontario. RCA Medal, 65; Centennial Medal, 67; Jubilee Medal, 77; Order of Canada, 87. Past President, DGC and Royal Canadian Academy. Has won film awards in Salerno, New York, Germany, Czechoslovakia. Has worked in 3-D film and Imax; 35 mm 3-D in permanent exhibit in Museum of Science and Industry, Chicago.
Selected Filmography: *Au Pays du Vent Leger* (Parc Asterix, Paris), Th, 88, F, Co-Prod/Dir/Ed/Cin; *U.S. Pavilion Film* (Expo 86), Th, 86, USA, Dir; *Chicago Museum of Science and Industry*, ED, 86, USA, Dir; *Wilderness*, Th, 84, CDN, Dir/Cin/Ed; *Pyramid of Roses*, Th, 82, CDN, Dir/Co-Prod/Ed; *Rome with Anthony Burgess*, "Cities", TV, 81, CDN, Dir/Ed/Cin; *Kelly*, Th, 80, CDN, Dir; *Volcano* (Imax), Th, 75, CDN, Dir/Ed; *Toronto the Good*, Th, 71, CDN, Dir/Ed; *Festival*, Th, 69, CDN, Dir/Prod/Cin/Ed; *A Place to Stand*, Th, 67, CDN, Dir/Prod/Cin/Ed, (OSCAR/CFA); *Loring and Wyle*, TV, 63, CDN, Dir/Ed/Cin; *The Persistent Seed*, Th, 61, CDN, Dir/Cin/Ed; *Quetico*, Th, 56, CDN, Dir/Prod/Cin/Ed, (CFA); *The Seasons*, Th, 52, CDN, Dir/Prod/Cin/Ed, (2 CFA).

CHAREST, Gaétan
- voir PRODUCTEURS

CHAREST, Louis
ARRQ. 613, rue Mercille, St-Lambert, PQ J4P 2M1 (514)672-2092. Radio-Québec, 1000, rue Fullum, Montréal, PQ H2K 3L7 (514)521-2424.
Types de production et générique: TV film-Réal; TV vidéo-Réal.
Types d'oeuvres: Drame-TV; Comédie-TV; Documentaire-TV.
Curriculum vitae: Né en 1937, Montréal, Québec. Etudes à l'Ecole des Beaux-Arts de Montréal, 57-62; études en musique, Université Laval, Québec. Enseignement en arts, 62-70. Production en télévision depuis 70.
Filmographie sélective: "La Soirée de l'impro" (15 eps), TV, 82-86, CDN/F, Réal, (GEMEAUX 87); La Déprime, TV, 84, CDN, Réal; "L'Objectif" (16 eps), TV, 81, CDN, Réal; "Neuf et demi" (3 eps), TV, 80, CDN, Réal; "Moi" (17 eps), TV, 78-79, CDN, Réal.

CHARTRAND, Alain
AQRRCT, ACCT, SACD, INIS, CQ. 256 Carré St-Louis, Montréal, PQ H2X 1A3 (514)848-9318. FAX: 843-2700. Lino Productions Inc., 205, chemin North-Hatley, Katevale, PQ J0B 1W0 (819)843-1944.
Types de production et générique: l métrage-Réal; c métrage-Réal;TV film-Réal
Types d'oeuvres: Drame-C; Comédie-C; Documentaire-C&TV; Education-C&TV.
Curriculum vitae: Né en 1946, Montréal, Québec. Etudes: Conservatoire de Musique de la Province de Québec, 63-67. Premier assistant réalisateur sur 23 films, dont 16 longs métrages, 70-86. *L'Etau-Bus* a gagné le Prix du Public, Belfort, 84, et à Clermont-Ferrand, France, 85, et le Prix Anik, Radio-Canada, 83. *Des Amis pour Vie*: 4 nominations aux Prix Gémeaux, 89. *Ding et Dong le film*: Prix Accueil du Public, Festival Baie Comeau.
Filmographie sélective: *Une Nuit a l'école*, C, CDN, 91, Réal; *Un Homme de Parole*, TV, CDN, 91, Réal/Sc; *Ding et Dong, le film*, C, CDN, 90, Réal; *Questions de drogue*, "Beaux Dimanches", TV, 89, CDN, Réal; *Des Amis pour la Vie*, C, 88, CDN, Réal; *L'Etau-Bus*, C, 83, CDN, Réal; *On est pas sorti du bois*, C, 82, CDN, Réal; *L'Estrie en Musique*, TV, 81, CDN, Réal/Sc; *Les Douces*, C, 80, CDN, Réal/Sc; *Images de l'Estrie*, TV, 80, CDN, Réal; *La XXe Olympiade*, C, 76, CDN, Réal ass; *La Piastre*, C, 74, CDN, Réal/Sc; *Isis au 8*, C, 72, CDN, Réal; *Ataboy*, C, 67, CDN, Réal.

CHAYER, Lise
AR, CAPAC, ARRFQ, ACCT. 5470, de

Repentigny, Montréal, PQ H1M 2G4 (514)597-4883. Radio-Canada, 1400 est, boul. René-Lévesque, Montréal, PQ H2L 2M2 (514)597-4883.
Types de production et générique: TV film-Réal; TV vidéo-Réal.
Types d'oeuvres: Drame-TV; Comédie-TV; Documentaire-TV; Enfants-TV.
Curriculum vitae: Née en 1943, Montréal, Québec. Langues: français et anglais. Etudes Lettres-Sciences à Montréal; Certificats: études juridiques, relations publiques, communications, Université de Montréal; Lauréat en musique, Ecole Vincent d'Indy; cours en réalisation, BBC Londres; atelier de théâtre Warren Robertson. Travaux de traduction, publicité sous le nom de Conceptel enrg.
Filmographie sélective: "Cormoran" (26 eps), TV, 90-91, CDN, Réal; "L'Héritage" (15 eps), TV, 88, CDN, Réal; "Paul, Marie et les enfants" (30 eps), TV, 85-87, CDN, Réal; "Traboulidon" (30 eps), TV, 83-85, CDN, Réal; "Le Trefle à quatre feuilles" (15 eps), TV, 82-83, CDN, Réal; "Du tac au tac" (45 eps), TV, 79-82, CDN, Réal; "Vedettes en direct" (30 eps), TV, 78-80, CDN, Réal; *Salut ben pis merci!*, TV, 77, CDN, Réal; "Les Coqueluches" (26 eps), TV, 76-77, CDN, Réal; *En récital-Nicole Croisille*, TV, 76, CDN, Réal; "Destination monde" (60 eps), TV, 74-76, CDN, Réal; *Ça s'pourrais-tu?*, TV, 75, CDN, Réal; *En récital Nana Mouskouri*, TV, 75, CDN, Réal; "Moi et l'autre" (100 eps), TV, 68-71, CDN, Ass réal.

CHAYER, Réjean
AR, ACCT. 1275 Laurier est, #106, Montréal, PQ H2J 1H2 (514)274-4320. Radio-Canada, 1400 est, boul. René-Lévesque, Montréal, PQ H2L 2M2 (514)285-2839.
Types de production et générique: TV film-Réal; TV vidéo-Réal.
Types d'oeuvres: Drame-TV; Variété-TV; Documentaire-TV; Enfants-TV.
Curriculum vitae: Né en 1945, Valleyfield, Québec. Langues: français et anglais. Maîtrise, sciences politiques, Université d'Ottawa. Trente ans d'expérience: 10 en informations, variétés; réalisateur, section dramatique, Radio-Canada, 86. Récipiendaire de quelques prix: Prix de l'Association nationale de Téléspectateurs, 86 et 87, prix CanPro, Meilleur Emission pour Enfants.
Filmographie sélective: "Tandem" (38 eps), TV, 89-90, CDN, Réal; "Bonjour Docteur" (18 eps), TV, 88-89, CDN, Réal; "A plein temps" (14 eps), TV, 87, CDN, Réal; "Flash Varicelle" (34 eps), TV, 87, CDN, Réal; "La Bonne Aventure" (7 eps), TV, 86, CDN, Réal; "Le Parc des braves" (1 eps), TV, 86, CDN, Réal; "L'Héritage" (5 eps), TV, 86, CDN, Réal; "Au jour le jour" (6 eps), TV, 84, CDN, Réal; *Congrès à la Chefferie - Parti Liberal du Canada*, TV, 84, CDN, Réal/Coor pro; *Congrès à la Chefferie - Par Conservateur du Canada*, TV, 83, CDN Réal; *Réunion du F.M.I. à Toronto*, TV, 83 CDN, Réal; *Sommet économique de Williamsburg*, TV, 83, CDN, Réal; *Visite du Pape en Grande-Bretagne*, TV, 82, CDN, Réal; *Visite du Premier ministre canadien en France*, TV, 82, CDN, Réal; *Sommet économique d'Ottawa*, TV, 82, CDN, Réal.

CHERCOVER, Murray
- see PRODUCERS

CHERNIACK, David
12 Thorburn Ave., Toronto, ON (416)536-3142. CBC, Man Alive, P.O. Box 500, Stn. A, Toronto, ON M5W 1E6 (416)975-6585.
Type of Production and Credits: TV Film-Prod/Dir.
Genres: Drama-TV; Documentary-TV; Experimental-TV.
Biography: Born 1946, Winnipeg, Manitoba. B.Sc., University of Manitoba; 4 years studying feature film direction at film school in Prague (FAMU), 68-72. Winner of awards at Columbus, New York, Yorkton, San Francisco.
Selected Filmography: *Heart of Tibet*, TV, 91, USA, Wr/Dir; *Josef Skvorecky: Keeper of the Flame*, "Man Alive", TV, 90, CDN, Prod/Dir; *Wheel of Rebirth*, "Man Alive", TV, 89, CDN, Prod/Wr/Dir; *The E.T. Hypothesis*, "Man Alive", TV, 88, CDN, Prod/Wr/Dir; *Circle of Healing, Parts 1 & 2*, "Man Alive", TV, 88, CDN, Prod/Wr/Dir; *Journey to Prague*, "Man Alive", TV, 87, CDN, Prod/Dir; *Stephen Hawking*, "Man Alive", TV, 86, CDN, Prod/Dir; *Mighty Quinn*, TV, 85, CDN, Prod/Dir; *Sharp and Terrible Eyes*, TV, 80, CDN, Prod/Dir; *Coming and Going*, "The Nature of Things", TV, 77, CDN, Prod/Dir.

CHETWYND, Lionel
- see WRITERS

CHICOINE, Nicole
ONF, ACCT. 10841 Laverdure, (2c), Montréal, PQ H3L 2L8 (514)385-0543.
Types de production et générique: m métrage-Réal/Sc.
Types d'oeuvres: Documentaire-C&TV; Education-C&TV; Enfants-C&TV.

Curriculum vitae: Conservatoire LaSalle, art dramatique; L'office national du film, coordonatrice au studio "B" de la Production française: *Partis pour la gloire, La Fleur aux dents, Tii-Mine Bernie pis la gang,* et documentaires: *La p'tite violence, Le Saint-Laurent, Derrière l'image,* 75, l'Atelier vidéo, co-réalise documentaire vidéo *Qui pére gagne,* 76, collabore à la réalisation de *Cordélia;* assiste à réaliser *L'Enfant fragile* et *Les Adeptes;* 80 assiste à réaliser *Les Beaux Souvenirs;* casting de *La quarantaine;* montage, *Maria Chapdelaine* (le film et la série télévisée) et *Mario;* correctrice de manuscrits pour la maison d'édition Québec/Amérique, *Le pouvoir? Connais pas!, L'enfant hyperactif, Pour la suite de l'Histoire,* 85-86, coordonnatrice nationale de Télé-Jeunesse Canada/Young Canada Television; 87-88, recherche, scénarisation, réalisation, et montage *Singulier Pluriel, On a pus les parents qu'on avait* (films documentaires); 89-91, direction de production *Joseph K.* A l'Office national du film, *Les Oursons Volants* à Ciné-Groupe, *Il était une fois....les Filles de Caleb* à Publi-Mages, scénarisation d'une série d'émissions pour les jeunes par Panacom, *Les Topinambus.*
Filmographie sélective: *Les Topinambus,* TV, 91, CDN, Ass réal; *Joseph K,* C, 90, CDN, Sc; *On a pus les parents qu'on avait,* C, 89, CDN, Rech/Sc/Réal; *Singulier Pluriel,* C, 88, CDN, Rech/Sc/Réal; *Mario,* C, 86, CDN, Ass montage; *Maria Chapdelaine,* C, 83, CDN, Ass montage; *Les beaux souvenirs,* C, 80, CDN, Ass réal; *Cordélia,* C, 76, CDN, Ass montage.

CHILVERS, Colin
DGA, DGC, AMPAS. P.O. Box 135, Ridgeway, ON L0S 1N0 (416)894-2963. GMS, 7025 Santa Monica Blvd., Hollywood, CA 90038 (213)856-4848. Shooters, 95 Berkeley St., Toronto, ON M5J 2W8 (416)862-1955. Maureen Lickhurst, London Management, 235 Regent St., London, W1A 2JT England (71)493-1610.
Type of Production and Credits: Th Film-Dir; TV Film-Dir.
Genres: Drama-Th; Science Fiction-Th&TV; Music Video-Th&TV; Commercials-TV.
Biography: Born 1945, England; graduated Hornsey College of Art. Winner of numerous awards including BMA Award, Best Video for *Smooth Criminal,* Oscar for *Superman: the Movie,* Clio for *Marching Band,* Friskies Buffet commmercial.
Selected Filmography: *Nightrider,* Sony, Cm, 90, USA, Dir; *Cinderella,* Dow Spiffits, Cm, 90, CDN, Dir; *Ladies Night,* Budweiser, Cm, 89, USA, Dir; "Superboy" (5 eps), TV, 89, USA, Dir; *Atomic City,* Holly Johnson, MV, 89, GB, Dir; *Madly in Love,* Bros, MV, 89, GB, Dir; *Michael Jackson's Moonwalker,* Th, 89, USA, Dir; *Smooth Criminal,* Michael Jackson, MV, 89, USA, Dir; *The Resurrection,* "War of the Worlds" (premier eps), TV, 88, CDN, Dir; *Marching Band,* Friskies Buffet, Cm, 83, USA, Dir; *Pippi Longstocking,* TV, 83, CDN, Dir; *Superman II,* Th, 81, USA/GB/CDN, Dir FX; *The Wars,* Th, 81, CDN, SFX Spv; *Superman: the Movie,* Th, 79, USA/GB/CDN, SFX Dir; *The Rocky Horror Picture Show,* Th, 74, SFX Spv.

CHRISTIE, Keith
110 - 19 St., #404, West Vancouver, BC V7V 3W8 (604)922-0263.
Type of Production and Credits: TV Film-Prod/Dir/Art Dir/Wr; TV Video-Prod/Dir/Art Dir/Wr.
Genres: Musical-TV; Documentary-TV; Educational-TV; Children's-TV.
Biography: Born Sydney, Australia. Studied Motion Picture Production, Graphic Arts, Stagecraft at Sydney College of Art. Has worked for CBC as design director, set designer; producer/director, CBC's first west coast mobile TV production and colour TV production; now independent producer and director.
Selected Filmography: *A Future-The Right of the Child,* Save the Children Fund of BC, TV, 90-91, CDN, Prod/Dir; *Audrey Hepburn: Gift of Music,* Unicef, TV, 88-89, CDN, Prod/Dir; *The Sinterklaas Fantasy,* TV, 87-88, CDN, Art Dir/Wr/Prod/Dir; *Anna in Graz,* TV, 80-81, CDN, Art Dir/Wr/ Prod/Dir; *Michelangelo and the Shoemaker,* TV, 81-82, CDN, Art Dir/Wr/Prod/Dir; *Maranatha* (Rock Mass), TV, 75-76, CDN, Prod/Dir; *Noel - Christmas Fantasy,* TV, 76-77, CDN, Prod/Dir; "Medical Explorers" (13 eps), TV, 74-75, CDN, Prod/Dir; "Suzuki on Science" (13 eps), TV, 70-71, CDN, Prod/Dir; *Klee Wyck,* TV, 75-76, CDN, Prod/Dir; *Prince Charles at Pearson College,* TV, 72-73, CDN, Prod/Dir; "Music to See" (6 eps), TV, 72-73, CDN, Prod/Dir; "Meeting Place" (25 eps), TV, 68-73, CDN, Prod/Dir; *Thank Heaven for Christmas,* TV, 66, CDN, Prod/Dir; "Vacation Time" (26 eps), TV, 66-70, CDN, Prod/Dir.

CICCORITTI, Gerard
DGC. 19 Tennis Cres., Apt. 8, Toronto, ON M4K 1J4 (416)465-6465. Lightshow

Communications, 77 Mowat St., Ste. 406, Toronto, ON M6K 3E3 (416)538-6815. Charles Northcote/The Core Group, 489 College St., Ste. 501, Toronto, ON M6G 1A5 (416)944-1093.
Type of Production and Credits: Th Film-Dir; TV Film-Dir.
Genres: Drama-Th&TV; Comedy-TV; Action-Th&TV; Horror-Th.
Biography: Born in 1956 in Toronto, Ontario. Canadian, eh...English. Italian. 1 year film at York University. Painter (on canvas, not walls).
Selected Filmography: "The Hidden Room" (3 eps), TV, 91, CDN/USA, Dir; "Sweating Bullets" (3 eps), TV, 90-91, CDN/USA/MEX, Dir; "Fly By Night" (1 eps), TV, 91, CDN/USA, Dir; "E.N.G." (6 eps), TV, 90-91, CDN, Dir; "The Hitchhiker" (4 eps), TV, 90, CDN/F, Dir; "Top Cops" (4 eps), TV, 90, CDN/USA, Dir; *Bedroom Eyes II*, Th, 88, CDN/USA, Wr; *A Whisper to a Scream*, Th, 88, CDN/USA, Wr/Co Prod; *Graveyard Shift II: The Understudy*, Th, 88, CDN, Dir/Wr; *Night of Retribution*, Th, 87, CDN, Wr/Co Prod; *Graveyard Shift*, Th, 86, CDN, Dir/Wr; *Psycho Girls*, Th, 85, CDN, Dir/Wr.

CIUP, Charles
NABET. 12810 Pacific Ave., #1, Los Angeles, CA 90066 (213)397-1903.
Type of Production and Credits: TV Video-Dir (Tech).
Genres: Comedy-TV; Variety-TV; Documentary-TV; Sports-TV.
Biography: Born in 1950 in Jerusalem. Canadian citizen. Fluent in French and English. Graduated Ryerson Polytechnical Institute in 1973 in Radio & Television Arts. School award for Outstanding Creative Ability in Television Production. Won 2 CanPro awards in 1986 for *When I Grow Too Old To Dream*. Has also won 2 RTNDA awards, 1 NATPE award and 1 Gabriel award.
Selected Filmography: "Hi Honey, I'm Home" (13 eps) TV, 91, USA, Tech Dir; "Supermarket Sweep" (195 eps), TV, 89-91, USA, Tech Dir; "Wake, Rattle & Roll", (130 eps), TV, 90-91, USA, Tech Dir; "Trial Watch" (50 eps), TV, 91, USA, Tech Dir; "Totally Hidden Video" (20 eps), TV, 90, USA, Tech Dir; "Fun House" (300+ eps), TV, 88-90, USA, Tech Dir.

CIUPKA, Richard ◆
(514)738-9996.
Type of Production and Credits: Th Film-Dir/DOP; TV Film-Dir/DOP.
Genres: Drama-Th&TV; Comedy-Th&TV; Action-Th&TV; Commercials-TV.
Biography: Born 1950, Liege, Belgium; Canadian citizenship. Languages: English, French, Polish. Education: Cours Classique and Diploma in Electronics. Worked 4 years in camera special effects with Wally Gentleman. Directed numerous commercials, 83-88. Has own production house, Ciupka Film, based in New York and Montreal.
Selected Filmography: *Hold-Up*, Th, 85, CDN/F, DOP; *Secret Weapons*, TV, 84, USA, DOP; *Heartsounds*, TV, 84, USA, DOP; *The Guardian*, TV, 83, CDN/USA, DOP; *The Blood of Others*, Th, 83, CDN/F, DOP; *The Terry Fox Story*, Th, 82, CDN, DOP; *Melanie*, Th, 80, CDN, DOP; *Curtains*, Th, 80, CDN, Dir; *Atlantic City*, Th, 79, CDN/F, DOP, (CSC/BSC); *Dirty Tricks*, Th, 79, CDN, DOP; *An American Christmas Carol*, TV, 79, USA, DOP; *Yesterday*, Th, 79, CDN, DOP; *It Rained All Night the Day I Left*, Th, 79, CDN/IL/F, DOP; *Violette Nozière*, Th, 77, CDN/F, DOP/Op; *Les Liens de sang*, Th, 77, CDN/F, Op.

CLAIROUX, Jacques
- voir MONTEURS

CLARK, Barry
- see PRODUCERS

CLARK, Bob ◆
(213)277-4545.
Type of Production and Credits: Th Film-Dir/Prod/Wr.
Genres: Drama-Th; Comedy-Th; Horror-Th.
Selected Filmography: *From the Hip*, Th, 86, USA, Dir/Co-Prod; *Turk 182!*, Th, 85, USA, Dir; *Rhinestone*, Th, 84, USA, Dir; *A Christmas Story*, Th, 83, CDN, Dir/Co-Prod, (GENIE); *Porky's II*, Th, 82, CDN, Dir/Co-Prod; *Porky's*, Th, 81, CDN, Dir/Co-Prod; *Tribute*, Th, 80, CDN, Dir/Co-Prod; *Murder by Decree*, Th, 78, CDN/GB, Dir/Co-Prod, (GENIE); *Breaking Point*, Th, 75, CDN/USA, Dir; *Black Christmas*, Th, 74, CDN, Dir/Co-Prod; *Deathdream*, Th, 72, CDN, Dir/Prod; *Children Shouldn't Play with Dead Things*, Th, 71, USA, Dir/Prod.

CLARK, Paulle
- see PRODUCERS

CLARK, Ron
- see WRITERS

COCHRAN, Andrew
- see PRODUCERS

COCK, Peter J. B. ◆
(613)745-4078.
Type of Production and Credits: Th Short-Dir/Prod/Ed/Wr; TV Video-

Dir/Prod/Wr.
Genres: Documentary-Th&TV; Educational-Th&TV; Commercials-Th&TV; Industrial-Th&TV.
Biography: Born 1918, England; Canadian and British citizenship. Languages: English and French. Seven and a half years in Royal Canadian Navy. Has directed, written and edited more than 400 films for public and private sectors; twenty-one years as staff producer with Crawley Films, Ottawa; freelance producer/director. Has lectured on film production internationally; 2 years as consultant on film to the Dean of Journalism at Carleton University; 2 years as professor, Algonquin College, Ottawa. Many consultancy positions.
Selected Filmography: *Walrus Hunt*, ED, 88, CDN, Ed/Prod; *After the Wars*, ED, 82, CDN, Prod/Dir; *A Visit to the Bank of Canada*, ED, 82, CDN, Prod/Dir; *Two-Way Window*, ED, 80, CDN, Prod/Dir; "There's No Place Like Home" (12 eps), ED, 80, CDN, Prod/Dir; *Indonesia: The Changing Face*, ED, 77, CDN, Prod/Dir; "Pregnanacy and Childbirth" (4 eps), ED, 76, CDN, Prod/Dir; *Safety-Oriented First Aid*, ED, 75, CDN, Prod/Dir; *National Role*, ED, 73, CDN, Prod/Dir; *Red, White and You*, ED, 72, CDN, Prod/Dir.

COHEN, Sidney M.
ATPD, ACCT. 21 Windsor Court Rd., Thornhill, ON L3T 4Y4 (416)731-1329. (416)361-0916. Harvey B. Sindle, 400 Madison Ave., New York, NY 10017 USA (212)935-5533.
Type of Production and Credits: TV Video-Dir/Prod; TV Video-Prod Cons.
Genres: Variety-TV; News-TV; Game Shows-TV.
Biography: Born 1947, Montreal, Quebec. Languages: English and French. President, S.P.P.L. Productions. Specializes in live or live-to-tape multicamera productions demanding little or no postproduction. In addition to listed credits, has directed and produced several TV pilots in Canada and the US, 72-91.
Selected Filmography: *Simcoe Solution*, "W5 Special", TV, 91, CDN, Dir; "Business World" (600 eps), TV, 91, CDN, Dir; "Pol's Minute" (130 eps), TV, 90-91, CDN, Prod/Dir/Creator; "Shirley" (50 eps), TV, 90-91, CDN, Dir; "Test Pattern" (130 eps), TV, 85-91, CDN, Prod/Dir; "Midday" (1100 eps), TV, 85-91, CDN, Dir; "Canada AM" (400 eps), TV, 84-91, CDN, Dir; "Thrill of a Lifetime" (150 eps), TV, 81-86, CDN, Creator/Dir; "The Mad Dash" (400 eps), TV, 79-81, CDN, Creator/Prod/Dir; "Say Powww" (19 eps), TV, 79-80, USA, Dir; "The Editors" (50 eps), TV, 78-79, USA, Dir; "It's Your Move" (400 eps), TV, 74-79, CDN, Prod/Dir; "The Art of Cooking" (400 eps), TV, 74-76, CDN, Prod/Dir; Elections (8), TV, 72-89, CDN, Prod/Dir; Political Conventions (4), TV, 72-88, CDN, Prod/Dir.

COLE, Frank
1785 Riverside Dr., #401, Ottawa, ON K1G 3T7 (613)736-8243.
Type of Production and Credits: Th Film-Prod/Dir; Th Short-Prod/Dir.
Genres: Documentary-Th; Drama-Th.
Biography: Born 1954, Saskatoon, Saskatchewan. Diploma of Film Production, Algonquin College, 80; B.A., Carleton University, 76.
Selected Filmography: *A Life*, Th, 86, CDN, Prod/Dir; *The Mountenays*, Th, 80, CDN, Prod/Dir; *A Documentary*, Th, 79, CDN, Prod/Dir.

COLE, Janis
- see PRODUCERS

COLLIER, Mike
- see PRODUCERS

COLLINS, Alan
CIFC. Nova Productions, 43 Metcalfe St., #20, Toronto, ON M4X 1R7 (416)920-8544.
Type of Production and Credits: TV Film-Dir/Ed; TV Video-Dir.
Genres: Drama-TV; Documentary-TV; Educational-TV; Children's-TV.
Biography: Born 1942, England; Canadian citizenship. Film and video editor. Won Best Director, North American Indian Film Festival for *Beauty of My People*.
Selected Filmography: *Killer Image*, Th, 91, CDN, Ed; *Le cri du silence*, TV, 90, CDN, Prod/Dir/Ed; *One Warm Line*, TV, 89, CDN, Dir; "Degrassi Junior High" (8 eps), TV, 87-88, CDN, Ed; *Covert Action*, TV, 86, CDN, Ed; *City Blues*, TV, 86, CDN, Dir/Ed; *October Stranger*, TV, 85, CDN, Dir; *Spirit of Turtle Island*, TV, 85, CDN, Dir; *Beauty of My People*, TV, 78, CDN, Dir; *The Brood*, Th, 78, CDN, Ed; *Love at First Sight*, Th, 75, CDN, Ed, (CFEG); *Von Richtofen and Brown*, Th, 70, USA, Ed.

COLLINS, Neil
- see WRITERS

COMEAU, Guy
AR. 12074, rue Dépatie, Montréal, PQ H4J 1W7. Radio-Canada, 1400 est, boul. René-Lévesque, Montréal, PQ H2L 2M2 (514)597-5616.
Types de production et générique: TV

film-Réal; TV vidéo-Réal.
Types d'oeuvres: Documentaire-C&TV; Education-C&TV; Enfants-C&TV; Animation-C&TV.
Curriculum vitae: Né à Montréal, Québec. Langues: français et anglais. Baccalauréat, Université de Montréal; licence en sciences commerciales, HEC; Diplôme d'expert audio-visuel, Centre audio-visuel de l'Ecole Normale Supérieure, St-Cloud, France. En distribution commerciale, ONF; réalisateur, Radio-Canada. "Klimbo" a gagné plusieurs prix internationaux: Paris, New York, Chicago, Banff, Montréal, Toronto.
Filmographie sélective: "La Semaine verte", TV, 85-88, CDN, Réal; "Michou et Pilo" (38 eps), TV, 84-85, CDN, Réal; "Klimbo" (39 eps)(13 eps produits avec France), TV, 80-83, CDN, Réal; "Tam-Tam" (90 eps), TV, 77-80, CDN, Réal; "Les Chibouskis" (90 eps), TV, 73-77, CDN, Réal.

COMEAU, Phil ◇
ARRFQ. (902) 425-3604.
Type of Production and Credits: Th Short-Dir/Wr/Ed; TV Film-Dir/Wr/Ed; TV Video-Dir/Wr.
Genres: Documentary-TV; Drama-Th&TV; Commercials-Th; Comedy-Th&TV.
Biography: Born 1956, Saulnierville, New Brunswick. Languages: English and French. Studied Drama, Moncton University; Cinema, Algonquin College; attended International Film and Television workshops, Rockport, Maine; apprenticed in Paris. His films won 2 awards at the Atlantic Film Festival and have been nominated at the Yorkton Short Film and Video Festival and at Chamrousse.
Selected Filmography: *Buskers: The Art of the Street Performer*, TV, 88, CDN, Dir/Ed; *People with a Mission*, 88, CDN, Dir; *Same Day Courier*, Cm, 88, CDN, Dir; *Le Creux de la vague*, TV, 87, CDN, Dir/Wr; *Le Deuxième Souffle*, TV, 87, CDN, Dir/Wr; *Le Tapis de Grand-Pré/The Hooked Rug of Grand-Pré*, TV, 86, CDN, Dir/Wr; *Touchons du bois/Knock on Wood*, ED, 85, CDN, Dir/Wr; *A l'image de la mer/Southwest Shore*, In, 84, CDN, Dir/Ed; *J'avions 375 ans*, C, 82, CDN, Dir/Wr; *La Femme Acadienne*, TV, 80, CDN, Dir/Ed; *La musique nous explique*, TV, 79, CDN, Dir/Wr; *Les Gossipeuses/The Gossips*, C, 78, CDN, Dir/Wr; *La Cabane*, C, 77, CDN, Dir/Wr/Ed.

CONDIE, Richard
ACCT, ASIFA, AMPAS. 220 Campbell St., Winnipeg, MB R3N 1B5 (204)489-8182.
Type of Production and Credits: Th Short-Dir/An/Wr.
Genres: Comedy-Th&TV; Educational-Th&TV; Animation-Th&TV; Experimental-Th.
Biography: Born 1942, Vancouver, BC. B.A., University of Manitoba. *The Big Snit* was nominated for an Oscar and won numerous awards at film festivals, including Montreal, Annecy, San Francisco, Krakow, Hiroshima; *Getting Started* won awards at Krakow, Zagreb and a Bijou.
Selected Filmography: *The Apprentice*, Th/TV, 91, CDN, Wr/Dir/Prod; *Expo 92*, Seville, Spain, In, 91, CDN, Dir; *The Cat Came Back*, Th/TV, 89, CDN, Prod, (GENIE); *Expo 88*, Brisbane, Australia, In, 88, CDN, Dir.

CONNOLLY, Phillip J.
Blackflight Filmwerks, 100 Roehampton Ave., #1312, Toronto, ON M4P 1R3 (416)440-0378.
Type of Production and Credits: Th Short-Wr/Dir/DOP; TV Video-Dir.
Genres: Commercials-TV; Drama-Th; Comedy-Th.
Biography: Born in 1965 in London, England. Canadian citizen. Attended the University of Western Ontario, London, and the Ryerson Polytechnical Institute Film School, Toronto. Presently exploring alternative perceptions of the frameline.
Selected Filmography: *The Answer*, Th, 90, CDN, Wr/Dir; *Priorities*, Cm, 90, CDN, Dir; *Woolgathering (Out In the Cold)*, Th, 89, CDN, Wr/Dir; *Flying*, Th, 88, CDN, Dir.

COOK, Heather
- see PRODUCERS

COOPER, Richard
- see WRITERS

COSMATOS, George P.
DGA, DGC, ACCT. Guy McElwaine/Peter Rawley, ICM, 8899 Beverly Blvd., Los Angeles, CA 90048 USA (213)550-4000.
Type of Production and Credits: Th Film-Dir/Prod/Wr.
Genres: Drama-Th; Action-Th; Horror-Th; Commercials-TV.
Biography: Born 1943; Canadian citizenship. Speaks 6 languages fluently. Attended London Film School; University of London (International Affairs). Victoria Film Commissioner. Grand Prize for *Of Unknown Origin*, Paris Film Festival, 83. Worked as assistant director on many features including *Exodus* and *Zorba the*

Greek. **Selected Filmography:** *Leviathan*, Th, 88, USA, Dir; *Cobra*, Th, 86, USA, Dir; *Rambo - First Blood Part II*, Th, 84, USA, Dir; *Of Unknown Origin*, Th, 82, CDN/USA, Dir; *Escape to Athena/Golden Raiders*, Th, 79, GB, Dir/Co-Story; *The Cassandra Crossing*, Th, 75, GB/D/I, Dir/Co-Wr/Co-Story; *Massacre in Rome*, Th, 73, I/F, Co-Wr/Dir; *Beloved/Restless*, Th, 69, GB, Prod/Wr/Dir.

COTE, François J.
ACCT. 3589, Décarie, Montréal, PQ H4A 3J4 (514)481-8385.
Types de production et générique: TV vidéo-Réal; TV film-Réal.
Types d'oeuvres: Drame-TV; Education-TV; Enfants-TV; Annonces-TV.
Curriculum vitae: Né à Québec. Langues: français et anglais. Bac., Université de Montréal, 66. Monteur de film, 67-69; réalisateur d'annonces, 69-74; directeur de la production, JPL Productions, 74-77; réalisateur pigiste depuis 79. "A plein temps" a gagné le Prix Maurice Proulx, 86; Grand Prix, ANT, 88.
Filmographie sélective: "Super Sans Plomb" (41 eps), TV, 89-90, CDN, Réal; "Maison Deschênes" (98 eps), TV, 87-88, CDN, Réal; "A plein temps" (56 eps), TV, 84-86, CDN, Réal; "Court Circuit" (15 eps), TV, 83-84, CDN, Réal; "Pop Citrouille" (50 eps), TV, 80-82, CDN, Réal; "Dynamique du lecteur" (3 eps), TV, 82, CDN, Réal; "Téléjeans" (15 eps), TV, 79-80, CDN, Réal; "Passe-Partout" (125 eps), TV, 77-79,

CRESSEY, John
- see CINEMATOGRAPHERS

CRONENBERG, David
DGC, ACCT. David Cronenberg Prod., 217 Avenue Rd., Toronto, ON M5R 2J3 (416)961-3432. Mike Marcus, CAA, 1888 Century Park E., Los Angeles, CA 90067 USA (213)288-4545.
Type of Production and Credits: Th Film-Dir/Wr.
Genres: Drama-Th.
Biography: Born 1943, Toronto, Ontario. One year Science and B.A., English, University of Toronto. Winner of many awards, including most recently L.A. Critics' Award for Best Director for *Dead Ringers*, 89.
Selected Filmography: *Regina vs. Horvath*, TV, 90, CDN, Dir; *Regina vs. Logan*, TV, 90, CDN, Dir; Nike, Cm, 90, CDN, Wr/Dir; Caramilk, Cm, 90, CDN, Dir; Hydro (4 cm), Cm, 89, CDN, Dir; *Dead Ringers*, Th, 88, CDN, Dir/Co-Prod/Co-Wr; *Faith Healer*, "Friday the 13th - The Series", TV, 88, CDN/USA, Dir; *The Fly*, Th, 86, USA, Dir/Co-Wr; *The Dead Zone*, Th, 83, USA, Dir; *Videodrome*, Th, 81, CDN/USA, Wr/Dir, (GENIE); *Scanners*, Th, 79, CDN, Dir/Wr; *Fast Company*, Th, 78, CDN, Dir/Co-Wr; *The Brood*, Th, 78, CDN, Dir/Wr; *Rabid Rage*, Th, 76, CDN, Dir; *The Parasite Murders/Shivers/They Came from Within*, Th, 74, CDN, Dir/Wr.

CROSSLAND, Harvey James
DGC, ACTRA, BCMPA. 3908 W. 51 Ave., Vancouver, BC V6N 5W1 (604)263-2256. Siren Films Inc., 827 W. Pender St., Vancouver, BC V6C 3G8 (604)662-8337. FAX: 263-7044.
Type of Production and Credits: Th Short-Wr/Dir; TV Film-Wr/Prod/Ed/Dir; TV Video-Prod/Dir/Wr.
Genres: Drama-Th&TV; Documentary-Th&TV; Educational-Th&TV; Commercials-Th&TV.
Biography: Born 1950, Ottawa, Ontario. Languages: English and Spanish. Honours B.A., Carleton University.
Selected Filmography: *A Different Dance*, "Family Pictures", TV, 88, CDN, Wr/Dir/Ed; *Walking in Pain*, Th, 88, CDN, Dir/Ed; *Asir Region*, "Saudi", TV, 87, SA, Wr/Dir; *Fishing for Trouble*, "The Beachcombers" (2 eps), TV, 87, CDN, Co-Wr; *If Asked to Serve*, "The Beachcombers", TV, 87, CDN, Co-Wr; *A Life of Independence*, TV, 86, CDN, Dir/Co-Wr; *Art of the Inuit*, Th, 85, D, Dir/Co-Wr; *Close to Home*, Th, 85, CDN, Co-Wr/Prod/Ed; *Somewhere Between*, Th, 83, CDN, Dir/Prod/Ed; *New Canadian Kid/New American Kid*, ED, 82, CDN, Prod; "Fliers: Pioneering Canadian Aviation" (18 eps), TV, 80, CDN, Wr/Prod/Dir.

CURNICK, David
P.O. Box 15560, Vancouver, BC V6B 5B3.
Type of Production and Credits: Th Film-Dir; Th Short-Dir.
Genres: Documentary-Th; Drama-Th; Comedy-Th; Educational-Th.
Biography: Born 1944, England; Canadian citizenship. B.A., History and English, University of British Columbia; P.B. Teaching Certificate (secondary school).
Selected Filmography: *The Dig*, ED, 90, CDN, Dir; *Let Me Sing*, Th, 76, CDN, Co Prod/Dir; *Summer Centre*, ED, 72, CDN, Dir/Wr/Ed; *The House That Jack Built*, Th, 71, CDN, Dir/Wr/Ed; *The Kind of September*, Th, 69, CDN, Dir/Wr/Ed.

CURRIE, Anthony
- see SOUND EDITORS

CURTIS, Dan
ACCT. Cygnus Communications, 186 Browning Ave., Toronto, ON M4K 1W5 (416)465-6684.
Type of Production and Credits: TV Film-Prod/Dir/Wr; TV Video-Wr.
Genres: Documentary-TV.
Biography: Born 1944, Vancouver, BC. M.Ed., University of Toronto. Worked at TVOntario as writer and project coordinator. Taught in Ghana, West Africa, with CUSO. Winner, Gold Award, Houston; Best Documentary, Yorkton; Best Documentary, CFTA; and Best Documentary, Atlantic Film Festival for *Alex Colville: The Splendour of Order.*
Selected Filmography: *In Advance of the Landing,* Th/TV, 90, CDN, Prod/Dir; *Words,* ED/TV, 90, CDN, Inter V; "Sketches of Our Town" (5 eps), TV, 87-88, CDN, Wr; *Stanley Knowles: By Word and Deed,* TV, 87, CDN, Prod/Dir/Wr; *Company of Adventurers,* TV, 85, CDN, Prod/Dir/Wr; *Alex Colville: The Splendour of Order,* TV, 85, CDN, Co-Prod; "Personal Spaces" (13 eps), TV, 77, CDN, Consult.

CUTHAND, Doug
- see PRODUCERS

CUTLER, Keith
- see PRODUCERS

CYNAMON, Helena
- see PRODUCERS

D'AIX, Alain
APFTQ. InformAction, 417 rue St-Pierre, bureau 403, Montréal, PQ H2Y 2M4 (514)284-0441. FAX: 845-0631.
Types de production et générique: l métrage-Réal; c métrage-Réal; TV film-Réal.
Types d'oeuvres: Documentaire-C&TV; Affaires publiques-TV.
Curriculum vitae: Né en 1938. Licence ès Lettres, Sorbonne; Maîtrise en Psychologie, Université de Montréal. Correspondant de presse en Afrique (AP), 60-64; enseignement en Communications, Université de Montréal; co-fondateur, Vice-président d'InformAction; réalise depuis 71 films documentaires, séries et reportages, en particulier sur les questions internationales; Président de Vues D'Afrique, organisme qui se consacre à favoriser par l'image les relations interculturelles avec les pays africains et créoles.
Filmographie sélective: *Le marché du couple,* TV, 90, CDN, Co réal/Co aut; "Vues d'Afrique" (9 eps), TV, 90, CDN, Réal; *Goute-sel, Haïti un soir d'hiver,* TV, 89, CDN, Réal; *Les îles ont une ame,* C, 88, CDN, Réal; *Nous près, nous loin,* TV, 86, CDN, Réal; *Zone de turbulence,* TV, 84, CDN, Co réal; *Mercenaires en quête d'auteurs,* TV, 83, CDN, Co réal; *Vivre en créole,* C, 82, CDN, Co réal; *Comme un bateau dans le ciel,* C, 81, CDN, Réal; *Le Dur Désir de dire,* C, 81, CDN, Réal; *Rasanbleman,* C, 79, CDN, Co réal; *La Danse avec l'aveugle,* C, 78, CDN, Co réal; *Contre censure,* C, 76, CDN, Co réal; *Yvongelisation,* C, 73, CDN, Co réal; *Tam-Tams et balafons,* C, 72, CDN, Réal.

DALE, Holly ◊
(416)967-6361.
Type of Production and Credits: Th Film-Dir/Prod/Ed; TV Film-Dir/Prod/Ed.
Genres: Drama-Th; Documentary-Th&TV; Educational-Th&TV.
Biography: Born in Toronto, Ontario. *Hookers on Davie* won the Gold Plaque, Chicago; Red Ribbon, American Film Festival; Genie nomination, 85. *P4W: Prison for Women,* Yorkton awards.
Selected Filmography: *Up on the Roof,* Th, 88, CDN, Dir; *Calling the Shots,* Th, 87, CDN, Co-Dir/Co-Prod/Co-Ed; *The Making of Agnes of God/Quiet on the Set: Filming Agnes of God,* TV, 85, CDN, Co-Dir/Co-Prod/Co-Ed; *Day in the Life of Canada: The Documentary* (Toronto seg), TV, 84, CDN, Dir; *Hookers on Davie,* Th, 83, CDN, Co-Dir/Co-Prod/Co-Ed; *P4W: Prison for Women,* Th, 80, CDN, Co-Dir/Co-Prod/Co-Ed, (GENIE); *Thin Line,* Th, 77, CDN, Co-Dir/Co-Prod/Co-Ed.

DALEN, Zale R.
DGC. Site 1, Comp. 23, R.R. #1, 546 Marine Dr., Gibsons, BC V0N 1V0 (604)886-8029. Natalie Edwards, 11 Dunbar Rd., Toronto, ON M4W 2X5 (416)922-4437.
Type of Production and Credits: Th Film-Wr/Dir/Ed; TV Film-Dir.
Genres: Drama-Th&TV; Comedy-TV; Action-TV; Horror-TV.
Biography: Born 1947, Iloilo, Philippines; Canadian citizenship. B.A., English, Simon Fraser University. Awards include certificates of merit from New York, London, Sydney, Australia, Thesalonica and Moscow film festivals. Nominated for Genie, 80, Best Director, for *The Hounds of Notre Dame.* Golden Plaque, Chicago, for *Phantom of the Auditorium,* an episode of "The Edison Twins." Best documentary award from the Festival of the Northwest. Creative Excellence award, U.S. Industrial Film Festival. Emmy nomination for "Wiseguy."

Selected Filmography: "Friday the 13th: The Series" (1 eps), TV, 88, USA/CDN, Dir; "Alfred Hitchcock Presents" (2 eps), TV, 87-88, CDN/USA, Dir; "J.J. Starbuck" (2 eps), TV, 87-88, USA/CDN, Dir; "The Beachcombers" (1 eps), TV, 87, CDN, Dir; "Airwolf" (1 eps), TV, 87, USA, Dir; "Wiseguy" (1 eps), TV, 87, CDN, Dir, (EMMY); "Danger Bay" (3 eps), TV, 85, CDN, Dir; "The Edison Twins" (5 eps), TV, 85, CDN, Dir; *Memories*, In, 84-85, CDN, Dir; "For the Record" (1 eps), TV, 82, CDN, Dir; "The Winners" (1 eps), TV, 81, CDN, Dir; *The Hounds of Notre Dame*, Th, 80, CDN, Dir; *Decision*, ED, 78, CDN, Wr/Dir/Ed; *Skip Tracer*, Th, 76, CDN, Wr/Dir/Ed, (CFA); *Granny's Quilts*, ED, 74, CDN, Wr/Dir/Ed.

DAMBERGER, Francis
- see WRITERS

DAMUDE, D. Brian
- see WRITERS

DANE, Lawrence
- see PRODUCERS

DANIS, Aimée
- voir PRODUCTEURS

DANSEREAU, Fernand
ARRFQ, ACCT. 5781 Deom, Montréal, PQ H3S 2M5 (514)524-7879.
Types de production et générique: l métrage-Réal; c métrage-Réal; TV film-Réal/Sc; TV vidéo-Réal/Sc.
Types d'oeuvres: Drame-C&TV; Documentaire-C&TV.
Curriculum vitae: Né en 1928. Nombreux prix dont le Prix Grierson, 77.
Filmographie sélective: "Les Filles de Caleb", TV, 89-90, CDN, Sc; "Le Parc des braves" (pl eps), TV, 84-86, CDN, Sc, (GEMEAUX 86); *Les Doux Aveux*, C, 82, CDN, Réal; *Thetford au milieu de notre vie*, C, 79, CDN, Réal; "L'Amour quotidien" (pl eps), TV, 76-77, CDN, Réal, (ANIK); *Simple Histoire d'amour*, TV, 74, CDN, Réal; *St-Jérôme*, C, 66, CDN, Réal; *Ça n'est pas le temps des romans*, TV, 66, CDN, Réal; *Astataïon/Le Festin des morts*, C, 64, CDN, Réal; "Temps présent" (pl eps), TV, 60-62, CDN, Prod; *Pour la suite du monde*, TV, 62, CDN, Prod, (CFA); *Les Mains nettes*, TV, 58, CDN, Sc; *Alfred J.*, TV, 56, CDN, Sc.

DANSEREAU, Jean
- voir PRODUCTEURS

DANSEREAU, Mireille ✧
(514)279-9114.
Types de production et générique: l métrage-Réal/Sc; TV film-Réal/Sc.
Types d'oeuvres: Drame-C&TV; Documentaire-TV.
Curriculum vitae: Née en 1943, Montréal, Québec. Langues: français, anglais, espagnol. Maîtrise, Royal College of Art, Londres; 18 ans de danse classique et jazz. A travaillé à l'ONF, Radio-Canada, Radio-Québec. "La Vie rêvée" a remporté le Prix du Meilleur Film, San Francisco; elle a remporté le Prix Wendy Michener, 72.
Filmographie sélective: *Le Sourd dans la ville*, C, 86, CDN, Réal; *Le Frère André*, TV, 82, CDN, Réal/Sc; *Un pays à comprendre*, TV, 81, CDN, Réal/Sc; *Germaine Guevremont*, "Visage", TV, 80, CDN, Réal/Sc; *L'Arrache-coeur*, C, 79, CDN, Réal/Sc; *Famille et variations*, TV, 77, CDN, Réal/Sc; *Rappelle-toi*, TV, 76, CDN, Co réal; *The Basement*, C, 74, CDN, Co prod; *Le Père idéal*, TV, 74, CDN, Réal; *J'me marie, j'me marie pas*, "En tant que femmes", TV, 73, CDN, Réal/Sc; *La Vie rêvée*, C, 71, CDN, Réal/Sc; *Forum*, C, 69, GB, Réal/Sc; *Moi, un jour*, C, 67, CDN, Réal/Sc.

DARCUS, Jack
ACTRA, ACCT. 8679 Cartier St., Vancouver, BC V6P 4T9 (604)266-3634. Exile Productions Ltd., 1219 Richards St., Vancouver, BC V6B 3G3 (604)669-9060. FAX: 669-9060.
Type of Production and Credits: Th Film-Dir/Prod/Wr; TV Film-Dir; TV Video-Dir.
Genres: Drama-Th&TV; Comedy-Th&TV.
Biography: Born 1941, Vancouver, BC. Languages: English, some French and German. B.A., Art History and Philosophy, University of British Columbia. Extensive work with animals and birds of prey. Many shows of paintings and many years of teaching painting and film.
Selected Filmography: *Kingsgate*, Th, 89, CDN, Dir/Wr/Prod; *Lunch Date*, "Lies from Lotusland" (1 eps), TV, 88, CDN, Dir; "Airwaves" (3 eps), TV, 87-88, CDN, Dir; *Overnight*, Th, 85, CDN, Dir/Wr/Prod; *Deserters*, Th, 82, CDN, Dir/Wr/Prod; *Wolfpen Principle*, Th, 73, CDN, Dir/Wr; *Great Coups of History*, Th, 70, CDN, Dir/Wr/Prod; *Proxyhawks*, Th, 70, CDN, Dir/Prod/Wr.

DARK, Randall Paris
- see PRODUCERS

DARLING, Gillian
- see PRODUCERS

DAVIDSON, Tom
3002-14 Ave., Regina, SK S4T 1R7 (306)525-3598. Film Crew Productions, 2345 Smith St., Regina, SK S4P 2P7 (306)777-0160. I.T.V. Prod., (403)436-1250.

Type of Production and Credits: TV Film-Dir; TV Video-Dir.
Genres: Comedy-TV; Documentary-TV; Commercials-TV.
Biography: Born in 1952 in Brandon, Manitoba. Educated at the University of Brandon, University of Winnipeg and M.I.T. (Degree in Photographic Technology). Won many T.V.B.s, Can-Pros and a 1989 'SAM' award for Best Overall Commercial.
Selected Filmography: "Tracks of Initiative" (3 eps), TV, 91, CDN, Dir; *Made in Saskatchewan*, TV, 91, CDN, Dir; *Dreams in the Dust*, TV, 91, CDN, Dir.

DAVIS, Bill
DGA, PGA. 854 - 5th St., Suite A, Santa Monica, CA 90212 (213)394-0063. C.A.A., 9830 Wilshire Blvd., Beverly Hills, CA 90212 USA.
Type of Production and Credits: TV Film-Dir; TV Video-Dir/Prod.
Genres: Comedy-TV; Variety-TV; Musical-TV.
Biography: Born 1931, Belleville, Ontario; US resident. B.A.A., Ryerson Polytechnical Institute. Began career CBC Toronto prior to broadcast in 52; moved to New York, 65, then Los Angeles, 67. Awards for TV shows include 2 Silver Rose at Montreux, Christopher Award.
Selected Filmography: *Anne Murray in Disneyworld*, TV, 91, CDN, Dir; "TV Bloopers & Practical Jokes" (62 eps), TV, 84-86, USA, Dir; *Glen Campbell's 25th Anniversary*, TV, 84, USA, Dir; *Paul Anka*, TV, 84, CDN, Dir; *Democratic National Telethon*, TV, 83, USA, Dir; "National Snoop" (pilot), TV, 83, USA, Dir; *Johnny Cash Special*, TV, 83, USA, Dir; *Joel Grey Live*, TV, 83, USA, Dir; *Sold Out* (Lily Tomlin in Vegas), TV, 83, USA, Dir, (EMMY); *The Carpenters' Special*, TV, 82, USA, Dir; *Cher*, TV, 81-82, USA, Dir; *John Denver Special* (7 shows), TV, 76-81, USA, Dir, (EMMY); *The Jacksons*, TV, 79, USA, Prod/Dir; *Superstunt* (3 shows), TV, 76-78, USA, Prod/Dir; *Julie Andrews*, TV, 72-73, USA, Dir, (EMMY).

DAVIS, Richard
- see PRODUCERS

DE CARUFEL, René
- voir DIRECTEURS-PHOTO

DE SILVA, Paul
- see PRODUCERS

DEFELICE, James
- see WRITERS

DELOREY, Walter J.
- see PRODUCERS

DEMEULE, Nadine
1670 boul. Rome, Brossard, PQ J4W 3A1 (514)672-7227.
Types de production et générique: c métrage-Réal/Prod/Mont/Sc.
Types d'oeuvres: Comédie-C&TV; Documentaire-C; Experimental-C; Enfants-C.
Curriculum vitae: Née à Montréal en 1968. Langues: français et anglais. Etudes collégiales et universitaires en communication (Brébeuf et Concordia). Travaille avec 16mm particulièrement et Hi-8. Film sur le point d'être distribué en France et en attente de sélection dans plusieurs festivals. Expérience majoritaire en conception d'éclairage et réalisation.
Filmographie sélective: *Elle*, C, 91, CDN, Prod/Réal/Mont/Sc; *Zucco*, C, 91, CDN, éclairage; *Jeux de Dames*, C, 91, CDN, éclairage; *Sergio et Margot*, C, 91, CDN, éclairage; *Julie et les jouets*, MV, 91, CDN, Réal/Prod/Mont/Sc; *Faites l'amour à la camera*, MV, 91, CDN, Réal/Prod/Mont/Sc; *Chambre à Souvenirs*, C, 90, CDN, Réal/Prod/Mont/Sc; *Piscis Delirium*, C, 90, CDN, éclairage; *About Annie*, C, 90, CDN, éclairage.

DENIKE, Brian
- see PRODUCERS

DENSHAM, Pen
- see PRODUCERS

DEROME, Gilles ✧
(514)667-0014.
Types de production et générique: c métrage-Réal; TV film-Réal; TV vidéo-Réal.
Types d'oeuvres: Documentaire-TV; Enfants-TV; Affaires publiques-TV.
Curriculum vitae: Né en 1928, Ste-Agathe-des-Monts, Québec. Langues: français et anglais. Cours classique; 3 ans d'études en céramique. A eu des expositions de céramique, de dessin, de peinture; a écrit 2 pièces de théâtre et 2 recueils de poèmes; a dirigé un ciné-club à Notre-Dame-de-Grâce.
Filmographie sélective: "Le Temps de vivre", TV, 75-82, CDN, Réal; "Femmes d'aujourd'hui", TV, 66-70, CDN, Réal; "Arts et lettre" (4 eps), TV, 64-66, CDN, Réal; *Champs libres*, "Faire la Terre", TV, 64, CDN, Réal; *Thetford Mines*, TV, 63, CDN, Prod.

DESBIENS, Francine
SGCT. 5095 ave. des Melèzes, Montréal, PQ H1T 2H8 (514)257-9546. ONF, 3155 Côte de Liesse, Montréal, PQ H4N 2N4 (514)283-9000.
Types de production et générique: c métrage-Réal/Prod.
Types d'oeuvres: Education-C; Enfants-C; Animation-C; Expérimental-C.

Curriculum vitae: Née en 1938, Montréal, Québec. Diplômée de l'Institut des Arts Appliqués. Prix à Téhéran et Bilbao, *Les Bibites de Chromagnon.*
Filmographie sélective: *Convention des Droits de l'Enfance-Voir le Monde,* C, 91, CDN, Réal/Conc vis/An/Phot; *Bande Annonce Ottawa 90* (vidéo-clips), C, 90, CDN, Réal/ Conc vis/An/Phot; *Dessine-moi une Chanson/Draw Me a Song,* C, 90, CDN, Réal/Conc vis/An/Phot; *Dessine-moi un mouton,* C, 88, CDN, Réal; *L'Homme de papier,* C, 87, CDN, An; *Ah! vous dirais-je, Maman,* C, 85, CDN, Réal; *L'Art du cinéma d'animation,* TV, 82, CDN, Réal; *Vivre en couleurs,* C, 81, CDN, Prod; *Luna Luna Luna,* C, 81, CDN, Prod; *Cogne-Dur,* C, 79, CDN, Prod; *Moi, je pense/This Is Me,* C, 79, CDN, Prod; *La Plage,* C, 78, CDN, Prod; *Dernier Envol,* C, 77, CDN, Réal; *Chérie ôte tes raquettes,* C, 75, CDN, Prod; *Du coq à l'âne,* C, 73, CDN, Réal.

DESCHENES, Clément
- voir SCENARISTES
DESJARDINS, Claude
- voir PRODUCTEURS
DESJARDINS, Jacques
- voir SCENARISTES
DEVINE, David
- see PRODUCERS
DEW, Simon Christopher
- see PRODUCERS
DEWALT, Kevin
- see PRODUCERS
DEWAR, David
- see PRODUCERS
DIMARCO, Steve
DGC, ACTRA. 7 Park Vista Dr., #412, Toronto, ON M4B 1A4 (416)285-9244. Great North Artists, 350 Dupont St., Toronto, ON (416)925-2051.
Type of Production and Credits: Th Film-Dir/Wr/Prod; TV Film-Dir/Wr/Prod.
Genres: Drama-TV; Comedy-Th; Action-TV; Children's-TV.
Biography: Born in 1958 in Toronto, Ontario. Has made Super 8 films; worked writing and directing for television. Has written, produced and directed 3 half-hour dramas and one feature, *Thick As Thieves.*
Selected Filmography: "Mom P.I." (4 eps), TV, 91, CDN, Dir; *Thick As Thieves,* Th, 90, CDN, Wr/Prod/Dir; "E.N.G." (3 eps), TV, 90, CDN, Dir; "My Secret Identity" (1 eps), TV, 90, CDN/USA, Dir; "Street Legal" (1 eps), TV, 89, CDN, Dir; "E.N.G." (3 eps), TV, 89, CDN, Dir.

DINEL, Pierre
- voir SCENARISTES
DION, Jean-Yves
- voir DIRECTEURS-PHOTO
DION, Yves
SGCT, (ONF). 6319- 3ème Avenue, Montréal, PQ H1Y 2X6 (514)721-0393. Office National du Film, C.P. 6100, Succursale A., Montréal, PQ H3C 3H5 (514)283-9345.
Types de production et générique: l métrage-Réal/Mont/Sc; c métrage-Réal/Mont/Sc.
Types d'oeuvres: Drame-C; Comédie-C; Documentaire-C; Enfants-C.
Curriculum vitae: Né à Montréal en 1947. Langues: français et anglais. Fait ses études à Montréal, Collège Ste-Croix. Com-mence à travailler dans le cinéma à L'O.N.F. en 1965. Sesterce D'Or du Festival de Nyon (Suisse), Sesterce d'Argent Festival de Nyon, Grand Prix Documentaire Festival de Lille (France).
Filmographie sélective: *20 Décembre,* C, 90, CDN, Mont; *Le Vendredi de Jeanne Robinson,* C, 90, CDN, Réal; "Pour Tout Dire Junior" (6 eps), ED, 90, CDN, Réal; *Perversion,* C, 89, CDN, Mont/Sc; *Sonia,* C, 88, CDN, Mont; *Danny,* C, 88, CDN, Mont/Réal; *L'Homme Renversé,* C, 87, CDN, Mont/Réal/Sc; *La Surditude,* C, 81, CDN, Mont/Réal; *Les Accidents,* C, 78, CDN, Mont/Réal; *Raison d'Etre,* C, 76, CDN, Mont/Réal; *Les Ordres,* C, 73, CDN, Mont; *Sur Vivre,* C, 72, CDN, Mont/Réal; *Wow,* C, 69, CDN, Mont.

DIXON, Will
ACCT, SMPIA, ACTRA. 2041 Rae St., Regina, SK S4T 2E6 (306)347-9988. Heartland Motion Pictures Inc., 2352 Smith St., Regina, SK S4P 2P6 (306)777-0888.
Type of Production and Credits: Th Short-Wr/Dir; TV Film-Wr/Dir; TV Video-Wr/Dir.
Genres: Drama-Th&TV; Comedy-Th&TV; Documentary-TV; Children's-TV.
Biography: Born in 1962 in St. Paul, Minnesota. Canadian citizen since 1975. B.F.A. in Film & Video from University of Regina, 1982-87. Graduating short drama, *Heartline,* earned an Honourable Mention at the 1987 Canadian Student Film Festival in Montreal. *Heartline* also won four awards at the 1987 Saskatchewan Showcase Awards including the Superchannel Best Script Award. More recently, directed *Home on the Range* for CBC series "Inside Stories", which won Gold Prize in Television Pilot category at the 1991 Houston International Film Festival, and *The Garden,* which was

awarded a Certificate of Merit at the 1991 Yorkton Short Film & Video Festival.
Selected Filmography: *The Garden*, TV, 90, CDN, Dir/Co Wr; *Home on the Range*, "Inside Stories", TV, 90, CDN, Dir; *Heart of Christmas*, TV, 90, CDN, Dir; *Roots and Wings*, TV, 90, CDN, Dir/Wr; *Zipper Club*, ED, 90, CDN, Dir/Wr; *For Whom The Bell Rings*, Th, 89, CDN, Dir/Wr; *Heartline*, Th, 87, CDN, Dir/Wr.

DODD, Marian
- see PRODUCERS

DONLON, Denise
- see PRODUCERS

DONOVAN, Paul
P.O. Box 2261, Stn. M, Halifax, NS B3J 3L8 (902)420-1577.
Type of Production and Credits: Th Film-Dir/Wr.
Genres: Drama-Th; Comedy-Th; Action-Th; Science Fiction-Th.
Biography: Born 1954, Canada. B.Sc., Physics; graduate of London Film School.
Selected Filmography: *George's Island*, Th, 89, CDN, Dir/Wr; *Squamish Five*, Th, 87, CDN, Dir; *Defcon-4*, Th, 84, CDN, Dir/Wr; *Siege*, Th, 81, CDN, Co-Dir/Wr; *South Pacific 1942*, Th, 79, CDN, Dir/Wr.

DORN, Rudi
- see ART DIRECTORS

DORRIS, Jocelyne
ACCT. 1812, boul. Pie IX, Montréal, PQ H1V 2C6 (514)521-1339. Les Productions La Fête, 225, rue Roy est, Suite 203, Montréal, PQ (514)848-0417.
Types de production et générique: l métrage-Réal; c métrage-Réal; TV film-Réal; TV vidéo-Réal.
Types d'oeuvres: Drame-C&TV.
Curriculum vitae: Née à Montréal en 1954. Langues: français et anglais. Diplômée en études Littéraires, UQAM. Expérience: animatrice et recherchiste T.V.
Filmographie sélective: *La Championne/Reach For The Sky*, C, 90, CDN/R, Réal; "Misère des Riches" (8 eps), TV, 89, CDN, Dir; *Vincent et Moi*, C, 89, CDN/F, Dir; *Pas de Répit pour Mélanie*, C, 89, CDN, Dir; *A Corps Perdu*, C, 89, CDN, Dir; "Lance et Compte" (13 eps), TV, 88, CDN, Réal; *La Grenouille et la Baleine*, C, 87, CDN, Dir; *Gaspard et Fils*, C, 87, CDN, Dir.

DOUGLAS, Michael
DGC, ACTRA. 32 Berryman St., Toronto, ON M5R 1M6 (416)972-6168.
Type of Production and Credits: TV Film-Wr/Dir; TV Video-Wr/Dr.
Genres: Drama-TV; Educational-TV; Industrial-TV.
Biography: Canadian citizen. Graduated from Ryerson and entered the film business through the assistant director ladder. Has worked as a director, writer or producer on over one hundred films and videos, primarily dramas. Considers directing drama to be an enjoyable privilege. Experienced in directing in French and has worked extensively in Alberta and Ontario. Was awarded the Red Ribbon for *Managing Performance Problems* at the 1988 American Film Festival.
Selected Filmography: "Top Cops", TV, 90, USA/CDN, Dir; *The Canadian Rangers*, ED, 90, CDN, Wr; *Mission Supremacy*, In, 90, CDN, Dir/Prod; *Commitment to Life*, TV, 89, CDN, Wr/Dir; "Degrassi Junior High", TV, 89, CDN/USA, Dir; *Managing Performance Problems*, In, 88, CDN/USA, Dir; *Airborne Saturday Night*, TV, 88, CDN, Wr.

DRAKE, Tom
- see WRITERS

DUBHE, Thérèse
AR. 6754, Drolet, Montréal, PQ H2S 2T2 (514)273-0791. Radio-Canada, 1400 est, boul. René-Lévesque, Montréal, PQ H2L 2M2 (514)597-4724.
Types de production et générique: TV vidéo-Réal.
Types d'oeuvres: Drame-TV; Education-TV; Enfants-TV.
Filmographie sélective: *Grande Visite*, MV, 88-89, CDN, Réal; "Au jour le jour", TV, 87-89, CDN, Réal; "Bobino" (quot.), TV, 75-85, CDN, Réal; "Cette nuit-là" (10 eps), TV, 80, CDN, Réal; "Donald Lautrec Show" (1 eps), TV, 70, CDN, Réal.

DUBRO, James R.
- see WRITERS

DUCKWORTH, Martin
CIFC, AQRRCT. 4618 rue Jeanne Mance, Montreal, PQ H2V 4J4 (514)849-4060.
Type of Production and Credits: Th Short-Dir/Cam; TV Film-Dir/Cam.
Genres: Drama-Th&TV; Documentary-Th&TV; Educational-TV; Experimental-Th&TV.
Biography: Born 1933, Montreal, Quebec; raised in Halifax. Languages: English and French. B.A., Yale University; M.A., University of Toronto. Director of Extension at Mount Allison University, New Brunswick, 58-63; staff cameraman, NFB, 63-70; now freelance cameraman, director. *No More Hiroshima* won a Genie,

86 and Peace Prize, Krakow; *Oliver Jones in Africa* won Mannheim Ducat; other awards at Festival of Films (Montreal), Yorkton, Troia, Leipzig, Tokyo, Chicago, and American Film Festival.
Selected Filmography: *Oliver Jones in Africa*, TV, 90, CDN, Dir; *Shared Rhythm/Rhythme du Monde*, TV, 90, CDN, Dir/Cam; *Crossroads: Three Jazz Pianists/le Jazz: Un Vaste Complot*, TV, 88, CDN, Dir/Ed; *Our Last Days in Moscow/Nos derniers jours à Moscou*, ED, 87, CDN, Dir/Ed; *Return to Dresden/Retour à Dresde*, TV, 86, CDN, Dir/Ed; *No More Hiroshima/Plus jamais d'Hiroshima*, TV, 85, CDN, Dir/Cam; *No More Hibakusha/Plus jamais d'Hibakusha*, TV, 84, CDN, Dir/Cam; *Back to Kampuchea/On l'appelait Cambadge*, TV, 82, CDN, Dir/Cam; *Wives' Tale/Une histoire de femmes*, TV, 80, CDN, Co-Dir/Cam; *12,000 Men*, ED, 78, CDN, Dir/Cam; *Temiscaming, Quebec/Temiscamingue, Québec*, TV, 76, CDN, Dir/Cam; *Cell 16*, TV, 72, Dir/Cam/Ed; *Accident*, Th, 72, CDN, Dir/Cam/Ed; *The Wish*, ED, 71, CDN, Dir/Cam; *Untouched & Pure*, TV, 70, CDN, Co-Dir/Cam.

DUFFELL, Greg ◆
(416)755-1741.
Type of Production and Credits: Th Film-Dir/An/Wr; TV Film-Dir/An/Wr.
Genres: Animation-Th&TV.
Biography: Born 1955, Toronto, Ontario. Trained at Richard Williams Animation, London, England, as apprentice in classical character animation. In 73, returned to Canada, worked on TV commercials; corporate films, USA, 76-77; writer, animator, director, Nelvana, Toronto, 77-82. Opened Lightbox Studios, 83.
Selected Filmography: Dare Cookies and Crackers/Crest/Magic Glass II, Cm, 84-85, CDN, An/An Dir; *Strange Animal*, MV, 85, CDN, An/An Dir; *A Criminal Mind*, MV, 84-85, CDN, An Dir/Co-An; "Inspector Gadget" (65 eps) (Wr 4 eps), TV, 83, CDN/USA, Voice; *Strawberry Shortcake: A Housewarming Surprise*, TV, 82, CDN, Co-An; *Rock & Rule/Ring of Power*, Th, 82, CDN, Contr Wr/Voice/Seg An Dir; *Easter Fever*, TV, 79-80, CDN, Co-An/Seg An Dir/Co-Wr; *Intergalactic Thanksgiving/Please Don't Eat the Planet*, TV, 79, CDN, Co-An/Co-Wr; *Romie-0 & Juliet-8*, TV, 78, CDN, Co-An/Voice; *The Devil and Daniel Mouse*, TV, 78, CDN, Co-An; *Magic of Cycloa*, In, 76-77, USA, Co-An; *Cougar Shoes*, Cm, 76, CDN, An/Dir; "Undresea World of Captain Nemo" (5 eps), TV, 75-76, CDN, Co-An; *12 Tasks of Asterix*, Th, 75, F, Co-An.

DUKE, Daryl
DGA, DGC. Jack Gilardi, International Creative Management, 8899 Beverly Blvd., Los Angeles, CA 90048 (213)550-4000.
Type of Production and Credits: Th Film-Dir/Prod; TV Film-Dir/Prod.
Genres: Drama-Th&TV.
Biography: B.A., English and Philosophy, University of British Columbia. Began career at NFB, then CBC; directed many feature films; launched the broadcast operations of CKVU-TV, Vancouver, 76, and was Chairman of the Board and Chief Executive Officer until 88. *Payday* won the National Society of Film Critics Award; *The Day the Lion Died*, Emmy; *The Thornbirds*, Emmy nomination; *I Heard the Owl Call My Name*, Christopher Award; *The Silent Partner*, CFA, 78.
Selected Filmography: *Columbo*, TV, 90-91, USA, Dir; *Tai-Pan*, Th, 86, USA, Dir; *The Thorn Birds* (mini-series), TV, 82-83, USA, Dir; *Hard Feelings*, Th, 80, CDN, Dir; *The Silent Partner*, Th, 77, CDN, Dir, (CFA); *Griffin Loves Phoenix*, TV, 75, USA, Dir; *A Cry for Help*, TV, 74, USA, Dir; *Forty Reasons to Kill*, "Harry O", TV, 74, USA, Dir; *I Heard the Owl Call My Name*, TV, 73, USA, Dir/Prod; *No Sign of the Cross*, "Banacek", TV, 72, USA, Dir; *Doorway to Death*, "Circle of Fear", TV, 72, USA, Dir; "The Bold Ones" (5 eps), TV, 69-72, USA, Dir; *Payday*, Th, 71, USA, Dir; *The Day the Lion Died*, "Senator", TV, 70, USA, Dir, (EMMY).

DUNCAN, Bob
- see WRITERS

EASTMAN, Allan
DGC. Labyrinth Film & Videoworks, 159 Westminster Ave., Toronto, ON M6R 1N8 (416)537-7455.
Type of Production and Credits: Th Film-Dir/Wr; TV Film-Dir/Wr.
Genres: Drama-Th&TV; Comedy-Th&TV; Musical-Th&TV; Action-Th&TV; Science Fiction-Th&TV; Horror-Th&TV.
Biography: Born 1950, Manitoba. 3 Camera VTR; Radio, Theatre, Music, Journalism; Graduate, University of Bristol Film School, B.A. Several original screenplays & rewrites including *Champagne Charlie*, "Danger Bay," *Teenage Vampire*, *Walesa Tape*, *Tradewinds East*, etc. Many story edits and rewrites on director assignments.
Selected Filmography: "Top Cops" (9 eps), TV, 90-91, CDN/USA, Dir; "Counterstrike" (pilot & 5 eps), TV, 90-

91, CDN/USA, Dir; "Dracula - The Series" (pilot & 5 eps), TV, 90, USA/CDN/L, Dir; "Friday the 13th - The Series" (2 eps), TV, 89, CDN/USA, Dir; "War of the Worlds" (2 eps), TV, 89, CDN/USA, Dir; *Champagne Charlie* (mini-series), TV, 88-89, CDN/F, Dir; *Ford: The Man & the Machine* (mini-series), TV, 86-87, USA, Dir; *Race for the Bomb* (mini-series), TV, 85-86, CDN/F, Dir; *Crazy Moon*, Th, 85, CDN, Dir; *The War Boy*, TV, 84-85, CDN/USA, Dir; "Night Heat" (6 eps), TV, 85-86, CDN/USA, Dir; "Hot Shots" (1 eps), TV, 85, CDN/USA, Dir; "Danger Bay" (10 eps), TV, 84-85, CDN/USA, Dir; "Edison Twins" (2 eps), TV, 84, CDN/USA, Dir; "Littlest Hobo" (44 eps), TV, 79-84, CDN, Dir.

ECKERT, John M.
- see PRODUCERS

EDWARDS, Cash
- see WRITERS

EGARHOS, Spyro
#7 - 6585 Rochdale Blvd., Regina, SK S4X 2Z1 (306)949-9741.
Type of Production and Credits: Th Film-Dir.
Genres: Drama-Th.
Biography: Born 1964, Regina, Saskatchewan.
Selected Filmography: *Bed and Breakfast*, Th, 91, CDN, Dir; *Her Boyfriend*, Th, 89, CDN, Dir; *4 Shots*, Th, 88, CDN, Dir; *1980 Volare*, Th, 87, CDN, Dir.

EGOYAN, Atom
490 Adelaide St. W., Suite 102, Toronto, ON M5V 1T3 (416)365-2137.
Type of Production and Credits: Th Film-Dir/Prod/Wr/Ed; Th Short-Dir/Prod/Wr/Ed; TV Film-Dir.
Genres: Drama-Th&TV.
Biography: Born 1960, Cairo, Egypt; Canadian citizenship. B.A., International Relations, University of Toronto, 82. Golden Ducat Award for *Next of Kin*. *Family Viewing* won Excellence in Canadian Production, Festival of Festivals, 87, as well as awards at Berlin Film Festival and Montreal Festival du Nouveau Cinéma. Both *The Adjuster* and *Speaking Parts* were selected for the Cannes Film Festival Directors' Fortnight, as well as other festivals internationally.
Selected Filmography: *The Adjuster*, Th, 91, CDN, Wr/Dir/Prod; *Speaking Parts*, Th, 89, CDN, Wr/Dir/Prod; *Temptation*, "Alfred Hitchcock Presents", TV, 88, CDN/USA, Dir; *Looking for Nothing*, "Inside Stories", TV, 88, CDN, Dir/Wr; *The Final Twist*, "Alfred Hitchcock Presents", TV, 87, CDN/USA, Dir; *Family Viewing*, Th, 86, CDN, Dir/Wr/Prod; *In This Corner*, TV, 85, CDN, Dir; *Men: A Passion Play Ground*, Th, 85, CDN, Dir/Cam/Ed; *Next of Kin*, Th, 84, CDN, Dir/Prod/Ed/Wr; *Open House*, "Canadian Reflections", TV, 82, CDN, Dir; *Peep Show*, Th, 81, CDN, Dir/Wr/Prod/Ed; *After Grad with Dad*, Th, 80, CDN, Dir/Wr/Prod; *Howard in Particular*, Th, 79, CDN, Dir/Prod/Wr/Ed.

EL-SISSI, Azza
- see PRODUCERS

ELDER, Bruce
Lightworks, 692 St. Clarens Ave., Unit 5, Toronto, ON M6H 3X1 (416)539-8612.
Type of Production and Credits: Th Film-Dir/Ed/Wr/DOP; Th Short-Dir/Wr/Ed/DOP.
Genres: Experimental-Th.
Biography: Born 1947, Hawkesbury, Ontario. Studied Philosophy, McMaster University, University of Toronto; Media, Ryerson Polytechnical Institute. Solo exhibitions at the Millennium, Museum of Modern Art, NY, Los Angeles, London and Berlin. Retrospectives of his film work have been mounted by the Art Gallery of Ontario, Innis College, Cinémathèque Québécoise and recently, by the NY Anthology Film Archives (88). Has written extensively on Canadian film, including a book *Image and Identity: Reflections on Canadian Film and Culture*. Has programmed Canadian films for the OKanada exhibition, Berlin, Art Gallery of Ontario and the Festival of Festivals. *The Art of Worldly Wisdom* won the L.A. Film Critics' Award as Best Independent/Experimental Film. *Flesh Angels* was selected for screening to mark the opening of the Museum of Contemporary Art (Bienal de la Imagen on Moviemiento), Spain, 90.
Selected Filmography: *Newton & Me*, Th, 91, CDN, Dir/DOP/Wr/Ed/Prod; *Flesh Angels*, Th, 90, CDN, Dir/DOP/Wr/Ed/Prod; *Consolations (Love Is an Art of Time)*(3 parts), Th, 88, CDN, Dir/Cin/Ed; *Lamentations: A Monument for the Dead World* (2 parts), Th, 84, CDN, Dir/Cin/Ed; *Illuminated Texts*, Th, 82, CDN, Dir/Cin/Ed; *1857 (Fool's Gold)*, Th, 81, CDN, Dir/Cin/Ed; *Trace*, Th, 80, CDN, Dir/Cin/Ed; *Sweet Love Remembered*, Th, 80, CDN, Dir/Cin/Ed; *The Art of Worldly Wisdom*, Th, 79, CDN, Dir/Cin/Ed; *Look! We Have Come Through*, Th, 78, CDN, Dir/Cin/Ed; *Unremitting Tenderness*, Th, 77, CDN, Dir/Cin/Ed;

Permutations and Combinations, Th, 76, CDN, Dir/Cin/Ed; *Barbara Is a Vision of Loveliness*, Th, 76, CDN, Dir/Cin/Ed, (CFA); *Breath/Light/Birth*, Th, 75, CDN, Dir/Cin/Ed; *She Is Away*, Th, 75, CDN, Dir/Cin/Ed.

ELDRIDGE, Scott
DGC. 12 Lynwood Ave., Toronto, ON M4V 1K2 (416)960-1258.
Type of Production and Credits: TV Film-Dir/Ed.
Genres: Documentary-TV; Music Video-TV.
Biography: Born 1956. B.A., University of Windsor, 78. *Lost Somewhere Inside Your Love* nominated for Gemini for Best Music Video, 86; *Crazy* won Canadian Reggae Music Association award for Best Music Video, 87.
Selected Filmography: *Old Bridges, New Friends*, Th, 91, CDN, Co-Dir; *Nothing in the World*, Jack de Keyzer, MV, 91, CDN, Dir; *That's The Way*, Jack de Keyzer, MV, 91, CDN, Dir; *Blue Train*, Jack de Keyzer, MV, 89, CDN, Dir; *Smalltown Bringdown*, The Tragically Hip, MV, 88, CDN, Co-Prod/Dir; *Deceiver*, China Blue, MV, 87, CDN, Co-Prod/Dir; *It's Been So Long*, Downchild, MV, 87, CDN, Co-Prod/Dir; *Crazy*, Messenjah, MV, 87, CDN, Co-Prod/Dir; *Diamonds and Pearls*, Sherry Kean, MV, 87, CDN, Co-Prod/Dir; *Everything Begins and Ends with You*, Sam Durrence, MV, 87, CDN, Co-Prod/Dir; *Good Old Rock and Roll*, MV, 85-86, CDN, Ed/Dir; *Lost Somewhere Inside Your Love*, Liberty Silver, MV, 86, CDN, Co-Prod/Dir; *Take Me As I Am*, MV, 84, CDN, Ed/Dir; *Introducing Ashley and Kimberly*, TV, 83, CDN, Ed.

ELLIOTT, William G.
ACCT. 350 Dennie Ave., Newmarket, ON L3Y 4M7 (416)895-1489. Global TV, 81 Barber Greene Rd., Don Mills, ON M3C 2A2.
Type of Production and Credits: TV Film-Dir/Prod; TV Video-Prod/Dir.
Genres: Drama-TV; Documentary-TV; Comedy-TV; Variety-TV.
Biography: Born 1951 in Ontario. Graduate, Broadcasting course, Conestoga College, 73. President, WRAP Television Film Productions Inc. Has directed numerous commercials.
Selected Filmography: "Jumbotron" (SkyDome), Th, 89-91, CDN, Spec Events Dir; "Beyond the Line" (26 eps), TV, 89, CDN, Dir; "Bumper Stumpers" (260 eps), TV, 88-89, CDN/USA, Dir; "Jackpot" (390 eps), TV, 87-89, CDN/USA, Dir; *1988 Olympic Winter Games* (6 domestic venues), TV, 88, CDN, Line Prod; "Citizens' Alert" (13 eps), TV, 82-86, CDN, Prod/Dir; "Terror - Politics of Terrorism" (2 eps), TV, 85, CDN/USA/GB/D/J, Dir; *Golden Age of Canadian Figure Skating*, TV, 84, CDN, Dir; *David Steinberg in Concert*, TV, 84, CDN/USA, Dir; "Frost Over Canada with David Frost" (6 eps), TV, 83, CDN, Dir; *Neil Sedaka in Concert at the Forum*, TV, 83, CDN/USA, Dir; "The Tommy Hunter Show" (6 eps), TV, 80, CDN/USA, Dir; "World Vision Specials", TV, 80, CDN/USA, Dir; "$128,000 Question" (26 eps), TV, 79, CDN/USA, Dir; "Code 10-78" (24 eps), TV, 77-79, CDN, Prod/Dir.

ERICKSON, Jim
16 Heman St., Toronto, ON M8V 1X5 (416)252-1026.
Type of Production and Credits: Th Film-Ed; TV Video-Dir/Prod/Ed.
Genres: Documentary-TV; Educational-TV; Children's-TV.
Biography: Born 1956. Canadian citizenship. Honours B.A., Film. Has received American Film and Video Association and Golden Sheaf nominations for his work.
Selected Filmography: *Kids and World Crisis*, "Positive Parenting", TV, 91, CDN, Field Prod; *Kids' Help Phone Benefit*, TV, 91, CDN, Dir (Vignettes); "Streetnoise" (26 eps), TV, 90, CDN, Dir; *Broken Trust*, ED, 90, CDN, Prod/Dir/Ed; *Human Rights, Human Wrongs*, ED, 89, CDN, Prod/Dir/Ed; *Reason to Live*, ED, 89, CDN, Prod/Dir/Ed; "It's Only Rock 'n' Roll" (13 eps), TV, 89, CDN, Ed; "OWL-TV" (30 eps), TV, 86-88, CDN, Ed; "Vid Kids" (13 eps), TV, 87, CDN, Ed; "Rocket Boy" (5 eps), TV, 86, CDN, Ed; *The Care Bear Movies*, Th, 86, CDN, Ed.

ERLICH, Alan
DGC, ACTT. 122 Garfield Ave., Toronto, ON M4T 1E1 (416)483-6665. Penny Noble, 2411 Yonge St., Toronto, ON M4P 2E7 (416)482-6556. Ron Lief, Contemporary Artists, 132 Lasky Dr., Beverly Hills, CA USA (213)278-8250.
Type of Production and Credits: TV Film-Dir; TV Video-Dir.
Genres: Drama-TV; Comedy-TV; Documentary-TV; Industrial-TV.
Biography: Born 1940, Plymouth, England; in Canada since 66. Co-winner, Michener Award for Journalism; CFTA Award for Best Educational Film. President, DGC, 84, 85 and 88. Film and multi camera.
Selected Filmography: *Mixed Blessings*,

"Stage on Screen", TV, 91, CDN, Dir; *National Environment Test and Telepoll*, TV, 91, CDN, Dir; *Letters from Wingfield Farm*, "Stage on Screen", TV, 91, CDN, Dir; *Local Talent*, "Stage on Screen", TV, 90, CDN, Dir; "Hangin' In" (108 eps), TV, 80-88, CDN, Dir; "Street Legal" (2 eps), TV, 86-88, CDN, Dir; "Check It Out!" (41 eps), TV, 85-88, CDN/USA, Dir; *The Body Test*, TV, 88, CDN, Dir; "Learning the Ropes" (20 eps), TV, 88, CDN, Dir; *Twelfth Night*, TV, 85, CDN, Dir; *One for the Pot*, TV, 85, CDN, Dir; "Littlest Hobo" (1 eps), TV, 84, CDN, Dir; *Tartuffe*, TV, 84, CDN, Dir; *Birds of a Feather*, TV, 84, CDN, Dir; "Birds in Paradise" (4 eps), TV, 83, CDN/USA, Dir.

ERNE, Andreas
- see PRODUCERS

ETHIER, Martial
- voir MONTEURS

FAIRE, Sandra
- see PRODUCERS

FARR, Gordon
- see PRODUCERS

FAUCHER, Jean
AR. Radio-Canada, 1400 est, boul. René-Lévesque, Montréal, PQ H3C 3A8 (514)597-4923.
Types de production et générique: l métrage-Réal; TV film-Réal; TV vidéo-Réal.
Types d'oeuvres: Drame-C&TV; Comédie-C&TV; Action-C&TV; Documentaire-C&TV.
Curriculum vitae: Né en 1924, Vesinet, France. A réalisé près d'une centaine de films. Prix de la Meilleure Réalisation, Gala des Splendeurs, *Les Frères Karamazov*, 60, et *Un mois dans la campagne*, 69.
Filmographie sélective: *Cyrano de Bergerac*, TV, 86, CDN, Réal; *Lorenzaccio*, TV, 85, CDN, Réal; *Les Noces de juin*, TV, 84, CDN, Réal; *Arioso*, TV, 82, CDN, Réal.

FAUCHER, Nicole ◆
(514)286-0231.
Types de production et générique: TV vidéo-Réal.
Types d'oeuvres: Drame-TV; Comédie-TV; Variété-TV.
Curriculum vitae: Née en 1946, Montréal, Québec. Langues: français et anglais. Bacc. en Communications, Université de Québec à Montréal.
Filmographie sélective: "Avec un grand A" (6 eps), TV, 87-88, CDN, Réal; "Pourquoi chanter" (6 eps), TV, 86-87, CDN, Réal; "Station Soleil" (20 eps), TV, 85-86, CDN, Réal.

FAVREAU, Robert
ARRFQ. 4424, rue Fabre, Montréal, PQ H2J 3V3 (514)521-4019. FAX: 521-4019.
Types de production et générique: l métrage-Réal/Sc/Mont; c métrage-Réal/Sc/Mont; TV film-Réal/Sc/Mont.
Types d'oeuvres: Documentaire-C&TV; Education-C&TV.
Curriculum vitae: Né en 1948, Montréal, Québec. Langues: français et anglais. Baccalauréat ès Arts. Expérience, autre que pédagogie. *Portion d'éternité* - Meilleur film canadien et Prix d'interprétation féminine, FFM, 89.
Filmographie sélective: *L'Ange Noir*, C, 91, CDN, Réal; *Portion d'éternité/Longing for Eternity*, C, 89, CDN, Réal/Aut; "Pour tout dire" (7 c métrages), C, 87, CDN, Réal/Aut; *La Ligne brisée*, C, 86, CDN, Sc/Réal; *Le Million tout puissant*, C, 85, CDN, Mont; *Les Coulisses de l'entraide*, C, 84, CDN, Réal/Sc/Mont; *La Vigie/Histoires de banlieue*, "Les Chocs de la vie", TV, 82, CDN, Réal/Sc/Mont; *Corridors*, C, 78, CDN, Réal/Sc/Mont; *La Longue Marche en institution/Une Chance sur mille*, "Les Exclus" TV, 77, CDN, Réal/Sc/Mont; *Le soleil a pas d'chance*, C, 75, CDN, Réal/Sc/Mont; *Vous savez-ça Monsieur le Ministre?*, TV, 73, CDN, Réal/Mont; *La Faim des caves*, C, 73, CDN, Réal/Mont; *Capables d'être un peu fous*, TV, 73, CDN, Réal/Sc; *Y'étand, Gaston*, C, 72, CDN, Réal/Sc.

FEARNLEY, Neill
DGC. Reel Possibilities Inc., 4475 Keith Rd., West Vancouver, BC V7W 2M4 (604)922-9148.
Type of Production and Credits: TV Film-Dir.
Genres: Drama-TV; Action-TV; Science Fiction-TV; Commercials-TV.
Biography: Born 1953, Liverpool, England; Canadian and British citizenship. B.A.A., Radio and Television Arts, Ryerson Polytechnical Institute.
Selected Filmography: *The Girl From Mars*, TV, 90-91, USA, Dir; "Neon Rider" (6 eps), TV, 90-91, CDN, Dir; "Bordertown, TV, 89-90, CDN, Dir; "Northwood" (pilot & eps #2), TV, 90, CDN, Dir; "Adventures of the Black Stallion" (2 eps), TV, 90, CDN/F, Dir; "War of the Worlds" (4 eps), TV, 88, CDN/USA, Dir; "21 Jump Street" (4 eps), TV, 88, CDN, Dir; "J.J. Starbuck" (1 eps), TV, 88, USA, Dir; "Wiseguy" (1 eps), TV, 88, USA, Dir; "The Beachcombers" (15 eps), TV, 84-88, CDN, Dir; "Danger Bay" (1 eps), TV, 87, CDN, Dir; "Hamilton's Quest" (3 eps), TV, 86, CDN, Dir.

FEDORENKO, Eugene
76 Durie St., Toronto, ON M6S 3E8 (416)762-6312.
Type of Production and Credits: Th Short-Dir/An.
Genres: Educational-Th; Animation-Th.
Biography: Born 1951, Vilnus, Lithuania. Languages: English, Polish, Russian. Attended Ontario College of Art. Film education: NFB. Held animated film workshop for children, 74-84; made 6 flip books jointly with David Suzuki; wrote and animated another flip book, *Origins*; now experimenting with stereo animation drawing. *Every Child* has won awards in Varna, Milan, New York, Krakow, Ottawa film festivals.
Selected Filmography: *Skyward* (1 seg), Th, 85, CDN, Dir/An; *This Is an Emergency* (1 seg), ED, 80, CDN, Dir/An; *Masterpiece Mystery Theatre* (opening), TV, 80, USA, An; "Market Place", TV, 80, CDN, Dir/An; *Every Child*, Th, 79, CDN, Dir/An, (GENIE/OSCAR).

FEINGOLD, Stan
- see WRITERS

FERGUSON, Graeme
Imax Corporation, 38 Isabella St., Toronto, ON M4Y 1N1 (416)960-8509. Fax: 960-8596.
Type of Production and Credits: Th Film-Prod/Dir/DOP; TV Film-Prod/Dir/DOP.
Genres: Documentary-Th; Educational-TV.
Biography: Born 1929, Toronto, Ontario. Honours B.A., Political Science and Economics, University of Toronto, 52. Began making films at the U. Of T. Film Society; apprenticed at the NFB and worked with Maya Deren, Swedish director Arne Sucksdorff in India and with documentarian Willard Van Dyke in the US. Co-founder and President of Imax Corporation, 67-90; currently active member of the board of directors. Environmental Achievement Award, for outstanding communications for environmental awareness, Canadian Ministry of the Environment, for *Blue Planet*, 91; *Aviation Week Magazine*, Laurel, for contribution to Awareness of the Space Program, 90; Royal Canadian Academy of the Arts Medal, 90; Special Achievement Award, Academy of Canadian Cienma & Television, 86. *North of Superior* won Special Jury Award, CFA, 71; *The Dream Is Alive* won Grand Prix du Public, La Geode International Film Festival, 87 and Special Jury Award, CFTA, 85.
Selected Filmography: *Blue Planet*, Th, 90, CDN, Prod/Dir; *The Dream is Alive*, Th, 85, CDN/USA, Prod/Dir/Cin, (CFTA); *Hail Columbia!*, Th, 82, CDN/USA, Prod/Dir/Cin; *Ocean*, Th, 77, CDN, Prod/Dir; *Snow Job*, Th, 74, CDN, Prod/Dir; *Man Belongs to the Earth*, Th, 74, CDN/USA, Prod/Dir/Cin; *North of Superior*.

FERNS, W. Paterson
- see PRODUCERS

FERRON, René
- voir PRODUCTEURS

FICHMAN, Niv
- see PRODUCERS

FINE, David
51A Tunley Rd., London SW17 7QH, England (081) 675-7648. Snowden Fine Prods., 105 The Chandlery, 50 Westminster Bridge Rd., London SE1 7QY England (071) 721 7474.
Type of Production and Credits: Th Short-Dir/Wr/An.
Genres: Documentary-Th; Drama-Th; Comedy-Th; Animation-Th.
Biography: Born 1960, Toronto, Ontario. Attended National Film and Television School, London, England. Worked at NFB, Montreal. Oscar nomination, 86, Annecy award for animated film *Second Class Mail*; Oscar nomination, 88, Gold Plaque, Chicago, 88, for *George and Rosemary*. Currently running Snowden Fine Productions in London, England.
Selected Filmography: *In and Out*, Th, 89, CDN, Co-Dir/Co-Wr/Co-Prod; *George and Rosemary*, Th, 87, CDN, Co-Wr/Co-Dir/Co-An/Co Des; *A Test of Time*, ED, 87, CDN, Co-Wr/Co-Dir/Co-Dir; *Second Class Mail*, Th, 84, GB, Co-Wr/Co-An; *The Day after the End of the World*, ED, 84, GB, Dir/Ed/Adapt; *The Man from Aldeberon*, Th, 83, GB, Adapt/Dir/Ed; *Viola*, TV, 80, CDN, Prod/Dir/Ed; *The Only Game in Town*, Th, 79, CDN, Wr/Dir/An; *Fit-Fat*, Cm, CDN, Dir/An.

FIRUS, Karen
4101 Grace Cres., North Vancouver, BC V7R 3Z9 (604)987-1999.
Type of Production and Credits: Th Short-Dir/Wr; Th Film-Wr/Dir; TV Film-Art Dir/Wr.
Genres: Drama-Th&TV; Musical-Th&TV; Commercials-TV; Music Video-TV.
Biography: Born 1959, Vancouver, BC. B.A., Film, University of British Columbia; M.F.A., Fine Arts, Film, U.B.C., 86. Won CBC Prize for playwriting, 83; *Fashion 99* was nominated for a Genie, 88, won numerous awards

including the Norman McLaren Award, 86, several festival awards and received special international screenings. Also an artist, skilled in painting and furniture design, and a non-fiction writer.
Selected Filmography: *Zig Zag*, TV, 88, CDN, Des/Art Dir; *Gnome, Sweet Gnome*, "Lies from Lotusland", TV, 88, CDN, Assist Art Dir; *Something Old, Something New*, "Lies from Lotusland", TV, 88, CDN, Assist Art Dir; *Homemade Vacations* (14 eps)(7 eps Dir), Cm, 87, CDN, Dir/Art Dir; *Fashion 99*, Th, 86, CDN, Dir/Wr/Ed; B.C. Children's Hospital, Cm, 86, CDN, Art Dir; *Canada's Wild Pacific Salmon*, In, 85, CDN, Art Dir; *Open Your Heart - West Coast Musicians Aid for Africa*, MV, 85, CDN, Dir/Ch; *Nuclear Follies*, Th, 85, CDN, Art Dir; *Spectrum Spectrum Spectrum*, Th, 81, CDN, Dir/Ch/Co-Ed; *Audition!*, ED, 80, CDN, Dir/Wr.

FLEMING, Susan K.
127 Langford Ave., Toronto, ON M4J 3E5 (416)461-9225.
Types of Production and Credits: TV-Film-Prod/Dir.
Genres: Drama-TV; Documentary-TV.
Biography: Born in 1962, Canadian citizen. Worked as a production manager on several award-winning dramas and documentaries before turning to producing and directing. Founder of Q Films Inc., 89. Producer and Director of the Gemini-nominated *Welcome Home*, which also won the Nettie Kryski Award at Yorkton, 91.
Selected Filmography: *Le Dortoir*, TV, 91, CDN/NL, Line Prod/PM; *Tectonic Plates*, TV, 91, GB/CDN/NL, Line Prod/PM; *Welcome Home*, TV, 90, CDN, Prod/Dir; *Nights in the Gardens of Spain*, TV, 90, CDN/GB/E, Line Prod/PM; *Master Peter's Puppet Show*, TV, 90, E/GB/CDN, Assoc Dir/Line Prod; *When the Fire Burns*, TV, 90, E/GB/CDN, Line Prod/PM.

FLOQUET, François
- voir PRODUCTEURS

FOLLOWS, E.J.(Ted) ◊
(416)961-7766.
Type of Production and Credits: TV Film-Dir; TV Video-Dir.
Genres: Drama-TV; Comedy-TV.
Biography: Born 1926, Ottawa, Ontario. Honours B.A., Psychology, University of Toronto, 50. Actor for 40 years in Canada, England and US; stage director; directing for TV since 81. "Hooked on Reading" won International Reading Association Broadcast Media Award, San Diego, 87, and was finalist in New York, Yorkton and Birmingham, Alabama, festivals.
Selected Filmography: "Family Matters" (101 eps), TV, 87, CDN, Dir; *To Serve and Protect* (3 parts), TV, 85-86, CDN, Dir; "Hooked on Reading" (6 eps), TV, 86, CDN, Dir; "Judge" (11 eps), TV, 81-84, CDN, Dir; "Backstretch" (2 eps), TV, 84, CDN, Dir; *Joey*, TV, 82, CDN, Dir.

FOREST, José
- see PRODUCERS

FORTIER, Bob
SGCT. 4835 Bessborough Ave., Montreal, PQ H4V 2S2 (514)482-5339. NFB, 3155 Côte de Liesse, Montreal, PQ H4N 2N4 (514)283-9558.
Type of Production and Credits: Th Film-Dir/Prod/Ed; Th Short-Dir/Ed; TV Film-Dir/Prod/Wr/Ed.
Genres: Drama-TV; Documentary-Th&TV; Educational-TV.
Biography: Born 1945, New Glasgow, Nova Scotia. Languages: English and French. Attended Loyola College and Concordia University. *The Last Right* won the Grand Prix de Varna.
Selected Filmography: *The Ticket Back*, TV, 90, CDN, Dir/Co-Prod/Co-Ed; "Battle for the Planet" (1 eps), TV, 87, CDN/GB, Dir; *Out of a Job*, TV, 86, CDN, Dir/Prod/Ed; *One Step Away*, TV, 85, CDN, Dir/Prod; *A Gift for Kate*, TV, 85, CDN, Prod; *Running Scared*, TV, 84, CDN, Dir/Ed/Wr/Prod; *The Last Right*, TV, 83, CDN, Dir/Prod/Wr/Ed; *A Single Regret*, TV, 82, CDN, Dir/Wr/Ed; *The Deadly Game of Nations*, "War", TV, 82, CDN, Ed; *The Devil at Your Heels*, Th, 80, CDN, Ed/Dir/Co-Prod, (GENIE); *Harmonium in California*, TV, 79, CDN, Dir/Ed; *The Mad Canadian*, Th, 76, CDN, Dir/Ed; *Metal Workers - Artisans des métaux*, TV, 76, CDN, Dir/Ed; *Eastern Graphic*, "Atlantic", TV, 75, CDN, Ed; *All the Years of Her Life*, TV, 74, CDN, Dir/Wr/Ed.

FORTIN, Armand
ARRQ. 837, Maisonneuve, St-Hubert, Chambly, PQ J3Y 7T1 (514)656-2655. Radio-Canada, 1400 est, boul. René-Lévesque, Montréal, PQ H3C 3A8 (514)597-5970.
Types de production et générique: TV film-Réal/Mont.
Types d'oeuvres: Documentaire-TV.
Curriculum vitae: Né en 1923 à Québec. Etudes à l'Académie commerciale de Québec et à l'Ecole d'entraînement de l'Armée canadienne, section cinéma. A fait plusieurs reportages tournés à Los Angeles pour "Ciné-Magazine" de cinéastes

américains (George Cukor, Sidney Pollack, Martin Scorcese, etc.).
Filmographie sélective: *A tout bout d'champ*, "Semaine verte", TV, 88, CDN, Réal; "La Semaine verte" (13 eps), TV, 82-88, CDN, Réal; *Biographie de l'Abbé M. Proulx/Le cinéaste d'un Québec*, Beaux Dimanches (2 eps), TV, 79, CDN, Réal; "Ciné-Magazine" (145 eps), TV, 75-76, CDN, Réal; "Cinéma d'ici" (13 eps), TV, 70, CDN, Mont.

FOSTER, John C.
- see PRODUCERS

FOURNIER, Claude
ACTRA, SAF, SARDEC, ACCT. C.P. 40, St-Paul d'Abbotsford, PQ J0E 1A0 (514)379-5304. Rose Films Inc., 86, de Brésoles, Montréal, PQ H2Y 1V5 (514)285-8901. FAX: 285-8936.
Types de production et générique: l métrage-Réal/Mont/Sc/D photo; c métrage-Réal/Mont/Sc/D photo; TV film-Réal/Mont/Sc/D photo; TV vidéo-Réal/Mont/Sc/D photo.
Types d'oeuvres: Drame-C&TV; Comédie-C&TV; Action-C&TV; Documentaire-C&TV.
Curriculum vitae: Né en 1931 à Waterloo, Québec. Journaliste, 48-53; publications: *Les Armes à faim*, 54, *Le Ciel fermé*, 56. Création du clown, Sol; 100 textes, 57-63; ONF, longs métrages et films pour la TV.
Filmographie sélective: *Golden Fiddles* (mini-series), TV, 90, CDN/AUS, Réal; *Les Tisserands du pouvoir* (aussi 6 ém TV), C, 87, CDN/F, Co sc/Cam/Réal; *Lavalin Industrie*, In, 86, CDN, Co sc/Réal/Cam; *Un Ordinateur au coeur*, "Page trois" (pilote), TV, 85, CDN, Réal/Sc/D phot/Mont; *Bonheur d'occasion/The Tin Flute* (aussi 5 ém TV, tourné simul-tanément fr. et angl.), C, 82, CDN, Co sc/Réal/Cam; *Cops and Other Lovers*, C, 79, CDN, Réal/Co sc; "The New Avengers" (1 eps), TV, 77, CDN/GB /F, Réal; *Je suis loin de toi mignonne*, C, 75, CDN, Réal/Co sc/Cam; *La Pomme, la queue...et les pépins!*, C, 74, CDN, Réal/ Dial/Cam; *Alien Thunder*, C, 72, CDN, Réal/Cam; *Les Chats bottés*, C, 71, CDN, Réal/Co sc/Cam; *Deux femmes en or*, C, 70, CDN, Réal/Co sc/Cam.

FOURNIER, Jacques ◆
(514)282-1505.
Types de production et générique: TV film-Réal.
Types d'oeuvres: Annonces-TV.
Curriculum vitae: Né en 1953, Sherbrooke, Québec. Président de La Fabrique d'Images Ltée. Réalisateur de messages publicitaires ayant gagné plusieurs prix dont 2 Certificats d'Excellence, 2 Coqs d'Or et 1 Coq de Bronze du Publicité Club de Montréal, 88; 1er prix Habitas; Best Commercial Award, Hollywood.

FOURNIER, Robert
981, rue des Ormes, Trois-Rivières, PQ G8Y 2P5 (819)375-0305.
Types de production et générique: c métrage-Réal/Prod; TV film-Réal/Prod; TV vidéo-Réal/Prod.
Types d'oeuvres: Documentaire-C&TV; Animation-C&TV.
Curriculum vitae: Né en 1953, Trois-Rivières, Québec. Diplôme en photographie professionnelle, Ecole des Arts et Métiers, Trois-Rivières, 72. Prise de vue d'animation et effets spéciaux jusqu'en 79; depuis, réalisateur, producteur.
Filmographie sélective: *Deux hommes aux mains liées*, MV, 88, CDN, Réal; *Le visage de Jésus*, ED, 86, CDN, Mont; *La bicyclette blanche*, ED, 86, CDN, Mont; *Le C.P.F. à votre service*, In, 85, BUR, Réal; *Oue, Monsieur le Directeur!*, ED, 85, BUR, Co réal; *Philippe Aubert de Gaspé/Elizabeth Bégon*, "Manuscrits", TV, 84, CDN, Réal/Prod/Mont; *Marie de l'Incarnation/Nerée Beauchemin*, "Manuscrits", TV, 84, CDN, 82-83, CDN, Réal/Prod; *Antoine Gerin Lavoie/Pamphile Lemay/Octave Crémazie*, "Manuscrits", TV, 82-83, CDN, Co prod; *Albert Lozeau/Laure Conan/Louis Frechette/ Charles Gill*, "Manuscrits", TV, 80-82, CDN, Co prod; *Arthur Buies/ Olivar Asselin*, "Manuscrits", TV, 80-81, CDN, Réal/Prod; *Chevauchée*, TV, 79, CDN, Co réal; *Pierre Guimond: entre Freud et Dracula*, TV, 79, CDN, Cam; *Commu-nauté urbaine de Montréal*, In, 79, CDN, Cam; *Nous vous aimons en santé*, ED, 79, CDN, Cam; *Au rythme du Québec*, TV, 77, CDN, Cam.

FOURNIER, Roger
- voir SCENARISTES

FOX, Beryl
- see PRODUCERS

FOX, Liz
- see PRODUCERS

FRANCON, Georges
AR. 1227 ouest, rue Sherbrooke, #63, Montréal, PQ H3G 1G1 (514)288-5878. Radio-Canada, 1400 est, boul. René-Lévesque, Montréal, PQ H2L 2M2 (514)285-2847.
Types de production et générique: TV film-Réal; TV vidéo-Réal.
Types d'oeuvres: Documentaire-TV.
Curriculum vitae: Né en 1924, France; citoyenneté canadienne. Langues: français

et anglais. Réalisateur, reporter, annonceur, scénariste à la radio et à la télévision.
Filmographie sélective: *Ceux qui ont tourné le dos à la vie,* TV, 82, CDN, Réal; *Livres d'artistes,* TV, 80, CDN, Réal; *Odanak,* TV, 79, CDN, Réal; *Théâtre pour enfants,* TV, 78, CDN, Réal; *Mitiarjuk,* TV, 77, CDN, Réal; *La Fin d'une époque,* "Canada Rural", TV, 70, CDN, Réal; *Joe Smallwood,* TV, 68, CDN, Réal; *Robert Stanfield,* TV, 67, CDN, Réal; *Lester B. Pearson,* TV, 67, CDN, Réal; *Aux frontières de la Terre promise,* TV, 66, CDN, Réal; *Alfred Pellan,* TV, 61, CDN, Réal; *Jeunesses musicales,* TV, 60, CDN, Réal.

FRASER, Louis
ARRQ. 3471 Chapleau, Montréal, PQ H2K 3H7 (514)527-2424. Radio-Québec, 1000 Fullum, Montréal, PQ H3K 2L7 (514)522-6331.
Types de production et générique: l métrage-Réal/Sc/Prod; c métrage-Réal/Sc/Prod; TV film-Réal/Sc/Prod; TV vidéo-Réal/Sc/Prod.
Types d'oeuvres: Comédie-C&TV; Documentaire-C&TV; Education-TV; Vidéo-clips-C&TV.
Curriculum vitae: Né en 1947. Pendant 15 ans, il a été à l'emploi de Radio-Québec. A travaillé comme réalisateur sur des documents corporatifs, des émission jeunesse, culturellles, scientifiques et de fiction; réalisateur-pigiste, 87; a réalisé, une émission pilot, le "Sushi Show" pour diffusion à Radio-Canada avec la maison de production Vision 4. A fait la mise en scène et la réalisation du film *Le Marché du Couple,* un docu-fiction qui a été diffusé à Radio-Québec en février, 90 et pré-selectionné pour "Input 91", à Florence. De mai 88, a réalisé la partie "dramatique réalité" du "Club des 100 Watts"; il travaille à la réalisation de sketches humoristiques, janvier, 90. Prix Gémeaux, 90, pour le meilleur émission ou série jeunesse variétés et/ou information pour "Le club des 100 watts."
Filmographie sélective: "Le Club des 100 Watts" (200 eps), ED, 87-88/89-90, CDN, Réal, (GEMEAUX); *Le Marche du Couple,* C, 89, CDN, Réal; *Radio-Québec par lui-même,* TV, 84-85, CDN, Réal; *Vendredi chaud* (pl ém), TV, 84, CDN, Réal; *Vivre le théâtre,* TV, 83, CDN, Réal; *Conarac le robot,* TV, 83, CDN, Mont; "Bozéjeunnes" (pl ém), TV, 81-82, CDN, Réal; "Neuf et demi" (7 eps), TV, 80-81, CDN, Réal; "Moi" (4 eps), TV, 79, CDN, Réal; *Planète,* TV, 79, CDN, Co réal; "L'Expérience aidant" (12 eps), TV, 76, CDN, Réal.

FRECHETTE, Michel ◊
(418)722-6609.
Types de production et générique: TV film-Réal; TV vidéo-Réal.
Types d'oeuvres: Documentaire-TV; Animation-TV; Industriel-TV.
Curriculum vitae: Né en 1950, Montréal, Québec. Réalisateur depuis 73; se spécialise dans l'animation 2D et 3D; copropriétaire d'une entreprise de production vidéo et film d'animation, 85.
Filmographie sélective: *Cégep plus,* TV, 88, CDN, Réal/Sc; *Tremplin,* C, 88, CDN, Réal; *19 mars 1980,* TV, 86, CDN, Réal; *Les Acteurs du loisir,* TV, 86, CDN, Réal; *Télémar,* TV, 85, CDN, Réal; *Dickner Inc.,* TV, 85, CDN, Réal; *Une admission chaleureuse,* TV, 85, CDN, Réal; *Melina,* TV, 84, CDN, Réal/Prod; *Les Temponautes,* TV, 83, CDN, Réal/Sc/Prod; *25 ans de télévision,* TV, 79, CDN, Réal; *Le Théâtre d'occasion,* TV, 79, CDN, Réal/Sc; *Coeur atout/Forêt y penser/La légende du Petouk-Petouk,* "Tout près d'ice", TV, 77, 78, CDN, Réal/Sc; *Samedi tout,* TV, 75, CDN, Réal; *Cabriole,* "Enersage", TV, 75, CDN, Réal/Prod.

FROST, F. Harvey
ACTT, DGC. 162 Westminster Ave., Toronto, ON M6R 1N7 (416)588-1096. Silbury Hill MPC Inc., 162 Westminster Ave., Toronto, ON M6R 1N7 (416)535-1468. Colleen Dolan, Credentials, 387 Bloor St. E., Toronto, ON M4W 1H7 (416)926-1507.
Type of Production and Credits: Th Film-Dir; TV Film-Dir/Wr; TV Video-Dir.
Genres: Drama-TV; Comedy-TV; Action-TV; Horror-Th.
Biography: Born 1947, London, England; Canadian and British citizenship. B.A., Hons. Sociology, Durham University, 69. Produced, directed commercials, 69-78. Immigrated to Canada, 74. Drama director since 78.
Selected Filmography: "Road to Avonlea" (6 eps), TV, 89-90, USA/CDN, Dir; "My Secret Identity" (10 eps), TV, 88-90, USA/CDN, Dir; "The Campbells" (4 eps), TV, 87-88, USA/CDN/GB, Dir; "T and T" (3 eps), TV, 87-88, CDN/USA, Dir; "Friday the 13th - The Series" (1 eps), TV, 88, CDN/USA, Dir; "Adderly" (1 eps), TV, 87, CDN/USA, Dir; "Max Haines' Crime Flashbacks" (pilot), TV, 87, CDN, Dir/Co-Wr; "Edison Twins" (2 eps), TV, 86-87, CDN/USA, Dir; "Front Runners" (3 eps), TV, 84, CDN, Dir/Co-Wr; "In Good Company" (pilot), TV, 84, CDN, Dir; "Romance" (15 eps)(Co-Prod 30 eps),

TV, 81-82, CDN, Dir; *Passion of the Patriots*, "Some Honourable Gentlemen", TV, 82, CDN, Dir; "The Great Detective" (9 eps), TV, 79-81, CDN, Dir; "High Hopes" (30 eps), TV, 78, USA/CDN, Dir; *Something's Rotten*, Th, 78, CDN, Dir.

FRUET, William
DGC, ACTRA. 51 Olive Ave., Toronto, ON M6G 1T7 (416)535-3569.
Type of Production and Credits: Th Film-Dir/Wr/Prod; Th Short-Dir/Wr/Prod; TV Film-Dir/Wr/Prod.
Genres: Drama-Th&TV; Action-Th&TV; Science Fiction-Th&TV; Horror-Th&TV.
Biography: Born 1933, Lethbridge, Alberta. Began his career in photography and directing on medical films; UCLA Film School; sponsored teaching films, California, 60-65; was editor, CBC, Film Arts, while also working on screenplays. Awards include: Etrog, Canadian Film Awards, 70 - Best Original Screenplay for *Goin' Down the Road*; Etrog, Canadian Film Awards, 72 - Best Picture for *Wedding in White*; Directors' Award, Spanish International Horror Festival for *Death Weekend*. *Wedding in White* presented at Directors' Fortnight, Cannes 72.
Selected Filmography: "Scene of the Crime" (1 eps), TV, 91, US/CDN, Dir; "Top Cop" (6 eps), TV, 90-91, USA/CDN, Dir; "My Secret Identity" (3 eps), TV, 90, USA/CDN, Dir; "War of the Worlds" (8 eps), TV, 88-89, US/CDN, Dir; "Friday the 13th - The Series" (10 eps), TV, 87-89, USA/CDN, Dir; *The Blue Monkey*, Th, 87, US, Dir; *The Playground*, "Ray Bradbury Theatre", TV, 85, US/CDN, Dir; *The Killer Party*, Th, 84, USA, Dir; *Bedroom Eyes I*, Th, 83, USA/CDN, Dir; *Spasms*, Th, 81, USA/CDN, Dir; *The Killer Instinct*, Th, 80, USA/CDN; *Search & Destroy*, Th, 78, USA/CDN, Wr/Dir; *Death Weekend/House By The Lake*, Th, 75, CDN, Wr/Dir; *Wedding in White*, Th, 71, CDN, Wr/Dir/Prod; *Goin' Down the Road*, Th, 69, CDN, Wr.

FRUND, Jean-Louis ✧
(819)228-9222.
Types de production et générique: TV film-Réal.
Types d'oeuvres: Documentaire-TV.
Filmographie sélective: "Connaissance du milieu" (12 films), TV, 80-86, CDN, Réal/Rech/Cam; "Faune nordique" (7 films), TV, 80-86, CDN, Réal/Rech/Cam; *Le Grand Héron*, TV, 77-78, CDN, Réal/Sc; *La Volée des neiges/L'oie blanche*, In, 74-75, CDN, Sc/Réal; *La Vie selon Félix Leclerc*, TV, 67, CDN, Co réal; *Jean Gauquet Larouche*, TV, 66, CDN, Réal/ Prod.

FUREY, Lewis
- see COMPOSERS

FURIE, Sidney J. ✧
(213)550-4000.
Type of Production and Credits: Th Film-Dir/Prod/Wr.
Genres: Drama-Th.
Biography: Born 1933, Toronto, Ontario. Trained in scriptwriting and directing, Carnegie Institute of Technology, Pittsburgh. Director/writer, CBC-TV, 54; moved on to feature films, directing/writing/producing in Canada, 57; England, 60; USA, 66.
Selected Filmography: *Superman IV*, Th, 86, USA, Dir; *Iron Eagle*, Th, 85, USA, Dir/Co-Wr; *Purple Hearts*, Th, 83, USA, Dir/Co-Wr/Prod; *The Entity*, Th, 82, USA, Dir; *The Boys in Company C*, Th, 78, USA, Dir/Co-Wr; *Gable and Lombard*, Th, 76, USA, Dir; *Sheila Levine Is Dead and Living in New York*, Th, 75, USA, Dir; *Little Fauss and Big Halsy*, Th, 70, USA, Dir; *The Lawyer*, Th, 70, USA, Dir/Co-Wr; *The Naked Runner*, Th, 67, GB, Dir; *The Appaloosa*, Th, 66, USA, Dir; *The Ipcress File*, Th, 65, GB, Dir; *Wonderful Life*, Th, 64, GB, Dir; *The Leather Boys*, Th, 64, GB, Dir; *The Boys*, Th, 62, GB, Dir/Prod.

FUSCA, Martha
- see PRODUCERS

GAGLIARDI, Laurent ✧
(514)288-5669.
Types de production et générique: c métrage-Réal/Prod; TV film-Réal/Prod/Sc; TV vidéo-Réal/Prod/Sc.
Types d'oeuvres: Documentaire-TV; Animation-C&TV.
Curriculum vitae: Né en 1948, Montréal, Québec. Critique de la cinéma et écrivain. *Charles Gill* de la série "Manuscrits" remporte le Prix de l'aide à la création, Festival des Films sur l'Art, 82.
Filmographie sélective: *Pamphile Lemay/ Albert Lozeau/Antoine Gerin Lajoie*, "Manuscrits", TV, 83-84, CDN, Réal/Sc/Co prod; *Octave Crémazie/Laure Conan/ Louis Frechette/Charles Gill*, "Manuscrits", TV, 79-82, CDN, Réal/Sc/Co prod; *Chevauchée*, C, 79, CDN, Co réal/Prod; *Jacques Hétu*, compsiteur, TV, 78, CDN, Réal/Sc; *André Gagnon*, TV, 77, CDN, Réal/Sc; *Une artisane: Yvonne Leclerc-Daigle*, TV, 76, CDN, Réal/Sc/Prod.

GAGNÉ, Pier
ACCT, AQBRCT. 1500 boul de Maisonneuve est, Bureau 401, Montréal, PQ H2L 2B1 (514)525-0366.

Types de production et générique: TV vidéo.
Types d'oeuvres: Industriel-TV; Documentaire-TV; Affaires Publiques-TV; Variété-TV.
Curriculum vitae: Né en 1957 à Jonquière, Québec. Langues: français, anglais, et connaissance de l'espagnol. Grand Prix pour "Vidéotour", 1988.
Filmographie sélective: "Desjardins" (3 eps), In, 91, CDN, Réal; "Sortir" (25 eps), TV, 90, CDN, Réal; "Routes des vacances" (18 eps), TV, 88-90, CDN, Réal; "Première Ligne" (23 eps), TV, 88-90, CDN, Réal; "Feu-Vert" (8 eps), TV, 89-90, CDN, Réal; "Info 5 et Parcours" (2 eps), TV, 89-90, CDN, Réal; "Info 5 et Parcours" (2 eps), TV, 90, CDN, Réal/Journ; "Nord-Sud" (1 eps), TV, 89, CDN, Réal/Journ; C.I.L., In, 89, CDN, Réal; "Vidéotour" (11 eps), TV, 87-88, CDN, Réal; *Médecine apprivoisée*, TV, 87, CDN, Réal; "Expression", TV, 86, CDN, Réal/Journ; *Prévost car*, In, 87, CDN, Réal.

GAGNON, Claude
APFVQ, ARRFQ, DGA, ACCT, ACTRA. 824, des Colibris, Longueuil, PQ J4G 2C1. Aska Film International Inc., 1600 av. de Lorimier, Suite 211, Montréal, PQ H2K 3W5 (514)521-7103. FAX: 521-6174.
Types de production et générique: l métrage-Réal/Prod/Sc/Mont; c métrage-Réal/Prod/Sc/Mont.
Types d'oeuvres: Drame-C; Comédie-C; Documentaire-C; Enfants-C.
Curriculum vitae: Né en 1949, St-Hyacinthe, Québec. Langues: français, anglais, japonais. Vit au Japon où il réalise ses premiers films; de retour au Canada, fonde la Compagnie Yoshimura-Gagnon inc. Nombreux prix dont le Prix spécial du jury et le Prix de la réalisation de l'Association des réalisateurs de films du Japon pour *Keiko*, 78; le Grand Prix des Amériques, le Prix de l'Unesco et Mention spéciale de l'Unicef (Berlin) pour *The Kid Brother*.
Filmographie sélective: *The Pianist*, C, 91, CDN/J, Réal/Prod; *Rafales*, C, 90, CDN, Prod; *The Kid Brother*, C, 86, CDN/USA/J, Réal/Sc; *Visage pâle*, C, 85, CDN/J, Réal/Co prod/Sc/Mont; *Larose, Pierrot et la Luce*, C, 81, CDN, Réal/Co prod/Sc/Mont; *Keiko*, C, 78, J, Réal/Co prod/Sc/Mont; *Yui to Hi*, C, 77, J, Réal/Mont; *Geinin*, C, 76, J, Réal/Mont; *Essai filmique sur musique japonaise*, C, 74, J, Réal/Sc.

GAGNON, Pierre ✧
(514)765-7422.
Types de production et générique: TV vidéo-Réal.
Types d'oeuvres: Variété-TV; Enfants-TV; Annonces-TV; Sports-TV.
Curriculum vitae: Né en 1954, Alma, Lac-St-Jean, Québec. Langues: français et anglais. DEC en électronique audio-visuelle, 75. Cinéaste, Gouvernement du Québec, 75; caméraman, éclairage, réalisateur commercial, Télécapitale Québec, 76-78; réalisateur pigiste, programme et commercial; directeur de production commercial, Pathonic Québec, 87; réalisateur pigiste, 88.
Filmographie sélective: "Le Hockey" (175 eps), TV, 83-88, CDN, Réal; "La Fourchette d'or" (60 eps), TV, 87-88, CDN, Réal; "Le Village de Nathalie" (85 eps), TV, 86-87, CDN, Réal; Sonnet francosonique, TV, 87, CDN, Réal; "Les Carnets de Louise" (3 eps), TV, 87, CDN, Réal; "Les Groupes parlementaires" (16 eps), TV, 84-86, CDN, Réal; *Concert au Grand Théâtre*, TV, 86, CDN, Réal; *Gala Miss Québec*, TV, 85, CDN, Réal; "Héritage 2001" (13 eps), TV, 84, CDN, Réal.

GALLUS, Maya
Travelling Light Productions Ltd., 19 Tennis Cres., #5, Toronto, ON M4K 1J4 (416)466-9079.
Type of Production and Credits: Th Short-Dir; TV Film-Dir;.
Genres: Documentary-Th&TV; Current Affairs-TV.
Biography: Born in 1959. Completed Journalism programme, Ryerson Polytechnical Institute, 1981. Worked in TV current affairs since 1983. Director, industrial and educational videos. Has written magazine articles for *The Globe & Mail, Toronto Life, Canadian Art* and *Chatelaine*. Completed first film, *On The Side Of The Angels*, combining documentary and dramatic techniques, in 1991.
Selected Filmography: *Elizabeth Smart: On The Side Of The Angels*, Th/TV, 91, CDN, Dir/Wr/Co Prod; "Live It Up", TV, 85-87, CDN, Field Prod; "CTV National News", TV, 89, CDN, Field Prod; "The Journal", TV, 87, CDN, Story Prod; "Canada AM", TV, 87/88, CDN, Story Prod.

GANDOL, Pedro B.
STCQ. 121 Irvine Ave., Westmount, PQ H3Z 2K3 (514)935-7249.
Type of Production and Credits: Th Film-1st AD/Dir; TV Film-1st AD; TV Video-1st AD.
Genres: Drama-Th&TV; Documentary-Th&TV; Educational-Th&TV; Commercials-Th&TV.

Biography: Born 1949, Montreal, Quebec. Languages: English, French and Spanish. B.A., Loyola College, 72. Extensive world travel including work in the U.S., Europe, the Arctic, and China. Guest lecturer on the topic of the AD in the film industry.
Selected Filmography: *Map of the Human Heart*, Th, 91, CDN/AUS/GB/F, 1st AD; *Blackrobe*, Th, 90, CDN/AUS, 1st AD; *Descending Angel*, TV, 90, USA, 1st AD; *Falling Over Backwards*, Th, 89, CDN, 1st AD; *Eddie Lives*, Th, 89, USA, 1st AD/2nd U Dir; *Bethune*, Th, 87-88, CDN/RC, 1st AD; *Liberace*, TV, 88, USA, 1st AD; *Jackknife*, Th, 88, USA/GB, 1st AD; *L'Emprise*, TV, 88, CDN, 1st AD; *Shades of Love*, TV, 87, CDN/USA, 1st AD; *Miles to Go*, TV, 86, USA, 1st AD; *Time for Miracles*, "Wonder Works", TV, 85, USA, 1st AD; *Joshua Then and Now*, Th, 84, CDN/USA, 1st AD; *Race to the Pole*, TV, 83, USA, 1st AD.

GAREAU, John
- see PRODUCERS

GAUTHIER, Fred
- see EDITORS

GAUVIN, Paul
- voir PRODUCTEURS

GAUVREAU, Gil
ACCT. 21 Dale Ave., #247, Toronto, ON M4W 1K3 (416)920-2479.
Type of Production and Credits: Th Short-Wr/Prod/Dir/Ed; TV Film-Wr/Dir; TV Video-Wr/Prod/Dir/Ed.
Genres: Drama-Th; Comedy-Th; Documentary-Th&TV; Industrial-Th.
Biography: Born 1946, Toronto, Ontario. Honours B.A., English Language and Literature, University of Windsor. Graduate School, UCLA Motion Picture Department. Received the Alex Pavlini Award. *Ex Cathedra* won the Eugene Keefer Award and 3rd prize, Kenyon Film Festival. *Neon: The Night Is Their Canvas* won a Chris Plaque, Columbus; *Helpless* won a Cinestud Award, Amsterdam; *Sheetfed Printing Inks* won Gold (Marketing) and Grand Prize, Quasar Awards, NY, Chris Plaque, Columbus, Certificate for Creative Excellence, US Film & Video Festival, Chicago, Certificate of Merit, International Film and TV Festival of New York.
Selected Filmography: *Sheetfed Printing Inks*, In, 89, CDN, Prod; *Dancer*, TV, 87, CDN, Wr/Prod/Dir/Ed; *Neon: The Night Is Their Canvas*, TV, 87, CDN, Wr/Prod/Dir/Ed; "Downstairs with Jimmy King" (6 eps), TV, 87, CDN, Dir; "Friday Night" (4 eps), TV, 87, CDN, Dir; *The Prairie Landscape*, TV, 86, CDN, Wr/Prod/Dir/Ed; *On the Publishing Trail*, TV, 86, CDN, Wr/Prod/Dir/Ed; "The Music Room" (14 eps), TV, 86, CDN, Prod/Dir; *Timothy Findley*, TV, 85, CDN, Wr/Prod/Dir/Ed; "The Phobia Series" (4 eps), ED, 81, CDN, Prod/Dir/Ed; *Ex Cathedra*, Th, 75, CDN, Wr/Prod/Dir/Ed; *Angel Glands*, Th, 69, CDN, Wr/Prod/Dir/Ed; *Supreme Sacrifice*, Th, 68, CDN, Wr/Prod/Dir/Ed; *Segments*, Th, 67, CDN, Wr/Prod/Dir/Ed; *Helpless*, Th, 65, CDN, Wr/Prod/Dir/DOP.

GÉLINAS, Michel
- voir PRODUCTEURS

GÉLINAS, Michel F. ✧
(514)845-0531.
Types de production et générique: TV film-Réal; TV vidéo-Réal/Sc.
Types d'oeuvres: Drame-TV; Variété-TV; Documentaire-TV; Affaires publiques-TV.
Curriculum vitae: Né en 1949. Langues: français, anglais, italien. Etudes universitaires avec stage de formation à la BBC, Londres; à Radio-Canada, Montréal, depuis 78; organisation et direction de stages intenationaux en France et au Sénégal (radio, TV).
Filmographie sélective: "Iniminimagimo" (195 eps), TV, 86-89, CDN, Réal, (GEMEAUX 87); "Traboulidon" (40 eps), TV, 83-87, CDN, Réal, (GEMEAUX 86); *L'Expérience*, TV, 87, CDN, Réal; *L'Agression sexuelle des jeunes* (4 ém), TV, 85, CDN, Réal; *La Justice et les jeunes*, TV, 85, CDN, Réal/Sc; "Bof et Cie" (20 eps), TV, 82-83, CDN, Réal; "Pierre et Cie" (15 eps), TV, 81-82, CDN, Réal; "Allô Boubou" (45 eps), T, 81-82, CDN, Réal; "Les Coqueluches" (39 eps), TV, 79-80, CDN, Réal; "L'Heure de pointe" (39 eps), TV, 78-79, CDN, Réal.

GERBER, Sig
- see PRODUCERS

GERRETSEN, Peter ✧
(416)484-9671.
Type of Production and Credits: Th Film-Dir/Wr; TV Film-Dir/Wr; TV Video-Dir/Wr.
Genres: Drama-Th&TV; Industrial-Th&TV; Commercials-Th&TV; Educational-Th&TV.
Biography: Born 1939, The Netherlands; Canadian citizenship. Graduate, Regiopolis College, Kingston. Director/writer of feature films, educational drama, commercials and industrials since 64. Co-founded own production company, 75. Has won awards of merit from the Art Directors' Club of Ontario, Canadian Film Awards, American, Columbus and New

York film festivals.
Selected Filmography: *Night Friend*, Th, 87, CDN, Dir/Wr; *The Kidnapping of Baby John Doe*, TV, 85, CDN, Dir/Wr.

GERVAIS, Suzanne
ASIFA, SGCT. ONF, C.P. 6100, Succ. A, Montréal, PQ H3C 3H5 (514)283-9302.
Types de production et générique: c métrage-Réal.
Types d'oeuvres: Animation-C.
Curriculum vitae: Née à Montréal, Québec. Etudes à l'Ecole des Beaux-Arts, Montréal. Peintre et illustrateur; a travaillé presque exclusivement en cinéma d'animation. *Climats* remporte des prix aux festivals de San Francisco, Columbus et Lubbock; *Premiers Jours*, Festival de Annecy, Columbus, New York, Londres et Ottawa; *Tchou-Tchou*, Annecy, New York, Los Angeles et Salerne (Italie).
Filmographie sélective: *Les Iris/The Irises*, C, 91, CDN, Co réal/An/Cam; *L'Atelier*, C, 87, CDN, Réal; *Trêve*, C, 83, CDN, Réal; *Premiers Jours*, C, 80, CDN, Co réal; *La Plage*, C, 78, CDN, Réal; *Climats*, C, 75, CDN, Réal; *Tchou-Tchou*, C, 72, CDN, Co an; *Cycle*, C, 71, CDN, Réal.

GIBBONS, Bob
ATPD. 1202 Greening Ave., Mississauga, ON L4Y 1H4 (416)277-4067.
Type of Production and Credits: TV Film-Dir/Prod; TV Video-Dir/Prod.
Genres: Comedy-TV; Variety-TV; Documentary-TV; Children's-TV.
Biography: Born 1939, London, Ontario. B.A., University of Toronto; presently studying for M.A. at the Ontario Institute for Studies in Education. Thirty-five years at CBC as Producer/Director/Technician. Awards include Anik award and Gemini nomination for "Under the Umbrella Tree", YTV Award nomination for "Wild Guess" and Gemini nomination for *The Great Gathering*.
Selected Filmography: "Under the Umbrella Tree" (195 eps), TV, 88-90, CDN, Prod, (ANIK); "Wild Guess" (26 eps), TV, 90, CDN, Prod; *Canada Day Special* (3 shows), TV, 82/83/88, CDN, Prod/Dir; "Adrienne Clarkson Festival" (11 eps), TV, 88, CDN, Prod/Dir; *The Great Gathering-Roy Thomson Hall Classical Music Special*, TV, 87, CDN, Prod/Dir; *The Messiah*, TV, 87, CDN, Prod; *Christmas Telethon*, TV, 87, CDN, Dir; *Genie Awards*, TV, 82/87, CDN, Prod/Dir; *Calgary Centre for Performing Arts Gala Opening*, TV, 85, CDN, Dir; *Queen's Gala Special*, TV, 84, CDN, Dir/Prod; *Gala: Premier Zhao of China*, TV, 84, CDN, Prod/Dir; *Gala: President Reagan*, TV, 83, CDN, Dir/Prod; "Trivia Quiz" (13 eps), TV, 78, CDN, Prod/Dir; "The Friendly Giant" (150 eps), TV, 75, CDN, Prod; "Mr. Dressup" (200 eps), TV, 74, CDN, Prod.

GILBERT, Tony
- see PRODUCERS

GILDAY, Katherine
- see WRITERS

GILDAY, Leonard
- see CINEMATOGRAPHERS

GILLARD, Stuart
ACTRA, AFTRA, SAG, WGAw, ACCT. P.O. Box 421, Pacific Palisades, CA 90272. Lynn Kinney, Credentials, 387 Bloor St. E., Toronto, ON (416)926-1507. A.P.A., 9000 Sunset Blvd., Los Angeles, CA 90069 USA (213)273-0744.
Type of Production and Credits: Th Film-Wr/Dir/Prod/Act; Th Short-Wr/Dir/Prod/Act; TV Video-Wr/Dir/Prod/Act.
Genres: Drama-Th&TV; Comedy-Th&TV; Variety-TV; Action-Th.
Biography: Born 1946, Coronation, Alberta. B.A., University of Alberta; Acting, National Theatre School of Canada; Special Acting Program, University of Washington. Received an Emmy nomination, writing for "Sonny and Cher."
Selected Filmography: "Max Glick" (1 eps), TV, 90, CDN, Dir; "My Secret Identity" (3 eps), TV, USA, 90, Dir; "Fly By Night" (2 eps), TV, 90, USA, Dir; "Adventures of the Black Stallion" (2 eps), TV, 90, USA/F, Dir; "Bordertown" (16 eps), TV, 88-90, USA, Dir; "Road to Avonlea" (4 eps), TV, 89-90, CDN/USA, Dir; *Return of the Shaggy Dog*, TV, 87, USA, Dir; *Indigo Autumn*, TV, 87, USA, Dir/Wr; "Check It Out" (44 eps), TV, 85-86, CDN/USA, Prod/Co-Wr; *Honeymoon Haven*, TV, 83, CDN, Prod/Wr; *Paradise*, Th, 81, CDN, Dir/Wr; "Mork and Mindy" (25 eps), TV, 79-80, USA, Exec Story Ed; "Donny and Marie" (25 eps), TV, 78-79, USA, Co-Dir/Head Wr; "Excuse My French" (50 eps), TV, 74-76, CDN, Act; *Why Rock the Boat?*, Th, 74, CDN, Act, (CFA/ACTRA).

GILLIS, Kevin
- see PRODUCERS

GILLSON, Malca
ACCT. 105 Gloucester St., Toronto, ON M4Y 1M2 (416)920-0732.
Type of Production and Credits: TV Film-Dir/Ed.
Genres: Documentary-TV.
Biography: Born in Yorkton, Saskatchewan. Studied voice, Royal Conservatory of Music; German Lieder,

Salzburg, Austria. Founded Baie d'Urfée Little Theatre, Montreal, 61; joined NFB, 54, worked on over 80 productions. *Last Days of the Living* won the Gold Plaque, Chicago International Film Festival.
Selected Filmography: *Make the Words Sing*, TV, 91, CDN, Dir/Ed; *The Joy of Singing*, TV, 90, CDN, Dir/Ed; *Musical Magic: Gilbert and Sullivan in Stratford*, TV, 84, CDN, Dir/Ed; *Time for Caring*, TV, 83, CDN, Dir/Ed; *Singing: A Joy in Any Language*, TV, 83, CDN, Dir/Ed; *Reflections on Suffering*, TV, 82, CDN, Dir/Ed; *A Choice of Two*, TV, 81, CDN, Assoc Prod; *The Last Days of the Living*, TV, 81, CDN, Dir/Ed; *It Wasn't Easy*, TV, 78, CDN, Ed; *The War Is Over*, TV, 77, CDN, Prod; *Alberta Girls*, Th, 75, CDN, Dir; *Musicanada*, TV, 75, CDN, Dir/Ed; *You're Eating for Two*, TV, 74, CDN, Dir; *Nell and Fred*, TV, 71, CDN, Ed; *The Question of Television Violence*, TV, 70, CDN, Ed.

GINSBERG, Donald
- see PRODUCERS

GIRALDEAU, Jacques
SGCT, ASIFA. 850, av. Wiseman, Outremont, PQ H2V 3L1 (514)273-1832. Office National du Film, 3155, ch. de la Côte de Liesse, Montréal, PQ H4N 2N4 (514)283-9360.
Types de production et générique: l métrage-Sc/Réal/Prod; c métrage-Sc/Réal/Prod; TV film-Sc/Réal/Prod.
Types d'oeuvres: Documentaire-C&TV; Animation-C; Expérimental-C.
Curriculum vitae: Né en 1927. Langues: français et anglais. Etudes en sciences sociales, Université de Montréal. Co-fondateur du premier ciné-club au Québec à l'Université de Montréal, 48; membre fondateur de la Commission Etudiante du Cinéma; journaliste cinématographique au *Front ouvrier* et écoupages; co-fondateur de la Cinémathèque québécoise, 63; membre fondateur de l'Association Professionnelle des Cinéastes, a commencé sa carrière de cinéaste à l'ONF, 50; a dirigé sa compagnie, Studio 7 Ltée, pendant 10 ans; est également peintre et graveur dont les oeuvres ont été exposées à Montréal, Ottawa, Boston, New York, etc.; a réalisé de nombreux films sur l'art au Québec et au Canada qui ont été remarqués dans les festivals internationaux dont Venise.
Filmographie sélective: *Les Iris/The Irises*, C/TV, 91, CDN, Co réal; *La toile blanche*, C/TV, 89, CDN, Sc/Réal; *Le tableau noir*, C/TV, 89, CDN, Sc/Réal; *L'Homme de papier*, C, 87, CDN, Sc/Réal; *Opéra Zéro*, C, 84, CDN, Réal/An; *Un Québécois retrouvé*, TV, 80, CDN, Prod; *La toile d'araignée*, C, 79, CDN, Réal/Sc/D phot/Prod dél; *Puzzle*, C, 76, CDN, Réal/An; *La Fougère et la Rouille*, C, 74, CDN, Réal; *Zoopsie*, C, 73, CDN, Réal/An/Mont; *Faut-il se couper l'oreille*, TV, 70, CDN, Réal; *Bozarts*, C, 69, CDN, Sc/Réal; *Les fleurs c'est pour Rosemont*, TV, 68, CDN, Réal; *Gros-Morne*, C, 66, CDN, Réal/Prod; *Eléments 3*, C, 65, CDN, Sc/Réal.

GIRARD, Hélène
- voir MONTEURS

GIRARD, Simon ◊
(514)483-3502.
Types de production et générique: TV vidéo-Réal.
Types d'oeuvres: Nouvelles-TV.
Curriculum vitae: Né en 1947, Montréal. Licence en Sciences politiques, Université Laval. A fait de l'animation, 3 ans; recherche, 3 ans; journaliste, affaires publiques, Radio-Canada, TV et radio, 4 ans.
Filmographie sélective: *Onu de jeunes.Live Aid québécois/Lorraine Guay/Procès au Pérou*, "Nord-Sud", TV, 85-86, CDN, Réal; *Femmes de Coopérant/Pena Gomez/Special République Dominicaine*, "Nord-Sud", TV, 85, CDN, Réal; *Ecole de coopération/Organisation canadienne de solidarité*, TV, 85, CDN, Réal; *Les Juifs à Sosua/Saco/Les Bateys/Forum-Afrique/Toto Bissainthe*, "Nord-Sud", TV, 85, CDN, Réal; *Jumelage Burlington - Nicaragua/La Lèpre/Socodevi/Ova*, "Nord-Sud", TV, 85, CDN, Réal.

GIROTTI, Ken
DGC. 45 Breadalbane St., #2, Toronto, ON M4Y 1C2 (416)928-5962.
Type of Production and Credits: TV Film-Dir; TV Video-Prod.
Genres: Drama-TV; Comedy-TV; Musical-TV; Action-TV.
Biography: Born 1956, Pictou, Nova Scotia. Languages: English and Spanish.
Selected Filmography: "Top Cops" (2 eps), TV, 90, CDN, Dir; "E.N.G." (3 eps), TV, 89-90, CDN, Dir; "My Secret Identity" (1 eps), TV, 90, CDN, Dir; "T and T" (3 eps), TV, 89-90, CDN, Dir; "The Campbells" (7 eps), TV, 88, CDN/GB/USA, Dir; "Captain Power" (1 eps), TV, 88, CDN, Dir; "Danger Bay" (1 eps), TV, 87, CDN, Dir.

GJERSTAD, Ole
- see PRODUCERS

GOETZ, Ron
- see PRODUCERS

GOLDBERG, Howard
4350 Melrose, Montreal, PQ H4A 2S6

(514)369-1701. Maximage Productions, 3981 boul. St. Laurent, Suite 801, Montreal, PQ H2W 1Y5 (514)987-1818. FAX: 987-1819.
Type of Production and Credits: Th Short-Dir/Ed; TV Film-Dir/Ed; TV Video-Dir/Ed.
Genres: Drama-Th&TV; Commercials-Th&TV.
Biography: Born in 1957 in Montreal, Quebec. Studied filmmaking at Concordia University. Languages: English and French. Has directed and edited award-winning dramatic shorts. *Metropolis* was nominated for two Prix Gémaux. *Meet Chagall* won a Coq Bronze from the Publicity Club of Montreal, and an Award of Merit from the Art Directors' Club of New York. *Moïse* was nominated for a Golden Sheaf Award. Won a Musique Plus Award for Best Editing for the music video *Ton amour est trop lourd.*
Selected Filmography: PetroCanada (2 spots), Cm, 91, CDN, Dir/Ed; *Moïse*, TV, 91, CDN, Dir/Ed; Humpty Dumpty, Cm, 90, CDN, Dir/Ed; *Les Trembley's*, PetroCanada, Cm, 90, CDN, Dir/Ed; *Ton amour est trop lourd*, MV, 90, CDN, Ed; Expotech (3 spots), Cm, 90, CDN, Dir/Ed; *Grand Canyon*, Imax, Cm, 89, CDN, Dir/Ed; *Japon des Shoguns*, Th, 89, CDN, Dir/Ed; *Meet Chagall*, Th, 88, CDN, Co Dir/Ed; *Metropolis*, TV, 87, CDN, Co Dir/Ed; "Vidéotour" (12 eps), TV, 87-88, CDN, Dir/Ed; *Trendsetters*, Th, 81, CDN, Dir/Ed.

GOLDSTEIN, Allan
DGA, DGC, ACCT, ACTRA, WGA. 2509 Green Valley Rd., Los Angeles, CA 90046 USA (213)461-1601. Debra Lieb, Triad Artists, 10100 Santa Monica, Los Angeles, CA USA (213)556-2727.
Type of Production and Credits: Th Film-Dir; Th Short-Dir; TV Film-Dir; TV Video-Dir.
Genres: Drama-TV; Comedy-Th&TV; Action-TV; Science Fiction-Th&TV.
Biography: Born 1951, Montreal, Quebec; US resident alient. Languages: English and French. B.A., Honours Psychology, McGill University; M.A., Design, York University. Directs dramas in Europe, US and Canada. Trained at NFB; trained in multiple-camera direction at BBC. Has written and directed over 40 television productions in US and Canada: episodics, movies-of-the-week, mini-series, specials. Has had 2 Emmy nominations and awarded Best Director of a Network Special for *True West*, 85. *The Outside Chance of Maximilian Glick* won Best Canadian Film award at Festival of Festivals and Vancouver Film Festival, 88.
Selected Filmography: *No Return*, 91, USA, Dir/Wr; *Chaindance*, Th, 90, USA, Dir; *Cold Front*, Th, 88, CDN, Dir; *Rooftops*, Th, 88, USA, Dir; "Survival Guides", TV, 87, USA, Dur; "Deadline", Th, 87, USA, Dir; *Moving Up*, Th, 87, USA, Dir; *The Outside Chance of Maximilian Glick*, Th, 87, CDN, Dir; "Wonderworks" (2 eps), TV, 86, USA, Dir; "Great Performances" (1 eps), TV, 86, USA, Dir; "Rockit Records" (1 eps), TV, 86, CDN, Dir; "Crossbow" (4 eps), TV, 86, GB/F/USA, Dir; *True West*, TV, 85, USA, Dir; "American Playhouse" (2 eps), TV, 85, USA, Dir.

GOLDSTEIN, Roushell
- see EDITORS

GOODMAN, Paul W.
- see PRODUCERS

GORDON, Lee
IATSE 873. 4 Deer Park Cres., #2C, Toronto, ON M4V 2C3 (416)925-6682.
Type of Production and Credits: Th Short-Dir/Prod; TV Film-Dir/Prod.
Genres: Drama-Th&TV; Educational-Th&TV; Children's-TV; Documentary-Th&TV;.
Biography: Canadian citizen. Attended University of Iowa and Columbia University. Partner in Westminster Films, Toronto for 25 years; has produced and directed over 200 titles. Has won awards at New York, Prague and American film festivals.
Selected Filmography: *Maximizing Production*, ED, 84, CDN/USA, Dir; *Irrigation/The Profit Paradise*, In, 79-80, CDN/USA, Dir; *Canwel/A Way Out*, ED, 70-74, CDN, Prod; *Here's Looking at You/Engineering Is for People*, ED, 71-74, CDN, Dir; *The Last Act of Martin Weston*, Th, 70, CDN/CS, Prod; *The Trouble With Words*, ED, 70, CDN, Prod; *Putting It Together*, ED, 70, CDN, Prod/Dir; *Rye on the Rocks*, In, 69, CDN, Prod, (CFA); *An Irish Touchstone*, In, 68, CDN/IRL, Prod/Dir; *Nikki Wild Dog of the North*, Th, 60, CDN/USA, Co-Prod; *The Lost Missile*, Th, 58, USA, Prod.

GOUDSOUZIAN, Hagop
- see PRODUCERS

GOUGH, William
- see PRODUCERS

GOULET, Stella
ARRFQ, FPRRTC. Les Films plein cadre inc., 3013, Boulogne, Ste-Foy, PQ G1W 2C4 (418)653-4219.
Types de production et générique: c métrage-Réal/Sc/Mont; TV film-Réal/

Sc/Mont; TV vidéo-Réal/Mont/Sc.
Types d'oeuvres: Drame-C&TV; Documentaire-C&TV; Enfants-C&TV.
Curriculum vitae: Née en 1947 à Québec. Baccalauréat multidisciplinaire, mineures en Cinéma et Théâtre, 82. *Pic et Pic et Contredanse* remporte un prix au Palmarès canadien du court métrage indépendant et *Elise et la mer*, la Gerbe d'or à Yorkton et le Gémeau du meilleur court métrage, 87.
Filmographie sélective: *Le festin de Coquette*, TV, 91, CDN, Sc/Réal/Mont; *Pas de répit pour Mélanie*, C, 90, CDN, Sc; *Yves Goulet, poésie d'ombre et de lumière*, TV, 87, CDN, Sc/Co réal/Co mont/Co prod; *Elise et la mer*, TV, 86, CDN, Sc/Réal; *Le gros de la classe*, TV, 86, CDN, Sc; *La Tirelire*, TV, 85, CDN, Réal/Prod/Sc; *Mélodie, ma grand-mère*, TV, 83, CDN, Réal/Sc; *Les chevaux d'Acier*, TV, 83, CDN, Co réal/Co mont/Prod; *Trois petits tours*, TV, 82, CDN, Réal/Prod/Mont/Sc; *Pic et Pic et Contredanse*, C, 78-79, CDN, Réal/Prod.

GRAVELLE, Raymond
- voir PRODUCTEURS

GREEN, Howard
- see PRODUCERS

GREENWALD, Barry
CIFC. 242 Delaware Ave., Toronto, ON M6H 2T6 (416)536-0655.
Type of Production and Credits: Th Film-Dir/Prod/Ed/Wr; Th Short-Dir/Prod/Ed/Wr; TV Film-Dir/Prod/Ed/Wr; TV Video-Dir/Prod/Wr.
Genres: Documentary-Th&TV; Drama-Th&TV; Educational-Th&TV.
Biography: Born 1955, Toronto, Ontario. Film major, Conestoga College; NFB, Directors' Training Unit (drama workshop), 76-78. Awards include Palme d'Or, Cannes Film Festival, for *Metamorphosis*; Best Documentary Direction Award, Silver Boomerang, Melbourne for *Taxi!*; Silver Medal, Houston, for *Pitchmen*; Blue Ribbon, American Film Festival; Genie nomination, ACCT, for *Who Gets In?*; Sesterce d'Argent, 22e Festival International du Film Documentaire, Nyon, Switzerland; Gold Apple, First Prize, NEFVF, Oakland; Second Prize of the Geneva International Television Award and Prix Pierre-Alain Donnier, Geneva; Golden Sheaf, Yorkton (Best Documentary for Broadcasters) for *Between Two Worlds*. Founding member of the Canadian Independent Film Caucus.
Selected Filmography: *Between Two Worlds*, TV, 90, CDN/AUS/GB/S, Dir; *Who Gets In? - An Inside Look at Canadian Immigration*, Th, 89, CDN, Dir; *What's New at School*, ED, 86, CDN, Dir/Co-Prod; *Pitchmen*, Th, 85, CDN, Dir/Co-Ed; *Falasha: Agony of the Black Jews*, "Man Alive", TV, 83, CDN, Ed; *Taxi!*, Th, 82, CDN, Dir/Wr; *Arctic Spirits/The New Shamans*, Th, 82, CDN, Ed/Snd Ed; *Hot Wheels*, Th, 79, CDN, Co-Ed, (CFEG); *Careers for Everyone*, ED, 77, CDN, Dir/Prod/Ed/Cam; *Metamorphosis*, Th, 75, CDN, Dir/Prod/Wr/Ed, (CFA); *Willamette, Mormot and Priest*, Th, 74, CDN, Dir/Prod; *Tangents*, Th, 73, CDN, Dir/Prod/Wr/Cam; *Agamemnon the Lover*, Th, 71, CDN, Co-Dir/Co-An; *Etude*, Th, 70, CDN, Dir/Wr/Ed/Cam.

GRENIER, Henriette ◊
(514)465-1303.
Types de production et générique: TV film-Réal.
Types d'oeuvres: Variété-TV; Sports-TV.
Curriculum vitae: Née en 1938, Montréal, Québec. Langues: français et anglais. Diplômée de l'Université McGill. A Radio-Canada depuis 63; nommée réalisatrice, 77, coordinatrice, 78; actuellement coordonnatrice des projets spéciaux et coproductions avec les pays francophones (CTF).
Filmographie sélective: "Les Insolences d'une caméra" (36 eps), TV, 86, CDN, Coord pro; *Gala des Grandes Ecoles*, "Les Beaux Dimanches", TV, 85, CDN/F, Coord pro; *Super Star*, "Les Beaux Dimanches", TV, 83-84, CDN, Réal; *Si on chantait*, "Les Beaux Dimanches", TV, 84, CDN/F/L/CH, Réal/Coord pro; *Gala des étoiles du Maurier*, "Les Beaux Dimanches", TV, 84, CDN, Prod dél; "Allô Boubou" (quot), TV, 78-83, CDN, Réal/Coord pro; *Fête de la St-Jean*, TV, 82, CDN, Coord pro; *Gala 25ième année télé Jonquière/Avec vous depuis 25 ans*, "Les Beaux Dimanches", TV, 81, CDN, Réal; "Heure de pointe" (quot), TV, 77-78, CDN, Réal; *Fête du Canada*, TV, 78, CDN, Coord pro.

GROULX, Sylvie ◊
(514)524-1420.
Types de production et générique: l métrage-Réal; c métrage-Réal; TV vidéo-Réal.
Types d'oeuvres: Documentaire-C&TV.
Curriculum vitae: Née en 1953, Montréal, Québec. Langues: français, anglais, espagnol. Baccalauréat en Communica-tions, Université Concordia, Montréal. Productions indépendantes et ONF; distribution de films, Cinéma Libre Inc.; animatrice à la radio.
Filmographie sélective: *Chronique d'une*

temps flou, C, 88, CDN, Réal/Sc/Rech; *Entre deux vagues*, TV, 85, CDN, Co réal; *Le Grand Remue-ménage*, Th, 78, CDN, Réal/Prod/Rech; *Une bien belle Ville*, Th, 76, CDN, Rech.

GRUBEN, Patricia ◊
(604)874-9450.
Type of Production and Credits: Th Short-Dir/Ed/Wr; TV Video-Wr.
Genres: Drama-Th&TV; Experimental-Th.
Biography: Born in Chicago, Illinois; landed immigrant Canada. Graduate film study, University of Texas. Art director, prop master and set decorator on feature films and television, 72-82. Independent filmmaker since 77. *Low Visibility* won special Jury Prize at Athens Film Festival; First Prize for dramatic feature, Atlanta Film Festival. *Sifted Evidence* showed in New York Film Festival, won First Prize for Experimental Narrative in Athens, received honourable mention on *Village Voice* list of Top Ten Films of 83. Instructor, film production at Simon Fraser University; Director of Praxis Film Development Workshop.
Selected Filmography: *Low Visibility*, Th, 84, CDN, Wr/Dir/Ed; *Sifted Evidence*, Th, 82, CDN, Wr/Dir/Ed; *Spasms*, Th, 81, CDN, Set Dec; *A Choice of Two*, TV, 81, CDN, Assist Art Dir; *Heartaches*, Th, 80, CDN, Set Dec; "Big City Comedy" (13 eps), TV, 80, CDN/USA, Set Dec; *Virus*, Th, 79, J, Spv Set Dec; "Littlest Hobo" (6 eps), TV, 79, CDN, Set Dec; *An American Christmas Carol*, TV, 79, CDN, Set Dec; *Morocco, A Berber Profile*, "People and Places", TV, 78, CDN, Wr; *Happy Arabia*, "People and Places", TV, 78, CDN, Wr; *The Central Character*, Th, 78, CDN, Wr/Dir/Ed; "Celebritiy Cooks" (26 eps), TV, 78, CDN, Set Dec; "SCTV" (52 eps), TV, 77-78, CDN, Props.Set Dec; *Good Day Care: One Out of Ten*, ED, 78, CDN, PM.

GUERTIN, Micheline ◊
(514)465-7768.
Types de production et générique: TV vidéo-Réal.
Types d'oeuvres: Drame-TV; Comédie-TV; Variété-TV; Annonces-TV.
Curriculum vitae: Née en 1944, Montréal, Québec. Langues: français et anglais. Etudes: Lettres françaises, Costumes de théâtre.
Filmographie sélective: "Beau et chaud" (25 eps), TV, 88, CDN, Réal; *Les 9 heures de Jean Lapointe*, TV, 88, CDN, Réal; "Station Soleil" (21 eps), TV, 87, CDN, Réal; *Les Voisins*, TV, 86, CDN, Réal; *Au de la nuit*, TV, 86, CDN, Réal; *Victor le vampire*, TV, 85, CDN, Réal; *Ecaille*, TV, 84, CDN, Réal; *Je persiste et signe...Brel*, TV, 84, CDN, Réal; "Bozéjeunnes" (pl ém), TV, 81-83, CDN, Réal.

GUILBEAULT, Luce ◊
(514)271-3784.
Types de production et générique: l métrage-Réal/Com; TV film-Com.
Types d'oeuvres: Drame-C&TV.
Curriculum vitae: Née en 1935 à Montréal, Québec. Baccalauréat en Philosophie, Université de Montréal; Conservatoire de la Province de Québec. Réalisatrice, comédienne, théâtre et cinéma; enseignement de théâtre, Université du Québec à Montréal, Ecole Nationale de Théâtre du Canada. Fonde Les Reines du Foyer (production cinéma), Montréal, 77. Comédienne, Théâtre de 4 sous, *Névrose à la carte*, janvier, 88.
Filmographie sélective: "Des Dames de coeur" (26 eps), TV, 86, CDN, Com; "Le Temps d'une paix" (4 eps), TV, 85, CDN, Com; *Qui a tiré sur nos histoires d'amour?*, C, 85, CDN, Com; *Pense à ton désir*, C, 84, CDN, Com; *Albédo*, C, 83, CDN, Com; *La Quarantaine*, C, 81, CDN, Com; *L'Echantillon*, "Contrejour", TV, 79, CDN, Com; *D'abord ménagères*, C, 78, CDN, Réal; *Mourir à tue-tête*, C, 78, CDN, Com; *Some American Feminists*, C, 77, CDN, Réal; *Some American Feminists*, C, 77, CDN, Réal; *Bargain Basement*, C, 76, CDN, Com, (CFA); *Denyse Benoît, comedienne*, C, 75, CDN, Réal; *Le Temps de l'avant*, "En tant que femmes", TV, 74, CDN, Com; *Mustang*, C, 74, CDN, Com; *Par une belle nuit d'hiver*, C, 74, CDN, Com.

GUNN, John
70 Charles St. E., #15, Toronto, ON M4Y 1T1 (416)924-7594.
Type of Production and Credits: Th Short-Wr/Dir/Prod; TV Video-Dir.
Genres: Drama-TV; Documentary-TV; Commercials-TV; Music Video-TV.
Biography: Born 1955, Halifax, Nova Scotia. Writer ATV Moncton, New Brunswick, 78-79; Writer/Director CKVR-TV Barrie, Ont., 80; Director, On-Air Promotion, Citytv/MuchMusic, Toronto, 81-88; Reporter, CityPulse News, 85; Director, FashionTelevision, 85-87; Resident, Canadian Centre for Advanced Film Studies, 88-89.
Selected Filmography: "Frontiers of the Unknown" (3 eps), TV, 90, CDN, Field Prod; *Someone Like You*, Th, 88, CDN, Wr/Dir; *The Grace of God*, Th, 88, CDN, Prod; *Blue Moon*, Th, 88, CDN, Prod;

Citytv's 15th Anniversary Special, TV, 87, CDN, Prod/Dir; *Spadina Bus*, MV, 86, CDN, Prod/Co-Dir; "FashionTelevision", TV, 85-87, CDN, Dir.

GUNNARSSON, Sturla
DGC, ACCT. 43 Glenwood Ave., Toronto, ON M6P 3C7 (416)769-0254. (416)604-4658. Suzanne Depoe, (416)466-4173.
Type of Production and Credits: Th Film-Dir/Prod; TV Film-Dir.
Genres: Drama-Th&TV; Documentary-Th&TV.
Biography: Born 1951, Iceland; moved to Canada as a young man; Canadian citizenship. Languages: English, Icelandic and Spanish. B.A., English Literature, University of British Columbia, 74. Has directed and produced many internationally celebrated films. *Final Offer* won Genie, Grand Prize (Banff), Prix Italia, Golden Gate Award (San Francisco) and Chris Award (Columbus); *After the Axe* was nominated for an Academy Award, won Golden Sheaf (Yorkton) and Blue Ribbon, American Film Festival; *Bamboo Brush* won First Prize, Chicago Festival; *A Day Much Like the Others* won Norman McLaren Award, Grand Prize, Canadian Student Film Festival and Special Jury Prize, Rencontres Henri Langois. Extensive assignment work directing for Canadian, British and US television. Feature film *Diplomatic Immunity* is scheduled for theatrical release in the fall of 91.
Selected Filmography: *Diplomatic Immunity*, Th, 91, CDN/MEX, Dir/Prod; "Scales of Justice", TV, 91, CDN, Dir; *Where Is Here?*, TV, 89, CDN/USA, Dir/Prod; "E.N.G.", TV, 89, CDN, Dir; "Street Legal", TV, 86-89, CDN, Dir; "Ray Bradbury Theatre", TV, 88, CDN/GB, Dir; "Alfred Hitchcock Presents", TV, 88, CDN/USA, Dir; "Beachcombers", TV, 84-88, CDN, Dir; *Final Offer*, Th, 87, CDN, Dir/Prod; "Twilight Zone", TV, 87, CDN/USA, Dir; *Bamboo Brush*, "Sons & Daughters", TV, 84, CDN, Dir; *After the Axe*, TV, 83, CDN, Dir/Prod; *A Day Much Like the Others*, Th, 78, CDN, Dir/Prod.

HALDANE, Don ✧
(416)279-8461.
Type of Production and Credits: Th Film-Dir; TV Film-Dir.
Genres: Drama-Th&TV; Action-TV; Science Fiction-Th; Children's-TV.
Biography: Born 1914, Edmonton, Alberta. Graduate of Yale Drama School, 41; after WWII, attended Columbia University and New School of Social Research. Past President of DGC; 25 years as President of Westminster Films. Recipient of Quen's Silver Jubilee Medal.
Selected Filmography: "The Way We Are" (1 eps), TV, 88, CDN, Dir; "Red Serge" (1 eps), TV, 87, CDN, Dir; "The Campbells" (4 eps), TV, 85-86, CDN/USA/GB, Dir; "The Edison Twins" (6 eps), TV, 85-86, CDN, Dir; "The Beachcombers" (12 eps), TV, 81-86, CDN, Dir; "Ritter's Cove" (6 eps), TV, 78-79, CDN, Dir; "For the Record" (3 eps), TV, 77-78, CDN, Dir; "Sidestreet" (6 eps), TV, 74-76, CDN, Dir; "Swiss Family Robinson" (7 eps), TV, 74-75, CDN, Dir; *The Reincarnate*, Th, 70, CND, Dir; "Forest Rangers" (14 eps), TV, 63-64, CDN, Dir; *Drylanders*, Th, 61, CDN, Dir; *Nikki Wild Dog of the North*, Th, 60, CDN/USA, Co-Dir.

HALL, Mark
1036 Beech Tree Lane, Brentwood, TN 37027 (615)331-6276. Hallway Productions Inc., 214 Second Ave. N., Ste. 100-A, Nashville, TN 37201 (615)254-7087. FAX: 254-6989.
Type of Production and Credits: TV Video-Dir/Wr.
Genres: Musical-TV; Documentary-TV.
Biography: Born in 1955. 1988 Gemini nominated for Best Writing in an Information/Documentary Program or Series for *Jerry Lee Lewis: I Am What I Am*. Director and co-writer of *Straight Shooter: The Mamas & Papas* which won a 1989 Gemini for Best Documentary and won Best Documentary at the American Film Institute/American Video Conference Awards. Director and co-writer of *George Jones: Same Ole Me*, which won the Best Profile & Personality award at the 1990 American Film Institute/American Video Conference Awards.
Selected Filmography: *Loretta Lynn: Honky Tonk Girl*, TV, 90, USA, Dir/Wr; *Waylon*, TV, 90, USA, Dir/Wr; *George Jones: Same Ole Me*, TV, 89, USA, Dir/Wr; *Straight Shooter: The Mamas & Papas*, TV, 88, USA, Dir/Wr, (GEMINI); *Jerry Lee Lewis: I Am What I Am*, TV, 87, USA, Dir/Wr; *Thanks, Troubadour, Thanks: The Ernest Tubbs Story*, TV, 86, USA, Dir/Wr; *The Real Patsy Cline*, TV, 85, USA, Dir/Wr.

HALLÉ, Roland
AMPAS. 44 Camelot Dr., Bedford, NH 03102 (603)472-3019. Unique Film Productions Inc., 44 Camelot Dr., Bedford, NH 03102.
Type of Production and Credits: Th

Film-Wr/Prod/Dir.
Genres: Drama-Th; Documentary-Th&TV.
Biography: Born in 1930 in Levis, Quebec. B.A. Collège de Lévis, 1951, M.B.A., Laval University, Quebec, 1954. Involved in the life insurance industry from 1954 to 1972. Registered at the School of Public Communications, Boston University, 1976. M.S. in Filmmaking, Boston University, 1980. Joint thesis with Peter W. Laude, a 26-minute film *Karl Hess: Toward Liberty*. This film has won many awards including a Hugo from the Chicago Film Festival; Blue Ribbon from the Amercian Film Festival in New York; Silver Cindy, Information Film Producers of America. *Urge to Build* was nominated for an Academy Award.
Selected Filmography: *The First Killing Frost*, Th, 87, USA, Dir/Prod/Wr; *Urge to Build*, ED, 81, USA, Dir/Prod/Wr; *Karl Hess: Towards Liberty/Karl Hess: Vers la liberté*, ED, 80, USA, Co Prod, (OSCAR).

HALLEE, Céline
AR. 5877, rue de Terrebonne, Montréal, PQ H4A 1B4. Radio-Canada, 1400 est, boul. René-Lévesque, Montreal, PQ H2L 2M2 (514)597-4867.
Types de production et générique: TV film-Réal; TV vidéo-Réal.
Types d'oeuvres: Drame-TV; Comédie-TV; Variété-TV; Documentaire-TV.
Curriculum vitae: Née en 1950, Ville-Marie, Québec. Baccalauréat en Musique et Expression dramatique, Université de Montréal et du Québec. Huit ans de mise en scène au théâtre; réalisatrice télévision depuis 83; scénariste. Mise en scène de la pièce L'Amérique à sec," 86. Atelier direction des acteurs avec Warren Robertson.
Filmographie sélective: "Jamais deux sans toi" (15 eps), TV, 90-91, CDN, Réal/Coord pro; "Robert et Compagnie" (67 eps), TV, 88-89, CDN, Réal; "Le Parc des braves" (26 eps), TV, 87, CDN, Réal; "La Vie promise" (26 eps), TV, 84-85, CDN, Réal; "L'Argent fait le bonheur" (20 eps), TV, 85, CDN, Réal; "Monsieur le Ministre" (2 eps), TV, 83-84, CDN, Réal; "Avis de recherche" (20 eps), TV, 83-84, CDN, Réal.

HALLIS, Ron
Hallis Media Inc., 122, rue de Touraine, St-Lambert, PQ J4S 1H4 (514)465-9571.
Type of Production and Credits: TV Film-Prod/Dir/Wr; TV Video-Prod/Wr/Dir.
Genres: Documentary-Th&TV; Educational-Th&TV; Industrial-Th&TV; Current Affairs-Th&TV.
Biography: Born 1945, Montreal, Quebec. Languages: English, French and Portuguese. Educated at McGill University. Independent filmmaker for 20 years; 5 years under contract in Mozambique, training young Mozambicans in film production and helping set up regular documentary production, 77-82. Special areas of interest as a filmmaker are southern Africa and the Middle East.
Selected Filmography: *Music of the Spirits/La Musique des Esprits*, ED, 90, CDN/ZM, Prod/Dir/Wr/Cin/Ed; *Samora Michael*, ED, 89, CDN/MZ, Prod/Dir/Wr/Cin/Ed; *Chopi Music of Mozambique*, ED, 87, CDN, Prod/Dir/Cam; *Iran Report*, TV, 86, CDN, Prod/Dir/Cam; *Iran: Adrift in a Sea of Blood*, TV, 86, CDN, Prod/Dir/Cam; *Documenting the Bomb*, ED, 85, CDN, Prod/Cam/Dir; *Zimbabwe: The New Struggle*, TV, 85, CDN, Prod/Dir/Cam; *Nkuleleko Means Freedom*, TV, 84, CDN, Prod/Dir/Cam; *I Can Hear Zimbabwe Calling*, TV, 80, CDN, Prod/Dir/Cam; *Mozambique before the Darkness*, TV, 79, CDN, Dir/Prod/Cam; *A Wile Mu Colonyi*, TV, 78, CDN, Prod/Dir/Cam; *Mukwai*, TV, 77, CDN, Dir/Prod/Cam; *Pride of the Panthers*, Th, 76, CDN, Prod/Dir/Cam; *Bull*, Th, 75, CDN, Prod/Dir/Cam; *Zaida*, Th, 75, CDN, Prod/Dir/Cam.

HAMILTON BROWN, Alex
- see PRODUCERS

HANUS, Otta ◊
(416)461-6064.
Type of Production and Credits: TV Film-Dir.
Genres: Drama-TV; Comedy-TV; Action-TV; Science Fiction-TV.
Biography: Born 1953, Cornwall, Ontario. Languages: English, French and Czech. Degrees in Economics, Film and Theatre, Concordia University. Worked for 10 years as assistant director and location manager; now directing.
Selected Filmography: "Captain Power and the Soldiers of the Future" (9 eps), TV, 87, CDN, Dir; "Airwaves" (4 eps), TV, 87, CDN, 1st AD; "Airwaves" (1 eps), TV, 87, CDN, Dir; *The Believers*, Th, 86, USA, 2nd Unit AD; *Burnin' Love*, Th, 86, USA, 1st AD; *Doing Life*, TV, 86, USA, 1st AD; *Many Happy Returns*, TV, 86, USA, 1st AD; "Airwaves" (7 eps), TV, 86, CDN, 1st AD; "Airwaves" (1 eps), TV, 86, CDN, Dir; "The Hitchhiker", TV, 85, USA, 1st AD; "Anne of Green Gables" (4 eps), TV, 85, CDN, 1st AD; "Airwaves" (1

eps), TV, 85, CDN, 1st AD; *Reckless Disregard*, TV, 84, USA/CDN, 1st AD; *Paper Castles*, TV, 84, USA, 1st AD; *Mrs. Soffel*, Th, 84, USA, 2nd Unit AD/2nd AD.

HARBURY, Martin
- see PRODUCERS

HAREL, David
ACCT. 18 Lebos Rd., Willowdale, ON M2H 2L9 (416)497-8706.
Type of Production and Credits: Th Film-Prod/Dir; TV Film-Prod/Dir; TV Video-Prod/Dir.
Genres: Documentary-Th&TV; Educational-Th&TV; Commercials-Th&TV; Current Affairs-TV.
Biography: Born 1947, Hungary; Israeli and Canadian citizenship. Languages: English, Hungarian and Hebrew. Design and Photography, Academy of Art, Jerusalem, Israel; B.A.A., Film Studies, Ryerson Polytechnical Institute. Winner of several awards, including Genie, Chicago, New York.
Selected Filmography: *My Happy Days in Hell*, TV, 91, CDN, Prod/Dir/Wr; *Promises to Keep: The Canadians in Palestine*, TV, 88, CDN, Dir; *The Twice Promised Land*, TV, 86, CDN, Co-Prod/Co-Dir; *Nations at Crossroads: Angola*, TV, 86, CDN, Dir; *Raoul Wallenberg: Buried Alive*, TV, 82, CDN, Co-Prod/Dir/Co-Wr; Mitsubishi Electronics (4), Cm, 81, CDN, Prod/Dir/Wr.

HARRIS, Les
ACFTP, ACCT. 16 Servington Cres., Toronto, ON M4S 2J3 (416)485-0874. Canamedia Productions Ltd., 189 Dupont St., Toronto, ON M5R 1V6 (416)324-9190. FAX: 968-9092.
Type of Production and Credits: TV Film-Dir/Prod; TV Video-Dir/Prod.
Genres: Drama-TV; Comedy-TV; Variety-TV; Documentary-TV.
Biography: Born 1947, England; British and Canadian citizenship. Educated in India and England; B.A.(Honours), Economics, Sheffield University. Editor, BBC TV; producer, director, CBC, CTV; TV distributor, consultant; Vice-President, ACFTP. *Escape from Iran: The Canadian Caper* won a Silver Medal, New York; *The King of Friday Night*, Gold Medal (NY), Silver Hugo (Chicago), Rockie (Banff), The Athens Award (Ohio).
Selected Filmography: "Take Off" (13 eps), TV, 91, CDN, Exec Prod/Co-Prod/Spv Ed; "Take Off", TV, 90, CDN, Prod/Exec Prod; *Padre Pablo: Fighter for Justice*, TV, 89, CDN, Dir/Prod/Co-Wr/Ed; *By the Seat of Their Pants*, TV, 88, CDN/GB, Dir/Prod/Wr/Ed, (GEMINI); *Frontier Footlights*, TV, 88, CDN, Prod/Dir; "Adderly" (11 eps), TV, 87, CDN, Prod; *Voices on the Water*, TV, 87, CDN, Exec Prod; "Gzowski & Co.", TV, 86, CDN, Prod/Dir; *444 Days to Freedom: What Really Happened in Iran*, TV, 86, CDN/USA, Dir/Prod/Ed, (GEMINI 86); *The King of Friday Night*, TV, 85, CDN, Prod, (2 CFTA); *Agents of Deception*, TV, 84, CDN, Dir; "W5" (50 seg), TV, 79-84, CDN, Dir/Prod; *Escape from Iran: The Inside Story*, TV, 81, CDN, Dir/Prod; *Escape from Iran: The Canadian Caper*, TV, 80, CDN, Prod; *Chabot Solo* (3 parts), TV, 79, CDN, Dir/Prod.

HARRIS SCHIPPER, Jayne
26 Birdsall Ave., Toronto, ON M4R 2B8 (416)440-1933.
Type of Production and Credits: TV Film-Dir; TV Video-Dir.
Genres: Drama-TV; Comedy-TV; Variety-TV; Musical-TV.
Biography: Born 1959, Toronto, Ontario; in L.A. 63-83; has U.S. green card. Languages: English and French. B.A., Sarah Lawrence College.
Selected Filmography: "Learning the Ropes" (4 eps), TV, 88, USA/CDN, Assoc Dir; *Rendez-vous 87 Gala - Quebec City*, TV, 87, USA/CDN, Assoc Dir; "Check It Out", TV, 85-87/87-88, CDN/USA, Assoc Dir/Dir; *A Long Day's Journey Into Night/Master Harold and the Boys/Grown Ups/Breakfast with Les and Bess*, "American Playhouse, 84-86, USA, Assoc Dir; *The Molson Indy Race*, TV, 86, USA/CDN, Assoc Dir; *Gala Evening at Expo 86*, TV, 86, USA/CDN, Assoc Dir; *As Is*, "American Playhouse, Th, 86, USA, Assoc Dir/Cont; *PMS: The Film*, TV, 85, USA, Assoc Dir; *Comedy Factory*, (4 eps), TV, 85, USA, Assoc Dir; *50th American Presidential Inaugural Gala*, TV, 85, USA, Assoc Dir; *The Shmenges' Last Polka*, TV, 84, USA, Assoc Dir; "Sharon, Lois and Bram's Elephant Show" (13 eps), TV, 84, CDN, Cont; *Anne Murray: Winter Carnival from Quebec*, TV, 84, CDN/USA, *Supertramp Concert at the CNE*, TV, 83, USA/CDN, Assoc Dir; *The Magic of David Copperfield*, TV, 83, USA/CDN, Assoc Dir; "Loving Friends and Perfect Couples" (80 eps), TV, 83, USA/CDN, Assoc Dir.

HARRISON, Jim
831 Richmond St. W., #213, Toronto, ON M6J 3P7 (416)367-5284. Rova Productions, 99 Queen St. E., Suite 303, Toronto, ON (416)362-6199.

Type of Production and Credits: TV Film-Dir/Ed; TV Video-Dir/Ed.
Genres: Drama-TV; Documentary-TV; Sports-TV.
Biography: Born 1941, Britain; landed immigrant Canada. Studied at London Film School, 70. Moved to Canada, 78.
Selected Filmography: "Sports Weekend" (40 seg), TV, 78-86, CDN, Dir/Ed/Wr; "Wide World of Sports" (12 seg), TV, 80-85, CDN, Dir/Ed/Wr; "Olympic Journey" (1 seg), TV, 84, CDN, Wr; "Country Canada" (1 eps), TV, 80, CDN, Ed; *Silence of the North*, Th, 79, CDN, Co-Snd Ed.

HAUKA, David
DGC. 43 - 784 Thurlow St., Vancouver, BC V6E 1V9 (604)685-4511.
Type of Production and Credits: Th Film-Prod/PM/Wr; Th Short-Prod/Dir/Wr.
Genres: Drama-TV; Comedy-TV; Music Video-TV.
Biography: Born in 1956 in Gibson's Landing, British Columbia. Canadian citizen. Simon Fraser University Film Workshop, 1982. Lighting Designer/T.D., Karen Jamieson Dance Company, 1983-84. Festival awards: Gold Plaque, Chicago International Film Festival, 1985; New York Dance on Camera Festival, 1984; Film Producer's Grant, Canada Council, 1984.
Selected Filmography: *Home Movie*, Th, 91, CDN, Prod Exec; "Max Glick" (7 eps), TV, 90, CDN, PM; *Day Glow Warrior*, TV, 90, CDN, PM; *The Comic Book Chase*, TV, 90, CDN, PM; *Head Down*, Moev, MV, 90, CDN, Dir; *Ben's Song*, Sarah McLachlan, MV, 90, CDN, Dir; *Steaming*, Sarah McLachlan, MV, 90, CDN, Dir; *Stoneman*, Hilt, MV, 90, CDN, Dir; *Disfunctional Relationship*, Consolidated, MV, 90, CDN, Dir; *Won't Matter* and *Baby*, Lava Hay, MV, 90, CDN, Dir/Prod; *All The Things You Are, Do You Want to Come, What Was Going Through My Head* , The Grapes of Wrath, MV, 89-90, CDN, Prod; *Baby Blues*, TV/ED. 89, CDN, PM; *What's Wrong With Neil?*, TV, 88, CDN, PM; *Quarantine*, Th, 88, CDN, PM; *Solus*, Th, 85, CDN, Prod/Dir/Wr.

HAWKINS, Crawford W.
- see PRODUCERS
HAWLEY, Gay
- see WRITERS
HAZZAN, Ray
- see PRODUCERS
HEBB, Brian R.R.
- see CINEMATOGRAPHERS

HEBERT, Bernar ✧
(514)397-1414.
Types de production et générique: c métrage-Réal/Sc; TV vidéo-Réal/Sc; Vidéo-Réal/Sc.
Types d'oeuvres: Danse-C; Vidéo clips-C&TV; Expérimental-C&TV.
Curriculum vitae: Né en 1961. A travaillé au sein de la troupe de théâtre l'Eskabel; co-fondateur des Productions Agent Orange inc., 82; produit et réalise quelques pièces de théâtre et plusieurs productions film et vidéo; co-fondateur de la compagnie de distribution Antenna, 87. Récipiendaire de plusieurs prix et mentions internationaux.
Filmographie sélective: *Rooms*, C, 88, CDN, Réal/Sc; *Commitment: Two Portraits*, TV, 88, CDN, Réal; *Georgia l'odeur des nuages*, TV, 88, CDN, Réal; *Anémique Cinéma*, MV, 87, CDN, Réal/Conc; *Lalala Human Sex Duo No. 1*, C, 87, CDN, Réal/Conc; *House*, MV, 87, CDN, Réal/Sc; *Tentations danse musique Montréal*, TV, 87, CDN, Réal; *En plein coeur d'été*, MV, 86, CDN, Réal/Conc; *Fiction* (vidéo), C, 85, CDN, Réal/Sc; *Exhibition*, C, 85, CND, Réal/Conc; *Air*, MV, 85, CDN, Réal/Conc; *Kidnapping*, C, 84, CDN, Réal/Sc; *Le Chien de Luis et Salvador* (vidéo), C, 83, CDN, Réal/Sc.

HEINEMANN, Michelle
- see WRITERS
HELLIKER, John
ACTRA. 184 Wright Ave., Toronto, ON M6R 1L2 (416)532-1969.
Type of Production and Credits: TV Film-Dir/Wr/Prod; TV Video-Dir/Wr/Prod; Th Film-Dir/Wr/Prod.
Genres: Documentary-Th&TV; Educational-Th&TV; Drama-Th&TV; Animation-Th&TV.
Biography: Languages: English and Chinese (Mandarin). Ph.D., Political Thought; M.A., Economics; 2 years study in People's Republic of China (Philosophy and Chinese Language Diploma). *Don't Call Me Stupid*, winner at Columbus and American Film Festivals. 1990 Resident at Canadian Centre for Advanced Film Studies.
Selected Filmography: *Norha and the Microbabe*, Th, 91, CDN, Dir/Co-Prod; *Beach Story*, Th, 90, CDN, Prod; *Killing Time*, TV, 88, CDN, Prod; *Target*, ED, 88, CDN, Line Prod; "OWL-TV" (20 eps), TV, 86-87, CDN, PM; "Indonesia: A Generation of Change" (5 eps), TV, 86, CDN, Wr; *Don't Call Me Stupid*, TV, 83, CDN, Wr/Co-Prod; "Kids of Degrassi Street" (6 eps), TV, 79-82, CDN, PM;

Patience Please, ED, 83, CDN, Dir/Wr.

HENAUT, Dorothy Todd
SGCT. 5045 Esplanade, Montreal, PQ H2T 2Y9 (514)276-5333. NFB, Box 6100, Stn. A, Montreal, PQ H3C 3H5 (514)283-9544.
Type of Production and Credits: Th Film-Prod/Dir; TV Film-Prod/Dir.
Genres: Documentary-Th&TV; Educational-Th&TV.
Biography: Born 1935, Hamilton, Ontario. Languages: English and French. Graduated from the Sorbonne, 54. Founded magazine *The Craftsman/ L'Artisan*, 65; edited newsletter *Access*, 68-74, and created regional community video programs, 72, for "Challenge for Change," NFB; Studio D, NFB, 77-89; currently in Studio C.
Selected Filmography: *Pour faire une histoire courte*, TV, 91, CDN, Dir; *Québec..un peu..beaucoup...passionnément*, TV, 89, CDN, Dir; *A Song for Quebec*, TV, 88, CDN, Dir; *Les Terribles Vivantes/Fireworks*, Th, 85, CDN, Dir; *Not a Love Story*, Th, 80, CDN, Prod; *Horse-Drawn Magic*, TV, 79, CDN, Dir; *Sun, Wind and Wood*, TV, 78, CDN, Dir; *Témiscamingue, Québec*, TV, 76, CDN, Prod; *The New Alchemists*, TV, 74, CDN, Dir; *VTR St-Jacques*, TV, 69, CDN, Assoc Dir; *Opération boule de neige*, TV, 69, CDN, Assoc Dir.

HENDERSON, Clark ◆
Box 8943, Saskatoon, SK S7K 6S7 (306)665-7250.
Type of Production and Credits: Th Film-Dir; Th Short-Cam.
Genres: Drama-Th&TV; Experimental-TV; Music Video-TV.
Biography: Born 1961, Saskatchewan. Languages: English, semifluent in French and Ameslan and some knowledge of Japanese. Winner, Best Video, Neutral Ground Film and Video Competition, Regina, 84.
Selected Filmography: *Coincidential Oppositorum*, Th, 88, CND, Prod/Cam; *Subkonscio Maligna*, Th, 87, CND, Prod/Dir/Cam/Ed; *Understanding of Process*, ED, 86, CDN, Prod/Dir/Cam/Ed; *Scientia Sexualis*, Th, 86, CDN, Ed; *Sinfonia Domestica*, Th, 85, CDN, Prod/Dir/Ed; *Microtsuwanoba*, Th, 84, CDN, Ed/Cam; *Brainfire Ritual*, Th, 84, CDN, Cam; *Dance of the Baby Vacuii*, Th, 84, CDN, Ed/Mus Ed; *Seventh Avenue Liaison*, Th, 84, CDN, Prod/Ed/Cam; *Sporadic Hemmorhoid Is Squalid*, Th, 83, CDN, Prod/Ed/Cam; *Anhanger*, Th, 83, CDN, Prod/Dir/Ed; *Rivals uber Riel*, MV, 83, CDN, Prod/Dir/Ed; *Spanghew Decorum*, Th, 83, Prod/Dir/Ed; *Border*, MV, 81, CDN, Prod/Dir/Ed/Cam.

HENLEY, Gail
- see WRITERS

HENSHAW, Helen
- see PRODUCERS

HÉROUX, Denis
- voir PRODUCTEURS

HERRON, J. Barry
- see CINEMATOGRAPHERS

HESLIP, Dale
30 Beaconsfield Ave., Toronto, ON M6J 3H9 (416)588-7955. Champagne Pictures, 437 Sherbourne St., Toronto, ON M4X 1K5 (416)928-3001. Vast Productions, 67 Mowat St., Toronto, ON M6K 3E3 (416)534-9914. Allan Weinrib (416)534-9914.
Type of Production and Credits: TV Video-Dir/Art Dir.
Genres: Variety-TV; Commercials-TV; Music Video-TV.
Biography: Born in 1958 in Galt, Ontario. Has worked in the music business for 7 years. 2 Juno nominations for LP Cover. 1982 U-Know for Best LP Cover. Won a Golden Sheaf, Yorkton Short Film & Video Festival for Best Music Video, 1991, *The Superman Song*, Crash Test Dummies. Bessie Award of Merit and Best TV Commercial, Ottawa for *Eviction Notice*.Golden Craft Award for *No Panic Christmas*. Gemini Nomination for *1990 Juno Awards*.
Selected Filmography: *The Superman Song*, Crash Test Dummies, MV, 91, CDN, Dir/Art Dir; *Labatt's Blue Band Warz*, TV, 90-91, CDN, Dir/Art Dir; *1991 Juno Awards*, TV, 91, CDN, Pro Des; *Eviction Notice*, Care Canada, Cm, 90, CDN, Dir/Art Dir; "Test Pattern" (130 eps), TV, 90, CDN, Art Dir; *No Panic Christmas*, Robinsons, Cm, 90, CDN, Dir/Art Dir; *1990 Juno Awards*, TV, 90, CDN, Pro Des; *Still Lovin' You*, Honeymoon Suite, MV, 90, Dir/Art Dir; *Seventh Son*, She's Insane, MV, 90, CDN, Dir/Art Dir; *1989 Juno Awards*, TV, 89, CDN, Art Dir.

HILLER, Arthur
DGA, DGC. Phil Gersh, Gersh Agency, 232 Canon Dr., Beverly Hills, CA 90210 USA (213)274-6611.
Type of Production and Credits: Th Film-Dir/Prod.
Genres: Drama-Th; Comedy-Th; Musical-Th; Action-Th.
Biography: Born 1923, Edmonton, Alberta. M.A., Psychology, University of Toronto. Served on National Board of

DGA and Board of Governors, Academy of Motion Picture Arts and Sciences. President, 2nd term, Directors Guild of America. Commander, Sursum Corda (Brussels); D.Litt., London Institute for Applied Research; Doctor Laureate, Imperial Order of Constantine, Lisbon; Flying Officer, RCAF (overseas) WWII. MECLA Award for *Making Love*; Yugoslav Film Festival Award for *Hospital*; Golden Globe Award, Oscar nomination for *Love Story*.
Selcted Filmography: *Married to It*, Th, 91, USA, Dir; *Taking Care of Business*, Th, 89, USA, Dir; *Hear No Evil, See No Evil*, Th, 88, USA, Dir; *Outrageous Fortune*, Th, 86, USA, Dir; *Teachers*, Th, 84, USA, Dir; *Author! Author!*, Th, 82, US, Dir; *Making Love*, Th, 81, USA, Dir; *The In-Laws/ Don't Shoot the Dentist*, Th, 79, USA, Dir; *Silver Streak*, Th, 76, USA, Dir; *Man in the Glass Booth*, Th, 75, USA, Dir; *Man of La Mancha*, Th, 72, I, Dir/Prod; *Hospital*, Th, 71, USA, Dir; *Plaza Suite*, Th, 70, USA, Dir; *Love Story*, Th, 70, USA, Dir, (DGA); *The Out of Towners*, Th, 70, USA, Dir; *The Americanization of Emily*, Th, 64, USA, Dir; "Route 66" (many eps), TV, 60-64, USA, Dir; "The Naked City" (sev eps), TV, 55-62, USA, Dir.

HOEDEMAN, Co
SGCT. 2183 Old Orchard, Montréal, PQ H4A 3A7 (514)484-7045. ONF, (514)283-9292.
Types de production et générique: c métrage-Réal/An; TV film-Réal/An.
Types d'oeuvres: Animation-C; Education-C; Enfants-C; Expérimental-C.
Curriculum vitae: Né en 1940, Amsterdam, Pays-Bas; au Canada depuis 65; immigrant reçu. Education: général, photographie, beaux-arts et surtout autodidacte. Dix ans d'expérience dans l'industrie du cinéma aux Pays-Bas comme assistant à la caméra et film d'animation; à l'ONF depuis 65 comme animateur et réalisateur de films d'animation; spécialisé en animation en volume (puppet films). Membre du conseil de ASIFA Canada et Président pendant 4 ans. Ses films ont reçu 57 prix internationaux.
Filmographie sélective: *La Boîte/The Box*, C, 89, CDN, Conc sc/Réal an; *Charles et François*, C, 87, CDN, Réal; *Mascarade*, C, 80-84, CDN, Réal/An/Sc; *Le Trésor des Grotocéans*, C, 77-80, CDN, Réal/An/Sc; *Co Hoedeman Animateur*, TV, 79-80, CDN, An; *Le Château de sable*, C, 75-77, CDN, Réal/An/Sc; *L'Homme et le géant*, C, 74-75, CDN, Réal/An; *Lumaaq*, C, 75, CDN, Réal/An; *Tchou-Tchou*, C, 71-72, CDN, Réal/Co an/Sc; *Le Hibou et le corbeau*, C, 72, CDN, Réal/An; *Matrioska*, C, 69-70, CDN, Réal/An; *Le Hibou et le lemming*, C, 70, CDN, Réal/An; *Oddball*, C, 68-69, CDN, Réal/An/Sc; *La Dérive des continents/Continental Drift*, ED, 67-68, CDN, Réal/An.

HOFFMAN, Philip
CAMERA, CSC. 76 Stafford St., Flr. 2, Toronto, ON (416)845-9430. Canadian Filmmakers Dist. Centre, (416)593-1808.
Type of Production and Credits: Th Short-Dir; Th Short-DOP.
Genres: Drama-Th; Experimental-Th; Music Video-TV.
Biography: Born in Kitchener, Ontario. B.A., English Literature, Wilfrid Laurier University; Diploma, Film, Sheridan College. Works as film teacher at Sheridan. Has won a number of American film festival awards (Athens and Ann Arbor), a Genie nomination, 87, and invitations/retrospectives at international film festivals (Sydney, Australia; Salso, Italy; Osnabruck, Germany; Rotterdam, Holland).
Selected Filmography: *Kitchener-Berlin*, Th, 90, CDN, Dir/DOP; *river*, Th, 89, CDN, Dir/DOP; *passing through/torn formations*, Th, 88, CDN, Dir/DOP, ?*O, Zoo! (The Making of a Fiction Film)*, Th, 86, CDN, Dir/DOP; *Sexual Intelligence*, MV, 85, CDN, DOP; *Somewhere Between Jalostotitlan and Encarnacion*, Th, 84, CDN, Dir/DOP; *On Land, Over Water*, Th, 84, CDN, DOP; *The Road Ended at the Beach*, Th, 82, CDN, Dir/DOP; *Krieghoff*, Th, 81, CDN, DOP; *Megan Carey*, Th, 79, CDN, DOP; *On the Pond*, Th, 78, CDN, Dir/DOP.

HOLENDER, Jacques
- see PRODUCERS

HOPE, Kathryn Ruth
- see PRODUCERS

HORNE, Jerry
- see PRODUCERS

HORNE, Tina ◊
(514)598-8095.
Type of Production and Credits: TV Film-Dir/Prod/Wr.
Genres: Documentary-TV; Educational-TV; Children's-TV; Industrial-TV.
Biography: Born 1947, London, England. Languages: English, French, German, Spanish. B.A., Communication Studies, Concordia University. Co-founder, 84, Les Nouvelles Cinéastes Montréal Inc., specializing in documentaries and dramas of particular interest to women; co-founder, 76, Aquilon Film Inc., producing educational and industrial films. Winner

of several awards, including CFTA, Houston, Columbus.
Selected Filmography: *Betty Goodwin*, TV, 88, CDN, Dir/Prod; *Cole Palen's Flying Circus*, TV, 87, CDN, Prod; *Speaking of Nairobi*, TV, 85-87, CDN, Dir/Wr; "Counselling the Sexual Abuse Survivor" (3 eps), ED, 84-85, CDN, Co-Dir; *Sylvie's Story*, ED, 83-85, CDN, Dir/Co-Prod/Wr; *A Safe Distance*, ED, 83-85, CDN, Dir/Co-Prod/Wr; *Moving On*, ED, 83-85, CDN, Dir/Prod/Co-Prod; *Si jamais tu pars*, ED, 83-85, CDN, Dir/Co-Prod/Wr; *J'osais pas rien dire*, ED, 83-85, CDN, Dir/Co-Prod/Wr; *Fallait que ça change*, ED, 83-85, CDN, Dir/Co-Prod/Wr; *In Good Company*, In, 82, CDN, Prod/Co-Wr; *Stop Bird Strikes!*, ED, 81, CDN, Dir/Wr; *Spirit of the Land*, ED, 79, CDN, Dir/Co-Wr.

HOUDE, Jean-Claude ◇
(418)681-2588.
Types de production et générique: TV vidéo-Réal.
Types d'oeuvres: Education-TV; Sports-TV.
Curriculum vitae: Né en 1930. Plus de trente ans de télévision, la plupart comme réalisateur.
Filmographie sélective: "Jour du Seigneur" (20 eps), TV, 87-88, CDN, Réal; "Génies en herbe", TV, 86-88, CDN, Réal; *Jeux Canada/Sydney*, TV, 87, CDN, Réal; "Pures Laine" (13 eps), TV, 86, CDN, Prod; *Cup du monde mont St-Anne*, "Univers des sports", TV, 84, CDN, Réal; *Grands Voiliers, Transit Québec/St-Malo*, TV, 84, CDN, Réal; *Jeux du Canada*, TV, 83, CDN, Réal; *Jeux du Québec* (réal 6 ans/coord pro 2 ans), TV, 73-83, CDN, Réal/Coord pro; "En mouvement" (quot), TV, 74-81, CDN, Réal; "Défilé du nuit, Carnaval de Québec (4 seg), TV, 65-80, CDN, Réal; "Les Héros du samedi" (8 seg), TV, 74-79, CDN, Réal; "Sport détente" (150 eps), TV, 73-77, CDN, Réal; "Jeux olympiques Montréal 1976", TV, 76, CDN, Réal; *Tennis Coupe Davis*, TV, 74, CND, Réal; "La Bohème" (2 eps), TV, 69-70, CDN, Réal.

HOWARD, Christopher
- see PRODUCERS
HUCULAK, William
- see EDITORS
HUG-VALERIOTE, Joan F.
- see WRITERS
HUNT, Bill
- see PRODUCERS
HUNT, Graham
DGC. 1967 Barcley St., #902, Vancouver, BC V6G 1L1 (604)685-2120.
Type of Production and Credits: TV Film-Dir; TV Video-Dir.
Genres: Children's-TV; Commercials-TV; Music Video-TV.
Biography: Born 1942, England; British and Canadian citizenship. B.A.A., Ryerson Polytechnic Institute; B.F.A., Communications. Director, producer, writer of many TV commercials, Canada, Australia; won numerous awards including NY Art Directors' Club, Bessies and Clios.

HUNTER, John
- see WRITERS
HUTTON, Douglas
- see PRODUCERS
HYDE, Steve
- see WRITERS
IANZELO, Tony ◇
(514)737-4357.
Type of Production and Credits: Th Short-Dir/Cam; TV Film-Dir/Cam.
Genres: Drama-Th&TV; Action-Th&TV; Documentary-Th&TV; Educational-Th&TV.
Biography: Born 1935, Toronto, Ontario. B.A.A., Radio and TV Arts, Ryerson Polytechnic Institute, 58. Member of Royal Canadian Academy; numerous awards at international film festivals including Yorkton, Berlin, Brussels, Columbus, San Francisco and Oscar nominations for *Blackwood* and *High Grass Circus*.
Selected Filmography: *Emergency*, Th, 88, CND, Co-Dir; *Give Me Your Answer True*, TV, 86, CDN, Dir/Co-Dir; *Transition*, Th, 86, CDN, Co-Dir; *Making Transitions*, TV, 86, CDN, Dir/Cam; *From Ashes to Forest*, "Parks Centennial", TV, 85, CDN, Dir/Cam; *Singing: A Joy in Any Language*, TV, 82, CDN, Co-Dir/Cam; *The Concert Man*, TV, 82, CDN, Dir/Cam/Ed; *China: A Land Transformed/North China Factory/North China Commune*, TV, 79-80, CDN, Co-Dir/Cam; *Viking Visitors to North America*, ED, 79, CDN, Co-Dir/Cam; *The Mighty Steam Calliope*, TV, 78, CDN, Dir/Cam; *High Grass Circus*, TV, 78, CDN/GB, Co-Dir/Cam; *Hunters of Mistassini*, TV, 74, CDN, Co-Dir/Cam, (CFA); *Don't Knock the Ox*, Th, 70, CDN, Dir/Cam; *The Best Damn Fiddler from Calabogie to Kaladar*, TV, 69, CDN, CAm, (CFA).

IRISH, William A.
RR #1, Thomasburg, ON K0K 3H0. Circle Productions, 174 Bedford Rd., Toronto, ON M5R 2K9 (416)922-9900.
Type of Production and Credits: TV Film-Dir.
Genres: Commercials-TV.

Biography: Born in Calgary, Alberta. Studied at Alberta Art College. Worked in advertising 67-75; one of original 7 founders of The Partners Film Company; has directed more than 2,500 commercials and has won numerous awards, including Cannes, San Francisco, Bessies; winner of Fritz Spiess Award for contributions to the industry.

ISACSSON, Magnus
CIFC. 5827 Jeanne Mance, #4, Montreal, PQ H2V 4K9 (514)276-9460.
Type of Production and Credits: Th Short-Dir; TV Film-Dir; TV Video-Dir.
Genres: Documentary-Th&TV; Educational-Th&TV; Current Affairs-Th&TV; Training Videos-Th&TV.
Biography: Born in 1948 in Sweden. Canadian citizen. Languages: English and French; working knowledge of Spanish. Independent filmmaker since 1986. Works for CBC, Radio-Canada, Radio-Québec, NFB as well as independent production companies, in particular, Alter-Ciné Inc. Directed NFB film *Uranium*, which won the Golden Sheaf award for Best Documentary over 30 Minutes at the Yorkton Festival, 1991. Specialties: environmental and social issues, Third World, human rights, development. TV producer for English and French networks of the CBC, 80-86; radio producer, 73-80.
Selected Filmography: *The Horn of Misery*, "the fifth estate", TV, 91, CDN, Field Prod; *Kanada 2000*, TV, 90, CDN, Co-Dir; *Les Attikameks* (pilot), TV, 90, CDN, Dir; *Uranium*, Th/TV, 90, CDN, Dir/ Res; *Tovio: Child of Hope*, Th, 90, CDN, Dir; *Portable Video Production*, ED, 89, CDN, Dir; *Les Jeunes Immigres*, TV, 88, CDN, Dir; *Prison Riots*, "Contrechamp", TV, 87, CDN, Dir; *Food Waste*, "Contrechamp", TV, 87, CDN, Dir.

IVESON, Rob
- see PRODUCERS

IZZARD, Dan ◇
Type of Production and Credits: TV Film-Dir/DOP.
Genres: Documentary-Th&TV; Commercials-TV; Industrial-TV.
Biography: Born 1949, Ireland; Canadian citizenship. Languages: English, French, Spanish. 7 years as grip and scenic painter; 4 as AD and production manager on feature films; 12 years with TDF Films, Toronto; 10 years with IATSE; has directed more than 300 commercials.
Selected Filmography: *Izzard: Master Impressionist*, TV, 84, CDN, Dir/DOP.

JACKSON, Doug ◇
(514)937-6870.
Type of Production and Credits: Th Film-Dir/Wr; Th Short-Dir/Wr; TV Film-Dir/Prod/Wr.
Genres: Drama-Th&TV; Comedy-Th&TV; Action-Th&TV; Documentary-Th&TV.
Biography: Born 1940, Montreal, Quebec. Languages: English and French. B.A., Sir George Williams (Concordia) University. Has lectured in film at American Film Institute, University of Oregon, McGill. Semi-pro baseball pitcher and football quarterback. Oscar nomination and numerous awards including Berlin and London Film Festival for *Blake*.
Selected Filmography: "Vulcan" (pilot), TV, CDN, Dir; *Extra Innings*, "The Twilight Zone" (1 eps)(premiere), TV, 88, CDN/USA, Dir; *Banshee*, "Ray Bradbury Theatre", TV, 86, CDN, Dir; *Uncle T/ Bambinger*, "Bell Canada Playhouse", TV, 84-85, CDN, Dir; *The Front Line*, "For the Record", TV, 84, CDN, Dir; *Empire Inc.*, (eps 1,3,4), TV, 82-83, CDN, Dir; *The Art of Eating*, Th, 81, CDN, Dir; *Why Men Rape*, TV, 79-80, CDN, Dir/Prod/ Wr; *The Heatwave Lasted Four Days*, TV, 74, CDN, Wr/Dir/Prod; *The Sloane Affair*, TV, 73, CDN, Dir/Co-Wr/Prod, (3 CFA); *The Huntsman*, Th, 72, CDN, Dir/Prod/ Wr; *La Gastronomie*, "Adieu Alouette", TV, 72, CDN, Wr/Dir; *Norman Jewison, Filmmaker*, TV, 71, CDN, Dir/Wr/Prod; *Danny and Nicky*, TV, 69-70, CDN, Dir/Wr/Prod; *Blake*, Th, 69, CDN, Prod, (CFA).

JACKSON, G. Philip
Lightscape Motion Picture Co. Ltd., Suite 216, Cine Village, 65 Heward Ave., Toronto, ON M4M 2T5 (416) 462-9741.
Type of Production and Credits: Th Film-Dir/Prod; TV Film-Dir/Prod; TV Video-Dir/Prod.
Genres: Drama-Th&TV; Documentary-TV; Educational-TV; Science Fiction-Th&TV;.
Biography: Born 1954. Honours B.A., Film, York University. Film editor, Radio-Canada/CBC, 4 years. *The Music of the Spheres* won Most Promising Feature, Atlantic Film Festival.
Selected Filmography: *Strange Horizons*, Th, 90-91, CDN, Dir/Prod/Wr; *Fateful Balance*, Th, 90-91, CDN, Dir/Prod; *The Reluctant Detectives*, "Splitz" (pilot), TV, 91, CDN, Prod/Co-Dir; *Hero Weather*, Th, 88, CDN, Prod/Dir; *Smoke Signals*, Th, 88, CDN, Prod/Dir; *Platinum*, Th, 86, CDN, Assoc Prod; *Pedestals*, TV, 85, CDN, Dir/Co-Prod/Ed; *Reflective*, TV,

85, CDN, Co-Dir/Co-Prod; *Rail Yard*, TV, 85, CDN, Dir/Co-Prod/Ed; *Shifting*, TV, 85, CDN, Co-Prod/Ed; *Colette*, TV, 85, CDN, Co-Prod/Cam; *Travelling Shot*, TV, 85, CDN, Dir/Prod/Ed; *The Music of the Spheres*, Th, 82, CDN, Prod/Dir/Co-Wr; *Circle of Recrimination*, ED, 80, CDN, Prod/Ed; *Rites of Passage*, TV, 80, CDN, Dir/Prod/Ed; *The Sorcerer's Eye*, TV, 80, CDN, Dir/Prod/Ed.

JACOBOVICI, Simcha
Associated Producers, 957 Broadview Ave., Unit A, Toronto, ON M4K 2R5 (416)422-1270.
Type of Production and Credits: Th Film-Dir/Prod/Wr; TV Film-Dir/Prod/Wr; TV Video-Dir/Prod/Wr.
Genres: Documentary-Th&TV; Current Affairs-Th&TV; Educational-Th&TV; Commercials-Th&TV.
Biography: Born in 1953 in Israel. Canadian citizen. Political analyst, writer and award-winning film producer. *Burden on the Land* won a Silver Medal, Houston International Film Festival, 1990; a Red Ribbon award at the American Film Festival and the Silver Screen award, U.S. Film & Video Festival. *AIDS in Africa* won the Gold Award at the John Muir Medical Film Festival; the Gold Hugo at Intercom 90; the Silver Hugo, Chicago International Film Festival; a Silver Medal at the International Film & Television Festival of New York and a Bronze Plaque at the Columbus International Film Festival. *Meeting the Challenge* awarded the Certificate for Creative Excellence, U.S. Film & Video Festival. *Hemophilia: In Perspective* won the Silver Medal, 1989 International Film & Television Festival of New York. *A Question of Time* awarded 1988 First Place Chris award, Columbus. *Falasha: Exile of the Black Jews* awarded Best Film, Hemisfilm; Certificate of Special Merit, Academy of Motion Picture Arts and Sciences; Red Ribbon, American Film Festival.
Selected Filmography: *Deadly Currents*, Th/TV, 91, CDN, Dir/Prod; *Burden on the Land*, TV, 90, CDN, Prod; *AIDS in Africa*, TV, 90, CDN, Prod; *Meeting the Challenge*, TV, 89, CDN, Prod; *Hemophilia: In Perspective*, ED, 89, CDN, Dir/Wr/Prod; *Canadian Red Cross Corporate Video*, ED, 88, CDN, Dir/Wr/Prod; *A Question of Time*, Cm/Th, 88, CDN, Dir/Wr/Prod; *Unfinished Exodus: Anatomy of an Airlift*, TV, 86, CDN, Dir/Wr/Prod; *Wings of Eagles*, TV, 86, CDN, Dir/Wr/Prod; *Journey's End: The Forgotten Refugees*, TV, 85, CDN, Dir/Wr/Prod; *Revolution and the Cross*, TV, 84, CDN, Dir/Wr/Prod; *Falasha: Agony of the Black Jews*, TV, 83, CDN, Wr/Prod; *Falasha: Exile of the Black Jews*, Th, 83, CDN, Dir/Wr/Prod.

JACQUES, Alain
ACCT. 1600, av. DeLorimier, Montréal, PQ H2K 3W5. Télé-Concept Montréal inc., 1600, av. DeLorimier, Montréal, PQ H2K 3W5 (514)521-3905.
Types de production et générique: TV vidéo-Réal.
Types d'oeuvres: Drame-TV; Comédie-TV; Annonces-TV; Industriel-TV.
Curriculum vitae: Né en 1959, Trois-Rivières, Québec. Baccalauréat en Communications (Spécialisation en TV), Université d'Ottawa, 85. Préposé aux opérations techniques, ensuite réalisateur, CKTM-TV, Trois-Rivières, 80-84; fonde Télé-Concept Montréal inc., 86; réalise et conçoit des vidéos corporatifs, commerciaux et dramatiques. Membre de l'Association Québécois des Réalisateurs et Réalisatrices de Cinéma et de Télévision depuis 90.
Filmographie sélective: *Les premières relations sexuelles* (titre travail), ED, 91, CDN, Réal; *L'éducation populaire autonome*, ED, 91, CDN, Réal/Sc; *Un défi au coeur du monde*, ED, 91, CDN, Réal; *Un été chaud sur l'A-40*, In, 90, CDN, Réal; *La maison au poils*, Cm, 90, CDN, Réal; *Condamné à mieux travailler*, In, 90, CDN, Réal; *Le monde des sens* (eps I&II), TV, 90, CDN, Réal; *Rafales, document de ventes*, Cm, 90, CDN, Réal; *Spécial amitié*, ED, 90, CDN, Réal; *Faire du chemin sans trop déranger*, In, 89, CDN, Réal; *Les déchets dangereux, un enjeu collectif*, ED, 89, CDN, Réal; *Montréal: ville cyclable d'Amérique*, Cm, 89, CDN, Réal; *Le Tour de l'Ile de Montréal*, In, 88, CDN, Réal; *La Folie de l'été Métro*, Cm, 88, CDN, Réal; *Vidéo Cube*, Cm, 88, CDN, Réal.

JARROTT, Charles
DGA, ACTT. c/o Jess Morgan & Co. Inc., 5750 Wilshire Blvd., Suite 590, Los Angeles, CA 90036 USA (213)937-1552. Tom Chasin & Associates, 190 N. Canon, Suite 210, Beverly Hills, CA 90210 USA (213)278-7505.
Type of Production and Credits: Th Film-Dir; TV Film-Dir; TV Video-Dir.
Genres: Drama-Th&TV; Comedy-Th&TV; Musical-Th&TV; Action-Th&TV.
Biography: Born 1927, London, England; Canadian citizenship; US resident. Originally an actor, commenced directing for CBC, Toronto in 57; worked at ABC-

TV and BBC-TV in the 60s. Won BAFTA Best Director Award, 62; won Prix Italia First Prize; feature films have received 14 Academy Award nominations and 8 Golden Globe nominations. Won Best Director-Motion Picture, Golden Globe, 70; Golden Globe, Best mini-series, *Poor Little Rich Girl*.
Selected Filmography: *Yes, Virginia, There is a Santa Claus*, TV, 91, USA, Dir; *Changes*, TV, 91, USA, Dir; *Lucy and Desi: Before the Laughter*, TV, 90, USA, Dir; *Till We Meet Again*, TV, 89, USA, Dir; *Night of the Fox*, TV, 89, USA, Dir; *The Woman He Loved*, TV, 88, USA, Dir; *Poor Little Rich Girl*, TV, 88, USA, Dir; *The Amateur*, Th, 81, USA, Dir; *The Other Side of Midnight*, Th, 77, USA, Dir; *The Dove*, Th, 73, USA/GB, Dir; *Mary, Queen of Scots*, Th, 71, USA, Dir; *Anne of a Thousand Days*, Th, 69, USA, Dir.

JAVAUX, Pierre
332, rue Laurier, Sherbrooke, PQ J1H 4Z5 (819)563-3292. Les Productions Kébel, 1612 ouest, rue King, Sherbrooke, PQ J1J 2C3 (819)822-4131.
Types de production et générique: TV vidéo-Réal/Sc.
Types d'oeuvres: Comédie-TV; Annonces-TV; Documentaire-TV; Education-TV.
Curriculum vitae: Né en 1947, Ampsin, Belgique; citoyenneté canadienne. Dix huit ans d'expérience en réalisation TV et communications.
Filmographie sélective: "Médicine apprivoisée" (7 eps), TV, 90-91, CDN, Réal/Sc; *Quarte à jouer*, MV, 90, CDN, Réal; *Des mots pour chanter*, MV, 89, CDN, Réal; CKSH-TV, CFKS-TV (200 cm), Cm, 88-89, CDN, Réal; "Vidéotour" (12 eps), TV, 87-88, CDN, Réal; "L'Estrie évidemment" (26 eps), TV, 86, CDN, Réal; "Sur la scène" (4 eps), TV, 86, CDN, Réal; "Reflets d'un pays" (8 eps), TV, 84-85, CDN, Réal; "Des gens que je connais" (5 eps), TV, 84, CDN, Réal; "Les Ateliers" (5 eps), TV, 84, CDN, Réal; *Le Nez dans le courant*, TV, 84, CDN, Réal; *L'Etonnoir du néant*, TV, 82, CND, Réal; "Les Immigrés" (3 eps), ED, 80, B, Réal; "La Santé" (3 eps), ED, 79, B, Réal; "La troisième âge" (2 eps), ED, 78, B, Réal.

JAY, Paul
ACCT. High Road Productions, 52R Badgerow Ave., Toronto, ON M4M 1V4 (416)461-3089.
Type of Production and Credits: TV Film-Dir/Prod/Wr/Ed.
Genres: Documentary-Th&TV; Sports-Th&TV; Educational-Th&TV.
Biography: Born 1951, Toronto, Ontario. Has worked in the Canadian film industry since 79. Films have appeared internationally including CBC, Global, TVOntario, Discovery Channel (USA), London Weekend (UK), Thames Television (UK), Central Television (UK), Disney Channel (USA), Swiss TV and others. Awards include the Chicago International Film Festival for *Here's to the Cowboy*, and Best Educational Film of 1987, TV Movie Awards (US) for *The Birth of Language*. Has recently completed *Albanian Journey: End of an Era* in association with CBC, TVOntario, Manitoba Broadcasting Network, CKVR, Access (Alberta), Knowledge Network, Telefilm Canada, and Ontario Film Development Corp. Executive producer for *The Famine Within* in association with Kandor Productions, N.F.B., TVOntario, Telefilm Canada and the OFDC. Executive producer, *Modern Slavery*, now in development. Past Chairman, Canadian Independent Film Caucus.
Selected Filmography: *Little League Baseball Canada*, Best Western/American Express, Cm, 91, CDN, Dir/Wr; *Albanian Journey: End of An Era*, TV, 91, CD, Exec Prod/Dir/Wr; *Albanian Journey*, TV, 90, CDN, Dir/Wr; *Arctic Red in Midnight Sun*, TV, 87, CDN, Dir/Wr; *The Birth of Language*, ED, 86, CDN, Wr/Dir/Prod/Ed; *Do It Or Die!*, TV, 83, CDN, Wr/Dir/Prod/Ed; *Olympic Portraits*, TV, 84, CDN, Wr/Dir/Prod/Ed; *Schooner II*, TV, 84, CDN, Wr/Dir/Prod/Ed; *Here's to the Cowboy*, TV, 83, CDN, Wr/Prod/Dir/Ed; *Squamish Days*, TV, 83, CDN, Wr/Prod/Dir/Ed; *The Smoky River*, TV, 82, CDN, Wr/Prod/Dir/Ed; *Supercross Spectacular*, TV, 81, CDN, Prod/Wr/Dir/Ed; *Baggots Difference*, In, 80, CDN, Dir/Wr; *Horton*, Th, 69, CDN, Dir/Wr.

JEAN, Jacques
193 de l'Epée, Outremont, PQ H2V 3T1 (514)270-3275. 8255 Mountain Sight, #506, Montreal, PQ H4P 2B5 (514)739-1642.
Type of Production and Credits: Th Film-Ed; Th Short-Dir; TV Film-Ed; TV Video-Dir/Prod.
Genres: Drama-Th&TV; Action-Th; Documentary-TV; Commercials-Th&TV.
Biography: Born 1948, Amqui, Québec. Languages: French and English. Classical Studies. Film Editor, 69-75; TV Director, 75-83; film and documentaries Producer/Director, 83-91.
Selected Filmography: *Whispers*, Th, 90, USA/CDN, Ed; *Snake II*, Th, 89, CDN,

Ed; *100 Ans Vincent*, TV, 89, CDN, Prod; *SnakeEaster*, Th, 88, CDN, P Pro Spv; *Les Yeux fermés*, 88, CDN, Prod; *Making It Safe*, 87, CDN, Assoc Prod; *State Park*, Th, 86, CDN, P Pro Spv; *Scoop*, Th, CDN/F, Assoc Prod; *Junior*, Th, 84, CDN, Ed; "Le Crime d'Ovide Plouffe" (2 eps), TV, 83, CDN/F, Ed; "Le Téléjournal" (quot), TV, 79-83, CDN, Dir; *Un mariage royal*, TV, 83, CDN, Dir; "Ce Soir" (quot), TV, 77-78, CDN, Ed; *Construction du Complexe Olympique*, Th, 76, CDN, Dir; *Ballad of Eskimo Nell* (seg Can), Th, 75, CDN/AUS, Dir.

JEWISON, Norman
OC. DGC, DGA, ACCT. Yorktown Productions Ltd., 18 Gloucester St., Toronto, ON M4Y 1L5 (416)923-2787. Sam Cohn, ICM (212)556-6810.
Type of Production and Credits: Th Film-Dir/Prod.
Genres: Drama-Th; Comedy-Th.
Biography: Born 1926, Toronto, Ontario. B.A., University of Toronto. Directed at BBC, 50-52; CBC, 52-58; CBS, 58-61; Universal Studios, 61-64. Named Officer, Order of Canada, 82. Over 30 Oscar nominations for films he has directed; Emmy Award for *Tonight with Harry Belafonte*; DGA nominations and a Golden Globe Award for *The Russians Are Coming, the Russians Are Coming*. Oscar nomination for Best Director, *Moonstruck*, 88.
Selected Filmography: *In Country*, Th, 89, USA, Prod/Dir; *The January Man*, Th, 88, USA, Prod; *Moonstruck*, Th, 87, USA, Dir/Prod; *Agnes of God*, Th, 85, CDN, Dir/Prod; *A Soldier's Story*, Th, 84, USA, Dir/Prod; *Iceman*, Th, 83, USA, Exec Prod; *Best Friends*, Th, 82, USA, Dir/Prod; *Academy Awards Show*, TV, 81, USA, Prod; *The Dogs of War*, Th, 80, USA, Exec Prod; *...And Justice for All*, Th, 79, USA, Dir/Prod; *F.I.S.T.*, Th, 77, USA, Dir/Prod; *Rollerball*, Th, 74, USA, Dir/Prod; *Billy Two Hats*, Th, 73, USA, Prod; *Jesus Christ Superstar*, Th, 72, USA, Dir/Prod; *Fiddler on the Roof*, Th, 70, USA, Dir/Prod; *In the Heat of the Night*, Th, 67, USA, Dir/Prod, (OSCAR).

JOHNSON, Andrew
- see PRODUCERS

JOHNSON, John A. ✧
ACFTP. (416)923-1345.
Type of Production and Credits: TV Film-Prod/Dir; TV Video-Prod/Dir/Wr.
Genres: Variety-TV; Musical-TV; Documentary-TV.
Biography: Born 1937, London, England; Canadian citizenship. Languages: English and working knowledge of French. Diploma, Capitol Institute of Technology, Washington, D.C. TV producer, director, writer since 60: telethons, superspecials, specials, daily series; CTV/CFTO-TV and CBC-TV, live-to-air, live-to-tape, segment shooting, EFP Multi-Cam(8) pre and post-production, studio/mobile, on and off-line editing, digital FX equipment. Production formats include fully--rehearsed ad lib, special events coverage; credits for over 3,000 shows.
Selected Filmography: "Video Hits" (1,000+ eps), TV, 84-88, CDN, Dir; "Coming Attractions" (120 eps), TV, 82-84, CDN, Prod/Dir; "Country in My Soul" (15 eps), TV, 82-83, CDN, Dir; "McLean at Large" (350 eps), TV, 80-82, CDN, Prod/Dir; *Carlton Show Band Special*, "McLean Series" (2 eps), TV, 82, CDN, Prod/Dir; *ACTRA Awards*, "Bob McLean Show" (2 eps), TV, 78-82, CDN, Prod/Dir; *Fraggle Rock*, "Bob McLean Show" TV, 78-82, CDN, Prod/Dir; *Juno Awards*, "Bob McLean Show" (2 eps), TV, 78-82, CDN, Prod/Dir; *Pacific Song Festival*, "Bob McLean Show", TV, 78-82, CDN, Prod/Dir; *Anne Murray in Jamaica*, "Bob McLean Show" (2 eps), TV, 78-82, CDN, Prod/Dir; *Magic on Ice*, TV, 81, CDN, Prod/Dir; *Bob McLean Show*, "Bob McLean Show", TV, 77-80, CDN, Prod/Dir; *Super Specials*, TV, 80, CDN, Prod/Dir; "Video Album", (12 eps), TV, 80, CDN, Dir' "Bob McLean Show" (350 eps), TV, 77-80, CDN, Prod/Dir.

JOHNSON, Richard
- see PRODUCERS

JOHNSTON, William
- see PRODUCERS

JUBENVILL, Ken
DGC, ACCT. 233 Roche Point Dr., North Vancouver, BC V7G 2G4 (604)929-3817. Allscreen Productions Ltd., #304-990 Homer St., Vancouver, BC V6B 2W7 (604)669-3543.
Type of Production and Credits: Th Short-Dir/Prod; TV Film-Dir/Prod.
Genres: Drama-TV; Documentary-TV; Commercials-TV; Industrial-TV.
Biography: Born 1937, Dauphin, Manitoba. Diploma, Commerce and Business Administration, University of British Columbia; spent 10 years studying music and art. Entered the film industry in Winnipeg, 56; worked in Austria for 4 years as a director and editor. Won US International Film Festival's Gold Camera Award 4 consecutive years for Best Documentary; winner of Gold Camera and Houston Special Jury Award for Theatre Short and One Hr Documentary;

One Boy, One Wolf, One Summer was nominated for 3 Gemini awards.
Selected Filmography: *Come Fly With Us/Snowbirds*, Th, 90, CDN, Dir; *Canada's Magnificent Snowbirds*, TV, 90, CDN, Dir; "Bordertown" (5 eps), TV, 90, CDN, Dir; "The Black Stallion" (2 eps), TV, 90, CDN, Dir; "Danger Bay" (18 eps), TV, 86-89, CDN, Dir; "Airwolf II" (8 eps), TV, 86-87, CDN/USA, Dir; "Seahunt" (4 eps), TV, 87, CDN/USA, Dir; *This Wouldn't Happen in Sarabar*, "Family Pictures", TV, 89, CDN, Prod/Dir; *One Boy, One Wolf, One Summer*, "Family Pictures", TV, 88, CDN, Prod/Dir; *B.C. at Expo 85*, Th, 85, CDN, Prod/Dir.

JUDGE, Maureen
WGC (ACTRA), DGC, LIFT. 1472 King St. W., #2, Toronto, ON M6K 1J1 (416)534-5077.
Type of Production and Credits: TV Film-Dir/Wr/Ed.
Genres: Drama-TV; Comedy-TV; Music Video-TV.
Biography: Independent Toronto writer/editor. M.A., Cinema Studies, New York University. Has co-written, directed and edited several comedic films with partner Martin Waxman, including *Family Business*, 84 and *A Venerable Occasion*, 86; both were broadcast on CBC TV and screened at numerous festivals. Directed and edited *Altered Ego*, her most recent film, an hour-long featurette, co-written with Martin Waxman; aired on CBC in prime time, 91. Has also directed films for the NFB, produced and contributed items to CBC radio, was a founding member of *cineAction!* film magazine. Former chair of the Board of Directors of the Liaison of Independent Filmmakers of Toronto (LIFT). Currently developing several film and TV projects for her production company, Makin' Movies Inc.
Selected Filmography: *Altered Ego*, TV, 90, CDN, Co-Wr/Dir/Ed; *Unnatural Causes*, MV, 90, CDN, Dir/Ed; *A Venerable Occasion*, TV, 86, CDN, Co-Wr/Dir/Ed; *Family Business*, TV, 84, CDN, Co-Wr/Dir/Ed.

KABELIK, Vladimir
- see PRODUCERS

KACZENDER, George ◆
DGC, DGA, AMPAS. (213)203-0710.
Type of Production and Credits: Th Film-Dir/Prod/Wr/Ed; Th Short-Dir/Prod/Wr/Ed; TV Film-Dir.
Genres: Drama-Th; Action-TV; Documentary-Th; Educational-TV.
Biography: Born 1933. Worked on 75 films at the NFB. *Don't Let the Angels Fall* won Best Foreign Feature Film, Ceylon and was official Canadian entry, Cannes, 69; Chris Award, Columbus, Silver Bear, Berlin for *Nahanni*; *U-Turn* was also entered Berlin, 73.
Selected Filmography: "Night Heat" (7 eps), TV, 85-88, CDN, Dir; "Falcon Crest" (2 eps), TV, 87, USA, Dir; *Chanel solitaire*, Th, 81, USA, Dir; *Your Ticket is No Longer Valid*, Th, 80, CDN, Dir; *Agency*, Th, 79, CDN, Dir; *In Praise of Older Women*, Th, 77, CDN, Dir/Ed; *U-Turn*, Th, 72, CDN, Dir; *Freud: The Hidden Nature of Man*, ED, 70, CDN, Dir; *Sabre and Foil*, Th, 60, CDN, Dir; *Don't Let the Angels Fall*, Th, 68, CDN, Dir/Wr; *You're No Good*, Th, 67, CDN, Dir/Ed; *The World of Three*, Th, 67, CDN, Dir; *The Game*, Th, 67, CDN, Dir; *Little White Crimes*, Th, 67, CDN, Dir; *Phoebe*, Th, 64, CDN, Dir/Ed.

KANDALAFT, Pierre ◆
(514)733-0750.
Types de production et générique: c métrage-Réal.
Types d'oeuvres: Documentaire-C&TV; Education-C&TV; Industriel-TV.
Curriculum vitae: Né en 1941, Beyrouth, Liban; citoyenneté canadienne. Langues: français, anglais, arabe. Licencié en Sciences politiques, Faculté de Lyon, France; Brevet en Psycho-pédagogie, Université du Québec à Montréal. Caméraman TV, Liban; assistant réalisateur, Paris; fonde sa propre compagnie de production au Canada, 79.
Filmographie sélective: *Le Ski en fête/Alupco/Polyfab - maisons modulaires*, In, 83-85, CDN, Prod/Réal; *Changeons le mode d'emploi*, TV, 85, CDN, Prod/Réal; *Les Chemins de l'espoir*, TV, 85, CDN, Prod/Réal; *The Mechanical Service Shops/Budgeting/Owens Corning Int'l*, In, 82-83, CDN, Prod/Réal; *A Boy from Saudi Arabia*, TV, 83, CDN, Co sc; *Quenching the Desert's Thirst/Zamil Soule Steel Buildings*, In, 81-82, CDN, Prod/Réal; *The Zamil Group of Companies/Tools and Heavy Equipment*, In, 82, CDN, Prod/Réal; *Living in Aramco Communities/Bathing Your Baby*, In, 82, CDN, Prod/Réal; *Why Accidents Happen/Shortcuts to the End*, In, 82, CDN, Prod/Réal; *Emergency/Hazardous Chemical/ Industrial Maintenance at Aramco*, In, 82, CDN, Prod/Réal; *Saudi Training and Career Development /Information Please*, In, 82, CDN, Prod/Réal; *Amiantit/Water in the Desert/Ameron Pipes/Fiberglass*, In, 79-80, CDN, Prod/Réal; *Venture in Solid Paint/Solid Paint*

Marketing, In, 76-77, CDN, Prod/Réal; *Do It Yourself with Solid Paint*, In, 76, CDN, Prod/Reeal.

KARDASH, Virlana
- see WRITERS

KAUFMAN, David
- see PRODUCERS

KAUFMAN, James T.
DGC. J.T.K. Productions, 241 Clarke Ave., Montreal, PQ H3Z 2E3 (514)931-7463. Charles Northcote, The Core Group Talent Agency, 489 College St., Suite 501, Toronto, ON M6G 1A5 (416)944-0193. The Agency, 10351 Santa Monica Blvd., Suite 211, Los Angeles, CA 90025 USA (213)551-3000.
Type of Production and Credits: Th Film-Wr/Prod/Dir; TV Film-Dir.
Genres: Drama-Th&TV; Comedy-TV; Documentary-TV; Children's-TV.
Biography: Born 1949, Montreal, Quebec; Canadian citizenship. Languages: English, French and Spanish. BS & BA, Babson College, Babson, Massachusetts. Eastern Canada representative, DGC, 79; National First Vice-President and Eastern Canada representative, 80; currently Director and member. *Here Comes the Groom* nomin-ated for a Golden Sheaf Award at Yorkton.
Selected Filmography: *A Star for Two*, Th, 90-91, F, Wr/Dir; *Here Comes the Groom*, "Inside Stories", TV, 90, CDN, Dir; *Backstab*, Th, 89, CDN, Dir; *The Thriller*, TV, 89, CDN/F, Dir; "My Secret Identity" (4 eps), TV, 88, CDN, Dir; *Last Days of Canada*, "Danger Bay", TV, 88, CDN, Dir; *Forgiving Harry*, "Inside Stories", TV, 87, CDN, Dir; *Moonlight Flight*, "Shades of Love", TV, 87, CDN/USA, Dir; *Make Mine Chartreuse*, "Shades of Love", TV, 86, CDN/USA, Dir; *Children of a Lesser God*, Th, 85, USA, 1st AD.

KEATING, Lulu
ACCT. 2125 Brunswick St., Halifax, NS B3K 2Y4 (902)423-3880. Red Snapper Films Ltd. (902)422-2427.
Type of Production and Credits: Th Film-Wr/Dir; TV Film-Dir/Wr; TV Video-Dir.
Genres: Drama-Th&TV; Documentary-TV.
Biography: Born 1952, Antigonish, Nova Scotia. Languages: English and French. Attended St. Francis Xavier University, 69-72; Fine Arts, Vancouver School of Art, 74-76; Ryerson Polytechnical Institute, 76-77. Experience as TV host, actor; President, Atlantic Filmmakers' Co-operative, 84-86. President, Linda Joy Busby Media Arts Foundation, 90 to present.
Selected Filmography: *In Service*, TV, 90, CDN, Dir/Co-Wr; *The Midday Sun*, Th, 89, CDN, Wr/Dir; *Enterprising Women*, Th, 87, CDN, Wr/Co-Dir; *Starting Right Now*, ED, 85, CDN, Co-Wr/Dir/Co-Ed; *Rita MacNeil in Japan*, TV, 85, CDN, Dir; *City Survival*, TV, 83, CDN, Prod/Co-Wr/Dir/Ed.

KEATLEY, Philip
- see PRODUCERS

KEELAN, Matt ✧
CTPDA. (519)945-8490.
Type of Production and Credits: TV Film-Dir/Prod; TV Video-Dir/Prod.
Genres: Variety-TV; Documentary-TV; Children's-TV; Commercials-TV.
Biography: Born 1930, Windsor, Ontario. Thirty-six years experience in radio, television; 30 years as TV director, producer.
Selected Filmography: "Freedom Festival Parade and Flag Raising" (6 eps), TV, 80-85, CDN, Dir/Prod; *Very Special Person*, TV, 84, CDN, Dir/Prod; "Around Town" (52 eps), TV, 84, CDN, Dir/Prod; *This is Hollywood*, TV, 80-82, CDN, Dir/Prod; "Legal Factor" (4 eps), TV, 81, CDN, Dir/Prod; "Summer Festival" (2 eps), TV, 80, CDN, Dir/Prod; "Columbo Quotes" (1 eps), TV, 77, CDN, Dir/Prod; "Bozo the Clown", TV, 66-74, CDN, Dir/Prod; "Wrestling", TV, 68-74, CDN, Dir/Prod; *Harness Racing*, TV, 73, CDN, Dir/Prod.

KELLNER, Lynne
- see PRODUCERS

KELLY, Peter
- see PRODUCERS

KEMP, Laurie Roy ✧
SMPIA. (306)242-9097.
Genres: Documentary-TV; Educational-TV; Industrial-TV; Sports-TV.
Biography: Born 1955, Saskatoon, Saskatchewan. B.Ed., University of Saskatchewan; Diploma, Recreation Technology, Kelsey Institute. Has taken classes at University of Saskatchewan in Still Photography Production as well as Audiovisual Production.
Selected Filmography: *Rendezvous in Saskatchewan*, ED, 88, CDN, Wr/Prod; *The Expanding Universe*, ED, 88, CDN, Wr/Prod; *Exhibition Grounds Redevelopment*, In, 87, CDN, Wr/Prod; *Team Saskatchewan Baseball - 87*, ED, 87, CDN, Prod/Cam; *Wood Siding Renovations*, ED, 86, CDN, Wr/Prod.

KENDALL, Nicholas
DGC, ACCT. 3425 W. 2 Ave., Vancouver, BC V6R 1J3 (604)732-9387.

Northern Lights Entertainment, 1020 Mainland St., #100, Vancouver, BC V6B 2T4 (604)684-2888. FAX: 681-3299.
Type of Production and Credits: TV Film-Dir/Prod/DOP/Wr; TV Video-Dir/Prod/DOP/Wr.
Genres: Drama-TV; Children's-TV; Documentary-TV; Educational-TV.
Biography: Born 1949, Manchester, England; Canadian and British citizenship. Bachelor of Arts (Theatre), University of British Columbia; Diploma, London Film School. Has won numerous awards for his films, including awards at Yorkton, American Film Festival, Krakow Film Festival, the Gemini Awards, etc. and others.
Selected Filmography: *Baby Pinsky*, TV, 90, CDN, Prod/Dir; "Danger Bay" (2 eps), TV, 89, CDN, Dir; "The Beachcombers" (2 eps), TV, 89, CDN, Dir; *Paper Route*, TV, 88, CDN, Prod/Dir; *First Harvest*, TV, 88, CDN, Dir/Prod/DOP; "The Fabulous Festival" (7 eps), TV, 85, CDN, Dir; *Valleys in Transition*, TV, 84, CDN, Dir/DOP; *Rape: Face to Face*, TV, 82, CDN/USA, Co-Dir/DOP; *The Lost Pharoah: The Search for Akhenaton*, TV, 80, CDN, Dir/DOP/Co-Prod; "This Land" (3 eps), TV, 78, CDN, Dir/Prod.

KENNEDY, Michael
ACCT. 614 Sweetwater Place, Port Credit, ON L5H 3Y8 (416)278-5830. Great North Artists Management, 350 Dupont St., Toronto, ON M5R 1V9 (416)925-2051.
Type of Production and Credits: Th Film-Dir/Wr; TV Film-Dir/Wr.
Genres: Drama-Th&TV; Comedy-Th&TV; Documentary-TV; Commercials-Th&TV; Corporate-Th&TV.
Biography: Born 1954, Prince Edward Island. B.A.A., Film Production, Ryerson Polytechnical Institute, 78. Associate Professor, Film Production, York University, 80-84. Social development film/video production, New Delhi, India, 83-84. Director of short films that have won awards at festivals in NY, Chicago, Athens, Ann Arbour, Rochester, Banff and Toronto. Feature film and television director and writer since 86. *Erik* premiered at Montreal Film Festival, then distributed in 43 countries. Husband, father, snowdome collector, and President of Appealing Productions Inc.
Selected Filmography: *In Search of Alexander*, Th, 91, CDN, Dir/Wr; "The Kids in the Hall" (8 eps), TV, 91, CDN, Dir; *The Achievement of Excellence*, In, 91, CDN, Prod/Dir/Wr/Ed; *The Seeds of Hope*, In, 90, CDN, Prod/Dir/Wr; *Foster Parents Plan of Canada* (series of 24 psa's), Cm, 90, CDN, Prod/Dir/Wr; *One Man Out/Erik*, Th, 89, CDN, Dir/Wr; *Sealed With a Kiss*, "Degrassi Jr. High", TV, 87, CDN, Wr; *Caribe*, Th, 87, CDN, Dir/Wr; *The Search for Intimacy*, ED, 86, CDN, Dir/Wr; *The Pink Chiquitas*, Th, 85, CDN, PM/1st AD; *The Aging of North America*, ED, 85, CDN, Dir/Wr/Ed; *The Study of Fine Arts* (6 eps), ED, 85, CDN, Prod/Dir/Wr/Ed; *The Volunteer*, TV, 83, IND, Prod/Dir/Wr/Ed; *Surface Tension*, TV, 82, CDN, Prod/Dir/Wr/Ed; *Jim and Muggins Tour Toronto*, Th, 78, CDN, Prod/Dir/Wr/Ed.

KERRIGAN, Bill
3471 Hingston Ave., Montreal, PQ H4A 2J5 (514)486-8456.
Type of Production and Credits: TV Film-Dir; TV Video-Dir; Video-Dir.
Genres: Drama-Th&TV; Documentary-Th&TV; Children's-TV; Industrial-Th&TV.
Biography: Born 1945, Ottawa, Ontario. Languages: English and French. B.A.A., Motion Picture major, TV Production option, Ryerson Polytechnical Institute. Two years as staff cameraman for Crawley Films; 9 years as freelance director/cameraman; 3 years as freelance director; has worked on more than 600 films, videos, commercials in over 30 countries. Winner of Gold Cindy, L.A., 87; US Industrial film award, 86.
Selected Filmography: "Météo Media/Weather Now", TV, 88, CDN, Dir/Prod/Pro Coord; *Custom Calling Project*, Northern Telecom & Bell Canada, TV, 88, CDN, Dir; "Pivot III" (12 eps), Northern Telecom & Bell Canada, ED, 87, CDN, Dir; *The Gold Standard*, In, 86, CDN, Dir; *Government Travel*, Enroute, In, 86, CDN, Dir; *Shock Absorber*, Royal Bank, In, 86, CDN, Dir: "Bats" (pilot), TV, 85, CDN, Dir.

KEUSCH, Michael
2014 North Hoover St., Los Angeles, CA 90027 (213)665-8443. Barb Alexander/Media Artists Group, 6255 Sunset Blvd., Hollywood, CA 90029 USA. (213)463-5610.
Type of Production and Credits: Th Film-Dir/Wr/Ed; Th Short-Dr/Wr/Ed; TV Film-Dir/Wr/Ed.
Genres: Drama-Th&TV; Comedy-Th&TV; Action-Th&TV; Science Fiction-Th&TV; Horror-Th&TV; Commercials-TV; Music Video-TV.
Biography: Born in 1955 in Calgary,

Alberta. Raised and educated in Germany. Worked in photography and theatre before studying film at the Southern Alberta Institute of Technology (SAIT). Made two award-winning documentaries then, in 1983, *Romantic Maneuvers*, his first feature film. Studied at the American Film Institute (A.F.I.), 1983-84. Since 1985 has lived permanently in Los Angeles. Has since worked in Canada for the National Film Board and Atlantis, among others. Fluent in German.
Selected Filmography: *Lena's Holiday*, Th, 90, USA, Wr/Dir; *Night Club*, Th, 89, USA, Wr/Dir/Ed; *Hacker John*, TV, 86, CDN, Dir; *I Can Do It*, ED, 84, CDN, Prod/Dir/Ed; *Romantic Maneuvers*, TV, 83, CDN, Wr/Prod/Dir; *Pieces of Anger*, ED, 80, CDN, Prod/Dir.

KIEFER, Douglas
- see CINEMATOGRAPHERS

KING, Allan
DGC, ACCT. 965 Bay St., Suite 2209, Toronto, ON M5S 2A3 (416)964-7284. FAX: 964-7997. Ralph Zimmerman, Great North Artists Mgmt., 350 Dupont St., Toronto, ON M5R 1V9 (416)925-2051.
Type of Production and Credits: Th Film-Dir/Prod; TV Film-Dir/Prod; TV Video-Dir/Prod.
Genres: Drama-Th&TV; Comedy-Th&TV; Educational-TV; Children's-Th&TV.
Biography: Born 1930, Vancouver, BC. Honours B.A., Philosophy, UBC; joined CBC, 54; began independent production, Spain, 58; formed Allan King Associates Ltd., Toronto, London, 61. Past President, DGC; Board of Directors, CCA; Chairman of the Mengen Institute. *Who Has Seen the Wind?* won the Grand Prix, Paris Film Festival; *A Married Couple* was shown in Directors' Fortnight, Cannes; *Warrendale* won the Cannes and New York Critics' Awards; also won awards at San Francisco, Melbourne, Mannheim, Edinburgh, Leipzig, Salerno, Sydney and Vancouver Film Festivals.
Selected Filmography: "Road to Avonlea" (3 eps), TV, 90, CDN, Dir; *All The Kings' Men*, "Vonnegut Theatre", TV, 90, CDN, Dir; "Dracula, The Series" (4 eps), TV, 90, CDN, Dir; "Danger Bay" (14 eps), TV, 87-90, CDN, Dir; *Termini Station*, Th, 89, CDN, Prod/Dir; "Alfred Hitchcock Presents" (13 eps), TV, 87-88, CDN/USA, Dir; "Twilight Zone" (1 eps), TV, 87, CDN/USA, Dir; *Tucker & the Horsethief*, "Family Playhouse", TV, 84, CDN/USA, Dir; *Who's In Charge?*, TV, 83, CDN, Prod/Dir; *Ready for Slaughter*, "For the Record", TV, 83, CDN, Dir; *Silence of the North*, Th, 81, CDN, Dir; *One Night Stand*, TV/Th, 78, CDN, Prod/Dir; *Who Has Seen the Wind?*, Th, 77, CDN, Prod/Dir; *A Married Couple*, Th, 70, CDN, Prod/Dir; *Warrendale*, Th, 67, CDN, Prod/Dir.

KING, Durnford
- see WRITERS

KING, Robert
- see WRITERS

KINSEY, Nicholas
ARRFQ, STTCQ, ACCT. 970 Chemin St-Louis, Sillery, PQ G1S 1C7 (418)683-2543. Les Productions Cinégraphe inc., 970, Chemin St-Louis, Sillery, PQ G1S 1C7 (418)683-2543.
Types de production et générique: l métrage-Réal/D phot/Prod; c métrage-Réal/D phot/Prod; TV film-Réal/D phot/Prod.
Types d'oeuvres: Drame-C&TV; Comédie-C; Documentaire-C.
Curriculum vitae: Né en 1948. Langues: français et anglais. Clifton College, Bristol, Angleterre (secondaire); Université du Texas; Université de Heidelberg, Allemagne; Université de Yale; Université du Québec. Prix de l'Excellence à la Création, U.S. Industrial Film Festival, Chicago, *On regardait toujours vers la mer*. Silver Apple Award, Oakland, California, *Theatre Magic*.
Filmographie sélective: *Short Change*, C, 91, CDN, Réal/Prod/D phot; *Stowaway*, C, 89, CDN, Réal/Prod/D phot; *Theatre Magic*, TV, 87, CDN, Réal/Prod/D phot; "Video Tours" (12 eps), TV, 87, CDN, Réal/D phot; *Le Passager*, TV, 84, CDN, Réal/D phot; *We Always Looked Out to Sea*, ED, 82, CDN, Réal/D phot; *Portraits d'une ville*, TV, 80, CDN, Co réal/Prod; *L'Archipel de Mingan*, TV, 78, CDN, Réal/DOP.

KISH, Albert ✧
SGCT. (514)933-8065.
Type of Production and Credits: Th Short-Dir.
Genres: Documentary-Th; Educational-Th; Experimental-Th.
Biography: Born 1937, Eger, Hungary; Canadian citizenship, 62. Senior film editor, CBC Toronto, 64-67; senior grant, Canada Council, 73-74. *Los Canadienses* won awards at New York, Mannheim, Chicago, Los Angeles, Melbourne film festivals; *The Age of Invention* received a Blue Ribbon, New York.
Selected Filmography: *Age of the Rivers*, "Hertiage", TV, 85, CDN, Dir/Ed; *The*

Age of Invention, Th, 84, CDN, Dir/Ed/Prod; *The Scholar in Society: Northrop Frye/Rhyme and Reason: F.R. Scott*, "Canadian Writers", TV, 83-84, CDN, Ed; *Bread*, Th, 83, CDN, Dir/Ed; *The Image Makers*, Th, 80, CDN, Dir/Ed; *Paper Wheat*, TV, 79, CDN, Dir/Ed; *Hold the Ketchup*, Th, 77, CDN, Dir/Ed; *Bekevar Jubilee*, Th, 76, CDN, Dir/Ed; *Los Canadienses*, TV, 75, CDN, Dir/Ed/Wr, (BFA); *Our Street Was Paved with Gold*, Th, 73, CDN, Dir/Ed; *In Praise of Hands*, Th, 73, CDN, Ed; *This Is A Photograph*, Th, 71, CDN, Dir/Ed, (CFA); *Banner Film*, Th, 71, CDN, ED; *Atomic Juggernaut*, Th, 71, CDN, Prod/Ed; *Bighorn*, Th, 70, CDN, ED.

KLEIN, Bonnie ◊
(514)283-9545.
Type of Production and Credits: Th Short-Dir/Prod; TV Film-Dir/Prod; TV Video-Dir/Prod.
Genres: Documentary-Th&TV.
Biography: Born 1941, Philadelphia; US and Canadian citizenship. Languages: English and French. B.A., Barnard College; M.A., Film, Communications, Stanford University. Part of original Challenge for Change Program, NFB. Woman of the Year, Salon de la Femme, 83. Consulting director, International Youth Year Training Program, NFB, 85-86. *Dark Lullabies* won Best Documentary, Mannheim Film Festival.
Selected Filmography: *Mile Zero: The SAGE Tour*, Th, 88, CDN, Dir/Co-Prod; *A Writer in the Nuclear Age/A Conversation with Margaret Laurence*, TV, 86, CDN, Prod; *Nuclear Addiction: Dr. Rosalie Bertell on the Cost of Deterrence*, TV, 86, CDN, Prod; *A Love Affair with Politics: A Portrait of Mario Dewar*, Th, 86, CDN, Prod; *Children of War*, Th, 86, CDN, Cons Dir; *Thin Dreams*, Th, 86, CDN, Cons Dir; *Speaking Our Peace*, TV, 86, CN, Co-Dir/Co-Prod; *Dark Lullabies*, Th, 85, CDN, Co-Prod; *Not a Love Story*, Th, 80, CDN, Dir; *Right Candidate for Rosedale*, TV, 79, CDN, Co-Dir/Co-Prod; *Patricia's Moving Picture*, Th, 78, CDN, Dir; *Harmonie*, TV, 77, CDN, Dir/Prod; *A Workng Chance*, TV, 76, CDN, Dir/Prod; *Citizen's Medicine*, TV, 70, CDN, Dir/Prod; *La Petite Bourgogne*, TV, 68, CDN, Dir/Ed.

KONOWAL, Charles
- see CINEMATOGRAPHERS
KOOL, Allen
- see PRODUCER
KOTCHEFF, Ted
DGA. c/o Teresa Deane, 2516 Via Tejon, #217, Palos Verdes Estates, CA 90274 USA. Todd Smith, CAA, 1888 Century Park E., Los Angeles, CA 90067 USA (213)277-4545.
Type of Production and Credits: Th Film-Dir/Prod/Wr; TV Film-Dir; TV Video-Dir/Wr.
Genres: Drama-Th&TV; Comedy-Th&TV; Action-Th.
Biography: Born 1931, Toronto, Ontario. B.A., English Language and Literature, University of Toronto, 52. Worked at CBC, 52-57; went to England, 57, directed TV, theatre, film; returned to Canada to make *The Apprenticeship of Duddy Kravitz*, which won the Golden Bear, Berlin; moved to Los Angeles, 74. *Joshua Then and Now* and *Outback* were both invited entries to the Cannes Film Festival.
Selected Filmography: *Weekend at Bernie's*, Th, 89, USA, Dir; *Joshua Then and Now*, Th, 84, CDN, Dir; *Uncommon Valor*, Th, 83, USA, Dir/Exec Prod; *First Blood*, Th, 82, USA, Dir; *Split Image*, Th, 82, USA, Dir/Prod; *North Dallas Forty*, Th, 79, USA, Dir/Scr; *Someone Is Killing the Great Chefs of Europe*, Th, 78, USA, Dir; *Fun with Dick and Jane*, Th, 76, USA, Dir; *The Apprenticeship of Duddy Kravitz*, Th, 73, CDN, Dir; *Billy Two Hats*, Th, 73, USA, Dir; *Outback*, Th, 71, AUS, Dir; *Edna, the Inebriate Woman*, TV, 71, GB, Dir; *Two Gentlemen Sharing*, Th, 70, GB, Dir; *Life at the Top*, Th, 65, GB, Dir; *Tiara Tahiti*, Th, 62, GB, Dir.

KOTTLER, Les
- see PRODUCERS
KOZAK, Sherry
- see PRODUCERS
KREPAKEVICH, Jerry
- see PRODUCERS
KRIZSAN, Les
- see CINEMATOGRAPHERS
KROEKER, Allan
DGC, WGC (ACTRA). 633 Bay St., #2701, Toronto, ON M5G 2G4 (416)593-5138.
Type of Production and Credits: Th Film-Dir; Th Short-Dir/Cin/Wr/Ed; TV Film-Dir/Wr; TV Video-Dir/Wr.
Genres: Drama-Th&TV; Action-Th&TV; Comedy-TV; Horror-TV; Documentary-TV; Children's-TV.
Biography: Born 1951, St. Boniface, Manitoba. Honours B.A., Fine Arts, York University, 74. Background as cameraman and editor. Also as writer for films, specializing in literary adaptation. His films have won over 50 awards internationally; *Age Old Friends* won 2 Emmys

and an ACE; *Heaven on Earth* won awards at Houston, Banff and Columbus; *Red Shoes* won at Columbus and Chicago; *Tramp at the Door* won New York, CFTA (Canadian Film and Television Association), Chicago, Iris, Houston, American Film Festival and Gabriel awards; "Trilogy" won Yorkton, ACTRA, Iris, American Film Festival, Banff, Columbus, CFTA, New York, Chicago, Gabriel, Houston, Michigan State and Gemini awards.
Selected Filmography: "Two for Joy" (pilot), TV, 91, CDN, Dir; *Kootenai Brown*, Th, 90, CDN, Dir; "Dracula - The Series" (2 eps), TV, 90, CDN/USA/LUX, Dir; "E.N.G." (1 eps), TV, 90, CDN, Dir; "Friday the 13th - The Series" (2 eps), TV, 89, CDN, Dir; "Ray Bradbury Theatre" (1 eps), TV, 89, CDN/USA, Dir; *Age Old Friends/A Month of Sundays*, TV, 89, USA/CDN, Dir; "Twilight Zone" (1 eps), TV, 88, CDN/USA, Dir; "T and T" (3 eps), TV, 87-88, CDN, Dir; "The Campbells" (3 eps), TV, 87-88, CDN, Dir; "Street Legal" (2 eps), TV, 87, CDN, Dir; *Heaven on Earth*, TV, 86, CDN/GB, Dir; *Red Shoes*, "Bell Canada Playhouse", TV, 85, CDN, Co-Wr/Dir; *Tramp at the Door*, TV, 85, CDN, Wr/Dir; *Capital, The Prodigal, In the Fall*, "Trilogy", TV, 81-83, CDN, Wr/Dir.

KROITOR, Roman
- see PRODUCERS

KUPER, Jack
301 Forest Hill Rd., Toronto, ON M5P 2N7 (416)782-4553. Kuper Productions Ltd., 179 Carlton St., Toronto, ON M5A 2K3 (416)961-6609.
Type of Production and Credits: Th Short Dir/Prod/Wr; TV Film-Dir/Wr/Prod; TV Video-Dir/Wr/Prod.
Genres: Educational-Th&TV; Animation-Th&TV; Industrial-TV; Commercials-Th&TV.
Biography: Born 1932, Pulawy, Poland; Canadian citizenship. Languages: English and Yiddish. Graphic artist, television play-wright, novelist (*Child of the Holocaust* published in US, Canada, GB, France) and art director. Many awards including Graphica, American TV Commercial Festival, Venice Film Festival; Art Director of the Year, Canada. Director of numer-ous commercials, instructional, industrial, experimental and documentary films.
Selected Filmography: *A Day in the Warsaw Ghetto, A Birthday Trip in Hell*, Th, 91, CDN, Wr/Dir/Prod; *Mehane Yehuda/Jerusalem Market*, TV, 70, CDN, Wr/Dir; *It's a Big, Wide, Wonderful World*, TV, 67, CDN, Wr/Dir; *Dawn*, TV, 65, CDN, Adapt/Dir; *I've Got My Eye On You*, TV, 65, CDN, Wr/Dir; *The Wounded Soldier*, TV, 62, CDN, Wr; *The Police*, TV, 61, CDN, Adapt; *Sun in my Eyes*, TV, 60, CDN, Wr; *Run!*, TV/Th, 60, CDN, Wr/Dir; *Street Music*, TV, 59, CDN, Wr; *Lost in a Crowd*, TV, 57, CDN, Wr; *On a Streetcar*, TV, 55, CDN, Wr.

LABERGE, Pierre
- voir PRODUCTEURS

LABREQUE, Jean-Claude
ACCT. 1566, Van Horne, Montréal, PQ H2V 1L5 (514)271-7694.
Types de production et générique: l métrage-Réal/D photo; c métrage-Réal/D photo.
Types d'oeuvres: Drame-C&TV; Documentaire-C&TV.
Curriculum vitae: Né en 1938, Québec. Fondateur de la Société Jeune Cinéma, 61. Directeur de la photographie, réalisateur, opérateur, monteur. Séjour en Italie dans le cadre d'un échange de techniciens, 64. Récipiendaire du Prix Wendy Michener, 69.
Filmographie sélective: *Leveillée - Piaf*, C, 91, CDN, D phot/Réal; *La Nuit de la Poésie*, C, 91, CDN, Co-Réal/D phot; *L'Histoire des Trois*, C, 89, CDN, D phot/Réal; *Bonjour Monsieur Gauguin*, C, 88, CDN, Réal/Cam; *Les Trois Montréals de Michel Tremblay*, C, 88, CDN, D phot; *Le Frère André*, C, 87, CDN, Réal; *Le Million Tout-Puisant*, C, 85, CDN, D phot; *Sacré Tango*, C, 84, CDN, D phot; *Les Années de Rêve*, C, 83, CDN, Réal.

LABROSSE, Sylvain
- voir DIRECTEURS-PHOTO

LAFOND, Jean-Daniel
ARRFQ, SARDEC. Majda Films International Inc., 2245 Quesnel, Montreal, PQ H3J 1G3 (514)937-7718.
Types de production et générique: l métrage-Réal; c métrage-Réal.
Types d'oeuvres: Documentaire-C; Education-C.
Curriculum vitae: Né en 1944, France; citoyenneté canadienne et française. Licence en Psychologie; D.E.A. en Science de l'Education; agrégé de Philosophie. Expérience de l'enseignement universitaire, du théâtre, de la critique au cinéma. Collaborateur et membre du comité de rédaction de la revue *Lumières*. Essayiste; auteur de nombreux films radiophoniques (Radio-Canada, Radio-France). *Les Traces du rêve*, en nomination pour Meilleur Réalisation Documentaire, Prix Génie.
Filmographie sélective: *La manière nègre/Aimé Césaire, chemin faisant*, C, 91,

CDN, Réal/Sc/Rech; *Le visiteur d'un soir*, C, 89, CDN, Réal/Sc/Rech; *Le Voyage au bout de la route/La ballade du pays qui attend*, C, 87, CDN, Réal/Sc/Rech; *Les Traces du rêve*, C, 86, CDN, Réal/Sc/Rech; *La Grande Allure*, C, 84, CDN, Rech; *Beyrouth: à défaut d'être mort*, C, 83, CDN, Dial/Adapt; *La Bête lumineuse*, C, 83, CDN, Adapt; *A Calculated Extinction*, C, 81, CDN, Adapt; *Man of the Tundra*, C, 81, CDN, Adapt.

LAFORÊT, Megan
- see PRODUCERS

LAMARRE, Louise ◇
(514)276-3970.
Types de production et générique: TV film-Réal.
Types d'oeuvres: Comédie-TV; Science-fiction-TV; Documentaire-TV.
Curriculum vitae: Née en 1960. Langues: français et anglais. Baccalauréat (Film Production), Université Concordia; Certificat en Etudes cinématographiques, Université Laval.
Filmographie sélective: *Alter Ego*, C, 88, CDN, Réal; *Le Cap sur l'essentiel*, ED, 88, CDN, Réal; *Nouvelle Mémoire*, TV, 86, CDN, Réal/Sc; *Growing Wild*, TV, 86, CDN, Réal; *Where Are You My Lovelies?*, C, 86, CDN, Réal; *Loose Page*, TV, 85, CDN, Sc; *L'Elue*, TV, 85, CDN, Réal/Prod; *Error...Error*, "Technological Change", TV, 85, CDN, Réal; *Les communications ça se soigne*, TV, 84, CDN, Réal; *Je me souviens de Charlevoix*, TV, 82, CDN, Sc/Réal/Prod; *Les Anciens Domaines de Sillery*, TV, 81, CDN, Co réal/Mont; *Le Vernissage*, TV, 80, CDN, Sc/Réal/Prod.

LAMOTHE, Arthur
APFVQ, ARRFQ. 194, av. de l'Epée, Outremont, PQ H2V 3T2 (514)277-8787. Ateliers audio-visuels du Québec, 194, av. de l'Epée, Outremont, PQ H2V 3T2 (514)277-2299. FAX: 277-0193.
Types de production et générique: l métrage-Réal/Aut/Prod; c métrage-Réal/Aut/Prod; TV film-Réal/Aut/Prod.
Types d'oeuvres: Drame-C&TV; Documentaire-C&TV; Education-C&TV; Enfants-C&TV.
Curriculum vitae: Né en 1928, Saint-Mont (Gers), France; citoyenneté canadienne. Maîtrise en économie politique, Université de Montréal, 58. A travaillé pour Radio-Canada, l'ONF; co-fondateur, Festival International du Film de Montréal, l'Association des producteurs de film du Québec; membre fondateur et rédacteur des revues *Images* et *Format Cinéma*; Président, ARRFQ, 81-83; Président et fondateur, Ateliers audio-visuels du Québec. Ses films ont remporté plusieurs prix dont le Prix de l'Association québécoise des critiques de cinéma, Sesterce d'Or (Nyon) pour "Carcajou et le péril blanc"; *Les Bûcherons de Manouane* remporte le Prix de la Critique française et le Grand Prix, Festival du Film canadien. L'ensemble de son oeuvre lui a valu la remise par le gouvernement du Québec du Premier Prix Albert Tessier en 1980.
Filmographie sélective: "La Conquête de l'Amérique" (2 eps), C, 91, CDN, Réal; *Ernest Livernois, Photographe*, C, 88, CDN, Réal; *Equinoxe*, C, 86, CDN, Réal; *Mémoire battante*, C, 82, CDN, Réal; "La terre des hommes" (5 eps), TV, 77-80, CDN, Réal; "Carcajou et le péril blanc" (8 eps), C, 73-76, CDN, Réal; *A bon pied, bon oeil*, In, 73, CDN, Réal; *La route du fer*, ED, 72, CDN, Réal; *Les gars de Lapalme*, ED, 71, CDN, Réal; *Le mépris n'aura aucun temps*, C, 69, CDN, Réal; "Actualité Québec" (5 eps), ED, 69, CDN, Réal; *Au delà des murs*, C, 68, CDN, Réal; *Le Train du Labrador*, C, 67, CDN, Réal; *Poussière sur la ville*, C, 65, CDN, Réal; *Bûcherons de la Manouane*, C, 62, CDN, Réal.

LANCTOT, Micheline ◇
(514)465-9014.
Types de production et générique: l métrage-Réal/Com/Sc; TV film-Com; TV vidéo-Com.
Types d'oeuvres: Drame-C&TV; Action-C; Comédie-C&TV; Animation-C.
Curriculum vitae: Née en 1947, Montréal, Québec. Langues: français et anglais. Etudes classiques et universitaires - lauréate en musique (piano). Débute comme animatrice, ONF, puis chez Potterton Productions. Nomination pour un Oscar, *The Selfish Giant*; *L'Homme à tout faire* gagne le Médaille d'Argent, Festival de San Sebastian. *Sonatine*, le Lion d'Argent, 2e Prix au Festival de Venise et Plaque d'Argent, Festival de Figueira da Foz (Portugal); récipiendaire du Prix d'Excellence de l'Académie du cinéma canadien, 80.
Filmographie sélective: *Onzième Spéciale*, TV, 88, CDN, Réal; *La Poursuite du bonheur*, C, 87, CDN, Sc/Réal; *La Ligne de chaleur*, C, 86, CDN, Co sc; *Sonatine*, C, 82, CDN, Sc/Réal, (GENIE); *L'Affaire Coffin*, C, 79, CDN, Com; *L'Homme à tout faire*, C, 79, CDN, Réal/Sc; *Mourir à tue-tête*, C, 78, CDN, Com; *Blood & Guts*, C, 77, CDN/USA, Com; *Fun with Dick and Jane*, C, 76, USA, Conc gén; *A Token Gesture*, C, 76, CDN, Réal/An; *Voyage en Grande Tartairie*, C, 74, F, Com; *Les Corps*

célestes, C, 73, CDN, Com; *Noël et Juliette*, C, 73, CDN, Com; *Souris tu m'inquiètes*, "En tant que femmes", TV, 73, CDN, Com; *The Apprenticeship of Duddy Kravitz*, C, 73, CDN, Com; *The Selfish Giant*, TV, 71, CDN, An; *La Vraie Nature de Bernadette*, C, 71, CDN, Com, (CFA).

LANDERS, Ivan
- see PRODUCERS

LANG, Robert
- see PRODUCERS

LANGLOIS, Yves
ARRFQ, FRRFQ. 18, 8ieme ave, St-Armand, PQ J0J 1T0. Les Productions Lany, 1760, Charles, app. 4, St-Hubert, PQ J4T 1L3.
Types de production et générique: TV film-Réal; TV vidéo-Réal.
Types d'oeuvres: Documentaire-TV; Education-TV; Animation-TV.
Curriculum vitae: Né en 1951, Montréal, Québec. Langues: français, anglais, espagnol, compréhension du créole et portugais. Expérience en journalisme et en photographie. Meilleur Reportage canadien sur l'Afrique, Le Festival Vues d'Afrique, *La Patrie de l'homme fier*, 87; *Le Batey*, 86.
Filmographie sélective: *Contes colombiens* (tourné simul. en français et espagnol), TV, 88, CDN/COL, Réal/Cam/Mont; *Le Coton* (tourné simul. en fran. et esp.), C, 88, CDN/COL, Réal/Cam/ Mont; *L'Invasion* (tourné simul. en français et espagnol), C, 87, CDN/COL, Réal/Cam/Mont; *Le Poisson se meurt* (tourné simul. en fran. et esp.), C, 87, CDN/COL, Réal/Cam/Mont; *La Patrie de l'homme fier*, TV, 85, CDN, Réal/Cam/ Mont; *Le Batey*, TV, 85, CDN, Réal; *Pedro Machete*, TV, 85, CDN, Réal; *Las Brujas del Cerrito*, TV, 85, CDN, Réal; *Patacamaya Prise I*, TV, 84, CDN, Réal; *Chambellan Chambellan*, TV, 83, CDN, Réal; *Noirs et blanches*, TV, 82, CDN, Réal; *Une histoire de lutte*, TV, 82, CDN, Réal; *Domitila*, TV, 81, CDN, Réal; *A Baie Comeau ce soir*, TV, 81, CDN, Réal; *Les Patenteux d'énergie*, TV, 81, CDN, Réal.

LANK, Barry
681 Cordova St., Winnipeg, MB R3N 1A9 (204)488-2590. Lank/Beach Productions, 341 Wardlaw Ave., Winnipeg, MB R3L 0L5 (204)452-9422.
Type of Production and Credits: Th Short-Dir.Wr; TV Film-Dir.
Genres: Commercials-TV; Documentary-Th&TV.
Biography: Born 1946. Graduate, London School of Film, England, 73; Certificate of Education, University of Manitoba, 71; Honours B.A., Sociology, Psychology, University of Winnipeg, 70. Has produced and directed over 400 TV commercials and several industrial films. *Kelekis 50 Years in the Chips* won the Canadian Showcase; *It's a Hobby for Harvey* won Golden Sheaf Award, Yorkton Film Festival, Chris Plaque, Columbus; *First A Dream* awarded Certificate of Excellence, US Industrial Film/Video Awards, 91.
Selected Filmography: *First A Dream/H.I.D.I.*, In, 91, CDN, Dir/Cin; *Dory*, TV, 89-90, CDN, Cin; *Babysitting Basics*, In, 89-90, CDN, Cin; *Independent Living*, ED, 88, CDN, Dir/Cin; *Investing in Manitoba*, ED, 88, CDN, Dir/Cin; *Not a Bad Year*, Th, 85, CDN/I, DOP; *Muscle*, Th, 84, CDN, Dir/Wr; *Kelekis 50 Years in the Chips*, Th, 82, CDN, Dir/Cin; *It's a Hobby for Harvey*, Th, 80, CDN, Prod/Dir/Cin.

LANSING, Floyd
CTPDA, DGC, ACCT. Lansing Productions, 1840 Garden Ave., North Vancouver, BC V7P 3A8 (604)988-2824.
Type of Production and Credits: TV Film-Dir/Prod; TV Video-Dir/Prod.
Genres: Drama-TV; Comedy-TV; Variety-TV; Sports-TV.
Biography: Born 1951, High River, Alberta. Diploma, Television, Stage and Film Arts, Southern Alberta Institute of Technology. Producer/director for 12 years. Four Gold Medals, CanPro, for live variety, music shows, dramas, sports. Won the National Award of Excellence (School Board) for *Back to Basics*. "Whoopties" won Best Children's Series, CanPro, 88.
Selected Filmography: "Airborne 911" (1 eps), TV, 91, CDN, Prod/Dir; "Kids' Zone" (1 eps), TV, 91, CDN, Dir; "Legends of Rock" (1 eps), TV, 91, CDN, Prod/Dir; "Whoopties" (4 eps), TV, 87-88, CDN, Prod/Dir; *Heart Disease: #1 Killer*, TV, 88, CDN, Prod/Dir; "On Your Side", TV, 87-88, CDN, Prod/Dir; *Life after Dark*, TV, 86, CDN, Prod/Dir; *Sleepless Nights*, TV, 84, CDN, Dir; *Nut Cracker*, TV, 83, CDN, Prod/Dir; *In Motion*, TV, 83, CDN, Dir; *Super Sunday* (Heart), TV, 82, CDN, Dir; *World Popular Song Festival*, TV, 82, CDN, Prod/Dir; *L.R.B.*, TV, 80, CDN, Prod/ Dir; *Discothon*, TV, 80, CDN, Prod/Dir; *Confessin' the Blues*, TV, 80, CDN, Prod/Dir.

LANTHIER, Stephen
- see PRODUCERS

LAPOINTE, Yves ◊
(514)735-1297.

Types de production et générique: l métrage-Réal/Sc/Prod; c métrage-Réal/Sc/Prod; TV film-An.
Types d'oeuvres: Education-C&TV; Enfants-C&TV; Animation-C&TV.
Curriculum vitae: Né en 1961, Rimouski, Québec. Langues: français et anglais. DEC, Art général avec études en cinéma, Cégep de St-Jérôme, Québec, 83; quelques cours universitaires en cinéma d'animation. Producteur, réalisateur, animateur, scénariste, directeur artistique en production 16 mm court métrage; animateur-cinéma 3D; fabrication de personnages animés; conception d'articulation pour personnages animés.
Filmographie sélective: *Bino Fabule*, TV, 88, CDN/B/F, An; *Une Pof?...Bof!*, ED, 85, CDN, Prod/Sc/Réal/An; *Turlupinade*, C, 84, CDN, Co prod/Co réal/Co sc/Co An.

LARIVIÉRE, Jean Marc
47 Milverton Blvd., Toronto, ON M4J 1T5 (416)466-7722. Osmosis Communications Inc., 47 Milverton Blvd., Toronto, ON M4J 1T5 (416)466-7722.
Type of Production and Credits: Th Film-Dir; Th Short-Dir.
Genres: Drama-Th&TV; Documentary-Th&TV; Experimental-Th&TV; Music Video-Th&TV.
Biography: Born and raised in Hawkesbury, Ontario. University education in mathematics and physics. Professional experience in theatre (director, actor, lighting); film (writer, director, producer, editor); electronic music; dubbing and subtitling (adaptation, translation, dubbing director). *Divine Solitude* won a Silver Plaque, Dance on Camera, New York and was a finalist at the American Film & Video Festival, New York.
Selected Filmography: *The Top of His Head*, Th, 89, CDN, Assist to Dir; *Sweet Jane*, Cowboy Junkies, MV, 88, CDN, Prod/Dir/Ed; *Divine Solitude*, Th, 86, CDN, Prod/Dir/Ed; *Révolutions*, Th, 82, CDN, Prod/Dir/Ed/Wr.

LAROCHELLE, André
- voir PRODUCTEURS

LARRY, Sheldon
DGA, DGC, ACTT. 3010 Paulcrest Dr., Los Angeles, CA 90046 USA (213)650-1004. FAX: 650-0954. Rob Lee/Devra Leib, Triad Artists Agency, 10100 Santa Monica Blvd., Los Angeles, CA 90067 USA (213)556-2727.
Type of Production and Credits: Th Film-Prod/Dir; TV Film-Prod/Dir; TV Video-Dir.
Genres: Drama-Th&TV; Comedy-Th&TV; Action-Th&TV.
Biography: Born 1948, Toronto, Ontario; Canadian citizenship; US resident. Languages: English and French. B.A., Political Science, York University. Worked for BBC, with over 100 credits, 68-78. US theatre experience includes: Shakespeare Festival, Playwrights Horizons, Mark Taper Forum. Has won Humanitas, ACE, Scott Newman and Emmy awards.
Selected Filmography: *The First Circle* (mini-series), TV, 90-91, CDN/F, Dir/Prod; *Burning Bodies*, TV, 89-90, USA, Dir; "Doogie Howser, M.D." (sev eps), TV, 89, USA, Dir; "Studio 5B" (pilot), TV, 88, USA, Dir; *Trying Times*, TV, 87, USA, Dir; "Shelley Duvall's Faerie Tale Theater", TV, 87, USA, Dir; *Hot Paint*, TV, 87, USA, Dir; "Remington Steele" (sev eps), TV, 84-86, USA, Dir; "Hill Street Blues" (sev eps), TV, 84-86, USA, Dir; "Knot's Landing" (sev eps), TV, 84-86, USA, Dir; *Behind Enemy Lines*, TV, 85, USA, Dir; *First Steps*, TV, 84, USA, Dir; *Popular Neurotics*, "American Playhouse", TV, 84, USA, Dir; *Terminal Choice*, Th, 82, CDN, Dir; *Secret of Charles Dickens*, TV, 81, USA, Dir, (EMMY).

LARTIGAU, Yvonne ◆
(819)771-3753.
Types de production et générique: TV vidéo-Réal.
Types d'oeuvres: Variété-TV; Comédie musicale-TV; Annonces-TV; Affaires publiques-TV.
Curriculum vitae: Née en 1940, Ottawa, Ontario. Langues: français et anglais. Diplômée du Collège commercial Lafortune; licence en diction du Conservatoire de Musique et de Diction de Montréal. Spécialisée dans le domaine musical; réalisatrice TV en publicité, 87, et à l'information, 88, pour "Ce Soir."
Filmographie sélective: "Ontario fête" (4 ém), TV, 87, CDN, Réal; "Ce Soir" (segments culturels), TV, 80-85, CDN, Réal; "Les Beaux Dimanches" (8 eps), TV, 74-80, CDN, Réal.

LAURENDEAU, Jean Pierre
- voir REGISSEURS
LAVOIE, Claude
5596 de l'Esplanade, Montreal, PQ H2T 3A1 (514)279-5323.
Type of Production and Credits: TV Film-Prod/Dir/Wr/Ed; TV Video-Prod/Dir/Wr/Ed.
Genres: Documentary-TV; Educational-TV; Animation-TV; Industrial-TV.

Biography: Born 1953, Montreal, Quebec. Languages: French and English. B.A., Music, M.Ed., University of Montreal. Freelance producer, director, editor of animated motion films, reports, educational programs, documentaries; manager/instructor, film training workshop; pedagogical counsellor; French teacher; music teacher; consultant for editing, video productions, animated films, educational programs and documentaries.

LAVOIE, Michel C.
ACCT. 1400 René-Lévesque E., Montreal, PQ H2L 2M2 (514)597-5252.
Type of Production and Credits: TV Film-Dir/Prod; TV Video-Dir/Prod.
Genres: Drama-TV; Children's-TV; Industrial-Th; Current Affairs-TV.
Biography: Born 1943, St. Boniface, Manitoba. Languages: English and French. B.A., Literature and Philosophy, University of Manitoba, 64; M.A., Philosophy, Université du Québec, 68; postgraduate degree, Communications, Concordia University, 72; M.Ed., Educational Psychology, McGill University, 84. Spent 2 years in Addis Ababa on contract with Ethiopian government. Joined Radio-Canada, 72; has produced, directed and been executive producer of series for current affairs, news and drama; Area Producer of Information programming (CBWFT) before entering field of children's television; Executive Producer, "Sesame Street Canada," 75; expanded award-winning series coast to coast, working in administrative and creative capacities; with Jim Henson Associates, New York, assisted in creation of original Canadian Muppets, 85; responsible for development of CBC Testing Centre, 76, to research TV programming elements; coordinator/director, Preschool Series, 89-90; currently Manager, Children's & Youth TV Programs, CBC. Has published theoretical material about TV and has taught Communications.
Selected Filmography: *Buried Treasure*, TV, 88, CDN, Dir; *I Love You Cowboy*, TV, 87, CDN, Dir/Prod; *Le Rêve de Pierre*, TV, 82, CDN, Dir/Prod; *Made in Quebec: The Referendum*, TV, 80, CDN, Dir; *Four Summers*, TV, 78, CDN, Dir/Prod; *Ethiopia, Architect of Light*, ED, 70, ETH, Co-Prod.

LAVOIE, Patricia
- see PRODUCERS

LAVUT, Martin
ACTRA, DGC, WGA, ACCT. 367 Sackville St., Toronto, ON M5A 3G5 (416)929-9677. Charles W. Northcote, The Core Group Talent Agency, 489 College St., Suite 501, Toronto, ON M6G 1A5 (416)944-0193.
Type of Production and Credits: Th Film-Dir/Wr; Th Short-Dir/Prod/Wr; TV Film-Dir/Wr; TV Video-Dir.
Genres: Drama-Th&TV; Documentary-TV; Children's-TV.
Biography: Born 1939, Montreal, Quebec. Has worked at NFB; writer, director, with Foster and J. Walter Thompson Advertis-ing Agencies; directed over 30 commercials (awards); actor, Second City; night club comic: *Maclean's, Young Canadian Issue,* Canadian Comic of the Year; co-writer and director of *Mr. Bach Comes to Call*, children's auditory tape released in 88.
Selected Filmography: "Counterstrike", TV, 91, CDN/USA, Dir; *Inventors Aren't Crazy*, TV, 91, CDN, Dir/Wr/Prod; "E.N.G." (3 eps), TV, 89-90, CDN, Dir; "Friday the 13th - The Series" (1 eps), TV, 89-90, CDN/USA, Dir; "Diamonds" (1 eps), TV, 89-90, CDN/USA, Dir; *The Cold Equations*, "The Twilight Zone", TV, 88, CDN/USA, Dir; *Palais Royale*, Th, 87, CDN, Dir; *The Marriage Bed*, TV, 86, CDN, Dir, (GEMINI); "Philip Marlowe, Private Eye" (1 eps), TV, 85, CDN, Dir; *Red River*, TV, 85, CDN, Dir; *Charlie Grant's War*, TV, 84, CDN, Dir; "Fraggle Rock" (1 eps), TV, 84, CDN, Dir; *Maggie and Pierre*, TV, 83, CDN, Dir; *Rumours of Glory: Bruce Cockburn Live*, TV, 82, CDN, Dir; "Landscape of Geometry" (12 eps), TV, 82, CDN, Dir.

LAWRENCE, Pierre
678 de la Métairie, Ile des Soeurs, PQ H3E 1T1 (514)768-4513.
Type of Production and Credits: TV Video-Dir.
Genres: Drama-TV; Documentary-TV; Educational-TV; Industrial-TV.
Biography: Born in 1956 in Montreal, Quebec. Languages: French and English. Director since 1979, mainly in documentary, drama, educational and industrial. Coordinating director since 1988 on "Comment ça va?", a series on health and lifestyle, Radio-Canada; prizes at Prix Gémeaux, 1990; Prix Jean-Charles Pagé, 1990; Prix Association des Infirmiers et Infirmières du Canada, 1990 and Prix Association des Rédacteurs Scientifiques du Canada, 1989.
Selected Filmography: *Les Mains Libres*, In, 91, CDN, Dir/Ed; *Publicité Club de Montreal/La Pub est tombée sur la tête*, In, 91, CDN, Dir; "Comment ça va?" (86

eps), TV, 88-91, CDN, Coord Dir; "La Grande Visite" (26 eps), TV, 26, CDN, Dir; "Au jour le jour" (26 eps), TV, 86, CDN, Dir; *Louis Hemon*, TV, 85, CDN, Wr/Dir; *Le Surviethon*, TV, 85, CDN, Wr/Dir; *Le decloisonnement des services financiers*, In, 88, CDN, Wr/Dir; "A Votre Rythme" (65 eps), TV, 84, CDN, Dir; "Le Grand Circuit" (13 eps), TV, 84, CDN, Dir; "Chasseurs, sachez chasser/Idem", TV, 82, CDN, Dir; *Jean Narrache*, TV, 82, CDN, Dir.

LE BOURHIS, Dominique
- voir SCENARISTES

LE BOUTILLIER, Geoff
- see WRITERS

LEACH, David
- see EDITORS

LEANEY, Cindy
- see PRODUCERS

LECKIE, Keith Ross
- see WRITERS

LECLERC, Jean ✧
(514)742-6007.
Types de production et générique: c métrage-Réal/Mont; TV vidéo-Réal/Mont.
Types d'oeuvres: Drame-C; Documentaire-C&TV; Education-TV; Annonces-C.
Curriculum vitae: Né en 1948, St-Roch-sur-Richelieu, Québec. Langues: français et anglais. Baccalauréat ès arts (lettres). Récipiendaire de plusieurs prix (Chicago, New York); nominations pour la réalisation et le montage, Prix Gémeaux, 86 et 87.
Filmographie sélective: *Paul-Emile Borduas*, TV, 88, CDN, Réal/Mont; *Le mieux c'est de regarder Radio-Québec*, Cm, 88, CDN, Réal/Mont; *Franc-Parler*, TV, 87, CDN, Réal/Mont; *Attends, t'as pas tout vu!*, Cm, 87, CDN, Réal/Mont; *Playback*, TV, 86, CDN, Réal/Conc; *Jeuness ad-lib*, TV, 85, CDN, Sc/Réal/Mont; *Mini Doc*, Cm, 84, CDN, Réal/Mont; *Jalousie*, C, 80, CDN, Réal/Sc/Mont.

LEDUC, Lucile ✧
(514)523-7181.
Types de production et générique: TV vidéo-Réal.
Types d'oeuvres: Drame-TV.
Curriculum vitae: Née en 1928, Verdun, Québec. Langues: anglais et français. Cours de photographie; 6 ans d'art dramatique. *La Bonne Aventure* remporte le Prix de l'Association national des téléspectateurs.
Filmographie sélective: "Des dames de coeur" (15 eps), TV, 86-88, CDN, Réal; "La Bonne Aventure" (48 eps), TV, 82-85, CDN, Réal; "Boogie-Woogie 47" (40 eps), TV, 80-81, CDN, Réal; "Caroline" (26 eps), TV, 79, CDN, Réal; "Grand-Papa" (40 eps), TV, 77-78, CDN, Réal; *Monsieur Zero*, TV, 76, CDN, Réal.

LEDUC, Yves
- voir PRODUCTEURS

LEFEBVRE, Jean Pierre
AQRRCT, FPRRTC. 1313, ch. Guthrie, C.P. 260, Bedford, PQ J0J 1A0 (514)248-3295.
Types de production et générique: l métrage-Réal/Sc.
Types d'oeuvres: Drame-C; Comédie-C; Documentaire-C; Expérimental-C.
Curriculum vitae: Né en 1941, Montréal, Québec. Langues: français et anglais. Maîtrise en Littérature française, Université de Montréal, 62. Critique de cinéma, 58-67; plusieurs publications dont *Parfois quand je vis*. *Les Fleurs sauvages* gagne le Prix Critique internationale, Cannes; Plaque d'Argent, Festival International de Figueira da Foz, Portugal; *Il ne faut pas mourir pour ça* remporte le Prix de la Critique québécoise et le Prix du Meilleur Film étranger, Hyères, France; récipiendaire du Prix Wendy Michener, 70.
Filmographie sélective: *Le fabuleux Voyage de l'Ange*, C, 90, CDN, Réal/Sc; *La Boîte à soleil*, C, 87, CDN, Réal/Prod; *Alfred Laliberté, sculpteur 1878-1953*, C, 86, CDN, Sc/Réal; *Le Jour "S..."*, C, 83, CDN, Réal/Co sc; *Au rythme de mon coeur*, C, 82-83, CDN, Réal/Sc/Comp; *Les Fleurs sauvages*, C, 82, CDN, Réal/Sc; *Avoir 16 ans*, C, 78, CDN, Réal/Co sc; *Le Gars des vues*, C, 76, CDN, Réal/Co sc; *Le Vieux Pays où Rimbaud est mort*, C, 76, CDN/F, Réal/Co sc; *L'Amour blessé/Confidences de la nuit*, C, 75, CDN, Réal/Sc; *Les Dernières Fiançailles*, C, 73, CDN, Réal/Sc; *On n'engraisse pas les cochons à l'eau claire*, C, 73, CDN, Réal/Sc; *Les Maudits Sauvages*, C, 71, CDN, Réal/Sc; *Ultimatum*, C, 71, CDN, Réal/Sc; *Q-bec My Love*, C, 69, CDN, Réal/Sc.

LEITERMAN, Richard
- see CINEMATOGRAPHERS

LENNICK, Michael
- see WRITERS

LENTE, Miklos
- see CINEMATOGRAPHERS

LEPAGE, Marquise
APFVQ, ARRFQ, ACCT. 1912 est, Laurier, Montréal, PQ H2H 1B4 (514)522-2192. Les Productions du Lundi Matin, C.P. 157, succ. de Lorimier, Montréal, PQ H2H 2N6 (514)271-5357.
Types de production et générique: l métrage-Réal/Sc; c métrage-Réal/Sc.
Types d'oeuvres: Drame-C; Comédie-C;

Documentaire-C&TV.
Curriculum vitae: Née en 1959. Baccalauréat en communications, spécialisé en cinéma.

LESEWICK, Robert
- see PRODUCERS

LESS, Henry ✧
(416) 536-9059
Type of Production and Credits: TV Film-Dir/Prod; TV Video-Dir/Prod.
Genres: Musical-TV; Documentary-TV; Industrial-TV.
Biography: Born 1947. Has won 2 Gold Camera Awards, US Industrial Film Festival for *Talkto* and *Dominos*.
Selected Filmography: *Nahanni: River of Gold*, TV, 88, CDN, Dir/Cin; *Dreams of Glory*, TV, 87, CDN, Dir/Cin; *Different Worlds*, TV, 86, CDN, Dir/Wr/Ed; *The Hawk Express*, TV, 81, CDN, Prod; *Gino Vanelli*, TV, 79, CDN, Prod, (CFTA).

LETOURNEAU, Diane
ARRFQ, SGCT. 125 Elmire, #403, Montréal, PQ H2T 1J9 (514)284-2610. ONF, 3155, Côte de Liesse, Montréal, PQ H4N 2N4 (514)283-9353.
Types de production et générique: l métrage-Réal/Sc; c métrage-Réal/Sc.
Types d'oeuvres: Documentaire-C&TV.
Curriculum vitae: Née en 1942, Sherbrooke, Québec.
Filmographie sélective: *Pas d'amitié à moitié*, C/TV, 91, CDN, Rech/Sc/Réal; *Comme deux gouttes d'eau*, ED, 87-88, CDN, Réal/Sc; *A force de mourir*, C, 86, CDN, Réal/Sc; *Une guerre dans mon jardin*, TV, 85, CDN, Réal/Sc; *En scène*, C, 82, CDN, Réal/Sc; *La Passion de danser*, C, 81, CDN, Réal/Sc; *Le Plus Beau Jour de ma vie...*, C, 80, CDN, Réal/Sc; *Les Statues de monsieur Basile*, C, 79, CDN, Réal/Sc; *Les Servantes de bon Dieu*, C, 78, CDN, Réal/Sc; *Les Oiseaux blancs de l'île d'Orléans*, C, 77, CDN, Réal/Sc; *Au bout de mon âge*, C, 75, CDN, Rech/1er ass réal/Ass mont; *Les Jardins d'hiver*, C, 74, CDN, Rech/1er ass réal/Ass mont; *A votre santé*, C, 73, CDN, Rech/1er ass réal/Ass mont.

LEVY, Joanne T.
- see WRITERS

LEWIS, Jefferson
- see WRITERS

LHOTSKY, Antonin
- see CINEMATOGRAPHERS

LICCIONI, Jean-Pierre
- voir SCENARISTES

LIIMATAINEN, Arvi
- see PRODUCERS

LINDO, Eleanore
DGC. 297 Waverley Rd., Toronto, ON M4L 3T5 (416)698-0412. Great North Artists Management Inc., 350 Dupont St., Toronto, ON M5R 1V9 (416)925-2051.
Type of Production and Credits: TV Film-Dir/Prod; TV Video-Dir/Prod.
Genres: Drama-TV; Comedy-TV; Documentary-TV.
Biography: Born in Toronto, Ontario. M.A., Graduate Centre for the Study of Drama, University of Toronto, 71; graduate of Directing program, American Film Institute, 86. Producer/director/writer for CBC, 75-85; freelance director, 86-91. *Talkin' About AIDS* won Best TV Special, Women in Film Festival.
Selected Filmography: "E.N.G." (2 eps), TV, 91, CDN, Dir; "Street Legal" (10 eps), TV, 87-91, CDN, Dir; "The Hitchhiker" (1 eps), TV, 91, CDN, Dir; "The Hidden Room" (1 eps), TV, 91, CDN, Dir; "Northwood" (4 eps), TV, 90-91, CDN, Dir; "Degrassi High" (3 eps), TV, 89-90, CDN, Dir; "Material World" (1 eps), TV, 90, CDN, Dir; *Thunder in My Head*, "Saying Good-Bye", TV, 89, CDN, Dir; *Talkin' About AIDS*, TV, 89, CDN, Dir; "Degrassi Junior High" (3 eps), TV, 88, CDN, Dir; "The Campbells", TV, 87-88, CDN/USA/GB, Dir; "The Beachcombers" (1 eps), TV, 87, CDN, Dir.

LIPSEY, Stan
- see PRODUCERS

LISHMAN, Eda Lever
- see PRODUCERS

LIU, Harrison
2466 Eglinton Ave. E., Ste. 605, Toronto, ON M1K 5T8 (416)269-5750. FAX: 269-5709.
Type of Production and Credits: Th Short-Dir/Wr; TV Film-Dir/Wr; TV Video-Dir.
Genres: Drama-Th&TV; Action-Th.
Biography: Born in Northeast China. Has worked in film and television for over 15 years. Immigrated to Canada in 1989. Has acted in over 30 features and television series. Passion is directing; has made 2 short films since his arrival in Canada. Preparing Canadian feature debut next spring. Speaks Mandarin and English.
Selected Filmography: *Birthday*, Th, 91, CDN, Co Wr/Co Dir; *Strange Dialogue*, Th/TV, 90, CDN, Co Wr/Dir; *Special Task Force*, Th, 88, RC, Wr; *Desert Under the Sun*, TV, 88, RC, Dir; *Breaking the Ground*, Th, 88, RC, Dir; *Alarm Bell*, Th, 87, RC, Wr; "Da-Mo Prisoner Escort Team" (4 eps), TV, 87, RC, Dir; "Isn't Winter After Fall" (2 eps), TV, 87, RC, Wr.

LIVINGSTON, Neal
Black River Productions Ltd., Box 55, Mabou, NS B0E 1X0 (902)258-3354.
Type of Production and Credits: Th Short-Dir; TV Film-Dir/Prod/Cam.
Genres: Documentary-TV; Educational-Th&TV; Experimental-Th.
Biography: Born 1955, Hamilton, Ontario. Attended Nova Scotia College of Art and Design, 75-76; B.F.A., York University. President, Black River Hydro Limited. Winner of CanPro awards and at Atlantic Film Festival.
Selected Filmography: *The Cape Breton Endangered Spaces,* ED, 90, CDN, Prod/Dir/Cam/Ed/Narr; *The Disappearance of John Ashby,* ED, 90, CDN, Cam/Ed/Dir; *Trees and Elevators,* ED, 90, CDN, Prod/Dir/Co-Ed; *John Dunsworth - The Candidate,* ED, 89, CDN, Prod/Dir/Cam/Ed; *John Nesbitt - Sculptor,* TV, 87, CDN, Dir/Prod/Ed; *Off to Work,* MV, 87, CDN, Dir/Prod/Ed; *Herbicide Trials,* TV, 84, CDN, Dir/Cam/Ed.

LOCK, Keith ✧
(416)429-7399.
Type of Production and Credits: Th Short-Dir/Wr/Prod; TV Film-Dir/Wr.
Genres: Drama-Th&TV; Action-TV; Documentary-Th&TV; Experimental-Th.
Biography: Born 1951, Toronto, Ontario. M.F.A., Film, York University, 81. Student awards include UNESCO Tenth Muse International, Super 8 Award, Amsterdam, 69; Sir George Williams University Film Festival, Best Documentary Award, Montreal, 70. Award nominations include Yorkton, 83, 87; Gemini, 87.
Selected Filmography: *A Brighter Moon,* Th, 86, CDN, Prod/Dir/Wr; *Chinatown,* "Neighbourhoods", TV, 84, CDN, Dir/Wr; *The Highway,* TV, 83, CDN, Prod/Wr; *Jeannie Goes Shopping,* Th, 81, CDN, Wr/Dir; *Everything Everywhere Again Alive,* Th, 75, CDN, Prod/Dir/Wr; *Work Bike And Eat,* Th, 71, CDN, Prod/Dir/Wr; *Base Tranquility,* Th, 69, CDN, Co-An.

LONGLEY, Richard
- see PRODUCERS

LORD, Jean-Claude ✧
(514)466-2602.
Types de production et générique: l métrage-Réal/Sc; TV film-Réal.
Types d'oeuvres: Drame-C; Horreur-C.
Curriculum vitae: Né en 1943, Montréal, Québec. Critique de film pour la télévision québécoise, 69-72; chroniqueur de film, 71-74.
Filmographie sélective: *La Grenouille et la Baleine,* C, 87, CDN, Réal; "Lance et compte" (13 eps), TV, 85-86, CDN, Réal, (GEMEAUX 87); *Toby McTeague,* C, 85, CDN, Réal; *The Vindicator,* C, 84, CDN, Réal; *Covergirl,* C, 81, CDN, Réal; *Visiting Hours,* C, 80, CDN, Réal; *Eclair au chocolat,* C, 78, CDN, Réal/Sc/Mont; *Parlez-nous d'amour,* C, 76, CDN, Co prod/Réal/Sc/Mont; *Panique,* C, 76, CDN, Co prod/Réal/Sc/Mont; *Bingo,* C, 73, CDN, Co prod/Réal/Co sc/Mont; *Les Colombes,* C, 72, CDN, Co prod/Réal/Sc/Mont; *Trouble-Fête,* C, 63, CDN, 1er ass réal.

LORD, Roger
ARRQ. 227, boul. Riel, Hull, PQ J8X 5Y9 (819)770-7085.
Types de production et générique: c métrage-Réal; TV film-Réal; TV vidéo-Réal.
Types d'oeuvres: Drame-TV; Documentaire-TV; Education-TV; Enfants-TV.
Curriculum vitae: Né en 1946.
Filmographie sélective: *Acheter la Boulangerie,* "A la recherche de l'homme invisible", C, 91, CDN, Sc/Réal; *SOS: Génération en Détresse* (3 eps), C, 89, CDN, Prod/Réal; "Bloc Notes" (122 eps), TV, 84-87, CDN, Réal; *Choeurs et Cordes Pascals,* TV, 87, CDN, Réal; "Les 100 Coups de Théâtre" (6 eps), C/TV, 87, CDN, Prod/Réal; "Contour" (38 eps), TV, 83, CDN, Réal; "A Tire d'Aile" (78 eps), TV, 81-82, CDN, Réal; "Actualité", TV, 77-80, CDN, Réal.

LORTI, Claude
av. de Lorimier, Montréal, PQ H2G 2P5 (514)386-0778. FAX: 725-2779.
Types de production et générique: TV film-Réal/Prod; TV vidéo-Réal/Prod.
Types d'oeuvres: Documentaire-TV; Industriel-TV; Affaires publiques-TV.
Curriculum vitae: Né en 1947, Montréal, Québec. Langues: français, anglais, espagnol et portugais. Participe comme réalisateur à des séries comme "Le Defi Mondial," "Laissez-passer," "Poste Frontière," "Cinq Milliards d'Hommes" et des magazines d'affaires publiques comme "the fifth estate," "The Journal," "Le Point," et "Table Rase." Ses dernières réalisations l'ont amené en Afrique du Sud, en Israel, en Jordanie et aux Etats-Unis.
Filmographie sélective: "Contact" (7 eps), TV, 90-91, CDN, Réal; *Les Plaintes reliées aux Droits de la Personne,* In, 91, CDN, Réal; "Tes Choix, ta Santé" (2 eps), ED, 90, CDN, Réal; *Le Métro de Montréal,* In, 90, CDN, Réal; *Norsk Hydro,* In, 90, CDN, Réal; "Table Rase" (36 eps), TV, 89, CDN, Réal; *La Carte Environnement Steinberg,* Cm, 90, CDN, Réal; *Une*

Question d'Image, ED, 90, CDN, Réal; "Le Défi mondial" (6 eps), TV, 86, CDN, Réal/Journ.

LOSIER, Aurel
- voir REGISSEURS

LOWER, Robert
- see EDITORS

LUNNY, Shane
- see PRODUCERS

LUSSIER, Jo
- voir MONTEURS

LYNCH, Paul
DGC, DGA. Questcan Inc., 1720 Pacific Ave., Suite 303, Los Angeles, CA 90291 USA (213)392-2621. Barry Perelman Agency, 9200 Sunset Blvd., Suite 531, Hollywood, CA USA (213)274-5999.
Type of Production and Credits: Th Film-Dir; TV Film-Dir.
Genres: Drama-Th&TV; Action-Th; Horror-Th&TV; Documentary-TV.
Biography: Born in Liverpool, England; Canadian citizenship.
Selected Filmography: "Top Cops" (4 eps), TV, 91, CDN/USA, Dir; *Drop Dead Gorgeous*, TV, 91, USA, Dir; "Dark Shadows" (2 eps), TV, 90, USA, Dir; "Sons and Daughters" (2 eps), TV, 90, USA, Dir; "In the Heat of the Night" (2 eps), TV, 90, USA, Dir; "Tour of Duty" (1 eps), TV, 90, USA, Dir; *Murder By Night*, TV, 89, USA, Dir; *Double Your Pleasure*, TV, 89, USA, Dir; *She Knows Too Much*, TV, 89, USA, Dir; "Star Trek - The Next Generation" (3 eps), TV, 87-88, USA, Dir; "The Twilight Zone" (10 eps), TV, 86-88, USA, Dir; "Moonlighting" (2 eps), TV, 87, USA, Dir; *Bullies*, Th, 85, CDN, Dir; *Cross Country*, Th, 82, CDN, Dir; *Prom Night*, Th, 80, CDN, Dir.

MacADAM, William I.
- see PRODUCERS

MacDONALD, Ramuna
CFTPA. Doomsday Studios Ltd., 212 James St., Ottawa, ON K1R 5M7 (613)230-9769. FAX: 230-6004.
Type of Production and Credits: Th Short-Dir/Ed; TV Film-Dir/Prod/Ed.
Genres: Drama-Th&TV; Comedy-Th&TV; Documentary-Th&TV; Animation-Th&TV.
Biography: Canadian citizenship. B.A., B.Sc., special courses, Nova Scotia College of Art and Design. Interim Acting Director, Atlantic Film and Video Festival, 84. *Spirits of an Amber Past* won Chris Bronze Plaque, Columbus International Film Festival; Best Editing Award, Atlantic Film Festival for *Sarah Jackson*. Writer, *Silver Water, Golden Sand* and Executive Producer/Writer, *A Man in the Elevator*, slated for late fall 91/early 92 production.
Selected Filmography: *Silent Conversations*, Th, 91, CDN, Exec Prod; *Rent*, Th, 91, CDN, Ed/Assist Prod; *Hoax*, Th, 91, CND, Assist Prod; *Window*, TV, 87, CDN, Dir/Exec Prod; *La Fenêtre*, TV, 87, CDN, Dir/Exec Prod; "Success" (pilot), TV, 86, CDN, Exec Prod; *Nobody's Perfect*, TV, 86, CDN, Dir/Prod/Wr; *Sarah Jackson*, TV, 80, CDN, Dir/Ed; *God's Island*, Th, 80, CDN, Dir/Ed; *Spirits of An Amber Past*, TV, 78, CDN, Dir/Co-Ed.

MacGILLIVRAY, William D.
Picture Plant Limited, P.O. Box 2465, Stn. M, Halifax, NS B3J 3E8 (902)423-3901.
Type of Production and Credits: Th Short-Dir/Prod/Wr/Mus Ed; TV Film-Dir/Prod/Wr/Mus Ed.
Genres: Drama-Th; Documentary-Th; Educational-Th&TV.
Biography: Born 1946, St. John's, Newfoundland. Founding member, First President, Atlantic Filmmakers Co-operative, the Atlantic Independent Film and Video Association. *Life Classes* was nominated for five Genie Awards, and won four Awards of Excellence, Atlantic Film Festival. *Linda Joy* won Blue Ribbon, American Film and Video Festival, and Special Jury Award, Yorkton Short Film and Video Festival; *Understanding Bliss* won Moonsnail Award (Best Feature Film), Atlantic Film Festival, 90.
Selected Filmography: *Understanding Bliss*, Th, 90, CDN, Dir/Wr/Ed; *No Apologies*, Th, 89-90, CDN, Exec Prod/Ed/Mus Ed; *The Vacant Lot*, Th, 88-89, CDN, Dir/ Wr/Ed; *My Brother Larry*, Th, 88, CDN, Dir; *I Will Not Make Any More Boring Art*, Th, 88, CDN, Exec Prod/Dir/Wr/Mus Ed; *Life Classes*, Th, 86, CDN, Dir/Wr/ Exec Prod; *Linda Joy*, Th, 85, CDN, Dir; *Abraham Gesner*, TV, 85, CDN, Dir; *Alistair MacLeod*, TV, 84, CDN, Dir/Wr/Prod; *Stations*, TV, 81, CDN, Dir/Wr/Prod/Ed; *The Author of These Words*, Th, 80, CDN, Dir/Wr/Prod; *Aerial View*, Th, 79, CDN, Dir/Wr/Prod/ Ed; *Breakdown*, TV, 77, CDN, 2nd AD; *7:30 A.M.*, Th, 71, CDN, Dir/Wr; *Talkautobanden*, Th, 70, CDN, Dir/Co-Wr/Cin.

MACKAY, Bruce
SGCT. 100 Ballantyne S., Montreal West, PQ H4X 2B3 (514)484-5668.
Type of Production and Credits: Th Short-Dir/Wr/Ed; TV Film-Dir/Prod/Ed.
Genres: Drama-Th&TV; Documentary-

Th&TV; Educational-Th&TV; Children's-Th&TV.
Biography: Born 1945, Montreal, Quebec. Languages: English and French. Produced playwright and songwriter/singer with 2 albums. *Gulf Stream* won the Grand Prize, Rio de Janeiro Science Film Festival; *Life on Ice* won 4 awards (including Best Film) at the 10th International Wildlife Film Festival; *Equatorial River* won Silver Apple Award, National Educational Film & Video Festival.
Selected Filmography: *The Safe Program*, ED, 90, CDN/USA, Wr/Dir; *Audition*, Th/TV, 89, CDN, Wr/Dir; *Eugene Levy Discovers Home Safety*, TV, 88, CDN, Prod/Wr/Dir/Ed; *Reznikoff's Revenge*, Th, 88, CDN, Dir/Wr/Ed; *Life on Ice*, ED, 87, CDN, Prod/Ed; *Equatorial River*, ED, 86, CDN, Dir/Ed; *Arctic River*, ED, 86, CDN, Dir/Ed; *Edge of Ice*, TV, 85, CDN, Prod/Ed; *Starbreaker*, Th, 85, CDN, Dir/Co-Ed/Wr; *Uncertain Future*, TV, 84, CDN, Snd Des; *Mozambique: Communal Village*, TV, 81, CDN, Prod; *Gulf Stream*, TV, 81, CDN/USA, Prod/Dir/Ed; *Northern Composition*, TV, 79, CDN, Prod/Dir/Ed; *Sail Away*, TV, 79, CDN/USA, Dir/Prod/Ed; Energy Conservation, Cm, 76, CDN, Dir/Ed.

MACKAY, David
- see PRODUCERS

MACKEY, Clarke
ACCT. 260 College St., Kingston, ON K7L 4M2 (613)547-6623. Telltales Ltd., Film Studies, Queen's University, Kingston, ON K7A 3N6 (613)545-2178.
Type of Production and Credits: Th Film-Dir/Prod/Wr/Ed; TV Film-Dir/Wr/Ed.
Genres: Drama-Th&TV; Comedy-TV; Documentary-Th&TV; Children's-TV.
Biography: Born 1950, Welland, Ontario. Trained as an assistant editor with Tony Lower, Vincent Kent and others at CBC, 68-70. Visiting Lecturer in Film at York University, 75-77. *Taking Care* won CFTA Award, 87, for New Feature Production and Kate Lynch was nominated for Best Actress, Genie, 88. Currently Assistant Professor, Dept. of Film Studies, Queen's University.
Selected Filmography: "Degrassi Junior High" (3 eps), TV, 86-87, CDN, Dir; *Taking Care*, Th, 86, CDN, Exec Prod/Dir, (CFTA); *Pulling Flowers*, TV, 85, CDN, Wr/Dir; *All Day Long*, TV, 84, CDN, Wr/Dir; *As We Are*, ED, 84, CDN, DOP; *Not One of the Crowd*, TV, 81, CDN, ED; *A Right to Live*, ED, 77, CDN, Prod/Dir/Wr/Ed; "The Peep Show" (1 eps), TV, 75, CDN, Dir; "Police Surgeon" (3 eps), TV, 73-74, USA, Ed; *Janis*, Th, 74, CDN/USA, Cam; *The Megantic Outlaw*, TV, 71, CDN, Co-Ed; *The Only Thing You Know*, Th, 71, CDN, Prod/Dir/Wr/Ed; *Mr. Pearson*, TV, 69, CDN, Co-Ed.

MACNEE, Rupert
- see PRODUCERS

MALLET, Marilu
ARRFQ. 743, Davaar, Outremont, PQ H2V 3B3 (514)272-0292.
Types de production et générique: c métrage-Réal/Prod/Mont; TV film-Réal/Mont.
Types d'oeuvres: Drame-C&TV; Documentaire-C&TV.
Curriculum vitae: Née en 1944, Santiago, Chili; citoyenneté canadienne. Maîtrise en Cinéma, Université de Montréal, 85; Ecole d'Etudes Cinématographiques de l'O.C.I.C., Santiago, Chili, Initiation au cinéma, 67-69; Architecture, Université du Chili, 64-69. *Journal inachevé* remporte le Prix de la Critique Québécoise et le Prix Spécial, Festival de Biarritz, France; Fellow de la Société John Guggenheim, New York; *Chère Amérique* a gagné Prix au meilleur documentaire essaie et création SCAM, FIPA, Cannes, 91; *Mémoires d'une enfant des Andes* a gagné Bronze Apple, catégorie Social Studies (Elementary), 21 Festival de films et vidéos en éducation, Oakland, 91.
Filmographie sélective: *Chère Amérique*, "Parler d'Amérique", TV, 90, CDN, Rech/Réal; *Mémoires d'une enfant des Andes/Child of the Andes*, C, 85, CDN, Réal/Rech; *Journal inachevé*, C, 83, CDN, Réal/Prod/Mont; *Hommage à Jordi Bonet/Pierre et le Capitaine*, "Planète", TV, 80, CDN, Réal/Mont; *Les "Borges"*, C, 79, CDN, Réal/Rech.

MALTBY, David
DGC. P.O. Box 448, Madoc, ON K0K 2K0 (613)473-4579.
Type of Production and Credits: TV Film-Dir; TV Video-Dir.
Genres: Drama-TV; Musical-Th&TV; Documentary-TV; Commercials-TV.
Biography: Born in 1945 in Hull, East Yorkshire, England; Canadian citizen. Film Festival awards: New York, San Francisco, Houston, Ohio, Yorkton.
Selected Filmography: *The Breakfast Club*, ED, 90, CDN, Dir; *Only Croît*, Cm, 90, CDN, Dir; *In Concert*, In, 89, CDN, Dir; *Remembrance*, TV/MV, 89, CDN, Dir; *Greenwing*, TV, 84, CDN, Dir; *Janis*, Th, 74, CDN, Ed.

MANATIS, Janine ◆
(416)691-1010.
Type of Production and Credits: Th Film-Dir/Wr; Th Short-Dir/Act; TV Film-Dir/Act.
Genres: Drama-Th; Documentary-Th&TV.
Biography: Born in US; landed immigrant Canada. Trained at Actors Studio, New York, as actor, director. Dialogue coach for film and individual lyricist.
Selected Filmography: *Iron Eagle II*, Th, 88, CDN/IL, Act; "Tuesday Night Dramas" (26 eps), TV, 87-88, CDN, Host; "Wednesday Night Specials" (26 eps), TV, 87, CDN, Host; *Intensive Care*, TV, 85, USA, Act; *Teen Mother: A Story of Coping*, Th, 83, CDN, Dir/Co-Wr; *The Hotel New Hampshire*, Th, 83, USA, Act; *Breaking Out*, Th, 82, CDN, Dir; *In a Far Country*, "Jack London's Tales of the Klondike", TV, 81, CDN, Dir; *After the Axe*, Th, 81, CDN, Act; *I, Maureen*, Th, 78, CDN, Dir/Wr; *Ottawa Valley*, TV, 76, CDN, Dir; "The Times They Are A-Changin'" (3 eps), TV, 75, CDN, Dir/Prod.

MANGAARD, Annette
TWIFT, LIFT, CFDC. Three Blondes Inc., 72 Rusholme Rd., Toronto, ON M6J 3H7.
Type of Production and Credits: Th Film-Wr/Prod/Dir; Th Short-Wr/Prod/Dir.
Genres: Drama-Th; Comedy-Th; Documentary-Th&TV; Experimental-Th&TV.
Biography: Born in 1956 in Lille Vaerlose, Denmark. Canadian citizen. Speaks English and Danish. Ontario College of Art (A.O.C.A. Honours), 76-80. Selected solo screenings: Edmonton, 91; Berlin, 90; Toronto, 1990; Vancouver, 89; Sao Paolo, Brazil, 88. Chairman, Board of Directors, Canadian Filmmakers Distribu-tion Centre, 90-91. Director: Images Festival of Independent Film & Video, 88-91; Toronto Arts Council, 89-90; The Funnel Experimental Film Theatre, 86-87.
Selected Filmography: *Let Me Wrap My Arms Around You*, Th, 91, CDN, Wr/Prod/Dir; *A Dialogue With Vision*, Th, 90, CDN, Dir/Co Prod; *Northbound Cairo*, Th, 87, CDN, Wr/Dir/Co Prod; *The Iconography of Venus*, Th, 87, CDN, Wr/Prod/Dir; *The Tyranny of Architecture*, Th, 87, CDN, Wr/Prod/Dir; *Her Soil Is Gold*, Th, 86, CDN, Wr/Prod/Dir; *There Is In Power...Seduction*, Th, 85, CDN, Wr/Prod/Dir; *She Bit Me Seriously*, Th, 84, CDN, Dir; *Nothing By Mouth*, Th, 84, CDN, Dir.

MANKIEWICZ, Francis
711, Stuart, Montréal, PQ H2V 3H4 (514)495-8055. Great North Artists Mgmt., 350 Dupont St., Toronto, ON M5R 1V9 (416)925-2051.
Types de production et générique: l métrage-Réal/Sc; c métrage-Réal; TV film-Réal; TV vidéo-Réal.
Types d'oeuvres: Drame-C&TV; Documentaire-C&TV; Education-C&TV; Annonces-TV.
Curriculum vitae: Né en 1944, Chang-Hai, Chine; citoyenneté canadienne. Baccalauréat en Sciences (Géologie), Université de Montréal; London School of Film Techniques, Angleterre (2 ans). Caméraman pigiste, Angleterre, 68; *Le temps d'une chasse* a été invité au Festival du Film de Cannes, a remporté un prix au Festival du Film de Venise et un Prix Spécial aux Palmarès du film canadien; *Les Bons Débarras* remporte 8 Génies dont Meilleur Film, a aussi été sélectionné comme entrée officielle du Canada aux Academy Awards; *Les Portes tournantes*, sélection officielle du Festival de Cannes, France, a reçu une mention oecuménique, 88, a gagné 2 Prix Génies, Prix le Permanent, 88, Prix France-Canada, Sélection canadienne officielle aux Academy Awards; *Love and Hate* gagnant de 7 Prix Gémeaux dont Prix Gémeau pour Meilleur Réalisateur, et Prix Anik du Meilleur Réalisateur.
Filmographie sélective: *Conspiracy of Silence* (mini-série), TV, 90, CDN,; *Love and Hate* (mini-série), TV, 89, CDN,; *Les Portes tournantes*, C, 87, CDN/F, Réal; *And Then You Die*, TV, 86, CDN, Réal; *The Sight*, "Bell Canada Playhouse", TV, 85, CDN, Réal; *Les Beaux Souvenirs*, C, 80, CDN, Réal; *Les Bons Débarras*, C, 78, CDN, Réal, (GENIE); *I Was Dying Away*, ED, 77, CDN, Réal; *A Matter of Choice*, "For the Record", TV, 77, CDN, Réal; *Une amie d'enfance*, C, 77, CDN, Réal; *Pointe Pelee*, C, 76, CDN, Réal; *Expropriation*, TV, 75, CDN, Réal; *Procès criminel/Orientation/Cause civile*, ED, 74, CDN, Réal; *Les Allées de la terre*, C, 73, CDN, Prod exéc; *Valentin*, TV, 73, CDN/CH/F, Réal.

MANN, Danny
- see WRITERS

MANN, Ron
ACCT. Sphinx Productions, 24 Mercer St., Toronto, ON M5V 1H3 (416)971-9131. FAX: 971-6014. The Colbert Agency, 303 Davenport Rd., Toronto, ON M5R 1K5 (416)964-3302.
Type of Production and Credits: Th

Film-Dir/Prod/Wr; Th Short-Dir/Prod/Wr; TV Film-Dir/Prod/Wr.
Genres: Drama-Th; Documentary-Th.
Biography: Born 1958, Toronto, Ontario. B.A., University of Toronto. Films he has produced and/or directed have won numerous prizes including Silver Hugo, Chicago, *Imagine the Sound*; Gold Plaque, Chicago, *Poetry in Motion* and Genie Award, *Comic Book Confidential*. Board member, United States Film Festival (Sundance Institute).
Selected Filmography: *Twist*, Th, 91, CDN, Prod/Dir/Wr; *Special of the Day*, TV, 89, CDN, Exec Prod; *Comic Book Confidential*, Th, 88, CDN, Prod/Dir/Wr; *Hoods in the Woods*, Th, 86, USA, Wr; *Making Legal Eagles*, TV, 86, USA, Dir; *Marcia Resnick's Bad Boys*, Th, 85, CDN, Prod/Dir; *New Cinema*, TV, 84, CDN, Assoc Prod; *Listen to the City*, Th, 84, CDN, Prod/Dir/Co-Wr; *Echoes without Saying*, TV, 83, CDN, Prod/Dir; *Imagine the Sound*, Th, 81, CDN, Co-Prod/Dir; *Poetry in Motion*, Th, 81, CDN, Prod/Dir; *Sshhh!*, Th, 80, CDN, Prod/Dir; *Feels So Good*, Th, 80, CDN, Prod/Co-Dir; *The Only Game in Town*, Th, 79, CDN, Co-Prod/Co-Dir/Co-Wr; *Dépôt*, Th, 78, CDN, Co-Prod/Co-Dir.

MARCOUX, Royal
AR. 740, Victoria, Longueuil, PQ J4H 2K3 (514)677-3147. Radio-Canada, 1400 est, boul. René-Lévesque, Montréal, PQ H3C 3A1 (514)597-5970.
Types de production et générique: TV film-Réal; TV vidéo-Réal.
Types d'oeuvres: Drame-TV; Comédie-TV; Variété-TV; Documentaire-TV.
Curriculum vitae: Né en 1944, Thetford-Mines, Québec. Baccalauréat ès Arts, Université de Sherbrooke; stage en technique télévisuelle, Ryerson Polytechnical Institute.
Filmographie sélective: "Jamais deux sans toi" (10 eps), TV, 90-91, CDN, Réal; "Un Signe de Feu" (8 eps), TV, 89-90, CDN, Réal; "Ma Tante Alice" (36 eps), TV, 88-89, CDN, Réal; "L'Autobus du Show Business" (30 eps), TV, 87-88, CDN, Réal; "Superstar" (10 eps), TV, 85-87, CDN, Réal; "Le 101 ouest, av. des Pins" (24 eps), TV, 84-85, CDN, Réal; *Super Star*, "Les Beaux Dimanches", TV, 85, CDN, Réal; "Allô Boubou" (80 eps), TV, 82-84, CDN, Réal; "Du tac au tac" (8 eps), TV, 81-82, CDN, Réal; "L'Observateur" (24 eps), TV, 78-81, CDN, Réal; "L'Heure de pointe" (65 eps), TV, 77-78, CDN, Réal; "Mesdames et Messieurs" (15 eps), TV, 76-77, CDN, Réal; "Lise Lib" (22 eps), TV, 75-76, CDN, Réal; "Appelez-moi Lise" (85 eps), TV, 72-75, CDN, Réal.

MARION, Jean-Claude
AR. 3542 Marcil, Montréal, PQ H4A 2Z3 (514)483-1755. Radio-Canada, 1400 est, boul. René Lévesque, Montréal, PQ H2L 2M2 (514)597-4959.
Types de production et générique: TV film-Réal.
Types d'oeuvres: Documentaire-TV.
Curriculum vitae: Né en 1940, Marionville, Ontario. Langues: français, anglais et allemand. Baccalauréat avec spécialisation en Sciences politiques, Université d'Ottawa. Trois ans de réalisation radio; réalisateur TV, CBOFT, Ottawa, 66-75; directeur de la radio des Forces Canadiennes en Europe (R.F.A.), 75-82; retour à la réalisation TV, Montréal. *Les Maladies mentales*, refait pour "Les Beaux Dimanches", a gagné le Prix Media du Canadian Nurses Association.
Filmographie sélective: *Lalkali: Doigts d'acier, pieds d'ébène*, "Partenaires", TV, 90-91, CDN, Réal; *Lalkali: Woman of Nepal*, "Partners", TV, 90-91, CDN, Réal; *Les Enfants du Divorce*, "Les Beaux Dimanches", TV, 89, CDN, Réal; *Les Maladies mentales*, "Au jour le jour" (13 eps), TV, 88, CDN, Réal; *Les Maladies mentales*, "Les Beaux Dimanches" (2 eps), TV, 88, CDN, Réal; "Ici Radio Canada" (14 eps), TV, 86, CDN, Réal; *Inceste*, "Les Beaux Dimanches", TV, 86, CDN, Réal; *Les Infants du Cancer*, "Les Beaux Dimanches", TV, 84, CDN, Réal; *New York, Délinquence juvenile*, TV, 84-85, CDN/F/CH/B, Réal.

MARKIW, Gabriel
- see PRODUCERS

MARKIW, Jancarlo
442 Marion St., Winnipeg, MB R2H 0V7 (204)233-1930. O'Meara Productions Ltd., 63 Albert St., Suite 200, Winnipeg, MB R3B 1G4 (204)943-3133.
Type of Production and Credits: Th Film-Wr; Th Short-Prod/Dir; TV Film-Dir/Wr/Prod; TV Video-Dir/Wr.
Genres: Drama-TV; Documentary-Th&TV; Educational-TV; Experimental-Th.
Biography: Born 1956, San Benedetto de Tronto, Italy; Canadian citizenship. Languages: English and Italian. B.A., Film Studies, University of Manitoba. Former musician and freelance journalist. Awards include Best Short, Yorkton; nominated for Best Drama, Yorkton; Best TV Drama, Italy.

Selected Filmography: *Mob Story*, Th, 89, CDN, Dir/Wr/Prod; *Not a Bad Year*, TV, 86, CDN, Co-Dir/Co-Wr/Co-Prod; *Rising Image*, TV, 85, CDN, Co-Dir/Co-Wr; *Concertante: Arnold Spohr and the Royal Winnipeg Ballet*, TV, 84, CDN, Co-Prod; *Carlo*, TV, 83, CDN, Co-Dir/Co-Wr; *Kelekis*, Th, 82, CDN, Prod; *All Work, No Play*, ED, 80, CDN, Dir/Wr/Prod.

MARKSON, Morley
Morley Markson & Assoc. Ltd., 2900 Bathurst St., Suite 208, Toronto, ON M6B 3A9 (416)784-1229.
Type of Production and Credits: Th Film-Dir/Prod; TV Video-Dir/Prod.
Genres: Drama-Th; Comedy-Th; Documentary-Th&TV.
Biography: Born Toronto, Ontario. Designer, photographer, filmmaker. Designed *Kaleidoscope*, Expo 67. International Photography Exhibition: *Man and his World*, Holocaust Museum & Educational Center. Filmmaking: *Breathing Together: Revolution of the Electric Family* was French Film Critics' Selection, Cannes, and First Prize Winner, Ann Arbor Film Festival; *The Tragic Diary of Zero the Fool* was First Prize winner, Ann Arbor Film Festival; *Monkeys in the Attic*, was Best Foreign Film, Toulon Film Festival; *Growing Up in America* was Best Documentary, Mannheim Film Festival.
Selected Filmography: *Growing Up in America*, Th, 89, CDN, Dir/Prod; *From Out of the Depths*, Th, 85, CDN, Dir/Prod; *Off Your Rocker*, Th, 80, CDN, Co-Wr/Co-Dir; *Monkeys in the Attic*, Th, 74, CDN, Dir/Prod; *Breathing Together: Revolution of the Electric Family*, Th, 71, CDN, Dir/Prod; *The Tragic Diary of Zero the Fool*, Th, 70, CDN, Dir/Prod; *Man and Colour: Kaleidoscope* (Expo 67), Th, 67, CDN, Dir/Prod.

MARR, Alan
16 Apsley Rd., Toronto, ON M5M 2X8 (416)485-5155.
Types of Production and Credits: Th Short-Dir/Wr.
Genres: Comedy-Th; Commercials-TV; Corporate-TV.
Biography: Born in 1945. Canadian citizen. Graduated from the University of Guelph, 86. Worked for 8 years as a copywriter and creative group head at 5 different ad agencies in Toronto; won many national and international awards. Became a TV commercial director, 76; has since directed over 500 commercials and won several Clios and numerous international and national recognitions. Wrote and directed *Edsville*, a 14-minute short that premiered at the 1990 Festival of Festivals and is currently being theatrically released.
Selected Filmography: *Edsville*, Th, 90, CDN, Dir/Co-Wr; Ontario Wine Council (3 spots), Cm, 91, CDN, Dir; *Grampa's Computer*, Senior Citizens, Cm, 88, CDN, Dir; *Hospital Beds*, Philishave, Cm, 85, CDN, Dir, (CLIO).

MARR, Leon G. ✧
(416)691-1215.
Type of Production and Credits: Th Film-Dir/Wr; TV Film-Dir/Prod.
Genres: Drama-Th&TV.
Biography: Born 1948, Toronto, Ontario. B.A.A., Photographic Arts, Ryerson Polytechnical Institute. *Dancing in the Dark* was invited to Directors' Fortnight, Cannes, 86, and Festival of Festivals and New York Film Festival.
Selected Filmography: *Dancing in the Dark*, Th, 85, CDN, Dir/Scr, (GENIE 87); *Flowers in the Sand*, TV, 80, CDN, Dir/Co-Prod; *Clare's Wish*, TV, 79, CDN, Dir/Co-Prod.

MARSHALL, Peter D.
DGC. 21 - 3939 River Dr., North Vancouver, BC V7G 2P5 Carole Bennett, 150 South Barrington Ave., Suite 1, Los Angeles, CA 90049 (213)471-2251.
Type of Production and Credits: Th Film-1st AD; TV Film-Dir/1st AD.
Genres: Drama-Th&TV; Documentary-TV; Educational-TV; Commercials-TV.
Biography: Born 1951, Hamilton, Ontario. B.A.A., Motion Picture, Ryerson Polytechnical Institute, 73. Awards for *Aeromedical Transportation* include First Prize, John Muir Medical Film Festival; Second Prize, Health Sciences Communication.
Selected Filmography: "Scene of the Crime" (1 eps), TV, 90, USA/CDN/F, Dir; "21 Jumpstreet" (1 eps), TV, 90, USA, Dir; "Wiseguy" (2 eps), TV, 90, USA, Dir; "Booker" (1 eps), TV, 90, USA, Dir; "The Black Stallion" (2 eps), TV, 90, CDN/F, Dir; "Mom P.I." (1 eps), TV, 90, CDN, Dir; *The Fly II*, Th, 88, USA, 1st AD; "Wiseguy" (6 eps), TV, 87-88, CDN, 1st AD; "J.J. Starbuck" (5 eps), TV, 87, USA, 1st AD; "Stingray" (4 eps), TV, 87, USA, 1st AD; *By Your Side*, MV, 86, CDN, 1st AD; "Hamilton's Quest" (1 eps), TV, 86, CDN, Dir; *Walsh*, TV, 86, CDN, 1st AD; *On the Edge*, TV, 85, CDN, 1st AD; *Aeromedical Transportation*, ED, 80, CDN, Wr/Dir.

MARTIN, Maude ✧
(514)272-7647.
Types de production et générique: TV

vidéo-Réal.
Types d'oeuvres: Drame-TV; Comédie-TV.
Curriculum vitae: Née en 1944, Montréal, Québec. Langues: français et anglais. A travaillé comme assistant réalisatrice et réalisatrice à Radio-Canada depuis plus de 20 ans.
Filmographie sélective: "Des dames de coeur" (26 eps), TV, 86-88, CDN, Réal; "Poivre et sel" (37 eps), TV, 83-86, CDN, Réal, (GEMEAUX 86); "Métro-Boulot-Dodo" (22 eps), TV, 82-83, CDN, Réal; "Chez Denyse" (40 eps), TV, 80-82, CDN, Réal; "Caroline" (13 eps), TV, 79-80, CDN, Réal; "Grand-Papa" (10 eps), TV, 79, CDN, Réal; "A cause de mon oncle eps), TV, 78, CDN, Réal.

MARTIN, Susan ◆
(213)463-3743.
Type of Production and Credits: Th Film-Dir/Wr/Ed; TV Film-Dir/Wr/Ed.
Genres: Drama-Th&TV; Comedy-Th&TV; Variety-TV; Children's-TV.
Biography: Born in Baltimore, Maryland; Canadian citizenship. Attended Ontario College of Art, 2 years; Goddard College, Vermont, York University and UCLA Film School. Films she has worked on have won awards at New York, San Francisco, Chicago and Berlin film festivals.
Selected Filmography: "Danger Bay" (1 eps), TV, 86, CND, Dir; "Airwaves" (3 eps) (Wr 2 eps), TV, 85-86, CDN, Dir; "Fraggle Rock" (5 eps) (Co-Wr 1 eps), TV, 85, CDN, Dir; *The Ovaltine Café*, Th, 85, USA, Co-Wr; *Rosedale*, "Neighbourhoods", TV, 84, CDN, Dir; *Parallel Tracks*, "For the Record", TV, 83, CDN, Co-Wr; *The Glitter Dome*, TV, 83, CDN/USA, Ed; *Is Anyone Home on the Range*, TV, 83, USA, Ed; *Threshold*, Th, 80, CDN, Ed; *First Family*, Th, 80, USA, Ed; *Blow Job*, "Saturday Night Live", TV, 78, USA, Dir; *The Black Stallion*, Th, 78, USA, Co-Ed; *Days of Heaven*, Th, 77, USA, Co-Ed; "Flakes" (pilot), TV, 77, USA, Ed; *Beachboys Special*, TV, 76, USA, Co-Ed.

MATHUR, Vishnu
- see PRODUCERS

MATTHEWS, Bill ◆
(819)684-8698.
Type of Production and Credits: TV Film-Dir; TV Video-Dir.
Genres: Variety-TV; Documentary-TV; Animation-TV; News-TV.
Biography: Born 1947, Montreal, Quebec. Languages: English and French. Has worked in Canada, USA, Great Britain, France, Italy, China, Japan, Hong Kong;
Selected Filmography: "Entertainment Tomato" (3 eps), TV, 86, CDN, Dir; *1984 Democratic Convention*, TV, 84, USA, Dir; "Niteline", TV, 83-84, USA, Dir; "Space Shuttle Challenger" (8 eps), TV, 83-84, USA, Dir; "World News Tonight", TV, 83-84, USA, Dir; *America's Cup*, TV, 83, USA, Dir; "The Journal" (175 eps), TV, 80-82, CDN, Dir; *Federal Elections*, TV, 79-80, CDN, Dir; *Oh, What a Feeling*, TV, 80, CDN, Dir.

McANDREW, Jack
- see WRITERS

McBREARTY, Don
DGC. 117 Niagara St., Toronto, ON M5V 1C6 (416)365-1810. (416)769-0540. Pamela Paul, 1778 Bloor St. W., Suite 14, Toronto, ON M6P 3K4 (416)975-9334.
Type of Production and Credits: TV Film-Dir.
Genres: Drama-Th&TV.
Biography: *A Child's Christmas in Wales* awarded the 1988 Gemini for Best Short Drama; Gold Special Jury Award, Houston International Film Festival, 1988; Special Jury Award, Chicago International Festival of Children's Films, 1987; Gold Plaque, 23rd Chicago International Film Festival; Best Production for Children, 24th Yorkton Short Film and Video Festival. *Boys & Girls* won the 1984 Oscar award for Best Short Live Action. *An Ounce of Cure* won the CFTA Award, 1984, for Best Drama and Best Overall Production.
Selected Filmography: "The Road to Avonlea" (5 eps), TV, 89-91, CDN, Dir; "E.N.G." (5 eps), TV, 89-91, CDN/USA, Dir; "21 Jump Street" (2 eps), TV, 90, USA, Dir; *The Private Capital*, TV, 89, CDN, Dir; "My Secret Identity" (pilot), TV, 87, CDN/USA, Dir; *A Child's Christmas in Wales*, TV, 87, CDN/USA, Dir, (GEMINI); "V.H. Adderly" (pilot, 2 eps), TV, 86-87, CDN/USA, Dir; *Cursed With Charisma*, "Really Weird Tales", TV, 86, CDN/USA, Dir; *The Town Where No One Got Off*, "Ray Bradbury Theatre", TV, 86, CDN/USA, Dir; *And Miles To Go*, TV, 85, CDN/USA, Dir; *I Love a Man in a Uniform*, TV, 83, CDN/USA, Dir; *An Ounce of Cure*, "Sons and Daughters", TV, 83, CDN/USA, Dir; *Boys & Girls*, "Sons and Daughters", TV, 83, CDN/USA, Dir; *American Nightmare*, Th, 82, CDN/USA, Dir; *Coming Out Alive*, TV, 79, CDN, Dir.

McCOWAN, George
DGA. Mark Lichtman, Shapiro-

Lichtman Agency, 1800 Ave. of the Stars, Los Angeles, CA 90067 USA (213)859-8877.
Type of Production and Credits: Th Film-Dir; TV Film-Dir; TV Video-Dir.
Genres: Drama-Th&TV; Comedy-Th&TV.
Biography: Born in Winnipeg, Manitoba; US resident alien. B.A., University of Toronto. Has directed hundreds of episodes for TV series and movies for TV in US and Canada. *Run Simon Run* won the Cowboy Hall of Fame Award.
Selected Filmography: "Seeing Things" (60 eps), TV, 81-88, CDN, Dir; "Hart to Hart" (10 eps), TV, 82-84, USA, Dir; "Starsky and Hutch" (20 eps), TV, 75-79, USA, Dir; "Charlie's Angels" (15 eps), TV, 75-79, USA, Dir; "Streets of San Francisco" (20 eps), TV, 71-75, USA, Dir; "Cannon" (40 eps), TV, 71-75, USA, Dir; *The Magnificent Seven Ride*, Th, 72, USA, Dir; *Carter's Army*, TV, 70, USA, Dir; *Face-Off*, Th, 70, CDN, Dir; *Frogs*, Th, 70, USA, Dir; "F.B.I." (20 eps), TV, 67-69, USA, Dir; *Ballad of Andy Crocker*, TV, 69, USA, Dir; *Run Simon Run*, TV, 69, USA, Dir; "Run for Your Life" (6 eps), TV, 67-69, USA, Dir.

McCURDY, Mark
CSC. 35 Cowan Place, London, ON N5W 3W6 (519)519-6006. FAX: 686-1714. Lockwood Films London Inc., 365 Ontario St., London, ON N5W 3W6 (519)434-6006.
Type of Production and Credits: TV Film-Dir/Prod/Wr; TV Video-Dir/Prod.
Genres: Documentary-TV; Educational-TV; Commercials-TV; Industrial-TV; Corporate-Th.
Biography: Born 1950, Montreal, Quebec. Attended St. Francis Xavier University. Started professional career in news and documentary programming; has worked for CBC and CTV National News. Founding partner, Lockwood Films; versatile director with production of over 1500 training/educational/public relations/ sales videos, films and multi-image shows, as well as TV commercials and document-aries. Has shot on location across Canada, the US, Europe, Peru, Bolivia and the Caribbean. Has won many national and international awards for his work, including awards at the New York Film Festival, US Industrial Film & Video Festival, Columbus Film Festival, the Canadian Film & Television Festival and the American Film Festival.
Selected Filmography: *Heart to Heart*, ED, 91, CDN, Prod/Dir; *Mine Launcher*, In, 91, CDN, Prod/Dir; *Back Doctor*, In, 90, CDN, Prod/Dir; *Headache*, In, 90, CDN, Prod/Dir; *Kids' Play*, Cm, 90, CDN, Prod/Dir; *It Works for Us*, In, 90, CDN, Prod/Dir; *The Summit*, In, 90, CDN, Prod/Dir; *Zebra Mussels*, Cm, 90, CDN, Prod; *Champions for Change*, In, 90, CDN, Prod/Dir; *Big V School*, In, 90, CDN, Prod/Dir; *Living the Vision*, In, 90, CDN, Prod; *A Symbol of Excellence*, In, 89, CDN, Prod/Dir; *Physical Activity*, ED, 89, CDN, Prod/Dir; *Burn Prevention*, ED, 89, CDN, Prod/Dir; *Doctor Woman*, TV, 79, CDN, Prod/Dir.

McEWEN, Mary Anne
- see WRITERS

McGLYNN, Gordon Paul
CSC. 180 Kirkpatrick St., Kingston, ON K7K 2P5 (613)544-0942. GT Video & Film Productions, 180 Kirkpatrick St., Kingston, ON K7K 2P5 (613)544-0942.
Type of Production and Credits: Th Short-Dir/Ed/Cin; TV Video-Dir/Ed/Cin.
Genres: Comedy-TV; Animation-Th&TV; Industrial-TV; Promotional-Th&TV.
Biography: Born 1963, Kingston, Ontario. B.A. (Honours), Film Studies, Queen's University. Currently, along with three other Queen's grads, owns and operates a film and video production company, GT Video & Film Productions, specializing in the production of industrial and com-mercial films and videos. As a student at Queen's, produced - with two other students - an award-winning short film, *A Symphony of Toys;* awarded first place in CBC's Telefest (animation category), first place in the SWATCH Festival (prize included the transferring of the film to 35mm and a national theatrical release by MGM), and second place in First Choice/Superchannel's *Great Canadian Shorts* contest. It has also appeared in festivals from Moscow to San Francisco.
Selected Filmography: *Excerpts from Dave Broadfoot's Comedy Crusade*, In, 91, CDN, Ed/Cin; *Chamber News*, Intro, TV, 90, CDN, Ed/Dir/Cin; *1,000 Islands Tours & Travel: Your Vacation Destination!*, In, 90, CDN, Dir/Ed/Cin; *It's All Here in Frontenac County!*, In, 89, CDN, Ed/Dir/Cin; *Room To Grow*, In, 89, CDN, Ed/Dir/Cin; *The Next Move*, In, 89, CDN, Dir/Cin; *Watch Us Grow in Frontenac County!*, In, 89, CDN, Ed/Dir/Cin; *A Symphony of Toys*, Th, 85, CDN, Co Dor/Co-Ed/Set Des/Light.

McGREEVY, John
- see PRODUCERS

McILVRIDE, David
2078 Dickson Rd., Mississauga, ON L5B 1Y6 (416)848-6417.
Type of Production and Credits: Th Film-Assoc Prod; TV Video-Dir/Prod.
Genres: Documentary-TV; Commercials-TV; Industrial-TV; Sports-TV.
Biography: Born in 1951 in London, Ontario. Canadian citizen. Graduate of Niagara College, majoring in film. Taught both college (television production) and, in a cross-cultural setting, Inuit students in the far north (television production). An award winner at the U.S. Industrial Film and Video festival. Has won EVA awards from I.T.V.A. Over 250 industrial (corporate) videos produced, written and directed over the past 13 years.
Selected Filmography: *The Spirit Soars*, TV, 91, CDN, Prod/Wr/Dir; *Canadian National Wheelchair Championship*, TV, 91, CDN, Prod/Wr/Dir; *Same Old Song*, MV, 91, CDN, Dir; *Whodunit*, Th, 85, CDN, Assoc Prod.

McINTYRE, JoAnn
ACTRA, DGC. Equity, 1305 St. Clair Ave. W., Toronto, ON M5E 1C2 (416)658-9242. Oscars & Abrams, 59 Berkeley St., Toronto, ON M5A 2W5 (416)860-1790.
Type of Production and Credits: Th Film-Wr/Ed; TV Film-Wr/Ed.
Genres: Drama-Th&TV; Documentary-Th.
Biography: Born 1949, Windsor, Ontario. Bachelor of Fine Arts, University of Alberta. Pauline McGibbon Award for Best New Director in Theatre Medium, 88; Dora Mavor Moore Award for Best Direction, 90. Professional playwright/director/performer for theatre. Also works as script consultant.
Selected Filmography: *Palais Royale*, Th, 87, CDN, Assoc Prod; *Salud*, ED, 84, CDN, Co-Dir/Wr; *That's My Baby!*, Th, 82, CDN, Act.

McKEOWN, Bob
- see PRODUCERS
McKEOWN, Brian
- see PRODUCERS
McKNIGHT, Bruce E.
- see PRODUCERS
McLACHLAN, Robert B.
- see CINEMATOGRAPHERS
McLAREN, Ian
- see PRODUCERS
McLELLAN, Doug
- see CINEMATOGRAPHERS
MEDAK, Peter ✧
(213)662-2411.
Type of Production and Credits: Th Film-Dir; TV Film-Dir; TV Video-Dir.
Genres: Drama-Th&TV; Comedy-Th&TV; Musical-Th&TV; Action-Th&TV; Horror-Th; Commercials-Th&TV; Music Video-TV.
Biography: Born 1939, Budapest, Hungary; landed immigrant Canada; US resident alien. Entered film industry as trainee with APBC Studios, England, and worked in editing, sound and camera departments to become assistant director, 2nd unit director and associate producer; began directing for television, 63, and features, 67.
Selected Filmography: *Fatal Charm*, Th, 88, USA, Dir; "Crime Story", TV, 87, USA, Dir; "Beauty and the Beast" (1 eps), TV, 87, USA, Dir; "Mount Royal" (pilot), TV, 87, CDN/F, Dir; *The Men's Club*, Th, 86, USA, Dir; *Nabokov*, TV, 85, USA, Dir; "The Twilight Zone" (6 eps), TV, 85, CDN/USA, Dir; "Faerie Tale Theater" (5 eps), TV, 84, USA, Dir; "Magnum P.I." (1 eps), TV, 84, USA, Dir; "St. Elsewhere" (1 eps), TV, 84, USA, Dir; *Cry from a Stranger*, TV, 83, USA, Dir; *Mistress of the Paradise*, TV, 82, USA, Dir; *Zorro, the Gay Blade*, Th, 81-82, USA, Dir; *The Baby Sitter*, TV, 81, USA, Dir; *The Changeling*, Th, 79, CDN, Dir; *Odd Job*, Th, 77, GB, Dir.

MELCHIOR, Klaus
- see PRODUCERS
MELLANBY, Ralph
- see PRODUCERS
MENARD, Robert
APFVQ, ACCT. Les Productions Vidéofilms, 296 ouest, rue St-Paul, Montréal, PQ H2Y 2A3 (514)844-8611.
Types de production et générique: l métrage-Réal/Prod/Sc; c métrage-Réal/Prod/Sc; TV film-Réal/Prod/Sc.
Types d'oeuvres: Drame-C; Comédie-C&TV.
Curriculum vitae: Né en 1947. Génie civil, Université de Montréal. Président des Productions Vidéofilms limitée; Secrétaire-trésorier de l'APFQ, 79-82; Directeur exécutif, 78. Prix d'Excellence du Publicité Club (Place Laurier); 7 nominations au Prix Génie pour *Une Journée en Taxi* qui a aussi été sélectionné par le Festival du Film de Toronto et pour représenter le Canada au Festival International du Film de Manile; *T'es Belle Jeanne* a gagné un Gémeaux, Meilleur Dramatique et un Gémeaux, Meilleur Réalisation.
Filmographie sélective: *Pepe Volcano*, TV, 91, CDN, Réal/Prod; *Amoureux Fou*, C, 90, CDN, Réal/Prod; *L'homme de rêve*,

TV, 90, CDN, Réal/Prod; *Blue, la magnifique*, TV, 89, CDN, Prod; *Cruising Bar*, C, 88, CDN, Réal/Prod/Sc; *Coeur de Nylon*, TV, 88, CDN, Prod; *T'es Belle Jeanne*, TV, 87, CDN, Réal/Prod; *Exit*, C, 86, CDN, Réal/Prod; "Un Amour de Quartier" (26 eps), TV, 84-85, CDN, Réal/Prod; *Une Journée en Taxi*, C, 80, CDN, Réal/Prod; *L'Affaire Coffin*, C, 79, CDN, Prod; *L'Arrache Coeur*, C, 79, CDN, Prod; *Eclair au chocolat*, C, 78, CDN, Prod; *Parlez nous d'amour*, C, 76, CDN, Prod; *Portraits de Femmes*, C, 75, CDN, Réal/Prod.

MENDELUK, George
ACCT. World Classic Pix Inc., 62633 Tapia Dr., Malibu, CA 90265 USA (213)457-9911. Michael Margules, Irv Schecter Co., 9300 Wilshire Blvd., Suite 410, Beverly Hills, CA 90212 USA (213)278-8070.
Type of Production and Credits: Th Film-Dir/Prod/Wr; Th Short-Dir/Prod/Wr; TV Film-Dir/Prod/Wr; TV Video-Dir/Prod/Wr.
Genres: Drama-Th&TV; Comedy-Th&TV; Variety-TV; Children's-Th&TV.
Biography: Born 1948, Augsburg, West Germany; Canadian citizenship; US resident alien. Languages: English, Ukranian and French. B.A., English and Humanities, York University. Trained in production at the CBC. Chris Award, Columbus Film Festival and Silver Medal, NY Film & TV Festival for *Christmas Lace*.
Selected Filmography: "Moment of Truth" (1 eps), TV, 91, CDN/USA, Dir; "Top Cops" (7 eps), TV, 90-91, CDN/USA, Dir; "Young Riders" (6 eps), TV, 89-90, USA, Dir; "Neon Rider" (1 eps), TV, 90, CDN, Dir; "Counterstrike" (2 eps), TV, 90, USA/CDN, Dir; "True Blue" (2 eps), TV, 89, USA, Dir; *Gideon Oliver*, TV, 88, USA, Dir; "Alfred Hitchcock Presents" (1 eps), TV, 88, USA/CDN, Dir; "Miami Vice" (2 eps), TV, 88, USA, Dir; "Night Heat" (10 eps), TV, 86-88, USA/CDN, Dir; *Meatballs III*, Th, 84, CDN, Dir; *Doin' Time*, Th, 83, USA, Prod/Dir; *The Kidnapping of the President*, Th, 80, CDN, Prod/Dir; *Stone Cold Dead*, Th, 78, CDN, Prod/Dir; *Christmas Lace*, TV, 78, CDN, Prod/Dir.

MERCEL, Edward L.
- see PRODUCERS

METCALFE, Bill
CSC. 25 Dundonald St., Toronto, ON M4Y 1K3 (416)925-8952.
Type of Production and Credits: TV Film-Dir/Cam; TV Video-Dir/Cam.
Genres: Drama-TV; Commercials-TV; Industrial-TV.
Biography: Born 1951, Toronto, Ontario. Director/cameraman working in sponsored and commercial productions. TVB retail, Gemini award.

METTLER, Peter
Grimthorpe Film Inc., 14 Grimthorpe Rd., Toronto, ON M6C 1G3 (416)653-2088.
Type of Production and Credits: Th Film-Wr/Dir/Prod/DOP; TV Film-Dir/DOP.
Genres: Drama-Th&TV; Musical-TV; Documentary-Th&TV; Experimental-Th&TV.
Biography: Born 1958, Toronto, Ontario; Canadian and Swiss citizenship. Languages: English, Swiss-German, German, French. B.A.A., Film, Ryerson Polytechnic Institute; Acting, New School of Drama. Has travelled extensively in Europe, North Africa, Asia.
Selected Filmography: *Tectonic Plates*, TV, 91, CDN/GB, Dir; *Standards*, TV, 90, CDN, DOP; *Red Wagon*, Jane Siberry, MV, 90, CDN, DOP; *The Top Of His Head*, Th, 89, CDN, Wr/Dir/DOP/Co Ed; *Lolita*, Th, 87, CDN, DOP/Dir; *Family Viewing*, Th, 86, CDN, DOP; *Artist on Fire*, Th, 86, CDN, DOP; *Eastern Avenue*, Th, 85, CDN, Dir/DOP/Prod/Ed; *You Don't Need*, Jane Siberry, MV, 85, CDN, DOP; *Passion*, Th, 85, CDN, DOP; *Divine Solitude*, Th, 85, CDN, DOP; *Knock Knock*, Th, 84, CDN, DOP; *Next of Kin*, Th, 84, CDN, DOP; *Scissere*, Th, 82, CDN, Dir/DOP/Wr/Ed/Prod.

MICAY, Jack
131 Albany Ave., Toronto, ON M5R 3C5 (416)977-0569. FAX: 977-0569.
Type of Production and Credits: TV Film-Dir/Prod/Wr; TV Video-Dir/Prod/Wr.
Genres: Documentary-TV; Educational-TV; Current Affairs-TV.
Biography: Born 1949, Winnipeg, Manitoba. B.A., M.D., University of Manitoba. Practising physician; has produced, directed and written many documentaries on science and medicine for TV, also a series on Sherpas of Nepal. Awards include Banff Festival of Mountain Films, 86; Telluride Mountain Film Festival, 87; International Adventure Film Festival, New Zealand, 88; John Muir Medical Film Festival, California, 84; *Oxygen: What A Gas!* won Golden Apple, US National Educational Film & Video Festival, 91, and Gold Medal, International Festival of Red Cross Health Films, Sofia, Bulgaria, 91; *Lobbying for Lives* won

Golden Sheaf, Yorkton, 89, and Golden Apple, US National Educational Film & Video Festival, 90.
Selected Filmography: *Oxygen: What A Gas!*, ED, 91, CDN, Prod/Dir/Wr; *Lobbying for Lives: Lessons from the Front*, ED, 89, CDN, Prod/Dir/Wr; *Tengboche: A Threatened Sanctuary*, TV, 88, CDN, Prod/Dir/Wr; *The Cigarette Underworld*, ED, 87, CDN, Prod/Dir; *Rescuing Everest*, TV, 86, CDN, Prod/Dir/Wr; *Kunde Hospital*, TV, 85, CDN, Prod/Dir; *Prenatal Surgery*, TV, 85, CDN, Prod/Dir.

MIGNEAULT, Hughes ◊
(514)651-6341.
Types de production et générique: l métrage-Réal/Sc/Pren son; c métrage-Réal/Sc/Pren son; TV film-Réal/Sc/Pren son; TV vidéo-Réal/Sc/Pren son.
Types d'oeuvres: Drame-C&TV; Comédie-C&TV; Science-fiction-C&TV; Documentaire-C&TV.
Curriculum vitae: Né en 1944, Montréal, Québec. Baccalauréat ès arts, Université de Montréal. Président et Directeur général, Les Films de la Rive.
Filmographie sélective: *Le Choix d'un peuple*, C, 80, CDN, Réal/Sc; *Les Adeptes*, C, 80, CDN, Pren son; *Le Québec est au monde*, C, 79, CDN, Réal/Sc/Rech; *12 Nov*, C, 76, CDN, Réal/Pren son.

MILINKOVIC, Gerry
5 Cameron Ave., Dundas, ON L9H 1P4 (416)627-7275. Hill's Video Productions, 2440 Industrial St., Burlington, ON L7P 1A5 (416)335-1146. (416)847-6058.
Type of Production and Credits: TV Film-Prod; TV Video-Prod/Dir/Cam.
Genres: Educational-TV; Music Video-TV; Sports-TV.
Biography: Born 1961, Hamilton, Ontario.
Selected Filmography: "Raceline" (13 eps), TV, 90-91, CDN, Dir/Prod/Ed/PM; "OHL Game of the Week" (10 eps), TV, 91, CDN, Features Prod; *Match-to-Win Garden Game*, C.I.L., Cm, 91, CDN, Dir/Prod; *Wild Waterworks*, Cm, 91, CDN/USA, Dir/Prod/PM; *Young Drivers of Canada* (10), ED, 88-91, CDN, Dir/Ed; *Brantford Makes It!*, In, 90, CDN, Dir/Prod/PM; *Amity: I Can Do It!*, In, 89, CDN, Dir/Ed.

MILLER, Bob
- see PRODUCERS

MILLS, Michael
ACTRA, CAPAC, CFTA, SMPTE. Michael Mills Productions, 4492 St. Catherine St. W., Montreal, PQ H3Z 1R7 (514)931-7117.
Type of Production and Credits: Th Short-Prod/Dir/An; TV Film-Prod/Dir.
Genres: Children's-Th&TV; Animation-Th&TV; Commercials-TV.
Biography: Born 1942, London, England; Canadian citizenship, 73. Producer/director/animator, London, 59-66; NFB, Canada, 66-69; joined Potterton Productions, 69; formed Michael Mills Productions Ltd., 74. Animator/director of award-winning commercials; *Evolution* won over 35 prizes at international film festivals including New York, London, San Francisco, Melbourne; it was also nominated for an Oscar. *History of the World In 3 Minutes Flat* won a Golden Bear Award, Berlin, a Blue Ribbon, New York, and was nominated for an Oscar. Won several marketing awards for Levi's, Volkswagon, and Nicorette commercials, 87.
Selected Filmography: *Constant Acceleration/Uniform Motion* (Expo 86), Th, 85-86, CDN, Prod/Dir; *Circular Motion/Occilatory Motion* (Expo 86), Th, 85-86, CDN, Prod/Dir; *History of the World in Three Minutes Flat*, Th, 80, CDN, Prod/Dir/Wr; *The Happy Prince*, TV, 74, CDN, Co-Prod/Dir/Wr; *Man the Polluter*, Th, 73, CDN, Dir/An; *Evolution*, Th, 72, CDN, Prod/Dir/Wr/An, (CFA); *Tiki Tiki*, Th, 69, CDN, An.

MINNIS, Jon
- see PRODUCERS

MITCHELL, Ken
- see WRITERS

MITTON, Susan Young
- see PRODUCERS

MONTESI, Jorge
DGC, DGA, IATSE. 50 Quebec Ave., #1601, Toronto, ON M6P 3B4 (416)259-7684. (416)766-0264. Lee Dinstman, Contemporary Artists, 132 Lasky Dr., Beverly Hills, CA 990212 USA (213)273-0744.
Type of Production and Credits: Th Film-Dir/Prod/Wr/DOP; TV Film-Dir/Prod/Wr/DOP.
Genres: Drama-Th&TV; Science Fiction-Th&TV; Documentary-TV; Action-Th&TV.
Biography: Canadian citizen. Languages: English, French, Spanish and Italian. Oscar nomination, 80; Gemini nomination. Awards at Yorkton, Chicago, Houston.
Selected Filmography: *Omen in the Awakening*, TV, 91, USA, Dir; "Jelly Bean Odyssey" (pilot), TV, 91, CDN, Dir; "The Hitchhiker" (sev eps), TV, 90-91, USA/CDN, Dir; "21 Jump Street" (sev eps), TV, 88-91, USA, Dir; "Street Legal" (sev eps), TV, 89-91, CDN, Dir; "Top

Cops" (sev eps), TV, 90-91, USA, Dir; "Scene of the Crime" (sev eps), TV, 90-91, USA, Dir; "Wiseguy" (sev eps), TV, 88-90, USA, Dir; "Friday the 13th: The Series" (sev eps), TV, 88-90, USA/CDN, Dir; "Booker" (sev eps), TV, 89, USA, Dir; "UN Sub" (sev eps), TV, 89, USA, Dir; "Alfred Hitchcock Presents" (sev eps), TV, 88, USA, Dir; "Night Heat" (sev eps), TV, 86-88, CDN, Dir/Wr; *Sentimental Reasons*, TV, 85, CDN, Dir/Prod/Wr; *Birds of Prey*, TV, 84, CDN Dir/Prod/ Wr.

MOORE-EDE, Carol
ATPD, ACCT. 156 Winchester St., Toronto, ON M4X 1B6 (416)962-9139. CBC, Box 500, Stn. A, Toronto, ON M5W 1E6 (416)979-3244.
Type of Production and Credits: TV Film-Dir/Prod; TV Video-Dir/Prod.
Genres: Drama-TV; Musical-TV; Documentary-TV; Experimental-Th&TV.
Biography: Born 1943, Tunbridge Wells, England; Canadian citizenship. Languages: English and French. B.A., Art and Archaeology, University of Toronto; postgraduate work at University of Paris; Film Animation, Vancouver School of Art. Author of *Canadian Architecture 1960-70*, which won Best Canadian Book of the Year, 71, and *The Lives and Works of Canadian Artists*. Photographer, TV and magazine writer, reviewer. Executive Producer, CBC-TV Arts and Music, "Music on a Sunday Afternoon;" "Adrienne Clarkson's Summer Festival." Has won awards for *The Canadian Brass Video Show*, including Bronze Medal, New York, 86; Best Set Design and Best Costume Design, Prix Anik.
Selected Filmography: *Cardiff Singer of the World*, "Video Visions" (1 eps), TV, 88, CDN, Dir; *Going to War*, "Bell Canada Playhouse", TV, 85, CDN, Dir; *The Canadian Brass Video Show*, "Thursday Night", TV, 85, CDN, Prod/Dir; *Where the Heart Is*, "For the Record", TV, 84, CDN, Dir; *But I'm Just a Kid* (video show/ concert), TV, 84, CDN, Dir; *Thy Servant Arthur/A Flush of Tories/King's Gambit*, "Some Honourable Gentlemen" TV, 83-84, CDN, Dir; *Veronica Tennant: A Dancer of Distinction*, "Spectrum", TV, 83, CDN, Dir/Prod; *Getting into the Act: Theatre for the Young*, TV, 82, CDN, Dir/ Prod; "Home Fires" (1 eps), TV, 82, CDN, Dir; *Drak: Circus Unikum*, TV, 81, USA, Dir; *Puppets, Masks and Men*, TV, 81, USA, Dir; *Drak: Sleeping Beauty*, TV, 81, USA, Dir; *Here Come the Puppets*, TV, 81, CDN/USA, Dir/Prod; "A Gift to Last" (1 eps), TV, 80, CDN, Dir; *Journeys through Illusion/ Mermaids & Manticores*, TV, 80, CDN, Dir/Prod; *The Garden and the Cage*, TV, 79, CDN, Dir/Prod; *Cyrus Eaton: The Prophet from Pugwash*, TV, 78, CDN, Dir/Prod; "Images of Canada" (prod 5eps/dir 4 eps), TV, 74-78, CDN, Dir/Prod.

MOREAU, Michel ◆
(514)271-6529.
Types de production et générique: l métrage-Réal; c métrage; TV film-Réal.
Types d'oeuvres: Documentaire-C&TV; Education-C&TV; Enfants-C.
Curriculum vitae: Né en 1931, France; citoyenneté canadienne. Etudes classiques; études en graphisme; Maîtrise en Psychologie. Rédacteur, concepteur en publicité; réalisateur de films fixes et diapositives. Création de l'équipe de films éducatifs français à l'ONF (responsable de la production). Réalisation pour la SGME de films sur la formation des professeurs; enseignement à l'Université du Québec à Montréal (psychologie et audio-visuel). Fondation de la compagnie Educfilm. Depuis 87, réalisateur pigiste.
Filmographie sélective: *Les Voisines venues d'ailleurs*, C, 86, CDN, Réal; *Le Million tout puissant*, C, 85, CDN, Réal; "Chocs de la vie" (5 eps), TV, 82-83, CDN, Réal; *En passant par Mascouche*, ED, 81, CDN, Réal; *Les Traces d'un homme*, TV, 81, CDN, Réal; *Le Dur Métier de frère*, TV, 80, CDN, Co réal; *Première pages du journal d'Isabelle*, TV, 80, CDN, Co réal; *Enfants du Québec*, TV, 79, CDN, Réal/ Prod/Sc; *Une naissance apprivoisée*, ED, 79, CDN, Réal; "L'Envers du jeu" (4 eps), ED, 78, CDN, Co réal; "Les Exclus" (5 eps), TV, 75-77, CDN, Réal; *Trois cents sourds*, ED, 75, CDN, Réal; *Les Débiles légers/Le Combat des sourds*, ED, 74, CDN, Réal; *La Leçon des Mongoliens/A l'aise dans ma job*, ED, 72, CDN, Réal.

MORETTI, Pierre ◆
(514)667-7898.
Types de production et générique: c métrage-Réal/Prod.
Types d'oeuvres: Documentaire-C; Animation-C; Expérimental-C.
Curriculum vitae: Né en 1931, Montréal, Québec. Langues: français et anglais. Cours classique; études en design. 10 ans comme concepteur visuel en spectacle et théâtre; 21 ans comme réalisateur et producteur à l'ONF. Plusieurs prix en graphisme et en cinéma documentaire et animation dont la Médaille d'Argent au Festival de Venise pour *Bronze*.
Filmographie sélective: *Bioscope*, C, 83,

CDN, Réal; *Variations graphiques sur Telidon*, C, 81, CDN, Réal; *Démons et merveilles*, C, 77, CDN, Prod; *L'Homme et le géant*, C, 75, CDN, Prod; *Lumaag*, C, 75, CDN, Prod; *Le Mariage du hibou*, C, 75, CDN, Prod; *Climats*, C, 75, CDN, Prod; *Modulo*, C, 74, CDN, Réal; *Ceci est un message enregistré*, C, 73, CDN, Prod; *Tchou-Tchou*, C, 73, CDN, Prod; *Air*, C, 72, CDN, Prod; *L'Oeil*, C, 72, CDN, Prod; *Le Bleu perdu*, C, 72, CDN, Prod; *L'Oeuf*, C, 72, CDN, Prod; *Le Hibou et le corbeau*, C, 72, CDN, Prod; *Meta-Data*, C, 71, CDN, Prod; *N'ajustez pas*, C, 70, CDN, Réal; *Bronze*, C, 70, CDN, Réal; *Cerveau gelé*, C, 70, CDN, Réal; *Le Hibou et le lemming*, C, 70, CDN, Prod; *Un enfant...un pays*, C, 67, CDN, Réal.

MORIN, Bertrand
ARRFQ, STCQ. 1252, Plessis, Montréal, PQ H2L 2W9 (514)525-2424. Bertrand Morin, 1600, av. de Lorimier, Montréal, PQ H2K 2W5 (514)521-1984.
Types de production et générique: TV film-Réal/Mont; TV vidéo-Réal/Mont/Sc.
Types d'oeuvres: Documentaire-C&TV; Annonces-TV; Industriel-TV.
Curriculum vitae: Né en 1955, Montréal, Québec. Langues: français et anglais. Baccalauréat ès arts, Université Laval, 78. Plus de 10 ans d'expérience comme assistant caméraman, réalisateur, producteur exécutif, Ciné-Mundo inc.; grande connaissance du Moyen-Nord québécois (4 ans à la Baie James), de l'Ungava et de la Terre de Baffin; expérience de tournage en Afrique (Togo, Ziare, Rwanda), au Hong Kong, et au Sri Lanka.
Filmographie sélective: *Hong Kong '97*, TV, 91, CDN, Réal; *Gorille de Volcans*, TV, 90, CDN, Réal; *Laniel, Ricoh Fax 20/Laniel, Toxedo*, Cm, 88, CDN, réal; *Rwanda, les collines de l'effort*, C, 87, RWA, Cam; *Stella Artois*, In, 87, CDN, Réal/Mont; *Caisse de dépot et placement du Québec*, In, 87, CDN, Réal/Sc/Mont; *Energie et Développement*, In, 87, CDN, Réal/Sc/Mont; *Shelling Is Believing*, TV, 87, CDN, Mont; *Casse-Noisettes*, Cm, 87, CDN, Réal/Mont; *Le Frère André*, C, 86, CDN, Phot de plat; *Le Géant du meuble*, Cm, 86, CDN, Réal/Mont; *Centre de réadaption Constance Lethbridge*, In, 86, CDN, Prod exéc/Mont; *Contes des 1001 nez*, TV, 86, CDN, Prod exéc; *Orphelins sans défenses* (Sri Lanka), TV, 86, CDN, Prod exéc/Cam; *Femmes sans frontières*, In, 86, CDN, Réal/Mont.

MORIN, Pierre
AR. 44, chemin Academy, #11, Westmount, PQ H3Z 1N6 (514)989-9192. Radio-Canada, 1400 est, boul. René-Lévesque, Montréal, PQ H2L 2M2 (514)597-4076.
Types de production et générique: TV film-Réal/Prod; TV vidéo-Réal/Prod.
Types d'oeuvres: Comédie musicale-TV; Documentaire-TV; Danse-TV.
Curriculum vitae: Né en 1932. Réalisateur à Radio-Canada depuis 56; spécialité: ballet, danse, opéra, musique (concerts, récitals). *Le Mandarin Merveilleux* remporte le Prix Iris et représente le Canada dans les ambassades à travers le monde.
Filmographie sélective: *Grossmann, Jones, Brassard et Compagnie*, TV, 90, CDN, Réal/Prod; *Renata Scotto*, TV, 87, CDN, Réal/Prod; *The Taylor Company: Recent Dances*, TV, 84, CDN/USA, Réal/Prod; *Pavlova*, TV, 83, CDN, Réal/Prod/Adapt; *Quant 1200 enfants s'accordent...*, TV, 83, CDN, Réal/Prod/Adapt; *Pilobolus*, TV, 81, CDN, Réal/Prod; *Le Mandarin merveilleux/The Miraculous Mandarin*, TV, 81, CDN, Réal/Prod, (ANIK); *The Medium*, TV, 79, CDN, Réal/Prod; *New York City Ballet* (2 ém), TV, 78-79, CDN, Prod/Réal; *Les Grands Ballets Canadiens*, TV, 78, CDN, Prod/Réal; *La Belle Hélène*, TV, 76, CDN, Réal/Prod; *Loves* (Les Grands Ballets Canadiens), TV, 75, CDN, Réal/Prod; *L'Heure espagnole*, TV, 75, CDN, Réal/Prod; *Messe pour le temps présent*, TV, 72, CDN, Réal/Prod/Adapt; *Le Barbier de Séville*, TV, 65, CDN, Réal/Prod, (INT'L EMMY).

MORRONE, Tony
- see PRODUCERS

MOSSANEN, Moze
ACCT. Mossanen Productions, 181 First Ave., Toronto, ON M4M 1X3 (416)461-6717.
Type of Production and Credits: Th Film-Dir/Prod/Wr; TV Film-Dir/Prod/Wr; TV Video-Dir/Prod/Wr.
Genres: Drama-Th&TV; Musical-Th&TV; Documentary-Th&TV.
Biography: Born 1958, Tehran, Iran; Canadian citizenship, 75. Languages: English, French and Farsi. Background in theatre and dance.
Selected Filmography: *Shades of Blue*, TV, 91, CDN, Dir/Prod/Ed; "The Dancemakers" (6 eps), TV, 87, CDN, Dir/Prod/Wr; *Dance for Modern Times*, Th, 87, CDN, Dir/Prod/Wr; *The Chicago Knockers*, TV, 83, CDN, Dir/Prod/Ed; *Illegal Acts*, Th, 82, CDN, Dir/Prod/Wr; *Haideh and Viguen*, TV, 82, CDN, Dir/Prod.

MOZER, Richard
- see PRODUCERS

MULLER, Helmfried
- see CINEMATOGRAPHERS

MULLER, John
CFTPA, ACCT. 475 Deloraine Ave., Toronto, ON M5M 2C1 (416)782-2552. FAX: 768-9092. M & M Film Productions Ltd., 189 Dupont St., Toronto, ON M5R 1V6 (416)968-9300.
Type of Production and Credits: Th film-Prod; Th Short-Prod/Dir; TV Film-Prod/Dir; TV Video-Prod/Dir.
Genres: Drama-TV; Variety-TV; Documentary-Th&TV; Educational-TV.
Biography: Born 1942, The Netherlands; Canadian citizenship. Came to Canada in 78 to develop a TV series with Marshall McLuhan. Graduate of San Francisco State, UCLA and the University of Amsterdam. Produced films in Europe. *A Fragile Tree Has Roots* was a winner at Columbus Film Festival.
Selected Filmography: *Twice in a Lifetime, Elgin/Winter Garden Theatres,* ED, 90, CDN, Dir; *Hidden Heritage: Mining in Ontario* (8 eps), ED, 89, CDN, Dir; *Welcome to the National Gallery of Canada,* ED, 89, CDN, Dir; "Dance Mix" (13 eps), TV, 89, CDN, Exec Prod; "Vid Kids" (26 eps), TV, 85-88, CDN, Co-Prod/Dir, (CFTA); "Challenge Yourself to New Heights" (7 eps), TV, In, 88, CDN, Dir; *Let's Talk,* ED, 88, CDN, Dir; *Food Choices: The Cancer Connection,* ED, 87, CDN, Dir/Co-Prod; *A Fragile Tree Has Roots,* TV, 85, CDN, Dir/Co-Prod; *Vincent Price's Dracula,* TV, 83, CDN, Dir/Co-Prod; *Money to Burn,* TV, 83, CDN, Co-Prod; *Warming to Wood,* TV, 83, CDN, Co-Prod; *Sunshine for Sale,* TV, 83, CDN, Co-Prod; *Taking a Leap,* In, 83, CDN, Dir/Co-Prod; *Thanks a Lot,* TV, 82, CDN, Dir/Co-Prod.

MULLINS, Ronald G. ✧
(604)986-7932.
Type of Production and Credits: TV Film-dir/Prod; TV Video-Dir/Prod/PM.
Genres: Drama-TV; Variety-TV; Children's-TV; Commercials-TV.
Biography: Born 1943. Directed, produced more than 2,500 commercials over the past 20 years.
Selected Filmography: "Family Theatre" (sev eps), TV, 85, CDN, PM; *Canada in an Information Age,* TV, 85, CDN, Dir/Prod; *Bathing Your Babies,* TV, 85, CDN, Dir/Prod; "The Minikins" (sev eps), TV, 84, CDN, Dir; *The Vancouver Show,* TV, 84, CDN, Prod; "Nuggets" (sev eps), TV, 82-83, CDN, Dir; "MacPherson" (sev eps), TV, 82, CDN, Dir; "Hour Music" (sev eps), TV, 82, CDN, Dir; "Canadian Express" (sev eps), TV, 81-82, CDN, Dir/Prod; *The Original Caste,* TV, 82, CDN, Dir/Prod.

MURPHY, Michael D.
- see PRODUCERS

MURRAY, James
- see PRODUCERS

NANTEL, Louise
- voir SCENARISTES

NASON, Kent
- see CINEMATOGRAPHERS

NELSON, Barrie
5555 Busch Dr., Malibu, CA 90265 (213)457-2523.
Type of Production and Credits: Th Film-Dir(An)/Wr; Th Short-Dir(An)/Wr; TV Film-Dir(An)/Wr; TV Video-Dir(An)/Wr.
Genres: Drama-Th&TV; Comedy-Th&TV; Variety-Th&TV; Musical-Th&TV.
Biography: Born 1933, Winnipeg, Manitoba. Diploma in Art, University of Manitoba. Familiar with all aspects of animated film. Animation on 4 Oscar-nominated films for John and Faith Hubley (one winner). Independent films have won awards at Annely, France; Zagreb, Ottawa and other festivals. Currently working on fourth film for IBM Corporation. Work on commercials including 7-Up.
Selected Filmography: *About Compensation,* IBM (2), In, 88/90, CDN, An; *About Information,* IBM, In, 86, CDN, An; *Opens Wednesday,* Th, 82, CDN, Wr/An/Des/Prod/Dir; *Twins,* Th, 74, CDN, Wr/An/Dir/Prod; *Doonesbury Special,* TV, 73, USA, An; *Keep Cool,* Th, 72, CDN, Wr/An/Des/Prod/Dir; *Propaganda Message,* Th, 72, CDN, Des/An/Dir; *Of Men and Demons,* Th, 70, CDN, An; *Windy Day,* Th, 68, CDN, An; *Herb Alpert: Double Feature,* Th, 66, CDN, An.

NELSON, Dale C.
- see PRODUCERS

NEUBACHER, Roman M.
- see PRODUCERS

NEW, David
- see EDITORS

NEWLAND, Marv
International Rocketship Ltd., 1168 Hamilton St., Suite 203, Vancouver, BC V6B 2S2 (604)681-2716.
Type of Production and Credits: Th Film-Dir; Th Short-Dir/Prod.
Genres: Comedy-Th; Variety-Th; Musical-Th; Animation-Th.
Biography: Born 1047, South Korea.

Graduate Art Center College of Design, L.A., 69. Staff designer, Spungbuggy Works, L.A., 69-70; freelance animation designer, director, Toronto, 71-72. Crawley Films (Ottawa), Phos-Cine (New York), Toonder Studios (Holland): commercials, educational and theatrical films. Founder, International Rocketship Ltd., 74. His films have won prizes at various film festivals including International Animation Festival, Toronto, (Jury Prize) for *Anijam*; Silver Hugo, Chicago, and Best Children's, Annecy, for *Sing Beast Sing*; Golden Gate Award, San Francisco for *Black Hula*. Retrospective, Telluride Film Festival, 84.
Selected Filmography: *Pink Komkommer*, Th, 90, CDN, Dir/Prod; *Let's Chop Soo-E*, Th, 89, CDN/USA, Prod; *Waddles*, Th, 88, CDN, Prod; *Dog Brain*, Th, 88, CDN, Prod; *Black Hula*, Th, 88, CDN, Dir/Prod; *Lupo the Butcher*, Th, 86, CDN, Prod; *Hooray for Sandboxland*, ED, 85, CDN, Prod/Dir; *Dry Noodles*, Th, 85, CDN, Prod; *Anijam*, Th, 84, CDN, Prod/Dir; *The Butterfly*, Th, 83, CDN, Prod; *Points*, Th, 83, CDN, Prod; *Sing Beast Sing*, Th, 80, CDN, Prod/Dir; *Bambi Meets Godzilla*, Th, 69, USA, Prod/Dir/An.
NEWTON, John ◊
(604)738-6482.
Type of Production and Credits: TV Film-Dir/Prod/Wr/Ed.
Genres: Drama-TV; Comedy-TV.
Biography: Born 1939, Bakersfield, California; Canadian citizenship. Languages: English and some Spanish. Has taught Film Production at the University of British Columbia since 71. Winner of award, University of Indiana Film Festival and Ecology Film Festival, for *Rabbit Hunt*; won American Film Institute fellowship for *Mystery of B. Traven*.
Selected Filmography: "Blue's Folly", TV, 86, CDN, Dir; *Mystery of B. Traven*, ED, 77, CDN, Dir/Wr/Ed; *Rabbit Hunt*, ED, 77, CDN, Dir/Wr/Ed.
NICHOL, Gary
- see PRODUCERS
NICOLLE, Douglas
109 North Holdom Ave., Burnaby, BC (604)294-2379. Spectra Communications Inc., #222 - 119 West Pender St., Vancouver, BC V6B 1S5 (604)682-4366.
Type of Production and Credits: Th Short-Dir; TV Film-Dir; TV Video-Dir.
Genres: Drama-Th&TV; Documentary-Th&TV; Commercials-TV; Industrial-TV.
Biography: Born 1952, Vancouver, BC. Honours B.A., Philosophy, Simon Fraser University. Spent 2 years as News/Public Affairs Editor, CBC Vancouver; 10 years in partnership, Spectra Media. *Over the Line* won PIMA. Certificate of Excellence; *Time of Wonder* won Award of Merit.
Selected Filmography: *Yoho: Now and Forever*, TV, 91, CDN, Dir; *Over the Line*, MV, 90, CDN, Dir; *Time of Wonder*, ED, 90, CDN, Prod; *Learning for Living*, ED, 89, CDN, Dir; *Classroom Reflections*, ED, 89, CDN, Prod; *People Connecting*, ED, 89, CDN, Prod; *Taking a Second Look*, ED, 88, CDN, Dir.
NIRENBERG, Les
- see PRODUCERS
NOEL, Jean-Guy ◊
(514)521-0538.
Types de production et générique: l métrage-Réal/Prod/Sc; c métrage-Réal/Prod/Sc; TV film-Sc.
Types d'oeuvres: Drame-C; Comédie-C; Action-C&TV.
Curriculum vitae: Né en 1945 à Montréal, Québec. Baccalauréat ès Arts, Collège St-Laurent, Montréal, 66; Philosophie, Université de Louvain, Belgique, 67-68; études à l'Institut National des Arts du Spectacle, Belgique, 68-69. Assistant réalisateur, Radio-Télévision Belge, 69; conseiller à la scénarisation, ONF, 78. *Ti-Cul Tougas* remporte le Grand Prix de la Critique québécoise et plusieurs autres.
Filmographie sélective: *L'Amelanchier*, TV, 84, CDN, Adapt; *Labrador 1905*, TV, 84, CDN, Sc; *Caméléon*, C, 84, CDN, Réal/Co sc; *Le Lion en cage* (3 films), C, 82-83, CDN, Réal/Sc/Prod; *Grief 81*, C, 81, CDN, Réal; *Contrecoeur*, C, 79, CDN, Réal/Co sc; *Fleur de mai/The Apprentice*, C, 77, CDN, Réal/Sc; *Ti-Cul Tougas*, C, 74, CDN, Réal/Sc; *Tu brûles...tu brûles...*, C, 72, CDN, Réal/Sc; *Elle était une fois...une autre fois*, C, 71, CDN, Réal/Sc/Prod; *Zeuzère de Zègouzie*, C, 70, CDN, Réal/Sc/Prod/Com.
NOVAK, Allan Z.
ACCT. 721 Manning Ave., Toronto, ON M5G 2W5 (416)534-1222. Suzanne Depoe, Creative Technique Inc., Box 311, Stn. F, Toronto, ON M4Y 2L7 (416)924-0341.
Type of Production and Credits: TV Video-Dir/Wr/Ed.
Genres: Comedy-TV; Children's-TV.
Biography: Born 1959, Winnipeg, Manitoba. B.F.A., Specialized Honours, Film and Videotape, York University. Co-founder and principal of Suite One Video

Inc. Gemini nominee for Best Editing/ Documentary for *In Fashion*, 87; Gemini nominee Besting Editing, Comedy/Variety Series for "It's Only Rock 'n' Roll," 88; Gemini nominee Best Writing, Variety Program for *1988 Genie Awards* telecast.
Selected Filmography: "Codco" (11 eps), TV, 91, CDN, Seg Dir; "OWL-TV" (5 eps), TV, 91, CDN/GB, Seg Dir/Wr; "Dealing with Drugs" (6 eps), TV, 90, CDN, Dir; "The Elephant Show" (2 eps), TV, 89, CDN, Dir; "Kids in the Hall" (20 eps), TV, 89, CDN/USA, Ed; *1988 Gemini Awards*, TV, 88, CDN, Dir; *1988 Genie Awards*, TV, 88, CDN, Wr; "It's Only Rock 'n' Roll" (15 eps), TV, 87, CDN, Field Prod/Dir; "Buried Alive" (Paris Black), MV, 87, CDN, Dir; "Vid Kids" (13 eps), TV, 85-86, CDN, Dir; *In Fashion*, TV, 86, CDN, Ed; *California Dream*, TV, 85, CDN, Dir; *The Rise and Fall of Tony Trouble*, TV, 83, CDN, Dir/Ed.

NOWLAN, John
- see PRODUCERS

O'CONNELL, Maura
- see PRODUCERS

O'DWYER, Michael J.
- see WRITERS

OBOMSAWIN, Alanis
OC. NFB, Box 6100, Montreal, PQ H3C 3H5 (514)283-9536.
Type of Production and Credits: Th Short-Dir/Prod/Wr; TV Film-Dir/Prod/Wr.
Genres: Variety-Th; Documentary-Th&TV; Educational-Th&TV; Children's-Th&TV.
Biography: Born 1932; raised on the Odanak Reserve. Writes and sings her own songs. Received the Order of Canada, 83; Arts and Humanities Education Award, 82. "Mother of Many Children" won Best Documentary, American Indian Film Festival and Grand Prize, Dieppe, France. *Richard Cardinal: Cry of a Metis Child* won Best Documentary, American Indian Film Festival, 85; *Poundmaker's Lodge: A Healing Place* won the Certificate of Merit, Golden Sheaf Award, Yorkton, 87. Record, *Bush Lady* was released October, 88, by WaWa Productions.
Selected Filmography: *No Address*, ED, 88, CDN, Dir/Prod/Wr; *A Place of Learning*, ED, 88, USA, Dir/Prod/Wr; *Poundmaker's Lodge: A Healing Place*, ED, 87, CDN, Dir/Wr/Prod; *Richard Cardinal: Cry of a Metis Child*, ED, 86, CDN, Dir/Prod/Wr; *Incident at Restigouche*, Th, 84, CDN, Dir/Co-Prod/Wr; *Gabriel Goes to the City*, TV, 79, CDN, Dir/Prod/Wr; "Sounds from Our People" (6 eps), TV, 79, CDN, Dir/Prod/Wr; *Amisk*, TV, 77, CDN, Dir/Co-Prod; *Old Crow*, TV, 77, CDN, Dir/Prod/Wr; *Mother of Many Children*, TV, 76, CDN, Dir/Prod/Wr; *Christmas at the Moose Factory*, TV, 71, CDN, Dir.

OLIVER, Ron
- see WRITERS

OLSEN, Stan
- see PRODUCERS

ONDA, Stephen
- see PRODUCERS

ORD, Cathy
Ordinary Film Productions Inc., 403 - 680 Queen's Quay West, Toronto, ON M5V 2Y9 (416)340-7660.
Type of Production and Credits: Th Film-Prod/Wr/Dir/Ed.
Genres: Drama-Th.
Biography: Born in 1955 in Ft. Lauderdale, Florida. Canadian citizenship. Education: B.F.A. from University of British Columbia, M.F.A. from York University, Diploma in Visual Arts from Emily Carr College of Art, Diploma in Film & TV from University of BC. As a visual artist, has worked in drawing and mixed media. Attended the Montreal International Film Festival and the Vancouver Film Festival with *Dear John*.
Selected Filmography: *Dear John*, Th, 87-88, CDN, Prod/Wr/Dir/Ed; *Dear John*, Th, 85, CDN, Co-Dir/Co-Wr/Co-Ed; *Hockey Night in Canada*, Th, 84, CDN, Prod/Dir/Wr; *Dirty Laundry*, Th, 83, CDN, Wr.

ORR, James
- see WRITERS

ORWIN, J. Graham
DGC. Graham Orwin Productions Ltd., 193 Seaton St., Toronto, ON M5A 2T5 (416)964-9321.
Types of Production and Credits: Th Short-Dir; TV Film-Dir; TV Video-Dir.
Genres: Drama-TV; Comedy-TV; Commercials-TV; Industrial-Th.
Biography: Born in 1939 in Bradford, England. Some French spoken. Musician. Awards: ITVA (2); CFTA (2); Canadian Radio TV Awards (2); Canadian Art Directors' Club award; New York Film Festival (for Creative Excellence); Clio statues (3); Clio certificates (10); Hollywood Commercial Festival (4); Houston International Film Festival; Philadelphia Addys (2); Washington/Baltimore Commercial Film Festival, awards (3). *Architecture of Newfoundland* won a North American Tourism award.
Selected Filmography: *Drive Smart*,

ED/TV, 90, USA, Dir; *Wake Up America*, TV, 85, USA/CDN, Dir; *Cry For Help*, Ed/TV, 85, CDN, Dir; *Ben Franklin*, ED/TV, 85, USA/CDN, Dir; *Architecture of Newfoundland*, Th/TV, 81, CDN, Dir; *Hospitality*, ED/TV, 80, CDN, Dir; "Nick's Place" (pilot), TV, 79, CDN, Dir; *Haiti Blind Musicians*, TV, 79, CDN/USA, Dir.

ORZARI, Lorenzo
- see WRITERS

OUHILAL, Iskra D. ✧
(514)481-7114.
Types de production et générique: l métrage-Réal; c métrage-Réal; TV vidéo-Réal.
Types d'oeuvres: Drame-TV; Documentaire-TV; Annonces-TV.
Curriculum vitae: Née en 1943, Sofia, Bulgarie; citoyenneté canadienne. Diplôme en réalisation, Ecole du Cinéma de Prague; Doctorat en cinématographie. A réalisé plusieurs courts métrages et messages publicitaires à l'extérieur du Canada.
Filmographie sélective: *Violence et cinéma*, TV, 87-88, CDN, Réal; *Guide*, C, 69, CS, Réal/Sc.

OWEN, Don ✧
(416)294-5163.
Type of Production and Credits: Th Film-Dir/Prod/Wr/Ed; Th Short-Dir/Prod/Wr/Ed; TV Film-Dir/Prod/Ed; TV Video-Dir.
Genres: Drama-Th&TV; Comedy-Th&TV; Action-Th&TV; Documentary-Th&TV.
Biography: Born 1935, Toronto, Ontario. Studied English and Anthropology, University of Toronto. Began in film as a grip; has worked in all departments, eventually directing, editing, producing, NFB, moving on to freelance. *You Don't Back Down* won the Robert Flaherty Award; *Runner*, First Prize, Tours; *High Steel*, Golden Bear, Berlin.
Selected Filmography: *Jan*, "Danger Bay", TV, 87, CDN, Dir; *Turnabout*, Th, 86, CDN, Prod/Dir/Wr; *Unfinished Business*, Th, 83, CDN, Dir/Wr/Co-Prod; "The Journal" (3 seg), TV, 82, CDN, Dir; *Tanya's Moscow Puppets*, TV, 81, CDN, Dir/Wr; *Holstein*, Th, 77, CDN, Dir/Wr/Ed; "Ontario Towns and Villages" (19 short films), TV, 72-77, CDN, Dir/Prod/Ed; *Partners*, Th, 75, CDN, Dir/Co-Wr/Co-Prod; "The Collaborators" (3 eps), TV, 74, CDN, Dir; *Not Far from Home*, TV, 73, CDN, Dir/Prod/Ed; *Canada: The St. Lawrence*, TV, 73, CDN, Dir/Prod; *Cowboy and Indian*, Th, 72, CDN, Dir/Ed; *Coughtry in Ibiza*, TV, 77, CDN, Dir; *Richler of St. Urbain*, TV, 71, CDN, Dir; *The Ernie Game*, Th, 67, CDN, Wr/Dir, (CFA); *High Steel*, Th, 65, CDN, Wr/Ed/Dir, (CFA).

PAABO, Iris
564 Logan Ave., Toronto, ON M4K 3B7 (416)465-2188.
Type of Production and Credits: Th Short-Dir; TV Film-Dir; TV Video-Dir.
Genres: Children's-Th&TV; Animation-Th&TV; Music Video-TV.
Biography: Born in Sweden; Canadian citizenship. Animation specialist: direction, design, storyboards, 3-D plasticiene stop-motion, cutouts, cels, 3-level plasticiene relief techniques. Film composer; also writer of children's songs, music theatre. Has received Honourable Mention, American Film Festival, and TV awards; Thea Award for Best New Musical 87, for *Projections*.
Selected Filmography: *Leaving the Poisons Behind*, Th, 91, CDN, An/Prod/Dir; *Wake Up/Wake Up*, Th, 90, CDN, Prod/Dir/An; *Oxygen - What a Gas!*, ED, 90, CDN, An; *Imagine*, Cm, 90, CDN, Art Dir; *Eight Ways*, Amway, In, 89, CDN, An; *Write Stuff*, TV, 87-88, CDN, Illustr; *Bozo the Killer*, MV, 86, CDN, An/Dir; *Dentyne*, Cm, 86, CDN, An Des; *The Lost Creature*, ED, 86, CDN, An Des; *Trudeau*, TV, 85, CDN, An Des; *Bon Vivant*, Th, 85, CDN, An/Dir; *Local Government Week*, Cm, 85, CDN, An Des; *Pri-Maths*, ED, 85, CDN, An Des; "Sesame Street" (5 eps), TV, 84-85, CDN, An Des; *I've Got A Little Brother*, Th, 82, CDN, An/Prod/Dir.

PAAKSPUU, Kalli
- see PRODUCERS

PACHECO, Bruno Lazaro
BLP Films, 67 Brookfield Ave., Toronto, ON M6J 3A8 (416)532-6253.
Type of Production and Credits: Th Film-Dir/Prod/Wr/Ed; Th Short-Dir/Wr; TV Film-Dir/Prod/Wr/Ed; TV Video-Dir/Prod.
Genres: Drama-Th&TV; Documentary-TV; Educational-TV; Experimental-Th&TV.
Biography: Born 1957, Madrid, Spain; Canadian citizenship. B.A., Film and Literature, Simon Fraser University. *Swingspan* won an award at the Northwest Film/Video Festival, Portland; *Sentencing Dilemma* won Best Educational Film, Toronto; *Hate to Love* won awards at Chicago, Toronto, Edmonton, Bilbao and Yorkton, and was invited to Quinzaine des Réalisateurs, Cannes, 83; *The Traveller*

premiered at the Festival of Festivals, Toronto, 89.
Selected Filmography: *The Traveller,* Th, 89, CDN, Prod/Wr/Dir/Ed; *The Hammer, the Sickle and the Maple Leaf,* TV, 88, CDN, Prod/Dir; *Swingspan,* TV, 86, CDN, Wr/Dir; *Sentencing Dilemma,* ED, 85, CDN, Prod/Wr/Dir/Ed; *Hate to Love,* Th, 82, CDN, Wr/Dir/Ed.

PALL, Larry
IATSE 644, IATSE 667, DEA, DGC. R.R. #1, Orton, ON L0N 1N0 (519)855-6734.
Type of Production and Credits: Th Film-Dir; TV Film-Dir; TV Video-Dir.
Genres: Drama-Th&TV; Comedy-Th&TV; Action-Th&TV; Commercials-TV.
Biography: Born Bridgeport, Connecticut; landed immigrant Canada. Studied Cinematography and Directing in New York City.
Selected Filmography: *Death in Hollywood,* TV, 85, CDN, Dir; *Strange Brew,* Th, 82, CDN, 2nd U Dir; *Off Your Rocker,* Th, 79, CDN, Dir; *The Kidnapping of the President,* Th, 79, CDN, 2nd U Dir.

PALMER, John
Cameron and Palmer Prod. Inc., 80 Wellesley St. E., #701, Toronto, ON M4Y 1H3 (416)967-7455. Ronda Cooper, Characters Talent, 150 Carlton St., Toronto, ON M5A 2K1 (416)964-8522.
Type of Production and Credits: Th Film-Wr/Dir.
Genres: Drama-Th; Comedy-Th.
Biography: Born 1943, Sydney, Nova Scotia. Has written and directed extensively for the stage in Canada, Britain and US. *Monkeys in the Attic* won Best Foreign Film, Toulon Film Festival, France.
Selected Filmography: *Me,* Th, 74, CDN, Dir; *Monkeys in the Attic,* Th, 73, CDN, Co-Wr.

PAQUET, Denis
ARRQ, FPRTC. 1555, rue Guay, Val d'Or, PQ (819)825-8640. Radio-Québec, 1032, 3e avenue, Val d'Or, PQ (819)825-5132.
Types de production et générique: TV Vidéo-Réal.
Types d'oeuvres: Documentaire-TV; Affaires publiques-TV; Corporatif-TV.
Curriculum vitae: Né en 1955, Ville-Marie, Québec. Langues: français et anglais. Baccalauréat spécialisé en Communications, Université Concordia. 10 ans d'expérience à la télévision éducative, maisons de production privée et télévision d'état.
Filmographie sélective: *Feu Vert,* TV, CDN, Réal; *Première Ligne,* TV, CDN, Réal; *Québec inc.,* TV, CDN, Réal; *L'Info5,* TV, CDN, Réal; *Ski Tips,* Coors Light, Cm, CDN, Réal.

PARE, Constance
AR. 1400 est René Lévesque, Montréal, PQ H2L 2M2 (514)597-4897.
Types de production et générique: TV film-Réal; TV Vidéo-Réal.
Types d'oeuvres: Drame-TV; Variété-TV; Enfants-TV; Affaires publiques-TV.
Curriculum vitae: Née en 1946, Ste-Anne-de-Beaupré, Québec. Baccalauréat en Pédagogie; Baccalauréat ès Arts; Maîtrise en administration. Réalisatrice depuis 10 ans.
Filmographie sélective: "Ciel Variable", TV, 91-92, CDN, Réal; "Le Grand Remous", TV, 89-91, CDN, Réal; "Robert et Compagnie", TV, 87-89, CDN, Réal; "La Clé des champs", TV, 86-87, CDN, Réal; *Quilico et Pellignini,* "Les Beaux Dimanches", TV, 85, CDN, Réal; "Reflets d'un pays" (1 eps), TV, 85, CDN, Réal; *Musique Jeunesse,* TV, 85, CDN, Réal; "Génies en herbe" (115 eps), TV, 81-85, CDN, Réal; *Les Ethnies d'ici,* TV, 84, CDN, Réal; "Québec, mer et monde" (40 seg), TV, 84, CDN, Réal; *Orchestre de Radio-Canada,* TV, 82, CDN, Réal; "Félix et Ciboulette" (51 eps), TV, 81, CDN, Réal; *Eva et Evelyne,* "Les Beaux Dimanches", TV, 80, CDN, Réal; "Québec Magazine" (200 eps), TV, 79-80, CDN, Réal; *Au temps des goélettes,* "Reflets d'un pays", TV, 78, CDN, Réal.

PARENT, Karl
AR. 906 est, Henri-Bourassa, Montréal, PQ H2C 1E9 (514)384-7538. Radio Canada, 1400 est, boul. René Lévesque, Montréal, PQ H2L 2M2 (514) 597-5650.
Types de production et générique: TV film-Réal; TV vidéo-Réal.
Types d'oeuvres: Documentaire-TV; Education-TV; Enfants-TV; Variété-TV.
Curriculum vitae: Né en 1941. Langues: français et anglais. A l'emploi de Radio-Canada depuis 74; réalisateur à la télévision éducative de l'Ontario. Enseignement aux universités de Dakar, Port-au-Prince et Montréal. *Juste un rêve du passé* fut sélectionné pour Input 83; *De Scheherazade à Selima* gagne le Prix Madea à Tokyo; Prix Judith Jasmin, 85, pour *Toronto Unlimited;* *Le Sahara algérien,* Plaque de Bronze, Columbus.
Filmographie sélective: *Quand la chanson dit bonjour au country,* TV, 90, CDN, Réal; *Algerie,* "Le Point", TV, 90, CDN, Réal; *Gerald Bull,* "Le Point", TV, 90,

CDN, Réal; *Rendez-vous avec Gerry*, TV, 89, CDN, Réal, (FELIX); *Arafat: L'Intifada*, "Le Point", TV, 89, CDN, Réal; *Les Palestiniens en territoire occupé/ Arafat*, "Un peuple sans état" (2 eps), TV, 88, CDN, Réal; *Pâques à Belfast*, TV, 88, CDN, Réal; *Les Cris de la Baie James*, "Le Point", TV, 87, CDN, Réal; *L'intelligence artificielle/La guerre des étoiles*, "Le Point", TV, 87, CDN, Réal; *Le crack à New York*, "Le Point", TV, 87, CDN, Réal, (GEMEAUX); *Les Sick au Punjab/ L'Euthanasie/Liszt*, "Le Point", TV, 86, CDN, Réal.

PARISEAU, Marcel ◊
(514)667-7615.
Types de production et générique: TV film-Mont; TV vidéo-Réal.
Types d'oeuvres: Documentaire-TV; Education-TV; Enfants-TV.
Curriculum vitae: Né en 1939, Montréal, Québec. Langues: français et anglais. A remporté le Prix du RTNDA (national et est du Canada) pour le montage de *One Year to Go*.
Filmographie sélective: "La Semaine verte", TV, 87-88, CDN, Réal/Coord; "Grand Air", TV, 87-88, CDN, Réal/ Coord; "Hockey Night in Canada", TV, 86-87, CDN, Réal; "Major League Baseball", TV, 86-87, CDN, Réal; "Steppin' Out", TV, 84-85, CDN, Réal' "Switchback", TV, 84-85, CDN, Réal; "News Watch", TV, 79-81, CDN, Réal' "The City at Six" (pl eps), TV, 80, CDN, Réal, (ANIK); *This Land Is Not for Sale*, TV, 78, CDN, Mont; *One Year to Go*, TV, 75, CDN, Mont.

PARKER, Fred
65 Lauder Ave., Toronto, ON M6H 3E2 (416)975-6300. CBC, Box 500, Stn. A, Toronto, ON M5W 1E6 (416)975-7819.
Type of Production and Credits: TV Video-Dir/Prod.
Genres: News-TV.
Biography: Born 1955, Montreal, Quebec. Educated in Ottawa and Toronto. Joined CBC as a Film Assistant, later a Production Assistant, then Director. Senior Director/Producer, CBC National News, 84; now Senior Director/ Producer, CBC National News and CBC News Specials, and Senior Director/ Producer and Program Consultant, "the fifth estate."

PARTINGTON, Lawrence
- see PRODUCERS

PATEL, Ishu
386, Touzin Ave., Dorval, PQ H9S 2N2 (514)631-0668. NFB, 3155 Côte de Liesse, Montreal, PQ H3C 3H5 (514)283-9634.
Type of Production and Credits: Th Short-An/Dir/Prod; TV Film-Dir/An.
Genres: Educational-Th&TV; Children's-Th&TV; Animation-Th&TV; Experi-mental-Th.
Biography: Born 1942, India. Received training at the Faculty of Fine Arts, Baroba; postgraduate training in graphic design, typography, photography and exhibition design, National Institute of Design, Ahmedabad, India; advanced graphic design course, Switzerland. After winning a Rockefeller Scholarship, 70, went to NFB to explore art of animation; since then, has directed, produced several international award-winning shorts such as *Paradise*, *The Bead Game* and *Afterlife*. *The Wanderer* won Special Jury Award, Montreal Film Festival.
Selected Filmography: *Divine Fate*, Th, 91, CDN, Dir/An; *Ottawa Festival Logo*, Th, 89, CDN, Co-Dir; *N.F.B. Logo*, Th, 89, CDN, Dir/Prod; *The Wanderer*, Th, 88, CDN, Prod; *The Talisman*, TV, 85-86, CDN, Dir/Prod; "Sesame Street" (60 CDN seg), TV, 75-85, USA, An/Dir/Wr; *A Special Letter*, Th, 82, CDN, Prod; *Sound Collector*, Th, 82, CDN, Prod; *Top Priority*, Th, 81, CDN, An/Dir/Prod; *Tournée titles*, Th, 81, CDN, An/Dir; *Paradise*, Th, 81, CDN, Creator/Dir/An/Prod; *This Is Me*, TV, 80, CDN, An; *Ottawa Festival Logo*, Th, 80, CDN, An/Dir; *Afterlife*, Th, 79, CDN, Creator/Des/An, (CFA); *The Bead Game*, Th, 78, CDN, Creator/Des/An/Dir, (BFA).

PATTERSON, Carol
- see CINEMATOGRAPHERS

PAYETTE, Jacques
- voir PRODUCTEURS

PEARSON, Peter ◊
Type of Production and Credits: Th Film-Dir/Wr; Th Short-Dir/Wr; TV Film-Dir/Prod/Wr; TV Video-Dir/Wr.
Genres: Drama-Th&TV; Documentary-Th&TV; Current Affairs-TV.
Biography: Born 1938, Toronto, Ontario. Languages: French, English, Italian. Attended Centro Sperimentale di Cinematografia, Rome; Political Science, University of Toronto; Radio and TV Arts, Ryerson Polytechnical Institute. Associate professor, Film Studies, Queen's University. Past President, DGC. Director of Broadcast Funds, Telefilm Canada, 83-85; Executive Director, Telefilm Canada, 85-87. Films he has directed have won awards at numerous international film festivals.
Selected Filmography: *Heaven on Earth*, TV, 86, CDN/GB, Co-Wr; *Quebec:*

Economy in Crisis, "The Journal", TV, 82, CDN, Prod/Dir; *National Crime Test*, TV, 82, CDN, Dir/Wr; *Snowbird*, "For the Record", TV, 81, CDN, Dir/Co-Wr; *The Unexpected*, "Jack London's Tales of the Klondike", TV, 81, CDN, Dir; *The Chairman: A Portrait of Paul Desmarais*, "The Canadian Establishment" TV, 81, CDN, Dir/Prod/Wr; "The Challengers" (6 eps), In, 78, CDN, Dir; *The Tar Sands*, "For the Record", TV, 77, CDN, Dir/Co-Wr; *Kathy Karuks is a Grizzly Bear*, "For the Record", TV, 77, CDN, Dir; *One Man*, Th, 76, CDN, Co-Wr, (ACTRA/CFA); *Insurance Man from Ingersoll*, TV, 76, CDN, Dir/Co-Wr, (ACTRA); "Sidestreet" (2 eps), TV, 76, CDN, Dir; *Only God Knows*, Th, 74, CDN, Dir; *Along These Lines*, Th, 74, CDN, Dir, (CFA); *Paperback Hero*, Th, 72, CDN, Dir.

PEDERSON, Larry V.
- see WRITERS

PELLETIER, Vic ✧
(418)566-2040.
Types de production et générique: TV film-Réal/Prod; TV vidéo-Réal.
Types d'oeuvres: Documentaire-TV; Education-TV.
Curriculum vitae: Né en 1948. Professeur de cinéma au Cégep de Matane depuis 76.
Filmographie sélective: "Vidéotours du Québec" (12 vidéogrammes), TV, 88, CDN, Réal; *Séduction de paysage*, TV, 88, CDN, Réal; *Gaspésie*, TV, 87, CDN, Réal; *Paysages gaspésiens*, TV, 87, CDN, Réal; *Le Bas St-Laurent/Gaspésie en image*, TV, 87, CDN, Réal; *Portrait du fou*, TV, 87, CDN, Réal; *Vidéotours du Québec*, TV, 87, CDN, Réal; *Cégep de Matane*, In, 87, CDN, Réal; *Présence amérindienne en Gaspésie*, TV, 86, CDN, Réal; *Option Photo*, In, 86, CDN, Réal; *Un emploi s.v.p.*, TV, 86, CDN, Réal; *Deuxième Biennale des arts visuels*, TV, 86, CDN, Réal; "Cité des jeunes" (1 eps), TV, 85, CDN, Réal; *Voyage en Union Soviétique*, TV, 85, CDN, Réal; *L'Ecole de rang*, TV, 85, CDN, Réal; *Les Oiseaux de la Gaspésie*, TV, 84, CDN, Réal.

PERKINS, Kenneth G.
MMPIA. 56 Galbraith Cres., Winnipeg, MB R2Y 1L3 (204) 889-0879. Kenn Perkins & Associates Ltd., 21 - 1313 Border St., Winnipeg, MB R3H 0X4 (204) 633-4545.
Types of Production and Credits: TV Film-Wr//Prod/Art Dir/Dir; TV Video-Wr/Prod/Art/Dir.
Genres: Educational-TV; Animation-TV; Commercials-TV; Industrial-TV.
Biography: Born 1942, Winnipeg, Manitoba; Canadian citizenship. Fine Arts, University of Manitoba. Areas of expertise include: computer & classical animation, motion control & special effects, live-action film & video, creative services. Has won many awards for his work including, CFA, 69; Gold Medal WPG, Art Directors Club, 69 & 70; Bronze Bessie, 71; Creative Excellence Award, US TV Commercial Festival, 74; TVB Award, 77; Sam Award, 80; International Broadcast Award, Hollywood Radio & TV, 88; 2 Sam Awards, 89; Signature Award, 90. Kenn Perkins & Associates incorporated, 69.
Selected Filmography: *Crystal Casino*, Cm, 91, CDN, Dir/Prod; *Cajun Wings*, Chicken Delight of Canada, Cm, 91, CDN, Wr/Dir/Prod; *Bombay Bicycle Club/Clancy's*, Cm, 91, CDN, Wr/Dir/Prod; *2 for $119*, Shopper's Optical, Cm, 91, CDN, Wr/Prod/Dir; *Caterpillar*, Finning, Cm, 91, CDN, An/P Prod; *Buy 1, Get 1 Free*, Stewart N. King, Cm, 91, CDN, Wr/Dir/Prod; *Hydro Bonds*, Manitoba, Cm, 91, CDN, An; *Advance Electronics*, Cm, 91, CDN, An; *Designated Driver*, Alberta, Cm, 91, CDN, An/P Prod; *Rate Reduction*, Manitoba Telephone, Cm, 91, CDN, Prod/Dir; *Sooter Studios*, Cm, 91, CDN, Wr/Dir/Prod; *Robin's Donuts*, Cm, 90, CDN, An/P Prod; *Silver Tag Sale*, Steart N. King, Cm, 90, Wr/Dir/Prod; *Since '52/Choices/'Round the World*, Chicken Delight of Canada, Cm, 90, Wr/Dir/Prod; *Knock, Knock*, Benylin, Cm, 90, CDN, An/Cam/P Prod.

PERRIS, Anthony
ATPD. 654 Markham St., Toronto, ON M6G 2L9 (416)534-1084. Charles Northcote, The Core Group, 489 College St., Suite 501, Toronto, ON M6G 1A5 (416)944-0193. FAX: 944-0446.
Type of Production and Credits: Th Short-Dir/Wr; TV Film-Dir; TV Video-Dir.
Genres: Drama-Th&TV; Action-TV; Educational-TV; Industrial-Th&TV.
Biography: Born 1939, Athens, Greece; Raised in South Africa. Student at 20th Century Fox Talent School, 58-59; production assistant to George Stevens, 59-65; assistant to *Life* magazine photographer, Eliot Elisofon, 65. *Honour Thy Father* won Best TV Drama, Yorkton, 77; *Being* won Most Outstanding Short Subject, Hoyts Theatres Film Festival (Australia); various awards at NY International Film & TV Festival, 69-74.

Selected Filmography: "Wonderstruck" (20 items), TV, 87-91, CDN, Prod/Wr/Dir; *A Grief Shared*, "Saying Goodbye", TV, 90, CDN, Dir; various corporate/industrial (25), In/Corp, 69-90, CDN, Prod/Dir/Wr; various educational (30), ED, 69-90, CDN, Prod/Dir/Wr; *Accident*, "9B", TV, 89, CDN, Dir; *Hiccups*, "You and Your Body" (OWL-TV), ED, 87, CDN, Dir; *Tug of War*, "Ritter's Cove", TV, 79, CDN, Dir; *The Defector*, "Littlest Hobo", TV, 79, CDN, Dir; *The Submarine*, "The Beach-combers", TV, 76, CDN, Dir; *Honour Thy Father*, "Here to Stay" (pilot), TV, 75, CDN, Dir; "To See Ourselves" (5 eps), TV, 71-74, CDN, Dir; *Scoop*, "For the Record", TV, 74, CDN, Dir; *The Contract*, "The Collaborators", TV, 73, CDN, Dir; *Being*, Th/TV, 71-72, CDN, Dir/Wr.

PERRON, Clément
- voir SCENARISTES

PERZEL, Anthony
- see PRODUCERS

PETERSEN, Curtis
- see CINEMATOGRAPHERS

PETKOVSEK, Danny S.
- see PRODUCERS

PETRIE, Daniel M.
DGA, DGC, SAG, ACCT. Donner, Schrier & Zucker, 15233 Ventura Blvd., #1100, Sherman Oaks, CA 91403 USA. Frek Specktor, CAA, 1888 Century Park E., #1400, Los Angeles, CA 90067 USA (213)277-4545.
Type of Production and Credits: Th Film-Dir/Wr; TV Film-Dir.
Genres: Drama-Th&TV.
Biography: Born in Glace Bay, Nova Scotia. B.A., Saint Francis Xavier University; later awarded honorary D.Litt.; M.A., Columbia University. Has taught at Northwestern University, Creighton University (head of Theatre Department). Won a Peabody Award for *Sybil* and a Special Award, Cannes Film Festival, for *A Raisin in the Sun*.
Selected Filmography: *My Name Is Bill W.*, TV, 89, USA, Dir; *Rocket Gibralter*, Th, 88, USA, Dir; *Cocoon: The Return*, Th, 88, USA, Dir; *Square Dance*, Th, 87, USA, Dir; *The Execution of Raymond Graham*, TV, 85, CDN, Dir; *The Bay Boy*, Th, 83, CDN, Dir/Wr, (GENIE); *The Dollmaker*, TV, 83, USA, Dir, (DGA); *Fort Apache, The Bronx*, Th, 79, USA, Dir; *Resurrection*, Th, 78, USA, Dir; *Harry Truman: Plain Speaking*, TV, 77, USA, Dir; *Sybil*, TV, 76, USA, Dir, (PEABODY); *Eleanor & Franklin: The White House Years*, TV, 76, USA, Dir, (EMMY); *Eleanor & Franklin*, TV, 75, USA, Dir, (EMMY); *Lifeguard*, Th, 74, USA, Dir; *Buster & Billy*, Th, 73, USA, Dir.

PETRIE, Robert J.
- see PRODUCERS

PICK, Anne
- see PRODUCERS

PINSENT, Gordon
OC, ACTRA, SAG. 130 Carlton St., PH 8, Toronto, ON M5A 2K1 (416)926-8778.
Type of Production and Credits: Th Film/Act/Wr; TV Film-Dir/Act; TV Video-Wr/Act.
Genres: Drama-Th&TV.
Biography: Born 1930, Grand Falls, Newfoundland. Attended Grand Falls Academy; honorary LL.D., University of Prince Edward Island, 75, Queen's University, 88; honorary D.Litt., Memorial University, 88. Officer, Order of Canada.
Selected Filmography: *Two Men*, TV, 88, CDN, Dir; *John and the Missus*, Th, 86, CDN, Scr/Dir/Act; *The Exile*, TV, 85, CDN, Dir; *And Miles to Go*, TV, 85, CDN, Wr/Act; "Airwaves" (2 eps), TV, 85, CDN, Dir; *Ready for Slaughter*, "For the Record", TV, 83, CDN, Act; *The Life and Times of Alonzo Boyd*, TV, 83, CDN, Act; *Once*, TV, 80, CDN, Dir; "A Gift to Last" (Wr 18 eps/Act 21 eps), TV, 76-80, CDN, Creator/Wr/Act, (ACTRA); *A Far Cry From Home*, TV, 80, CDN, Dir; *Escape from Iran: The Canadian Caper*, TV, 80, CDN, Act; *Klondike Fever*, Th, 79, CDN, Act, (GENIE); *Silence of the North*, Th, 79, CDN, Act; *Who Has Seen the Wind*, Th, 76, CDN, Act; *Horse Latitudes*, TV, 75, CDN, Act; *The Heatwave Lasted Four Days*, TV, 74, CDN, Act; *Michael in the Morning*, TV, 73, CDN, Wr; *The Rowdyman*, TH, 71, CDN, Wr/Act, (ACTRA/CFA); "Quentin Durgens, M.P." (30 eps), TV, 65-68, CDN, Act.

PIRKER, Roland K.
- see CINEMATOGRAPHERS

PITTMAN, Bruce
DGC. Worthwhile Movies Inc., 191 Logan Ave., Toronto, ON M4M 2N2 (416)469-0459.
Type of Production and Credits: Th Film-Dir; TV Film-Dir; TV Film-Dir.
Genres: Drama-Th&TV; Comedy-TV; Action-Th&TV; Horror-Th&TV.
Biography: Born 1950, Toronto, Ontario. Director of diverse projects. *The Painted Door* was nominated for an Oscar, 85; *Where the Spirit Lives* won 22 international awards and Gemini, 90 (Best TV Movie); *Maniac Mansion* on list of "1990 Ten Best," *Time* magazine.

Selected Filmography: "Street Legal" (1 eps), TV, 90, CDN, Dir; *The Meeting Place*, Th, 89, CDN, Dir; *Tools of the Deal*, TV, 88, CDN, Dir; *Scales of Justice*, TV, 88, CDN, Dir; "Chasing Rainbows" (7 eps), TV, 88, CDN, Dir; "Adderly" (4 eps), TV, 87, CDN, Dir; *The Screaming Woman*, "Ray Bradbury Theatre", TV, 86, CDN, Dir; *Hello Mary Lou, Prom Night II*, Th, 86, CDN, Dir; "Airwolf II" (2 eps), TV, 86, CDN, Dir; *Legs of the Lame*, "Bell Canada Playhouse", TV, 85, CDN, Dir/T'play; *The Painted Door*, "Bell Canada Playhouse", TV, 85, CDN, Dir; *Confidential*, Th, 85, CDN, Wr/Dir/Ed; *The Chorus of Xmas*, TV, 85, CDN, Dir; "Moviemakers" (25 eps), TV, 84, CDN, Dir/Prod; *Four to Four*, TV, 82, CDN, Dir.

PLAMONDON, Louis

ACCT. 1545 Docteur Penfield, #809, Montreal, PQ H3G 1C7 (514)932-2800.
Types de production et générique: TV film-Réal/Sc; TV vidéo-Réal/Sc.
Types d'oeuvres: Drame-TV; Comédie-TV; Variété-TV; Education-TV; Enfants-TV.
Curriculum vitae: Né en 1949 à Québec. Etudes: Collège des Jésuites de Québec; Loyola, Montréal, B.A.; Loyola, Los Angeles, M.A. Assistant réalisateur, Radio-Canada de 1973-84. Réalisateur, Radio-Canada, 1984-86. Réalisateur indépendant depuis 1986.
Filmographie sélective: "Les Grandes Vacances" (16 eps), TV, 89-91, CDN, Conc/Réal; *La Maison sur la Lune*, TV, 89, CDN, Conc/Réal; *Le Bar Ouvert*, TV, 89, CDN, Réal; *Bonjour ches vous*, TV, 89, CDN, Conc/Réal; "Bonjour Docteur" (10 eps), TV, 87-88, CDN, Réal; "Bon Dimanche" (2 eps), TV, 88, CDN, Réal; "Premières" (2 eps), TV, 88, CDN, Réal; "La Bonne Aventure" (5 eps), TV, 84, CDN, Réal; "Sesame Street", TV, 75-80, CDN, Sc; *Adieu Françoise*, "Les Beaux Dimanches", TV, 78, CDN, Sc.

PLOUFFE, Jean-Paul ✧

(514)982-9099.
Types de production et générique: TV film-Réal; TV vidéo-Réal.
Types d'oeuvres: Documentaire-TV.
Curriculum vitae: Né en 1933, Montréal, Québec. Langues: français et anglais. Baccalauréat en Sciences politiques.
Filmographie sélective: *Les 50 ans d'Agrepur*, TV, 88, CDN, Réal; *Amélioration génétique par ordinateur*, TV, 88, CDN, Réal; *Le Mérite agricole*, TV, 88, CDN, Réal; "L'Agriculture dans les pays de l'Est" (20 eps), TV, 87, CDN, Réal; *Veaux en fécondation in vitro*, TV, 87, CDN, Réal; "La Semaine verte" (6 eps), TV, 83-86, CDN, Réal; *Travaux correcteurs à la baie James/Radisson ville ouverte*, "Baie James", TV, 85, CDN, Réal; *Chasse à l'oie/Les insectes piqueurs*, "Baie James", TV, 85, CDN, Réal; *Relocalisation de Fort-Georges à Chisasibi*, "Baie James", TV, 85, CDN, Réal; *Visite Jean-Paul II*, TV, 84, CDN, Réal; La Mer et ses princes, TV, 83, CDN/F, Réal

PODESWA, Jeremy

DGC. 494 Euclid Ave., #3, Toronto, ON M6G 2S9 (416)963-8692. Rebelfilms Inc., 345 Adelaide St. W., #606, Toronto, ON M5V 1R5 (416)593-1616.
Type of Production and Credits: Th Film-Unit Pub; Th Short-Dir/Prod; TV Film-Dir/Prod.
Genres: Drama-Th&TV; Comedy-Th; Musical-TV; Documentary-TV.
Biography: Born in 1962 in Toronto, Ontario. Education includes Bachelor of Applied Arts, Ryerson Polytechnical Institute and a post-graduate directing fellowship at the American Film Institute's Center for Advanced Film Studies in Los Angeles. Has also served in an Academy apprenticeship as a director-observer on Filmline's *Bethune* in China. Worked as a unit publicist on numerous features. Honours include: 1986 Genie nominee for Best Live Action Short for *Nion*; the Norman Jewison Award for Best Film; the Blue Ribbon, American Film Festival in New York and Best Short Subject, Frameline S.F. for *David Roche Talks To You About Love*, 1983. Produced and directed the electronic press kits for *Prom Night IV, Masala, Dead Ringers* and *Some Girls*.
Selected Filmography: *Standards*, TV, 91, CDN, Dir/Co-Prod; *Profile: Betty Oliphant*, Toronto Arts Awards, TV, 90, CDN, Dir; *Car 54, Where Are You?*, Th, 90, USA, Unit Pub; *Masala*, Th, 90, CDN, Unit Pub; *Sing*, Th, 89, USA, Unit Pub; *Dead Ringers*, Th, 89, CDN/USA, Unit Pub; *Nion*, Th, 86, CDN, Dir/Prod; *David Roche Talks to You About Love*, Th, 83, CDN, Dir/Prod.

POIRIER, Anne Claire ✧

(514)270-2020.
Types de production et générique: l métrage-Réal/Prod/Sc; c métrage-Réal/Prod/Sc.
Types d'oeuvres: Drame-C; Documentaire-C.
Curriculum vitae: Née en 1932, St-Hyacinthe, Québec. Licenciée en Droit de l'Université de Montréal, 58;

Conservatoire d'Art Dramatique de Montréal (Théâtre). ONF, assistante réalisatrice, 60; tient une chronique et collabore à "Femmes d'aujourd'hui," Radio-Canada, 64-65; productrice à l'ONF, 70; productrice exécutive et Chef de Studio à la production française et responsable du programme Société Nouvelle, 75-78; retourne à la réalisation. Récipiendaire de l'Ordre du Québec, 85.
Filmographie sélective: *Salut Victor!*, C, 88, CDN, Réal/Co sc; *La Quarantaine,* C, 81, CDN, Réal/Co sc; *Mourir à tue-tête,* C, 78, CDN, Réal/Co sc/Prod; *Famille et variations,* C, 77, CDN, Prod; *Raison d'être,* C, 77, CDN, Prod; *La Maladie,* C, 77, CDN, Prod; *La Thérapie,* C, 77, CDN, Prod; *Québec à vendre,* C, 77, CDN, Prod; *Shakti,* C, 76, CDN, Prod; *Surtout L'hiver,* TV, 76, CDN, Prod; *Les Héritiers de la violence,* C, 76, CDN, Prod; *La P'tite Violence,* C, 76, CDN, Prod; *Le Temps de l'avant,* "En tant que femmes", TV, 75, CDN, Réal/Sc/Co prod; *A qui m'appartient ce gage?/J'me marie, j'me marie pas,* "En tant que femmes", TV, 73-74, CDN, Prod.

POOL, Léa ◊
SARDEC. 5964, rue Hutchison, Outremont, PQ H2V 4C1 (514)273-9351.
Types de production et générique: l métrage-Réal/Sc; TV Vidéo-Réal.
Types d'oeuvres: Drame-C; Documentaire-TV.
Curriculum vitae: Née à Soglio, Suisse; immigrante au Canada, 75. Diplôme ès Arts, Université du Québec, 78. Réalisatrice de documentaires et d'émissions de variétés, Radio-Québec. Prix: Festival de Sceaux, France pour *Strass Café*; Prix de la Presse, Festival International du Film du Monde, Montréal, Prix d'Excellence, Festival of Festivals, Toronto, et nominations au César et au Prix Génie pour *La Femme de l'hôtel.*

POTTERTON, Gerald
R.R. #3, Brome Lake, Cowansville, PQ J2K 3G8 (514)263-3282. Crayon Animation Inc., 4030 St-Ambroise, Suite 333, Montreal, PQ H4C 2C8 (514)933-6396. FAX: 933-0200.
Type of Production and Credits: Th Film-Dir/Wr; Th Short-Dir/Wr; TV Film-Dir/Wr.
Genres: Drama-Th; Comedy-Th; Animation-Th&TV.
Biography: Born 1931, London, England; Canadian citizenship. Studied Art, Hammersmith College, London; 2 years service in RAF. Assistant animator on *Animal Farm,* GB; animator, director, writer, NFB, 54-68; formed Potterton Productions, 68; worked in London, New York, Los Angeles. Member, Royal Canadian Academy. *Pinter People* won Gold and Silver Hugos, Chicago; *The Railrodder* won the Prix Femina, Belgium and a Special Award, Berlin; Oscar nominations for *Christmas Cracker,* 63, and *My Financial Career,* 62.
Selected Filmography: "The Real Story" (3 eps), TV, 90-91, F, Dir; "Smoggies" (52 eps), TV, 87-90, CDN/F, Dir/Creator; *The Ghost Ship,* TV, 86, CDN, Dir; *George and the Star,* TV, 85, CDN, Dir/Wr; *Melpomenus Jones,* Th, 83, CDN, Dir; *Heavy Metal,* Th, 81, CDN, Dir; *Raggedy Ann,* Th, 77, USA, Co-Dir; *The Remarkable Rocket,* TV, 75, CDN, Dir; *The Rainbow Boys,* Th, 72, CDN, Dir/Wr; *Tiki Tiki,* Th, 70, CDN, Dir/Wr; *Pinter People,* "Experiments in Television", TV, 68, CDN, Dir; *The Railrodder,* Th, 65, CDN, Dir/Wr; *Christmas Cracker,* Th, 63, CDN, Co-Dir/Wr; *My Financial Career,* Th, 62, CDN, Dir/An Des.

PRESTON, David
- see WRITERS
PRICE, Roger Damon
- see WRITERS
PRIETO, Claire
- see PRODUCERS
PROCOPIO, Frank
- see PRODUCERS
PURDY, Brian E.
- see PRODUCERS
PURDY, Jim
ACTRA, ACCT. 170 Courcelette Rd., Scarborough, ON M1N 2T2 (416)690-9331.
Type of Production and Credits: TV Film-Wr/Dir; TV Video-Wr/Dir; Th Film-Wr/Dir.
Genres: Drama-Th&TV; Documentary-TV; Educational-TV; Children's-TV.
Biography: Born 1949, Toronto, Ontario. Studied English Literature, University of Toronto, 67-69; Film & Theatre Studies, York University, 69-72. Actor, journalist, photographer, painter before co-authoring the book, *The Hollywood Social Problem Film,* published in US, 80. Now a freelance writer/director.
Selected Filmography: *The Big Fix,* "The Black Stallion", TV, 90, F/USA, Dir; *Dark Horse,* TV, 89, CDN, Wr/Dir; *Destiny to Order,* Th, 88, CDN, Wr/Dir/Assoc Prod; *20/20 Vision,* "The Twilight Zone", TV, 88, CDN/USA, Dir; *Concrete Angels,* Th, 87, CDN, Wr; *When This Man Dies,* "Alfred Hitchcock Presents", TV, 87,

CDN/USA, Dir; *Taking Care of Terrific*, "PBS Wonderworks", TV, 87, USA, Dir; *Where's Pete?/Left Out*, "Home Movies", TV, 85-86, CDN, Dir/Wr; *The Dream and the Triumph*, "Bell Canada Playhouse", TV, 85, CDN, T'play; "Home Fires" (19 eps) (Co Creator/Wr 8 eps), TV, 80-83, CDN, Wr; *The Morning Man*, In, 83, CDN, Wr/Dir; *The Disease is Arthritis*, In, 82, CDN, Wr; *Plenty Room in Pakistan*, ED, 79, CDN, Wr/Dir.

PYKE, Roger
58 Cartier Cres., Richmond Hill, ON L4C 2N2 (416)884-5957. Roger Pyke Prods. Ltd., 957 Broadview Ave., Unit A, Toronto, ON M4K 2R5 (416)422-1270. FAX: 422-4678.
Type of Production and Credits: Th Film-Ed; Th Short-Ed; TV Film-Dir/Ed; TV Video-Dir.
Genres: Drama-Th&TV; Comedy-Th&TV; Documentary-TV; Educational-TV; Commercials-TV; Corporate-Th.
Biography: Born 1940, London, England; Canadian citizenship. Languages: English, working knowledge of French and Spanish. B.A.A., Ryerson Polytechnic Institute, 63. Has worked in Toronto, Montreal, London (BBC), Guatemala, Nicaragua, Berlin, Washington, New York, Los Angeles, Malawi, Mozambique, Uganda, Rwanda, Burundi, Ethiopia, Zaire, Ivory Coast and Mali. Directors awards include: Chris Award, Columbus, 89; Special Jury Award, Golden Sheaf, Yorkton, 89; "Creative Excellence," US Film & Video Festival, 90; Silver Medal, C.A.S.E. Awards, Washington, 86; two Silvers and two Golds, Retail Comp. Awards, Toronto, 89; Bronze Award, Columbus, 90; Silver Hugo, Chicago, 91; Silver Medal, International Film & TV Festival, New York, 90; Silver Screen Award, US Film & Video Festival, 91; *Burden on the Land* won Silver Award, Houston International Film Festival and Red Ribbon, American Film Festival, 91.
Selected Filmography: *Burden on the Land* (documentary), TV, 91, CDN, Dir; *AIDS in Africa* (documentary), TV, 90, CDN, Dir; *Meeting the Challenge* (documentary), TV, 89, CDN, Dir; *Canadian Red Cross* (corp. video), TV, 88, CDN, Dir/Prod; *Wings of Eagles*, Th, 86, CDN, Dir; *These Few Years*, In, 86, CDN, Prod/Dir; *Canadian Connection*, TV, 85, CDN, Dir/Prod; *Crude Awakening*, TV, 84, CDN, Dir; *Energy: Search for an Answer*, TV, 84, CDN, Dir; *Bring 'em On*, Th, 82, CDN, Dir; *The Playing Fields of Brock*, Th, 82, CDN, Dir; *Gilberto's Dream*, TV, 80, CDN, Dir.

RABINOVITCH, David
- see PRODUCERS

RACINE, Pierre
- voir DIRECTEURS-PHOTO

RADFORD, Tom
- see PRODUCERS

RAKOFF, Alvin
ACTT, DGC, WGGB. 1 The Orchard, Chiswick, London, GB W4 1JZ (081)994-1269. Douglas Rae Management, 28 Charing Cross Rd., London, WC2H ODB England. (071)836-3903.
Type of Production and Credits: Th Film-Dir/Prod/Wr; TV Film-Dir/Prod/Wr; TV Video-Dir/Prod/Wr.
Genres: Drama-Th&TV; Action-Th&TV.
Biography: Born 1937, Toronto, Ontario. B.A., University of Toronto. On staff at BBC London, 4 years; seconded to French TV in Paris; worked in Germany, Spain, Italy, US, etc.
Selected Filmography: *The Best of Friends*, TV, 91, GB, Prod/Dir; *Gas & Candles*, TV, 90, GB, Dir; "Paradise Postponed" (12 eps), TV, 85-86, GB, Dir; *The First Olympics - Athens 1896*, TV, 85, USA/GB, Dir; *Mr. Halpern and Mr. Johnson*, TV, 83, GB, Dir; *A Voyage 'round My Father*, TV, 81, GB, Dir/Prod, (INT'L EMMY); *Dirty Tricks*, Th, 79, CDN, Dir; *City on Fire*, Th, 78, CDN/USA, Dir; *Romeo and Juliet*, "Shakespeare", TV, 78, GB, Dir; *The Kitchen*, TV, 77, GB, Dir; *The Dame of Sark*, TV, 76, GB, Dir; *In Praise of Love*, TV, 75, GB, Dir/Adapt; *The Nicest Man in the World*, TV, 75, GB, Dir.

RANSEN, Mort
ACTRA, DGC, CFTPA, CIFC. 837 Isabella Point Rd., R.R. #1, Fulford Harbour, BC V0S 1C0 (604)653-4755. Ranfilm Productions Inc., P.O. Box 411, Ganges, BC V0S 1C0 (604)653-9100. FAX: 653-4511. Ralph Zimmerman, Great North Management, 350 Dupont St., Toronto, ON M5R 1V9 (416)925-2051. FAX: 925-3904.
Type of Production and Credits: Th Film-Dir/Wr/Prod; TV Film-Dir/Wr/Prod.
Genres: Drama-Th&TV; Comedy-Th&TV; Documentary-Th&TV; Children's-Th&TV.
Biography: Has been making films since 61; director/writer with the National Film Board, 61-84; made 17 films; since 84, has written/directed 77 dramas, 4 of these feature-length; participated in cultural exchange to work in Sweden and made several award-winning films for Swedish

television, 69; has won 15 international awards as director and writer. Formed his own production company, Ranfilm, in 88, now with first feature in distribution (written, directed and co-produced by Ransen).
Selected Filmography: *Falling Over Backwards/Cul par-dessus tête*, Th, 90, CDN, Wr/Dir/Co-Prod; *Morris and Muush*, TV, 88, CDN, Wr/Dir; *Emerald Tear*, TV, 87, CDN, Dir; *Tangerine Taxi*, Th, 87, CDN, Wr/Dir; *Sincerely Violet*, TV, 86, CDN, Dir; *A Question of Honour*, "Street Legal", TV, 86, CDN, Dir; *Time Bomb*, ED, 85, CDN, Co-Wr/Dir; *Mortimer Griffin and Shalinsky*, TV, 85, CDN, Co-Wr/Dir; *Bayo*, Th, 84, CDN, Wr/Dir; *The Russells*, TV, 87-88, CDN, Co-Dir; *Untouched and Pure*, ED, 69, CDN, Dir; *You're On Indian Land*, ED, 69, CDN, Dir; *Chistopher's Movie Matinee*, Th, 67, CDN, Dir/Ed; *The Circle*, TV, 66, CDN, Wr/Dir; *No Reason to Stay*, TV, 65, CDN, Wr/Dir/Ed.

RASKY, Harry
ACTRA, DGA, WGA, ACCT. CBC, Box 500, Stn. A, Toronto, ON M5W 1E6 (416)975-6888.
Type of Production and Credits: Th Film-Dir/Prod/Wr; TV Film-Dir/Prod/Wr; TV Video-Dir/Prod/Wr.
Genres: Drama-Th&TV; Variety-Th&TV; Documentary-Th&TV.
Biography: Born 1928, Toronto, Ontario. B.A., University of Toronto. Has worked as a journalist, author, lecturer, host/interviewer. Granted honorary degree by University of Toronto. Won many awards for his films including International Critics Prize, Montreal, for *Arthur Miller on Home Ground*; Grand Prize, New York TV/Film Festival; Oscar nomination for *Homage to Chagall: The Colours of Love*; Academy Award Certificate of Merit for *Stratasphere*; selected as Top Non-Fiction Director, TV Directors' Guild of America, 86. CBC presented retrospective of 12 "Raskymentries" (*Rasky's Gallery*), 88. The Mayor of Toronto named June 2, 88, as Harry Rasky Day. Honoured with a special prize at the Moscow International Film Festival, 91, in recognition of his "contribution to the spiritual life of the 20th century."
Selected Filmography: *The Magic Season of Robertson Davies*, TV, 90, CDN, Prod/Wr/Dir; *The Great Teacher: Northrop Frye*, TV, 89, CDN, Prod/Wr/Dir; *To Mend the World*, Th, 87, CDN, Prod/Dir/Wr; *Karsh: The Searching Eye*, TV, 86, CDN, Prod/Dir/Wr; *Stratasphere*, TV, 82, CDN, Dir/Prod/Wr; *The Song of Leonard Cohen*, TV, 79, CDN, Dir/Prod/Wr; *Homage to Chagall*, Th, 75, CDN, Dir/Prod/Wr; *Next Year in Jerusalem*, TV, 73, CDN, Dir/Prod/Wr, (ACTRA); *Tennessee Williams' South*, TV, 73, CDN, Dir/Prod/Wr; *The Wit and World of George Bernard Shaw*, TV, 72, CDN/GB, Dir/Prod/Wr; *Upon This Rock*, Th, 71, USA, Dir/Wr; *Hall of Kings*, TV, 67, USA, Dir/Prod/Wr, (EMMY); *Cuba and Castro Today*, TV, 65, USA, Dir/Prod/Wr; *The Lion and the Cross*, "The 20th Century", TV, 61, USA, Dir/Wr, (EMMY); "Newsmagazine" (100 films), TV, 52-55, CDN, Dir/Prod/Wr.

RASTELLI, Maryse
- voir PRODUCTEURS

RATTAN, Amarjeet S.
- see PRODUCERS

RAWI, Ousama
ACTT, DGA, IATSE 667, ACCT. Rawi Sherman, 567 Queen St. W., Toronto, ON M5V 2B6 (416)777-1234. FAX: 777-0876.
Type of Production and Credits: Th Film-Dir/DOP; TV Film-Dir/DOP.
Genres: Drama-Th&TV; Comedy-Th; Action-Th; Commercials-TV.
Biography: British and Canadian citizenship. Entered film industry in UK, 65; started as newsreel, TV drama and commercials cameraman, then feature film DOP; started directing commercials, 79; first feature, 86. Has won numerous awards including Clios and awards at NY, Cannes and UK commercials festivals.
Selected Filmography: *A Judgement in Stone*, Th, 86, CDN, Dir; *Charlie Muffin*, TV, 79, GB, DOP; *Story of Princess Grace*, TV, 78, USA, DOP; *Girl in Blue Velvet*, Th, 78, F, DOP; *Zulu Dawn*, Th, 78, USA, DOP; *Power Play*, Th, 77, CDN/GB, DOP; *Bovver Boots*, TV, 77, GB, DOP; *Sky Riders*, Th, 76, USA, DOP; *Human Factor*, Th, 76, USA, DOP; *Rachel's Man*, Th, 74, GB, DOP; *Alfie Darling*, Th, 74, GB, DOP; *Black Windmill*, Th, 73, USA, DOP; *Gold*, Th, 73, GB, DOP; *The 14/Wild Little Bunch*, Th, 72, GB, DOP; *Pulp*, Th, 71, GB, DOP.

RAYMONT, Peter
ACCT, DGC, CIFC. 125 Havelock St., Toronto, ON M6H 3B7. Investigative Productions Inc., 490 Adelaide St. W, Suite 302, Toronto, ON M5V 1TZ (416)594-0580. FAX: 594-1691. (416)593-5969.
Type of Production and Credits: Th Film-Dir/Prod; TV Film-Dir/Prod/Wr/Narr; TV Video-Dir/Prod/Wr/Narr.

Genres: Action-Th&TV; Documentary-Th&TV; Educational-TV.
Biography: Born 1959, Ottawa, Ontario. B.A., Film, Politics, Economics, Queen's University. Worked at CBC, NFB; producer of radio documentaries for CBC's "Sunday Morning;" writer of articles for the *Globe and Mail, Canadian Business.* Winner, Red Ribbon, American Film Festival; Gold Plaque, Chicago, for *Magic in the Sky*; *On to the Polar Sea: A Yukon Adventure,* Yorkton; Special Jury Peace Prize, Krakow, for *With Our Own Two Hands.* Between Two Worlds won Sesterce d'Argent, Nyon Documentary Film Festival, 90; two awards, Media Nord/Sud Geneva, 91; Gold Apple, Educational Film & TV Awards, California, 90. *The World is Watching Us* won Genie, Best Documentary, 89; Red Ribbon, American Film Festival; Gold Hugo, Best Social/Political documentary, Chicago, 88; Ecumenical Prize/Public Jury Prize, Nyon, 88; Bronze Apple Award, U.S. Educational Film & Video Festival, 90. Produced and directed at WGBH-TV and Christian Science Monitor TV, Boston, 86-87. Resident (Director), Canadian Centre for Advanced Film Studies, 88. Founding member and past chairperson, Canadian Independent Film Caucus. Executive Producer and Producer of 5-hour TV documentary series: *As Long as the Rivers Flow -The Native Canadian Search for Self-Government.*
Selected Filmography: "As Long as the Rivers Flow" (5 parts), TV, 91, CDN, Exec Prod/Prod; *Between Two Worlds,* Th/TV, 90, CDN/GB/AUS, Prod; *The World is Watching Us,* Th/TV, 88, CDN/GB/S, Dir/Prod/Co-Wr; *Haiti - The Politics of Aid,* TV, 87, USA, Prod/Wr; *Jamaica - Broken Promises,* TV, 87, USA, Prod/Dir/Wr; "The Nuclear Age", TV, 86, USA/J, Prod/Dir/Wr; *With Our Own Two Hands,* Th, 85, CDN, Dir/Prod; "Venture" (weekly), TV, 85, CDN, Prod/Report; *The Brokers,* Th, 84, CDN, Dir/Prod/Narr; *On to the Polar Sea: A Yukon Adventure,* Th, 83, CDN/USA, Dir/Co-Prod/Co-Wr; *Prisoners of Debt,* Th, 82, CDN, Dir/Narr; *Falasha: Agony of the Black Jews,* Th, 82, CDN, Dir/Co-Wr/Narr; *Falasha: Exile of the Black Jews,* Th, 82, CDN, Loc Dir; *The Forgotten Refugees,* Th, 82, CDN, Loc Dir; *Arctic Spirits,* Th, 82, CDN, Dir/Prod/Wr.

READ, Merilyn
- see PRODUCERS

REED-OLSEN, Joan
ACCT. 12 Hazel Ave., Toronto, ON M4E 1C5 (416)694-0589.
Type of Production and Credits: TV Film-Dir/Prod; TV Video-Dir/Prod.
Genres: Documentary-TV.
Biography: Born 1923, Toronto, Ontario; Norwegian and Canadian citizenship; lived in Norway for 25 years. Languages: English and Norwegian. Worked as freelance writer/broadcaster in Norway; returned to Canada, 70; research, writing, hosting, directing, producing documentaries, TVOntario, 71-86; now retired but freelances.
Selected Filmography: "Hands Over Time" (48 eps), TV, 80-91, CDN, Prod/Dir/Host; "People Patterns" (126 eps), TV, 80-88, CDN, Prod/Dir/Host.

REGAN, Ted
- see PRODUCERS

REID, William
- see PRODUCERS

REISENAUER, George ◊
(416)962-0678.
Type of Production and Credits: TV Film-Dir.
Genres: Documentary-TV; Educational-TV; Commercials-TV.
Biography: Born 1947, Prague, Czechoslovakia. Languages: Czech and English. Educated to grade 12 level in Prague; studied photography, then filmmaking at Ryerson Polytechnical Institute, Toronto, 70-74. Has been producing TV commercials, short films, industrials and documentaries since 66.

REITMAN, Ivan
DGA. 100 Universal City Plaza, Bungalow 64, Universal City, CA 91604 (818)777-8080. FAX: 777-0467. Michael Ovitz, C.A.A., 1888 Century Park E., Suite 1400, Los Angeles, CA, USA 90067 (213)277-4545.
Types of Production and Credits: Th Film-Dir/Prod
Genres: Comedy-Th; Horror-Th.
Biography: Born 1947, Komano, Czechoslovakia; Canadian citizenship. Attended McMaster University where he set up a film society. After graduation, started New Cinema of Canada; producer for Cinépix Inc.; also experienced in the production of Broadway shows. Received Special Award from the Academy of Canadian Cinema, 84.
Selected Filmography: *Stop! Or My Mom Will Shoot,* Th, 91, USA, Prod; *Beethoven,* Th, 91, USA, Exec Prod; *Kindergarten Cop,* Th, 90, USA, Prod/Dir; *Ghostbusters II,* Th, 89, USA, Prod/Dir; *Twins,* Th, 88, USA, Dir/Prod; *Legal Eagles,* Th, 86, USA, Dir/Prod; *Ghostbusters,* Th, 84, USA,

Dir/Prod; *Spacehunter*, Th, 83, CDN, Prod; *Stripes*, Th, 81, USA, Dir; *Heavy Metal*, Th, 81, CDN, Prod; *National Lampoon's Animal House*, Th, 78, USA, Co-Prod; *Meatballs*, Th, 78, CDN, Dir; *Rabid*, Th, 76, CDN, Exec Prod; *Death Weekend*, Th, 75, CDN, Prod.

REMEROWSKI, Ted
- see PRODUCERS

REPKE, Ron
- see PRODUCERS

REUSCH, Peter ✧
(604)688-1772.
Type of Production and Credits: TV Film-Dir/Prod.
Genres: Drama-TV; Action-TV; Documentary-Th&TV; Educational-TV.
Biography: Born 1930, Hamburg, Germany; has lived in Canda since 55. After graduation from art college, worked as art director, photojournalist, special effects cameraman; DOP on many feature films, TV series, TV commercials and documentary films. Opened film/video production houses in Vancouver and Seattle, 73.
Selected Filmography: *Canadian Coast Guard*, (Expo 86), Th, 86, CDN, Dir/Prod; *The Leading Edge*, TV, 85, CDN, Dir/Prod/Cam/Ed; *Unity Canada*, TV, 84, CDN, Dir/Prod/Cam/Ed; *Vacation*, TV, 84, CDN, Dir/Prod/Cam/ Ed; *A Visit to Purdy's*, TV, 83, CDN, Dir/Prod/Cam/ Ed; *It's Your Money*, TV, 82, USA, Dir/Prod/Cam.

REYNOLDS, Gene
DGA, WGA, PGA. 2034 Castilian Dr., Los Angeles, CA 90068 (213)969-0703. Mike Rosenfeld/CAA, (213)277-4545.
Type of Production and Credits: TV Film-Prod/Dir; TV Video-Dir.
Genres: Drama-TV; Comedy-TV.
Biography: Has won 6 Emmy awards and 3 DGA awards.
Selected Filmography: *Whereabouts of Jenny*, TV, 90, USA, Prod/Dir; *Doing Life*, TV, 87, USA, Prod/Dir; *In Defense of Kids*, TV, 82, USA, Prod/Dir; "Lou Grant" (5 years), TV, USA, Prod; "M.A.S.H." (5 years), TV, USA, Prod.

REYNOLDS, Stephen P.
- see PRODUCERS

RICH, Ron
ACCT, DGA, DGC. 91 Post Rd., Don Mills, ON M3B 1J3 (416)446-1886. L.T.B. Productions, 137 Berkeley St., Toronto, ON M5A 2W7 (416)360-0053.
Type of Production and Credits: TV Film-Dir.
Genres: Drama-Th&TV; Variety-TV; Action-TV; Commercials-TV;

Biography: Born 1940, London, England; landed immigrant Canada; H1 status, US. Graduate of Wimbledon College of Art, St. Martin's School of Art, England. Began professional career in advertising. Started as a film director, 71, winning a Lion d'Argent, Cannes, with his first commercial; later won international awards, including Lion d'Or (Cannes), Gold Award (US TV Commercial Festival), Tokyo Silver, Hollywood Broadcast Award.
Selected Filmography: *Driving Impaired*, Cm, 88, CDN, Dir; *Play It Smart*, Cm, 88, CDN, Dir; *Body Heat*, Cm, 88, CDN, Dir; Alfred Sung Fashions, Cm, 88, CDN, Dir; Pepto Bismal campaign, Cm, 87, CDN, Dir; *Boardwalk*, Black's Photography, Cm, 85, CDN, Dir; *Telephone*, Dentyne Gum, Cm, 85, CDN, Dir; *New Star*, Texaco, Cm, 85, CDN, Dir; *Going Out*, Hochtaler, Cm, 84, CDN, Dir; *Mess*, Lestoil, Cm, 84, USA, Dir; *Desert*, Levi Strauss, Cm, 84, CDN, Dir, (CMA/TVB); *Early Morning*, Velour, Cm, 84, CDN, Dir; *No Caffeine*, Dr. Pepper, Cm, 84, USA, Dir; *Touch Me*, Johnson's Baby Powder, Cm, 83, CDN, Dir; *Chew-Chew*, Hershey, Cm, 83, CDN, Dir.

RICHER, Simon
(514)294-2544.
Types de production et générique: TV film-Réal/Sc; TV vidéo-Réal/Sc.
Types d'oeuvres: Documentaire-TV; Education-TV; Religion-TV.
Curriculum vitae: Né en 1929, Montréal, Québec. Langues: français, anglais, italien.
Filmographie sélective: *Mariage grec*, TV, 88, CDN, Réal; *Les Croix de chemins*, ED, 80, CDN, Réal/Sc; "La Semaine Verte" (50 eps), TV, 74, CDN, Sc; "Les Travaux et les jours" (300 eps), TV, 55-73, CDN, Réal.

ROBBINS, Karen
- see PRODUCERS

ROBERGE, Hélène
ACCT. 1814 ouest, rue Sherbrooke, #5, Montréal, PQ H3H 1E4 (514)937-3350. Société Radio-Canada, 1400 est, boul. René-Lévesque, Montréal, PQ H3C 3A8 (514)597-4336.
Types de production et générique: TV film-Prod; TV vidéo-Réal.
Types d'oeuvres: Drame-TV; Comédie-TV; Documentaire-TV; Enfants-TV.
Curriculum vitae: Née au Québec. Langues: français et anglais. Baccalauréat, Littérature anglaise, Université Laval. Oeuvre en télévision depuis 54 à titre de

réalisatrice; Directrice, émissions dramatiques, Radio-Canada, 86-90; Directrice des relations internationales et des ventes d'émissions (TV) depuis 90. Gagne le Children's TV Workshop Award pour "Nic et Pic."
Filmographie sélective: "Le Parc des braves" (30 eps), TV, 83-86, CDN, Réal; "Monsieur le Ministre" (25 eps), TV, 82-83, CDN, Réal; "Terre humaine" (30 eps), TV, 80-82, CDN, Réal; "Nic et Pic" (60 eps), TV, 72-80, CDN, Réal; "Femmes d'aujourd'hui", TV, 64-70, CDN, Réal.

ROBERT, Vincent
- see WRITERS

ROBERTSON, David M.
DGC, ACCT. 39 Lincoln St., Ajax, ON L1S 6C4 (416)683-2473. Actorfone West, 6565 Sunset Blvd., Suite 318, Hollywood, CA 90028 USA. (213)462-6565. Barry Perelman Agency, 9200 Sunset Blvd., Suite 531, Los Angeles, CA 90069 USA. (213)274-5999.
Type of Production and Credits: Th Film-Dir/1st AD/Line Prod; TV Film-Dir/1st AD/Line Prod.
Genres: Drama-Th&TV; Action-Th&TV; Horror-Th; Children's-TV.
Biography: Born 1941, Scotland; British and Canadian citizenship; US resident alien. Attended art school; Creative Writing, School of Continuing Education, University of Toronto; Theatre Drama, Department of Extension, University of British Columbia.
Selected Filmography: *Final Judgement/The Reckoning*, TV, 90, CDN, Dir; *Uncut Gem*, TV, 89, CDN, Dir; *Midday Sun*, Th/TV, 88, CDN, 1st AD; *Blindside*, Th, 87, CDN, 1st AD; "Adderly" (2 eps), TV, 87, CDN, 1st AD; "Friday the 13th: The Series" (6 eps), TV, 87, CDN/USA, 1st AD; *Hello Mary Lou - Prom Night II*, Th, 86, CDN, 1st AD/2nd U Dir; *Nowhere to Hide*, Th, 86, CDN, 2nd Unit AD; *Hostage: Dallas*, Th, 85, USA, 1st AD; *Limousine/My Chauffeur*, Th, 85, USA, 1st AD; *Letting Go*, TV, 85, USA, 1st AD; *Friday the 13th, Part V*, Th, 85, USA, 1st AD; "Mania" (1 eps), TV, 85, CDN, Dir; *The Return of the Living Dead*, Th, 84, USA, 1st AD/2nd U Dir; *Doin' Time*, Th, 83, USA, 1st AD/2nd U Dir.

ROBINSON, John Mark
WGA, DGA. (213)452-1554. Modern Productions, 4112 Del Rey Ave., Venice CA (213)578-1112. Peter Turner, (213)315-4772.
Type of Production and Credits: Th Film-Dir/Wr; Th Short-Dir/Wr.
Genres: Drama-Th; Musical-Th&TV; Experimental-Th&TV.
Biography: Born 1949, Toronto, Ontario. Has produced, written and directed over 80 rock videos; MTV Video Award and Houston Film Festival Award for Tina Turner's *What's Love Got to Do With It*, 87.
Selected Filmography: *Kid*, Th, 90, USA, Dir; *Motown's Mustang*, Th, 88, USA, Wr/Dir; *What's Love Got to Do With It*, Tina Turner, MV, 87, USA, Dir; *Roadhouse 66*, Th, 85, USA, Dir.

ROBISON, Michael
DGC, IATSE. 2627 Balaclava St., Vancouver, BC V6K 4E3 (604)734-7111. Robison Productions Ltd., 314 W. Pender St., Vancouver, BC V6B 1T3 (604)669-8890.
Type of Production and Credits: TV Film-Dir.
Genres: Drama-TV.
Biography: Born 1955, Toronto, Ontario; Canadian and US citizenship. B.A., Communications, Simon Fraser University. First film editor in Canada to work with Montage and Ediflex on series. Works as director of commercials and documentaries.
Selected Filmography: "Mom P.I." (1 eps), TV, CDN, Dir; "Neon Rider" (1 eps), TV, CDN/USA, Dir; "Bordertown" (2 eps), TV, CDN/F, Dir; "Danger Bay" (1 eps), TV, CDN/USA, Dir; "The Hitchhiker" (1 eps), TV, CDN/F, Dir; "21 Jump Street" (2 eps), TV, CDN, Dir.

ROCHON, Gerard O.
- see PRODUCERS

RODGERS, Bob
- see PRODUCERS

ROGAN, N. (Bert)
- see WRITERS

ROGERS, Allen
- see PRODUCERS

ROLAND, Herb
- see PRODUCERS

ROLLASON, Steve ✧
(416)454-4810.
Type of Production and Credits: TV Video-Dir.
Genres: Documentary-TV; Industrial-TV.
Biography: Born 1951, Toronto, Ontario. Received Top Honour Student Award at graduation from Media Arts, Sheridan College. Twenty years media experience: Citytv, Film House, National Advertising, Panasonic, Sony; President of Canadian Corporate Productions.
Selected Filmography: *World of Magnetic Recording*, In, 87, CDN, Dir/Prod; *Ontario Surveying*, In, 87, CDN, Dir/Prod; *Allied Packing* In, 87, CDN, Dir/

Prod; *Crowd Management/Crowd Control/ Crime Scene Management/T.R.U. Team*, In, 84-85, CDN, Dir; *Transport Truck Inspection/Directing Traffic/Computer Services*, In, 84, CDN, Dir; *Finger Printing/ Death Notification/A.L.E.R.T./Young Offenders*, In, 83-84, CDN, Dir; *B.O.S.S./ Baton/Hand Cuffs/Foreign Weapons*, In, 83, CDN, Dir; *Search and Seizure/Form X-37/Vehicle Registration/ House Search*, In, 82, CDN, Dir; *Consider the Source/The O.P.P. Academy/Telecommunication*, In, 81-82, CDN, Dir; *Alf Neilsen/A Taste of Disbelief*, In, 70-74, CDN, Dir.

ROMANOFF, Sergei
- see WRITERS

ROSCOE, Stephen G.
Point of View Productions Inc., 106 - 199 Upper Canada Dr., Willowdale, ON M2P 1T3 (416)224-5751.
Type of Production and Credits: Th Short-Dir/Prod; TV Film-Dir; TV Video-Dir.
Genres: Drama-Th&TV; Comedy-Th&TV; Documentary-Th&TV; Music Video-TV.
Biography: Born in 1963 in Ottawa, Ontario. Canadian citizen. B.F.A. in Film/Video Production, York University, 86. *Odyssey In August* received Genie Award nomination, 90, as Best Short Drama. *Thanatos* received the Grand Prize, Best Direction and Best Drama awards at Cinegrad Showcase and Forum 87. *She Waits* received Second Prize in the Music Video category at CBC Telefest, 85. *Slay the Dragon* received the Best Youth Film award at the Canadian International Amateur Film Festival, 81.
Selected Filmography: *Odyssey In August*, TH, 89, CDN, Dir/Co Prod; *Moving Day*, Th, 87, CDN, Dir/Ed; *Music in the Midnight Sun*, Th, 87, CDN, 2nd Unit Dir; *Thanatos*, Th, 86, CDN, Dir/Prod; *She Waits*, MV, 85, CDN, Wr/Dir/ Prod; *Slay the Dragon*, Th, 81, CDN, Wr/Dir/ Prod; *The Grand Illusion*, Th, 80, CDN, Wr/Dir/Prod.

ROSE, Hubert-Yves
ARRFQ, SARDEC. 241, rue Maple, St-Lambert, PQ J4P 2S1 (514)465-9014.
Types de production et générique: l métrage-Réal/Sc; c métrage-Réal/Sc.
Types d'oeuvres: Drame-C.
Curriculum vitae: Né en 1944, Verdun, Québec. Langues: français et anglais. Licence en lettres, Université de Montréal, 70. Travaille comme scénariste et assistant réalisateur pour l'ONF et Radio-Québec. Enseigne la scénarisation à l'Université du Québec à Montréal. *La Ligne de Chaleur* a gagné de Claude Jutra Award, 89 pour meilleur premier long métrage (Directors' Guild of Canada); mention de la Fipresci Festival International Figueira da Foz, 88.
Filmographie sélective: *La Ligne de Chaleur*, C, 88, CDN, Réal/Co sc; *Voyageur*, C, 83, CDN, Réal/Sc; *L'Heure bleue*, C, 76, CDN, Réal/Sc.

ROSEMOND, Perry
DGC, DGA, ACTRA. The Rosemond Co., 4 Lowther Ave., #407, Toronto, ON M5R 1C6 (416)923-5394. Lynn Kinney/Credentials, 387 Bloor St. E., 5th Floor, Toronto, ON M4W 1H7 (416)926-1507.
Type of Production and Credits: TV Film-Dir/Prod/Wr; TV Video-Dir/ Prod/Wr.
Genres: Drama-TV; Comedy-TV; Variety-TV; Action-TV.
Selected Filmography: *Dog House*, TV, 91, CDN/USA, Dir; "Maniac Mansion", TV, 91, CDN/USA, Dir.

ROSS, Rodger W.
- see PRODUCERS

ROULEAU, Mario
FPRRTC. 5380, 15 Ave, Apt. 102, Montreal, PQ H1X 3G2 (514)725-5656. (514)521-2424.
Types de production et générique: TV vidéo-Réal.
Types d'oeuvres: Variété-TV; Documentaire-TV.
Curriculum vitae: Né en 1953. Langues: français, anglais. Réalisateur d'émissions de variété et de documentaire à la télévision avec Radio-Quebec, Productions Scéno Vision, Productions Pixart inc, Films Vision-4 et Productions 24-30. Remporte prix Gémeaux pour "Beau et Chaud", 90, (meilleure réalisation, série de variétés); "Lumières", 89 (meilleure émission d'information service) et "WOW", 87, (meilleure émission jeunesse).
Filmographie sélective: "Beau & Chaud" (44 eps), TV, 90-91, CDN, Réal, (GEMEAUX); "Lumieres" (120 eps), TV, 88-91 CDN, Real (GEMEAUX); *L'Empire des futures stars*, TV, 90, CDN, Réal; "La Route des Vacances" (65 eps), TV, 88, CDN, Prod rél; "WOW" (60 eps), TV, 87-88, CDN, Réal, (GEMEAUX); "Fan Club" (120 eps), TV, 86-87, CDN, Réal; "Graffiti" (30 eps), TV, 86-87, CDN, Réal.

ROWE, Peter
DGC. Rosebud Films, 435 The Thicket, Port Credit, ON L5G 4P6 (416)271-5757. FAX: 278-7871 Charles Northcote, The Core Group, 489 College St., # 501, Toronto, ON M6G 1A5 (416)944-0193.

Type of Production and Credits: Th Film-Dir/Prod; TV Film-Dir/Prod; TV Video-Dir/Prod.
Genres: Drama-Th&TV; Comedy-Th&TV; Horror-Th&TV; Action-Th&TV.
Biography: Born 1947, Winnipeg, Manitoba.
Selected Filmography: "E.N.G." (5 eps), TV, 89-91, CDN, Dir; "The Black Stallion" (2 eps), TV, 90, CDN/F, Dir; "Katts & Dog" (4 eps), TV, 89-90, CDN/F, Dir; "Oceans Adventure Video Magazine", TV, 88, USA, Prod; *Take Two*, Th, 88, USA, Dir; *Personal Exemptions*, Th, 88, CDN, Dir; *The Architects of Fear*, Th, 86, CDN, Dir; "The Campbells" (4 eps), TV, 86, CDN/USA/GB, Dir; *Lost!*, Th, 85, CDN, Dir/Prod/Wr; "The Edison Twins" (2 eps), TV, 84-85, CDN, Dir; *Adventures on Shark Reef*, TV, 84, CDN, Wr/Cin; "Vanderberg" (3 eps), TV, 83, CDN, Dir; *Micronesia: The Winds of Change*, TV, 83, CDN, Dir; *Reasonable Force/Final Edition*, "For the Record", TV, 81-83, CDN, Dir; "Takeover", TV, 81, CDN, Dir.

ROY, Robert L.M.
Stornoway Productions Inc., 160 Bloor St. E., Suite 1220, Toronto, ON M4W 1B9 (416)923-1104. FAX: 923-1122.
Type of Production and Credits: TV Video-Dir.
Genres: Documentary-TV; Current Affairs-TV.
Biography: Born 1955, Toronto, Ontario; US and Canadian citizenship. Honours B.A., Political Science, University of Western Ontario. Honourable mention, Columbus Film Festival; finalist, Golden Sheaf Awards, 88.
Selected Filmography: *Caught in the Crossfire*, TV, 91, J/A, Prod; *Out of Control*, TV, 90, CDN, Prod; "End of An Empire" (4 eps)(Wr 3 eps/Prod 1 eps/Dir 1 eps), TV, 89, CDN/USA, Wr/Dir/Prod; "At the Crossroads" (4 eps), TV, 87-88, CDN, Wr/Res/Dir; *The Twice Promised Land*, TV, 86, CDN, Assoc Prod; *Agents of Deception*, TV, 84, CDN, Co-Wr/Assoc Prod; *The KGB Connections*, TV, 80, CDN, Res.

ROY-DECARIE, Matthieu
- voir MONTEURS SON

ROZEMA, Patricia
212 Robert St., Toronto, ON M5S 2K7.
Type of Production and Credits: Th Short-Dir/Prod/Wr; TV Video-Dir/Wr.
Genres: Drama-Th.
Biography: Born 1958. Languages: English and Dutch. B.A. (Honours), English and Philosophy, Journalism minor, Calvin College, Michigan, 81; Dean's List for scholastic achievement. *I've Heard the Mermaids Singing* won Prix de la jeunesse, Cannes, 87, and several other prizes at 26 festivals; film released in 34 countries; *White Room* won L'Antenne d'Or and La Prix de la Commission Superieure Technique at Avoriaz Film Festival, 91.
Selected Filmography: *White Room*, Th, 90, CDN, Dir/Wr/Ed/Exec Prod; *I've Heard the Mermaids Singing*, Th, 86, CDN, Dir/Co-Prod; *Passion: A Letter in 16mm*, Th, 85, CDN, Dir/Wr/Prod; "The Journal" (sev seg), TV, 82-83, CDN, Assoc Prod.

RUBBO, Michael
- see WRITERS
RUSSELL, Paul
- see WRITERS
RUTHERFORD, John T.
- see WRITERS
RUVINSKY, Morrie
- see WRITERS

SADR, Seyyed ◆
(416)498-0883.
Type of Production and Credits: Th Short-Dir/Cam; TV Film-Dir/Cam/Snd Rec.
Genres: Drama-Th&TV; Documentary-Th&TV; Educational-Th&TV; Industrial-Th&TV.
Biography: Born 1944, Bobul, Iran; landed immigrant Canada. A.A. (Associated Arts degree), Photography, Phoenix College, Arizona; B.A., Theatre Arts, UCLA; M.F.A., Motion Picture, UCLA. Winner of awards at Berlin (76), San Francisco (72) and Frankfurt (72).
Selected Filmography: *Our Elders Remember*, TV, 86, In, Cam/Snd Rec; *Licence to Kill*, TV, 85, F, Snd Rec; *Iran: A Revolution Betrayed*, TV, 83-84, GB, Dir/Cam; *Traffic Cop*, Th, 83, IRN, Dir; *Teamsters' Strike*, Th, 72, USA, Dir/Cam.

SAHASRABUDHE, Deepak
- see PRODUCERS

SAINT-LAURENT, Francine
UDA. 6099, ave. de l'Esplanade, Montréal, PQ H2T 3A2. (514)273-1484.
Types de production et générique: TV film-Réal; TV vidéo-Réal.
Types d'oeuvres: Documentaire-TV.
Curriculum vitae: Née en 1954, Ottawa, Ontario. Baccalauréat en Communications, Université du Québec à Montréal, 81.
Filmographie sélective: "La route de vacances", TV, 91, CDN, Réal; "La vie en couleurs", TV, 91, CDN, Réal; *Coorporatif Caisse Desjardins*, In, 90, CDN, Réal;

"Dossier Mystère", TV, 90, CDN, Réal; *Medecine apprivoisé*, Th, 90, CDN, Réal; "Première Ligne", TV, 89, CDN, Réal; "S.O.S. Télé", TV, 89, CDN, Réal; "Caméra 86-87", TV, 86-87, CDN, Réal.

STE-MARIE, Pierre
FPRRTC. 921 Notre Dame, Répentigny, PQ J5Y 1C6 (514)585-4510. Télé Métropole inc., 1600 boul. Maisonneuve est, Montréal, PQ (514)598-3967.
Types de production et générique: TV vidéo-Réal.
Types d'oeuvres: Comédie-TV; Variété-TV; Affaires Publiques-TV; Sports-TV.
Curriculum vitae: Né en 1939 à Montréal, Québec. Citoyenneté canadienne. Langue: français. Formation Beaux Arts de Montréal. Début dans le domaine à Radio-Canada, Montréal. Formation mise en scène avex Jean Doat, experience en télé romans, variétés, reportages, émissions speciales. Responsable comme producteur délégué Jeux Olympiques de Barcelone, Espagne et prochains Jeux Olympiques d'hiver en Norvège (1994) et preparation du Metro Star 92.
Filmographie sélective: *Gala Griffe d'or*, TV, 91, CDN, Réal; *Gala Metro Star*, TV, 91, CDN, Réal; *Avis de Recherche/Charles Aznavour*, TV, 90, F, Prod dél; *Gala Metro Star*, TV, 90, CDN, Réal; "Ferland/Nadeau" (65 eps), TV, 89-90, CDN, Réal; Jeux Olympiques Calgary 88, TV, 88, CDN, Réal coord; *Gala Artis*, TV, 86, CDN, Réal; "Michel Jasmin" (210 eps), TV, 81-83, CDN, Réal; "Dominique" (90 eps), TV, 77-80, CDN, Réal; *Georges Guetary en chanson*, TV, 78, CDN, Conc/Réal; "Cre-Basile" (150 eps), TV, 64-68, CDN, Réal.

SALTZMAN, Deepa Mehta
ACCT. Sunrise Films Limited, 160 Perth Ave., Toronto, ON M6P 3X5 (416)535-2900.
Type of Production and Credits: TV Film-Dir/Prod/Wr.
Genres: Documentary-TV; Drama-Th&TV; Action-Th&TV.
Biography: Born 1949, Amritsar, India; Canadian citizenship. Degree in Philosophy from the University of New Delhi. Writer of youth section of the *New Delhi Statesman*. Executive Vice-President of Sunrise Films Limited since 73. Winner of numerous awards at international film festivals, including Chicago, San Francisco, New York, Lyon, Krakow, Columbus; *Sam & Me* closed "Critics' Week", Cannes, 91 and earned honourable mention du Camera d'Or.
Selected Filmography: *Sam & Me*, Th, 90, CDN, Dir/Prod; "Danger Bay" (3 eps), TV, 88-89, CDN/USA, Dir; "Inside Stories", TV, 88, CDN, Dir; *Martha, Ruth & Edie*, Th, 87, CDN, Prod/Co-Dir; *Travelling Light: The Photojournalism of Dilip Mehta*, TV, 86, CDN/GB, Dir; *K.Y.T.E.S. How We Dream Ourselves*, TV, 85, CDN, Prod/Dir; *The Annex*, "Toronto Neighbourhoods", TV, 84, CDN, Dir/Wr; *Reasonable Force*, "For the Record", TV, 82, CDN, Act; "Spread Your Wings" (8 eps), TV, 76-81, CDN, Co-Prod/Co-Wr/Snd Rec; *What's the Weather Like Up There*, TV, 77, CDN, Dir/Prod; *To Be a Clown*, TV, 76, CDN, Co-Prod/Co-Wr; *Indira Gandhi: The Heritage of Power*, ED, 75, CDN, Co-Prod; *At 99: A Portrait of Louise Tandy Murch*, TV, 74, CDN/USA, Dir/Co-Prod; *Father Bill Mackey: Son of Beloved Bhutan*, TV, 74, CDN, Co-Wr/Co-Ed/Snd Rec; *The Perlmutter Story*, TV, 73, CDN, Co-Wr/Assist Ed.

SALTZMAN, Paul
- see PRODUCERS

SALZMAN, Glen ◊
Cineflics Ltd., 215 Albany Ave., #302, Toronto, ON M5R 3C7 (416)531-2612.
Type of Production and Credits: TV Film-Dir/Prod.
Genres: Drama-TV; Children's-TV.
Biography: Born 1951, Montreal, Quebec. Honours B.F.A., York University, 74. Since 76, has been directing and producing original TV drama with partner, Rebecca Yates. Has won awards at film festivals, including American, Yorkton, Columbus and Childfilm.

SANCHEZ-ARIZA, José
ARRFQ. 3 Armstrong Dr., Dollard des Ormeaux, PQ H9G 1B6 (514)620-6441.
Types de production et générique: c métrage-Réal/Prod.
Types d'oeuvres: Drame-C; Documentaire-C&TV; Annonces-TV.
Curriculum vitae: Né en 1943; citoyenneté espagnole et canadienne. Langues: espagnol, anglais, français et polonais. Education: Ecole Supérieure de Cinéma, Théâtre et TV de Lodz, Pologne.
Filmographie sélective: *La Flûte à Bec*, ED, 91, CDN, Prod; *Les memoires de mon violin*, "Batir mon Canada", TV, 90, CDN, Réal/Prod/Cam; *Gregor*, "Batir mon Canada", TV, 89, CDN, Réal/Prod/Cam; *Nitrex*, In, 89, CDN, Réal/Prod/Cam; *Sahara: la détermination d'un peuple*, C, 76, E, Réal/D phot/Prod; *Séminariste*, C, 70, PL, Réal/Sc; *Déserteurs*, TV, 69, S, Réal/Sc; *Olympique de Mexico*, C, 68, MEX, Co réal; *Le chat est mort de faim*, C, 68, PL,

Réal/Sc; *Lalka 594*, C, 67, PL, Réal/Sc; *Entracte*, C, 66, PL, Réal/Sc; *Passage à niveau*, C, 66, PL, Réal/Sc; *Tir à la cible*, C, 66, PL, Réal/Sc; *Barro*, C, 64, MEX, D phot; *Bread and Puppets*, C, 64, USA, Cam; *Quand la nuit tombe*, C, 64, MEX, Réal/Sc.

SANDERS, Ed
- see PRODUCERS

SARIN, Victor
CSC, ACCT, DGC. 84 Hillsdale Ave. E., Toronto, ON M4S 1T5 (416)484-8415. FAX: 484-9273.
Type of Production and Credits: Th Film-DOP; TV Film-Dir/DOP.
Genres: Drama-Th&TV; Comedy-TV; Musical-TV; Documentary-Th&TV.
Biography: Born 1941, Srinagar, Kashmir; Canadian citizenship. Diploma in TV Techniques, Sydney Technical School, Australia; 2 years of Fine Arts, University of Melbourne. *Solitary Journey* won Best Film & Best Documentary over 30 minutes at Yorkton; People's Choice, Best Picture and Best Social/Political Documentary at Banff; Red Ribbon at American Film Festival (NY); Best Film at Villa de Torello, Italy; Silver Gentian at Turrin, Italy; and Best Film at Colorado Festival.
Selected Filmography: *Millennium*, TV, 91, CDN, Dir/DOP; *On My Own*, Th, 91, CDN/AUS/I, DOP; *Love and Hate*, TV, 90, CDN, DOP, (ANIK/GEMINI); *Solitary Journey*, TV, 89, CDN, Dir/DOP, (Prod - Suzanne Cook); *Moving Pictures*, TV, 88, CDN, DOP, (GEMINI); *Bethune*, Th, 88, CDN/RC/F, 2nd U DOP; *Cold Comfort*, Th, 88, CDN, Dir/DOP; *Bye Bye Blues*, Th, 88, CDN, DOP; *Family Reunion*, TV, 87, CDN, Dir/DOP; *Shoot Me*, Th, 87, CDN, DOP; "Alfred Hitchcock Presents" (5 eps)(4 eps DOP/1eps Dir), TV, 87, CDN/USA, Dir/DOP; "Mr. T" (1 eps), TV, 87, CDN, Dir; *So Many Miracles*, TV, 87, CDN, Dir/DOP, (GEMINI 87/ANIK); *Island Love Song*, TV, 86, CDN, Dir/DOP; *War Brides*, TV, 80, CDN, DOP, (ANIK).

SAROSSY, Paul
- see CINEMATOGRAPHERS

SARRAZIN, Pierre
- see PRODUCERS

SAURIOL, Brigitte ◊
(514)522-2507.
Types de production et générique: l métrage-Réal/Sc; c métrage-Réal/Sc; TV film-Réal/Sc; TV vidéo-Réal/Sc.
Types d'oeuvres: Drame-C&TV; Comédie-C; Variété-C&TV.
Curriculum vitae: Née en 1945.

Filmographie sélective: *Laura Laur*, C, 88, CDN, Réal/Sc; *L'Eau noire*, C, 86, CDN/F, Réal/Sc; *Bleue Brume*, C, 82, CDN, Réal/Sc; *Rien qu'un jeu*, C, 82, CDN, Réal/Sc; "Une ville que j'aime" (1 eps), TV, 81, B, Réal/Sc; *L'Absence*, C, 75, CDN, Réal/Sc; *Le Loup blanc*, C, 73, CDN, Réal/Sc.

SAUVE, Alain
- voir MONTEURS SON

SAVOIE, Elie
- see PRODUCERS

SCAINI, Stefan
DGC, ACTRA. 3274 Ivernia Rd., Mississauga, ON L4Y 3E8 CBC, 790 Bay St., 5th Fl., Toronto, ON M5G 1N8 (416)975-7104. Charles Northcote/The Core Group, 489 College Street, Ste. 501, Toronto, ON M6G 1A5 (416)944-0193.
Type of Production and Credits: TV Film-Prod/Dir; TV Video-Dir/Wr.
Genres: Drama-TV; Comedy-TV; Children's-TV; News-TV.
Biography: Born in 1955 in Toronto Ont. Languages: English and Italian. 7 years experi-ence directing live news and current affairs. 8 years experience directing film. ACTRA Awards, CanPro, New York, Film Festival Award, Yorkton Film Awards and others.
Selected Filmography: *I'll Never Get To Heaven*, TV, 91, Dir; "Street Legal" (9 eps), TV, 88-91, Dir; "Max Glick" (6 eps), TV, 90, Dir; "My Secret Identity" (6 eps), TV, 89-90, Dir; "Northwood" (2 eps), TV, 90, Dir; *Gracie*, TV, 89, Dir (GEMINI); *Cement Soul*, TV, 89, Dir; "Adderly" (2 eps), TV, 88, Dir; *The Calendar Girl*, TV, 87, Wr/Prod/Dir; *The Silent Bell*, TV, 86, Wr/Prod/Dir; "The Haunting" (4 eps), TV, 85-87, Wr/Prod/Dir; *Family Matter*, TV, 88, Wr/Prod/Dir; *One Enchanted Evening*, TV, 88, Wr/Prod/Dir; *The Silver Cloud*, TV, 86, Wr/Prod/Dir.

SCANLAN, Joseph L. ◊
(213)275-2911.
Type of Production and Credits: Th Film-Dir; TV Film-Dir.
Genres: Drama-Th&TV; Comedy-TV; Action-TV.
Selected Filmography: "Adderly" (1 eps), TV, 86, CDN, Dir; "Knot's Landing" (7 eps), TV, 86, USA, Dir; "Falcon Crest" (1 eps), TV, 86, USA, Dir; "Hot Shots" (2 eps), TV, 86, CDN, Dir; "Night Heat" (1 eps), TV, 86, CDN, Dir; "Loving Friends and Perfect Couples" (40 eps), TV, 82-83, USA, Dir; *Spring Fever*, Th, 81, CDN, Dir; "Matt and Jenny" (10 eps), TV, 78-79, CDN/GB/D, Dir; *Our Man Flint*, TV,

78, USA, Dir; "Search and Rescue" (10 eps), TV, 78, CDN/USA, Dir.

SCARFF, Clive
ACCT. 6 Forest Laneway, #1002, Willowdale, ON M2N 5X9 (416)229-1759.
Type of Production and Credits: TV Video-Dir/Wr.
Genres: Comedy-TV; Commercials-TV; Industrial-TV; Sports-TV.
Biography: Born 1964, Toronto, Ontario. Attended high school in Melbourne, Australia; studied theatre/television. Appearance on the "Paul Hogan Show". Canadian and Australian citizenship. Returned to Toronto in 1982 to attend Ryerson Polytechnical Institute (RTA); graduated in 1985. Was Head Writer for the Ryerson Comedy Revue and won award for comedy writing. Utilizes comedy in writing (especially in corporate video work). Directing experience includes multicam mobiles; solid technical background in TV.
Selected Filmography: *I'm a Customer Too*, Country Style Donuts, Cm, 91, CDN, Dir/Wr; *Fish'n Canada Show* (50 eps), TV, 89-91, CDN, Dir/Wr.

SCHADT, Christa
- see WRITERS

SCHERBERGER, Aiken M.
DGC. 28 Roxborough St. W., Toronto, ON M5R 1T8 (416)922-1375.
Type of Production and Credits: TV Film-Dir/Wr; TV Film-Dir/Wr.
Genres: Drama-TV; Documentary-TV; Industrial-Th.
Biography: Born 1955, Freiburg, West Germany; Canadian citizenship. Languages: English and working knowledge of Italian and German. Attended the Canadian Centre for Advanced Film Studies, 88. Awards for documentaries and industrials, including Best PR Film, CFTA, 79, and Creative Excellence Award at US Industrial Film Festival. Currently writing, directing and producing "For the Love of the Game," a 10-part TV documentary series for The Sports Network (TSN).
Selected Filmography: *A White Man's Game?*, "For the Love of the Game", TV, 91, CDN, Wr/Dir/Prod; *For Whom the Bell Rings*, "For the Love of the Game", TV, 91, CDN, Wr/Dir/Prod; *Special Olympics*, TV, 90, CDN, Wr/Dir/Prod; "Passport to Skiing" (6 eps), TV, 90, CDN, Wr/Dir/Prod; "Captain Power" (22 eps), TV, 87, CDN, 2nd U Dir; *Wayne Gretzky: Hockey My Way*, TV, 86, CDN, Dir; *Whodunit*, TV, 85, CDN, Dir/Wr; "Captain Power" (1 eps), TV, 85, CDN, Dir.

SCHERER, Karl
- see CINEMATOGRAPHERS

SCHONBERG, Pasia
- see PRODUCERS

SCHULZ, Bob
DGC. 56 Russell Hill Rd., Toronto, ON M4V 2T2 (416)961-6160.
Type of Production and Credits: Th Film-Dir; TV Film-Dir/Prod; TV Video-Dir/Prod.
Genres: Drama-Th&TV; Comedy-Th&TV; Action-Th&TV; Commercials-Th&TV.
Biography: Born 1931; came to Canada as Hungarian refugee. Graduate of Academy of Cinematography, Budapest. Has directed more than 2000 commercials in over 30 countries; has won major international awards for directing TV commercials. Feature debut as a director, *Robbers of the Secret Mountain*, was shown on "Showtime", "CBS," and "First Choice."
Selected Filmography: *OHM*, Dan Hill, MV, 83-84, CDN, Dir; *European World Cup Soccer Championship*, TV, 84, CDN, Dir; *Falcon's Gold*, Th, 82, CDN, Dir; *ACTRA's Live Command Performance*, TV, 81, CDN, Dir; *Grown Up Tomorrow*, TV, 81, CDN, Dir; *Near and Far*, TV, 80, CDN, Prod; *Exploding the Myth*, TV, 80, CDN, Co-Dir/Prod; *The Glove*, TV, 79, CDN, Dir; *House on Front Street*, TV, 79, CDN, Dir; *1976 Canada Cup Hockey*, TV, 76, CDN, Prod; *Ave Luna*, TV, 73, CDN, Dir; *Come Away, Come Away*, TV, 72, CDN, Dir.

SCHUURMAN, Hubert ✧
(902)542-9248.
Type of Production and Credits: Th Short-Dir/Wr/DOP/Ed; TV Film-Dir/Wr/DOP/Ed.
Genres: Documentary-Th; Educational-Th; Children's-Th.
Biography: Born 1932, The Netherlands; Canadian citizenship. Languages: English, Dutch, Norwegian; knowledge of Danish, Swedish, French and Inuktitut. Honours B.A., Sociology, Memorial University of Newfoundland; M.A., Sociology and Economics, University of Minnesota; additional studies in Anthropology of Development. Has produced documentaries on people of the Arctic, poverty and the underprivileged; generally does own cinematography. Winner of awards at Chicago, Columbus and New York.
Selected Filmography: *Mudnificent*, ED, 87, CDN, Dir/Cam/Ed; *The Church and the Hearth*, ED, 87, CDN, Dir/Cam; *Enterprising Women*, ED, 87, CDN,

Dir/Cam/Ed; *A Ballad of South Mountain*, ED, 86, CDN, Dir/Cam/Wr/Ed; *The Power and the Tide*, ED, 85, CDN, Dir/Cam/Wr/Ed; *The Last Log Drive*, ED, 85, CDN, Ed; *The Arctic: Our Common Responsibility*, ED, 85, CDN, Wr/Ed; *A Touch of Alice*, ED, 84, CDN, Dir/Cam; *Unitas Fratricum*, ED, 83, CDN, Dir/Cam/Ed; *Sami Herders*, ED, 78, CDN, Dir/Cam; *Sami: Four Lands, One People*, ED, 78, CDN, Dir/Cam.

SCHWARTZ, Nadine
75 Markham St., #13, Toronto, ON M6J 2G4 (416)594-1426.
Type of Production and Credits: TV Video-Dir/Prod.
Genres: Drama-TV; Educational-TV; Children's-TV.
Biography: Born in 1964. Canadian citizen. Languages: French and English. B.A. Applied Arts, Interior Design. Multimedia artist, painting, sculpture, video art. Independent director and producer.
Selected Filmography: "Raconte Moi" (11 eps), TV/ED, 91, CDN, Dir/Prod; "Flash Français" (45 eps), TV/ED, 91, CDN, Dir/Prod; "Ciné pour Toi" (2 eps), TV, 90, CDN, Dir/Prod.

SCOTT, Cynthia
225 Clarke, Montreal, PQ H3Z 2E3. NFB, Box 6100, Montreal, PQ H3C 3H5 (514)283-9536. FAX: 283-5487.
Type of Production and Credits: Th Film-Dir; Th Short-Dir/Prod; TV Film-Dir/Prod; TV Video-Dir/Prod.
Genres: Drama-Th&TV; Variety-Th&TV; Documentary-Th&TV.
Biography: Born 1939, Winnipeg, Manitoba. B.A., University of Manitoba; also studied music and art. Producer, director for CBC Toronto for 8 years. Member, Royal Canadian Academy. Films have won many awards, including Oscar for *Flamenco at 5:15*; *The Company of Strangers* won Grand Prix, Mannheim Film Festival, 90 and Prix du Public, Creteil, France, 91; was official selection at Venice Biennale, 90. Other awards from film festivals at San Francisco, New York, Salerno, Krakow.
Selected Filmography: *The Company of Strangers/Strangers in Good Company*, Th, 90, CDN, Dir/Co-Wr; *A Chronic Problem*, "Discussions in Bioethics", TV, 85, CDN, Dir; *Jack of Hearts*, "Bell Canada Playhouse", TV, 85, CDN, Dir; *Flamenco at 5:15*, Th, 83, CDN, Dir/Co-Prod/Co-Ed, (OSCAR); *For the Love of Dance*, TV, 81, CDN, Co-Dir; *First Winter*, Th, 81, CDN, Co-Wr; *Gala*, Th, 81, CDN, Co-Dir; *Don Arioli Fitness and Nutrition* (11 clips), TV, 78-79, CDN, Prod; *Listen, Listen, Listen*, TV, 76, CDN, Prod; *Scoggie*, "Atlantic Canada", TV, 74, CDN, Dir; *Some Natives of Churchill*, "West", TV, 73, CDN, Dir; "West" (12 eps), TV, 73, CDN, Co-Prod; *The Ungrateful Land*, "Adieu Alouette", TV, 72, CDN, Dir, (CFA).

SCOTT, Michael J.F.
ASIFA, ACCT, MIMPIA. 275 Harvard Ave., Winnipeg, MB R3M 0K2 (204)453-6005. Muddy River Films, 120 Sherbrook St., Winnipeg, MB R3C 2B4 (204)786-5909.
Type of Production and Credits: Th Film-Prod; Th Short-Prod/Dir; TV Film-Prod/Dir.
Genres: Drama-Th&TV; Comedy-Th&TV; Action-Th&TV; Documentary-Th&TV; Educational-Th&TV; Children's-Th&TV; Animation-Th&TV.
Biography: Born 1942, Winnipeg, Manitoba. Graduated from Ryerson Polytechnical Institute, Radio & Television Arts. Directed and/or produced over 60 feature length dramas, documentaries and animated shorts. Worked at NFB as a producer/director for 23 years and helped to establish its regionalization program as Executive Producer of the Prairie Region; now an independent filmmaker. Founding member, National Screen Institute; has received many awards including Genies for *Get a Job*, *The Big Snit* and *Ted Baryluk's Grocery*; Gemini for *Daughters of the Country*; American Blue Ribbons for *Cages* and *Whistling Smith*; Emmy nomination for *Lost in the Barrens*; Academy award nominations for *Whistling Smith* and *The Big Snit*; 3 Etrogs for *For Gentlemen Only*.
Selected Filmography: *Curse of the Viking Grave*, TV, 91, CDN, Dir/Prod; *Lost in the Barrens*, TV, 90, CDN, Dir/Prod; *Flowers in the Sky* (Imax), Th, 89, J, Dir; *Who Gets In*, TV, 88, CDN, Prod; *Karate Kids*, ED, 88, CDN, Prod; *Get a Job*, Th, 86, CDN, Prod, (GENIE 87); *Daughters in the Country*, TV, 86, CDN, Prod, (GEMINI 87); *The Big Snit*, Th, 85, CDN, Prod, (GENIE 86); *Ted Baryluk's Grocery*, Th, 84, CDN, Prod, (GENIE 84); *Cages*, TV, 84, CDN, Dir; *Whistling Smith*, "Pacific Canada", TV, 75, CDN, Dir/Prod; *For Gentlemen Only*, TV, 75, CDN, Dir, (3 ETROGS).

SCOTT, T.J.
DGC, ACTRA, SAG. Magic-Motion Pictures, 4 Woodycrest Ave., Toronto, ON M4J 3A6 (416)469-2409.
Type of Production and Credits: Th

Film-Wr/Dir/2nd Unit Dir; TV Film-Wr/Dir/2nd Unit Dir.
Genres: Drama-Th&TV; Comedy-Th&TV; Action-Th&TV; Horror-Th&TV.
Biography: Born 1961, Penticton, British Columbia. Began his career as a successful child actor. During teens, actor/stunt performer in various projects including *My American Cousin, Police Academy*, "Night Heat" etc. Credit on over 30 features and 250 TV episodes as stunt coordinator. York University Film School, 81-84. Became a 2nd unit director; writer and director of action sequences on a wide variety of projects including "Friday The 13th: The Series", "One Life to Live" and *Car 54, Where Are You?*. Has written 2 feature film scripts, *In-Line* and *Bat Cave*, both optioned. Currently directing television.
Selected Filmography: "Top Cops" (2 eps), TV, 91, CDN/USA, Dir; "Top Cops" (39 eps), TV, 91, CDN/USA, 2nd Unit Dir; "One Life to Live", TV, 91, USA, 2nd Unit Dir; "Moment of Truth" (pilot), TV, 91, USA/CDN, 2nd Unit Dir; *Car 54, Where Are You?*, Th, 90, USA, 2nd Unit Dir; "Dog House" (pilot), TV, 90, CDN/USA, 2nd Unit Dir; *Replicator*, Th, 90, CDN, 2nd Unit Dir; "Friday The 13th: The Series" (50 eps), TV, 89-90, USA/CDN, 2nd Unit Dir; *Just U.N. Me Babe*, Th, 89, USA, 2nd Unit Dir; "T and T" (7 eps), TV, 89, USA/CDN, 2nd Unit Dir; *Hearts of Fire*, Th, 88, USA/GB, 2nd Unit Dir.

SECRETAN-COX, Michael
P.O. Box 91372, West Vancouver, BC V7V 3P1 (604)926-2786.
Type of Production and Credits: Th Film-Wr/Dir; Th Short-Wr/Dir; TV Film-Wr/Prod/DOP.
Genres: Drama-Th&TV; Documentary-TV.
Biography: Born in 1955 in London, Ontario. British and Canadian citizenship. Education includes studies in theatre and anthropology; broadcast journalism; television production; motion picture producing. Skills: writing screenplays and narration; directing; documentary director of photography; documentary location sound recordist; acting and teaching acting.
Selected Filmography: *U.V.*, Th, 92, CDN, Wr/Dir; *Cold Hands*, Th, 91, CDN, Wr/Dir; *Dance Essence*, Th, 91, CDN, DOP; *Slowly Fasting*, TV, 90, CDN, Prod/Dir; *In the Eyes of a Panther*, Th, 90, CDN, Assist Dir; *Picker's Alley*, TV, 90, CDN, DOP; *Songlines*, TV, 90, CDN, DOP.

SEDAWIE, Gayle Gibson
- see PRODUCERS

SEDAWIE, Norman
- see PRODUCERS

SEGUIN, Jean-Gaétan ✧
(514)276-6867.
Types de production et générique: TV vidéo-Réal.
Types d'oeuvres: Variété-TV; Documentaire-TV; Education-TV; Expérimental-TV.
Curriculum vitae: Né en 1940, Montréal, Québec. Etudes en linguistique et en psychologie. Un des idéateurs de la série "Les Oraliens;" à Radio-Québec depuis 71; a participé à Input 81; travaille surtout sur les émissions culturelles.
Filmographie sélective: *L'Univers de Armand Vaillancourt/Carbone 14/L'Ecran humain*, TV, 86, CDN, Réal; *L'Univers de 6 peintres actuels*, TV, 86, CDN, Réal; *L'Univers de Jean-Guy Moreau/Michel Lemieux/Margie Gillis*, TV, 84-85, CDN, Réal; *L'Univers de Charles Dutoit/Juliette Huot/Lucien Francoeur*, TV, 84, CDN, Réal; *Fous...comme dans foufounes*, TV, 83, CDN, Réal; *To Be or Not to Be*, TV, 82, CDN, Réal; *Demi-Tour*, TV, 81, CDN, Réal; "Neuf et demi" (30 eps), TV, 81, CDN, Prod dél; "L'Envers du décor" (37 eps), TV, 78-80, CDN, Réal; "Moi, mes chansons" (27 eps), TV, 76-77, CDN, Réal.

SELZNICK, Arna
ACCT. 387 Kingswood Rd., Toronto, ON M4E 2P2 (416)690-4242. FAX: 690-2504.
Type of Production and Credits: Th Film-Dir; TV Film-Dir.
Genres: Musical-Th&TV; Action-TV; Children's-Th&TV; Animation-Th&TV.
Biography: Born 1948, Toronto, Ontario. Working graphic artist and illustrator; teacher/designer of a course on storyboarding, Ryerson Polytechnical Institute, 85. Main focus of professional attention: concept design, scripting, story development and film direction for feature films, specials and series work for TV in both animation and live action.
Selected Filmography: "Beetlejuice" (91 eps), TV, 90-91, CDN/USA, St'board; "Captain Zed and the Zee Zone" (13 eps), TV, USA/GB, St'board; *Hot Dog at the Zoo*, "The Family Dog", TV, 90, USA/CDN, St'board; "Little Rosie" (13 eps), TV, 90, USA/CDN, St'board; "Babar" (cycles I, II, III, IV, V&VI), TV, 88-91, CDN/F, St'board; *Babar: The*

Movie, Th, 89, CDN/F, St'board; *The Care Bears Movie II & III*, Th, 85-87, CDN/USA, Spv Layout; "My Pet Monster" (13 eps), TV, 87, CDN/USA, Spv St'board; *Madballs*, Th, 86, CDN/USA, Spv Layout; "Johnny Quest", TV, 86, CDN/USA, Spv Layout;"Ewoks & Droids Adventure Hour" (39 eps), TV, 85-86, CDN/USA, Spv St'board; *The Care Bears Movie*, Th, 84-85, CDN/USA, Dir; "Inspector Gadget" (64 eps), TV, 83, CDN/USA/F, Spv St'board; *Strawberry Shortcake I*, TV, 82, CDN/USA, Spv Layout.

SENECAL, Gilles
AR. 223 bas de la rivière sud, Rg. 5, St-Césaire, PQ J0L 1T0 (514)469-4189.
Types de production et générique: TV film-Réal/Prod; TV vidéo-Réal/Prod.
Types d'oeuvres: Variété-TV; Documentaire-TV; Enfants-TV.
Curriculum vitae: Né en 1926. Baccalauréat ès Arts, Université de Laval; études en médicine (1 ans à l'Université de Montréal); à Paris; pédiatrie, Hôpital des Enfants Malades de Paris, 3 ans. Réalisateur à Radio-Canada depuis 56; professeur: Atelier de télévision, Université du Québec à Montréal, 73-86; cours de production de télévision, l'institut Teccart, 88; conférencier sur la production à la télévision à Radio Québec et l'Université de Sherbrooke; Chargé de Cours à l'UQAM, "interprétation devant la caméra", 89. Ses films ont gagné plusieurs prix aux festivals de films internationaux.
Filmographie sélective: *Hamlet en Québec*, TV, 91, CDN, Prod/Réal; *Sortie de Secours*, "Les Beaux Dimanches", TV, 91, CDN, Prod/Réal; "Jeux de Sociéte" (2 eps), TV, 89, CDN, Réal; *La dernière Demeure de Mme Rose*, TV, 89, CDN, Prod/Réal; *La Fin des Jeux* (mini-série), TV, 88, CDN, Prod/Réal; "Monsieur le Ministre" (15 eps), TV, 65-86, CDN, Réal; "La Vie promise" (hebdo), TV, 83-84, CDN, Réal; *Tu rêves, Adrienne*, "Les Beaux Dimanches", TV, 83, CDN, Réal; *Catherine Provost, fille du Roy*, TV, 82, CDN, Réal; *C'est à cause d'elle*, TV, 82, CDN, Réal; "Race de monde" (11 eps), TV, 81, CDN, Réal; *Entre le soleil et l'eau*, "Les Beaux Dimanches", TV, 80, CDN, Réal, (ANIK); "Pop Citrouille" (10 eps), TV, 80, CDN, Réal; "Psst-psst aie-là!" (76 eps), TV, 79-80, CDN, Réal; *La Mémoire cassée*, "Scénario" (4 seg), TV, 78, CDN, Réal; *Le Quartrième Age*, "Scénario", TV, 77, CDN, Réal.

SENECAL, Marguerite
- see PRODUCERS

SENKYIRE, Opong
- see PRODUCERS

SENS, Al
- see PRODUCERS

SHAFFER, Beverly
508 Lansdowne, Westmount, PQ H3Y 2V2 (514)932-1347. NFB, Box 6100, Montreal, PQ H3C 3H5 (514)283-9509.
Type of Production and Credits: TV Film-Dir/Prod.
Genres: Documentary-TV; Educational-TV; Children's-TV.
Biography: Born 1945, Montreal, Quebec. Languages: English, French, Hebrew and Yiddish. B.A., McGill University, Hebrew University, Jerusalem; M.Sc., Film, Boston University. Has won numerous inter-national awards, most recently a Best Film of the Festival award for *To a Safer Place* at the American Film and Video Festival, 88; *I'll Find a Way* won 9 awards inter-nationally, including an Oscar, 78; "Children of Canada" series won several prizes: among the winners were *Benoît*, *My Friends Call Me Tony*, *It's Just Better* and *The Way It Is*.
Selected Filmography: *Half the Kingdom*, TV, 89, CDN, Prod; *To a Safer Place*, TV, 87, CDN, Dir; *Who Will Decide*, "Discussions in Bioethics", TV, 86, CDN, Dir; *I Want to Be an Engineer*, TV, 83, CDN, Dir; *Julie O'Brian/It's Just Better/The Way It Is/Veronica/ Benoît*, "Children of Canada", TV, 75-82, CDN, Dir/Prod; *I'll Find a Way*, "Children of Canada", TV, 78, CDN, Dir/Prod, (OSCAR); *Gurdeep Singh Bains/Kevin Alec/Beautiful Lennard Island*, "Children of Canada", TV, 77, CDN, Dir/Prod; *My Name Is Susan Lee/My Friends Call Me Tony*, "Children of Canada," TV, 76, CDN, Dir/Prod.

SHAPIRO, Paul
ACTRA, DGC. Decal Film Inc., 41 Shanly St., #10, Toronto, ON M6H 1S2 (416)461-3614. Suzanne Depoe, Creative Technique, 483 Euclid Ave., Toronto, ON M6G 2T1 (416)466-4173. Bernie Weintraub, Stu Robinson, Ken Gross, Robinson, Weintraub, Gross & Assoc., 8428 Melrose Place, Suite C, Los Angeles, CA 90069 USA (213)653-5802.
Type of Production and Credits: TV Film-Dir/Wr.
Genres: Drama-TV; Comedy-TV; Action-TV; Children's-TV.
Biography: Born 1955, Regina, Saskatchewan. B.A.A., Photographic Arts, Motion Picture, Ryerson Polytechnical Institute, 75; NFB directors' training units, 76-78; violin, Conservatory of Music, Regina (6 years); 15 years guitar training,

music composition. Playwright: *The True Story of Frankenstein*, 82. *Hockey Night* won a CFTA; *The Truth about Alex* won several awards, 88; *The Umpire* won a Blue Ribbon at American Film Festival; *Miracle at Moreaux* won awards at Columbus, Houston, New York and others.
Selected Filmography: "Mom P.I." (5 eps), TV, 90-91, CDN, Dir; *Next Door*, "Welcome to the Monkey House", TV, 90, CDN, Dir; "Max Glick" (3 eps), TV, 90, CDN, Dir; *Rookies*, TV, 90, CDN, Dir/Co-Wr; *The Journey Begins*, "Road to Avonlea", TV, 89, CDN, Dir; *A Proposal of Marriage/Comfort and Joy*, "The Campbells", TV, 87, CDN/USA/GB, Dir; *Just One Kiss*, "Street Legal", TV, 87, CDN, Dir; *The Truth about Alex*, TV, 86, CDN/USA, Dir, (GEMINI); *Critical Mass*, "Adderly", TV, 86, CDN, Dir; *Miracle at Moreaux*, TV, 85, CDN, Dir/Co-T'play; *The Umpire*, TV, 84, CDN, Dir/Co-Wr; *Hockey Night*, TV, 84, CDN, Dir/Co-Wr; "The Edison Twins" (5 eps), TV, 83-84, CDN, Dir/Co-Wr; *R.W.*, "Sons and Daughters", TV, 82, CDN, Dir/Co-Wr; *Clown White*, TV, 80, CDN, Dir/Co-Wr.

SHATALOW, Peter ◊
(416)461-3614.
Type of Production and Credits: Th Film-Dir/Wr; TV Film-Dir/Wr; TV Video-Dir/Wr.
Genres: Variety-TV; Documentary-Th&TV.
Biography: Born in Brussels; Canadian citizenship. Attended Seneca College. Joined CBC as film editor; formed own production company in the mid-70s. *Challenge: The Canadian Rockies* won CFTA award.
Selected Filmography: *Blue City Slammers*, Th, 87, CDN, Dir/Co-Prod/Co-Wr; The *Making of La Cage*, TV, 85, CDN, Dir/Wr; *The Papal Visit: Behind the Scenes*, TV, 84, CDN, Wr; *Caroline*, "Sons and Daughters", TV, 83, CDN, Dir; *Heart of an Artist*, TV, 83, CDN, Dir/Wr; "Heart of Gold" (3 eps), TV, 82, CDN, Dir/Wr; *Challenge: The Canadian Rockies*, Th, 81, CDN, Dir/Wr/Ed; *Laroussi and the Fantasia*, "Spread Your Wings", TV, 81, CDN, Co-Dir/Ed; *Black Ice*, Th, 80, CDN, Dir/Ed.

SHEBIB, Don
DGC. Evdon Films Ltd., 312 Wright Ave., Toronto, ON M6R 1L9 (416)536-8969.
Type of Production and Credits: Th Film-Dir/Prod/Ed; Th Short-Dir/Ed/Cam; TV Film-Dir/Ed/Cam.
Genres: Drama-Th&TV; Comedy-Th; Action-Th; Documentary-TV.
Biography: Born 1938, Toronto, Ontario. B.A., University of Toronto, 60; M.F.A., UCLA, 65.
Selected Filmography: "Night Heat" (6 eps), TV, 86-88, CDN, Dir; "Diamonds" (4 ps), TV, 87-88, CDN, Dir; "The Edison Twins" (8 eps), TV, 85-86, CDN, Dir; *The Climb*, Th, 85, CDN/GB, Dir; *Running Brave*, Th, 83, CDN/USA, Dir; *Slim Obsession*, "For the Record", TV, 83, CDN, Dir; *Heartaches*, Th, 80, CDN, Dir; *Fish Hawk*, TH, 78, CDN, Dir; *Fighting Men*, "For the Record", TV, 77, CDN, Dir; *Second Wind*, Th, 75, CDN, Dir/Ed, (CFA); *We've Come a Long Way Together*, TV, 75, CDN, Dir/Ed; *Born Hustler*, TV, 72, CDN, Dir; *Between Friends*, Th, 72, CDN, Dir; *Rip-Off*, Th, 71, CDN, Dir; *Goin' Down the Road*, Th, 69, CDN, Dir/Ed/Prod, (CFA).

SHEKTER, Louise ◊
46 Muriel Ave., Toronto, ON M4J 2X9 (416)469-3104. French Media Solutions, 67 Mowat, #242, Toronto, ON M6K 3E3 (416)964-3302.
Type of Production and Credits: Th Short-Dir; TV Film-Dir.
Genres: Documentary-Th&TV; Educational-TV; Children's-TV.
Biography: Born 1950, Montreal, Quebec. Languages: English and French. Active as a translator/writer; specializes in audio-visual and broadcast work; experience in all aspects of dubbing production; musical background. *Making a Difference* won awards at American, San Francisco and Yorkton festivals.

SHENKEN, Lionel
- see PRODUCERS

SHERRIN, Robert
- see PRODUCERS

SHILTON, Gilbert ◊
(213)553-0171.
Type of Production and Credits: TV Film-Dir.
Genres: Drama-TV; Action-TV.
Biography: Born 1945; raised and educated in Montreal. Has worked for TV stations in Montreal, Toronto; worked in L.A. for CBS, Metromedia, 75-79; self-employed as a director, writer, 79 to date.
Selected Filmography: *Spearfield's Daughter* (mini-series), TV, 85, CDN/USA/AUS, Dir; "V" (3 eps), TV, 84-85, USA, Dir; "Danger Bay" (dir 5 eps/wr 1 eps), TV, 84, CDN, Dir/Wr; *Arm's Race*, "Blue Thunder", TV, 84, USA, Dir; "The A-Team" (3 eps), TV, 83-84, USA, Dir; "This Is the Life" (2 eps),

TV, 83-84, USA Dir; *Second Thunder*, "Blue Thunder" (pilot), TV, 83, USA, Dir; "Magnum P.I." (sev eps/dir 1 eps), TV, 79-82, USA, Assoc Prod.

SHRAGGE, Sherv
- see PRODUCERS

SIEGEL, Lois
ACCT. 88 Argyle Dr., Kirkland, PQ H9H 3H8 (514)426-4218.
Type of Production and Credits: Th Short -Dir/Prod/Ed; TV Film-Dir/Prod/Ed.
Genres: Drama-Th; Documentary-Th&TV; Experimental-Th.
Biography: Born 1946, Milwaukee, Wisconsin; Canadian citizenship. Languages: English and French. B.Sc. (Honours in English), Journalism; M.A., Comparative and English Literature, Ohio University. *Stunt People* won Genie, Best Short Documentary, 90.
Selected Filmography: *Harmonie Raciale*, Cm, 91, CDN, Cast Dir; *Government in Canada*, ED, 91, CDN, Cast Dir; *Le Patro*, Th, 91, CDN, Voice Cast; *Penifield/Heritage Minute*, TV, 91, CDN, Voice Cast; *I Won't Dance*, TH, 91, CDN, Cast Dir; *Pancake on a Hot Tin Roof*, Th, 90, CDN, Ed/Dir/Prod; *Fipsi*, Th, 90, CDN, Ed/Dir/Prod; *Open for Business*, TV, 90, CDN, Cast Dir (Montreal); *Falla*, MV, 90, CDN, Extras Cast; *Kids on Parents/Listen to Me*, ED, 90, CDN, Cast Dir; *Prokofiev By Two*, MV, 90, CDN, Extras Cast; *Kafka* (pilot), Th, 90, CDN, Cast; *Stunt People*, TV, 89, CDN, Ed/Dir/Prod, (GENIE); *Vincent and Me*, Th, 89, CDN, Cast Dir; *Princes in Exile*, TV, 89, CDN, Cast Dir.

SILVER, Jonny
Silverfilm Inc., 863 King St. W., Toronto, ON M5V 1P2 (416)360-1838. FAX: 360-7799.
Type of Production and Credits: Th Film-Dir/Prod/Wr/Ed; TV Film-Dir/Wr; TV Video-Dir/Wr.
Genres: Drama-Th&TV; Musical-TV; Documentary-TV; Experimental-Th.
Biography: Born 1950, Toronto, Ontario. Languages: English and French. Ontario College of Art, 71-75.
Selected Filmography: *Enigma Mimara*, TV, 90, CDN/YU, Co-Dir; *Lonely Child*, Th/TV, 88, CDN, Dir/Prod/Co-Wr; *Music*, "Trade Secrets", TV, 86, CDN, Dir /Wr; *Queen-Spadina*, "Neighbourhoods", TV, 84, CDN, Dir/Wr; *Ubu Etude*, TV, 84, CDN, Dir/Prod/Wr/Ed; *Kubota*, Th, 83, CDN, Dir/Wr/Ed.

SIMANDL, Lloyd
- see PRODUCERS

SIMARD, Cheryl
Peartree House Productions Inc., 2 Jean St., Toronto, ON M4W 3A7 (416)923-6408. Paul Simmons, 125 Dupont Ave., Toronto, ON (416)920-1500.
Type of Production and Credits: TV Film-Dir/Prod; TV Video-Dir/Prod.
Genres: Drama-TV; Comedy-TV; Documentary-TV; Educational-TV.
Biography: Born 1946, Quebec City. Languages: English and French. Studied at Marymount College. Has been directing since 75. Cordon Bleu Diploma, London; La Varenne Diploma, Paris. Director of many commercials.
Selected Filmography: "C'est ton droit" (65 eps), TV, 83-88, CDN, Prod/Dir/Wr; "17 rue Laurier" (39 eps), TV, 85-88, CDN, Dir; "Live at the Forum" (20 eps), TV, 88, CDN, Isolation Dir; Petro Canada/GM/Gulf, In, 85-86, CDN, Dir; "A votre service" (64 eps), TV, 84-85, CDN, Dir.

SIMMONDS, Alan Francis ◊
(416)763-4529.
Type of Production and Credits: Th Film-Prod; TV Film-Dir; TV Video-Dir.
Genres: Drama-Th&TV; Action-Th&TV; Documentary-TV; Children's-TV.
Biography: Born in 1942 in London, England. Bachelor of Applied Arts, Communications and Fine Arts, Ryerson Polytechnical Institute, Toronto, Ontario, 1965.
Selected Filmography: "Danger Bay" (10 eps), TV, 86, CDN, Dir; *Striker's Mountain*, TV, 85, CDN, Dir; "The Edison Twins" (7 eps), TV, 84-85, CDN, Dir; "The Beachcombers" (5 eps), TV, 82-85, CDN, Dir; "Littlest Hobo" (6 eps), TV, 83-84, CDN, Dir; "Lorne Greene's New Wilderness (sev eps), TV, 83, CDN, Dir; "The Hitchhiker" (sev eps), TV, 83, USA, Line Prod; *Harry Tracy*, Th, 80, CDN, Line Prod; *Ticket to Heaven*, Th, 80, CDN, Line Prod; *Head On*, Th, 79, CDN, Co-Prod.

SIMONEAU, Guy
ARRFQ, STCQ. C.P. 333, Place du Parc, Montreal, PQ H2W 2N8 (514)288-5022.
Types de production et générique: c métrage-Réal/Sc/Mont; TV film-Réal/Sc/Mont; TV vidéo-Réal/Sc/Mont.
Types d'oeuvres: Drame-C&TV; Documentaire-C&TV.
Curriculum vitae: Né en 1953 à Québec. Langues: français et anglais. *David Chez Les Coréens*, Gemeaux (Prix multi-culturalisme); *La Symphonie Fantastique*, Chicago Film Award ("Short"); *Plusieurs*

Tombent en Amour, Genie, 80 ("Best Feature Documentary").
Filmographie sélective: *Super Trio*, TV, 90, CDN, Sc/Réal; *David Chez Les Coréens*, TV, 89, CDN, Sc/Réal; "Ken Dryden's Home Game" (6 eps), TV, 89, CDN, Mont; *Mario et Gretzky: Les Magnifiques*, TV, 88, CDN, Sc/Réal; *Mario Myke and Mr. Greatness*, TV, 88, CDN, Mont; *Les contes des 1001 nez*, TV, 86, CDN, Sc/Réal; *La Symphonie Fantastique*, C/TV, 86, CDN, Sc/Réal; *E = ROCK²*, TV, 84, CDN, Sc/Réal; *On n'est pas des anges*, C/TV, 82, CDN, Sc/Réal; *Plusieurs tombent en amour*, TV, 78, CDN, Sc/Réal/Mont; *Je suis en même temps maudit et classique*, TV, 78, CDN, Sc/Réal/Mont.

SIMONEAU, Yves
5046 rue Clark, Montréal, PQ H2T 2T8 (514)939-0128.
Types de production et générique: l métrage-Réal/Sc; c métrage-Réal/Sc.
Types d'oeuvres: Comédie-C; Action-C; Drame-C; Documentaire-C&TV; Commerciaux-C&TV.
Curriculum vitae: Travaille d'abord comme cameraman de reportage puis devient monteur et réalisateur de documentaires et de films de fiction; scénarise, co-scenarise, réalise et produit depuis 78.
Filmographie sélective: *Memphis*, TV, 90-91, USA, Réal; *Perfectly Normal*, C, 90, CDN, Réal; *Dans le ventre du dragon*, C, 88, CDN, Réal/Sc; *Les fous de Bassan*, C, 86, CDN/F, Réal/Co sc; *Pouvoir intime*, C, 85, CDN, Réal/Co sc; *Pourquoi l'étrange Monsieur Zolock s'intéressait-il tant à la bande dessinée*, C, 83, CDN, Réal/Sc, (GENIE); *Les yeux rouges*, C, 82, CDN, Réal/Sc; *Dernier Voyage*, TV, 82, CDN, Réal/Sc; *Les célébrations*, C, 78, CDN, Réal/Adapt.

SIMPSON, Dee E.
- see PRODUCERS

SINGER, Gail
82 Willcocks St., Toronto, ON M5S 1C8 (416)923-4245. FAX:924-3938.
Type of Production and Credits: Th Film-Dir/Wr/Prod; TV Film-Dir/Wr/Prod.
Genres: Drama-TV; Documentary-Th&TV; Educational-Th&TV; Children's-Th&TV.
Biography: Born 1943, Winnipeg, Manitoba. M.A., English and Zoology, Univeristy of Manitoba. Has received a number of awards for documentary films.
Selected Filmography: *True Confections*, Th, 91, CDN, Dir/Wr; *Wisecracks*, Th, 91, CDN, Prod/Dir/Wr; *Hailey's Home Movie*, TV, 87, CDN, Dir/Wr; *Abortion: Stories from North and South*, TV, 84, CDN, Co-Prod/Dir/Wr; *Portrait of the Artist as an Old Lady* (Parakeyva Clark), TV, 82, CDN, Dir/Prod; *Loved, Honoured and Bruised*, TV, 80, CDN, Dir/Wr.

SIRETEANU, Ion-Dragos
- see PRODUCERS

SKERRETT, Bill
- see PRODUCERS

SKOGLAND, Kari
197 Chaplin Cres., Toronto, ON M5P 1B1 (416)483-5736. Skogland Films Ltd., 31 Atlantic Ave., Toronto, ON M6K 3E7 (416)588-3324.
Type of Production and Credits: Th Short-Ed; TV Film-Ed; TV Video-Ed.
Genres: Drama-Th&TV; Documentary-Th&TV; Commercials-TV; Music Video-TV.
Biography: Born 1959. Owner, Skogland Films Ltd. Director of film and TV commercials and music videos. Awards include Bessies, Monitor, International Film & TV Awards (NY), Coq d'Or and Juno nomination.
Selected Filmography: *Girlsmoke*, ED, 91, CDN, Dir; *Lipton's*, Cm, 91, CDN, Dir; *Miller Lite*, Cm, 91, CDN, Dir; *Frito Lay*, Cm, 91, USA, Dir; *AT&T*, Cm, 91, USA, Dir; *Labatts*, Cm, 90, CDN, Dir; *Kellogg's*, Cm, 90, CDN, Dir; *Canadian Airlines*, Cm, 90, CDN, Dir; *Waterline*, Spoons, MV, 90, CDN, Dir; *American Express*, Cm/Th, 90, CDN, Dir/Des; *McDonalds*, Cm, 90, CDN, Dir; *Haywire*, MV, 90, CDN, Dir; *Sheree*, MV, 90, CDN, Dir; *Noxema*, Cm, 89, CDN, Dir; *Le Chateau*, Cm, 89, CDN, Dir.

SKY, Laura
566 Palmerston Ave., Toronto, ON M6G 2P7 (416)536-6581. FAX: 536-7728.
Type of Production and Credits: Th Film-Dir/Prod.Wr; TV Film-Dir/Prod/Wr; TV Video-Dir/Prod/Wr.
Genres: Documentary-Th&TV; Educational-Th&TV.
Biography: Born 1946, Montreal, Quebec. Languages: English and French. Has designed and taught several advanced courses in Film and Social Science at post-secondary institutions, including York University, Queen's University, Swedish Film Institute, University of Toronto, Sheridan College, University of Windsor, and Humber College. Numerous nominations and awards including Athens, Columbus, Houston, Lille, Yorkton, New York and Mannheim film festivals.

Selected Filmography: *The Right to Care*, ED, 91, CDN, Prod/Dir; *Crying for Happiness* (3 parts), ED, 90, CDN, Prod/Dir/Wr; *More Than Just A Job*, ED, 90, CDN, Exec Prod; *Eight Hours a Day* (2 eps), ED, 88, CDN, Prod/Dir; *A Vision of Dignity*, ED, 88, CDN, Prod/Dir; *Proud Women, Strong Steps*, ED, 87, CDN, Prod/Dir; *To Hurt & To Heal* (2 parts), ED, 86, CDN, Prod/Dir/Wr/Res; *Yes, We Can!*, ED, 84, CDN, Prod/Dir; *All of Our Lives*, TV/ED, 83, CDN, Dir/Co-Prod; *Good Monday Morning*, ED, 82, CDN, Prod/Dir; *Houdaille: Days of Courage, Days of Rage*, ED, 81, CDN, Prod/Dir; *Moving Mountains*, TV/ED, 80, CDN, Prod/Dir; *Shutdown*, TV/ED, 79, CDN, Wr/Dir.

SLIPP, Marke
- see EDITORS

SMALLEY, Katherine
ATPD, ACCT. Katherine Smalley Productions, 368 Brunswick Ave., Toronto, ON M5R 2Y9 (416)961-8907. FAX: 324-8253.
Type of Production and Credits: Th Film-Prod; TV Film-Dir/Prod.
Genres: Drama-TV; Documentary-TV; Educational-TV.
Biography: McGill Univeristy, 67; CBC, 70-87. Formed Katherine Smalley Productions Inc., independent producer, producing and developing features, movies for TV, documentaries and series. Producer of features; producer/director of TV documentaries and docudramas. Has won various awards including Gold Medal, New York for *All That Glistens*; Gabriel Award and Special Jury Award, San Francisco, for *So Many Miracles*, 87.
Selected Filmography: *Libertad*, Th, 91, USA, Prod; *So Many Miracles*, TV, 87, CDN, Prod/Dir; *Glimpse of Heaven - Easter in the Soviet Union*, 86, CDN, Prod/Dir; *Profile of Aga Khan*, "Man Alive", TV, 86, CDN, Dir/Prod; *Pornography/Ethiopia/Shrine Under Seige*, "Man Alive", TV, 84, CDN, Dir/Prod; *One Foot in Heaven*, TV, 84, CDN, Dir/Prod; *All That Glistens/Against Oblivion*, "Man Alive", TV, 83, CDN, Dir/Prod; *The Shroud of Turin*, TV, 82, CDN, Dir/Prod; *Leaving Early/Saints or Subversires/Ethiopia*, "Man Alive", TV, 81, CDN, Dir/Prod; *Soaps: The Love Business/Mission from China*, "Man Alive", TV, 80, CDN, Dir/Prod; *Does Faith Kill?/A Legacy of Hate*, "Man Alive", TV, 79, CDN, Dir/Prod; *Politics and the Pope/Listen to the Children*, "Man Alive", TV, 78, CDN, Dir/Prod; *Must Freedom Fail?*, TV, 78, CDN, Dir/Prod; *A Church under the Cross/No Easy Walk to Freedom/Fields of Vision*, "Man Alive", TV, 77, CDN, Dir/Prod; *The Good Life*, TV, 76, CDN, Dir/Prod.

SMILSKY, Peter
Centaur Films Inc., P.O. Box 5108, Vancouver, BC V6B 4A9 (604)228-1815.
Type of Production and Credits: Th Short-Prod/Dir/Ed; TV Film-Prod/Dir/Ed; TV Video-Prod/Dir/Ed.
Genres: Documentary-Th&TV; Educational-Th&TV; Current Affairs-Th&TV.
Biography: Born 1947, Hamilton, Ontario. Languages: English, French, Ukrainian. B.A., University of Toronto, 68; LL.B., University of British Columbia, 71. Winner of several awards including Yorkton and American Film Festival.
Selected Filmography: *At the Frontiers of Health*, ED, 87, CDN, Dir/Wr; *Broadcasting in Saudi Arabia*, TV, 87, CDN/SA, Dir/Wr/Ed; *With Both Eyes Open*, ED, 87, CDN, Dir/Wr; *Wall to Wall*, TV, 85, CDN, Dir/Co-Ed; *Inside/Out*, TV, 82, CDN, Prod/Snd Ed.

SMITH, Arthur
- see PRODUCERS

SMITH, John N. ✧
(514)933-4885.
Type of Production and Credits: Th Film-Dir/Wr/Prod/Ed; TV Film-Dir/Prod/Wr/Ed; TV Video-Prod.
Genres: Drama-Th&TV; Dance-Th&TV; Documentary-Th&TV; Current Affairs-TV.
Biography: Born 1943, Montreal, Quebec. Languages: English and French. B.A., McGill University; postgraduate studies in Political Science. Oscar nomination for *First Winter*; Emmy and film festival awards at Montreal, Toronto, New York, Atlanta, Germany, Spain, Chicago, Columbus, France and others.
Selected Filmography: *Train of Dreams*, Th, 86, CDN, Dir/Wr/Ed; *Sitting in Limbo*, Th, 85, CDN, Dir/Wr/Co-Prod; *First Stop China*, TV, 85, CDN, Dir/Prod; *The Rebellion of Young David*, "Northern Lights", TV, 85, CDN, Dir/Wr; *A Gift for Kate*, "Families in Crisis", TV, 85, CDN, Dir; *The Masculine Mystique*, Th, 83, CDN, Co-Dir/Co-Prod/Co-Wr; *River Journey* (Imax), Th, 83, CDN, Dir; *For the Love of Dance*, TV, 82, CDN, Co-Dir/Co-Prod; *First Winter*, Th, 81, CDN, Dir/Prod; *Gala*, Th, 81, CDN, Dir/Prod; *Acting Class*, TV, 80, CDN, Dir/Prod; *Revolution's Orphans*, "Adventures in History" (1 eps), TV, 79, CDN, Dir/Co-Wr; *No Day of Rest*, TV, 78, CDN, Dir/Ed; *Happiness Is Loving Your Teacher*,

TV, 77, CDN, Dir/Wr/Ed; *The 51st State*, TV, 71-72, USA/A, Prod, (EMMY).
SMITH, Robert F.
- see PRODUCERS
SMOFSKY, Lenny ✧
(514)683-5348.
Type of Production and Credits: Th Film-DOP; Th Short-Dir/DOP; TV Video-Dir/DOP.
Genres: Comedy-Th; Action-TV; Commercials-TV; Industrial-TV.
Biography: Born 1959, Montreal, Quebec. Languages: English and French. B.A.A., Motion Picture, Ryerson Polytechnical Institute, 82.
Selected Filmography: *Stranger Among Friends*, TV, 88, CDN, Dir; *Society for the Prevention of Cruelty to Children*, Cm, 88, CDN, DOP; *Ontario Lung Association*, Cm, 88, CDN, Dir/DOP; *Luggage Survival*, In, 88, CDN, Dir; *Friend Go Up Higher*, Th, 87, CDN, DOP; *Foodshare*, Cm, 87, CDN, Dir/DOP; *Mr. Nice Guy*, Th, 85, CDN, DOP.

SNOW, Michael
Canadian Filmmakers Dist. Centre, 67A Portland St., Toronto, ON M5V 2M9 (416)593-1808.
Type of Production and Credits: Th Film-Dir/Ed/Wr/DOP; Th Short-Dir/Wr/Ed/DOP.
Genres: Experimental-Th.
Biography: Born 1929, Toronto, Ontario. Ontario College of Art, 52; received an honorary degree from Brock University, 74. Began film career at George Dunning's Graphic Associates, Toronto, 55-56; based in New York in the 60s. Also painter, sculptor and musician; solo exhibitions world-wide. Retrospective of work held in Hara, Tokyo, October, 88. Recipient of Toronto Arts Award, 86.
Selected Filmography: *Seated Figures*, Th, 88, CDN, Creator/Dir/Prod; *So This Is*, Th, 83, CDN, Dir/Wr/Ed/Cin; *Presents*, Th, 81, CDN, Dir/Wr/Ed/Cin; *Breakfast/Table Top Dolly*, Th, 72-76, CDN, Dir/Wr/Ed/Cin; *Rameau's Nephew by Diderot Thanx to Dennis Young by Wilma Schoen*, Th, 74, CDN, Dir/Wr/Ed/Cin; *La Région centrale*, Th, 71, CDN, Dir/Wr/Ed/Cin; *Side Seat Paintings Slides Sound Film*, Th, 70, USA, Dir/Wr/Ed/Cin; *Back and Forth*, Th, 69, USA, Dir/Wr/Ed/Cin; *One Second in Montreal*, Th, 69, USA, Dir/Wr/Ed/Cin; *Dripping Water*, Th, 69, USA, Co-Dir/Wr/Ed/Cin; *Wavelength*, Th, 67, USA, Dir/Wr/Ed/Cin; *Standard Time*, Th, 67, USA, Dir/Wr/Ed/Cin; *Short Shave*, Th, 65, USA, Dir/Wr/Ed/Cin; *New York Eye and Ear Control*, Th, 64, USA, Dir/Wr/Ed/Cin; *A to Z*, Th, 56, CDN, Dir/Wr/Ed/Cin.

SNOWDEN, Alison
51A Tunley Rd., London SW17 7QH England (081) 675-7648. Snowden Fine Prods., 105 The Chandlery, 50 Westminster Bridge Rd., London SE1 7QY (071) 721 7474.
Types of Production and Credits: Th Short-Dir/Wr/An.
Genres: Animation-Th; Drama-Th; Comedy-Th.
Biography: Born 1959, Arnold, Nottingham, England. Degree in Graphic Design, Coventry, 80; attended National Film and Television School, London, 80-84. Oscar nomination and Annecy Award for *Second Class Mail*; Oscar nomination, Gold Plaque, Chicago, Montreal Film Festival Award for *George and Rosemary*; Genie nomination, awards at Berlin, Athens and Ohio for *In and Out*. Presently running Snowden Fine Productions in London, England.
Selected Filmography: *In and Out*, Th, 89, CDN, Co-Dir/Co-Wr/Co-Prod; *George and Rosemary*, Th, 87, CDN, Co-Dir/Co-Wr/Co-An; *Second Class Mail*, Th, 84, CDN, Co-Dir/Co-Wr/Co-An; *Norman*, Th, 84, GB, Dir/Wr.

SOBEL, Mark
DGA, DGC. Cinecan Film Prod., P.O. Box 8601, Universal City, CA 91608 USA. Victoria Wisdom, Chasin/Becsey Agency, 190 N. Canon Dr., #201, Beverly Hills, CA 90210 USA (213)278-7505.
Type of Production and Credits: Th Film-Dir/Prod; TV Film-Dir/Prod.
Genres: Drama-Th&TV; Action-Th&TV.
Biography: Born in Canada; US resident. Winner of Chicago International Film Festival Award for *Chrissy and Me*.
Selected Filmography: *little secrets*, Th, 91, USA, Dir/Prod; "The Commish" (pilot), TV, 91, USA, Dir; "Dark Shadows", TV, 91, USA, Dir; "Gabriel's Fire", TV, 91, USA, Dir; "Equal Justice", TV, 91, USA, Dir; "Quantum Leap" (premiere eps), TV, 90, USA, Dir; "The Equalizer", TV, 88, USA, Dir/Prod; *Chrissy and Me*, Th, 80, USA, Dir/Wr/Prod; *Mon Ame*, Th, 75, CDN, Dir/Wr/Prod.

SOBELMAN, David
- see WRITERS
SPIESS, Fritz
- see CINEMATOGRAPHERS
SPRINGBETT, David
Asterisk Productions, 110 Spadina Ave.,

#703, Toronto, ON M5V 2K4 (416)868-1175.
Type of Production and Credits: Th Short-Prod; TV Film-Dir/Prod; TV Video-Dir/Prod.
Genres: Documentary-Th&TV; Educational-Th&TV; Children's-Th&TV.
Biography: Born 1944. Attended the University of Manitoba. Specializes in documentary production in developing countries and difficult environments. Produced 6 films for NFB, Ontario Region, 78-80. Awards include Blue Ribbon, 3 Red Ribbons from American Film Festival; Bronze Chris Award; Audubon Environmental Film Festival.
Selected Filmography: *Growing Up in the World Next Door*, TV, 88, CDN, Co-Prod/Dir; *Heart of the Lotus*, ED, 87, CDN, Dir/Prod; *Roots of Hunger, Roots of Change*, TV, 85, USA, Co-Prod/Dir; *Michael Gets Water/Women & Water*, Cm, 83-84, USA, Dir/Ed; *What Do You Do When...*, Cm, 83, CDN, Dir/Ed; *Old House, New House*, ED, 82, CDN, Prod; "World's Children" (13 eps), TV, 79-80, CDN, Co-Prod; *Black Ice*, Th, 79, CDN, Prod.

SPRY, Robin
- see PRODUCER

STAMPE, Bill
123 Rao Cres., Saskatoon, SK (306)242-6581. Cinepost Productions, 1937 Ontario Ave., Saskatoon, SK (306)244-7788.
Type of Production and Credits: TV Film-Dir/Prod; TV Video-Dir/Prod.
Genres: Documentary-Th&TV; Drama-Th&TV; Commercials-Th&TV; Industrial-TV.
Biography: Born 1957, St-Hubert, Quebec. Mechanical Engineer; attended University of Alberta, 75-77. Developed SRTV Productions, film and video business, in Saskatoon, 83; name changed to Cinepost Productions, 89. Has produced and directed hundreds of TV commercials for regional and national clients. Awards include a Bronze Bessie for public service; 2 top Saskatchewan commercials, 88-90. 1/2 hour drama purchased by CBC National; also documentaries and corporate films.

STAVRIDES, Stavros
ACCT. Arto-Pelli Motion Pictures, 33 Hazelton Ave., 3rd Flr., Toronto, ON M5R 2E3 (416)928-0164. FAX: 928-3399.
Type of Production and Credits: Th Film-Dir/Prod; Th Short-Dir/Prod; TV Film-Dir/Wr; TV Video-Dir/Wr.
Genres: Documentary-Th&TV; Drama-Th.
Biography: Born 1954, Montreal, Quebec. B.A.A., Motion Picture, Ryerson Polytechnical Institute, 79. *H* won Citytv Award, 90; *God Rides a Harley* won Genie, 88.
Selected Filmography: "Venture" (15 eps), TV, 86-91, CDN, Prod/Dir/Wr; *On My Own*, Th, 91, CDN/I/AUS, Co-Prod; *H*, Th, 90, CDN, Prod; *God Rides a Harley*, Th, 85, CDN, Prod/Dir, (GENIE); *Tukak*, ED, 83, CDN, Prod/Ed; *In Whiteman's Land, Qallunaani*, ED, 82, CDN, Dir/Ed; *Open Circle*, ED, 82, CDN, Prod/Ed.

STEELE, Fraser
ACCT. Stainless Productions Ltd., 948 Logan Ave., Suite 2, Toronto, ON M4K 3E5 (416)465-4906.
Type of Production and Credits: TV Film Dir/Prod/Wr; TV Video-Dir/Prod/Wr.
Genres: Drama-TV; Documentary-TV; Educational-TV.
Biography: Born 1949, Montreal, Quebec. Honours B.A., Film and English Litt., Sir George Williams (Concordia) University. Directing and producing since 77. "Beyond Stress" won Gold Medal, Houston, 88; "Science of Architecture" won 5 awards including 1st place at AMTEC, 89 and the American Film & Video Festival, 89, and Silver Medal, Houston, 89.
Selected Filmography: "A Sense of Design" (7 eps), TV, 90-91, CDN, Dir/Prod/Wr; "Marketing for Everyone" (8 eps), TV, 89-90, CDN, Dir/Prod; "The Science of Architecture" (8 eps), TV, 88, CDN, Dir/Prod/Wr; "Beyond Stress" (6 eps), TV, 87, CDN, Dir/Prod/Wr; "the fifth estate" (2 seg), TV, 86, CDN, Dir/Prod; "Automating the Office" (9 eps), TV, 85, CDN, Dir; "Futurework" (10 eps), TV, 84, CDN, Dir; *Rogers and Salazar*, "World's Greatest Athletes", TV, 83, CDN, Dir/Prod/Wr; *Inside TV News*, TV, 82, CDN, Dir/Prod; "Turning Point" (8 eps), TV, 81, CDN, Dir/Prod; "Beyond the Fridge" (26 eps), TV, 77-78, CDN, Prod; *King Koncert: The Boffo World of Donald K. Donald*, TV, 77, CDN, Dir/Prod/Wr; *The Battle for Montreal*, TV, 77, CDN, Dir/Prod.

STEELE, Michael
- see PRODUCERS

STEIN, Allan
- see WRITERS

STERN, Sandor
DGA, PGA, WGAw. 521 North Camden Dr., Beverly Hills, CA 90210 (213)278-

0688. Jamson Productions Inc., 9116 1/2 Pico Blvd., Los Angeles, CA 90035 USA. (213)275-0180. Broder, Kurland & Webb, 8439 Sunset Blvd., #402, Los Angeles, CA 90069 USA. (213)656-9262.
Type of Production and Credits: Th Film-Wr; TV Film-Dir/Prod/Wr; TV Video-Dir/Wr.
Genres: Drama-Th&TV; Comedy-Th&TV; Variety-TV; Horror-Th&TV.
Biography: Born 1936, Timmins, Ontario. B.A. and M.D., University of Toronto. Practised medicine for 5 years in Toronto. Has written, directed TV movies, series since 60. Winner of NAACP Image Award, Best Screenplay for *Fast Break*, 80.
Selected Filmography: *Web of Deceit*, TV, 90, USA, Wr/Dir/Prod; *Without Her Consent*, TV, 89, USA, Dir; *Dangerous Pursuit*, TV, 89, USA, Wr/Dir/Prod; *Amityville: The Evil Escapes*, TV, 88, USA, Wr/Dir/Prod; *Glitz*, TV, 88, USA, Dir; *Pin*, Th, 87, CDN, Dir/Wr; *Shattered Innocence*, TV, 87, USA, Dir/Co-Wr; *Assassin*, TV, 86, USA, Dir/Wr/Exec Prod; *Easy Prey*, TV, 86, USA, Dir/Co-Wr; *John and Yoko: A Love Story*, TV, 85, USA/GB, Dir/Wr; *Passions*, TV, 84, USA, Dir/Co-Wr; *Cutter to Houston*, TV, 83, USA, Dir/Wr; *Memories Never Die*, TV, 82, USA, Dir/co-Wr; *Muggable Mary: Street Cop*, TV, 81, USA, Dir/Wr; *The Amityville Horror*, Th, 78, USA, Scr.

STERN, Steven ◊
(818)788-3607.
Type of Production and Credits: Th Film-Dir/Wr; TV Film-Dir/Prod/Wr.
Genres: Drama-Th; Comedy-Th; Variety-TV; Action-Th.
Biography: Born 1937, Timmins, Ontario. B.A.A., Radio and TV Arts, Ryerson Polytechnical Institute. Over 40 writing and directing awards for commercials including Cannes, Venice, New York. *Neither by Day Nor by Night* won Grand Peace Prize, European Critics Award, International Writers Guild Award.
Selected Filmography: *Love and Murder*, Th, 88, CDN, Wr/Prod/Dir; *Philly Boy*, Th, 88, USA, Dir; *Man against the Mob*, TV, 87, USA, Dir; *Many Happy Returns*, TV, 86, USA, Dir/Prod; *Rolling Vengeance*, Th, 86, USA, Dir/Prod; *Weekend War*, TV, 86, USA, Dir; *Terror in the Sky*, TV, 85, USA, Dir; *Young Again*, TV, 85, USA, Dir/Wr/Prod; *The Park Is Mine*, TV, 84, CDN/USA, Dir; *The Undergrads*, TV, 84, USA, Dir/Prod; *Obsessive Love*, TV, 84, USA, Dir; *Getting Physical*, TV, 84, USA, Dir; *Draw!*, TV, 83, CDN/USA, Dir; *Uncommon Love*, TV, 83, USA, Dir; *Portrait of a Showgirl*, TV, 82, USA, Dir.

STEWART, Gordon
- see PRODUCERS
STILMAN, Philip Samuel
- see EDITORS
STINSON, Fred T.
- see PRODUCERS
STIRLING, Michelle G.
- see PRODUCERS
STOCKTON, Brian
ACTRA. 120 Shannon Rd., Regina, SK S4S 5B1 (306)584-9165.
Type of Production and Credits: Th Film-Dir/Wr/Ed; Th Short-Dir/Wr/Ed.
Genres: Drama-Th; Comedy-Th; Science Fiction-Th; Music Video-TV.
Biography: Born 1964, North Battleford, Saskatchewan. B.F.A., Film & Video, University of Regina. Writer/producer/director of low budget features including *Wheat Soup* which won Best Production at Sask. Showcase, and *The 24 Store* which won Best Script at the same festival. Numerous short films including animated film, *The Blob Thing*.
Selected Filmography: *The 24 Store*, Th, 90, CDN, Wr/Prod/Dir; *The Blob Thing*, Th, 88, CDN, Wr/Dir/An; *Wheat Soup*, Th, 87, CDN, Co-Wr/Co-Dir/Co-Prod/Co-Ed.

STOLLER, Bryan M.
B.M.S. Film Productions, 11101 Aquavista, Suite 103, Studio City, CA 91602 USA. (818)980-8880.
Type of Production and Credits: Th Film-Dir/Wr; TV Film-Dir.
Genres: Drama-Th; Comedy-TV; Science Fiction-Th Documentary-Th.
Biography: Born 1960, Peterborough, Ontario. Attended the American Film Institute as a director fellow; won 11 international film awards including Gold Award, Bronze Award, Houston.
Selected Filmography: *The American Comedy Awards*, TV, 91, USA, Seg Dir; *Sunday Comics*, TV, 91, USA, Seg Prod/Dir; *Undershorts - The Movie*, Th, 88, USA, Prod/Dir/Wr; *The Bitterest Pill*, "Tales from the Dark Side", TV, 86, USA, Dir; "Hands Across America" (3 seg), TV, 86, USA, Dir; *The Frog Prince*, "TV Bloopers & Practical Jokes", TV, 85, USA, Dir/Wr/Ed/Prod; *The Shadow of Michael/Encounter with an E.T./Don't Walk*, TV, 84, USA, Dir/Wr/Ed/Prod; *Incredible Bulk/The Karate Guy*,Foul-Ups, Bleeps & Blunders, TV, 84, USA, Dir/Wr/Ed/Prod; "Greenlight", MV, 84, USA, Dir/Wr/Ed; *Storytime*, TV, 83, USA, Dir/Wr; *Just Like*

Magic, TV, 82, USA, Dir/Wr; *The Making of Slapstick*, TV, 82, USA, Dir/Wr; *Just Joking*, TV, 82, USA, Dir/Wr/Ed/Prod.

STONEMAN, John
- see CINEMATOGRAPHERS

STRATYCHUK, Perry Mark
ACCT. 3790 Ness Ave., Winnipeg, MB R2Y 1T4 (204)888-6277.
Type of Production and Credits: Th Short-Prod/Dir/DOP/Ed; TV Film-Prod/Dir/DOP/Ed/Wr; TV Video-Dir/DOP/Ed/Wr.
Genres: Science Fiction-Th&TV; Documentary-Th&TV; Experimental-TV; Music Video-Th&TV.
Biography: Born 1962, St. Boniface, Manitoba. Studied Film, University of Winnipeg; Media, Red River Community College; Directing, Algonquin College. Independent filmmaker since 80. Worked at NFB Winnipeg as Production Coordinator. Winner of awards at various film and video festivals including: Houston, Chicago, Toronto, Orlando. Freelance cameraperson, director, editor and writer. Experienced in model and miniatures construction.
Selected Filmography: *The Stealer Breed*, "R.O.C. Saga", TV, 91, CDN, Prod/Dir/DOP/Ed; *The Orphan God of Sand*, "R.O.C. Saga", TV, 91, CDN, Prod/Dir/DOP/Ed; *Shifters Anonymous*, "R.O.C. Saga", TV, 91, CDN, Prod/Dir/DOP/Ed; *A Metal Bouquet*, "R.O.C. Saga", TV, 91, CDN, Prod/Dir/DOP/Ed; *Infinity on a Wasted World*, "R.O.C. Saga", TV, 91, CDN, Prod/Dir/DOP/Ed; *Passion Wrap*, TV, 91, CDN, Prod/Dir/DOP/Ed/Comp; *The Traveller*, MV, 88, CDN, Dir/DOP/Ed; *The Half-Life of Bernard Blanda*, TV, 88, CDN, Prod/Dir/DOP/Ed; *Take What You Want*, MV, 87, CDN, DOP/Light Tech; *The Point on the Hill*, MV, 86, CDN, DOP; *Savannah Electric*, TV, 86-87, CDN, Prod/Dir/DOP/Ed; *A Game of Death*, Th, 86, CDN, DOP/Light Tech; *A Soft Look*, TV, 84, CDN, Prod/Dir/DOP/Ed/Comp; *His First Million*, Th, 82, CDN, Prod/Dir/DOP/Ed; *Room Four Memory*, Th, 80, CDN, Prod/Dir/Ed/Comp.

STRAYER, Colin J.
- see PRODUCERS

STREET, Bill
(416)277-2685.
Type of Production and Credits: TV Film-Dir.
Genres: Documentary-TV; Educational-Th&TV; Sports-TV.
Biography: Born Ottawa, Ontario. Sound department, Briston Films Ltd., Montreal, 55-59, Chetwynd Films Ltd., Toronto, 60; picture editing, 62; became director/producer, 65.
Selected Filmography: *On Camera '81 and '82*, In, 80-83, CDN, Dir; *Some of Those Newcomers*, TV, 82, CDN, Dir; *On Computer and Television*, In, 80, CDN, Ed; "Small Is Beautiful" (pilot), TV, 80, CDN, Ed; "I've Got a Story" (pilot), TV, 79, CDN, Dir; *Ravages of David*, TV, 79, CDN, ED; *Grey Cup '77*, TV, 77, CDN, Ed, (CFTA); *Canadian Parachute Jumping Championship*, TV, 76, CDN, Dir; *Heritage Canada*, TV, 75, CDN, Dir; *Marcia Longa*, TV, 75, CDN, Dir; *The Stanley Cup* (3 times), TV, 60-70, CDN, Dir; "Instructional Hockey" (9 eps), ED, 69, CDN, Dir; *Life is Worth the Living*, In, 67, CDN, Dir/Prod, (CFA); *Grand Prix Canada*, TV, 67, CDN, Dir; *Player's 200* (sports car racing), TV, 62-65, CDN, Dir.

SUISSA, Danièle J.
APFTQ, ACTRA, CFTPA, ACCT, DGC. 3 Westmount Square, Apt. 1712, Westmount, PQ H3Z 2S5 (514)937-7171.
Type of Production and Credits: Th Film-Dir/Prod/Wr; TV Film-Dir/Prod/Wr.
Genres: Drama-Th&TV; Comedy-Th&TV; Action-Th&TV; Commercials-TV.
Biography: Born 1940, Casablanca, Morocco; Canadian and E.C. citizenship. Educated in Europe and New York; speaks 5 languages. Co-produced 16 films for television with Hamster Productions, France, 89; has directed over 30 plays, classical to contemporary, both in English and in French; director of hundreds of television commercials. *The Rosé Cafe* was nominated for 2 Gemini Awards; *No Blame* won awards internationally including New York, Banff, Houston and Monte Carlo. Past President, Quebec Film Producers Association and past national Vice-President and Quebec President, Academy of Canadian Cinema and Television; presently on the Board of Directors, Canadian Film and Television Producers Association.
Selected Filmography: *The Secret of Nandy*, TV, 89, CDN/F, Dir; *Double Identity*, TV, 89, CDN/F, Prod; *Doubles Jeux*, TV, 89, CDN/F, Prod; *Justice Express*, TV, 89, CDN/F, Prod; *The Thriller*, TV, 89, CDN/F, Prod; *The Phone Call*, TV, 89, CDN/F, Prod; *No Blame*, TV, 88, CDN/F, Prod; *Martha, Ruth & Edie*, Th, 88, CDN, Dir; *Morning Man*, Th, 85, CDN, Dir; *Garnet Princess*,

"Shades of Love", TV, 86, CDN, Dir; *The Rose Café*, "Shades of Love", TV, 86, CDN, Dir; *Evangeline the Second*, TV, 83, CDN, Dir; *Divine Sarah*, TV, 83, CDN, Dir; *Kate Morris: Vice-President*, TV, 83, CDN, Dir; "The Judge", TV, 81-83, CDN, Dir.

SULLIVAN, Kevin R.
- see PRODUCERS

SULYMA, Michael H.
- see PRODUCERS

SURJIK, Stephen
DGC. 15A Rusholme Dr., Toronto, ON M6J 3K1 (416)535-2844.
Type of Production and Credits: TV Film-Dir.
Genres: Drama-TV; Comedy-TV; Commercials-TV; Music Video-TV.
Biography: Born in 1958. Canadian citizen. B.F.A. (Film), Concordia University. Has directed short films, music videos and commercials.
Selected Filmography: "Mom P.I.", TV, 91-92, CDN, Dir; "Maniac Mansion", TV, 91-92, USA/CDN, Dir; *Grand Larceny*, TV, 90, CDN, Dir; "Kids in the Hall" (film segments), TV, 90, CDN/USA, Dir.

SUTHERLAND, Neil
- see PRODUCERS

SUTHERLAND, Paul
ACTRA, DGC. Quantum Creative Ltd., 50 Vicora Linkway, Don Mills, ON M3C 1B1 (416)423-7070. Characters, 150 Carlton St., 2nd Flr., Toronto, ON (416)964-8522.
Type of Production and Credits: TV Film-Dir/Prod; TV Video-Dir/Prod; Interact V-Dir/Prod.
Genres: Drama-TV; Documentary-TV; Educational-TV; Children's-TV.
Biography: Born 1930, Toronto, Ontario. Attended University of Toronto and Ryerson Polytechnical Institute. Worked at CBC, ran "Riverbank Productions" (Hammy Hamster); worked at Foster Advertising (copywriter, producer, director); IBM Canada (industrials, commercials, marketing videos); currently runs Quantum Video Marketing. Awards: IBM Outstanding Achievement, Silver Birch, Houston Gold and 2 ITVA Evas.

SWAN, James
ATPD. 136 Waverley Rd., Toronto, ON M4L 3T3 (416)690-4572. CBC, Box 500, Stn. A, Toronto, ON M5W 1E6 (416)975-7164.
Type of Production and Credits: TV Film-Dir/Prod; TV Video-Dir/Prod.
Genres: Drama-TV; Comedy-TV; Musical-TV; Horror-TV.
Biography: Born 1941, Gainsborough, Great Britain; British and Canadian citizenship. Fifteen years of stage experience as performer, director, designer, stage manager (mainly in England); dialect coach, story editor, CBC. Recent episodes of "Sunday Arts Entertainment" produced include, *A Voyage Around R.H. Thomson*, *Once Upon a "G" String* and *Con Brio*.
Selected Filmography: "Sunday Arts and Entertainment" (sev eps), TV, 89-91, CDN, Prod; "9B" (5 eps) (Dir 1 eps), TV, 88-89, CDN, Co-Creator/Exec Prod; *Smokedown*, TV, 88, CDN, Dir/Prod; *Hero of the Family*, TV, 87, CDN, Dir/Prod; *Lonely Hearts Club*, "Street Legal", TV, 87, CDN, Dir; *The Oatman*, TV, 86, CDN, Dir/Prod; *9B*, TV, 85, CDN, Dir/Prod; *And Miles to Go*, TV, 85, CDN, Prod; *The Job*, TV, 84, CDN, Dir; *The Regiment*, TV, 84, CDN, Dir; "Home Fires" (8 eps), TV, 83, CDN, Prod; *Once*, TV, 80, CDN, Prod; "A Gift to Last" (18 eps) (Dir eps 15,18,21), TV, 78-80, CDN, Assoc Prod.

SWEETMAN, Bill
- see PRODUCERS

SWERHONE, Elise
1096 Wolseley Ave., Winnipeg, MB R3G 1G7 (204)783-9108.
Type of Production and Credits: Th Short-Dir/Prod; TV Film-Dir/Prod.
Genres: Drama-TV; Comedy-TV; Documentary-TV; Educational-TV; Children's-TV.
Biography: *Kamik* won a Silver Apple award, Oakland, California, 1991. *Tommy Douglas: Keeper of the Flame* won an Award of Excellence, Yorkton Short Film and Video Festival, 1988, and Amtec Award of Excellence. *Ester Warkow: A Spy in the House* won Amtec Award of Merit, 1982. *Joe's Gym* awarded an Amtec Award of Merit, 1981.
Selected Filmography: *The Mayor of Odessa*, TV, 91, CDN, Dir/Co Prod; *Sandra's Garden*, ED, 90, CDN, Pict Ed; *Now & Then*, TV, 90, CDN, Dir/Co Prod; *Miss Manitoba*, TV, 89, CDN, Dir/Co Prod; *Kamik*, ED, 89, CDN, Dir; *Swift Fox*, TV, 88, CDN, Pict Ed; *Tommy Douglas: Keeper of the Flame*, TV, 86, CDN, Dir/Co Prod; *Sniff*, ED, 83, CDN, Dir/Prod; *Caught in the Middle*, ED, 83, CDN, Dir; *Ester Warkow: A Spy in the House*, ED/TV, 82, CDN, Dir; *Joe's Gym*, ED, 81, CDN, Dir; *No Noonse*, ED/TV, 80, CDN, Dir; *Havakeen Lunch*, Th/TV, 78, CDN, Dir/Prod; *A Place That I Call Home*, ED, 76, CDN, Dir/Prod; *The First Step*, ED, 75, CDN, Dir/Prod.

TABORSKY, Vaclav
DGC, ACCT. 70 Parkview Ave., Willowdale, ON M2N 3Y2 (416)222-3385. York University, Film/Video Department, 4700 Keele St., North York, ON M3J 1P3 (416)667-3729.
Type of Production and Credits: Th Film-Dir/Wr; Th Short-Dir/Wr; TV Film-Dir/Wr.
Genres: Comedy-Th&TV; Documentary-Th; Educational-TV.
Biography: Born 1928, Prague, Czechoslovakia; Canadian citizenship. Graduate FAMU. Directed, wrote feature films, TV comedies, 80 documentaries and educational films. Won the Golden Lion, Venice, for *Mud Covered City*; Silver Lion, Venice, for *Escape in the Wind*. Currently Associate Professor, Film Department, York University.
Selected Filmography: *Miraculous Puzzle*, Th, 67, CZ, Dir/Prod/Co-Wr; *Escape in the Wind*, Th, 65, CZ, Dir/Prod/Co-Wr; *Mud Covered City*, Th, 63, CZ, Dir/Wr.

TAKACS, Tibor
DGA, DGC. Image Pictures, 104 Richview Ave., Toronto, ON M5P 3E9 (416)483-7301. (213)938-8337. Donald Kopaloff, 1930 Century Park W., Los Angeles, CA 90067 USA. (213)203-8430.
Type of Production and Credits: Th Film-Dir/Prod; Th Short-Dir/Prod.
Genres: Drama-Th&TV; Science Fiction-Th&TV; Horror-Th&TV.
Biography: Born 1954, Budapest, Hungary; Canadian citizenship. *Snow* won an award at Chicago and was the Official Entry at Berlin Film Festival; *I Madman* won at Avoriaz, 90.
Selected Filmography: *The Gate II*, Th, 90, CDN, Dir; *I, Madman*, Th, 87, USA, Dir; *The Gate*, Th, 86, CDN, Dir; *Snow*, Th, 82, CDN, Co-Prod/Ed/Dir; *The Tomorrow Man*, TV, 78, CDN, Dir/Co-Prod/Ed, (CFTA); *Metal Messiah*, Th, 76, CDN, Dir/Co-Prod/Ed.

TAYLOR, Rick
CFTA. R T Productions Inc., Box 30, Glencairn Manor, Glencairn, ON L0M 1K0 (705)424-2741.
Type of Production and Credits: Th Film-Snd Ed; Th Short-Prod/Dir; TV Film-Ed; TV Video-Dir.
Genres: Documentary-TV; Educational-TV; Commercials-TV; Industrial-TV.
Biography: Born in 1952 in Toronto, Ontario. Canadian citizen. University formal education. Motion picture studies in Toronto and Los Angeles. 18 years professional experience. Feature film/television series: sound editor, foley artist. 7 years broadcast television commercials as editor and director. 9 years documentary/industrial as director and editor. Maintains own videotape production and post production equipment. Experience with all visual production media, from slides to discs. Special effects and exhibit production. Specializes in film/tape/animation. Numerous editing and production awards.
Selected Filmography: *The Majesty of Sail: A Legacy of Valor*, Th, 91, CDN, Dir/Ed; *Relocation* (3), In, 90, CDN, Dir/Ed; *Needle Alley*, Cm, 89, CDN, Dir; *The Job* (3), ED, 89, CDN, Dir/Ed; "Ripley's San Francisco", Th, 88, USA, Ed/Dir; *Montreal*, Sun Life, In, 87, CDN, Dir; *Water Park Place*, Campeau, In, 86, CDN, Dir.

TERRY, Christopher
DGC. 37 Hiltz Ave., Toronto, ON M4L 2N6 (416)461-8150.
Type of Production and Credits: Th Film-Dir; TV Film-Dir/DOP; TV Video-Dir/DOP/Prod.
Genres: Documentary-TV; Children's-TV; Corporate-Th&TV; Industrial-Th&TV; Music Video-TV.
Biography: Born 1952, Hornchurch, Essex, England; Canadian and British citizenship. B.F.A., Film, York University. Part-time instructor, Film, Ontario College of Art. Director/DOP/writer of numerous music videos including Perfect World, Exchange, Bowkun Trio, Manteca, Anvil, Helix, Honeymoon Suite, Nylons; Director/cinematographer on several corporates/industrials including Ontario Ministries of Transportation, Labour, Tourism, Agriculture, Corporations; Fairweather, Shell, IBM, Dupont, Pepsi, Canada Dry, Cantel, CIBC, Royal Bank, Bank of Nova Scotia, and others. Winner of numerous awards.
Selected Filmography: "Distant Journeys" (18 eps), ED, 91, CDN, Dir; Various music videos, MV, 84-91, CDN, Dir/DOP/Wr; Various corporates/industrials, In/Corp, 84-91, CDN, Dir/Cin; *Glory! Glory!* (2 eps), TV, 89, CDN, 2nd U Dir/P Pro Spv; *Toronto: Struggle for Neighbourhood* "Cities Fit to Live In", ED, 88, CDN, Dir/Cin; *Leave Only Footprints*, TV, 87, CDN, Dir/Cin; "Vid Kids" (26 eps), TV, 85-86, CDN, Dir; *Freeloading*, Th, 84, CDN, Co-Dir; *Peru, The Hidden Empires*, Th, 78, CDN, Dir/Ed/Snd.

TETREAULT, Roger
AR. 2145, Barclay, Montréal, PQ H3S 1J4 (514)738-3438.

Types de production et générique: c métrage-Réal; TV film-Réal; TV vidéo-Réal.
Types d'oeuvres: Documentaire-C&TV; Drame-TV; Education-TV; Enfants-TV.
Curriculum vitae: Né en 1941, Farnham, Québec. Langues: français et anglais. Baccalauréat ès Arts; class de réalisation à l'Institut des Hautes Etudes Cinématographiques, Paris; études musicales (piano), physique nucléaire et archéologie.
Filmographie sélective: "Sommes-Nous Préparés?", TV, 89, CDN, Sc/Réal; *Looking Forward with Canadians*, In, 88-89, CDN, Sc/Réal; "Les Enfants de la rue" (3 eps), TV, 88, CDN, Réal; "Les Enfants mal-aimés" (3 eps), TV, 84, CDN, Réal; "Vivre en prison" (3 eps), TV, 80, CDN, Réal; "La Science en question" (30 eps), TV, 77-78, CDN, Réal; *A l'autre bout de mon âge*, C, 75, CDN, Réal.

THEBERGE, André
SOGIC, 1755, boul. René-Lévesque est, 2e étage, Montréal, PQ H2K 4P6 (514)873-7768.
Types de production et générique: l métrage-Réal/Sc/Mont; c métrage-Réal/Sc/Mont; TV film-Réal/Sc/Mont.
Types d'oeuvres: Documentaire-C&TV; Drame-C.
Curriculum vitae: Né en 1945, Kamouraska, Québec. Langues: français, anglais, allemand, danois. Baccalauréat ès Arts, Collège de Saint-Laurent; Licence ès Lettres, Université de Montréal, 69 (Certificat d'Etudes Cinématographiques). Directeur des Opérations-film, Société Générale des Industries Culturelles.
Filmographie sélective: *La Petite Nuit*, C, 83, CDN, Réal; *Ca peut pas être l'hiver on n'a même pas eu d'été*, C, 79, CDN, Mont; *Le Réseau*, C, 79, CDN, Mont/Mont son; *Les Quais*, C, 79, CDN, Moont/Mont son; *La Nuit des clairons*, C, 79, CDN, Mont; *La Belle Apparence*, C, 78, CDN, Mont/Mont son; *Jeanne Moreau*, "Visage", TV, 78, CDN, Sc; *Papeterie St-Gilles*, C, 78, CDN, Mont; *La Quadrille acadienne*, C, 78, CDN, Mont/Mont son; *Quicksilver*, "Teleplay", TV, 76, CDN, Réal/Sc; *Close Call*, "Peep Show", TV, 75, CDN, Réal; *Un Fait accompli* "Toul'monde parle français", C, 74, CDN, Réal/Sc; *La Dernière Neige*, "Toul'monde parle français", C, 73, CDN, Réal/Sc/Mont; *Les Allées de la terre*, C, 72, CDN, Réal/Sc; *Question de vie*, C, 69, CDN, Réal/Sc/Mont.

THEOBALD, Geoff
4391 Capilano Rd., North Vancouver, BC V7R 4J8 (604)987-2518. FAX: 987-2518.
Type of Production and Credits: TV Video-Dir/Prod.
Genres: Drama-TV; Comedy-TV; Variety-TV; Game Shows-TV.
Biography: Born 1934, Chilliwack, BC. Stage and TV actor prior to 60. Staff producer/director at BCTV, 60-71. Has since been Vice-President/Creative Director of two advertising agencies. Writer, producer, director of award-winning film and TV commercials. Now specializing in game-show production.
Selected Filmography: "Lingo" (70 eps), TV, 87, CDN/USA, Dir/Prod; "Pitfall" (130 eps), TV, 80-81, CDN, Dir; "Let's Make a Deal" (200 eps), TV, 80-81, CDN, Dir; "Stan Kann" (52 eps), TV, 77-79, CDN, Dir/Prod; *Handel's Messiah*, TV, 79, CDN, Dir; "Cosmopolitan Kitchen" (sev eps), TV, 77, CDN, Dir/Pro Spv; "Celebrity Revue" (sev eps), TV, 76, CDN, Dir/Pro Spv; "Mantrap" (sev eps), TV, 70-71, CDN, Dir; "Windfall" (sev eps), TV, 63-70, CDN, Dir; *Workshop 30*, TV, 65, CDN, Dir/Prod; *Tides and Trails*, TV, 60, CDN, Dir/Prod; *Audition*, TV, 60, CDN, Dir/Prod.

THIBAULT, Gilles
3218 Cherrier, Ile Bizard, PQ H9C 1E2 (514)620-1116. Radio-Canada, 1400 est, boul. René-Lévesque, Montréal, PQ H2L 2M2 (514)597-5970.
Types de production et générique: TV film-Réal; TV vidéo-Réal.
Types d'oeuvres: Documentaire-TV; Nouvelles-TV.
Curriculum vitae: Né en 1937, Hull, Québec. Langues: français et anglais. Etudes à l'Université d'Ottawa. Vice-président national de l'Association des Réalisateurs de Radio-Canada. Prix Wilderness pour la série "Dossier."
Filmographie sélective: *Funérailles de René Lévesque*, TV, 88, CDN, Réal; *Election présidentielles françcaises*, TV, 88, CDN, Réal; *Sommet de la Francophonie*, TV, 87, CDN, Réal/Coord; *Visite du Pape à Fort Simpson*, TV, 87, CDN, Réal; *Expo 86 Vancouver*, TV, 86, CDN, Réal; "Sommet économique" (6 ém), TV, 78-85, CDN, Rál/Coord pro; "Congrès politiques" (12 ém), TV, 73-85, CDN, Réal/Coord pro; *Conférence des Premiers ministres*, TV, 73-85, CDN, Réal/Coord pro; *Budget fédéral*, TV, 74-75, CDN, Réal/Coord pro; *Elections provinciales*, TV, 85, CDN, Réal; *Visiste du Pape*, TV, 83-84, CDN, Co réal; "Elections" (12 ém), TV, 72-84, CDN, Réal/Coord pro; *Visite du Président Reagan*, TV, 84, CDN, Réal/Coord pro; "Visiste royale" (6 ém), TV, 76-83, CDN,

Réal/Coord pro.

THOMAS, Dave
The Brillstein Co., 9200 Sunset Blvd., Suite 428, , Los Angeles, CA 90069 USA. (213)275-6135. FAX: 275-6180.
Type of Production and Credits: Th Film-Wr/Dir/Act; TV Film-Prod/Wr/Dir/Act; TV Video-Wr/Act/Dir/Prod.
Genres: Comedy-Th&TV; Variety-TV; Children's-Th&TV; Commercials-TV.
Biography: Born in St. Catharines, Ontario; currently resides in Santa Monica, California. Comedian with "SCTV" series, 76-82; one of the McKenzie Brothers whose *Great White North* record sold over 1 million copies and received a Grammy nomina-tion; started career as copywriter for McCann-Erickson Advertising, joined Second City Stage, went on to Emmy-winning TV series, then films in USA and Canada as actor, writer and director.
Selected Filmography: "The Dave Thomas Comedy Show", TV, 89, USA, Exec Prod/ Co-Wr/Act; *Moving*, Th, 88, USA, Act; *B-Men*, TV, 87, USA, Wr/Prod; *The Experts*, Th, 87, USA, Dir; *Incredible Time Travels of Henry Osgood*, TV, 86, USA, Prod, (ACE); *Burnin' Love*, Th, 86, USA, Act; *Spies Like Us*, Th, 86, USA, Act; *Follow That Bird*, Th, 85, USA, Act; "The New Show" (13 eps), TV, 84, USA, Wr/Act; "SCTV" (186 eps), TV, 76-84, CDN/ USA, Wr/Act, (ACTRA/ EMMY); *Strange Brew*, Th, 82, CDN, Co-Wr/Co-Dir/Act; *Stripes*, Th, 81, USA, Act; *From Cleveland*, TV, 80, USA, Wr/Act.

THOMAS, R.L.
DGA, WGAw, DGC.   David Wardlow, Camden Artists, 822 S. Robertson Bllvd., #200, Beverly Hills, CA 90035 USA (213)289-2706.
Type of Production and Credits: Th Film-Dir/Wr; TV Film-Dir/Prod/Wr.
Genres: Drama-Th&TV.
Biography: Born in Sao Luiz, Brazil; Canadian citizenship; US resident. Won a Special Award, Canadian Film Awards, 77; *Tyler* won the International Critics Award, Montreal Film Festival; Ace Award for *The Terry Fox Story*.
Selected Filmography: *A Burning Desire*, Th, 91, USA, Wr/Dir; *Green Fire*, Th, 90, USA, Wr; *Apprentice to Murder*, Th, 87, USA, Dir; *The Crowd*, "Ray Bradbury Theatre", TV, 84, CDN, Dir; *The Terry Fox Story*, Th, 82, CDN, Dir; *Ticket to Heaven*, Th, 80, CDN, Dir/Co-Scr; *Every Person Is Guilty*, "For the Record", TV, 79, CDN, Co-Wr, (ACTRA); *They're Drying Up the Streets*, "For the Record", TV, 78, CDN, Prod, (ACTRA); *Tyler*, TV, 77, CDN, Dir/Prod; *Dreamspeaker*, "For the Record", TV, 76, CDN, Prod, (CFA).

THOMPSON, Jane
DGC. 170 Lippincott St., Toronto, ON M5S 2P1 (416)964-7949.
Type of Production and Credits: Th Film-Dir/Ed.
Genres: Drama-Th; Documentary-Th.
Biography: Born 1952, Montreal, Quebec. B.A., Film Studies, Queen's University. Film editor and producer, documentary and industrial films, 74-85. Additional studies included Dramalab, Director, 85; Masterclass Theatre, Director-Observer, 86. Films have won several awards, including New York and Chicago; *At the Lake* won Silver Plaque, Chicago, and Bronze, Houston.
Selected Filmography: *At the Lake*, Th, 90, CDN, Wr/Dir; *Bush Pilot: Reflections on a Canadian Myth*, Th, 80, CDN, Ed.

THOMSON, Andy
- see PRODUCERS

THOMSON, Brian
- see CINEMATOGRAPHERS

THORNE, John
CTPDA. 8049 Argyle St., Vancouver, BC (604)324-1302.
Type of Production and Credits: TV Film-Dir/Prod; TV Video-Dir/Prod.
Genres: Drama-TV; Comedy-TV; Educational-TV; Children's-TV.
Biography: Born 1922, Punnichy, Saskatchewan. M.A., Northwestern University, 52. Taught at the Summer School of Theatre, University of British Columbia; directed stage productions. Director, producer, CBC, 54-85.
Selected Filmography: "The Beachcombers", TV, 80-85, CDN, P Prod; *Mon ami*, TV, 76-78, CDN, Dir/Prod; *Music to See*, TV, 70, CDN, Dir/Prod; *Shoestring Theatre*, TV, 70, CDN, Dir/Prod.

THURLING, Peter
DGC. Schafer/Thurling Productions, 8480 Harold Way, Los Angeles, CA 90069 (213)656-6635. FAX: 656-8993.
Type of Production and Credits: TV Film-Dir/Wr; TV Video-Dir/Wr.
Genres: Drama-TV; Music Video-TV; Documentary-TV.
Selected Filmography: "African Story" (3 eps), TV, 91, USA, Dir; "Beyond the Line" (pilot), TV, 89, CDN/USA, Dir; "The Campbells", TV, 87, CDN/USA/GB, Dir; *Floating Over Canada*, TV, 85, CDN, Dir/Wr, (ACTRA); "Behind the Scene" (2 eps), TV, 80, CDN, Dir; *Gopher Broke*, TV, 79, CDN, Dir/Wr; *Breakdown*, TV, 78, CDN, Dir; "Target the

Impossible" (26 eps), TV, 73-74, CDN/USA, Exec Dir/Dir/Wr; "Here Come the 70s" (100 eps), TV, 70-73, CDN/USA, Dir/Wr; "The Seasons" (3 eps), TV, 69-70, CDN/USA, Dir/Wr.

TICHENOR, Harold
- see PRODUCERS

TILL, Eric
DGA, DGC. Coquihala Films, 62 Chaplin Cres., Toronto, ON M5P 1A3 (416)488-4068. Christine Foster, Shapiro-Lichtman, 8827 Beverly Blvd., Los Angeles, CA 90048 (213) 859-8877.
Type of Production and Credits: Th Film-Dir; TV Film-Dir.
Genres: Drama-Th&TV; Comedy-Th.
Biography: Born 1929, London, England; Canadian citizenship. Came to Canada as a manager with the National Ballet of Canada, 54; directed first TV program at CBC, 57. Has since directed feature films in Canada and England and award-winning TV dramas.
Selected Filmography: *To Catch a Killer* (mini-series), TV, USA/CDN, Dir; *Getting Married in Buffalo Jump*, TV, 90, CDN, Dir; *Glory Enough for All* (mini-series), TV, 89, GB/CDN, Dir; *Glenn Gould: A Portrait*, TV, 87, CDN, Dir/Prod; *Case of Libel*, TV, 86, USA, Dir; *All Things Bright and Beautiful*, Th, 76, GB/USA, Dir; *Hot Millions*, Th, 68, GB, Dir.

TKACH, Alex
- see PRODUCERS

TODD, Michael
- see EDITORS

TOSONI, Joan
ACCT. Joan Tosoni Productions Inc., 111 Latimer Ave., Toronto, ON M5N 2M3 (416)596-8118.
Type of Production and Credits: TV Film-Dir; TV Video-Dir.
Genres: Variety-TV; Documentary-TV.
Selected Filmography: *Kurt Browning: Tall in the Saddle*, TV, 91, CDN, Dir; "The Tommy Hunter Show" (Dir 80-85), TV, 85-90, CDN, Prod/Dir; "Test Pattern", TV, CDN, 90, Dir; *George Fox's New Country*, TV, 90, CDN, Dir; "The Judge" (2 eps), TV, 90, CDN, Dir; "Eric's World" (1 eps), TV, 90, CDN, Dir; *The Opening of Skydome - A Celebration*, TV, 89, CDN, Prod/Dir; *A David Foster Christmas Card*, TV, 89, CDN, Dir; "Sensations" with David Foster, TV, 89, CDN, Dir; *Big Valley Jamboree/Songs of the Big Valley*, TV, 89, CDN, Dir; *From the Heart - A Gala on Ice*, TV, 89, CDN, Prod/Dir; *The Irish Rovers Silver Anniversary*, TV, 89, CDN, Dir; *Celebration '89*, TV, 89, CDN, Dir; *1989 Genie Awards/1988 Genie Awards*, TV, 88-89, CDN, Dir; *1988, Gemini Awards/1986 Gemini Awards*, TV, 88/86, CDN, Dir.

TOUGAS, Kirk
- see CINEMATOGRAPHERS

TOVELL, Vincent ◊
(416)925-4006.
Type of Production and Credits: TV Film-Dir/Prod; TV Video-Dir/Prod.
Genres: Drama-TV; Documentary-TV; Educational-TV.
Biography: Born 1922, Toronto, Ontario. Languages: English and French. B.A. and M.A., University of Toronto, Columbia University. Director, Hart House Theatre, 46-48; producer, director, announcer, writer, United Nations radio/TV/film, 50-53; producer, CBC New York, 53-57, Toronto, 57-85. Member of Royal Canadian Academy; Centennial Medal, 67; Queen's Jubilee Medal, 78; has won various television awards including, the Canadian Film Award (CFA), Anik and Wilderness awards.
Selected Filmography: "Glenn Gould Plays" (23 eps), TV, 87, CDN, Exec Prod/Prod/Dir; *Glenn Gould: A Portrait*, TV, 85, CDN, Exec Prod/Co-Prod/Co-Dir, (GEMINI 86); "Hand and Eye" (7 eps), TV, 84, CDN, Exec Prod/Co-Prod/Co-Dir; *The Owl and the Dynamo: George Grant*, TV, 79, CDN, Prod/Dir; *The Masseys*, TV, 78, CDN, Exec Prod/Prod/Co-Dir; *Must Freedom Fail*, TV, 78, CDN, Prod/Dir; "Images of Canada" (10 eps), TV, 70-76, CDN, Exec Prod/Co-Prod/Co-Dir.

TREMBLAY, Robert
136 Côte Bellevue, C.P. 315, Pointe-au-Pic, PQ G0T 1M0 (418)665-3555.
Types de production et générique: l métrage-Réal/Prod/Sc/Mont; c métrage-Réal/Prod/Sc/Mont.
Types d'oeuvres: Documentaire-C; Education-C; Enfants-C.
Curriculum vitae: Né en 1946, Pointe-au-Pic, Québec. Baccalauréat spécialisé en information culturelle, Université du Québec à Montréal. Réalisateur et monteur depuis 70; producteur pour les Films d'Aventure du Québec depuis 74.
Filmographie sélective: *Enfants d'école*, C, 88, CDN, Prod/Réal/Sc/Mont; *Le gars qui chante sua jobbe*, C, 86, CDN, Co prod/Mont; *Pow Pow té mort ou ben j'joue pu*, C, 80, CDN, Prod/Réal/Sc/Mont; *Du mauvais côté de la clôture*, C, 79, CDN, Mont; *Belle Famille*, C, 78, CDN, Prod/Réal/Sc/ Mont; *A maison*, C, 78, CDN, Co mont; *Toul Québec au monde sua jobbe/Le Québec sua jobbe*, C, 75, CDN, Prod/ Réal/Sc/ Mont.

TROFYMOW, L.A.
- see WRITERS

TROSTER, David
ITVA. David Troster Productions Inc., 7 Jackes Ave., Suite 902, Toronto, ON M4T 1E3 (416)922-2437. FAX: 962-0288.
Type of Production and Credits: TV Film-Prod/Dir; TV Video-Dir; Video-Dir/Prod.
Genres: Documentary-TV; Educational-TV; Children's-TV; Industrial-TV.
Biography: Born in 1949, Toronto, Ontario. Participant in Grierson documentary film seminars, 86 and 87. Founded David Troster Productions Inc. to create films and videotape programs for business and public institutions. Winner of several awards, including Silver Leaf, International Association of Business Com-municators; *Re-opening the Therapeutic Window* won an award at the US Industrial Film & Video Festival, Chicago; other awards in Chicago and Los Angeles.
Selected Filmography: *Re-opening the Therapeutic Window*, ED, 91, CDN, Prod/Dir; *Pneumonia and the Compromised Host*, In, 89, CDN, Prod/Dir; *Putting a Stop to Money Laundering*, In, 90, CDN, Prod/Dir; *Royal Bank of Canada: A Portrait*, In, 88, CDN, Prod/Dir; *Managing C.O.P.D.*, Boehringer Ingelheimer Ltd., In, 87, CDN/D, Prod/Dir; *Robbery: It Could Happen to You*, In, 86, CDN, Prod/Dir/Ed; *Spadina*, TV, 84, CDN, Prod/Dir/Wr/Ed; *Energy for the Future*, Ontario Hydro, In, 82, CDN, Dir/Ed; *Back from the Edge*, Boehringer Ingelheim Ltd., In, 81, CDN/USA/D, Prod/Dir/Wr/Ed; "Mr. Roger's Neighborhood" (film seg), TV, 70-75, CDN/USA, Dir/Cam/Ed.

TRUDEL, Yvon
AR, ACCT. Les Productions Yvon, 6, 21e Avenue, Melocheville, PQ J0S 1J0 (514)429-4865.
Types de production et générique: TV vidéo-Réal.
Types d'oeuvres: Drame-TV.
Curriculum vitae: Né en 1934 à Montréal, Québec. Trente trois ans à Radio-Canada, 21 ans comme réalisateur, TV drame.
Filmographie sélective: "Cormorain" (26 eps), TV, 89-90, CDN, Réal; "Le Temps d'une paix" (236 eps), TV, 80-88, CDN, Réal, (3 ANIK/2 GEMEAUX 86); "Terre humaine" (60 eps), TV, 79-80, CDN, Réal; "Rue des Pignons" (hebdo), TV, 70-78, CDN, Réal; "Les Belles Histoires des pays d'en haut" (hebdo), TV, 66-69, CDN, Réal.

TUNNICLIFFE, Jack
743 Bard Cres., Regina, SK S4X 2G1 (306)543-2485. Film Crew Productions, 2345 Smith St., Regina, SK S4P 2P7 (306)777-0160. FAX: 352-8558.
Type of Production and Credits: Th Short-Dir/Prod; TV Film-Prod/Dir; TV Video-Prod/Dir.
Genres: Commercials-TV; Documentary-Th&TV; Music Video-TV; Sports-TV.
Biography: Born in 1954. Studio Camera Operator, Studio Lighting Technician, Set Designer and Video-Tape Operator, CKCK-TV, 71-76; Program Producer/Director, 78-79. Producer/Director, Armadale Communications, Harvard Creative Services and Sunspirit Productions, 79-86; Production Manager, CKCK-TV, Regina, 86-88; Vice-President, Operations, 88-89. Co-owner of Film Crew Productions, Regina, 89 to date. Many award-winning productions.
Selected Filmography: "The Complete Angler" (13 eps), TV, 90-91, CDN, Prod/Dir; *The Heart of Canada's Old Northwest*, In, 90-91, CDN, Dir; "Putnam's Prairie Emporium", TV, 88-89, CDN, Exec Prod; Winter Olympics, Calgary, TV, 88-89, CDN, Prod/Dir/ Host; *CTV and ABC Sports World Indoor Speed Skating Championships*, TV, 87, CDN/USA, Dir; *CTV Sports, Canadian Football League*, TV, 86-87, CDN, Prod; *CTV Sports, Canadian Football League*, TV, 83-86, CDN, Dir; *CTV Sports, Winter Olympics, Sarejevo*, TV, 86, CDN, Dir; *CTV Sports, Winter Olympics, Lake Placid*, TV, 80, CDN, Prod/Dir.

TURNER, Brad
DGC, ACCT. 4568 Strathcona Rd., North Vancouver, BC V7G 1G3 (604)929-4233. FAX: 929-0418.
Type of Production and Credits: Th Film-Dir; TV Film-Dir.
Genres: Drama-TV; Comedy-Th&TV; Action-TV; Science Fiction-TV.
Biography: Born 1954, Bayfield, Ontario. 20 years experience in film and television. 4 Gemini nominations for Best Director.
Selected Filmography: "21 Jump Street" (3 eps), TV, 90, USA, Dir; "Scene of the Crime" (1 ep), TV, 90, USA, Dir; "Mom P.I." (pilot & 6 eps), TV, 90, CDN, Dir; "Northwood" (pilot), TV, 90, CDN, Dir; "Ray Bradbury Theatre" (3 eps), TV, 87-90, USA/CDN, Dir; *Pray for Me Paul Henderson*, TV, 90, CDN, Dir; *The Prom*, TV, 90, CDN, Dir; "Street Legal" (6 eps), TV, 88-90, CDN, Dir; "The Twilight Zone", TV, 88, USA, Dir; "Neon Rider", TV, 89, CDN, Dir; "Airwolf" (3 eps), TV,

87, USA, Dir; "Adderly" (1 eps), TV, 87, USA, Dir; "Danger Bay" (12 eps), TV, 85-89, USA/CDN, Dir; "The Beachcombers" (8 eps), TV, 86-90, CDN, Dir; *Goofballs*, Th, 85, CDN, Dir.

TURNER, Robert
Circle Productions Limited, 1700 Cypress St., Vancouver, BC V6J 4W2 (604)733-5727.
Types of Productions and Credits: TV Film-Dir.
Genres: Commercials-TV; Music Videos-Th&TV.
Biography: Born 1951, Vancouver, BC. Educated at the University of British Columbia and Simon Fraser University. Director of Zargon, the Showscan format film for BC's pavilion at Expo 86. *Playback* magazine's "Director of the Year", 88. Awards include: Golde Bessies, 87, 88, 89; Chicago Mobius Gold Award; London International Film And Television Awards, Hollywood Film and Television Association Awards; *Marketing* Judge's Choice Award.
Selected Filmography: Zargon, Th, 86, CDN, Dir.

TUSTIAN, Jim
- see PRODUCERS

VAITIEKUNAS, Vincent
DGC. 263 Spring Garden Ave., Willowdale, ON M2N 3H1 (416)223-4297. York University, Film/Video Dept., 4700 Keele St., North York, ON M3J 1P3 (416)736-5149.
Type of Production and Credits: Th Film-Wr; Th Short-Dir; TV Film-Dir.
Genres: Documentary-Th&TV; Drama-Th&TV; Children's Th&TV; Educational-Th&TV
Biography: Born in Lithuania; Canadian citizenship. Began his career in acting, stage design and film editing, then moved on to directing and screenwriting. Has won several film awards. Currently teaches Editing, Acting and Directing for Film and TV at York University, Film and Video Department.
Selected Filmography: *To Birthplace with Film Camera*, TV, 88, CDN, Dir/Wr/Ed; *Ontario Surprise*, Th, 79, CDN, Dir; *Fine Arts at York*, ED, 77, CDN, Dir/Wr/Prod/Ed; "The White Oaks of Jalna" (eps #10), TV, 71, CDN, Dir; *Canada at 8:30*, Th, 70, CDN, Dir/Ed; *Multiplicity*, Th, 70, CDN, Dir/Wr/Co-Prod/Ed; *The Sun Don't Shine on the Same Dawg's Back All the Time*, Th, 69, CDN, Dir, (CFA); *Mr. Flim-Flam*, "McQueen", TV, 69, CDN, Dir; *The Want of a Suitable Playhouse*, Shaw Festival, Th, 68, CDN, Dir/Wr/Prod/Ed; *Explore* (Expo 67), Th, 67, CDN, Dir/Ed; *Motion*, Th, 66, CDN, Dir/Ed; "This Hour Has Seven Days" (sev seg), TV, 65-66, CDN, Co-Dir/Ed; "Mr. Piper" (sev eps), TV, 63, CDN, Dir.

VALCOUR, Pierre
- voir PRODUCTEURS

VALLÉE, Jean-Marc
9532 rue Foucher, Montréal, PQ H2M 1W4 (514)389-4207. SVP Agence, 305 Ave. Elm, Westmount, PQ H3Z 1Z4 (514)937-1057.
Types de production et générique: l métrage-Réal/Mont/D phot; c métrage-Réal/Mont/D phot; TV vidéo-Réal/Mont/D phot.
Types d'oeuvres: Comédie-C; Vidéo-Clips-C&TV; Affaires Publiques-TV.
Curriculum vitae: Né en 1963 à Montréal, Québec. Citoyenneté canadienne. Langues parlées et écrites: français et anglais. D.E.C. en Cinéma au Cégep Ahuntsic et majeur en Cinéma à l'Université de Montréal.
Filmographie sélective: *Stéréotypes*, C, 91, CDN, Réal/Mont; *La Femme de Pablo Ruiz*, C, 91, CDN, Mont; *Maria Ouellette*, MV, 90, CDN, Réal/Cam/Mont; *Dossiers Mystères/OUNI*, TV, 90, CDN, Réal/Cam/Mont; *Camera 89-90*, TV, 89-90, CDN, Réal/Cam/Mont; *System-A*, In, 88, CDN, Real/Cam; *Ripping Headache*, MV, 86, CDN, Réal/Cam; *Soft Blue Veins*, MV, 86, CDN, Réal/Mont; *Herman*, C, 86, CDN, D phot/Cam; *Les Aventures de la Force Obscure*, C, 86, CDN, D phot; *Mr. Montréal*, MV, 86, CDN, Réal/Mont; *Wild Touch*, MV, 85, CDN, Réal/Mont; *New News*, MV, 85, CDN, Réal/Mont; *Angel*, MV, 85, CDN, Réal/Mont; *Park Avenue*, MV, 85, CDN, Réal/Mont.

VAN DE WATER, Anton
- see PRODUCERS

VAN DER HEYDEN, Jan
FPRRTC. 9055 de Reims, Montréal, PQ H2N 1T2 (514)388-2674.
Types de production et générique: TV vidéo-Réal.
Types d'oeuvres: Variété-TV; Documentaire-C&TV; Affaires Publiques-TV; Nouvelles-TV.
Curriculum vitae: Né en 1944 au Pays Bas. Citoyenneté canadienne et néerlandaise. Langues: français, anglais et néerlandais. B.A. et scolarité de maîtrise en communication. 15 ans d'expérience en production télévisée (studio, mobile, vidéo légère). Travaille en français et en anglais, Radio Canada, Radio Québec, CFCF (CTV), CKSH (COGECO). Finaliste Prix Gémeaux 1987 et 1990. Finaliste Banff

Television Festival, 1988. Prix Judith Jasmin-TV, 1987. Premier Prix CanPro, 1977.
Filmographie sélective: "Droit de Parole" (76 eps), TV, 89-91, CDN, Réal; "Questions d'Argent" (74 eps), TV, 89-91, CDN, Réal; *Soiree d'Elections* (provinciales) 1985 et 1989, TV, 85/89, CDN, Prod dél; "Les Jeux de la Vie" (184 eps), TV, 88-89, CDN, Prod dél; "Le Magazine" (74 eps), TV, 86-88, CDN, Prod dél; "Arrimage" (74 eps), TV, 84-86, CDN, Prod dél; "Hi Noon" (65 eps), TV, 84, CDN, Réal; *Telethon des Etoiles*, TV, 79/84, CDN, Réal; "Pulse" (1200 eps), TV, 79-84, CDN, Réal; "Hockey Magazine" (37 eps), TV, 80, CDN, Réal; "As It Is" (74 eps), TV, 80-82, CDN, Réal; "Regets d'un Pays" (6 eps), TV. 77-79, CDN, Réal; "Le Jour du Seigneur" (2 eps), TV, 77-79, CDN, Réal; "Morning Exercise" (250 eps), TV, 79, CDN, Réal; "Frederic" (39 eps), TV, 77-78, CDN, Réal.

VAN DER VEEN, Milton
Miscellaneous Productions, Manfred's Meadow, R.R. #1, Grand Valley, ON L0N 1G0 (519)925-5306. FAX: 484-4742.
Type of Production and Credits: TV Film-Prod/Dir/Wr; TV Video-Prod/Dir/Wr.
Genres: Drama-TV; Documentary-TV; Educational-TV; Children's-TV.
Biography: Born 1945, The Netherlands; Canadian citizenship. Executive producer, "TVO Daytime" since 90; Producer/director, children's programming, 78-90. "Take a Look" won prizes at Agro Film Festival, Czechoslovakia, 91; NAEB Award, Oakland, 86; and AMTEC, Saskatoon, 87; "Voyageurs" won prizes at Film & Video Festivals in New York City, 90; La Grange (Illinois), 89; Oakland, 89, Houston, 89 and AMTEC, Edmonton, 89.
Selected Filmography: "TVO Daytime" (96 eps), TV, 90-91, CDN, Exec Prod/Dir/Prod; "Nature Watch Digest" (20 eps), TV, 90-91, CDN/J, Prod/Wr; "Take a Look" (10 eps), ED, 89-90, CDN, Prod/Dir/Wr; "Full Circle: Native Way" (4 eps), TV, 89, CDN, Dir; "Voyageurs" (40 eps) (Eng & Fr), ED, 87-88, CDN, Dir/Prod/Wr; "Excursions" (12 eps), ED, 87-88, CDN, Prod/Dir; "Habitat" (40 eps) (Eng and Fr), ED, 86-87, CDN, Prod/Dir/Wr; "Take a Look" (20 eps), TV, 85-86, CDN, Prod/Dir/Wr; "The Computer Room" (10 eps), ED, 84-85, CDN, Prod/Dir; "It's Your World" (20 eps), ED, 83-84, CDN, Prod/Dir/Wr; "Artscape" (8 eps), ED, 82-83, CDN, Prod/Dir; "The Science Alliance" (10 eps), ED, 80-82, CDN, Prod/Dir/Wr; "The Body Works" (40 eps), ED, 78-80, CDN, Prod/Dir; "Kidsworld" (52 eps), TV, 78-79, CDN, Prod.

VANDERBURGH, Clive
- see PRODUCERS

VARUGHESE, Sugith
ACTRA, ACCT, WGC. 123 Scadding Ave., #806, Toronto, ON M4A 4J3 (416)360-7321. FAX: 360-4601.
Type of Production and Credits: Th Short-Wr/Dir; TV Film-Wr; TV Video-Wr.
Genres: Drama-Th&TV; Comedy-TV; Action-TV; Children's TV.
Biography: Born 1957, Cochin, India; raised in Saskatoon, Saskatchewan; Canadian citizenship. B.A., summa cum laude, University of Minnesota; M.F.A., Film, York University. Director resident/senior resident, Canadian Centre for Advanced Film Studies. York Trillium Award, Most Promising Writer (TV), 89. Also TV and film actor.
Selected Filmography: *Mela's Lunch*, ED, 91, CDN, Wr/Dir; *Kumar and Mr. Jones*, Th, 90, CDN, Wr/Dir; "Mount Royal" (1 eps), TV, 87, CDN/F, Wr; "Fraggle Rock" (10 eps), TV, 83-86, CDN, Wr; *Best of Both Worlds*, TV, 82, CDN, Wr; *The Crush*, Th, 80, CDN, Wr/Dir; "The Phoenix Team" (1 eps), TV, 80, CDN, Wr.

VERDY, Paul
ACCT. 802 Lusignan, Montreal, PQ H3C 1Y9 (514)935-5565.
Type of Production and Credits: Th Film-Dir; Th Short-Dir; TV Film-Dir.
Genres: Drama-Th&TV; Comedy-Th; Variety-TV; Commercials-Th&TV.
Biography: Born 1959, Ann Arbor, Michigan; Canadian and US citizenship. Languages: English and French. B.A., Communication Arts, Concordia University.
Selected Filmography: Opto Plus, Cm, 91, CDN, Dir; Loto-Québec, Cm, 90, CDN, Dir; Petro Canada, Cm, 90, CDN, Dir; Ikea, Cm, 90, CDN, Dir; Cinarron, Cm, 88, CDN, Dir; *Sonnet francosonique*, TV, 87, CDN, Dir; *Nuit Blanche*, TV, 86, CDN, Dir/Wr; *Feu de paille*, TV, 80, CDN, Dir/Wr.

VERGE, Robert ✧
(514)465-9557.
Types de production et générique: c métrage-Réal; TV film-Réal; TV vidéo-Réal.
Types d'oeuvres: Documentarie-C&TV;

Education-C&TV; Industriel-C&TV; Affaires publiques-C&TV.
Curriculum vitae: Né en 1950, Valleyfield, Québec. Langues: français et anglais; connaissance de l'espagnol et de l'allemand. Baccalauréat ès Arts, Cinéma et Littérature, Université de Montréal. Travail en doublage, sonorisation, adaptation, scénari-sation, recherche et réalisation depuis 69; fondation de Publiciné, 76.
Filmographie sélective: "Actuel" (15 eps), TV, 87-88, CDN, Réal; *Daniel Tremblay,* "Sens des affaires", TV, 87, CDN, Réal; SR Télécom, In, 87, CDN, Réal; "Foundation" (5 eps), TV, 87, CDN, Réal/Mont; "Desjardins" (14 eps), TV, 87, CDN, Réal/Sc/Mont; Laurentienne (4 eps), In, 87, CDN, Réal/Sc/Mont; *Contraception*, Wyeth, ED, 87, CDN, Réal/Sc/Mont.

VIALLON, Claudine
- see WRITERS

VON PUTTKAMER, Peter ✧
660 Wildwood Blvd. S.W., #B16, Issaqua, WA 98027 (206)391-5407. Gryphon Productions Ltd., 2272 Folkestone Way, #4, West Vancouver, BC V7S 2X7 (604)922-7025.
Type of Production and Credits: Th Short-Dir/Ed; TV Video-Dir/Ed/DOP.
Genres: Drama-Th; Documentary-TV; Educational-TV.
Biography: Born 1957, Bonn, West Germany; Canadian citizenship. Languages: English, German, French. B.A., Film and TV Productions, University of British Columbia. Has produced video programs for Health and Welfare Canada; formed Gryphon Productions, 83.

WACHNIUC, Michel
DGC. 231 Notre Dame W., Suite 102, Montreal, PQ H2Y 1T4 (514)845-0727. (514)989-1714.
Type of Production and Credits: Th Film-Dir; TV Film-Dir/Prod.
Genres: Drama-Th&TV; Comedy-Th&TV; Action-Th&TV; Commercials-Th&TV.
Biography: Born in 1952 in Montreal, Quebec. Graduated Cum Laude, Department of Communications, Loyola, 1974. Languages: English and French. A documentary produced as student project, *First Steps* amassed several international awards. Has worked as a editorial assistant, French News Services of Radio-Canada; freelance journalist for CBC Radio and radio interviewer (most notably with rock artists such as Mick Jagger, Frank Zappa and Alice Cooper). Has worked as a production manager and line producer on over 200 commercials. Completed the Directors' Guild of America tutorial in Los Angeles, 82. Has directed rock videos for CBS and Capital Records. Currently Chairman of the Quebec District Council of the Directors' Guild of Canada; member of the Canadian Preselection Committee at Telefilm (for Canadian entries in world film festivals including Cannes, Berlin and the Academy Awards).
Selected Filmography: *More Than Friends*, MV, 91, CDN, Dir; *You're Driving Me Crazy*, TV, 90, CDN, Dir; *Laugh Riot*, "Dangerous Dreams", TV, 89-90, CDN, Dir/Spv Prod; *Flip Side*, "Dangerous Dreams", TV, 89-90, CDN, Dir/Spv Prod; *Alienation*, "Dangerous Dreams", TV, 89-90, CDN, Dir/Spv Prod; *The Scorpio Factor*, Th, 88-89, CDN, Dir; *Rebel High*, Th, 86, CDN, 2nd Unit Dir; *Victim of a Fantasy*, MV, 85, CDN, Dir; *Elf Bloo*, Cm, 85, USA/CDN, Dir/Prod; *Gaz Metropolitain*, Cm, 84, CDN, Dir/Prod; *Evil Judgement*, Th, 82, CDN, 2nd Unit Dir; *Money Money*, MV, 82, CDN, Dir; *Je t'aime*, MV, 81, CDN, Dir; *Si tu l'aimes*, MV, 81, CDN, Dir.

WALKER, Giles
SGCT, ACCT. 4039 Grand Blvd., Montreal, PQ H4B 2X4 (514)483-3270. NFB, Box 6100, Montreal, PQ H3C 3H5 (514)283-9537. Jerry Kalajian, APA, 9000 Sunset Blvd., 12th Flr., Los Angeles, CA 90069 USA (213)273-0744.
Type of Production and Credits: Th Film-Dir/Prod/Wr; TV Film-Dir/Prod/Wr.
Genres: Drama-Th&TV; Comedy-Th&TV; Children's-TV.
Biography: Born 1946, Dundee, Scotland; Canadian citizenship. B.A., University of New Brunswick, 70; M.A., Stanford University Film School, 72. Films have won over 20 national and international awards: *Bravery in the Field* was nominated for an Oscar, won Silver Hugo, Chicago; *Princes in Exile* won Golden Nymph and Prix Amade at Monte Carlo, 90; *90 Days* (seen in over 40 countries) received 6 Genie nominations, Gold Plaque, Chicago, Gold Ducat, Mannheim and Gold Toucan, Rio de Janeiro; *A Good Tree* won ACTRA award for Best Children's TV, 86; *The Concert Stages of Europe* won Golden Sheaf, Yorkton, 87.
Selected Filmography: *Princes in Exile*, Th, 90, CDN, Dir; *Caddie Woodlawn*, TV, 89, USA, Dir; *The Last Straw*, Th, 87, CDN, Dir/Co-Wr/Co-Prod; *90 Days*, Th,

85, CDN, Dir/Co-Wr/Co-Prod; *Jack of Hearts*, "Bell Canada Playhouse", TV, 85, CDN, Dir/Co-Wr/Co-Prod; *The Concert Stages of Europe/A Good Tree*, "Bell Canada Playhouse", TV, 84, CDN, Dir; *The Masculine Mystique*, Th, 83, CDN, Co-Dir/Co-Wr, Co-Prod; *Harvest*, "For the Record", TV, 80, CDN, Dir; *Twice Upon A Time*, Th, 79, CDN, Dir; *Bravery in the Field*, TV, 78, CDN, Dir/Co-Wr, (GENIE); *I Wasn't Scared*, TV, 77, CDN, Dir/Co-Wr; *Descent*, Th, 75, CDN, Dir.

WALKER, John
CSC. 730 Euclid Ave., Toronto, ON M6G 2T9 (416)531-5252. 490 Adelaide St. W., #304, Toronto, ON M5V 1T2 (416)368-1338. FAX: 362-3608.
Type of Production and Credits: Th Film-Prod/Dir; Th Short-DOP; TV Film-Dir/DOP.
Genres: Drama-Th; Musical-TV; Documentary-Th&TV; Children's-TV.
Biography: Born 1952, Montreal, Quebec. Has had many photographic exhibitions of his work and received numerous Canada and Ontario Arts Council grants. *Chambers - Tracks and Gestures* won several awards including CFTA, Golden Sheaf at Yorkton and Blue Ribbon at the American Film Festival; *On to the Polar Sea: A Yukon Adventure* also won a Golden Sheaf at Yorkton, and was nominated for a CSC award; *Making Overtures* was nominated for a Gemini, 1986; *Whalesong* received a Gemini nomination, 1988; *Strand - Under the Dark Cloth* won a Genie, 1990, for Best Feature Documentary.
Selected Filmography: *Distress Signal*, TV, 90; *Leningradskaya: A Village in South Russia*, "The Hand of Stalin", TV, 90, GB/CDN, Dir; *Leningrad*, "The Hand of Stalin", TV, 90, GB/CDN, Dir; *Strand - Under a Dark Cloth*, Th/TV, 89, CDN, Prod/Dir; *Winter Tan*, Th, 87, CDN, Co-Prod/Co-Dir/Dir; *Calling the Shots*, Th, 87, CDN, DOP; *Blue Snake*, TV, 85, CDN, DOP, (CSC); *A Fragile Tree Has Roots*, TV, 84, CDN, Dir/DOP, (GEMINI 86); *Making Overtures*, TV, 84, CDN, DOP; *America and Lewis Hine*, TV, 83, USA, DOP; *On to the Polar Sea: A Yukon Adventure*, TV, 83, CDN, DOP; *Chambers: Tracks and Gestures*, TV, 82, CDN, Dir/Cin, (CSC); *Acid Rain: Requiem or Recovery*, TV, 81, CDN, DOP; "The World's Children" (7 eps), TV, 80, CDN, DOP; *Song for a Miner*, Th, 75, CDN, DOP.

WALTON, Lloyd A.
- see PRODUCERS

WARREN, Mark
AFTRA, DGA. 3528 10th Ave., Los Angeles, CA 90018 Mew Prod./BNW Prod. Consultants, 1954 Roscomare Rd., Los Angeles, CA 90024 USA (213)476-1462. Sue Goldin Talent, 6380 Wilshire Blvd., #1600, Los Angeles, CA 90048 USA (213)852-1441.
Type of Production and Credits: Th Film-Dir; TV Film-Dir/Prod; TV Video-Dir/Prod.
Genres: Drama-Th&TV; Comedy-Th&TV; Variety-TV; Action-TV.
Biography: Born 1938. Directed and/or produced "Juliette," "In Person," "The World of Music," CBC, 62-68; TV series and specials in the US. NAACP Image Award winner for "The New Bill Cosby Show;" LAPD Commendation for "Get Christie Love."

WATSON, John
- see PRODUCERS

WATT, Michael
CTPDA. 3805 Hamber Place, North Vancouver, BC V7G 2K2 (604)929-5534. Michael Watt Productions, 3805 Hamber Place, North Vancouver, BC V7G 2K2 (604)929-7124.
Type of Production and Credits: TV Video-Dir.
Genres: Comedy-TV; Variety-TV; Musical-TV; Music Video-TV.
Biography: Born in 1948 in Vancouver, British Columbia. Member of the American Federation of Musicians for 24 years. Can work in Canada or the US (green card).
Selected Filmography: "The Tommy Hunter Show" (26 eps), TV, 89-90, CDN, Dir; *The Canadian Country Music Awards*, TV, 87-90, CDN, Dir; *The 1990 Genie Awards*, TV, 90, CDN, Dir; *Mike MacDonald On Target*, TV, 90, CDN/USA, Dir; *The 1989 Gemini Awards*, TV, 89, CDN, Dir; "Talkabout" (260 eps), 88-89, CDN/USA, Dir; "Pilot 1" (11 eps), TV, 89, CDN, Dir; "Secret Lives" (130 eps), TV, 88-89, CDN/USA, Dir; *Colin James: 5 Long Years*, TV, 88, CDN, Dir; "Lingo" (70 Eps), TV, 88, CDN/USA, Dir; "5-4-3-2-Run" (17 eps), TV, 88, CDN/USA, Dir; *XV Olympic Games*, TV, 88, CDN, Dir; *The Vancouver Awards*, TV, 87-88, CDN, Dir; "Fifteen" (13 eps), TV, 87, CDN/USA, Dir; *Jerry Lee Lewis in Concert*, TV, 87, CDN/USA, Dir.

WAXMAN, Al
ACTRA, DGA, DGC, DAG, ACCT. The Brillstein Co., 9200 Sunset Blvd., Suite 428, Los Angeles, CA 90069 USA

(213)275-6135. Catherine McCartney Enterprises, Toronto, Canada. Harris & Goldbert, 2121 Avenue of the Stars, Suite 950, Los Angeles, CA, USA 90067 (213)553-5200.
Type of Production and Credits: Th Film-Dir/Act; TV Film-Dir/Act; TV Video-Dir/Act.
Genres: Drama-Th&TV; Comedy-Th&TV; Action-Th&TV.
Biography: Born 1935, Toronto, Ontario. B.A., University of Western Ontario; London School of Film Technique, England; Neighborhood Playhouse School of Theatre, N.Y.; Actors Studio, N.Y.; N.Y. School of Motion Picture Production. Has directed over 100 episodic TV shows, theatrical features and shorts, commercials, documentaries and industrials. Has acted in over 300 TV shows and features films. Chairman, Academy of Canadian Cinema and Television, 88-91. Awarded the Queen's Silver Jubilee Medal; Luminous Award from American Women in Film, 86; Nancy Susan Reynold Award, 88; Scott Newman Award, 90.
Selected Filmography: *White Light*, Th, USA, 90, Dir; *Maggie's Secret*, TV, 90, USA, Dir; *Diamond Fleece*, 90-91, USA, Dir; *Scream of Stone*, Th, 90-91, USA, Act; *Hit Man*, Th, 91, USA, Act; "Cagney and Lacy" (120 eps) (Dir 7 eps), TV, 81-88, USA, Act; "King of Kensington" (111 eps), TV, 75-80, CDN, Act.

WEINSTEIN, Larry
CFTA, ACCT, CIFC. 134 Hogarth Ave., Toronto, ON M4K 1K5 (416)466-3672. Rhombus Media Inc., 339 King St. W., Suite 102, Toronto, ON M5V 1L3 (416)971-7856. FAX: 971-9647.
Type of Production and Credits: Th Short-Dir/Prod; TV Film-Dir/Prod; TV Video-Dir.
Genres: Musical-Th&TV; Documentary-Th&TV; Variety-TV; Educational-TV.
Biography: Born 1956, Toronto, Ontario. Canadian and US citizenship. Honours B.F.A., Film, York University. Formed Rhombus Media, 79, with Niv Fichman and Barbara Willis Sweete. Past Chairman, Board of Canadian Filmmakers' Distribution Centre. Winner of several awards, including Quebec-Alberta, Banff, San Francisco, Yorkton, Birmingham, Australia, New York, Oakland, Houston, as well as Oscar, Emmy nominations.
Selected Filmography: *When the Fire Burns: The Life and Music of Manuel de Falla*, TV, 91, CDN/E/GB/NL/SF/DK/S/NOR, Dir/Wr/Prod; *Master Peter's Puppet Show*, TV, 91, CDN/E/GB/NL/SF/DK/S/NOR, Dir/Wr/Prod; *Nights in the Garden of Spain*, TV, 91, CDN/E/GB/NL/SF/DK/S/NOR, Dir/Prod; *The Radical Romantic - John Weinzweig*, TV, 89, CDN, Dir/Prod, (GEMINI 90); *For the Whales*, TV, 89, CDN, Dir/Prod; *Ravel*, TV, 88, CDN/USA/E/NL/S/NOR /DK/SF, Dir/Prod, (GEMINI 89); *A Moving Picture*, TV, 87, CDN, Prod, (GEMINI 87); *Eternal Earth*, ED, 87, CDN, Dir/Prod; *All That Bach*, TV, 85, CDN, Dir; *Making Overtures: The Story of a Community Orchestra*, TV, 84, CDN, Dir, (GEMINI 86).

WEINSTEIN, Les
- see PRODUCERS

WEINTHAL, Eric
- see WRITERS

WELDON, John ◊
(514)484-2753.
Type of Production and Credits: Th Short-Dir.
Genres: Animation-Th&TV.
Biography: Born 1945, Belleville, Ontario. Wrote *Genius Is a Four-Letter Word*, 67 (Green & Gold Revue); *Pipkin Papers*, a comic book, 69. NFB animation department, 70-86. Developed Weldon Animaster System, computer animation software. *Real Inside* won a Silver Hugo, Chicago.
Selected Filmography: *Of Dice and Men*, Th, 88, CDN, Dir; *Giordano*, "Charter", TV, 85, CDN, Wr; *Elephantrio*, TV, 85, CDN, Co-Dir; *Piece of the Action*, TV, 84, CDN, Co-Dir; *Real Inside*, Th, 84, CDN, Co-Dir; *Ice*, "Vignettes", TV, 84, CDN, Prod; *Log Driver's Waltz*, "Vignettes", TV, 80, CDN, Dir; *Special Delivery*, Th, 79, CDN, Co-Dir, (OSCAR); *Spinnolio*, Th, 77, CDN, Dir, (CFA).

WEYMAN, Peter (Bay)
- see PRODUCERS

WHALEY, Ronald T.
- see PRODUCERS

WHEELER, Anne
ACTRA, DGC, ACCT. Wheeler Hendren Enterprises Ltd., R.R. 1, 212 Sunset Dr., Ganges, BC V0S 1E0 (604)537-9916. FAX: 537-9463.
Type of Production and Credits: Th Film-Dir/Prod/Wr/Ed; Th Short-Dir/Prod/Wr/Ed; TV Film-Dir/Prod/Wr/Ed.
Genres: Documentary-Th&TV; Drama-Th&TV; Educational-Th&TV; Children's-Th&TV.
Biography: Born 1946, Edmonton, Alberta. B.Sc., Mathematics, 67; Professional Teaching Certificate, Music, 69. Musician, Performer, Secondary

School Teacher, 69-71; co-owner, Filmwest Associates Ltd., 71-76; Freelance Filmmaker, Broadcaster, Media Instructor, Writer and Performer, 76-78; Producer/Director/Writer, NFB Northwest Studio, 78-82; Shareholder/Director, Wheeler-Hendren Enterprises Ltd., Loyalties Films Ltd., True Blue Films Ltd., Rendez-vous Films Ltd., to date. Awards include: AMPIAS for *Cowboys Don't Cry*, *Loyalties*, *A Change of Heart*, *From Bears to Bartok* and *A War Story*; Alberta-Quebec Prize (Best Direction) for *Loyalties*; numerous other awards at Houston, Creteil, Portugal, American and other film festivals. Alberta Achievement Award in Filmmaking, 88; CFTA Achievement Award, 89; Honorary Member, Women in Film, L.A. and Toronto.
Selected Filmography: *Angel Square*, Th, 89-90, CDN, Co-Wr/Dir; *Bye Bye Blues*, Th, 88-89, CDN, Wr/Dir/Prod; *Cowboys Don't Cry*, TV, 87-88, CDN, Wr/Dir/Assoc Prod; *Loyalties*, Th, 85-86, CDN/GB, Dir/Co-Prod; *To Set Our House in Order*, TV, 84, CDN, Wr/Dir; *One's A Heifer*, TV, 84, CDN, Co-Wr/Dir; *A Change of Heart*, TV, 83, CDN, Dir; *Children of Alcohol*, TV, 83, CDN, Prod; *From Bears to Bartok*, TV, 82, CDN, Prod; *A War Story*, Th, 81, CDN, Wr/Dir/Prod; *Never A Dull Moment*, TV, 79, CDN, Prod; *Teach Me to Dance*, TV, 78, CDN, Dir; *Welfare Mothers*, TV, 78, CDN, Cin; *Triangle Island*, TV, 78, CDN, Prod; *Priory: The Only Home I've Got*, Th, 77, CDN, Prod, (GENIE).

WHITE, Helene B.
CFTA, AMPIA, ACTRA. 1135 Sifton Blvd. S.W., Calgary, AB T2T 2K8 HBW Film Productions Inc., 1724 - 10 Ave. S.W., Calgary, AB T3C 0K1 (403)228-1900. FAX: 228-1110.
Type of Production and Credits: Th Short-Dir/PRod; TV Film-Dir/Prod.
Genres: Comedy-Th; Documentary-Th&TV; Educational-Th&TV.
Biography: Born Western Canada. B.F.A., Drama, University of Calgary; attended Banff Centre, Alberta College of Art, UCLA. *Lady in Motion* won Bronze Medal, New York; "Connecting," a TV series for teens, won Bronze Medal, New York and earned Finalist Status, 89 and 90, New York.
Selected Filmography: "Connecting", TV, 85/88/89, CDN, Prod/Dir/Creator; "World Class" (pilot), TV, 88, CDN, Prod/Dir; "Jr. High..." (5 eps), Th, 88, CDN, Dir/Co-Prod; *Freedom of Choice*, Th, 83, CDN, Dir/Wr; *Lady in Motion*, Th/TV, 82, CDN, Prod/Dir/Wr; *Rocky Mountain Trickle*, Th, 82, CDN, Dir/Prod.

WIELAND, Joyce
497 Queen St. E., Toronto, ON M5A 1V1 (416)366-2986.
Type of Production and Credits: Th Film-Dir/Prod/Wr/Ed.
Genres: Experimental-Th.
Biography: Born 1931, Toronto, Ontario. Studied Commercial Art, Central Technical School, toronto, 55-57. Animator, George Dunning Associates; worked in New York, 62-69; filmmaker and artist; numerous solo art and film exhibitions around the world. Received the Order of Canada, 83. Two awards for *Rat Life and Diet in America*, 3rd Independent Filmmakers Festival, New York. Subject of film *Artist on Fire*, 87.
Selected Filmography: *Peggy's Blue Skylight*, Th, 85, CDN/USA, Dir/Wr/Ed/Prod; *Birds at Sunrise*, Th, 85, CDN, Dir/Wr/Ed/Prod; *A and B in Ontario*, Th, 84, CDN, Co-Dir/Co-Wr/Co-Ed/Co-Prod; *The Far Shore*, Th, 75, CDN, Dir/Co-Wr/Co-Prod; *Solidarity*, Th, 73, CDN, Dir/Wr/Ed/Prod; *Pierre Vallières*, Th, 72, CDN, Dir/Wr/Ed/Prod; *Dripping Water*, Th, 69, USA, Co-Dir/Co-Wr/Co-Ed/Co-Prod; *La Raison avant la passion*, Th, 69, ISA. Dir/Wr/Ed/Prod; *Sailboat*, Th, 67-68, USA, Dir/Wr/Ed/Prod, *1933*, Th, 67-68, USA, Dir/Wr/Ed/Prod; *Handtinting*, Th, 67-68, USA, Dir/Wr/Ed/Prod; *Rat Life and Diet in North America*, Th, 68, USA, Dir/Wr/ Ed/Prod; *Bill's Hat*, Th, 67, USA, Dir/Wr/ Ed/Prod; *Barbara's Blindness*, Th, 67, USA, Dir/Wr/Ed/Prod; *Water Sark*, Th, 64-65, USA, Dir/Wr/Ed/Prod; *Patriotism, Part One*, Th, 64, USA, Dir/Wr/Ed/Prod; *Patriotism, Part Two*, Th, 64, USA, Dir/Wr/Ed/Prod.

WILKINSON, Charles
DGC, ACCT. Apple Pie Pictures, 617 Beachview Dr., Deep Cove, North Vancouver, BC V7G 1P8 (604)929-8280.
Type of Production and Credits: Th Film-Dir; Th Short-Dir/Wr; TV Film-Dir.
Genres: Drama-Th&TV; Documentary-Th&TV.
Biography: Born 1952, Calgary, Alberta. B.A., Film and Communications, Simon Fraser University, 77. Has won several awards as director, editor and composer; *The Little Town That Did* won Best Documentary, Northwest Film Festival, 86; *Blood Clan* won AMPIA, Best Feature, 91; "Magic Hour" won AMPIA for Best Drama Under 60 Minutes, 91.
Selected Filmography: *Blood Clan*, Th,

90, CDN, Dir, (AMPIA); *High Country*, "Magic Hour", TV, 90, CDN, Dir; "The Dragon" (24 eps), TV, 83-88, D, Co-Prod; *Quarantine*, Th, 88, CDN, Dir/Prod/Wr; "The Beachcombers" (3 eps), TV, 85-86, CDN, Dir; *My Kind of Town*, Th, 84, CDN, Dir/Wr; *The Little Town That Did*, Th, 84, CDN, Co-Prod/Wr; *Tiers...A Story of the Penitentiary*, Th, 81, CDN, Dir/Wr.

WILLIAMS, Don S. ◊
(604)929-2766.
Type of Production and Credits: Th Film-Dir; TV Film-Dir/Prod; TV Video-Dir/Prod.
Genres: Drama-Th&TV; Comedy-TV; Variety-TV; Documentary-TV.
Biography: Born 1939, Edmonton, Alberta. Stage, film and videotape director, choreographer; past President, DGC; past President and a founder of CTPDA; teacher of short courses at British Columbia Insitute of Technology (BCIT), the Film and Theatre School, Vancouver, and on tour. Winner of 2 Ohio State Awards and 2 Wilderness Awards.
Selected Filmography: *Free Enterprise*, TV, 88, CDN, Dir; *Market Forces*, TV, 87, CDN, Dir; *Harry*, TV, 87, CDN, Dir; *Punchline*, TV, 87, CDN, Dir; *Music Lessons*, TV, 87, CDN, Dir; *New Tricks*, TV, 87, CDN, Dir; "The Beachcombers", TV, 81-86, CDN, Exec Prod; *Chung Chuck*, TV, 85, CDN, Dir/Exec Prod; "Constable, Constable" (2 pilots), TV, 83, CDN, Dir/Exec Prod; "Mayonnaise" (3 pilots), TV, 83, CDN, Dir/Exec Prod; *Last Call*, TV, 83, CDN, Dir/Exec Prod; "The Bush Pilot Company" (3 pilots), TV, 83, CDN, Dir; "The Beachcombers" (30 eps), TV, 71-81, CDN, Dir; "Ritter's Cove" (7 eps), TV, 79-80, CDN, Dir; "Huckleberry Finn and His Friends" (4 eps), TV, 79, CDN, Dir.

WILLIAMS, Douglas
DGC. 98 Fulton Ave., Toronto, ON M4K 1X8 (416)423-8714.
Type of Production and Credits: TV Film-Dir; TV Video-Dir.
Genres: Drama-TV; Comedy-TV; Action-TV; Science Fiction-TV; Children's-TV.
Biography: Born Windsor, Ontario; Canadian citizenship. Languages: French and English. Fine Arts, Wayne State University, London International Film School. Writer of short stories and articles. President, Ananda Productions Inc.
Selected Filmography: "Movin' On Up" (2 eps), TV, 90, CDN, Dir; "Eric's World" (1 ep), TV, 90, CDN, Dir; "Join In" (26 eps), TV, 88-89, CDN, Dir; "The Elephant Show" (2 eps), TV, 88, CDN, Dir; "Polka Dot Door" (20 eps), TV, 88, CDN, Dir; "T and T" (1 ep), TV, 87, CDN/USA, Dir; "Captain Power" (2 eps), TV, 87, CDN/USA, Dir; "The Wee Wonders" (pilot), TV, 86, USA, Dir; *The Molson Story*, In, 86, CDN, Dir; *Overdrawn at the Memory Bank*, TV, 85, CDN, Dir; "Fraggle Rock" (4 eps), TV, 85, CDN/USA, Dir; *The Disability Myth*, TV, 85, CDN, Dir; *Art in the Corporate Environment*, In, 85, CDN, Dir; *Best of Both Worlds*, TV, 84, CDN/USA, Dir; *Jarvis Clark*, In, 83, CDN, Dir.

WILLIAMS, Roger
- see CINEMATOGRAPHERS

WILSON, Sandra ◊
(604)734-4688.
Type of Production and Credits: Th Film-Dir/Wr; Th Short-Dir/Wr; TV Film-Dir/Wr.
Genres: Drama-Th&TV; Documentary-TV; Educational-TV.
Biography: Born 1947, Penticton, BC. B.A., English and History, Simon Fraser University, 69. *My American Cousin* won International Critics' Choice Award, Festival of Festivals, Toronto, 85; won 6 Genie Awards including Best Picture, 86; *He's Not the Walking Kind* won at award at Yorkton, Blue Ribbon, New York, Chris Statuette, Columbus.
Selected Filmography: *My American Cousin*, Th, 84, CDN, Co-Prod/Wr/Dir, (2 GENIES 86); *Going All The Way*, Th, 80, CDN, Dir/Ed/Co-Prod; *Mount Chopaka Easter Sunday Jackpot Rodeo*, TV, 79, CDN, Dir; *Growing Up at Paradise*, Th, 77, CDN, Dir/Prod/Ed; *Pen-hi Grad*, Th, 74, CDN, Dir; *Raising the Gilhast Pole*, Th, 73, CDN, Dir/Ed; *He's Not the Walking Kind*, Th, 72, CDN, Dir; *The Bridal Shower*, Th, 71, CDN, Dir/Wr/Prod/Ed; *Penticton Profile*, Th, 70, CDN, Dir/Ed; *Garbage*, Th, 69, CDN, Prod/Dir/Ed.

WINEMAKER, Mark Joesph
- see PRODUCERS

WINKLER, Donald
SGCT. 3640 Clark St., Montreal, PQ H2X 2S2 NFB, Box 6100, Montreal, PQ H3C 3H5 (514)283-9495.
Type of Production and Credits: Th Short-Dir; TV Film-Dir.
Genres: Documentary-Th&TV; Educational-TV; Experimental-Th.
Biography: Born 1940, Winnipeg, Manitoba. B.A., Honours, University of Manitoba; Woodrow Wilson Fellowship; postgraduate study, Yale Drama School. Films he has directed have won numerous

award; awards at Krakow, Melbourne and Yorkton for *Travel Log.*
Selected Filmography: *Still Waters: The Poetry of P.K. Page,* TV, 90, CDN, Dir; *Winter Prophecies: The Poetry of Ralph Gustafson,* TV, 88, CDN, Dir; *Al Purdy: A Sensitive Man,* TV, 88, CDN, Dir; *Poet: Irving Layton Observed,* TV, 86, CDN, Dir; *A Tall Man Executes a Jig,* TV, 86, CDN, Dir; *The Scholar in Society: Northrop Frye in Conversation,* TV, 84, CDN, Dir; *F.R. Scott: Rhyme and Reason,* TV, 82, CDN, Dir/Wr; *Earle Birney: Portrait of a Poet,* TV, 81, CDN, Dir/Wr; *Bookmaker's Progress,* TV, 79, CDN, Dir/Wr; *Travel Log,* Th, 78, CDN, Dir/Wr/Stills; *In Praise of Hands,* TV, 74, CDN, Dir; *One Man's Garden,* TV, 74, CDN, Dir/Wr; *Bannerfilm,* Th, 72, CDN, Dir; *Doodle Film,* Th, 70, CDN, Dir/Wr/Ed.

WINKLER, Melta
3 - 314 Lonsdale Rd., Toronto, ON M4V 1X4 (416)440-0215. Musemedia Inc., 1342 Pape Ave., Toronto, ON M4K 3X2 (416)696-6123. Ray Wickens & Associates, (416)693-6404.
Type of Production and Credits: Th Short-Dir/Prod/Wr.
Genres: Drama-Th; Experimental-Th&TV; Comedy-TV; Children's-Th&TV.
Biography: Born in 1962 in Toronto, Ontario. Attended B.C.I.T., Vancouver and Vancouver Community College. 8 years of acting experience and 5 years of production experience. Specially skilled in guerilla shooting.
Selected Filmography: *Stealer,* ED, 91, CDN, Dir/Prod; *Blessed Boy,* Th, 91, CDN, 1st Assist Dir; *The Better Way,* TV, 90, CDN, Prod/Dir; *Sunday Morning Blues,* TV, 90, CDN, Dir/Prod; *The Muse,* Th, 90, CDN, Wr/Dir.

WINNING, David
Groundstar Entertainment Corp., 918 - 16 Ave. N.W., Suite 4001, Calgary, AB T2M 0K3 (403)284-2889. FAX: 282-7797.
Type of Production and Credits: Th Film-Dir/Prod/Wr; Th Short-Dir/Wr; TV Video-Dir.
Genres: Drama-Th; Comedy-TV; Action-TV; Horror-Th.
Biography: Born 1961, Calgary, Alberta. Award-winning film and television director. Three nominations for Best Director, 1989/90 Gemini Awards; two Silver Hugo Awards, Chicago International Film Festival; *Storm* received five AMPIA awards including Best of Festival and was New York Festival finalist, 91. Currently directing for Paramount.
Selected Filmography: *Killer Image,* Th, 91, CDN, Prod/Dir/Wr; "Friday the 13th: The Series" (3 eps), TV, 89-90, CDN/USA, Dir; *Storm,* Th, 87, CDN, Prod/Dir/Wr; *Storm: In the Making,* TV, 85, CDN, Prod; "Profile" (25 eps), TV, 82, CDN, Dir; "All Star Comedy" (pilot), TV, 82, CDN, Dir/Act; *Rat Patrol,* Cm, 80, CDN, Dir/Wr; *Sequence,* Th, 80, CDN, Dir/Wr; *In Search of the Last Frame,* Th, 78, CDN, Prod/Wr; *Game Over,* Th, 78, CDN, Dir/Wr; *The Visitors,* Th, 77, CDN, Dir/Wr; *Return,* Th, 76, CDN, Dir/Wr; *Canadian Ski Patrol,* Th, 76, CDN, Prod.

WINTONICK, Peter
- see EDITORS

WODOSLAWSKY, Stefan
- see PRODUCERS

WOLOSCHUK, Walter
see - PRODUCERS

WOODLAND, James
- see WRITERS

WRIGHT, Charles R.D. R.
- see PRODUCERS

WRONSKI, Peter
DGC. Via Trezzo, 42A, Mestre, Venice, Italy, (041)610-034. Ocean Corporation, 686 Richmond St. W., Main Floor, Toronto, ON M6J 1C3 (416)363-4051. Joanne Smale Production, 686 Richmond St. W., Main Floor, Toronto, ON M6J 1C3 (416)363-4051.
Type of Production and Credits: Th Film-Dir/Wr/Prod; TV Film-Dir/Wr/Prod; TV Video-Dir/Wr/Prod.
Genres: Drama-Th&TV; Action-Th&TV; Documentary-Th&TV; Music Video-Th&TV.
Biography: Born in 1956 in Toronto, Ontario. Languages: English, Russian and Italian. Studied History and Economics, Trinity College, University of Toronto. Freelance work on "W-5" and "the fifth estate". Artist-In-Residence, Sony Corporation, 1983. Assigned to Rome Bureau, CNN (Cable News Network), 1986. President, Ocean Corporation.
Selected Filmography: *Sorcerer's Apprentice: The Secret Life of Lee Harvey Oswald,* Th, 91, CDN/USR/I, Wr/Dir/Prod; *Mondo Moscow,* TV, 91, CDN/I, Wr/Prod/Dir; *Russian Rock Underground,* TV, 88, CDN/I, Dir.

XALIMAN, Don ✧
(604)255-4575.
Type of Production and Credits: TV Video-Prod/Dir/Wr/Comp.
Genres: Experimental-Th&TV; Music Video-TV; Animation-Th&TV.
Biography: Born 1950, Vancouver, BC. Mainly a composer of music that has a

visual dimension. Special FX photography and electronic-generated imagery. Has also worked with theatrical and projected-lighting effects.
Selected Filmography: *Haida Warrior*, TV, 87, CDN, Wr/Art Dir; *NORKARA*, MV, 82, CND, Prod/Dir; *Crossing the Sacred Seas*, MV, 81, CDN, Comp/Art Dir.

YALDEN-THOMSON, Peter
83 Langley Ave., Toronto, ON M4K 1B4 (416)466-6630. The Core Group, 489 College St., Toronto, ON M6G 1A5 (416)944-0193.
Type of Production and Credits: Th Short-Dir; TV Film-Dir; TV Video-Dir.
Genres: Drama-TV; Action-TV; Commercials-TV; Industrial-Th&TV.
Biography: Born Cleveland, Ohio; Canadian citizenship. Languages: French, Spanish and English. Education: McGill University, Bethany College, Universidad de Salamanca, Western Reserve University. Has won several commercial awards including Bessies in various categories, Best Canadian Commercial Director, Clios; recognition in Osaka, Hollywood, Chicago, Virgin Islands, and other places. Various special projects including multi-image/multi-screen spectacle for the SkyDome and a 90 minute mime special for CBC French Network. Co-writer of various scripts including *God Loves Ya, Jesse* which is currently in development.
Selected Filmography: *Shellgame*, "Street Legal" (pilot), TV, 85, CDN, Dir; *Tools of the Devil/Rough Justice*, "For the Record", TV, 83-84, CDN, Dir; *Clowns of Christmas*, TV, 80, CDN, Dir; *Four to Four*, TV, 78, CDN, Dir; *Race Home to Die*, Th, 72, CDN, Co-Wr.

YATES, Rebecca
- see PRODUCERS

YOLLES, Edie
CSC, ACCT, ACTRA, CFTPA. Gemini Film Productions Ltd., 163 Queen St. E., Suite 200, Toronto, ON M5A 1S1 (416)862-9031.
Type of Production and Credits: Th Film-Dir/Prod/Wr/Ed; TV Film-Dir/Prod/Wr/Ed.
Genres: Drama-Th&TV; Comedy-Th&TV; Documentary-Th&TV; Educational-Th&TV.
Biography: Honours B.A.A., Film and Photography, Ryerson Polytechnical Institute; Gold Medal and Honours B.A. in Sociology, University of Toronto; Diploma, Town Planning, University of Toronto; Painting and Sculpture, Ontario College of Art. *That's My Baby!* won Finalist Award, Int'l Film and TV Festival, 2 Genie nominations (Best Actress, Best Sound); *Angels* won Red Ribbon, American Film Festival, Chris Statuette, Columbus, Gold Medal (MIFED), Milan International Competi-tion, Gold Medal, International Film and TV Festival.
Selected Filmography: *That's My Baby!*, Th, 82, CDN, Prod/Co-Dir/Co-Ed/Co-Wr; *Angels*, TV, 79, CDN, Dir/Ed/Prod.

YOUNG, Stephen ✧
(604)385-2480.
Type of Production and Credits: TV Film-Prod/Dir; TV Video-Prod/Dir.
Genres: Drama-TV; Documentary-TV; Educational-Th&TV; Children's-TV.
Biography: Born 1943, England; came to Canada in 56. Began career in broad-casting, 62; has been involved with several aspects of the industry, including sales, marketing and producing.
Selected Filmography: *Root Rot Disease*, In, 85, CDN, Prod; *Canada-British Columbia F.R.D.A./Decisions*, ED, 85, CDN, Prod; *Working Well*, In, 85, CDN, Prod/Dir; *Oly's*, Cm, 85, CND, Prod/Dir; *Treasure Hunters*, TV, 85, CDN, Tech Dir; Woodgrove Centre/Qualicum Inn/U.I. Ford Mrecury, Cm, 83-84, CDN, Dir; *Death from Sex*, MV, 84, CND, Dir; *Scrapbook*, TV, 83, CDN, Dir; Tom Harris Chev-Olds/Beach Garden Resort/Granite Industries, Cm, 80-83, CDN, Dir; *David Barrett: Address to the Province*, TV, 82, CDN, Dir.

ZALOUM, Alain
- see WRITERS

ZARITSKY, John
ACCT. K.A. Productions Inc., 49 Cavell Ave., Toronto, ON M4J 1H5 (416)466-8202.
Type of Production and Credits: Th Film-Dir/Prod; TV Film-Dir/Prod/Wr.
Genres: Drama-TV; Variety-Th&TV; Documentary-TV.
Biography: Born 1943, St. Catharines, Ontario. Langugages: English and French. B.A., University of Toronto. National Newspaper Award, 70; Ford Foundation Fellowship, Washington Journalism Centre, 70. Awards for *Just Another Missing Kid* include Gold Medal, NY; Gold Medal, Hemisfilm; Rocky, Banff; Blue Ribbon, American Film Festival; *I'll Get There Somehow* won the Wilderness Award, Bronze Plaque, Columbus; *Rapists: Can They Be Stopped?* won ACE Award, Best Information Special, Academy Cable Broadcasting, 87; *The Real Stuff* won Bronze Award, Columbus, 87.

Selected Filmography: *My Doctor, My Lover*, "Frontline", TV, 91, USA, Dir/Wr; *Born in Africa*, "Frontline", TV, 90, USA, Dir/Wr, (2 GEMINIS); *Extraordinary People*, "Frontline", TV, 89, USA, Dir/Wr; *My Husband Is Going to Kill Me*, "Frontline", TV, 88, USA, Dir/Co-Prod/Wr; *Broken Promises*, TV, 88, CDN, Dir/Wr; *The Real Stuff*, TV, 86, CDN, Exec Prod/Prod/Dir/Wr; *Tears Are Not Enough*, Th, 85, CDN, Dir/Prod; *Rapists: Can They Be Stopped?*, "America Undercover", TV, 85, USA/CDN, Dir/Prod/Wr; *The Boy Next Door*, "For the Record", TV, 84, CDN, Prod; *I'll Get There Somehow*, TV, 84, CDN, Dir/Prod/Wr; *Bjorn Borg*, "Champions", TV, 83, CDN, Dir/Prod/Wr; *Just Another Missing Kid*, "the fifth estate", TV, 81, CDN, Dir/Prod/Wr, (ACTRA, OSCAR); *Caring for Chrysler/Charity Begins At Home/The Loser's Gam*, "the fifth estate", TV, 77-80, CDN, Dir/Prod/Wr; *Gord S./I Did Not Kill Bob/Betsy's Last Chance*, "the fifth estate, TV, 76-78, CDN, Dir/Prod/Wr; *The Making of a Martyr/Steeltown Star*, "the fifth estate", TV, 76, CDN, Dir/Prod/Wr.

ZELDIN, Toby
- see WRITERS

ZEMLA, Ed
The Annex Studios Ltd., 174 Bedford Rd., Toronto, ON M5R 2K9 (416)922-7100. FAX: 922-0548.
Type of Production and Credits: Th Short-Dir; TV Film-Dir.
Genres: Commercials-Th&TV; Industrial-Th; Music Video-TV; Sports-TV.
Biography: Born 1939, Windsor, Ontario. Languages: English and Polish. B.A.; 2 years at Royal Academy of Dramatic Arts, London. Worked and trained in film business in London for 7 years; started own production house in Canada, 71; director for 14 years with awards including: NY, Hollywood Radio and TV Festival, NY Art Directors', Clios and several Bessies, including Best of Show. Now principally directs commercials.

ZIELINSKA, Ida Eva
- see WRITERS

ZIELINSKI, Rafal
Neo Modern Entertainment Corp., 8033 Sunset Blvd., Suite 640, Hollywood, CA 9046 (213)650-1642. FAX: 650-1642.
Type of Production and Credits: Th Film-Dir; TV Film-Dir.
Genres: Drama-Th; Comedy-Th; Action-Th.
Biography: Born 1957, Warsaw, Poland. Studied and lived in US, Europe, Middle East and India. B.Sc., Art and Design, Massachusetts Institute of Technology, 74. Directed and produced commercials, Montreal. Michel Pellus was entry at Cannes, 79; won Silver Medal, Australian Film Festival.
Selected Filmography: *Under Surveillance*, Th, 91, USA, Dir; "Veronica Claire" (1 eps), TV, 91, USA, Dir; *Night of the Warrior*, Th, 90, USA, Dir; *Ginger Ale Afternoon*, Th, 89, Dir/Prod; *Screwball Hotel*, Th, 88, USA, Dir; *State Park*, Th, 87, USA, Dir; *Spellcaster*, Th, 86, USA, Dir; *Valet Girls*, Th, 86, USA, Dir; *Recruits*, Th, 85, USA, Dir; *Loose Screws*, Th, 84, USA, Dir; *Breaking All the Rules*, Th, 84, USA, Co-Wr; *Screwballs*, Th, 83, USA, Dir.

Editors
Monteurs

ADAMAKOS, Peter
- see PRODUCERS

APPLEBY, George
DGC, IATSE 891, ACCT. 3536 West 28 Ave., Vancouver, BC V6S 1S1 (604)733-8159.
Type of Production and Credits: Th Film-Ed; TV Film-Ed/Dir; TV Video-Ed/Dir.
Genres: Drama-Th&TV.
Biography: Born 1939, Toronto, Ontario; grew up in South America. Languages: English and Spanish. Honorary life member DGC and ACCT.
Selected Filmography: "Neon Rider" (21 eps), TV, 89-91, CDN, Ed; *Girl from Mars*, TV, 90-91, CDN/USA, Ed; "Adventures of the Black Stallion" (13 eps), TV, 90, CDN/USA, Ed; *Neon Rider*, TV, 90, CDN, Ed.

ARCAND, Michel
SNTT. 377, rue Murray, Greenfield Park, PQ J4V 1N6 (514)466-5369. (514)951-2004.
Types de production et générique: l métrage-Mont/Comp; c métrage-Mont/Comp; TV film-Mont/Comp; TV vidéo-Mont/Comp.
Types d'oeuvres: Drame-C&TV; Action-C&TV; Documentaire-C&TV; Enfants-TV; Expérimental-C&TV; Annonces-TV; Vidéo-Clips-TV; Comédie-TV
Curriculum vitae: Né en 1949, Val d'Or (Abitibi), Québec. Langues: français et anglais. Sciences humaines, Cégep. Prix Gémeaux, "Lance et Compte"; Prix Génie, *Un Zoo la Nuit*; 3 étoiles CMAS, *Plongée sous-marine*.
Filmographie sélective: *Amoureux Fou*, C,

424 Adelaide St. E., 2nd Floor, Toronto M5A 1N4
Telephone (416) 368-9925

91, CDN, Mont/Dir p pro; *Love Moi*, C, 90, CDN, Mont; *Moody Beach*, C, 90, CDN, Mont; *Le Party*, C, 90, CDN, Mont; *Cruising Bar*, C, 90, CDN, Mont; *La nuit du visiteur*, C, 90, CDN, Comp; *67° Nord*, TV, 90, CDN, Comp; *Un zoo la nuit*, C, 89, CDN, Mont, (GENIE); *A corps perdue*, C, 89, CDN, Mont; "Lance & Compte II", TV, 89, CDN/F, Mont, (GEMEAUX); *La Guèpe*, C, 88, CDN, Mont; *Exit*, C, 88, CDN, Mont/Mont son; *Night Magic*, C, 88, CND/F, Mont; *Maria Chapdeleine*, C/TV, CDN, Mont; *La femme de l'hôtel*, C, 87, CDN, Mont.

AUCKLAND, Geoff
SMPIA. 1806 Wiggins Ave. S., Saskatoon, SK S7H 2K2 (306)956-3013. Cinepost Productions, 1937 Ontario Avenue, Saskatoon, SK S7K 1T5 (306)244-2288.
Type of Production and Credits: TV Film-Ed; TV Video-Ed.
Genres: Commercials-TV; Industrial-TV.
Biography: Born in 1960 in Regina, Saskatchewan. Canadian citizen. Editor of over 200 local commercials and provincial commercials and industrial videos. Edited two half-hour television series running province-wide. Awards include two Saskatchewan Showcase Best Commercial awards, a Saskatchewan Showcase award for Best Editing and a Bronze Bessie award.
Selected Filmography: *Winter Seasoned*, TV, 90-91, CDN, Ed; *Knowing Each Other*, TV, 90-91, CDN, Ed; *In Perfect Harmony*, TV, 90, CDN, Assist Ed; *Take a Vacation In Your Own Backyard*, Tourism vignettes, (11 spots), TV, 91, CDN, Ed; *Lightbridge*, In, 91, CDN, Ed; *New Kids on the Farm*, In, 91, CDN, Ed; Community Bonds (12 spots), Cm, 90-91, CDN, Ed; United Way (3 spots), Cm, 90, CDN, Ed.

AUDY, Michel
- voir REALISATEURS

BACKUS, Barry
- see POSTPRODUCTION SOUND MIXERS

BAKER, Bob
- see DIRECTORS

BALSER, Dean
DGC, ACCT. 21 Elmer Ave., Toronto, ON M4L 3R6 (416)699-3678. XTO Productions Ltd., 21 Elmer Ave., Toronto, ON M4L 3R6 (416)520-3897.
Type of Production and Credits: TV Film-Ed; TV Video-Ed.
Genres: Drama-TV; Action-TV; Comedy-TV; Variety-TV.
Biography: Born in Wingham, Ontario. Canadian citizen. 22 years production experience. Was regular editor on "Night Heat". Series was best drama and most popular Canadian show. Has worked on prime time shows for all major networks. Now edits with laser-optical disks, from any original medium.
Selected Filmography: "Top Cops" (16 eps), TV, 90-91, USA/CDN, Ed; "Counterstrike" (2 eps), TV, 90, USA/CDN/F, Ed; "True Blue" (6 eps), TV, 89-90, USA, Ed; "Diamonds" (14 eps), TV, 88-90, USA/CDN/F, Ed; "Night Heat" (30 eps), TV, 84-88, USA/CDN, Ed; "Hot Shots" (6 eps), TV, 86, USA/CDN, Ed; "The Campbells" (3 eps), TV, 86, CDN/GB, Ed; "The Comedy Factory" (4 eps), TV, 85, USA/CDN, Ed; "Littlest Hobo" (30 eps), TV, 81-84, CDN, Ed; "Just Kidding" (22 eps), TV, 83, CDN, Ed; "The Magic of David Copperfield" (1 eps), TV, 81, USA/CDN, Ed; "Circus" (40 eps), TV, 77-80, CDN, Ed; "Evening at the Improv" (8 eps), TV, 80, USA, Ed; "Grand Ol' Country" (26 eps), TV, 79-80, CDN, Ed; "Stars on Ice" (26 eps), TV, 79, CDN, Ed.

BARCLAY, John
- see DIRECTORS
BARRIE, Scott
- see WRITERS
BATTISTA, Franco
- see PRODUCERS
BAUMAN, Larry
- see DIRECTORS

BEAUDOIN, Jean
4577, av. Hingston, Montréal, PQ H4A 2K2 (514)488-6081. Baude Films, 5169, av. King Edward, Montréal, PQ H4V 2J8 (514)488-1855.
Types de production et générique: l métrage-Mont; c métrage-Réal/Mont; TV film-Mont/Réal; TV vidéo-Réal/Mont/Sc.
Types d'oeuvres: Comédie-C&TV; Action-C&TV; Docu-mentaire-C&TV; Drame-C&TV.
Curriculum vitae: Né en 1959, Drummondville, Québec. Langues: français, anglais et connaissance usuelle de l'espagnol. D.E.C., études en lettres, 78. Autodidacte, produit et réalise des courts métrages dès 73. Fonde Baude Films inc. en 1985, compagnie oeuvrant dans le domaine cinématographique et télévisuel.
Filmographie sélective: "Urban Angel" (4 eps), TV, 91, CDN, Mont; *Persona Non Grata*, "Madame", M, 91, CDN, Mont; *Chauffeur, tu es toute ma vie*, TV, 91, CDN, Réal; *Milena*, C, 90, CDN/F, Mont; *The Secret of Nandy*, TV, 90, CDN/F, Mont; *Doubles-Jeux*, TV, 90, CDN, Mont; *The Journey Home*, C, 90, CDN, Mont; *Guetteurs des saisons*, TV, 90, CDN, Prod/Mont; *La force de la paix*, TV,

90, CDN, Réal/Mont; *Dracula: Live from Transylvania*, TV, 89, CDN/USA, Mont; *The Thriller*, TV, 89, CDN, Mont; *The Phone Call*, TV, 89, CDN, Mont; *Challenge and Commitment: Canada in NATO*, TV, 89, CDN, Réal/Mont.

BELANGER, Fernand
- voir REALISATEURS

BERGERON, Guy
- voir PRODUCTEURS

BJORNSON, Michelle
- see WRITERS

BOCKING, Robert V.
- see CINEMATOGRAPHERS

BOISVERT, Dominique
DGC. 3371 Jean-Brillant, #306, Montréal, PQ H3T 1N9 (514)731-0919.
Type of Production and Credits: Th Film-Ed/Snd Ed; TV Film-Ed; TV Video-ED.
Genres: Drama-Th&TV; Documentary-TV; Educational-TV; Commercials-TV.
Biography: Born in 1946 in Montréal, Québec. Fluently bilingual. Joined pioneering shooting crews in the sixties. Attended the National Theatre School in 1967. Became freelance editor in 1971. Award for education film, Boston Festival, 1973. Award from 'Les Rendez-vous d'Automne', 1981.
Selected Filmography: Loto-Québec, Cm, 90, CDN, Ed; *Mike's Pan-Pizza*, Cm, 90, CDN, Ed; *Prinivil*, ED, 90, CDN, Ed; *Whispers*, Th, 90, CDN/USA, Snd Ed; *Le cratère du Nouveau-Québec*, TV, 89, CDN, Ed; *Snakeeater II*, Th, 89, CDN/USA, Snd Ed; *S.A.R.A.*, In, 89, CDN, Wr/Ed; *Vive la banlieue*, TV, 88, CDN, Ed; "Lance et Compte II", TV, 87, CDN, Ed; *Black Mirror*, Th, 82, CDN/USA, Ed; *C'est pour Mathieu*, Th/TV, 81, CDN, Ed/Dir; *Jeanius Jeans*, Cm, 80, CDN, Dir; *Hog Wild*, Th, 79, CDN, Ed; *La Belle de Cassis*, TV, 79, CDN/F, Ed/Wr; *Phillips Milk of Magnesia*, Cm, 78, CDN, Dir.

BOND, Richard
DGC, CIFC. Bondfast Productions Inc., 92 Stafford St., Toronto, ON M6J 2S1 (416)361-5950.
Type of Production and Credits: Th Film-Ed/Snd Ed; TV Film-Ed/Snd Ed.
Genres: Drama-Th&TV; Documentary-Th&TV; Animation-Th&TV; Action-Th.
Biography: Born in 1956 in Stettler, Alberta. Canadian citizen. English speaking with limited French and Italian. Bachelor of Applied Arts, Motion Picture Studies, Ryerson. In the process of producing a one hour documentary on a Canadian painter living in Italy. Planning to produce more. Was Co-editor on *H*, which won the 1990 Festival of Festivals Best Canadian Feature Award.
Selected Filmography: "Rupert the Bear" (13 eps), TV, 91, GB/CDN, Ed; "Tin Tin" (13 eps), TV, 91, F/CDN, Ed; "Babar" (30 eps), TV, F/CDN, Ed; "Little Rosey" (13 eps), 90, USA/CDN, Ed; "Beetlejuice" (22 eps), TV, 89-90, USA/CDN, Ed; *H*, Th, 89, CDN, Co Ed; *A Whisper To A Scream*, Th, 89, CDN, Ed/Snd Ed; "Degrassi Junior High" (4 eps), TV, 86-88, CDN, Ed; "Degrassi Junior High" (11 eps), TV, 86-88, CDN, Snd Ed; *Care Bears 3: Adventures in Wonderland*, Th, 87, CDN/USA, Dial Ed; *Droids: The Great Heep*, TV, 86, CDN/USA, Dial Ed; *Care Bears 2: A New Generation*, Th, 86, CDN/USA, Dial Ed; "Ewoks" (13 eps), TV, 85-86, CDN/USA, Dial Ed; "Droids" (13 eps), TV, 85-86, CDN/USA, Dial Ed.

BOURASSA-DUTTON, John
- see DIRECTORS

BRASIER, Fabrice
ACCT. 874, rue Des Colibris, Longueuil, PQ J4G 2C4 (514)442-2193. Télé-Métropole Inc., 1600, boulevard de Maisonneuve est, Montréal, PQ H2L 4P2 (514)598-2863.
Types de production et générique: TV vidéo-Réd en chef/Prod.
Types d'oeuvres: Documentaire-TV; Affaires Publiques-TV; Nouvelles-TV.
Curriculum vitae: Né à Châlons-Sur Marne (France). Citoyenneté canadienne et française. Langues: anglais et français. Bacc. science politique (relations int'l.), Maîtrise science politique, Université du Québec à Montréal, D.E.A. (3ème cycle) études politiques(Université de Nancy, France). Prix CanPro 1990-1991 (*Le Match de la Vie*), Prix Gémeaux 1990 (*Le Match de la Vie*), Prix de l'association nationale des téléspectateurs du Québec (*Le Match de la Vie*), Prix Canada-Europe 1983 (prix universitaire).
Filmographie sélective: "Le Match de la Vie" (74 eps), TV, 89-91, CDN, Réd en chef/Prod; *Commission Bélanger Campeau*, TV, 91, CDN, Réd en chef; *Crise d'Octobre: 20 Ans Après*, TV, 90, CDN, Prod.

BREDIN, James
DGC. 2 Boulton Ave., Ste. 9, Toronto, ON M4M 2J3 (416)463-4782.
Type of Production and Credits: Th Film-Assist Ed; TV Film-Ed; TV Video-Ed.
Genres: Drama-Th&TV; Documentary-TV; Industrial-TV; Music Video-TV.
Biography: Born in 1957 in Calgary,

Alberta. Attended TSR program at Southern Alberta Institute of Technology (SAIT) for one year. B.F.A. (Hons.) in film production from York University. Charter member of the Rocky Alpine Free Athletic Club. Member of the Board of Directors, Ontario Seventh Step Society.
Selected Filmography: *Hidden Room*, TV, 91, Ed; "Sweating Bullets", TV, 90-91, CDN/USA/MEX, Ed; "The Hitchiker", TV, 90, CDN/US/F, Ed; *CIBC - "On the Line"*, In, 90, CDN, Ed; "Live It Up" (13 eps), TV, 86-88, CDN, Ed; "The Canadians" (2 eps), TV, 87, CDN, Ed.

BRONSARD, Louis
- see DIRECTORS

BROWN, Barbara
- see WRITERS

BROWNE, Colin
- see DIRECTORS

BRUNJES, Ralph
DGC, ACCT. 26 Brownstone Circle, Thornhill, ON L4J 7P4 (416)881-6770. Inverclyde Film Prods. Ltd., 79 Berkeley St., Toronto, ON (416)941-9412.
Type of Production and Credits: Th Film-Ed; TV Film-Ed; TV Video-Ed.
Genres: Drama-Th&TV; Comedy-Th&TV; Action-Th&TV.
Biography: Born in Dunoon, Scotland; Canadian citizenship. Twenty-seven years film editing experience; credits on numerous dramas, features, documentaries and specials. Winner of many awards for film and sound editing.
Selected Filmography: *To Catch a Killer* (mini-series), TV, 91, CDN/USA, Ed; *Conspiracy of Silence* (mini-series), TV, 91, CDN, Ed; *The Bruce Curtis Story: Journey Into Darkness*, TV, 90, CDN, Ed; *Defence of a Married Man*, TV, 90, USA, Ed; "African Journey" (3 eps), TV, 89, CDN/USA, Spv Ed; *Tom Alone*, TV, 89, CDN, USA, Ed; "The Challengers", TV, 89, CDN, Ed; "The Twilight Zone" (30 eps), TV, 88, CDN/USA, Spv Ed; *Hoover vs the Kennedys: The Second Civil War* (mini-series), TV, 87, CDN/USA, Ed; *Glory Enough For All* (mini-series), TV, 87, CDN/UK, Ed; *Cursed with Charisma*, "Really Weird Tales", TV, 86, CDN, Ed, (ACE); "Oakmount High", TV, 85, CDN, Ed, (GEMINI, 86); *The Playground*, "Ray Bradbury Theatre", TV, 85, CDN, Ed, (GEMINI, 86); "Love & Larceny", TV, 84, CDN, Ed; *Cries in the Night*, Th, 80, CDN, Ed, (CFEG).

BUCHAN, Bob◊
(416)698-4815.
Genres: Commercials-TV.
Biography: Born in 1947. 18 years experience in film: feature, drama, documentary, 70-89; edited and directed mostly commercials and short films since 75.

BUSH, Bert
SMPTE. Bush Edit House, P.O. Box 86352, North Vancouver, BC V7L 4K6 (604)987-5115.
Type of Production and Credits: TV Film-Ed; TV Video-Ed.
Genres: Documentary-TV; Educational-TV; Children's-TV; Animation-TV.
Biography: Born in Toronto, Ontario. Started in film, Hollywood, 1956; laboratory (film) background during the 60s in Vancouver; has owned post-production facility since 71. Extensive experience editing, sound editing and doing Foley work.
Selected Filmography: *Attack of the Grizzly*, Th, 90, CDN, Ed; *Empire of Ash III*, Th, 88, CDN, Ed.

CARTMER, Debbie
- see PRODUCERS

CASTRAVELLI, Claudio
- see DIRECTORS

CEREGHETTI, Jean-Pierre
STCQ. 317, rue Rivermere, St-Lambert, PQ J4R 2G3 (514)672-3296.
Types de production et générique: l métrage-Mont/Mont son/Mont mus; c métrage-Mont; TV film-Mont.
Types d'oeuvres: Drame-C&TV; Action-TV; Documentaire-TV; Animation-C.
Curriculum vitae: Né en 1946, Binche, Belgique; au Canada depuis 73. Langues: français et anglais. Etudes en beaux-arts musique, cinéma, TV (I.A.D., Bruxelles), philosophie.
Filmographie sélective: *Bombardier* (mini série), TV, 91, CDN, Mont; "Super Sans Plomb II", TV, 90, CDN, Mont; "Super Sans Plomb", TV, 89, CDN, Mont; *Le Palanquin des Larmes*, C, 88, CDN, Mont mus; *La Ligne de Chaleur*, C, 87, CDN, Mont mus; *Les Somnambules*, TV, 86, CDN, Mont; *Le Matou*, C, 85, CDN/F, Sup mont; *Du rêve au défi*, Sofati-Soconav-Québec, TV, 84, CDN, Mont; *Communications*, L'Ordinateur, TV, 83, CDN, Mont; *Maladies Héréditaires*, Les Grands Maladies, TV, 83, CDN, Mont; *Obésité/Infertilité*, "Dossier Santé", TV, 83, CDN, Mont; *Un W.E. Heureux*, TV, 82, CDN, Réal; *J. de Tonnancourt/Paul David/Maurice Proulx*, "Visage", TV, 81-82, CDN, Mont; *Les Sons/Le Conte/Le Cancer*, "Dossier", TV, 79-82, CDN, Mont; *De jour en jour*, TV, 80, CDN, Sup mont.

CHAPMAN, Christopher
- see DIRECTORS

CHICOINE, Nicole
- voir REALISATEURS

CLAIROUX, Jacques M.
SARDEC. 339 de la Rabastalière est, St-Bruno-de-Montarville, PQ J3V 2A7 (514)653-7746.
Types de production et générique: l métrage-Mont; TV film-Mont.
Types d'oeuvres: Variété-TV; Documentaire-TV.
Curriculum vitae: Né en 1945, Verdun, Québec. Langues: français et anglais. Onze ans comme monteur à Radio-Canada. Publication: *Coeur de hot-dog.* Recherchiste sur l'histoire du théâtre; recherche sur vaudeville au Québec 1880 - 1930; recherchiste iconographique. *LG4-plus que de l'énergie*, US Industrial Film Festival, Chicago, 85; *Quand 1200 enfants s'accordent...*, "Meilleur documentaire musical télévisé en 1983," Conseil de la musique à Ottawa.
Filmographie sélective: *LG4 - plus que de l'énergie*, TV, 84, CDN, Mont; *Du quêteux au joueur d'orgue de barbarie*, TV, 83, CDN, Réal/Prod; *Quand 1200 enfants s'accordent...*, TV, 81, CDN, Mont/Sc; *'77 juin*, C, 79, CDN, Mont; *Tristan und Isolde*, TV, 77, CDN, Mont; *La Superfrancofête*, TV, 76, CDN, Mont; *Raoul Duguay*, TV, 75, CDN, Mont.

CLARK, Alison
- see SOUND EDITORS

COCK, Peter J.
- see DIRECTORS

COLE, Janis
- see PRODUCERS

COLE, Stan◊
IATSE 771, IATSE 776, ACCT. (416)483-7034.
Type of Production and Credits: Th Film-Ed; TV Film-Ed; TV Video-Ed.
Genres: Drama-Th&TV; Comedy-Th; Musical-Th; Action-Th&TV.
Biography: Born 1936, Toronto, Ontario.
Selected Filmography: *From the Hip*, Th, 86, USA, Ed; *Turk 182!*, Th, 85, USA, Ed: *Rhinestone*, Th, 84, USA, Ed; *A Christmas Story*, Th, 83, CDN, Ed; "The Hitchhiker" (pilot), TV, 83, CDN/F/ USA, Ed; *Porky's*, Th, 81, CDN, Ed; *Phobia*, Th, 79, CDN, Ed; *Murder By Decree*, Th, 78, CDN/GB, Ed, (GENIE); *Why Shoot the Teacher?*, Th, 76, CDN, Ed; *Jacob Two Two Meets the Hooded Fang*, Th, 75, CDN, Ed; *Black Christmas*, Th, 74, CDN, Ed, (CFA); "Salty" (12 eps), TV, 73, CDN, Ed; *The Neptune Factor*, Th, 72, CDN, Ed.

COLLIER, Mike
- see PRODUCERS

COLLINS, Alan
- see DIRECTORS

COMEAU, Phil
- see DIRECTORS

CONTENT, Phil
IATSE 776. 507 11th St., Santa Monica, CA 90402 (213)394-8911.
Type of Production and Credits: Th Short-Ed; TV Film-Ed/Prod/Dir; TV Video-Ed.
Genres: Documentary-Th&TV; Educational-Th&TV; Children's-Th&TV; Industrial-Th&TV.
Biography: Born in 1943 in Montreal, Quebec. Canadian citizen, U.S. resident. English-speaking. B.A. (Honours) English from Loyola, Montreal; M.F.A. in Cinema from The Univ. of Southern California. Started at the National Film Board of Canada in 1963. Has recently edited 10 or so "Behind the Scenes/The Making of...", 6-minute featurettes tied to current theatrical feature releases (for electronic press kits). Has also edited music videos, comedy, drama, animated TV shorts and commercials. 3 Cine Golden Eagle awards and 1 Silver Screen award have been awarded to films.
Selected Filmography: *Monkeys on the Edge*, "Nature", TV, 90, USA, Ed; *Yellowstone on Fire*, "Nature", TV, 90, USA, Ed; "Adventures in Diving" (13 eps), TV, 89-90, USA, Ed; "Dive to Adventure" (26 eps), TV, 86-89, USA/CDN, Ed; *The Only Word Was "Win"*, "Secret Intelligence", ED, 89, USA, Ed; "The Animal Life" (3 eps), TV, 89, USA, Ed; *The Magellan Flight*, ED, 88, USA, Ed; *Return to the Titanic*, TV, 87, USA/F, Ed; "The Secret World" (18 eps), TV, 87, USA/CDN, Ed; *The Climate Puzzle*, "Planet Earth", TV, 86, USA, Ed; "Photoplay" (40 eps), TV, 86, USA, Ed; "Marketing" (4 eps), TV, 84-85, USA, Ed; "Playboy on the Scene" (2 eps), TV, 83-84, USA, Ed; "Real People" (2 eps), TV, 83, USA, Ed; "Special Edition" (26 eps), TV, 82, USA, Ed.

COPEMAN, Bruce◊
(416)863-0459.
Type of Production and Credits: TV Film-Ed; TV Video-Ed.
Genres: Commercials-TV.
Biography: Born 1954, Quebec, Quebec. Studied Film, Algonquin College, 78-79. For past 6 years has worked on hundreds of commercials for TV and has won several awards; expertise in special effects with both film and tape opticals.

CORNFORD, Darryl
ACCT. 35 Frances Ave., Toronto, ON

M8Y 3K8 (416)252-0653. Film Arts, 424 Adelaide St. E., Toronto, ON M5A 1N4 (416)368-9925.
Type of Production and Credits: Th Film-Ed/Snd Ed; TV Film-Ed/Snd Ed.
Genres: Drama-Th&TV; Documentary-Th&TV; Animation-TV; Current Affairs-TV.
Biography: Born 1949, Edmonton, Alberta. B.A., Economics, University of Calgary; Diploma with Honours, Media Communications, Emily Carr College of Art.
Selected Filmography: *Poor Man/Rich Man*, "Millennium", TV, 90-91, CDN, Ed; *Defy Gravity*, Th, 89-90, CDN, Ed; "the fifth estate", TV, 82-89, CDN, Ed; *Carry On Sergeant*, (1928-restoration, Nat'l Archives of Canada), Th, 89, CDN, Mus Ed; *Mob Story*, Th, 89, CDN, Snd Ed; "Inside Stories" (4 eps), TV, 88, CDN, Snd Ed; *Night Friend*, Th, 87, CDN Snd Ed; *The Discovery of Penicillin*, ED, 87, CDN, Ed.

CORRIVEAU, André
STCQ, ACCT. 590, Labonté, Longueuil, PQ J4H 2R3 (514)679-3098.
Types de production et générique: l métrage-Mont; c métrage-Mont.
Types d'oeuvres: Drame-C; Comédie-C; Action-C; Documentaire-C.
Curriculum vitae: Né en 1946, Longueuil, Québec. Langues: français et anglais. Diplôme de l'Institut des Hautes Etudes Cinématographiques, Paris, 68.
Filmographie sélective: *L'Homme de Rêve*, TV, 91, CDN, Mont; *The Pianist*, C, 91, CDN/J, Mont; *Rafales*, C, 90, CDN, Mont; *Vincent and Me*, C, 90, CDN, Mont; *Blue La Magnifique*, TV, 89, CDN, Mont; *Les Heures Précieuses*, TV, 89, CDN, Mont; *Fierro, L'été des Secrets*, C, 89, CDN/AR, Mont; *Laura Laur*, C, 88, CDN, Mont; *Dans le Ventre du Dragon*, C, 88, CDN, Mont; *Les Bleus au Coeur*, TV, 87, CDN, Mont, (GEMEAUX); *Les Portes tournantes*, C, 87, CDN/F, Mont; *Tommy Tricker and the Stamp Traveller*, C, 87, CDN/A/RC, Mont; *Le Jeune Magicien*, C, 86, CDN/PL, Mont; *Bach et Bottine*, C, 86, CDN, Mont; *Le Frère André*, C, 86, CDN, Mont.

CRAIGEN, Geoff
DGC. 277 Wolverleigh Blvd., Toronto, ON M4C 1S3 (416)421-3724.
Type of Production and Credits: TV Film-Ed; TV Video-Ed/P Prod Spv.
Genres: Drama-TV; Comedy-TV; Variety-TV; Documentary-TV.
Biography: Born in 1945 in Alice Springs, Australia. Moved to Canada in 1970.

Canadian citizen.
Selected Filmography: "Sweating Bullets" (3 eps), TV, 91, CDN/USA/MEX, Ed; *Dead Time*, TV, 91, CDN, Ed; "The Super Dave Osborne Show" (80 eps), TV, 86-90, USA/CDN, Ed; "War of the Worlds" (5 eps), TV, 89-90, USA/CDN, Ed; "Friday The 13th - The Series" (1 eps), TV, 88, USA/CDN, Ed; "Night Heat" (3 eps), TV, 88, CDN/USA, Ed; "The Campbells" (5 eps), TV, 87, CDN/GB, Ed; *Christmas Toy*, TV, 86, USA/CDN, Ed.

CROSSLAND, Harvey James
- see DIRECTORS

CUTLER, Keith
- see PRODUCERS

CYNAMON, Helena
- see PRODUCERS

DAMUDE, D. Brian
- see WRITERS

DANDY, Michael
- see SOUND EDITORS

DE BAYSER, Eric
STCQ. 1303 ouest, Bernard, #2, Outremont, PQ H2V 1W1 (514)276-5914.
Types de production et générique: l métrage-Mont; c métrage-Mont; TV film-Mont/Réal.
Types d'oeuvres: Drame-C&TV; Documentaire-C&TV; Comédie-C&TV;
Curriculum vitae: Né en 1937, Paris, France; citoyenneté française et canadienne. ONF, 63-73; plus de 77 films. Remporte le prix du meilleur film canadien au Festival du film de Vancouver, 67, pour *La Télévision est là*. Cart professionnelle de monteur à Paris.
Filmographie sélective: *Freedom to Move*, (Omnimax-film officiel de l'Expo 86 de Vancouver), C, 85, CDN, Mont; *Le Choix d'un peuple*, C, 80, CDN, Mont son; *Envoyez d'l'avant nos gens*, "Le Son des Français en Amérique", TV, 75, CDN, Moont; *Denis Vanier*, "La vie qu'on mène", TV, 74, CDN, Mont; *Les Filles du Roy*, "En tant que femmes", TV, 73-74, CDN, Mont; *Etes-vous seuls?*, "Témoignage P", TV, 73, CDN, Mont; *The Netsilik Eskimo Today*, "Netsilik", C, 72, CDN/USA, Sup mont; *Voudou-Haïti 1972*, TV, 72, F, Mont; *Conteneurs*, C, 71, CDN, Mont; *Les Rochassiers*, C, 69, CDN, Mont; *Vertige*, C, 68, CDN, Mont; *La Télévision est là*, C, 67, CDN, Mont/Co réal; *Regards sur l'occultisme*, C, 65, CDN, Sc; *Percé on the Rocks*, C, 64, CDN, Mont; *La Fin des étés*, C, 63, CDN, Mont.

DELEUZE, Marc◊
(416)595-9624.

Type of Production and Credits: TV Video-Ed; TV Video-Cam.
Genres: Documentary-TV; Industrial-TV.
Biography: Born 1954, Martinique; landed immigrant Canada. Languages: French and English. Studied Television Production, Seneca College. Works as editor and camerman on *Fashion Moods*. Won 2nd Place in the Best Promotional Video category, Festival of Canadian Fashion, 86, and 2nd Place, ITVA awards, 86; *Models on the Move* won 2nd Place, Best Promotional Video category, ITVA, 87.
Selected Filmography: *Fashion Moods*, In, 87, CDN, Ed/Cam; *Models on the Move*, In, 86, CDN, Ed.

DELOREY, Walter J.
- see PRODUCERS

DEMEULE, Nadine
- voir REALISATEURS

DESHARNAIS, Jacques
- voir DIRECTEURS-PHOTO

DESJARDINS, Jacques
- voir SCENARISTES

DI CIAULA, Pia
DGC. 2010 Bloor St. W., #22, Toronto, ON M6P 3L1 (416)763-5380.
Type of Production and Credits: Th Film-Ed; TV Film-Ed; TV Video-Ed.
Genres: Drama-Th&TV; Musical-TV; Action-Th&TV; Industrial-TV.
Biography: Born in Toronto, Ontario. Languages: English and Italian. B.A.A., Motion Picture, Ryerson Polytechnical Institute; Cert., CSC Camera Assistant course.
Selected Filmography: "My Secret Identity" (12 eps), TV, 90-91, CDN/USA, Ed; "T and T" (4 eps), TV, 90, CDN, Ed; "Danger Bay" (26 eps), TV, 86-89, CDN/USA, Ed; "Live Wires", TV, 89, CDN/USA, Ed; *Iron Eagle II*, Th, 88, CDN/IL, Assoc Ed; "C.I.B.C." (6 eps), In, 87-88, CDN, Ed; "Danger Bay" (57 eps), TV, 84-88, CDN/USA, Assist Ed/Assist Snd Ed; *Blindside*, Th, 86, CDN, Assist Ed; *Oklahoma Smugglers*, Th, 86, CDN/USA, Assist Ed; *Joshua Then and Now*, Th, 85, CDN, Assist Snd Ed; *Vancouver: A Portrait by Arthur Erickson*, TV, 84, CDN, Assist Ed; *Dancemakers*, "Canciones", TV, 84, CDN, Snd Ed.

DION, Jean-Yves
- voir DIRECTEURS-PHOTO

DION, Yves
- voir REALISATEURS

DOUGHTY, Robert
DGC, AFM. Robert Doughty Productions Ltd., 127 Soudan Ave., Toronto, ON M4S 1V5 (416)484-0248.
Type of Production and Credits: Th Film-Ed; TV Film-Ed; TV Video-Ed.
Genres: Drama-Th&TV; Comedy-Th&TV; Musical-Th&TV; Action-Th&TV.
Biography: Born in 1950 in Toronto, Ontario. Canadian citizen. Graduated community college in 1971. Musician: guitars and brass instruments. Worked and recorded in Los Angeles, 1971-72. Toured the US extensively. Specializes in offline editing TV series work, online and special FX, post audio supervision.
Selected Filmography: *Breakthru*, Canada Trust, Cm, 91, CDN, Dir; "Top Cops" (3 eps), TV, 90, CDN/USA, Ed; "Eric's World" (6 eps), TV, 90, CDN/USA, Ed; "My Secret Identity" (12 eps), TV, 89-90, CDN/USA, Ed; "Captain Power" (7 eps), TV, USA, 87-88, Ed; "SCTV" (24 eps), TV, 78-79, CDN, Ed; *City in Panic*, Th, 86, CDN/USA, Ed.

DREW, Rick
- see WRITERS

DROT, Jean-Marie
STCVQ. 700 Outremont, Outremont, PQ H2V 3N1 (514)274-9341.
Types de production et générique: c métrage-Mont; TV film-Mont; TV vidéo-Mont.
Types d'oeuvres: Drame-C&TV; Comédie-C&TV; Variété-C&TV; Documentaire-C&TV.
Curriculum vitae: Né en 1950, Livry-Gargan, France. Langues: français, anglais. Certificat en comm. de l'Université de Montréal; formation en tant qu'assistant-monteur, compagnie Neyrac Films, Paris; étude de la photo à Paris à l'Institut Français de Photographie. Monteur de film et vidéo pour documentaires, drames, comédies et variété. Série "Lance et Compte": Lauréat du prix Gémeaux pour meilleur montage, série dramatique en 1988 et 1989.
Filmographie sélective: "Lance et Compte" (5 eps), TV, 90, CDN, Mont; "Alphonse Desjardins" (2 eps), TV, 89-90, CDN, Mont; "Justice Express" (3 eps), TV, 89-90, CDN, Mont; "La Misère des Riches" (4 eps), TV, 89, CDN, Mont; Bell Canada, Cm, 89, CDN, Mont; Esso (3), Cm, 89, CDN, Mont; "Lance et Compte" (6 eps), TV, 88-89, CDN, Mont; "Formule 1" (2 eps), TV, 87-88, CDN, Mont; "Lance et Compte" (3 eps), TV, 87-88, CDN, Mont; "La Femme et le Développement" (4 eps), TV, 86-87, IND/BR/UAE/RC, Mont; "Opération Ypsilon" (8 eps), TV, 86, CDN, Mont.

DUCKWORTH, Martin
- see DIRECTORS

DUPUIS, Raymond
- voir DIRECTEURS ARTISTIQUES
ELDRIDGE, Scott
- see DIRECTORS
ERICKSON, Jim
- see DIRECTORS
ETHIER, Martial
4461, de l'Esplanade, #4, Montréal, PQ H2W 1T2 (514)284-1786.
Types de production et générique: l métrage-Mont; c métrage-Mont; TV film-Mont.
Types d'oeuvres: Drame-C; Documentaire-TV; Expérimental-C.
Curriculum vitae: Né en 1954, Montréal, Québec. Langues: français et anglais. Baccalauréat, majeur en cinéma, Université Concordia, 79.
Filmographie sélective: *Tant pis pour le reste*, MV, 90, CDN, Réal/Mont; *Swimsuit 90*, TV, 90, CDN, Mont; *Cursed*, C, 89, CDN, Mont; First Choice Haircut, Cm, 89, CDN, Mont; *Welcome to Canada*, C, 88, CDN, Mont; *Bye, Johnny, Bye*, C, 87, CDN, Mont; *Train of Dreams*, MV, 87, CDN, Mont; *Maria Carmen's Story*, TV, 86, CDN, Mont; *A Long Way From Home*, "Defence of Canada", TV, 85, CDN, Mont; *Liban*, TV, 85, CDN, Mont; *Télé-Festival*, "Festival des films du monde", TV, 85-86, CDN, D photo; 666, C, 84, CDN, Réal/D photo/Mont; *Deux sucres dans mon café*, TV, 83, CDN, Mont; *Amour et violence*, C/TV, 90, CDN, Réal/D photo/Mont; *Guys & Dolls*, TV, 80, CDN, D photo.
FANFARA, Stephan
DGC. 97 Earl Grey Rd., Toronto, ON M4J 3L6 (416)461-7010.
Type of Production and Credits: Th Film-Ed; TV Film-Ed; TV Video-Ed.
Genres: Drama-Th&TV; Comedy-TV; Action-Th; Music Video-TV.
Biography: Born 1950.
Selected Filmography: "Maniac Mansion" (22 eps), TV, 90-91, CDN/USA, Ed; *Johann's Gift to Christmas*, TV, 91, CDN, Ed; *Coca Cola Countdown*, opening, Cm, 89, CDN, Prod; *George's Island*, Th, 89, CDN, Ed; *Confidence Man*, The Jeff Healey Band, MV, 88, CDN, Prod; *High On You*, Iggy Pop, MV, 88, CDN, Prod; *Life's Tough*, Silkience, Cm, 88, USA, Prod; *Got a Hole In My Heart*, Cyndi Lauper, MV, 88, USA, Prod; *Sing*, Th, 88, USA, Co-Ed; *Normanicus*, Th, 87, CDN, Ed; *Higher Education*, Th, 86, CDN, Ed; *Police Academy 4*, Th, 86, USA, Co-Ed; *Recruits*, Th, 85, USA, Ed; *Wave Babies*, Honeymoon Suite, MV, 85, CDN, Prod.

FAVREAU, Robert
- voir REALISATEURS
FORTIN, Armand
- voir REALISATEURS
FORTIN, Dominique
512 boul. Brassard, Chambly, PQ J3L 1S6 (514)658-2101.
Types de production et générique: l métrage-Mont/Sc; c métrage-Mont/Sc; TV film-Mont/Sc; TV vidéo-Mont/Sc.
Types d'oeuvres: Drame-C&TV; Documentaire-C&TV.
Curriculum vitae: Née en 1961, Montréal, Québec. Citoyenneté canadienne. Langues: français et anglais. Monteuse et scénariste pour film. Gagnante du prix du meilleur documentaire pour *Uranium*, Festival Yorkton en 91 et mention honorable pour *Entre l'effort et l'oubli*, Alberta Film and TV awards, 1989.
Filmographie sélective: *City of Champion*, C, 90, CDN, Mont/Mont son; *Uranium*, C, 89-90, CDN, Mont; *Chaindance*, C, 90, CDN, 1ère ass mont; *Bloodclan*, C, 90, CDN, 1ère ass mont; *Franc Ouest*, C, 89, CDN, Mont/1ère ass mont; *Entre l'effort et l'oubli*, C, 89, CDN, Mont/co réal; *The Edmonton Fringe*, C, 89, CDN, Mont/Mont son; *The Unspoken*, C, 88, CDN, Mont; *First Take - Double Take*, C, 86, CDN, Mont; *Les Enfants de la Guerre*, C, 86, CDN, Mont; *On The Edge*, C, 85, CDN, Mont.

FULLER, Michael
73 Catherine Ave., Aurora, ON L4G 1K6 (416)841-8872. Film Arts, 424 Adelaide St. E., 2nd Flr., Toronto, ON M5A 1N4 (416)368-9925.
Type of Production and Credits: Th Film-Ed/Dir; Th Short-Ed/Dir; TV Film-Ed/Dir; TV Video-Ed/Dir.
Genres: Drama-TV; Documentary-Th&TV; Educational-TV; Children's-TV.
Biography: Born 1949, London, Ontario. B.A., English, Philosophy, Film, Queen's University, 70. Worked extensively as cameraman; professional musician with film recording experience, 70-74. Films he has edited have won major awards at Chicago and New York Festivals; *Magic in the Sky* won Etrog, Best Documentary over 30 min.; *Les Canadiens* was a finalist for Best Sports Production, Prix Gémeaux, 86; *Solitary Journey* won awards at Banff, Yorkton, Italy and others.
Selected Filmography: *Millennium* (4 eps), TV, 90-91, CDN/USA/GB, Series Spv Ed; *30 Years - Special*, "The Nature of Things", TV, 90, CDN, Ed; "Man Alive" (2 eps), TV, 90, CDN, Ed; *Carlos Ott: The*

Will to Win, TV, 89-90, CDN, Ed; *Solitary Journey*, TV, 88, CDN, Ed; "the fifth estate" (140 eps), TV, 76-88, CDN, Sr Ed; *Everest: The Solitary Journey*, TV, 88, CDN, Ed; *Great Lakes Salmon Adventure*, Th, 86, CDN, Dir/Ed; *Les Canadiens*, TV, 85, CDN, Co-Ed; *The Beach with John Sewell*, "Neighbourhoods", TV, 84, CDN, Dir/Wr; *The Brokers*, TV, 84, CDN, Ed; *Alberto Salazaar and Bill Rogers*, "World's Great Athletes", TV, 83, CDN, Ed; *Magic in the Sky*, TV, 81, CDN, Ed, (ETROG); *Ice Flight*, TV, 78, CDN, Dir/Ed/Cam/Wr; *Dene*, TV, 72, CDN, Dir/Co-Prod/Ed/Cam.

GAREAU, John
- see PRODUCERS

GAUTHIER, Fred
NABET. 5 Rathfon Cres., Richmond Hill, ON L4C 5B6 (416)883-9832. CBC, P.O. Box 500, Stn. A, Toronto, ON M5W 1E6 (416)975-7640.
Type of Production and Credits: Th Film-Ed; TV Film-Ed/Dir.
Genres: Documentary-TV; Children's-TV; Experimental-Th; Current Affairs-TV.
Biography: Born in Montreal, Quebec. Languages: English and French. Honours Diploma, TV and Film, Sheridan College, 73.
Selected Filmography: *Population*, "The Nature of Things", TV, 91, CDN, Ed; "the fifth estate" (30 segs), TV, 89-91, CDN, Ed; *The Curtain Rises*, TV, 90, GB/CDN, Ed; "The Struggle for Democracy" (3 eps), TV, 88, CDN/GB, Ed; "Man Alive" (4 eps), TV, 86-87, CDN, Ed; "Sesame Street" (20 eps), TV, 86-87, CDN, Ed; "Everyman", TV, 86, CDN/GB, Ed; *Shifting*, TV, 86, CDN, Dir; "This Land" (1 eps), TV, 85, CDN, Ed; "Neighbourhoods" (4 eps), TV, 84, CDN, Ed; "Ce Soir" (50 eps), TV, 83-84, CDN, Ed; *La Nuit sur l'étang*, TV, 82-83, CDN, Ed; *The Music of the Spheres*, Th, 82, CDN, Ed.

GÉLINAS, Michel
- voir PRODUCTEURS

GEROFSKY, Susan
- see SOUND EDITORS

GIBB, Alan D.◊
(416)928-9687.
Type of Production and Credits: TV Film-Ed/Prod.
Genres: Drama-TV; Documentary-TV; Educational-TV; Children's-TV.
Biography: Born 1947, Lisburn, Northern Ireland; landed immigrant Canada. Languages: English and French. Studied Journalism, Centennial College. Nine years at CBC; co-founded Film Images, 80. Main prize at EKO film festival, Czechoslovakia, 88; *Gold: The Hemlo Story* won Silver Medal, NY, 85; *Wild Goose Jack* won Blue Ribbon, American Film Festival, 83.
Selected Filmography: "A Science Walk with David Suzuki" (3 eps), TV, 87-88, CDN, Prod/Ed; "People of Our World" (6 eps), ED, 87, CDN, Ed; "Indonesia: A Generation of Change" (6 eps), TV, 86-87, CDN, Ed; *Science Is Happening Here*, ED, 87, CDN, Ed/Prod; "Modern Times" (4 eps), In, 87, CDN, Ed; *Endangered Species*, In, 87, CDN, Ed; "Man Alive" (1 eps), TV, 86, CDN, Ed; *From Inside Out*, In, 86, CDN, Ed; "Market Place" (38 eps), TV, 85-86, CDN, Ed; *Mr. Neverlearn Meets the Firefighter*, TV, 85, CDN, Prod/Ed; *Scouts!*, TV, 85, CDN, Ed; *Gold: The Hemlo Story*, TV, 84, CDN, Ed; *Quest for the City of David*, TV, 84, CDN, Ed; *Everbody*, TV, 84, CDN, Ed; *Wild Goose Jack*, TV, 83, CDN, Ed.

GILLSON, Malca
- see DIRECTORS

GINSBERG, Donald
- see PRODUCERS

GIRARD, Hélène
STCQ. 650, de l'Epée, Outremont, PQ H2V 3T8 (514)276-5126.
Types de production et générique: l métrage-Mont/Réal; c métrage-Mont/Réal; TV vidéo-Mont/Réal.
Types d'oeuvres: Drame-C&TV; Documentaire-C&TV; Education-C&TV.
Curriculum vitae: Née en 1945. Langues: français, anglais et espagnol. Bacc., Collège Français, Montréal; B.Sc., anthropologie, Université de Montréal. Organisatrice du premier Festival la Femme et le Film, 73.
Filmographie sélective: *Bulle*, C, 91, CDN, Mont; *Nelligan*, C, 90-91, CDN, Mont; *Comme un voleur*, C, 90, CDN, Mont; *Les amazones*, C, 90, CDN, Mont; *Reach for the Sky*, C, 90, CDN/R, Mont; *Pas de répit pour Mélanie*, C, 89, CDN, Mont; *Portion d'éternité*, C, 88, CDN, Mont; *Coeur de nylon*, C, 88, CDN, Mont; *T'es belle, Jeanne*, TV, 88, CDN, Mont; *The Dumb Waiter*, C, 87, CDN, Mont/Mont son; *La Grenouille et la Baleine*, C, 87, CDN, Mont; *The Great Land of Small*, C, 86, CDN, Mont; *Fuir*, C, 78, CDN, Réal/Co mont; *J.A. Martin photographe*, C, 76, CDN, Mont, (CFA); *Les filles c'est pas pareil*, "En tant que femmes", TV, 74, CDN, Réal/Mont

GODDARD, Bill
DGC. 116 Scarborough Rd., Toronto, ON M4E 3M5 (416)698-5110.

Type of Production and Credits: TV Video-Ed.
Genres: Drama-TV; Comedy-TV; Documentary-TV; Industrial-TV.
Biography: Born 1956, Lucan, Ontario. Languages: English and some French. Diploma, Radio and TV, Fanshawe College, 76. Emmy nomination for Individual Achievement, Special Visual Effects, 83 for work on "SCTV Network." Edits exclusively on video (linear or non-linear); practised in negative matchback.
Selected Filmography: "Sweating Bullets" (3 eps), TV, 91, CDN/USA/MEX, Ed; "Dracula - The Series" (21 eps), TV, 90, CDN/USA, Spv Ed; "Friday the 13th - The Series" (10 eps), TV, 89-90, CDN/USA, Ed; *Return of the Six Million Dollar Man and Bionic Woman II*, TV, 89, USA, Ed/Assoc Prod; "Alfred Hitchcock Presents" (21 eps), TV, 87-88, CDN/USA, Ed; *Taking Care of Terrific*, TV, 87, CDN/USA, Ed; "Captain Power" (6 eps), TV, 87, CDN/USA, Ed; *Shades of Love - Ballerina and the Blues*, TV, 87, CDN, Ed; *All My Sons*, TV, 86, USA, Ed; *The Incredible Time Travels of Henry Osgood*, TV, 86, CDN/USA, Ed; *4 on the Floor*, "The Frantics" (13 eps), TV, 85-86, CDN, Ed; *The Last Polka*, TV, 83, CDN/USA, Ed; *The First Howie Mandel Special*, TV, 83, CDN/USA, Ed; "SCTV Network" (18 eps), TV, 82-83, CDN/USA, Assoc Ed; "The Littlest Hobo" (3 eps), TV, 79, CDN, Ed.

GODDARD, Eric
DGC, ACCT. 50 Garnock Ave., Toronto, ON M4K 1M2 (416)461-6901. Shodan Productions Inc., 50 Garnock Ave., Toronto, ON M4K 1M2.
Type of Production and Credits: TV Film-Ed; TV Video-Ed.
Genres: Drama-TV; Action-TV; Documentary-TV; Current Affairs-TV.
Biography: Born in 1952. Canadian citizen. Went to Ryerson Polytechnical Institute, Toronto. Won a Golden Sheaf Award while working as the editor on "the fifth estate".
Selected Filmography: "E.N.G" (23 eps), TV, 89-91, CDN, Ed; *Clowns in Convention*. "Adrienne Clarkson Presents", TV, 91, CDN, Ed; "the fifth estate" (21 eps), TV, 80-91, CDN, Ed; Medical Video Library (40 eps), ED, 87-88, CDN, Dir/Ed; "Adderly" (4 eps), TV, 86-88, CDN/USA, Ed; *The Last Resort*, "the fifth estate", TV, 86, CDN, Ed; "Gzowski & Co." (7 eps), TV, 86, CDN, Ed; "Peter Ustinov's Russia" (6 eps), TV, 85, CDN, Snd Ed, (GEMINI); *Red Deer Challenge*, TV, 84, CDN, Ed; "World's Greatest Athletes" (3 eps), TV, 84, CDN, Assoc Dir/Ed.

GOLDBERG, Howard
- see DIRECTORS

GOLDSTEIN, Roushell
DGC. 322 Clinton St., Toronto, ON M6G 2Y8 (416)535-5393.
Type of Production and Credits: Th Film-Ed; Th Short-Ed; TV Film-Ed/Dir.
Genres: Drama-TV; Musical-TV; Documentary-TV; Educational-TV; Children's-Th&TV; Current Affairs-TV.
Biography: Born 1947, Ottawa, Ontario. Languages: English, Hebrew and some French. Editor since 70; trained at Israel Television Network, 69-74; recently began directing. Winner of several awards, including Chicago and New York.
Selected Filmography: *Tribal Wisdom and the Modern World*, "Millennium", TV, 91-92, CDN, Ed; *Welcome Home*, TV, 90, CDN, Ed; *Playing For Keeps*, "Feminization of Poverty", ED/TV, 89, CDN, Ed; *Half the Kingdom*, TV, 89, CDN, Dir/Ed; *For Richer, For Poorer*, "The Feminization of Poverty", ED/TV, 88, CDN, Ed; *No Way! Not Me!*, "The Feminization of Poverty", ED/TV, 87, CDN, Ed; "Degrassi Jr. High" (3 eps), TV, 86-97, CDN, Ed.

GOOREVITCH, David S.
535 Rushton Rd., Toronto, ON M6C 2Y6 (416)651-4229. Goorevitch Electric Film & Video, 535 Rushton Rd., Toronto, ON M6C 2Y6 (416)651-4229.
Type of Production and Credits: Th Short-Ed/Wr; TV Film-Wr/Ed; TV Video-Ed/Wr.
Genres: Drama-TV; Action-TV; Documentary-Th&TV; Children's-TV.
Biography: Born in 1951 in Edmonton, Alberta. Canadian citizen. English speaking with a working knowledge of French. B.A. in English Lit. from the University of Alberta; Diploma in Music Studies; B.A.A. in Motion Picture Studies from Ryerson, 1982. Varied background included careers as a musician, tour-organizer and still photographer. Past-President of the Edmonton Jazz Society. *Black Rage* has won awards at the American Film Festival and CBC Telefest and was screened at/on PBS, The Museum of Modern Art, Canadian Images & the Festival of Festivals. Nominated for an Emmy in 1984 for editing on "Lorne Greene's New Wilderness". Currently has several projects and has read, consulted and story edited for several producers and agencies including OFDC, FUND, Cinexus, Owl

Centre, Alliance, Screenwrite and Beaver Creek.
Selected Filmography: "Sketches of our Town" (6 eps), TV, 90-91, CDN, Ed; "The Last Frontier" (6 eps), TV, 89-90, CDN, Wr/Ed; *Bonaparte*, "Owl TV" (2 eps), TV, 90, CDN/GB, Wr; "Danger Bay" (3 eps), TV, 89, CDN, Ed; *Superconductor*, TV, 88, CDN, Ed/Story Ed/PM; *Stranger Among Friends*, TV, 88, CDN, PM/Story Ed; *Come Spy With Me*, TV, 88, CDN, PM/Story Ed; *Negative Image*, TV, 87-88, CDN, Co Wr/Ed; *Streetgames*, TV, 87, CDN, Ed/Post Spv; *Cowboy*, TV, 87, CDN, Post Spv; *Where There's A Will*, TV, 87, CDN, Post Spv; "Lorne Greene's New Wilderness" (6 eps), TV, 84-86, CDN, Ed; "Lorne Greene's New Wilderness" (61 eps), TV, 83-86, CDN, SFX/Narr/Ed; *Black Rage*, Th, 82, CDN, Wr/Dir.

GRADIDGE, Havelock
DGC, IATSE 891. 3536 West 28 Ave., Vancouver, BC V6S 1S1 (604)733-8159.
Type of Production and Credits: Th Film-Ed; TV Film-Ed; TV Video-Ed.
Genres: Drama-Th&TV; Documentary-TV; Educational-TV.
Biography: Born 1933 in South Africa. Moved to Canada in 1957; Canadian citizenship.
Selected Filmography: "Free the Horses" (11 eps), TV, 91, USA, Ed; "Vonnegut Theatre" (1 eps), TV, 90, CDN/USA, Ed; *The Quarrel*, TV, 90, CDN/USA, Ed.

GREENWALD, Barry
- see DIRECTORS

GRUBEN, Patricia
- see DIRECTORS

GULKIN, Cathy
DGC. 56 Wellesley St. E., Unit 7, Toronto, ON M4Y 1G2 (416)920-5347.
Type of Production and Credits: Th Short-Ed; TV Film-Ed.
Genres: Drama-TV; Variety-TV; Documentary-TV; Educational-TV.
Biography: Born 1954, Montreal, Quebec. Languages: English, French and some Spanish. A graduate of the London International Film School, England. Films she has edited have won various awards: *Strand: Under the Dark Cloth*, Genie, 89; *I Need a Man Like You*, Genie, 87; *Flight For Freedom*, Gold Ribbon, Houston; *To Hurt and To Heal*, Blue Ribbon, American Film Festival; *All of Our Lives*, Blue Ribbon American Film Festival; *Houdini Never Died...*, Blue Ribbon, American Film Festival; *Breakthrough*, Bijou; *Best for Us*, Golden Sheaf, Yorkton Short Film and Video Festival; *No Looking Back*, International Film and Television Festival of New York.
Selected Filmography: *Flight for Freedom*, TV, 90, CDN, Ed; *Borrowed Time*, TV, 90, CDN, Ed; *Good Medicine*, MV, 89, CDN, Ed; *Best of Us*, ED, 89, CDN, Ed; *No Looking Back*, ED, 88, CDN, Ed; *Strand: Under the Dark Cloth*, Th, 85-88, CDN, Ed; *To Hurt and to Heal*, Th, 86, CDN, Ed; *I Need a Man Like You to Make My Dreams Come True*, Th, 86, CDN, Ed; *Women and Drugs/Crib Design*, "Marketplace", TV, 86, CDN, Ed; *The Best Time of My Life*, Thm 85, CDN, Ed; *All of Our Lives*, Th, 83, CDN, Ed; *Heart of Gold*, TV, 81-82, CDN, Ed; *Those Flying Canucks*, TV, 81, CDN, Ed; *Moving Mountains*, Th, 81, CDN, Ed; *Breakthrough*, TV, 80, CDN, Ed.

HALL, Ray◊
IATSE 891, ACCT. (604)263-0247.
Type of Production and Credits: Th Film-Ed; Th Short-Ed/Snd Ed; TV Film-Ed/Dir; TV Video-Ed.
Genres: Drama-Th&TV; Documentary-Th&TV; Educational-TV; Children's-TV.
Biography: Born 1932, Norfolk Island, Australia; Canadian citizenship, 62. Languages: English, French and German. Attended University of British Columbia. Professor, Film Studies, UBC. *Dance and Kids* won a Blue Ribbon, American Film Festival, New York.
Selected Filmography: *Differences*, TV, 86, CDN, Ed/Snd Ed; *North West Territories* (Expo 86), Th, 86, CDN, Ed/Snd Ed; *Dance and Kids*, TV, 85, CDN, Ed/Snd Ed; *Jacks or Better*, TV, 82, CDN, Ed/Prod; *On Top of the World*, TV, 80, CDN, Dir; *Sing Beast Sing*, Th, 80, CDN, Ed/Snd Ed; *Nails*, Th, 79, CDN, Ed/Snd Ed, (CFEG); *One Cyclist*, TV, 79, CDN, Prod; *One Tree*, TV, 79, CDN, Dir; *Spartree*, Th, 77, CDN, Ed/Snd Ed, (CFA); *B.T.O.*, TV, 76, CDN, Ed/Snd Ed; *How to Break a Quarter Horse*, TV, 65, CDN, Ed/Snd Ed; *Torch to Tokyo*, TV, 64, CDN, Ed/Snd Ed.

HALLIS, Ophera
122 de Touraine, St. Lambert, PQ J4S 1H4 (514)465-9571.
Type of Production and Credits: Th Film-Ed/Prod; Th Short-Ed; TV Film-Ed; TV Video-Prod.
Genres: Drama-Th&TV; Documentary-Th&TV; Educational-Th&TV; Musical-Th&TV;
Biography: Born in 1949 in Montreal, Quebec. Languages: English, French, Portuguese, Hebrew and German. Educated at McGill University, seminar

student of John Grierson. Independent filmmaker for 20 years, chiefly editor and producer; 4 years under contract in Mozambique training young Mozambicans in film production and editing. Edited first Mozambique newsreel series as well as numerous feature-length documentaries, 1977-81. Editor of *L'Ange et la Femme* by Gilles Carle, winner of the prix Festival d'Avoriaz. Editor and director of *Pamberi ne Zimbabwe*, Leipzig Film Award winner. Subtitler and translator of *L'Ange et la Femme* and *Mueda* by Ruy Guerra, a Portuguese-English production. *Chopi Music of Mozambique* was a Blue Medal Finalist at the 1987 American Film Festival.
Selected Filmography: *The Ancient Kingdom of Great Zimbabwe*, ED, 90, CDN/ZB, Wr/Prod/Dir/Ed; *Chopi Music of Mozambique*, ED, 87, CDN/MZ, Prod/Ed; *Zimbabwe: The New Struggle*, ED, 85, CDN/ZB, Prod/PS; *Nkuleleko Means Freedom*, ED, 84, CDN/ZB, Prod/Dir/Ed/Snd Ed; *Dancas de Mozambique*, Th, 82, MZ, Ed; *I Can Hear Zimbabwe Calling*, Th, 80, CDN/ZB, Prod/Dir/Ed/PS; *Pamberi Ne Zimbabwe*, Th, 80, MZ/ZB, Ed/Dir; *Mozambique Before The Darkness*, Th, 79, CDN/MZ, Prod/Dir/Ed/PS; *A Wile Mu Colonyi*, Th, 78, CDN, Prod/Dir/Ed/PS; *L'Ange et la Femme*, Th, 77, CDN, Ed; *Pride of the Panthers*, Th, 76, CDN, Prod/Ed; *Bull*, Th, 75, CDN, Prod/Ed; *Zaida*, Th, 74, CDN, Prod/Ed; *Toni, Randi & Marie*, Th, 73, CDN, Prod/Ed; *Nightshift*, Th, 71, CDN, Prod/Ed.

HANNIGAN, Teresa
1303 King St. W., Toronto, ON M6K 1G9 (416)534-2003.
Type of Production and Credits: TV Film-Ed/Snd Ed; Th Film-Ed/Snd Ed.
Genres: Drama-Th&TV; Documentary-TV; Children's-TV; Animation-TV.
Biography: Born 1957, Kingston, Ontario. Diploma, Media Arts, Sheridan College, 80.
Selected Filmography: *Waiting for You: Christiane Pflug*, TV, 91, CDN, Ed; *The Right to Care*, ED, 91, CDN, Snd Ed; "Nancy Drew & Daughter", TV, 90, CDN, Pict Ed; *Beach Story*, Th, 90, CDN, Co-Ed; *The Greening of Ian Elliot*, TV, 89, CDN, Pict Ed/Snd Ed; *Taking Care/Prescription for Murder*, Th, 87, CDN, Pict Ed/Snd Ed; "The Edison Twins" (18 eps), TV, 85-86, CDN, Pict Ed; *Spirit Bay*, TV, 86, CDN, Pict Ed/Snd Ed; *My Pet Monster*, TV, 86, CDN, Co-Pict Ed; *Dancing in the Dark*, Th, 86, CDN, Snd Ed; "the fifth estate" (2 eps), TV, 85, CDN, Pict Ed/Snd Ed; *On the Polar Sea: A Yukon Adventure*, TV, 85, CDN, Snd Ed; *The Other Kingdom* (mini-series), TV, 84, CDN, Co-Pict Ed/Co-Snd Ed; "Inspector Gadget" (64 eps), TV, 83, USA/CDN, Dial Ed/Mus Ed; *Chautauqua Girl*, TV, 82, CDN, Snd Ed/Assist Pict Ed.

HARDING, John
2116 Dunvegan Ave., Oakville, ON L6J 6N5 (416)845-0449. John Harding Editing Ltd., 23 Fraser Ave., Toronto, ON M6K 1Y7 (416)538-4283.
Type of Production and Credits: Th Film-Ed/Prod; Th Short-Ed/Prod; TV Film-Ed/Prod; TV Video-Ed/Prod.
Genres: Drama-Th&TV; Commercials-Th&TV; Industrial-Th&TV; Documentary-Th&TV.
Biography: Born in 1944 in England; Canadian citizenship. Languages: English and French. Twenty-two years experience as editor and postproduction supervisor. Various awards, including Cannes, US commercials festivals, Clio.

HAWKES, Kirk◇
(416)691-8186.
Type of Production and Credits: Th Short-Ed; TV Film-Ed/Snd Ed/Mus Ed; TV Video-Ed/Snd Ed/Mus Ed.
Genres: Drama-Th&TV; Horror-Th; Commercials-TV; Industrial-TV.
Biography: Born in 1951 in Winnipeg, Manitoba. Studied Creative Electronics, Fanshawe College.
Selected Filmography: "Shades of Love" (16 eps), TV, 87-88, CDN, Mus Ed; "GM10 Story" (4 eps), In, 87-88, USA, Ed; "Race for the Bomb" (3 eps), TV, 86-87, CDN/F, Mus Ed.

HECTOR, Nick
ACCT. 162 Fairview Ave., Toronto, ON M6P 3A5 (416)767-8933. MPI Productions, 57 St. Nicholas St., Toronto, ON M4Y 1W6 (416)967-1288.
Type of Production and Credits: TV Video-Ed/Snd Ed.
Genres: Documentary-Th&TV; Eduational-TV; Current Affairs-TV.
Biography: Born in 1963. Edited many programs that have won awards at the Festival international du film documentaire, Nyon, Switzerland; Vues d'afrique, Montreal and the Canadian Association of Journalists. Nominated for a Gemini award for *Electronic Jam*, 1989.
Selected Filmography: *The People's Accord*, TV, 91, CDN, Ed; "the fifth estate" (32 eps), TV, 87-91, CDN, Ed; *The Children Shall Lead*, TV, 91, CDN, Ed/Snd Ed; "Earth Journal" (2 eps), TV,

91, CDN/USA, Ed; *Nuit et silence*, TV, 90, CDN, Ed/Snd Ed; "The Journal" (2 eps), TV, 90, CDN, Ed; *Tovio! Child of Hope*, TV, 90, CDN, Ed/Snd Ed; *Namibie: A l'aube de l'indépendance*, TV, 89, CDN, Ed/Snd Ed; *Electronic Jam*, TV, 89, CDN, Ed/Snd Ed; *Le pays interdit*, TV, 89, CDN, Ed/Snd Ed; "W5" (10 eps), TV, 86-89, CDN, Ed; "Gzowski & Co." (2 eps), TV, 86-87, CDN, Ed.

HEYDON, Michael
- see PRODUCERS

HOLE, Jeremy
- see WRITERS

HOPE, Kathryn Ruth
- see PRODUCERS

HOWARD, Christopher
- see PRODUCERS

HUCULAK, William
SMPIA. 523 - 21 St. S.E., Prince Albert, SK S6V 1M5 (306)764-5805.
Type of Production and Credits: Th Short-Ed/Dir/Prod; TV Video-Ed/Dir /DOP.
Genres: Science Fiction-Th; Documentary-Th; Educational-Th&TV; Experimental-Th.
Biography: B.A.A., Photographic Arts, (Film Studies), Ryerson Polytechnical Institute. Functional in a computerized video editing environment.
Selected Filmography: *150 Circuses*, Th, 91, CDN, Prod/Dir/Ed/DOP; *505-506, Descending*, Th, 90, CDN, Dir/Ed; *Prairie Phoenix*, ED, 86, CDN, DOP/Ed; *Pregnancy: A New Life*, ED, 86, CDN, DOP/Ed.

IRVINE, Frank
IATSE 891. #10 - 1415 Lamey's Mill, Vancouver, BC V6H 3W1 (604)736-9296.
Type of Production and Credits: Th Film-Ed; Th Short-Ed; TV Film-Ed.
Genres: Drama-Th&TV; Documentary-Th& TV. Action-Th&TV; Comedy-Th&TV.
Biography: Born 1938, Edmonton, Alberta. *Marathon* won Best First Production; *The Grey Fox* won CFE Best Editor; Genie nominations for *First Season*, *My Kind of Town*, and *The Grey Fox*; Emmy nomination for *Next Door*.
Selected Filmography: *The Learning Path*, ED, 91, CDN, Ed; *Omen IV*, Th, 91, USA/CDN, Ed; *Next Door*, "Kurt Vonnegut Theatre", TV, 91, CDN, Ed; "Black Stallion" (7 eps), TV, 90, F/CDN, Ed; "Neon Rider" (10 eps), TV, 90, USA/CDN, Ed; *First Season*, Th, 89, CDN, Ed; *Beyond the Stars*, Th, 89, CDN/USA, Ed; *High Stakes*, Th, 85, CDN, Ed; *My Kind of Town*, Th, 84, CDN, Ed; *Marathon*, Th, 83, CDN, Ed; *The Grey Fox*, Th, 81, CDN, Ed; *Lotomania*, Th, 80, CDN, Ed; "Ritter's Cove" (13 eps), TV, 79-80, CDN, Ed; "The Beachcombers" (71 eps), TV, 70-80, CDN, Ed; *Canada's Water Sale*, ED, 69, CDN, Ed.

JAN, Miume
DGC, ACCT. 30 Victor Ave., #3, Toronto, ON M4K 1A8 (416)461-3646.
Type of Production and Credits: Th Film-Ed/Mus Ed; Th Short-Ed/Mus Ed; TV Film-Ed/Spv Ed.
Genres: Drama-Th; Comedy-Th; Documentary-Th&TV; Musical-Th&TV;
Biography: Born in 1959 in Hong Kong. Canadian citizen. Languages: English and Chinese. Supervised editing on *The Peggy*, which won Best Short Drama at Calgary's Canadian Celebrations '91. Edited *The Making of Monsters* which won a Teddy at the Berlin Festival ,1991.
Selected Filmography: *Norha & The Microbabe*, Th, 91, CDN, Ed; *R.S.V.P.*, Th/TV, 91, CDN, Ed/Mus Ed; *Just Like Me*, ED, 91, CDN, Ed/Snd Ed; *The Making of Monsters*, Th, 90, CDN, Ed/Mus Ed; *In Service*, "Inside Stories", TV, 90, CDN, Ed; *The Peggy*, "Inside Stories", TV, 90, CDN, Spv Ed; *Strange Dialogue*, Th/TV, 90, CDN, Ed/Mus Ed; *Thick As Thieves*, Th, 90, CDN, Ed; *Alan Bean: Art Off This Earth*, TV, 89, CDN, Ed; *The Midday Sun*, Th, 89, CDN, Ed/Mus Ed; *Heart to Heart*, MV, 88, CDN, Ed; "The Space Experience" (6 eps), TV, 86, CDN, Assoc Ed; *No Sad Songs*, Th, 85, CDN, Ed/Snd Ed.

JAY, Paul
- see DIRECTORS

JEAN, Jacques
- see DIRECTORS

JUDGE, Maureen
- see DIRECTORS

KABELIK, Vladimir
- see PRODUCERS

KARDASH, Virlana
- see WRITERS

KAREN, Debra
ACCT. Final Cut Enterprises Ltd., 5207 Globert, Montreal, PQ H3W 2E6 (514)489-0657.
Type of Production and Credits: Th Film-Ed; TV Film-Ed.
Genres: Drama-Th&TV; Comedy-Th; Action-Th; Horror-Th.
Biography: Born 1952, Montreal, Quebec. Languages: English and French. B.A., Magna cum laude, Communication Arts, Concordia University.

Selected Filmography: *The First Circle* (mini-series), TV, 91, CDN/F, Ed; *The Love She Sought*, TV, 90, USA, Ed; *The Last Elephant*, TV, 90, USA, Ed; *The Incident*, TV, 89, USA, Ed; *Day One*, TV, 88, USA, Ed; *First Offender*, TV, 86, CDN/USA, Ed; *Spearfield's Daughter* (mini-series), TV, 85, CDN/USA/AUS, Ed; *Happy Birthday to Me*, Th, 80, CDN, Ed; *Yesterday*, Th, 79, CDN, Ed; *Meatballs*, Th, 78, CDN, Ed; *Blackout*, Th, 77, CDN/F, Ed; *Rabid*, Th, 76, CDN, Ed; *Death Weekend*, Th, 75, CDN, Ed.

KEATING, Lulu
- see DIRECTORS

KENT, Vincent
DGC, BECTU, ACCT. 910 - 31 Alexander St., Toronto, ON M4Y 1B2 (416)968-0407.
Type of Production and Credits: TV Film-Ed; TV Video-Ed.
Genres: Drama-TV; Comedy-TV; Action-TV; Documentary-TV.
Biography: Born in 1938 in Ipswich, Australia. Educated at St. Mary's College. Completed army training in Royal Australian Artillery. Began editing career as an assistant on Stanley Kramer's *On The Beach*, shot in Melbourne. Moved to London, England in 1960. Worked for numerous production companies. Became a writer and editor with the Film Producers' Guild, London. Moved to Canada in 1966 to work on centennial projects. Former President of the Canadian Film Editors' Guild. British and Australian credits available on request. Gemini award nominee for *Sanity Clause* and "Seeing Things". Genie award winner for "Seeing Things".
Selected Filmography: *Sanity Clause*, TV, 89, CDN, Ed; *Breaking All The Rules*, TV, 88, CDN, Ed; *Coming & Going*, TV, 88, CDN, Ed; "Seeing Things" (43 eps), TV, 81-87, CDN, Exec Ed, (GEMINI); "Matt & Jenny" (26 eps), TV, 80-81, CDN, Spv Ed; "Swiss Family Robinson" (26 eps), TV, 74-75, CDN/USA, Spv Ed; "Police Surgeon" (104 eps), TV, 70-74, USA/CDN, Spv Ed; "Adventures in Rainbow Country" (5 eps), TV, 70, CDN/GB, Ed; "Telescope" (14 eps), TV, 68-69, CDN, Ed; *Walk, Do Not Run*, TV, 69, CDN, Ed; *Delightful Monster*, TV, 68, CDN, Ed; *The Secret of Spaniards Rock*, TV, 68, CDN, Ed; "Album of History" (6 eps), TV, 67, CDN, Ed; *Countdown to a Gold Medal*, TV, 66, CDN, Ed.

KEUSCH, Michael
- see DIRECTORS

KISH, Albert
- see DIRECTORS

KRAVSHIK, Marty◊
(416)425-3167.
Type of Production and Credits: TV Film-Ed; TV Video-Ed.
Genres: Documentary-TV; Commercials-TV; Industrial-TV.
Biography: Born 1951, Toronto, Ontario. On-line video editor for 3 years; has edited more than 1,500 commercials in 11 years. Has won various awards. Also produced and edited several industrials (Xerox, Esso).

KREPAKEVICH, Jerry
- see PRODUCERS

LAHTI, James◊
DGC, ACCT. (416)537-6123.
Type of Production and Credits: TV Film-Ed; TV Video-Ed.
Genres: Action-TV; Children's-TV; Drama-TV.
Biography: Born in northern Ontario. B.F.A., Film, York University. Film and tape editor since 76; has also edited music videos, sponsored films and dozens of documentaries.
Selected Filmography: *Anne of Green Gables - The Sequel* (mini-series), TV, 86, CDN, Co-Ed; "Adderly" (2 eps), TV, 86, CDN, Ed; "Spirit Bay" (1 eps), TV, 86, CDN, Ed: *Anne of Green Gables* (mini-series), TV, 85, CDN, Co-Ed; *Hockey Night*, TV, 84, CDN, Ed; *Coming Apart*, TV, 84, CDN, Ed; *The Umpire*, TV, 84, CDN, Ed; *Introducing...Janet*, TV, 81, CDN, Co-Ed; *Reaching Out*, TV, 80, CDN, Co-Ed; *Clown White*, TV, 80, CDN, Co-Ed.

LANDIS, Evan
DGC. 156 Glenholme Ave., Toronto, ON M6E 3C4 (416)653-8491.
Type of Production and Credits: Th Film-Spv Ed; TV Film-Spv Ed; TV Video-Spv Ed.
Genres: Drama-Th&TV; Comedy-Th&TV; Animation-Th&TV; Music Video-TV.
Biography: Canadian, born and raised in Ottawa. Fine Arts Degree in Film Production, York University, 1981. Began his professional career as an assistant picture and sound editor; worked on almost a dozen features in this capacity. Picture editor on a number of short documentaries, 1984. Within a year was editing the award-winning Jim Henson/Warner Bros. feature *Follow That Bird*. Cut several feature length films and almost a hundred episodes for TV, including "Danger Bay", "T and T", "The Nancy Drew Mysteries" and the George Lucas

production, "The Ewoks and Droids Adventure Hour". He is presently supervising editor on the Steven Spielberg/Tim Burton television series, "Family Dog". Evans has extensive experience in all facets of post-production.
Selected Filmography: "Nancy Drew Mysteries" (2 eps), TV, 91, CDN/USA, Spv Ed; *Queensryche Live*, concert video, MV, 91, USA, Spv Ed; "Dealing With Drugs" (6 eps), TV, 90, CDN, Spv Ed; "T and T" (12 eps), TV, 90, CDN/USA, Spv Ed; *Baby X*, Look People, MV, 90, CDN, Ed; *Babar: The Movie*, Th, 89, CDN/USA, Ed; *Straight Line*, TV, 89, CDN/USA, Ed; *Personal Exemptions*, Th, 88, CDN, Spv Ed; "T and T" (24 eps), TV, 87-88, CDN/USA, Ed; *Care Bears Adventure in Wonderland*, Th, 87, CDN, Ed; "Danger Bay" (2 eps), TV, 86, CDN, Ed; "Dennis the Menace" (10 eps), TV, 86, USA, Ed; *Follow That Bird*, Th, 86, USA, Ed; "The Ewoks and Droids Adventure Hour" (13 eps), TV, 86, USA, Ed.

LANGE, Bruce◊
DGC. (604)669-1333
Type of Production and Credits: Th Film-Ed.
Genres: Drama-Th; Comedy-Th; Action-Th; Horror-Th.
Biography: Born 1951, Jasper, Alberta. B.Sc., Dalhousie University.
Selected Filmography: *The Big Town*, Th, 86, USA, Assoc Ed; *Agnes of God*, Th, 85, CDN, Assoc Ed; *Abducted*, Th, 85, CDN, Ed; *Blue Snake*, TV, 85, CDN, Ed; *Mrs. Soffel*, Th, 84, USA, Assist Ed; *The Glitter Dome*, TV, 83, CDN/USA, 2nd Assist Ed; *Martin's Day*, Th, 83, CDN/GB, Assist Ed; *Strange Brew*, Th, 82, CDN, Assist Ed; *The Amateur*, Th, 81, CDN, Assist Ed; *Pure Escape*, Th, 80, CDN, Assist Ed; *Hot Touch*, Th, 80, CDN/USA, Assist Ed; *Klondike Fever*, Th, 79, CDN, Assist Ed; *Phobia*, Th, 79, CDN, Assist Ed; *The Shape of Things to Come*, Th, 78, CDN, Assist Ed.

LANK, Barry
- see DIRECTORS

LAWRENCE, Stephen
ACTT, DGC, ACCT. Merlin Films Inc., 30 Holloway Rd., Etobicoke, ON M9A 1G1 (416)233-3570.
Type of Production and Credits: Th Film-Ed/Snd Ed; Th Short-Ed/Snd Ed; TV Film-Ed/Snd Ed; TV Video-Ed/Snd Ed.
Genres: Drama-Th&TV; Documentary-Th&TV; Comedy-Th&TV; Action-Th&TV;
Biography: Born in the United Kingdom; British and Canadian citizenship. Started in film business in 66 with National Screen Services; freelance since 70.
Selected Filmography: "Sweating Bullets" (3 eps), TV, 91, USA/CDN/MEX, Ed; "My Secret Identity" (22 eps), TV, USA/CDN, Spv Pix Ed; *Bethune: The Making of a Hero*, Th, 90, CDN/RC, Snd Ed; "Danger Bay" (110 eps), TV, 83-89, CDN/ USA, Spv Pix Ed; "The Jim Henson Hour" (2 eps), TV, 89, USA, Snd Ed; *Sesame Street Anniversary*, TV, 89, USA, Snd Ed; *Day One*, TV, 89, CDN/USA, Snd Ed; *Blindside*, Th, 87, CDN, Pix Ed; *Oklahoma Smugglers*, Th, 86, USA, Pix Ed; *Agents of Deception*, TV, 84, CDN, Spv Pix Ed; *Gold Lust*, TV, 84, CDN, Spv Pix Ed; *A Matter of Sex*, Th, 83, USA/CDN, Snd Ed; "Jack London's Tales of the Klondike" (6 eps), TV, 81, CDN, Pix Ed; *A Man Called Intrepid*, TV, GB/CDN, Snd Ed.

LEACH, David
DGC. 7 Frasco Way, Santa Fe, NM 87505 (505)983-8037.
Type of Production and Credits: TV Film-Ed/Dir.
Genres: Drama-TV; Documentary-TV; Educational-TV; Commercials-TV.
Biography: Born in 1952 in Montreal, Quebec. Languages: English and French. Attended McGill University; Honours B.A., Film, York Univ., 74. *Replanting the Tree of Life* won the Golden Sheaf award Yorkton Short Film and Television Festival, Chris Plaque, Ohio, and Arbor Day, Education Award, US.
Selected Filmography: "Your Green Home" (6 eps), TV, 90, Dir; *Your Community*, "Your Green Home", TV, 90, Dir/Wr/Ed; *Kitchen Cabinets Made Easy* (4 eps), TV, 90, Wr/Dir; "Home Brew" (3 eps), TV, 90, Wr/Dir; *Medium Rare, Hold the Cottage*, Th, 89, Co-Dir/Co-Ed; "Street Legal" (8 eps), TV, 89, CDN, Ed; *Straight Line*, TV, 88, Spv Ed; "T and T" (32 eps), TV, 87-88, CDN/USA, Ed, (Spv Ed 24 eps; "Danger Bay" (15 eps), TV, 86-88, CDN/USA, Ed; *Growing Up in the World Next Door*, ED, 86-87, CDN, Ed; *Replanting the Tree of Life*, ED, 86-87, CDN, Prod/Dir/Ed; *Race Against the Wind*, ED, 86, CDN, Ed; *Life Insurance*, "Money Smart", TV, 85, CDN, Dir; *P & L Insurance*, "Money Smart", TV, 85, CDN, Dir/Ed.

LECLERC, Jean
- voir REALISATEURS

LEDUC, Yves
- voir PRODUCTEURS

LEE, Mike
DGC, ACCT. 117 Hiltz Ave., Toronto, ON M4L 2N7 (416)466-0900. Blue Gates Productions Inc., 117 Hiltz Ave., Toronto, ON M4L 2N7 (416)466-0900.
Type of Production and Credits: TV Film-Ed; TV Video-Ed.
Genres: Drama-TV; Action-TV; Documentary-TV; Children's-TV.
Biography: Born in 1955 in Marlborough, Wiltshire, England. British citizen, Canadian landed immigrant (currently applying for Canadian citizenship). B.A. (Honours) in Sociology and Social Anthropology, University of Hull, North Humberside, England.
Selected Filmography: "Counterstrike" (20 eps), TV, 90-91, CDN/USA/F, Ed; "Top Cops" (5 eps), TV, 91, USA/CDN, Ed; "Katts and Dog" (15 eps), TV, 88-90, CDN/F/USA, Ed; "Diamonds" (4 eps), TV, 89, CDN/F/USA, Ed; "Just a Chance" (1 eps), TV, 89, CDN, Ed; "Night Heat" (1 eps), TV, 88, CDN/USA, Ed; "Wonderstruck" (126 eps), TV, 85-88, CDN, Ed.

LESEWICK, Robert
- see PRODUCERS

LIGHT, Peter F.
DGC. Contact: DGC, Ontario District Council.
Type of Production and Credits: TV Film-Spv Ed; TV Video-Spv Ed.
Genres: Drama-TV; Comedy-TV; Documentary-TV.
Biography: Over 20 years of television experience from studio work to post production. Experience on CMX & compatible systems as well as editdroid.
Selected Filmography: "E.N.G" (21 eps), TV, 89-91, CDN/USA, Ed; *Same Ole Me*, TV, 89, CDN, Ed; *Teen Gangs*, TV, 89, CDN, Spv Ed; "Diamonds" (1 eps), TV, 88, CDN/USA/F, Ed; "Night Heat" (1 eps), TV, 88, CDN/USA, Ed; "Friday The 13th - The Series" (8 eps), TV, 87, USA/CDN, Ed; *Beyond The Blues*, TV, 88, CDN, Ed.

LOWER, Robert
ACCT, ACTRA (WGC). 1096 Wolseley Ave., Winnipeg, MB R3G 1G7 (204)783-9108.
Type of Production and Credits: TV Film-Wr/Dir/Ed.
Genres: Drama-TV; Action-TV; Documentary-TV; Commercials-TV.
Biography: Born in 1946 in Winnipeg, Manitoba. Educated at the University of Manitoba. Trained in editing in Toronto, 1966-71. Lived in Winnipeg since 1971 with occasional working stints in Montreal and Toronto. Director, writer, editor of documentaries with particular talent and skill at story structure and commentary/narration writing.
Selected Filmography: *Millennium: Tribal Wisdom and the Modern World*, TV, 91, CDN/USA/GB, Ed; *Lost in the Barrens*, TV, 90, CDN/USA, Ed/Narr Wr; *Carl Ott: The Will To Win*, "Adrienne Clarkson Presents", TV, 90, CDN/F, Wr; *The Wings of September*, Imax, Th, 89, CDN/J, Wr/Ed; *Canada: Another Government Movie*, Th, 87, CDN, Wr/Ed; *Riding The Tornado*, "Reckoning", TV, 86, CDN, Dir/Wr/Ed; *After the Big One*, TV, 83, CDN, Dir/Wr; *Something Hidden/The Biography of Wilder Penfield*, TV, 80, CDN, Dir/Ed.

LUHOVY, Yurij G.
ACCT, SMPTE. La Maison du Montage, 2330 Beaconsfield Ave., Montreal, PQ H4A 2G8 (514)481-5871.
Type of Production and Credits: Th Film-Ed/Prod/Dir; Th Short-Ed/Prod/Dir; TV Film-Ed/Dir.
Genres: Drama-Th&TV; Industrial-Th; Action-Th&TV; Documentary-Th&TV.
Biography: Born in 1949 in Belgium; Canadian citizenship. Languages: English, French and Ukrainian. B.A., Literature and Cinema, Sir George Williams (Concordia) University. Has own editing house. Awards for *Harvest of Despair* are as follows: first prize Grand Award Silver Bowl Trophy for Best Overall and the first prize, Gold Medal for Best Documentary from the International Film and Television Festival of New York, 1985; first prize- Gold Lone Star award for Best Documentary from the Houston International Film Festival; Chris award for Best Social Documentary from the 33rd Annual Columbus International Film Festival; the Special Jury award and the Antoinette Kryski award from the Yorkton Short Film and Video Festival.
Selected Filmography: *The Dance Goes On*, Th, 90-91, CDN, Ed; *50th Anniversary of the Allied Jewish Community Services*, In, 90, CDN, Cam/Ed; *Camp B'Nai B'Rith*, In, 90, CDN, Dir/Ed; *Harold Greenberg, the Montreal World Film Festival's Merit Award*, In, 89, CDN, Dir/Ed; *La Cosecha de la Desseperanza*, Th, 89, RA, P Prod Dir; *Harold Greenberg's 60th Birthday Celebration*, In, 89, CDN, Dir/Ed; *Harold's Tribute*, ED, 87, CDN, Ed; *Captive Hearts*, Th, 87, USA, Ed; "Les Tisserands du pouvoir" (6 eps), TV, 87, CDN/F, Ed; *Astral - A Great Canadian Company*, In, 86, CDN, Ed; "Race for the

Bomb" (6 eps), TV, 86, CDN/F, Spv Ed; *Harvest of Despair*, Th, 85, CDN, Prod/Assoc Dir/Ed/P Prod Spv; "WWII - Educational Conference" (15 eps), ED, 85, CDN, Prod/Dir/Ed; "1933 Ukrainian Famine Symposium" (20 eps), ED, 84, CDN, Prod/Dir; *The Year of the Hungry Horse*, ED, 84, CDN, Ed.

LUSSIER, Jo
223 St. Joseph ouest, Montréal, PQ (514)495-9067. Coscient Inc., 300 Leo-Parizeau, CP 1145, Suite 2400, Montréal, PQ H2W 2P4 (514)284-2525.
Types de production et générique: TV film-Mont; TV vidéo-Mont/Réal.
Types d'oeuvres: Variété-TV; Documentaire-TV; Enfants-C&TV.
Curriculum vitae: Née à Ottawa en 1957. Langues: français et anglais. Bacc. Arts Visuels, comm. graphique, Université Laval. Monteur TV de 1984 `a 1991.
Filmographie sélective: *La Coccinelle Tigrée La Livraison*, "La Saga d'Archibald," (13 eps), TV, 91, CDN/F, Mont; "Omni Science" (78 eps), TV, 88-91, CDN, Mont; "The Science Show" (55 eps), TV, 89-90, CDN, Mont; *spécial La Tournée Des Fêtes Molson/O'Keefe*, TV, 89, CDN, Mont; "L'Aventure" (5 eps), TV, 89, CDN, Mont; *spécial Les Grandes Vacances*, TV, 89, CDN, Mont/Scripte; *spécial Bonjour Chez-Vous*, TV, 89, CDN, Mont; "Les Carnets de Louise" (37 eps), TV, 87-88, CDN, Mont/Réal; "Playback" (39 eps), TV, 86-87, CDN, Mont; " Les Canadiens"(mini-documentaire) (8 eps), TV, 85, CDN, Mont; "Série Rock Etc..." (3 eps), TV, 84-85, CDN, Mont.

MacDONALD, Ramuna
- see DIRECTORS

MacGILLIVRAY, William D.
- see DIRECTORS

MacINTYRE, Rod
- see WRITERS

MACKAY, Bruce
- see DIRECTORS

MACKEY, Clarke
- see DIRECTORS

MacLAVERTY, Michael
DGC, ACCT. 37 Corley Ave., Toronto, ON M4E 1T8 (416)690-6405.
Type of Production and Credits: Th Film-Ed; TV Film-Ed; TV Video-Ed.
Genres: Drama-Th&TV; Variety-TV; Action-Th&TV; Horror-Th&TV.
Biography: Born in 1947 in England; immigrated to Canada, 64; Canadian citizenship, 78. Started in film business, 67. Supervising picture editor for series of 20 TV movies, 80-86, for Visual Productions in association with CHCH-TV.
Selected Filmography: "E.N.G." (pilot &

NUMBERS (416) 598-0722
EDGE CODING AND EDITING SUPPLIES

FILM EDITORS
SOUND EDITORS
ASSISTANT EDITORS

WE CARRY ALL YOUR EDITING SUPPLIES

16/35 SPLICING TAPE – PERFORATED 35 TAPE – WHITE LEADER – BLACK LEADER – SOUNDTRACK FILL – COTTON GLOVES – FREON – BLACK VELVETS – WEBRIL WIPES – SYNC BEEPS – READY EDDYS – CORES – MOVILA – FLATBED LAMPS – SHARPIES – GREASE PENCILS – TRIM I.D. CARDS – TRIM BOXES – PAPER TAPE – CAMERA TAPE – GAFFER TAPE – PACKING TAPE – SMILES AND GREAT SERVICE.

79 BERKELEY ST., TORONTO ONTARIO M5A 2W5

44 eps), TV, 89-91, CDN, Spv Snd Ed; "Night Heat" (8 eps), TV, 88, CDN, Snd Ed; "Friday the 13th - The Series" (8 eps), TV, 88, CDN/USA, Snd FX Ed; *Mania*, TV, 85, CDN, ED; "Just Jazz" (52 eps), TV, 84-85, CDN, Spv Ed; "Niagara Repertory Theatre" (24 eps), TV, 83-84, CDN, Ed/Spv Ed; *Survival 1990*, TV, 83, CDN, Spv Ed; *Firebird 2015 AD*, Th, 80, CDN, Ed; *Curtains*, Th, 80, CDN, Ed; *The Kidnapping of the President*, Th, 79, CDN, Ed; *Tanya's Island*, Th, 79, CDN, Ed; *Running*, Th, 78, CDN, 1st Assist Ed; *Just Jessie*, Th, 78, CDN, Ed; *Ragtime Summer*, Th, 76, CDN/GB, 1st Assist Ed.

MANNE, M.C.
ACTRA. 546 Old Orchard Gr., Toronto, ON M5M 2G9 (416)781-3837.
Type of Production and Credits: Th Film-Ed; TV Film-Ed/Dir/Wr.
Genres: Drama-Th&TV; Comedy-Th&TV; Documentary-TV; Educational-TV.
Biography: Born 1931. Languages: English, French, German and Spanish.
Selected Filmography: "Man Alive" (19 eps), TV, 67-68, CDN, Ed; *The Fatal Itch*, TV, 86, CDN, Ed; "the fifth estate" (25 eps), TV, 80-85, CDN, Ed; "Quarterly Report" (16 eps), TV, 70-84, CDN, Spv Ed; "Images of Canada" (4 eps), TV, 69-82, CDN, Ed; *Summer's Children*, Th, 78, CDN, Ed; *Obit: Gordon Sinclair*, TV, 77, CDN, Ed/Co-Dir; *Songs and Tales of Yesterday*, TV, 77, CDN, Ed/Wr; *Along the Whoopup Trail*, TV, 76, CDN, Ed/Wr; *Slopes of the Rockies*, TV, 77, USA, Ed; *Ruffled Grouse Riddle*, TV, 75, USA, Ed; *Dance of the Whooping Crane*, TV, 75, USA, Ed; *Carpathian Tales*, TV, 75, CDN, Ed/Wr; *Pastorale*, TV, 75, CDN, Ed/Wr; "Police Surgeon" (10 eps), TV, 72-74, CDN, Ed.

MARKIW, Gabriel
- see PRODUCERS

MARTIN, Susan
- see DIRECTORS

MATTIUSSI, Roger
DGC, ACCT. MOM P.I. Productions Inc., 3737 Napier St., Burnaby, BC V5C 3E4 (604)298-9866. FAX: 298-9830.
Type of Production and Credits: TV Film-Ed; TV Video-Ed.
Genres: Drama-TV; Comedy-TV; Action-TV; Documentary-TV.
Biography: Born in 1951 in Vancouver, British Columbia. Has edited more than 75 films, from animation to documentaries; a number of these have won international awards.
Selected Filmography: "Mom P.I." (25 eps), TV, 90-91, CDN, Assoc Prod; *Welcome to the Monkey House* (3 eps), TV, 90, CDN/USA, P Pro Spv; *Five in a Row*, MV, 89, AUS, PM; "MacGyver" (18 eps), TV, 87-88, USA, 2nd U Dir; *Where Is Here?*, TV, 86-87, CDN/USA, Ed; *At the Brink*, "The Nuclear Age", TV, 86, USA, Ed; "Adderly" (2 eps), TV, 86, CDN, Ed; "Airwaves" (4 eps), TV, 85-86, CDN, Ed; *Showstoppers*, TV, 85, CDN, Ed/Snd Ed; *The Crowd*, "Ray Bradbury Theatre", TV, 85, CDN, Ed; *The Front Line*, "For the Record", TV, 84, CDN, Ed/Snd Ed; *All the Years*, "Bell Canada Playhouse", TV, 84, CDN, Ed; *White Lies/An Ounce of Cure*, "Sons and Daughters", TV, 83-84, CDN, Ed; "Spirit Bay" (pilot), TV, 83, CDN, Ed; *Thanks for the Ride*, TV, 82, CDN, Ed.

MAZUR, Lara
ACCT. 5581 Dundas St., Burnaby, BC V5B 1B3 (604)291-1117.
Type of Production and Credits: Th Film-Ed; TV Film-Elec Ed/P Prod Spv.
Genres: Drama-Th&TV; Comedy-Th&TV; Documentary-Th&TV.
Biography: BFA, University of Manitoba; 13 years experience, with over 40 films as an editor and 28 films as a sound editor to her credit, winning over 70 awards throughout the world.
Selected Filmography: *Curse of the Viking Grave*, TV, 91, CDN, Ed; *Bordertown Café*, Th, 91, CDN, Ed/P Prod Spv; *Kootenai Brown*, Th, 91, CDN, Ed; *Deep Sleep*, Th, 90, CDN, Ed; *The Last Winter*, Th, 89, CDN, Ed; *American Boyfriends*, Th, 89, CDN, Ed; *Martha, Ruth & Edie*, Th, 87, CDN, Ed; "Ramona Q" (5 eps), TV, 87, F/USA/CDN, Ed; *Heaven on Earth*, TV, 86, GB/CDN, Ed; *Daughter of the Country* (mini-series), TV, 85-86, CDN, Ed/P Prod Spv; *Tramp at the Door*, TV, 84, CDN, Ed; *Get a Job*, Th, 85, CDN, Snd Ed; *Cages*, TV, 84, CDN, Ed; *The Prodigal*, TV, 83, CDN, Ed; *In the Fall*, TV, 82, CDN, Ed.

McCLELLAN, Gordon
DGC, ACCT. Interframe Productions Inc., 3424 Grand Forks Rd., Mississauga, ON L4Y 3M9 (416)238-2820.
Type of Production and Credits: Th Film-ED; TV Film-Ed.
Genres: Drama-Th&TV; Documentary-Th&TV.
Biography: Born 1949, Ottawa, Ontario. B.A., Film, Queen's University, 71. Film and video picture editor since 71. *Love and Hate* won Best Mini-Series Gemini, 90, and *A Marriage Made in Hell* was number one Neilsen-rated show in US.

Squamish Five won Best TV Movie Gemini, 89; *Skate!* won Best TV Movie Gemini 88. Edited 3 of 4 Best TV Movie nominees in 88. *Just Another Missing Kid* won an Oscar, 82. Won an Ace award in 1986, for editing *Rapists: Can They Be Stopped?*
Selected Filmography: *Grand Larceny*, TV, 91, CDN, Ed; "Road to Avonlea" (6 eps), TV, 90, CDN, Ed; "Maggie's Secret" (1 eps), TV, 90, CDN, Ed; *Wisecracks*, Th, 90, CDN, Ed; *Love and Hate/A Marriage Made in Hell* (mini-series), TV, 89, CDN, Ed; *The Private Capital*, TV, 89, CDN, Ed; *Termini Station*, Th, 89, CDN, Ed; *The Squamish Five*, TV, 88, CDN, Ed; *Skate!*, TV, 87, CDN, Ed; *Family Reunion*, TV, 87, CDN, Ed; *And Then You Die*, TV, 87, CDN, Ed; *The Real Stuff*, TV, 86, CDN, Ed; *Tears Are Not Enough*, Th, 85, CDN, Ed/Assoc Prod; *Alex Colville: The Splendour of Order*, TV, 84, CDN, Ed; *Just Another Missing Kid*, TV, 81, CDN, Ed.

McEWEN, Mary Anne
- see WRITERS

McGLYNN, Gordon Paul
- see DIRECTORS

McILVRIDE, David
- see DIRECTORS

MERRITT, Judith
3730 Coloniale Ave., Montreal, PQ H2X 2Y6 (514)849-1561. NFB, Box 6100, Station A, Montreal, PQ H3C 3H5 (514)283-9474.
Type of Production and Credits: TV Film-Ed.
Genres: Documentary-Th&TV.
Biography: Born 1937. Educated in London, England; came to Canada, 54. Received professional training at the NFB.
Selected Filmography: *Burning Times*, TV, 89, CDN, Ed/Assoc Dir/Prod; *Goddess Remembered*, TV, 89, CDN, Ed/Assoc Dir/Prod; *See No Evil*, TV, 87, CDN, Ed; *Apprenticeship of Mordecai Richler*, TV, 86, CDN, Ed; *After the Crash*, "At the Wheel", TV, 85, CDN, Ed; *Anybody's Son Will Do*, "War", TV, 84, CDN, Ed; *Goodbye War*, "War", TV, 84, CDN, Ed; *See You in the Funny Papers*, TV, 83, CDN, Ed; *Lost Pharoah*, TV, 82, CDN, Ed; *Arthritis: A Dialogue With Pain*, TV, 81, CDN, Ed; *Loved, Honoured and Bruised*, TV, 80, CDN, Ed; *Paintings of the 1930's*, TV, 77, CDN, Ed.

MILINKOVIC, Gerry
- see DIRECTORS

MONDION, Denis
NABET, SMPTE. 115, boul. Goyer, St-Eustache, PQ J7P 5E4 (514)491-1639 Supersuite, 4 Westmount Square, bur. 200, Westmount PQ (514)933-1161. FAX: 933-1706.
Types de production et générique: TV film-Mont; TV vidéo-Mont; TV-post-production-Mont.
Types d'oeuvres: Drame-TV; Comédie-TV; Annonces-TV; Vidéo-clips-TV.
Curriculum vitae: Né en 1957, Montréal, Québec. Langues: français et anglais. Etudes en techniques de l'électronique, Cégep de Maisonneuve, 79. Expérience: Télé-Métropole de 79-84; depuis 1984, Supersuite (Les Productions Champlain Inc.) Monteur senior et superviseur. Se spécialise dans les effets visuels en montage en ligne et dans les animations élecroniques. 6 nominations aux prix Gémeaux. Gagnant du Gémeaux 1988 du meilleur montage, série de comédie. Commerciaux: Laurentide, Budweiser, Labatt 50, Loto-Québec, Via Rail, Hydro-Québec.
Filmographie sélective: "Juste pour rire" (vers fr et angl), TV, 87-88, CDN, Mont; "Rock et Belles Oreilles", TV, 86-87, CDN, Mont, (GEMEAUX); "Shades of Love", TV, 87, CDN, Mont; "D'amour et de théâtre" (3 eps), TV, 85-87, CDN, Mont; "Passe-Partout" (21 eps), TV, 86, CDN, Mont.

MONTPETIT, Jean-Guy
STCQ. 3711, Drolet, Montréal, PQ H2X 3H7 (514)845-4837.
Types de production et générique: l métrage-Mont/Mont son; TV film-Mont; TV vidéo-Mont.
Types d'oeuvres: Drame-C&TV; Comédie-C&TV; Enfants-C&TV; Anmation-C&TV.
Curriculum vitae: Né à Québec en 1951. Baccalauréat en journalisme, Univ. Laval.
Filmographie sélective: "Les Filles de Caleb" (20 eps), TV, 89-90 CDN, Mont; *A Star for Two*, C, 90, F/CDN, Mont; *Eddie and the Cruisers II/Eddie Lives*, C, 89, USA, Mont; *Gaspard et Fils*, C, 88, CDN, Mont; *Tinamer*, C, 87, CDN, Mont; *The Peanut Butter Solution*, C, 85, CDN, Mont; "Transit" (1 eps), TV, 86, CDN, Mont; "Getting to Work" (1 eps), TV, 86, CDN, Mont; "Cap Lumière", TV, 86, CDN, Mont; "Georges and the Star" (1 eps), TV, 85, CDN, Mont son; *Killing Them Softly*, C, 85, CDN, Mont; *Maria-Chapdelaine*, TV, 82, CDN, Mont son; *Les Plouffes*, TV, 80, CDN, Mont son; *The Lucky Star*, C, 80, CDN, Mont son, (GENIE); *Quest for Fire/La Guerre du Feu*, C, 81, F/CDN, 2e mont.

MOORE, James◊
(416)690-4269.

Type of Production and Credits: Th Short-Ed/Snd Rec/Snd Ed/Comp; TV Video-Ed/Snd Ed/Comp.
Genres: Documentary-TV; Commercials-TV; Industrial-TV; Music Video-TV.
Biography: Born in 1959 in Boulder, Colorado; landed immigrant Canada, 70. Hons. B.A., Philosophy and Psychology, University of Western Ontario. Musicians since age 10; has worked in video for past 6 years; started own production services business in 86; specializes in composing and producing music videos using unusual motion control techniques.
Selected Filmography: Cheerios Bananas, Cm, 88, CDN, Snd Ed; *Burlington Cultural Centre*, In, 88, CDN, Comp; *Video Zone*, MV, 88, CDN, Dir/Comp/Ed; Colgate Palmolive, Cm, 86-88, CDN, Snd Rec; *Boysie and Imogene*, TV, 88, CDN, Ed; *McGarvey*, TV, 88, CDN, Ed; *IBM - Building Solutions*, In, 87, CDN, Ed/Comp; *York University*, ED, 87, CDN, Snd Rec; *Ontario Heritage Foundation*, In, 87, CDN, Ed; *Schwarzkopf*, In, 87, CDN, Snd Rec; *Discount - The Movie*, In, 87, CDN, Snd Rec; *Co-op - The Wizard*, In, 87, CDN, Snd Rec/Ed; *Nabisco Vice*, In, 86, CDN, Snd Rec/Ed; *BMX Racing*, In, 86, CDN, Ed; *C.A.P.E.*, Frito Lay, In, 86, CDN, Ed.

MORIN, Bertrand
- voir REALISATEURS

MORNINGSTAR, Michael
NABET 72. Morningstar Films, 76 Ferrier Ave., Toronto, ON M4K 3H4 (416)469-1729.
Type of Production and Credits: TV Film-Ed/Prod/Dir.
Genres: Drama-Th&TV; Documentary-Th&TV.
Biography: Born 1954, Niagara Falls, Ontario. Studied Theatre and Film, Brock University; Film Production, York University. VTR Editor, TVOntario.
Selected Filmography: "A Question of Justice" (4 eps), TV, 91, CDN, Ed; "the fifth estate" (40 eps), TV, 83-87, CDN, Ed; *Strangers in a Strange Land*, Th, 87, CDN, Ed; *The Street Where We Live*, TV, 87, CDN, Ed; *Dream Merchants/The Fastest Man on Wheels*, "the fifth estate", TV, 81-82, CDN, Assoc Prod; *A.J. Casson - The Only Critic Is Time*, TV, 80, CDN, Dir/Prod/Wr.

MORRONE, Tony
- see PRODUCERS

MOSSANEN, Moze
- see DIRECTORS

MULLER, Helmfried
- see CINEMATOGRAPHERS

MUNN, Michael
19 Olive Ave., Toronto, ON M6G 1T7 (416)536-9835. Grimthorpe Film, 14 Grimthorpe Rd., Toronto, ON M6C 1G3 (416)653-2088.
Type of Production and Credits: Th Film-Ed; Th Short-Ed; TV Film-Ed.
Genres: Drama-Th; Comedy-Th; Experimental-Th; Musical-Th; Industrial-Th.
Biography: Born in 1959. Canadian citizen. Graduate of Film Studies, Ryerson Polytechnical Institute, 1984. Has travelled extensively in Europe and Asia as well as working one year in Japan.
Selected Filmography: *Tectonic Plates*, TV, 91, CDN/GB, Ed; *Masala*, Th, 90, CDN, Ed; *The Secret Goldfish*, Th, 90, CDN, Ed; *Roadkill*, Th, 89, CDN, Ed; *The Pride of Duntroon*, Th, 88, CDN, Ed.

MYERS, Toni
41 Amelia St., Toronto, ON M4X 1E3 (416)961-7961.
Type of Production and Credits: Th Film-Ed; Th Short-Ed/Wr/Narr; TV Film-Ed.
Genres: Drama-Th&TV; Musical-Th; Documentary-Th&TV; Educational-Th.
Biography: Spent six years in England working on films with Canadian director Allan King and with the Beatles' former company, Apple. Has worked with John Lennon, Yoko Ono, Donovan, and created various film segments for the BBC's "Top of the Pops". Worked at the BBC with associate directors and cameramen and formed Tattoist Int'l., an independent group working on experimental films in London and Los Angeles. Upon returning to Canada, worked on "This Hour has Seven Days, "Forest Rangers" and "Seaway". Went on to edit several dramas for CBC TV's "For the Record", working with directors Gilles Carle, Francis Mankiewicz and Claude Jutra. Began an association with wide-screen films in 1967 as assistant editor on Graeme Ferguson's multi-screen film, *Polar Life*. *Abortion: Stories from the North and South*, won Best Editing, Quebec Film Festival.
Selected Filmography: *North of Superior* (Imax), Th, CDN, Ed; *Snow Job* (Imax), Th, CDN, Ed; *Ocean* (Imax), Th, CDN, Ed; *Nomads of the Deep* (Imax), Th, CDN, Ed; *Hail Columbia* (Imax), Th, CDN, Ed; *The Dream is Alive* (Imax), Th, CDN, Ed; *By Design*, Th, CDN, Ed; *Surfacing*, Th, CDN, Ed; *A Thousand Moons*, TV, CDN, Ed; *What We Have Here is a People Problem*, TV, CDN, Ed; *Dreamspeaker*, TV, CDN, Ed; *A Matter of Choice*, TV, CDN, Ed; *Abortion: Stories from the North*

and South, ED, CDN, Ed; *Arts Cuba*, ED, CDN, Ed; *Shadows of Bliss*, ED, GB, Ed.

NEW, David
887 Dovercourt Rd., Toronto, ON M6H 2X6 (416)516-0469.
Type of Production and Credits: Th Short-Wr/Prod/Ed; TV Film-Ed; TV Video-Dir/Ed; Interactive V/Disc-Ed.
Genres: Drama-Th&TV; Musical-Th&TV; Industrial-Th&TV; Documentary-Th&TV;.
Biography: Born in 1961 in Toronto, Ontario. Canadian citizen. B.I.S., 1984. Studied music and computer graphics. Speaks fluent French and some Spanish and Portuguese. Has worked on HDTV and interactive videodisc formats, among others. Founding member of BEAM 103, an alternative music recording studio and distribution company. Computer graphics and blue-screen matte experience.
Selected Filmography: *Memories of Jets*, TV, 91, CDN, Dir/Wr; *Canadian Brass: Home Movies*, TV, 91, CDN/GB, Ed; *Nights in the Gardens of Spain*, TV, 90, CDN/E/GB, Ed; *When the Fire Burns*, TV, 90, CDN/GB/E, Ed/Wr; *Breaking Through*, Cm, 90, CDN, Dir; *Riders of the Pig*, Th, 89, CDN, Wr/Prod/Ed; *The Best We Have To Give?*, TV, 89, CDN/GB, Ed; *The Adventure Begins*, "The Spacewatch Club", TV, 89, CDN/USA, Ed; *Space Pioneers*, TV, 88, CDN, Ed; "Spacewatch" (pilot), TV, 87, CDN/USA, Ed; *The Bartletts*, ED, 86, CDN, Ed; *Incompatibilities*, TV, 85, CDN, Wr/Prod/Ed; *The Hospital*, ED, 85, CDN, Ed.

NEWTON, John
- see DIRECTORS

NICHOL, Gary
- see PRODUCERS

NICOL, Eric
- see WRITERS

OLDENBURG, Gunter◇
(416)961-5839.
Type of Production and Credits: Th Film-Ed; TV Film-Ed.
Genres: Drama-Th&TV; Comedy-Th&TV; Variety-TV; Documentary-TV; Commercials-TV; Industrial-TV.
Biography: Born 1937, Berlin, Germany; landed immigrant Canada. Started work in film with Pathé Nouvelle, Paris; to Canada, 59; worked with CBC; joined CFTO, 61; to Europe with Disney Films; returned to Canada and joined TDF Productions, 56; President of Central Film Services, 68; bought assets, 70; produced, directed and edited many TV commercials; now production consultant.
Selected Filmography: "Seaway" (39 eps), TV, 66, CDN, Ed; *Ballerina*, Th, 65, USA, Assist Ed; "Forest Rangers" (13 eps), TV, 65, CDN, Ed; *Emil and the Detectives*, Th, 63, USA, Assist Ed; "Heritage" (4 eps), TV, 59, CDN, 1st Assist Dir/Assist Ed; "Face of Labour" (4 eps), TV, 59, CDN, 1st Assist Dir/Assist Ed; *Man on a String*, Th, 57, USA, 1st Assist Dir; *Fraulein*, Th, 56, USA, 2nd Assist Dir.

ORD, Cathy
- see DIRECTORS

PAAKSPUU, Kalli
- see PRODUCERS

PACHECO, Bruno Lazaro
- see DIRECTORS

PAPILLON, Denis
ACCT. 2551 boul. Cantin, Longueuil, PQ J4M 2N9 (514)468-7307.
Types de production et générique: l métrage-Mont; c métrage-Mont; TV film-Mont; TV vidéo-Mont.
Types d'oeuvres: Comédie-C&TV; Variété-C&TV; Annonces-C&TV; Drame-C&TV.
Curriculum vitae: Né à Québec. Citoyenneté canadienne. Langue: maternelle, français. Education: Dec en communications, certificat en communications, certificat en publicité, Univ. de Montréal. Monteur depuis 1975. Plusieurs documentaires, films industriels; plus de mille commerciaux, un long métrage, series télé (dramatique et de variété).Prix Gémeaux (RBO, 1988). Grand intérêt pour les vins.
Filmographie sélective: *Fire and Ice*, "Urban Angel", TV, 90, CDN, Mont; *Postcard From the Past*, "Urban Angel", TV, 90, CDN, Mont; *Le Choix*, "Lance et Compte", TV, 90, CDN, Mont; *Here Comes The Groom*, "Inside Stories", TV, 90, CDN, Mont; "Le festival juste pour rire" (10 eps), TV, 89-90, CDN, Chef Mont; "Rock et Belles Oreilles" (44 eps), TV, 88-89, CDN, Mont, (GEMEAUX).

PARISEAU, Marcel
- voir REALISATEURS

PATE, Brent◇
ACCT. (416)766-3607.
Type of Production and Credits: TV Video-Ed.
Genres: Comedy-TV; Children's-TV; Commercials-TV; Music Video-TV.
Biography: Born 1957, London, Ontario. Studied TV Broadcasting, Fanshawe College.
Selected Filmography: Wintario/E40/Woodies/Kraft/Crispy Crunch/Pork, Cm, 86, CDN, Ed; *Project Leapfrog*, In, 86, CDN, Ed; *Madame*, MV, 86, CDN, Ed; Texaco/Klondike Days/Trappers Baseball/

Silverwing Travel, Cm, 85, CDN, Ed; *Butt-Out*, In, 85, CDN, Ed; *Bopolina/Polly-anne*, MV, 85, CDN, Prod/Dir/Ed; *Good Friends*, MV, 85, CDN, Ed; "SCTV" (160 eps)(re-edit for syndication), TV, 84-85, CDN, Co-Ed; "Native Heritage" (26 eps), TV, 85, CDN, Ed; "The Little Vampire" (13 eps), TV, 85, CDN/GB/D, Ed; *Apartment on the Dark Side of the Moon*, TV, 84, CDN, Ed; "Rendezvous" (13 eps), TV, 84, CDN, Ed; *Bonnie Doon*, Cm, 84, CDN, Ed; "Living Today" (26 eps), TV, 84, CDN, Ed.

PATERSON, Sally
DGC, CFEG, ACCT. 321 Crawford St., Toronto, ON M6J 2V7 (416)535-6687.
Type of Production and Credits: TV Video-Ed.
Genres: Drama-Th&TV; Comedy-Th&TV; Documentary-Th&TV; Musical-Th&TV;
Biography: Born in 1946 in England; Canadian citizenship. Taught film editing at Toronto Film Cooperative; President of Canadian Film Editors' Guild, 83. Resident Editor for United Nations Audio-Visual Information Centre, Vancouver. *Chambers: Tracks and Gestures* won Best Editing, CFEG; *Overnight*, nominated, Best Picture Editing, Genie Awards, 86.
Selected Filmography: *Talk 16*, Th, 91, CDN, Ed; *The Tai Babilonia Story*, TV, 90, USA, Ed; "Magic Hour" (3 eps), TV, 90, CDN, Ed; "The Twilight Zone" (10 eps), TV, 88, CDN/USA, Ed; *A Child's Christmas in Wales*, TV, 87, CDN/USA/GB, Ed; "Life Revolution" (3 eps), TV, 87, CDN, Ed; "Street Legal" (3 eps), TV, 86, CDN, Ed; "Ramona" (5 eps), TV, 86, CDN/USA, Ed; *Overnight*, Th, 85, CDN, Ed; "Airwaves" (8 eps), TV, 85, CDN, Ed; "Danger Bay" (6 eps), TV, 85, CDN, Ed; *Class of Promise*, TV, 85, CDN, Ed; "American Caesar" (3 eps), TV, 83, CDN, ED; "Going Great" (26 eps), TV, 81-32, CDN, Ed; *Chambers: Tracks and Gestures*, TV, 82, CDN, Ed, (CFEG).

PERZEL, Anthony
- see PRODUCERS

PILON, France
STCQ. 3942, rue Berri, Montréal, PQ H2L 4H1 (514)849-5091.
Types de production et générique: l métrage-Mont; c métrage-Mont; TV film-Mont/Sc.
Types d'oeuvres: Drame-C&TV; Documentaire-C&TV; Education-C&TV; Enfants-C&TV.
Curriculum vitae: Née en 1947, Kapuskasing, Ontario. Langues: français et anglais. Baccalauréat ès arts, Collège St-Maurice, Québec. A participé à des jury pour l'Institut québécois du cinéma.
Filmographie sélective: *Pellan*, C, 86, CDN, Sc/Rech/Mont; *Toutes les photos finissent par se ressembler*, C, 84-85; CDN, Mont; *Bateau blue, maison verte*, C, 84-85, CDN, Mont; **Marc-Aurèle Fortin**, 1988-1970, C, 82, CDN, Mont/Sc; *Ces étrangers nos amis*, C, 80, CDN, Mont; "Portraits d'un été" (2 eps), TV, 79-80, CDN, Mont; *La Point du moulin*, C, 79, CDN, Mont; *Thetford au milieu de notre vie*, C, 78, CDN, Mont; *Clara, d'amour et de révolte*, C, 78, CDN, mont; *La Tradition de l'orgue au Québec*, C, 78, CDN, Mont; "Un pays, un goût, une manière" (10 eps), TV, 76-77, CDN, Mont; "Passe défini" (5 eps), TV, 76, CDN, Mont; "L'Amout quotidien" (6 eps), TV, 75, CDN, Mont; *Autopsie d'une exclusion*, "Les Exclus", TV, 75, CDN, Mont; *Histoire de pêche*, C, 74, CDN, Mont.

PINDER, Chris◇
DGC. (416)690-3262.
Type of Production and Credits: TV Film-Ed/Snd Ed.
Genres: Drama-Th&TV; Documentary-Th&TV; Educational-TV; Industrial-TV.
Biography: Born in Canada. Languages: English and French. Honours B.A., English Language and Literature, Glendon College, York University. Editing since 78; previous experience in educational film distribution; published writer/researcher for national trade magazine. Editor on award-winning documentaries.
Selected Filmography: "The Feminization of Poverty" (2 eps), TV, 88, CDN, Snd Ed; *The Real Stuff*, TV, 87, CDN, Snd Ed; *Working for Tomorrow and Ways of Winning*, In, 87, CDN, Ed; *The Birth of Language*, TV, 86, CDN, Ed; "Durrell in Russia" (4 eps), TV, 85, CDN, Snd Ed; *By Our Own Hands*, TV, 85, CDN, Snd Ed; "The Olympians" (6 eps), TV, 84, CDN, Ed; *Sunshine for Sale*, In, 84, CDN, Snd Ed; "The Chinese" (4 eps), TV, 82, CDN, Snd Ed; *Raoul Wallenberg: Buried Alive*, Th, 82, CDN, Snd Ed; *The Battle of Beech Hall*, "Man Alive", TV, 81, CDN, Ed; "The Ten Thousand Day War" (3 eps), TV, 80, CDN, Snd Ed; *It's in Every One of Us*, In, 79, CDN, Ed; *Can Canada Compete?*, In, 78, CDN, Ed.

PIRKER, Roland K.
- see CINEMATOGRAPHERS

POTHIER, Marcel
ACCT. Productions Cinébulle Inc., 2619 De Soissons, Montréal, PQ H3S 1V7 (514)738-5106. 522-9828.

Types de production et générique: l métrage-Mont/Mont son; TV film-Mont/Mont son; c métrage-Mont/Mont son.
Types d'oeuvres: Drame-C&TV; Variété-TV; Action-C; Documentaires-C&TV.
Curriculum vitae: Né en 1948, St-Hyacinthe, Québec. Etudes classiques. Début de formation cinéma, Onyx Films (Montréal), 69-72. Boursier du Conseil des Arts, stage à Paris en bruitage et postsyncro au Studio de Boulogne, 77. Plusieurs nominations aux Prix Génie.
Filmographie sélective: *Un enfant sur le lac*, C, 91, CDN, Mont son; "Urban Angel" (6 eps), TV, 91, CDN, Mont son; *Une nuit à l'école*, C, 91, CDN, Mont son; *Ding & Dong*, C, 90, CDN, Mont son; *Une histoire inventée*, C, 90, CDN, Mont son; *Moody Beach*, C, 90, CDN, Mont son; *Impasse de la vignette*, C, 89, CDN, Mont son; *Sous les draps les étoiles*, C, 89, CDN, Mont son; *Jésus de Montréal*, C, 89, CDN, Mont son, (GENIE); *Vent de galerne*, C, 88, CDN, Mont son; *Gaspard & Fils*, C, 88, CDN, Mont son; *A corps perdu*, C, 88, CDN, Mont son; *The Jeweller's Shop*, C, 87, CDN/I/F, Mont son; *Le Million tout puissant*, TV, 86, CDN, Mont son; *Un zoo la nuit*, C, 86, CDN, Conc son, (GENIE); *Le Frère André*, C, 86, CDN, Mont son.

PRESANT, Donald A.
166 Wheeler Ave., Toronto, ON M4L 3V4 (416)694-9499. Loki Film & Video, P.O. Box 341, Adelaide Stn., Toronto, ON M5C 2J4 (416)429-1928.
Type of Production and Credits: Th Short-Ed; TV Video-Ed.
Genres: Drama-TV; Documentary-TV; Industrial-Th.
Biography: Born in 1956 inToronto, Ontario. Languages: English, French, some German and Spanish. Bachelor of Arts, Communications, Concordia University.
Selected Filmography: "The Global Family" (20 eps), TV, 91, CDN, Ed; *Making It Happen*, TV, 91, CDN, Wr/Dir/Ed; *Bicycles: Not Just for Fun*, TV, 90, CDN, Wr/Dir/Ed; "Medical Video Library" (4 eps), ED, 88, CDN, Ed; *Electrotech*, In, 88, CDN, Ed; "Captain Power's Greatest Hits" (4 eps), MV, 88, CDN, Ed; *The Lurking Threat*, In, 87, CDN, Ed; *Trial by Fire*, In, 87, CDN, Ed; *The Black Box*, Th, 86, CDN, Ed.

PYKE, Roger
- see DIRECTORS

RACINE, Pierre
- voir DIRECTEURS-PHOTO

RAVOK, Brian
DGC, ACTT. 111 Davisville Ave., PH 18, Toronto, ON M4S 1G5 (416)485-3100.
Type of Production and Credits: Th Film-Ed/Snd Ed; Th Short-Ed/Snd Ed; TV Film-Ed/Snd Ed; TV Video-Ed/Snd Ed.
Genres: Drama-Th; Comedy-Th; Documentary-Th&TV; Commercials-TV.
Biography: Born in 1942 in England; Canadian citizenship. Languages: English and French. Started at BBC; immigrated to Montreal under contract to Onyx Film Inc. as supervising editor, 74; to TVOntario; then freelance, 77; has edited commercials, documentaries, docudramas since 64. Supervising editor on animation series in Korea (K.K. DIC), 85; Japan (K.K. DIC), 86.
Selected Filmography: *Termini Station*, Th, 89, CDN, Snd Ed; "T and T" (13 eps), TV, 88-89, CDN/USA, Snd Ed; *Straightline*, TV, 88, CDN, Snd Ed; *Screwballs*, Th, 82, CDN, Ed; *Melanie*, Th, 80, CDN, Ed; *Prom Night*, Th, 79, CDN, Ed; *Something's Rotten*, Th, 78, CDN, Ed; *Quebec the Good Earth*, Th, 75, CDN, Ed, (CFEG).

REED, Tony
ACCT. 5334 Esplanade, Montreal, PQ H2T 2Z7 (514)279-0461.
Type of Production and Credits: Th Film-Dial Ed; TV Film-Snd Ed; TV Video-Dial Ed.
Genres: Drama-Th&TV; Documentary-TV; Commercials-Th&TV.
Biography: Born in 1948 in Montreal, Quebec. Canadian citizen with a British "Right of Abode". Educated at UBC and London Film School. Fluently bilingual. Has worked in London, New York, Montreal and Hong Kong.
Selected Filmography: *Citizenship in Action/Government in Action*, ED, 91, CDN, Ed.

REIART, Arvo
31 Bellefair Ave., Toronto, ON M4L 3T7 (416)699-2704. CBC, 790 Bay St., Toronto, ON M5G 1N8 (416)975-7627.
Type of Production and Credits: TV Film-Ed/Snd Ed.
Genres: Drama-TV; Comedy-TV; Documentary-TV.
Biography: Born 1950, Goteborg, Sweden. Languages: English and Estonian. B.A., English and Fine Arts, University of Guelph.
Selected Filmography: *Oil Spills*, "The Nature of Things", TV, 91, CDN, Ed; *Captive of Conscience/Dr. Giannou*, "Man

Alive", TV, 91, CDN, Snd Ed; *Not Your Average Lawyer/Clayton Ruby*, "Man Alive", TV, 91, CDN, Ed/Snd Ed; *Day of Reckoning* "The Nature of Things", TV, 91, CDN, Ed; *Leonard (Leonard Cohen)*, "Adrienne Clarkson's Summerfest", TV, 90, CDN, Ed/Snd Ed; *Eye of the Needle/Martin Connell*, "Man Alive", TV, 90, CDN, Ed/Snd Ed; *From the Heart/Country Music*, "Man Alive", TV, 90, CDN, Ed/Snd Ed; *Update/Planet for the Taking*, "The Nature of Things", TV, 90, CDN, Snd Ed; *A Family Affair, I & II*, "Man Alive", TV, 89, CDN, Ed/Snd Ed; *Endless Journey/Lesley Parrott*, "Man Alive", TV, 89, CDN, Ed/Snd Ed; *Cracking the Shell/By Reason of Insanity/June Callwood*, "Man Alive", TV, 85-88, CDN, Ed/Snd Ed; *Stein/Russia/Bat*, "The Nature of Things", TV, 88, CDN, Snd Ed; *Murder Sees the Light*, TV, 86, CDN, Assist Snd Ed; *Asylum*, TV, 86, CDN, Assist Ed/Snd Ed; *Prison Mother, Prison Daughter*, TV, 86, CDN, Assist Ed/Snd Ed.

REID, Brian
ITS, SMPTE, ACCT, CFTPA. 189 Millwood Rd., Toronto, ON M4S 1J6 Magnetic North, 70 Richmond St. E, Toronto, ON M5C 1B8 (416)365-7622.
Type of Production and Credits: TV Film-Ed; TV Video-Ed.
Genres: Drama-TV; Variety-TV; Commercials-TV; Music Video-TV.
Biography: Born 1957, Calgary, Alberta. Graduate, Southern Alberta Institute of Technology, (Television, Stage & Radio Arts). EVA Award, 90; nominated for ITS Monitor Award, 91. Special effects editor for many commercials.
Selected Filmography: "You Can't Do That on Television" (13 eps), ED, 84-85, CDN/USA, Ed/FX Ed; *They Went to Fight for Freedom*, TV, 85, CDN, Spv Ed; "The Magic Ring" (5 eps), ED, 84, CDN, Ed; "Medical Legal Issues" (4 eps), ED, 83, CDN, Ed; "The Parent Puzzle" (10 eps), ED, 83, CDN, Co-Ed.

RODECK, Ken
- see PRODUCERS

ROSS, Rodger W.
- see PRODUCERS

ROTUNDO, Nick
DGC. 83 Arlington Ave., Toronto, ON M6G 3L2 (416)654-1277.
Type of Production and Credits: Th Film-Ed; TV Film-Ed.
Genres: Drama-Th; Comedy-Th&TV; Action-Th&TV; Horror-Th&TV.
Biography: Born 1954, Toronto, Ontario. Honours B.F.A., Film Studies, York University, 78.
Selected Filmography: *Carwars*, Toyota, In, 91, CDN, Ed; *Drop Dead Gorgeous*, TV, 91, CDN, Ed; *The Big Slice*, Th, 90, CDN, Ed/Snd Spv; *Red Blooded American Girl*, Th, 90, CDN, Ed/Mus Ed/Spv Snd; *Cold Comfort*, Th, 90, CDN, Ed/Snd Ed/Mus Ed/Assoc Prod; *Prom Night III*, Th, 90, CDN, Ed; *Murder By Night*, TV, 89, CDN, Ed.

ROULSTON, George P.
11 Keystone Ave., Toronto, ON M4C 1G9 (416)690-2738.
Type of Production and Credits: TV Film-Ed; TV Video-Ed.
Genres: Drama-TV; Comedy-TV; Documentary-TV; Musical-TV;
Biography: Born 1946, England; British and Canadian citizenship. B.A., Sir George Williams (Concordia) University. Camera/sound assist., BBC TV; film sound assist., Film House Ltd.; technical prod., Champlain Productions, Montreal; staff ed. at Champlain Productions, MPV, Magnetic North and Glen Warren Productions and Amsterdam Film and Video, The Netherlands.
Selected Filmography: "Sweating Bullets" (5 eps), TV, 91, CDN/MEX/USA, Ed; "The Hidden Room" (2 eps), TV, 91, CDN, Ed; "African Journey", TV, 90, CDN/USA, Ed; "The Hitchhiker" (21 eps), TV, 89-90, CDN/F, Ed; "Diamonds" (2 eps), TV, 88, CDN, Ed; "My Secret Identity" (11 eps), TV, 88, CND/USA, Ed; "Night Heat" (17 eps), TV, 87-88, CDN, Ed; *Ford: The Man and the Machine*, TV, 87, CDN/USA, Ed; *One Night Love Affair*, Bryan Adams, MV, 87, CDN, Ed; *Somebody*, Bryan Adams, MV, 87, CDN, Ed.

ROY, Rita◊
(514)484-5383.
Type of Production and Credits: Th Film-Ed; Th Short-Ed; TV Film-Ed/Dir.
Genres: Drama-Th&TV; Comedy-Th&TV; Variety-Th&TV; Educational-TV.
Biography: Born 1937, Bourlamaque, Quebec. Languages: English and French. Studied Arts and Languages, Cinematography, Concordia University, McGill University, Sorbonne. Lived in Europe for 5 years. Worked for CBC Ottawa, 1 year; joined NFB, 72.
Selected Filmography: *Champlain/Micmac*, "Rendezvous", TV, 88, CDN, Ed; *The King Chronicles* (mini-series), TV, 88, CDN, Co-Ed; *Richard Cardinal: Cry of a Metis Child*, Th, 87, CDN, Ed; *Poundmaker's Lodge: A Healing Place*, Th, 87, CDN, Ed: *Jenny*, "Wednesday's Child",

TV, 87, CDN, Ed; *The Dream and the Triumph/Mortimer Griffin & Shalinsky*, "Bell Canada Playhouse", TV, 85-86, CDN, Ed; *The Job Offer*, TV, 86, CDN, Ed; *Rebellion of Young David/The Trumpetter/Uncle T.*, "Bell Canada Playhouse", TV, 85, CDN, Ed; *Critical Choice/Happy Birthday*, "Bioethics", TV, 85, CDN, Ed; *Canada's Sweetheart: The Saga of Hal C. Banks*, TV, 85, CDN, Ed; *All About Bears*, TV, 84, CDN, Ed/Dir; *Bayo*, Th, 84, CDN, Assist Ed; *Bambinger*, "Bell Canada Playhouse", TV, 84, CDN, Co-Ed; "The Tin Flute"/"Bonheur d'occasion" (5 eps)(Assist Ed, "Bonheur d'occasion"/Fr. and Eng. shot simult.), TV, 82, CDN, Ed; *The Tin Flute/Bonheur d'occasion* (Spv Assist Ed-Bonheur d'occasion/Fr. and Eng. shot simult.), Th, 82, CDN, Assist Ed.

ROY-DECARIE, Matthieu
- voir MONTEURS SON

ROZEMA, Patricia
- see DIRECTORS

RUBBO, Michael
- see WRITERS

RUSSELL, Robin
DGC. 96 Palmerston Blvd., Toronto, ON M6J 2J1 (416)363-3288.
Type of Production and Credits: Th Short-Ed; TV Film-Ed; TV Video-Ed.
Genres: Drama-TV; Comedy-TV; Documentary-TV; Educational-TV.
Biography: Born 1954. Honours B.A., Film, Queen's University, 78.
Selected Filmography: "Tarzan - The Series" (12 eps), TV, 91, USA/CDN/MEX, Spv Ed; "Maniac Mansion" (11 eps), TV, 90, USA/CDN, Ed; *F/X 2*, Th, 90, USA, Assoc Ed; *Survivors of The Titanic*, TV, 89, CDN, Ed; *The Freshman*, Th, 89, USA, 1st Assist Ed; *Speedzone /Cannon Ball Run III*, Th, 89, USA/CDN, Assoc Ed; "The Twilight Zone" (9 eps), TV, 88, USA/CDN, Ed; *Short Circuit II*, Th, 87, USA, 1st Assist Ed; *Hoover vs The Kennedys*, TV, 87, USA/CDN, 1st Assist Ed; *Three Men and a Baby*, Th, 87, USA, Assoc Ed; *Suspect*, Th, 87, USA, Assoc Ed; *Adventures in Babysitting*, Th, 87, USA, 1st Assist Ed; *The Big Town*, Th, 86, USA, 1st Assist Ed; *Dead of Winter*, Th, 86, USA, 1st Assist Ed; *Courage*, TV, 86, USA, 1st Assist Ed.

SANDERS, Ed
- see PRODUCERS

SANDERS, Ronald
DGC. 181 Carlaw Ave., Toronto, ON M4M 2S1 (416)465-3031. FAX: 465-6959. Smith, Gosnell, Nicholson & Asssoc., (213)459-0307. FAX: 454-7987.
Type of Production and Credits: Th Film-Ed; TV Film-Ed.
Genres: Drama-Th&TV; Action-Th; Science Fiction-Th; Horror-Th.
Biography: Born in 1945 in Winnipeg, Manitoba. Bachelor of Arts, English, Political Science, History, University of Manitoba.
Selected Filmography: *Naked Lunch*, Th, 91, GB/CDN, Ed; *Perfectly Normal*, Th, 90, CDN, Ed; *The Gate II*, Th, 89, CDN, Ed; *Age Old Friends*, TV, 89, USA, Ed; *Dead Ringers*, Th, 88, CDN, Ed; "Mariah State" (1 eps), TV, 87, USA, Ed; "Friday the 13th: The Series", TV, 87, CDN/USA, Spv Ed/Coord Prod; *The Fly*, Th, 86, USA, Spv Ed; "Alfred Hitchcock Presents" (6 eps), TV, 86, CDN/USA, Ed; *Striker's Mountain*, TV, 85, CDN, Ed; "Phillip Marlowe Private Eye" (2 eps), TV, 85, CDN, Ed; *The Park Is Mine*, TV, 84, CDN/USA, Ed; *Firestarter*, Th, 83, USA, Ed; *The Dead Zone*, Th, 83, USA, Ed; *Videodrome*, Th, 81, CDN/USA, Ed.

SAUNDERS, Peter◊
ACTT, DGC. (416)536-1360.
Type of Production and Credits: Th Film-Ed/Dir/Wr; Th Short-Dir/Prod/Wr/Ed; TV Film-Ed/Dir/Wr.
Genres: Drama-Th&TV; Documentary-Th&TV; Comedy-Th&TV; Variety-Th&TV;
Biography: Born in 1930 in London, England; landed immigrant, Canada, 1982. Has been in the film industry since 1945. Has had 10 short stories and *The Serbian Triangle*, his first novel, published. Has worked in the Middle East, Africa, Europe, Canada and the US; supervising editor for many British series, including "International Detective," "Glencannon," "Ghost Squad." Co-writer and director of episodes of "Swallows and Amazons;" has directed over 50 commercials.
Selected Filmography: "Street Legal" (4 eps), TV, 87-88, CDN, Snd Ed; *The Man Who Loved Birds*, TV, 86, CDN, Ed; "Profiles of Nature" (11 eps), TV, 85, CDN, Ed; *Parole Dance*, TV, 84, CDN, Ed; *Birds in Paradise*, Th, 83, CDN/USA, 1st Assist Dir; *Cabin Fever*, Th, 83, CDN, 1st Assist Dir; "Lorne Greene's New Wilderness" (9 eps), TV, 82-83, CDN, Ed; *Heavenly Bodies*, Th, 83, CDN, Dial Ed; *Light on a Dark Continent*, Th, 80-81, GB, Ed/Dir/Wr; *North Sea Oil*, Th, 80, GB, Dir; *Ten Seconds to Knockdown*, Th, 79, GB, Dir; *Pyrene Protects*, Th, 79, GB, Dir; *Housewives' Choice*, Th, 78, GB, Dir; *The Lonely Places*, Th, 76, GB, Dir; *Targo Florio*, TV, 74, GB/I, Dir; *Parker Pen*, Th,

73, F, Dir; *Rocket to the Moon*, Th, 67, GB, 2nd Unit Dir; *The African Queen*, Th, 51, USA, Assist Ed.

SAUVE, Alain
- voir MONTEURS SON

SAVOPOL, Adrian
P.O. Box 964, Snowdon Stn., Montréal, PQ H3X 3Y1 (514)529-6512.
Types de production et générique: TV film-Mont/Cam/Pren son; TV vidéo-Mont/Cam/Pren son.
Types d'oeuvres: Drame-TV; Documentaire-TV; Education-TV.
Curriculum vitae: Né en 1958, Roumanie; citoyenneté canadienne. Langues: français, anglais, roumain. Mineur en communications, Univ. de Montréal, 86-87; mineur en cinéma, Univ. de Montréal, 86-87; spécialité cinéma, Ecole d'art de Bucharest, 81-83; spécialité photographie, Univ. culturelle, Bucharest, 79-81. Monteur (film 16 mm), caméraman, technicien du son, assistant réalisateur, Radio-Télévision roumaine, Bucharest, 79.
Filmographie sélective: *Haricana*, TV, 91, CDN, Mont; "Les Jeunes Contrevenants dans la communauté" (13 eps), TV, 88, CDN, Dir tech; *Un contrevenant ça s'arrête*, In, 88, CDN, Ass pro; *Avant après le délit, réagis*, In, 88, CDN, Ass pro; *Le Richelieu des arts*, TV, 87-88, CDN, Dir tech; "Le Droit des gens", TV, 87-88, CDN, Dir tech; "Escales", TV, 87-88, CDN, Dir tech; "Le Monde dans nos mains", TV, 86-87, CDN, Cam; *La Sentimentale entre le discours et la réalité*, TV, 86, CDN, Dir tech; "Lance et Compte" (13 eps) (en double version fr/angl), TV, 86, CDN/F/CH, Ass mont.

SAWCHYN, Norm
NABET. 2441 Wallace St., Regina, SK S4N 4B2 (306)525-2948.
Type of Production and Credits: Th Short-Ed; TV Video-Ed.
Genres: Drama-Th&TV; Documentary-Th&TV; Current Affairs-TV; News-TV.
Biography: Born in Regina, Saskatchewan, 48. Studied Motion Picture Production at the University of Regina from 70-74. Produced, directed and edited TV commercials, industrial and educational films after joining Camera West Film Associates Ltd. in 1978. Also taught production classes at the University of Regina's Film & Video Dept. and held film editing workshops during this period. Joined the CBC as a video editor in 1983, and has remained there to the present. In addition to the perpetual grind of daily news items, has cut innumerable dramatic, documentary and current affairs stories. Occasionally enjoys freelancing and will take on any interesting and challenging project. Won Best Achievement in Editing, Sask. Showcase Awards.
Selected Filmography: *Choices You Make*, ED, 91, CDN, Ed; "The Dreamseekers" (4 eps), TV, 90, CDN, Ed; "The New Immigrants" (3 eps), TV, 89, CDN, Ed; "Countryside" (12 eps), TV, 87-89, CDN, Ed; *The Medicine Line*, Th, 85, CDN, Ed; *The Shipbuilder*, Th, 85, CDN, Ed; *Everyone's Business*, Th, 82, CDN, Ed; *Grain Elevator*, Th, 81, CDN, Ed; *In The Spirit of Our Forefathers*, Th, 76, CDN, Ed.

SCHADT, Christa
- see WRITERS

SCHUURMAN, Hubert
- see DIRECTORS

SILVER, Jonny
- see DIRECTORS

SIMONEAU, Guy
- voir REALISATEURS

SKOGLAND, Kari
- see DIRECTORS

SLIPP, Marke
DGC, ACCT. Pegasus Productions Ltd., 11313 - 123 St., Edmonton, AB T5M 0G1 (403)488-2287.
Type of Production and Credits: Th Film-Ed; TV Film-Ed/Dir/Prod; TV Video-Ed/Dir/Prod.
Genres: Drama-Th&TV; Variety-TV; Documentary-TV; Educational-TV.
Biography: Born 1949, Sackville, New Brunswick. 56-58, actor in TV; in commercials, 69-present; editor on more than 200 documentaries, TV dramas, features, rock videos and educational films; worked in Toronto and Vancouver before establishing Pegasus Productions Ltd., Edmonton, 78; also producer and director. Won Best Editing award at Alberta Film and TV Awards, 88 and 89.
Selected Filmography: *Sylvan Lake Summer*, TV, 90, CDN, Ed; *To the Chicago Abyss*, "Ray Bradbury Theatre" (4 eps), TV, 89, CDN/USA/NZ, Ed/P Pro Cons; *CanadArts*, TV, 88, CDN, Ed/Dir/Prod, (AMPIA); *The Rope/ Anniversary*, "Family Matters" (2 eps), TV, 88, CDN, Ed; *Get Back the Night*, Connie Kaldor, MV, 87, CDN, Ed, (AMPIA); *Winter Olympics Hall of Fame*, TV, 87, CDN, Ed/Dir/Prod; *Paper Marriage*, Th, 86, CDN/HK, Ed; *Frozen Music*, TV, 85, CDN, Wr/Dir; *To the Ends of the Earth*, TV, 84, CDN/USA, Ed; *Snowbirds 81*, Th, 82, CDN, Ed; "Sacred Circle" (2 eps), TV, 80, CDN, Ed; *Latitude 55*, Th, 80,

CDN, Ed; *Do What You Want, Mama,* MV, 79, CDN Ed/Prod, (CFEG); *Music Therapy,* "Come Alive", TV, 75, CDN, Dir/Wr/Ed; "Adventures in Rainbow Corner" (sev eps), TV, 69, CDN/GB/AUS, Asst Ed/Ed.

SLOAN, Anthony◊
(416)925-1070.
Type of Production and Credits: Th Short-Prod/Dir; TV Film-Ed/DOP; TV Video-Ed/DOP.
Genres: Drama-TV; Comedy-Th&TV; Musical-TV; Documentary-TV.
Biography: Born in 1958 in Montreal, Quebec. Bachelor of Fine Arts, Specialized Honours, Film Production, York University, 80; awarded the Famous Players Theatres Maple Leaf Award for Outstanding Achievement. Training and experience in various aspects of the performing arts.
Selected Filmography: *Canadian Odyssey,* TV, 88, CDN, Co-Cin; *Ravel,* TV, 87, CDN, Co-Ed; *The Diplomat,* "Motley Tales", TV, 86, CDN, Dir; Amnesty International, Cm, 86, CDN, DOP; *The Mighty Quinn,* "Man Alive", TV, 85, CDN, Snd Ed; *All That Bach,* TV, 85, CDN, Ed; *Making Overtures,* TV, 84, CDN, Ed; *Cowboys Don't Cry,* TV, 84, CDN, Snd Ed; *Thrillkill,* Th, 83, CDN, 1st Assist Cam; *Bay Street Tap,* Th, 82, CDN, Co-Prod/Co-Dir; *Door-Desh,* Th, 81, CDN/IND, Assist Cam/Assist Ed.

SMILSKY, Peter
- see DIRECTORS

SMITH, Derek◊
(416)884-1240.
Type of Production and Credits: Th Film-Ed; Th Short-Ed; TV Film-Ed; TV Video-Ed.
Genres: Documentary-Th&TV; Educational-Th&TV; Commercials-TV; Industrial-Th&TV.
Biography: Born 1929, London, England; Canadian citizenship.
Selected Filmography: *Popeye Doyle,* TV, USA, Ed; "Encounter with Disaster" (13 eps), TV, CDN, Ed; *Summer in Canada,* Th, CDN, Ed; "Survivors" (13 eps), TV, CDN, Ed; "Mad Avenue" (pilot), TV, 88, USA, Ed; Toyota, Cm, 88 CDN, Ed; Buffalo Zoo, Cm, 88, USA, Ed; *Echoes in the Darkness,* TV, 87, USA, Ed; *Bluffing It,* TV, 87, USA, Ed; *Sticky Fingers,* Th, 87, USA/CDN, Ed; *Secret Passions,* TV, 87, USA, Ed; *After Midnight,* TV, 87, USA, Ed; "Street Justice", TV, 87, USA, Ed; *The Fierce Dreams of Jackie Watson,* TV, 87, USA, Ed; *Unnatural Causes,* TV, 86, USA, Ed.

SOBELMAN, David
- see WRITERS

STILMAN, Philip Samuel
DGC, ACCT. 36 Earl Haig Ave., Toronto, ON M4C 1E1 (416)691-9770.
Type of Production and Credits: Th Film-Ed/Snd Ed; Th Short-Dir/Prod/Dir.
Genres: Drama-Th&TV; Horror-TV; Children's-Th&TV; Animation-Th&TV.
Biography: Born in 1958 in Montreal, Quebec. Cégep degree in pure & applied sciences. Bachelor of fine arts, Concordia University, 1983, major in film production and photography. Moved to Toronto in 1984, working primarily in editing, post production management and project development. President of Philip Stilman Productions Inc. since 1987. *Autoerotica* was screened at the Montreal World Film Festival, 1983 and won Best Short Film award at MediaByte, 1983.
Selected Filmography: "Dog House" (26 eps), TV, 90-91, USA/CDN, P Prod Spv; "Power Pack" (pilot), TV, 90-91, USA/CDN, P Prod Spv; *Held Hostage: The Sis and Jerry Levin Story,* TV, 90-91, USA/IL, P Prod Spv; "Friday The 13th - The Series" (52 eps), TV, 88-90, USA/CDN, P Prod Spv; "T and T" (24 eps), TV, 87-88, USA/CDN, P Prod Coord; *Carebears in Wonderland,* Th, 87, USA/CDN, Ed/Snd Ed; "Carebears Family" (13 eps), TV, 86, USA/CDN, Ed/Snd Ed; "The Ewoks and Droids Adventure Hour" (39 eps), TV, 85-86, USA/CDN, Assist Ed; "The Edison Twins" (1 eps), TV, 85, CDN/USA, Trainee Assist Dir; *Carebears Movie,* Th, 85, USA/CDN, Assist Ed; "The Kids of Degrassi Street" (6 eps), TV, 84-85, CDN, Assist Ed; *Monkey Up,* MV, 83, CDN, Ed; *The Surrogate,* Th, 83, CDN, Prod Assist; *Autoerotica,* Th, 83, CDN, Prod/Dir/Ed; *Tango,* Th, 82, CDN, Prod/Dir/Ed.

STOCKTON, Brian
- see DIRECTORS

STODDARD, Gordon
NABET, ACCT. 227 Jeffrey St., #19, Whitby, ON (416)668-0463. The Magnetic North Corp., 70 Richmond St. E., Toronto, ON M5C 1N9 (416)365-7622.
Type of Production and Credits: TV Video-Ed.
Genres: Drama-TV; Variety-TV; Science Fiction-TV; Documentary-TV.
Biography: Born 1946, Sherbrooke, Quebec. Diploma, Radio College of Canada. Monitor award nomination, 88, Best Editing, Entertainment Special.
Selected Filmography: "Alfred Hitchcock

Presents" (13 eps)(post liaison), TV, 87-88, CDN/USA; *The Muppet Family Christmas*, TV, 87, USA, Ed; "The Hitchhiker" (23 eps), TV, 85-86, CDN/F, Ed; *The Future is Now*, In, 86, CDN, Ed; "Trends" (2 eps), In, 86, USA, Ed; *Federal Express 10th Anniversary*, In, 85, USA, Ed; *A Point in the Sun*, In, 85, CDN, Ed; *Rise Up*, The Parachute Club, MV, 85, CDN, Ed; *The Band/Who*, "First Choice Rocks" (2 eps), TV, 84, CDN, Ed; *The Good Brothers in Concert*, TV, 84, CDN, Ed; "Office Girls" (15 eps), TV, 83, CDN/USA, Ed; *Jewel of the Caribbean*, In, 82, CDN, Ed; "Bizarre" (52 eps), TV, 81-82, CDN/USA, Ed; "Billy Graham Crusades", TV, 72-82, USA, Ed; "Billy Graham Christmas Specials", TV, 79-81, USA, Ed.

STOLLER, Bryan M.
- see DIRECTORS

STRATYCHUK, Perry Mark
- see DIRECTORS

STRAUGHAN, Brent
- see COMPOSERS

STREET, Bill
- see DIRECTORS

SVAB, Lenka
DGC, ACCT. 18604 - 95a Ave., Edmonton, AB T5T 4A5 (403)484-0577.
Type of Production and Credits: Th Film-Ed; TV Film-Ed; TV Video-Ed.
Genres: Drama-Th&TV; ; Documentary-Th&TV; Educational-Th&TV; Variety-Th&TV
Biography: Born in 1949 in Prague, Czechoslovakia. Canadian citizen. Languages: English, Czech and Russian. Graduate of Charles University, Prague.
Selected Filmography: *Solitaire*, Th, 91, CDN, Ed; *Living with Dying*, TV, 90, CDN, Ed; *The Garden*, TV, 90, CDN, Ed; *Angel Square*, Th, 90, CDN, Ed; *Hail & Farewell*, "The Ray Bradbury Theatre", TV, 89, CDN/USA, Ed; *In Her Chosen Field*, ED, 89, CDN, Ed; *Bye Bye Blues*, Th, 89, CDN, Add Ed; *Movie Showman*, Th, 88, CDN, Ed; *Cowboys Don't Cry*, Th, 87, CDN, 1st Assist Ed.

SVAB, Peter
DGC, ACCT. Crown Films Inc., 18604 - 95A Ave., Edmonton, AB T5T 4A5 (403)484-0577. FAX: 444-3364.
Type of Production and Credits: Th Film-Ed; TV Film-Ed/Snd Rec.
Genres: Drama-Th&TV; Comedy-Th; Documentary-Th&TV.
Biography: Born in 1947 in Tabor, Czechoslovakia; Canadian citizen. Speaks English, Czech, Slovak and Russian. Graduate of University of Music and Dramatic Art (FAMU), Prague., Czechoslovakia. Won an AMPIA award, 87, for Best Editing, *A Sick Call* and *Long Lance*; won again in 1991 for *Return of the Whirlwind*.
Selected Filmography: *Return of the Whirlwind*, TV, 91, CDN, Ed; *Living With Dying*, TV, 90, CDN, Ed; *The Garden*, TV, 90, CDN, Ed; *Angel Square*, Th, 90, CDN, Ed; *Hail and Farewell*, "Ray Bradbury Theatre", TV, 89, CDN/USA, Ed; *Life After Hockey*, TV, 89, CDN, Ed; *Movie Fieldman*, Th, 88, CDN, Ed/Snd Rec; *Bordertown Café*, "Family Pictures", TV, 88, CDN, Ed; *Cowboys Don't Cry*, Th, 87, CDN, Ed; *Prairie Women*, ED, 87, CDN, Ed; *A Sick Call/Hotwalker*, "Short Stories", TV, 85-86, CDN, Ed; *Long Lance*, TV, 86, CDN, Ed; *Not Another Hero*, In, 85, CDN, Ed/Snd Rec; *Maharishi*, Th, 83, CDN, Ed/Snd Rec.

SWEETMAN, Bill
- see PRODUCERS

TATE, Christopher◊
DGC, IATSE 210, ACCT. (403)451-2152.
Type of Production and Credits: Th Short-Ed; TV Film-Ed.
Genres: Drama-Th&TV; Documentary-Th&TV; Children's-Th&TV.
Selected Filmography: *Polynesia* (Imax), Th, 88, USA, Key Grip; *Canada Tourism*, TV, 87, CDN, Key Grip; "Wiseguy", TV, 87, USA, Dolly Grip; *Horse Safety*, TV, 87, CDN, Ed; *Rat Tales*, TV, 86, CDN, Ed; *Niagara Miracles* (Imax), Th, 86, CDN, Key Grip; *A Sick Call*, TV, 86, CDN, Key Grip; *Paper Marriage*, Th, 86, CDN/HK, Key Grip; *Eastern Condors*, Th, 86, RC, Snd Mix; *Laughing Matters*, TV, 85, CDN, Key Grip; *Harry Osgoode*, TV, 85, CDN, Key Grip; *The Canadian Conspiracy*, TV, 85, CDN/USA, Key Grip; *Hypersapien*, Th, 85, GB, Dolly Grip; *Another Naked Night*, TV, 85, CDN, Ed; *Bridge to Terabithia*, "Wonderworks", TV, CDN, Snd Ed.

TAYLOR, Rick
- see DIRECTORS

TETRAULT, Cameron
- see CINEMATOGRAPHERS

THEBERGE, André
- voir REALISATEURS

THOMPSON, David
DGC. Toronto, ON (416)930-5062.
Type of Production and Credits: TV Video-Ed.
Genres: Drama-Th&TV; Comedy-Th&TV; Action-Th&TV; Music Video-TV.
Biography: Born in 1949 in Brussels,

Ontario. Canadian citizen. English. Nominated for 2 Geminis for editing.
Selected Filmography: "Top Cops" (21 eps), TV, 91, CDN/USA, Ed; "True Blue" (7 eps), TV, 90, USA, Ed; "Diamonds" (20 eps), TV, 89, USA/CDN/F, Ed; "Night Heat" (30 eps), TV, 84-89, CDN/USA, Ed; "The Gunfighters" (pilot), TV, 87, CDN/USA, Ed; "Littlest Hobo" (50 eps), TV, 78-84, CDN/USA, Ed; "Circus" (48 eps), TV, 76-77, CDN, Ed; *Cult of Lion*, TV, 79, CDN/USA, Ed; *Rhino War*, TV, 79, CDN/USA, Ed.

THOMPSON, Don◊
(604)435-4007.
Type of Production and Credits: TV Video-Ed/Prod.
Genres: Musical-TV; Documentary-TV; Sports-TV.
Biography: Born in 1962. News and magazine background; works in model/fashion industry, including fashion videos.
Selected Filmography: *Wonder Why They're Lonely*, MV, 85, CDN, Ed; *Challenge of Change*, TV, 85, CDN, Ed/Co-Prod; *Swiftsure 85*, TV, 85, CDN, Tech Dir; *Discovery*, TV, 84, CDN, Prod; "the fifth estate" (1 eps), TV, 84, CDN, Snd Rec; *North American WKA Kickboxing*, TV, 84, CDN, Ed; "Understanding the Stockmarket" (10 eps), TV, 83 CDN, Dir.

THOMPSON, Jane
- see DIRECTORS

THORNE, Gordon
Gordon Thorne Films, 9 Mountjoy Ave., Toronto, ON M4J 1J4 (416)466-7988.
Type of Production and Credits: TV Video-Ed.
Genres: Documentary-TV; Educational-TV; Industrial-Th&TV.
Biography: Born in 1958 in Vancouver, British Columbia. Canadian citizen. Graduated from Ryerson Polytechnical Institute, Dept. of Film & Photography, 1981, B.A.A. Final film won third place award, CBC Telefest. 3-1/2 years experience in multi-image presentations. Edited for Northern Telecom, a 36-screen videowall presentation. 4-1/2 years corporate video experience. 17 programs with CMX & TurboTrace Systems.
Selected Filmography: "Your Green Home" (5 eps), TV, 90-91, CDN, Ed; "Well Being" (8 eps), TV, 91, CDN, Ed; "HomeBrew" (3 eps), TV, 90, CDN, Ed; *Walking Fit*, TV, 90, CDN, Ed; *The Making of the Phantom of the Opera*, Th, 89, CDN, Ed; "Learn to Navigate" (6 eps), TV, 89, CDN, Ed; *Overboard*, ED, 88, CDN, Ed; *Networking*, videowall, In, 87, CDN, Ed; *C.A.P. Intro Video*, In, 87, CDN, Ed; *Molson Indy*, Cm, 87, CDN, Ed; *Be Bike Smart*, Cm, 86, CDN, Ed; "Inspector Gadget" (30 eps), TV, 83, CDN/F/J, Dial Ed.

TILDEN, Annette
1666 Queen St. E., #32, Toronto, ON M4L 1G3 (416)699-1829. Unicorn Concepts, 181 Carlaw Ave., Ste. 305, Toronto, ON M4M 2S1 (416)461-5530.
Type of Production and Credits: TV Film-Ed.
Genres: Drama-TV; Documentary-TV; Educational-TV; Children's-TV.
Biography: Born 1940, Harriston, Ontario. Graduate of Radio and TV Arts, Ryerson Polytechnical Institute; University of Toronto. 20 years film experience. Was the editor on the electronic press kits for *White Room*, *Clearcut* and *Bordertown Café*.
Selected Filmography: *My Happy Days in Hell*, TV, 91, CDN, Ed; "OWL-TV" (sev segs), TV, 84-87, CDN, Ed; *Our Roots Run Deep*, Th, 86-87, CDN, Ed; *Playing for Keeps*, TV, 87, CDN, Ed; *See Saw Marjorie Daw*, TV, 86, CDN, Ed; *The Simulator Challenge*, ED, 83-84, CDN, Co-Ed; "Hockey Night in Canada Features" (29 seg), TV, 76-82, CDN, Ed; *Special Olympics*, Th, 81, CDN, Ed; "Sport Fishing" (13 eps), TV, 80-81, CDN, Ed; *Sports Hall of Fame Inductees*, ED, 90, CDN, Ed; "Personal Spaces" (13 eps), TV, 78-79, CDN, Ed; "Fish Tales" (13 eps) TV, 77-78, CDN, Co-Ed; *Bad Paint Story*, "Market Place", TV, 76, CDN, Ed; "Sidestreet" (1 eps), TV, 75, CDN, Ed; "Police Surgeon" (5 eps), TV, 74, CDN, Ed.

TINGLEY, Cameron
DGC. 377 Milverton Blvd., Toronto, ON M4J 1W1 (416)469-3033.
Type of Production and Credits: TV Film-Ed/Assoc Prod; TV Video-Ed/Assoc Prod.
Genres: Drama-TV; Comedy-TV; Documentary-TV; Industrial-TV.
Biography: Born in 1953 in London, Ontario. Studied Film Production, Conestoga College. Owns film and video editing equipment.
Selected Filmography: "Profiles of Nature Specials" (22 eps), TV, 89-91, CDN, Assoc Prod/Ed; *A String of Perils*, In, 91, CDN, Ed/Snd Ed; *Desperation Quality*, In, 90, CDN, Ed/Snd Ed; *Who's Looking After My Forests?*, ED, 89, CDN, Ed/Snd Ed; "Profiles of Nature" (64 eps), TV, 84-88, CDN, Ed/Assoc Prod; *Wellington County Courthouse*, ED, 84, CDN, Ed; *Celly and*

Friends, TV, 84, CDN, Ed/Snd Ed; *Rock, Ice and Oil*, TV, 83, CDN, Ed; *Safe Strangers*, ED, 82, CDN, Ed/Snd Ed; *Canada: On the Leading Edge of Science*, TV, 82, CDN, Snd Ed; *Canada: Coast to Coast/The House Next Door*, ED, 81, CDN, Ed/Snd Ed; "Wild Canada" (3 eps), TV, 80, CDN, Ed; *Jason and the Champs*, ED, 79, CDN, Ed/Snd Ed; *The Imbalance of Nature*, TV, 77, CDN, Ed/Snd Ed; *A Midnight Snack*, TV, 75, CDN, Ed/Snd Ed.

TKACH, Alex
- see PRODUCERS

TODD, Michael
DGC. 36 Wimbleton Rd., Etobicoke, ON M9B 3R8 (416)236-0763.
Type of Production and Credits: Th Film-Ed; Th Short-Ed/Dir; TV Film-Ed/Dir; TV Video-Ed/Dir.
Genres: Drama-Th&TV; Documentary-Th&TV; Educational-TV; Current Affairs-TV.
Biography: Born 1951, Toronto, Ontario. Diploma, Media Arts, Sheridan College, 76. *The Edit* won a CFTA award, 85, and was selected for screening at the Toronto Festival of Festivals; *A Helping Hand* won Red Ribbon, American Film Festival, 83, and Gold Plaque, Chicago, 83.
Selected Filmography: "Millennium: Tribal Wisdom and the Modern World" (4 eps), TV, 90-91, CDN/USA, GB, Ed; "Road To Avonlea" (6 eps), TV, 90-91, CDN, Ed; *Blood Sport*, TV, 89, CDN/IRL/USA/D, Ed; *Mob Story*, Th, 89, CDN, Ed; *Where the Spirit Lives*, TV, 88-89, CDN, Ed; *Medical Video Library*, ED, 88, CDN, Ed/Dir; *Buying Time*, Th, 87-88, CDN/USA, Ed; *Night Friend*, Th, 87, CDN, Ed; *Home is Where the Heart Is*, Th, 86-87, CDN, Ed; *Turnabout*, Th, 86, CDN, Ed; *The Kidnapping of Baby John Doe*, Th, 86, CDN, Ed; "the fifth estate", TV, 79-86, CDN, Ed; *The Edit*, Th, 85, CDN, Dir; *Those Roos Boys and Friends*, TV, 84, CDN, Ed; *A Helping Hand*, "The Nature of Things", TV, 82, CDN, Dir/Ed.

TODD, Richard
1431 Canora Rd., Town of Mount Royal - Montreal, PQ H3P 2J7 (514)731-1085. National Film Board, P.O. Box 6155, Station A, Montreal, PQ H3C 3H5 (514)283-9472.
Type of Production and Credits: Th Film-Ed; Th Short-Ed; TV Film-Ed.
Genres: Drama-Th&TV; Documentary-TV; Educational-TV; Children's-TV; Interact V
Biography: Born in 1936. Worked as a photojournalist/fashion photographer in New York. Also an actor. Two of the films he directed won awards.
Selected Filmography: *Princes in Exile*, TV, 90, CDN, Ed; *Perspectives in Science*, Interact V, 87-88, CDN, Ed; *Jack of Hearts*, TV, 86, CDN, Ed; *Canada's Sweetheart: The Saga of Hal C. Banks*, TV, 85, CDN, Ed; *Concert Stages of Europe*, TV, 85, CDN, Ed; *The Sight*, TV, 85, CDN, Ed; *A Good Tree*, TV, 84, CDN, Ed; *Keeping the Old Game Alive*, TV, 83, CDN, Ed; *The Party is Over*, "Empire, Inc.", TV, 83, CDN, Ed; *The Inheritance*, TV, 80, CDN, Ed; *Paperland: The Bureaucrat Observed*, TV, 79, CDN, Ed; *The Sunny Munchy Crunchy Natural Food Shop*, TV, 73, CDN, Ed/Dir; *Nell & Fred*, TV, 71, CDN, Dir.

TOUSSAINT, Jurgen
DGC. 19 Smithfield Dr., Toronto, ON M8Y 3M1 (416)251-6801. Jatco Film Services Inc., 266 Adelaide St. W., Toronto, ON (416)591-6761.
Type of Production and Credits: TV Film-Ed.
Genres: Documentary-TV; Educational-TV; Commercials-TV.
Biography: Born 1941, Berlin, Germany; landed immigrant Canada. Languages: English and German. Self-employed since 78; founded Jatco Film Services Inc., 78; editor on numerous commercials and industrial films.
Selected Filmography: *Goofballs*, Th, 85, CDN, P Pro Spv/Ed.

TRAEGER, Tracy
- see PRODUCERS

TREMBLAY, Robert
- voir REALISATEURS

TUSTIAN, Jim
- see PRODUCERS

VAITIEKUNAS, Vincent
- see DIRECTORS

VALLÉE, Jean-Marc
- voir REALISATEURS

VAN EERDEWIJK, Margaret
ACCT. 564 Palmerston Ave., Toronto, ON M6G 2P7 (416)536-4680. FAX: 538-7095.
Type of Production and Credits: Th Film-Ed; TV Film-Ed.
Genres: Drama-Th&TV; Musical-TV; Documentary-TV; Children's-TV.
Biography: Born in The Netherlands; Canadian citizenship. A.O.C.A., Painting, Ontario College of Art, 70; B.A., East Asian Studies, University of Toronto, 91. Nominated for Gemini, 87, for *The Truth About Alex*; nominated for Gemini, 89, for *The Eternal Earth*. Awarded Best Editing

Award, Yorkton, 90, for *The Radical Romantic*.
Selected Filmography: *El Retablo de Maese Pedro/Master Peter's Puppet Theatre*, TV, 90, CDN/GB/E, Ed; *The Radical Romantic - John Weinzweig*, TV, 89, CDN, Ed; *The Top of His Head*, Th, 88, CDN, Co-Ed; *World Drums*, TV, 87, CDN, Ed; *The Eternal Earth*, TV, 87, CDN, Ed; *The Truth About Alex*, TV, 86, CDN, Ed; *Magnificat*, TV, 85, CDN, Ed; *The Painted Door*, TV, 84, CDN, Ed; *The Mark of Cain*, Th, 84, CDN, Ed; *Cornet at Night*, TV, 83, CDN, Ed; *Storytelling*, TV, 83, CDN, Ed; *Bamboo Brush*, TV, 82, CDN, Ed; *I Know a Secret*, TV, 82, CDN, Ed; *David*, TV, 82, CDN, Ed; *A Private World*, Th, 81, CDN, Co-Ed.

VAN VELSEN, Hans◇
DGC. (416)979-7810.
Type of Production and Credits: Th Film-Ed; TV Film-Ed.
Genres: Drama-Th&TV; Comedy-TV; Documentary-TV; Commercials-TV.
Biography: Born 1926, The Netherlands. Has worked in Canada since 56; editing commercials since 79.
Selected Filmography: "Matt and Jenny" (6 eps), TV, 79, CDN/GB/D, Ed; "Search and Rescue" (7 eps), TV, 76, CDN/USA, Ed; "Swiss Family Robinson" (5 eps), TV, 74-75, CDN, Ed; "George" (15 eps), TV, 74, CDN, Ed; "Police Surgeon" (18 eps), TV, 67-70, CDN, Ed; "The Collaborators" (5 eps), TV, 68, CDN, Ed; "Dr. Simon Locke" (16 eps), TV, 66, CDN/USA, Ed; "Forest Rangers" (17 eps), TV, 62, CDN, Ed; "Hudson's Bay" (4 eps), TV, 60, CDN, Ed.

WARREN, Jeff
DGC. 249 Armour Blvd., Toronto, ON M3H 1N1 (416)636-8661.
Type of Production and Credits: Th Film-Ed; TV Film-Ed; TV Video-Ed.
Genres: Drama-TV; Documentary-Th&TV; Educational-TV; Children's-TV.
Biography: Born 1950; Canadian citizen. Studied Photographic Arts, Ryerson Polytechnical Institute. Has been a full-time editor since 72; edited award-winning dramas, documentaries and educational programs; *Final Offer - Bob White and the United Auto Workers Fight for Independence* won a Genie award and the Prix Italia, 86; awarded a Gemini, 89, Best Editing in a Dramatic Program or Series for premiere episode of "9B" series.
Selected Filmography: *Diplomatic Immunity*, Th, 90, CDN/GB, Ed; *Rookies*, TV, 90, CDN, Ed; "T and T" (8 eps), TV, 89-90, CDN/USA, Ed; "Adderly" (14 eps), TV, 86-88, CDN, Ed; "9B" (3 eps), TV, 88, CDN, Ed; *Where's Pete?*, TV, 86, CDN, Ed; *Final Offer*, Th, 85, CDN, Ed/Snd Ed; "Going Great" (20 eps), TV, 83, CDN, Ed; "American Caesar" (2 eps), TV, 83, CDN, Ed; *Pretty Babies*, TV, 82, CDN, Ed; *National Crime Test*, TV, 81, CDN, Ed; *Away from Home*, TV, 81, CDN, Ed; *Escape from Iran: The Canadian Caper*, TV, 80, CDN, Ed, (CFEG); "Maclear" (23 eps), TV, 74-77, CDN, Ed; "Here Come the Seventies" (2 eps), TV, 71, CDN, Ed.

WEBSTER, Ion
DGC, STCVQ, ACCT. 80 Quebec Ave., Apt. 510, Toronto, ON M6P 4B7 (416)762-9485.
Type of Production and Credits: Th Film-Ed; TV Film-Ed; TV Video-Ed.
Genres: Drama-Th&TV; Comedy-Th&TV; Documentary-TV; Industrial-TV.
Biography: Born in 1950 in Ottawa, Ontario. Languages: English, French with a working knowledge of Greek and Russian. Has travelled in Europe, the USSR and the Far East.
Selected Filmography: *Acheter la boulangerie*, "L'homme invisible", Th, 91, CDN, Ed; *Sous le signe du poisson*, TV, 90, CDN/F, Ed; *Lady from Berlin* (mini-series), TV, 90, CDN/F, Ed; *Destiny to Order*, Th, 89, CDN, Ed; *Indigo Autumn*, TV, 87, CDN, Ed; *Emerald Tear*, TV, 87, CDN, Ed; *Indigo Autumn*, TV, 87, CDN, Video Ed; *Emerald Tear*, TV, 87, CDN, Video Ed; "Jeunesse" (2 eps), TV, 86, CDN, Ed; *State Park*, Th, 86, CDN, Spv Ed; *Material Girl*, "Discussions in Bioethics", TV, 85, CDN, Ed; *The Prodigal*, "Lifestudies", TV, 85, CDN, Ed; *Alice Munro/Al Purdy/Michel Tremblay/Janice Rapoport*, "Canadian Literature". TV, 85, CDN, Dir; *Conseil des arts de l'Ontario/Orléans/Alcide*, "Mosaïque", TV, 85, CDN, Ed; *Mr. Nice Guy*, Th, 85, CDN, Ed.

WEINTHAL, Eric
- see WRITERS

WELLS, Richard
189 Church St., Toronto, ON M5B 1Y7 (416)863-6414.
Type of Production and Credits: TV Film-Ed; TV Video-Ed.
Genres: Drama-TV; Variety-TV; Documentary-TV; Industrial-TV.
Biography: Born in 1948 in Toronto, Ontario. After a brief career as a dancer in Toronto and Montreal, entered the television industry as a producer/director on *Through the Eyes of Tomorrow* in 1969.

Started editing for Don Haig in 1971. Has since edited many award-winning shows for PBS, CBC, CTV and BBC. Won the Best Editing Award, 1981 Yorkton Film Festival for *Shroud of Turin*.
Selected Filmography: *My Doctor - My Lover*, TV, 91, USA, Ed; "Street Legal" (24 eps), TV, 89-91, CDN, Ed; *Born in America*, TV, 90, USA/CDN, Ed; *Broken Promises*, TV, 89, USA/CDN, Ed; "9B" (3 eps), TV, 89, CDN, Ed; *My Husband's Going to Kill Me*, TV, 88, USA/CDN, Ed; "Adderly" (16 eps), TV, 86-88, USA/CDN, Ed; "The Race for Gold" (13 eps), TV, 86, CDN, Ed; "Peter Ustinov in China" (2 eps), TV, 84, CDN/GB, Ed; "Peter Ustinov's Russia" (6 eps), TV, 83, CDN/GB, Ed; *Shroud of Turin*, TV, 81, CDN, Ed; "Man Alive", TV, 76-80, CDN, Ed; "Live It Up" (1 yr), TV, 75-76, CDN, Ed; "the fifth estate" (5 yrs), TV, 73-75, CDN, Ed; "CBC Weekend" (2 yrs), TV, 71-73, CDN, Ed.

WERTH, Michael
- see SOUND EDITORS

WESLAK, Steve
DGC. 16 Forsyth Cres., Toronto, ON M4S 2R1 (416)489-5398. 181 Carlaw Ave., Toronto, ON M4M 2S1 (416)469-2961.
Type of Production and Credits: Th Film-Ed; TV Film-Ed; TV Video-Ed.
Genres: Drama-Th; Documentary-TV; Educational-TV; Children's-TV.
Biography: Born 1947. Has worked in film business since 69; staff editor, CBC, 70-72; Kingcroft Films, Sydney, Australia, 72-74; now freelance in Toronto.
Selected Filmography: *Deadly Currents*, Th, 90, CDN, Ed; "War of the Worlds" (16 eps), TV, 89, CDN/USA, Ed; *Gate II*, Th, 89, CDN, Add'l Ed; *Dead Ringers*, Th, 88, CDN, Assoc Ed; *Guitar*, TV, 87 CDN, Ed; *The Fly*, Th, 86, CDN, Assemb Ed; "Durrell in Russia" (6 eps), TV, 85, CDN/USR, Ed; "Amateur Naturalist" (6 eps), TV, 83, CDN, Ed; *Home Feeling*, TV, 82, CDN, Ed; "Ark on the Move" (13 eps), TV, 81, CDN, Ed; *The Last Chase*, Th, 80, CDN, Ed; "Connections: An Investigation into Organized Crime in Canada" (6 eps), TV, 77, CDN, Spv Ed; "The Stationary Ark" (13 eps), TV, 75, CDN, Sr Ed; "Wild Country" (2 eps), TV, 74, AUS, Ed; "Weekend", TV, 70-72, CDN, Ed.

WEYMAN, Peter (Bay)
- see PRODUCERS

WHITE, Bryon◊
DGC. (416)488-0550.
Type of Production and Credits: Th Film-Ed; TV Film-Ed; TV Video-Ed.
Genres: Drama-Th&TV; Commercials-TV.
Biography: Born 1952, Toronto, Ontario. B.Sc. Pioneered the use of electronic film editing system on *Murder in Space*, acts as a consultant/liaison with PFA and editors. Distribution Manager, Robert Cooper Productions, 84-86; formed own syndication company, Vialla Cinematics Ltd., 1987.
Selected Filmography: "T and T" (1 eps), TV, 88, CDN, Ed; "Philip Marlowe, Private Eye" (3 eps), TV, 86, CDN, Ed/P Pro Spv; *Playing the Odds*, TV, 86, CDN, PM; "Hot Shots" (13 eps), TV, 86, CDN, P Pro Spv; "Airwaves" (4 eps), TV, 86, CDN, Ed; *Murder in Space*, TV, 85, CDN/USA, P Pro Spv; *Rapists - Can They Be Stopped?*, "America Undercover", TV, 85, USA/CDN, PM; *Las Aradas*, TV, 84, CDN, Ed/Snd Ed; *A Matter of Sex*, TV, 83, CDN/USA, Co-Ed; *Kelly*, Th, 80, CDN, Ed; *Thunder*, TV, 79, CDN, Ed/Snd Ed; *Circle of Two*, TV, 79, CDN, Assist Ed/Mus Ed.

WILKINSON, Mairin
DGC, ACCT. 194 Howland Ave., Toronto, ON M5R 3B6 (416)537-6123.
Type of Production and Credits: Th Film-Ed; TV Film-Ed; TV Video-Ed.
Genres: Drama-Th&TV; Documentary-TV; Children's-TV.
Biography: Born in England; landed immigrant, Canada. Studied Film, York University. Film, tape and Ediflex editor.
Selected Filmography: "Road To Avonlea" (7 eps), TV, 90, CDN, Ed; "Road To Avonlea" (11 eps), TV, 90, CDN, Assoc Prod; *Jane of Lantern Hill*, TV, 89, CDN, Ed; "War of the Worlds" (pilot), TV, 88, USA, Ed; *The Lawrenceville Stories*, TV, 87, CDN, Ed; *Anne of Green Gables - The Sequel*, TV, 86, CDN, Co-Ed; "Adderly" (1 eps), TV, 86, CDN, Ed; "Spirit Bay" (1 eps), TV, 86, CDN, Ed; *Anne of Green Gables*, TV, 85, CDN, Co-Ed; *Isaac Littlefeathers*, Th, 84, CDN, Ed; *Jen's Place*, TV, 82, CDN, Ed; *Introducing...Janet*, TV, 81, CDN, Co-Ed; *Clown White*, TV, 80, CDN, Co-Ed; *Corletto & Son*, TV, 80, CDN, Ed; *Reaching Out*, TV, 80, CDN, Co-Ed.

WINEMAKER, Mark Joseph
- see PRODUCERS

WINTONICK, Peter
CIFC, AIVF. 5110 rue Jeanne-Mance, Montreal, PQ H2V 4K1 (514)273-5330. Necessary Illusions Inc., 10 Pine Ave. W., Suite 315, Montreal, PQ H2W 1P9 (514)287-7337. 4371 Avenue de

L'Esplanade, Montreal, PQ H2W 1T2 (514)287-7620.
Type of Production and Credits: Th Film-Ed/Dir; TV Film-Ed; TV Video-Ed/Prod/Dir.
Genres: Drama-Th&TV; Documentary-Th&TV; Educational-TV; Experimental-Th.
Biography: Born 1953, Trenton, Ontario. Carleton University, Ottawa; Algonquin College Film Production Course. 20 years as a professional writer, producer, director and editor of film, video and audio-visual productions; has written about film for national and int'l. cinema magazines. and worked as post-production consultant on many independent productions; was recently part-time Prof. of Documentary Film, Concordia University, Montreal. Founding member and Secretary of the National Exec., Canadian Independent Film Caucus, Association of Independent Video and Filmmakerrs (USA), former member, the Directors' Guild of Canada. Nominated for Canadian Film Award for editing; *The New Cinema* won Blue Ribbon, best video documentary, American Film Festival, and best Canadian video documentary at the Atlantic Festival.
Selected Filmography: *The Street* (documentary), Th, 91, CDN, Exec Prod; *Manufacturing Consent: Noam Chomsky on Mass Media*, Th, 91, CDN, Co-Prod/Co-Dir/Co-Ed; *Harbour Symphony*, Th, 90, CDN, Ed; *A Rustling of Leaves*, Th, 88, CDN, Ed/Assoc Prod; *Comic Book Confidential*, Th, 88, CDN, Spv Ed; *Ben Johnson: The Inside Story*, Th, 88, CDN, Dir/Ed; *The Journey: A Film for Peace*, Th, 84-87, CDN, Prod/P Pro Coord/Co-Ed/Co-Res/2ndU; *The Media Project* (video-projects), Th, 84, CDN, Dir; *Filmmaker/Peacemaker*, Th, 84, CDN, Prod/Dir/Ed; *Listen to the City*, Th, 84, CDN, Line Prod/1st AD; *The Bay Boy*, Th, 84, CDN, Co-Ed; *The New Cinema*, Th, 83-84, CDN, Wr/Prod/Dir/Ed; *Doctor Tilley and His Guinea Pigs*, Th, 82, CDN, Ed/Assoc Prod; *Poetry in Motion*, Th, 82, CDN, Ed/Assoc Prod; *Portrait by Implication*, TV, 82, CDN, Ed.

WISMAN, Ron
DGC, ACCT. 41 Cheston Rd., Toronto, ON M4S 2X4 (416)486-9339. FAX: 486-6068.
Type of Production and Credits: Th Film-Ed; Th Short-Ed; TV Film-Ed.
Genres: Drama-Th&TV; Comedy-Th; Science Fiction-Th; Horror-Th.
Biography: Born in 1943. Associated with many award-winning documentaries and commercials over the past 26 years. *Tyler*, "For the Record" (78) won, CFED; *Along These Lines* won CFTA; *The Violin* was nominated for an Oscar, Short Film.
Selected Filmography: *Young Catherine* (mini-series), TV, 90, USA/CDN /GB/ USR, Ed; *The Little Kidnappers*, TV, 90, USA/CDN, Ed; *Beautiful Dreamers*, Th, 89, CDN, Ed; *Millennium*, Th, 88, CDN, Ed; *The Sword of Gideon* (mini-series), TV, 86, CDN, Ed, (GEMINI 87/ACE); *The Climb*, Th, 85, CDN/GB, Ed; *Joshua Then and Now* (also 4 eps TV), Th, 84, CDN, Ed; *The Undergrads*, TV, 84, USA, Ed; *Draw!*, TV, 83, CDN/USA, Ed; *A Matter of Sex*, TV, 83, CDN/USA, Spv Ed; *The Terry Fox Story*, Th, 82, CDN, Ed, (GENIE); *Ticket to Heaven*, Th, 80, CDN, Ed, (CFEG/GENIE); *An American Christmas Carol*, TV, 79, USA, Ed; *The High Country*, Th, 79, CDN, Ed/P Pro Spv; *Fish Hawk*, Th, 78, CDN, Ed.

WOLINSKY, Sidney
DGC, IATSE 776, MPEG. 2121 Hill St., Santa Monica, CA 90405 USA (213)450-1634. Barbara Halperin, The Gersh Agency, 222 N. Canon Dr., Beverly Hills, CA 90210 USA (213)274-6611.
Type of Production and Credits: Th Film-Ed; TV Film-Ed.
Genres: Drama-Th&TV; Comedy-Th; Action-Th&TV.
Biography: Born 1946, Winnipeg, Manitoba. B.A., English, American Literature, Brandeis University, 69; M.A., Film, San Francisco State University, 74.
Selected Filmography: *Red Wind*, TV, 91, USA, Ed; *Perfect Harmony*, TV, 90, USA, Ed; *The China Lake Murders*, TV, 89, USA, Ed; *Worth Winning*, Th, 88, USA, Ed; *Maid to Order*, Th, 87, USA, Ed; "Almost Grown" (pilot), TV, 87, CDN/USA, Ed; *Howard the Duck*, Th, 86, USA, Co-Ed; *One Magic Christmas*, Th, 85, CDN/USA, Ed; *Best Defense*, Th, 84, USA, Ed; *Terms of Endearment*, Th, 83, USA, Add'l Ed; *My Tutor*, Th, 83, USA, Ed; *Young Doctors in Love*, Th, 82, USA, Add'l Ed.

WRATE, Eric
SMPTE, ACCT. 200 Silverbirch Ave., Toronto, ON M4E 3L5 (416)694-0827. Post Production Services, 181 Carlaw Ave., Toronto, ON M4M 2S1 (416)466-5870.
Type of Production and Credits: Th Film-Ed; TV Film-Ed; TV Video-Ed.
Genres: Drama-Th&TV; Comedy-Th&TV; Documentary-TV; Children's-Th&TV.
Biography: Born in London, England; Canadian citizenship. Owner, Post

Production Services Ltd. Trained in the British film industry, working with directors such as Alfred Hitchcock.
Selected Filmography: "Degrassi Junior High" (20 eps), TV, 85-88, CDN, Ed; "Street Legal" (9 eps), TV, 86-87, CDN, Spv Ed/Ed, (GEMINI); "Philip Marlowe Private Eye" (1 eps), TV, 86, CDN, Ed; *Special Delivery*, TV, 85, CDN, Ed; "Shell Game" (pilot), TV, 85, CDN, Ed; *Cuckoo Bird*, TV, 85, CDN, Ed; "Kids of Degrassi Street" (6 eps), TV, 85, CDN, Ed; *Bridge to Terabithia*, "Wonderworks", TV, 84, CDN, Ed; *Shocktrauma*, TV, 83, CDN, Spv Ed; *If You Could See What I Hear*, Th, 82, CDN, Ed; *Highpoint*, Th, 79, CDN, Ed; "A Man Called Intrepid" (mini-series), TV, 78, CDN/GB, Spv Ed; *The Courage of Kavik the Wolf Dog*, TV, 78, CDN, Ed; *High-Ballin'*, Th, 77, CDN, Ed; "The Newcomers" (2 eps), TV, 77, CDN, Ed, (CFEG), *Second Wind*, Th, 75, CDN, Ed.

ZALOUM, Alain
- see WRITERS

ZAMARIA, Charles
- see PRODUCTION MANAGERS

ZANDER, Ildy
32 Saybrook Ave., Etobicoke, ON M8Z 2V4 (416)233-7804.
Type of Production and Credits: Th Short-Ed/Prod; TV Film-Ed; TV Video-Ed/Prod.
Genres: Drama-Th&TV; Documentary-Th; Educational-TV; Industrial-TV.
Biography: Born in 1944 in Budapest, Hungary; Canadian citizen. Languages: English, French, Hungarian, working knowledge of German and Spanish. B.A., University of Toronto.
Selected Filmography: IBM videos, In, 75-90, CDN, Ed/Prod; *Menopause*, TV, 82, CDN, Ed; *Brooke: A New Generation*, Th, 81, CDN, Ed/Prod; *The July Group*, TV, 80, CDN, Ed; *Coming Home Alive*, TV, 79, CDN, Ed; *Raising Cane*, ED, 78, CDN, Ed/Assoc Prod; *The Fighting Men* (re-cut for Th release), Th, 78, CDN, Ed; *Silent Sky*, Th, 77, CDN, Ed; *Paperback Hero*, Th, 71, CDN, Assist Ed; *The Rowdyman*, Th, 71, CDN, Assist Ed; *A Fan's Notes*, Th, 70, CDN, Assist Ed.

ZIPURSKY, Arnie
- see PRODUCERS

ZLATARITS, Harvey◈
DGC. (416)588-7763.
Type of Production and Credits: Th Film-Ed; TV Film-Ed/Prod; TV Video-Ed/Prod.
Genres: Variety-TV; Documentary-Th&TV; Educational-TV; Children's-TV.
Biography: Born in 1946 in Regina, Saskatchewan; B.Environmental Studies, University of Manitoba; Film, Ryerson Polytechnical Institute. Also works as cameraman, architectural designer, draughtsman, still photographer.
Selected Filmography: *Time After Time*, Th, 87-88, CDN, Ed; *Dixie Lanes*, Th, 86, CDN/USA, Ed; *Into the Fire*, Th, 86, CDN, Ed; "Quest" (13 eps), TV, 85, CDN, P Pro Spv/Prod; "Celebrations" (5 eps), TV, 85, CDN, P Pro Spv/Prod; *Olympic Moments*, TV, 84, CDN, Ed; *Star Song*, TV, 84, CDN, Ed; *Disability Myth* (parts I & II), TV, 83-84, CDN, Ed; "Alpine Ski School" (5 eps), TV, 83, CDN, Ed; *The Hawk*, Th, 82, CDN, Ed, (BIJOU/CFEG); *Deadline*, Th, 81, CDN, Ed; *Gino*, TV, 80, CDN, Ed, (CFEG).

Music Editors
Monteurs musique

BRONSKILL, Richard
- see COMPOSERS

CEREGHETTI, Jean-Pierre
- voir MONTEURS

CLYNE, Dale
- see POSTPRODUCTION SOUND MIXERS

CORNFORD, Darryl
- see EDITORS

FORMAN, Howard
- see COMPOSERS

GILLSON, Malca
- see DIRECTORS

GORBACHOW, Yuri
- see PRODUCTION SOUND MIXERS

HALL, Grant
- see POSTPRODUCTION SOUND MIXERS

HANNIGAN, Teresa
- see EDITORS

HAWKES, Kirk
- see EDITORS

JAN, Miume
- see EDITORS

KLIS, Danuta
- see SOUND EDITORS

MacGILLIVRAY, William D.
- see DIRECTORS

MORRONE, Frank
- see PRODUCTION SOUND MIXERS

NYZNIK, Bruce
- see POSTPRODUCTION SOUND MIXERS

QUAN, Donald
- see COMPOSERS

RAVOK, Brian
- see EDITORS

ROTUNDO, Nick
- see EDITORS

SANDERS, Ronald
 - see EDITORS
SEREDA, John
 - see COMPOSERS
TINGLEY, Cameron
 - see EDITORS
WISMAN, Ron
 - see EDITORS

Postproduction Sound Mixers
Mixeurs son postproduction

APPLEBY, David
ACCT. 11 Sandalwood Dr., Ballinafad, ON N0B 1H0 (416)873-3333. Film House, 424 Adelaide St. E., Toronto, ON M5A 1N4 (416)364-4321.
Type of Production and Credits: Th Film-Re-record Ed; Th Short-Re-record Ed; TV Film-Re-record.
Genres: Comedy-Th; Musical-Th; Horror-Th; Drama-Th.
Selected Filmography: *Perfectly Normal,* Th, 90, CDN, Re-record Ed; *Love & Hate,* Th, 90, CDN, Re-record Ed; *Divided Loyalties,* TV, 90, CDN, Re-record Ed; *One Magic Christmas,* Th, 86, USA/CDN, Re-record Ed; *The Bay Boy,* Th, 85, CDN, Re-record Ed; *A Christmas Story,* Th, 84, CDN, Re-record Ed; *Follow That Bird,* Th, 83, USA/CDN, Re-record Ed; *Ticket To Heaven,* Th, 82, CDN, Re-record Ed.

BACKUS, Barry
2438 Hoskins Rd., North Vancouver, BC V7J 3A3 (604)984-6316. Film Arts, 424 Adelaide St. E., 2nd Flr., Toronto, ON M5A 1N4 (416)368-9925.
Type of Production and Credits: Th Short-Dir; TV Film-Ed; TV Film-Snd Ed.
Genres: Documentary-Th&TV; Educational-TV; Children's-TV; Animation-TV.
Biography: Born 1951, Sudbury, Ontario. Faculty of Engineering, Carleton Univ., 70/71; Photo Arts and Motion Pictures, Ryerson Polytechnical Institute, 75.
Selected Filmography: "The Adventures of the Black Stallion" (26 eps), TV, 90-91, CDN/F, P Pro Snd Spv; "Neon Rider" (24 eps), TV, 89-90, CDN, P Pro Snd Spv; *Anything to Survive,* TV, 89-90, USA, P

Pro Snd Spv; *Cold Front*, Th, 89-90, CDN, Snd Ed; *California Dreamin'*, Th, 89-90, CDN, Snd Ed; "The Beachcombers" (special), TV, 87-88, CDN, Snd Ed; "T and T" (special), TV, 87-88, CDN, Snd Ed; "21 Jump Street" (33 eps), TV, 87-88, USA, Snd Ed; "Wheeled Warriors" (8 eps)(Snd Ed 7 eps), TV, 85-86, USA, FX Ed; "Masked Heroes" (8 eps)(Snd Ed 3 eps), TV, 85-86, USA, FX Ed; "the fifth estate" (8 eps), TV, 80-86, CDN, Ed; *Proceed with Caution*, In, 86, CDN, Ed; *Turning to Stone*, TV, 86, CDN, FX Ed; "Kid Video" (6 eps), TV, 86, USA, FX Ed; "Hulk Hogan" (2 eps), TV, 86, USA, FX Ed.

BERNS, Marvin
ACCT. 62 Westmount Ave., Toronto, ON M6H 3K1 (416)656-2402.
Type of Production and Credits: Th Film-Snd Mix; TV Film-Snd Mix; TV Video-Snd Mix.
Genres: Drama-Th&TV; Documentary-TV; Animation-Th&TV; Current Affairs-TV.
Biography: Born 1950, Toronto, Ontario. B.Sc., University of Toronto. Genie nominee, Best Overall Sound, 87, *Hello Mary Lou, Prom Night II*; Genie nominee, Best Overall Sound, 90, *Millennium*.
Selected Filmography: "Nature Connection" (13 eps), TV, 91, CDN, Re-record Mix; *Cold Comfort*, Th, 89, CDN, Re-record Mix; *Where the Spirit Lives*, Th, 89, CDN, Re-record Mix; "Beetlejuice" (16 eps), TV, 89, CDN, Re-record Mix; *Millennium*, Th, 88, CDN/USA, Re-record Mix; *Shadow Dancing*, Th, 88, CDN, Re-record Mix; "Babar" (26 eps), TV, 88, CDN, Re-record Mix; *Buying Time*, Th, 87, CDN, Re-record Mix; *Blindside*, Th, 87, CDN, Re-record Mix; *The Care Bears Adventures in Wonderland*, Th, 87, CDN, Re-record Mix; "Care Bears" (30 eps), TV, 86-87, CDN, Re-record Mix; "My Pet Monster" (24 eps), TV, 86-87, CDN, Re-record Mix; *Life Classes*, Th, 86, CDN, Re-record Mix; *Taking Care*, Th, 86, CDN, Re-record Mix; *Hello Mary Lou - Prom Night II*, Th, 86, CDN, Re-record Mix.

BOUCHER, Diane
ACADEMIE. 201 chemin du Club Marin, #405, Ile des Soeurs, PQ H3E 1T4 (514)761-6286.
Types de production et générique: TV Film-Post-synchro; l métrage-Post-synchro; c métrage-Post-synchro.
Types d'oeuvres: Drame-C&TV; Action-C&TV; Comédie-C&TV; Enfants-C&TV.
Curriculum vitae: Née au Québec. Langues: français et anglais. Radio-Canada, Assistante au montage. Diplôme, Académique Conservatoire Lassalle, montage image, montage sonore dialogue. Directeure technique en post-synchronisation de fiction. Propriétaire (Associée) d'une salle de montage 35mm. Prix "Génie" montage sonore pour: *Le déclin de l'empire américain*, *Un zoo la nuit* et *Jésus de Montréal*. Personne ressource stage de post production de Parle-Image.
Filmographie sélective: *L'Ange Noir*, C, 91, CDN, Post-synchro/Dir tech; *La Sarrasine*, C, 91, CDN, Post-synchro/Dir tech; *La Demoiselle Sauvage*, C, 91, CDN, Post-synchro/Dir tech; *Fabuleux Voyage de L'Ange*, C, 91, CDN, Post-synchro/Dir tech; *The Pianist*, C, 91, CND/J, Post-synchro/Dir tech; *Autopsie de la Violence/Love Moi*, C, 90-91, CDN, Post-synchro/Mont dial; *On a marché sur la lune*, TV, 90, CDN, Post-synchro/Mont dial; *Ding & Dong Le Film*, C, 90, CDN, Post-synchro/Dir tech; *Rafale*, C, 90, CDN, Post-synchro/Dir tech; *Une histoire inventée*, C, 90, CDN, Post-synchro/Dir tech; *Blue la Magnifique*, TV, 89, CDN, Post-synchro/Dir tech; *Impasse de la Vignette*, C, 89, CDN/F, Post-synchro/Dir tech/Mont dial; *Jésus de Montréal*, C, 89, CDN/F, Post-synchro/Dir tech/Mont dial; *Un zoo la nuit*, C, 87, CDN, Mont dial; *Le déclin de l'empire américain*, C, 85, CDN, Mont dial.

BUCHANAN, Jack
- see PRODUCTION SOUND MIXERS
BURKE, Dennis
- see COMPOSERS
CARUSO, Elius◊
(416)690-0989.
Type of Production and Credits: Th Film-Snd Mix; Th Short-Snd Mix; TV Film-Snd Mix; TV Video-Snd Mix.
Genres: Drama-Th&TV; Horror-Th; Documentary-Th&TV; Commercials-Th&TV.
Biography: Born 1950, Italy; Canadian citizenship, 60. Languages: English and Italian. Studied at Ryerson Polytechnical Institute. Has also done some location recording. Two Gemini nominations, 86.
Selected Filmography: "Danger Bay" (57 eps), TV, 84-87, CDN, Snd Mix; *Traveling Light*, TV, 86, CDN, Snd Mix; *Shell Game*, TV, 85, CDN, Snd Mix; *Neon*, TV, 85, CDN, Snd Mix; *No Sad Songs*, TV, 85, CDN, Snd Mix; *Roots of Hunger, Roots of Change*, TV, 84, CDN, Snd Mix; *The Other Kingdom*, TV, 84, CDN, Snd Mix; "The Edison Twins" (13

eps), TV, 83, CDN, Snd Mix; "Inspector Gadget" (35 eps), TV, 83, CDN/USA, Snd Mix; *Hookers on Davie*, Th, 83, CDN, Snd Mix; *American Nightmare*, Th, 82, CDN, Snd Mix; *Inward Passage*, Th, 82, CDN, Snd Mix; *Rock & Rule/Ring of Power*, Th, 82, CDN, Snd Mix; *Poetry in Motion*, Th, 81, CDN, Snd Mix; *Track Stars*, Th, 79, CDN, Snd Mix, (GENIE).

CLYNE, Dale
373 Lawrence Ave. W., Toronto, ON M5M 1B8 (416)789-7775. Emmanuel Productions, 31B Industrial St., Toronto, ON M4G 1Z2 (416)423-7131. FAX: 423-7151.
Type of Production and Credits: Th Film-Snd Ed/Snd Mix; TV Film-Snd Ed/Snd Mix; TV Video-Snd Ed/Snd Mix.
Genres: Drama-Th&TV; Action-Th&TV; Horror-Th&TV; Industrial-Th&TV.
Biography: Born 1963, Ottawa, Ontario. Studied at the Institute of Communicating Arts, Vancouver, BC.
Selected Filmography: *Alex Trebek Walks the World*, TV, 91, CDN/USA, Snd FX Ed/Snd Mix; *Rhoda's Breakfast*, Th, 90, CDN, Snd FX Ed/Snd Mix; *Family Coalition Party, Election '90*, Cm, 90, CDN, Snd FX Ed/Snd Mix; *Cleared for Take-Off*, TV, 89, CDN, Mus Engin; *The Angel*, Th, 89, CDN, Snd FX Ed; *Starvation*, World Vision, Cm, 89, CDN, Snd FX Ed; *The Metro Toronto Zoo* (documentary), Th, 88, CDN, Snd FX Ed; *Don't Look Cow*, TV, 88, CDN, Snd FX Ed/Snd Mix; *To Die For*, Th, 88, CDN/USA, Mus Engin; *Chambers of Terror*, Th, 87, CDN, Post Audio Spv/Snd Mix; *Shuttle Command*, TV, 87, CDN, Snd FX Ed/Snd Mix; *Fight Back*, TV, 87, CDN, Snd FX Ed/Snd Mix.

COLE, Steven
DGC, IATSE 771. 293 Wychwood Avenue, Toronto, ON M6C 2T6 (416) 651-0555.
Type of Production and Credits: Th Film-P Pro Spv/Spv Snd Ed/Snd Ed; TV Film-P Pro Spv/Spv Snd Ed/Snd Ed; TV Video-P Pro Spv/Spv Snd Ed/Snd Ed.
Genres: Drama-Th&TV; Comedy-Th&TV; Action-Th&TV; Horror-Th&TV; Animation-TV.
Biography: Born in Toronto, Ontario in 1960. Has been working in post audio for over 14 years. Experienced in 35mm and 16mm film; Synclavier, Soundmaster, Adam Smith and Atari tape.

CORNFORD, Darryl
- see EDITORS

CORRIVEAU, Jean
- voir COMPOSITEURS

DESCOMBES, J. Michel
203, rue Châteauguay, B/P 1319, Huntington, PQ J0S 1H0 (514)264-4720. Sonolab inc., 1500, Papineau, Montréal, PQ H2K 4L9 (514)527-8671.
Types de production et générique: l métrage-Mix s post; c métrage-Mix s post; TV film-Mix s post; TV vidéo-Mix s post.
Types d'oeuvres: Action-C&TV; Comédie-C&TV; Documentaire-C&TV; Animation-C.
Curriculum vitae: Né en 1942, Suisse; citoyenneté canadienne. Langues: français et anglais. Enregistrement de musique, RCA Victor; prise de son TV, mixage de plus de 1,000 films depuis 67.
Filmographie sélective: *La Sarrazine*, C, 90, CH/CDN, Mix; *La Demoiselle Sauvage*, C, 90, CDN, Mix; *The Pianist*, C, 90, CDN, Mix; *Amoureux Fou*, C, 90, CDN, Mix; "Golden Fiddle" (2 eps), TV, 90, CDN/AUS, Mix; *Love Moi*, C, 90, CDN, Mix; "Lance et Compte IV", TV, 90, CDN, Mix; "Alphonse Desjardins" (6 eps), TV, 90, CDN, Mix; *Melanie*, C, 90, CDN, Mix; *Le Party*, C, 89, CDN, Mix; "La Misère des Riches" (6 eps), TV, 89, CDN, Mix; *Eddie Lives/Eddie and the Cruisers II*, C, 89, USA, Mix; *Cruising Bar*, C, 89, CDN, Mix; *Les Matins Infidèles*, C, 88, CDN, Mix; *Dans le ventre du dragon*, C, 88, CDN, Mix.

ELLIOTT, Keith
19 Wales Ave., Toronto, ON M5T 1J2 (416)599-8479. The Film House, 424 Adelaide St. E., Toronto, ON M5A 1N4 (416)364-4321.
Type of Production and Credits: Th Film-P Prod Snd Mix/Comp; Th Short-P Prod Snd Mix/Comp; TV Film-P Prod Snd Mix; TV Video-P Prod Snd Mix.
Genres: Drama-Th&TV; Experimental-Th.
Biography: Born in 1960 in Hamilton, Ontario. Grew up in Stoney Creek. In 1984, participated in the Festival of Festivals with the short experimental film *The Fear of Cancer*, which also won 1st Prize (Experimental Images Category) at the Athens International Film & Video Festival. Enjoys composing music, scoring for film and playing guitar in pop bands. Was a Genie nominee for the 1988 feature *The Kiss*.
Selected Filmography: *Abraxas*, Th, 91, CDN, Re-record Mix; *Hell Night/Blood Rush*, Th, 91, CDN, Re-record Mix; *Jimmy's Coming*, Th, 91, CDN, Re-record Mix; *Battle of the Bulge*, Th, 91, CDN, Re-record Mix; *Moose Jaw*, Th, 91, CDN, Re-record Mix; "Top Cops" (2 eps), TV, 91,

USA/CDN, Re-record Mix; *The Flipbook Movie*, Th, 90, CDN, Comp; *O.K. But..I've Got To Get To Work!*, Th, 90, CDN, Comp; *The Last Season*, Th, 89, CDN, Re-record Mix; *Babar: The Movie*, Th, 89, CDN, Re-record Mix; *Special of the Day*, Th, 89, CDN, Re-record Mix/Comp; *Comic Book Confidential*, Th, 88, CDN, Comp; *Murderers Among Us: The Simon Weisenthal Story*, Th, 88, CDN/USA, Re-record Mix; *The Kiss*, Th, 88, CDN, Re-record Mix; "Street Legal" (10 eps), 87, CDN, Re-record Mix.

ELLIS, Rick
MPSE. 1042 Falgarwood Dr., Unit 95, Oakville, ON L6H 2P3 (416)338-0254. The Masters' Workshop Corp., 306 Rexdale Blvd., Unit 7, Rexdale, ON M9W 1R6 (416)741-1312.
Type of Production and Credits: Th Film-Re-record Mix; Th Short-Re-record Mix; TV Film-Re-record Mix.
Genres: Drama-Th&TV; Comedy-TV; Variety-TV; Horror-Th&TV.
Biography: Born in Toronto, Ontario, in 1956. 2 years dialogue editor and ADR recording. Currently Re-recording Mixer at Masters' Workshop. Winner of 2 Golden Reel Awards (MPSE) for *Day One* and *Ford: The Man & The Machine*. Nominated for a Gemini in 1989. Eats a lot of pizza.
Selected Filmography: *Scanners II - The New Order*, Th, 90, CDN, Re-record Mix; *Simone Les Nuages*, Th, 90, CDN, Re-record Mix; "The Hitchhiker" (3 seasons), TV, 88-90, CDN/USA/F, Re-record Mix; "Friday The 13th - The Series" (2 seasons), TV, 89-90, CDN/USA, Re-record Mix; *The Last Elephant/Ivory Hunters*, Th, 89, USA, Re-record Mix; *Day One*, TV, 89, USA, Re-record Mix; "The Jim Henson Hour" (4 eps), TV, 89, USA, Re-record Mix; *Andrea Martin Special*, TV, 89, USA, Re-record Mix; "Ray Bradbury Theatre" (5 eps), TV, 89, CDN, Re-record Mix; *Small Sacrifices*, TV, 89, USA, Re-record Mix; *Secrets of the Muppets*, TV, 89, USA, Re-record Mix; "The Campbells" (4 seasons), TV, 86-89, CDN/GB, Dial Ed; *Glory! Glory!*, TV, 88, CDN/USA, Re-record Mix; *Ford: The Man & The Machine*, TV, 87, CDN/USA, Dial Ed; *Sword of Gideon/Vengence*, TV, 86, CDN/USA, Dial Ed.

FERNANDES, Gavin
5005 Leger, Pierrefonds, PQ H8Z 2H1 (514)684-8002. Studio Place Royale, 640 St. Paul W., Montreal, PQ H3C 1L9 (514)866-6074.
Type of Production and Credits: Th Film-P Prod Snd Mix; TV Film-P Prod Snd Mix.
Genres: Drama-Th&TV; Documentary-TV; Industrial-Th&TV; Current Affairs-TV.
Biography: Born in 1965 in London, England. Fluent in English and French. Canadian citizen since 1972.
Selected Filmography: *Le Dortoir/Excerpts from Le Dortoir*, TV, 90-91, CDN, P Prod Snd Mix; *Léa*, Th/TV, 1991, CDN, P Prod Snd Mix; *Moïse*, Th, 91, CDN, Foley Rec; *A la Belle Vie*, Th/TV, 90, CDN, P Prod Snd Mix/Foley Rec/Snd Mix; "Molson Tournée des Fêtes" (2 eps), TV, 87/90, CDN, P Prod Snd Mix; "North South" (20 eps), TV, 89, CDN, P Prod Snd Mix; "Omniscience" (26 eps), TV, 88-89, CDN, P Prod Snd Mix; "L'Aventure" (15 eps), TV, 89, CDN, P Prod Snd Mix; *Cursed*, Th, 89, CDN, Foley Rec/Re-record Mix; *Power Games*, Th, 89, CDN, Foley Rec/P Post Snd Mix.

FRANK, Jim
91 Chudleigh Ave., Toronto, ON M4R 1T4 (416)486-7929. Master's Workshop, 306 Rexdale Blvd., Unit 7, Rexdale, ON M9W 1R6 (416)741-1312.
Type of Production and Credits: Th Film-Snd Mix; Th Short-Snd Mix/Snd Ed; TV Film-Snd Mix/Mus Ed; TV Video-Snd Mix/Mus Ed.
Genres: Drama-Th&TV; Comedy-Th&TV; Musical-Th&TV.
Biography: Born 1948, New York, New York; landed immigrant, Canada. B.Sc., State University of New York; Certificate of Audio Technology, Institute of Audio Research, New York, NY. Assistant Engineer, Record Plant, New York; album, scoring and jingle engineer, Nimbus Studios, Toronto; Editor, Re-recording Engineer, Director of studio operations, Master's Workshop, Toronto; recorded tracks for Harry Chapin, Peter Gabriel, The Guess Who, Alice Cooper, Rough Trade, Murray McLaughlan and others. Received Gemini and various film festival awards.
Selected Filmography: *Bethune: The Making of a Hero*, Th/TV, 90-91, CDN, Post Audio; *Scanners II/III*, Th, 90-91, CDN, Post Audio; *Switzerland*, Th (Imax), 91, CH, Post Audio; *Echoes of the Sun*, Th (Omnimax), 90, CDN/J, Snd Mix; "Profiles of Nature" (84 eps), TV, 85-88, CDN, Snd Mix; "4 on the Floor" (12 eps), TV, 86, CDN, Snd Mix; *John and the Missus*, Th, 86, CDN, Snd Mix; *A Judgement in Stone*, Th, 86, CDN, Snd Mix; *Whalesong*, TV, 86, CDN, Snd Mix,

(GEMINI 87); "Laughing Matters" (13 eps), TV, 85, CDN, Snd Mix; *Last Polka*, TV, 85, CDN, Snd FX Ed; "The Campbells" (26 eps), TV, 85, CDN/USA/GB, Snd Mix; "The Hitchhiker" (13 eps), TV, 85, USA, Mus Ed; *Tears Are Not Enough*, Th, 85, CDN, Snd FX Ed; *The Canadian Conspiracy*, TV, 85, CDN/USA, Snd Mix.

GELDART, Alan
- see SOUND EDITORS

GORDICA, Terry◊
ACCT. (416)858-2228.
Type of Production and Credits: TV Film-Snd Mix/Snd Ed; TV Video-Snd Mix/Snd Ed/Snd Rec.
Genres: Drama-TV; Comedy-TV; Action-TV; Science Fiction-TV.
Biography: Born 1957, Edmonton, Alberta. Specialized in ADR; currently Director of Tele-Division/Senior Mixer at Master's Workshop Corp. Twice nominated for MPSE Golden Reel Award; recipient of Golden Reel Award, Best Sound Television Half Hour Series, 86.
Selected Filmography: *Beavers* (Imax), Th, 88, CDN, Snd Mix; "Adderly" (44 eps), TV, 86-88, CDN, Snd Mix; "Diamonds" (22 eps), TV, 86-88, CDN/F, Snd Mix; *Chasing Rainbows* (mini-series)(6 eps), TV, 87, CDN, Snd Mix/Snd Ed; "Alfred Hitchcock Presents" (13 eps), TV, 87, CDN/USA, Snd Mix; *Gunfighters*, TV, 87, CDN, Snd Mix; *Beautiful Korea* (Imax), Th, 87, CDN/K, Snd Mix; "The Hitchhiker" (22 eps), TV, 85-86, CDN/USA, Snd Mix/Snd Ed; "The Campbells" (54 eps), TV, 84-86, CDN/GB, Snd Mix/Snd Ed; "Check It Out!" (13 eps), TV, 85, CDN/USA, Snd Mix; "The Frantics" (13 eps), TV, 85, CDN, Snd Mix/Snd Ed; *Joshua Then and Now*, Th, 84, CDN, Snd Mix; "SCTV" (87 eps), 82-84, CDN, Post Audio Spv/Snd Ed; "In Concert" (6 eps), TV, 79-82, CDN/USA, Snd Rec/Snd Mix; "Rock It" (22 eps), TV, 79, CDN/USA, Snd Mix.

GOULD, Derek◊
NABET. (306)586-1029.
Type of Production and Credits: TV Video-Snd Mix.
Genres: Variety-TV; Musical-TV; Commercials-TV; News-TV.
Biography: Born 1956, Winnipeg, Manitoba. Languages: French and English. Graduate of Collège Mathieu, Gravelbourg, Saskatchewan. Five years of radio and 4 with TV, CBC Regina; has specialized in live sound reinforcement for the past 10 years.

Selected Filmography: *Easter Seal Telethon*, TV, 85-88, CDN, Snd Mix; "Contact" (52/yr), TV, 86-87, CDN, Snd Mix; "Ce Soir plus" (104/yr), TV, 86-87, CDN, Snd Mix; "Country West" (26 eps), TV, 85-86, CDN, Snd Mix; "Tour à tour" (26 eps), TV, 85-86, CDN, Snd Mix; "Pile ou face" (13 eps), TV, 85, CDN, Snd Mix; "Génies en herbe" (26 eps), TV, 83-84, CDN, Snd Mix.

GRIMALDI, Austin
ACCT. 192 Markland Dr., Etobicoke, ON M9C 1P7 (416)621-2956. McClear Pathé, 121 St. Patrick St., Toronto, ON M5T 1V3 (416)598-2521.
Type of Production and Credits: Th Film-Snd Re-record; Th Short-Snd Re-record; TV Film-Snd Re-record; TV Video-Snd Re-record.
Genres: Drama-Th&TV; Action-Th&TV; Horror-Th&TV; Documentary-Th&TV.
Biography: Born in 1934 in Toronto, Ontario. Radio College of Canada, Radio & TV course. Built and wired mixing consoles and maintained magnetic and film equipment. 35 years in the film and television industry with Queensway Film Studios, Shelly Films, Pathé Deluxe, Pathé Humphries, Astral Bellevue Pathé and presently McClear Pathé. Nominated and received awards for sound re-recording for features and television.
Selected Filmography: *The Girl From Mars*, TV, 91, CDN/USA, Re-record Mix; "The Nature of Things" (30 years), TV, 61-91, CDN, Re-record Mix; *Young Catherine*, TV, 90, CDN/USA/GB/USR, Re-record Mix; *Secret of Nandy*, TV, 90, CDN, Re-record Mix; *Primo Baby*, Th, 89, CDN, Re-record Mix; *The Kiss*, Th, 88, CDN/ USA, Re-record Mix; *Skate*, TV, 88, CDN, Re-record Mix, (GEMINI); "Street Legal" (3 years), TV, 87-89, CDN, Re-record Mix; "Seeing Things" (40 eps), TV, 84-86, CDN, Re-record Mix; *Agnes of God*, Th, 85, CDN/USA, Re-record Mix; *The Terry Fox Story*, Th, 84, CDN/USA, Re-record Mix, (GENIE); *Quest For Fire*, Th, 83, CDN/USA, Re-record Mix, (GENIE); *Heavy Metal*, Th, 82, CDN/USA, Re-record Mix (GENIE); *The Changeling*, Th, 80, CDN/USA, Re-record Mix, (GENIE); "The Last Cause" (6 eps), TV, 76, CDN, Re-record Mix (ETROG).

GRIMALDI, Joseph P.
ACCT., SMPTE. 25 Golf Valley Lane, Etobicoke, ON M9C 2K2 (416)620-9496. 121 St. Patrick St., Toronto, ON M5T 1V3 (416)598-2521.

Type of Production and Credits: Th Film-P Prod Snd Mix; Th Short-P Prod Snd Mix; TV Film-P Prod Snd Mix; TV Video-P Prod Snd Mix.
Genres: Drama-Th&TV; Action-Th& TV; Documentary-Th&TV; Current Affairs-TV.
Biography: Born in 1928 in Toronto, Ontario. Specialized in theatrical and TV post production mixing (re-recording), ADR foley and production mixing. 7 Etrog-Genie awards, 73-78; 2 Gemini awards; 3 CBC Wilderness awards; 1 Prix Anik (CBC) award; 1 Golden Reel award; 1 International Film and Television Festival award. In sound work since 1953, VP of McClear Pathé Studio's (formally Pathé Sound) since 1976.
Selected Filmography: *True Confections*, Th, 90-91, CDN, P Prod Snd Mix; *And The Dance Goes On*, Th, 90-91, CDN, P Prod Snd Mix; *Diplomatic Immunity*, Th, 90, CDN, P Prod Snd Mix; "Young Catherine", TV, 90, CDN/GB, P Prod Snd Mix; "The Nature of Things", TV, 50-90, CDN, P Prod Snd Mix; "Little Kidnappers", TV, 89, CDN/USA, P Prod Snd Mix; *Iron Eagle II*, Th, 88-89, CDN/USA, P Prod Snd Mix; *Murderers Among Us: The Simon Weisenthal Story*, TV, 89, CDN/US/I/GB, P Prod Snd Mix; *Moonstruck*, Th, 87, CDN/USA, P Prod Snd Mix; *Agnes of God*, Th, 85, CDN/USA, P Prod Snd Mix; *One Magic Christmas*, Th, 85, USA, P Prod Snd Mix; "The Edison Twins" (32 eps), TV, 84-85, CDN, P Prod Snd Mix; *The Terry Fox Story*, Th, 83, CDN, P Prod Snd Mix, (GENIE); *Heavy Metal*, Th, 82, CDN/USA, P Prod Snd Mix, (GENIE); *Quest for Fire*, Th, 82, CDN/F, P Prod Snd Mix, (GENIE).

GRIMALDI, Sal
2901 Kipling Ave., Ste. 1508, Etobicoke, ON M9V 5E5 (416)748-6659. 121 St. Patrick St., Toronto, ON M5T 1V3 (416)598-2521.
Type of Production and Credits: Th Film-P Prod Snd Mix/Foley; Th Short-P Prod Snd Mix/Foley; TV Film-P Prod Snd Mix/Foley; TV Video-P Prod Snd Mix/Foley.
Genres: Drama-Th&TV; Action-Th& TV; Educational-TV; Commercials-Th&TV.
Biography: Born in 1965 in Toronto, Ontario. Specialized in theatrical and TV re-recording. Also does Foley. Genie nomination for *Termini Station*. Has been in the business since 1983.
Selected Filmography: *True Confections*, Th/TV, 90-91, CDN, P Prod Snd Mix; *And The Dance Goes On*, Th, 90-91, CDN, P Prod Snd Mix; *Diplomatic Immunity*, Th, 90, CDN, P Prod Snd Mix; *Ice Princess*, TV, 90, USA, P Prod Snd Mix; *Thick As Thieves*, Th, 90, CDN, P Prod Snd Mix; *Boat in the Grass*, Th, 90, CDN, P Prod Snd Mix/Foley; *Double Daniel*, TV, 89, CDN, P Prod Snd Mix; *Terminal City Ricochet*, Th, 89, CDN, P Prod Snd Mix; *Complex World*, Th, 89, USA, P Prod Snd Mix; *Termini Station*, Th, 89, CDN, P Prod Snd Mix; *The Christmas Wife*, TV, 89, USA, P Prod Snd Mix; "Street Legal", TV, 86-88, CDN, P Prod Snd Mix; *Vent de Galerne*, Th, 88, CDN, P Prod Snd Mix; *The Jeweller's Shop*, Th/TV, 88, CDN/I, P Prod Snd Mix; "Shades of Love", TV, 86, CDN, P Prod Snd Mix.

HALL, Grant
562 Rink Ave., Regina, SK S4X 2E9 (306)949-6621. Touchwood Recording Studios, Box 794, Regina, SK S4P 3A8 (306)775-1929.
Type of Production and Credits: TV Video-Snd Mix.
Genres: Drama-TV; Musical-TV; Commercials-TV; Variety-TV.
Biography: Born 1961, Weyburn, Saskatchewan. Educated at Saskatchewan Technical Institute. 4 years background in recording/audio production and post-production for TV and commercial jingles.
Selected Filmography: *Once Upon a Knight*, "Shawn Shields", MV, 91, CDN, Audio Prod; *Hurray for Hollywood*, TV, 91, CDN, Post Audio Spv/Snd Mix; "Miss Regina 89-90" (2 eps), TV, 89-90, CDN, Post Audio Spv/Snd Mix; "Puttnam's Prairie Emporium" (52 eps), TV, 87-90, CDN, Post Audio Spv/Audio Dir; *Marching for Freedom*, "Cinema X", MV, 90, CDN, Prod; *Saskatchewan Rough Riders*, "Hall of Fame" (3 eps), TV, 88-90, CDN, Snd Mix; *1988 CanPro Awards*, TV, 88, CDN, Snd Mix; *70th Anniversary, Queen City Kinsmen*, TV, 88, CDN, Snd Mix; *Saskatchewan RoughRiders Ticket Telethon*, TV, 87, CDN, Snd Mix.

HANNIGAN, Teresa
- see EDITORS

HONE, Louis
SGCT, AES. C.P. 185, St-Joseph du Lac, PQ J0N 1M0 (514)623-0410. ONF, 3155, Côte de Liesse, Montréal, PQ (514)283-9222.
Types de production et générique: l métrage-Mix son/Pren son; c métrage-Mix son/Pren son; TV film-Mix son/Pren son; TV vidéo-Mix son/Pren son.

Types d'oeuvres: Drame-C&TV; Action-C&TV; Documentaire-C&TV; Animation-C&TV.
Curriculum vitae: Né en 1950, Montréal, Québec. Langues: français et anglais. B.A.A., Radio and Television Arts, Ryerson Polytechnical Institute, 71-74; Eastman School of Music, Rochester, 80; acoustique, Université de Montréal, 77. Producteur, ingénieur de son, CJRT FM, Toronto, 73-75; ingénieur de son, Studio Switch, COJO, Studio Expérience, Studio Jean Sauvageau, 75-79; mixeur, ONF Montréal, depuis 79. Récipiendaire du Prix CJON, Excellency in FM production, 73, et du Prix Anik, Music Recording, 85. Gemini 88, "Best Sound," *King Chronicle*.
Filmographie sélective: *La Sarrazine*, C, 91, CDN, Mix Mus; *Company of Strangers*, C, 89, CDN, Mix Mus; *The First Emperor of China*, C (Imax), 89, CDN, Mix Mus; *Juke Bar*, C, 89, CDN, Mix Mus; *Beautiful Dreamers*, C, 89, CDN, Mix Mus; *George's Island*, C, 89, CDN, Mix Mus; "King Chronicle" (3 eps), TV, 88, CDN, Mix Mus; *Charles et François*, C, 87, CDN, Mix Mus; *Le déclin de l'empire américain*, C, 86, CDN, Mix Mus; *Transitions*, C (Imax), 86, CDN, Mix Mus; *Un zoo la nuit*, C, 86, CDN, Bruit; *Anne Trister*, C, 85, CDN, Mix Mus; *Mario*, C, 83, CDN, Bruit; *Narcisse*, C, 83, CDN, Mix Mus; *L'Homme à tout faire*, C, 80, CDN, Mix Mus.

HUNT, Catherine
DGC. 156 Sunnyside Ave., Toronto, ON M6R 2P2 (416)532-0535. FAX: 532-2537.
Type of Production and Credits: Th Film-Snd Ed/P Pro Spv; TV Film-Snd Ed/P Pro Spv; Th Short-Snd Ed; TV Video-Snd Ed/P Pro Spv.
Genres: Drama-Th&TV; Documentary-Th.
Biography: Born in 1956 in Toronto, Ontario. Languages: English and conversational French. B.A.A., Motion Picture, Ryerson Polytechnical Institute. Experience creating postproduction budgets for film and tape and subsequent cost reporting.
Selected Filmography: *Clearcut*, Th, 90-91, CDN, P Pro Spv; *Perfectly Normal*, Th, 90, CDN, Postprod Coord; "Alfred Hitchcock Presents" (41 eps), TV, 87-88, CDN/USA, P Pro Spv; *A Switch in Time*, Th, 87, CDN, Dial Ed; "Alfred Hitchcock Presents" (13 eps), TV, 86-87, CDN/USA, Postprod Coord; *Sword of Gideon*, TV, 86, CDN, Spv ADR Ed, (GEMINI 87); "The Campbells" (4 eps), TV, 86, CDN/USA/GB, Dial Ed; *The Town Where No One Got Off*, "Ray Bradbury Theatre", TV, 85, CDN, Snd Ed; *Anne of Green Gables* (mini-series), TV, 85, CDN, Dial Ed; *Making a Difference*, ED, 84, CDN, Snd Ed; *Downside Adjustments*, ED, 83, CDN, Snd Ed; *The Making of Rock and Rule*, Th, 83, CDN, Ed/Snd Ed; "Inspector Gadget" (30 eps), TV, 83, F/USA, FX Ed; "The Blood of Others" (3 eps), Th, 83, CDN/F, Jr ADR Ed; *The Grey Fox*, Th, 80, CDN, Assist Snd Ed.

JONES, Barry P.✧
(416)694-0452.
Type of Production and Credits: Th Film-Snd Mix; TV Film-Snd Mix; Th Short-Snd Mix; TV Video-Snd Mix.
Genres: Drama-Th&TV; Documentary-Th&TV; Commercials-TV; Industrial-TV.
Biography: Born 1943, Winchester, England; Canadian and British citizenship. Studied Cinematography, London Polytechnic, 1962-65. Five years with film department, BBC London, 65-70. Credits as dubbing mixer on more than 1,000 productions. Creative craft award, Chicago, 87; AMPIA awards for sound.
Selected Filmography: "The Beachcombers" (300 eps), TV, 71-87, CDN, Snd Mix; *Regeneration*, TV, 87, CDN, Snd Mix; *Shooting Stars*, TV, 87, CDN, Snd Mix; *Frozen in Time*, TV, 87, CDN, Snd Mix; "Red Serge" (12 eps), TV, 86, CDN, Snd Mix; *Discovery* (Showscan), Th, 86, CDN, Snd Mix; *Which Way to Carnegie Hall?*, TV, 86, CDN, Snd Mix; *Paper Marriage*, Th, 86, CDN/HK, Snd Mix; "Red Serge Wives" (4 eps), TV, 85, CDN, Snd Mix; *Walls*, Th, 84, CDN, Snd Mix; "Bush Pilots" (13 eps), TV, 83, CDN, Snd Mix; *Deserters*, Th, 82, CDN, Snd Mix; *Sculptor in Steel*, TV, 82, CDN, Snd Mix; *Dead Wrong*, Th, 81, CDN, Snd Mix; "Stony Plain Ranch" (13 eps), TV, 81, CDN, Snd Mix.

KELLY, Peter
5 Greystone Walk Dr., Scarborough, ON M1K 5J5 (416)261-5216. The Film House Group Inc., 424 Adelaide St. E., Toronto, ON M5A 1N4 (416)364-4321.
Type of Production and Credits: Th Film-Snd Mix/Snd Rec; Th Short-Snd Mix/Snd Rec; TV Film-Snd Mix/Snd Rec; TV Video-Snd Mix/Snd Rec.
Genres: Drama-Th&TV; Documentary-Th&TV; Industrial-Th&TV. Experimental-Th&TV;
Biography: Born in Montreal, Quebec. Languages: English and French. Attended Concordia University; Diploma, Media

Arts, Sheridan College. Experienced in postproduction sound mixing for film and tape; has worked as a recording engineer in Montreal, Toronto and Vancouver.
Selected Filmography: *The Adjuster*, Th, 91, CDN, Re-record Mix; *Highway 61*, Th, 91, CDN, Re-record Mix; *The Grocer's Wife*, Th, 91, CDN, Re-record Mix; *Masala*, Th, 91, CDN, Re-record Mix; *The Big Slice*, Th, 90, CDN, Re-record Mix; *Swan Lake/The Zone*, Th, 90, CDN, Re-record Mix; *The Last Winter*, Th, 90, CDN, Re-record Mix; *The Greening of Ian Elliott*, TV, 90, CDN, Re-record Mix; *At the Lake*, Th, 90, CDN, Re-record Mix; "Street Legal", TV, 90, CDN, Re-record Mix; *Bye Bye Blues*, Th, 89, CDN, Re-record Mix; *Love and Hate*, TV, 89, CDN, Re-record Mix, (ANIK); *The Private Capital*, TV, 88, CDN, Re-record Mix; *Champagne Charlie*, TV, 88, CDN, Re-record Mix; "T & T", TV, 88, CDN, Re-record Mix.

KOYAMA, Andrew
189 Mutual St., Toronto, ON M5B 2B4 (416)597-0762. The Film House Group Inc., 424 Adelaide St. E., Toronto, ON M5A 1N4 (416)364-4321.
Type of Production and Credits: TV Film-Re-record Mix; TV Video-Re-record Mix.
Genres: Drama-TV; Action-TV; Documentary-Th&TV; Animation-TV.
Biography: Born in 1962 in Toronto, Ontario. Album production and engineering credits, "The Love Cows" and "The Lowest of the Low". Assistant engineer on the *Dirty Dancing* Soundtrack and Shirley Eikhard-*Taking Charge*.
Selected Filmography: "Top Cops" (29 eps), TV, 90-91, USA/CDN, Re-record Snd Mix; "Sweating Bullets" (22 eps), TV, 91, USA/CDN/MEX, Re-record Snd Mix; "Counterstrike" (20 eps), TV, 90, USA/CDN/F, Re-record Snd Mix; "Street Legal" (1 eps), TV, 90, CDN, Re-record Snd Mix; "Maniac Mansion" (1 eps), TV, 90, USA/CDN, Re-record Snd Mix; *Born in Africa*, "PBS AIDS Quarterly", TV, 90, USA/CDN, Re-record Snd Mix; "Babar" (1 eps), TV, 90, USA/CDN, Re-record Snd Mix; "T and T" (2 eps), TV, 89, USA/CDN, Re-record Snd Mix.

LIOTTA, Michael
ACCT. (416)621-2509.
Type of Production and Credits: Th Film-Snd Mix; Th Short-Snd Mix; TV Film-Snd Mix; TV Video-Snd Mix.
Genres: Drama-Th&TV; Comedy-Th&TV; Action-Th&TV; Documentary-Th&TV.
Biography: Born 1954, Italy; Canadian citizenship. Languages: English, Italian and some French. Honours B.A., Fine Arts, York University.
Selected Filmography: *Guitar Festival*, TV, 88, CDN, Snd Mix; *Masterclass with Menuhin*, TV, 88, CDN, Snd Mix; *Moonstruck*, Th, 87, USA, Snd Mix: *A Winter Tan*, Th, 87, CDN, Snd Mix; *A Nest of Singing Birds*, Th, 87, CDN, Snd Mix; "Shades of Love" (7 eps), TV, 87, CDN, Snd Mix: *Obsessed/Hitting Home*, Th, 86, CDN, Snd Mix; *Nowhere to Hide*, Th, 86, CDN, Snd Mix; *9B*, TV, 86, CDN, Snd Mix; *Show Stopper*, TV, 86, CDN, Snd Mix; *Les Fous de Bassan*, Th, 86, CDN, Snd Mix; *The Gate*, Th, 86, CDN, Snd Mix: *The Morning Man*, Th, 86, CDN, Snd Mix; "The Edison Twins" (32 eps), TV, 84-86, CDN, Snd Mix: *State Park*, Th, 86, CDN, Snd Mix.

LUKE, Corby
SMPTE, AES. 166 Borden St., Toronto, ON M5S 2N3 (416)535-9608. The Film House Group Inc., 424 Adelaide St. E., Toronto, ON M5A 1N4 (416)364-4321.
Type of Production and Credits: Th Film-Re-record Mix; Th Short-Re-record Mix; TV Film-Re-record Mix; TV Video-Re-record Mix.
Genres: Drama-Th&TV; Variety-Th&TV; Musical-Th&TV; Docu-mentary-Th&TV.
Biography: Born in 1958 in Montreal, Quebec. Languages: English and French. Education: University of Ottawa, Engineering; Fanshawe College, Music Production and Audio Engineering. Primarily mixes audio for film and television; freelances as music recording engineer and saxophone player.
Selected Filmography: *Ten Musicians*, Th, 91, USA, Re-record Mix; *Don't Take My Sunshine*, Th, 91, CDN, Re-record Mix; *Love Clinic*, Th, 91, CDN, Re-record Mix; *Bon Appetit*, Th, 91, CDN, Re-record Mix; "Street Legal" (46 eps), TV, 91, CDN, ADR/Foley/Mix; "Top Cops" (41 eps), TV, 91, CDN/USA, ADR/Foley /Mix; "Road to Avonlea" (26 eps), TV, 91, CDN/USA, ADR/Foley/Mix; "Sweating Bullets" (22 eps), TV, 91, CDN/USA/MEX, ADR/Foley/Mix; *South of Wawa*, Th, 91, CDN, ADR Rec; *The Exorcist III*, Th, 90, USA, ADR Rec; *Driving Miss Daisy*, Th, 90, USA, ADR Rec; *The Gate II*, Th, 89, CDN/USA, ADR Rec; *Twin Dragons*, Th, 89, CDN, Re-record Mix; *Deal Easy*, Th, 89, CDN, Re-record Mix; *Red Blooded American Girl*, Th, 89, CDN/USA, ADR Rec.

MacLAVERTY, Michael
- see EDITORS

McCLEMENT, Doug
- see PRODUCTION SOUND MIXERS

MITCHELL, Brian
306 Seaton St., Toronto, ON M5A 2T7 (416)968-2306.
Type of Production and Credits: TV Video-Snd Mix/Snd Rec.
Genres: Action-Th&TV; Documentary-TV; Commercials-TV; Industrial-Th&TV.
Biography: Born, 1946, Fredericton, New Brunswick. Elect. Eng., Univ. of NB; Music Theory, Univ. of Toronto; owner/ manager of Studio 306 in Toronto, audio post and recording for jingles, corporate videos, TV and film programs.
Selected Filmography: *Ontario Place Waterfall Show*, Th, 88, CDN, Snd Mix; *Hyundai*, Cm, 88, CDN, Snd Mix; *Mission Specialists*, Union Carbide, In, 88, CDN, Snd Mix; *Wardair*, In, 88, CDN/USA, Snd Mix; *Pepsi*, In, 88, CDN, Snd Mix; *Rothmans*, In, 88, CDN, Snd Mix; "The Maples and the Crown" (3 eps), TV, 86, CDN, Snd Mix.

MONK, Roger J.
- see SOUND EDITORS

MORRONE, Frank
- see PRODUCTION SOUND MIXERS

NICOLOV, Yordan
APFVQ, ACCT. 1818 ouest, rue Sherbrooke, Montreal, PQ H3H 1E4 (514)932-4439. FAX: 931-7155.
Types de production et générique: l métrage-Mix son/Pren son; c métrage-Mix son/Pren son; TV film-Mix son/Pren son; TV vidéo-Mix son/Pren son.
Types d'oeuvres: Drame-C&TV; Action-C&TV; Science-fiction-C&TV; Documentaire-C&TV.
Curriculum vitae: Né en 1923 Bulgarie. Langues: Bulgare, français et anglais. Etudes à l'Institut des Hautes Etudes cinématographiques de Paris, 49.
Filmographie sélective: *Drop Dead Fred/Fais de l'air Fred*, TV, 91, GB, Trad; "Dog House"/"Parole de chien", TV, 91, CDN, Trad; "Chicken Minute"/"Cocotte Minute", TV, 91, CDN, Trad; *Scanners II*, C, 90, CDN, Trad; *Prancer*, C, 90, USA, Trad; *Opportunity Knocks/ Coup Double*, C, 90, USA, Trad.

NYZNIK, Bruce◊
DGC, ACCT. (416)977-3177.
Type of Production and Credits: Th Film-Snd Ed/Ed/Mus Ed; TV Film-Snd Ed/Ed/Mus Ed.
Genres: Drama-Th&TV; Musical-Th&TV; Documentary-Th&TV.
Biography: Born in Dauphin, Manitoba. Winner of several awards for sound and editing, including 4 Genies.
Selected Filmography: *Glory! Glory!*, TV, 88, CDN/USA, Snd Spv; *Milk and Honey*, Th, 87, CDN, Ed/Snd Des; *John and the Missus*, Th, 86, CDN, Snd Des; *Zargon*, Th, 85, CDN, Dir/Snd Des; *One Magic Christmas*, Th, 85, CDN/USA, Snd Des, (GENIE); *I Am a Hotel*, Leonard Cohen, MV, 84, CDN, Snd Des, (ANIK); *Mario*, Th, 83, CDN, Snd Des, (GENIE); *The Wars*, Th, 81, CDN/D, Snd Spv, (GENIE); *The Grey Fox*, Th, 80, CDN, Snd Spv, (CFE); *The Italians*, "The Newcomers", TV, 79, CDN, Snd Ed/Ed; *The Silent Partner*, Th, 77, CDN, Snd Spv, (CFA); *Renaldo and Clara*, Th, 77, USA, Snd Ed/Mus Ed; *The Man Who Skied Down Everest*, Th, 73, CDN/J, Snd Ed.

ORMEROD, Allen
50 Cordova Ave., #3608, Toronto, ON M9A 4X6 (416)234-8693. The Film House Group Inc., 424 Adelaide St. E., Toronto, ON M5A 1N2 (416)364-4321.
Type of Production and Credits: Th Film-Re-record; Th Short-Re-record; TV Film-Re-record; TV Video-Re-record.
Genres: Drama-Th&TV; Comedy-TV; Action-Th&TV; Documentary-TV.
Biography: Born in 1958 in Toronto, Ontario. Canadian citizen. Entered the business, Microphonic Sound, 78; Pathé Sound, 84; Film House, 88 to date.
Selected Filmography: "Sweating Bullets" (22 eps), TV, 91, USA/CDN/MEX, Lead Eng; "Street Legal" (32 eps), TV, 89-91, CDN, Lead Eng; "Top Cops" (3 eps), TV, 90-91, CDN/USA, Lead Eng; *Dream Like Me/Clear Cut*, Th, 91, CDN, Assist Eng; *Portable Phone; Bouncer; Bear*, Labatt's Blue, Cm, 91, CDN, Lead Eng; "Maniac Mansion" (22 eps), TV, 90, CDN/USA, Lead Eng; "Rookies" (8 eps), TV, 89-90, CDN, Lead Eng; "The Ray Bradbury Theatre" (4 eps), TV, 90, CDN/USA/NZ, Lead Eng; "Counterstrike" (3 eps), TV, 90, CDN/USA, Lead Eng; *Born in Africa*, ED, 90, CDN, Lead Eng; *Talk About AIDS*, ED, 90, CDN, Lead Eng; *Speed Zone*, Th, 90, CDN/USA, Assist Eng; "The Twilight Zone" (26 eps), TV, 88-89, CDN/USA, Assist/Lead Eng; "Alfred Hitchcock" (44 eps), TV, 88-89, CDN/USA, Assist Eng; *In Country*, Th, 89, CDN/USA, Assist Eng.

PELLERIN, Daniel
2 Hector Ave., Toronto, ON M6N 2M1 (416)767-9221. The Film House Group Inc., 424 Adelaide St. E., Toronto, ON M5A 1N4 (416)364-4321.

Type of Production and Credits: Th Film-Snd Mix/Snd Rec; Th Short-Snd Mix/Snd Rec; TV Film-Snd Mix/Snd Rec; TV Video-Snd Mix/Snd Rec.
Genres: Drama-Th&TV; Variety-Th& TV; Musical-Th&TV; Documentary-Th&TV.
Biography: Born 1956, Ottawa, Ontario. Languages: English and French. Diploma, Film Studies, Algonquin College, with specialization in sound recording and editing and production. Producer of various music projects (live and studio), recording engineer and mixer (live and studio). Sound engineer at Film House since 88.
Selected Filmography: "Road to Avonlea" (26 eps), TV, 89-91, CDN/USA, Snd Mix/Mus Engin; *The Adjuster*, Th, 91, CDN, Snd Mix/Mus Engin; *Highway 61*, Th, 91, CDN, Snd Mix/Mus Engin; *The Nutcracker Prince*, Th, 91, CDN/USA, Snd Mix/Mus Engin; *Masala*, Th, 91, CDN, Snd Mix/Mus Engin; *La nuit d'été*, "R.S.V.P.", TV/Th, 91, CDN, Snd Mix; *Musicians in Exile*, Th/TV, 90, CDN, Snd Mix/Mus Engin; *Anne of Green Gables* (mini-series, orig & sequel), Th/TV, 85-87/88-90, CDN/USA/D, Snd Mix; *Entry in a Diary*, Th, 90, CDN, Snd Mix; *Jane of Lantern Hill*, TV/Th, 88, CDN/USA, Snd Mix/Mus Engin; *Speaking Parts*, Th, 89, CDN/USA, Snd Mix/Mus Engin; *Road Kill*, Th, 89, CDN, Snd Mix/Mus Engin; *The Railway Dragon*, TV, 89, CDN, Snd Mix; *Looking for Miracles*, TV/Th, 88, CDN/USA, Snd Mix/Mus Engin; *Comic Book Confidential*, Th, 88, CDN, Snd Mix/Mus Eng.

PREDOVICH, Robert
89 Barford Rd., Rexdale, ON M9W 4H8 (416)741-1117. Master's Workshop, 306 Rexdale Blvd., Suite 7, Rexdale, ON M9W 1R6 (416)741-1312.
Type of Production and Credits: Th Film-Snd Mix; Th Short-Snd Mix; TV Film-Snd Mix; TV Video-Snd Mix.
Genres: Drama-Th&TV; Variety-TV; Documentary-TV.
Biography: Born 1954, Toronto, Ontario. Honours B.F.A., Film and Television, York University, 76. After 6 years with Global Television Network, joined Master's Workshop Corp.; converted recording studio into an audio for film and video postproduction; also involved in system design and is a co-designer of the Soundmaster Integrated Editing System; currently Vice-President and General Manager of the Master's Workshop division of Maclean Hunter Ltd. Award winner at New York Festival of TV and Cinema.
Selected Filmography: "Profiles of Nature" (100 eps), TV, 85-91, CDN, Snd Mix; *Tears Are Not Enough*, Th, 85, CDN, Snd Mix; *A Freedom to Move*, Th, 85, CDN, Snd Mix; *Earthwatch*, Th, 85, CDN, Snd Mix; "The Hitchhiker" (26 eps), TV, 84-85, USA, Snd Mix; *Skyward*, Th, 84, CDN, Snd Mix; *The Last Polka*, TV, 84, CDN/USA, Snd Mix; *Claus Mission*, TV, 84, CDN, Snd Mix; "First Choice Rocks" (12 eps), TV, 83-84, CDN, Snd Mix; *A Case of Libel*, TV, 84, CDN, Snd Mix; *I Am a Hotel*, TV, 84, CDN, Snd Mix; "King of Friday Night" (1 eps), TV, 84, CDN, Snd Mix; *Magic Planet*, TV, 83, CDN/USA, Snd Mix; *Balconville*, TV, 83, CDN, Snd Mix; *Pygmalion*, TV, 83, CDN/USA, Snd Mix.

PURDY, Scott
51 Alexander St., #1119, Toronto, ON M4Y 1B3 (416)923-7239. The Film House Group Inc., 424 Adelaide St. E., Toronto, ON M5A 1N4 (416)364-4321.
Genres: Drama-Th&TV; Comedy-Th&TV; Action-Th&TV; Experimental-Th&TV.
Biography: Born in 1960 in Charlottetown, Prince Edward Island. Nominated for a Gemini for "Street Legal", 1990.
Selected Filmography: *Carnival of Shadows*, Th, 90, CDN, Re-record Mix, (GEMINI); "Top Cops" (22 eps), TV, 90, CDN/USA, Re-record Mix; "Counterstrike", (22 eps), TV, 90, USA/CDN, Re-record Mix; "Sweating Bullets" (5 eps), TV, 91, USA/MEX/CDN, Re-record Mix; "Maniac Mansion", TV, 90, CDN/USA, Re-record Mix; *Pas de Deux*, Th, 90, CDN, Re-record Mix; "Street Legal", TV, 90, CDN, Re-record Mix; *Behind the Mask*, TV, 90, CDN, Re-record Mix; "Diamonds" (10 eps), TV, 89, CDN/USA/F, Re-record Mix; *Shadow Dancing*, Th, 88, USA/CDN, Re-record Mix/Foley-ADR rec.

RAVOK, Brian
- see EDITORS

REIART, Arvo
- see EDITORS

ROSIN, Urmas John✧
ACFC. (416)921-6394.
Type of Production and Credits: Th Film-Snd Mix; Th Short-Snd Mix; TV Film-Snd Mix; TV Video-Snd Mix.
Genres: Drama-Th&TV; Action-Th& TV; Science Fiction-Th&TV; Horror-Th&TV.
Biography: Born 1957, Toronto, Ontario. B.F.A., Film Production, York University.

Selected Filmography: "T and T" (25 eps), TV, 88, CDN, Snd Mix; *Sadie and Son*, TV, 88, USA, Snd Mix; *Night Friend*, Th, 87, CDN, Snd Mix; *Calhoun*, Th, 87, USA, Snd Mix; *Blue Monkey*, Th, 87, Snd Mix; *City of Shadows*, Th, 86, CDN, Snd Mix: *Higher Education*, Th, 86, CDN, Snd Mix; *Hello Mary Lou - Prom Night II*, Th, 86, CDN, Snd Mix; *Recruits*, Th, 85, CDN, Snd Mix; *Dancing in the Dark*, Th, 85, CDN, Snd Mix; *Confidential*, Th, 85, CDN, Snd Mix; *Thrillkill*, Th, 84, CDN, Snd Mix; *Twin Dragon Encounter*, Th, 84, CDN, Snd Mix; *Flying*, Th, 84, CDN, Snd Mix.

TATE, Christopher
- see EDITORS

van den AKKER, Tony✧
(416)278-3739.
Type of Production and Credits: Th Film-Snd Mix; TV Film-Snd Mix.
Genres: Drama-Th&TV; Horror-Th&TV; Documentary-TV; Animation-Th&TV.
Biography: Born 1936, The Netherlands; Canadian citizenship. Languages: English and Dutch. Winner of Genies for *Track Stars* and *Three Card Monte*.
Selected Filmography: "The Care Bears" (136 eps), TV, 86-88, CDN, Snd Mix; "Last Frontier" (52 eps), TV, 86-88, CDN, Snd Mix; "T and T" (26 eps), TV, 87, CDN, Snd Mix; *Palais Royale*, Th, 87, CDN, Snd Mix; *Night Friend*, Th, 87, CDN, Snd Mix; *The Care Bears Adventure in Wonderland*, Th, 87, CDN, Snd Mix; *Hello Mary Lou - Prom Night II*, Th, 86, CDN, Snd Mix; *The Care Bears Movie II*, Th, 86, CDN, Snd Mix; "Lorne Greene's New Wilderness" (104 eps), TV, 81-85, CDN, Snd Mix; *Dancing in the Dark*, Th, 85, CDN, Snd Mix; *Mr. Patman*, Th, 80, CDN, Snd Mix; *Track Stars*, Th, 80, CDN, Snd Mix, (GENIE); *An American Christmas Carol*, TV, 79, USA, Snd Mix; *Nothing Personal*, Th, 79, CDN/USA, Snd Mix; *Three Card Monte*, Th, 77, CDN, Snd Mix, (GENIE).

Producers
Producteurs

A'COURT, Susan
- see WRITERS

ABASTADO, Lise
Abastado Films Inc., 294 Carré St. Louis, Br. #301, Montréal, PQ H2X 1A4 (514)284-3681.
Types de production et générique: l métrage-Prod.
Types d'oeuvres: Drame-C&TV; Comédie-C&TV; Documentaire-C&TV; Action-C&TV.
Curriculum vitae: Née à Montréal; Citoyenneté Canadienne. Langues: français, anglais et espagnol - parlés et ecrits. Début au cinéma en 1965. Participation à une centaine de films, à titres divers: Producteur Directeur de Production, 1er Ass't Réalisateur. Directeur de casting.
Filmographie sélective: *La Sarrazine*, C, 90, CDN, Prod dél; *Une Histoire Inventée*, C, 89-90, CDN, Prod dél; *Les Loups*, TV, 88, CDN/USA, Prod dél; *Comment Faire L'Amour*, C, 88, CDN/F Ass réal; *Les Portes Tournantes*, C, 87, CDN/F, Ass réal; *Normanicus*, C, 87, CDN, Ass réal; *La Ligne de Chaleur*, C, 86, CDN, Ass réal; *Keeping Track*, C, 85, CDN, Ass réal; *Les Beaux Souvenirs*, C, 80, CDN, Dir Casting; *Les Bons Debarras*, C, 79, CDN, Ass réal; *Au Claire De La Lune*, C, 79, CDN, Dir Casting; *Panique*, C, 76, CDN, Dir prod; *L'Eau Chaude L'Eau Frette*, C, 75, CDN, Dir Casting; *Les Ordres*, C, 74, CDN, Dir prod; *Lies My Father Told Me*, C, 73, CDN, Cast; *Kamouraska*, C, 70, Ass Réal/Cast.

ABONYI, Susan
11 Nanaimo Dr., Nepean, ON K2H 6X6

Whether you're flying across North America or halfway around the world, Air Canada goes above and beyond to serve you better.

Par l'ensemble de ses destinations, par l'élégance de son service, Air Canada vous démontre sa passion du monde.

ABOVE AND BEYOND
LA PASSION DU MONDE™

Air Canada

(613)820-1343. Senderlea Communications Inc., 437 Gilmour St., 2nd Floor, Ottawa, ON K2P 0R5 (613)236-7518.
Type of Production and Credits: TV Video-Prod.
Genres: Documentary-TV; Children's-TV; Industrial-Video.
Biography: Born in 1951 in Montreal, Quebec. Received a B.Sc. Nursing degree from McGill University and spent 10 years in community and public health as a nurse practitioner prior to entering the video production business as a producer. Established Senderlea Communications Inc. in 1986 and developed a solid reputation for award-winning sponsored government and corporate productions. In 1990, officially went into broadcast development with a 13 part children's series, a 24 episode health information program and a 4 part documentary series on divorce.
Selected Filmography: *Bend With the Wind*, "Active Living", ED, 90, CDN, Prod; *Who's the Parent, Who's the Child*, "Active Living", ED, 90, CDN, Prod; *Doctor/Self*, "Active Living", ED, 90, CDN, Prod; *Canada: The Opportunity Next Door*, In, 90, CDN, Prod; *Canada's GST*, In, 90, CDN, Prod; *Harassment in the Workplace*, In, 90, CDN, Prod; *The Human Rights at Employment & Immigration Canada*, In, 90, CDN, Co-Prod.

ADAMAKOS, Peter
Disada Productions Ltd., 5788 Notre Dame de Grace, Montreal, PQ H4A 1M4 (514)489-0527.
Type of Production and Credits: Th Short-Prod/Dir/Wr; TV Video-Prod/Dir/Wr.
Genres: Children's-Th&TV; Animation-Th&TV; Commercials-Th&TV; Industrial-Th&TV.
Biography: Born 1946, Montreal, Quebec. Honours B.A., Concordia University. Founded Disada Productions, 1971. Professional English and French work as producer, director, writer in theatrical and TV work, live action and animation, TV commercials; syndicated comic strip, daily and weekend newspapers Canada and USA. Industry positions have included President, Society of Film Makers; V.P., ASIFA-Canada; writer of scripts, film articles, children's books; founded Disada Productions for live-action and animation production. Retrospectives in Canada, US, Europe; Animation Guest of Honour, London and Atlanta. *Bibite II* won Silver Screen Award, Chicago.
Selected Filmography: *Disada: 20 Years of Animation 1971-1991*, In, 91, CDN, Prod/Wr; *Bibite III*, In, 91, CDN, Prod/Dir/Wr; *Bibite II*, In, 89, CDN, Prod/Dir/Wr.

ADAMS, G. Chalmers
CFTPA, ACCT. 251 Glencairn Ave., Toronto, ON M5N 1T8. Clearwater Film Limited, 1255 Yonge St., Toronto, ON M4T 1W6 (416)929-7232. FAX: 929-7225.
Type of Production and Credits: Th Film-Prod; TV Film-Prod.
Genres: Drama-Th&TV.
Biography: Born in Toronto, Ontario. Manager, CFDC, (Toronto), 69-72; Founding President of CAMPP, 72; now a lawyer.
Selected Filmography: *Horse Latitudes*, TV, 75, CDN, Exec Prod/Co-Prod; *Brethren*, Th, 75, CDN, Exec Prod/Prod; *Partners*, Th, 75, CDN, Exec Prod/Prod; "Sidestreet" (2 eps), TV, 74, CDN, Prod; *The Canary*, TV, 74, CDN, Prod; *Between Friends*, Th, 72, CDN, Exec Prod.

ADETUYI, Alfons
CIFC, CFTPA, BFVN. 10 - 33 Wasdale Cres., Toronto, ON M6A 1W9 (416) 588-9824. Inner City Films Inc., 67 Mowat Ave., Suite 341, Toronto, ON M6K 3E3.
Type of Production and Credits: Th Film-Prod; Th Short-Prod/Dir.
Genres: Drama-Th&TV; Comedy-Th&TV; Documentary-TV; Industrial-TV.
Biography: Born 1956, Sudbury, Ontario. 3 year Diploma in Film Arts, Fanshawe College, 79. Producer/Director of Corporate Video, Telelight Entertainment Corp., 81. Initiated the production of regionally-based drama in Northern Ontario with the production of *Lawyers' Suite*, a situation comedy, produced in association with CHCH-TV and Mid-Canada Television. Established Inner City Films, 87, and has since developed licenced feature-length drama to Pay-TV and private broadcasters. Actively developing co-productions with West Africa (mainly Nigeria) and Germany.
Selected Filmography: *Where's the Colour? - Racial Minorities & the Media*, ED, 91, CDN, Dir/Prod/Wr; *We Are Here For You*, In, 89, CDN, Dir/Prod; *People Helping People*, In, 89, CDN, Dir/Prod; *A.C.T.*, In, 88, CDN, Dir/Prod; *Lawyers' Suite*, TV, 86, CDN, Dir/Prod; *Artist Proof*, ED, 82, CDN, Dir/Prod.

ADETUYI, Robert
- see WRITERS

ALEXANDER, Andrew
ACCT. Second City, 110 Lombard St., Toronto, ON M5C 1M3 (416)863-1162.
Type of Production and Credits: TV Film-Prod.
Genres: Comedy-TV; Experimental-Th&TV.
Biography: Born 1944, London, England. Tri-State College; Ryerson Polytechnical Institute, 65. Owner, Second City Inc., since 74; acquired Chicago Second City, 85. "SCTV" received 13 Emmy nominations and won 2 (writing). Currently co-venturing prime time television projects with The Walt Disney Company.
Selected Filmography: "My Talk Show" (65 eps), TV, 90, CDN, Exec Prod; *110 Lombard*, TV, 88, CDN, Exec Prod; *15th Anniversary - The Second City Toronto*, TV, 88, CDN, Exec Prod; "SCTV" (185 eps), TV, 76-84, CDN, Creator/Exec Prod; *25th Anniversary of Second City*, TV, 84, CDN, Exec Prod/Prod.

ALEXANDER, Vince
106 Scarboro Beach Blvd., Toronto, ON M4E 2X1 (416)698-3826.
Type of Production and Credits: TV Video-Prod.
Genres: Variety-TV; Children's-TV; Industrial-TV; Music Video-TV.
Biography: Born 1952, Toronto, Ontario. Ten years experience in music/variety TV with demographic coverage, pre-teen to adult viewers; also writer/journalist for entertainment trade publications for 6 years - coverage includes video, film, TV and music video; has recently done several corporate videos.
Selected Filmography: "Street Noise" (26 eps), ED, 90, CDN, Prod; "It's Only Rock 'n' Roll" (13 eps), TV, 87, CDN, Field Prod; "Vidkids" (13 eps), TV, 86, CDN, Mus Cons; "Rockline" (26 eps), TV, 84-85, CDN/GB, Prod; "Flipside" (130 eps), TV, 84-85, CDN, Prod; "Something Else" (65 eps), TV, 85, CDN, Prod; "Video Singles" (195 eps), TV, 83-84, CDN, Prod; "Jukebox" (13 eps), TV, 83, CDN, Prod; "Metro Music" (26 eps), TV, 80-81, CDN, Prod.

ALIX, Stephen
- see WRITERS

ALLAN, Don
- see DIRECTORS

ALLAN, Sean
ACTRA, SAG, AEA, AFTRA, ACCT. Beacon Group Productions, Ste. 640, 999 Canada Place, Vancouver, BC V6C 3E1 (604)641-1323 EXT: 1323.
Type of Production and Credits: Th Film-Prod/Wr.
Genres: Drama-Th&TV; Comedy-Th&TV; Action-Th&TV.
Biography: Born in Victoria, B.C. Canadian citizen. San Francisco State University.
Selected Filmography: *Cold Front*, Th, 89, CDN, Prod/Dir.

ALMOND, Paul
- see DIRECTORS

ALVAREZ, Paco
24 Doddington Dr., Etobicoke, ON M8Y 1S4 (416)503-9130.
Type of Production and Credits: Th Film-Prod/PM.
Genres: Drama-Th; Comedy-Th; Action-Th.
Biography: Born in 1959 in Montreal, Quebec. Canadian citizen. Speaks English, French and Spanish. Graduated from Concordia University. Has worked in development as VP Production. Has filmed in Central America and Mexico. Has scouted in Iceland and Greece.
Selected Filmography: *Big Slice*, Th, 90, CDN, Co-Prod; *Red Blooded American Girl*, Th, 90, CDN, Co-Prod; *Stillife*, Th, 89, CDN, Co-Prod; *One Man Out*, Th, 88, M, Co-Prod; *Office Party*, Th, 88, CDN, Line Prod; *Blood Relations*, Th, 88, CDN, Line Prod; *Murder One*, Th, 87, CDN/USA, PM; *Caribe*, Th, 86, BL, PM.

AMITAY, Jonathan
CUPE. 931 Logan Ave., Toronto, ON M4K 3E3 (416)469-2989. CBC Graphic Design Dept., P.O. Box 500, Stn. A, Toronto, ON M5W 1E6 (416)975-7084.
Type of Production and Credits: Th Short-Wr/Prod/An; TV Film-Wr/Dir/An.
Genres: Educational-Th&TV; Children's-Th&TV; Animation-Th&TV; Experimental-Th&TV.
Biography: Born 1940, Israel; immigrated to Canada, 68; Canadian and Israeli citizenship. Worked as cartoonist, stage designer, fine artist in Canada since 68; self-taught in animation. With the CBC since 78: hundreds of animated shorts for various CBC programs. Produces own films in spare time. Has participated in most major animation film festivals around the world with own films and CBC films; winner of several awards including 1st Prize at Vermont International Peace Film Festival, 87 for *Oh Dad!* and Gold Plaque, Chicago Film Festival, 89 for *Oh Dad!, Part II*.
Selected Filmography: *Nukie Takes a Valium*, Th, 91, CDN, Prod/An; *Flags*, Th, 90, CDN, Prod/An; *Oh Dad, Part II*, Th/ED, 88, CDN, Prod/Wr/An; *Nukie's*

Sermon from the Bottle, Th, 88, CDN, Wr/Prod/An; *Of Lines and Men*, Th, 87, CDN, Wr/Prod/An; *A Moving Picture* (animated segment), TV, 87, CDN, An; *Oh Dad!*, Th, 86, CDN, Wr/Prod/An; *Musical Instruments*, TV, 86, CDN, Wr/Dir/An; *Chiplicks* (animated segment), TV, 86, CDN, An, (ANIK); *Nukie's Lullaby*, Th, 85, CDN, Wr/Prod/An; "Sesame Street" (animated shorts), TV, 85, CDN, Wr/Dir/An, (ANIK); *Spirit of the Olympics*, Th, 84, CDN, Wr/Dir/An; "Sesame Street", TV, 80, CDN, Wr/Dir/An, (ANIK).

ANDERSON, Jon C.
DGC, DGC, WGA, SAG. RR #1, Winlaw, BC V0G 2J0 The Bennett Agency, (213)471-2251.
Type of Production and Credits: TV Film-Prod/Dir.
Genres: Drama-TV; Action-TV; Science Fiction-TV; Horror-TV.
Biography: Born in 1939 in Los Angeles, California. Work experience: Supervising Producer, Associate Producer, Unit Production Manager, Assistant Director. Studios and production companies: Columbia, Fox, Universal, Paramount, Alliance, EMI and Warner Bros. Producer of "Friday The 13th - The Series", winner of the 1989 and 1990 International New York Film & Television Awards in photography, editing, art direction and achievement (drama).
Selected Filmography: "Fly By Night" (13 eps), TV, 90-91, CDN/F, Spv Prod; "Friday The 13th - The Series" (44 eps), TV, 88-90, USA/CDN, Spv Prod; "War of the Worlds" (13 eps), TV, 89, USA, Spv Prod; "Mickey Spillane's Mike Hammer" (48 eps), TV, 85-88, USA, Prod/Dir; *The Blue & The Grey*, TV, 83, USA, Assoc Prod/PM; *From Here to Eternity*, TV, 81, USA, Assoc Prod/Prod; *High Country*, Th, 80, CDN, 1st Assist Dir; *Brubaker*, Th, 79, USA, 1st Assist Dir; *The Competition*, Th, 78, USA, 1st Assist Dir; *Heroes*, Th, 77, USA, 1st Assist Dir; *The Big Fix*, Th, 76, USA, 1st Assist Dir.

ANDERSON, Michael
- see DIRECTORS

ANDREWS, Neil
ATPAD. 319 Wellesley St. E., Toronto, ON M4X 1H2 (416)924-0888.
Type of Production and Credits: TV Film-Prod/Dir/Wr; TV Video-Prod/Dir/Wr.
Genres: Variety-TV; Documentary-TV; Educational-TV; Current Affairs-TV.
Biography: Born 1930, Toronto, Ontario. Languages: English, some French and German. B.A.A., Radio and Television Arts, Ryerson Polytechnical Institute. Has produced work in Sydney, Australia, Winnipeg, Halifax, St. John's and Toronto; location work in the US, Great Britain, France, Germany and Switzerland.
Selected Filmography: "Market Place" (150 eps), TV, 83-91, CDN, Prod; "Worldwide" (20 eps), TV, 82-83, CDN, Prod/Wr; "Country Canada" (117 eps), TV, 78-81, CDN, Exec Prod; "This Land" (19 eps), TV, 71-77, CDN, Prod/Wr; "The New Wave" (3 eps), TV, 76-77, CDN, Prod/Wr; "Fortunes" (2 eps), TV, 77, CDN, Prod/Wr; "Land and Sea" (20 eps), TV, 74, CDN, Exec Prod; "Vacation Canada" (18 eps), TV, 71-74, CDN, Prod; "Music Album" (17 eps), TV, 70, CDN, Prod/Dir; "Weekend" (12 eps) (Saturday Edition), TV, 69-70, CDN, Exec Prod; "Through the Eyes of Tomorrow" (63 eps), TV, 65-69, CDN, Exec Prod; "Reach for the Top" (49 eps), TV, 65-66, CDN, Exec Prod; "Razzle Dazzle" (390 eps), TV, 64-65, CDN, Prod; "Swingalong" (74 eps), TV, 61-63, CDN, Prod/Dir/Wr.

ANGELOVICI, Gaston André
ACCT. CP. 503, Succ. Outremont, Montréal, PQ H2V 4N4 (514)738-2594.
Types de production et générique: l métrage-Dir; TV film-Prod/Réal; TV vidéo-Prod/Réal.
Types d'oeuvres: Documentaire-C; Affaires Publiques-TV.
Curriculum vitae: Né en 1945, Santiago, Chile; citoyenneté Canadienne. Langues: anglais, français, espagnol et italien. Université de Bordeaux, France, Institut de Communications Audio-visuelles; Ecole d'Urbanisme et Architecture, Université du Chili/Chile. Producteur-réalisateur, TV et Cinéma. Président de la maison de production Imaginavision Inc. Co-auteur du livre *Cinémas d'Amérique Latine* (France). Auteur de plusieurs articles sur le cinéma latino-américain publiés en France et Espagne. Prix du Festival du Film de Nyon et Festival de Bilbao.
Filmographie sélective: *Chile In Transition*, TV, 91, CDN/Pays Bas, Prod/Réal; *Onward Christian Soldiers/Les Nouveaux Croisés*, TV, 89, CDN, Prod/Réal; *The Electronic Preacher*, TV, 88, CDN, Prod/Réal; *Memoirs Of An Everyday War/Récits d'une guerre quotidienne*, TV, 86, CDN/F, Prod/Réal; *Chile, I Do Not Take*, TV, 84, F, Prod/Réal; *Latin American Writers*, TV, 83, F, Réal.

APOR, Gabor
114A Bedford Rd., Toronto, ON M5R 2K2 (416)923-9228. FAX: 923-1610.

Type of Production and Credits: TV Film-Dir/Prod; TV Video-Dir/Prod.
Genres: Drama-TV; Variety-TV; Documentary-TV; Commercials-TV.
Biography: Born in Hungary; Canadian citizenship. B.A., Theatre Arts, Budapest; studies towards B.Comm., Montreal; TV Arts degree, Toronto. Communications & media consultant, producer of national, provincial and municipal election campaigns. Producer, director of over 3000 commercials; 8 Clio Awards, 3 Gold Lions (Cannes) and many other awards for production excellence. Worked in Toronto, New York; previously Director and Senior V.P. of major advertising agency.
Selected Filmography: *What Is to Be Done*, TV, 84, CDN, Prod/Exec Prod; "Chal-lengers" (13 eps), TV, 78-81, CDN, Dir/Prod/Exec Prod; "It's Up to You!" (26 eps), TV, 72-74, CDN, Dir/Prod.

ARCHIBALD, Nancy
ATPD. 30A Victoria Park Ave., Toronto, ON M4E 3R9. CBC, 790 Bay St., Toronto, ON M5G 1N8 (416)975-6898.
Type of Production and Credits: TV Film-Prod/Dir.
Genres: Documentary-TV.
Biography: Born 1934, Toronto, Ontario. Has produced and directed films on many science subjects and on children's poetry. Interest in anthropology and natural history has led to focus on ethnographic and biology/conservation programming. Winner of numerous international awards including prizes for wildlife and environmental films.
Selected Filmography: *James Bay: The Wind That Keeps Blowing*, "The Nature of Things", TV, 90-91, CDN, Prod/Dir; *Amazonia:The Road to the End of the Forest*, "The Nature of Things", TV, 89-90, CDN, Prod/Dir; "The Nature of Things", TV, 69-91, CDN, Prod/Dir; "A Planet for the Taking", TV, 82-84, CDN, Prod/Dir; *The Mendi*, TV, 73, CDN, Prod/Dir; "The Last Stand", TV, 70-72, CDN, Prod/Dir; *The Lacandons*, TV, 71, CDN, Prod/Dir; "Man at the Centre", TV, 67-70, CDN, Prod/Dir.

ARMSTRONG, Antony
104 Queensbury Ave., Toronto, ON M1N 2X7 (416)698-0788. FAX: 967-1292.
Type of Production and Credits: Th Film-PM/1st AD; TV Video-Prod/Dir.
Genres: Drama-Th; Comedy-Th; Variety-TV; Commercials-TV.
Biography: Born 1959, Toronto, Ontario. B.A., York University.
Selected Filmography: "The People Speak" (8 eps), TV, 91, CDN, Wr/Prod/Dir; *The Forum in Prison*, TV, 91, CDN, Prod; *Macleans* (television specials), TV, 91, CDN, Creator; *Ingenuity*, TV, 88, CDN, Prod; *Blue City Slammers*, Th, 87, CDN, PM/1st AD; "50 Plus" (26 eps) (seg), TV, 86, CDN, Prod; "Heroes of the Golden West" (pilot), TV, 86, CDN, Prod/Dir; *Dentufication*, In, 86, CDN, Dir; "Your Health Quiz" (6 eps), TV, 85, CDN, Prod Coord; "Parenting" (65 eps), TV, 84-85, CDN, PA; *The Man Who Fell to Earth*, Th, 75, GB, PA; "Nakia" (26 eps), TV, 74, USA, PA.

ARMSTRONG, Mary
APFVQ, AQRRCT. Cinéfort inc., 3981 St-Laurent, #205, Montreal, PQ H2W 1Y5 (514)289-9477. FAX: 289-1963.
Type of Production and Credits: TV Film-Prod/Dir.
Genres: Drama-TV; Documentary-TV; Children's-TV.
Biography: Born 1953, Winnipeg, Manitoba. Languages: English, French, Spanish. B.A., Film, Concordia University. Films have won awards at the American, US industrial and national educational film festivals.
Selected Filmography: "On the Eighth Day" (2 eps), TV, 91, CDN, Prod/Co-Dir; *Just Before Dawn/Le jour se leve*, TV, 90, CDN, Prod/Dir; *Images for Export*, TV, 87, CDN, Prod/Dir; *Aid for Whose Benefit*, TV, 87, CDN, Prod/Dir; *Season on the Water*, "A Life's Work", TV, 86, CDN, Co-Prod/1st AD; *Billion Dollar Loan Shark*, MV, 86, CDN, Prod; *Welcome to the Public Service*, In, 85, CDN, Wr/Dir; *Non-Traditional*, In, 83, CDN, Dir/Prod; *Music Therapy*, ED, 83, CDN, Co-Prod/Dir; *Patients' Rights*, In, 83, CDN, Prod/Dir; *Everyone's Business*, TV, 82, CDN, Prod/Dir; *You Could Save a Life*, TV, 80, CDN, Prod/Wr/Dir; *Our House*, TV, 78, CDN, Prod/Dir; *Native Document*, ED, 78, CDN, Prod/Dir; *Aislin*, TV, 76, CDN, Prod/Dir.

ARNOTT, Duane S.
- see WRITERS

ARRON, Wayne
CFTPA, ACCT. 13 Watford Ave., Toronto, ON M6C 1G4 (416)656-6290. OWL TV, 56 The Esplanade, #302, Toronto, ON M5E 1A7 (416)863-1661. FAX: 868-6009.
Type of Production and Credits: Th Film-Prod; TV Film-Prod; TV Video-Prod.
Genres: Drama-Th&TV; Horror-Th&TV; Documentary-Th; Children's-

TV.
Biography: Born 1949, Ottawa, Ontario. M.A., B.A., University of Toronto. Sixteen years experience in film and TV production. Senior Producer, Owl Centre for Children's Film and Television, 88-91. *Raoul Wallenberg: Buried Alive* won a Cerficate of Merit, Academy Awards, Red Ribbon, American Film Festival and a Silver Plaque, Chicago. Winner, Nielsen-Ferns award, 1981 CFTA Awards; *Exposure* won Best Film, Best TV Drama, Best Art Direction and Best Actress, 1981 Yorkton International Film & TV Festival.
Selected Filmography: "OWL-TV" (10 eps), TV, 88, CDN, Prod; "OWL-TV" (10 eps), TV, 87, CDN, Assoc Prod; "Owl TV" (10 eps), TV, 86, CDN, Spv Pro Acc't; *The Park Is Mine*, TV, 84, CDN/USA, Pro Acc't; *Evergreen* (mini-series), TV, 84, USA, Assist Pro Acc't; *Mrs. Soffel*, Th, 84, USA, Assist Pro Acc't; "The Chinese" (6 eps), TV, 81-82, CDN, Spv Pro Acc't; *Raoul Wallenberg Buried Alive*, Th, 82, CDN, Prod, (GENIE); *Exposure*, TV, 80, CDN, Prod; *Gas*, Th, 80, CDN, Pro Acc't; *The Funny Farm*, Th, 80, CDN, Pro Acc't; *Ariane*, TV, 79, CDN, Prod; *Head On*, Th, 79, CDN, Pro Acc't; *Tanya's Island*, Th, 79, CDN, Pro Acc't; *The Brood*, Th, 78, CDN, Pro Acc't.

ARSENAULT, Yvon
- voir REALISATEURS
AYLWARD, Alan W.
- see DIRECTORS
AZZOPARDI, Anthony
- see DIRECTORS
AZZOPARDI, Mario
- see DIRECTORS
BACHMAN, Kay
ACCT. 292 Indian Rd., Toronto, ON M6R 2X5 (416)769-7229. Source Productions, 99 Atlantic Ave., Ste. 415, Toronto, ON M6K 1Y2 (416)516-0200. Lee Sacks, Sacks & Zweig, (213)451-3113.
Type of Production and Credits: Th Film-Prod; TV Video-Prod.
Genres: Drama-Th&TV; Children's-TV; Variety-TV.
Biography: Born Portland, Oregon; landed immigrant, Canada, 72. Has produced television shows in Detroit, Chicago, Boston and Los Angeles. "Quiz Kids" nominated for ACE Award, 81.
Selected Filmography: *Shadow Dancing*, Th, 88, CDN, Prod; "Quiz Kids" (44 eps), TV, 80-81, USA, Prod; *A Lady out of Lizzie*, TV, 81, CDN/USA, Prod/Dir; *Good for You*, TV, 81, CDN, Prod; *Everybody Loves a Hero*, TV, 80, CDN, Prod/Dir; *Lyrics, Lyricists*, TV, 79, CDN, Prod;

Who's Minding the Zoo?, TV, 79, CDN, Prod; *Auto Repair for Dummies*, TV, 78, CDN, Prod; "The New Quiz Kids" (2 seasons), TV, 78, CDN, Prod; *Dream Machine*, TV, 76, CDN, Prod/Creator; "Any Woman Can...Fix It" (65 eps), TV, 75, CDN, Prod; "Eye Bet" (4 seasons), TV, 70-74, CDN, Prod/Creator; *Chicago Show*, TV, 71, USA, Assoc Prod; "Morning Show", TV, 70, USA, Assoc Prod; "Anniversary Show", TV, 69, USA, Assoc Prod.

BACKUS, Barry
- see POSTPRODUCTION SOUND MIXERS
BAILEY, Norma
- see DIRECTORS
BAKER, Bob
- see DIRECTORS
BALL, Christopher
- see DIRECTORS
BANNING, Everett
WGC (ACTRA). 26 Westwood Lane, Richmond Hill, ON L4C 6X9 (416)764-1029. Everett Banning Media Corp., 550 Queen St. E., Ste. 310, Toronto, ON M5A 1V2 (416)369-9455. Penny Noble Talent Management, (416)482-6556.
Genres: Educational-Th&TV; Industrial-Th&TV; Current Affairs-TV; News-TV.
Biography: Born in 1949 in Rotterdam, The Netherlands. Citizenship: Holland, Ireland and Canada. Immigrant work visa (green card) for the United States. Experienced news anchor; writer; producer for Global Television Network (Canada), Biznet, ESPN (United States), First Business, national syndication (United States). Winner of the Selkirk Award, Charlie Edward Award and the Dan McArthur Award.
Selected Filmography: "Blue Chip Enterprise" (65 eps), TV, 91, USA, Prod/Wr/Host; "Holt Economics Series" (12 eps), ED, 91, CDN, Prod/Host; "The Winning Edge" (6 eps), In, 90-91, CDN, Prod/Wr/Host; "Businessline" (94 eps), TV, 89-90, USA, Prod/Wr/Host; "Canada Business Week" (39 eps), TV, 88-89, CDN, Prod/Wr/Host; "Global Newsweek" (400 eps), TV, 80-88, CDN, Wr/Host; "Everybody's Business" (325 eps), TV, 78-87, CDN, Wr/Host.

BARCLAY, Robert
- see DIRECTORS
BARDE, Barbara
ACCT. 58 Winchester St., Toronto, ON M4X 1A9 (416)925-8258. Why Not Productions Inc., 700 King St. W., Ste. 606, Toronto, ON M5V 2Y6 (416)594-0059. FAX: 594-0550.

Type of Production and Credits: TV Film-Prod/Dir; TV Video-Prod/Dir.
Genres: Drama-TV; Documentary-TV; Educational-TV; Children's-TV.
Biography: Born 1947, St. Paul, Minnesota; Canadian citizenship. Languages: English and French. B.A., Journalism and Political Science, Syracuse University; M.A., Mass Communications. Eleven years at TV Ontario as director/producer; President, Why Not Productions Inc.; has filmed in Asia, Africa, Latin America. *North of 60, Destiny Uncertain* awarded at American Film Festival, 83; *The Africa File*, Japan Prize, 75; *Tanah Air: Our Land, Our Water*, Main Prize, Eko Film Festival, 87.
Selected Filmography: *It's Our Future*, TV, 91, CDN, Prod/Dir; *To Heal the Spirit*, TV, 90, CDN, Prod/Dir; *Sustainable Development: Global Challenge, Global Change*, TV, 90, CDN, Prod/Dir; *Briefing Programs of Teenagers Living Overseas* (2 eps), TV, 90, CDN, Prod/Dir; *Entrepreneurship You Can Bank On*, TV, 89, CDN, Prod/Dir; *The Spirit of Entrepreneurship*, TV, 89, CDN, Prod/Dir; *The Way Forward*, TV, 89, CDN, Prod/Dir; *The Queen Charlottes: Islands in the Web of Life*, TV, 88, CDN, Prod/Dir; *From a Small Beginning*, TV, 88, CDN, Prod; *Seeds of Hope*, TV, 88, CDN, Prod/Dir; *Favourable Exchange: International Students in Canada*, TV, 87-88, CDN, Prod; *SADCC: The Struggle for Self-Reliance*, TV, 87, CDN, Prod; *Indonesia: A Generation of Change* (5 eps), TV, 85-86, CDN, Prod/Dir; *Briefing Programs for Canadians Working in Indonesia*, In, 85-86, CDN, Prod/Dir; *Paths of Development*, TV, 83-85, CDN, Prod/Dir.

BARLOW, David
ACTRA, DGC, ATPD, WGAw, ACCT. 28 Henry Lane Terrace, Toronto, ON M5A 4A1 (416)366-0605. Charles Northcote, The Core Group, 489 College St., Suite 501, Toronto, ON M6G 1A5 (416)944-0193. FAX: 944-0446.
Type of Production and Credits: TV Film-Prod/Wr/Dir; TV Video-Prod/Wr/Dir.
Genres: Drama-TV; Comedy-TV; Action-TV.
Biography: Born 1946, Hamilton, Ontario. B.A., Queen's University; M.A., Theatre, Northwestern University. Theatre Administrator, Stage Manager, 70-75. Wrote, story-edited sit-coms in U.S., 78-80. TV productions have received 13 Gemini and ACTRA awards, 24 other nominations, sold to over 50 countries.
Selected Filmography: *The Prom*, TV, 90, CDN, Wr; *Sanity Clause*, TV, 89, CDN, Co-Dir/Co-Prod; *Breaking all the Rules*, TV, 87, CDN, Dir/Co-Prod; "Seeing Things" (43 eps) (Co-Wr 3 eps), TV, 80-86, CDN, Co-Creat/Co-Exec Story Ed/Co-Prod, (ANIK/2 GEMINIS 86 & 87); "King of Kensington" (45 eps), TV, 76-78, CDN, Assoc Prod; "King of Kensington" (18 eps), TV, 75-76, CDN, Unit M.

BARTON, Natalie
APFTQ. InformAction, 417, rue St-Pierre, bureau 403, Montréal, PQ H2Y 2M4 (514)284-0441. FAX: 845-0631.
Types de production et générique: TV film-Prod; TV vidéo-Prod.
Types d'oeuvres: Documentaire-TV; Education-TV; Current Affairs-TV.
Curriculum vitae: Née en 1948, Londres, Angleterre. Langues: français et anglais. Maîtrise en lettres, McGill University, 71. Co-Fondatrice, Présidente d'InformAction. Réalise et produit des films documentaires, séries et vidéos educatifs depuis 71. Depuis 7 ans se consacre surtout à la production.
Filmographie sélective: *Le marché du couple*, TV, 90, CDN, Prod; "Vues d'Afrique" (9 eps), TV, 90, CDN, Prod; *Goute-sez, Haiti un soir d'hiver*, TV, 89, CDN, Prod; *Les îles ont une Ame*, C, 88, CDN, Prod; *Nous près, nous loin*, C, 86, CDN, Prod; *Justice blanche*, C, 85, CDN, Co réal; "Recours", TV, 79-81, CDN, Réal; *La Danse avec l'aveugle*, C, 78, CDN, Co réal; *Anyanya*, C, 71, CDN, Co réal.

BATTISON, Jill
393 Shaw St., Toronto, ON M6J 2X4 (416)538-6326.
Type of Production and Credits: TV Film-Prod.
Genres: Drama-Th&TV; Documentary-TV; Industrial-Th.
Biography: Born in 1958 in England. Holds dual citizenship (Canada and UK). Educated at Ware College of Graphic Design, England; Ryerson Polytechnical Institute, Film, Toronto. Awards include Silver AMI 1987, Silver AMI 1988, Bronze AMI 1985. Published author in magazines and books. Special skill in television program development.
Selected Filmography: *Going Home*, ED, 91, CDN, Prod/Dir; *Thirty*, Th, 89, CDN, Prod/Dir.

BATTISTA, Franco
12523 Leon Binguet, Montreal, PQ H1E 2B1 (514)643-4086. Allegro Films Inc., 2187 Lariviere, Montreal, PQ H2K 1P5 (514)529-0320.
Type of Production and Credits: Th

Film-Prod/Ed/Line Prod.
Genres: Drama-Th&TV; Comedy-Th; Science Fiction-Th; Horror-Th.
Biography: Born in 1955 in Larino, Italy. Canadian citizen. Languages: English, French, Italian.
Selected Filmography: *Scanners II - The New Order*, Th, 91, CDN, Co Prod/Line Prod; *Backstab*, TV, 90, CDN, Prod; *Amityville Curse*, Th, 90, CDN, Prod/Ed; *Blind Fear*, Th, 89, CDN, Prod/Ed; *Mindfield*, Th, 89, CDN, Exec Prod; *Something About Love*, Th, 88, CDN, Prod/Ed; *Crazy Moon*, Th, 87, CDN, Line Prod/Ed.

BAUMAN, Larry
- see DIRECTORS

BAZAY, David
ATPD. 54 Beaconsfield, Toronto, ON M6J 3H9 (416) 530-4748. CBC, P.O. Box 500, Stn. A, Toronto, ON M5W 1E6 (416) 975-6319.
Type of Production and Credits: TV Video-Prod.
Genres: News-TV.
Biography: Born 1939, Winnipeg, Manitoba. Languages: French and English. B.A., University of Western Ontario; attended McGill University and University of Montreal. Foreign correspondent, France (70-72, 80-83), CBC TV National News. Recipient of the Duke University Journalism Fellowship, 87.
Selected Filmography: "The National" (sev eps), TV, 85-91, CDN, Exec Prod; *Runaways: 24 Hours on the Street*, TV, 87, CDN, Area Head Prod.

BEARDE, Chris
ACTRA, AFTRA, DGA, WGAw. Chris Bearde Television, 11150 West Olympic Blvd., Ste. 1030, Los Angeles, CA 90064. William Morris Agency, 131 El Camino Dr., Beverly Hills, CA (213)274-7451.
Type of Production and Credits: TV Video-Prod/Wr.
Genres: Comedy-TV; Variety-TV; Musical-TV; Children's-TV.
Biography: Born in UK; emigrated to Canada, 62. Has received 12 Emmy nominations, 4 Writers' Guild nominations; won the Golden Globe Award for "Sonny & Cher Comedy Hour".
Selected Filmography: "Night Rap", TV, 90-91, USA, Exec Prod/Wr; "Truth or Con-sequences" (72 eps), TV, 87-88, USA, Exec Prod/Wr; "Gong Show II" (170 eps), TV, 88, USA, Exec Prod/Wr; "Puttin' on the Hits" (80 eps), TV, 81-85, USA, Creator/Co-Exec Prod; *Hysterical*, MV, 80, USA, Dir; *Bob Hope in Australia*, TV, 79, USA, Prod; "The Gong Show" (120 eps), TV, 75-78, USA, Co-Prod/Creator; *Bob Hope Christmas Special*, TV, 78, USA, Prod; "Bill Cosby" (7 eps), TV, 78, USA, Prod; "Bobby Vinton" (48 eps), TV, 75-77, CDN/USA, Prod; "Sonny & Cher Comedy Hour" (90 eps), TV, 71-74, USA, Co-Prod; "Sonny & Cher Show" (13 eps), TV, 71, USA, Co-Prod; "Andy Williams" (48 eps), TV, 69-70, USA, Co-Prod; "Laugh In" (48 eps), TV, 68-69, USA, Wr, (EMMY); *Elvis/Singer Presents Elvis*, TV, 68, USA, Wr; "Nightcap" (60 eps), TV, 63-67, CDN, Wr; "Tommy Hunter" (sev eps), TV, 64-67, CDN, Wr; "Julliette" (1 eps), TV, 67, CDN, Wr; "Front & Centre" (13 eps), TV, 63, CDN, Wr; "Network", TV, 62, CDN, Wr.

BEAUBIEN, Conrad
526-C Palmerston Blvd., Toronto, ON M6G 2P5 (416)539-0676. FAX: 539-0676. Beaver Creek Pictures, 81 Main Street, Unionville, ON L3R 2E6 (416)477-3821. FAX: 470-0410.
Type of Production and Credits: TV Film-Prod/Dir; TV Video-Prod/Dir.
Genres: Drama-TV; Documentary-TV; Variety-TV.
Biography: Born 1947; Canadian. 25 year career in film, TV and music.
Selected Filmography: "Sketches of Our Town" (50 eps), TV, 85-91, CDN, Prod/Dir/Wr; *And There Were Seven: The Story of A.J. Casson*, TV, 90, CDN, Prod/Dir/Wr; *The Shantymen*, TV, 89, CDN, Prod/Dir/Wr; "Second Chance" (13 eps), TV, 89, CDN, Prod/Dir/Wr; "Women & Success" (13 eps), TV, 88, CDN, Prod; Sun Life/Agincourt Interiors/Alex Colville, Cm, 82-85, CDN, Prod/Dir; "Strange but True" (26 eps), TV, 83, CDN/USA/GB, Co-Prod; *Fred Dobbs Goes to Hollywood*, TV, 83, CDN/USA, Exec Prod; *Energy, a Time for Learning*, ED, 81-82, CDN, Prod/Dir; *Adjustment*, ED, 80, CDN, Dir.

BEAUBIEN, Joseph F.
377, rue Roslyn, Westmount, PQ H3Z 2N7 (514)935-3955.
Types de production et générique: l métrage-Prod; TV film-Prod.
Types d'oeuvres: Drame-C; Action-C; Documentaire-TV.
Curriculum vitae: Né en 1938, Montréal, Québec. A étudié le Droit à l'Université McGill. Avocat; conseiller juridique, SDICC (maintenant Téléfilm), 70-78; producteur exécutif, longs métrages, 78-84; Président, Vidéo Globe I Inc., 84-85; depuis 85, Directeur général de l'Association québécoise des distributeurs et exportateurs de films et de vidéo.

Depuis 90, avocat-conseil chez Colby, Rioux & Demers.
Filmographie sélective: *You've Come a Long Way Lady: Women in Sports in Canada*, TV, 84, CDN, Prod exéc; *Heartaches*, C, 80, CDN, Co prod exéc; *Une journée en taxi*, C, 80, CDN/F; *Atlantic City*, C, 79, CDN/F; *A nous deux*, C, 79, CDN/F, Prod exéc.

BEAUDET, Michel
- voir REALISATEURS

BECKMAN, Henry
- see WRITERS

BEDEL, Jean-Pierre
- see DIRECTORS

BEEFORTH, Doug
ACCT. CTV Television Network, 42 Charles St. E., Toronto, ON M4Y 1T5 (416)928-6000.
Type of Production and Credits: TV Video-Prod.
Genres: Sports-TV.
Biography: Born in 1955 in Hamilton, Ontario. Canadian citizen. Bachelor of Applied Arts, Radio & Television, Ryerson Polytechnical Institute, Toronto. Winner of a 1988 Emmy award for work with NBC on the Seoul Olympics. Nominated for a 1988 Emmy award for work with ABC on the Calgary Olympics. Nominated for a 1990 ACE Award for work with TBS on the Seattle Goodwill Games. Currently Executive Producer, CTV Sports. Projects as Executive Producer, CTV include: 1991 Pan-Am Games, Cuba; 1992 Summer Olympics, Barcelona, Spain; 1994 Winter Olympics, Lillehammer, Norway.
Selected Filmography: *World Curling Championships*, TV, 91, CDN, Exec prod; "Canadian Figure Skating Championships" (4 seg), TV, 91, CDN, Exec Prod; "Goodwill Games" (2 seg), TV, 90, USA, Prod; "Canadian Open Golf Championship" (4 seg), TV, 90, CDN, Exec Prod; *Nicki Bear Christmas Special*, TV, 89, CDN, Exec Prod; "Coca-Cola Hockey Matchups with Wayne Gretzky" (26 eps), TV, 89, CDN, Exec Prod; "World Alpine Ski Championships" (14 seg), TV, 89, USA, Prod; *World Cup of Figure Skating*, TV, 88, CDN, Exec Prod; "Seoul Summer Olympic Games" (16 seg), TV, 88, USA, Prod, (EMMY); "Calgary Winter Olympic Games" (16 seg), TV, 88, CDN, Spv Prod; "Hockey Night in Canada", TV, 80-86, CDN, Prod.

BELANGER, André A.
- voir REALISATEURS

BELEC, Marilyn A.
- see DIRECTORS

BELEC, Philip
- see DIRECTORS

BELISLE, Pierre
- voir REALISATEURS

BELL, John G.
- see DIRECTORS

BENOIT, Ted
25 Ambleside Blvd., Winnipeg, MB (204)895-1934. Spectra Video Productions Ltd., 1253 Clarence Ave., Bay 3, Winnipeg, MB R3T 1T4 (204)452-9832.
Type of Production and Credits: TV Video-Prod.
Genres: Variety-TV; Documentary-TV; Educational-TV; Children's-TV.
Biography: Born 1924. CBC TV producer for 22 years; involved in all facets of TV production. Since opening Spectra Video, 79, has been involved with commercial, documentary and industrial videotape production.
Selected Filmography: New Flyer Industries (7 films), In, 88, CDN, Prod; Manitoba Dept. of Tourism (10 films), ED, 87, CDN, Prod; *Mercury, Fish and You*, ED, 87, CDN, Prod; *Canada Breeds the Best Swine Product*, ED, 87, CDN, Prod; *Freshwater Fish*, In, 87, CDN, Prod; "Athletes and Injury" (6 eps), ED, 84, CDN, Exec Prod; "Explorations" (13 eps), ED, 83, CDN, Exec Prod.

BERGERON, Guy
3783 rue St-André, Montréal, PQ H2L 3V6 InformAction, 417 rue St-Pierre, Montréal, PQ H2Y 2M4 (514)284-0441. FAX: 523-3163.
Types de production et générique: l métrage-Prod; c métrage-Prod/Réal; TV film-Prod/Réal; TV vidéo-Prod/Réal.
Types d'oeuvres: Drame-C&TV; Comédie-TV; Documentaire-C&TV; Enfants-C&TV; Affaires Publiques-TV.
Curriculum vitae: Né en 1945, Montréal, Québec. Langues: français et anglais. Etudes en administration, Ecole nationale d'administration publique, depuis 82.
Filmographie sélective: "Le spasme de vivre" (2 eps), C/TV, 91, CDN, Prod; *Voodoo Taxi*, "Inside Stories", TV, 91, CDN, Line Prod; *Le marche du couple*, TV, 90, Prod dél; "Les petits Debrouillards, TV, 89, CND, Prod dél; "Cinéastes à l'écran" (20 eps), TV, 85, CDN, Réal; "Les lundis de Pierre Nadeau" (30 eps), TV, 79-81, CDN, Prod; "L'objectif" (39 eps), TV, 79-81, CDN, Prod; "Une vie en prison" (3 eps), TV, 80, CDN, Prod; *Guitare*, C, 74, CDN, Prod; *Une nuit en Amérique*, C, 74, CDN, Prod; *La vie rêvée*, C, 72, CDN, Prod; *Le semaine dernière pas loin du pont*, C, 67, CDN, Réal.

BERGMAN, Robert
- see DIRECTORS

BERMAN, Brigitte
- see DIRECTORS

BERRY, Michael J.
- see DIRECTORS

BERTOLINO, Daniel
APFVQ, UDA, ACCT. Les Productions Via le Monde Inc., 326 St-Paul ouest, Montréal, PQ H2Y 2A3 (514)285-1658. FAX: 285-1970.
Types de production et générique: c métrage-Prod/Réal; TV film-Prod/Réal; TV vidéo-Prod/Réal.
Types d'oeuvres: Documentaire-C&TV; Enfants-TV.
Curriculum vitae: Né en 1942; au Canada depuis 67. Fondateur des Productions Via le Monde Inc. A écrit et réalisé 158 films tournés dans presque tous les pays du globe. Directeur de l'information de l'Unicef au Québec pour l'Année de l'enfance, 79; Vice-président de l'APFVQ depuis 82.
Filmographie sélective: "Vie Privée" (22 eps), TV, 90-91, CDN, Co prod; "Journal de l'Histoire/Stopwatch" (65 eps), TV, 89-91, CDN/F, Co prod/Réal; "Fortunes d'ici et d'ailleurs" (8 eps), TV, 89-90, CDN, Co prod; "Bien dans sa Peau" (26 eps), TV, 89-90, CDN, Prod; "Education: Option 2000" (2 eps), TV, 89-90, CDN, Prod/Co réal; "Points chauds", TV, 87-88, CDN, Prod/Co réal, (GEMEAUX 88); "Légendes du monde", TV, 83-86, CDN, Prod/Co réal; "Défi mondial", TV, 85-86, CDN, Prod/Co réal, (3 GEMEAUX 86); *Légendes indiennes*, TV, 81-82, CDN, Prod; "Les Grands Reportages" (Réal 1 eps/Prod 1 eps), TV, 79-80, CDN, Réal/Prod; *A coeur battant*, TV, 78-79, CDN, Réal; *Les Amis de mes amis*, TV, 79, CDN, Réal; *Nosotros Cubanos*, C, 78, CDN, Co réal; "Poste frontière", TV, 74-77, CDN, Prod/Réal; *Ahô...au coeur du monde primitif*, C, 76, CDN, Prod, (CFA).

BESSADA, Milad
ACCT. 5 Cassels Ave., Toronto, ON M4E 1X9 (416)694-1956.
Type of Production and Credits: Th-Prod/Dir/Wr; TV Video-Prod/Dir/Wr.
Genres: Drama-Th&TV; Comedy-TV; Variety-Th&TV; Musical-TV; Documentary-Th&TV; Educational-Th&TV.
Biography: Born in 1934. Canadian citizen.
Selected Filmography: "Santa Claus Parade" (annual), TV, 86-91, CDN, Prod; "Variety Club Telethon" (annual), TV, 87-91, CDN, Prod.; "Wintario" (510 eps), TV, 76-90, CDN, Prod; "Easy Country" (30 eps), TV, 79-80, CDN, Prod; "SCTV" (40 eps), TV, 79-80, CDN, Prod/Dir; *A Quiet Day in Belfast*, Th, 74, CDN, Prod/Dir.

BIENSTOCK, Ric Esther
1679 Bathurst St., #3, Toronto, ON M5P 3J8 (416)487-9373. Associated Producers, 957 Broadview Ave., Unit A, Toronto, ON M4K 2R5 (416)422-1270.
Type of Production and Credits: Th Film-Prod/PM; TV Film-Prod/PM; TV Video-Prod/PM.
Genres: Documentary-Th&TV; Educational-Th&TV; Industrial-Th&TV.
Biography: Born in 1959 in Montreal, Quebec. Languages: English, French, Hebrew. McGill University. Worked in feature film industry in Israel for four years, providing production services for Para-mount, Warner Bros, Swiss TV. On location experience in Africa and Israel. *Burden on the Land* won a Red Ribbon award at the American Film Festival, Silver Medal, Houston International Film Festival and the Silver Screen Award, U.S. Film & Video Festival; *AIDS in Africa* won Gold Award, John Muir Medical Film Festival; Gold Hugo, Intercom 90, Silver Medal, International Film & Television Festival of New York, Bronze at the Columbus International Film Festival and Silver Hugo, Chicago International Film Festival; *Meeting the Challenge* was awarded the Certificate for Creative Excellence, U.S. Film & Video Festival.
Selected Filmography: *Deadly Currents*, Th/TV, 91, CDN, Prod; *Burden on the Land*, TV, 90, CDN, Prod/PM; *AIDS in Africa*, TV, 90, CDN, Assoc Prod/PM; *Meeting the Challenge*, TV, 89, CDN, Assoc Prod/PM; *Unfinished Exodus: Anatomy of an Airlift*, TV, 86, Pro Coord.

BITTMAN, Roman
CFTA, ACCT. 127 Eastville Ave., Scarborough, ON M1M 2P2 (416)265-7459. Mobius Media Corporation, 39 Baywood Rd., Rexdale, ON M9V 3Y8 (416)745-6270. FAX: 745-7179.
Type of Production and Credits: Th Short-Dir/Prod/Wr; TV Film-Dir/Prod/Wr; TV Video-Dir/Prod/Wr.
Genres: Drama-TV; Documentary-TV; Educational-TV.
Biography: Born 1941. Journalism Program, Ryerson Polytechnical Institute, 67; B.A.A., Radio and Television Arts, Ryerson Polytechnical Institute, 64. More than 20 years experience as director, writer and producer. Has worked for CBC, NFB and private sector production companies; has written for, directed and produced

programs including "The Nature of Things," "Man Alive," "CBC News," and documentary specials with the NFB's Environment and International Affairs Studio. Has created and produced award-winning film and video programs with Mobius Media Corporation since 84; clients include federal and provincial government departments. Awards include CFTA - Best Overall TV Program, Best in Category, Best Actor and Best Cinematography; American Film Festival - 2 Blue and 3 Red Ribbons; Yorkton Film Festival - Golden Sheaf Award; Columbus Film Festival - Chris Statuette; The New York Advertising Club - Andy Award. Works in progress include "Anglosea", a 10-part series of films co-funded by the U.N., for use in training merchant marine officers in the use of navigational English; and *The Devil's Punchbowl*, a feautre film for television.
Selected Filmography: *Lache pas!*, ED, 91, CDN, Prod; *Smoke Rings*, Th, 86, CDN, Wr/Dir; *The Sea is at Her Gates*, Th, 85, CDN, Wr; "CBC Access", TV, 81-82, CDN, Prod/Dir; *Castles in the Air*, TV, 80, CDN, Wr/Dir; "Seeing for Ourselves", TV, 78, CDN, Wr/Prod; "National Film Board Environment Program" (20 films), TV, 74-77, CDN, Exec Prod; "The Nature of Things" (40 eps), TV, 67-74, CDN, Wr/Dir/Prod.

BJORNSON, Michelle
- see WRITERS

BLACK, Jennifer
112 Hudson Dr., Toronto, ON M4T 2K5 (416)489-4989. Alliance Communications, 920 Yonge St., Ste. 400, Toronto, ON M4W 3C7 (416)967-1174.
Types of Production and Credits: Th Film-Postprod Spv; TV Film-Prod.
Genres: Drama-Th&TV; Comedy-Th&TV; Action-Th&TV.
Biography: Born in Montreal, Quebec. Canadian citizen. Languages: English and French.
Selected Filmography: "E.N.G." (62 eps), TV, 89-91, CDN, Co-Prod; "Mount Royal" (16 eps), TV, 88, CDN/F, Assoc Prod; *Nowhere To Hide*, Th, 87, P Pro Spv; *Control*, Th/TV, 87, CDN/I, P Pro Spv; "Sword of Gideon" (2 eps), TV, 86, P Pro Spv; *Joshua Then and Now*, Th, 85, CDN, P Pro Spv; *Night Magic*, Th, 85, P Pro Spv; "Night Heat" (6 eps), TV, 84, CDN/USA, P Pro Spv; *Overdrawn At The Memory Bank*, TV, 83, CDN/USA, P Pro Spv; "Loving Friends & Perfect Couples" (80 eps), TV, 82, USA, P Pro Spv; *Threshold*, Th, 81, CDN, P Pro Spv; *Utilities*, Th, 81, USA, P Pro Spv; *Nothing Personal*, Th, 80, CDN, Postprod Coord; "The Challengers" (3 eps), TV, CDN, Assoc Prod.

BLAIS, Micheline ◆
APFVQ. (819)322-6013.
Types de production et générique: l métrage-Prod; c métrage-Prod; TV film-Prod; TV video-Prod/Réal.
Types d'oeuvres: Variété-TV; Documentaire-C&TV; Education-TV.
Curriculum vitae: Née en 1944, Longueuil, Québec. Langues: français et anglais. Etudes universitaires en linguistique; cours de gestion pour la petite et moyenne entreprise. Fonde Les Productions La Sterne, 80; assistante à la réalisation pour tous les produits de La Sterne; se spécialise dans les archives du Grand Nord; auteur, *Trois Compagnons sur les traces de Jacques Cartier*, volume pour enfants, Editions Héritage, 84.
Filmographie sélective: *Partenaires dans le crime*, TV, 88, CDN, Prod; "Gamelle et Sac à dos" (13 eps), TV, 87, CDN, Prod; *Un homme, un piano*, TV, 86, CDN, Sc/Réal/Prod; *Femmes de la mer*, TV, 86, CDN, Prod; "Intermèdes (17 c métrages), C, 86, CDN, Prod; *Aventure Torngat*, TV, 85, CDN, Prod; *Mes Voyages en Canada de Jacques Cartier*, ED, 84, CDN, Prod; *Torngat*, C, 83, CDN, Réal; *Histoire de l'exploration polaire*, ED, 77, CDN, Prod; *Défi arctique Ellesmere*, C, 77, CDN, Prod; *Arctique: défi de tous les temps*, C, 76, CDN, Prod/Rech.

BLANCHARD, André
- voir SCENARISTES

BLOUIN, C. Denis
ACCT. Euro American Pictures, 1444 Queens Rd., Los Angeles, CA 90069 USA. (213)656-2042.
Type of Production and Credits: Th Film-Prod; TV Film-Prod.
Genres: Drama-Th&TV; Action-Th&TV.
Biography: Born in 1954. Canadian citizen. Member of both the Quebec and Canadian Bar Associations. Fluent in English and French. In 1980-81, was an associate lawyer working for Stikeman, Elliott in Montreal, as an assistant to Stanley Hart, Senior Partner, Tax & Entertainment Department. From 1981-88, was VP, Business Affairs for Keith Barish Productions, Inc. and was responsible for film rights, budgets and contracts. In 1988, formed Euro American Pictures, Inc. as an international film company dedicated to co-productions with European, Canadian and American film

production companies.
Selected Filmography: *The Fugitive*, Th, 91, USA, Co Prod; *Ironweed*, Th, 87, USA, Exec Prod; *The Serpent and the Rainbow*, Th, 87, USA, Prod Assoc; *The Running Man*, Th, 87, USA, Prod Assoc; *9 1/2 Weeks*, Th, 86, USA *A Streetcar Named Desire*, TV, 85, USA, Assoc Prod; *Sophie's Choice*, Th, 82, USA, Prod Assoc.

BLUM, Jack
- see WRITERS

BLYE, Garry
ACTRA. Chestnut Park Productions, 163 Queen St. E., #300, Toronto, ON M2P 1A9 (416)480-2808. Catherine McCartney, (416)250-6541.
Type of Production and Credits: TV Video-Prod.
Genres: Comedy-TV; Variety-TV; Musical-TV; Documentary-TV.
Biography: Born 1944, St. Boniface, Manitoba. Attended Univ. of Manitoba, L.A. Valley College, UCLA. Administrative assistant to Col. Tom Parker, 68; agent, Television/Variety, William Morris Agency, 69; talent coordinator, Andy Williams Show, 69-71; has produced specials for Kate Smith, Dick Van Dyke, Ringling Bros Circus, and others.
Selected Filmography: "Super Dave Osborne" (97 eps), TV, 87-91, CDN, Pro Exec; *1990 Gemini Awards*, TV, 90, CDN, Prod/Wr; "The Judge" (175 eps), TV, 89-90, CDN, Prod; *Rich Little Christmas Special*, TV, 89, CDN, Prod; *Genie Awards*, TV, 89, CDN, Prod; *Elizabeth Manley Special*, TV, 89, CDN, Pro Exec; *Guess Who Special*, TV, 88, CDN, Prod/Wr; *Olympic Gala, Calgary 88*, TV, 88, CDN, Prod; "Molson Indy Race" (3 eps), TV, 86-88, CDN, Prod; "Starting from Scratch" (22 eps), TV, 87-88, CDN, Pro Exec; *Rendezvous for Peace*, TV, 87, CDN, Prod; *Juno Awards* (annual), TV, 85-87, CDN, Prod; *Wayne Gretzky's Hockey My Way*, ED, 87, CDN, Creat Cons; *Expo 86 Gala*, TV, 86, CDN, Prod.

BOARD, John
DGC, ACCT. The Original Motion Picture Company, 37 Sussex Ave., Toronto, ON M5S 1J6 (416)979-2518. FAX: 944-8475.
Type of Production and Credits: Th Film-Prod/1st AD; TV Film-1st AD.
Genres: Drama-Th&TV; Comedy-Th&TV; Horror-Th.
Biography: Born 1934, Hamilton, Ontario. Bachelor of Arts, University of Western Ontario, London. Currently in development, *Eyes That Went Away* (91).
Selected Filmography: *Scales of Justice*, TV, 91, CDN, 1st AD; "Top Cops", TV, 91, CDN/USA, 1st AD; *Naked Lunch*, Th, 90-91, CDN, 1st AD; *Dead Ringers*, Th, 88, CDN, 1st AD/Assoc Prod; *Shadow Dancing*, Th, 88, CDN, 1st AD; *Christmas Wife*, TV, 87, USA 1st AD; *The Fly*, Th, 86, USA, 1st AD; *Pippi Longstocking* (2 parts), TV, 85, USA, 1st AD; *Overnight*, Th, 85, CDN, Co-Prod/1st AD; *A Letter to Three Wives*, TV, 85, USA, 1st AD; *Agnes of God*, Th, 85, CDN, 1st AD; *Evergreen* (mini-series), TV, 84, USA, 1st AD; *The Dead Zone*, Th, 83, USA, 1st AD; *The Grey Fox*, Th, 80, CDN, Assoc Prod/1st AD; *Atlantic City*, Th, 79, CDN/F, 1st AD.

BOBET, Jacques
SARDEC. 4121, av. Harvard, Montréal, PQ H4A 2W8 (514)489-9986.
Types de production et générique: l métrage-Prod/Sc; c métrage-Prod/Sc.
Types d'oeuvres: Documentaire-C; Education-C; Enfants-C; Sports-C&TV.
Curriculum vitae: Né en 1919, Saumure, France; citoyenneté canadienne. Scénariste, réalisateur, producteur, ONF, 47-84; joue un rôle clef comme producteur des films québécois importants aux années 60; Directeur de la Production Française, ONF, 68; Producteur exécutif, Studio C, 83. En cours: *Les Enfants du Déluge*, *I Want to be an Astronaut*, *Making It*, et *Charles le mal lavé/Le Roi mal lavé*. (Scénariste/Co scénariste).
Filmographie sélective: *La Grenouille et la Baleine*, C, 87, CDN, Sc; *Les Enfants des normes post scriptum*, C, 83, CDN, Prod; *Comme en Californie*, C, 83, CDN, Prod exéc; *Mario*, C, 83, CDN, Prod exéc; *Le Crime d'Ovide Plouffe*, C, 83, CDN/F, Prod exéc; *Du grand large aux Grands Lacs*, C, 81, CDN, Prod exéc; *Les Pièges de la mer*, C, 81, CDN, Prod; *La Nuit de la poésie 28 mars 1980*, C, 80, CDN, Prod; *La Bête lumineuse*, C, 80, CDN, Prod; *Les Adeptes*, C, 80, CDN, Prod exéc; *L'Enfant fragile*, C, 79, CDN, Prod; *Fermont, P.Q.*, C, 79, CDN, Prod; *Going the Distance*, C, 78, CDN, Prod exéc; *Le Pays de la terre sans arbre ou le Mouchouânipic*, C, 77, CDN, Prod; *Jeux de la XXIe Olympiade*, C, 76, CDN, Prod exéc.

BOCKING, Richard C.
5341 Parker Ave., Victoria, BC V8Y 2N1 (416)658-2993.
Type of Production and Credits: TV Film-Prod/Dir/Wr.
Genres: Musical-TV; Documentary-TV; Current Affairs-TV.
Biography: Born Thunder Bay, Ontario.

Graduated from the University of Manitoba. For more than 20 years a producer/director for CBC; now operates a television and film production company; based in Victoria, BC and Montreal, he has produced, directed and written many feature documentary films for both the English and French networks of the CBC, primarily related to music and the environment. His productions have won ANIK awards and Gemini nominations. Has worked in several cities in Canada and Europe.
Selected Filmography: *Nelligan: The Making of an Opera/Nelligan: La création d'un opéra*, "Adrienne Clarkson Presents", TV, 90, CDN, Prod/Dir/Wr; *Lanaudiere: A Summer of Music/Lanaudière: Un été en musique*, "Adrienne Clarkson Presents", TV, 89, CDN, Prod/Dir/Wr; *Ida Haendel: Voyage of Music/Ida Haendel: La voie de la musique*, "Adrienne Clarkson Presents", TV, 88, IL/PL/SF, Prod/Dir/Wr; *Vivaldi*, TV, 86, I/D, Prod/Dir/Wr, (ANIK); *Electricity: The Cost of Too Much Power/ Electricité: le coût de l'abondance*, TV, 84, CDN, Prod/Dir/Wr; *The Heritage of Marius Barbeau/L'heritage de Marius Barbeau*, TV, 83, CDN, Prod/Dir; *Marconi: Sparks That Shook the World/Marconi*, TV, 82, CDN/I, Prod/Dir; *After the Flood*, TV, 81, CDN, Prod/Dir/Wr; *The New West*, TV, 80, CDN, Prod/Dir; "The Music of Man/L'homme et la musique" (8 eps), TV, 79, CDN/USA, Prod/Dir, (ANIK).

BOCKING, Robert V.
- see CINEMATOGRAPHERS
BODOLAI, Joe
- see WRITERS
BOIRE, Roger
9435 Foucher, Montréal, PQ H2M 1W1
L'Oeil fou inc., 1600, av. de Lorimier, #295A, Montréal, PQ H2K 3W5
Types de production et générique: c métrage-Real/Prod/Mont.
Types d'oeuvres: Drame-C; Comédie-C; Comédie musicale-C; Education-C.
Curriculum vitae: Né en 1948, Montréal, Québec. Langues: français et anglais. Baccalauréat en Philosophie, Université du Québec à Montréal; Cinéma, London Film School, Angleterre. Monteur sonore sur plusieurs longs métrages, 85-86.
Filmographie sélective: *Le pied tendre*, C, 88, CDN, Réal; *Il faut chercher pour apprendre*, TV, 81, CDN, Prod/Mont; *Histoire vécue*, C, 79, CDN, Ass réal; *Jeux de portes*, C, 79, CDN, Prod/Cam; *Au bout du doute*, C, 78, CDN, Cam; *Un gars ben chanceux*, C, 77, CDN, Réal; *La Ceuillette du tabac d'hier à demain*, C, 76, CDN, Prod/Mont.

BOISVERT, Nicole M.
3924 rue Henri Julien, Montréal, PQ H2W 2K2 (514) 286-0222.
Types de production et générique: l métrage-Prod; c métrage-Prod.
Types d'oeuvres: Drame-C; Horreur-C; Animation-C.
Curriculum vitae: Citoyenne canadienne. Responsables des ventes, achats et de la distribution de films européens au Québec jusqu'en 76; Présidente, Les Productions Agora Inc., 76-83; Présidente, APFVQ, et Vice-présidente, producteur exécutif, SDA Productions Ltée., 82; Présidente directrice-générale, Société générale du cinéma du Québec, 84-85; Productrice, Fondation de la Société Cinemaginaire inc., 89; Scenariste, 88-91. *Pourquoi l'étrange M. Zolock s'intéressait-il tant à la bande dessinée?* a gagne le Prix Special du Jury à Banff.
Filmographie sélective: *Pourquoi l'étrange M. Zolock s'intéressait-il à la bande desinée?*, C, 83, CDN, Prod dél, (GENIE); *Heartaches*, C, 80, CDN, Co prod exéc; *Au revoir...à lundi*, C, 79, CDN/F, Co prod; *Blackout*, C, 77, CDN/F, Co prod.

BOITEAU, Denise
- see WRITERS
BOLAND, Deborah
ACTRA. 880 Dundas St. W., Ste. 1509, Mississauga, ON L5C 4H3 (416)275-1233. CFTO-TV, P.O. Box 9, Stn. O, Toronto, ON M4A 2M9 (416)299-2314. Kareer Artists, 508B Lawrence Ave. W., Toronto, ON M6A 1A1 (416)785-3073.
Types of Production and Credits: TV Video-Assoc Prod.
Genres: Current Affairs-TV; News-TV; Talk Shows-TV.
Biography: Born in 1960 in Toronto, Ontario. Canadian citizen. B.A.A., Broadcast Journalism, Ryerson Polytechnical Institute. Television Production, Humber College. Awards: Citytv Scholarship, 1984; CBC Telefest award for Best Short Documentary, 1985; C.A.P. Communications award, Best Reporter, 1984; Rogers, Outstanding Host, 1987/89/90.
Selected Filmography: "The Dini Petty Show" (2 yrs), TV, CDN, Assoc Prod; "Lifetime" (4 yrs), TV, CDN, Sr Story Ed; "The Shirley Show" (pilot), TV, CDN, Seg Prod; "Cityline", TV, CDN, Field Prod.

BOLEN, Norm
ACCT. 573 Roosevelt Ave., Ottawa, ON K2A 2A2 (613)761-1880. CBC TV, P.O.

Box 3220, Station C, Ottawa, ON K1Y 1E4 (613)724-5270.
Type of Production and Credits: TV Video-Prod/Wr.
Genres: Documentary-TV; Current Affairs-TV; News-TV.
Biography: Born in 1948 in Regina, Saskatchewan. Director, English TV Programming, Nation's Capital Region, CBC, Ottawa. Chairman of the National Training Committee, CBC TV, 1989 to date. Golden Sheaf and Saskatchewan Cable TV Association award winner. Co-winner, CBC Anik award, 1978.
Selected Filmography: "CBC Newsday, Regina" (5 eps/wk), TV, 83-85, CDN, Exec Prod; *Colony Trek - A Trip Through the Past*, TV, 81, CDN, Prod/Wr.

BONIN, Claude
APFTQ. 10860, rue Esplanade, Montréal, PQ H3L 2Y6 (514)336-3111. Les Films Vision 4 inc., 3575, boul. St-Laurent, bureau 411, Montréal, PQ H2X 2T7 (514)844-2855.
Types de production et générique: l métrage-Prod; TV film-Prod.
Types d'oeuvres: Drame-C&TV; Comédie-C&TV; Varieté-TV; Enfants-C&TV.
Curriculum vitae: Né à Montréal, Québec. Langues: français et anglais. Diplômé des Hautes Etudes Commerciales. Travaille plusieurs années dans l'industrie privée comme directeur de production. Devient le directeur du secteur de la production à l'Institut québécois du cinéma en 79. Durant les trois années de son mandat à l'IQC, il met sur pied les programmes *Premières oeuvres* et *Court métrage de fiction*, et aussi un plan de financement pour le long métrage à partir de fonds publics et privés. Il est producteur de films depuis maintenant près de 10 ans. Les plus récentes oeuvres qu'il a produites sont *Amoureux fou*, *Cruising bar*, *Simon les nuages*, *Henri*, *Pouvoir intime* et *Anne Trister*, et certaines de ces oeuvres ont été primées dans différents festivals inter-nationaux. Il a aussi produit depuis quelques années une série de téléfilms et la très populaire télésérie *Super sans plomb*.
Filmographie sélective: *Amoureux fou*, C, 91, CDN, Prod; *Un léger vertige*, TV, 91, CDN, Prod exéc; "Super sans plomb" (68 eps), TV, 89-91, CDN, Prod exéc; *Cuervo*, TV, 90, CDN, Prod exéc; *Cruising Bar*, C, 90, CDN, Prod; *Simon les nuages*, C, 90, CDN, Prod; *Gaspard et fils*, C, 88, CDN, Prod assoc; *Des amis pour la vie*, TV, 88, CDN, Prod; *Bonjour Monsieur Gauguin*, TV, 88 CDN, Prod; *Candy Mountain*, C, 86, CH/CDN/F, Prod assoc; *Henri*, C, 86, CDN, Prod; *Pellan*, C, 86, CDN, Prod; *Pouvoir intime*, C, 85, CDN, Prod; *Anne Trister*, C, 85, CDN, Prod; *Les années de rêves*, C, 84, CDN, Prod.

BONIN, Jacques
APFTQ, ACCT. 177 est., boul. Gouin, Montréal, PQ H2C 1C3 (514), 383-5325. Téléfiction inc., 355 Ste-Catherine ouest, Montréal, PQ, H3B 1A5.
Types de production et générique: TV film-Prod.
Types d'oeuvres: Drame-C&TV; Comédie-C&TV; Documentaire-TV; Enfants-TV.
Curriculum vitae: Né en 1951, Montréal, Québec. Langues: français et anglais. Baccalauréat en Communications (cinéma et TV), Université du Québec à Montréal.
Filmographie sélective: *Bombardier* (mini-série), TV, 91, CDN, Prod; "Super sans plomb" (68 eps), TV, 89-90, CDN, Prod; "Labo Labo" (26 eps), TV, 88, CDN, Prod; "Wow" (54 eps), TV, 87, CDN, Prod; "Fan Club" (250 eps), TV, 86-87, CDN, Prod; "Graffiti" (26 eps), TV, 96-87, CDN, Prod; "Télégrammes" (22 eps), TV, 86, CDN, Prod; *Henri*, Th, 85, CDN, Prod assoc; *Pouvoir intime*, C, 85, CDN, Prod assoc; "L'Argent des jeunes", TV, 85, CDN, Prod; "Emploi jeunesse" (17 eps), TV, 85, CDN, Prod; "Mémoires d'insectes" (20 eps), TV, 85, CDN, Prod; "Leurs héritiers" (13 eps), TV, 84, CDN, Prod; "La Sexualité inachevée" (13 eps), TV, 84, CDN, Prod; "Astrologie avec Marylène" (20 eps), TV, 84, CDN, Prod.

BOUCHARD, Michel
- voir REALISATEURS

BOURDON, Laurent
APFTQ. 10015 Verville, Montréal, PQ H3L 2E4 (514)381-2791. Les Productions Prisma Inc., 5253, ave. du Parc, #330, Montréal, PQ H2V 4P2 (514)277-6686.
Types de production et générique: l métrage-Prod; TV vidéo-Prod.
Types d'oeuvres: Drame-TV; Documentaire-C; Education-C; Enfants-TV.
Curriculum vitae: Bacc. Pédagogie, Université de Montréal; Certificat en Géographie, Université de Montréal. Stage intensif de formation en communication ONF, 1969 (production-réalisation de vidéos). Experiences de travail: Producteur, Novalis, Ottawa, 1969-71; Directeur du Marketing, Novalis, Ottawa, 1971-73; Producteur, Adimec, Montréal, 1973-79; Producteur et administrateur, Groupe Multi-média

du Canada, Montréal, 1979-87; fondation d'une compagnie de distribution, Montréal, 1988; Producteur chez Les Productions Prisma, Montréal.
Filmographie sélective: "Pacha et les chats" (65 eps), TV, 90-91, CDN, Prod; "Zone interdite" (21 eps), TV, 89-90, CDN, Prod; "Bonne Table" (110 eps), TV, 89, CDN, Prod.

BOURNE, Lindsay
- see WRITERS

BOURQUE, Paul
ACCT. 103 Blainville ouest, Ste-Thérèse, PQ J7E 1Y1 (514)437-4247. Les Productions SDA Ltée, 1425 boul. René-Lévesque ouest, 10e etage, Montréal, PQ H3G 1T7
Types de production et générique: TV video-Prod.
Types d'oeuvres: Documentaire-TV; Enfants-TV; Annonces-TV; Industrial-TV.
Curriculum vitae: Né au Québec en 1959. Langues: français et anglais. Animateur, Radio, Journaliste sportif, Asst de Production/film; Régisseur; Directeur de Production; Directeur de Production; Directeur de Post Production/Video; Asst Réalisateur/Video; Producteur délégué.
Filmographie sélective: *Chauffeur Le Soir T'es Toute Ma Vie*, In, 91, CDN, Prod dél; *Human Rights Complaints EIC*, In, 91, CDN, Prod dél; "Sault Martin" (39 eps), TV, 90, CDN, Prod dél; *Pédibus*, In, 90, CDN, Prod dél; "Video Théatre" (13 eps), TV, 90, CDN, Prod dél; *La Table Ronde National Sur L'environnement et l'énergie*, Cm, 90, CDN, Prod dél; *Où va l'argent de vos taxes?*, In, 90, CDN, Prod dél; *Commissaires aux Langues Officielles* (3), Cm, 90, CDN, Prod dél; "Impôt 89" (2 eps), TV, 90, CDN, Dir pro.

BOWLBY, Barbara
ACCT, CFTPA. 40 Davean Dr., North York, ON M2L 2R7 (416)449-2174. Insight Productions, 489 King St. W., Ste. 401, Toronto, ON M5V 1L3 (416)596-8118.
Type of Production and Credits: TV Film-Assoc Prod; TV Video-Assoc Prod.
Genres: Drama-TV; Variety-TV; Documentary-TV; Game Shows-TV.
Biography: Born in Toronto, Ontario. P&OT, University of Toronto. Eight years experience in business affairs for television production.
Selected Filmography: *Kurt Browning: Tall in the Saddle*, TV, 91, CDN, Assoc Prod; "Test Pattern" (65 eps), TV, 90, CDN, Assoc Prod; "Saying Good-Bye" (5 eps), TV, 90, CDN; *A David Foster Christmas Card*, TV, 89, CDN.

BOYCE, M. Susanne ◊
ATPD, ACCT. (416)782-7593.
Type of Production and Credits: TV Video-Prod.
Genres: News-TV; Current Affairs-TV; Sports-TV.
Biography: Born 1949, New Brunswick. B.A., Carleton University.
Selected Filmography: "Midday", TV, 86-88, CDN, Sr Prod; "The Journal", TV, 86, CDN, Sr Prod; "The Journal", TV, 82-84, CDN, Prod; "Webster", TV, 78-82, CDN, Prod; "CTV Sports" (26 eps), TV, 76-82, CDN, Prod/Assoc Dir; "BCTV Newshour", TV, 773-78, CDN, Prod.

BOYDEN, Barbara
ACTRA. 165 Shaw St., Toronto, ON M6J 2W6 (416)531-7864. TVOntario, 2180 Yonge St., Toronto, ON M4S 2C1 (416)484-2600.
Type of Production and Credits: Th Film-Prod/Wr; TV Film-Prod/Dir/Wr; TV Video-Prod/Dir/Wr.
Genres: Documentary-Th&TV; Educational-TV; Children's-TV.
Biography: Born 1944, Toronto, Ontario.
Selected Filmography: "Report Canada" (150/yr), TV, 74-92, CDN, Prod/Dir; "Many Voices" (9 eps), TV, 90-91, CDN, Prod/Dir; "Write Stuff" (30 eps), TV, 87-88, CDN, Dir; *Those Roos Boys and Friends*, TV, 87, CDN, Prod/Dir/Wr; *The Seaway*, "It's Your World", TV, 84, CDN, Wr; *Keep the Beat*, "It's Mainly Music", TV, 84, CDN, Wr; "Music Box" (2 eps)(Co-wr pilot), TV, 80-81, CDN, Wr; *The View from Vinegar Hill*, TV, 80, CDN, Prod/Dir/Wr; "Owl Magazine" (pilot), TV, 78, CDN, Prod; *The Doll Factory*, TV, 78, CDN, Co-Prod/Co-Wr; "Get It Together" (20 eps), TV, 77, CDN, Dir.

BRANDT, C.V. (Caryl)
CTPDA. Box 1709, Canmore, AB T0L 0M0 (403)678-2987.
Type of Production and Credits: TV Film-Prod/Dir; Th Film-PM; TV Video-Prod/Dir.
Genres: Drama-Th&TV; Documentary-TV; Children's TV; Current Affairs-TV.
Biography: Born 1949, Swan Lake, Manitoba. Radio and Television Arts, Northern Alberta Institute of Technology; Film Criticism and Theory, University of Manitoba. More than 20 years experience as producer, director, production manager for film and videotape production, both freelance and on contract with organizations such as CBC, NFB, MTV; Executive Director, National Screen

Institute-Canada, 87-90; from 85-87, Vice-President of Alberta Motion Picture Development Corporation, responsible for project development and promotion. *A Grand Opening* won AMPIA 76 for Best of Festival, Best Industrial, Best Script, Best Music and Best Cinematograpy; *Challenge for '78* won CFTA 78 and CanPro 78 for Best Sports Special; "Points West" won Certificate of Merit at Yorkton, 81, for "On-going Series Quality;" "Edmonton Extra Special" won Prix Anik, 82, for Best Regional Information Series; *Prairie Women* won award at Yorkton, 87, for Best Documentary Over 30.
Selected Filmography: *Prairie Women*, Th, 87, CDN, Prod; "Mr. Wizard's World" (26 eps), TV, 84-85, CDN, USA, Assoc Prod; "Edmonton Extra Special" (13 eps), TV, 81-82, CDN, Exec Prod, (ANIK); "Points West" (36 eps), TV, 79-82, CDN, Prod/Dir; *Challenge for '78*, TV, 78, CDN, Prod/Dir; *Fast Company*, Th, 78, CDN, PM; *A Grand Opening*, In, 76, CDN, Dir.

BRASIER, Fabrice
- voir MONTEURS

BRASSEUR, Raymond ✧
(514)935-8521.
Types de production et générique: TV film-Prod; TV vidéo-Prod.
Types d'oeuvres: Drame-C&TV; Education-TV; Industriel-C&TV.
Curriculum vitae: Né en 1945; citoyenneté canadienne. Langues: français et anglais.
Filmographie sélective: *A Matter of Cunning*, TV, 83, CDN, Co prod; *New Orleans*, TV, 83, CDN, Co prod; "A plein temps" (pilote), TV, 83, CDN, prod; "Faut voir à son affaire" (13 eps), ED, 80, CDN, Prod; "Forano" (2 ém), TV, 80, CDN, Prod; "That's It" (26 eps), TV, 80, CDN, Prod; *Chauffeur, Chauffard*, In, 78, CDN, Prod; *City on Fire*, C, 78, CDN/USA, Co prod.

BRAULT, Michel
- voir REALISATEURS

BRINTON, Donald C.
5296 Meadfield Rd., West Vancouver, BC V7W 3C4 (604)922-9192. CanWest Broadcasting, 180 - W. 2nd Ave., Vancouver, BC (604)876-1344.
Type of Production and Credits: TV Film-Prod.
Genres: Drama-TV.
Biography: Born 1927, Alberta. B.Sc, University of Alberta. Has worked in radio and television for 38 years. Broadcaster of the Year Award, WAB, 80; Canadian Association of Broadcasters Gold Medal for Excellence in Broadcasting, 87; many other awards and nominations including Yorkton, New York, San Francisco, Houston, Banff, CanPro, Columbus, Gemini and ACTRA.
Selected Filmography: *Tramp at the Door*, TV, 85, CDN, Exec Prod; *The Prodigal*, TV, 84, CDN, Exec Prod; *Hunting Season*, TV, 83, CDN, Exec Prod; *Reunion*, TV, 83, CDN, Exec Prod; *In the Fall*, TV, 83, CDN, Exec Prod/Co-Prod; *The Catch*, TV, 82, CDN, Exec Prod.

BROCHU, Pierre
- voir SCENARISTES

BRONFMAN, Paul
Comweb Corporation, 1200 Bay St., Ste. 703, Toronto, ON M5R 2A5 (416)920-7050.
Type of Production and Credits: Th Film-Prod; TV Film-Prod.
Genres: Drama-Th&TV; Action-Th&TV; Horror-Th&TV; Children's-Th&TV.
Biography: Born in 1957 in Montreal, Quebec. Canadian citizen. Speaks English and French. Graduated from the University of Toronto with a B.A., Commerce. Member of the Board of Directors for The Canadian Centre for Advanced Film Studies.
Selected Filmography: *The Quarrel*, Th, 90, CDN, Co-Exec Prod; *Golden Fiddles*, TV, 90, AUS, Co-Exec Prod; "Katts & Dog" (23 eps), TV, 90, CDN/F, Co-Exec Prod; *The Last Kiss - Prom Night III*, Th, 90, CDN, Co-Prod; 'Neon Rider" (14 eps), TV, 89, CDN, Assoc Prod.

BROUSSEAU, Pierre
ACTRA, CAPAC, UDA, ACCT. 1, Wood Ave., Ste. 211, Westmount, PQ H3Z 3C5 (514)989-7500.
Types de production et générique: l métrage-Prod/Sc.
Types d'oeuvres: Drame-C; Comédie-C; Action-C.
Curriculum vitae: Né en 1945, Québec. Langues: français et anglais. Correspondant (radio et revue) au Festival de Cannes; journaliste d'arts et spectacles pendant 15 ans. Publie *La Vie secrete de Marilyn Monroe* et *La fantastique histoire du film E.T.*; devient adjoint au Président de Films Mutuels; correspondant au Québec pour le *Hollywood Reporter*, 82-84; critique de cinéma, 84-85; secrétaire du jury au Festival des Films du Monde depuis 81; publiciste pour films, *Le Matou*, *Jean de Florette*, *Manon des sources*, *Au revoir les enfants*, *Les Aventures de Chatran*, *Les Portes tournantes*, *Le déclin de l'empire américain*, *La Lectrice*, *Cruising Bar*, *Cyrano*

de Bergerac, et *Le Festin de Babette*; retour à la production, 92.
Filmographie sélective: *Tanya's Island*, C, 79, CDN, Prod/Sc; *Après-Ski*, C, 70, CDN, Sc; *James Bagatelle*, C, 69, CDN, Prod/Sc/Réal; *Narcissus*, C, 68, CDN, Prod/Sc/Réal.

BROWN, Alexandra
TWIFT, ITVA. 448 Spadina Rd., #201, Toronto, ON M5P 2W4 (416)488-5040.
Type of Production and Credits: TV Video-Prod/Wr; Corp Video-Prod/Wr.
Genres: Documentary-TV; Educational-TV; Industrial-TV; Current Affairs-TV.
Biography: Born 1957, Toronto, Ontario. B.A. English, University of Toronto. Writer/on-camera, TVOntario, 3 years. Producer/on-camera, 5 series on health and issues affecting the human condition. Producer, corporate video/live events, 3 years. Specializes in work for the corporate sector. Clients include: Kraft/General Foods Canada, Kellogg's Canada, Bata International, Ortho Pharmaceutical, Royal Bank.

BROWN, Jamie
ACTRA, WGAw, ACCT. 174 Beacon Hill Rd., Beaconsfield, PQ H9W 1T6 (514)694-6928. Telescene Film Group Inc., 5510 Ferrier St., Montreal, PQ H4P 1M2 (514)737-5512. FAX: 737-7945.
Type of Production and Credits: Th Film-Prod/Wr; Th Short-Wr; TV Film-Wr.
Genres: Drama-Th&TV; Comedy-Th&TV; Action-Th; Documentary-Th.
Biography: Born 1945, Brantford, Ontario. Published 5 novels including *Superbike*, the Young Adult Canadian Book of the Year, 83. Executive Vice-President of Telescene Film Group Inc.
Selected Filmography: "Urban Angel" (6 eps), TV, 90-91, CDN, Exec Co-Prod; *Une Histoire Inventée*, Th, 90, CDN, Exec Co-Prod; *Malarek*, Th, 88, CDN, Co-Prod; "Morris & Muush" (pilot), TV, 88, CDN, Exec Prod; *Obsessed/Hitting Home*, Th, 86-87, CDN, Co-Prod; *A corps perdu*, Th, 87, CDN/SH, Exec Prod; *Keeping Track*, Th, 85, CDN, Co-Prod/Wr; *Toby McTeague*, Th, 85, CDN, Co-Wr; *You've Come a Long Way Ladies*, TV, 84, CDN, Wr; "The Winners" (1 eps), TV, 81, CDN, Wr; *The War Is Over*, Th, 77, CDN, Co-Wr.

BROWNE, Christene
BUPD, BFVN, BFF, CIFC. Syncopated Productions, 517 Delaware Ave. N., Toronto, ON M6H 2V3 (416)531-0857. Syncopated Productions Inc., 517 Delaware Ave. N., Toronto, ON M6H 2V3 (416)531-0857.
Type of Production and Credits: TV Video-Prod/Dir; Th Film-Prod/Dir/Ed/Wr.
Genres: Documentary-TV.
Biography: Born 1965, St. Kitts, West Indies; came to Canada at age 4. Languages: English and French. Studied film at Ryerson Polytechnical Institute, 1985-87. *No Choice* was part of the historical Five Feminist Minutes film package of the NFB's Studio D, 1990. *Brothers in Music* was nominated for Best Documentary Under 30 mins at the 1991 Yorkton Short Film and Video Festival. Special skills include producing, directing, picture/sound editing.
Selected Filmography: *Jodie Drake: Blues in My Bread*, "Adrienne Clarkson Presents", TV, 91, CDN, Prod/Dir; *Brothers in Music*, ED/TV, 90, CDN, Prod/Dir/Ed; *No Choice*, ED, 90, CDN, Prod/Dir/Ed; *From Nevis To...*, ED, 1987, CDN, Prod/Dir/Ed/Wr.

BRUNELLE, Wendy A.
- see WRITERS

BRUNTON, John
CFTA, ACCT. Insight Production Co. Ltd., 489 King St. W., Ste. 401, Toronto, ON M5V 1L3 (416)596-8118. FAX: 596-8270.
Type of Production and Credits: TV Film-Prod; TV Video-Prod.
Genres: Drama-TV; Comedy-TV; Variety-TV; Documentary-TV.
Biography: Born 1953, Toronto, Ontario. Background and schooling in business; worked for Insight Productions; took control of the company, 76. *Tucker and the Horse Thief* won a Silver Medal, International Film and TV Festival, NY; *My Father, My Rival* won a Bronze Medal, NY; *The Truth about Alex* won Best Short Drama, ACE Award, Los Angeles, 88; *It's Only Rock 'n' Roll* won a Gemini, 87, for Best Sound.
Selected Filmography: *Kurt Browing: Tall in the Saddle*, TV, 90, CDN, Exec Prod/Prod; *A David Foster Christmas Card*, TV, 89, CDN, Prod; "Saying Good-bye" (5 eps), TV, 89-90, CDN, Exec Prod (GEMINI 90); "The Big Valley Jamboree" (2 eps), TV, 89, CDN, Prod; *David Foster Sensations*, TV, 89, CDN, Prod; *1989 Juno Awards*, TV, 89, CDN, Prod; "It's Only Rock 'n' Roll" (13 eps), TV, 87, CDN, Exec Prod, (GEMINI 88); *The Wesselys*, TV, 87, CDN, Co-Exec Prod; *Crystal Comedy Pageant*, TV, 87, CDN, Exec Prod; *The Truth About Alex*, TV, 86, CDN, Exec Prod, (GEMINI 87); "Rockit

Records" (pilot), TV, 86, CDN, Exec Prod/Co-Creator; *Tucker and the Horse Thief/Working for Peanuts/My Father, My Rival,* "Family Playhouse", TV, 84, CDN, Exec Prod; *Indigo!,* TV, 83, CDN, Exec Prod; *Heart of Gold* (3 parts), TV, 82, CDN, Prod.

BRYDON, Loyd
DGC, BECTU (UK). Distribudata International Inc., 30 Fontenay Court, #1207, Islington, ON M9A 4W5 (416)242-7629.
Type of Production and Credits: Th Short-Wr/Narr; TV Film-Dir/Wr.
Genres: Drama-Th; Variety-Th; Documentary-Th; Commercials-Th.
Biography: Born 1925, Toronto, Ontario. Served in Canadian Army in WWII; on discharge concluded degree in Political Science and Economics, University of British Columbia; graduate of Motion Picture Film Production and Television (Advanced Award; Professional Designation), Advanced Sequential Award for Writing, UCLA, 81; studied computer editing, computer graphics, Univesity of Santa Barbara. In a career of more than 40 years, has worked as actor, writer, producer, director in radio, theatre, film, video and golden years of television in many countries including Australia, Jamaica, Europe, England and North America and has won awards in ballet-documentary and drama. Currently President of Distribudata International Inc. and Brydon Aero Cam Associates Inc.

BUDGELL, Jack ✧
ATPD, ACCT. (416)462-0560.
Type of Production and Credits: TV Video-Prod/Dir.
Genres: Comedy-TV; Variety-TV; Documentary-TV; Children's-TV.
Biography: Born Toronto, Ontario. Technical Studies; Radio and TV Arts, Ryerson Polytechnical Institute. Extensive experience in audio production. Credits include production of album, "Rich Little on Broadway", for Columbia Records.
Selected Filmography: "Super Dave Osborne Show" (13 eps), TV, 88, USA, Prod; NHL Awards, TV, 86, CDN, Prod; "Super Dave Osborne Show" (13 eps), TV, 86, CDN/USA, Prod/Dir; *Crystal Comedy Pageant,* TV, 86, CDN, Dir; *CBC New Year's Special,* TV, 85, CDN, Exec Prod; "Country West" (6 eps), TV, 85, CDN, Dir; "Fraggle Rock" (45 eps), TV, 85, CDN, Line Prod; "Bizarre" (100 eps), TV, 82-85, CDN/USA, Dir; *ACTRA Awards* (3 shows), TV, 81-85, CDN, Prod; "Carroll Baker Jamboree" (12 eps), TV, 84, CDN, Exec Prod; *Juno Awards* (5 shows), TV, 78-83, CDN, Prod; "Bob McLean Show" (1400 eps), TV, 76-82, CDN, Exec Prod; *Stage Band Festival,* TV, 80, CDN, Prod; "Jazz Canada" (12 eps), TV, 80, CDN, Prod/Dir; *Maynard Ferguson Concert,* TV, 80, CDN, Prod.

BURKE, Alan
ATPD, ACCT. 111 Hilton Ave., Toronto, ON M5R 3E8 (416)533-4463. CBC, Box 500, Stn. A, Toronto, ON M5W 1E6 (416)975-7100.
Type of Production and Credits: TV Film-Prod/Dir.
Genres: Drama-TV; Documentary-TV; Educational-TV; Animation-TV.
Biography: Born 1943, Woodstock, Ontario. B.A. Produced/directed animation, documentary shorts in London, England for 9 years. Has won awards at New York and Brighton film festivals.
Selected Filmography: *Attila Lukcas,* "Adrienne Clarkson Presents", TV, 91, CDN, Prod/Dir; *It's Back,* "the fifth estate", TV, 89, CDN, Prod/Dir; *Skate,* TV, 87, CDN, Prod, (GEMINI 88); *Michael and Kitty,* TV, 85, CDN, Prod; *In This Corner,* TV, 85, CDN, Prod; *Till Death Do Us Part,* "The Lawyers", TV, 84, CDN, Dir; *Where the Heart Is/Hide and Seek,* "For the Record", TV, 84, CDN, Prod; *Out of Sight, Out of Mind/By Reason of Insanity,* "For the Record", TV, 82-83, CDN, Prod; *Yen for You/Shroud/Trucks/Test Tube Town,* "the fifth estate", TV, 80-81, CDN, Prod/Dir; "the fifth estate" (20 eps), TV, 80, CDN, Prod; *Drug Resistance,* In, 75, GB, Dir; *Ling Sur Ling,* In, 75, GB, Prod.

BURMAN, Tony ✧
ATPD, ACCT. (416)483-4575.
Type of Production and Credits: TV Film-Prod/Wr; TV Video-Prod/Wr.
Genres: Documentary-TV; Current Affairs-TV; News-TV.
Biography: Born 1948, Montreal, Quebec. Languages: English and French. Attended Loyola College, Montreal. Documentary producer, CBC "Journal", 85; senior editor, CBC National TV News 75-85; producer, executive producer, "The National", 80-82; earlier, producer CBC Radio Current Affairs and reporter, the *Montreal Star.* Best Report TV Award, Centre for Investigative Journalism, 87, for *Mandela,* "The Journal".
Selected Filmography: *Life after Death: Ethiopia,* "The Journal", TV, 88, CDN, Prod/Dir; *Legacy of Death: The Air India Crash,* "The Journal", TV, 87, CDN, Prod/Dir; *Battle for Central America,* "The

Journal", TV, 87, CDN, Sr Prod; *Last Great Cause: Spanish Civil War*, "The Journal", TV, 86, CDN, Prod/Dir; "The Journal" (2 eps), TV, 86, CDN, Prod/Narr.

BURNS, Michael
AME Productions, 261 Davenport Rd., Toronto, ON M5R 1S1 (416)961-9977. FAX: 924-4169. Bialystock & Bloom Ltd., 181 Carlaw Ave., #222, Toronto, ON M4M 2S1 (416)463-8124. FAX: 463-1471.
Type of Production and Credits: Th Film-Prod; TV Film-Prod; TV Video-Prod.
Genres: Drama-Th; Documentary-Th&TV.
Biography: Born 1947, Toronto, Ontario. B.A., Philosophy, Antioch College.
Selected Filmography: *Perfectly Normal*, Th, 91, CDN/UK, Prod; *Threshold*, Th, 83, CDN, Co-Prod; *Days of Heaven*, Th, 78, USA, Pro Assoc; *Who is Guru Maharaj-ji?*, "Rogers Report", TV, 77, CDN, Dir/Prod; "Barbara Frum" (39 eps), TV, 76, CDN, Prod; *Hearts and Minds*, Th, 75, USA, PM/Assoc Prod; *Five Easy Pieces*, Th, 70-71, USA, PA; *The Last Picture Show*, Th, 71, USA, PA; *Head*, Th, 70, USA, Assoc Prod; "The Monkees" (51 eps), TV, 66-69, USA, Assoc Prod.

BURTON, Robert H.
ACCT. 422 Castlefield Ave., Toronto, ON M5N 1L5 (416)484-6217.
Type of Production and Credits: TV Film-Prod/Dir/Wr; TV Video-Prod/Dir/Wr.
Genres: Drama-TV; Comedy-TV; Documentary-TV; Children's-TV.
Biography: Born 1946, USA; Canadian citizenship. Languages: English, Spanish, French. B.A., University of New Mexico; M.S., Columbia University. Several awards at NY International Film and TV Festival and CanPro award for Lorne Greene's *They Went to Fight for Freedom*.
Selected Filmography: "Nancy Drew" (2 eps), TV, 90, CDN/F, Assoc Prod; "YTV Rocks" (260 eps), TV, 88-90, CDN, Exec Prod, (CBI); *YTV Achievement Awards*, TV, 89, CDN, Exec Prod, (CBI); *Canada's Search for Missing Children*, TV, 89, CDN, Exec Prod, (CBI); "Deke Wilson's Mini Mysteries" (13 eps), TV, 89, CDN, Network Exec, (CBI); "Alfred Hitchcock Presents" (13 eps), TV, 88, CDN/USA, PM; *Taking Care of Terrific*, TV, 87, CDN/USA, PM, (ACE); "Don't Stop Now!" (13 eps), TV, 86, CDN, Exec Prod; "Turkey TV" (65 eps), TV, 85, CDN/USA, Mng Prod; *Latch Key Kids*, TV, 85, CDN, Exec Prod; *They Went to Fight for Freedom*, TV, 84, CDN, Prod/Dir/Wr; *Cosmic Fire*, TV, 83, CDN, Prod/Dir/Wr; "CBOT News" (520 eps), TV, 82, CDN, Prod; "Hands That Heal" (18 eps), TV, 79, CDN, Prod/Dir/Wr; "Marketplace" (39 eps), TV, 72, CDN, Ed.

BUSATO, Paul
- see WRITERS

BUTTIGNOL, Rudy
ACC&TV, CFPTA, WGC (ACTRA), ASWA. Rudy Inc., 40 Glengarry Ave., Toronto, ON M5M 1C9 (416)489-7115. FAX: 489-7760. Production Office:, 31 Lawrence Ave. W., Toronto, ON M5M 1A3 1710 Albans, Houston, TX 77005 USA. (713)520-6712.
Type of Production and Credits: Th Short-Prod/Dir/Wr; TV Film-Prod/Dir/Wr.
Genres: Drama-TV; Documentary-Th&TV; Educational-TV.
Biography: Born 1951, Italy; Canadian citizenship, 75. B.F.A., York University. Has produced over 70 independent film and video programs for television, industry and government; worked for the NFB; received numerous grants from the Canada Council, Ontario Arts Council and Science Culture Canada. Co-founder and first Chairman of the Canadian Independent Film Caucus; ACC&TV board member, 85-present.
Selected Filmography: "The Spacewatch Club" (4 eps), TV, 90-91, CDN/USA, Prod/Wr/Story Ed; *Videocosmos*, "Soviet Space Program Library" (6 eps), TV, 91, CDN/USA/USSR, Prod/Wr/Host; *Alan Bean, Art Off This Earth*, TV, 90, CDN/USA, Prod/Wr; *Space Pioneers, A Canadian Story*, TV, 88, CDN, Prod/Dir/Narr; *Spacewatch*, TV, 87, USA, Wr/Prod; "The Space Experience" (6 eps), TV, 87, CDN, Wr/Dir; *Bangladesh from the River*, TV, 85, CDN, Prod/Dir/Ed; *The Bartletts*, ED, 85, CDN, Prod; *Neon: An Electric Memoir*, Th, 84, CDN, Prod/Dir; *An Arm in Space/Un Bras Spacial*, In, 82, CDN, Prod/Dir/Wr; *Inward Passage*, Th, 82, CDN, Prod/Dir; *Shipyard*, TV, 80, CDN, Prod/Dir; *Jack Bush*, TV, 79, CDN, Prod; *The Dairy*, TV, 78, CDN, Prod; *Where's Topper*, TV, 76, CDN, Prod/Dir.

CAHILL, T.J.
- see WRITERS

CAMPBELL, Harry
85 Roe Ave., Toronto, ON M5M 2H6 (416)485-8063. Espial Productions Ltd., Box 624, Stn. K, Toronto, ON M4P 2H1 (416)485-8063.

Telefilm Canada

Avec vous on tourne!

En apportant notre appui à l'entreprise privée, nous contribuons au développement du film, de l'industrie canadienne de la télévision et de la vidéo.

Notre action sur les marchés internationaux vise à promouvoir les réalisations d'ici.

Par l'entremise de nos bureaux à l'étranger, nous suscitons des ententes de coproductions, apport important au dynamisme et à la vitalité de l'industrie.

Action!

By providing support to the private sector, Telefilm Canada contributes to the development of the Canadian television, film and video industry.

As well, Telefilm is committed to promoting Canadian productions on the international scene.

By maintaining offices abroad, the Corporation paves the way to co-production agreements that are key elements of a vigorous and dynamic industry.

Head Office
Siège social
Montréal
Tour de la Banque Nationale
14e étage
600, de la Gauchetière Ouest
Montréal (Québec) H3B 4L2
Téléphone : (514) 283-6363
Télex : 055-66598
Télécopieur : (514) 283-8212

Offices in Canada
Bureaux au Canada

Toronto
2 Bloor Street West
22nd Floor
Toronto, Ontario
M4W 3E2
Telephone : (416) 973-6436
Fax : (416) 973-8606

Vancouver
350-375 Water Street
Vancouver, British Columbia
V6B 5C6
Telephone : (604) 666-1566
Fax : (604) 666-7754

Halifax
5525 Artillery Place
Suite 220
Halifax, Nova Scotia
B3J 1J2
Telephone : (902) 426-8425
Fax : (902) 426-4445

International Offices
Bureaux à l'étranger

Los Angeles
144 South Beverly Drive
Suite 400
Beverly Hills, California
U.S.A. 90212
Telephone : (213) 859-0268
Fax : (213) 276-4741

Paris
15 rue de Berri
75008 Paris, France
Téléphone : (1) 45.63.70.45
Télécopieur : (1) 42.25.33.61

Londres
59/59 Oxford Street
Fourth Floor
London, W1R 1RD
England
Telephone : (44-71) 437-8308
Telex : 923753
Fax : (44-71) 734-8586

Type of Production and Credits: TV Film-Prod/Dir.
Genres: Documentary-TV; Educational-TV.
Biography: Born 1919. Entered film production as head of Foreign Language Unit, NFB Ottawa, 44. Adviser on educational and instruction material, United Nations Film & Sound Archives, New York, 46-48. Head of Clearing House for Publications, UNESCO, 50-56; Chief Librarian, Toronto Public Library, 56-78; film and library consultant, 79-86; documentary film producer, China, 86-91.
Selected Filmography: *Tillson Lever Harrison, a Canadian Hero*, ED, 90, RC, Prod/Dir; *Canadian Study Tours in China*, ED, 86, CDN/RC, Prod/Dir.

CAMPBELL, Norman
- see DIRECTORS

CAMPBELL, Peg
- see DIRECTORS

CANELL, Marrin
4700 Bonavista Ave., #210, Montreal, PQ H3C 2C5 (514)482-2856.
Type of Production and Credits: Th Film-Dir/Prod/Ed; Th Short-Dir/Prod/Ed; TV Film-Dir/Prod/Ed; TV Video-Dir/Prod.
Genres: Drama-Th&TV; Variety-TV; Documentary-Th&TV; Educational-Th&TV.
Biography: Born 1943, Montreal, Quebec. Studied Economics, Political Science and Communications, Sir George Williams (Concordia) University; postgraduate work Film and Television, Loyola University; Law, University of Montreal. Film work in public and private sectors over a span of twenty years; topics ranging from political and social documentaries to sports. Films have won numerous awards, including 7 Genie Awards, 3 Red Ribbons (NY), British Film Academy Award and Academy Award nomination.
Selected Filmography: "God's Dominion" (4 eps), TV, 91-92, CDN, Dir; *Le Patro*, ED, 90-91, CDN, Prod; *Penfield*, "Heritage Minutes", TV, 90-91, CDN, Dir; *Princes in Exile*, TV, 89-90, CDN, Prod; *No Address*, TV, 88, CDN, Prod; *The New North*, TV, 87, CDN, Prod; *The Outfoxed Tiger/A Dog's Tale*, "Parables", TV, 85-86, CDN, Prod; *Richard Cardinal: Cry of a Metis Child*, TV, 86, CDN, Prod; *Poundmaker's Lodge: A Healing Place*, TV, 86, CDN, Prod; *Legs of the Lame*, "Bell Canada Playhouse", TV, 85, CDN, Co-Prod; *Overtime*, TV, 84, CDN, Prod/ Dir/Ed; *The Sweater*, Th, 82, CDN, Prod, (BFA); *The New Establishment*, "The Canadian Establishment", TV, 81, CDN, Prod/Dir; *Paperland: The Bureaucrat Observed*, TV, 80, CDN, Co-Prod, (GENIE); *Whistling Smith*, "Pacific Canada", TV, 75, CDN, Co-Dir/Ed.

CAPPE, Syd
CFTA, ACCT. SC Entertainment International Incorporated, 434 Queen St. E., Toronto, ON M5A 1T5 (416)363-6060. FAX: 363-2305.
Type of Production and Credits: Th Film-Prod.
Genres: Drama-Th; Documentary-Th&TV.
Biography: Born 1952, Toronto, Ontario. B.PHE., University of Toronto; M.HK., University of Windsor. Producer of theatrical features and feature documentaries through SC Entertainment since 81.
Selected Filmography: *Stepping Razor*, Th, 91, CDN, Exec Prod; *Pump Up the Volume*, Th, 90, USA, Exec Prod; *Red Blooded American Girl*, Th, 90, CDN, Exec Prod; *The Big Slice*, Th, 90, CDN, Exec Prod; *Blood Relations*, Th, 88, CDN, Exec Prod; *Friends Lovers and Lunatics*, Th, 88, CDN, Exec Prod; *Murder One*, Th, 87, CDN, Exec Prod; *One Man Out*, Th, 88, CDN, Exec Prod; *Hostile Takeover*, Th, 88, CDN, Exec Prod; *Caribe*, Th, 87, CDN, Exec Prod; *The Sexiest Animal*, Th, 87, CDN, Exec Prod; *Into the Fire*, Th, 86, CND, Exec Prod; *The Pink Chiquitas*, Th, 85, CDN, Exec Prod.

CARMODY, Don
DGC, DGA, PGA. Don Carmody Productions, 8275 Mayrand St., Montreal, PQ H4P 2C8 (514)342-2340. Stephen Gray, Gray-Goodman, (213)276-7070.
Type of Production and Credits: Th Film-Prod; TV Film-Prod.
Genres: Drama-Th&TV; Comedy-Th; Horror-Th.
Biography: Born 1951, Providence, Rhode Island; Canadian citizenship. B.A., Communications, Loyola University; 2 years Law, McGill University. Has owned production company since 78. *Porky's* won the Golden Reel Award.
Selected Filmography: *Hitman*, Th, 91, USA, Prod/Wr; *Payoff*, Th, 90, USA, Prod; *Whispers*, Th, 89, CDN, Prod/Wr; *Welcome Home*, Th, 88, USA, Exec Prod; *Physical Evidence*, Th, 87, USA, Exec Prod; *Switching Channels*, Th, 87, USA, Exec Prod; *The Big Town*, Th, 86, USA, Co-Prod; *Meatballs III*, Th, 84, CDN, Prod; *Spacehunter*, Th, 83, USA, Prod; *Christmas Story*, Th, 83, USA, Prod Cons; *Porky's II*, Th, 82, USA, Prod; *Porky's*, Th, 81, USA,

Prod; *Rabid*, Th, 76, CDN, Assoc Prod; *Death Weekend*, Th, 75, CDN, Assoc Prod; *They Came From Within/Shivers*, Th, 74, CDN, Assoc Prod. 1958, Simcoe, Ontario. B.A.A.,

CARR, Warren H.
DGC. 691 - W. 32 Ave., Vancouver, BC V5Z 2J8 (604)872-4777. Coast Production Services Ltd., 150 - 555 Brooksbank Ave., North Vancouver, BC V7J 3S5 (604)983-5307.
Type of Production and Credits: Th Film-Prod/Exec Prod/PM; TV Film-Prod/Exec Prod/PM.
Genres: Drama-Th&TV; Comedy-Th&TV; Action-Th&TV; Horror-Th&TV.
Biography: Born 1950.
Selected Filmography: *Bingo*, Th, 90, USA, Exec Prod/PM; *The Russia House*, Th, 89, USA, PM (Cdn. seg); *Anything to Survive*, TV, 89, USA/CDN, Prod/PM; *We're No Angels*, Th, 88-89, USA, PM; *Cousins*, Th, 88, USA, PM; *The Accused*, Th, 87, USA, PM; *Distant Thunder*, Th, 87, USA, PM; *Roxanne*, Th, 86, USA, PM; *The Boy Who Could Fly*, Th, 85, USA, PM; *Going for Gold: The Bill Johnson Story*, TV, 85, CDN, PM; *The Stepfather*, Th, 85, USA, PM; *The Clan of the Cave Bear*, Th, 84, USA, 2nd AD; *Secrets of a Married Man*, TV, 84, USA, 2nd AD; *Labatt 1984 Rock Express Award*, TV, 84, CDN, Assoc Prod; *Year of the Dragon*, Th, 84, USA, 2nd AD.

CARTMER, Debbie
- see DIRECTORS

CASEY, Bill
- see CINEMATOGRAPHERS

CASTONGUAY, Viateur
4833, rue de Grandpré, Montréal, PQ H2H 2H9 (514) 287-9709. Les Films Tango, 1600 ave de Lorimier, Bureau 396, Montréal, PQ H2K 3W5 (514) 521-1984, #338.
Type de production et générique: l métrage-Prod; c métrage-Prod; TV film-Prod; TV vidéo-Prod.
Types d'oeuvres: Drame-C; Comédie-C; Documentaire-C&TV; Industriel-TV.
Curriculum vitae: Né à Montréal, Québec en 1949. Baccalauréat en communication à l'Université du Québec à Montréal, 76. μembre du conseil d'administration de la compagnie de distribution Cinéma Libre, 78-81. Président et producteur de Les Films Tango depuis 87. Nomination au Genie 89 pour meilleur court métrage dramatique, *Le Pied Tendre*.
Filmographie sélective: *L'Amour Volé*, C, 90, CDN, Prod; *Le Pied Tendre*, C, 88, CDN, Prod; *Le Gardien de l'Ile*, C, 85, CDN, Prod; *Une Histoire a se Raconte*, C, 79, CDN, Réal/Prod.

CASTRAVELLI, Claudio
- see DIRECTORS

CAULFIELD, Paul
ACCT. Mirus Communications Inc., 22 Rogers Rd., Brampton, ON L6X 1L8 (416)457-5117.
Type of Production and Credits: Th Short-Prod/Wr; TV Film-Prod/Dir; TV Video-Prod/Dir.
Genres: Drama-Th&TV; Documentary-TV; Educational-TV; Children's-TV.
Biography: Born 1950, Toronto, Ontario. Journalism Diploma, Humber College; Honours B.A., Film, York University. Editor, 7 years; produced for Film Arts, 3 years; formed Mirus Films, 76; Mirus Communications Inc., 86; Mirus Video (post production house), 86 . Has won 8 CFTA Awards; Gold Plaque, Chicago; Red Ribbon, American Film Festival.
Selected Filmography: *Getting Married, Staying Married/Marriage: The Early Years*, Ed, 85, CDN, Prod; *The Ordinary Bath*, Ed, 85, CDN, Prod/Dir; *Margaret Laurence*, Ed, 85, CDN, Prod/Dir; *The Edit*, Th, 84, CDN, Wr/Prod, (GENIE 86/CFTA); *Finding Out*, Ed, 84, CDN, Prod; *A Storyteller's Story*, TV, 84, CDN, Prod/Dir; *Sky High*, TV, 84, CDN, Prod; *John Doe*, TV, 82, CDN, Prod; *A Helping Hand*, "The Nature of Things", TV, 82, CDN, Prod; *Highwinding*, TV, 82, CDN, Prod; *New Tomorrow*, TV, 82, CDN, Assoc Prod; *Jimmy and Luke*, TV, 82, CDN, Assoc Prod; *The Only Critic Is Time*, TV, 81, CDN, Co-Wr/Co-Prod; *Reaching Out, Letting Go*, TV, 80, CDN, Co-Prod/Co-Dir; *Alligator Shoes*, Th, 80, CDN, Assoc Prod.

CAVAN, Susan
Accent Entertainment Corporation, 151 John St., Ste. 502, Toronto, ON M5V 2T2 (416)348-8722. FAX: 348-8721.
Type of Production and Credits: Th Film-Prod; TV Film-Prod.
Genres: Drama-Th&TV; Comedy-Th&TV.
Biography: Born 1952, Toronto, Ontario. LL.B., Queen's University, 76; called to Ontario Bar, 78; practised entertainment law with Roberts and Drabinsky; Vice-President, Business Affairs, Cineplex Corporation, 80; General Counsellor, International Cinema Corporation, 82; Partner and Senior Vice-President of Business and Legal Affairs, Alliance Entertainment Corp., 85 to 87; President, 87 to 89; Co-chairperson, Accent

Entertainment Corporation, 89 to present.
Selected Filmography: "Sweating Bullets" (22 eps), TV, 90-91, CDN/MEX, Exec Prod; *Wisecracks*, Th, 90, CDN, Exec Prod; *South of Wawa*, Th, 90, CDN, Prod; "Bordertown" (54 eps), TV, 89-90, CDN/F, Exec Prod; *The Bay Boy*, Th, 83, CDN/F, Exec Prod.

CHAMBERLAIN, David
4 Foxden Rd., Don Mills, ON M3C 2A9 (416)484-2600.
Type of Production and Credits: TV Film-Prod/Dir/Wr; Animation-TV.
Genres: Documentary-TV; Educational-TV; Children's-TV; Animation-TV.
Biography: Born 1941, St. Thomas, Ontario. B.A., Psychology, Geology, University of Western Ontario, 68; Honours B.A., Psychology, Geology, University of Toronto, 71. Has won numerous film awards including: Gold Medals, Houston for *The Final Chapter*; Bronze Medal, Blue Ribbon, New York, for *Landscape of Geometry*; Bronze Medals, New York and Houston, for *N.A.: Growth of a Continent*.
Selected Filmography: "Planet Under Pressure" (10 eps), TV, 91, CDN, Prod/Dir; "Conic Sections" (6 eps), TV, 90, CDN, Prod/Dir; "Trigonometric Functions" (12 eps), TV, 89, CDN, Prod/Dir; "Organic Chemistry" (12 eps), TV, 88, CDN, Prod/Dir; "Vectors" (6 eps), TV, 87, CDN, Prod/Dir; "Electromagnetism" (6 eps), TV, 87, CDN, Prod/Dir; "Photosynthesis" (6 eps), TV, 87, CDN, Prod/Dir; "Organic Evolution" (6 eps), TV, 86, CDN, Prod; "Electrochemistry" (6 eps), TV, 86, CDN, Prod; "Nuclear Physics" (6 eps), TV, 86, CDN, Prod; "Electron Arrangement and Bonding" (6 eps), TV, 85, CDN, Prod; "Geography Skills" (12 eps), TV, 85, CDN, Prod; *The Final Chapter?*, TV, 85, CDN/J/F, Co-Prod/Wr; "Landscape of Geometry" (8 eps), TV, 82, CDN, Prod/Dir; "N.A.: Growth of a Continent" (13 eps), TV, 80, CDN, Prod/Dir.

CHAMMAS, Robert
SMPTE, STLD, EPS, CSC. R.C. Productions, 132 Kingsley Ave., Dollard des Ormeaux, PQ H9B 1M9 (514)683-2527.
Type of Production and Credits: TV Film-DOP; TV Video-Prod/Dir/DOP; Th Film-DOP.
Genres: Drama-Th&TV; Comedy-Th&TV; Documentary-Th&TV; Current Affairs-TV; Education-TV; Commercials-Th&TV.
Biography: Born 1934, Guizeh, Egypt; Canadian citizenship. Languages: Arabic, French and English. Graduated from Cairo University and Ecole Universelle de Paris; diploma in Cinematography (motion picture). DOP, Egyptian Television, Cairo, 60-65; lighting director, CFCF TV, Montreal, 65-89; founder and director/producer of *Egyptian Television in Canada* since 73, and *The Greek Show* CFCF TV, 68-70. Has taught film production and motion picture camera technique, Algonquin College and University of Montreal; conducts seminars on lighting for TV and theatre.
Selected Filmography: "Egypt, Land of the Pharaohs" (weekly), TV, 79-91, CDN, Prod/Dir/DOP; "Snow Job", TV, 77-80, CDN, Light Dir; "Excuse My French", TV, 71-73, CDN, Light Dir; "John Allen Cameron", TV, 69-70, CDN, Light Dir; EXPO 67, In, 67, CDN, DOP; Fetina, Cm, 67, CDN, DOP; Star Hellas, Cm, 68, CDN, COP; Sursis, Cm, 69, CDN, Dop/Prod; *Pavillion - Ramses II*, TV, 80, CDN, DOP; *Visit of President Murbarak to Canada*, TV, 83, CDN, DOP/Prod/Dir.

CHAMPAGNE, Edith
CTPD. 39 Austin Ave., Toronto, ON M4M 1V7 (416)466-3103. CBC, 303 Mutual St., 5th Flr., Toronto, ON M5W 1E6 (416)975-7865.
Type of Production and Credits: TV Film-Prod; TV Video-Prod.
Genres: Documentary-TV; Current Affairs-TV; News-TV.
Biography: Born 1953, Winnipeg, Manitoba. Languages: English and French. B.A., University of Manitoba. Has worked in television production for 16 years and with the CBC National News since 87. Topics covered include: 1988 federal election; crumbling of the Berlin Wall; war in Panama; crisis at Oka; Meech Lake Accord; San Francisco earthquake.
Selected Filmography: *Runaways: 24 Hours on the Street*, TV, 87, CDN, Prod; "News" (items: Zundel, malpractice suits, elderly abuse), TV, 84-86, CDN, Prod; "Adoption" (5 eps), TV, 83, CDN, Prod/Pro Coord.

CHAMPAGNE, François
APFVQ, CFTA, ACCT. 566 Claremont, Westmount, PQ H3Y 2P1 (514)487-5384. Productions S.D.A., 1425 René-Lévesque, 10e étage, Montréal, PQ H3G 1T7 (514)866-1761.
Types de production et générique: c métrage-Prod; TV film-Prod; TV vidéo-Prod.
Types d'oeuvres: Drame-C&TV; Documentaire-C&TV; Education-C&TV;

Industriel-C&TV.
Curriculum vitae: Né en 1941. Etudes en administration, Université McGill; études RIA, H.E.C. Vice-Président, administrateur, 72-78; Président, administrateur depuis 78; producteur (projets spéciaux); producteur exécutif (documentaires), Productions S.D.A.
Filmographie sélective: "A plein temps" (132 eps), TV, 84-88, CDN, Prod; *La Faune au Québec I & II/O Québec*, In, 78-81, CDN, Prod; *Souffle du Nord*, ED, 81, CDN, prod; "Ecologie" (12 eps), ED, 80-81, CDN, Prod; "Ader" (42 eps), ED, 80-81, CDN Prod; "J'ai une histoire" (26 eps), ED, 80, CDN, Prod; *How to Start a Small Business*, ED, 79, CDN, Prod; *L'Espace d'un été*, C, 79, CDN, Co prod; "Français III - c'est-à-dire", ED, 74, CDN, Prod; *Ti-Mine Goulet Inc.*, In, 74, CDN, Prod; "Language Arts" (3 eps), ED, 73, CDN, Prod; "La Géographie" (4 eps), ED, 73, CDN, Prod; *L'Electricité/Churchill Falls/Face au défi*, In, 71-72, CDN, Prod; *La Motoneige au Québec*, ED, 72, CDN, Prod.

CHAN, David
Golden Harvest Communications (Ont.) Inc., 390 Bay St., Ste. 707, Toronto, ON M5H 2T6 (416)862-7880.
Type of Production and Credits: Th Film-Prod.
Genres: Comedy-Th; Action-Th; Children's-Th.
Biography: Born in 1951 in Hong Kong. Landed immigrant. Languages: English and Chinese. Education: M.A. in Radio-TV-Film from the University of Kansas. Awards: The Movie Awards, 1991.
Selected Filmography: *Teenage Mutant Ninja Turtles II*, Th, 91, USA, Prod; *Teenage Mutant Ninja Turtles*, Th, 90, USA, Prod; *The Proctector*, Th, 85, USA, Prod.

CHAPELLE, Nancy
306 Lonsdale Rd., Apt. 3, Toronto, ON M4V 1X4 (416)488-6997. Catalyst Entertainment Inc., 11 Bathurst St., Ste. 100, Toronto, ON M5V 2N8 (416)586-9634.
Type of Production and Credits: TV Video-Prod.
Genres: Comedy-TV; Documentary-TV; Children's-TV.
Biography: Born in 1959.
Selected Filmography: *'Tis A Gift*, "Shining Time Station", TV, 90, USA, Line Prod; "Spatz" (13 eps), TV, 89/90, CDN/GB, PM; *S.A.F.E., Substance Abuse Family Education*, ED, 90, CDN/USA, Prod; "Mosquito Lake" (19 eps), TV, 89, CDN, Co-Prod; "In Opposition" (6 eps), TV, 89, CDN, Co-Prod.

CHAPMAN, Christopher
- see DIRECTORS

CHAREST, Gaétan
3895, Edouard Montpetit, #1, Montréal, PQ H3T 1L1 (514)733-2093. FAX: 739-8798.
Types de production et générique: l métrage-Prod/Réal/Sc; TV film-Prod/Réal/Sc; TV vidéo-Prod/Réal/Sc.
Types d'oeuvres: Drame-C&TV; Documentaire-C&TV; Education-C&TV; Enfants-C; Annonces-TV; Affaires Publiques-TV.
Curriculum vitae: Né en 1951. Producteur, réalisateur, scénariste depuis 69. Travail à Radio Canada dès 77 comme pigiste, monteur film à l'information. En 84, obtient un statut de réalisateur à la Société Radio Canada. Entre temps, il fait diverses productions et réalisations tant pour le cinéma que pour la télévision ou la publicité. Travail dans des co-productions canadienne et américaines de 83 jusqu'à présent. Producteur d'émissions télévisuelles.
Filmographie sélective: "Bricolo Déco & Cie" (37 eps), TV, 91-92, CDN, Prod/Conc; "Québec en marche" (39 eps), TV, 91-92, CDN, Prod/Conc; *Annabelle*, C, 91-92, CDN, Sc/Réal; *Satellite Broadcast*, ED, 90, USA, Réal; *First Basri of Sant Darshan Singh Ji*, ED, 90, USA, Mont p pro/Réal; *Conference on Human Integration*, ED, 90, USA/IND/CDN, Sc; *El Paradisio*, TV, 88, USA, Réal; *San Juan de la Cruz*, TV, 88, USA, Réal; *Land of Love*, TV, 88, USA, Réal; *Best of Both Worlds*, TV, 88, USA, Réal; *The Divine Musician*, TV, 88, USA, Réal; *Quand on y pense...*, Ligue d'Epilepsie du Québec, In, 88, CDN, Réal/Sc; *Golden Age*, "Morning of the Golden Age" (pilot), TV, 88, CDN/USA/IND, Réal; *I Can Sing*, Marv Jonesi, MV, 88, USA, Sc; "Les Sages-Femmes", TV, 87, CDN, Réal/Sc.

CHAREST, Micheline
ACCT. 734 Lansdowne Ave., Montreal, PQ H3Y 1J7 (514)484-7469. Cinar Films Inc., 1207 St-André, Montreal, PQ H2L 3S8 (514)843-7070. FAX: 843-7080.
Type of Production and Credits: Th Film-Prod; TV Film-Prod; TV Video-Prod.
Genres: Variety-Th&TV; Children's-Th&TV.
Biography: Born 1953, London, England; Canadian citizenship. Distributor of features and TV for 15 years. President of

Cinar Films Inc.
Selected Filmography: "Young Robin Hood" (13 eps), TV, 91, CDN/F, Exec Prod; "A Bunch of Munsch" (7 eps), TV, 91, CDN, Exec Prod; "Les Intrépides" (26 eps), TV, 91, CDN/F, Exec Prod; "C.L.Y.D.E." (26 eps), TV, 91, CDN/F, Exec Prod; "The Real Story" (13 eps), TV, 91, CDN/F, Exec Prod; "Madeline" (13 eps), TV, 91, CDN/F, Exec Prod; *Stand-in for Danger*, TV, 90, CDN, Exec Prod; "Happy Castle" (13 eps), TV, 90, CDN, Exec Prod; "Smoggies" (52 eps), TV, 89, CDN/F, Exce Prod/Co-Prod(Cda); "The Wonderful Wizard of Oz" (52 eps), TV, 87, CDN, Exec Prod.

CHEIKES, Stephen
BCMPA, ACCT. 4497 Marine Dr., West Vancouver, BC V7W 2N8 (604)925-3141. The Beacon Group of Companies, 640 - 999 Canada Place, Vancouver, BC V6C 3E1 (604)641-1323.
Type of Production and Credits: Th Film-Exec Prod.
Genres: Drama-Th&TV; Comedy-Th.
Biography: Born in New York City in 1949. US citizen. State University of New York at Buffalo, B.A., 1971; Cornell Law School, J.D., 1974. President of Beacon Group Releasing Ltd. and Vice-President of Beacon Group Productions Ltd.
Selected Filmography: *Cold Front*, Th, 88-89, CDN, Exec Prod; *Quarantine*, Th, 88-89, CDN, Exec Prod; *The Heavenly Kid*, Th, 85, USA, Exec Prod.

CHERCOVER, Murray
34 Dunbar Rd., Toronto, ON M4W 2X6 (416)923-4113. Chercover Communications, 80 Bloor St. E., Ste. 3606, Toronto, ON M4W 3G9 (416)968-7876.
Type of Production and Credits: TV Film-Prod/Dir/PM/Dist; TV Video-Prod/Dir/PM/Dist.
Genres: Drama-Th&TV; Comedy-Th&TV; Action-Th&TV; Documentary-Th&TV.
Biography: Born 1929, Montreal, Quebec. Attended Academy of Radio and TV Arts, Toronto; School of Theatre, Neighbour-hood Playhouse, New York. 44-46. CFPA Radio, Port Arthur, Ont., 44-46; radio & theatre, Toronto, 46-48; Executive Director, Equity Library Theatre, NY, Director of various stock companies, 48-52; CBC, Toronto, Producer/Director, Drama, Special Programs & Comm'l Productions, 52-60; Exec. Producer, Baton Broadcasting, 60; Director of Program-ming, 61; V.P. Programming, 61; Chair-man of Programming, ITO (later CTV Network), 61; Chairman of Program Committee, CTV, 61; Exec. V.P and General Manager, 66; President & C.O.O., 67; President & Managing Director, 68; President & C.E.O., 86; Special Consultant, 90. Now President & C.E.O., Chercover Communications, President & Director, Avanti Manage-ment Ltd. Fellow and Founding Director, International Council, National Academy of Television Arts and Sciences; Founding Director, Children's Broadcast Institute; Co-Chairman, International Board of the Banff Television Festival; Director, International Film and TV Festival of New York; Vice-Chairman, General Assembly, Prix Italia Television Festival.

CHERNIACK, David
- see DIRECTORS

CHETWYND, Lionel
- see WRITERS

CHETWYND, Robin J. ✧
CFTA, SMPTE. (416)893-2522.
Type of Production and Credits: Th Film-Prod; TV Film-Prod/Dir/Wr; TV Video-Prod/Dir.
Genres: Variety-TV; Documentary-Th&TV; Industrial-TV; Sports-Th&TV.
Biography: Born 1941, Vancouver, BC. Business Administration, Journalism, Ryerson Polytechnical Institute. Past President, CFTA; Co-chairman, Co-producer, Annual Variety Club of Ontario Telethon, 83-85; Chetwynd Productions Inc. has received more than 350 national and international awards for industrial/ sponsored documentary and television production through thirty-seven years of operation.
Selected Filmography: *Kaptesting 1988*, In, 88, CDN, Prod/Dir; "Player's/GM Motorsport Series" (7 eps), TV, 88, CDN, Prod/Dir; *Schenley Awards* (3 shows), TV, 84-87, CDN, Prod; *Schweppes*, In, 87, CDN, Prod; *Playing for Keeps*, In, 87, CDN, Prod/Dir; *...Just for Living*, In, 87, CDN, Prod; *Sticks & Stones*, TV, 87, CDN, Prod/Dir; *Uniroyal World Junior Curling*, In, 87, CDN, Prod/Dir; *Schwepping 86*, In, 85-86, CDN, Prod; *The Good Life*, TV, 85-86, CDN, Prod; *Grey Cup*, In, 85, CDN, Prod/Dir; *No Place to Go*, TV, 85, CDN, Prod; "CFL Stars of the Week" (20 eps), TV, 85, CDN, Prod; *Kaptesting/Uniroyal*, In, 85-85, CDN, Prod; *Play Your Hand*, In, 85, CDN, Prod.

CHILCO, Cathy ✧
CTPDA. (604)986-4662.
Type of Production and Credits: TV Film-Prod; TV Video-Prod.

Genres: Comedy-TV; Variety-TV; Documentary-TV; Children's-TV.
Biography: Born Toronto, Ontario. B.A., University of Toronto. Taught for 2 years; 6 years experience as performer, stage/radio/TV; 9 years as associate producer at TVOntario.
Selected Filmography: "Venture" (52 eps), TV, 85-86, CDN, Prod; "Sesame Street" (sev seg), TV, 81-86, USA, Prod; "Futurescan" (7 eps), TV, 84, CDN, Prod; "Fabulous Festival" (7 eps), TV, 84, CDN, Co-Prod; *Rick Scott: Feet First*, TV, 84, CDN, Prod; *Ann Mortifee: Born to Live*, TV, 84, CDN, Prod; *Sessions*, TV, 83, CDN, Prod; *Super Variety Live with David Steinberg*, TV, 83, CDN, Prod; *Raffi's Really Big Show*, TV, 82, CDN, Prod; *David Steinberg Presents the Comedians*, TV, 82, CDN, Prod; *Flying Fruit Fly Circus*, TV, 81, CDN, Prod; *Raffi, Belugas and Friends*, TV, 81, CDN, Prod; *A Special Place*, TV, 80, CDN, Prod; "Canada after Dark" (daily), TV, 78-79, CDN, Prod; "90 Minutes Live" (5/wk), TV, 77-78, CDN, Prod.

CHRISTIE, Keith
- see DIRECTORS

CHURCH, Babs ✧
(416)962-5863.
Type of Production and Credits: Th Film-Prod; TV Film-Prod; TV Video-Prod.
Genres: Drama-Th&TV; Documentary-TV; Educational-TV.
Biography: Born 1929, Calgary, Alberta. B.A., B.Ed., University of Manitoba; M.A., Education, McGill University. Winner of several awards including Gold at New York, Columbus, B'nai B'rith Human Rights Award.
Selected Filmography: *All in Together*, TV, 87-88, CDN, Prod; "Passion for Food" (5 eps), TV, 86-87, CDN, Prod; *Taking Care*, Th, 86, CDN, Assoc Prod; *By Our Own Hands*, TV, 85-86, CDN, Prod; "Men in Transition" (3 eps), TV, 84-85, CDN, Prod; "Changing Paces" (4 eps), TV, 84-85, CDN, Prod; *Don't Take It Easy*, TV, 83-84, CDN, Prod; "Everybody's Children" (8 eps), TV, 80-84, CDN, Prod; *Nothing to Be Sorry About*, TV, 82-83, CDN, Prod/Dir; "One and All" (4 eps), TV, 82—83, CDN, Prod; "Not One of the Crowd" (5 eps), TV, 81-82, CDN, Prod; *Away from Home*, TV, 80-81, CDN, Prod.

CICCORITTI, Gerard
- see DIRECTORS

CLARK, Barry
WGAw. Barry Clark Productions, 11811 West Olympic Blvd., Los Angeles, CA 90064 (213)478-7878. FAX: 477-7166.
Type of Production and Credits: Th Film-Wr/Dir/Prod; Th Short-Wr/Dir/Prod; TV Film-Wr/Dir/Prod; TV Video-Wr/Dir/Prod.
Genres: Documentary-TV; Educational-TV; Drama-Th; Action-Th&TV.
Biography: Born 1937, Lethbridge, Alberta. B.Sc., Chemistry, McGill University, 57; M.A., Physics, Harvard University, 59. Board Member, Jackson Hole Wild Life Film Festival. *The Big Six* won 8 awards, Hollywood TV Festival, 78; *American Diary* won a Cine Golden Eagle, Golden Babe, Chicago, 84; *The Wild World* won Silver Award, Houston Film Festival, 89, Bronze Award, New York Film Festival, 89; *Martin Luther King: The Letter from Birmingham Jail* won Cine Golden Eagle, 88; "Animal Life" series won Cine Golden Eagle, 91 and Silver Screen Award, US Industrial Film & Video Festival, 91.
Selected Filmography: *Monkeys on the Edge*, TV, 90, USA, Prod/Wr; *Yellowstone on Fire*, TV, 90, USA, Wr; *Wild Colorado*, TV, 90, USA, Wr; *Land of the Llamas*, "Nova", TV, 90, USA, Wr; *Under the Emerald Sea*, TV, 89, USA, Prod/Wr; "Adventures in Diving" (26 eps), TV, 88-90, USA, Prod/Wr; *Martin Luther King: The Letter from Birmingham Jail*, TV, 88, USA, Prod/Dir/Wr; "The Wild World" (5 eps), ED, 88, USA, Prod/Dir/Wr; "American Diary" (5 eps), TV, 84, USA, Prod/Dir/Wr; "American Chronicles" (12 eps), TV, 87, USA, Prod/Dir/Wr; "Danger Bay" (2 eps), TV, 85, CDN, Wr; *Eleanor Roosevelt: An Uncommon Woman*, "Legends", TV, 80, USA, Dir/Wr; "Wonderful World of Disney" (5 eps), TV, 72-78, USA, Wr; *Mysteries, Myths, & Legends*, "Encyclopaedia Brittanica Presents", TV, 81, USA, Dir/Wr; "Salty" (2 eps), TV, 75, USA, Wr.

CLARK, Bob
- see DIRECTORS

CLARK, Louise ✧
DGC. (416)962-5092.
Type of Production and Credits: Th Film-PM/Prod; TV Film-PM/Prod.
Genres: Drama-TV; Comedy-Th; Documentary-Th&TV.
Biography: Born 1954, Sarnia, Ontario. Production manager, associate producer on 35 documentaries since 76; producer/line producer, 85-86. Has worked on many award-winning films.
Selected Filmography: *A Winter Tan*, Th, 87, CDN, Prod/Co-Dir; *A Dance for*

Modern Times, TV, 87, CDN, Prod; "The Dance Makers" (6 eps), TV, 87, CDN, Prod; *World Drum Festival*, TV, 86, CDN, Line Prod; "Brothers by Choice" (6 eps), TV, 86, CDN, Co-Prod; *Blue Snake*, TV, 85, CDN, Prod; *Magnificat*, TV, 85, CDN, Co-Prod; *All That Bach*, TV, 85, CDN, Co-Prod; *Hockey Night*, TV, 84, CDN, PM; *After the Axe*, Th, 81, CDN, PM.

CLARK, Paulle
SAG, AFTRA, BAE, ACTRA, ACCT. Horus Productions Inc., P.O. Box 6118, El Prado, NM 87529 (505)758-4423.
Type of Production and Credits: Th Film-Prod; Th Short-Prod/Dir; TV Film-Prod/Dir; TV Video-Prod/Dir.
Genres: Drama-Th&TV; Documentary-Th&TV; Educational-Th&TV; Children's-Th&TV.
Biography: Born in Prince Rupert, BC; US resident alien. Winner of many awards, including Columbus, Chicago, New York, Birmingham, Yorkton.
Selected Filmography: *The Sante Fe Symphony*, TV, 91, USA, Prod/Dir; "OWL-TV" (30 eps), TV, 84-88, CDN/USA, Prod/Dir/Wr; *Easter in Igloolik*, TV, 87, CDN/USA, Prod/Dir; *Free Dive*, TV, 80, CDN, Prod/Dir; "Fishtales" (13 eps), TV, 77, CDN, Prod/Dir; *The October Crisis* (Fr and Eng), TV, 74, CDN, Pro Spv; *The Pyx*, Th, 72, CDN, Assoc Prod; *What's the Matter with Helen?*, Th, 69, USA, Assist to Prod; *How Awful about Alan*, Th, 69, USA,, Assist Prod; *Oedipus the King*, Th, 67, GB, Assist to Prod.

CLARK, Ron
- see WRITERS

CLARKSON, Adrienne
ACTRA, ACCT, ATPD. CBC, Box 500, Station A, Toronto, ON M5W 1E6 (416)975-6885. Michael Levine, Goodman & Goodman, 20 Queen St. W., Toronto, ON M5H 1V5 (416)979-2211.
Type of Production and Credits: TV Film-Wr/Host/Exec Prod; TV Video-Wr/Host/Exec Prod.
Genres: Documentary-TV; Current Affairs-TV.
Biography: Born in 1939. 4 ACTRA awards, plus others too numerous to mention. Has hosted over 2,000 television programmes and written many.
Selected Filmography: "Adrienne Clarkson Presents", TV, 89-91, CDN, Host/Prod; "Adrienne Clarkson's Summer Festival", TV, 88-89, CDN, Host/Prod; "the fifth estate", TV, 76-82, CDN, Host/Prod, (ACTRA); "Adrienne At Large", TV, 75-76, CDN, Host, (ACTRA); "Take 30" (10 seasons), TV, 65-75, CDN, Host, (ACTRA).

CLERMONT, Nicolas
ACFTP, APFVQ, ACCT. Filmline Group Inc., 410 St. Nicolas, Ste. 600, Montreal, PQ H2Y 2P5 (514)288-5888. FAX: 288-8083.
Type of Production and Credits: Th Film-Prod; TV Film-Prod.
Genres: Drama-Th; Children's-Th; Drama-TV.
Biography: Born in France; Canadian resident since 68. Started as assistant director in France; producer/director in educational television, Montreal. Co-founder, Can-America Film Corporation, 80; co-founder, Filmline International Inc., 84; co-founder, Filmline Group Inc., 90.
Selected Filmography: *Bethune - The Making of a Hero*, Th, 90, CDN/F/RC, Prod; *Le Palanquin des Larmes*, Th, 89, CDN/F, Co-prod; *Wild Thing*, Th, 86, USA/CDN, Prod; *Toby McTeague*, Th, 85, CDN, Prod; *The Blue Man*, Th, 85, CDN, Exec Prod; *Riding Fast*, Th, 80, CDN, Prod.

COACH, Ken
CTPDA. 4158 W. 15th Ave., Vancouver, BC V6R 3A5 (604)222-3743. Damn Good Productions Ltd., PO Box 2865, Vancouver, BC V6B 3X4 (604)662-6868.
Type of Production and Credits: TV Film-Wr/Prod/Report/Narr.
Genres: Documentary-Th&TV; Educational-Th&TV; Current Affairs-TV; News-TV.
Biography: Born in 1951 in Manitoba but raised on the west coast. More than 21 years experience in documentary, news and current affairs in newspapers, TV and magazines. Spent 2 years as a freelancer in New York City. "The Best Years" received an Honorable Mention at Columbus. "Diversity", the pilot, received a Media Human Rights award and as a reporter/producer, received 2 Can-Pro awards while working at CITV News in Edmonton.
Selected Filmography: "The Best Years" (54 eps), TV, 89-91, CDN, Exec Prod; "Diversity" (pilot), TV, 90, CDN, Exec Prod; "Diversity (5 eps), TV, 90, CDN, Exec Prod; *The Dream Fields of W.P. Kinsella*, TV/ED, 89, CDN/USA, Exec Prod; "Newscentre", CBC Vancouver (daily), TV, 87-89, CDN, Sr Prod; "CTV National News" (daily), TV, 86, CDN, Assign Prod; "Calgary Newshour", CBC Calgary (daily), TV, 84-86, CDN, Exec

Prod; CITV News (daily), TV, 80-83, CDN, Report/Prod.
COATSWORTH, David
- see PRODUCTION MANAGERS
COCHRAN, Andrew
ACCT, CFTPA, NSFVPA, WGC. 5157 Morris St., #101, Halifax, NS B3J 3P2 (902)423-7273. Andrew Cochran Associates Limited, 1820 Hollis St., Ste. 300, Halifax, NS B3J 1W4 (902)421-9777. FAX: 425-8659.
Type of Production and Credits: TV Video-Prod/Wr/Dir; TV Film-Prod/Wr.
Genres: Documentary-TV; Children's-TV; Drama-TV; Current Affairs-TV.
Biography: Born 1952, Halifax, Nova Scotia. CJCH Radio & Television news reporter/writer, 70-72 (Halifax); news/current affairs producer/writer, CTV Network, 72-79 (Toronto); Executive Producer, CBC Network, 79-80, (Winnipeg); business development consultant, 80-84 (Toronto); established Atlantic Canada's first independent production facility, Studio East Limited, 1984 (Halifax); President, Andrew Cochran Associates Limited, 84-present (Halifax).
Selected Filmography: *Discoveries*, TV, 91, CDN, Exec Prod/Wr/Dir; *Characters Incorporated: The Friendship Tour*, TV, 90, CDN, Exec Prod/Wr/Dir; *Welcome to Ceilidh*, TV, 89, CDN, Exec Prod/Wr; *The Argon Quest*, TV, 89, CDN, Exec Prod; "Blizzard Island" (14 eps), TV, 87-88, CDN, Exec Prod/Prod; *Nova Scotia Videowall*, In, 86, CDN, Exec Prod/Wr; "The Medicine Show", TV, 79-80, CDN, Exec Prod/Series Prod; "CTV National News" & "CTV News Specials" (daily), TV, 77-78, CDN, Exec Prod; "CTV Reports", TV, 77, CDN, Sr Prod; "Canada AM" (daily), TV, 74-77, CDN, Series Prod; "W5" (weekly), TV, 72-74, CDN, Field Prod.
COCK, Peter J.
- see DIRECTORS
COHEN, Annette
CFTPA, ACCT. 447 Ontario St., Toronto, ON M5A 2V9 (416)920-3745. 25 Imperial St., Ste. 500, Toronto, ON M5P 1C1 (416)483-8018.
Type of Production and Credits: Th Film-Prod/Wr; TV Film-Prod/Wr; TV Video-Prod/Wr.
Genres: Drama-Th&TV.
Biography: Born 1935, Toronto, Ontario. B.A., M.A., University of Toronto. Feature film producer. Began working in film and television 14 years ago writing scripts for CBC television and TVO. Has directed several documentaries and dramas. President and C.E.O. of Primedia Pictures. Divides time between film producing and other business activities.
Selected Filmography: *Unfinished Business*, Th, 83, CDN, Co-Prod; "Romance" (6 eps), TV, 82, CDN, Co-Prod; *Love* (1 part), Th, 80, CDN, Dir; *The Doll Factory*, TV, 78, CDN, Co-Prod/Dir/Co-Wr; *One People, One Destiny*, TV, 77, CDN, Prod/Dir; *Nellie McClung*, TV, 77, CDN, Wr; "Royal Suite" (1 eps), TV, 77, CDN, Wr; "King of Kensington" (1 eps), TV, 76, CDN, Wr; *The Visible Woman*, ED, 76, CDN, Co-Prod/Co-Dir; *True North* (3 seg), TV, 75, CDN, Wr; *Report Metric* (100 seg), TV, 75, CDN, Wr.
COHEN, Ronald I.
The Ronald Cohen Film Co., 410, rue St-Nicholas, Suite 600, Montréal, PQ J2Y 2P5 (514) 288-5888.
Type of Production and Credits: Th Film-Prod; TV Film-Prod.
Genres: Drama-Th&TV; Comedy-Th&TV.
Biography: Born 1943, Montreal, Quebec. Languages: English and French. B.A., cum laude, Government, Harvard University, 64; B.C.L., (first class honours), McGill University, 68; member, Quebec Bar Association. Taught Law, 4 years, McGill University. Vice-President, Consumers Association of Canada, 5 years; then Senior Counsel, to Quebec Police Commission Inquiry into Organized Crime, 74-77. Started producing feature films, 77; Chairman, Academy of Canadian Cinema & Television, 80-82, 85-87; Director, Centaur Theatre, Montreal; Director, Geordie Productions, Montreal. *Ticket to Heaven* won Best Picture, Taormina, Italy.
Selected Filmography: *Champagne Charlie* (mini-series), TV, 89, CDN, Co-Prod; *Race for the Bomb* (mini-series), TV, 85-86, CDN/F, Co-Prod; *Draw!*, TV, 83, CDN/USA, Prod; *Cross Country*, Th, 82, CDN, Exec Prod; *Ticket to Heaven*, Th, 80, CDN, Exec Prod, (GENIE); *Harry Tracy*, Th, 80, CDN, Prod; *Middle Age Crazy*, Th, 79, CDN/USA, Co-Prod; *Running*, Th, 78, CDN, Co-Prod; *Power Play*, Th, 77, CDN/GB, Co-Exec Prod.
COHEN, Sidney M.
- see DIRECTORS
COLE, Janis
Spectrum Films, P.O. Box 5613, Stn. A, Toronto, ON M5W 1N8 (416)967-6361.
Type of Production and Credits: Th

Film-Prod/Dir.
Genres: Documentary-Th; Educational-TV.
Biography: Born 1954, Chatham, Ontario. Studied Media Arts, Sheridan College, 2 years. *Hookers on Davie* won a Gold Plaque, Chicago, Red Ribbon, American Film Festival and was nominated for a Genie, 85. *P4W: Prison for Women* won Best Film of Festival at Yorkton, Red Ribbon, American Film Festival and a 1982 Genie.
Selected Filmography: *Shaggie*, Th, 90, CDN, Prod/Dir/Wr/Ed; *Calling the Shots*, Th, 88, CDN, Co-Prod/Co-Dir/Co-Ed; *The Making of Agnes of God*, TV, 85, CDN, Co-Prod/Co-Dir/Co-Ed; *Hookers on Davie*, Th, 84, CDN, Co-Prod/Co-Dir/Co-Ed; *P4W: Prison for Women*, Th, 81, CDN, Co-Prod/Co-Dir/Co-Ed, (GENIE 82); *Thin Line*, Th, 77, CDN, Co-Prod/Co-Dir/Co-Ed; *Minimum Charge No Cover*, Th, 76, CDN, Co-Prod/Co-Dir/Co-Ed.

COLLEY, Peter
- see WRITERS

COLLIER, Mike
DGC. 1915 W. 35 Ave., Vancouver, BC V6M 1H1 (604)266-2878. Yaletown Productions Inc., 990 Horner St., Ste. 304, Vancouver, BC V6B 2W7 (604)669-3543.
Type of Production and Credits: TV Film-Ed.
Genres: Drama-TV; Documentary-Th&TV; Educational-Th&TV; Industrial-Th&TV.
Biography: Born 1947, London, England; Canadian citizenship. Bachelor of Science., Simon Fraser University. Twenty-three years experience in Vancouver film industry; created special colour tinting for *McCabe and Mrs. Miller*. Has won over forty awards for his films, including Gold Award, Chicago; Gold Screen Awards, US Industrial Film Festival; Gold Award, Houston; Gold Camera, US Industrial Film & Video Festival; Silver, ITVA; Bronze, National Educational Film & Video Festival.
Selected Filmography: *Canada's Magnificent Snowbirds*, TV, 91, CDN, Prod; *Come Fly With Us*, Th, 91, CDN, Prod; *Speedy Auto Glass*, In, 90, CDN, Prod/Dir; *A Sense of Wonder*, ED, 89, CDN, Prod/Dir; *Land Above the Trees*, Th, 88, CDN, Dir; *Earthquakes in Canada?*, TV, 87, CDN, Dir; *Canadian Pacific*, Th, 86, CDN, Dir; *B.C., The Rockies to the Pacific*, TV, 86, CDN, Dir; *The World in a City*, TV, 85, CDN, Dir/Ed; *An Exchange of Value*, TV, 84, CDN, Dir, (CFTA); *Salmon Spectacular*, TV, 82, CDN, Ed; "Huck Finn" (8 eps), TV, 81, CDN, Ed; *Valley of the Grizzly*, In, 80, CDN, Dir/Ed; *Winter Survival*, In, 79, CDN, Dir/Ed; *Pacific Celebration*, TV, 78, CDN, Dir/Ed.

COLLINS, Alan
- see DIRECTORS

COLLINS, Neil
- see WRITERS

CONNOLLY, Bea Broda
8 Lisa St., #807, Bramalea, ON L6T 4S7 (416)796-3446. BC Pictures, 245 Britannia Rd. E., Mississauga, ON L4Z 2Y7 (416)890-3400.
Type of Production and Credits: TV Video-Prod/Wr.
Genres: Drama-Th&TV; Musical-Th&TV; Documentary-TV; Industrial-TV.
Biography: Born in Winnipeg, Manitoba. B.A., Psychology and English; studies toward B.F.A., University of Manitoba. Grade 10 piano; grade 9 voice; 8 years dance. 4 years as Host-Coordinator of "CKND Magazine" and "Manitoba Morning". 1-1/2 years as weather announcer, "CKND 6:00 News" and 2-1/2 seasons as Host of "The Music Room". Several acting courses in Winnipeg, Toronto and Los Angeles; some small acting parts. Host of "Discover Your World" and Associate Producer for 1-1/2 years. For 3 years has produced, written, narrated and hosted for her company, BC Pictures, which are producers of "Passport To Adventure," a travel show on many PBS stations and Vision TV.
Selected Filmography: "Passport To Adventure" (13 eps), TV, 89-90, CDN, Co-Prod/Wr/Host; *Canoe Ontario*, TV, 90, CDN, Co-Prod/Wr/Host; *Colour Painting on the Desktop*, In, 90, CDN/USA, Host/Narr; *Aruba Bonbini*, In, 90, CDN, Co-Prod/Wr/Host; *Panorama of the USSR*, In, 90, CDN, Co-Prod/Wr/Host; *CUBA*, In, 89, CDN, Co-Prod/Wr/Host.

COOK, Heather
ATPD. 74 Spruce Hill Rd., Toronto, ON M4E 3G3 (416)975-6902. CBC, Box 500, Stn. A, Toronto, ON M5E 1E6 (416)975-6902.
Type of Production and Credits: TV Film-Prod/Dir/Wr.
Genres: Drama-TV; Documentary-TV.
Biography: Born in Montreal, Quebec. Languages: English, French and some Spanish. B.A., Bishop's University. Has been journalist, feature writer and was host and writer of own radio program. Joined CBC TV, 68, as researcher; now works

there as writer/ director/producer on series "The Nature of Things". Has won several awards, including Columbus and N.Y.
Selected Filmography: *You Must Have Been a Bilingual Baby,*"The Nature of Things", TV, 90, CDN, Prod/Dir/Wr; *I Never Planned on This*, "The Nature of Things", TV, 89, CDN, Prod/Dir; *The Children Who Learned to Listen (Ears to Hear, 76)*, "The Nature of Things", TV, 87, CDN, Prod/Dir/Wr; *The Familiar Face of Love,* "The Nature of Things", TV, 86, CDN, Prod/Dir; "A Planet for the Taking" (2 eps), TV, 85, CDN, Prod/Dir; *Bring Back My Bonnie,* "The Nature of Things", TV, 82, CDN, Prod/Dir; *Twins,* "Nova", TV, 82, CDN/USA, Prod/Dir; *Twins: And Then There Were Two,* "The Nature of Things", TV, 81, CDN, Prod/Dir; *Skin - The Bare Necessity,* "The Nature of Things", TV, 80, CDN, Prod/Dir; *Poisoned Playgrounds/One, Two, Three-Zero,* "The Nature of Things", TV, 79, CDN, Prod/Dir/Wr; "Science Magazine", TV, 75-79, CDN, Prod/Dir/Wr; *Dreams/Sleep,* "The Nature of Things" (2 eps), TV, 78, CDN, Prod/Dir; *Newborn,* "The Nature of Things", TV, 77, CDN, Prod/Dir; *Children's Hospital,* "The Nature of Things", TV, 75, CDN, Prod/Dir/Wr; *Out of the Mouth of Babes*, "The Nature of Things", TV, 74, CDN, Prod/Dir/Wr.

COOKE, Lindsay Ann
Yellowknife Films, Box 2562 - 3501 Ingraham Dr., Yellowknife, NT X1A 2P9 (403)873-8610.
Type of Production and Credits: Th Short-Prod/Wr; TV Film-Prod/Wr; TV Video-Prod/Wr.
Genres: Documentary-TV; Educational-TV; Animation-TV; Commercials-TV; Industrial-TV.
Biography: Born 1952, Renfrew, Ontario. Canadian citizen. Educated in Political Science at the University of Toronto. Has lived in the Northwest Territories since 1973. Lived in the bush as a fisherman for two years. Began writing for TV, 1978, for CBC North; started producing films for TV, 1983. Is a partner in Yellowknife Films. Has produced and written three award-winning films, *The Emerging North* for Expo 86, *A Fishing Tale* and *Whole Language - A Northern Experience.*
Selected Filmography: *The Northern Lights,* TV, 91, CDN, Prod/Wr; *Whole Language - A Northern Experience,* ED, 90, CDN, Prod/Wr; *Spirit Run,* Cm, 91, CDN, Dir; *Nursing North of 60,* In, 90, CDN, Prod/Wr; *Kingalik Jamboree,* TV, 89, CDN, Dir/Wr; *Firearm Safety,* Cm, 88, CDN, Prod/Wr; *Get an Education,* Cm, 88, CDN, Prod/Wr; *The Sky's the Limit,* In, 87, CDN, Prod/Wr; *The Emerging North,* Th, 86, CDN, Prod/Wr; *A Fishing Tale,* TV, 85, CDN, Prod/Wr.

COOPER, Richard
- see WRITERS

COOPER, Robert
ACCT. H.B.O., 2049 Century Park E., Suite 4100, Los Angeles, CA 90067 USA. (213)201-9405.
Type of Production and Credits: Th Film-Prod; TV Film-Prod.
Genres: Drama-Th&TV; Comedy-Th&TV; Action-TV, Documentary-TV.
Biography: Born 1944. Sr. Vice-President, HBO Pictures. *The Terry Fox Story* won an ACE Award, Best Dramatic Presenta-tion; *Murderers Among Us: The Simon Wiesenthal Story* won an ACE award, Best Dramatic Presentation; *Rapists: Can They Be Stopped?* won an ACE award, Best Documentary.
Selected Filmography: *Murderers Among Us: The Simon Wiesenthal Story,* TV, 88, GB, Prod; *Glitz,* TV, 88, USA, Prod; *Vanishing Act,* TV, 86, USA, Prod; "Adderly" (11 eps), TV, 86, CDN, Co-Exec Prod; *Murder in Space,* TV, 85, CDN/USA, Prod; *Rapists - Can They Be Stopped?,* "America Undercover", TV, 85, USA, Exec Prod; *Between Friends,* TV, 83, CDN, Co-Prod; *The Guardian,* TV, 83, CDN/USA, Prod; *The Terry Fox Story,* Th, 82, CDN, Prod, (GENIE); *Middle Age Crazy,* Th, 79, CDN/USA, Co-Prod; *Running,* Th, 78, CDN, Co-Prod.

COPELAND, Greg
DGC, ACCT. 42 Gainsborough Rd., Toronto, ON M4L 3C2 (416)465-3520. 9 Channel 9 Court, Scarborough, ON M1S 4B5 (416)299-2360.
Type of Production and Credits: TV Film-Assoc Prod/PM; TV Video-PM.
Genres: Drama-TV; Comedy-TV; Variety-TV; Action-TV.
Biography: Born in Toronto, Ontario. Has worked in both film and videotape. Has also worked on animation (children's), commercials, music video, educational, sports and news. Completed work in various capacities on over 200 episodes for TV and 2 MOWs.
Selected Filmography: "E.N.G." (62 eps), TV, 90-91, CDN, Assoc Prod; "E.N.G." (pilot), TV, 89-90, CDN, PM; "T and T" (20 eps), TV, 89, USA, Assoc Prod; "T and T" (pilot), TV, 89, USA, PM; "Diamonds" (22 eps), TV, 88, USA/CDN/F, PM; "Raccoons" (3 eps), TV, 88,

USA, Assoc Prod; *Hotdiggety*, TV, 87, Assoc Prod; "Loving Friends & Perfect Couples" (80 eps), TV, 85-86, USA, Prod Spv; *A Case of Libel*, TV, 85, USA, Prod Spv.

CORDER, Sharon
- see WRITERS

COUELLE, Marcia
ACCT. 165 Côte Ste-Catherine, #1112, Outremont, PQ H2V 2A7 (514)271-4933. FAX: 271-9705.
Type of Production and Credits: Th Film-Prod; Th Short-Prod; TV Film-Prod; TV Video-Prod.
Genres: Drama-Thh&TV; Documentary-Th&TV; Children's-Th&TV.
Biography: Born 1943, Philadelphia, Pennsylvania; US citizen; landed immigrant, Canada. Languages: English, French and Italian. Began film career in distribution, 69; co-owner, Vice-President, Les Productions Prisma Inc., 74-86; has served on Board of Directors of Cinématheque Québécoise, APFQ, CFI, ACCT Montreal, FUND; board member, Banff Television Foundation and pre-selection committee, Banff Television Festival. *Les Bons Débarras* won 8 Genie Awards including Best Picture, 80; *Comme les six doigts de la main* won le Prix de la Critique Québécoise. Since 86, freelance consultant on matters related to film and television.
Selected Filmography: "Livre ouvert" (26 eps), TV, 84-85, CDN, Co-Prod; *Earthwatch* (Expo 86), Th, 85, CDN, Co-Prod; "Profession: écrivain" (13 eps), TV, 83, CDN, Co-Prod; "Zigzag" (6 eps), TV, 83, CDN, Co-Prod; *Le Cahier Noir*, "Secrets diplomatiques", TV, 82, F, Co-Prod; *Le Plus Beau Jour de ma vie...*, Th, 80, CDN, Co-Prod; *On n'est pas des anges*, Th, 80, CDN, Co-prod; *Thetford au milieu de notre vie*, Th, 79, CDN, Co-Prod; *Les Servantes du bon Dieu*, Th, 78, CDN, Co-Prod; *Les Bons Débarras*, Th, 78, CDN, Co-Prod, (GENIE); *Montréal*, "Les Grandes Villes du monde", TV, 78, F, Co-Prod; *Corridors*, Th, 78, CDN, Co-Prod; *Comme les six doigts de la main*, Th, 77, CDN, Co-Prod; *Le St-Laurent*, "Les Grands Fleuves du monde", TV, 76, F, Co-Prod; "L'Amour quotidien" (13 eps), TV, 75, CDN, Co-Prod.

COUSINEAU, Gaston
ACCT. 234 Lakeside, Ville de Lac Brome, PQ J0E 1V0 (514) 242-1389. Les Productions Via Le Monde (DB) Inc., 326 rue St-Paul ouest, Montréal,PQ H2Y 2A3 (514) 285-1658.
Types de production et générique: l metrage-Prod; c metrage-Prod; TV film-Prod; TV video-Prod.
Types d'oeuvres: Drame-C&TV; Documentaire-C&TV; Education-TV.
Curriculum vitae: Né en 1942, Sturgeon Falls, Ontario. Langues: français et anglais. Plus de 25 années d'expérience dans le domaine des communications dont les 15 dernières consacrées à la production cinématographique et télévisuelle. Fonde sa propre compagnie de production, Les Productions Vidéodio Inc.; Directeur général, APFTQ, 83; reprend activités de producteur à temps complet, Productions SDA, 85; entre au service des Productions Via le Monde (Daniel Bertolino) Inc. en décembre, 88.
Filmographie sélective: "Journal de l'histoire" (65 eps), TV, 90-91, CDN, Prod; "Les Années Pilule" (2 eps), TV, 91, CDN, Prod dél; "Vie Privée" (22 eps), TV, 90-91, CDN, Prod; "Education: Option 2000" (2 eps), TV, 90, CDN, Prod; "Bien dans sa peau" (26 eps), TV, 89-90, CDN, Prod; "Fortunes d'ici et d'ailleurs" (8 eps), TV, 89-90, CDN/F, Prod; "Rock" (5 eps), TV, 88, CDN, Prod, (GEMEAUX); *Et l'enfant alors...*, ED, 87, CDN, Prod; *The Morning Man*, C, 85, CDN, Prod; "Kamouraska" (4 eps), TV, 83, CDN, Dir p pro; *Doux Aveux*, C, 81, CDN, Prod; "Les P 'tits Plats du Québec" (13 eps), TV, 80, CDN, Prod; *Les Montagnais*, TV, 79, CDN, Prod; "Un Pays, Un goût, Une Manière" (28 eps), TV, 76-79, CDN, Prod; *Le Dernier des Coureurs de Bois*, TV, 78, CDN, Prod.

COUTURE, Suzette
- see WRITERS

COWLING, Barry
ACTRA, ACCT, CFTPA. 1166 Waterloo St., Halifax, NS B3H 3L4 (902)422-2209. Citadel Communications, 1652 Barrington St., Halifax, NS B3J 2A2 (902)421-1326.
Type of Production and Credits: Th Film-Prod/Wr; TV Video-Prod/Wr.
Genres: Drama-TV; Variety-TV; Documentary-TV; Commercials-TV.
Biography: Born 1943, Cornwall, England; Canadian citizenship. Vice-President, Advertising, 69; Executive Producer NFB Atlantic Region Studio, 82-85; President, Citadel Communications since 85. Wrote *Blackwood* which was nominated for an Oscar, 76. Many radio, TV and print advertising awards including Art Directors Club of New York for TV commercial, 70. Has written, produced and directed more than 100 documentary films and numerous commercials.
Selected Filmography: *Bruce Curtis:*

Journey Into Darkness, TV, 91, CDN, Prod; *The Joy of Singing*, TV, 90, CDN, Exec Prod/Wr; *Buskers: The Art of the Street Performer*, TV, 88, CDN, Prod/Wr; "Imperfect Union" (5 eps), TV, 88, CDN, Wr; *Margaret Perry*, ED, 88, CDN, Exec Prod; *Black Mother, Black Daughter*, ED, 88, CDN, Prod Cons/Script Cons; "Aquaculture Videos", In, 87, CDN, Wr/Prod; *Dawn of the Dinosaurs*, In, 87, CDN, Prod/Wr; *Musical Magic*, TV, 85, CDN, Wr; *Herbicide Trials*, TV, 84, CDN, Exec Prod; *Singlehanders*, TV, 82, CDN, Exec Prod; *Miller Britain*, TV, 81, CDN, Wr/Prod; *Last Days of Living*, TV, 80, CDN, Wr.

COX, Kirwan
WGC (ACTRA). Box 338, Rigaud, PQ J0P 1P0 (514)451-4664.
Type of Production and Credits: TV Film-Prod; TV Video-Prod.
Genres: Documentary-TV.
Biography: Born in 1946 in Boston, Mass. Canadian citizen. B.A. History, McGill University, 1969. Organized the Association of Canadian Film Cooperatives in 1970. Executive Director, Canadian Filmmakers Dist. Centre, 1971-73. Lecturer on Canadian TV and cinema, Seneca College and McGill University, 1972-76. On the Board of Toronto Filmmakers Cooperative, Canadian Film Institute and the Council of Canadian Filmmakers, 1973-79. Director of Research and Policy Development, NFB, 1980-84. Freelance policy consultant and independent TV documentary producer, 1985 to date. *America, Love It or Leave It* won 1st Prize, Politics and Government Category, American Film & Video Festival, 1991.
Selected Filmography: *America, Love It or Leave It*, TV, 90, CDN, Prod/Res; *My Children Are Going To Be Something/Courage to Change*, TV, 86, CDN, Prod; *Has Anybody Here Seen Canada?*, TV/ED, 78, CDN, Prod; *Home Movies*, "Great Canadian Culture Hunt", TV, 77, CDN, Res/Interv; *Dreamland*, TV/ED, 74, CDN, Prod; *Montreal Main*, Th, 73, CDN, Assoc Prod.

CROSLEY, Lawrence (Larry)
- see COMPOSERS

CROSSLAND, Harvey James
- see DIRECTORS

CULBERT, Bob
ATPD. 16 Oakdene Cres., Toronto, ON (416)465-4114. CBC, 100 Carlton St., 3rd Flr., Toronto, ON M5W 1E6 (416)975-7904.
Type of Production and Credits: TV Film-Prod; TV Video-Prod.
Genres: Documentary-TV; Current Affairs-TV.
Biography: Born 1945. Worked at CBC, Winnipeg as Executive Producer, Current Affairs, 77-79; CBC Halifax as area producer overseeing News and Current Affairs, 79-81; CBC Toronto, since 81, Senior Producer, "The Journal."

CURTIS, Dan
- see DIRECTORS

CUTHAND, Doug
3633 John A. MacDonald Rd., Saskatoon, SK S7L 4X7 (306)382-9787. (306)978-0728.
Type of Production and Credits: TV Video-Prod/Dir/Wr.
Genres: Documentary-TV; Children's-TV.
Biography: Born in 1946 in northern Saskatchewan. Native Canadian, Cree, member of the Little Pine Band. Attended Simon Fraser University, 3 years. Twenty years working journalist in the print media. Co-produced *Theatre for Change*, which won 4 Showcase awards including Best Documentary and Best Overall. Produced and wrote *No Laughing Matter* which won Best Documentary at the 1990 Showcase awards. Has done freelance work for the series, "My Partners, My People". In 1976 won the Unity Award for minority journalists, Best Political Reporting, USA.
Selected Filmography: *No Laughing Matter*, ED, 90, CDN, Prod/Wr; *Theatre for Change*, ED, 89, CDN, Co-Prod.

CUTLER, Keith
DGC. New Communications Concepts Ltd., 5 - 23260 Dyke Rd., Richmond, BC V6V 1E2 (604)520-0272. FAX: 526-3351.
Type of Production and Credits: Th Short-Wr; TV Video-Dir/Prod.
Genres: Documentary-Th&TV; Educational-TV; Industrial-Th&TV; Current Affairs-TV.
Biography: Born 1926, Vancouver, BC. Entered television commercial production, 53, from radio broadcasting; progressed through film crafts of sound recording, editing, directing and writing. Working with Art Jones at Artray Film Productions, he was part of the creative team that assembled Vancouver's first private-sector television station, CHAN (now BCTV); moved to administration at Canawest Film Productions and formed his own production company, New Communications Concepts, 74. Twice served as president of the BC Film Industry Association and was National President of

DGC, 86-87; life member, DGC. Now engaged primarily in corporate film/video, as well as working on television/feature projects.
Selected Filmography: "Security" (4 eps), ED, 87, CDN, Dir/Wr; *Payback: The Rewards of Good Science*, In, 87, CDN, Dir/Wr; *Bread on the Table*, ED, 80, CDN, Dir/Wr; *The Tall Country*, Th, 57, CDN, Dir/Wr.

CYNAMON, Helena
Forefront Productions Corp., 609 - 402 W. Pender, Vancouver, BC V6B 1T6 (604)682-7910.
Type of Production and Credits: TV Film-Prod/Dir/Wr/Ed; TV Video-Prod/Dr/Wr/Ed.
Genres: Documentary-TV; Educational-TV.
Biography: Born in 1954 in Oshawa, Ontario. English with a knowledge of French. Graduated with Bachelor of Education degree in Special Education, University of Alberta, 1977. Completed Extended Studies Diploma in Film, Simon Fraser University, 1982. Completed Electronic and Film Media Program, The Banff Centre, School of Fine Arts, 1982. *Working It Out* won Bronze Apple, National Education Film & Video Festival, Honourable Mention, American Film & Video Festival, and a Certificate of Merit, the Yorkton Film Festival. *Journey Into Self Esteem* won 3rd prize at the American Film & Video Festival. *Women and the Nicaraguan Revolution* was the Entry Selection at the Women in the Directors Chair Film Festival. *This Should Not Have Happened* won the CALM award.
Selected Filmography: *Working It Out*, ED/TV, 90, CDN, Exec Prod/Prod; *Journey Into Self Esteem*, "Inside Stories", ED/TV, 90, CDN, Prod/Wr; *Caught in a World of Pesticides*, ED, 88, CDN, Prod/Dir/Wr/Ed; *Women and the Nicaraguan Revolution*, ED, 88, CDN, Prod/Dir/Wr/Ed; "Women & Politics" (2 eps), ED/TV, CDN, 87, Prod/Dir/Ed; *Learning Peace*, ED, 85, CDN, Prod/Dir/Ed/Wr; *This Should Not Have Happened*, ED, 84, CDN, Prod/Dir/Ed; *Media Watch: Images of Women*, ED, 83, CDN, Prod/Wr/Ed.

D'AGOSTINO, Len
- see PRODUCTION MANAGERS

DAGENAIS, Bernard
APFTQ, UDA. Les Prod. Télé-Script Inc./Les Prod. ZAP Inc., 335, boul. de Maisonneuve est., 2e étage, Montréal, PQ H2X 1K1 (514)987-9671 EXT: 514. FAX: 987-9675.
Types de production et générique: c métrage-Prod.
Types d'oeuvres: Drame-C&TV; Animation-C.
Curriculum vitae: Né à Montréal en 1945. Langues: français et anglais
Filmographie sélective: *Le Visiteur*, C/TV, 90, CDN, Prod; *Les Amazones*, C/TV, 90, CDN, Prod; "Phobius" (100 eps), TV, 90, CDN, Prod; "Inventions" (150 eps), TV, 89, CDN, Prod; "Cocologie" (26 eps), TV, 88, CDN, Prod; "ZAP" (250 eps), TV, 88, CDN, Prod.

DAIGLE, Marc
APFTQ. 3564B rue Clark, Montréal, PQ H2X 2R8 (514)842-3444. ACPAV, 1050, boul. René-Lévesque est, bureau 200, Montréal, PQ H2L 2L6 (514)849-2281.
Types de production et générique: l métrage-Prod; c métrage-Prod.
Types d'oeuvres: Drame-Th&TV; Comédie-Th&TV; Documentaire-Th&TV;.
Filmographie sélective: *La Sarrazine*, C, 90, CDN, Prod; *Le Fabuleux Voyage de L'ange*, C, 90, CDN, Prod assoc; *Le Party*, C, 89, CDN, Prod assoc; *Les Martins Infidèles*, C, 88, CDN, Prod assoc; *Les Portes Tournantes*, C, 88, CDN, Prod assoc; *La Linge de Chaleur*, C, 88, CDN, Prod assoc; *Tinamer*, C,, 88, CDN, Prod assoc; *Le Dernier Havre*, C, 86, CDN, prod; *Caffe Italia, Montréal*, C, 85, CDN, prod; *O Picasso*, C, 85, CDN, Prod assoc; *La Femme de L'Hôtel*, C, 83, CDN, Prod assoc; *Lucien Brouillard*, C, 82, CDN, Prod, assoc; *Les Grands Enfants*, C, 79, CDN, Prod; *Ti-Cul Tougas*, C, 73, CDN, Prod; *Noel et Juliette*, C, 73, CDN, Prod.

DALE, Holly
- see DIRECTORS

DALE, Miles
ACCT, DGC. Demilo Productions Ltd., 73 Albany Ave., Toronto, ON M5R 3C2 (416)588-2809. FAX: 588-1828.
Type of Production and Credits: Th Film-Prod: TV Film-PM; TV Video-PM.
Genres: Drama-Th&TV; Comedy-TV; Variety-TV; Musical-TV.
Biography: Born Toronto, Ontario. Worked as a radio programmer (CITR-FM) while at University of British Columbia. Qualified to work in the US or Europe
Selected Filmography: "Moment of Truth" (pilot), TV, 91, USA/CDN, Prod; "Top Cops" (48 eps), TV, 90-91, USA/CDN, Prod; "Friday the 13th: The Series" (72 eps), TV, 87-90, USA/CDN, Line Prod; "True Confessions" (25 eps), TV,

87, USA, Prod; "It's Only Rock 'n' Roll", TV, 87, CDN, Line Prod; *Easter Seal Telethon*, TV, 86, CDN, Line Prod; *Gemini Awards*, TV, 86, CDN, Assoc Prod; *Gordon Pinsent Special*, TV, 86, CDN, Assoc Prod; *Timing*, Th, 85, CDN, Co-Prod; *The Executive of Raymond Graham*, TV, 85, CDN, Pro Spv; "The Comedy Factory" (8 eps), TV, 85, CDN/USA, Assoc Prod; *FT/Fashion Television*, TV, 85, CDN, Assoc Prod; *Juno Awards*, TV, 84, CDN, PM; *Anne Murray in Quebec*, TV, 84, CDN, PM; "Office Girls" (45 eps), TV, 83, CDN, PM.

DALEN, Laara
DGC. 546 Marine Dr., Site 1, #23, Gibsons, BC V0N 1V0 (604)886-8029.
Type of Production and Credits: Th Film-PM/Prod; Th Short-Prod; TV Film-PM.
Genres: Drama-Th; Industrial-Th&TV; Current Affairs-TV.
Biography: Born in British Columbia. B.A., University of British Columbia. Producer of numerous industrial films with Highlight Productions, Vancouver, since 70.
Selected Filmography: "The Vancouver Show" (daily), TV, 85, CDN, PM; *Skip Tracer*, Th, 76, CDN, Prod; *Sally Fieldgood & Co.*, Th, 74, CDN, PM.

DALTON, Chris
ACCT. 2879 Forks of Credit Rd., Caledon, ON L0N 1C0 (416)927-5522. Dalton Films Ltd., 26 Soho St., #300, Toronto, ON M5T 1Z7 (416)599-0000. FAX: 599-4224.
Type of Production and Credits: Th Film-Prod; TV Film-Prod.
Genres: Drama-Th&TV.
Biography: Born 1946, Toronto, Ontario. Owner, Dalton Films Ltd.
Selected Filmography: *The Beast*, Th, 87, USA, Assoc Prod/PM; *Rites of Summer*, Th, 86, USA, Assoc Prod; *Remo Williams*, Th, 85, USA, Pro Spv; *Reckless Disregard*, TV, 84, CDN/USA, Prod; "20 Minute Workout", TV, 83, CDN, Prod; *Utilities*, Th, 80, CDN, Co-Prod; *Power Play*, Th, 77, CDN/GB, Prod; *Separation*, Th, 77, CDN, Prod; *The Clown Murders*, Th, 75, CDN, Prod; *Me*, Th, 74, CDN, Co-Prod.

DAMBERGER, Francis
- see WRITERS

DAMUDE, D. Brian
- see WRITERS

DANE, Lawrence
ACTRA, AFTRA, DGC, SAG. P.O. Box 310, Stn. F, Toronto, ON M4Y 2L7 (416)923-6000.
Type of Production and Credits: Th Film-Wr/Dir/Prod/Act; TV Film-Prod/Dir/Act.
Genres: Drama-Th&TV; Comedy-Th&TV; Musical-Th; Action-Th&TV.
Biography: Born 1937, Masson, Quebec. Has acted in over 20 movies and over 200 TV shows worldwide, as well as producing, directing and writing.
Selected Filmography: *Heavenly Bodies*, Th, 83, CDN, Dir/Co-Wr; *Rituals*, Th, 76, CDN, Prod; *Only God Knows*, Th, 73, CDN, Prod; *The Rowdyman*, Th, 71, CDN, Prod; *Action, Cut and Print*, TV, 71, CDN, Prod.

DANIELS, David J.
CFTPA, ACTRA, ACCT. Metaphor Productions Inc., 788 King St. W., Toronto, ON M5V 1N6 (416)363-3887. FAX: 363-2674. 925 14th St., Ste. 28, Santa Monica, CA 90403 (213)451-9277. FAX: 451-9277.
Type of Production and Credits: Th Film-Prod; TV Film-Prod; TV Video-Prod.
Genres: Drama-Th&TV; Comedy-Th&TV.
Selected Filmography: *Smokescreen*, Th, 91, CDN, Exec Prod/Prod; *Palais Royale*, Th, 89, CDN, Exec Prod/Prod; *Reckless Disregard*, TV, 85, CDN/USA, Assoc Prod.

DANIS, Aimée
AR, APFQ, APFVQ, ACCT. Les Productions du Verseau, 225 Roy est, bur. 200, Montréal, PQ H2W 1M5 (514)848-9814.
Types de production et générique: l métrage-Prod; c métrage-Réal.
Types d'oeuvres: Documentaire-TV; Drame-TV, Industriel-C&TV.
Curriculum vitae: Née à Maniwaki, Québec. Langues: français et anglais. Diplôme d'enseignement spécialisé du ministère de l'Education de l'Ontario. Débute sa carrière au cinéma comme script-girl, Radio-Canada; ensuite, monteuse, Films Claude Fournier, et réalisatrice, Onyx Films inc., 68; Présidente, Les Productions Verseau, depuis 76; Présidente, APFVQ, 88-89; a également réalisé environ 300 messages publicitaires dont Air Canada, Ministère des Affaires sociales, General Foods, Le Gouvernement du Québec, Banque de Montréal, Kraft Ltd. A gagné de nombreux prix aux festivals internationaux - Italie, Chicago, Budapest, Marseille, Cannes.
Filmographie sélective: *L'Emprise*, C, 88, CDN, Prod; "Les Tigres du Papier" (26 eps), TV, 88, CDN, Prod; "A première

vue" (hebdo/Festival des films du monde), TV, 83-87, CDN, Prod; "Les Enfants de la rue" (3 eps), TV, 86-87, CDN, Prod; *Les Bleus au coeur*, C, 87, CDN, Prod; "Jolis à croquer" (130 eps), TV, 86, CDN, Prod; "Enquête sur les enfants mal-aimés" (12 eps), TV, 85, CDN, Prod; "Manon" (48 eps), TV, 85, CDN, Prod; "Les Enfants mal-aimés" (3 eps), TV, 84, CDN, Prod; "Le Temps des choix" (11 eps), TV, 82, CDN, Réal; "L'Age de l'énergie" (13 eps), TV, 79, CDN, Réal; *Joie de vivre*, TV, 73, CDN, Réal; *Souris, tu m'inquiètes*, "En tant que femmes", C, 72, CDN, Co réal; *Gaspésie, oui j'écoute*, TV, 71, CDN, Réal; *KW* + Pavillon du Québec à Osaka, In, 69, CDN, Réal.

DANSEREAU, Jean ◆
APFVQ, ACCT. (514)672-7117.
Types de production et générique: l métrage-Prod; c métrage-Prod/Réal; TV film-Prod/Réal; TV vidéo-Prod/Réal.
Types d'oeuvres: Drame-C&TV; Variété-C&TV; Documentaire-C&TV; Industriel-C&TV.
Curriculum vitae: Né en 1930, Montréal, Québec. Langues: français et anglais. Stages successifs à la caméra, au montage et à la réalisation, ONF, 57; co-fondateur et Directeur général des Cinéastes Associés, 65; Directeur général des Ateliers du Cinéma québécois, 71; producteur, ministère de l'Education, 75; producteur exécutif, Studio D, ONF, 78; producteur/ réalisateur, Les Ateliers du Cinéma québécois, 86.
Filmographie sélective: *Kalamazoo*, C, 86, CDN, Prod; *Le Dernier Glacier*, C, 83, CDN, Prod; *La Dame en Couleurs*, C, 83, CDN, Co prod exéc; *Le Confort et l'Indifférence*, C, 81, CDN, Co prod; *On est rendu devant le monde!*, C, 80, CDN, Co prod; *Les Beaux Souvenirs*, C, 80, CDN, Co prod dél; *Au pays de Zom*, C, 80, CDN, Prod; *La Surditude*, C, 80, CDN, Prod; *Gui Daà* (3 films su la Chine), C, 79-80, CDN, Prod; *Debout sur leur terre*, C, 80, CDN, Prod; *Au clair de la lune*, C, 79, CDN, Co prod; *M'en revenant par les épinettes*, C, 74, CDN, Prod/Sc/Mont; *Bar Salon*, C, 73, CDN, Prod Exéc; *Montreal Blues*, C, 71, CDN, Prod; *Le Martien de noël*, C, 70, CDN, Prod.

DANYLKIW, John
DGC, ACCT. 23 Summerhill Gardens, Toronto, ON M4T 1B3 (416)964-1468. Heartstar Productions Ltd., 629 Eastern Ave., Ste. 101, Toronto, ON M4M 1E4 (416)778-8612. FAX: 778-8617. 939 Palm Ave., Ste. 406, Los Angeles, CA 90069 USA (213)854-5646. FAX: 854-5646. (604)688-1437. FAX: 688-7205.
Type of Production and Credits: Th Film-PM; TV Film-PM/Prod; TV Video-PM/Prod.
Genres: Drama-Th&TV; Action-Th&TV; Documentary-TV; Children's-Th&TV.
Biography: Born 1949; Canadian citizen. Languages: English and French. B.A., Communication Arts, Loyola College. President, Heartstar Productions Ltd., 79-present; producer of many commercials in Canada and internationally. *Maggie's Secret* won Best Children's, Scott Newman Drug Abuse Prevention Awards and was nominated for 3 daytime Emmys; *A Time for Miracles* won Grand Award at NY Int. Film & TV Awards, Pres. C. Columbus Award at Coluumbus International Film Festival, Gold Award at Houston International Film Festival, and Best TV Drama, Non-comm., Domestic at Samuel Angle International Festival.
Selected Filmography: *Honor Bright*, TV, 91, USA, Prod/Unit PM; *Last Wish*, TV, 91, USA, Prod/Unit PM; *Enchantment: Mark Twain & Me*, TV, 90, USA, Assoc Prod/Unit PM; *In Defense of a Married Man*, TV, 90, USA, Co-Prod/Unit PM/P Pro Spv; *Maggie's Secret*, TV, 90, USA, Prod/Unit PM; *Personals*, TV, 89, USA, Assoc Prod/Unit PM; *Sorry Wrong Number*, TV, 89, USA, Unit PM; *Final Notice*, TV, 89, USA, Unit PM; *The Ladykiller*, TH, 88, Assoc Prod/Unit PM/P Pro Spv; "Captain Power and the Soldiers of the Future" (22 eps), TV, 87, USA, Assoc Prod/Unit PM; *Ghost of a Chance*, TV, 86, USA, Unit PM; *Many Happy Returns*, TV, 86, USA, Line Prod/Unit PM/P Pro Spv; *Alex, The Life of a Child*, TV, 85, USA, Unit PM; *Young Again*, TV, 85, USA, Line Prod/Unit PM; *A Time for Miracles*, TV, 85, USA, Line Prod/Unit PM.

DARCUS, Jack
- see DIRECTORS
DARK, Randall Paris
ACCT, SMPTE, CSC. 445 West 54th St., Apt. 5B, New York, NY 10019 (212)956-4230. Captain New York, Ed Sullivan Theatre, 1697 Broadway, New York, NY 10019 USA (212)307-4388.
Type of Production and Credits: Th Film-Prod; Th Short-Prod; TV Film-Prod; TV Video-Prod/Dir.
Genres: Drama-Th&TV; Comedy-Th&TV; MusicalTh&TV; Music Video-Th&TV.
Biography: Canadian citizen. Baccalaureatus in Artibus cum Honore.

Member of Playwrights Union of Canada. Vice-President of Captain New York, Inc., the first commercial High Definition company in the world. Has been involved in over 50 High Definition projects, from *Chasing Rainbows* to *Jackie Mason*. Winner of an Astrolabium at the Montreux Festival for *Moscow Melodies*. *Nobody's Fault* won a Citation Award at Montreux, 1991.
Selected Filmography: *Nobody's Fault*, MV, 91, USA, Prod; *Tall Wars*, Th, 91, USA, Prod; *Hangin' on a Heart Attack*, MV, 91, USA, Prod; *I Love a Parade*, TV, 91, USA, Prod; *The Accordian and HDTV*, In, 91, USA, Prod; *Journey to Beyond Excellence*, In, 91, USA, Assist Dir; *Manhattan Melodies*, Th, 91, USA, Prod; "Jackie Mason's Town Meeting" (5 eps), TV, 90, USA, Assist Dir; *Where Did the Magic Go*, MV, 90, USA, Prod; *Moscow Melodies*, Th, 89, USR/USA, Prod, (ASTROLABIUM); *Sugar Bowl 89*, TV, 89, J/USA, Dir; *Delores Schwartz*, Cm, 89, USA, Dir; *Pretentious Pictures*, TV, 89, USA, Assist Dir.

DARLING, Gillian
Sarus Productions, 5537 Toronto Rd., Vancouver, BC V6T 1L1 (604)222-0005. FAX: 222-0036.
Type of Production and Credits: TV Film-Prod/Wr; TV Video-Prod/Wr.
Genres: Documentary-TV; Educational-TV.
Biography: Born 1949, Vancouver, BC. B.A., Anthropology/Art History/ Museology, University of British Columbia, 75; Language Diploma (Shastri scholarship), Central Institute of Hindi Language, Delhi, India, 74; M.A., Anthropology, University of British Columbia, 79; Canadian/Indian government Shastri scholarship, Eastern Regional Language Institute, Orissa, India, 81. Media Associate, Video/Multi AV/Docu-Educ. Programming, Media Resources Department, Capilano College, North Vancouver, 83-85. Producer, assistant producer, translator and writer, Northern Lights Media Corporation, 85; involvement in production includes scriptwriting, on-location preproduction research (Africa, South Asia), line production, assistant direction, translation/ translation co-ordination in 10 foreign languages; also producer/writer for made-for-TV nature specials. Currently producer, *Battle for the Trees* (in pre-production).
Selected Filmography: *Island of Whales/Swimming with Whales*, TV, 90, CDN, Prod/Exec Prod; *First Harvest*, ED, 88, CDN, Assist Prod/Trans; *Aga Khan Canada Film*, ED, 88, CDN, Prod; *With Both Eyes Open*, ED, 87, CDN, Assist Prod/Trans; *At the Frontlines of Health*, ED, 87, CDN, Assist Prod/Trans.

DAVID, Pierre
AMPAS, ACCT. 2373 Century Hill, Los Angeles, CA 90067. Image Organization, Inc., 9000 Sunset Blvd., Ste. 915, Los Angeles, CA 90069 USA (213)278-8751.
Type of Production and Credits: Th Film-Prod/Exec Prod; TV Film-Prod/Exec Prod.
Genres: Drama-Th&TV; Action-Th&TV, Science Fiction-Th&TV; Horror-Th&TV.
Biography: Born in Montreal; moved to Los Angeles, 83. In Canada, established, with Roger Corman, New World Mutual Pictures of Canada, Ltd. President, Film Packages International, 83; later with the Larry Thompson organization; Chairman of the Board and Chief Executive Officer, Image Organization, 87 to present.
Selected Filmography: *Deep Cover*, Th, 91, USA, Prod; *Twin Sisters*, Th, 91, CDN, Exec Prod; *Martial Law Undercover*, Th, 91, USA, Exec Prod; *Scanners: The Takeover*, Th, 91, CDN, Exec Prod; *The Perfect Weapon*, Th, 91, USA, Prod; *Dolly Dearest*, Th, 91, USA, Exec Prod; *Desire & Hell at Sunset Motel*, Th, 90, USA, Exec Prod; *Martial Law*, Th, 90, USA, Exec Prod; *The Perfect Bride*, Th, 90, USA, Prod; *Scanners II, The New Order*, Th, 90, USA, Exec Prod; *Internal Affairs*, Th, 90, USA, Exec Prod; *Blind Fear/A Long Dark Night*, Th, 89, CDN, Prod; *Pin*, Th, 88, CDN, Exec Prod; *My Demon Lover*, Th, 87, USA, Exec Prod; *Hot Pursuit*, Th, 86, USA, Prod.

DAVIS, Richard ✧
DGC. (604)253-5378.
Type of Production and Credits: Th Film-Prod/Line Pro; TV Film-Prod/Dir/Wr.
Genres: Drama-Th&TV; Comedy-Th&TV; Documentary-TV.
Biography: Born 1940, England; emigrated to Australia, 51; immigrated to Canada, 86; British and Australian citizenship; landed immigrant, Canada. Background as journalist, covering news and current affairs as reporter, producer, director; press secretary and executive producer of New South Wales Film Commission, Australia; producer, line producer, director, writer on features, television and documentaries; more than 100 productions, 76-81.
Selected Filmography: *The Outside Chance of Maximilian Glick*, Th, 87,

CDN, Co-Prod; "Comedy College" (3 eps), TV, 87, CDN, PM; "Quest for Healing" (6 eps), TV, 86, GB/AUS, PM; "Butterfly Island" (8 eps), TV, AUS, Exec Prod; "The Maestro's Company" (13 eps), TV, 84, AUS, Prod; *Grave for the President*, TV, 84, AUS, Exec Prod; *Out of Darkness*, TV, 84, AUS, Exec Prod; *The Flying Vet*, TV, 84, AUS, Exec Prod; *Phar Lap*, Th, 83, AUS, Line Prod; *The Pirate Movie*, Th, 82, AUS, Line Prod.

DAY, Deborah
TWIFT. 2466 Eglinton Ave. E., Ste. 605, Scarborough, ON M1K 5J8 (416)269-5750. FAX: 269-5709.
Type of Production and Credits: Th Short-Wr/Prod/Dir; TV Film-Wr/Prod/PM; TV Video-PM.
Genres: Drama-Th&TV.
Biography: Born in Toronto, Ontario and grew up in Montreal and Toronto. Studied communications and business administration at Concordia University in Montreal. Has worked in film and television production for 6 years, most recently producing and writing original material.
Selected Filmography: *Birthday*, Th, 91, CDN, Dir/Prod/Wr; *RSVP*, TV, 91, CDN, Prod Spv; *Strange Dialogue*, TV, 90, CDN, Prod/Co-Wr; *Kumar & Jones*, TV, 90, CDN, PM.

DE CARUFEL, René
- voir DIRECTEURS-PHOTO

DE ROCHEMONT, Nicole
ACCT, APFVQ. 5405 Grovehill Place, Montréal, PQ H4A 1J8 (514)488-0395. Télé-Action, 1338 est, rue Ste-Catherine, Montréal, PQ H2L 2H5 (514)524-1118. FAX: 524-2041.
Types de production et générique: l métrage-Prod/Sc/Rech; TV film-Prod/Sc; TV vidéo-Prod/Rech.
Types d'oeuvres: Drame-C&TV; Variété-TV; Science fiction-TV; Documentaire-TV; Education-TV; Enfants-TV; Industriel-C; Affaires publiques-TV.
Curriculum vitae: Neé en 1939, Montréal, Québec. Langues: français et anglais. Expérience professionnelle: concepteur, scénariste, relationniste, producteur. Formation professionnelle: Columbia School of Journalism, NYC, cours d'un an en journalisme, 62. Université McGill, Département des communications, la réalisation pour le théâtre, le cinéma et la télévision. ACCT: collaboratrice du comité Gala, 87-88; membre du comité exécutif, 86-89; Directrice comité des finances, conseil exécutif, 89. APFVQ: membre du conseil d'administration, 84-85. Scénariste, recherchiste, assistant réalisateur, réalisateur, Radio-Québec, 73-76; Producteur délégué, Direction générale du cinéma, Ministère des Communications du Québec, 76-78; Agent d'information professionnel, Ministère des Affaires Intergouvernementales du Québec, 78-83; Vice-présidente, SDA Productions, 83-89; Présidente, Télé-Action, 89 à présent.
Filmographie sélective: "Une faim de loup" (26 eps), TV, 91, CDN, Prod; "Les Dimanches de Clémence" (14 eps), TV, 87, CDN, Prod; "Claude Albert et les autres" (26 eps), TV, 86-87, CDN, Prod; "Bonjour Docteur" (30 eps), TV, 87, CDN, Prod; *Les Bottes*, TV, 86, CDN, Prod; "Pour une chanson" (6 eps), TV, 84-85, CDN, Prod.

DE SILVA, Paul ✧
CFTA, ACTRA, ACCT. 362 Gladstone Ave., Toronto, ON M6H 3H6 (416)537-8507.
Type of Production and Credits: Th Short-Prod/Dir; TV Film-Prod/Dir; TV Video-Prod/Dir.
Genres: Drama-TV; Documentary-Th&TV; Educational-TV.
Biography: Born 1950, Calcutta, India. B.A., English Literature and Political Science, York University. Worked at Radio HSA, Bangkok, 69; joined Ontario Human Rights Commission, 73; Producer and News Director, CKWR-FM, Kitchener-Waterloo; reporter for CBC Winnipeg, 78; later host/reporter of CBC Toronto series "Canadians"; multicultural program consultant CBC, 80-81; co-ordinated recruitment for CBC's broadcast trainee program for visible minorities, 83; currently Executive Producer of "Inside Stories", a multicultural drama anthology series.
Selected Filmography: "The Nature of Things" (2 eps), TV, CDN, Dir; "Inside Stories" (13 eps), TV, 87-88, CDN, Exec Prod; *In Support of the Human Spirit*, ED, 87, CDN, Exec Prod; "Trade Secrets" (4 eps), TV, 85, CDN, Exec Prod; "Neighbourhoods" (13 eps), TV, 85, CDN, Exec Prod; *Two Families*, TV, 85, CDN, Prod/Dir; *Fantastic Visions*, Th, 80, CDN, Co-Prod/Dir.

DELMAGE, John A.
CFTPA, ACCT. 25 Langford Ave., Toronto, ON M4J 3E4 (416)463-6833. J.A. Delmage Productions Ltd., 550 Queen St. E., Ste. M107, Toronto, ON (416)363-8034. FAX: 363-8919.
Type of Production and Credits: TV Film-Prod; Th Film-Prod; TV Video-Prod.

Genres: Drama-TV&Th; Action-TV; Children's-TV.
Selected Filmography: "Two for Joy" (pilot), TV, 91, CDN, Prod; *Brown Bread Sandwiches*, Th, 89, I, Exec Prod; "My Secret Identity" (24 eps), TV, 89, US, Prod; "The Campbells" (100 eps), TV, 85-89, CDN/USA/GB, Prod; *World Theatre Day*, TV, 84, CDN, Prod; *But I'm Just a Kid*, TV, 84, CDN, Prod; "The Claus Mission", TV, 84, CDN, Prod; *A Case of Libel*, TV, 84, CDN, Co-Prod; "Some Honourable Gentlemen" (7 eps), TV, 82-84, CDN, Prod.

DELOREY, Walter J. ✧
(902)945-2052.
Type of Production and Credits: Th Short-Prod/DOP/Ed; TV Video-Dir/Wr.
Genres: Documentary-Th&TV; Educational-Th; Experimental-Th; Industrial-Th.
Biography: Born 1945, Quebec City, Quebec. Languages: English and French. Courses at Ryerson Polytechnical Institute. Professional artist; award-winning art films; Best Cinematography, Atlantic Film Festival, 82; special award of merit for creative use of media, International Wildlife Film Festival, 84. Specialties: nature filming, art film footage.
Selected Filmography: *Airships*, Th, 85, CDN, Wr/Dir; *River of Light*, Th, 82, CDN, Prod/Cam/Ed; *Green Feathered Sea*, Th, 75, CDN, Prod/Cam/Ed; *Shaman*, Th, 74, CDN, Prod/Cam/Ed; *Cold August Wind*, Th, 73, CDN, Prod/Cam/Ed; *Blue Sleep*, Th, 73, CDN, Prod/Cam/Ed; *Great Rain Mountain*, Th, 73, CDN, Prod/Cam/Ed.

DEMERS, Rock
APFVQ, ACCT. 320, Carré St-Louis, Montréal, PQ H2X 1A5 (514)288-5603. Les Productions La Fête, 2306 est, rue Sherbrooke, Montréal, PQ H2K 1E5 (514)521-8303.
Types de production et générique: l métrage-Prod.
Types d'oeuvres: Enfants-C.
Curriculum vitae: Né en 1933. A travaillé dans plusieurs branches de l'industrie dont la production/distribution, program-mation. Collabore à l'institution du Festival International du Film et devient le Directeur général de 62 à 67; fondateur, Président, Directeur exécutif de Faroun Films; participe à la formation de l'Institut Québécois du Cinéma, 77-79; co-fondateur de la Cinémathèque québécoise. Ses films ont gagné de nombreux prix internationaux; récipiendaire de la Médaille du Gouverneur Général, le Prix Albert-Tessier, 87 (la plus haute distinction accordée par le gouvernement du Québec dans le domaine du cinéma) et le Prix Air Canada pour sa contribution exceptionnelle à l'industrie cinéma-tographique canadienne, 88.
Filmographie sélective: *Why Havel?*, C, 91, CDN/CS, Prod; *Le Championne*, C, 91, CDN/R, Prod; *Vincent and Me*, C, 90, CDN/F, Prod; *Pas de répit pour Mélanie*, C, 90, CDN, Prod; *Bye Bye Chaperon Rouge*, C, 89, CDN/H, Prod; *Fierro... l'été des secrets*, C, 89, CDN/ARG, Prod; *Tommy Tricker and the Stamp Traveller*, C, 88, CDN, Prod; *La Grenouille et la baleine*, C, 88, CDN, Prod; *The Great Land of Small*, C, 87, CDN, Prod; *The Young Magician*, C, 86, CDN/PL, Prod; *Bach et Bottine*, C, 86, CDN, Prod; *The Peanut Butter Solution*, C, 85, CDN, Prod; *La guerre des tuques*, C, 84, CDN, Prod.

DEMEULE, Nadine
- voir REALISATEURS

DENIKE, Brian
100 Roehampton Ave., #710, Toronto, ON M4H 1R3 (416)322-6281. CBC-TV, The Journal, 100 Carlton St., 3rd Flr., Toronto, ON (416)975-7920.
Type of Production and Credits: TV Film-Prod/Dir; TV Video-Prod/Dir.
Genres: Documentary-TV; Current Affairs-TV; News-TV; Sports-TV.
Biography: Born 1939 Flin Flon, Manitoba. Attended Carleton University and University of New Brunswick.
Selected Filmography: *Kuwait Today*, "The Journal", TV, 91, CDN, Prod; *The Fires of Kuwait*, "The Journal", TV, 91, CDN, Prod; *Valley of Despair*, "The Journal", TV, 91, CDN, Prod; *The Arab Mind*, "The Journal", TV, 91, CDN, Prod; *Bhagdad Diary*, "The Journal", TV, 91, CDN, Prod; *Panama - 1 Year After*, "The Journal", TV, 90, CDN, Prod; *The Baron*, "The Journal", TV, 90, CDN, Prod; *Voices of the Revolution*, "The Journal", TV, 90, CDN, Prod; "The Journal", TV, 85-91, CDN, Field Prod; "Midday", TV, 84-85, CDN, Prod; *Olympic Games*, TV, 84, CDN, Sr Prod; *Olympic Journey*, TV, 83-84, CDN, Sr Prod; "The Journal", TV, 80-83, CDN, Sr Ed; "the fifth estate", TV, 77-80, CDN, Sr Prod; "24 Hours" (Winnipeg), TV, 74-77, CDN, Exec Prod.

DENSHAM, Pen ✧
ACTRA, DGA, WGAw. (213)277-5662.
Type of Production and Credits: Th Film-Prod/Dir/Wr.
Genres: Drama-Th; Comedy-Th; Action-Th.

Biography: Born 1947, UK; immigrated to Canada, 66; Canadian citizenship. Formed Insight Productions Canada with John Watson, 70; directed/wrote 100 films; TV dramas, specials, documentaries, educational films etc. *If Wishes Were Horses* won 12 international awards; films have won over 70 awards, including 2 Oscar nominations. Received Queen's Silver Jubilee Medal. Moved to L.A., 79.
Selected Filmography: *The Kiss*, Th, 87, CDN, Prod/Dir/Wr; *The Zoo Gang*, Th, 85, USA, Prod/Co-Dir; *Quicksilver*, Th, 85, USA, Creat Cons; *Nighthawks*, Th, 81, USA, Creat Cons; *Victory*, Th, 81, USA, Creat Cons; *Rocky II*, Th, 80, USA, Creat Cons.

DESCHAMPS, Yvon ✦
UDA. (514)845-5131.
Types de production et générique: l métrage-Sc/Com; c métrage-Com; TV film-Prod/Sc/Com; TV Vidéo-Prod/Sc/Com.
Types d'oeuvres: Drame-C&TV; Comédie-C&TV; Variété-C&TV; Enfants-C&TV.
Curriculum vitae: Né en 1935, Montréal, Québec. Langues: français et anglais. Etudes en théâtre avec Georges Groulx, François Rozet et Paul Buissonneau. Comédien; débute sa carrière au théâtre, 58, et à la télévision, 59; co-fondateur, Théâtre de Quat'sous, 64; présente son premier monologue, *Les Unions, qu'ossa donne*, 68; sortie de son premier album du même titre, 69; 11 albums, 74-84; tous ses spectacles *one man* ont été enregistrés sur vidéo et diffusés par Radio-Canada.
Filmographie sélective: "Samedi de rire", TV, 85-88, CDN, Co prod; *Le p'tit vient vite*, C, 72, CDN, Sc.

DESJARDINS, Claude ✦
UDA. (514)842-5333.
Types de production et générique: TV film-Prod/Réal; TV vidéo-Prod/Réal.
Types d'oeuvres: Education-TV; Annonces-TV.
Curriculum vitae: Né en 1952, Montréal, Québec. Comédien, producteur, réalisateur; éditeur de *Qui fait quoi*.
Filmographie sélective: Les Serres Rosaire Pion (4 annonces), Cm, 83-88, CDN, Prod/Réal; Ecole de Danse Louise Lapierre, Cm, 85, CDN, Prod/Réal.

DEVINE, David
ACCT, CFTA. Devine Video and Filmworks, 100 Cambridge Ave., Toronto, ON M4K 2L6 (416)465-4499. FAX: 465-5827.
Type of Production and Credits: TV Film-Prod/Dir; TV Video-Prod/Dir.
Genres: Comedy-TV; Variety-TV; Children's-TV.
Biography: Born 1952, Toronto, Ontario. B.A., University of Toronto; M.F.A., UCLA Graduate Film School. Production manager, producer, director for Glen-Warren Productions before forming Devine Video and Filmworks. *A Young Children's Concert with Raffi* won Parents' Choice Award, US, 86; *Raffi: In Concert* nominated for 1990 Grammy Award, ACE award, and won Gemini award and US Parent's Choice Gold award. *Indian Time* won the 1989 NY Film and Video Festival award for Best Variety Program.
Selected Filmography: "Lifetime" (20 eps), TV, 90, CDN, Dir; *A Coca-Cola Day*, In, 90, CDN, Dir; *Raffi: In Concert*, TV, 88, USA/CDN, Prod/Dir; *Indian Time*, TV, 88, CDN, Dir; "The Comedy Mill" (24 eps), TV, 87, CDN, Dir; *A Young Children's Concert with Raffi*, TV, 85, CDN, Prod/Dir; *The Stray Cats Live*, TV, 83-84, CDN, Prod/Dir; *The Getaway*, MV, 84, CDN, Prod/Dir; *The Making of Strange Brew*, TV, 82, CDN, Prod/Dir; *Jeeves Takes Charge*, TV, 81, CDN/GB, Prod/Dir; "Big City Comedy" (7 eps), TV, 80, CDN/USA, Assoc Prod; *The Joe-Bob Walker Show*, TV, 79, CDN/USA, Assoc Prod; "Rich Little Salutes" (2 eps), TV, 79, CDN/USA, Assoc Prod.

DEW, Simon Christopher
ACTRA, CFTPA. 11 Winchester St., Toronto, ON M4X 1A6 (416)923-3432.
Type of Production and Credits: TV Film-Prod/Dir/Wr/Ed; TV Video-Prod/Dir/Wr/Ed.
Genres: Drama-TV; Variety-TV; Documentary-TV; Commercials-TV.
Biography: Born 1938, London, England; Canadian citizenship. Producer, director, writer, editor in drama, documentaries, commercials and sports. Has won numerous awards, including 2 Gold at New York, CanPro, Clios.
Selected Filmography: *Hockey My Way* (Wayne Gretzky), TV, 87, CDN, Prod; *Jimmy Valentine*, TV, 85, CDN, Prod; "Littlest Hobo" (78 eps), TV, 79-84, CDN, Prod; "Loving Friends and Perfect Couples" (20 eps), TV, 84, CDN, Prod; *Cult of the Lion*, TV, 83, CDN, Prod/Dir; *The Rhino War*, TV, 83, CDN, Prod/Dir.

DEWALT, Kevin
ACCT, SMPIA, CFTPA, IQ. 83 Angus Crescent, Regina, SK S4T 6N1 (306)522-9719. Minds Eye Pictures, Division of Regina Motion Picture, 1212A Winnipeg Street., Regina, SK (306)359-7618. FAX: 359-3466.

Type of Production and Credits: Th Short-Prod; TV Film-Prod/Dir; TV Video-Prod/Dir.
Genres: Documentary-TV; Commercials-TV; Industrial-TV; Music Video-TV.
Biography: Born 1959, Moose Jaw, Saskatchewan. Educated University of Regina, BA, Music Education. President, Minds Eye Pictures since 86. Chairman, Sask Showcase 1990. Best Drama Award, Sask Showcase, 89 for *The Great Electrical Revolution*. CPRS Award for Best Corporate Video, Denro Holdings 1990. Business Excellence Award (ABEX). In addition to listed credits, producer/director of various corporate/industrial projects, 84-86.
Selected Filmography: *Eli's Lesson*, TV, 91, CDN, Prod; *The Energy Arc*, TV, 91, CDN, Prod/Dir; "It Starts At Home" (13 eps), TV, 91, CDN, Exec Prod; *It's Your Right*, ED, 91, CDN, Prod; *See What You Wanna See*, ED, 91, CDN, Prod; "Lost and Found" (2 eps), In, 90, CDN, Prod; *Winter Seasoned*, TV, 90, CDN, Exec Prod; Department of National Defence, In, 90, CDN, Prod; *The Great Electrical Revolution*, TV, 89, CDN, Prod; *The Heart of the Matter*, MV, 88, CDN, Prod; *Communicating at the Speed of Light*, TV, 87, CDN, Prod; *Who Calls*, In, 87, CDN, Prod/Dir; Unisource System, In, 87, CDN, Prod/Dir; *Western Canada Summer Games*, TV, 87, CDN, Prod/Dir; *The Western Canadian Exhibition*, In, 87, CDN, Prod/Dir.

DEWAR, David
DGC. 502 St. George St., New Westminster, BC V3L 1L1 (604)525-160. The Dewar Group, 502 St. George St., New Westminster, BC V3L 1L1 (604)525-1160. FAX: 521-8790. Pager: 667-3632.
Type of Production and Credits: TV Video-Prod/Dir/P Prod Spv.
Genres: Drama-TV; Variety-TV; Documentary-TV; Children's-TV.
Biography: Canadian born, BC bred. Graduate of UBC in Physical Education and Theatre. Worked as an actor, singer and dancer in BC and Alberta. Joined CBC in Vancouver in 1975. Worked as a set decorator and assistant designer. Prix Anik Award for Set Design on Claud Jutra's *Dreamspeaker*, 1976, one of two Jutra films he did. Wrote sketch comedy for "Dr. Bondolo" and "Downtown Saturday Night". Became producer and director in CBC TV Drama Department in 1986. Developed first all tape random access post system ever at CBC. Trained as montage editor. Left CBC in 1990. Produced new series called "Hillside", a teen soap at BCTV, and 3 pilots for a new series with writer James Barber. Currently producer in development with a new sitcom series, "Ferry Tales" for New City Productions and WIC.
Selected Filmography: Drake Beam Morin (2 spots), In, 91, CDN, Ed; "Hillside" (13 eps), TV, 90, CDN/USA, Prod; "The Urban Peasant" (3 eps), TV, 90, CDN, Prod; "P.A.T.A. '90" (3 eps), TV, 90, USA, PM; *The Young Performers*, TV, 89, CDN, P Pro Spv; *The Manin Chance*, "The Way We Are", TV, 89, CDN, Prod; "Lies From Lotus Land" (13 eps), TV, 88, CDN, P Pro Spv; "Trying Times" (6 eps), TV, 88, CDN/USA, P Pro Spv; *Wheels*, "Lies From Lotus Land", TV, 87, CDN, Prod/Dir; "Bailey's Law" (6 eps), TV, 86, CDN, P Pro Spv; *Timmy's Teleathon*, TV, 86, CDN, Dir; "Downtown Saturday Night" (13 eps), TV, 85, CDN, Assoc Prod; *Super Holiday Air Band Special*, "Switchback", TV, 85, CDN, Dir/Assoc Prod; *The Storytellers*, TV, 85, CDN, Prod/Dir.

DEWAR, Stephen W. ✧
ACCT. Stephen Dewar Productions Ltd., 27 Tyrrel Ave., M6G 2G1 (416)651-2530.
Type of Production and Credits: TV Film-Prod/Dir/Wr.
Genres: Documentary-TV; Educational-TV.
Biography: Has worked for National Film Board of Canada, Heritage Films, Mediavision, CTV. Formed Stephen Dewar Productions Ltd., 79. *Jet Speed at Ground Zero* won Best Science Film, Bell Northern Prize, 74.
Selected Filmography: "Lorne Greene's New Wilderness" (104 eps), TV, 81-86, CDN, Co-Prod; "Man of the North" (12 eps) (Dir 6 eps), TV, 77-78, CDN, Wr; "Last of the Wild" (9 eps) (Co-Wr 6 eps), TV, 76, CDN/USA, Wr; "Behind the Scenes with Jonathan Winters" (9 eps)(Co-Wr 8 eps), TV, 75, CDN/USA, Wr/Dir; "Glenn Ford's Friends of Man" (18 eps), TV, 73-74, CDN/USA, Co-Wr; "W5" (sev seg), TV, 68-71, CDN, Dir/Report; *Jet Speed at Ground Zero*, TV, 71, CDN, Dir/Wr.

DEY, Wendy E.
ACCT. 44 Belsize Dr., Toronto, ON M4S 1L4 (416)489-7434. CTV Television Network Ltd., 9 Channel 9 Court, Scarborough, ON M1S 4B5 (416)609-7372.
Type of Production and Credits: TV Video-Prod.
Genres: News-TV.

Biography: Born 1943, Ottawa, Ontario. English, Philosophy, Queen's University; Ontario College of Art; Journalism, Carleton University. Reporter, *Ottawa Citizen, Toronto Star*; editor, *Victoria Times, Toronto Star*; assignment editor, reporter, Producer and Executive Producer, News and Current Affairs, Global TV; currently Producer, News and Current Affairs, CTV.
Selected Filmography: "Canada AM", TV, 86-91, CDN, Prod; "Newsweek"/"News at Noon"/"Saturday Edition", TV, 83-86, CDN, Exec Prod; "First News", TV, 84-85, CDN, Exec Prod/Prod; "6 O'Clock News"/"11 O'Clock News" (national edition), TV, 84-85, CDN, Exec Prod/ Prod; "Evening Edition", TV, 83-84, CDN, Exec Prod/Prod; "News at Noon", TV, 81-83, CDN, Prod.

DIBAI, Nastaran
- see CINEMATOGRAPHERS

DICK, Jacques ✧
APFVQ. (514)288-6113.
Types de production et générique: TV film-Prod; TV vidéo-Prod.
Types d'oeuvres: Annonces-TV; Industriel-TV; Drame-TV.
Curriculum vitae: Né en 1943, Montréal, Québec. Langues: français et anglais. H.E.C., 72; CMA. Chef des services administratifs de la Société de développement de l'industrie cinématographique canadienne, 68-80; administration de la participation canadienne au Festival International du Film de Cannes, 78-84; Vice-président, Productions Vidéofilms ltée, 80-84; Président, Productions Diva inc., 84.
Filmographie sélective: *Une journée en taxi*, C, 80, CDN/F, Prod exéc.

DIEHL, Barrie
Barrie Diehl Productions, 20 Jondan Cres., Thornhill, ON L3T 3Z5 (416)886-1613. The Core Group Talent Agency Inc., 489 College St., Ste. 501, Toronto, ON M6G 1A5 (416)944-0193.
Type of Production and Credits: TV Film-Prod; TV Video-Prod/PM.
Genres: Drama-Th&TV; Variety-TV; Children's-TV; Sports-TV.
Biography: Born in 1938 in Sqouris, Manitoba. Worked at CKBI-TV, Prince Albert, 1958-61; CFRN-TV, Edmonton, 1961-68, producing and directing. Was Program Manager, CKSO-TV, Sudbury, 1969-70; Production Manager/Producer, CFTO-TV, 1971-89. Produced and directed many documentaries on special events for local stations. Much experience in studio and remote field shoots throughout the U.S. and Canada. Produced the "Littlest Hobo" from 1982-86 which won the Silver in 1983 and the Bronze in 1984 at the New York Film Festival.
Selected Filmography: "Canada's Best" (6 eps), TV, 91, CDN, Prod; "Thrill of a Lifetime" (55 eps), TV, 86-88, CDN, Prod; "Littlest Hobo" (66 eps), TV, 82-86, CDN, Prod; *The Nutcracker*, TV, 79, USA, PM; *F.D.R.*, TV, 78, USA, PM.

DIMARCO, Steve
- see DIRECTORS

DINEL, Pierre
- voir SCENARISTES

DION, Jean-Yves
- voir DIRECTEURS-PHOTO

DIONNE, Francine
C.P. 39, Succ. Westmount, Westmount, PQ H3Z 2T1
Types de production et générique: l métrage-Prod.
Types d'oeuvres: Drame-C.
Filmographie sélective: *Salut! J.W.*, C, 80, CDN, Prod; *L'Inconnu*, C, 74, CDN, Prod.

DODD, Marian
ACTRA. 8382 Victoria Dr., Vancouver, BC V5P 4A9 (604)324-7277. The Eyes Multi-Media Productions Inc., 505 - 1168 Hamilton St., Vancouver, BC V6B 2S7 (604)876-3937. 21st Century Talent Management, 201 - 1224 Hamilton St., Vancouver, BC (604)669-7486.
Type of Production and Credits: Th Film-Pub; TV Video-Prod/Dir/Wr/Pub.
Genres: Drama-Th; Documentary-TV; Industrial-TV; Current Affairs-TV; News-TV.
Biography: Has a decade of professional experience in broadcast journalism, film, print and corporate communications. Has worked as a news and features reporter at Vancouver radio station CFOX FM99 and CJJR Country FM and as a news and entertainment reporter/editor at CKVU (UTV) Television. Has interviewed over 500 celebrities. Exclusive B.C. field producer/correspondent for "Entertainment Tonight", and host of the syndicated program "On Location", 89 to date. Print writer. Publicist: TV series including "21 Jump Street" and "Wiseguy". Wrote press package and produced audio-visual press kit for the feature film *K2*. Produced, directed and wrote a 60-minute documentary, *K2, The Making of the Movie*, which premiered at the Cannes Film Festival, 91, and has since been invited to numerous film and video festivals worldwide.
Selected Filmography: *K2, The Making of*

the Movie, TV, 91, CDN/USA/GB, Dir/Wir/Prod; *K2*, Th, 91, CDN/USA, GB, Unit Pub; "Entertainment Tonight" (150 eps), TV, 89-91, USA, Corr/Field Prod; Mapleglade/Parkview, Strongbases Real Estate, In, 91, CDN/J, Wr/Prod; "Personalities", TV, 90-91, USA, PM; "On Location" (400 eps), TV, 89-91, CDN, Wr/Host; "BCAA Today" (5 eps), In, 90-91, CDN, Wr/Prod/Dir/Host; "Variety Club Telethon", TV, 89-91, CDN, Host/Vignette Prod; *Canadian Helicopters/Helilogging*, In, 90, CDN, Wr/Prod; *BC Rail/On Track with BC Rail*, In, 90, CDN, Wr/Prod/Dir; *Quality Plus*, Canadian Homebuilders Association, In, 90, CDN, Wr/Prod; PCL Packaging/Shopping Bag Recycling, In, 90, CDN, Wr/Host/Prod/Dir; "21 Jump Street" (13 eps), TV, 88-89, USA, Pub; "Wiseguy" (13 eps), TV, 88-89, USA, Pub; "Unsub" (13 eps), TV, 88-89, USA, Pub.

DONLON, Denise
ACTRA, CARAS, ACCT. 246 Bain Ave., Toronto, ON M4K 1G2 Citytv/MuchMusic, 299 Queen St. W., Toronto, ON M5V 2Z5 (416)591-5757. Sam Wilson, The Talent Group, 387 Bloor St. E., 3rd Floor, Toronto, ON M4W 1H7 (416)961-3304.
Type of Production and Credits: TV Video-Prod/Host/Dir/Wr.
Genres: Documentary-TV; Educational-TV; Music Video-TV; Current Affairs-TV.
Biography: Born in 1956. Voted the 1989 Video Programmer/Personality of the Year by *The Record*.
Selected Filmography: "The New Music" (7 years), TV, 85-91, CDN, Prod/Host; *Real Roots: A Native Perspective*, "The New Music", TV, 91, CDN, Prod/Host; *Rock n Roll n Reading*, "The New Music" (2 eps), TV, 91, CDN, Prod/Host; *Your Place or Mine*, "The New Music", TV, 91, CDN, Co-Prod/Host; *Earth to Ground Control*, "The New Music", TV, 90, CDN, Prod/Host; *Artists of the Decade: RUSH*, k.d. lang, Bryan Adams, "The New Music", TV, 90, CDN, Prod/Host; *Dance: One Hour of Attitude Music*, "The New Music", TV, 90, CDN, Prod/Host.

DONOVAN, Michael
2354 Moran St., Halifax, NS (902)429-6870. Salter Street Films Ltd., 2507 Brunswick St., Halifax, NS B3K 2Z5 (902)420-1577.
Type of Production and Credits: Th Film-Prod.
Genres: Drama-Th&TV; Action-Th.
Biography: Born 1953, Nova Scotia.
Selected Filmography: "Codco" (49 eps), TV, 87-91, CDN, Exec Prod, (2 GEMINIS); *Diplomatic Immunity*, Th, 90, CDN, Exec Prod; *Defcon-4*, Th, 84, CDN, Prod; *Siege*, Th, 81, CDN, Prod; *South Pacific 1942*, Th, 79, CDN, Prod.

DOYLE, Patrick
DGC. Pandemonium Productions Limited, 52 Van Dusen Blvd., Toronto, ON M8Z 3G1 (416)233-3891.
Type of Production and Credits: Th Film-Prod; TV Film-Prod/PM.
Genres: Drama-Th&TV; Comedy-Th&TV; Action-Th&TV; Horror-Th.
Biography: Born Toronto, Ontario. Three years, Business Administration and Marketing, University of Toronto. Languages: English and French.
Selected Filmography: "My Secret Identity" (24 eps), TV, 90, CDN, Prod; "My Secret Identity" (24 eps), TV, 89, CDN, Assoc Prod; "Bordertown" (16 eps), TV, 89, CDN, Line Prod; "The Campbells" (100 eps), TV, 85-89, CDN/USA/GB, Co-Prod.

DRAKE, Tom
- see WRITERS

DRYSDALE, Alyson
Tamarac Filmworks Ltd.,3495 West 28th Ave., Vancouver, BC V6S 1R8 (604)737-6260.
Type of Production and Credits: Th Short-Prod/Dir/Wr; TV Film-Prod.
Genres: Drama-Th&TV; Comedy-Th&TV; Documentary-Th&TV; Educational-TV.
Biography: Has lived in BC, Alberta and Colorado. Languages: English, some French and Spanish. Graduate, Arts, University of British Columbia, 81. Has worked in the film industry for ten years, the past five as a producer, writer, director and script editor. Winner, Short Drama competition, National Screen Institute.
Selected Filmography: *High Country*, "Magic Hour" (1 eps), TV, 90-91, CDN, Assoc Prod; *The Mailboat Doesn't Stop Here Anymore*, TV, 90, CDN, Exec Prod; *Skookumchuck-in-the-Rockies*, Th, 89, CDN, Prod/Dir; "The Beachcombers" (26 eps), TV, 89-90, CDN, Script Ed.

DUBRO, James R.
- see WRITERS

DUDINSKY, Donna
40 Soudan Ave., Ste. 1501, Toronto, ON M4S 1V7 (416)485-4269.
Type of Production and Credits: TV Film-Prod/Dir/Ed; TV Video-Prod.
Genres: Variety-TV; Documentary-TV; Educational-TV; Children's-TV.
Biography: Born in St. Jean, Quebec. Languages: English and French. B.A.

Honours English, McGill University. Editorial board, *Take One*; editor, *Interlock*; articles, reviews and interviews for newspapers and magazines; film critic for CBC Intl; assessed scripts, NFB; consultant to Secretary of State; production and location manager on documentaries and dramas; archival film expert; researched over 50 programs; film and research consultant: Washington, Toronto, Montreal, Vancouver; Managing Director, Television Division, Academy of Canadian Cinema and Television, 87-89. Has won awards for *Goodbye War*.
Selected Filmography: "Beyond the Line" (13 eps), TV, 89-90, CDN/USA, Prod; *1988 Gemini Awards*, TV, 88, CDN, Co-Exec Prod; "Durrell in Russia" (13 eps), TV, 84-86, CDN/GB/USR, Prod; *Daly*, ED, 84, CDN, Dir; *Goodbye War*, "War", TV, 82-83, CDN, Dir/Prod; "War" (7 eps), TV, 80-83, CDN, Assoc Prod/Res/Interv; "10,000 Day War" (26 eps), TV, 79-80, CDN, Res; *The Image Makers*, TV, 79, CDN, Assoc Prod/Res.

DUFRESNE, Hélène
APFTQ. 3994, Parc Lafontaine, Montréal, PQ H2L 3M7 (514)527-8616. Les Productions Télémagik Inc., 1217 rue Notre-Dame est, Montréal, PQ H2L 2R3 (514)522-2324.
Types de production et générique: l métrage-Prod; c métrage-Prod; TV Vidéo-Prod.
Types d'oeuvres: Drame-C; Comédie-TV; Variété-TV; Documentaire-C&TV.
Curriculum vitae: Née à Trois-Rivières. Langues: français et anglais. Travaillé à la pige comme technicienne au cinéma, 81-84. A participé à l'organisation de la Fête Foraine de Baie St-Paul, 82, 83, 84, puis à la naissance du Cirque du Soleil. Court séjour a Télévision Quatre Saisons, 87. Fondation des Productions Télémagik, division Film et Vidéo du Groupe du Soleil, 88.
Filmographie sélective: *Le Cirque réinventé*, Le Cirque du Soleil, TV, 89, CDN, Prod; *Jasmin Spécial-Rentrée*, TV, 87, CDN, Dir prod; "Jasmin Centre-Ville" (112 eps), TV, 87, CDN, Dir prod; "Jolis à Croquer" (15 eps), TV, 87, CDN, Dir prod; *La Magie Continue, Le Cirque du Soleil*, TV, 86, CDN, Dir prod.

DUNCAN, Bob
- see WRITERS

DUNDAS, Sally
190 Crawford St., Toronto, ON M6J 2V6 (416)531-1461. Imax Corporation, 38 Isabella St., Toronto, ON M4Y 1N1 (416)960-8509.
Type of Production and Credits: Th Film-Prod; TV Film-Prod.
Genres: Drama-Th&TV; Documentary-Th; Children's-TV.
Biography: Born 1953, England; British and Canadian citizenship. Educated in England. Freelance production manager since 73; senior production executive, First Choice, 82-83; on staff at Imax Corp. since 86. *The Last Buffalo*, Best Audio-Visual Production, World Expo; *Echoes of the Sun*, Best Pavillion, World Expo.
Selected Filmography: *Mountain Gorilla* (Imax), Th, 90-91, CDN, Prod; *The Last Buffalo* (Imax 3D), Th, 89-90, CDN, Co-Prod; *Echoes in the Sun* (Imax), Th, 88-89, Co-Prod; *Heartland* (Imax), Th, 87, CDN, Co-Prod; "The Edison Twins" (26 eps)(Cycles IV & V), TV, 84-85, CDN, PM; *Skyward* (Imax), Th, 84, CDN, PM; *Freedom to Move*, Th, 84, CDN, Pro Exec; *Ticket to Heaven*, Th, 80, CDN, PM; *Escape from Iran: The Canadian Caper*, TV, 80, CDN, PM; *Clown White*, TV, 80, CDN, PM; *Head On*, Th, 79, CDN, PM; *Summer's Children*, Th, 78, CDN, PM; *I Miss You, Hugs and Kisses*, Th, 77, CDN, PM; *The Shoe Fits*, TV, 76, CDN, Assoc Prod.

DUNNING, John
ACTRA. Cinépix Inc., 8275 Mayrand, Montreal, PQ H4P 2C8 (514)342-2340. FAX: 342-1944.
Type of Production and Credits: Th Film-Prod/Wr.
Genres: Drama-Th; Comedy-Th; Science Fiction-Th; Horror-Th; Action-Th.
Biography: Born Montreal, Quebec. Languages: English and French. Co-founder and Chairman of the Board, Cinépix Inc. *Princes in Exile* won Golden Nymph, Monte Carlo and Gold Award, Houston Film Festival; *Meatballs* won Golden Reel.
Selected Filmography: *Princes in Exile*, TV, 89, CDN, Prod; *Snakeeater II - The Drug Buster*, Th, 89, CDN, Prod/Wr; *Whispers*, Th, 89, CDN, Prod; *Snakeeater*, Th, 88, CDN, Prod/Wr; *The Vindicator*, Th, 84, CDN, Co-Prod; *Meatballs III*, Th, 84, CDN, Co-Prod; *Spacehunter*, Th, 83, CDN, Co-Prod; *Happy Birthday to Me*, Th, 80, CDN, Co-Prod; *Yesterday*, Th, 79, CDN, Co-Prod/Co-Wr; *Meatballs*, Th, 78, CDN, Co-Exec Prod; *Rabid*, Th, 76, CDN Prod; *Death Weekend*, Th, 75, CDN, Co-Exec Prod; *Shivers/They Came from Within-The Parasite Murders*, Th, 74, CDN, Co-Prod; *L'Initiation*, Th, 69, CDN, Co-Prod; *Valerie*, Th, 68, CDN, Co-Prod.

DUPUIS, François G.
APFVQ, ARRFQ, STCQ. 1069 Route 219, Hemmingford, PQ J0L 1H0 (514)247-2579. ACPAV, 1050 est, boul. René-Lévesque, bur. 200, Montréal, PQ H2L 2L6 (514)849-2281.
Types de production et générique: l métrage-Prod; c métrage-Réal; TV film-Mont.
Types d'oeuvres: Drame-C&TV; Documentaire-C&TV; Education-TV.
Curriculum vitae: Né en 1947. Prix remporté: *Raili Minkanen* gagne le Wilderness Award; meilleur film expérimental, Yorkton, pour *Les oiseaux ne meurent pas de faim*; Un Makhila d'Argent pour *O Picasso*, festival de Biarritz, 87; Prix de la Critique pour *Lamento pour un homme de lettres*, festival du Nouveau Cinéma de Montréal, 88.
Filmographie sélective: *Lamento pour un homme de lettres*, C, 88, CDN, Prod; *Le Marchand de jouets*, C, 88, CDN, Prod; *Le trou du diable*, C, 88, CDN, Prod; *Le Dernier Havre*, C, 86, CDN, Mont; *O Picasso*, C, 86, CDN, Prod; *Pluie d'été*, C, 84, CDN, Mont; *Pourquoi l'étrange M. Zolock' s'intéressait-il tant à la bande dessinée*, C, 83, CDN, Mont; *Les Candidats*, C, 81, CDN, Prod; *En plein coeur*, TV, 81, CDN, Réal/Co sc; *T'étais belle avant*, TV, 80, CDN, Mont; *Cogne-Dur*, C, 79, CDN, Mont; *Les oiseaux ne meurent pas de faim*, C, 79, CDN, Réal/Sc; *Les "Borges"*, TV, 77, CDN, Mont; *Jos Carbone*, C, 75, CDN, Mont; *Les aventures d'une jeune veuve*, C, 74, CDN, Mont.

DYS, Hans J.
- see WRITERS

EARL, Morgan
ACTRA, CFTA, ACCT. 179 Bellefair Ave., Toronto, ON M4L 3V1 (416)698-4042. McCartney Enterprises, P.O. Box 128, Stn. Z, Toronto, ON M5N 2Z3 (416)250-6541. Phil Kent, Creative Artists, 1888 Century Park E., Ste. 1400, Los Angeles, CA 90067 USA (213)277-4545.
Type of Production and Credits: TV Film-Prod/Wr; TV Video-Prod/Wr; Th Film-Prod/Wr.
Genres: Drama-Th&TV; Comedy-Th&TV; Variety-TV.
Biography: Born 1934; Canadian citizen. Languages: English and French. B.Comm., McGill University. Broadcast producer, 25 years experience: commercials, documentary, TV specials and series. Winner of 13 Clio awards; *Billboard* award for Best Radio Program, 75.
Selected Filmography: *Brian Orser - Night Moves*, TV, 91, CDN, Prod/Wr; *1989 Gemini Awards*, TV, 89, CDN, Prod/Wr; *Brian Orser: Skating Free*, TV, 89, CDN, Prod/Wr; "Just for Laughs" (6 eps), TV, 89, CDN, Prod; *1988 Gemini Awards*, TV, 88, CDN, Prod/Wr; "4 on the Floor - The Frantics", TV, 86, US/CDN, Prod/Story Ed; *One Fine Weekend: The Lighthouse Reunion*, TV, 82, CDN, Prod.

ECKERT, John M.
CFTPA, DGA, DGC, ACCT. John M. Eckert Prod. Ltd., 385 Carlton St., Toronto, ON M5A 2M3 (416)960-4961.
Type of Production and Credits: Th Film-Prod; TV Film-Prod.
Genres: Drama-Th&TV; Comedy-Th&TV; Action-Th&TV; Horror-Th&TV.
Biography: Canadian citizen. Studies in Photographic Arts, Motion Picture, Ryerson Polytechnical Institute, 71. *Special People* won Christopher Award, 85. Involved in producing feature films, made for television movies and television series in Canada since 71; co-production ventures with partners in USA, USSR and UK; postproduction in Toronto, LA, NY and London, UK; has performed consulting services for the Motion Picture Bond Company Inc. and Film Finances Inc.; member of Film Studies Advisory Committee, Ryerson Polytechnical Institute, since 85; currently developing projects for film and television production.
Selected Filmography: *Car 54, Where Are You*, Th, 90, USA, Spv Prod; *Deep Sleep*, Th, 89, CDN, Prod; *Millennium*, Th, 88, CDN, Spv Prod/2nd U Dir; "Danger Bay" (66 eps)(Dir 1 eps, 2nd U Dir 4 eps), TV, 85-87, CDN, Spv Prod; *Home Is Where the Hart Is*, Th, 86, CDN, Prod; *Silver Bullet*, Th, 84-85, USA, Assoc Prod; *Cat's Eye*, Th, 84, USA, Pro Exec; *Special People*, TV, 83, CDN/USA, Prod; *The Dead Zone*, Th, 83, USA, PM; *The Terry Fox Story*, Th, 82, CDN, Assoc Prod; *Middle Age Crazy*, Th, 79, CDN/USA, Co-Prod; *Running*, Th, 78, CDN, Co-Prod; *Power Play*, Th, 77, CDN/GB, Assoc Prod; *Home Free*, Th, 72, CDN, Dir/Prod; *Three Films: Toronto*, Th, 70, CDN, Dir/Prod.

EDMONDS, Alan
33 Roxborough St. W., Toronto, ON M5R 1T9 (416)926-0220. Deja Communications Inc., 56 The Esplanade, Ste. 503, Toronto, ON M5E 1A7 (416) 360-0995. Stephen Waddell, Talent Associates, 387 Bloor St. E., Toronto, ON M4W 1H7 (416)961-3304.
Type of Production and Credits: TV

Video-Prod/Wr/Host.
Genres: Documentary-TV; Industrial-TV; Current Affairs-TV; News-TV.
Biography: Born in 1938 in London, England. In Canada since 1960. Newspaper special correspondent and editor in England, Canada and the United States. Subsequently magazine writer and editor. Co-founder, co-host, producer and writer of CTV Network current affairs show, "Live It Up". Guest host on other network news and public affairs shows. Writer of several documentaries. Winner of a Producer's Gemini, 1987.
Selected Filmography: "Live It Up", TV, 77-88, CDN, Prod/Wr/Co-Host.

EDWARDS, Cash
- see WRITERS

EGOYAN, Atom
- see DIRECTORS

EIGENMANN, Jean-Daniel
ADISQ, ACCT. 4091 Hingston, Montreal, PQ H4A 2J6 (514)486-0213. Poly-Productions (Entr. Phot. Eigenmann Inc.), 1583 St. Laurent Blvd., Montreal, PQ H2X 2S9 (514)288-4823. FAX: 288-4039.
Type of Production and Credits: TV Video-Prod.
Genres: Variety-TV; Documentary-TV; Educational-TV; Current Affairs-TV.
Biography: Born 1948, Fribourg, Switzerland. Languages: English and French. Ecole des Arts & Métiers, Photography, Veney, Switzerland. Opened photo studio, Montreal, 78; developed new optical technique for photographic special effects. Specializes in slide shows and multi media (multi-screens, panorama, multi-projectors, etc.), 83 to date. Still photography for animation of *Sam Borenstein*, 90. Prix de la Ville de Bièvres Phot-Univers (photographs in the permanent collection of the Musée de la photographie, Bièvres, France), 78. Graphisme Québec, Grand Distinction, category: posters of 3 colours or more, 88.
Selected Filmography: *Le Monde selon Clémence*, TV, 90, CDN, Prod; *Tête à Tête Avec J.-G. Moreau*, TV, 90, CDN, Prod; *Olivier*, TV, 89, CDN, Prod, (FELIX).

EL-SISSI, Azza
ATPD. 331 Seaton St., Toronto, ON M5A 2T6 (416)923-3166. CBC TV - Current Affairs, P.O. Box 500, Stn. A, Toronto, ON M5W 1E6 (416)975-6574.
Type of Production and Credits: TV Film-Prod/Dir/Wr; TV Video-Prod/Dir/Wr.
Genres: Drama-TV; Documentary-TV; Current Affairs-TV.
Biography: Born 1942, Cairo, Egypt; Canadian citizenship. Languages: English and Arabic. B.Sc., Electrical Engineering; diploma in teaching technologists; Canadian Studies, University of Toronto. Worked in broadcasting since 64 as an engineer, maintenance engineer, videotape editor before joining CBC drama as service producer, 75. With TV Current Affairs as documentary producer since 78. *The Price Tag* won the Gold Medal, NY. *Men, Sex and the Strait Jacket* won Best Videotape at Film Festival of the American Association for Counselling and Development, Houston, Texas. *For All the Good Intentions* won Chris Plaque at Columbus Film Festival. *Asylum* won Best Director, Anik 88.
Selected Filmography: *Asylum*, TV, 88, CDN, Prod/Dir/Wr, (ANIK); "Man Alive" (4 eps), TV, 87-88, CDN, Prod/Dir; *Cracking the Shell*, TV, 86, CDN, Prod/Dir; *For All the Good Intentions*, TV, 84, CDN, Prod/Dir; "Market Place" (2 eps), TV, 83, CDN, Prod/Dir/Wr; *Preemies, The Price Tag*, TV, 83, CDN, Prod/Dir; "The Journal" (2 eps), TV, 83, CDN, Prod/Dir; "Man Alive" (11 eps), TV, 78-82, CDN, Prod/Dir/Wr; *Pretty Babies/Men, Sex and the Strait Jacket*, "Man Alive", TV, 81-82, CDN, Prod/Dir; "A Gift to Last" (pilot), TV, 76, CDN, Serv Prod, (ANIK).

ELLIS, R. Stephen
CFTA. 182 Fulton Ave., Toronto, ON (416)421-3930. KEG Productions Ltd., 1231 Yonge St., Ste. 201, Toronto, ON M4T 2T8 (416)924-2186. FAX: 924-6115.
Type of Production and Credits: TV Film-Prod.
Genres: Documentary-TV; Children's-TV.
Biography: Born 1954, Ottawa, Ontario. Managing director, since 83, of KEG Productions Ltd., independent TV program production house affiliated with Maclean Hunter; President of Ralph C. Ellis Enterprises, independent TV program distributor (previously General Manager, 77-85); designed and implemented computer software package for distributors, 78-81; former CFTA President, 84-85; founding President CRC (Canadian Retransmission Collective), a non-profit cable royalty-collecting body for producers; currently Treasurer, CFTPA. Has won several awards in the field.
Selected Filmography: *A Passion for Canoes*, TV, 91, CDN, Exec Prod; *In Praise of Wolves*, TV, 90, CDN, Exec Prod;

Man of the Wilderness, TV, 90, CDN, Exec Prod; *Around the Inland Sea*, TV, 90, CDN, Exec Prod; *Treasure of Madera Canyon*, TV, 89, CDN, Exec Prod; "Wild Guess, Series 2" (26 eps), TV, 89, CDN, Exec Prod; *The Unpredictable Prairie*, TV, 88, CDN, Exec Prod; *From the Pacific Rim to the Serengheti*, TV, 88, CDN, Exec Prod; *Nature in Close-up*, TV, 87, CDN, Exec Prod; *Animal Aliens*, TV, 87, CDN, Exec Prod; *Camera in the Wilderness*, TV, 87, CDN, Exec Prod.

ELLIS, Ralph C.
CFTPA, ACCT. 211 Queen's Quay, #1015, Toronto, ON M5J 2M6 (416)363-4623. KEG Productions Ltd., 1231 Yonge St., Ste. 201, Toronto, ON M4T 2T8 (416)924-2186. FAX: 924-6115.
Type of Production and Credits: Th Film-Prod; TV Film-Prod.
Genres: Drama-Th&TV; Documentary-TV; Children's-TV.
Biography: Born 1924, Milton, Nova Scotia. Served in RCAF, 43-45; joined NFB as field representative in Halifax, 46; co-ordinator of theatrical distribution, Ottawa, 49-52; assist. regional supervisor, Toronto, 52-54; commercial representative, NY, 54-56; returned to Canada to specialize in international TV program distribution. Received the Jack Chisholm Award, CFTA, and Lifetime Achievement Award, Children's Broadcast Institute (CBI). Awards at many film festivals, including Yorkton, Chicago, New York, Cork, Moscow, Houston.
Selected Filmography: *Polar Bridge*, TV, 91, CDN, Prod; "Profiles of Nature Specials" (22 eps), TV, 87-91, CDN, Prod; *Spirit of the Wilderness*, TV, 89, CDN, Prod; *World of Baby Animals*, TV, 89, CDN, Prod; *Baby Animals*, TV, 87, CDN, Prod; "Profiles of Nature" (65 eps), TV, 84-87, CDN, Prod; *The Man Who Loved Birds*, TV, 86, CDN, Prod; *Images of the Galapagos*, TV, 83, CDN, Prod; "Wild Canada" (12 eps), TV, 78-81, CDN, Exec Prod, (CFTA); "Matt & Jenny" (26 eps), TV, 79, CDN/GB/D, Exec Prod, (CBI); "To the Wild Country" (10 eps), TV, 72-74, CDN, Exec Prod; *Wings in the Wilderness*, Th, 74, CDN, Exec Prod; "Wildlife Cinema" (26 eps), TV, 72, CDN, Exec Prod; "Audubon Wildlife Theatre" (78 eps), TV, 67-72, CDN, Exec Prod; "Adventures in Rainbow Country" (26 eps), TV, 69, CDN/GB/AUS, Exec Prod.

ELSON, Richard
ACCT, CIFC. 336 Longueuil, Longueuil, PQ J4H 1H5 (514)674-4453. Imageries PB Ltée, 816 est, rue de la Gauchetière, Montréal, PQ H2L 2N2 (514)845-0868.
Types de production et générique: l métrage-Prod; c métrage-Prod; TV film-Prod; TV vidéo-Prod.
Types d'oeuvres: Documentaire-C&TV; Education-C&TV; Animation-C&TV; Industriel-C&TV.
Curriculum vitae: Né en 1949, Etats Unis. Citoyenneté américaine, immigrant reçu au Canada. Langues: français, anglais. Etudes en Science Politique à Wabash College, BFA (cinéma) de l'Université Concordia et études cinématographiques à l'Université de New York. Producteur de documentaires, d'émissions d'éducation, d'animation et de films industriels pour long et court métrage ainsi que pour télévision et vidéo.
Filmographie sélective: *Lucien Francoeur L'Amérique Inavouable*, C/TV, 91, CDN, Prod; *Bonjour! Shalom!*, C/TV, 91, CDN, Prod; *The Colours of My Father/Les Couleurs de mon Père*, C/TV, 91, CDN, Prod; *La Complainte du Béluga/The Cry of the Beluga*, C/TV, 89, CDN, Prod; *Inventer!*, C/TV, 86, CDN, Prod.

ENGEL, Paul David
AR, CTPDA, RTNDA, SMPTE. 4065 av. de Vendôme, Montreal, PQ H4A 3N2 (514)487-7639. CBC/Radio-Canada, 1055 René-Lévesque Blvd., Montreal, PQ H2L 4S5 (514)597-7500.
Type of Production and Credits: TV Film-Prod/Dir; TV Video-Prod/Dir.
Genres: Variety-TV; Documentary-TV; Educational-TV; Sports-TV.
Biography: Born 1949, Tacoma, Washington; Canadian citizen. Languages: English and French. B.F.A., Concordia University. Began as a freelance photographer; producer/director of News, Current Affairs and Sports since 79; supervisor, English News, 86; Manager, Current Affairs/Actualités, 87-91, Radio-Canada International, Montreal.
Selected Filmography: *Open Skies Verification Talks*, Ottawa, TV, 90, CDN, PM; *Francophone Summit*, Dakar, TV, 89, CDN, PM; *G-7 Economic Summit*, Toronto, TV, 88, CDN, PM; *Federal Election 1988*, TV, 88, CDN, PM; "Compass" (PEI), TV, 84-86, CDN, Prod/Dir; *Gold Cup 85*, TV, 85, CDN, Prod/Dir/Wr; *Gold Cup Parade*, TV, 85, CDN, Prod/Dir; *Health Care for the Handicapped*, TV, 85, CDN, Prod/Dir; *Sing Noel*, TV, 84, CDN, Prod/Dir; "Newswatch" (Montreal), TV, 79-84, CDN, Prod/Dir; *Steppin' Out*, TV, 84,

CDN, Prod/Dir; *PC Leadership Review*, TV, 83, CDN, Prod/Dir; "In the Public Eye", TV, 83, CDN, Prod/Dir; *Montreal Municipal Election*, TV, 82, CDN, Prod/Dir.

ENNIS, Bob
- see CINEMATOGRAPHERS

ERICKSON, Jim
- see DIRECTORS

ERLICH, Alan
- see DIRECTORS

ERNE, Andreas
174 Lakeshore Rd. W., Oakville, ON L6K 1E6 (416)842-9747. FAX: 842-9747.
Type of Production and Credits: Th Film-Prod; Th Short-Prod/Dir/Wr.
Genres: Drama-Th; Comedy-Th; Documentary-Th; Action-Th.
Biography: Born 1951, Luzern, Switzerland; landed immigrant, Canada. Languages: English and German. Motion picture studies, Ryerson Polytechnical Institute.
Selected Filmography: *H*, Th, 89, CDN, Dir/Prod; *God Rides a Harley*, Th, 87, CDN, Prod, (GENIE 88); *The Rocky Horror Picture Short*, Th, 80, CDN, Prod/Dir/Wr; *Skyprose*, Th, 79, CDN, Prod/Dir/Wr.

EVANS, Janet
CTPDA. 404 Athlone, Ottawa, ON K1Z 5M5 (613)722-3587.
Type of Production and Credits: Th Short-Dir; TV Film-Dir; TV Video-Prod.
Genres: Drama-TV; Variety-TV; Documentary-Th&TV.
Biography: Born 1939, U.K.; landed immigrant, Canada. Attended Central School, Stage Management course; worked for Granada TV, BBC London and Glasgow in Drama departments; immigrated to Canada, 66; writer/director, Crawley Films, 67; CBC Ottawa, writer/broadcaster; contract producer since 77.
Selected Filmography: "Switchback" (30 eps), TV, 86, CDN, Prod; Ice Time, "The Way We Are", TV, 85, CDN, Prod/Dir; "Local Drama" (3 eps), TV, 83, CDN, Dir/Prod, (ACTRA); "Scene from Here" (52 eps), TV, 79-81, CDN, Prod; "Country Report" (52 eps), TV, 77-79, CDN, Prod; Ottawa: The Nation's Capital, Th, 74, CDN, Dir, (CFA).

EVANS, Margaret
- see WRITERS

FAIRE, Sandra
ACCT, ACTRA. S.F. Productions, (416)975-6991.
Type of Production and Credits: TV Film-Prod/Wr; TV Video-Prod/Dir/Wr.
Genres: Comedy-TV; Variety-TV; Musical-TV; Documentary-Th&TV.
Biography: Produced and co-wrote top-rated specials for Anne Murray, k.d. lang, Bryan Adams, George Fox and Corey Hart. Produced and co-wrote *Anne Murray's Family Christmas*, CBC-TV's highest-rated variety special in over a decade. Executive Producer of Canada's "Live Aid" music documentary, *Tears Are Not Enough*. Created Canada's longest running video series for CBC-TV, "Video Hits." Has received numerous awards including 2 Gemini Awards, San Francisco Film Festival Honorary Award, Casby Award, as well as gold and platinum albums in recognition of support for Canadian recording artists. Produced 3 albums including the 'gold-selling' *Video Hits, Volume II*. Prior to CBC-TV, produced and directed "The Joyce Davidson Show" for CFTO-TV; directed "Canada AM" and "W5" for CTV/CFTO-TV; and was executive producer of entertainment and daytime programming for CBLT-TV.
Selected Filmography: *George Fox on Campus*, TV, 91, CDN, Wr/Prod; *Anne Murray in Disney World*, TV, 91, CDN, Wr/Prod; *George Fox's New Country*, TV, 90, CDN, Wr/Prod; "Video Hits" (1820 eps), TV, 84-91, CDN, Exec Prod; "Video Hits Presents" (12 eps), TV, 90, CDN, Exec Prod; *k.d. lang's Buffalo Cafe*, TV, 89, CDN, Wr/Prod, (GEMINI); *Anne Murray's Greatest Hits, Volume II*, TV, 89, CDN, Wr/Prod; *Bryan Adams: Live in Belgium*, TV, 89, CDN, Wr/Prod; *Anne Murray's Family Christmas*, TV, 88, CDN, Wr/Prod; *Corey Hart*, TV, 87, CDN, Wr/Prod; *Casby Rock Show*, TV, 87, CDN, Wr/Prod; *Ian and Sylvia Re-union*, TV, 86, CDN, Wr/Prod, (GEMINI); *Carole Pope & Rough Trade Farewell Concert*, TV, 86, CDN, Wr/Prod; *Toronto Arts Awards*, TV, 86, CDN, Wr/Prod; *Tears Are Not Enough*, TV, 85, CDN, Exec Prod.

FALZON, Charles
571 DeLoraine Ave., Toronto, ON M5M 2C7 (416)782-9989. Catalyst Entertainment Inc., 11 Bathurst St., Ste. 100, Toronto, ON M5V 2N8 (416)586-9634. FAX: 586-1295.
Type of Production and Credits: TV Video-Prod.
Genres: Comedy-TV; Drama-TV; Children's-TV.
Biography: Born 1956; Canadian citizen. Attended York University; Ryerson Radio & TV Arts Program. Has distributed programs as Sales Manager for CBC

Enterprises and MCA-TV; 3 years in New York as V.P. International for D.L. Taffner Ltd., distributing and packaging foreign co-productions; co-founded and formerly President, Producers Group International; currently President, Catalyst Entertainment Inc., a Toronto-based development and production packaging company; also President, Producers Group Distribution Inc., a subsidiary of Catalyst, specializing in the distribution of television programs in the international marketplace; Chairman of the Board of Directors, CFTPA.
Selected Filmography: "Sweating Bullets" (22 eps), TV, 91, CDN/USA/MEX, Co-Exec Prod; "Shining Time Station" (PBS & YTV) (20 eps), TV, 91, USA, Exec Prod; "Mosquito Lake" (19 eps), TV, 90, CDN, Exec Prod; "Spatz" (13 eps), TV, 90, GB, Exec Prod; "Learning the Ropes" (24 eps), TV, 88, CDN, Prod; "Check It Out!" (22 eps), TV, 85-86, CDN/USA, Pro Exec.

FANFARA, Stephan
- see EDITORS

FARR, Gordon
ACCT, ACTRA, WGA, DGA. Twenty Paws Prod. Inc., 502 N. June St., Los Angeles, CA 90004 USA (213)467-1828. The Barry Perelman Agency, 9200 Sunset Blvd., Los Angeles, CA 90069 USA (213)274-5499.
Type of Production and Credits: TV Film-Prod/Wr/Dir; TV Video-Prod/Dir/Wr.
Genres: Drama-TV; Comedy-TV; Variety-TV; Sports-TV.
Biography: Born in 1942 in Toronto, Ontario. Canadian citizen. Producer, director, writer for CTV, 1964-67. Writer and/or producer of 8 variety series (USA) and approximately 10 variety specials, 67-71. Writer and/or producer for several hundred television shows.
Selected Filmography: "American Dreamer" (3 eps), TV, 91, USA, Wr; "Dog House" (9 eps), TV, 91, CDN/USA, Wr; "Diamonds" (1 eps), TV, 90, CDN/USA/F, Wr; "We Got It Made" (44 eps), TV, 88/89, USA, Exec Prod/Wr; "New Love American Style" (110 eps), TV, 87, USA, Exec Prod/Wr; "The Love Boat" (90 eps), TV, 75-80, USA, Prod/Wr/Dir; "The Bob Newhart Show" (50 eps), TV, 74-75, USA, Prod/Wr; "Maude" (3 eps), TV, 72-74, USA, Wr; "Doc" (1 eps), TV, 74, USA, Wr; "The Glen Campbell Show" (26 eps), TV, 74, USA, Wr; "Bridget Loves Bernie" (24 eps), TV, 73, USA, Prod/Wr; "Dianna" (24 eps), TV, 73, USA, Prod/Wr; "The Jeffersons" (3 eps), TV, 73, USA, Wr; "Rhoda" (1 eps), TV, 73, USA, Wr; "This Is Tom Jones" (pilot), TV, 72, USA, Prod/Wr.

FEINGOLD, Stan
- see WRITERS

FENSKE, Wayne
CFTA, DGC, ACCT. 456 Ontario St., Toronto, ON M5A 2W1 (416)964-0194. LTB Productions, 137 Berkeley St., Toronto, ON M5A 2X1 (416)360-0053. FAX: 360-1253.
Type of Production and Credits: TV Film-Prod; TV Video-Prod.
Genres: Drama-TV; Variety-TV; Musical-TV; Commercials-TV.
Biography: Born 1947, Toronto, Ontario. B.A.A., Radio and TV Arts, Ryerson Polytechnical Institute. Has worked as Executive Producer on over 2000 commercials and won over 500 international awards.
Selected Filmography: *Full Circle Again*, TV, 84, CDN, Prod; *The Rich Little Show*, TV, 83, CDN, Prod; *Shocktrauma*, TV, 82, CDN, Prod; *The Magic Show*, TV, 80, CDN, Prod.

FERGUSON, Graeme
- see DIRECTORS

FERNS, W. Paterson
ACTRA, CFTPA, ACCT. 78 Manor Rd. E., Toronto, ON M4S 1P8 (416)484-4882. Primedia, 219 Front St. E., Toronto, ON M5A 1E5 (416)361-0306.
Type of Production and Credits: TV Film-Prod/Wr; TV Video-Prod.
Genres: Drama-TV; Musical-TV; Documentary-TV; Children's-TV.
Biography: Born 1945, Winnipeg, Manitoba. B.A., Cambridge University (First Class Honours/Wrenbury Scholar); M.Soc.Sc., Birmingham University. President, Banff TV Foundation, 84-89; President, CFTA, 79-81; President ACFTP, 84-85. President: Primedia Entertainment Inc; Primedia Productions Limited; Comedia Entertainment Inc.; Primedia Releasing Inc.; Primedia/Héroux Productions Inc. Vice-President: Primedia Pictures Inc.; Soapbox Productions Inc. CFTPA Personal Achievement Award, 90; first recipient, Chetwynd Award. Numerous other awards include the Quebec/Alberta Prize, 87, and Gold and Bronze (Houston) for *Heaven on Earth* and *Going Home* respectively; Padua Award for *Bold Steps*; First Prize (Venice) for *Countdown to Looking Glass*; Gold (Chicago) for *Lynn Seymour: In a Class of Her Own*; and Emmy nominations for "The Newcomers" and *Onegin*.

Selected Filmography: *Young Catherine*, (mini-series), TV, 90, CDN/USA/GB/USR, Exec Prod; "Stage on Screen" (8 eps), TV, 90-91, CDN, Exec Prod; "Northwood" (6 eps), TV, 90, S, Exec Prod; *Glory Enough for All*, TV, 87, GB, Exec Prod; *Passion and Paradise*, (mini-series), TV, 87, GB, Exec Prod; "Life Revolution" (6 eps), TV, 87, CDN, Exec Prod; "Talkabout" (260 eps), TV, 88-89, CDN, Exec Prod; *Heaven on Earth*, TV, 86, GB, Exec Prod/Prod; *Going Home*, TV, 86, GB, Exec Prod; *Onegin*, TV, 86, CDN, Prod; *Countdown to Looking Glass*, TV, 84, CDN, Co-Prod; "The Amateur Naturalist" (13 eps), TV, 83, GB, Exec Prod; *Billy Bishop Goes to War*, TV, 82, GB, Co-Prod; "Newcomers"/"Les Arrivants" (7 eps), TV, 76-78, CDN, Prod; "A Third Testament", TV, 73, CDN, Prod/Dir.

FERRETTI, Nina
CTPDA. 735 Bidwell St., Ste. 5B, Vancouver, BC V6G 3B9 (604)685-5140.
Type of Production and Credits: TV Video-Prod/Dir/Wr/Res/Interv.
Genres: Variety-TV; Children's-TV; Commercials-TV; News-TV.
Biography: Born 1949, France; French and Canadian citizenship. Languages: English and French. Two years of university studies in Arts/Drama. Twelve years experience in television production from live news broadcast to children's stories. Directed and produced 2-hour live variety special, broadcast simultaneously on radio and television.
Selected Filmography: "Génies en Herbe"/"Reach for the Top", TV, CDN, Prod/Dir; "SMAC", TV, CDN, Prod/Dir; "Video Club", TV, CDN, Prod/Dir; "Aujourd'hui Pour Demain", TV, CDN, Prod/Dir; "Ce Soir" (regional newscast), TV, CDN, Prod/Dir; "Le Point"/"The Journal" (sev seg), TV, CDN, Prod/Dir; "Le Telejournal"/"The National" (sev seg), TV, CDN, Prod/Dir; "Le Sens des Affaires", TV, CDN, Prod/Dir; "Vendredi Vingt Heure", TV, CDN, Prod/Dir; "La Semaine Verte", TV, CDN, Prod/Dir; "Autoroute Electronique", TV, CDN, Prod/Dir; "Au jour le jour", TV, CDN, Prod/Dir; "Le Lien", TV, CDN, Prod/Dir.

FERRON, René ✧
UDA, SARDEC, ACCT. (514)844-4504.
Types de production et générique: TV film-Prod/Réal; TV vidéo-Prod/Réal.
Types d'oeuvres: Documentaire-TV; Variété-TV;
Curriculum vitae: Né en 1935, Trois-Rivières, Québec. Baccalauréat ès Arts, Université d'Ottawa; études en sciences politiques, la Sorbonne, Paris, France.
Filmographie sélective: "Caméra 88", TV, 86-88, CDN, Prod/Réal/Conc; "SOS Télé", TV, 86-88, CDN, Prod; "Coup de foudre", TV, 86-88, CDN, Prod/Conc/Cam; "Au jour le jour", TV, 80-85, CDN, Journ; "Télémag", TV, 77-80, CDN, Journ; "Magazine économique", TV, 80, CDN, Journ.

FERSTMAN, Brian
- see PRODUCTION MANAGERS

FICHMAN, Ina
ACTRA. 4350 Melrose, Montreal, PQ H4A 2S6 (514)369-1701. Maximage Productions, 3981 boul. St. Laurent, Ste. 801, Montreal, PQ H2W 1Y5 (514)987-1818. FAX: 987-1819.
Type of Production and Credits: Th Short-Prod; TV Film-Prod; TV Video-Prod/Dir.
Genres: Drama-Th&TV; Documentary-TV; Commercials-Th&TV.
Biography: Born in 1961 in Montreal, Quebec. Degree in Communications, Carleton University. Worked for CBC Radio and Television. Founding member of Montreal Women in Film. Vice-President of Maximage Productions. *La Deroute* nominated as Best Short Film by the Rendez-Vous du Cinéma Quebecois. *Moïse* nominated for a Golden Sheaf Award. Languages: English and French
Selected Filmography: *Moïse*, TV, 91, CDN, Prod; *Okanada*, ED, 91, CDN, Pro; *Humpty Dumpty*, Cm, 90, CDN, Co Prod; *Moving Mountains: Yiddish Theatre in Russia*, TV, 90, CDN, Prod/Dir; *Les Trembleys*, Petro-Canada, Cm, 90, CDN, Co Prod; *La Déroute*, Th, 90, CDN, Prod; *Expotech* (3 spots), Cm, 90, CDN, Prod; *La Fleuve D'Energie*, TV, 90, CDN, Spv Producer; *Grand Canyon*, IMAX, Cm, 89, CDN, Prod; *Japon des Shoguns*, Th, 89, CDN, Prod; *Sida et Jeunes*, In, 89, CDN, Line Prod; *Dédale et Icare*, ED, 89, CDN, Prod; *Women Who Kill*, TV, 88, CDN, Res; *Puzzles*, TV, 87, CDN, Res; *Fringes*, ED, 84, CDN, Assist Dir.

FICHMAN, Niv
CFTA, ACCT. Rhombus Media Inc., 489 King St. W., Ste. 102, Toronto, ON M5V 1L3 (416)971-7856. FAX: 594-0153.
Type of Production and Credits: Th Film-Prod; TV Film-Prod/Dir/Ed; TV Video-Prod/Dir.
Genres: Drama-Th; Variety-TV; Musical-TV; Documentary-TV.
Biography: Born 1958, Tel Aviv, Israel;

Canadian and Israeli citizenship. Moved to Toronto, 67. B.A., Film Studies, York University. Founded Rhombus Media Inc. in 79 with Barbara Willis Sweete and Larry Weinstein. Currently on board of directors, Toronto Arts Council. Several awards including Chicago, New York, San Francisco, Yorkton, Banff and Nyon.
Selected Filmography: *Canadian Brass: Home Movies*, TV, 91, CDN/GB, Prod/Dir; *Le Dortoir*, TV, 91, CDN, Prod; *When the Fire Burns*, TV, 90, CDN/GB/E/D, Prod; *Prokofiev by Two*, TV, 90, CDN/CH/GB/D, Prod; *The Radical Romantic*, TV, 89, CDN, Prod, (GEMINI 90); *Ravel* (CDN/USA/E/NL/S/NOR/DK/SF), Th, 88, CDN, Exec Prod/Prod, (GEMINI 89); *Masterclass with Menuhin*, TV, 88, CDN, Prod/Dir, (GEMINI 88); *The Top of His Head*, Th, 87, CDN, Prod; *World Drums*, TV, 87, CDN, Prod; *A Moving Picture*, TV, 87, CDN, Prod, (GEMINI 87); *Guitar*, TV, 87, CDN, Prod/Dir; *A Moving Picture*, TV, 87, CDN, Prod, (GEMINI 87); *Guitar*, TV, 87, CDN, Prod; *Whalesong*, TV, 86, CDN, Prod; *All That Bach*, TV, 85, CDN, Prod.

FILTHAUT, Fred
3514 Edinburgh Dr., Regina, SK S4V 2G7 (306)789-4470. SaskWest Television Inc./STV Regina, 370 Hoffer Dr., Regina, SK S4N 7A4 (306)721-2211.
Type of Production and Credits: TV Video-Prod.
Genres: Children's-TV.
Biography: Born 1946, Maple Creek, Saskatchewan. Mount Royal College, Calgary. Started in television, CJLH-TV, Lethbridge, Alberta, 66. Chairman of CanPro, 84. Signed new independent station STV (CFRE-TV) on air, 87. Currently President of WAB (Western Association of Broadcasters). CanPro winner for "The Great Spelling Bee", 89.
Selected Filmography: "The Great Spelling Bee" (39 eps), ED/TV, 90-91, CDN, Exec Prod; *ABEX Awards*, TV, 90-91, CDN, Exec Prod.

FLAK, George ◊
(416)538-2666.
Type of Production and Credits: Th Film-Prod.
Genres: Drama-Th.
Biography: Born 1948, Dangan Luka, Yugoslavia; Canadian citizenship. LL.B., University of Toronto, 70. Joined CBC's legal department; became Executive Assistant to Vice-President and General Manager; set up own law practice, 76; later moved to film production.
Selected Filmography: *The Office Party*, Th, 88, CDN, Prod; *Crazy Horse*, Th, 88, CDN, Exec Prod; *Murder One*, Th, 87, CDN, Assoc Prod; *Dixie Lanes*, Th, 86, CDN/USA, Exec Prod; *Into the Fire*, Th, 86, CDN, Assoc Prod; *The Pink Chiquitas*, Th, 85, CDN, Assoc Prod; *Into the Minds of Men*, Th, 81, CDN, Exec Prod; *MGM Christmas Story*, Th, 81, CDN, Exec Prod.

FLOQUET, François ◊
APFVQ. (514)488-3437.
Types de production et générique: l métrage-Prod/Réal; TV film-Prod/Réal.
Types d'oeuvres: Documentaire-C&TV; Drame-C;
Curriculum vitae: Né en 1939, France; citoyenneté canadienne, 67. Doctorat en Géographie, Sorbonne, Paris. Fondation de Productions Via le Monde Inc., Montréal, 67. Président de l'APFQ, 79; ouverture de Productions Via le Monde François Floquet Inc., 84. Remporte la Médaille d'or et le Prix Spécial du Jury à Atlanta pour *Brésil* de la série "Aventure humaine".
Filmographie sélective: "Les Nouveaux Scientifiques" (13 eps), TV, 87-88, CDN, Réal/Cam; *Les Explorateurs de la mort*, TV, 88, CDN/F, Prod; *La Guêpe*, C, 85-86, CDN, Prod; *Les Aventures du grand écran*, TV, 85, CDN, Prod/Réal/Cam; "Le Paradis des chefs" (13 eps)(Cam et Réal 12 eps), TV, 79-83, CDN, Prod; *Chateau de Chapultepes*, "Les Histoires de l'histoire", TV, 81, CDN, Co réal/Cam; "Les Amis de mes amis" (13 eps)(Cam et Réal 4 eps), TV, 77-80, CDN, Co prod; *Le Grand Désert blanc*, TV, 80, CDN, Réal; *Spécial Baie James*, TV, 78-79, CDN, Prod/Réal; "Aventure humaine" (2 eps), TV, 73-77, CDN, Co prod/Réal/Cam; "Des idées, des pays, des hommes" (10 eps)(Réal 3 eps), TV, 77, CDN, Co prod; "Défi" (39 eps)(Réal et Cam 12 eps), TV, 74-77, CDN, Co prod; *Ahô...au coeur du monde primitif*, C, 76, CDN, Co prod/Co réal, (CFA); "Les Primitifs" (6 eps)(Cam et Réal 2 eps), TV, 70-74, CDN, Co prod; "Plein feu...l'aventure" (37 eps)(Cam et Réal 2 eps), TV, 70-74, CDN, Co prod.

FLOREN, Russell
PO Box 5961, Station A, Toronto, ON M5W 1P4 (416)969-9777. Lynx Images Releasing, 174 Spadina Ave., #606, Toronto, ON M5T 2C2 (416)777-9333. FAX: 777-1407.
Type of Production and Credits: Th Short-Prod.
Genres: Drama-Th; Comedy-Th; Documentary-Th&TV; Educational-Th&TV; News-TV.

Biography: Born 1965, Halifax, NS. Graduate, Film Program, Ryerson Polytechnical Institute. Academy of Canadian Cinema Apprenticeship Program. Recipient of Norman Jewison Award for *In 1956...*. Formed Lynx Images, 88, for production and distribu-tion. Company produced compilation tape of short films from across Canada and has produced the short films, *Alienation, Blue, In 1956..., Monumental, Studio* and the documentary *Ghosts of the Bay*. Partners in Lynx Images are Andrea Gutsche (director) and James Flaherty (DOP).
Selected Filmography: *Ghosts of the Bay*, ED/TV, 91, CDN, Prod/Dir; *Studio*, Th, 91, CDN, Prod; *In 1956...*, Th, 90, CDN, Prod; *See Bob Run*, ED, 90, CDN, Dist; *Scorched Earth - Film Distribution in Canada*, ED, 90, CDN, Dist; *Backstage - Canadian Short Films - Volume 2*, ED, 90, DN, Dist; *Catharsis - Canadian Film Shorts - Volume I/Canadian Independent & Student Film Shorts*, ED, 89, CDN, Dist.

FODOR, Thomas C.
On/Q Corporation, 1405 Bishop St., Ste. 101, Montreal, PQ H3G 2E4 (514)842-1183.
Type of Production and Credits: TV Video-Prod; InteractV-Prod.
Genres: Industrial-TV.
Biography: Born in Hungary. M.A., English, Concordia University. Winner of several awards, including Gold Cindy for Best Level 3 Interactive Video Training Program and Best Show Cindy, Outstanding Production for *Interact: Meridian Business Services*, 87; Best Industrial/Military Training Achievement, Nebraska Video Disc Awards for *PIVOT-1*, 86.
Selected Filmography: *Call Management Services II*, In, 91, CDN, Co-Prod; *Call Management Services I*, In, 90, CDN, Co-Prod; *Custom Calling Services*, In, 88, CDN, Co-Prod; *Interact*, Meridian Business Services, In, 87, CDN, Co-Prod; *Talking P.C. Data Demo*, Northern Telecom, In, 87, CDN, Co-Prod; *PIVOT-1*, In, 86, CDN, Co-Prod.

FOLDY, Peter
- see WRITERS

FOREST, Claude ✧
CFTA, ACCT. (204)786-2145.
Type of Production and Credits: TV Film-Prod; TV Video-Prod.
Genres: Documentary-TV; Music Video-TV; Current Affairs-TV.
Biography: Born 1954, Canada. Languages: French and English. CUPE cameraman, CBC, Current Affairs, 78-80; freelance researcher, "The Medicine Show", CBC, "24 Hours", numerous news features for "Téléjournal", 80-85; owner and general manager, Studio Forest Inc., 80; President and production manager, Les Productions de la Seine, 88.
Selected Filmography: *Main Street* (French adapt.), Th, 87, CDN, Dir; *Les Entre-prises Folle Entreprises inc.*, In, 86, CDN, Prod/Ed; *Le Cercle Molière* (French and English), Cm, 86, CDN, Prod/Ed; *Galaxy Garments Intl*, In, 86, CDN, PM.

FOREST, José
ACCT. 460 Abélard, #1C, Ile des Soeurs, Verdun, PQ H3E 1B5 (514)761-6261. Projet IMAGE, Centre de recherche, Centre hospitalier Côte-des-Neiges, 4565 ch. de la Reine-Marie, Montréal, PQ H3W 1W5.
Types de production et générique: TV film-Prod/Conc/Réal; TV vidéo-Prod/Conc/Réal.
Types d'oeuvres: Documentaire scientifique-C&TV/ED; Documentaire-C&TV/ED; Affaires publiques-C&TV; Drame-C&TV.
Curriculum vitae: Né à Montréal. Citoyenneté canadienne. Langues parlées et écrites: français et anglais. Nombreuses années d'expérience en audiovisuel (1960-91) dont la plus grande partie (1970-91) en production et réalisation professionnelle de films, d'émissions de télévision ou de vidéos en technologie de qualité "broadcast". Plus d'une dizaine d'années à des postes impliquant des responsabilités de planification, d'organisation de direction, de contrôle, d'évaluation, de gestion et d'administration. Formation en production cinématographique (caméra, éclairage, prise de son, montage) à l'Office National du Film du Canada, 1960. CanPro 89 (Prix télévisuel) et Showcase award pour *Une image à chaque nouveau chagrin*. CanPro 87 (Premier prix promotion) pour *Le Petit Prince de l'Estrie*. CanPro 85 (Premier prix documentaire dramatique) pour *Pourquoi*.
Filmographie sélective: *Une image à chaque nouveau chagrin*, TV/ED, 89, CDN, Prod/Conc/Réal; *Le Petit Prince de l'Estrie*, Cm, 88, CDN, Prod/Conc/Réal; *Pourquoi*, TV/ED, CDN, Prod/Conc/Réal; "Pascale et Martin découvrent", TV/ED, 82, CDN, Prod/Conc/Réal.

FORTIER, Bob
- see DIRECTORS

FOSTER, John C.
CSC, DGC. 77 Huntley St., Ste. 905, Toronto, ON M4Y 2P3 (416)963-4992.
Type of Production and Credits: Th

Film-Dir/DOP; Th Short-Dir/DOP; TV Video-Prod/Dir/DOP/Wr.
Genres: Drama-Th&TV; Variety-TV; Documentary-Th&TV; Current Affairs-Th&TV.
Biography: Born 1929. Worked at the National Film Board of Canada, 43-59: engineering department, 1 year; camera department (assistant cameraman, operating cameraman, director of photography), 15 years. Developed 35mm multi-camera studio systems and innovative location systems for drama filming.
Selected Filmography: "McGovern Campaign: Democrats Try Democracy" (6 eps), TV, 72, USA, Dir/Cam; "Bill Moyers Journal", TV, 68-72, USA, Dir/Cam; *The Master Blasters*, "60 Minutes", TV, 68-69, USA, Prod/Dir/Cam; "The Fifth Estate", TV, 62-69, CDN, Dir/Cam; *Hugh Hefner - The Most*, Th/TV, CDN, Dir/Cam; *Summer in Mississippi*, "CBC Compass", TV, 65-66, CDN, Dir/Cam; "CBC Close Up", TV, 59-63, CDN, Dir/Cam; *Ground Crew*, Th, 54, CDN, DOP; *The Rising Tide*, Th, 48-49, CDN, DOP/Cam.

FOSTER, Stephen
Fosterfilm Productions Ltd., 3556 W. 12th Ave., Vancouver, BC V6R 2N4 (604)731-5005.
Type of Production and Credits: Th Film-Prod; TV Film-Prod.
Genres: Drama-Th&TV; Comedy-Th&TV.
Biography: Born 1950, Toronto, Ontario. B.Sc., Biology and Neuropsychology, University of Victoria. Public affairs - CBC, host of "Through the Eyes of Tomorrow"; for TVO, host of "Whatever Turns You On." Performed at Stratford Festival, Theatre New Brunswick, Young People's Theatre and others. *The Outside Chance of Maximilian Glick* won Best Canadian Film, Toronto and Vancouver Film Festivals; "Max Glick" awarded for Achievement in Children's Television, Washington, DC.
Selected Filmography: "Max Glick" (26 eps), TV, 90-91, CDN, Exec Prod/Co Creator; *The Outside Chance of Maximilian Glick*, Th, 88, CDN, Prod.

FOURNIER, Eric
APFVQ, ACCT, ADISQ. 557, av. Davaar, Outremont, PQ H2V 3A7 (514)277-6271. Productions Téléféric inc., 3575 St-Laurent, bureau 812, Montréal, PQ H2X 2T6 (514)843-3297.
Types de production et générique: l métrage-Prod; c métrage-Prod; TV film-Prod; TV vidéo-Prod.
Types d'oeuvres: Drame-TV; Variété-TV; Documentaire-TV; Annonces-TV.
Curriculum vitae: Né en 1952, Sherbrooke, Québec. Langues: français et anglais. Baccalauréat en Administration des affaires, Université de Montréal (H.E.C.), 79; Maîtrise en Administration des affaires, H.E.C., 86. Producteur et administrateur, Productions du Verseau inc., 85-87; Président et producteur, Productions Téléféric inc., depuis 87 et compte à son actif des émissions de variété, documentaires, séries dramatiques ainsi que des courts-métrages. nombreux annonces et films industriels; conseil d'administration de Télépoint inc., 82-84; Les Studios Marko inc., 82-84; Les Productions du Verseau inc., depuis 81; Le Groupe Télécopro inc., depuis 86; Napoléon Télévision inc., depuis 88.
Filmographie sélective: "Libre-échange" (27 eps), TV, 90-91, CDN, Prod; *Signé, Charlotte S.*, TV, 90, CDN, Prod; "Tanzi", TV, 86-87, CDN, Prod; *Les Gars*, TV, 87, CDN, Prod; *Jasmin Spécial Rentrée*, TV, 87, CDN, Prod; "Manon" (46 eps), TV, 85-86, CDN, Prod; Pétro Canada, In, 86, CDN, Prod; "Les Enfants mal-aimés", TV, 84-85, CDN, Prod; Coca Cola/Alcan Institutionnel, Cm, 82-83, CDN, Prod; *Fantastica*, C, 79, CDN/F, Prod.

FOURNIER, Lili
DGC, IATSE. 165 Lascelles Blvd., Toronto, ON M5P 2E7 (416)482-0052.
Type of Production and Credits: Th Film-1st AD; TV Film-1st AD; TV Video-Prod.
Genres: Drama-Th&TV; Comedy-Th&TV; Variety-Th&TV; Action-Th&TV.
Biography: Born in Transylvania, Romania; Canadian citizenship. B.A., Urban Studies, York University. Experience in live television and multiple camera drama; lifestyle and travel writer and columnist, 81-83; President, Zolar Entertainment Corp., 87-present, feature film development.
Selected Filmography: "Kay O'Brien", TV, 86, USA, Script Spv; *Alex, the Life of a Child*, TV, 85, USA, Script Spv; *Police Academy III*, Th, 85, USA, Script Spv; *A Case of Libel*, TV, 84, CDN, Script Spv; *Pygmalion*, TV, 83, USA, Assoc Dir; *What Is to Be Done?*, TV, 83, USA, Assoc Dir; *Pyjama Tops*, TV, 83, USA, Assist Dir/Script Spv; *Shocktrauma*, TV, 82, CDN, Assoc Dir/Assist Dir; *If You Could See What I Hear*, Th, 82, CDN, Script Spv; "Time to Quit", TV, 80, CDN, Assoc Dir/Assist Dir; *Death Hunt*, Th, 80, USA,

Script Spv; *Silence of the North*, Th, 79, CDN, Script Spv; *White Christmas*, TV, 79, USA, Script Spv; *James Robinson*, TV, 79, USA, Assoc Prod; "Spectrum" (13 eps), TV, 79, CDN, Prod/Host.

FOX, Beryl
14 Birch Ave., Toronto, ON M4V 1C9 (416)968-0595.
Type of Production and Credits: Th Film-Prod; Th Short-Prod.
Genres: Drama-Th&TV; Comedy-Th&TV; Documentary-TV; Current Affairs-TV.
Biography: Born Winnipeg, Manitoba. B.A., History, University of Toronto; honorary LL.D., University of Western Ontario. Awards at Atlanta, Vancouver and Columbus film festivals. Polk Journalism Award for *Mills of the Gods*.
Selected Filmography: *By Design*, Th, 80, CDN, Co-Prod; *Surfacing*, Th, 79, CDN, Prod; "Wild Refuge" (26 eps), TV, 74-75, CDN, Co-Prod/Dir/Wr; *Towards the Year 2000*, TV, 70-74, CDN, Co-Prod/Dir/Wr; "Here Come the Seventies" (78 eps), TV, 70-72, CDN, Co-Prod/Dir; *North with the Spring*, TV, 70, CDN/USA, Prod/Dir/Wr; *In Memoriam: Martin Luther King*, TV, 70, CDN/USA, Prod/Dir/Wr; *Last Reflections on a War*, TV, 68, CDN/USA, Prod/Dir/Wr; *View from the 21st Century*, TV, 68, USA, Prod/Dir/Wr; *Saigon: Portrait of a City*, TV, 67, USA, Prod/Dir/Wr; "This Hour Has Seven Days" (52 eps), TV, 64-66, CDN, Dir/Wr; *Mills of the Gods: Viet Nam*, "This Hour Has Seven Days", TV, 65, CDN, Prod/Dir/Wr, (ANIK/CFA); *One More River*, TV, 64, CDN/USA/GB, Co-Prod/Co-Dir; *Summer in Mississippi*, "This Hour Has Seven Days", TV, 64, Prod/Dir/Wr, (CFA); *NFB Toronto Studio*, ED, 64, CDN, Exec Prod.

FOX, Liz
ATPD, ACCT. 122 Ferrier Ave., Toronto, ON M4K 3H4 (416)465-2148. CBC, Box 500, Stn. A, Toronto, ON M5W 1E6 (416)975-6776.
Type of Production and Credits: TV Film-Prod/Wr; TV Video-Prod/Dir.
Genres: Documentary-TV; Educational-TV; Children's-TV; Current Affairs-TV.
Biography: Born in St. Catharines, Ontario. Has worked in radio, advertising and television, initially as writer and later as producer. Since 85, Executive Producer of "Wonderstruck," a series she developed for CBC.
Selected Filmography: "Wonderstruck" (179 eps), TV, 85-91, CDN, Exec Prod; *The Vortex*, "The Nature of Things", TV, 85, CDN, Prod/Dir; "Market Place", TV, 77-85, CDN, Wr/Prod; *Palaeontologist's Paradise/Burgess Shale Fossils*, "The Nature of Things", TV, 83, CDN, Prod/Dir/Wr; *Children Take Care*, TV, 83, CDN, Dir; *Irradiated Food*, "Country Canada", TV, 83, CDN, Prod.

FRANK, Anne
ACCT. 190 Bayview Heights Dr., Toronto, ON M4G 2Z2 (416)696-7939.
Type of Production and Credits: TV Film-Prod/Exec Script Cons.
Genres: Drama-TV.
Biography: M.A., Drama, University of Alberta, 72. B.A., French, Spanish. Producer, CBC TV drama, 74-89; Executive Script Consultant, Atlantis Films, 89-90; now independent producer. Winner, Silver Medal - New York, Blue Ribbon - American Film Festival, ACTRA award, Columbus Film Festival.
Selected Filmography: *Lost in the Barrens/Pray for Me Paul Henderson/Tom Alone*, TV, 90, CDN, Exec Script Cons; *A Change of Heart*, "For the Record", TV, 83, CDN, Prod; *Kate Morris, Vice-President/Becoming Laura/High Card*, "For the Record", TV, 82-83, CDN, Co-Prod; *A Far Cry from Home/Harvest*, "For the Record", TV, 81, CDN, Prod; *Homecoming/A Matter of Choice/Seer Was Here*, "For the Record", TV, 78-80, CDN, Prod; *Dreamspeaker/The Tar Sands/Hank*, "For the Record", TV, 77, CDN, Assoc Prod.

FRANK, Ilana
Norstar Entertainment Inc., 86 Bloor St. W., 5th Flr., Toronto, ON M5S 1M5 (416)961-6278.
Type of Production and Credits: Th Film-Prod; TV Film-Prod.
Genres: Drama-Th&TV; Comedy-Th&TV; Action-Th&TV; Horror-Th&TV.
Biography: Born Toronto, Ontario. B.A., York University. Worked in theatre for 8 years in Toronto, London. Partner in Stratton/Frank Associates.
Selected Filmography: *Intimate Delusions*, Th, 91, CDN, Co-Prod; *Prom Night III - The Last Kiss*, Th, 90, CDN, Exec Prod; *Cold Comfort*, Th, 88, CDN, Prod; *Blindside*, Th, 87, CDN, Assoc Prod; *A Switch in Time*, Th, 87, CDN, Pro Exec; *Hello Mary Lou - Prom Night II*, Th, 86, CDN, Assoc Prod; *Higher Education*, Th, 86, CDN, Co-Prod; "Mania" (4 eps), TV, 85, CDN, Co-Prod; *High Stakes*, Th, 85, CDN, Assoc Prod; *Bullies*, Th, 85, CND, Assoc Prod; *Burton Cummings: My Own Way to Rock*, TV, 84, CDN, Prod; *Curtains*, Th, 80, CDN, Assoc Prod; *Born*

to Run, TV, 80, CDN, Prod.

FRANKLIN, Elsa
3 Hillcrest Ave., Toronto, ON M4X 1W1 (416)961-6031. My Country Productions Inc., 21 Sackville St., Toronto, ON M5A 3E1 (416)868-1972.
Type of Production and Credits: TV Film-Prod; TV Video-Prod.
Genres: Drama-TV; Documentary-TV.
Biography: Born 1930, Ottawa, Ontario. Studied at Queen's University; Academy of Radio Arts and Sciences, Toronto; Neighbourhood Playhouse, New York; Martha Graham School of Modern Dance, New York. Founding Director of MCTV, Toronto; Director of McClelland and Stewart since 68; independent television producer for 23 years.
Selected Filmography: "The Secret of My Success", TV, 88, CDN, Prod/Dir; "Heritage Theatre" (26 eps), TV, 84-85, CDN, Prod; *I Married the Klondike*, TV, 83, CDN, Co-Creator/Prod; "The Great Debate" (234 eps), TV, 73-82, CDN, Prod; *Klondike Quest*, TV, 82, CDN, Prod/Dir; *Beginnings*, TV, 80, CDN, Wr/Dir/Prod; "Female Imperative" (24 eps), TV, 79, CDN, Wr/Prod/Dir; *Joso in Yugoslavia*, TV, 79, CDN, Wr/Dir/Prod; "Under Attack" (150 eps), TV, 68-76, CDN, Prod; "My Country" (52 eps), TV, 74, CDN, Prod; "A Day in the Life of" (2 eps), TV, 73-74, CDN, Creator/Prod; "Gallery", TV, 73-74, CDN, Creator/Prod; "Pierre Berton Show" (3000 eps), TV, 64-72, CDN, Prod; *55 North Maple*, TV, 70-71, CDN, Exec Prod.

FRAPPIER, Roger
APFTQ. Max Films inc., 5130, boul. St-Laurent, 4e étage, Montréal, PQ H2T 1R8 (514)272-4425. FAX: 274-0214.
Types de production et générique: l métrage-Prod; TV film-Prod.
Types d'oeuvres: Drame-C&TV; Comédie-C&TV; Action-C&TV; Documentaire-C&TV.
Curriculum vitae: Né en 1945, St-Joseph-de-Sorel, Québec. Langues: français et anglais. Producteur, monteur, réalisateur. Bien qu'il ait commencé sa carrière comme monteur et réalisateur, c'est surtout comme producteur qu'il fait sa marque. Associé à plusieurs des principaux succès du cinéma québécois de fiction des années 80 et 90. *Jésus de Montréal* a gagné 2 Prix, Festival de Cannes, 89; a été mis en nomination aux Oscars, 89; a gagné Prix Genie, 89: 12 Prix. *Un zoo la nuit* a gagné Prix Genie, 88: 13 Prix. *Le déclin de l'empire américain* a gagné Prix Genie, 87: 8 Prix; a été mis en nomination aux Oscars, 87; a gagné Prix de la Critique, Festival de Cannes, 86.
Filmographie sélective: *Ding et Dong, le film*, C, 91, CDN, Prod; *L'enfant sur le lac*, TV, 91, CDN, Prod; *A Lapse of Memory*, C, 90, CDN/F, Co prod; *Jésus de Montréal*, C, 88, CDN, Co prod; *Onzième spéciale*, TV, 88, CDN, Prod; *Un zoo la nuit*, C, 86, CDN, Co prod; *Le déclin de l'empire américain*, C, 85, CDN, Co prod; *Pouvoir intime*, C, 85, CDN, Co prod; *Sonia*, C, 84-85, CDN, Co prod; *Anne Trister*, C, 85, CDN, Co prod; *Le dernier glacier*, C, 83, CDN, Co réal/Co sc; *Le confort et l'indifférence*, C, 81, CDN, Co prod; *L'infonie inachevée*, C, 72, CDN, Réal/Mont; *Le grand film ordinaire*, C, 70, CDN, Prod/Réal.

FRASER, Fil
- see WRITERS
FREWER, Terry
- see COMPOSERS
FRUET, William
- see DIRECTORS

FUSCA, Martha
TWIFT, ACCT, CIPC. 37 Knightswood Rd., North York, ON M4N 2H2. Stornaway Productions Inc., 160 Bloor St. E., Ste. 1220, Toronto, ON M4W 1B9 (416)923-1104.
Type of Production and Credits: TV Film-Prod/PM/Dir.
Genres: Drama-TV; Documentary-TV; Current Affairs-TV.
Biography: Born 1955, Italy; Canadian citizenship. Languages: English and Italian.
Selected Filmography: *Caught in the Crossfire*, TV, 91, CDN, Dir/Prod; *Out of Control*, TV, 90, CDN, Prod; *Angola*, TV, 89, CDN, Prod/PM; *The Shattered Dream*, TV, 89, CDN, Prod/PM; *Ethiopia and the Horn of Africa*, TV, 89, CDN, Prod/PM; *Witnesses: What Happened in Afghanistan*, TV, 89, CDN, Prod/PM; *Promises to Keep*, TV, 88, CDN, Prod; *The Twice Promised Land*, TV, 86, CDN, Prod/PM; *Agents of Deception*, TV, 84, CDN, Prod.

GABOURIE, Richard
ACTRA, ACCT. Richard Gabourie Productions, 111 Poynter Dr., Weston, ON M9R 1L7 (416)248-8934.
Type of Production and Credits: Th Film-Prod/Wr; TV Film-Prod.
Genres: Drama-Th&TV; Comedy-Th&TV; Action-Th&TV; Documentary-Th&TV.
Biography: Born 1939, Moose Jaw, Saskatchewan. Has been an actor, writer and producer in television and feature film for more than 20 years. Winner "Best Film Actor" (Canadian Film Awards) for

Three Card Monte, 1978 Wendy Michener Award for Outstanding Achievement. *Silent Witness* and *The Long Walk* are currently in development.
Selected Filmography: *Buying Time*, Th, 87, CDN, Prod/Co-Wr; "The Achievers" (13 eps), TV, 85-86, CDN, Prod; *Show Biz Bally Hoo*, TV, 83, CDN, Exec Prod; *The Time Machines*, TV, 81, CDN, Exec Prod; *Treasures*, TV, 80, CDN, Exec Prod; *Title Shot*, Th, 79, CDN, Act/Wr/Exec Prod; *Three Card Monte*, Th, 77, CDN, Act/Wr/Prod, (CFA).

GABRIELE, Vincent
Prod. SDA Ltée, 1425 ouest, boul. René-Lévesque, Montréal, PQ H3G 1T7 (514)866-1761.
Types de production et générique: TV film-Prod; TV vidéo-Prod.
Types d'oeuvres: Drame-C&TV; Comédie-TV; Variété-TV.
Curriculum vitae: Né à Montréal, Québec. Diplôme en Communications, Université de Montréal, 69. BeP Publicité, 72-78: Chef de Publicité; Chef de Groupe; VP, Service Clientèle. Télé Métropole inc., 78-88: Chef des Programmes; Directeur de Programmation; VP, Programmation et Production. Prod. SDA Ltée, 88 à aujourd'hui: Producteur.
Filmographie sélective: "Sortir", TV, 90, CDN, Prod; *Denise Aujourd'hui*, TV, 90, CDN, Prod; *7e Ciel*, TV, 89, CDN, Prod.

GAD, Ezz E.
10 Grenoble Dr., #1208, Don Mills, ON M3C 1C7 (416)429-0055. Universal Horizons TV Prod., P.O. Box 375, Stn. P, Toronto, ON M5S 2S9 (416)340-0914. FAX: 260-0417. Ajman Ind. Studio, P.O. Box 4442, Ajman, UAE (971)642-4000.
Type of Production and Credits: TV Video-Prod.
Genres: Documentary-TV; Educational-TV.
Biography: Born 1932, Egypt; Canadian citizenship. Languages: English and Arabic. Educated at Cairo University, Ryerson Polytechnical Institute, School of Modern Photography, Centennial College.
Selected Filmography: "Reflections on Islam" (340 eps), TV, 83-90, CDN, Prod/Host; "Islamic Horizons" (650 eps), TV, 83-89, CDN/UAE, Prod/Host.

GAGNON, Claude
- voir REALISATEURS

GANDER, Mogens
CSC, ACCT. R.R. #5, Madoc, ON K0K 2K0 (613)473-2891.
Type of Production and Credits: Th Film-DOP; TV Film-DOP.
Genres: Drama-Th&TV; Documentary-Th&TV; Educational-Th&TV.
Biography: Born 1933, Denmark; Canadian citizenship. Languages: English and Danish. Initial employment at NFB; freelance cameraman for CBC and independent producers in Toronto; produced, directed and acted in many documentaries, commercials and CBC dramas.
Selected Filmography: *The Man That Wouldn't Die*, TV, 75, USA, 2nd U DOP; *The Chicago Seven*, Th, 72, USA, DOP; *The Long Way Home*, Th, 66, CDN, DOP.

GAREAU, John
CUPE. 68 Eastmount Ave., Toronto, ON M4K 1V1 CBC, P.O. Box 500, Stn. A, Toronto, ON M5W 1E6 (416)975-7631.
Type of Production and Credits: TV Film-Ed.
Genres: Drama-TV; Documentary-TV.
Biography: Born in 1947 in Montreal, Quebec. Graduated, Bachelor of Arts, Communication Arts, Concordia University,
Selected Filmography: "Adrienne Clarkson Presents" (49 eps), TV, 89-90, CDN, Assoc Prod; "Man Alive" (4 eps), TV, 89, CDN, Ed; "The Struggle for Democracy" (3 eps), TV, 88, CDN/GB, Ed; "The Nature of Things" (20 eps), TV, 77-86, CDN, Ed; *Up the Down Elevator*, "Quarterly Report", TV, 86, CDN, Ed; "A Planet for the Taking" (3 eps), TV, 85, CDN, Ed; "The Phoenix Team" (3 eps), TV, 79-80, CDN, Ed; "Toronto Jam" (pilot), TV, 79, CDN, Ed; "Sidestreet" (7 eps), TV, 76-77, CDN, Ed; "Adrienne At Large", TV, 76-77, CDN, Ed; "Hard Times" (4 eps), TV, 75-76, CDN, Ed; "the fifth estate" (10 eps), TV, 70s, CDN, Ed; "Take 60" (10 eps), TV, 70s, CDN, Ed; "Take 30" (20 eps), TV, 70s, CDN, Ed.

GAUVIN, Paul
4236 Fabre, Montréal, PQ H2J 3T6 (514)525-2739. G.R.A.A.V. inc., 1600 Delorimier, Montréal, PQ H2K 3W5 (514)521-1584.
Types de production et générique: c métrage-Prod; TV vidéo-Réal.
Types d'oeuvres: Variété-TV; Documentaire-TV; Enfants-C&TV; Expérimental-TV; Industriel-TV.
Curriculum vitae: Né en 1960. Langues: français, anglais. Citoyenneté canadienne. Maîtrise en histoire l'art programme d'étude cinématographique, Université de Montréal; programme d'étude supérieure, cours sur la communication et les nouvelles technologies, Université Concordia; Baccalauréat en beaux-Arts, production

cinématographique, Université Concordia; Baccalauréat général, Université Laval. Réalisateur et producteur depuis 1982.
Filmographie sélective: *Petit Théâtre Musical,* "Série Blanche, TV, 91, CDN, Réal/Prod; *Chi,* "Série Blanche", TV, 91, CDN, Réal/Prod; *Nellie,* C, 91, CDN, Prod; *Men Gen,* In, 89, CDN, Co prod; *Cela prend plus que du coeur,* In, 89, CDN, Cam montage; *Chauve-souris,* C/TV, 89, CDN, Prod; *Puzzle,* TV, 86, CDN, Réal; *Enfant: XIe siècle: Infans: Qui ne parle pas,* TV, 84, CDN, Réal.

GAUVREAU, Gil
- see DIRECTORS

GÉLINAS, Michel
4650 Garnier, Montréal, PQ H2J 3S7 (514)524-2521.
Types de production et générique: c métrage-Prod/Réal/Mont/D phot.
Types d'oeuvres: Expérimental-C&TV.
Curriculum vitae: Né à St-Jean-sur-Richelieu en 1958. Langues: français, anglais. M.A. Histoire de l'art - orientation études cinématographique (1990). Certificat d'études cinématographiques (1985), B.Sc. sociologie (complément en communication), 1983. Chargé de cours à l'Université de Montréal. Enseigne les techniques cinématographiques et la production depuis 1989. Meilleur sélection FIFREC 90 à Nîmes et nomination pour meilleur court-métrage au 8ième Rendez-vous du cinéma Québécois pour *Objets Perdus. En train de danser sur une musique de M. Muybridge* en nomination pour le meilleur court métrage expérimental au 26ième Festival de Yorkton (juin 90). Bronze Apple Award au "20th National Educational Film and Video Festival" dans la catégorie film et vidéo expérimental (Oakland, 90), Red Ribbon award au "31st American Film and Video Festival" dans la catégorie "Film as Art" (Chicago, 89), et mention spéciale, catégorie expérimentale au FFEC à Montréal en 88 pour *Sales Images.*
Filmographie sélective: *Duciel, une poussière d'ange,* C, 91, CDN, Prod/Co D phot; *20 octaves au dessous du Do moyen,* C, 90, CDN, Prod/Co réal/Mont; *Objets perdus,* C, 90, CDN, Prod/Co réal/Montage; *En train de danser sur une musique de M. Muybridge,* C, 90, CDN, Prod/Co réal/Montage; *Chutes,* C, 89, CDN, Prod/Co réal/Montage; *Sales Images,* C, 88, CDN, Prod/Co réal/Montage; *A votre service,* In, 87, CDN, Prod/D phot/Réal/Montage; *Meanwhile/en tretemps,* C, 87, CDN, Prod/Co réal/D phot/Montage.

GENDRON, Pierre
APFVQ, ACCT. 318 rue Sherbrooke est, Montréal, PQ H2X 1E6 (514)982-9770.
Types de production et générique: l métrage-Prod; TV film-Prod; TV vidéo-Prod.
Types d'oeuvres: Drame-C&TV; Comédie-C&TV; Expérimental-C&TV.
Curriculum vitae: Né en 1952, Grand-mère, Québec. Langues: français et anglais. Baccalauréat en Communications, Collège Loyola (Concordia), 74.
Filmographie sélective: *Ding et Dong,* Th, 90, CDN, Prod exéc; *Un Autre Homme,* TV, 89, CDN, Prod; *Moody Beach,* Th, 89, CDN, Prod; *Le Chemin de Damas,* C, 88, CDN, Prod; *Jésus de Montréal,* C, 88, CDN, Prod; *Un zoo la nuit,* C, 86, CDN, Prod (GENIE 88); *Lune de miel,* C, 85, CDN/F, Prod dél; *Le Déclin de l'Empire américain,* C, 85, CDN, Prod dél; *Sonatine,* C, 82, CDN, Prod.

GERBER, Sig
ATPD, ACCT. 26 Albertus Ave., Toronto, ON M4R 1J4 CBC, Box 500, Stn. A, Toronto, ON M5W 1E6 (416)975-6716.
Type of Production and Credits: TV Film-Prod/Dir; TV Video-Prod/Dir.
Genres: Drama-TV; Documentary-TV; Current Affairs-TV.
Biography: Born 1940, Germany; Canadian citizenship. Languages: English and German. B.A., Ryerson Polytechnical Institute. Worked as radio reporter in commercial radio and briefly for German TV before starting career at CBC, 64, as an editor. Studied Fine Arts; had paintings exhibited. *Life before Birth* and *To Be Truly Human* each won a Gabriel Award; *Ready for Slaughter* won Best TV Drama, Banff, and Bronze Medal, International Film and TV Festival, NY, 87; "Market Place" won Bronze at International TV & Film Festival, NY, 87; *Turning to Stone* won Red Ribbon, American Film Festival; *Oakmount High* won Gemini, Best Short Drama.
Selected Filmography: "Market Place" (136 eps), TV, 85-91, CDN, Exec Prod; *Turning to Stone,* TV, 85, CDN, Exec Prod; *Oakmount High,* TV, 85, CDN, Exec Prod; *Where the Heart Is/Tools of the Devil/The Front Line,* "For the Record", TV, 84, CDN, Exec Prod; *The Boy Next Door/Slim Obsession/Rough Justice,* "For the Record", TV, 83, CDN, Exec Prod; *Who's In Charge,* TV, 83, CDN, Dir; *Ready for Slaughter/Hide and Seek/Out of Sight,Out of Mind,* "For the Record", TV, 82-83, CDN, Exec Prod; "Take 30", TV, 79-78,

CDN, Prod/Dir; "Man Alive" (26 eps), TV, 78, CDN, Exec Prod; "Man Alive" (30 eps), TV, 72-78, CDN, Prod/Dir; *The Quiet Olympics*, TV, 76, CDN, Prod/Dir; *I Am Not What You See*, TV, 76, CDN, Prod/Dir; *Cuba: Faith in Revolution*, TV, 73, CDN, Prod/Dir; *Life Before Birth* (2 parts), TV, 72, CDN, Prod/Dir; *The Bittersweet Sounds: Bruce Cockburn*, TV, 71, CDN, Prod/Dir.

GERRETSEN, Patricia ◇
CFTA, ACCT. (416)484-9671.
Type of Production and Credits: Th Film-Prod/PM; TV Film-Prod/PM.
Genres: Drama-Th&TV; Educational-Th&TV; Commercials-Th&TV; Industrial-Th&TV.
Biography: Born 1942, London, Ontario. On-air talk show host on radio station WCAS, Cambridge, Mass., 68. Stringer for ABC's "Wide World of Sports." Produced for Foster Advertising Ltd., and Vickers and Benson. Own production house, 75.
Selected Filmography: *Night Friend*, Th, 87, CDN, Prod/PM; *The Kidnapping of Baby John Doe*, TV, 85, CDN, Prod/PM.

GIBB, Alan D.
- see EDITORS

GIBBONS, Bob
- see DIRECTORS

GILBERT, Tony
ACTRA, CTPDA. Togil Communications Inc., 3673 Loraine Ave., North Vancouver, BC V7R 4B9 (604)984-7011. FAX: 984-7011.
Type of Production and Credits: TV Film-Dir/Prod/Wr; TV Video-Dir/Prod/Wr.
Genres: Variety-TV; Musical-TV; Documentary-TV; Children's-TV.
Biography: Born 1940, Sydney, Australia; Canadian citizenship. Educated to university level. Twenty years in TV production with ABC (Sydney), BBC (London), CBC (Toronto, Vancouver); freelance producer/director/writer in Wester Canada and Australia since 78. Extensively trained in music; experienced private pilot.
Selected Filmography: *Return to Eagle Rock*, TV, 91, CDN, Prod/Dir/Wr; *Prizewinners*, TV, 90, CDN, Co Prod/Dir; "Inside Stories", TV, 90, CDN, Dir/Wr; "Children's Festival" (4 eps), TV, 90, J, Dir; *The Magic of Aladdin*, TV, 89, CDN/GB, Dir; *Don't Play Backstage*, TV, 89, CDN, Dir; *Die Fledermaus*, TV, 88, CDN, Prod/Dir; *The Cinderella Gang*, TV, 87, CDN/GB, Dir; *Rick Hansen: Sharing the Dream*, TV, 87, CDN, Dir;

TVONTARIO BOX 200 STATION Q
TORONTO M4T 2T1
CANADA

TELEPHONE
416/484-2600
FAX 416/484-6285
TELEX 06-23547

TVONTARIO C.P. 200 SUCCURSALE Q
TORONTO M4T 2T1
CANADA

TÉLÉPHONE
416/484-2600
TÉLÉCOPIEUR 416/484-628
TÉLEX 06-23547

"Worldstage 86" (42 eps), TV, 86, CDN, Prod/Wr; *Carmen*, TV, 86, CDN, Prod/Dir; *Canadance*, TV, 85, CDN, Prod/Dir; *Mozart at the Gallery*, TV, 84, CDN, Prod/Dir; *Vancouver Folk Festival*, TV, 83, USA, Dir; *Raffi's Really Big Show*, TV, 82, CDN, Dir.

GILDAY, Katherine
- see WRITERS

GILDAY, Leonard
- see CINEMATOGRAPHERS

GILLARD, Stuart
- see DIRECTORS

GILLIS, Kevin ✧
ACTRA, AFM, ACCT. (613)722-9115.
Type of Production and Credits: TV Film-Prod/Dir/Wr/Comp.
Genres: Variety-TV; Children's-TV; Animation-TV; Music Video-TV.
Biography: Born 1950, Ontario. Musical career includes writing themes for several television shows, as well as touring with Mary Travers of Peter, Paul and Mary; hosted television variety shows "Bang Bang, You're Alive!" and "Yes You Can!"; created the award-winning "Raccoons" specials and the television series; songs have been recorded by Rita Coolidge, Leo Sayer, Dottie West, Tom Schneider, Luba, Lisa Lougheed, Rupert Holmes.
Selected Filmography: "The Raccoons" (34 eps), TV, 84-88, CDN, Prod/Dir/Head Wr/Comp, (GEMINI 88); "Run with Us", MV, 87, CDN, Prod/Comp; "Raccoons- Let's Dance", MV, 84, CDN, Prod/Dir/Wr/Comp; *The Raccoons and the Lost Star*, TV, 83, CDN, Prod/Dir/Wr/Comp; *Raccoons on Ice*, TV, 81-82, CDN, Prod/Dir/Wr/Comp; "Yes You Can!" (46 eps), TV, 79-81, CDN, Comp; "Bang Bang, You're Alive!" (13 eps), TV, 79-81, CDN, Co-Prod; *The Christmas Raccoons*, TV, 80, CDN, Prod/Co-Dir/Co-Wr.

GINSBERG, Donald
77 Carlton St., #801, Toronto, ON M5B 2J7 (416)593-0753.
Type of Production and Credits: Th Film-Ed/Prod; Th Short-Ed/Prod; TV Film-Ed/Prod; TV Video-Prod/Dir/Ed.
Genres: Drama-Th&TV; Comedy-Th&TV; Action-Th&TV; Documentary-Th&TV.
Biography: Born in London, England; British and Canadian citizenship. Producer/director/editor of over 25 dramas and documentaries for the NFB and 100 TV commercials. Optioned the novel *The Man Without a Face* by Isabelle Holland; developed it into screenplay and sold all rights to Icon Productions/Warner Bros. Studios, to be filmed in summer of 92.
Selected Filmography: "Comedy Tonight" (13 eps), TV, 84-85, CDN, Creator/ Prod/Dir; *Search and Destroy*, Th, 78, CDN/USA, Ed, (CFEG); *To the Top*, Th, 75, CDN, Ed; *Making Nickel*, TV, 75, CDN, Ed, (CFEG); "The Collaborators" (13 eps), TV, 74, CDN, Ed; *Fortune and Men's Eyes*, Th, 71, CDN, Co-Prod; *The Earth Is Man's Home* (Expo 67), Th, 67, CDN, Dir/Ed; *Nobody Waved Good-Bye*, Th, 64, CDN, Ed; *The Most*, TV, 64, CDN, Ed; *Target for Tonight*, Th, 43, GB, Ed.

GIRALDEAU, Jacques
- voir REALISATEURS

GJERSTAD, Ole
ARRQ. 3524 Clark St., Montreal, PQ H2X 2R8 (514)281-8320. CBC, 1400 Réné-Lévesque Blvd. E., #1605, Montreal, PQ H2L 2M2 (514)597-6677.
Type of Production and Credits: TV Film-Prod/Wr; TV Video-Prod/Wr.
Genres: Documentary-TV; Educational-TV; Current Affairs-TV.
Biography: Born 1948, Bergen, Norway. Canadian citizen. Works in English, French, Portuguese and Norwegian. Has worked as a journalist since 1975 in print, radio and television. Has lived and worked in Africa, Europe and USA. *Mozambique: Riding Out The Storm* was a Golden Sheaf winner in 1989.
Selected Filmography: "Venture", TV, 91, CDN, Prod; "North-South", TV, 91, CDN, Prod; *Tovio: Child of Hope*, TV, 90, CDN, Wr/Loc Mgr; *Mozambique: Riding Out The Storm*, TV, 89, CDN, Wr/Dir.

GLASSBOURG, Michael
- see WRITERS

GLAWSON, Bruce
CFTA, ACCT. 129 Maitland St., Toronto, ON M4Y 1E5 (416)920-1897. Cambium Film & Video Prod. Ltd., 141 Gerrard St. E., Toronto, ON M5A 2E3 (416)964-8750. FAX: 964-1980.
Type of Production and Credits: TV Film-Prod/Dir/Ed; TV Video-Ed/Prod.
Genres: Variety-TV; Musical-TV; Documentary-TV; Children's-TV.
Biography: Born 1954, Brandon, Manitoba. B.A., Music, Brandon University, 75; recipient of the Silver Medal in music; B.F.A., (Specialized Honours in Film Production), York University, 77. Originally worked as a video and audio switcher/mixer at CBC Winnipeg and Toronto; formed Cambium Film & Video Productions Ltd., 82. Awards include Chris Plaques (Columbus) for *Contact* and *Michael, a Gay Son*, which

also won Best Documentary (Yorkton); "Elephant Show" won US Parents' Choice Award Television, 86, 87, and Silver Medal, (New York); *Jane Siberry, One More Colour*, Silver Medal, Annual Festival of the Americas, and Gold Medal, (New York); *Jane Siberry, I Muse Aloud*, Silver Medal, (New York) and Gold Hugo (Chicago).
Selected Filmography: *The Boy Who Dreamed Christmas*, "The Sandman", TV, 91, CDN, Prod; "Eric's World" (13 eps), TV, 90, CDN, Exec Prod/Co-Creator; "Sharon, Lois and Bram's Elephant Show" (65 eps), TV, 84-88, CDN, Co-Prod/Ed; *Luba, Between Earth and Sky*, MV, 88, CDN, Exec Prod; "Einstein Tonight", TV, 88, CDN, Co-Prod; *Eric Nagler: A Special for All Seasons*, TV, 88, CDN, Co-Prod; *Jane Siberry: I Muse Aloud*, MV, 87, CDN, Co-Prod; *Jane Siberry: One More Colour*, MV, 87, CDN, Co-Prod; "Sharon, Lois and Bram's Elephant Show" (12 eps), TV, 84, CDN, Co-Prod/Ed; *For Paul*, ED, 83, CDN, Prod/Dir; *Sharon, Lois and Bram at the Young People's Theatre*, TV, 83, CDN, Co-Prod/Co-Dir; *Michael, a Gay Son*, TV, 80, CDN, Prod/Dir; *Contact*, TV, 79, CDN, Co-Prod/Co-Dir/Cin.

GODBOUT, Claude
APFVQ, ACCT. 704 B, Champagneur, Outremont, PQ H2V 3P8 (514)276-8829. Les Productions Prisma Inc., 5253, av. du Parc, #330, Montréal, PQ H2V 4P2 (514)277-6686.
Types de production et générique: l métrage-Prod; TV film-Prod; TV vidéo-Prod.
Types d'oeuvres: Drame-C&TV; Documentaire-C&TV; Enfants-C&TV.
Curriculum vitae: Né en 1941, Montréal, Québec. Langues: français et anglais. Fondateur et Président directeur-général, Les Productions Prisma Inc. *Les Bons Débarras* a gagné 8 Prix Génie; *Servantes du Bon Dieu* fut invité à la Semaine de la Critique, Cannes; *Comme les six doigts de la main* remporte le Prix de la Critique Québécoise. *Les Ordres*, remporte le Prix de la Mise en Scène à Cannes.
Filmographie sélective: "Pacha et les chats" (65 eps), TV, 90-91, CDN, Prod exéc; "Tandem" (75 eps), TV, 89-90, CDN, Prod exéc; "Pachaison Deschênes" (394 eps), TV, 87-88, CDN, Co prod; "Marguerite et Compagnie" (390 eps), TV, 87-88, CDN, Co prod; "La Garderie des amis" (26 eps), TV, 88, CDN, Co prod; "Livre ouvert" (39 eps), TV, 84-87, CDN, Co prod; *La Rivière*, TV, 87, CDN, Co prod; "Profession: écrivain" (13 eps), TV, 83, CDN, Co prod; "Zigzag" (6 eps), TV, 83, CDN, Co prod; *Le Cahier Noir* "Screts diplomatiques", TV, 82, F, Co prod; *Le Plus Beau Jour de ma vie...*, C, 80, CDN, Co prod; *On n'est pas des anges*, C, 80, CDN, Co prod; *Thetford au milieu de notre vie*, C, 79, CDN, Co prod; *Les Servantes du bon Dieu*, C, 78, CDN, Co prod; *Les Bons Débarras*, c, 78, CDN, Co prod, (GENIE).

GOETZ, Ron
263 Fulton Dr., Regina, SK S4X 2N9 (306)545-8363. CKCR-TV Creative Service, Box 2000, Regina, SK (306)569-2000.
Type of Production and Credits: TV Film-Prod/Dir/Wr; TV Video-Prod/Dir/Wr.
Genres: Documentary-TV; Educational-TV; Children's-TV; Commercials-TV.
Biography: Born in 1958.
Selected Filmography: *Agriculture*, "Saskatchewan Resource Series" (6 eps), ED, 90, CDN, Prod/Dir; *Saskatchewan Day*, "Expo 86", TV, 86, CDN, Prod/Wr/Dir.

GOLD, Howard
ACCT. 23 Livingstone Rd., Thornhill, ON L3T 7B9 (416)731-0402. Palette, 340 Gerrard St. E., Toronto, ON M5A 2G7 (416)921-8987.
Type of Production and Credits: TV Video-Prod.
Genres: Drama-TV; Comedy-TV; Educational-TV; Industrial-TV.
Biography: Born 1951, Toronto, Ontario. Languages: English and some French. B.A.A., Radio and Television Arts, Ryerson Polytechnical Institute; studied Fine Arts, York University, 1 year.
Selected Filmography: "Video Dentistry" (45 eps), In, 84-85, CDN, Exec Prod.

GOODMAN, Paul W.
ATPD. 295 Belsize Dr., Toronto, ON M4S 1M7 (416)488-1977. CBC, P.O. Box 500, Stn. A, Toronto, ON M5W 1E6 (416)975-6780. FAX: 975-2945.
Type of Production and Credits: TV Film-Prod/Wr; TV Video-Prod/Wr.
Genres: Children's-TV; Current Affairs-TV; News-TV; Sports-TV.
Biography: Born 1951, Toronto, Ontario. Seneca College, Toronto. Experienced in research and with ENG camera.
Selected Filmography: "Wonderstruck", TV, 86-91, CDN, Prod; "Take 30", TV, 81-84, CDN, Prod; "For the Love of Sport", TV, 81, CDN, Assoc Prod; "Profiles" (5 eps), TV, 80, CDN, Prod.

GOODWILL, Jonathan
ACCT. 3324 W. 3rd Ave., Vancouver,

BC V6R 1L4 (604)734-8981. Small Blessings Pictures Ltd., 3324 W. 3rd Ave., Vancouver, BC V6R 1L4 (604)731-0566.
Type of Production and Credits: Th Film-Prod; TV Film-Prod; TV Video-Prod.
Genres: Drama-Th&TV; Comedy-Th&TV; Action-Th&TV.
Biography: Born 1956, Montreal, Quebec. B.A., Communication Arts, Loyola-Concordia University, 78. Extensive work in Montreal, Toronto, Vancouver, Edmonton, Calgary and New Zealand. Currently lives in Vancouver.
Selected Filmography: "Mom P.I." (25 eps), TV, 90-91, CDN, Prod; "Kurt Vonnegut's Monkey House" (3 eps), TV, 90, CDN, Prod; "Mom P.I." (pilot), TV, 90, CDN, Prod; "Ray Bradbury Theatre" (12 eps), TV, 90, CDN/NZ, Spv Prod; *Dark Horse*, TV, 89, CDN, Prod; "Ray Bradbury Theatre" (12 eps), TV, 89, CDN/NZ, Prod, (ACE); *Destiny to Order*, Th, 88, CDN, Prod; *Glory! Glory!*, TV, 88, CDN/USA, Co-Prod; "Ray Bradbury Theatre" (4 eps), TV, 87, CDN, Line Prod; *110 Lombard*, TV, 87, CDN, Pro Exec; "Airwolf" (24 eps), TV, 86-87, CDN, Prod; *Race for the Bomb*, TV, 86, CDN/F, Post Prod Spv; "Bell Canada Playhouse" (9 eps), TV, 85, CDN, PM/Line Prod; *Joshua Then and Now*, Th, 84, CDN, Pro Assoc; "Snow Job" (32 eps), TV, 82-84, CDN, Assoc Prod.

GORD, Ken
DGC. 5 Relmar Gardens, Toronto, ON M5P 1S1 (416)484-4496.
Type of Production and Credits: Th Film-PM/Prod; TV Film-PM/Prod.
Genres: Drama-Th&TV; Comedy-Th&TV; Action-Th&TV; Science Fiction-Th.
Biography: Born 1949, Toronto, Ontario. Educated at University of Toronto, 67-69. Has filmed in the Orient, India, USA, Hungary and Mexico. *Day One* awarded Emmy 89, Best Drama Special.
Selected Filmography: "Sweating Bullets" (9 eps), TV, 91, CDN/MEX, Prod; "Dog House" (pilot, 4 eps), TV, 90, CDN, Line Prod; *Iran* (mini-series), TV, 90, USA/F, Line Prod; *The World's Oldest Living Bridesmaid*, TV, 90, USA, Pro Exec; *Daughter of Darkness*, TV, 89, USA, Line Prod; *Day One*, TV, 88, USA, Pro Exec; *Criminal Law*, Th, 87, USA, Co-Prod; *The Brain*, Th, 87, CDN, Co-Prod; *The Housekeeper*, Th, 86, CDN, PM; "The Edison Twins" (13 eps), TV, 86, CDN, PM; *Recruits*, Th, 85, CDN, PM; "First Class with Patrick MacNee" (2 eps), TV, 83, CDN, Line Prod; *Deadly Eyes*, Th, 82, USA/CDN, PM; *The High Country*, Th, 79, CDN, Co-Prod; *Starship Invasions*, Th, 77, CDN, Co-Prod.

GORDON, Ben
- see WRITERS

GOUDSOUZIAN, Hagop
66 Roxborough St. W., Toronto, ON M5R 1T8.
Type of Production and Credits: TV Film-Prod/Dir; TV Video-Prod/Dir.
Genres: Documentary-TV; Educational-TV; Children's-TV.
Biography: Born in Egypt, of Armenian origin, 1949. Has been in Canada since 1961. Languages: Armenian, English, French and Spanish. Began his career at the age of four as an actor in commercials. Has photographed and worked with children in television. "Nouvelles Nouvelles" won a Prix de Mérite, L'Institute de Radiotélévision pour enfants.
Selected Filmography: "Actualité Pédagogique" (76 eps), ED/TV, 86-90, CDN, Prod/Dir; "Nouvelles Nouvelles" (31 eps), ED/TV, 90-92, CDN, Prod/Dir.

GOUGH, William
WGA, WGC, ATAS. Steve Weiss, William Morris Agency, (213)859-4423. Adam Berkowitz, William Morris Agency, (212)903-1153.
Type of Production and Credits: TV Film-Prod/Dir/Wr; TV Film-Prod/Dir/Wr.
Genres: Drama-TV; Comedy-TV; Documentary-TV.
Biography: Born Halifax, Nova Scotia. Attended The Film School, Boston, Mass.; Memorial University of Newfoundland. Publications include *Chips and Gravey*, *Maud's House*, *Finger Prints*, *The Proper Lover*, *The Last White Man in Panama*, *The Art of David Blackwood*. Winner of many international awards for producing, including Chris Plaque, Columbus International Film Festival; Blue Ribbon, American Film Festival.
Selected Filmography: "Tarzan - The Series" (25 eps), TV, 91, CDN/F/MEX, Creat Prod; *Stolen, One Husband*, TV, 90, USA, Wr; *Tarzan in Manhattan*, TV, 89, USA, Wr; *Two Men*, TV, 88, CDN, Prod, (ANIK/CHRIS); *Mama's Going to Buy You a Mockingbird*, TV, 88, CDN, Prod; "The Campbells" (2 eps), TV, 87, CDN/USA/GB, Wr; "Seeing Things" (9 eps), TV, 83-86, CDN, Co-Wr; *The Marriage Bed*, TV, 86, CDN, Prod, (GEMINI 87); *The Suicide Murders*, TV, 85, CDN, Prod/Lyrics; *Charlie Grant's War*, TV, 84, CDN, Prod, (ACTRA); *Anne's Story*, TV,

84, CDN, Prod/Lyrics; *The Accident*, TV, 83, CDN, Prod/Wr/Lyrics; *High Card*, "For the Record", TV, 78-81, CDN, Prod/Dir.

GRANT, Trudy
Sullivan Films Distribution Inc., 16 Clarence Square, Toronto, ON M5V 1H1 (416)597-0029.
Type of Production and Credits: TV Film-Prod.
Genres: Drama-TV.
Biography: Graduated with a degree in Sciences from the University of Western Ontario. Post-graduate work in Education. Met Kevin Sullivan in 1978 and became involved in his first production *The Fir Tree*. Has been involved in every Sullivan Films production, ranging from executive producing to distribution. Involvement in distribution prompted the formation of Sullivan Films Distribution in 1981.
Selected Filmography: "The Road to Avonlea" (26 eps), TV, 90-91, CDN/USA, Exec Prod; *Lantern Hill*, TV, 90, CDN/USA, Exec Prod; *Looking for Miracles*, TV, 89, CDN/USA, Exec Prod; *Anne of Green Gables - The Sequal*, TV, 87, CDN/USA, Exec Prod; *Anne of Green Gables*, TV, 85, USA/CDN, Exec Prod; *The Prodigious Hickey*, TV, 85, USA/CDN, Dist.

GRAVELLE, Raymond
SMPTE. Les Prods. LaGauchet inc., 816 est, de la Gauchetière, Montreal, PQ H2L 2N2 (514)845-8186. FAX: 843-8145.
Types de production et générique: c métrage-Prod/D photo; l métrage-Prod/D photo; TV film-D photo/Prod; TV vidéo-D photo/Prod.
Types d'oeuvres: Documentaire-TV; Education-TV; Enfants-TV.
Curriculum vitae: Né en 1947, Ottawa, Ontario. Langues: français et anglais. Baccalauréat, cours en gestion et administration. Rédacteur, CBOFT, Ottawa; caméraman pour CBC/Radio-Canada à la colline parlementaire; caméraman, journaliste, TVA et CTV en Chine; caméraman et administrateur, bureau de CTV à Washington. Fonde et dirige Les Productions LaGauchet inc., Montréal depuis 77.
Filmographie sélective: *I Won't Dance*, C, 91, CDN, Prod; *Tontines/Nous et les Assurances*, TV, 91, CDN/F/B, Prod; *L'ours Noir*, In, 91, CDN, D photo; *CAMCO*, In, 91, CDN, D photo/Prod; *L'Art est un Jeu*, TV, 90, CDN, Prod; *Screen Kids*, TV, 90, CDN, D photo/Prod; *Créations d'Enfants*, ED, 89, CDN, Réal/Prod; *D'Amour d'Amertume*, TV, 88, CDN, D photo/Prod; *Ces Jeunes Stars*, TV, 87, CDN, D photo/Prod; *Erythrée*, TV, 86, CDN, Prod.

GRAY, William
- see WRITERS

GREAN, Wendy
1252 King St. W., #10, Toronto, ON M6R 1G5 (416)538-9310.
Type of Production and Credits: Th Film-Prod; TV Film-Prod.
Genres: Drama-Th&TV; Action-Th&TV; Science Fiction-Th&TV.
Selected Filmography: "Hiddenroom"/ "Heartbreakers" (16 eps), TV, 91, USA, Spv Prod; "The Hitchhiker" (9 eps), TV, 90, USA, Spv Prod; "Dracula: The Series", TV, 90, USA, Pro Exec; *Last Best Year*, TV, 90, USA, Pro Exec; *Eddie & the Cruisers: Part II/Eddie Lives*, Th, 89, USA, Line Prod; *One for the Money/Cannonball Run III*, Th, 88, USA, Line Prod; *Spies, Lies & Naked Thighs/Just U.N. Me Babe*, TV, 88, USA, PM/Line Prod; *The Host*, Th, 87, USA, PM/Line Prod; *April Morning*, TV, 87, USA, PM/Line Prod; *Ford: The Man and the Machine* (mini-series), TV, 87, USA, PM/Line Prod; *Barnum*, TV, 86, USA, PM/Line Prod; *Broken Vows*, TV, 86, USA, PM/Line Prod; "C.A.T. Squad" (pilot), TV, 86, USA, PM; *Choices*, TV, 84, USA, PM/Line Prod; *Spearfield's Daughter*, (mini-series), TV, 84, USA, PM/Line Prod.

GREEN, Cari
ACCT. 107 - 2772 Spruce St., Vancouver, BC V6H 2R2 (604)731-8044.
Type of Production and Credits: TV Film-Prod.
Genres: Documentary-TV.
Biography: Born in 1947 in Montreal, Quebec. Educated in Psychology at McGill University. Graduated from the University of British Columbia in 1969 after moving to B.C. in 1966. Worked as a film distributor for six years at Canadian Filmmakers Distribution West (in Vancouver) before switching to producing in 1987. Appointed to the Non-Theatrical Film Industry Task Force in 1986. *Songololo: Voices of Change* won the Best Art Documentary at the San Francisco International Festival. A member of Women in Film, Vancouver.
Selected Filmography: "As Long as the Rivers Flow" (1 eps), ED, 91, CDN, Prod; *Awakening The Dragons*, ED, 91, CDN, Prod; *Songololo: Voices of Change*, ED, 90, CDN, Prod.

GREEN, Howard
ACTRA, CTPDA, ACCT. Howard &

Howard Productions, 55 Lombard St., Ste. 214, Toronto, ON M5C 2R7 (416)861-9875.
Type of Production and Credits: TV Film-Prod; TV Video-Prod.
Genres: Documentary-TV; Educational-TV; Children's-TV.
Biography: Born 1959, Halifax, Nova Scotia. B.Journalism, Carleton University. TV news reporter wtih CTV affiliates in the Maritimes and CBC, Newfoundland and Labrador, 80-83; producer and host of "What's New?", 83-88 (175 episodes); freelance director, TVOntario, 89; freelance reporter/producer, CBC "Venture", 88-91; freelance writer/producer, CBC "The Nature of Things", 90-91; freelance reporter/producer, PBS, 90-91. Chris Award, Columbus International Film Festival, 90.

GREEN, Joseph G.
349 St. Clair Ave. W., Ste. 107, Toronto, ON M5P 1N3 (416)922-8968. Fundamentally Film Inc., 349 St. Clair Ave. W., Ste. 107, Toronto, ON M5P 1N3 (416)928-1992.
Type of Production and Credits: TV Film-Exec Prod.
Genres: Drama-TV; Industrial-TV.
Biography: Born in 1934 in Philadelphia, Pennsylvania. Canadian citizen. B.A., M.A., Ph.D. in Dramatic Theory. Prof. of Theatre & Arts and Media Management, York University. Gemini award, 1988, for *Glory Enough For All*.
Selected Filmography: *F.A.S. Report*, In, 90, CDN, Prod; *Glory Enough For All*, TV, 87-88, CDN/GB, Exec Prod, (GEMINI); *Fine Arts at York*, In, 76, CDN, Prod.

GREENBERG, Brenda M.
DGA. 160 Ava Rd., Toronto, ON M6C 1W5 (416)787-8991. Street Legal, 420 Dupont St., Toronto, ON M5R 3P3 (416)588-4206. Suzanne Depoe/Creative Technique Inc., 483 Euclid Ave., Toronto, ON M6G 2T1 (416)466-4173.
Type of Production and Credits: TV Film-Prod.
Genres: Drama-TV; Comedy-TV; Educational-TV; Children's-TV.
Biography: Born in 1953 in the USA. Canadian landed immigrant. B.S. in Speech, Magna Cum Laude, Emerson College, Boston. Began career as assistant to the Director of Daytime Programs, NBC TV, New York. A member of the CBC Producer's Association.
Selected Filmography: "Street Legal" (50 eps), TV, 89-92, CDN, Exec Prod; "Street Legal" (19 eps), TV, 88-89, CDN, Sr Prod; "Street Legal" (13 eps), TV, 87-88, CDN, Exec Story Ed; *Rockit Records*, TV, 86, CDN, Prod; "What Every Baby Knows" (4 eps), TV, 85, USA, Prod; "As The World Turns" (795 eps), TV, 82-85, USA, Prod; "As The World Turns" (530 eps), TV, 80-82, USA, Assoc Prod

GREENBERG, Harold
CFTA, ACCT. Astral Inc., 2100 Ste-Catherine St. W., Montreal, PQ H3H 2T3 (514)939-5000.
Type of Production and Credits: Th Film-Prod; TV Film-Prod.
Genres: Drama-Th&TV; Horror-Th.
Biography: Born Montreal, Quebec. President & Chief Executive Officer, Astral Inc. Chairman of the Board, First Choice Canadian Communications Corporation and Premier Choix:TVEC. Has been involved as packager, producer or co-producer of over 35 feature films and TV projects. Received the Presidential Proclamation Award, SMPTE, 85; International Achievement Award, Montreal World Film Festival, 89; Air Canada Award, presented by the Academy of Canadian Cinema and Television, 90. *Porky's* won the Golden Reel Award.
Selected Filmography: *Porky's Revenge*, Th, 84, USA, Exec Prod; *Draw!*, TV, 83, CDN/USA, Co-Exec Prod; *Pygmalion*, TV, 83, CDN, Co-Exec Prod; *Porky's II*, Th, 82, CDN, Co-Exec Prod; *Tell Me that You Love Me*, Th, 82, CDN/IL, Co-Exec Prod; *Mary and Joseph*, TV, 82, CDN, Co-Exec Prod; *Maria Chapdelaine*, Th, 82, CDN/F, Prod; *Porky's*, Th, 81, CDN, Exec Prod; *Hard Feelings*, Th, 80, CDN, Co-Exec Prod/Prod; *Hot Touch*, Th, 80, CDN/USA, Co-Exec Prod/Prod; *Tulips*, Th, 80, CDN, Co-Exec Prod; *Death Ship*, Th, 79, CDN/GB, Co-Prod; *Terror Train*, Th, 79, CDN/USA, Prod; *A Man Called Intrepid* (mini-series), TV, 78, CDN/GB, Co-Exec, Prod; *City on Fire*, Th, 78, CDN/USA, Co-Exec Prod.

GREENE, Charles J. ◊
ACTRA, ACCT. (213)207-3417.
Type of Production and Credits: TV Film-Prod/Wr; TV Video-Prod/Wr.
Genres: Documentary-TV; Drama-TV; Action-TV.
Biography: Born Toronto, Ontario. Education: undergraduate, MIT (Political Science); graduate, Sloan School of Management (Systems Analysis). Has worked at CTV, CBC, A&M Records, TVOntario, Mediavision, Heritage Communications. "New Wilderness" has won numerous awards, including 3 Emmys.
Selected Filmography: "Lorne Greene's New Wilderness" (104 eps), TV, 81-86,

CDN, Co-Prod, (EMMYs); "Survivors" (5 eps), TV, 78, CDN, Wr; "Last of the Wild" (6 eps)(Wr 2 eps), TV, 76, CDN/USA, Wr; "Behind the Scenes with Jonathan Winters" (5 eps), TV, 75, CDN/USA, Wr; "Glenn Ford's Friends of Man" (18 eps), TV, 73-74, CDN/USA, Co-Wr; *Africa File*, ED, 74, CDN, Wr; Shoppers Drug Mart/Canadian Tire, In, 73, CDN, Wr; Procul Harem, Cm, 72, CDN, Prod/Wr; "Ideas" (5 eps), ED, 71, CDN, Prod/Wr; "W5" (52 seg), TV, 70-71, CDN, Wr/Res.

GREENLAW, Terry
Picture Plant Ltd., PO Box 2465, Stn M, Halifax, NS B3J 3E8 (902)423-3901.
Type of Production and Credits: Th Film-Prod/PM/Assist Dir/ Assist Ed; TV Video-Assist Dir; Th Video-Prod/Assist Dir/Ed.
Genres: Drama-Th&TV; Documentary-Th&TV; Experimental-Th; Commercials-TV.
Biography: Born in Montreal, Quebec. Theatre at Dalhousie University and mixed media at the Nova Scotia College of Art & Design. Has lived in Nova Scotia for the past 18 years. *Understanding Bliss* won the Moonsnail Award for Best Feature Film at the Atlantic Film Festival in 1990.
Selected Filmography: *Understanding Bliss*, Th, 90, CDN, Prod/Ed/Assist Dir; *No Apologies*, Th, 89-90, CDN, Prod; *The Vacant Lot*, Th, 88-89, Prod/PM; *My Brother Larry*, TV, 88, CDN, Assist Dir; *I Will Not Make Any More Boring Art*, Th, 87, CDN, Prod/PM/Assist Dir; *Life Classes*, Th, 76, CDN, PM/Assist Ed.

GREENWALD, Barry
- see DIRECTORS

GRITTANI, Ronald S.
58-1/2 Main St., Hillsburgh, ON N0B 1Z0 (519)855-4822. 567 Queen St. W., Toronto, ON M5V 2B6 (416)777-1234.
Type of Production and Credits: TV Film-Prod.
Genres: Documentary-TV; Commercials-TV.
Biography: Born 1934, Toronto, Ontario. Twenty-five years in the business; worldwide shooting experience. Commercials over 15-year period for: Nestle (Europe), Goodyear (Europe), Molson (Australia), G.M. (Canada), Esso (Canada), and others.
Selected Filmography: Wilkinson Sword, In, 86, GB, Prod.

GROBERMAN, Jeffrey
- see WRITERS

GROSS, Bonnie
ACCT. 107 Donwoods Dr., Toronto, ON M4N 2G7 (416)484-0610. 208 St. Clair W., Toronto, ON M4X 1R2 (416)323-3881.
Type of Production and Credits: TV Video-Prod/Host.
Genres: Documentary-TV.
Biography: Born in Toronto, Ontario. B.A., Psychology, University of Toronto; graduate work in Speech Pathology and Audiology, University of Toronto. Regular contributor to CJRT-FM radio's "News Journal" and "Sunday Journal." B'nai Brith Human Rights Award for media for "The Truth Behind the Iron Curtain" and awards from Canadian Cable Television Association and Ontario Cable Television Association.
Selected Filmography: "Second Chance" (26 eps), TV, 88, CDN, Prod/Host.

GULKIN, Harry
APFVQ, ACCT. Jape Film Services Inc., 111 ouest, boul. St-Joseph, Montreal, PQ H2T 2P7 (514)277-5307.
Type of Production and Credits: Th Film-Prod; TV Film-Prod.
Genres: Drama-Th&TV; Comedy-Th&TV.
Biography: Born, 1927, Montreal, Quebec. Canadian Army Reserve, 42-44; Canadian Merchant Marine, 44-49. Founding President of Motion Picture Institute of Canada, 77-79. Has won numerous awards at national and international film festivals, including Gold Medallion, Special Jury Award, Miami, for *Jacob Two-Two Meets the Hooded Fang*; a Golden Globe and Chris Awards, Columbus International Film Festival, for *Lies My Father Told Me*.
Selected Filmography: *Bayo*, Th, 84, CDN, Prod; *The Challenger*, TV, 79, CDN, Assoc Prod; *Two Solitudes*, Th, 77, CDN, Co-Prod; *Jacob Two Two Meets the Hooded Fang*, Th, 75, CDN, Prod; *Denny and Ann*, TV, 74, CDN, Prod; *Lies My Father Told Me*, Th, 72, CDN, Co-Prod, (CFA).

GUNN, John
- see DIRECTORS

GUNNARSSON, Sturla
- see DIRECTORS

HACKETT, Jonathan
DGC, ACCT. 212 Crawford St., Toronto, ON M6J 2V6 (416)535-1835.
Type of Production and Credits: Th Film-PM; TV Film-PM/1st AD; TV Video-PM/1st AD.
Genres: Children's-Th&TV; Commercials-TV.
Biography: Born in England; Canadian and British citizenship. Started in film

business, 70; worked mostly as key grip till 80; 1st assistant director/production manager on numerous commercials, 81-84; commercials producer, 85-86; TV producer, 87.
Selected Filmography: "The Adventures of the Black Stallion" (26 eps), TV, 90, CDN/F, Prod; *Bloodsport*, TV, 89, CDN/IRL, Prod; "War of the Worlds" (26 eps), TV, 88-89, USA, Prod; "Adderly" (39 eps), TV, 86-88, CDN, Prod.

HAIG, Don
ACCT, CFPTA. Film Arts, 424 Adelaide St. E., Toronto, ON M5A 1N4 (416)368-9925. FAX: 364-1310.
Type of Production and Credits: Th Film-Prod; TV Film-Ed/Prod.
Genres: Drama-Th&TV; Documentary-Th&TV; Educational-TV.
Biography: Born 1933, Winnipeg, Manitoba. Began in film at MGM Distribution, Winnipeg; film editor, CBC, 56-63; started own film editing firm, Film Arts, 63. Winner of the Academy of Canadian Cinema and Television's Air Canada Award, 85; Jack Chisholm Award, 85; CBC TV Producers Association Award, 87; Ontario Film Institute Award, 87.
Selected Filmography: *Shadow Dancing*, Th, 88, CDN, Exec Prod; *Stanley Knowles*, Th, 88, CDN, Exec Prod; *The Brain*, Th, 88, CDN, Exec Prod; *Comic Book Confidential*, Th, 88, CDN, Exec Prod; *Night Friend*, Th, 87, CDN, Exec Prod; *Turnabout*, Th, 86, CDN, Exec Prod; *I've Heard the Mermaids Singing*, Th, 86, CDN, Exec Prod; *Artie Shaw: Time Is All You've Got*, Th, 85, CDN, Assoc Prod; *Dancing in the Dark*, Th, 85, CDN, Exec Prod; *The Kidnapping of Baby John Doe*, TV, 85, CDN, Exec Prod; *Alex Colville: The Splendour of Order*, TV, 84, CDN, Exec Prod; *Samuel Lount*, Th, 84, CDN, Exec Prod; *Arnold Spohr Gala/Royal Winnipeg Ballet*, TV, 83, CDN, Exec Prod; *Unfinished Business*, Th, 83, CDN, Exec Prod; *Alligator Shoes*, Th, 80, CDN, Exec Prod.

HALLÉ, Roland
- see DIRECTORS

HALLIS, Ophera
- see EDITORS

HALLIS, Ron
- see DIRECTORS

HAMELIN, Christiane
La Fabrique d'Images inc., 318 est, rue Sherbrooke, Montreal, PQ H2X 1E6 (514)282-1505.
Types de production et générique: TV film-Prod.
Types d'oeuvres: Annonces-TV.
Curriculum vitae: Née en 1950, Montréal, Québec. Langues: français et anglais. Etudes en Arts, Institut des Arts appliqués. Productrice, Fabrique d'Images, depuis 13 ans; a produit plusieurs annonces publicitaires: General Motors, Pontiac, Chevrolet, MacDonald's, Loto Québec, O'Keefe, etc.

HAMILTON BROWN, Alex
ACCT. Hamilton Brown Productions Ltd., 123 Coady Ave., Toronto, ON M4M 2Y9 (416)469-1344.
Type of Production and Credits: Th Film-Prod/Dir; Th Short-Prod/Dir/Wr; TV Film-Prod/Dir/Wr; TV Video-Prod/Dir/Wr.
Genres: Drama-Th&TV; Documentary-Th&TV; Educational-TV; Industrial—TV.
Biography: Born in Scotland; Canadian citizenship. Graduate in Film and Television Production, New York University. Started in film industry with Pathé London and Elstree Studios. Worked in television drama as producer/director for NBC-TV, Boston. Wrote and directed documentaries in Africa for 2 years. Produced and directed over 70 dramas and documentaries for Canadian, British and US television. Founded Hamilton-Brown Productions Ltd., 78. Won 7 international awards for TVO, 70-76; 16 awards for Hamilton Brown Productions Ltd., including 3 festival winners, a jury award, 2 gold medals and 3 Gemini nominations.
Selected Filmography: *The Hauting of Esther Cox*, Th, 90-91, CDN, Prod; *The Agent*, ED, 89, CDN, Prod/Dir; "Hazards" (6 eps), TV, 87-88, CDN, Prod/Dir; *A Whole New Ball Game*, TV, 86-87, CDN, Prod/Dir; *From Inside Out*, ED, 86, CDN, Prod/Dir; *Closer to the Street*, ED, 85, CDN, Prod/Dir; *Affirmation of Life*, TV, 84, CDN, Prod/Dir; *Life Another Way*, TV, 83, CDN, Prod/Dir; "The Guild" (2 eps), TV, 82, CDN, Prod/Dir; *Axios*, TV, 81, CDN, Prod/Dir; *Pathway from Within*, TV, 80, CDN, Prod/Dir; *Changeover*, TV, 79, CDN, Prod/Dir; *The Ex*, TV, 78, CDN, Prod/Dir; "Thursday Night" (13 eps), TV, 78, CDN, Prod/Dir; "Dimensions in Science" (7 eps), TV, 75, CDN, Prod/Dir.

HAMON-HILL, Cindy
ACCT. 2455A Queen St. East, Toronto, ON M4E 1H7 (416)693-1087. FAX: 693-1087.
Type of Production and Credits: TV Film-Prod.

Genres: Drama-Th&TV; Documentary-TV; Children's-TV.
Biography: Born in Toronto, Ontario. Honours B.A., Film.
Selected Filmography: *Alligator Pie*, TV, 91, CDN, Prod; *The New North*, TV, 87, CDN, Assoc Prod; *Jack of Hearts/Connection*, "Bell Canada Playhouse", TV, 85, CDN, Prod.

HAMORI, Andras
82 Willcocks, Toronto, ON M5S 1C8 (416)923-4245. Accent Entertainment Corp., 151 John St., Ste. 502, Toronto, ON M5V 2T2 (416)348-8722. FAX: 348-8721.
Type of Production and Credits: Th Film-Prod; TV Film-Prod.
Genres: Drama-Th&TV; Comedy-Th&TV; Action-Th&TV.
Biography: Born 1953, Budapest, Hungary; Canadian citizenship. Ph.D., Law and Political Science, Budapest University; diploma, Film and Television Journalism. Theatre and film critic for Hungarian magazines and newspapers, London periodicals, *Theatre Quarterly* and *Theatrefacts*. Worked for Schulz Productions, developing feature films, 81; joined RSL Entertainment Corp., 83; producer, Alliance Entertainment Corporation 86; co-founded Accent Entertainment Corp., 89; currently Sr. Vice-President.
Selected Filmography: "Sweating Bullets" (22 eps), TV, 91, CDN/MEX, Exec Prod; *Storm and Sorrow*, TV, 90, USA, Prod; *Daughter of Darkness*, TV, 90, USA, Prod; *Gate 2*, TV, 89, CDN, Prod; *Iron Eagle II*, Th, 88, CDN, CDN/IL, Exec Prod; *God Bless the Child*, TV, 87, CDN, Prod; *After the Food of the Gods*, Th, 87, CDN, Exec Prod; "Night Heat" (96 eps) (Prod 51 eps), TV, 84-86, CDN, Prod/Spv Prod, (Gemini 87/Gemini 86); *The Gate*, Th, 86, CDN, Co-Prod; *Nowhere to Hide*, Th, 86, CDN, Prod; *Big Deal*, Th, 85, CDN, Prod; *Separate Vacations*, Th, 85, CDN, Assoc Prod; *One Night Only*, TV, 84, CDN, Assist Prod; *Joshua Then and Now*, Th, 84, CDN, Assoc Pro Exec; *Night Magic*, Th, 84, CDN/F, Pro Exec.

HANDEL, Alan
- see DIRECTORS

HARBURY, Martin
CFTPA, ACCT. Atlantis Films Ltd., 65 Heward Ave., Toronto, ON M4M 2T5 (416)462-0246. Martin-Paul Productions Ltd., Bar Harbour Films Inc., 74 Dagmar Ave., Toronto, ON M4M 1W1 (416)778-4491.
Type of Production and Credits: TV Film-Prod; TV Video-Prod/Dir.
Genres: Drama-TV; Documentary-TV; Educational-TV; Children's-TV.
Biography: Born 1945, Worthing, Sussex, England; Canadian and British citizenship. Languages: English and French. Author of *The Last of the Wild Horses*, 84.
Selected Filmography: "Gold" (10 hrs), TV, 90-91, CDN/NZ, Prod; *Rookies*, TV, 90, CDN, Prod; *Firing Squad/Le peloton d'execution*, TV, 89, CDN/F, Prod; *Comic Book Confidential*, Th, 88, CDN, Co-Prod; *Return of Hickey*, TV, 87, CDN, Prod; *The Truth About Alex*, TV, 86, CDN, Prod, (GEMINI/ACE); *Hockey Night*, TV, 84, CDN, Prod; *Clown White*, TV, 80, CDN, Prod.

HARDING, John
- see EDITORS

HARDING, Stewart
ACCT. Moving Image Productions Inc., 106 Florida Dr., Montreal, PQ H9W 1L9 (514)630-1946.
Type of Production and Credits: Th Film-Prod; TV Film-Prod/Exec Prod.
Biography: Born 1952, Montreal, Quebec. B.A., Communication Arts, Loyola University, 74. Entered motion picture business as production assistant, 74; rose through production manager, associate producer and line producer positions on theatrical features to producing TV and theatrical films with own company, Moving Image Productions Inc., 84-87 and 89-90. V.P., Production Investment, Astral Film Enterprises (Montreal), 88-89. Executive in Charge of Production, Alliance Communications Inc. (Toronto), 90-91. Returned to independent production, 91. *Half a Lifetime* was nominated for ACE and Gemini awards; *The Rose Cafe* was nominated for 2 Gemini awards; *Falling Over Backwards* was invited to festivals in Montreal, Toronto, Vancouver, Chicago, Fort Lauderdale, Palm Springs and Valladolid, Spain.
Selected Filmography: "Fly By Night" (13 eps), TV, 91, CDN, Exec Prod; *Falling Over Backwards*, Th, 90, CDN, Prod; *Midnight Magic*, TV, 88, CDN, Prod; *Indigo Autumn*, TV, 87, CDN, Prod; *The Man Who Guards the Greenhouse*, TV, 87, CDN, Prod; *Moonlight Flight*, TV, 87, CDN, Prod; *The Ballerina and the Blues*, TV, 87, CDN, Prod; *Sincerely Violet*, TV, 86, CDN, Prod; *Champagne for Two*, TV, 86, CDN, Prod; *The Rose Café*, TV, 86, CDN, Prod; *First Offender*, TV, 86, CDN, Prod; *Half a Lifetime*, TV, 85, CDN, Prod; "In Like

Flynn" (pilot), TV, 85, USA, Co-Prod; *Spacehunter*, Th, 83, USA, Assoc Prod/Story; *Happy Birthday To Me*, Th, 80, CDN, Line Prod.

HAREL, David
- see DIRECTORS

HARRIS, Jane ◊
(416)485-0874.
Type of Production and Credits: TV Film-Prod; TV Video-Prod.
Genres: Drama-TV; Musical-TV; Documentary-TV.
Biography: Born in Wolverhampton, England; British and Canadian citzenship.
Selected Filmography: *Aviation in the North*, TV, 88, CDN/GB, Exec Prod; *Frontier Footlights*, TV, 88, CDN/GB, Exec Prod; *444 Days to Freedom*, TV, 86, CDN/USA, Exec Prod; *The King of Friday Night*, TV, 85, CDN, Exec Prod.

HARRIS, Les
- see DIRECTORS

HARVEY, Daniel
APFTQ, ACCT, ADISQ. 7470, Bayard, Montréal, PQ H3R 3A9 (514)342-1093. Spectel Communication inc., 355 ouest, Ste-Catherine, #700, Montréal, PQ H3B 1A5 (514)288-5363.
Types de production et générique: TV vidéo-Prod; TV vidéo-Prod.
Types d'oeuvres: Comédie-TV; Variété-TV; Vidéo clips-TV.
Curriculum vitae: Né en 1950; citoyen canadien. Langues: français et anglais. Etude de Baccalauréat en Communications, Université d'Ottawa, 72-74. Vaste expérience en production comme assistant réalisateur, réalisateur, directeur de production, producteur, 74-79; Président de Spectel Communications inc.; V.P. Spectel Vidéo, Spectra Scène, Spectrum de Montreal; V.P., Studio Audiogram-Spectel (Morin Heigh). Gémeaux 87 - Série Humour & Spécial Humour pour "Rock et Belles Oreilles"; Gémeaux 88 - Spécial Humour pour *Grande Liquidation*; Gémeaux 89 - Spécial Variété pour *Un trou dans les nuages*; Gémeaux 90 - Série Variété pour *FrancoFolies de Montreal*.
Filmographie sélective: "Wattatow" (72 eps), TV, 91, CDN, Prod exéc; "Studio-Théâtre" (4 eps), TV, 91, CDN, Prod exéc; *Le rire démasqué*, TV, 91, CDN, Prod exéc; "FrancoFolies" (12 eps), TV, 90, CDN, Prod exéc; "Jazz 91" (6 eps), TV, 91, CDN, Prod exéc; *Grand liquidation des fêtes*, TV, 90, CDN, Prod exéc; *Un trou dans les nuages*, TV, 89, CDN, Prod exéc; "Rock et Belles Oreilles" (20 eps), TV, 86, CDN, Prod exéc.

HAUKA, David
- see DIRECTORS

HAWKINS, Crawford W.
DGA, ACCT. 1947 Fulton Ave., West Vancouver, BC V7V 1T2 (604)926-8221. Seahawk Communications Inc., 1947 Fulton Ave., West Vancouver, BC V7V 1T2 (604)926-5393.
Type of Production and Credits: TV Film-Prod/Dir; TV Video-Prod/Dir.
Genres: Drama-TV; Comedy-TV; Variety-TV; Children's-TV; Commercials-TV.
Biography: Born 1933, Brooklyn, New York; landed immigrant Canada. Attended St. Joseph's University, New York University. Winner of 2 Clio awards; 2 Hollywood Radio and TV Society Awards and 1 International Film and Television Festival, NY, award.
Selected Filmography: "Scene of the Crime" (22 eps), TV, 90-91, USA/CDN/F, Assoc Prod; "The Adventures of the Black Stallion" (26 eps), TV, 90-91, CDN/F, P Pro Spv; "Neon Rider" (24 eps), TV, 89-90, CDN, P Pro Spv; *Sweet Dreams*, TV, 83, USA, Dir; "School for Speed" (pilot), TV, 82, USA, Dir; *Pyramids and Prophets*, TV, 82, USA, Dir; "Your Car and Your Money" (pilot), TV, 81, USA, Prod; *Up River*, TV, 79, USA, Prod; *The Nixon/Frost Interviews* (6 eps, TV, 77, USA, PM; "The New Mickey Mouse Show" (165 eps), TV, 76-77, USA, Unit M; "Soap" (13 eps), TV, 76, USA, Unit M.

HAWLEY, Gay
- see WRITERS

HAZZAN, Ray
ATPD, ACCT. 111 Runnymede Cres., London, ON N6G 1Z7 CBC, Box 500, Stn. A, Toronto, ON M5W 1E6 (416)975-6888.
Type of Production and Credits: TV Film-Prod/Dir/Wr; TV Video-Prod/Dir/Wr.
Genres: Documentary-TV; Educational-TV; Children's-TV; Science-TV.
Biography: Born 1931, Alexandria, Egypt; Canadian citizenship. Languages: English and French. B.A.(Honours), M.A., Economics, Political Science, Cambridge University; Licence ès Lettres, Université de Paris et Lille. Journalist at British United Press; CBC Radio and TV, 56-90; has been head of CBC radio and TV national news; Executive Producer of "Newsmagazine", news specials, children's TV and "Quarterly Report", TV Current Affairs; President, Association of Television Producers and Directors (Toronto), 74-75

and 84-86. Awards include: Ekofilm Festival Award, Prague, for *Great Lakes, Troubled Waters*, 86; ACTRA nomination, Distinguished Journalism Award for *In the Name of Justice*, 84; Jury Award, Yorkton, for *The Electronic Web*, 83; Gold Medal, Varna International Film Festival and Gold Medal, John Muir Medical Film Festival for *The Dark Side of Hope*, 90; Award of Excellence, Canadian Nurses' Association for *Call for Help*, 88.
Selected Filmography: *Water*, ED, 90, CDN, Prod/Dir; *Life Cycle*, ED, 90, CDN, Prod/Dir; *Howe Sound: Poisoned Waters*, "The Nature of Things", TV, 89, CDN, Prod/Wr/Dir; *Call for Help*, "Man Alive", TV, 88, CDN, Prod/Dir/Wr; *The Dark Side of Hope*, "Man Alive", TV, 88, CDN, Prod/Dir/Wr; *Temples of Mammon*, "Man Alive", TV, 87-88, CDN, Prod/Dir/Wr; *Acid Rain: Clouds with a Sulphur Lining*, "The Nature of Things", TV, 86, CDN, Prod/Wr/Dir; *Great Lakes: Troubled Waters*, "The Nature of Things", TV, 86, CDN, Prod/Dir; *In the Name of Justice*, "Man Alive", TV, 84, CDN, Prod/Wr; *The Electronic Web*, "Quarterly Report", TV, 82, CDN, Prod/Dir/Wr.

HEINEMANN, Michelle
- see WRITERS

HELLIKER, John
- see DIRECTORS

HENAUT, Dorothy Todd
- see DIRECTORS

HÉNAUT, Suzanne
APFTQ. Les Productions ZANN Inc., 5041 Esplanade, Montréal, PQ H2T 2Y9 (514)273-4694.
Types de production et générique: l métrage-Prod; TV film-Prod.
Types d'oeuvres: Drame-C; Comédie-C.
Curriculum vitae: Née en 1956 au Canada. Débute dans le milieu en 75. De 78 à 81, participe à la mise au pied du Inuit Broadcasting Corporation. Administratice, Convergence (un forum sur les nouvelles technologies film et vidéo), 84/86/90. Devient associée de les Films Vision 4 inc. en 85 et produit ou co-produit 6 longs métrages. Travaille sur Le Festival international du nouveau cinéma et de la vidéo de Montréal, en 85 et 86. Se joint au conseil d'Administration de la Cinémathèque Québécoise/Musée du Cinéma en 88. Fonde les productions ZANN inc., 90.
Filmographie sélective: *Cuervo*, TV, 90, CDN, Prod; *Sous les Draps, les étoiles*, C, 89, CDN, Prod; *Gaspard & Fils*, C, 88, CDN, Prod; *Candy Mountain*, C, 87, CDN/F/CH, Prod; *Pellan*, C, 86, CDN, Prod; *Henri*, C, 86, CDN, Prod.

HENLEY, Gail
- see WRITERS

HENSHAW, Helen
111 Bath St., Oakville, ON L6K 1A7 (416)844-0787. Henshaw Productions, 111 Bath St., Oakville, ON L6K 1A7 (416)844-0787.
Type of Production and Credits: Th Film-PM; Th Short-Prod; TV Film-Prod; TV Video-Prod/Dir.
Genres: Documentary-Th&TV; Educational-TV; Industrial-TV; Current Affairs-TV.
Biography: Born in 1957. Canadian citizen. Fluent in both English and French. Bachelor of Applied Arts, Film, Ryerson Polytechnical Institute, 1978-82. Experience in budgeting and scheduling.
Selected Filmography: "Changing Worlds" (13 eps), ED/TV, 90, CDN, Prod/Dir; "North/South with Peter Trueman" (52 eps), TV, 88-89, CDN, Prod/Dir; *Canadian Tire - Oscar*, In, 89, CDN, PM; *CIBC*, In, 89, CDN, PM; *Office Party*, Th, 88, CDN, PM; *Birks*, In, 87, CDN, PM; *Dofasco*, In, 86, CDN, PM; *Celfortex*, In, 86, CDN, Prod; *Where Are You My Lovelies?*, Th, 86, CDN, Prod; *Loose Page*, Th, 85, CDN, Prod; *Old Fort William*, TV, 85, CDN, PM; *Motion* (8 spots), In, 85, CDN, PM; *Foreign Investment*, In, 85, CDN, PM; *Trash to Treasure*, TV, 84, CDN, Prod.

HERBERMAN, Lee
ATPD. 57 Donegail Dr., Toronto, ON M4G 3G8 (416)488-8387. FAX: 489-6293.
Type of Production and Credits: TV Video-Prod.
Genres: Variety-TV; Documentary-TV; Industrial-TV; Sports-TV.
Biography: Born 1957, Toronto. At CBC since 76; tech., 3 years; prod. assist., 4 years; producer/director 2 years; exec. prod., 1988 to date. President of Showcase Productions, established in 1988.
Selected Filmography: "CFL on CBC", TV, 89-91, CDN, Exec Prod; *World Athletic Championships, Tokyo* (8 seg), TV, 91, CDN, Sr Prod; *Benson & Hedges Inc. International Fireworks*, TV, 1988-91, CDN, Prod; *World Junior Hockey Championships*, TV, 89/90, CDN, Prod; *1988 Summer Olympics*, TV, 88, CDN, Prod; *1988 Queen's Plate*, TV, 88, CDN, Prod; *1988 Winter Olympics*, TV, 88, CDN, Prod; *1984 Summer Olympics*, TV, 84, CDN, Prod.

HEROUX, Claude
APFVQ. Communications Claude Héroux

Inc., 4542 boul. Décarie, Montréal, PQ H3X 2H5 (514)488-6633.
Types de production et générique: TV film-Prod.
Types d'oeuvres: Drame-TV.
Curriculum vitae: Né en 1942 à Montréal, Québec. Langues: français et anglais. Etudes universitaires à Montréal et à Québec en économie et en administration. Oeuvre dans l'industrie depuis 60; a produit plus de 30 films ainsi que plusieurs séries télévisées.
Filmographie sélective: "Lance et Compte" (43 eps), TV, 86/87/88/90, CDN, Prod; "La Misère des Riches" (eps 1 à 39), TV, 89/90, CDN, Prod; *Le Premier Cercle*, 90, Prod; *Alphonse Desjardins*, 89, Prod; *Les Trois Flacons*, C, 85, CDN, Co prod; *Clémence Aletti*, C, 84, CDN, Co prod; *Au nom de tous les miens*, C, 83, CDN/F, Co prod; *Of Unknown Origin*, C, 83, USA, Prod; *Going Berserk*, C, 82, CDN/USA, Prod; *Videodrome*, C, 81, CDN/USA, Prod; *Hog Wild*, C, 79, CDN, Prod; *Scanners*, C, 79, CDN, Prod; *City on Fire*, C, 78, CDN/USA, Prod; *In Praise of Older Women*, C, 77, CDN, Co prod; *Angela*, C, 76, CDN, Co prod; *Born for Hell*, C, 75, CDN/F/I/D, Co prod.

HÉROUX, Denis
ACCT. 28, rue Roskilde, Montréal, PQ H2V 2N5 (514)272-0526. Astral Europa Communications, 2100 Ste-Catherine Ouest, Montréal, PQ H3H 2T3 (514)939-5000.
Types de production et générique: l métrage-Prod/Réal; TV film-Prod/Réal.
Types d'oeuvres: Drame-C&TV; Comédie-C; Action-C.
Curriculum vitae: Né en 1940, Montréal, Québec. Maîtrise ès Arts, Université de Montréal; professeur à l'Université du Québec à Montréal. Auteur de 2 livres. Président du conseil d'administration, Académie du cinéma canadien, 83. Reçoit le Prix du Mérite de l'Université de Montréal; ses films ont remporté plusieurs prix dont le Grand Prix (Festival de Film de Venise) et le Prix du Meilleur Film (Los Angeles Film Critics Association) pour *Atlantic City*; *La Guerre du feu* remporte 7 Césars, le Gold Scroll Award, BFA, Oscar et 5 Génies; *Les Plouffe* remporte 7 Génies et fut projeté lors de l'ouverture de la Quinzaine des Réalisateurs au Festival de Film de Cannes.
Filmographie sélective: "Counterstrike" (22 eps), TV, 91, CDN/F, Prod exéc; *Black Robe*, C, 91, CDN, Prod exéc; *Le Matou*, C, 84, CDN, Prod; *The Bay Boy*, C, 83, CDN/F, Prod; *Lousiana*, C, 83, CDN/F, Prod; *The Blood of Others*, C, 83, CDN/F, Co prod; *Quest for Fire*, C, 81, CDN/F, Prod; *Les Plouffe*, C, 80, CDN, Prod; *Atlantic City*, C, 79, CDN/F, Prod; *Violette Nozière*, C, 77, CDN/F, Prod; *Jacques Brel is Alive and Well and Living in Paris*, C, 74, CDN/F, Dir; *Quelques Arpents de Neige*, C, 72, CDN, Réal; *L'initiation*, C, 69, CDN, Réal; *Valérie*, C, 68, CDN, Réal; *Seul ou avec d'autres*, C, 63, CDN, Réal.

HÉROUX, Justine
APFVQ, ACCT. 28, Roskilde, Outremont, PQ H2V 2N5 (514)272-0526. Cinévidéo Plus, 2100 Ste-Catherine Ouest, Suite 810, Montréal, PQ H3H 2T3 (514)937-7986. FAX: 937-8332.
Types de production et générique: l métrage-Prod; TV film-Prod.
Types d'oeuvres: Drame-C&TV; Comédie-C&TV; Action-C&TV.
Curriculum vitae: A l'emploi de Radio-Canada comme script-girl, 67-69; travaille activement dans le milieu du cinéma comme scripte, et comme assistante réalisatice; ensuite, directrice de production pour de nombreuses annonces publicitaires et quelques films; productrice, 79. *Atlantic City* remporte le Grand Prix du Festival de Film de Venise, Meilleur Film, Acteur et Scénario (Los Angeles Film Critics Association); *Les Plouffe* remporte le Prix International Press et plusieurs Prix Génie dont Meilleur Scénario, 82. En 90, fonde Cinévidéo Plus, prolongement naturel de Cinévidéo, maison de production dont elle occupe la présidence depuis 85.
Filmographie sélective: *Star for Two*, C, 91, F/CDN, Prod; *Sous le signe du poisson*, C, 91, F/CDN, Prod; *Dames Galantes*, C, 90, CDN/F/I, Prod; *Slog*, C, 87, F/CDN, Prod; *Les fous de Bassan*, C, 86, CDN/F, Prod; *Le Matou*, C/TV, 85, CDN/F, Prod; *Le Crime d'Ovide Plouffe*, C/TV, 84, CDN/F, Prod; *Hold Up*, C, 85, CDN/F; *Little Gloria...Happy At Last* (4 eps), TV, 82, CDN/USA, Prod; *Les Plouffe*, C/TV, 81, CDN/F, Prod; *Atlantic City*, C, 80, CDN/F, Prod; *The Little Girl Who Lived Down the Lane*, C, 75, CDN/F, 1er assist réal; *L'amour humain*, C, 70, CDN, 1er assist réal.

HÉROUX, Roger
ACCT. Les Productions Roger Héroux, 4056, Beaconsfield, Montréal, PQ H3X 2P8 (514)484-5574.
Types de production et générique: l métrage-Prod/Dir prod/Prod dél; c métrage-Prod/Réal; TV film-Prod/Dir prod/Réal; TV vidéo-Réal/Prod.
Types d'oeuvres: Drame-C; Annonces-

TV; Industriel-TV.
Curriculum vitae: Né en 1951. Citoyenneté canadienne. Langues: français et anglais. Etudie à l'Université du Québec; cours en Photographie, Académie des Arts du Canada. Président, Les Productions Roger Héroux inc., 79; Directeur de production et producteur de nombreux courts métrages; directeur de production de plusieurs annonces publicitaires dont Labatt, Sucrets, Loto-Québec, Eaton's, Simpsons, Banque de Commerce, etc.
Filmographie sélective: *Alphonse Desjardins*, TV, CDN, Prod dél; "Misère des Riches", TV, CDN, Prod dél; "Misère des Riches II", TV, CDN, Prod dél; "Lance et Compte", TV, CDN, Prod dél; *Formule I*, C, 87, CDN/F, Prod dél; *Les Fous de Bassan*, C, 86, CDN, Prod dél; *Popeye Doyle*, C, 86, USA, Dir pro; *Les Faiseurs d'étoile*, C, 86, CDN, Prod/Réal; *In Like Flynn*, TV, 85, USA,; *The Park Is Mine*, C, 84, CDN, Sup pro; *Clémence Aletti*, C, 83, CDN/I/F, Co prod; *Au nom de tous les miens*, C, 83, CDN/F, Dir pro; *Of Unknown Origin*, C, 82, CDN/USA, Prod; *Covergirl/Dreamworld*, C, 81, CDN, Dir pro; *The Funny Farm*, C, 80, CDN, Dir pro.

HERTZOG, Larry
ACCT. Lawrence Hertzog Productions, 62 Charles St. E., Toronto, ON M4Y 1T1 (416)921-9300.
Type of Production and Credits: Th Film-Prod; TV Film-Prod.
Genres: Drama-Th&TV; Comedy-Th&TV; Documentary-TV.
Biography: Born 1933, Hanna, Alberta. Attended University of Alberta; Banff School of Fine Arts. *Why Shoot The Teacher?* won the Golden Reel Award; his television documentaries have won numerous awards at Atlanta, New York, Chicago, Virgin Islands film festivals.
Selected Filmography: *The Mayan*, "Ticket to Adventure" (pilot), TV, 90, CDN, Prod; "Emu-TV" (24 eps), TV, 87, CDN, Prod/Wr; "Birds in Paradise" (4 eps), TV, 84, CDN, Prod; *Till Death Do Us Part*, Th, 81, CDN, Prod; *Final Assigment*, Th, 79, CDN, Prod; *Why Shoot the Teacher?*, Th, 76, CDN, Prod; "Police Surgeon" (78 eps), TV, 73-75, CDN, Assoc Prod; "Canada - Five Portraits" (5 eps), TV, 72-75, CDN, Exec Prod; "Window of the World" (7 eps), TV, 72-75, CDN, Exec Prod; "Heritage" (6 eps), TV, 74-75, CDN, Exec Prod; "Untamed World" (120 eps), TV, 71-75, CDN, Exec Prod; "George" (26 eps), TV, 72, CDN, Assoc Prod.

HEYDON, Michael ◊
(416)363-2345.
Type of Production and Credits: Th Short-Ed; TV Video-Ed/Prod.
Genres: Musical-TV; Music Video-TV.
Biography: Born 1950. B.A.A., Radio and TV Arts, Ryerson Polytechnical Institute.
Selected Filmography: "Much Music", TV, 84-86, CDN, Sr Prod; *I Am a Hotel*, TV, 84, CDN, Ed; "City Limits", TV, 83-84, CDN, Prod; "The New Music", TV, 82-83, CDN, Ed; *Booze Mothers: Doin' it Right on the Wrong Side of Queen*, TV, 82, CDN, Prod/Wr/Ed/Act; Mash/New Gun, Cm, 81, CDN, Prod/Dir/Wr/Ed.

HILL, Don
- see WRITERS

HIRSH, Michael
ACCT. Nelvana Ltd., 32 Atlantic Ave., Toronto, ON M6K 1X8 (416)588-5571.
Type of Production and Credits: Th Film-Prod; TV Film-Prod; TV Video-Prod.
Genres: Children's-Th&TV; Animation-Th&TV.
Biography: Co-founder, Vice-President, Nelvana Ltd. Recipient of numerous awards including Wilderness, Chris, a Special Award, Canadian Film Awards, 78; *The Care Bears Movie* won the Golden Reel Award, 86.
Selected Filmography: "Tintin" (26 eps), TV, 91, CDN/F, Prod; "Rupert" (26 eps), TV, 91, CDN/GB, Exec Prod; "Beetlejuice" (29 eps), TV, 89-91, USA/CDN, Prod; "Babar" (65 eps), TV, 88-91, CDN/F, Prod; "Little Rosey" (13 eps), TV, 90, USA/CDN, Prod; "Care Bears Family Series II" (26 eps), TV, 87-88, CDN, Co-Prod; "The Edison Twins" (78 eps), TV, 83-87, CDN, Co-Prod; "My Pet Monster" (13 eps), TV, 87, CDN, Co-Prod; *The Care Bears Adventure in Wonderland*, Th, 87, CDN, Co-Prod; *Burglar*, Th, 86, USA, Prod; *Mad Balls*, TV, 86, CDN, Co-Prod; "The Care Bears Family" (13 eps), TV, 86, CDN, Co-Prod; *The Care Bears Movie II*, Th, 86, CDN, Co-Prod; "Ewoks" (13 eps), TV, 85, CDN, Co-Prod; *Babar: The Movie*, Th, 82, CDN/F, Exec Prod.

HODGINS, Barbara L.
1908 - 2020 Bellevue Ave., West Vancouver, BC V7V 1B8 (604)926-7155. ViewPoint Productions, 1908 - 2020 Bellevue Ave., West Vancouver, BC V7V 1B8 (604)926-7155.
Type of Production and Credits: TV Video-Prod/Wr.

Genres: Documentary-TV.
Biography: Born in 1944 in Edmonton, Alberta. Educated as an economist (M.A.), University of British Columbia. Career in field of public policy including seven years in central agencies of the federal government in Ottawa and seven years in national research institutes, (C.D. Howe Institute and the Institute for Research on Public Policy). Began to pursue documentary filmmaking in 1987.
Selected Filmography: *Sustainable Development: Global Challenge, Global Change*, TV, 90, CDN, Wr/Prod; *Seeing the Forest*, ED, 87, CDN, Prod.

HOFFMAN, Kitty
TWIFT. 559 Melrose Ave., Toronto, ON M5M 2A4 (416)781-0311.
Type of Production and Credits: TV Video-Prod/Wr.
Genres: Drama-Th&TV; Documentary-Th&TV; Educational-Th&TV; Current Affairs-Th&TV.
Biography: Born 1949, Norway; Canadian citizenship. Languages: English, French and Yiddish. Ph.D., Communications/ American Literature. Ten years of senior government experience.
Selected Filmography: "N.E.W.S." (10 eps), TV, 89, CDN, Prod.

HOLENDER, Jacques
ACCT. Nemesis Productions, Main Floor, 317 Adelaide St. W., Toronto, ON M5V 1P9 (416)323-0577. FAX: 515-7934.
Type of Production and Credits: Th Short-Prod/Dir; TV Film-Prod/Dir.
Genres: Documentary-Th&TV.
Biography: Born 1953, Zambia; Canadian citizenship. Studied Fine Arts, University of Cape Town, and Film in London, England. Worked in the UK for 8 years; immigrated to Canada. Has been working as a producer/director since 79; Nemesis Productions established in 81.
Selected Filmography: *Musicians in Exile*, Th, 90, CDN, Prod/Dir/Ed; *Juju Music*, TV, 87, CDN, Prod/Dir/Ed; *Kodo*, Th, 84, CDN, Prod/Dir/Ed; *Traces*, Th, 83, CDN, Prod/Dir/Ed; *Echoes*, Th, 82, CDN, Prod/Dir/Ed.

HOMBERT, Madeline
Altasee Productions Inc./West Sky Entertainment Group Inc., 304 Birch Cres., Sherwood Park, AB T8A 1W9 (403)467-3570. FAX: 449-2067.
Type of Production and Credits: Th Film-Prod/Wr/Exec Prod.
Genres: Comedy-Th; Drama-Th; Action/Adventure-Th.
Biography: Born 1944, Shoal Lake, Manitoba. More than 15 years experience in writing; 6 years in producing. Currently developing *The Studhorse Man*, co-writing screenplay with Ches Dauphinee; executive producer and co-producer. As a writer, *Troubled Waters* and *British Prime Minister's Wife* are under option for feature films. *Troubled Waters* is in development for 1991 production (Producer and Co-Writer).
Selected Filmography: *The Ranch*, Th, 88, Prod/Wr; *Personal Exemptions*, Th, 88, CDN, Prod/Wr.

HOPE, Kathryn Ruth
KRH Productions, 100 Manor Rd. E., Toronto, ON M4S 1P8 (416)736-5149. FAX: 736-5710.
Type of Production and Credits: Th Film-Ed; TV Film-Prod/Dir/Wr; TV Video-Prod/Dir/Wr.
Genres: Drama-Th&TV; Documentary-TV; Children's-TV; Industrial-TV.
Biography: Born 1952, Toronto, Ontario. B.A., Film and Video, York University, 74; Executive M.B.A., University of Toronto, 87. Has won several awards, including medals at Chicago and New York Festivals.
Selected Filmography: *Spontaneous Combustion*, In, 90, CDN, Prod; *Bravo York*, In, 87, CDN, Prod/Dir/Wr; *Men in Transition* (mini-series), TV, 84-85, CDN, Prod/Dir; "Bailey Creek" (2 eps), In, 82-83, USA, Prod/Dir; *Money and Medicine*, TV, 81-82, USA, Assoc Prod/Ed; *Student Bodies*, Th, 81, USA, Ed; *A Different Understanding*, TV, 78-79, CDN, Prod/Dir/Ed; *Young and Just Beginning* (mini-series), TV, 76-77, CDN, Prod/Dir/Wr/Ed; *Total Coverage*, TV, 77, CDN, Ed; *A Certain Vision*, TV, 77, CDN, Ed; *Starship Invasions*, Th, 77, CDN, Ed; *Education*, Cm, 76, CDN, Prod/Dir; *Lacrosse is Everybody's Game*, TV, 75, CDN, Prod/Dir/Wr/Ed; *Table Tennis Champions*, TV, 75, CDN, Prod/Dir/Wr/Ed; *Point of No Return*, Th, 75, CDN, Snd FX Ed.

HORNE, Jerry
ACTRA. 2137 Wallace St., Regina, SK S4T 2E8 (306)525-6252. Birdsong Communications, 806 Victoria Ave., Regina, SK S4N 0R6 (306)359-3070.
Type of Production and Credits: Th Short-Wr/Dir; TV Film-Wr/Dir/Prod/DOP; TV Video-Wr/Dir/Prod/DOP.
Genres: Documentary-Th&TV; Educational-Th&TV; Current Affairs-Th&TV.
Biography: Born 1952, Swift Current, Saskatchewan. M.A., Communications, McGill University.
Selected Filmography: *Work Safe*, ED,

91, CDN, Dir; *Not Bad Kids*, ED, 90, Prod/Dir; "One World" (10 eps), ED, 87-88, CDN, Dir; *Jimmy's Game*, TV, 86, CDN, Dir.

HORNE, Tina
- see DIRECTORS

HOUSE, Bill
Telefilm Canada, 2 Bloor St. W., Toronto, ON M4W 3E2 (416)973-6436.
Type of Production and Credits: TV Film-Prod; TV Video-Prod.
Genres: Comedy-TV; Variety-TV; Musical-TV; Documentary-TV.
Biography: Born 1948, Windsor, Ontario. Honours B.A., University of Windsor; M.A., York University. 25 professional theatrical productions, especially at Theatre Second Floor, Toronto; Production Manager, Festival of Festivals, 77-81 (produced/directed the tributes to Martin Scorsese, Robert Duvall and Warren Beatty); Executive Coordinator of Production and Development, Ontario Film Development Corporation, until 88; currently Director of Operations and overall administrative head for Telefilm Canada, Province of Ontario.
Selected Filmography: *The Canadian Conspiracy*, TV, 84-85, CDN/USA, Co-Prod, (GEMINI 86); *The Making of Spacehunter*, TV, 83-84, CDN, Prod; *Rumours of Glory: Bruce Cockburn Live*, TV, 82, CDN, Prod; *Gongga Shan: White Peak Beyond the Clouds*, TV, 82, CDN, Prod; *The Little Paper That Grew*, TV, 81, CDN, Prod.

HOWARD, Christopher
31 Evans Ave., Toronto, ON M6S 3V7 (416)766-0846. OWL Centre for Children's Film and Television, 56 The Esplanade, Ste. 213, Toronto, ON M5E 1A7 (416)863-1661. FAX: 868-6009.
Type of Production and Credits: TV Video-Prod/Dir/Wr/SFX Des/Spv Ed/Foley; TV Film-Wr/Spv Ed/Foley; Th Film-Dir/Wr/Ed.
Genres: Children's-TV; Documentary-Th&TV; Educational-Th&TV; Music Video-TV.
Biography: Born 1954, Windsor, Ontario. M.A., English Literature.
Selected Filmography: "OWL-TV" (30 eps), TV, 89-91, CDN, Prod; "OWL-TV" (50 eps), TV, 86-91, CDN, Dir; "OWL-TV" (60 eps) TV, 85-91, CDN, Wr; "OWL-TV" (60 eps), TV, 85-91, CDN, Foley; "OWL-TV" (15 eps), TV, 85-87, CDN, SFX Des; "OWL-TV" (30 eps), TV, 85-87, CDN, Spv Ed; *A Walk in the Rainforest*, ED, 90, CDN, Prod/Dir/Wr/Foley; *My Ship/Riki Turofsky Sings Kurt Weil*, MV, 89, CDN, Dir/Wr/Ed; "Vid Kids" (13 eps), TV, 85, CDN, Co-Ed/SFX Des; "Earth Odyssey" (5 eps), TV, 84, CDN, Wr.

HOWARD, Dan
DGC, DGA. 70 Alcorn Ave., Toronto, ON M4V 1E4 (416)323-9881. FAX: 323-9732. David Gersh, The Gersh Agency, 222 N. Canon Dr., Beverly Hills, CA 90210 USA (213)274-6611. Ralph Zimmerman, 350 Dupont St., Toronto, ON M5R 1V9 (416)925-2051.
Type of Production and Credits: Th Film-PM/Prod; TV Film-Prod/PM.
Genres: Drama-Th&TV; Comedy-Th&TV; Action-TV; Children's-TV.
Biography: Born 1940, Morton, Ontario; Canadian citizenship; U.S. resident alien. Involved in productions which have won 5 Gemini awards, 1 Emmy; nominated for 5 Canadian Film Awards, won one Best Picture award.
Selected Filmography: *Terminal City Ricochet*, Th, 89-90, CDN, Exec Prod; *Gorillas in the Mist*, Th, 88-89, USA/GB, PM; *Palais Royale*, Th, 87, CDN, Line Prod; *Anne of Green Gables* (mini-series), TV, 86-87, CDN, Line Prod; *Heaven on Earth*, TV, 86, CDN/USA/GB, Prod; *Frontier* (mini-series), TV, 85, CDN/GB/F, Line Prod; *I'Maureen*, Th, 77, CDN, Prod; *Goldenrod*, Th, 73, USA/CDN, Assoc Prod; "Tales of the Klondike" (13 eps), TV, 84, GB/F/CDN, Assoc Prod; "SCTV" (12 eps), TV, 82-83, USA/CDN, Unit M.

HOWARD, Jeff
R.R. #1, Site 118, C-56, Parksville, BC V0R 2S0 (604)248-5446. Jeffrey Howard Productions Ltd., 893 Shorewood Dr., Parksville, BC V9P 1S6 (604)248-9311.
Type of Production and Credits: Th Short-Dir/Prod/Wr/Ed.
Genres: Documentary-TV; Educational-TV.
Biography: Born 1937, Lamont, Alberta. Has worked in television since 57 starting as host/announcer, becoming film producer/director; founded Jeffrey Howard Productions Ltd., 73; specializes in dramatic, motivational films for Native people.
Selected Filmography: *Fire Protection Connection*, ED, 91, CDN, Wr/Prod/Dir; *Healing Journey*, ED, 89-90, CDN, Wr/Prod/Dir/Ed; *The Winners*, TV, 88, CDN, Prod/Dir/Wr; *Champions*, TV, 88, CDN, Prod/Dir/Wr; *The Ridge*, TV, 87, CDN, Wr; *Somebody Called Ernestine*, ED, 86, CDN, Prod/Dir/Wr/Ed; *New Day - New Horizons/Guns for Life*, ED, 78-83,

CDN, Prod/Dir/Wr; *The Home Team*, Cm, 79, CDN, Prod/Dir/Wr/Ed; *Proline*, Cm, 78, CDN, Prod/Dir/Ed; *Chief Dan George Speaks*, TV, 77, CDN, Prod/Dir/Wr; *Tukusinuk/You're Hired/Job Wanted/Help Wanted*, ED, 75-77, CDN, Prod; *Name of the Game/What Did You Say?/A Matter of Choice*, ED, 74, CDN, Prod/Dir; *It Wasn't My Fault/Who's in Charge Here?*, ED, 74, CDN, Prod/Dir; *He Comes Without Calling*, ED, 74, CDN, Prod/Dir; *More Power to You/I Move/Many Voices*, ED, 72-73, CDN, Prod/Dir.

HUNT, Bill ◆
(416)699-4209.
Type of Production and Credits: TV Film-Prod/Dir; TV Video-Prod/Dir; Video-Dir.
Genres: Drama-TV; Comedy-TV; Educational-TV; Children's-TV.
Biography: Born in Ottawa, Ontario. Experience as film editor and production manager. Winner of several awards.
Selected Filmography: "Inside Stories", TV, 88, CDN, Assoc Prod; "Prescriptions for Health" (13 eps), TV, 87-88, CDN, Dir; "Seeing Things" (6 eps), TV, 86, CDN, Assoc Prod; "Going Great" (26 eps), TV, 83-84, CDN, Prod/Dir; "Yes, You Can" (37 eps), TV, 81-83, CDN, Prod; "Nuggets" (26 eps), TV, 80, CDN, Prod/Dir; *Someday, Sometime*, TV, 79, CDN, 1st AD; "Catch Up" (26 eps), TV, 76-78, CDN, Assoc Prod/Assist Dir; "Coming Up Rosie" (26 eps), TV, 73-75, CDN, 2nd U Dir.

HUNT, Graham
- see DIRECTORS
HUNTER, John
- see WRITERS
HUTTON, Douglas
RR #5, Stony Plain, AB T0E 2G0 (403)963-3604. King Motion Picture Corp., 1509, TD Tower, Edmonton Centre, Edmonton, AB T5J 2Z1 (403)424-2950.
Type of Production and Credits: Th Film-Prod; TV Video-Prod/Dir.
Genres: Variety-TV; Musical-TV; Documentary-TV; Music Video-TV.
Biography: Born in 1940. During a 25 year career, has been involved as an executive producer, producer/director, development consultant, promoter, associate producer, executive in charge and general consultant. Has been active in recording, publishing, songwriting, concert promotion and television production. Has produced over 139 television programs, 12 television series including "The Canada Heritage Series". Was a founding board member of The Banff Television Festival and has served as President and Board Member of the Edmonton Motion Picture and Television Bureau, Director of 373706 Alberta Ltd. (a corporate shareholder in Alberta Television Network, Inc.) and is President of Tennessee Entertainment Corporation, located in Nashville, Tenn.
Selected Filmography: "This Living World" (3 eps), TV, 90-91, CDN, Prod/Dir; *Centre Stage*, TV, 88, CDN, Prod/Dir; *Isaac Littlefeather*, TV, 84, CDN, Assoc Prod; *In The Dawning*, TV, 82, CDN, Prod; "Devils Lake" (9 eps), TV, 82, CDN, Prod; "Star Chart" (39 eps), TV, 80, CDN, Prod; "Rock It" (13 eps), TV, 78-79, CDN, Prod; "In Concert" (25 eps), TV, 75-77, CDN, Prod.

IVESON, Rob ◆
CFTA, DGC, ACTRA. (416)466-9436.
Type of Production and Credits: Th Film-Prod/Line Pro/PM; TV Film-Prod/Line Pro/PM/Wr; TV Video-Prod/ Line Pro/PM/Wr.
Genres: Drama-Th&TV; Documentary-Th&TV; Educational-TV; Current Affairs-TV.
Biography: Born 1942, Renfrew, Ontario. B.A., English, University of Toronto; Woodrow Wilson scholar in English. Film career with Allan King Associates; hands-on experience in every aspect of filmmaking, from researching the idea to selling the final film; past executive of the Canadian Association of Motion Picture Producers.
Selected Filmography: *Finding Mary March*, Th, 87, CDN, Co-Prod; *The Day They Came to Arrest the Book*, TV, 86, CDN/USA, PM/Line Prod; *Loyalties*, Th, 85, CDN/GB, Line Prod; "Lorne Greene's New Wilderness" (22 eps), TV, 83, CDN/USA, Line Prod/Prod Cons; *A Matter of Sex*, TV, 83, CDN/USA, Co-Prod; *Escape from Tehran*, TV, 81, CDN/USA, Co-Prod; *Title Shot*, TV, 79, CDN, Prod; *Three Card Monte*, TV, 77, CDN, Prod.

JACKSON, G. Philip
- see DIRECTORS
JACKSON, Joanne P.
502 Scarborough Rd., Toronto, ON M4E 3N2 (416)698-0169. YTV Canada Inc., 64 Jefferson Ave., Unit 18, Toronto, ON M6K 3H3 (416)534-1911.
Type of Production and Credits: TV Video-Prod.
Genres: Variety-TV; Documentary-TV; Children's-TV; Current Affairs-TV; News-TV.

Biography: Born in 1955 in New Liskeard, Ontario. Ryerson RTA Graduate, 1977. CBI Award for Excellence in Children's Broadcasting, "YTV Rocks", 1989. Gemini nomination, Youth category, 1989 for "YTV Hits". Gemini nomination, 1990 for "YTV Rocks". Developed and produced the talk shows "Contact!" and "Positive Parenting", both hosted by Debbie Van Kiekebelt. Associate Producer, CITY-TV, Toronto from 1979-85. Freelance researcher for "CBC National News", 1987-88. Currently Senior Co-ordinating Producer at YTV in Toronto.
Selected Filmography: "Rock'N Talk" (180 eps), TV, 90-91, CDN, Prod; *Kids Help Phone Benefit*, TV, 91, CDN, Prod; *Kids and World Crisis*, "Positive Parenting", TV, 91, CDN, Prod; "YTV'S Young Canada" (13 eps), TV, 91, CDN, Prod; "YTV Rocks" (215 eps), TV, 88-90, CDN, Prod; "YTV Hits", (26 eps) TV, 88-90, CDN, Prod; "Positive Parenting" (52 eps), TV, 90, CDN, Prod; *Stars Shine for Joe Philion*, TV, 89, CDN, Prod; "CBC National News" (100 eps), TV, 87-88, CDN, Svc Prod/Res; "Contact!" (120 eps), TV, 86, CDN, Prod; "CityPulse News" (160 eps), TV, 85, CDN, Assoc Prod; "CityLife" (200 eps), TV, 83-84, CDN, Assoc Prod; "You're Beautiful" (800 eps), TV, 79-83, CDN, Assoc Prod.

JACOBOVICI, Simcha
- see DIRECTORS

JACQUES, Blain
APFTQ. 212, rue du Dauphiné, St-Lambert, PQ J4S 1N1 (514)923-3783. Productions SDA Ltée, 1425 ouest, boul. René-Lévesque, 10e étage, Montréal, PQ H3G 1T7 (514)866-1761.
Types de production et générique: TV film-Prod; TV video-Prod.
Types d'oeuvres: Drame-TV; Enfants-TV.
Curriculum vitae: Né en 1947 au Québec. Langues: français et anglais. Membre du Barreau du Québec depuis 81. Conseiller juridique, Téléfilm Canada, 83-85. Chef production extérieures et acquisitions au réseau français de Radio-Canada, 86-87. Producteur exécutif chez SDA depuis 87.
Filmographie sélective: Les débrouillards II" (30 eps), TV, 91, CDN, Prod exéc; "Scoop" (23 eps), TV, 91, CDN, Prod exéc; "Les débrouillards I" (30 eps), TV, 90, CDN, Prod exéc; "Des Fleurs sur la Neige" (4 eps), TV, 90, CDN, Prod exéc; "Video-Théâtre" (13 eps), "Les Animaux Magiques" (26 eps); TV, 89, CDN, Prod exéc, "AZ" (26 eps); TV, 89, CDN, Prod exéc.

JAY, Paul
- see DIRECTORS

JEAN, Jacques
- see DIRECTORS

JEFFREY, Robert
ACTRA. 460 Palmerston Blvd., Toronto, ON M6G 2P1 (416)534-8115.
Type of Production and Credits: TV Video-Prod/Wr.
Genres: Educational-TV; Children's Th&TV.
Biography: Born in 1936 in Winnipeg, Manitoba. Studied at the Royal Conservatory of Music, Toronto (scholarship student). Performer in children's television and television music dramas. Co-author of "Queen On Moose Handbook".
Selected Filmography: "Reach For The Top" (48 eps), TV, 87-91, CDN, Assoc Prod; "Mr. Dressup" (10 eps), TV, 78, CDN, Wr; "Polka Dot Door" (6 eps), TV, 74, CDN, Wr.

JENNINGS, Christina
890 Queen St. W., Toronto, ON M6J 1G3 (416)516-2948.
Type of Production and Credits: Th Film-Prod; Th Short-Prod.
Genres: Drama-Th&TV; Documentary-TV; Children's-TV; Industrial-Th.
Biography: Born 1951, Northallerton, Yorkshire, England. Canadian citizenship. Languages: English and French. B.A. English and Geography, University of Toronto, 1974; Canadian Centre for Advanced Film, Resident 1990, 2nd Year Resident, 1991.
Selected Filmography: *Love Clinic*, Th, 91, Prod; *Pictures on Water*, TV, 90, Prod/Exec Prod; *A Funny Thing Happened on the Way to the Olympics*, TV, 88, Prod; *En Allant Aux Jeux*, TV, 88, Prod; *Dreams of Glory*, TV, 87, Prod; Communications Canada, In, 87, Prod; *Different Worlds*, TV, 86, Prod; Transportation Canada, In, 86, Prod; *Who Dunnit?*, Th/TV, 84, Assoc Prod.

JEPHCOTT, Samuel C.
ACTRA, BAE, CFTPA, DGC, ACCT. Cyclops Communications Corp., 44 Gibson Ave., Toronto, ON M5R 1T5 (416)926-8981. CFTA, 663 Yonge St., Ste. 404, Toronto, ON M4Y 2A4 (416)927-8942. FAX: 922-4038.
Type of Production and Credits: Th Film-Prod; TV Film-Prod; TV Video-Prod.
Genres: Drama-Th&TV; Comedy-Th; Documentary-TV; Children's-Th.
Biography: Born 1944, England;

Canadian citizenship. Director/General Manager, CFTPA since 90; President, CFTA, 87-90; Governor, ACTRA Fraternal, 84-88; Governor, Canadian Conference of the Arts, 86-92; Executive Director, CFTA, 84-87; President, Cyclops Communications Corp. since 78; former board member and National Executive Secretary, DGC; Director, CAMPP; extensive experience in foreign distribution of features and television with Quadrant Films, Nielsen Ferns International and CBC Enterprises; Publisher, *Action-The Voice of Independent Production* and *Action-Canadian Production Guide*; Maître d'Hôtel, CFTPA Awards for Personal and Corporate Achievement Presentations, 84 to present.
Selected Filmography: "The Last Frontier" (23 eps), TV, 85-88, CDN, Prod; *The Wars*, Th, 81, CDN/D, Pro Spv; "Man of the North" (7 eps), TV, 77-78, CDN, P Pro Spv; "The Newcomers" (1 eps), TV, 78, CDN, P Pro Spv; "The New Avengers" (2 eps), TV, 77, CDN/GB/F, PM; *Love at First Sight*, Th, 75, CDN, Pro Acc't; *A Sweeter Song*, Th, 75, CDN, Assoc Prod; *Find the Lady*, Th, 75, CDN/GB, Stills; *It Seemed Like a Good Idea at the Time*, Th, 74, CDN, Assist PM; *Lions for Breakfast*, Th, 74, CDN, PM; *Me*, Th, 74, CDN, PM; *The Hard Part Begins*, Th, 73, CDN, PM; *The Merry Wives of Tobias Rouke*, Th, 71, CDN, Co-Prod.

JESPERSEN, Rik
1500 South Dyke Rd., New Westminster, BC V3M 5A2 (604)525-5248. CBC-TV, 700 Hamilton St., Vancouver, BC (604)662-6800.
Type of Production and Credits: TV Video-Prod.
Genres: Documentary-TV; News-TV.
Biography: Born 1950, Gravenhurst, Ontario. Diploma in Journalism. Four years at Citytv as assignment editor, senior writer, producer; producer, CBC's "The Journal", 83-85; senior producer, Citytv News, 86-88; senior producer, CBC-TV News, Vancouver, 89 to present.

JEWISON, Norman
- see DIRECTORS

JOHNSON, Andrew
ACCT, CIFC. Open City Productions Ltd., 54 Manfield Ave., Toronto, ON M6J 2B2 (416)532-6892.
Type of Production and Credits: TV Video-Prod/Wr/Dir/Ed.
Genres: Documentary-TV; Drama-TV; Industrial-TV.
Biography: Born 1956, Toronto, Ontario. B.A., English Literature, 80; M.A., Drama, 82, University of Toronto; winner of Queen Elizabeth Scholarship. Freelance writer - *Globe and Mail*, *Cinema Canada*, *Toronto Star*. *Voices on the Water* won "Best Cultural Program," 1986 Paters Awards, Australia; "Chris Bronze," Columbus, Ohio 86. *By the Seat of Their Pants* was nominated for "Best Documentary Writing," Gemini 90.
Selected Filmography: *Padre Pablo*, TV, 89, CDN/GB, Co-Prod/Co-Dir/Co-Ed/Co-Wr; *By the Seat of Their Pants*, TV, 88, CDN/GB, Assoc Prod/Assist Dir/Co-Wr; *Frontier Footlights*, TV, 88, CDN, Assoc Prod/Assist Dir; *Voices on the Water*, TV, 87, CDN, Prod/Dir/Ed/Wr; *1987 International Children's Festival*, In, 87, CDN, Prod/Dir/Ed/Wr; *444 Days to Freedom*, TV, 86, CDN/USA, Assoc Prod/Assist Dir/Co-Wr; *The King of Friday Night*, TV, 85, CDN, 3rd AD/Post PM.

JOHNSON, Dan
ACCT, CFTPA. 62 Humewood Dr., Toronto, ON M6C 2W4 (416)653-0702. Alliance Communications, 920 Yonge St., Ste. 400, Toronto, ON M4W 3C7 (416)967-1174.
Type of Production and Credits: Th Film-Exec Prod.
Genres: Drama-TV.
Biography: Born in 1953 in Toronto, Ontario. Canadian citizen. Educated at York University (Honours Bachelor of Arts in Film Production, 1976). Law degree from Osgoode Hall Law School, 1978. Has practised entertainment law in Toronto since 1980. Founded the Business Affairs department and became Vice-President, Business Affairs at Norstar Entertainment (formerly Simcon Limited), Norstar Releasing and Norstar Home Video in May, 1987. Was Founding President of the Ontario Film Distributors Association, February 1990. Was appointed Vice-President, Production Finance & Distribution of Alliance Communications Corp., October 1990. On the Board of Directors of CFTPA, serving on the Executive Committee and as Chairman of the Broadcast Relations Committee.
Selected Filmography: *The Last Kiss - Prom Night III*, Th, 89, CDN, Exec Prod; *Cold Comfort*, Th, 88, CDN, Exec Prod.

JOHNSON, John A.
- see DIRECTORS

JOHNSON, Nancy
35 Cowan Place, London, ON N6C 2X4 (519)686-1714. Lockwood Film and Video Prod., 365 Ontario St., London, ON N5W 3W6 (519)434-6006.

Type of Production and Credits: TV Film-Prod/Wr; TV Video-Prod/Wr.
Genres: Documentary-TV; Educational-TV; Commercials-TV; Industrial-TV.
Biography: Born in Kirkland Lake, Ontario. B.A., University of Western Ontario, 69. President of Lockwood Film and Video Productions; founding member of London Film Commission; past member TV and Film Advisory Board, Centennial College, Toronto. Awards at American Film Festival, New York Film Festival, Columbus, CFTA.
Selected Filmography: *Multiculturalism: Rooted in Agriculture*, ED, 88, CDN, Prod; *Multiculturalism: Tracing Your Immigrant Roots*, ED, 88, CDN, Prod; *The Canadian Red Cross: People Helping People*, ED, 88, CDN, Prod; *Dentacare Plus*, London Life, In, 87, CDN, Prod; *Greg Curnoe*, TV, 83, CDN, Wr; *Always Be Careful*, ED, 81, CDN, Prod/Wr; *Doctor Woman*, TV, 79, CDN, Prod/Wr.

JOHNSON, Richard
12 Sullivan St., Toronto, ON M5E 1B9 (416)971-5674. TVOntario, 2180 Yonge St., 6th Flr., Toronto, ON M4S 2C1 (416)484-2700. After Image Video Prod., 12 Sullivan St., Toronto, ON M5E 1B9 (416)971-5674.
Type of Production and Credits: TV Film-Prod; TV Video-Prod/Dir.
Genres: Documentary-TV; Experimental-TV; Educational-TV; Music Video-TV.
Biography: Born 1940, Appleton, Wisconsin; landed immigrant Canada. M.F.A., University of Wisconsin. Has worked at TVOntario since 69. Won Gold Medal, Los Angeles Film Festival, 71, for film on Jack Nicholson; Gold Medal for *Nightmusic Concert FM*, Chicago, 77.
Selected Filmography: "Waves from the Pleasure Palace" (5 eps), MV, 90-91, CDN, Prod/Dir/Comp/Snd Ed; "Moving Images" (20 eps), TV, 87-88, CDN, Prod/Dir/Wr; "New Directions in Film" (2 eps), TV, 86, CDN, Prod/Dir; "Saturday Night at the Movies" (208 eps), TV, 78-86, CDN, Prod/Dir; "The Movie Show" (52 eps), TV, 83-85, CDN, Dir/Prod; "Rough Cuts" (104 eps), TV, 79-83, CDN, Prod/Dir; "Film International" (4 eps), TV, 82, CDN, Prod/Dir; "On Air" (8 eps), TV, 78, CDN, Prod/Dir; "After Image" (16 eps), TV, 78, CDN, Prod/Dir; "The Comedy Shoppe" (26 eps), TV, 78, CDN, Prod/Dir; "Nightmusic Concerts" (62 eps), TV, 76-78, CDN, Prod/Dir; "Nightmusic" (540 eps), TV, 73-77, CDN, Prod/Dir; "Calendar" (52 eps), TV, 71-73, CDN, Pro Coord; "Showcase" (52 eps), TV, 69-71, CDN, Pro Coord; "People Worth Knowing" (70 eps), TV, 70-71, CDN, Pro Coord.

JOHNSTON, William ◆
DGC, ACCT. (416)967-6503.
Type of Production and Credits: Th Film-Prod; TV Film-Dir/Prod.
Genres: Drama-Th; Documentary-Th&TV.
Biography: Born 1946, Winnipeg, Manitoba. Languages: English and French. Attended London International Film School, England; Institut des Arts de Diffusion, Brussels; Université Paul-Valéry, France; B.Sc., University of Manitoba. *The Fast and the Furious* won Blue Ribbon, American Film Festival; *Quilting: The Patterns of Love* won Chris Plaque, Columbus; *No Surrender* won International Critics Award, Toronto Festival of Festivals; *Loyalties* won 9 Genies.
Selected Filmography: *A Winter to Remember*, TV, 88, CDN, Dir/Exec Prod/Ed; *A Funny Thing Happened on the Way to the Olympics*, TV, 87, CDN, Dir/Exec Prod; *Dreams of Glory*, TV, 87, CDN, Exec Prod; *Shoot Me*, Th, 87, CDN, Dir/Prod; *Loyalties*, Th, 85, CDN/GB, Prod, (GENIES); *No Surrender*, Th, 85, CDN/GB, Co-Prod; *Drastic Measures*, Th, 84, CDN, Prod; *The Saga of Those Crazy Canucks*, TV, 84, CDN, Prod; *The Heroes of Summer*, TV, 84, CDN, Prod; *Beyond Words*, TV, 84, CDN, Prod; *The Disability Myth* (parts I, II & III), TV, 82-84, CDN, Prod; *The Fast and the Furious*, TV, 83, CDN, Dir; *The Heroes of Winter*, TV, 83, CDN, Prod; *It Takes a Champion*, TV, 83, CDN, Prod; *Three Against the World*, TV, 83, CDN, Prod.

JONAS, George
ATPD, ACTRA, CAPAC. MGA Agency, 10 St. Mary St., #510, Toronto, ON M4Y 1P9 (416)964-3302. FAX: 975-9209.
Type of Production and Credits: TV Film-Prod/Wr/Dir; TV Video-Prod/Wr/Dir.
Genres: Drama-TV; Action-TV; Documentary-TV; Children's-TV.
Biography: Born 1935, Budapest, Hungary; Canadian citizen. Languages: English, German, Hungarian. Attended Academy of Theatre and Film Arts, Budapest. Author of several books, including *By Persons Unknown, Vengeance, Final Decree* and *Greenspan: The Case for the Defence*. Produced over 100, directed 15 dramas, docudramas, 69-91; producer, CBC Radio and TV, "The Scales of Justice" (as well as writer/director of several

episodes). Two ACTRA Awards, Gabriel Award, Gold Award (NY) for radio shows; many literary awards, including National Magazine Award and Edgar Allan Poe Award for Best Fact Crime Book.
Selected Filmography: "The Scales of Justice" (5 eps), TV, 90-91, CDN, Wr/Prod; *The House on Front Street*, Th&TV, 77, CDN, Prod/Dir; *The Princess of Tombosa*, TV, 76, CDN, Wr/Prod/Dir; "The Play's the Thing" (12 eps)(Dir 2 eps), TV, 73-74, CDN, Prod; "Purple Playhouse" (9 eps), TV, 72-73, CDN, Prod; "Program X" (60 eps)(Dir 8 eps), TV, 69-72, CDN, Prod.

JONES, Cliff
ACTRA, AFM, ACCT. Cliff Jones Productions, 21 Bramble Dr., Don Mills, ON M3B 2E9 (416)924-2400. FAX: 510-0160.
Type of Production and Credits: TV Video-Wr/Prod/Comp; TV Film-Wr/Prod/Comp.
Genres: Drama-TV; Comedy-TV; Variety-TV; Musical-TV.
Biography: Born Toronto, Ontario. M.A., Psychology. Active in musical theatre: *Babies, Robin Hood - The Musical, Hey Marilyn, Hamlet - The Musical*. Best Writer, Best Composer, L.A. Dramalogue Awards.
Selected Filmography: *Rich's Video* (Rich Little), TV, 91, CDN/USA, Comp; *Rita MacNeil Christmas Special*, TV, 90, CDN, Prod/Wr/Comp; *Flying On Your Own* (Rita MacNeil), TV, 90, CDN, Prod/Wr; *Alexandra: The Last Empress*, TV, 88, CDN, Wr/Comp/Orch/Mus Dir; "Lifetime" (daily), TV, 85-86, CDN, Comp/Mus Dir; "Hangin' In" (120 eps), TV, 80-86, CDN, Mus Dir; "Thrill of a Lifetime" (60 eps), TV, 83-86, CDN/USA, Comp/Mus Dir; "Definition" (daily), TV, 83-86, CDN, Comp/Mus Dir; *The True Gift of Christmas*, TV, 85, CDN, Co-Wr; "Just Kidding" (40 eps), TV, 84-85, CDN, Comp/Mus Dir; "Sunday's Child" (14 eps), TV, 83, CDN/USA, Comp/Mus Dir; *Pygmalion*, TV, 83, CDN, Comp/Mus Dir; *Frank Mills Christmas Special*, TV, 82, CDN, Wr/Mus Dir; *Rich Little's Robin Hood*, TV, 82, CDN/USA, Co-Wr; *Anne Murray Specials* (4 shows), TV, 78-82, CDN, Co-Wr.

JONES, Dennis
DGA. 23612 Lund St., Woodland Hills, CA 91367 (818)704-9184. Deja View Productions Inc., 11845 W. Olympic Blvd., #645, Los Angeles, CA 90064 USA (213)312-8660. The Gray/Goodman Agency, 211 S. Beverly Blvd., Suite 100, Beverly Hills, CA 90212 USA (213)276-7070.
Type of Production and Credits: Th Film-PM/Prod; TV Film-PM/Prod.
Genres: Drama-Th&TV; Comedy-Th&TV; Action-Th&TV; Science Fiction-Th&TV.
Biography: Born 1943, Grimsby, Lincolnshire, England; Canadian citizenship; US resident alien. B.A., Economics, University of Toronto, 66; B.A.A., Radio and TV Arts, Ryerson Polytechnical Institute, 70.
Selected Filmography: *Pacific Heights*, Th, 89-90, USA, Co-Prod; *Prime Target*, Th, 89, USA, Prod; *Moonwalker*, TV, 86-88, USA, Prod; *Short Circuit*, Th, 86, USA, Co-Prod; *Back to the Future*, Th, 84-85, USA, PM; *Back to the Future*, Th, 84-85, USA, PM; *Mrs. Soffel*, Th, 84, USA, Assoc Prod/PM; *The Adventures of Buckaroo Banzai*, Th, 83, USA, Assoc Prod/PM; *The Twilight Zone - The Movie*, Th, 82, USA, PM; *Poltergeist*, Th, 81, USA, PM; *Rich and Famous*, Th, 80-81, USA, PM; *Fun and Games*, TV, 80, USA, PM; *Freedom Road*, TV, 79, USA, PM; *Love for Rent*, TV, 78-79, USA, PM; *Seizure: The Story of Kathy Morris*, TV, 78, USA, PM.

JORDAN, Eric
CFTPA, ACCT. The Film Works Ltd, 194 Sherbourne St., Toronto, ON M5A 2R7 (416)360-7968. FAX: 360-8569.
Type of Production and Credits: Th Film-Prod; TV Film-Prod/Dir; TV Video-Prod.
Genres: Drama-TV; Documentary-TV; Educational-TV; Children's-TV.
Biography: Born in 1946 in Toronto, Ontario. Formed The Film Works in 1975 with Paul Stephens. Produced documentary and educational films, then started producing drama in the early 1980s. "African Journey" won the Silver Hugo and Chris awards, "Spirit Bay" the Chris and *Where the Spirit Lives* has won many awards including a 1990 Gemini for Best Movie.
Selected Filmography: "Journey to Understanding" (6 eps), TV, 90, CDN, Exec Prod; "African Journey" (6 eps), TV, 89, CDN, Spv Prod; *Where the Spirit Lives*, TV, 88, CDN, Prod; "Spirit Bay" (13 eps), TV, 84-87, CDN, Prod/Dir/Wr.

JUBENVILL, Ken
- see DIRECTORS

KABELIK, Vladimir
ACCT, AMI, CCAIT, FITES. 2024 Glenada Cres., Oakville, ON L6H 4M6 (416)842-3967. Sheridan College, 1430

Trafalgar Rd., Oakville, ON L6H 2L1. Cutaway Prod. Ltd., 258 Wallace Ave., Toronto, ON M6P 3M9 (416)537-6501.
Type of Production and Credits: TV Film-Prod/Wr/Ed; TV Video-Prod/Wr/Ed.
Genres: Musical-TV; Documentary-Th&TV; Educational-TV; Industrial-Th&TV.
Biography: Born in 1951 in Zlin, Czechoslovakia. Studied at the Academy of Film and Television Arts in Prague. Employed as a motion picture director/writer by the "Short Film Studios", Prague. Also worked for Czechoslovak Television, Radio Prague and the musical agency Pragokoncert. Came to Canada in 1982. Has produced for CBC, CTV, TVO, Vision TV, SCN and Access Network. Has filmed on location in USA, Switzerland, Cuba, U.S.S.R. etc. Currently a Professor of Film and Television at Sheridan College and a Principal Partner in Cutaway Production Limited. *Boris* awarded the Silver Award, 1991, AMI; *Glass From the Attic* awarded Special Jury Award, 1989, Yorkton.
Selected Filmography: "Music From Castles and Chateaux" (26 eps), TV, 91, CDN/CS, Exec Prod; *Living With Asthma*, ED, 90, CDN, Prod/Dir; *Boris*, "Canadian Reflections", TV, 89, CDN, Prod/Dir/Wr; *Glass From the Attic*, "Canadian Reflections", TV, 88, CDN, Prod/Dir/Wr; *Mississauga*, Cm, 88, CDN, Prod/Dir; *Arts Card*, Cm, 88, CDN, Prod; *Environmental Statue/Sculptor of Dying Birds*, "The Nature of Things", TV, 84, CDN, Dir; *The Kellogg's Man*, Cm, 83, CDN, Dir/Ed; *Krystyna*, TV, 82, CDN, Prod/Dir; *Expedition Cuba*, Th/TV, 81, CS, Dir/Wr; *Drivers, Drugs and Spirits*, TV, 79, CS, Dir/Wr; *Generation 70!*, Th, 78, CS, Dir/Wr; *Attention, Children..!*, Th, 77, CS, Dir/Wr; *Man, Machine and Conscience*, Th, 76, CS, Dir/Wr.

KAHN, Mary
DGC. 22 Dartnell Ave., Toronto, ON M5R 3A4 (416)922-7562.
Type of Production and Credits: Th Film-Prod; TV Film-Prod.
Genres: Drama-Th&TV; Comedy-Th&TV; Commercials-TV.
Biography: Born in Toronto, Ontario. Documentary and advertising writer; producer or production manager for many commercials.
Selected Filmography: *The Girl from Mars*, TV, 91, CDN, Prod; *Clarence*, TV, 90, CDN, Prod; "Neon Rider" (24 eps), TV, 89-90, CDN, Prod; "Alfred Hitchcock Presents" (41 eps), TV, 87-88, CDN/USA, Prod; "T and T" (10 eps), TV, 87, CDN, PM; "Alfred Hitchcock Presents" (8 eps), TV, 86-87, CDN/USA, PM; "Weird Tales" (3 eps), TV, 86, CDN/USA, PM; "Stingray" (7 eps), TV, 86, CDN/USA, PM; "Ray Bradbury Theatre" (3 eps), TV, 85, CDN, PM; *Incubus*, Th, 81, CDN, PM.

KAIN, Robert
225 Davenport Rd., Toronto, ON M5R 3R2 (416)924-7177. Videoart Group, 100 Lombard St., Suite 202, Toronto, ON M5C 1M3 (416)360-1456.
Type of Production and Credits: TV Video-Prod.
Genres: Educational-TV; Children's-TV; Animation-TV; Industrial-TV.
Biography: Born 1932, Vancouver, BC. Attended Ontario College of Art and School of Visual Art (on scholarship), New York. Started Videoart Productions, 59. Creator of 2 syndicated comic strips. Won Creative Award at US Film and TV Festival for animated logos.

KARMAZYN, John ✧
(416)486-6059.
Type of Production and Credits: Th Short-Prod; Video-Prod.
Genres: Experimental-Th&TV; Documentary-Th&TV; Drama-Th&TV; Educational-Th&TV.
Biography: Born 1962, Toronto, Ontario. B.A.A., Film and Photographic Arts, Ryerson Polytechnic Institute, 86; Graduate Film Program, York University, 84; Cinematography and Photographic Arts, Independent Learning Centre, Ontario Ministry of Education.
Selcted Filmography: "Filmclips" (10 seasons), TV, 80-88, CDN, Prod/Dir/Wr; *Safelight*, Th, 82, CDN, Prod/Dir/Wr.

KAUFMAN, David
ATPD, ACCT. 60 Fontainbleau Dr., Willowdale, ON M2M 1N9 (416)221-3780. CBC, The 5th Estate, Box 500, Stn. A, Toronto, ON M5W 1E6 (416)975-6661.
Type of Production and Credits: TV Film-Prod/Dir/Wr.
Genres: Documentary-TV; Current Affairs-TV; News-TV.
Biography: Born 1948, Montreal, Quebec. Languages: English and Hebrew. Honours B.A., English, McGill University, 69. Winner Best Political/Social theme for *The Freedom Ride*, San Francisco Film Festival, 87.
Selected Filmography: *Violation of Trust*, "the fifth estate", TV, 91, CDN, Prod/Dir; *Company Town*, "the fifth estate", TV, 90,

CDN, Prod/Dir; *Aids and Society,* "The Journal", TV, 87, CDN, Prod; *The Reagan Doctrine,* "The Journal", TV, 87, CDN, Prod; *50 Years of Public Broadcasting,* "The Journal", TV, 86, CDN, Prod; *The Freedom Ride,* "The Journal", TV, 86, CDN, Prod; *Earthquake,* "The Journal", TV, 86, CDN, Prod; *A.M. Klein: The Poet as a Landscape,* TV, 79, CDN, Prod/ Dir/Wr.

KEATING, Lulu
- see DIRECTORS

KEATLEY, Philip
CTPDA. 844 West 13th Ave., Vancouver, BC V5Z 1P2 (604)874-8780.
Type of Production and Credits: TV Film-Dir/Prod; TV Video-Dir/Prod.
Genres: Drama-TV; Comedy-TV; Documentary-TV; Children's-TV.
Biography: Born 1929, British Columbia. B.A., University of British Columbia, 51; LAMDA, England. Actor, director in theatre and film; became producer/director CBC, 57; head of Vancouver drama department, 67-78; headed CBC production training program, 78-80 ; returned to head CBC Vancouver Drama, 82; Western development, Head of Drama, 87-90. Presently owner of Keatley Film Ltd. Awards as Producer/Director include 6 CFAs in drama and documentaries; Wilderness Award for *Antoine's Wooden Overcoat;* American Film Festival Award's Red Ribbon for *Glorious Mud.* Films shown at festivals in Edinburgh, Vancouver International Festival and San Francisco Film Festival. Specializes in development and production of television dramatic series including, "Cariboo Country" and "The Beachcombers." Television dramas and docu-mentaries include *Glorious Mud* and *How to Break a Quarterhorse.*
Selected Filmography: *Glorious Mud,* TV, 83, CDN, Wr/Dir/Prod; "Ritter's Cove", TV, 78, CDN/D, Wr/Prod; "The Magic Lie" (18 eps), TV, 75-78, CDN, Dir/Prod; "The Beachcombers" (120 eps), TV, 71-77, CDN, Dir/Prod; *Sacrament,* TV, 76, CDN, Prod; *How to Break a Quarterhorse,* TV, 68, CDN, Dir/Prod; "Cariboo Country" (22 eps), TV, 63-67, CDN, Dir/Prod; *The Education of Phyllistine,* TV, 65, CDN, Dir/Prod.

KEELAN, Matt
- see DIRECTORS

KELLNER, Lynne ◆
(204)775-8351.
Type of Production and Credits: TV Film-Prod/Dir; TV Video-Prod/Dir.
Genres: Variety-TV; Documentary-TV; Sports-TV.
Biography: Born 1943, Winnipeg, Manitoba.
Selected Filmography: "CBC Curling" (24 eps), TV, 86-88, CDN, Prod; "Body Talk" 947 eps), TV, 84-85, CDN, Prod/Dir; "Sports Weekend" (sev events), TV, 86, CDN, Prod; *Canadian National Darts Championship,* TV, 86, CDN, Prod/Dir; *Chai Is a Lucky Number,* TV, 85, CDN, Prod/Dir; *Opera Is for Everybody,* TV, 85, CDN, Prod/Dir; *Women of the Year,* TV, 83-85, CDN, Prod/Dir; *Symphony for Kids,* TV, 84, CDN, Prod/Dir; *Manitoba Marathon* (5 specials), TV, 79-84, CDN, Prod/Dir; *Los Angeles Olympics,* TV, 84, CDN, Prod; *Men of Medicine,* TV, 83, CDN, Prod/Dir; *Western Canda Summer Games* (2 shows), TV, 79-83, CDN, Exec Prod; *Universiade,,* TV, 83, CDN, Prod/ Dir; *Arnold Spohr Gala/Royal Winnipeg Ballet,* TV, 83, CDN, Prod/Dir; *Rusalka Dancers,* TV, 82, CDN, Prod/Dir; "International Raquetball Classic" (13 eps), TV, 79-82, CDN, Prod.

KELLY, Peter
ATPD, ACCT. 30 Brookdale Cres., Suite 212, Dartmouth, NS (902)464-0536. CBC, P.O. Box 3000, Halifax, NS B3J 3E9 (902)420-4293. FAX: 420-4414.
Type of Production and Credits: TV Film-Dir/Prod.
Genres: Drama-TV; Documentary-TV; Children's-TV.
Biography: Born 1929, England; Canadian citizenship. Lighting cameraman, England, Iraq, 50-56; NFB, 56-58; DOP, CBC, 58-62; director/ producer, 62-85; currently executive producer, CBC. "Five Years in the Life" won the Wilderness Medal; *Gentle Sinners* won Bronze, New York, and Chris award, Columbus; *Getting Married in Buffalo Jump,* Honourable Mention, Houston International Film Festival, Finalist, Banff Festival.
Selected Filmography: *Getting Married in Buffalo Jump,* TV, 90, CDN, Exec Prod; *A Nest of Singing Birds,* TV, 87, CDN, Exec Prod; *Gentle Sinners,* TV, 83, CDN, Exec Prod; "Some Honourable Gentlemen" (6 eps), TV, 83, CDN, Exec Prod; *I Married the Klondike* (3 parts), TV, 82-83, CDN, Exec Prod; "Ritter's Cove" (26 eps), TV, 79-81, CDN, Exec Prod; *The Dawson Patrol,* TV, 77, CDN, Dir/Prod; "Five Years in the Life" (30 eps), TV, 71-77, CDN, Exec Prod; *Ballad of the Bicycle,* TV, 75, CDN, Dir/Prod; *To the Sea in Ships,* TV, 74, CDN, Dir/Prod; *Two Arctic Tales,* TV, 72, CDN, Dir/Prod; *Flight 751,* TV,

70, CDN, Dir/Prod; *The Magnificent Gift*, TV, 70, CDN, Dir/Prod; "McQueen", TV, 70, CDN, Dir; *The White Christmas of Archie Nicotine*, "To See Ourselves", TV, 70, CDN, Dir;

KEMENY, John
PGA, ACCT. 2225 E. Adams, Tuscon, AZ 85319 (602)325-5757.
Type of Production and Credits: Th Film-Prod; Th Short-Prod; TV Film-Prod.
Genres: Drama-Th&TV; Action-Th; Documentary-Th&TV; Education-Th&TV.
Biography: Born in Budapest, Hungary. Graduated from Academy of Commerce. Worked at NFB, 57-69. Festival prizes: *Atlantic City*, Grand Prize (Venice), nominated for 5 Oscars including Best Picture; *The Apprenticeship of Duddy Kravitz*, Grand Prize (Berlin), Gold Medal and Jury Prize (Atlanta), Mermaid (Sorento); *Don't Let the Angels Fall*, Interfilm Festival Jury Award (Edinburgh), Best Foreign Feature Film (Ceylon). Decorated with Canadian Centennial Medal, "In Recognition of Valuable Service to the Nation." *The Bay Boy* won 6 Genie Awards, including Best Picture of the Year; *Quest for Fire* won Academy Award, Best Makeup; 3 Cesars including Best Film and Best Director. *Murderers Among Us: The Simon Wiesentahal Story* won Emmy, Best Script and Ace Award, Best Film.
Selected Filmography: *The Josephine Baker Story*, TV, 90, USA, Prod; *Red King, White Knight*, TV, 89, USA, Prod; *Murderers Among Us - The Simon Wisenthal Story*, TV, 88, CDN/USA, Prod, (EMMY/ ACE); *Iron Eagle II*, Th, 88, CDN/IL, Prod; *Nowhere to Hide*, Th, 86, CDN, Prod; *The Gate*, Th, 86, CDN, Prod; *The Boy in Blue*, Th, 84, CDN/USA, Prod; *The Bay Boy*, Th, 83, CDN/F, Prod, (GENIE); *The Blood of Others*, Th, 83, CDN/F, Co-Prod, (CESAR); *Louisiana*, Th, 83, CDN/F, Co-Prod; *La Guerre du feu*, Th, 81, CDN/F, Co-Prod, (CESAR); *Les Plouffes*, Th, 80, CDN, Co-Exec Prod; *Atlantic City*, Th, 80, CDN/F, Prod; *Ice Castles*, Th, 78, USA, Prod; *The Apprenticeship of Duddy Kravitz*, Th, 73, CDN, Prod, (CFA).

KENDALL, Nicholas
- see DIRECTORS
KENNEDY, Michael
- see DIRECTORS
KENT, Paul
- see DIRECTORS
KIMBER, Les
- see PRODUCTION MANAGERS

KING, Allan
- see DIRECTORS
KING, Jeff
DGC, ACCT. (416)467-0338. (416)299-2360.
Type of Production and Credits: TV Film-Prod.
Genres: Drama-Th&TV.
Biography: Born in Montreal, Quebec. Has produced two movies-of-the-week pilots and over 100 hours of episodic television programs.
Selected Filmography: "Top Cops" (sev eps), TV, USA/CDN, Prod/Wr; "Night Heat" (sev eps), TV, 84-88, CDN, Prod/Wr; "Diamonds" (sev eps), TV, 87-88, CDN, Prod; *The Gunfighter*, TV, 87, CDN, Prod; "Hot Shots" (13 eps), TV, 86, CDN, Assoc Prod; *Big Deal*, Th, 85, CDN, Assoc Prod; *Overdrawn at the Memory Bank*, TV, 83, CDN/USA, Unit M; *Heavenly Bodies*, Th, 83, CDN, PM/Loc M; *Bedroom Eyes*, Th, 83, CDN, Loc M/PM.

KINSEY, Nicholas
- voir REALISATEURS
KLEIN, Bonnie
- see DIRECTORS
KLEIN, Monika
3659 Kelton Ave., #2, Los Angeles, CA 90034 (213)559-9253. 324-2055 York Ave., Vancouver, BC V6J 1E5 (604)731-6442.
Type of Production and Credits: Th Film-PA; TV Film- PA; TV Video-Prod/Dir.
Genres: Drama-Th&TV; Documentary-Th&TV; Industrial-TV; Current Affairs-TV.
Biography: Born in 1957 in Winnipeg, Manitoba. Languages: English and German. B.A., University of Manitoba. Has worked on 3 International Film Festivals: Vancouver Film Festival 89, Women in Film Festival 90 (Los Angeles), Marketing Director, American Film Institute Film Festival, 91 (Los Angeles). Special Events Co-ordinating Assistant. 1984 Winner of Cable TV Award For Excellence in Programming-Historical Category for *Maillardville: A French Factor*.
Selected Filmography: *Hammer Down/Dancing for Time*, Th, 91, CDN, PA; *Pricewinners*, TV, 89, CDN, Prod Coord; *Dance Alive*, TV, 87, CDN, Prod/Dir; *The Up & Coming*, TV, 87, CDN, Prod/Dir; *Rock & Hyde*, MV, 87, CDN, PA; *Arthur Erikson - A Profile*, TV, 86, CDN, Prod/Wr; *Young Romantics*, TV, 85, CDN, Prod/Wr; *Maillardville - A French Factor*, TV, 84, CDN, Prod/Wr;

Gum San - Gold Mountain, TV, 84, CDN, Prod/Wr.

KLINCK, Elizabeth
ACCT, CIFC. 56 King St., Elmira, ON N3B 2R9 (519)669-2661. FAX: 669-2661.
Type of Production and Credits: Th Film-Prod/PM; TV Film-Prod/PM; TV Video-Prod/PM.
Genres: Drama-TV; Documentary-TV; Children's-TV; Animation-TV.
Biography: Born 1957, Kitchener, Ontario. Languages: English, French, German. B.A., B.Ed., Queen's University.
Selected Filmography: *See No Evil*, TV, 88, CDN, Assoc Prod; *Sitting in Limbo*, Th, 87, CDN, Assoc Prod; *First Stop China* (Eng & French), TV, 85, CDN, Assoc Prod/PM; *Earthwatch*, Th, 85, CDN, Assoc Prod/PM; *River Journey* (Imax), Th, 84, CDN, Assoc Prod/PM; "War" (7 eps), TV, 83, CDN, Res.

KONOWAL, Charles
- see CINEMATOGRAPHERS

KONYVES, Tom ✧
(604)538-8214.
Type of Production and Credits: TV Video-Prod/Dir.
Genres: Documentary-TV; Educational-TV; Experimental-TV.
Biography: Born 1947, Budapest, Hungary; Canadian citizenship. Languages: English, French. Published poet.
Selected Filmography: *BCMHP: A Case for Community Living*, ED, 88, CDN, Prod; *The Royal Hudson: A Steam Excursion*, In, 87, CDN, Exec Prod/Dir; *Profile of an Artist: Pnina Granirer*, TV, 86, CDN, Prod; *The Last Debate: Hoffman and Rubin*, TV, 86, CDN, Prod; *Dancing In the Street*, TV, 86, CDN, Prod/Dir; *O Vancouver!*, In, 86, CDN, Prod/Dir; *Canadian-Chinese Art Festival*, ED, 86, CDN, Prod/Dir; *Canadian-Japanese Art Festival*, ED, 85, CDN, Prod; *Bill Vazan: Cosmographe*, TV, 82, CDN, Prod/Dir; *The Best of the 3rd International Mime Festival*, ED, 82, CDN, Prod/Dir; *Chris Burden: An Interview*, TV, 82, CDN, Prod/Dir; *Leaving the House: Deborah Hay*, TV, 81, CDN, Prod/Dir; "Art Montréal" (6 eps), ED, 80, CDN, Prod.

KOOL, Allen
CFTPA, CARAS, CIRPA, ACTRA, DGA, LCC. R.R. #3, Granton, ON N0M 1V0 Bluestar Motion Pictures, 433 King St., Suite 101, London, ON N6B 3P3 (519)432-2015.
Type of Production and Credits: Th Film-Wr/Prod/Dir; Th Short-Wr/Prod/Dir; TV Film-Wr/Prod/Dir; TV Video-Wr/Prod/Dir.
Genres: Musical-Th&TV; Documentary-TV; Commercials-TV; Industrial-TV; Music Video-TV.
Biography: Born 1948, Holland; Canadian citizenship. Languages: English and French. Educated in Canada and US (B.F.A.). President, Futuremax Corp., Bluestar International Inc., Bluestar Motion Pictures, Bluestar Entertainment and Raw Diamond Music. *I Am Your Child* nominated for Gemini, Best Music Video and Best Sound Recording; *No* won Golden Venus, Miami International Film Festival, 1st Place: Santa Barbara, San Diego, Windsor, Milan and Krakow.
Selected Filmography: *Be A Power Saver* (12 eps), ED, 91, CDN, Wr/Prod/Dir; *Cry of Silence*, Th, 90-91, CDN, Prod/Dir; *A Bright Idea - Pass It On*, ED, 90, CDN, Wr/Prod/Dir; *Road to Success*, In, 90, CDN, Prod/Dir; *People Service People with Sensitivity*, In, 90, CDN, Wr/Prod/Dir; *Adapting to Change*, In, 89, CDN, Prod/Dir; Honeymoon Suite, MV, 84-85, CDN, Prod/Dir; "F.Y.I. First Edition" (200 eps), TV, 87-88, CDN, Prod/Dir; *I Am Your Child*, Th/MV, 86, CDN, Wr/Prod/Dir; *Floating Across Canada with Murray McLaughlin*, TV, 85, CDN, Exec Prod; *Shark Reef*, TV, 83, CDN, Wr/Prod/Dir; "CBC National News" (250 eps), TV, 81-82, CDN, Dir/Line Prod; "CBC Sat./Sun. Report" (50 eps), TV, 81-82, CDN, Dir; *No*, TV, 78-79, CDN, Prod; *Arabia Incident*, TV, 78-79, CDN, Prod.

KOTCHEFF, Ted
- see DIRECTORS

KOTTLER, Les
Adderley Productions Inc., 7 Granada Court, Thornhill, ON L3T 4V3 (416)886-3777. FAX: 886-3777.
Type of Production and Credits: TV Film-Dir/Prod; Video-Dir/Prod.
Genres: Documentary-TV; Educational-TV; Industrial-TV.
Biography: Born 1947, Cape Town, South Africa; Canadian citizenship. B.A., Economics; Diploma, African Government and Law, University of Cape Town; honour student, television, Lord Thomson Foundation, Glasgow, Scotland, 71. Joined CBC; producer/director, "Ombudsman," "Country Canada," "Man Alive," "Take 30," "Market Place," "Venture;" 75-85. On-camera and production training, CBC Training Department, 80-90. Adjunct Professor, University of Western Ontario, Faculty of

Journalism, 85-90. Professor, Broadcast Journalism, Ryerson Polytechnical Institute, and Professor, TV Production, Seneca College, 87. Producer, "Shirley," CTV Network, 89-91.
Selected Filmography: "Shirley" (271 eps), TV, 89-91, CDN, Prod; "Venture" (160 eps), TV, 85-88, CDN, Dir; "Talking Sex" (3 eps), ED, 88, CDN, Wr/Dir; *Missing,* TV, 85, CDN, Dir/Wr; *No Place to Hide,* TV, 85, CDN, Dir/Wr; *The Disappearing Land/Cholesterol: Myth or Fact,* "Country Canada", TV, 83-84, CDN, Dir/Prod; *The Poisoned Garden,* "the fifth estate", TV, 83, CDN, Dir/Prod; "Ombudsman" (45 seg), TV, 76-80, CDN, Dir/Prod; *A True and Faithful Account-The Diaries of Mackenzie King,* "Take 30", TV, 75, CDN, Dir/Prod.

KOZAK, Sherry
DGC. Missing Link Productions, 817 - 3 St. N.W., Calgary, AB T2N 1P1 (403)283-0011.
Type of Production and Credits: TV Film-Prod/Dir; TV Video-Prod/Dir.
Genres: Documentary-Th&TV; Educational-Th&TV; Children's-Th&TV.
Biography: Born in 1957. Ten years of film and television experience in Canada and internationally. Specialize in documentaries on social issues.
Selected Filmography: *Willing to Learn,* ED/TV, 91, CDN, Assoc Prod; *Our Own Voice,* ED/TV, 91, CDN/N, Exec Prod/Dir; *Coffee Break,* "A Taste for Trade", ED/TV, 91, CDN/TZ, Exec Prod/Dir; *Taking Control,* ED/TV, 90, CDN, Exec Prod/Dir; *Bigger Than A Basket,* "A Taste for Trade", ED/TV, 90, CDN/ZB, Exec Prod/Dir.

KRAMREITHER, Anthony
217 Arnold Ave., Thornhill, ON M4J 1C4 (416)881-5443. Brightstar Films Inc., 424 Adelaide St. E., Toronto, ON M5A 1N4 (416)362-1774.
Type of Production and Credits: Th Film-Prod/Exec Prod.
Genres: Drama-Th&TV; Comedy-Th&TV.
Biography: Born in Vienna, Austria; arrived in Canada, 54. Has acted in television shows and films in Europe and Canada.
Selected Filmography: *White Light,* Th, 90, CDN, Prod; *Dreams Beyond Memory,* Th, 87, CDN, Prod; *Concrete Angels,* Th, 85, CDN, Prod; *Confidential,* Th, 85, CDN, Prod; *Dancing in the Dark,* Th, 85, CDN, Prod; *Mark of Cain,* Th, 84, CDN, Prod; *Flying,* Th, 84, CDN, Prod; *Thrill Kill,* Th, 83, CDN, Prod/Co-Dir; *American Nightmare,* Th, 82, CDN, Exec Prod; *Humongous,* Th, 81, CDN, Prod; *All in Good Taste,* Th, 80, CDN, Prod/Dir; *Deadly Harvest,* Th, 76, CDN, Prod; *A Sweeter Song,* Th, 75, CDN, Exec Prod; *Lions for Breakfast,* Th, 74, CDN, Prod; "Famous Nobel Prize Winner" (4 ep), TV, 72, CDN/F/AUS/D.

KREPAKEVICH, Jerry
SGCT, ASIFA. Box 819, Beaumont, AB T0C 0H0 (403)986-1162. NFB, 120 - 9700 Jasper Ave., Edmonton, AB T5J 4C3 (403)495-3016.
Type of Production and Credits: Th Film-Prod; Th Short-Prod/Dir; TV Film-Prod/Dir/Ed/Snd Ed.
Genres: Drama-Th&TV; Documentary-Th&TV; Animation-Th&TV.
Biography: Born 1946, Yorkton, Saskatchewan. Studied Economics, University of Saskatchewan. Producer, director, writer, editor, NFB, since 68. Winner of many awards, including Yorkton, New York, Toulon, AMPIA, Bijou, Cork.
Selected Filmography: *The Spirit Within,* TV, 90, CDN, Prod; *Primo Baby,* Th, 90, CDN, Prod/Wr Cons; *Shooting Stars,* TV, 87, CDN, Prod; *Foster Child,* TV, 87, CDN, Prod; *Elk Island,* ED, 85, CDN, Prod; *Long Lance,* TV, 85, CDN, Prod/Dir/Snd Rec; *The Man from Petrocan,* TV, 84, CDN, Prod; *Beyond the Frontier,* ED, 83, CDN, Prod; *The Last Mooseskin Boat,* ED, 83, CDN, Prod; *Great Days in the Rockies,* Th, 83, CDN, Prod; *The Top Few Inches,* ED, 82, CDN, Prod/Dir/Wr/Narr; *Capital,* TV, 82, CDN, Prod; *Loved, Honoured and Bruised,* TV, 80, CDN, Prod; *Getting Started,* Th, 80, CDN, Prod; *Blowhard,* Th, 78, CDN, Prod/Ed.

KROITOR, Roman ◆
Imax Corporation, 45 Charles St., Toronto, ON (416)960-8509. FAX: 960-8596.
Type of Production and Credits: Th Film-Prod/Dir.
Genres: Documentary-Th.
Biography: Born 1926, Yorkton, Saskatchewan. M.A., Philosophy, Psychology, University of Manitoba, 49. Began career at NFB; worked for CBC (60s) as producer/director of "Candid Eye". Co-founder, Multi Screen Corporation, 67; returned to NFB in 75 to become Executive Producer of Studio B. Currently Producer/Director with Imax Corporation. Genie nomination for Best Short Documentary, 86; Academy of Canadian Cinema & Television Award for *Skyward;*

CFA, 65 for *Above the Horizon*; CFA, 62, *Lonely Boy*; CFA (two) 60, *Universe*.
Selected Filmography: *We Are Born of Stars*, Th, 85, CDN, Wr/Co-Prod; *Skyward*, Th, 84, CDN, Prod; *Freedom to Move*, Th, 84, CDN, Exec Prod; *Hail Columbia*, Th, 82, CDN, Co-Prod; *Man Belongs to the Earth*, Th, 74, CDN, USA, Co-Prod; *Circus World*, Th, 74, USA, Prod/Dir; *Tiger Child*, Th, 70, CDN, Prod; *Labyrinth* (Expo 67), Th, 67, CDN, Co-Dir; *Stravinsky*, TV, 66, CDN, Co-Dir, (CFA); *Above the Horizon*, Th, 65, CDN, Co-Dir, (CFA); *Lonely Boy*, Th, 62, CDN, Co-Dir, (CFA); *Universe*, Th, 60, CDN, Wr/Co-Dir, (2 CFA); *Paul Tomkowica: Street Railway Switchman*, Th, 54, CDN, Dir/Co-Wr.

KROONENBURG, Pieter
APFVQ, ACCT. 6266 Notre Dame de Grâce Ave., #12, Montreal, PQ H4B 1L3. 410 St. Nicolas, 6th Floor, Montreal, PQ H2Y 2P5 (514)288-8083. FAX: 288-5888
Type of Production and Credits: Th Film-Prod; TV Film-Prod.
Genres: Drama-Th&TV; Comedy-Th&TV; Action-Th&TV.
Biography: Born 1942, Castricum, Netherlands; landed immigrant Canada, 84. Languages: English, French, Dutch, German. Attended the Film Academy, Amsterdam. Lived in Brussels, Rome and Paris, making films, TV series and commercials; moved to Canada, 79.
Selected Filmography: *Bethune*, Th, 88, CDN/RC/F, Prod; *Le Palanquin des larmes*, Th, 87, CDN/F, Prod; *Wild Thing*, Th, 86, CDN/USA, Co-Prod; *The Blue Man*, Th, 85, CDN, Prod; *Toby McTeague*, Th, 85, CDN/USA, Co-Exec Prod; *Breaking All the Rules*, Th, 84, CDN, Co-Prod; *The Hotel New Hampshire*, Th, 83, USA, Co-Prod; *Cook & Peary: The Race to the Pole*, TV, 83, USA, Line Prod; *Cross Country*, Th, 82, CDN, Co-Prod; *The Lucky Star*, Th, 80, CDN, Line Prod; *Heartaches*, Th, 80, CDN, Co-Prod; *Girls*, Th, 79, CDN/F/D, Prod.

KROST, Roy
CFTA, ACCT. Roy Krost Productions Ltd., 9 Deer Park Cres., #1705, Toronto, ON M4V 2C4 (416)964-2838.
Type of Production and Credits: Th Film-Prod; TV Film-Prod; TV Video-Prod.
Genres: Drama-Th; Musical-TV; Educational-TV; Children's-Th&TV.
Biography: Born London, England. Has produced and directed numerous award-winning industrial and educational films: Chris Awards (Columbus) for *The Spirit Soars* and *Don't Take Chances*; *The Nutcracker, A Fantasy on Ice* was nominated for an Emmy, 85.
Selected Filmography: *True Confections*, Th, 90, CDN, Prod; *Too Outrageous!*, Th, 87, CDN, Prod; *Magical Musical Days*, TV, 85, CDN, Prod/Co-Dir; *Martin's Day*, Th, 83, CDN/GB, Co-Prod; *Nutcracker, a Fantasy on Ice*, TV, 83, CDN, Prod, (CFTA); *Nikki, Wild Dog of the North*, Th, 60, CDN/USA, Co-Prod.

KUPER, Jack
- see DIRECTORS

LABERGE, Pierre
1812 Boul. Pie IX, Montréal, PQ H1V 2C6 (514)521-1339. Productions Publi Mages, 393 Laurier ouest, Montréal, PQ H2V 2K3 (514)270-4044.
Types de production et générique: l métrage-Dir prod; TV film-Prod.
Types d'oeuvres: Drame-C&TV; Comédie-C&TV; Action-C&TV; Documentaire-C&TV; Commerciaux-C&TV.
Curriculum vitae: Né en 1950.
Filmographie sélective: *Esso* (5), Cm, 90-91, CDN, Prod/Réal; *Steinberg* (8), Cm, 90-91, CDN, Prod/Réal; *La Capitale* (2), Cm, 90-91, CDN, Prod/Réal; *O'Keefe* (4), Cm, 90-91, CDN, Prod/Réal; *Il était une fois...Les filles de Caleb*, TV, 90, CDN, Prod; *Oui, Allo Estelle*, TV, 89, CDN, Dir pro; "Lance et Compte" (39 eps), TV, 87-89, CDN, Dir pro; "Shades of Love" (6 eps), TV, 87, CDN, Dir pro; *Joshua Then and Now*, C, 86, CDN, Rég; *New Year's Eve*, C, 85, CDN, Rég; *Once Upon a Time in America*, C, 85, CDN, Rég; *St-Louis Square*, C, 83, CDN, Rég; *Les Plouffe*, C, 80, CDN, Rég.

LABROSSE, Sylvain
- voir DIRECTEURS-PHOTO

LAFERRIERE, Richard
ACCT. 300, Léo-Parizeau, #2400, C.P. 1145, Montréal, PQ H2W 2P4 (514)284-2525.
Types de production et générique: c métrage-Prod; TV vidéo-Prod.
Types d'oeuvres: Documentaire-TV.
Curriculum vitae: Né en 1954, Joliette, Québec.

LAFFEY, Barbara Joy
Life Artists Inc., 1027 Swarthmore Ave., Suite 201, Pacific Palisades, CA 90272 USA. (213)454-0101.
Type of Production and Credits: TV Film-Prod; Th Film-PM.
Genres: Drama-Th&TV.
Biography: Born in Chicago; landed immigrant Canada, 71. Attended University of Illinois and Ontario College

of Art. Vice-President, Production, Paragon Motion Pictures 85-87; Consultant, Sunrise Films 88-90; Production Executive, Lifetime Television 91. Currently President, Life Artists Inc., developing and producing theatrical feature films. ACE Award, Best Dramatic Series for "Alfred Hitchcock Presents."
Selected Filmography: "My Secret Identity", TV, 88-89, CDN, Cons Prod; "Alfred Hitchcock Presents" (27 eps), TV, 86-88, CDN/USA, Prod, (ACE); *Taking Care of Terrific*, "PBS Wonderworks", TV, 87, CDN/USA, Prod; "Philip Marlowe, Private Eye" (6 eps), TV, 85-86, CDN, Line Prod; *Threshold*, Th, 90, CDN, PM; *Improper Channels*, Th, 79, CDN, PM.

LAFORéT, Megan
2121 Bathurst St., #405, Toronto, ON M5N 2P3 (416)535-1033. Poor Alex Theatre, 296 Brunswick Ave., Studio 223, Toronto, ON M5S 2M7
Type of Production and Credits: TV Video-Prod/Dir/Wr.
Genres: Documentary-TV; Educational-TV; Children's-TV; Animation-TV.
Biography: M.A., Film and Communication, New York University.
Selected Filmography: "Caring for Young Children" (5 seg), TV, 91, CDN, Prod/Co Dir/Co Wr; *Bodyguard: The Immune System*, TV, 89, CDN, Prod/Co-Dir/Co-Wr; *Bodyguard: The Invisible Protector*, ED, 89, CDN, Prod/Co Dir/Co Wr; *Sexually Transmitted Diseases & AIDS*, ED, 89, CDN, Prod/Co-Dir/Co-Wr; *The Immune System: Mind/Body/Spirit Connection*, ED, 89, CDN, Prod/Co Dir/Co Wr.

LAGER, Martin
- see WRITERS

LAMB, Duncan
ATPD, ACCT. 300 Coxwell Ave., #302, Toronto, ON M4L 3W1 (416)465-2088. CBC, Box 500, Stn. A, Toronto, ON M5W 1E6 (416)975-7101.
Type of Production and Credits: TV Film-Prod; TV Video-Prod.
Genres: Drama-TV; Comedy-TV.
Biography: Born 1945, England; Canadian citizenship. Radio and Television Arts, Ryerson Polytechnical Institute, 68.
Selected Filmography: "Street Legal" (45 eps), TV, 86-91, CDN, Prod; "Seeing Things" (24 eps), TV, 83-86, CDN, Assoc Prod; *Ready for Slaughter/Moving Targets/Out of Sight, Out of Mind*, "For the Record", TV, 82, CDN, Assoc Prod; "Home Fires" (20 eps) (Assoc Prod 15 eps/Prod 5 eps), TV, 80-82, CDN, Assoc Prod; "The Phoenix Team" (8 eps), TV, 80, CDN, Pro Coord; "For the Record" (10 eps), TV, 77-80, CDN, Pro Coord; *Riel*, TV, 78, CDN, Pro Coord; "Sidestreet" (24 eps), TV, 75-78, CDN, Pro Coord; *Bethune*, TV, 76, CDN, Serv Prod; *The Victim/The Lie Chair/Microdramas*, "Peep Show", TV, 75, CDN, Serv Prod; *Overlaid*, TV, 75, CDN, Serv Prod; *Turncoat*, TV, 75, CDN, Serv Prod.

LAMBIN, Diane
APFTQ, ADISQ. 4141 Mentana, Montréal, PQ H2L 3S1 (514)524-0612. 1600, De Lorimier, Montréal, PQ H2K 3W5 (514)521-1984.
Types de production et générique: c métrage-Prod; TV film-Prod; TV vidéo-Prod.
Types d'oeuvres: Documentaire-TV; Annonces-C&TV; Vidéo-clips-TV.
Curriculum vitae: Née à Montréal en 1950. Langues: français et anglais. Administrateur de comptes publicitaires (1980-1988) pour Loto-Québec, Steinberg, Brasserie O'Keefe, Téléglobe Canada. 1988 à aujourd'hui: Producteur associé chez Les Productions Quai 32 Inc. : Vidéo-clips, publicité, documentaire.
Filmographie sélective: "Hong Kong - Macao" (5 eps.), TV, 92, CDN, Prod; "Archéologie" (13 eps.), TV, 91-92, CDN, Prod; *On The Outside*, MV, 91, CDN, Prod; *Darlin*, MV, 91, CDN, Prod; *Tshinanu*, MV, 90, CDN, Prod; *Une Dernière Fois*, MV, 90, CDN, Prod; *América #3*, Cm, 90, CDN, Prod; *Clef De Sol*, Cm, 89, CDN, Prod; *Hélène*, MV, 89, CDN, Prod.

LAMOTHE, Arthur
- voir REALISATEURS

LAMY, André
ACCT. 245 Outremont, Montréal, PQ H2V 3L9 (514)279-9381.
Types de production et générique: l métrage-Prod; TV film-Prod; TV vidéo-Prod.
Types d'oeuvres: Drame-C; Comédie-TV; Animation-TV.
Curriculum vitae: Né en 1932. Citoyenneté canadienne. Langues: français et anglais. Ecole de technologie médicale, Université de Montréal, 52-55; Faculté des Sciences, Université McGill; cours d'administration de l'entreprise et session intensive, Ecole des Hautes Etudes Commerciales, 69-71. Fondateur, Vice-président, producteur, réalisateur, directeur de production, Onyx Film, Montréal, 64-70; Commissaire adjoint et Directeur général, 70-75, et Commissaire du gouvernement à la cinématographie et Président, ONF, 75-79; Vice-président aux

Relations avec l'auditoire, CBC, 79-80; Directeur général, Téléfilm Canada, 80-85; producteur, réalisateur, Les Productions Stanké-Lamy, 86-87; producteur exécutif, directeur recherche et développement, Ciné-Groupe J.P. inc., 87. Présidente de l'Association des Producteurs de films et Télévision du Québec, 90-91.
Filmographie sélective: *The Valour and the Horror*, C, 91, CDN, Proc exéc; "Lucky Luke" (39 eps)(anim), TV, 87-89, CDN/ F, Prod exéc; "Les Oursons volants" (26 eps)(anim), TV, 88, CDN/F, Prod exéc; "L'Aventure de l'écriture" (anim), TV, 87-88, CDN, Prod exéc; "Les Insolences d'une caméra, TV, 86-87, CDN, Prod/ Réal; *Le Viol d'une jeune fille douce*, C, 67, CDN, Co prod.

LAMY, Pierre ◊
(514)525-9904. **Types de production et générique:** l métrage-Prod; TV film-Prod.
Types d'oeuvres: Drame-C; Comédie-C; Documentaire-TV.
Curriculum vitae: Né à Montréal, Québec. Langues: français et anglais. Récipiendaire du Prix Albert Tessier, 81; Prix Air Canada de l'Académie du Cinéma canadien, 82.
Filmographie sélective: *La Dame encouleurs*, C, 83, CDN, Prod; *La Terre de l'homme* (3 ém), TV, 78-80, CDN, Prod exéc; *Contrecoeur*, C, 79, CDN, Prod exéc/Prod dél; *Who Has Seen the Wind*, C, 76, CDN, Prod exéc; *Chanson pour Julie*, C, 75, CDN, Prod; *The Far Shore*, C, 75, CDN, Prod exéc; *La Tête de Normande St-Onge*, C, 75, CDN, Prod; *Le soleil se lève en retard*, C, 75, CDN, Prod; *Il était une fois dans l'Est*, C, 74, CDN, Prod exéc; *Gina*, C, 74, CDN, Prod; *Pour le meilleur et pour le pire*, C, 74, CDN, Prod; *Les Corps célestes*, C, 73, CDN, Prod exéc; *Kamouraska*, C, 72, CDN, Prod; *La Mort d'un bûcheron*, C, 72, CDN, Prod; *La Maudite Galette*, C, 71, CDN, Prod; *La Vraie Nature de Bernadette*, C, 71, CDN, Prod exéc; *Les Smattes*, C, 71, CDN, Prod; *Les Mâles*, C, 70, CDN, Prod; *Deux femmes en or*, C, 80, CDN, Prod.

LANDERS, Ivan ◊
ATPD. 52 Shudell Ave., Toronto, ON M4J 1C7
Type of Production and Credits: TV Video-Prod/Dir.
Genres: Documentary-TV; Industrial-TV; Current Affairs-TV; Sports-TV.
Biography: Born 1942, Budapest, Hungary; immigrated to Canada, 57; Canadian citizenship. Finished education in Toronto. Started work at CBC as electronic technician, 61; has worked as co-ordinating producer, production manager, director and producer/ director on numerous programs and several television series; now an independent producer. Produced corporate video programs in the fields of training, marketing and corporate communications, in English, French and Spanish, in Canada, Europe and South America. More than 25 years combined television production experience.
Selected Filmography: *Aerodynamics*, In, 88, CDN, Prod/Dir; *Finnair Sports and Tours*, In, 87, SF, Prod/Dir; *Playing It Safe*, In, 86, CDN, Prod/Dir; *Face to Face*, In, 85, CHI, Prod/Dir; *Quality Circles*, In, 84, CDN, Prod/Dir; "Reach for the Top" (160 eps), TV, 79-83, CDN, Prod/Dir; "Local and Federal Election Coverage" (3 eps), TV, 81-83, CDN, Prod/Dir; "From Now On" (300 eps), TV, 79-81, CDN, Prod/Dir; "Class of 8" (13 eps), TV, 81, CDN, Prod/Dir; "For the Love of Sport" (13 eps), TV, 80, CDN, Prod/Dir; "The Barbara McLeod Show" (300 eps), TV, 78-79, CDN, Dir.

LANG, Robert
CIFC. R.R. #1, Port Hope, ON L1A 3V5 (416)753-2383. Kensington Communications, 490 Adelaide St. W., Suite 304, Toronto, ON M5V 1T4 (416)362-9822. FAX: 362-3608.
Type of Production and Credits: TV Film-Prod/Dir/DOP.
Genres: Documentary-TV; Educational-TV; Drama-TV.
Biography: Born 1949, Montreal, Quebec. B.A., English and Theatre, Queen's University; postgraduate diploma, Communications, Concordia University, 70. Worked on more than 50 productions in 20 years as director, writer, cinematographer in North America, Europe, Africa and Asia; owned Kensington Communications since 80. Has won numerous international awards including Genies, CFTA, Columbus, Yorkton, American Film Festival, Birmingham, Berlin and Parma. Founding member and member of the executive, Canadian Independent Film Caucus.
Selected Filmography: "Earth Journal", TV, 91, CDN, Prod/Dir; *Mariposa: Under a Stormy Sky*, TV, 91, CDN, Prod/Dir; *Shared Rhythm/Rythme du monde*, TV, 90, CDN, Prod; *One Warm Line: The Legacy of Stan Rogers*, TV, 89, CDN, Prod/Dir; *Face Value*, TV, 88, CDN, Prod/Dir; *Out of the Past*, TV, 88, CDN, Prod/Dir; *Stepdancing: Portrait of a Remarried Family*, TV, 87, CDN, Prod/Dir/Cin; *Path to Nepal*, TV, 87, CDN, Prod/Dir; *Fragile*

ONTARIO FILM DEVELOPMENT CORPORATION

SOCIÉTÉ DE DÉVELOPPEMENT DE L'INDUSTRIE CINÉMATOGRAPHIQUE ONTARIENNE ▸ ▸ ▸ ▸ ▸

FINANCIAL ASSISTANCE
Project development
Production financing
Sales and distribution
Industry development

LOCATION PROMOTION AND SERVICES

Location scouting
Location library
Production facilitation/
liaison services

An Agency of the Ontario Ministry of Culture and Communications

AIDE FINANCIÈRE
Développement de projets
Financement de productions
Vente et distribution
Développement de l'industrie

PROMOTION ET SERVICES-LIEUX DE TOURNAGE

Recherche des lieux de tournage
Bibliographie des lieux de tournage
Services de liaison

Un organisme du ministère de la Culture et des Communications de l'Ontario

---

175 RUE BLOOR ST. E., NORTH TOWER/ÉDIFICE NORD, SUITE/BUREAU 300, TORONTO, ONTARIO M4W 3R8
TÉL. (416) 965-8393 • FAX/TÉLÉCOPIEUR (416) 965-0329 • TÉLEX 06-219728

Harvest, TV, 86, CDN, Prod/Dir; *Joe David - Spirit of the Mask*, TV, 82, CDN, Prod/Dir/Cin; *Childhood's End*, TV, 81, CDN, Prod/Dir; *Taking Chances*, ED, 79, CDN, Dir/Wr; *An Easy Pill to Swallow*, TV, 78, CDN, Dir/Wr; *Potatoes*, TV, 76, CDN, Dir/Ed; *A Great Tree Has Fallen*, TV, 73, CDN, Prod/Dir/Cin.

LANSING, Floyd
- see DIRECTORS

LANTHIER, Stephen
ACCT. 246 Braebrook, Pointe Claire, PQ H9R 1V9 (514)697-2257. CFCF Inc., 405 Ogilvy Ave., Montreal, PQ H3N 1M4 (514)273-6311.
Type of Production and Credits: TV Film-Prod; TV Video-Prod/Dir.
Genres: Documentary-TV; Music Video-TV; News-TV; Sports-TV.
Biography: Born 1952, Montreal, Quebec.
Selected Filmography: "Expos Summer '88" (13 eps), TV, 88, CDN, Prod/Dir; *Academy Awards Countdown*, TV, 88, CDN, Prod/Dir; "Dick Irvin's Hockey Magazine" (23 eps), TV, 88, CDN, Prod/Dir; *15th Winter Olympics* (alpine skiing), TV, 88, CDN, Prod; *The Making of a Champion* (Matthew Hilton), TV, 87, CDN, Prod/Dir; "Snow Job" (13 eps), TV, 85, CDN, Fl Dir.

LANTOS, Robert
ACCT. Alliance Entertainment Corp. 920 Yonge St., , Suite 400, Toronto, ON M4W 3C7 (416)967-1174. FAX: 960-0971.
Type of Production and Credits: Th Film-Prod; TV Film-Prod.
Genres: Drama-Th&TV; Comedy-Th&TV; Musical-Th&TV; Action-Th&TV.
Biography: Born 1949, Budapest, Hungary; emigrated to Uruguay, 58; to Canada, 63. B.A., Honours, McGill University. Co-founder, RSL Entertainment Corporation, 75; partner, producer, Alliance Entertainment Corp. since 85; also theatrical producer. Past Chairman, Academy of Canadian Cinema and Television. *Joshua Then and Now* and *Night Magic* were both official selections for Cannes; "Bordertown" and "Night Heat" each won Silver Medal at New York; Emmy nomination for *The Execution of Raymond Graham*.
Selcted Filmography: *Black Robe*, Th, 91, CDN/AUS, Prod; "E.N.G." (64 eps), TV, 89-91, CDN, Exec Prod, (3 GEMINIS); "Counterstrike" (44 eps), TV, 90-91, CDN/F, Exec Prod; "Fly By Night" (13 eps), TV, 90-91, CDN/F, Exec Prod; "Bordertown" (78 eps), TV, 88-91, CDN/F, Exec Prod; "Mount Royal" (17 eps), TV, 87, CDN/F, Exec Prod, (GEMINI); *The Sword of Gideon* (miniseries), TV, 86, CDN, Prod, (ACE/3 GEMINIS); "Night Heat" (96 eps), TV, 84-89, CDN, Co-Spv Prod, (5 GEMINIS); *The Execution of Raymond Graham*, TV, 85, CDN, Exec Prod; *Night Magic*, Th, 84, CDN,/F, Co-Prod, (GENIE); *Joshua Then and Now*, Th, 84, CDN, Co-Prod, (5 GENIES); *Overdrawn at the Memory Bank*, Th, 83, CDN/USA, Co-Prod; *Suzanne*, Th, 79, CDN, Co-Prod; *In Praise of Older Women*, Th, 77, CDN, Co-Prod; *L'Ange et la Femme*, Th, 77, CDN, Co-Prod.

LAPOINTE, Yves
- voir REALISATEURS

LAROCHELLE, André
APFTQ. Les Productions Impex inc., 353, rue St-Nicolas, bur. 401, Montréal, PQ H2Y 2P1 (514)284-0204. FAX: 284-9581.
Types de production et générique: TV film-Prod/Réal; TV vidéo-Prod/Réal.
Types d'oeuvres: Drame-TV; Vidéo clips-TV; Documentaire-TV; Industriel-TV; Variété-TV.
Curriculum vitae: Né en 1944, Trois-Rivières, Québec. Langues: français et anglais. Cinématographie, University of Southern California, 66-68. Président, Productions Impex inc., production et réalisation des films et vidéos (industriels, documentaires, docu-drames, vidéo-clips, série-tv); fondateur, Cipro-vidéos inc., 85; associé dans Télépro inc., production et réalisation de plus de 300 messages publicitaires et de 20 films documentaires, 78-85; réalisateur, Production Yves Hébert inc., 100 messages publicitaires et 9 films documentaires, 67-78. *D'hier à aujourd'hui* gagne le prix du meilleur documentaire, Palaiseau (France), 90; *Un lac venu de l'espace* a gagné à Festival International Film Scientifique, Palaiseau.
Filmographie sélective: *Un lac venue de l'espace*, TV, 90, CDN, Prod/Réal; *Les eaux coquillières*, TV, 90, CDN, Prod/Réal, (ITVA); *Bell 800 +*, In, 90, CDN, Prod/Réal; *French&Langlais*, In, 89, CDN, Prod/Réal; *5 règles de conduite préventive*, In, 89, CDN, Prod/Réal, (ITVA); *Risk of Ground Collision*, In, 89, CDN, Prod/Réal; *Véronique Béliveau*, MV, 88, CDN, Prod/Réal; *Picto* (vidéo interactif), In, 88, CDN, Prod/Réal; *S.C.A.A.*, In, 88, CDN, Prod/Réal, (ITVA); *Diner at the Ritz*, In, 88, CDN, Prod/Réal; *Claritine*, In, 88, CDN, Prod/Réal; *Le Client*, In, 87, CDN, Prod/Réal; *La paralysie cérébrale*, In, 87,

CDN, Prod/Réal; *The Geological Survey of Canada*, In, 87, CDN, Prod/Réal; Marie-Claire Séguin, MV, 87, CDN, Prod/Réal.
LARRY, Sheldon
- see DIRECTORS
LATRAVERSE, Guy
3962, av. Laval, Montréal, PQ H2W 2J2 (514)288-2743. Sogestalt 2001 Inc., 801, rue Sherbrooke est, Montréal, PQ H2L 1K7 (514)526-7090. FAX: 526-7873.
Types de production et générique: TV Vidéo-Prod.
Types d'oeuvres: Comédie-TV; Variété-TV.
Curriculum vitae: Né en 1939, à Chicoutimi, Québec. Langues: français et anglais. Cours classique au Collège Saint-Laurent, baccalauréat ès arts, 61. Directeur général des Artistes et Associés, producteur de spectacles sur scène et de télévision, 83-84; Président et actionnaire majoritaire de Kébec Films; producteur de plus de cent vingt-cinq heures d'émissions de télévision, 74-83; Impresario et producteur d'artistes tels Deschamps, Léveillé, Ferland, Charlebois, Diane Dufresne, etc., 62. Membre du conseil d'administration de l'Association de l'industrie du disque, du spectacle et de la vidéo québecoise (ADISQ), 87-88; membre fondateur et président de l'ADISQ, 80-81; président-fondateur du gala télévisé de l'ADISQ, 79; membre fondateur et président du Groupe Québec pour le marché international du disque et de l'édition musicale (MIDEM), 79; membre fondateur du Groupe Québec pour le marché international de productions de télévision MIP-TV, 78
Filmographie sélective: "Mission Apollo" (Gala de la Communauté des télévisions francophones), TV, 90, CDN, Prod; *20e anniversaire de Loto-Québec*, TV, 89-90, CDN, Prod; *Rendez-vous avec Gerry*, TV, 89, CDN, Prod, (FELIX); "Samedi P.M.", TV, 89-91, CDN, Prod; *Groupe Sanguin* (4 ém), TV, 88-90, CDN, Prod; "Samedi de Rire", TV, 86-89, CDN, Prod; *Rendez-vous '87*, TV, 87, CDN, Prod (FELIX); *Symphonic 'n' Roll*, TV, 88, CDN, Prod, *Mon royaume pour un bleuet*, TV, 88, CDN, Prod.
LAURIER, Nicole ✧
(514)522-2269.
Types de production et générique: c métrage-Prod/Réal/Sc; TV film-Prod/Réal/Sc; TV vidéo-Prod/Sc; V Interact-Prod/Sc.
Types d'oeuvres: Drame-C&TV; Documentaire-C&TV; Education-C&TV; Enfants-TV.
Curriculum vitae: Née en 1946, Montréal, Québec. Langues: français et anglais. Maîtrise, Sciences politiques, Université Laval; formation en scénarisation interactive et production de vidéodisque, Université du Nebraska; théâtrales, Université du Québec à Montréal . Productrice responsable d'une quarantine de documentaires; auteur de plusieurs articles et scénarios.
Filmographie sélective: *s*, Interactifs Niveau III, In, 87, CDN, Prod/Sc; *Les Infections intra-abdominales.Community-acquired*, In, 86, CDN, Prod; *Job Interviews: Strategies and Tactics/L'Entrevue*, ED, 85, CDN, Prod; *Au pays des fraises éternelles/Apprendre à apprendre*, ED, 85, CDN, Prod/Co réal/Sc; *Nouveaux voisins, voisins lointains*, ED, 85, CDN, Prod/Co réal/Sc; *La Coopération canadienne au Zaire*, ED, 85, CDN, Prod/Co réal/Sc; *Les Jeunes Contrevenants/Où la connaissance devient respect*, ED, 84, CDN, Prod; *La Médicine auscultée*, "Les Beaux Dimanches", TV, 82, CDN, Sc/Anim; *Le Travail à temps partiel/Résidentce: Biermans*, TV, 81, CDN, Rech/Interv; "Moi aussi, je parle français" (13 eps), TV, 77-79, CDN/F/S, Sc/Rech/Interv; "Consom-mateurs avertis" (26 eps), TV, 77, CDN, Interv; "Un maillon de la chaîne" (10 eps), TV, 76-77, CDN, Rech/Interv; "Femmes d'aujour 'hui" (40 eps), TV, 73-75, CDN, Rech/Interv; "La Superfrancofête" (8 eps), TV, 74, CDN, Interv; "Kaleidoscope" (7 eps), TV, 73, CDN, Rech/Interv.
LAVOIE, Michel C.
- see DIRECTORS
LAVOIE, Patricia
562 Chester, Mount Royal, PQ H3R 1W9 (514) 733-3624. Voilà Productions, 1334 Notre Dame West, Suite 200, Montreal, PQ H3G 1T7 (514)932-0147. FAX: 932-1809.
Type of Production and Credits: TV Film-Prod/Wr/Dir; TV Video-Prod/Wr/Dir.
Genres: Educational-TV; Children's TV; Industrial-Th&TV
Biography: Canadian citizenship. Languages: English and French. Honours B.A., French, Literature, University of Western Ontario and Université de Strasbourg, France; postgraduate diploma, Com-munication Arts, Concordia University. Experience at the CBC, in the private sector and at the National Film Board.
Selected Filmography: *AIDS* (2 parts), ED, 90, CDN, Prod/Wr; *CN* (2 parts), In, 90, CDN, Prod/Wr; "Happy Castle" (13 eps), TV, 87-88, CDN, Head Wr; *Stork*

Maternity, In, 87, CDN, Prod; *CRB Foundation Heritage Minutes*, Cm, 89, CDN, Prod; *A l'écoute de son corps*, TV, 87, CDN, Prod; "Sesame Street" (50 seg), TV, 72-86, USA, Dir/Wr; *Via Canada*, In, 85, CDN, Prod/Dir; "Now!" (20 eps), TV, 84-85, CDN, Prod/Dir; Familiprix/ Laissons-les-rire.savouplait, Cm, 85, CDN, Dir; "Moi aussi j'écrase" (3 eps), TV, 83, CDN, Prod.

LE BOUTILLIER, Geoff
- see WRITERS

LEANEY, Cindy
ACTRA, ACCT. Voyage Media Productions Inc., #14-1255 15th Ave. E., Vancouver, BC V5T 2S7 (604)879-7643. FAX: 530-1310.
Type of Production and Credits: TV Film-Prod/Dir/Wr; TV Video-Prod/Dir/Wr.
Genres: Drama-TV; Documentary-TV; Current Affairs-TV; Educational-TV.
Biography: Born 1959, Calgary, Alberta. B.A., Communications, Simon Fraser University; extended studies include French, Political Science, Broadcast Communications and Photography. President, Vancouver Firehall Theatre, Board of Directors, 91; Treasurer, Vancouver Women in Film and Video, 91-92. Specializes in broadcast documentary and dramatic writing; experienced in on-location directing throughout Canada and the US; has also worked on location in Eastern Europe (Czechoslovakia). Corporate and industrial credits. Portfolio and Reel available. Letter of Commendation, CBI; CanPro; American Film & Video Festival.
Selected Filmography: *East to West, The Goh Ballet*, TV, 91, CDN, Dir/Prod; *Too Close for Comfort*, Th, 91, CDN, Co-Wr; "Beyond the Line" (6 eps), TV, 90, CDN/USA, Prod/Field Dir; "OWL-TV" (13 eps), TV, 90, CDN/GB, Field Dir/Story Prod; *Live*, TV, 89, CDN, Assoc Prod; *En Vie*, TV, 89, CDN, Assoc Prod; *Working Together*, ED, 89, CDN, Dir/Prod; *Five Days in October: The Commonwealth Challenge*, TV, 87, CDN, Prod; *Asia Pacific Festival*, TV, 87, CDN, Prod/Dir/Wr; "Press Conference" (43 eps), TV, 86-87, CDN, Series Prod/Wr; "Newsmakers" (45 eps), TV, 86-87, CDN, Series Prod/Dir/Wr; *Earle Birney: A Maker of Words*, TV, 87, CDN, Prod/Dir/Wr; *Rick Hansen: The Journey Home*, TV, 87, CDN, Prod/Dir/Wr; "World Stage '86" (43 eps), TV, 85-86, CDN, Res/Wr; "Perspectives on Human Rights" (10 eps), TV, 80-81, CDN, Assist Prod/Wr.

LEBOWITZ, Michael
2750 West 14th Ave., Vancouver, BC V6K 2X2 (604)736-9100. Snackbar Film Corporation, 201 - 1750 West 14th Ave., Vancouver, BC V6K 2X2 (604)736-3234. FAX: 736-7639.
Type of Production and Credits: Th Film-Prod/Exec Prod; TV Film-Prod/Exec Prod; TV Video-Prod/Exec Prod.
Genres: Drama-Th&TV; Comedy-Th&TV; Variety-Th&TV; Action-Th&TV; Science Fiction-Th&TV; Horror-Th&TV.
Biography: Born in 1946 in New York City. Landed immigrant.
Selected Filmography: *Deep Sleep*, Th, 89, CDN, Prod; "Comedy College" (16 eps), TV, 87-88, CDN, Prod; *Good Times at the Rainbow Bar & Grill*, TV, 86, CDN, Prod; "In Motion" (21 eps), TV, 83, CDN, Prod; *Misdeal/Best Revenge*, Th, 80, CDN, Prod; *Fast Company*, Th, 78, CDN, Prod; "Three Dead Trolls in a Baggie" (5 eps), TV, Exec Prod.

LEDUC, Yves
SGCT, ASIFA. 9045, est, boul. Gouin, Montréal, PQ H1E 2P8 (514)648-0306. Office National du Film, C.P. 6100, Succ. A, Montréal, PQ H3C 3H5 (514)283-9296.
Types de production et générique: l métrage-Mont; c métrage-Prod/Mont/Réal.
Types d'oeuvres: Documentaire-C; Animation-C.
Curriculum vitae: Né en 1942, Saint-Hyacinthe, Québec. Baccalauréat ès Arts, 61; diplômé de l'IDHEC en montage, Paris, 63. A l'Office National du Film depuis 64; monteur de plus de 40 films; directeur de la production française, 72-76; producteur d'animation depuis 82 et directeur du studio d'animation depuis 89. 2 Prix ETROG pour *Les Philharmonistes*, 71.
Filmographie sélective: *L'Empire des Lumières*, C, 91, CDN, Prod; *Entre Deux Soeurs*, C, 90, CDN, Co-Prod; *Enfantillage/Kid Stuff*, C, 90, CDN, Prod; *Juke-Bar*, C, 89, CDN, Prod; *Le Colporteur/The Persistent Peddler*, C, 88, CDN, Prod; *Charles et François*, C, 87, CDN, Prod; *L'Homme de Papier*, C, 87, CDN, Prod; *Concerto Grosso Modo*, C, 85, CDN, Prod; *Jouer Sa Vie*, C, 82, CDN, Mont; *Les Enfants des Normes* (8 eps), C, 79, CDN, Mont; *Saint-Urbain-de-Troyes*, C, 72, CDN, Réal/Mont/Mont son; *Les Philharmonistes*, C, 71, CDN, Réal/Mont/Mont son, (2 ETROGS); *Un Pays Sans Bon Sens*, C, 70, CDN, Mont/Mont son;

Le Corbeau et le Renard, C, 69, CDN, Co-Réal; *Le Règne du Jour*, C, 67, CDN, Mont/Mont son.

LEE, Patrick ◊
(416)531-3896.
Type of Production and Credits: TV Film-Prod; TV Video-Prod.
Genres: Documentary-TV; Educational-TV; Children's-TV.
Biography: Born 1947, London, England; Canadian citizenship. B.A., University of Toronto, 68; London film School, 70. Editor, 72-80; producer, 80-91; also produces videodiscs. Has taught film production, Niagara College, 80; Media Arts, Sheridan College, 85-91. Blue Ribbon for "Healthwise", American Film Festival, 81; *Bartlett Family* won Golden Eagle Award, United States Film Festival. Interactive-multimedia producer.
Selected Filmography: *Bartlett Family*, TV, 86, CDN, Prod; *Shield of the Homeland*, TV, 84, CDN, Prod; "Working" (4 eps), ED, 83, CDN, Assoc Prod; "Healthwise" (13 eps), ED, 80, CDN, Prod/Dir.

LEE, Terrye
301 Forest Hill Rd., Toronto, ON M5P 2N7 (416)782-4553. Kuper Productions, (416)961-6609.
Type of Production and Credits: Th Short-Prod; TV Film-Prod; TV Video-Prod.
Genres: Documentary-Th&TV; Experimental-Th; Commercials-TV; Industrial-Th&TV.
Biography: Born 1936, Toronto, Ontario. Former dancer; now a producer of commercials, videos, films (both theatrical and non-theatrical).

LEEBOSH, Vivienne
CFTA, ACCT. 8480 Harold Way, Los Angeles, CA 90069 (213)650-5253.
Type of Production and Credits: Th Film-Prod; TV Film-Prod.
Genres: Drama-Th&TV; Action-Th&TV; Documentary-TV.
Selected Filmography: *Speed Zone*, Th, 89, USA, Co-Prod; *Ticket to Heaven*, Th, 80, CDN, Prod, (GENIE); *Every Person Is Guilty*, "For the Record", TV, 80, CDN, Prod; *Women in Cuba*, Th, 78, CDN, Prod.

LEGER, Claude
Transfilm Inc., 5862 Place Plantagenet, Montréal, PQ H3S 2K6 (514)738-1731. FAX: 345-9075.
Types de production et générique: l métrage-Prod.
Types d'oeuvres: Drame-C; Action-C.
Curriculum vitae: Né en 1945. Langues: français et anglais. Citoyenneté canadienne. Tournage complété en 90: *Agaguk*.
Filmographie sélective: *Eminent Domain*, C, 90, CDN/IL/F, Prod; *L'Amante*, C, 90, CDN/F, Prod.

LEIGH, Norman
- see CINEMATOGRAPHERS

LEIS, Hank ◊
(604)535-1393.
Type of Production and Credits: Th Film-Prod; TV Film-Prod; TV Video-Prod/Wr.
Genres: Drama-Th; Educational-TV.
Biography: Born 1943, Apsalu, Estonia; Canadian citizenship. Languages: English, French, Estonian. M.B.A., Simon Fraser University. Director and President, Image International Productions Inc. and Project Quasar Technologies Inc.
Selected Filmography: *Overnight*, Th, 85, CDN, Exec Prod; "Focus on Process" (40 eps), TV, 79-80, CDN, Prod/Wr.

LEITERMAN, Douglas
ACCT. Motion Picture Guarantors Inc., 14 Birch Ave., Toronto, ON M4V 1C9 (416)968-0577.
Type of Production and Credits: Th Film-Prod; Th Short-Prod; TV Film-Prod/Dir; TV Video-Prod/Dir/Wr.
Genres: Drama-Th&TV; Comedy-Th&TV; Action-Th&TV; Documentary-Th&TV.
Biography: Born in South Porcupine, Ontario. B.A., Economics, Political Science, University of British Columbia; postgraduate studies in Law and Economics as Nieman Fellow, Harvard, 53-54. Parliamentary and overseas correspondent, Southam News Service; reporter, editorial and business writer for the *Vancouver Province*. Chairman and CEO of Motion Picture Guarantors Inc. since 77; Chairman of Hobel Leiterman Communications Ltd., Document Associates Inc. of Toronto and New York, Entertainment Securities Ltd., The Mixing House Ltd., since 68; Board Chairman and CEO, Wired City Communications Ltd., 70-78. Has won 3 Wilderness Awards, 3 Ohio Awards, Gold Award (Atlanta). *Surfacing* was nominated for an Emmy.
Selected Filmography: *Millennium*, Th, 88, CDN, Prod; *By Design*, Th, 80, CDN, Exec Prod; *Surfacing*, Th, 79, CDN, Exec Prod; "The Sensational Seventies" (12 eps), TV, 77-78, CDN, Co-Prod; "Human Resources" (13 eps), TV, 77, CDN, Co-Prod; *Kennedys Don't Cry*, Th, 75, CDN, Co-Prod; "Here Comes the Seventies", TV, 70-73, CDN, Co-Prod; "North

American Seasons" (4 eps), TV, 72, CDN, Co-Prod; *The Crew*, TV, 69, USA, Dir; *CBS News*, TV, 66-69, USA, Prod; *Fasten Your Seatbelts*, TV, 68, CDN/USA, Dir/Prod; *Resurrection City*, TV, 68, CDN/USA, Co-Dir/Prod; *The Old College Try*, TV, 67, CDN, Dir/Prod, (EMMY); *Democrats in '66*, TV, 66, USA, Dir/Prod; *Youth in Search of Morality*, TV, 66, CDN, Co-Dir/Prod.

LENNON, Randy
Randy Lennon Productions, #1635, 10130-103 St., Edmonton, AB T5J 3N9 (403)420-1616. U.S. Office, 6363 Wilshire Blvd., Suite 610, Los Angeles, CA 90048 USA. (213)651-1634.
Type of Production and Credits: Th Short-Prod; TV Video-Prod/Wr/Act.
Genres: Comedy-TV; Variety-TV; Documentary-TV; Commercials-TV.
Biography: Born 1956, Edmonton, Alberta. Has hosted and produced TV programs in field of entertainment, comedy, interviewing, music and public affairs since 77. Newspaper publisher 77-79. Currently involved in talent management in Los Angeles.
Selected Filmography: "The Chat Channel" (pilot), TV, 90, USA, Exec Prod/Act; Gasland Roadtrip/Swizzlesticks (corporate), Cm, 88, CDN, Prod/Dir; Gasland/Smarty Mart/The Brick Warehouse/Akai (various), Cm, 87, CDN, Prod/Wr; Smarty Mart (various), Cm, 87, CDN, Prod; *Meanstreak*, MV, 87, CDN, Prod; *Listen for the Heartbeat*, MV, 87, CDN, Prod; "Midnight with Randy Lennon" (29 eps), TV, 86-87, CDN, Prod/Wr/Host; "Edmonton Live" (15 eps), TV, 85-86, CDN, Prod/Wr/Host.

LESEWICK, Robert
Freelance Productions, 20714-96 Ave., #116, Langley, BC V1M 1E4 (604)888-2368.
Type of Production and Credits: TV Video-Prod/Dir/Ed/Cam.
Genres: Commercials-TV; Industrial-TV; News-TV; Sports-TV.
Biography: Born 1948, Winnipeg, Manitoba. One year teachers' training; 1 year technical college; course in effective teaching strategies for adults. Nine years as a VTR production editor with Canadian networks and a private station. With own company and Infocam. Inc. acts as account executive, estimator, producer, director, cameraman, production manager, VTR production operator, stills photographer; teaches a VCR course.
Selected Filmography: *The Legends of Rock 'n' Roll*, In, 87, CDN, Assist Prod/Dir; Silver Cup Mines, In, 84, CDN, Prod/Dir/Wr; Freeway Chrysler, Cm, 82, CDN, Prod/Dir; "Let's Get Physical" (pilot), TV, 82, CDN, Prod/Dir.

LEVIN, Victor
176 Albany Ave., Toronto, ON M5R 3C6 (416)588-0716. School Services of Canada, 66 Portland St., Toronto, ON M5V 2M8 (416)366-0903.
Type of Production and Credits: TV Video-Prod.
Genres: Documentary-TV; Educational-TV.
Biography: Born in 1944 in Chicago, Illinois. B.A., University of Wisconsin, Madison; M.Ed., Columbia University. President and Treasurer of Educational Mediaproducts and Distributors of Canada, 1981-85. President, School Services of Canada, 1975 to date.
Selected Filmography: *Meet Paul Yee*, "Meet The Canadian Author", ED, 91, CDN, Prod; *Meet Martyn Godfrey*, "Meet The Canadian Author", ED, 91, CDN, Prod; *Meet Marilyn Halvorson*, "Meet The Canadian Author", ED, 91, CDN, Prod; *Meet Marie-Louis Gay*, "Meet The Canadian Author", ED, 91, CDN, Prod; *Meet Ian Wallace*, "Meet The Canadian Author", ED, 91, CDN, Prod; *Meet Camilla Gryski*, "Meet The Canadian Author", ED, 91, CDN, Prod; *Meet Barbara Reid*, "Meet The Canadian Author", ED, 90, CDN, Prod; *Meet Gordon Korman*, "Meet The Canadian Author", ED, 90, CDN, Prod.

LEVENE, Sam
BUPD, ACCT. 642 Shaw St., Toronto, ON M6G 3L7 (416)538-1241. CBC, Box 500, Stn. A, Toronto, ON M5W 1E6 (416)975-6598.
Type of Production and Credits: TV Film-Prod/Dir/Wr; TV Video-Prod/Dir/Wr.
Genres: Drama-TV; Documentary-TV; Music & Dance-TV.
Biography: Born 1936, Kitchener, Ontario. B.A. (Fine Arts), M.S.J. (Journalism), Northwestern University, Chicago, Illinois. Worked in radio, TV and theatre while student. CBC producer from mid-60s; executive producer form 73. "For the Record" dramas won numerous ACTRA and other awards; "Final Edition" won Best Drama Special at Banff TV Festival; *One of Our Own* and *A Far Cry From Home* won awards at American Film Festival; *Certain Practices* won a TV Genie; *Friends of a Feather* won a Chris Award, Columbus; 4 Gemini nominations 86-90 for Dramas and Performance-Documen-

taries. Joined "Man Alive," 91.
Selected Filmography: *Just Wanna Dance*, TV, 90, CDN, Prod/Dir/Wr; *Veronica Tennant: Completing the Circle*, TV, 89, CDN, Prod/Dir/Wr; *Oliver Jones: Jazz Pianist*, TV, 89, CDN, Prod/Dir/Wr; *Loreena McKennitt: Breaking the Silence*, TV, 88, CDN, Prod/Dir/Wr; *Murder Sees the Light*, TV, 86, CDN, Exec Prod; *9-B*, TV, 85, CDN, Exec Prod; *One for the Pot*, TV, 85, CDN, Exec Prod; *Twelfth Night*, TV, 85, CDN, Exec Prod; *Joshua Then and Now* (2 eps), TV, 84, CDN, Pro Exec; *Tartuffe*, TV, 84, CDN, Exec Prod; "Vanderberg" (6 eps), TV, 82-83, CDN, Exec Prod; "For the Record" (22 eps), TV, 78-82, CDN, Exec Prod; "Gallery" (22 eps), TV, 74-75, CDN, Exec Prod/Dir/Wr; "Telescope" (71 eps), TV, 70-73, CDN, Prod/Wr; "This Hour Has Seven Days" (26 eps), TV, 64-65, CDN, Story Ed.

LEVITAN, Steven
Sunrise Films Limited, 160 Perth Ave., Toronto, ON M6P 3X5 (416)535-2900.
Type of Production and Credits: Th Film-Prod; TV Film-Prod.
Genres: Drama-Th&TV.
Biography: Born in 1952 in Toronto, Ontario. Canadian citizen. Languages: English. Lawyer by profession. Founding Chairman, Desrosiers Dance Theatre, 1984-88. Chairman, Festival of Festivals Trade Forum, 1988. Vice-Chairman, Ontario, Academy of Canadian Cinema & Television, 1989. Member of the Board of Directors of Comic Relief Canada and the Canadian Retransmission Collective. "My Secret Identity" has received numerous awards including an Emmy and Act Award.
Selected Filmography: *Max Glick/The Outside Chance of Maximillian Glick"* (26 eps), TV, 90-91, CDN, Exec Prod; *Sam & Me*, Th, 90, CDN, Exec Prod; "My Secret Identity" (24 eps), TV, 90, CDN/USA, Exec Prod; *Palais Royale*, Th, 89, CDN, Exec Prod; *Stiker's Mountain*, TV, 85, CDN, Exec Prod.

LEVY, Joanne T.
- see WRITERS

LIIMATAINEN, Arvi
237 Westridge Rd., Edmonton, AB T5T 1B9 (403)487-8666. Kicking Horse Productions Ltd., 10022 - 103 St., 2nd Floor, Edmonton, AB T5J 0X2 (403)426-6441.
Type of Production and Credits: Th Film-Prod; Th Short-Dir; TV Film-Prod/Dir.
Genres: Drama-TV; Educational-TV; Industrial-TV; Current Affairs-TV.
Biography: Born 1949, Finland; Canadian citizenship. Worked in motion picture industry since 68. President of Alberta Motion Picture Industries Association (AMPIA), 80-82; Advisory Committee member for Alberta Motion Picture Development Corporation(AMPDC) 82-84. Executive Committee, National Screen Institute (NSI), 1989-92.
Selected Filmography: *Angel Square*, Th, 91, CDN, Prod; *Sylvan Lake Summer*, TV, 89, CDN, Co-Prod; "Ray Bradbury Theatre" (4 eps), TV, 89, CDN/USA/NZ, Co-Prod, (ACE); *Down Came The Rain*, TV, 89, CDN, Dir; *Bye Bye Blues*, Th, 88, CDN, Co-Prod; *Into The Fields*, TV, 88, CDN, Prod/Dir; *Cowboys Don't Cry*, TV, 87, CDN, Line Prod; *Stone Fox*, TV, 87, CDN, Prod Spv; "Hamilton's Quest" (3 eps), TV, 86, CDN, Dir; *Good Times at the Rainbow Bar & Grill*, TV, 86, CDN, Co-Prod; *Paper Marriage*, Th, 86, CDN, Prod Spv; "The Beachcombers" (6 eps), TV, 82-85, CDN, Dir; *Strikers Mountain*, Th, 85, CDN, Line Prod; *Great Days in the Rockies*, Th, 84, CDN, Dir; *Bridge to Terabithia*, TV, 84, CDN, Co-Prod.

LILLIE, Ronald ✧
(416)967-6503.
Type of Production and Credits: Th Film-Prod; Th Short-Prod; TV Film-Prod; TV Video-Prod.
Genres: Drama-Th&TV; Comedy-Th&TV; Action-Th&TV; Documentary-Th&TV.
Biography: Born 1938; Canadian citizenship. B.A.A., Radio and TV Arts, Ryerson Polytechnical Institute, 60. *No Surrender* won the Festival of Festivals International Critics Award.
Selected Filmography: *A Winter to Remember*, TV, 88, CDN, Prod; *Shoot Me*, Th, 87, CDN, Prod; *Dreams of Glory*, TV, 87, CDN, Prod; *Loyalties*, Th, 85, CDN/GB, Co-Prod; *No Surrender*, Th, 85, CDN/GB, Co-Prod; "Assignment Adventure: (13 eps), TV, 85, CDN/GB, Prod; *Isaac LIttlefeathers*, Th, 84, CDN, Exec Prod; *The Saga of Those Crazy Canucks*, TV, 84, CDN, Prod; *The Heroes of Summer*, TV, 84, CDN, Prod; *Beyond Words*, TV, 84, CDN, Prod; *The Disability Myth* (parts I, II and III), TV, 82-84, CDN, Prod; *The Fast and the Furious*, TV, 83, CDN, Prod; *The Heroes of Winter*, TV, 83, CDN, Prod; *It Takes A Champion*, TV, 83, CDN, Prod; *Three Against the Wind*, TV, 83, CDN, Prod.

LINDO, Eleanore
- see DIRECTORS

LINDSAY, Gillian
955 Braeside Ave., West Vancouver, BC V7T 2K7. Forefront Productions, 609 - 402 W. Pender St., Vancouver, BC V6B 1T6 (604)682-7910.
Type of Production and Credits: Th Film-2nd Assist Dir; Th Short-PM; TV Film-Prod/PM; TV Video-Assist Dir.
Genres: Drama-Th&TV; Documentary-Th&TV; Educational-Th&TV; Music Video-Th&TV.
Biography: Born in 1952 in Victoria, British Columbia. Prior to work in film industry, has worked in the accounting field. Graduated Vancouver Film School (Honours) in 1988. Producer with strong business background; has worked as PM, AD and in continuity. Partner in Forefront Productions for 2-1/2 years; company awards to date include: Bronze Apple, National Film Festival (CA); Third Place and Honorable Mention, American Film Festival (NY) and Certificate of Merit, Yorkton (Sask) for 2 educational productions (drama and documentary).
Selected Filmography: *Journey Into Self Esteem*, "Inside Stories", ED/TV, 89-90, CDN, Prod/Wr/PM; *Working It Out*, "High School Live", ED/TV, 90, CDN, Prod/PM; *Christmas Cowboy*, Th/TV, 90, CDN, PM/Cont; *Silhouette*, Th, 90, CDN, 2nd Assist Dir; United Way 1990, Cm, 90, CDN, Cont; NU 95.3, Cm, 89, CDN, Assist Dir; *And I Miss You*, Rocky Swanson, MV, 89, CDN, Assist Dir; *Good Ol' Boys*, Jess Lee/Rocky Swanson, MV, 89, CDN, Assist Dir; *Honky Tonk Affair*, Jess Lee, MV, 89, CDN, Assist Dir; *Shakin'*, The Jeans, MV, 89, CDN, Assist Dir; *Lorelei*, Montana, MV, 89, CDN, Assist Dir; *Humanimal*, Mark Hasselbach, MV, 89, CDN, Assist Dir; *Alice in Hell*, Annihilator, MV, 88, CDN, Assist Dir; *Fire Attack*, TV, 88, CDN, Prod Coord; *In a Minute*, Montana, MV, 88, CDN, Cont.

LINK, André
Cinépix Inc., 8275 Mayrand, Montreal, PQ H4P 2C8 (514)342-2340. FAX: 342-1922.
Type of Production and Credits: Th Film-Prod.
Genres: Drama-Th; Comedy-Th; Science Fiction-Th; Horror-Th; Action-Th.
Biography: Born Montreal, Quebec. Languages: English and French. Co-founder and President of Cinépix Inc.
Selected Filmography: *Princes in Exile*, TV, 89, CDN, Exec Prod; *Snakeeater II - The Drug Buster*, Th, 89, CDN, Exec Prod; *Whispers*, Th, 89, CDN, Exec Prod; *Snakeeater*, Th, 88, CDN, Exec Prod; *The Vindicator*, Th, 84, CDN, Co-Prod; *Meatballs III*, Th, 84, CDN, Exec Prod; *Spacehunter*, Th, 83, CDN, Co-Prod; *Happy Birthday to Me*, Th, 80, CDN, Co-Prod; *Yesterday*, Th, 79, CDN, Co-Prod; *Meatballs*, Th, 78, CDN, Co-Exec Prod; *Rabid*, Th, 76, CDN, Co-Exec Prod; *Death Weekend*, Th, 75, CDN, Co-Exec Prod; *Shivers/They Came From Within/The Parasite Murders*, Th, 74, CDN, Co-Prod; *L'Initiation*, Th, 69, CDN, Co-Prod; *Valerie*, Th, 68, CDN, Co-Prod.

LIPSEY, Stan
ACCT. Stan Lipsey Productions, 219 Belsize Dr., Toronto, ON M4S 3M1 (416)480-2430.
Type of Production and Credits: Th Short-Prod; TV Film-Prod; TV Video-Prod.
Genres: Variety-TV; Documentary-Th; Industrial-TV; Current Affairs-TV.
Biography: Born 1951, Montreal, Quebec. B.A., English and Communications, McGill University, 72. Brief acting and stage-managing stints in comedy; perform-ed and produced a weekly segment on "That's Life" called "Satin Stan's Moveable Movie Palace" for a season on Global.
Selected Filmography: "Workweek" (24 eps), TV, 91, CDN, Dir; "Imprint" (31 eps), TV, 90-91, CDN, Prod/Dir; "Imprint" (17 eps), TV, 89-90, CDN, Prod; "Lifetime" (580 eps), TV, 85-89, CDN, Prod; "Thrill of a Lifetime" (57 eps), TV, 83-85, CDN, Prod; "Market Place" (43 eps), TV, 81-83, CDN, Field Prod; "That's Life" (124 eps), TV, 80-81, CDN, Field Prod; "Canada AM" (520 eps), TV, 78-80, CDN, Story Ed/Field Prod; "In Search Of" (2 eps), TV, 77, USA, PM/Assist Dir; "90 Minutes Live" (150 eps), TV, 76-77, CDN, Story Ed; *The World Is Round*, Th, 75-76, CDN, Assist Ed.

LISHMAN, Eda Lever
DGC, ACTRA. The Producers Ltd., 5115 Crowchild Trail S.W., Calgary, AB T3E 1T9 (403)249-6212.
Type of Production and Credits: Th Film-Prod/Dir/Wr; TV Film-Prod.
Genres: Drama-Th&TV; Children's-Th&TV; Industrial-Th&TV.
Biography: Born in 1949 in Vigo Cavedine, Italy. Languages: English and Italian. Graduated from N.A.I.T. in Edmonton, Alberta with a degree in Radio and Television Arts. Instrumental in the founding of the Alberta Motion Picture Development Corporation and currently sits on the board for the Canadian Centre

for Advanced Film Studies. Production credits to date have included writing, producing and directing numerous industrial, commercial and television projects.
Selected Filmography: *Primo Baby*, Th, 89-90, CDN, Prod/Dir/Wr; *Western Canada Lottery*, In, 86, CDN, Dir; *The Wild Pony*, TV, 82, Prod/2nd Unit Dir; *The Grande Opening*, In, 78, CDN, Dir/Prod.

LIVINGSTON, Neal
- see DIRECTORS

LOCK, Keith
- see DIRECTORS

LOCKE, Jeannine
ATPD, ACCT. 12 Belmont St., Toronto, ON M5R 1P8
Type of Production and Credits: TV Film-Prod/Dir/Wr.
Genres: Drama-TV; Documentary-TV.
Biography: Born in Indian Head, Saskatchewan. M.A., English, University of Saskatchewan. Editorial writer, *Ottawa Citizen*; staff writer, *Chatelaine*; London Bureau Chief, *Toronto Star*; producer/director/writer, CBC. Her films have won awards at New York and Columbus film festivals.
Selected Filmography: *The Greening of Ian Elliot*, TV, 91, CDN, Prod/Wr; *The Private Capital*, TV, 88, CDN, Prod/Wr; *Island Love Song*, TV, 86, CDN, Prod/Wr; "The Other Kingdom" (mini-series), TV, 84, CDN, Prod/Wr; *All the Days of My Life*, TV, 81-82, CDN, Prod/Wr; *Chautauqua Girl*, TV, 82, CDN, Prod/Wr, (ACTRA); *You've Come a Long Way, Katie* (mini-series)(Wr parts 1,3), TV, 79-80, CDN, Prod; *The Quieter Revolution*, TV, 78, CDN, Prod/Dir; *The Canadian Monarchy*, TV, 77, CDN, Prod/Dir; *The Woodsworth Phenomenon*, TV, 76, CDN, Prod/Dir; *The Family Prince*, TV, 75, CDN, Prod/Dir; *A Celebration/Perceptions of France/Defending the Peaceable Isles*, "People of Our Time", TV, 74, CDN, Prod/Dir; *Too Much of a Terrible Beauty/In Remembrance: Stewart Alsor*, "People of Our Time", TV, 73-74, CDN, Prod/Dir; *The Vassar Girl/3 1/2 Cheers for Toronto/Guardian of Dreams*, "People of Our Time", TV, 73, CDN, Prod/Dir; *Goodbye Joey*, TV, 72, CDN, Prod/Dir.

LONGLEY, Richard
ATPD. 266 Markham St., Toronto, ON M6J 2G6 (416)961-2766. CBC-TV, The Nature of Things, P.O. Box 500, Stn. A, Toronto, ON M5W 1E6 (416)975-6896. FAX: 975-6887.
Type of Production and Credits: TV Film-Prod.
Genres: Documentary-TV.
Biography: Born 1943, Surrey, England; Canadian citizenship. B.Sc., Diploma in Education, University of London, 66. Science teacher 8 years: England, Kenya, Papua New Guinea, 66-73. Consultant, researcher, story editor, associate producer, producer with "The Nature of Things," "Science Magazine," 73 to date. *The Vision of the Blind* won Red Ribbon, American Film Festival and was a finalist at International Film Festival and John Muir Film Festival; *Pain in the Back* won Bronze Chris, Columbus, Media Award, American Journal of Nursing and Honourable Mention, American Film Festival; *Microscope - Making It Big* won Blue Ribbon, American Film Festival, Gold Election, International Educational Film Festival and Honourable Mention, National Educational Film Festival; *The Cathedral Engineers* won 1st place, National Educational Film Festival; *Japan* won Bell Northern Award. Produced over 100 segments of less than 20 minutes each on "Science Magazine" and "The Nature of Things" from 74-84.
Selected Filmography: *Day of Reckoning*, TV, 91, CDN, Prod; *The Balancing Act*, TV, 90, CDN, Prod; *The Vision of the Blind*, TV, 88, CDN, Prod; *Piercing the Dark*, TV, 87, CDN, Prod; *Jellyfish of the Sky*, TV, 87, CDN, Prod; *USSR* (2 eps), TV, 87, CDN, Res/Field Prod; *Comet of a Lifetime*, TV, 86, CDN, Prod; *Air Craft*, TV, 85, CDN, Prod; *Pain in the Back*, TV, 84, CDN, Prod; *Philip Morison on Nuclear War*, TV, 82, CDN, Prod; *Microscope - Making It Big*, TV, 82, CDN, Prod; *The Cathedral Engineers*, TV, 82, CDN, Prod; *Japan* (2 eps), TV, 82, Res; *China* (2 eps), TV, 80, CDN, Res/Wr.

LORD, Roger
- voir REALISATEURS

LORTI, Claude
- voir REALISATEURS

LOUBERT, Patrick
ACCT. Nelvana Ltd., 32 Atlantic Ave., Toronto, ON M6K 1X6 (416)588-5571.
Type of Production and Credits: Th Film-Prod; TV Film-Prod; TV Video-Prod.
Genres: Children's-Th&TV; Animation-Th&TV.
Biography: Co-founder and President, Nelvana Ltd. Recipient of many awards including Wilderness Award, Chris Award, and a Special Award at the Canadian Film Awards, 78; *The Care Bears Movie* won the

Golden Reel Award, 86; "Babar" won Gemini, 89 and 90; "Beetlejuice" won an Emmy 90, for Best Animated Program.
Selected Filmography: "Babar" (65 eps), TV, 89-91, F/CDN, Prod (GEMINI 89, 90); "Beetlejuice" (94 eps), TV, 89-91, CDN, Prod, (EMMY); "Tin Tin" (26 eps), TV, 90-911, F/CDN, Prod; "Rupert Bear" (13 eps), TV, 90-91, F/CDN, Prod; "Little Rosey" (13 eps), TV, 89-90, CDN, Prod; "T and T" (65 eps), TV, 87-89, CDN, Exec Prod; "The Care Bears Family" (67 eps), TV, 86-88, CDN, Co-Prod; *Babar: The Movie*, Th, 88, CDN, Co-Prod; "The Edison Twins" (78 eps), TV, 83-86, CDN, Co-Prod; "My Pet Monster", TV, 86, CDN, Co-Prod; *The Care Bears Movie II*, Th, 86, CDN, Co-Prod; *The Care Bears Movie*, Th, 85, CDN, Co-Prod; "Inspector Gadget" (13 eps), TV, 83, CDN/USA, Co-Prod; *Rock & Rule/Ring of Power*, Th, 82, CDN, Co-Prod.

LOWER, Peter
ACTRA, ACCT. 243 Waverley Rd., Toronto, ON M4L 3T4 (416)694-4652.
Type of Production and Credits: TV Film-Prod/Wr; Th Film-Wr.
Genres: Drama-TV; Action-TV.
Biography: Born 1943, Kingston, Ontario. B.A., English, University of Victoria; M.A., Drama, Carleton University. Currently Executive Producer, Drama, CTV Television Network.
Selected Filmography: *My Brother Larry*, TV, 89, CDN, Prod; "Street Legal", TV, 86-87, CDN, Exec Story Ed; "Oakmount High", TV, 85, CDN, Prod, (2 GEMINIS, 86); *The Exile*, TV, 85, CDN, Co-Wr; *Reasonable Force*, TV, 82, CDN, Co-Wr; *The Unexpected*, TV, 81, CDN, Wr; *The Last Season*, TV, 86, CDN, Story Ed; *Dreamspeaker*, TV, 77, CDN, Story Ed; "For the Record", TV, 81-85, CDN, Story Ed.

LOWRY, Christopher
ACCT. 46 Wales Ave., Toronto, ON M5T 1J4 (416)368-0407.
Type of Production and Credits: TV-Film-Prod/Wr; TV Video-Prod/Dir/Wr.
Genres: Drama-TV; Comedy-TV; Documentary-TV; Educational-TV.
Biography: Born 1955, London, Ontario. Languages: English, French and some Spanish. B.A., Honours English, University of Western Ontario. Began work in film with Insight Productions, Toronto, 79; edited the humour book, *The Best of Playboar*, 84. *Chambers: Tracks and Gestures* won a Bronze Award at the Houston Film Festival, Blue Ribbon, American Film Festival, and Best Film of Festival at Yorkton. Senior Editor, *The Journal of Wild Culture*, (a quarterly magazine of ecology and imagination), 87-88.
Selected Filmography: *Palais Royale*, Th, 87, CDN, Assist to Dir; *October Stranger*, TV, 85, CDN, Prod/Assoc Dir; *The People Want Meat*, MV, 85, CDN, Dir/Prod/Wr; *Ranch*, TV, 85, CDN, Co-Prod/Wr/Ed; *Doris McCarthy: Heart of a Painter*, TV, 83, CDN, Assoc Prod; *Chambers: Tracks and Gestures*, TV, 82, CDN, Prod/Co-Wr/Res, (CFTA); *Heart of Gold*, TV, 81, CDN, Res.

LUCA, Claudio
APFVQ. 352, av. Grenfell, Mont-Royal, PQ H3R 1G3 (514)340-1211. Productions C.M. Luca Inc./Prod. Télé-Action Inc., 1338 St. Catherine est, Montréal, PQ H2L 2H5 (514)524-1133/524-1133.
Types de production et générique: l métrage-Prod/D phot; c métrage-Prod/D phot; TV film-Prod/ phot; TV vidép-Prod/D phot.
Types d'oeuvres: Drame-C&TV; Comédie-C&TV; Documentaire-C&TV; Enfants-C&TV.
Curriculum vitae: Né en 1945, Rome Italie; citoyenneté canadienne. Langues: français et anglais. Diplôme du Germain School of Cinematography, New York, 65. Assistant-caméraman, 66-69; directeur-photo et cadreur, films publicitaires et émissions ("Le 60", "Télémag", "Dossier"), 70-81; producteur et producteur délégué depuis 82.
Filmographie sélective: "Une faim de loup" (26 eps), TV, 91, CDN, Co prod; *Une histoire inventée*, C, 90, CDN, Prod exéc; *Lalala Human Sex*, TV, 87, CDN, Prod; *CHO OYU - la Voie de l'impossible*, C, 86, CDN, Prod; *La Fleur de Noel*, TV, 86, CDN, Prod; *Esperanza*, TV, 85, CDN, Prod/Cam; *Léprosierie San Pablo*, TV, 85, CDN, Prod/Réal; *Pionniers de la brousse*, TV, 84, CDN, Prod/Cam; "Les risques du métier" (15 eps), TV, 82-83, CDN, Prod/Cam.

LUHOVY, Yurij
- see EDITORS

LUNNY, Shane
Shane Lunny Productions Inc., #305 - 560 Beatty St., Vancouver, BC V6B 2L3 (604)669-0333.
Type of Production and Credits: TV Film-Prod/Dir; TV Video-Prod/Dir; Interact Video-Prod.
Genres: Documentary-TV; Educational-Th&TV; Industrial-TV; Music Video-

Th&TV; Commercials-TV.
Biography: Born 1952, Kenora, Ontario. Languages: English and French. Diploma, Communications, Television and Film, Confederation College. Association of Visual Communicators Cindy Award, 86, for *Is Einstein Wrong?*, interactive laserdisc at the UN Pavilion, Expo 86; Silver Birch Award, ITVA, 87, for *Sona Systems Corporation*; I.T.V.A., Musical Score and Silver Birch for *The Dinosaur Project*.
Selected Filmography: *Ultimate Roller Coaster*, Th, 91, CDN, Prod/Dir; *The Dinosaur Project*, ED, 91, CDN, Prod; *Is Einstein Wrong?*, ED, 86, CDN, Prod; *Sona Systems*, In, 85, CDN, Prod/Wr/Dir; "Much Music West", TV, 84, CDN, Prod; *Cry from the Wild*, ED, 84, CDN, Prod/Dir; Cam-net, Cm, 84, CDN, Prod.

MACADAM, William I.
148 Collier St., Toronto, ON M4W 1M3 (416)922-7554.
Type of Production and Credits: TV Film-Prod.
Genres: Documentary-TV; Drama-TV; Children's-TV.
Biography: Born 1938, London, England; Canadian citizenship. Educated at Eton College, England, and the loggings camps of the West Coast. Founded Trans Mountain Air Services, 62; Vice-President, Progressive Conservative Party of Canada, 64-70; ran Robert Stanfield's national campaign, 68; founded Norfolk Group of Companies, 73; past Chairman, CFTA Film and Television Division; founding member ACFTP and Canadian Broadcasting League. President, Norfolk Productions. Films have won a number of awards including ACTRA, CFTA, ANIK Wilderness Awards.
Selected Filmography: *Winnie*, TV, 82, CDN, Prod; *The KGB Connection: An Investigation into Soviet Operations in North America*, TV, 81, CDN, Exec Prod; "Jack London's Tales of the Klondike" (7 eps), TV, 80-81, CDN, Prod; *Scorn of Woman*, TV, 81, CDN, Prod; *Race for Number One*, TV, 81, CDN, Prod; *Finis*, TV, 81, CDN, Prod; *Tales from a Toy Shop* (3 parts), TV, 81, CDN, Prod; "The Unexpected", TV, 81, CDN, Prod; *Love of Life*, TV, 80, CDN, Prod; *The One Thousand Dozen*, TV, 80, CDN, Prod; *In a Far Country*, TV, 80, CDN, Prod; *Connections: A Further Investigation into Organized Crime* (2 parts), TV, 79, CDN, Co-Prod; *The Tomorrow Man*, TV, 78, CDN, Co-Prod; *Connections: An Investigation into Organized Crime in Canada* (2 parts), TV, 77, CDN, Co-Prod, (ACTRA/ANIK); *The Fifth Estate: The Espionage Establishment*, TV, 74, CDN, Prod.

MacANDREW, Heather
Asterisk Productions, 490 Adelaide St. W., Suite 303, Toronto, ON M5V 1T2 (416)868-1175. FAX: 868-1176.
Type of Production and Credits: TV Film-Prod/Wr; TV Video-Prod/Wr.
Genres: Documentary; Educational.
Biography: Born 1949, Canadian citizen. Partner, Asterisk Productions. *The Best We Have to Give?* won Blue Ribbon, American Film Festival and Certificate of Merit Chicago; *That's Right!* won Silver Apple, National Educational Film & Video Festival; *Growing Up in the World Next Door* won Silver Apple and Certificate of Merit, Chicago; *Roots of Hunger, Roots of Change* won Red Ribbon, American Film Festival; *Replanting the Tree of Life* won Golden Sheaf, Yorkton; *Medium Rare, Hold the Cottage!* was selected for the Festival of Festivals, 90.
Selected Filmography: *Medium Rare, Hold the Cottage!*, Th, 90, CDN, Co-Prod; *Words: Four Stories About Becoming Literate*, ED, 90, CDN, Co-Prod; *The Best We Have to Give*, "Stolen Childhood", ED, 89, GB/NOR/S/I/E, Wr/Co-Prod; *That's Right*, ED, 89, CDN, Co-Prod/Co-Dir; *Growing Up in the World Next Door*, ED, 88, CDN, Wr/Co-Prod; *A Handcrafted History*, "The Nature of Things", TV, 86, CDN, Wr/Co-Prod; *Replanting the Tree of Life*, ED, 86, CDN, Exec Prod; *Roots of Hunger, Roots of Change*, ED, 85, CDN, Wr/Co-Prod; *A Moveable Feast*, ED, 81, CDN, Co-Prod; "The World's Children" (13 eps), ED, 78-80, CDN, Co-Prod.

MacDONALD, Ramuna
- see DIRECTORS

MACFARLANE, Douglas
- see PRODUCTION MANAGERS

MACKAY, Bruce
- see DIRECTORS

MACKAY, David
David Mackay Limited, 23 Fraser Ave., Toronto, ON M6K 1Y7 (416)538-7625. FAX: 538-3775.
Type of Production and Credits: Th Short-Prod/Dir; TV Film-Prod/Dir; TV Video-Prod.
Genres: Documentary-Th&TV; Experimental-Th&TV; Industrial-Th&TV.
Biography: Began communication and design career as art director for CBC television; founded TDF Film Productions; produced and directed many TV commercials and documentary films under a subcompany, Reason Associates;

formed own company, producing films in Imax for the Ontario Place Cinesphere and other Imax theatres, wide-screen films for expositions. Promotional work includes tourism films for provincial government, industries and corporate clients such as Olympia & York Devopments Ltd. A division of the company has developed several new 3-D concepts including 360 Circle-RAMA; another division works on script develop-ment for feature film and television productions. Has won many awards in the corporate, commercial and theatrical fields, including an Oscar for *A Place to Stand*, a 70mm multi-image film for the Ontario Pavilion, Expo 67.
Selected Filmography: *Ontari-Oh!* (Ontario Pavilion '86), Th, 86, CDN, Prod/Dir; *China: 7,000 Years of Discovery*, Th, 83, CDN, Prod/Dir; *Control of Asthma*, ED, 83, CDN, Prod/Dir; *Thin Ice Survival*, ED, 83, CDN, Prod/Dir; *Olympia & York series*, In, 82, CDN, Prod/Dir; *Search for Great Ideas*, In, 82, CDN, Prod/Dir; *Winter in Ontario with Hagood Hardy*, In, 81, CDN, Prod/Dir; *Tour/Ontario*, In, 79, CDN, Prod/Dir; *Tidewater Ontario*, Th, 78, CDN, Prod/Dir; *Silent Sky* (Imax), Th, 77, CDN, Prod/Dir; *Think About It*, In, 77, CDN, Prod/Dir; *Ontario/Summertide* (Imax), Th, 76, CDN, Prod/Dir; *The Giant's Club*, Th, 76, CDN, Prod/Dir; *St. Lawrence...More Than a River*, Th, 74, CDN, Prod/Dir; *Catch the Sun* (Imax), Th, 73, CDN, Prod/Dir.

MACKAY, Margaux
- see PRODUCTION MANAGERS

MACKENZIE, Scott
154 Langley Ave., Toronto, ON M4K 1B7 (416)462-1742.
Type of Production and Credits: Th Film-Prod/PM; TV Video-Prod/PM.
Genres: Variety-TV; Commercials-TV; Music Video-TV; Sports-TV.
Biography: Born in 1955. Canadian citizen. Has produced film and video shoots involving up to eight cameras with 24-track mobile sound. Freelance producer for television, commercials and corporate films. Won the Canadian Film Editor Guild Award for Best Sound Editing, Documentary 1979.
Selected Filmography: "Video Guide" (pilot), TV, 90, CDN, Prod; *Exposed*, Th, 89, CDN, 1st Assist Dir; "Video Preview" (6 eps), TV, 89, CDN, Prod; *Luba*, TV, 88, CDN, Line Prod; *In Fashion*, TV, 88, CDN, Line Prod; *The Revue*, TV, 87, CDN, Line Prod; *Jane Siberry*, TV, 87, CDN, PM; "Don Cherry's Grapevine" (56 eps), TV, 84-86, CDN, Prod; "The Orginal Six" (54 eps), TV, 84-86, CDN, Prod; "Bobby Orr Series" (26 epd), TV, 81-83, CDN, Prod/Ed.

MACKEY, Clarke
- see DIRECTORS

MACLEAR, Michael
Screenlife Incorporated, 112 - 114 Cumberland St., Toronto, ON M4R 1A6 (416)324-9837. FAX: 324-9843.
Type of Production and Credits: TV Film-Prod/Wr; TV Video-Prod/Wr.
Genres: Documentary-TV; Children's-TV.
Biography: Born in London, England; Canadian citizenship. Former foreign correspondent for CBC, CTV; travelled in 80 countries. President of Screenlife Inc. "Vietnam: The Ten Thousand Day War" won Best Documentary, National Education Association of America.
Selected Filmography: *The Greenpeace Years* (2 eps), TV, 91, CDN, Co-Exec Prod; *Ken Dryden's Homegame* (6 eps), TV, 90, CDN, Exec Prod; *Beautiful Dreamers*, Th, 89, CDN, Prod; "The Canadians" (2 eps), TV, 87, CDN, Co-Exec Prod; "The American Century" (6 eps), TV, 86, CDN, Exec Prod/Wr; "American Caesar" (5 eps), TV, 83, CDN, Exec Prod; "Going Great" (52 eps), TV, 81-82, CDN, Exec Prod; "Vietnam: The Ten Thousand Day War" (26 eps), TV, 80, CDN, Exec Prod/Wr; "Maclear" (60 eps), TV, 74-78, CDN, Wr/Host, (ACTRA).

MACLEOD, Douglas J.
DGC, WGC (ACTRA). 2 Varcourt Place N.W., Calgary, AB T3A 0G8 (403)288-8903. FAX: 288-8812. Bradshaw, MacLeod & Associates Ltd., 1700 Varsity Estates Dr. N.W., Calgary, AB T3B 2W9 (403)247-6067. FAX: 247-6440.
Type of Production and Credits: Th Film-Prod; TV Film-Prod.
Genres: Drama-Th&TV; Action-Th&TV; Educational-Th&TV; Children's-Th&TV.
Biography: Co-production specialist with several dramatic (theatrical and television) projects in active development.
Selected Filmography: "The Ray Bradbury Theatre" (12 eps), TV, 90-91, CDN/NZ, Prod.

MacMILLAN, Michael
CFTA, ACCT. Atlantis Films Limited, 65 Heward Ave., Toronto, ON M4M 2T5 (416)462-0246.
Type of Production and Credits: TV Film-Prod; Th Film-Prod.
Genres: Drama-Th&TV; Comedy-Th &TV; Science Fiction-TV; Children's-TV.

Biography: Born 1956, Scarborough, Ontario. B.A., Film Studies, Queen's University. Founded Atlantis Films Limited with partners Janice Platt and Seaton McLean; film and TV distribution company. Films he has produced have won Oscars and awards at the American, Chicago, and Yorkton film festivals, among others. Awards for "Magic Hour" series Daytime Emmy, 91, for *Lost in the Barrens*; AMPIA, 90, for *High Country*.
Selected Filmography: *Montreal Vu Par*, Th, 91, CDN, Co-Exec Prod; *Curse of the Viking Grave*, TV, 91, CDN/NZ, Co-Exec Prod; *The Sound and the Silence* (mini-series), TV, 91, CDN/NZ, Exec Prod; *The Boy from Andromeda*, TV, 91, CDN//NZ, Co-Exec Prod; "Kurt Vonnegut's Monkey House" (3 eps), TV, 90-91, CDN, Co-Exec Prod; "Gold" (20 eps), TV, 90-91, CDN/NZ, Co-Exec Prod; "Mom P.I." (26 eps), TV, 90-91, CDN, Exec Prod; "Neon Rider" (39 eps), TV, 89-91, CDN, Co-Exec Prod; *The Girl from Mars*, TV, 90, CDN/NZ, Co-Exec Prod; *Clarence*, TV, 90, CDN/NZ, Co-Exec Prod; *Star Runner*, TV, 90, CDN/NZ, Co-Exec Prod; *Raider of the South Seas*, TV, 90, CDN/NZ, Co-Exec Prod; "Magic Hour" (8 eps), 89-90, CDN, Co-Exec Prod; *All For One*, TV, 89, CDN./NZ, Co-Exec Prod; *Firing Squad*, TV, 89, CDN/F, Co-Exec Prod.

MACNEE, Rupert
DGC, ACCT, SIVA. 3114 Glenmanor Place, Los Angeles, CA 90039 (213)668-1334. FAX: 668-1877.
Type of Production and Credits: TV Film-Dir/Prod; TV Video-Prod.
Genres: Variety-TV; Documentary-TV; Educational-TV.
Biography: Born 1947, England. Educated at Princeton University. Has produced several series for syndication; now living in Los Angeles.
Selected Filmography: *The Making of "Dying Young"* (electronic press kit), Th, 90, USA, Dir; *Writing a Timed Essay*, Corp, 89, USA, Prod; *Diabetes: A Positive Approach*, ED, 89, USA, Prod; National Academy of Recording Arts & Sciences, Corp, 90, USA, Dir; *Saturday Night Harold!*, TV, 88, USA, Assoc Prod; *Vibrations...The Making of "Vibes"*, TV, 88, USA, Wr; *Triple Cross!*, Th, 88, CDN, Wr; *American Video Awards*, TV, 87, USA, Prod; *Technical Marketing and Proposal Preparation*, ED, 86, USA, Prod; "OWL-TV" (sev segs), TV, 85, CDN, Dir; "An Evening at the Improv" (52 eps), TV, 80-83, USA, Prod; *Suicide* (5 parts), TV, 79, CDN, Co-Wr/Co-Ed; "Behind the Scenes with Jonathan Winters"(46 eps)(Dir 8 eps), TV, 76-78, CDN/USA, Prod; "Friends of Man" (45 eps)(Dir 8 eps), TV, 74-75, CDN, Co-Prod; *Talk of the Devil*, TV, 73, CDN, Assoc Prod.

MAGDER, Zale
- see CINEMATOGRAPHERS

MALLEN, Bruce
PGA, ACCT. Filmcorp, 253 South Maple Dr., Beverly Hills, CA 90212 USA. (213)470-1433.
Type of Production and Credits: Th Film-Prod.
Genres: Drama-Th; Comedy-Th; Action-Th.
Biography: Born 1937, Montreal, Quebec. B.Comm., B.A., Concordia University; M.S., Columbia University, M.B.A., University of Michigan; Ph.D., New York University. Developer of Filmland Corporate Center, Culver City, California; Ford Foundation Fellow; former Professor & Dean, Faculty of Commerce, Concordia University; former visiting professor, University of Southern California, and visiting scholar, UCLA; economic consultant to major Canadian corporations and government agencies; member of board of directors for various associations, including Cinema Circulus (USC School of Cinema and TV), Los Angeles Arts Council; author of several business textbooks.
Selected Filmography: *Billy Galvin*, Th, 86, USA, Prod; *Doin' Time/Big House*, Th, 84, USA, Prod; *Killing 'em Softly*, Th, 82, CDN, Co-Prod; *Paradise*, Th, 81, CDN, Exec Prod; *Heartaches*, Th, 80, CDN, Co-Prod; *Odyssey*, Th, 80, CDN, Exec Prod; *The High Country*, Th, 79, CDN, Prod.

MALLEN, Carol
ACCT. Filmcorp, 253 South Maple Dr., Beverly Hills, CA 90212 USA. (213)470-1433.
Type of Production and Credits: Th Film-Prod.
Genres: Drama-Th; Comedy-Th.
Biography: Born 1942, Montreal, Quebec. Languages: English and French. B.A., Concordia University. Manager of Filmland Corporate Center, Culver City, California; creative consultant on several films; former educator of hearing impaired, Montreal Oral School for the Deaf.
Selected Filmography: *Doin' Time/Big House*, Th, 84, CDN, Exec Prod; *The High Country*, Th, 79, CDN, Creat cons.

MALO, René
APFVQ, ACCT. 372, Côte Ste-Catherine, Outremont, PQ. Groupe

Malofilm, 1207 rue Saint-André, 4e étage, Montréal, PQ H2L 3S8 (514)844-4555 FAX: 844-1471.
Types de production et générique: l métrage-Prod; c métrage-Prod.
Types d'oeuvres: Drame-C; Comédie-C.
Curriculum vitae: Né en 1942. Langues: français et anglais. Fondation de Corporation Image M & M Ltée, 70; producteur/réalisateur de plus de 50 courts et moyens métrages; fonde Les Films René Malo, 74, Malo Vidéo, 83; distributeur et producteur de films au niveau international; achète Mutual Films, 83, devenant un partenaire dans New World Mutual Pictures; achète, avec Pierre David, la totalité des parts de Image Organization, 89. *Sonatine* remporte le Lion d'Argent, Venise, 84; *Le Déclin de l'empire américain* gagne le Prix de la Critique Internationale, Cannes, le Prix John Labatt Classic pour le film le plus populaire et le Prix CITY, Meilleur Film Canadien au Festival of Festivals, Toronto, 86.
Filmographie sélective: *Money* (minisérie), TV, 90, USA, Co prod; *Scanners III: The Takeover*, C, 90, CDN, Prod; *Scanners II: The New Order*, C, 89, CDN, Prod; *Internal Affairs*, C, 89, USA, Prod exéc; *Les Portes tournantes*, C, 87, CDN/F, Prod; *Les Tisserands du pouvoir*, C, 87, CDN/F, Co prod; *Pin*, C, 87, CDN, Prod; *Le Déclin de l'empire américain*, C, 85, CDN, Prod, (GÉNIE 87); *Lune de miel*, C, 85, CND/F, Prod exéc; *Sonatine*, C, 82, CDN, Prod; *Le Ruffian*, C, 82, CDN/F, Prod; *L'Homme à tout faire*, C, 79, CDN, Prod; *L'Animal*, C, 77, F, Co prod; *Panique*, C, 76, CDN, Co prod; *L'aile ou la cuisse*, C, 75, F, Co prod.

MANGAARD, Annette
- see DIRECTORS

MANN, Ron
- see DIRECTORS

MARGELLOS, James
DGA, DGC. 1646 Michael Lane, Pacific Palisades, CA 90272 (213)454-1097. Pacific Rim Films Ltd., 1432 W. 45th Ave. Vancouver, BC V5Y 1K2 (604)983-5300.
Type of Production and Credits: Th Film-Prod/ Unit PM; TV Film-Prod/Unit PM.
Genres: Drama-Th&TV; Comedy-Th &TV; Action-Th&TV; Science Fiction-Th&TV; Children's-Th&TV.
Biography: Born 1946, Revelstoke, B.C. Selected Filmography: *Still Not Quite Human*, TV, 91, USA, Prod; *Four Eyes*, TV, 91, USA, Co-Prod; *Kaleidoscope*, TV, 90, USA, Co-Prod; "Checkered Flag" (pilot), TV, 90, Prod; "Shannon's Deal" (6 eps), TV, 90, USA, Co-Prod; *The Little Kidnappers*, TV, 89, USA/CDN, Prod; *Not Quite Human*, TV, 89, USA, Prod.

MARK, Gordon
DGC. 4001 West 32nd Ave., Vancouver, BC V6S 1Z5 (604)224-1750. Crescent Entertainment Ltd., 2 - 1163 Commercial Dr., Vancouver, BC V5L 3X3 (604)255-6488.
Type of Production and Credits: Th Film-Prod/PM; TV Film-Prod/PM.
Genres: Drama-Th&TV; Comedy-Th&TV; Action-Th&TV.
Biography: Born in 1951 in New Westminster, British Columbia. Attended University of British Columbia and BCIT. 18 years experience as a producer; production manager; assistant director; locations manager on features, MOWs and many series. Now partner in Crescent Entertainment.
Selected Filmography: *Knight Moves*, Th, 91, D/USA, Line Prod; "Kurt Vonnegut's Monkey House" (3 eps), TV, 90, CDN, Prod/PM; *Kootenai Brown*, Th, 90, CDN, Assoc Prod/PM; "Danger Bay" (44 eps), TV, 88-89, CDN, Assoc Prod/PM; *Penthouse*, TV, 89, USA, PM; *Neverending Story, I & II*, Th, 88, D, PM; "The Beachcombers" (22 eps), TV, 87, CDN, Prod.

MARKIW, Gabriel
652 Spruce St., Winnipeg, MB R3G 2Z1 (204)783-5182. O'Meara Productions, 63 Albert St., Suite 200, Winnipeg, MB R3B 1G4 (204)943-3133.
Type of Production and Credits: Th Film-Dir/Prod; TV Film-Dir/Prod; TV Video-Prod/Wr.
Genres: Drama-Th&TV; Comedy-Th; Documentary-TV; Educational-TV.
Biography: Born 1952, Italy; Canadian citizenship. Languages: English and Italian. Bachelor of Arts, University of Manitoba; attended University of Munich; Red River Community College; Winnipeg Ballet School. Best Television Film award at International Film Festival of Popular Traditions, Italy, for *Not a Bad Year*. *Mob Story* was nominated at American Film Institute Comedy Festival.
Selected Filmography: *Mob Story*, Th, 89, CDN, Co-Wr/Dir/Prod; *Not a Bad Year*, TV, 87, CDN, Co-Dir/Co-Prod; *A Rising Image*, TV, 85, CDN, Co-Prod/Co-Wr; *Concertante: Arnold Spohr and the Royal Winnipeg Ballet*, TV, 84, CDN, Co-Dir/Co-Prod; *Carlo*, TV, 84, CDN, Co-Prod/Co-Wr; "Players" (8 eps), TV, 81, CDN, Wr; "Live Weekend" (13 eps), TV, 80, CDN, Dir.

MARKIW, Jancarlo
- see DIRECTORS

MARKS, Julian
21 Elmsthorpe Ave., Toronto, ON M5P 2L5 (416)322-3482. Power Pictures Corp., 629 Eastern Ave., Toronto, ON M4M 1E4 (416)778-8766.
Type of Production and Credits: TV Film-Prod; TV Video-Prod.
Genres: Drama-Th&TV; Comedy-Th&TV; Action-Th&TV.
Biography: Born Montreal, Quebec. Languages: English and French. B.A., McGill University; M.A., Concordia University.
Selected Filmography: *Drop Dead Gorgeous*, TV, 91, CDN, Prod; "Counterstrike" (22 eps), TV, 90, CDN, Prod; "Mount Royal" (18 eps), TV, 88, CDN/F, Prod; *Return of Ben Casey*, TV, 87, CDN, Prod; "Mariah" (7 eps), TV, 87, USA, Prod; *Doing Life*, TV, 86, CDN, Prod; *The Execution of Raymond Graham*, TV, 85, CDN, Prod; *Separate Vacations*, Th, 85, CDN, Assoc Prod; *Joshua Then and Now*, Th, 84, CDN, Assoc Prod; *Les Carcasses*, TV, 83, CDN, Prod.

MARKSON, Morley
- see DIRECTORS

MARSHALL, William
ACCT. The Marshall Plan Television Inc., 260 Richmond St. E., Suite 2000, Toronto, ON M5A 1P4 (416)368-7300.
Type of Production and Credits: Th Film-Prod.
Genres: Drama-Th; Comedy-Th; Action-Th; Horror-Th.
Biography: Born 1939, Scotland; Canadian citizenship. Has been executive assistant to mayors of Toronto. Co-founder Festival of Festivals.
Selected Filmography: *You Gotta Come Back a Star*, Th, 86, CDN, Co-Prod; *The War Boy*, Th, 84, CDN, Prod; *Mr. Patman*, Th, 80, CDN, Co-Prod; *Hank Williams: "The Show He Never Gave"*, Th, 80, CDN, Co-Prod; *Circle of Two*, Th, 79, CDN, Exec Prod; *Wild Horse Hank*, Th, 78, CDN, Co-Prod; *Outrageous!*, Th, 77, CDN, Co-Prod; *Flick*, Th, 70, CDN, Prod.

MARSHALL, Heather A.
ACCT, TWIFT. Marshall Business Affairs Inc., 439 Montrose Ave., Toronto, ON M6G 3H2 (416)464-4162. FAX: 537-7660.
Type of Production and Credits: TV Film-Exec Prod/Prod.
Genres: Drama-Th&TV; Action-TV; Documentary-Th&TV; Educational-TV.
Biography: Born in 1952 in London, Ontario. Grew up in Windsor, Ontario. Hons B.F.A., (1973) and M.B.A. (1980), York University. After many years in commercial lending, returned to the film and television industry. In 1985, joined Sunrise Films as VP, Finance and Business Affairs; worked on "Danger Bay", *K.Y.T.E.S.* and *Travelling Light*. In 1987 incorporated Marshall Business Affairs Inc., providing freelance business affairs, production and executive production expertise to the film and television industry. *Half The Kingdon* was nominated for a Gemini for Best Documentary and won a Red Ribbon at the Amercian Film and Video Festival, 1991. Executive in Charge of Business Affairs for "Inside Stories", series 1, which won a Gemini for Best Short Drama and the Multi-culturalism Gemini, as well as an award at Yorkton.
Selected Filmography: *Shared Rhythm/Rythme du Monde*, TV, 90, CDN, Exec Prod; *Half The Kingdom*, TV, 89, CDN, Exec Prod/Prod; "Inside Stories", TV, 88, CDN, Exec Bus Affairs; *Hoover vs. the Kennedys: The Second Civil War*, TV, 88, CDN, Bus Affairs.

MARTIN, Marcia
ACFTP, ACCT. 240 Evelyn Ave., Toronto, ON M6P 2Z9 Citytv, 299 Queen St. W., Toronto, ON M5V 2Z5 (416)591-5757.
Type of Production and Credits: TV Video-Prod/Spv Prod.
Genres: Drama-TV; Commercials-TV; Variety-TV
Biography: Born Portland, Maine; Canadian citizenship. Sociology, American University, Washington, D.C. Director of General/Independent Production, Citytv; Chairperson of Gemini Awards committee, 88/89; board member, ACCT. *I Am A Hotel* won Golden Rose, Montreux, International Film & TV Festival, NY, Golden Gate.
Selected Filmography: "Fashion Television" (234 eps), TV, 85-91, CDN, Spv Prod; "Movie Television" (117 eps), TV, 88-91, CDN, Spv Prod; "Originals" (52 eps), TV, 90-91, CDN, Spv Prod; *I Am A Hotel*, TV, 84, CDN, Spv Prod; *Neighbours/Streetwise/Golden Promise*, "Toronto Trilogy", TV, 84, CDN, Prod; *1988 Gemini Awards*, TV, 88, CDN, Co-Exec Prod; "Titans" (13 eps), TV, 81, CDN, PM.

MARTINELLI, Gabriella
DGC, ACCT, CPA. 940 Lansdowne Ave., Bldg. 29, Toronto, ON M6H 4G9 (416)656-7273. #101 - 1525 Bellevue

Ave., West Vancouver, BC V7V 1A6 (604)922-0718.
Type of Production and Credits: Th Film-Prod.
Genres: Drama-Th; Documentary-Th.
Biography: Born in Italy; Canadian citizenship. Studied Art, Art History, Carleton University. Producer, production manager on TV commercials before entering feature film industry, 84; Supervised production and post for Toronto based Independent Pictures Inc. as well as co-producing 70mm Showscan docudrama for B.C. Pavilion at Expo 86. Line Producer/Producer from 88-90 for L.A. based Morgan Creek Productions filming in Toronto, Philadelphia, England and Los Angeles. Co-Producer of David's Cronenberg's *Naked Lunch*, a Canadian/British co-production with Jeremy Thomas, producer of *The Last Emperor*.
Selected Filmography: *Naked Lunch*, Th, 90-91, CDN/GB, Co-Prod; *Nightbreed*, Th, 89-90, USA, Prod; *Renegades*, Th, 88, USA, Line Prod/PM; *Dead Ringers*, Th, 88, CDN, PM/P Pro Spv; *Milk and Honey*, Th, 87, CDN, Line Prod/P Pro Spv; *John and the Missus*, Th, 86, CDN, Assoc Prod/PM; *Discovery* (Expo 86), Th, 85-86, CDN, Co-Prod/PM; *Western Canada Lottery Christmas*, TV, 84, CDN, PM; *My American Cousin*, Th, 84, CDN, Pro Coord; *Walls*, Th, 84, CDN, Pro Coord.

MATHUR, Vishnu
ATPD, IATSE, ACTT. Priya Films, 140 Brunswick Ave., Toronto, ON M5S 2M2 (416)969-9048.
Type of Production and Credits: Th Short-Prod/Dir/DOP; TV Film-Prod/Dir/DOP.
Genres: Drama-TV; Documentary-TV; Educational-TV; Current Affairs-TV.
Biography: Born 1934, Bombay, India; Canadian citizenship. Attended University in New Delhi. Twenty-five years experience in filmmaking; started as cameraman, BBC; joined UN Special Fund as director/cameraman; has worked freelance for major TV networks in Europe and North America. *The Knowing Nose* won a Gemini Award; *Return to the Land* won Bronze Ear, Berlin.
Selected Filmography: *Bugman of Ithaca*, "The Nature of Things", TV, 90-91, CDN, Prod/Dir; *Return to Land*, "The Nature of Things", TV, 90-91, CDN, Prod/Dir; *The Knowing Nose*, "The Nature of Things", TV, 88-89, CDN, Prod/Dir; *Pains of Performance*, ED, 88, CDN, Prod/Dir/DOP; *The Red Bindi*, TV, 87, CDN/IND, Prod; "The Nature of Things" (1 eps), TV, 87, CDN, Prod/Dir/DOP.

McANDREW, Jack
- see WRITERS

McCURDY, Mark
- see DIRECTORS

McDOUGALL, Ian
CFTA, DGC, ACCT. Ventura Pictures Inc., 185 Grace St., Toronto, ON M5G 3A7 (416)537-2641.
Type of Production and Credits: Th Film-Prod; TV Film-Prod.
Genres: Drama-Th&TV.
Biography: Born 1945, Toronto, Ontario. President, Abaton Pictures. Worked in theatre in England (67-70) before returning to Canada. *Anne of Green Gables* won Golden Gate Award (San Francisco), Emily Award (American Film Festival), 10 Geminis, and Emmy for Outstanding Children's Performance, 86. CFTA Chairman, 88-90.
Selected Filmography: *Clearcut*, Th, 91, CDN, Prod; *Passion & Paradise* (mini-series), TV, 89, CDN/GB/USA, Prod; "Captain Power" (22 eps), TV, 87, CDN, Prod; *Fight for Life*, TV, 87, USA, Prod; *Anne of Green Gables* (mini-series), TV, 85, CDN, Co-Prod, (EMMY/GEMINI 86); "The Edison Twins" (26 eps), TV, 83-84, CDN, Prod.

McEWAN, Duncan
ATPD. 23 Moore Ave., Toronto, ON M4T 1V4 (416)489-3258. CBC, Box 500, Stn. A, Toronto, ON M5W 1E6 (416)975-7501.
Type of Production and Credits: TV Film-Prod/Dir; TV Video-Prod/Dir.
Genres: Documentary-TV.
Biography: Born 1953, England. B.Sc., University of Toronto, 73. Artistic director, producer, lighting designer, theatre, 74-78. Joined CBC, 76; Executive Producer, CBC, 80-82; Manager of Programming and Development, The Star Channel (pay TV), 82-84; Executive Producer, CBC, 84-91.
Selected Filmography: "Venture" (weekly), TV, 85-91, CDN, Exec Prod, (GEMINI 88); "The Medicine Show" (19 eps), TV, 78-82, CDN, Exec Prod; *Cook County Hospital*, "the fifth estate", TV, 80, CDN, Prod/Dir; "Take-30" (sev items), TV, 76-78, CDN, Prod/Dir.

McEWAN, Maryke
ATPD. 112 Willow Ave., Toronto, ON M4E 3K3 (416)699-1517.
Type of Production and Credits: TV Film-Prod.
Genres: Drama-TV.
Biography: Born 1948, Oshawa, Ontario.

B.A., English, University of Toronto. *Ready for Slaughter,* Best TV Drama, Banff. Producer, *Diary of a Street Kid,* scheduled to begin shooting in fall 91.
Selected Filmography: "Street Legal" (39 eps), TV, 86-88, CDN, Exec Prod; *Shellgame,* TV, 85, CDN, Prod; *Tools of the Devil,* TV, 84, CDN, Prod; *Rough Justice/Ready for Slaughter/Blind Faith,* "For the Record", TV, 83, CDN, Prod; *Kate Morris, Vice President,* "For the Record", TV, 83, CDN, Co-Prod.

McEWEN, Mary Anne
- see WRITERS

McGAW, Jack
CFTA, ACCT. Documentary Productions Ltd., 66 Rowanwood Ave., Toronto, ON M4W 1Y9 (416)924-2020. MC Productions Inc., (416)924-2020.
Type of Production and Credits: TV Film-Prod; TV Video-Prod.
Genres: Action-TV; Documentary-TV; Education-TV; Children's-TV.
Biography: Born 1936. Winner of more than 30 film and TV awards world-wide, including Gold, Silver and Bronze Medals, International Film and TV Festival (NY) for "Live It Up"; *Children's Hospital* was nominated for an Emmy and won a Bronze Medal at the NY Festival. *The Ticker Test* won at Yorkton and was nominated for 2 Geminis. Currently Chairman, MC Productions Inc.
Selected Filmography: *The National Environment Test and Telepoll,* TV, 91, CDN, Prod; *The Bicycle Test,* TV, 89, CDN, Prod; "Live It Up" (250 eps), TV, 78-88, CDN, Prod, (GEMINI 88); *The National Drug Test,* TV, 88, CDN, Exec Prod/Wr/Host; *The Ticker Test,* TV, 87, CDN, Exec Prod/Prod; *The Body Test,* TV, 87, CDN, Prod; *The Red Deer Challenge,* TV, 84, CDN, Prod/Host; *The First National Attitude Test on Drinking Drivers,* TV, 83, CDN, Prod/Host; *The National Safety Drill,* TV, 82, CDN, Prod/Dir; *Yesterday's Children,* "Inquiry", TV, 78, CDN, Prod/Host, (CFTA); *The Failing Strategy/Hear No Evil, See No Evil, Speak No Evil,* "Inquiry", TV, 73-77, CDN, Prod/Host; *Children's Hospital,* "W5", TV, 76, CDN, Prod/Host; *Keep Out of the Reach of Adults,* "Inquiry", TV, 73, CDN, Prod/Host; *Give Us This Day Our Daily Bread/To Your Healt,* "Inquiry", TV, 73, CDN, Prod/Host; "W5" (46 eps), TV, 71-72, CDN, Prod/Host.

McGILLIVRAY, Derek
ACCT. Ironstar Communications Inc., 65 Heward Ave., Ste. 202, Toronto, ON M4M 2T5 (416)466-2522.
Type of Production and Credits: TV Film-Prod; TV Video-Prod.
Genres: Drama-TV; Comedy-TV.
Biography: Born in Vancouver, British Columbia. English and French. M.A. (Canadian Studies). Has been active in the television industry since 1972. He began in production at TVOntario and went on to become the marketing manager for Nielsen Ferns International until he formed his own company, Ironstar Communications Inc., in 1981. Member of the Broadcast Executives Society and the Canadian Film and Television Association. Ironstar is a television programme distribution company that has branched out into producing.
Selected Filmography: "No Place Like Home" (6 eps), TV, 91, CDN, Exec Prod; *Brothers By Choice,* TV, 86, CDN, Exec Prod.

McGREEVY, John
ACTRA, CFTA, DGC, ACCT. 36 Roxborough St. E., Toronto, ON M4W 1V6 (416)922-8625.
Type of Production and Credits: TV Film-Dir/Prod/Wr; TV Video-Dir/Prod.
Genres: Drama-TV; Documentary-TV.
Biography: Has won several television awards including 2 Gold Medals, New York International Film Festival, for *Cities*; Emmy nomination for *Hope Abandoned.* "Peter Ustinov's Russia" won CFTA Award for Outstanding Television Documentary, 87.
Selected Filmography: "Return Journey" (8 eps)(dir 5 eps), TV, 87-88, CDN/NZ/GB, Sr Prod/Exec Prod/Dir; *Secret of the Phantom of the Opera,* TV, 88, CDN/USA, Dir; *Pen '86,* TV, 86, CDN, Prod/Dir; *Beijing to Tibet/Tibet to Hong Kong,* "Peter Ustinov's Russia", TV, 86, CDN, Dir/Prod; "Peter Ustinov's Russia" (6 eps), TV, 85, CDN, Prod/Co-Exec Prod/Dir/Wr; *Quebec/Canada 1995,* TV, 84, CDN, Dir/Co-Prod; *American Caesar,* TV, 84, CDN, Dir/Prod; "Quintet: Vision of Five" (1 seg), TV, 84, CDN, Dir/Prod; "Cities" (13 parts), TV, 76-79, CDN, Dir/Co-Prod/Wr; *Beaverbrook-The Life and Times of Max Aitken,* TV, 76, CDN, Dir/Wr/Prod, (ACTRA); "People of Our Time" (18 eps), TV, 74-75, CDN, Dir/Prod; *Mendelstam's Witness,* TV, 75, CDN, Prod; *Hope Against Hope,* TV, 75, CDN, Prod; *Hope Abandoned,* TV, 75, CDN, Prod; *Three Women on Human Values,* "Man Alive", TV, 73, CDN, Dir/Prod/Wr.

McKEOWN, Bob
ACTRA, ACCT. 23 W. 69th St., Apt. A,

New York, NY 10023
Type of Production and Credits: TV Film-Prod/Dir/Wr; TV Video-Prod/Dir/Wr.
Genres: Documentary-TV; Educational-TV; Commercials-TV.
Biography: Born 1950, Ottawa, Ontario. B.A., Yale University, 71. Member of Ottawa Rough Riders, Canadian Football League, 71-76; journalist and filmmaker since 76; correspondent, CBS News, 90 to present.
Selected Filmography: *Hockey Night in Hollywood*, TV, 91, USA, Exec Prod/Dir; *Pas de Deux with Paul and Isabelle Duchesnay*, TV, 90, USA, Prod/Dir; "the fifth estate" (30 seg/year), TV, 81-88, CDN, Wr/Host; *Strangers in a Strange Land*, Th, 87, CDN, Prod; *The Boys on the Bus:A Teammate's View of the Edmonton Oilers*, TV, 86, CDN, Prod/Dir/Wr, (2 GEMINIS 88); *Les Canadiens*, TV, 85, CDN, Prod/Dir/Wr; Roots Algonquin, Cm, 85, CDN, Prod/Dir/Wr; Roots Athletics, Cm, 85, CDN, Prod/Dir; *Cleared for Take-Off/The U.N. and Civil Aviation*, ED, 84, CDN, Prod/Dir/Wr.

McKEOWN, Brian
DGC, WGC, CFTPA. Howe Sound Films Inc., 3539 West Third Ave., Vancouver, BC V6R 1L8 (604)731-2577. FAX: 731-9393.
Type of Production and Credits: TV Film-Exec Prod/Prod/Dir/Wr; TV Video-Prod/Dir/Wr.
Genres: Drama-TV; Comedy-TV; Variety-TV; Musical-TV; Educational-TV; Children's-Th&TV; Current Affairs-TV; News-TV.
Biography: Born 1944. "Drama Producer of the Year," TV Weekly Awards, 88 for "The Beachcombers."
Selected Filmography: "The Beachcombers" (65 eps), TV, 86-90, CDN, Exec Prod; "The Beachcombers" (40 eps), TV, 85-86, CDN, Prod; "Magee & Company" (150 eps), TV, 75-78, CDN, Dir; "The French Show" (8 eps), TV, 77, CDN, Dir; "Les aventures de Dorpp" (20 eps), TV, 71-72, CDN, Prod/Dir; "Child Life in Canada" (8 eps), TV, 70, CDN, Prod/Dir.

McKNIGHT, Bruce E.
5915 Gibbings Bay, Regina, SK S4X 4B3 (306)569-6412. CKCK-TV, Creative Serives, Hwy #1, East Regina, SK S4P 3E5 (306)569-2000.
Type of Production and Credits: TV Video-Prod.
Genres: Children's-TV; Current Affairs-TV; Sports-TV.
Biography: Born 1958, Regina Saskatchewan. Employed by CKCK-TV for the past 11 years, the last 4 as Creative Director, working on various film and video commercials and corporate videos.
Selected Filmography: *Straight Talk*, ED, 91, CDN, Prod; "Puttnam's Prairie Emporium" (26 eps), TV, 87-88, CDN, Tech Dir; *Master Effective Manners*, ED, 87, CDN, Prod/Dir; "Rankin File" (26 eps), TV, 86, CDN, Field Dir; "Government of Saskatchewan Educational Series" , ED, 86. CDN, Prod/Dir; "Hot Rock Video" (52 eps), TV, 84-85, CDN, Prod/Dir; "Video Country Style" (100 eps), TV, 85, CDN, Prod/Dir; *Babe*, Jack Green, MV, 84, CDN, Prod/Dir.

McLAREN, Ian
APFTQ, CFTA. 542 Lansdowne Ave., Westmount, PQ H3Y 2V2 (514)937-9955. Productions Grand Nord Québec Inc., 1600 ave de Lorimier, Ste. 121, Montréal, PQ H2K 3W5 (514)521-7433.
Type of Production and Credits: Th Film-Prod; TV Film-Prod/Dir; TV Video-Prod/Dir.
Genres: Drama-Th&TV; Comedy-TV; Documentary-Th&TV; Current Affairs-TV.
Biography: Born in 1943 in England; grew up in Canada. After working as a journalist in Paris, became public affairs producer, first in Toronto, and then for the CBC in Montreal. Joined the National Film Board as Producer of award-winning CBC TV series "Adieu Alouette", 1972; Director of English Production, 1977. From 1980 to 1984, worked at the Ministry of Com-munications in Ottawa, and developed the Government's National Film and Video Policy. Joined Telefilm Canada as Head of Distribution, 1984; later responsible for Strategic Planning. Has headed own independent production company, Productions Grand Nord, since 1987; company produces features and TV programming in both French and English.
Selected Filmography: *The Dance Goes On*, Th, 91, CDN, Exec Prod; *Here Comes the Groom*, "Inside Stories", TV, 90, CDN, Prod; *Life After Hockey*, TV, 89, CDN, Assoc Prod; *The Hecklers*, TV, 76, CDN, Prod/Dir; *Whistling Smith*, TV, 75, CDN, Exec Prod; "Adieu Alouette" (12 eps), TV, 73, CDN, Prod; *Une Job Steady - Un Bon Boss*, "Adieu Alouette", TV, 73, CDN, Prod/Dir; *The Ungrateful Land*, "Adieu Alouette", TV, 73, CDN, Prod; *Crisis - October Plus One*, TV, 72, CDN, Prod/Dir; *Separatism - A Decade in Perspective*, TV, 70, CDN, Prod/Dir.

McLEAN, Seaton
ACCT. Atlantis Films Ltd., 65 Heward Ave., Toronto, ON M4M 2T5 (416)462-0246.
Type of Production and Credits: TV Film-Prod.
Genres: Drama-TV; Documentary-TV; Children's-TV.
Biography: Born 1955, Clearwater, Florida; Canadian and US citizenship. Studied journalism, Carleton University; B.A., Film Studies, Queen's University. Producer, co-owner, Atlantis Films Ltd.; the company's productions have won many international awards. *The Painted Door*, "Bell Canada Playhouse," won CFTA; *Boys and Girls*, "Sons and Daughters," won CFTA and Oscar; *Lost in the Barrens*, "Magic Hour," won a Daytime Emmy, 91.
Selected Filmography: "Maniac Mansion" (44 eps), TV, 90-91, CDN/USA, Spv Prod; *Journey Into Darkness: The Bruce Curtis Story*, TV, 90, CDN, Co-Prod; *Clarence*, TV, 90, CDN/NZ, Spv Prod; "Magic Hour" (8 eps)(Co-Prod 1 eps), TV, 89-90, CDN, Spv Prod; *Destiny to Order*, Th, 88, CDN, Co-Prod; "Glory! Glory!" (2 eps), TV, 88, CDN/USA, Prod; "The Twilight Zone" (30 eps), TV, 88, CDN/USA, Prod; "Ray Bradbury Theatre" (18 eps), TV, 85-88, CDN/USA/ F/GB, Prod, (GEMINI 86); *A Child's Christmas in Wales*, TV, 87, CDN/USA/ GB, Prod, (GEMINI 88); "Really Weird Tales" (3 eps), TV, 86, CDN/USA, Prod (CFTA); "Bell Canada Playhouse" (25 eps), TV, 84-85, CDN, Co-Prod; "Brothers by Choice" (6 eps), TV, 85, CDN, Co-Prod/Ed, (CFTA/OSCAR); "Airwaves" (1 eps), TV, 85, CDN, Dir; "Sons and Daughters" (11 eps), TV, 82-83, CDN, Co-Prod (BIJOU/CFTA); *The Olden Days Coat*, TV, 81, CDN, Co-Prod/Ed, (BIJOU/CFTA).

McLEOD, Ian ✧
ACCT. 10 Balsam Ave., Toronto, ON (416)694-2737.
Type of Production and Credits: TV Film-Prod/Wr; TV Video-Prod/Wr.
Genres: Documentary-Th&TV; Educational-Th&TV; Industrial-Th&TV; Current Affairs-Th&TV.
Selected Filmography: *The National Drug Test*, TV, 88, CDN, Prod/Co-Wr; "The Canadians" (2 eps), TV, 87, CDN, Prod/Exec Prod; The New North, TV, 87, CDN, Prod; "The American Century" (6 eps), TV, 86, CDN, Prod; "Women of the World" (7 eps), TV, 86, CDN, Prod; "Going Great" (52 eps), TV, 81-84, CDN, Prod; "American Caesar" (5 eps), TV, 83, CDN, Prod; *Greatest Journey*, TV, 81, CDN, Prod; "Vietnam: The Ten Thousand Day War" (26 eps), TV, 80, CDN, Prod.

McMANUS, Mike
ACTRA. 58 Eleanora Circle, Richmond Hill, ON L4C 6K7 (416)881-0408. TVOntario, 2180 Yonge St., Toronto, ON M4S 2B9 (416)484-2600. The Characters, 150 Carlton St., Toronto, ON M5A 2K1 (416)964-8522.
Type of Production and Credits: TV Video-Prod.
Genres: Documentary-TV; Educational-TV.
Biography: Born 1935, Montreal, Quebec. Languages: English, French and Italian. Education: B.A., M.Sc. "Energy, Search for an Answer" was a winner at the New York International Film and TV Festival.
Selected Filmography: "Telefest 91" (5 eps), TV, 91, CDN, Wr/Prod; *With or Without Quebec: The Future of Ontario*, TV, 91, CDN, Wr/Prod; "Ontario Lottery Live" (52 eps), TV, 90-91, CDN, Prod; "Beyond Stress" (6 eps), TV, 87-88, CDN, Exec Prod; "The Successful Landlord" (5 eps), TV, 88, CDN, Exec Prod; "Artificial Intelligence" (4 eps), TV, 86-87, CDN, Exec Prod; "Women and Politics" (6 eps), TV, 86-87, CDN, Exec Prod; "Fitness Over 40" (7 eps), TV, 85-86, CDN, Exec Prod; "Frontrunners" (9 eps), TV, 85, CDN, Exec Prod; "Automating the Office" (9 eps), TV, 84, CDN, Exec Prod; "Energy - Search for an Answer" (9 eps), TV, 84, CDN, Exec Prod; "Futurework" (9 eps), TV, 84, CDN, Prod; "Bits and Bytes" (12 eps), TV, 81-83, CDN, Exec Prod; "The Academy on Computers" (12 eps), TV, 83, CDN, Prod; "The Academy on Moral Philosophy" (7 eps), TV, 82, CDN, Prod.

MEDINA, Ann
ACCT, ACTRA, ATPD. Medina Productions Inc., 112 Alcina Ave., Toronto, ON M6G 2E8 (416)656-8850 EXT: 8549.
Type of Production and Credits: Th Film-Prod; TV Video-Prod.
Genres: Documentary-TV; Current Affairs-TV; News-TV; Drama-Th&TV.
Biography: Born 1943, New York, New York. Herschel Fellow, M.A., Philosophy, University of Chicago; studied Philosophy at Harvard, University of Edinburgh. Taught Philosophy, University of Illinois; Producer, NBC Network; Network Correspondent, ABC News; Network

Documentary Producer, ABC News; Reporter, CBC, "Newsmagazine", Executive Producer, CBC "Newsmagazine"; CBC Beirut Bureau Chief, News and "The Journal"; Senior Foreign Journalist, "The Journal"; Anchor, CBC News; resident (producer), Canadian Centre for Advanced Film Studies, 88; National Vice-Chairman ACCT, 88-89; senior resident, CCAFS, 89. Winner of several awards, including Ohio State University, San Francisco State, Chicago, Yorkton.
Selected Filmography: *Bhopal*, "The Journal", TV, 85, CDN, Prod/Report; *Inflation*, "Close-Up", TV, 74, USA, Prod/Dir/Wr; *Trapped*, TV, 74, USA, Prod/Wr/Report; *Women in Prison*, "Close-Up", TV, 73, USA, Wr/Report/Co-Prod; "Housing Crisis" (5 eps), TV, 72, USA, Prod/Wr/Report, (2 EMMYS).

MEDJUCK, Joe
Warner Brothers, 4000 Warner Blvd., Producers Bldg. #7, Rm. 8, Burbank, CA 91522 USA. (818)954-1771.
Type of Production and Credits: Th Film-Prod; TV Film-Prod.
Genres: Comedy-Th; Children's-TV.
Biography: Born 1943, Fredericton, New Brunswick. McGill University; Ph.D., University of Toronto.
Selected Filmography: *Kindergarten Cop*, Th, 90, USA, Exec Prod; *Ghostbusters II*, Th, 89, USA, Exec Prod; *Twins*, Th, 88, USA, Exec Prod; "The Slimer Show", TV, 88, USA, Exec Prod; *Big Shots*, Th, 87, USA, Prod; *Legal Eagles*, Th, 86, USA, Exec Prod; "The Real Ghostbusters" (78 eps), TV, 85, USA, Exec Prod; *Ghostbusters*, Th, 84, USA, Assoc Prod; *Stripes*, Th, 81, USA, Assoc Prod; *Heavy Metal*, Th, 81, CDN, Pro Coord.

MELCHIOR, Klaus
IATSE 667, DGC. Molokai Productions Inc., 1260 Hornby St., Suite 3, Vancouver, BC V6Z 1W2 (604)681-2324. FAX: 681-2312.
Type of Production and Credits: Th Film-Unit PM; TV Video-Prod/Dir.
Genres: Drama-Th&TV; Action-Th&TV; Documentary-TV; Commercials-TV; Industrial-TV.
Biography: Born 1956, Lienz, Austria; Canadian citizenship. Languages: English and German. Specializes in motion picture video coordinations.
Selected Filmography: *Knight Moves*, Th, 91, D/F/USA, 24 FPS Video Playback (Vid PB); *Bingo*, Th, 90, USA, Vid Assist/24 FPS Vid PB; *Look Who's Talking, Part 2*, Th, 90, USA, Video Assist/24 FPS Vid PB; *Bird on a Wire*, Th, 89, USA, Video Assist/24 FPS Vid PB; *The Fly, Part II*, Th, 88, USA Video Assist/24 FPS Vid PB; *The Accused*, Th, 87, USA, Vid Assist; *Stakeout*, Th, 87, USA, Vid Assist; *Roxanne*, Th, 86, USA, Vid Assist; "Wiseguy" (50 eps), TV, 88-90, USA, 24 FPS/Vid PB; "Booker" (24 eps), TV, 89-90, USA, 24 FPS Vid PB; "UN Sub" (sev eps), TV, 89-91, USA, 24 FPS/Vid PB; "Top of the Hill" (sev eps), TV, 89-91, USA, 24 FPS Vid PB; *Betrayed*, Th, 87, USA, 24 FPS Vid PB; *The Experts*, Th, 87, USA, 24 FPS Vid PB.

MELLANBY, Ralph
ACCT, ATAS. 44 Charles St. W., Toronto, ON M4Y 1R7 (416)969-8552. Ralph Mellanby and Associates, 42 Charles St. E., Toronto, ON M4Y 1T5 (416)968-6050.
Type of Production and Credits: Th Film-Prod/Dir/Wr; TV Film-Prod/Dir/Wr; TV Video-Prod/Dir/Wr.
Genres: Drama-TV; Comedy:TV; Documentary-TV; Educational-Th; News-Th&TV; Sports-Th&TV.
Biography: Born 1936, Hamilton, Ontario. B.A., Communications, Wayne State University, Detroit; Doctor of Law, University of Windsor. Former Executive Producer, "Hockey Night in Canada" (17 years); Executive Producer (Host Broadcaster), 1988 Olympics, Calgary. 15 Emmy nominations, winner of 4 for sports directing/producing. Other awards include the Kennedy Award and the Ohio State Award. Productions include The Goalie, Gretzky's Classic Matchups, The Olympic River and the National Performing Arts Awards.

MENARD, Robert
- voir REALISATEURS

MENDELUK, George
- see DIRECTORS

MERCEL, Edward L. ✧
(416)489-1217.
Type of Production and Credits: TV Video-Prod/Dir.
Genres: Variety-TV; Children's-TV; News-TV; Sports-TV.
Biography: Born 1939, Toronto, Ontario. Studied Radio and TV, Ryerson Polytechnical Institute. Has produced and directed childen's shows, variety, sports; Executive Producer, 88 Olympics, CTV.
Selected Filmography: "1988 Winter Olympics" (120 eps), TV, 88, CDN, Exec Prod; *Variety Club Telethon* (annually), TV, 81-88, CDN, Exec Prod; "The Hobby Garden" (26 eps), TV, 84-88, CDN, Prod/Dir; "The Fitness People"

(130 eps), TV, 88, CDN, Prod/Dir; *OHL Game of the Week*, TV, 81-88, CDN, Prod/Dir; *Molson Indy* (annually), TV, 86-88, CDN, Exec Prod; *Canada Cup Hockey Tournament* (annually), TV, 76-86, CDN, Dir; *Blue Jays Baseball*, TV, 84-86, CDN, Dir; "CFL Games", TV, 71-85, CDN, Dir; *1984 Winter Olympics*, TV, 84, CDN, Prod/Dir; *Grand Prix du Canada*, TV, 79-82, CDN, Prod; *1976 Summer and Winter Olympics*, TV, 84, CDN, Prod/Dir; "Catherine McKinnon Show" (26 eps), TV, 69, CDN, Prod/Dir; "River Inn" (5 eps)(Catherine McKinnon), TV, 68, CDN, Dir.

MESSIER, H. Monique
APFVQ. 6770, 9e av. Rosemont, Montréal, PQ H1Y 2K9 (514)721-2339. Cité Amérique Inc, 5800, boul. St-Laurent, Montréal, PQ H2T 1T2 (514)278-8080.
Types de production et générique: l métrage-Prod/Sc; TV film-Prod/Sc.
Types d'oeuvres: Drame-C&TV; Action-C&TV.
Curriculum vitae: Née en 1946, Montréal, Québec. Langues: français et anglais. Consultante production et scénarisation.
Filmographie sélective: "Les Filles de Caleb" (20 eps), TV, 89-90, CDN, Prod; *Dans le ventre du dragon*, C, 88, CDN, Prod; "Rock" (5 eps), TV, 87, CDN, Sc; *Exit*, C, 85, CDN, Prod/Sc; "Amour de quartier" (13 eps), TV, 83, CDN, Prod; *Rien qu'un jeu*, C, 82, CDN, Prod/Sc; *Futur Intérieur*, TV, 81, CDN, Prod.

METTLER, Peter
- see DIRECTORS

MICAY, Jack
- see DIRECTORS

MICHAELS, Joel B.
ACTRA, AFTRA, SAG, ACCT. Lantana, 3000 Olympic Blvd., Suite 1300, Santa Monica, CA 90404 USA.
Type of Production and Credits: Th Film-Prod; TV Film-Prod.
Genres: Drama-Th&TV; Comedy-Th.
Biography: Born 1938, Buffalo, New York; American citizen; landed immigrant, Canada. President, Cineplex Odeon Films, 86-90; production/distribution slate during his tenure included the *The Glass Menagerie*(87), *Madame Sousatzka* (88), *Talk Radio* (88), *Prancer* (89), *Mr. and Mrs. Bridge* (90), and *The Grifters* (90). Producer, *Universal Soldier* (in development).
Selected Filmography: *Courage*, TV, 86, USA, Prod; *Harem* (mini-series), TV, 86, USA, Prod; *Black Moon Rising*, Th, 85, USA, Co-Prod; *The Philadelphia Experiment*, Th, 84, USA, Co-Prod; *Losin' It*, Th, 82, USA, Exec Prod; *The Amateur*, Th, 81, CDN, Co-Prod; *Tribute*, Th, 80, CDN, Co-Prod; *The Changeling*, Th, 79, CDN, Co-Prod, (GENIE); *The Silent Partner*, Th, 77, CDN, Co-Prod, (CFA); *Bittersweet Love*, Th, 76, USA, Co-Prod.

MICHAELS, Lorne
WGAe. Broadway Video, 1619 Broadway, New York, NY 10019 USA. (212)265-7621. Sandy Wernick, The Brillstein Co., 9200 Sunset Blvd., Los Angeles, CA USA. (213)276-6135.
Type of Production and Credits: Th Film-Prod/Wr; TV Video-Prod/Wr.
Genres: Comedy-Th&TV; Variety-TV; Musical-TV.
Biography: Born Toronto, Ontario. Writer/producer, comedy specials, drama, CBC TV, Toronto, 69-72.
Selected Filmography: "Saturday Night Live", TV, 85-91, USA, Exec Prod, (4 EMMYS); "Kids in the Hall", TV, 89-91, CDN/USA, Exec Prod; *Rolling Stones: Steel Wheels Concert*, TV, 90, USA, Exec Prod; *Rolling Stones Pay-Per-View Concert*, TV, 90, USA, Exec Prod; "Night Music", TV, 88-90, USA, Exec Prod; *Gilda Radner Live From New York*, TV, USA, Exec Prod; *Gilda Live*, Th, USA, Exec Prod; *Rolling Stone Magazine's 20 Years of Rock 'n' Roll*, TV, 88, USA, Exec Prod; *1988 Emmy Awards*, TV, 88, USA, Exec Prod; *Three Amigos*, Th, 86, USA, Prod/Wr; *Steve Martin's Best Show Ever*, TV, 81, USA, Prod; *Simon and Garfunkel's Concert in the Park*, TV, 81, USA, Exec Prod; *The Ruttles - All You Need Is Cash*, TV, 78, USA, Prod/Wr; *The Paul Simon Special*, TV, 77, USA, Prod/Wr, (EMMY); *The Beach Boys Special*, TV, 76, USA, Prod/Wr.

MIGNEAULT, Hughes
- voir REALISATEURS

MILINKOVIC, Gerry
- see DIRECTORS

MILLAR, Susan
22 Albermarle Ave., Toronto, ON M4K 1H7 (416)465-9644. Soma Film & Video, 345 Carlaw Ave., Ste. 200, Toronto, ON M4M 2T1 (416)466-0822.
Type of Production and Credits: TV Film-Prod/Wr; TV Video-Prod/Wr.
Genres: Documentary-TV; Educational-TV; Industrial-TV.
Biography: Born in 1951 in Deep River, Ontario. Canadian citizen. Bachelor of Journalism from Carleton University. Co-owner of Soma Film & Video. Co-producer/writer or supervising writer of all Soma productions whose specialty is adult

educational television programs. Primary customers are TVOntario, Knowledge Network and Access Alberta with ancillary markets in educational institutions and direct markets to individual customers. Productions have been given awards from: American Film & Video Festival, Blue Ribbon, Red Ribbon, Festival Finalist and 3 Honourable Mentions. National Educational Film & Video Festival, Bronze Apple. U.S. Film Festival, 2 Awards for Creative Excellence
Selected Filmography: "Your Green Home" (6 eps), TV, 90-91, CDN, Co-Prod/Wr; "Kite Crazy" (4 eps), TV, 90-91, CDN, Co Prod; "Walking Fit" (1 eps), TV, 90, CDN, Co-Prod; "Personal Finance" (10 eps), TV, 90, CDN, Co-Prod/Wr/Host; "Learn to Navigate" (6 eps), TV, 89, CDN, Co-Prod/Wr; "Homebrew" (4 eps), TV, 89, CDN, Co-Prod; "Kitchen Cabinets Made Easy" (4 eps), TV, 89, CDN, Co-Prod; *Overboard*, In, 88, CDN, Co-Prod; "Set Your Sails" (6 eps), TV, 87, CDN, Co-Prod/Spv Wr; *Managing Performance Problems*, ED, 87, CDN, Co-Prod/Spv Wr; "Money Smart" (13 eps), TV, 86, CDN, Co-Prod/Spv Wr; *Lifeline*, In, 85, CDN, Co-Prod/Spv Wr; *Termination Interview*, ED, 84, CDN, Co-Prod/Spv Wr; "Starting a Business" (13 eps), ED, 83, CDN, Co-Prod/Wr.

MILLER, Bob
Atlantic Mediaworks, 469 King St., Fredericton, NB E3B 1E5 (506)458-8806.
Type of Production and Credits: TV Video-Prod/Dir.
Genres: Documentary-TV; Educational-TV; Children's-TV; Commercials-TV.
Biography: Born 1948, Cardiff, Wales; has lived in Canada since 54. B.A., B.Ed., M.Ed., University of New Brunswick. President of Atlantic Mediaworks since 82.
Selected Filmography: "NB Tel: In Focus" (7 eps), In, 91, CDN, Prod/Dir; "Sophie Stories" (15 eps), TV, 90, CDN, Prod/Dir; *Special Olympics Run*, TV, 90, CDN, Prod/Dir; *Freedom*, ED, 90, CDN, Exec Prod; "Welcome Spoken Here" (6 eps), TV, 89, CDN, Prod/Dir; *Speaking of Language*, ED, 89, CDN, Prod/Dir; "Say Hello to Success" (26 eps), In, 88, CDN, Prod/Dir; "Our Best to You" (6 eps), In, 88, CDN, Prod/Dir.

MILLS, Michael
- see DIRECTORS

MINNIS, Jon
ACCT, CFTPA, AMPAS, ASIFA. 2356 Hampton Ave. #2, Montreal, PQ H4A 2K6 (514)482-8278. Filminnis Productions, 2356 Hampton Ave., #2, Montreal, PQ H4A 2K6 ()482-8278. FAX: 369-0183.
Type of Production and Credits: Th Short-Dir/Wr/An Prod.
Genres: Animation-Th&TV; Commercials-TV.
Biography: Born 1950, Birmingham, England. Travelled extensively throughout Europe, the Middle East, the South Pacific and North America before settling in British Columbia in 74; Canadian citizenship, 78. Attended Sheridan College's International Summer School of Animation; produced short animated film, *Charade* during final year. Moved to Montreal, 84, to work in commercial animation industry; work included many animated commercials for television; also directed and animated short film for Expo 86, Vancouver, BC. In 88, released second independent film, *Just a Cartoon*. Formed Filmminnis Productions in 89. Mostly involved in animated commercials for television. *Charade* won numerous awards including Best Animated Film, CFTA awards, 84; Best Short Film, Genie 85; Best First Film, International Festival of Animation, Toronto; Oscar, Best Animated Short Film; Outstanding Film of the Year at the following: London Film Festival, Sydney Film Festival, Wellington Film Festival.
Selected Filmography: *World Tour of Sports*, Gilette, Cm, 91, CDN, Prod/Dir/An; *Time Machine*, "In Search of the Dragon" (PBS special/NFB), TV, 90, CDN, Dir/Wr/An; *Participation "Vitality"*, Cm, 90, CDN, Co-Prod/Dir/An; *Breakaway*, Gilette, Cm, 90, CDN, Prod/Dir/An; *The AIDS Nerd*, "Talkin' About AIDS", ED, 89, CDN, Dir/Wr/An; *Just a Cartoon*, Th, 88, CDN, Prod/Dir/Wr/An; *Charade*, Th, 83, CDN, Prod/Dir/Wr/An.

MIRKIN, Lawrence S.
ACCT. 133 Fulton Ave., Toronto, ON M4K 1X9 (416)466-1704. Primedia Productions Ltd., 219 Front St. E., Toronto, ON (416)361-0306.
Type of Production and Credits: TV Film-Prod; TV Video-Prod.
Genres: Drama-TV; Comedy-TV; Variety-TV; Children's-TV.
Biography: Born 1947, Cumberland, Maryland; US and Canadian citizenship. B.A., Yale College, 69; M.F.A., Yale School of Drama, 73-75. Literary manager, Mark Taper Forum, Los Angeles, 73-75; Story Editor, Associate Producer, Producer for CBC-TV Drama, 75-82;

formed Lawrence S. Mirkin Productions, 83. Many awards for "Fraggle Rock" including 86 Gemini Award for Best Children's Series, 84-85 ACE Awards, Best Children's Program, and 84 International Emmy Award, Best Children's Program. "The Jim Henson Hour" received 8 Emmy nominations and the 1990 Monitor Award for Best Children's Program. Appointed Vice-President, Drama, Primedia Productions, June 91.
Selected Filmography: *La Maison Suspendue*, "Stage on Screen", TV, 91, CDN, Creat Prod; *Amigo's Blue Guitar*, "Stage on Screen", TV, 90, CDN, Creat Prod; *Farther West*, "Stage on Screen", TV, 90, CDN, Creat Prod; "The Jim Henson Hour" (13 eps), TV, 88, USA, Prod; "Mount Royal" (17 eps), TV, 87-88, CDN/F, Prod; "Fraggle Rock" (84 eps), TV, 82-86, CDN, Prod, (GEMINI 86); *Best of Both Worlds*, TV, 82, CDN, Prod; "The Phoenix Team" (9 eps), TV, 79-81, CDN, Prod; "For the Record" (1 eps), TV, 79, CDN, Prod, (ACTRA).

MITTON, Susan Young ◆
6053 Jubilee Rd., Halifax, NS B3H 2E3 (902)420-4360.
Type of Production and Credits: TV Film-Prod/Dir; TV Video-Prod/Dir.
Genres: Drama-TV; Variety-TV; Documentary-Th&TV.
Biography: Born 1951, Saint John, New Brunswick. B.A., English, Acadia University. Has worked in Montreal, PEI, Nova Scotia; travelled extensively.
Selected Filmography: "Land and Sea" (48 eps), TV, 86-88, CDN, Exec Prod; "Land and Sea" (50 eps), TV, 75-85, CDN, Prod/Dir, (ANIK); "Feeling Good" (60 eps), TV, 83, CDN, Prod/Dir; "MacIntyre File" (8 eps), TV, 76-77, CDN, Prod/Dir; "A Way Out" (104 eps), TV, 75-77, CDN, Host/Res; "Studio 13" (240 eps), TV, 73-75, CDN, Host/Res.

MONTESI, Jorge
- see DIRECTORS

MORAIS, Robert D.
- see PRODUCTION MANAGERS

MORIN, Bertrand
- voir REALISATEURS

MORIN, Francyne
APFTQ. 1530 Bernard ouest, Apt 8, Outremont, Montréal, PQ H2V 1W8 (514)270-0999. 1207 St-André, 4e étage, Montréal, PQ H2L 3S8 (514)844-4555.
Types de production et générique: l métrage-Prod; TV film-Prod.
Types d'oeuvres: Drame-C&TV; Comédie-C&TV; Action-C&TV.
Curriculum vitae: Née à Montréal en 1952. Langues: français et anglais. Diplômée du Ravensbourne College of Art en Londres Angleterre. VP Executive Malo Film Distribution et Malo Film Production; distributeur de film depuis 10 ans.
Filmographie sélective: *Les Portes Tournantes*, TV, 88, CDN/F, Prod; *Tinamer*, TV, 87, CDN, Prod ass.

MORIN, Pierre
- voir REALISATEURS

MORRONE, Tony
42 Swordbill Dr., Islington, ON M5A 4V5 (416)247-9509. Cinematic Music, 264 Seaton St., #203, Toronto, ON M5A 2T4 (416)925-8889.
Type of Production and Credits: Th Film-Prod/Dir; Th Short-Prod/PM/Ed; TV Film-Prod/PM/Ed; TV Video-Prod/Dir/Ed/Cin.
Genres: Documentary-TV; Commercials-TV; Music Video-TV.
Biography: Born in 1956 in Toronto, Ontario. Languages: English and Italian. Italian citizen. Has filmed on location in over 17 countries including Egypt, Italy, Brazil and various Caribean Islands. Specializing in location production since 1984. Experience in location sound and post production. Special skills on skis with cameras. Staff photographer for various magazines.
Selected Filmography: *Kinnip Drumbo*, Th, 91, CDN, Prod/Ed/Snd Ed/PM; "Discover Your World" (60 eps), TV, 87-91, CDN, Prod/Cin/Ed; Air China (2 spots), Cm, 91, CDN, Ed; *I Think I Love You*, MV, 90, CDN, Prod/Dir/Ed; BWIA Airlines (5 spots), Cm, 87-89, CDN, Dir/Ed; *She Does What She Wants*, MV, 89, CDN, Prod/Ed; *Canadian Dressage Championships*, TV, 87, CDN, Dir/Ed; Ting Grapefruit (3 spots), Cm, 86, JAM, Dir/Ed; *Antigua Windsurfing*, TV, 86, ANT, Dir/Ed; *Kovergirlz*, TV, 85, STK, Prod/Ed; *Highjacking Studio 4*, TV, 85, CDN, PM; *Sodaman*, TV, 85, CDN, Prod.

MORTIMER, Peter
176 Ava Rd., Toronto, ON M6C 1W5 (416)785-1668. 663 Yonge St., Suite 404, Toronto, ON M4Y 2A4 (416)927-8942.
Type of Production and Credits: TV Film-Prod/Wr; TV Video-Prod.
Genres: Drama-TV; Musical-TV; Action-TV.
Biography: Born 1937, UK; British and Canadian citizenship. Languages: English, French, Greek. TV and film production experience in UK; 6 years with Associated Rediffusion as producer and executive producer; 3 years with Yorkshire TV as

Deputy Head of Drama, manager of shows for "Playhouse" including *The Caretaker*, which won an Emmy. Experienced in co-productions with foreign partners; Canadian experience consulting between governments and film and TV industry and in policy formulation and research.
Selected Filmography: *Summer Sounds*, TV, 84, CDN, Prod; "Just Do It Yourself" (26 eps), ED, 78, CDN, Prod; "Kate" (26 eps), TV, 71, GB, Prod; *For Those in Peril...*, "Hadleigh", TV, 70, GB, Wr; "The Main Chance" (13 eps), TV, 69, GB, Creator; "Castle Haven" (52 eps), TV, 68, GB, Prod; "Double Your Money" (26 eps), TV, 67, GB, Exec Prod; "Ready, Steady, Go!" (26 eps), TV, 64, GB, Pro Coord; "This Week" (26 eps), TV, 63, GB, Pro Coord.

MOSSANEN, Moze
- see DIRECTORS

MOZER, Richard
56 Hampton Ave., Toronto, ON M4K 2Y6 (416)463-4467. Devine Videoworks Corp., 100 Cambridge Ave., Toronto, ON M4K 2L6 (416)465-4499.
Type of Production and Credits: Th Film-Prod; TV Film-Prod/Dir; TV Video-Prod/Dir/Wr.
Genres: Drama-Th&TV; Variety-Th&TV; Commercials-Th&TV; Industrial-Th&TV.
Biography: Born 1958, Caracas, Venezuela; Canadian citizenship. Cornell University; B.F.A., M.F.A., Film Production, USC Film School. Co-founder with David Devine of Devine Videoworks Corp., 82. *Raffi in Concert with the Rise and Shine Band* won Gemini, 90; *Indian Time* won Bronze Medal, NY Film & TV Festival; *Bell Canada Terminal Connections* won ITVA Silver Birch; *A Young Children's Concert with Raffi* won Gold Parents' Choice Award (US).
Selected Filmography: *Raffi in Concert with the Rise and Shine Band*, TV, 89, CDN/USA, Prod, (GEMINI 90); *Indian Time*, TV, 88, CDN, Co-Wr/2nd U Dir; *Bell Canada Terminal Connections*, In, 88, CDN, Dir/Wr; *Class Acts - You Never Can Tell*, ED, 88, CDN, Dir/Wr; *Make a Move*, Veronique Beliveau, MV, 86, CDN, Prod; *Go To Pieces*, Paul Janz, MV, 86, CDN, Prod; *Wild*, Sattalites, MV, 86, CDN, Prod; *A Young Children's Concert with Raffi*, TV, 85, CDN, Assoc Prod; *The Stray Cats Live at Massey Hall*, TV, 84, CDN, Assoc Prod; *Chris DeBurgh - The Getaway*, TV, 83, CDN, Assoc Prod; *Strange Brew* (video segs), Th, 82, CDN, Prod.

MULLER, Henia ◊
CFTA. (416)968-9300.
Type of Production and Credits: TV Film-Prod; TV Video-Prod.
Genres: Documentary-TV; Educational-TV; Children's-TV; Industrial-TV.
Biography: Born 1947, West Germany; grew up in Israel; Canadian citizenship. Graduate of Hebrew University, Jerusalem. Has been producing film and video since 70.
Selected Filmography: *Challenge Yourself to New Heights*, TV, 88, CDN, Prod; "Vid Kids" (26 eps), TV, 86-87, CDN, Co-Prod, (CFTA); *All the World's a Stage*, TV, 87, CDN, Prod; *Food Choices: The Cancer Connection*, TV, 87, CDN, Prod; *The Fragile Tree Has Roots*, TV, 85, CDN, Co-Prod; *Star Song*, TV, 84, CDN, Prod; *Celly and Friends*, TV, 84, CDN, Co-Prod; *Vincent Price's Dracula*, TV, 83, CDN, Co-Prod; *Money to Burn*, TV, 83, CDN, Co-Prod; *Warming to Wood*, TV, 83, CDN, Co-Prod; *Sunshine for Sale*, TV, 83, CDN, Co-Prod; *Taking a Leap*, In, 83, CDN, Co-Prod; *Thanks a Lot*, TV, 82, CDN, Co-Prod; *Water: Friend or Foe?*, TV, 82, CDN, Co-Prod; *The Greening of the North*, In, 82, CDN, Co-Prod; *You Don't Smoke, Eh?/Living Proof*, ED, 80-81, CDN, Co-Prod; *A Dove with Clipped Wings*, TV, 75, CDN, Co-Prod.

MULLER, John
- see DIRECTORS

MURPHY, Jack F.
3104 Brookdale Rd., Studio City, CA 91604 (213)654-2820. American Cinema Marketing, 3575 Cahuenga Blvd. W., Suite 455, Los Angeles, CA 90068 USA. (213)850-6300. FAX: 850-7117. 4141 Sherbrooke St. W., Suite 660, Westmount, PQ H3Z 1B8
Type of Production and Credits: Th Film-Prod.
Genres: Drama-Th; Comedy-Th; Action-Th; Science Fiction-Th.
Biography: Born 1943, Montreal, Quebec; US resident alien. Active as worldwide film distributor, specializing in feature films.
Selected Filmography: *Syngenor*, Th, 90, USA, Prod; *The Delos Adventure*, Th, 85, USA, Exec Prod; *Pinball Summer*, Th, 79, CDN, Prod; *Dark Star*, Th, 74, USA, Assoc Prod; *Pieds dans la même bottine*, Th, 73, CDN, Prod.

MURPHY, Michael D. ◊
CFTA. (416)927-1724.
Type of Production and Credits: TV Film-Prod/Dir/Wr; TV Video-Prod/Dir/Wr.

Genres: Drama-TV; Comedy-TV; Documentary-TV; Educational-TV.
Biography: Born 1951, Windsor, Ontario. Studied Film and TV Production. Founded Clear Horizon Films, 81; Cine-Visa International Media Distributors, 84; co-founded P.I.C. Entertainment, 85; President, ViaVideo Communications. Active internationally as export sales agent for Canadian-produced TV programs. *Wild Goose Jack*, Best Documentary, Nature or Wildlife, American Film Festival, and the Canadian Heritage Award, Yorkton.
Selected Filmography: "Max Haines Crime Flashback" (26 eps), TV, 86, CDN, Prod; "To Your Health" (5 eps), ED, 86, CDN, Exec Prod/Prod/Wr; *Scouts!*, TV, 84-85, CDN, Exec Prod/Prod/Dir/Wr, (CFTA); *Brentwood*, ED, 85, CDN, Exec Prod/Prod/wr; *Wild Goose Jack*, TV, 82-83, CDN, Exec Prod/Prod/Dir/Wr, (CFTA).

MURRAY, James
ACFTP, ACCT. CBC, P.O. Box 500, Stn. A, Toronto, ON M5W 1E6 (416)975-6904.
Type of Production and Credits: TV Film-Prod/Dir; TV Video-Prod/Dir.
Genres: Documentary-TV; Current Affairs-TV.
Biography: Born 1932, Toronto, Ontario. B.A., Indiana University, 54; M.A., Northwestern University, 57. Joined CBC in Toronto as radio producer of public affairs documentaries, 57; moved to TV, 60; became Producer of "The Nature of Things", 61; has been with the series for most of its 30 years, 17 of them as Executive Producer; the series has won hundreds of awards. Served as Executive Producer, "A Planet for the Taking", 81-84; the series has won several environmental awards including the United Nations' Environment Program Medal, 85, and the World Environment Festival Award, 85. Personal awards include the Distinguished Service Award from the North American Association for Environmental Education for outstanding contributions to the field of environmental education, 88, and an Outstanding Achievement Award from Wildscreen International Wildlife Film and Television Festival, 90.

NADEAU, Jacques
222, av. McDougall, Outremont, PQ H2V 3P2 (514)279-5289. Idéacom inc., 1000 Amherst, Bur. 300, Montréal, PA H2L 2K5 (514)849-6966. FAX: 849-0776.
Types de production et générique: TV film-Prod; TV vidéo-Prod.
Types d'oeuvres: Documentaire-TV; Education-TV; Enfants-TV; Industriel-TV.
Curriculum vitae: Né en 1939, Montréal, Québec. Langues: français et anglais. Maîtrise, Sciences politiques, Université de Montréal; boursier du gouvernement français, études à l'Institut d'études politiques, Université de Grenoble. Président de Idéacom inc. depuis 73.
Filmographie sélective: "Comment ça va?" (108 eps), TV, 88-91, CDN, Prod exéc/Prod; *Le grand test sur l'environnement*, TV, 91, CDN, Prod; *Les mains libres*, Société canadienne du cancer, In, 91, CDN, Prod; *Puzzle*, TV, 90, CDN, Prod exéc/Prod; *Le décloissonement des institutions financières*,Desjardins, In, 88, CDN, Prod; *Pour l'avenir du monde*, TV, 87, CDN, Prod exéc/Prod; "Prendre la route/At the Wheel" (4 eps), TV, 83-86, CDN, Prod exéc/Prod.

NADEAU, Pierre
1324 est, Ste-Catherine, Montréal, PQ H2L 2H5 (514)597-2211. FAX: 525-9551.
Types de production et générique: TV vidéo-Prod.
Types d'oeuvres: Documentaire-TV.
Curriculum vitae: Né en 1937. Oeuvre dans le domaine du journalisme depuis bientôt 30 ans. Débute comme animateur à Radio-Canada, 60; remporte le trophée Méritas (meilleur reporter TV) pour "Aujourd'hui," 64; correspondant de Radio-Canada à Paris, 65-68; animateur radio et TV, 68-86; animateur de l'émission "Le Point," Radio-Canada, 84-88.
Filmographie sélective: *L'illusion de Vivre*, TV, 91, CDN, Prod; *Montréal D'hier à demain*, TV, 90, CDN, Prod; *Sécurité Aérienne*, TV, 90, CDN, Prod; *Dans l'Oeil de l'Aigle*, TV, 90, CDN, Prod; *Le Canari est mort*, TV, 89, CDN, Prod.

NELSON, Dale C. ✧
ACCT. (204)269-6756.
Type of Production and Credits: Th Film-Prod; TV Film-Prod/Dir; TV Video-Prod/Dir.
Genres: Drama-Th&TV; Comedy-TV; Variety-TV; Musical-TV.
Biography: Born 1935, High Prairie, Alberta. B.A., University of Washington. Producer of many CKY telethons.
Selected Filmography: "Interprovincial Lottery Shows" (many), TV, 74-88, CDN, Prod; "George Dalgleish" (120 eps), TV, 79-84, CDN, Prod; Back Home with John

Vernon, TV, 83, CDN, Prod/Dir; Harry Belafonte Sings, TV, 80, CDN, Prod.

NEMTIN, Bill
CFTPA. 125 Dupont St., 2nd Floor, Toronto, ON M5R 1V4 (416)975-9768.
Type of Production and Credits: TV Film-Prod; TV Video-Prod.
Genres: Documentary-Th&TV; Drama-Th&TV.
Biography: Born in 1943. Has worked in film and television since 1964, including production, acquisition, distribution and government policy consultation. Began his career at the National Film Board of Canada where he trained in film production and distribution. From 1970 to 1976, was independent producer of feature films, television documentaries and consulting on government broadcasting policy for such clients as the CBC, CTV, NFB and the Federal Government. In 1977, began working full-time for PBS, setting up Canadian operations for its station KCTS/Seattle. Became Director of Canadian and International Operations for WTVS/Detroit, 1983. Executive Producer of the 4-part national PBS documentary, *Canada: True North* and the special *America: Love It or Leave It*. Incorporated own independent Ontario-based production company, PTV Productions Inc., 1989.
Selected Filmography: *The Hand of Stalin*, (mini-series), TV, 90, CDN/GB, Exec Prod; *America: Love It or Leave It*, TV, 90, CDN, Exec Prod; *Canada: True North* (mini-series), TV, 89, CDN/USA, Exec Prod.

NEUBACHER, Roman M.
ACFC, CSC, ACCT. 198 Woodbine Ave., Unit 3, Toronto, ON M4L 3P2 (416)690-7259. Neuro Productions, 198 Woodbine Ave., Unit 3, Toronto, ON M4L 3P2 (416)690-7259.
Type of Production and Credits: Th Film-Focus Pull/Prod; Th Short-D.O.P./Wr; TV Film-Focus Pull; TV Video-D.O.P./Dir/Wr.
Genres: Drama-Th&TV; Action-Th&TV; Documentary-Th&TV; Music Video-Th&TV.
Biography: Born in Wintertur, Switzerland in 1965; came to Canada in 1968. Ventured into the film business after attending Waterloo University and Ryerson Film School. Started as a clapper-loader in 1985 and proceeded to various positions within the industry, including a move to producing and directing in 1990. Neuro Productions has been involved in various TV and film projects. Upcoming ventures include an Imax production, and distribution contracts within the EEC.
Selected Filmography: *The Last Paladin*, Th, 91, CDN, Co-Prod; "Popculture" (4 eps), TV, 91, CDN, Co-Prod/Dir; *Cool*, TV, 90, CDN, Prod; "Dance Music Television", TV, 90, USA, Prod/Dir; *Between Two Worlds/Artic Dreams*, Th, 90, CDN, Assist Prod/Res; "Dog House" (16 eps), TV, 90, CDN/USA, 2nd Unit Cam Assist; *The Sun Comes Up, It's Tuesday Morning*, Cowboy Junkies, MV, 90, CDN, Cam Assist; *Cardinal Sins*, TV, 89, USA, Cam Assist; *Indian Summer*, Th, 89, CDN, Cam Op/2nd Unit D.O.P.; *Morningside*, Th, 89, CDN, Cam Op/2nd Unit D.O.P.; "Friday's Curse" (36 eps), TV, 89, USA, 2nd Unit Cam Assist; "War of the Worlds" (36 eps), TV, 89, USA, 2nd Unit Cam Assist; *Uncut Gem*, TV, 88, USA, Cam Assist; "Night Heat" (36 eps), TV, 88, CDN/USA, Cam Assist; *Cold Comfort*, Th, 87, CDN, Cam Assist.

NEWLAND, Marv
- see DIRECTORS

NEWTON, John
- see DIRECTORS

NICHOL, Gary
Gary Nichol Associates Ltd., 144 Glenholme Ave., Toronto, ON M6E 3C4 (416)654-6906.
Type of Production and Credits: Th Film-Wr; TV Film-Prod/Dir/Ed; TV Video-Prod/Dir/Ed.
Genres: Documentary-Th&TV; Educational-Th&TV; Commercials-Th&TV; Industrial-Th&TV.
Biography: Independent film producer for over 20 years. Incorporated Gary Nichol Associates Ltd. in 1972 with over 100 films produced for the National Film Board of Canada, CBC, PBS, Federal Government and numerous private sector clients. Work focuses on social and health issues, cross-cultural communication and native Canadian perspectives. Winner of Yorkton Festival Special Jury award in 1985 and 1984 for documentaries. Progressive interest in drama; first feature film script, *Double Trouble*, has O.F.D.C., Telefilm and Praxis support.
Selected Filmography: *Life Circles*, ED, 89, CDN, Prod; Parks Canada, (4 spots), ED/Th, 87, CDN, Prod/Dir/Wr; *An Act of God*, ED/TV, 85, CDN, Prod/Dir; *The Circle Moving*, ED/TV, 84, CDN, Prod; *The Only Gift*, ED/TV, 84, CDN, Prod; *A New Dawn*, ED, 83, CDN, Prod/Dir; *Trent-Severn Seasons*, ED/Th, 83, CDN, Prod; *Long and Lean*, ED, 81, CDN, Prod; *In The Chips*, In, 81, CDN, Prod/Wr;

Taking Care of Business, In/ED, 80, CDN, Prod/Dir; *Jean Luc Grondin*, TV/ED, 80, CDN/USA, Prod/Dir/Ed; *Michael Dumas*, TV/ED, 80, CDN/USA, Prod/Dir/Ed; *The Yerxas*, TV/ED, 79, CDN/USA, Prod/Dir/Ed; *Smiths Falls Carvers*, TV/ED, 79, CDN/USA, Prod/Dir/Ed; *Knacky People*, TV/ED, 79, CDN/USA, Prod/Dir/Ed.

NICHOLL, Jim
105 Beach Dr., Victoria, BC V8S 2L6 (604)592-8595. CHEK-TV, 780 Kings Rd., Victoria, BC V8T 5A2 (604)383-2435.
Type of Production and Credits: TV Film-Prod; TV Video-Exec Prod.
Genres: Drama-TV; Musical-TV; Commercials-TV; Music Video-TV.
Biography: Born in 1948 in London, England. Bachelor, Business Administration, University of Saskatchewan, 1970. 20 years experience as writer, producer and in management in the film and television industry. Currently Vice-President and General Manager of CHEK-TV, Victoria. Awards: TVB Top 10 Retail Commercials, 1973; TVB Top 10 Retail Commercials, 1977; CanPro Program Awards, 1983, 84, 86; CAB Gold Ribbon Award, 1989 for Canadian Talent Development.
Selected Filmography: "BC Music Project" (13 eps), TV, 88, CDN, Exec Prod; "Shake It Up" (13 eps), TV, 86, CDN, Exec Prod; "Highband" (13 eps), TV, 85, CDN, Exec Prod; *A New Look*, Cm, 77, CDN, Wr/Prod; *News In Action*, Cm, 73, CdN, Wr/Prod.

NIRENBERG, Les
ACTRA. 67 Ridge Hill Dr., Toronto, ON M6C 2J5 (416)785-1671. 335 Dundas St. E., Toronto, ON M5A 2A2 (416)876-1221.
Type of Production and Credits: TV Film-Prod/Wr; TV Video-Prod/Wr.
Genres: Documentary-TV; Educational-TV; Industrial-TV.
Biography: Born 1935, Toronto, Ontario. Languages: English and Yiddish. Writer/producer, CBC Current Affairs, 67-81. Producer, director, writer for corporate television, public service announcements, training video and promotional in-store film and video
Selected Filmography: *Living with Capital "L"*, In, 91, CDN, Prod/Dir; "Quelqueshow", TV, 69-74, CDN, Prod/ Host, (ANIK); *Propaganda Message*, Th, 73, CDN, Co-Wr; *La Québecoise*, "Adieu Alouette", TV, 73, CDN, Dir/Wr.

NOWLAN, John
BUPD. 1766 Beech St., Halifax, NS B3J 3E9 (902)425-3577. CBC, P.O. Box 3000, Halifax, NS B3J 3E9 (902)420-8311.
Type of Production and Credits: TV Film-Prod/Dir.
Genres: Children's-TV; Animation-TV; News-TV.
Biography: Born 1942, Toronto, Ontario. B.Sc., Acadia University. Experience: CBC announcer, radio producer, radio executive producer. Executive producer, Children's TV, Halifax, 85-91. Awarded the Centennial Medal, 67; "Switchback" won the Children's Broadcast Institute Award; CBC winner of Commonwealth Relations Trust Bursary for study in Britain; winner of 3 US-based awards for "Street Cents."
Selected Filmography: "Street Cents", TV, 89-91, CDN, Exec Prod; "Switchback" (weekly), TV, 81-88, CDN, Exec Prod/Prod/Dir, (ANIK); "Sesame Street" (sev seg), TV, 85-88, USA, Prod; "Moneypenny" (pilot), TV, 88, CDN, Exec Prod/Prod/Dir/Wr; "Blizzard Island" (12 eps), TV, 87-88, CDN/GB, Exec Prod; *Children's Miracle Network Telethon*, TV, 85, CDN, Exec Prod; *Pope's Tour - I.W.K. Children's Hospital*, TV, 84, CDN, Prod/Dir; "Compass" (daily), TV, 75-81, CDN, Exec Prod/Dir.

NYSTEDT, Colleen
DGC, ACCT, BCMPA. 2143 Stephens St., Vancouver, BC V6K 3W4 (604)732-7677. PAGER: 686-0036.
Type of Production and Credits: Th Film-Line Prod/PM; TV Film-Prod/PM.
Genres: Drama-Th&TV; Comedy-Th&TV.
Biography: Born, raised and educated in Vancouver, British Columbia. Canadian citizen. Languages: English, French and some German. Geography/Political Science; Urban Planning at the University of British Columbia and University of Victoria. Secretary and Treasurer of the DGC, 1989 to date. Also Production Department Representative, 1989 to date. President of New City Productions, Inc. Currently developing TV and motion picture projects.
Selected Filmography: *Christmas on Division St.*, TV, 91, CDN/USA, Prod/PM; *Crooked Hearts*, Th, 90, USA, PM; *Heartbreak Hoteru*, TV, 90, CDN, PM; *American Boyfriends/California Dreamin'*, Th, 88, CDN, PM; *Beyond the Stars/Personal Choice*, Th, 88, USA, Line Prod/PM; *Murphy's Law*, TV, 88, USA, Loc M; "MacGyver" (2 eps), TV, 87, USA, Loc M; *Return of the Sh. Dog*, TV,

87, USA, Loc M; *The Accused/Reckless Endangerment*, Th, 87, USA, Loc M; *Earth-Star Voyager*, TV, 87, USA, Loc M; *The Room Upstairs*, TV, 86, USA, Loc M; *Christmas Snow*, TV, 86, USA, Loc M; *Nobody's Child/The Marie Balter Story*, TV, 85, USA, Loc M; *Love is Never Silent/In This Sign*, TV, 85, USA, ALM; *April Fools' Day*, Th, 85, USA, Loc M.

OBOMSAWIN, Alanis
- see DIRECTORS

O'BRIAN, Peter
ACFTP, ACCT. Independent Pictures Inc., 111 Gore Vale Ave., Toronto, ON M6J 2R5 (416)363-5155. FAX: 363-1021.
Type of Production and Credits: Th Film-Prod.
Genres: Drama-Th.
Biography: Born 1947, Toronto, Ontario. B.A., Mass Communications and English Literature, Emerson College, Boston. *The Grey Fox* was nominated as Best Foreign Film, Golden Globe Awards; *My American Cousin* won the International Critics Award, Festival of Festivals, Toronto, 85. Executive Director, Canadaian Centre for Advanced Film Studies, 88-April, 91.
Selected Filmography: *Milk and Honey*, Th, 87, CDN, Prod/Exec Prod; *John and the Missus*, Th, 86, CDN, Exec Prod/Co-Prod; *One Magic Christmas*, Th, 85, CDN/USA, Prod; *Discovery* (Expo 86), Th, 85, CDN, Prod; *My American Cousin*, Th, 84, CDN, Prod, (GENIE 86); *The Grey Fox*, Th, 80, CDN, Prod, (GENIE); *Fast Company*, Th, 78, CDN, Co-Prod; *Blood & Guts*, Th, 77, CDN/USA, Co-Prod; *Outrageous!*, Th, 77, CDN, Assoc Prod; *Love at First Sight*, Th, 75, CDN, Prod; *Me*, Th, 74, CDN, Co-Prod.

O'BRIEN, Ann
ACCT, DGC. 85 Balmoral Ave., Toronto, ON M4V 1J5 (416)929-9684.
Type of Production and Credits: TV Film-Prod; TV Video-Prod.
Genres: Drama-TV; Comedy-TV; Variety-TV; Documentary-TV.
Biography: US citizen, landed immigrant, Canada. B.A. Tufts University, Boston. Ten years (81-91) as freelance Producer and Line Producer with: Primedia Productions (TV adaptations of theatrical plays), "Toronto Talkies"/CBC (drama anthology series), Green & Dewar New Wilderness (104 wildlife programs). Prior to this, worked as freelance Co-Producer/Associate Producer for Columbia Pictures TV (variety/comedy speicals), and PKO TV (romance mini-series), as well as Production Manager on over 50 film and television productions. Two Emmy awards for "Lorne Greene's New Wilderness", Gemini and Yorkton Festival awards for "Inside Stories".
Selected Filmography: "Stage on Screen" (8 eps), TV, 90-91, CDN, Prod; "Inside Stories" (13 eps), TV, 88, CDN, Co-Prod, (GEMINI); "Lorne Greene's New Wilderness" (104 eps), TV, 82-86, CDN, Line Prod; *The Country Wife*, TV, 83, CDN, Pro Spv; *Love at the Crossroads*, "Romance" (5 eps), TV, 82, USA, Assoc Prod; *Burley Q.*, TV, 81, CDN/USA, Co-Prod; *Oh Coward!*, TV, 80, CDN/USA, Assoc Prod; *Bon Voyage...But*, ED, 80, CDN, Co-Prod; *Heaven's Heroes*, Th, 80, USA, Assist Dir; *They Write the Songs*, TV, 79, CDN/USA, Assoc Prod; *Image of the Beast*, Th, 79, USA, Assist Dir; *Wilderness Christmas*, TV, 78, USA, PM/Assist Dir; *Flip Wilson's Salute to Football*, TV, 77, CDN, PM; *Jonathan Winter's Salute to Baseball*, TV, 77, CDN, PM; "Behind the Scene" (47 eps), TV, 75-76, CDN, PM.

O'CONNELL, Maura
1723 Centinela Ave., Santa Monica, CA 90404 (213)453-0298.
Type of Production and Credits: Th Film-Prod; Th Film-Wr.
Genres: Drama-Th.
Biography: Attended London International Film School.
Selected Filmography: *George's Island*, Th, 90, CDN, Prod/Wr; *Defcon-4*, Th, 84, CDN, Co-Prod/Co-Dir; *Siege/Self Defense*, Th, 81, CDN, Co-Prod.

O'CONNOR, Matthew
DGC. Pacific Motion Pictures Corp., 827 Hamilton St., Vancouver, BC V6B 2R7 (604)683-8811.
Type of Production and Credits: Th Film-Prod; TV Film-Prod; TV Video-Prod.
Genres: Drama-Th&TV; Comedy-Th&TV; Action-Th&TV; Science Fiction-Th&TV
Biography: Born in 1960. *Isn't Love Crazy* was winner of the 1987-88 West Coast Music Awards for Best Video. *Empty House* won in 1986-87.
Selected Filmography: *Lovebirds*, TV, 91, USA, Prod/Unit PM; *A Mother's Justice*, TV, 91, USA, Spv Prod/2nd Unit Dir; *And The Sea Will Tell* (mini-series), TV, 90, USA, Spv Prod/2nd U Dir; *It* (mini-series), TV, 90, USA, Spv Prod; *The First Season*, Th, 88, CDN, Co-Prod; *Isn't Love Crazy*, Tony Pappa & The Theory, MV, 87, CDN, Prod; *Empty House*, Art Bergman, MV, 86, CDN, Prod; *The Sun Ain't Gonna Shine*, Long John Baldry, MV,

86, CDN, Prod.
O'DELL, Dean A.
- see ART DIRECTORS
O'DWYER, Michael J.
- see WRITERS
O'REGAN, James
ACTRA. 547 Arlington Ave., Toronto, ON M6C 3A6 (416)652-1730.
Type of Production and Credits: Th Short-Prod/Wr; TV Video-Wr.
Genres: Comedy-Th&TV.
Biography: Born in 1952 in Ottawa, Ontario. Actor, writer, producer and theologian. Has acted in all-media since 1972, starring now in "Road to Avonlea" as Abner Jeffries. Has written for all media, directed theatre and produced in film and theatre. Received a Gold Medal for Best Short Comedy in Spain for *Edsville*. Holds a Pontifical License and a Master's degree in Theology. Interests include languages (reads 6, some speech in 5), book collecting, the sea, cooking and travel.
Selected Filmography: *Edsville*, Th, 90, CDN, Prod/Wr; "What's New", political satire, (5 eps), TV, 82-83, CDN, Wr.
OLIVER, Ron
- see WRITERS
OLSEN, Stan
DGA, DGC. 915 Lawn Dale Ave., Victoria, BC V8S 4C9 (604)595-7787. FAX: 595-7727.
Type of Production and Credits: TV Film-Dir/Prod; TV Video-Dir/Prod.
Genres: Drama-TV; Comedy-TV; Action-TV; Commercials-TV.
Biography: Born 1939, Berkeley, California; landed immigrant Canada since 74. Languages: English and Spanish. Attended University of California at Berkeley. Has produced and directed numerous commercials.
Selected Filmography: "T and T", TV, 88, CDN, Dir; "Sea Hunt" (22 eps), TV, 87, CDN/USA, Dir/Prod; "Danger Bay", TV, 84-86, CDN, Dir; "The Edison Twins", TV, 86, CDN, Dir; "The Beachcombers", TV, 75-85, CDN, Dir; "Littlest Hobo", TV, 80, CDN, Dir; "Sidestreet", TV, 77-80, CDN, Dir; *Artichoke*, TV, 78, CDN, Dir; "Swiss Family Robinson", TV, 75-76, CDN/USA, Dir.
ONDA, Stephen
2359 Montague, Regina, SK S4T 3K6 (306)525-6921. Heartland Motion Pictures Inc., 2352 Smith St., Regina, SK S4P 2P6 (306)777-0888.
Type of Production and Credits: TV Film-Prod; TV Video-Dir/Prod.
Genres: Drama-TV; Comedy-TV; Documentary-TV; Educational-TV; Children's-TV.
Biography: Born in 1958 in Moncton, New Brunsiwck. Canadian citizen. Working as an independent producer since 1983. Founder of Heartland Motion Pictures Inc. in 1987. Director of documentary programs for TV; Producer of dramas and documentaries for TV. Board member of the Banff TV Festival, 1986-88. Board member, Saskatchewan Motion Picture Association, 1985-88. Programs have won Canadian and American awards, including a Gold at the Houston International Film and Television Festival.
Selected Filmography: *The Garden*, TV, 90, CDN, Prod; *Home on the Range*, "Inside Stories", TV, 90, CDN, Prod; *Room Full of Men*, TV, 90, CDN, Prod; *Zipper Club*, TV, 90, Prod; *Theatre for Change*, TV, 89, CDN, Prod/Dir; *Nothing's Forever*, ED, 87, CDN, Prod/Dir; *Bottom Line*, ED, 86, CDN, Prod/Dir.
ORD, Cathy
- see DIRECTORS
ORR, James
- see WRITERS
ORZARI, Lorenzo
- see WRITERS
OSTRIKER, David M.
Stornaway Productions, 160 Bloor St. E., Suite 1220, Toronto, ON M4W 1B9 (416)923-1104.
Type of Production and Credits: Th Film-DOP; Th Short-DOP; TV Film-Exec Prod; TV Video-Exec Prod.
Genres: Documentary-TV; Current Affairs-TV.
Biography: Born 1947, New York City; Canadian and US citizenship. Educated at New York University, where he later taught film. Has received 13 national and international awards.
Selected Filmography: *Caught in the Crossfire* (2 eps), TV, 90-91, A/J, Exec Prod; *Out of Control*, TV, 90, CDN, Exec Prod; *The Shattered Dream*, "End of An Empire", TV, 89-90, CDN, Prod; *Angola*, "End of An Empire", TV, 89-90, CDN, Prod; *The Horn of Africa*, "End of An Empire", TV, 89-90, CDN, Prod; *Witnesses: What Happened in Afghanistan*, "End of an Empire", TV, 89-90, CDN, Prod; *Promises to Keep*, TV, 88, CDN, Prod; *The Twice Promised Land*, TV, 86, CDN, Prod; *Agents of Deception*, TV, 84, CDN, Prod/DOP; *Scorn of Women*, TV, 82, CND, DOP; *KGB Connections*, TV, 81, CDN, DOP; *The Intruder*, Th, 79, CDN, DOP; "Some-

thing Ventured" (13 eps), TV, 76, CDN, DOP; *Brethren*, Th, 75, CDN, DOP; "Here Come the Seventies" (39 eps), TV, 69-71, CDN, DOP.

OUELLETTE, Michel L.
- see CINEMATOGRAPHERS

OUELLETTE, Michel
Les Productions Agent Orange, 1178, Place Phillips, bur. 104, Montréal, PQ H3B 3C8 (514)397-1414. FAX: 397-0280.
Types de production et générique: c métrage-Prod; TV film-Prod; TV vidéo-Prod.
Types d'oeuvres: Expérimental-C&TV; Vidéo clips-C&TV.
Curriculum vitae: Né en 1948, Montréal, Québec. Baccalauréat en Pédagogie, 70; études théâtrales, Université du Québec à Montréal. Voyage, 76-78, Europe, Etats-Unis, Amérique centrale. Président, administrateur, Véhicule Art, 81-82; co-fondateur, Président, producteur, Agent Orange inc.
Filmographie sélective: *Ne plus jamais dormir*, C, 91, CDN/F, Prod; *Léa*, C/TV, 91, CDN, Prod; *A la belle vie!*, C/TV, 90, CDN, Prod; "Visions" (3 eps), TV, 89-90, CDN/USA, Prod; *Lalala Human Sex Duo No. 1*, C, 87, CDN, Prod; *House (Time Code)*, TV, 87, CDN, Prod; *Introducing Agent Orange*, C, 87, CDN, Prod; *Anémique Cinéma*, MV, 87, CDN, Prod; *Tentations*, TV, 87, CDN, Prod; *Fiction* (vidéo), C, 85, CDN, Prod; *Le Chien de Luis et Salvador* (vidéo), C, 83, CDN, Prod; *Kidnapping Kidnapping*, C, 83, CDN, Prod.

OWEN, Don
- see DIRECTORS

PAABO, Iris
- see DIRECTORS

PAAKSPUU, Kalli
4 Cathedral Bluffs Dr., Scarborough, ON M1M 2T7 (416)261-7889.
Type of Production and Credits: Th Short-Dir/Prod/Wr; TV Film-Dir/Prod/Wr; TV Video-Dir/Prod/Ed.
Genres: Drama-Th&TV; Documentary-Th&TV; Experimental-Th.
Biography: Born Vancouver, B.C. B.A., University of British Columbia; M.A., University of Toronto. Currently producing and directing *The Story In And Outside Exile* and *Big City Girls;* and developing *Suicide - a love story,* in co-production with the National Film Board of Canada.
Selected Filmography: *Goodbye to Two-Day Weekends*, Th, 87, CDN, Prod/Dir/Wr; *I Need a Man Like You to Make My Dreams Come True*, Th, 86, CDN, Co-Dir/Prod/Wr, (GENIE 87); *Set in Motion*, TV, 82, CDN, Dir/Prod; *Maypole Carving*, Th, 81, CDN, Dir/Wr/Prod/Ed; *Ceremonies of Innocence*, ED, 80, CDN, Dir/Prod/Ed/Cam; *The First Day of School/The Child's Conception of Age*, ED, 78-79, CDN, Dir/Cam/Ed; *October Alms*, Th, 78, CDN, Dir/Prod/ Wr; Passage, Th, 78, CDN, Wr/Prod/Dir; *Sacred Circle*, Th, 76, CDN, Snd Rec/Wr/Ed/Prod; *Solstanz*, TV, 75, CDN, Dir/Prod/Cam.

PACHECO, Bruno Lazaro
- see DIRECTORS

PARE, Rénald
ACCT, ADISQ. 171, Pierre Connefroy, Boucherville, PQ (514)449-2001. Sogestalt 2001 inc., 801 Sherbrooke est, #801, Montréal, PQ H2L 1K7 (514)526-7090.
Types de production et générique: l métrage-Prod/Prod exéc; TV Vidéo-Prod/Prod exéc.
Types d'oeuvres: Drame-C; Comédie-TV; Variété-TV; Documentaire-TV.
Curriculum vitae: Né en 1942, Joliette, Québec. Langues: français et anglais. L.Sc., Economie, Université de Montréal, 68; M.B.A., Université de Sherbrooke, 70.
Filmographie sélective: "Samedi P.M." (32 eps), TV, 89-91, CDN, Prod exéc; "Groupe Sauguin" (4 eps), TV, 88-91, CDN, Prod exéc; *Scanners III*, C, 90, CDN, Prod exéc; *Mission Apollo*, TV, 90, CDN, Prod exéc; *Loto 20 ans*, TV, 90, CDN, Prod exéc; *Célébration '90*, TV, 90, CDN, Prod exéc; *Nelligan*, TV, 90, CDN, Prod exéc; *Scanners II*, C, 89, CDN, Prod exéc; "Samedi de Rire" (80 eps), TV, 85-89, CDN, Prod exéc; *Rendez-vous avec Gerry*, TV, 88, CDN, Prod exéc.

PARK, Alex
131 Silverbirch Ave., Toronto, ON M4E 3L3 (416)690-3545.
Type of Production and Credits: TV Video-Prod.
Genres: Variety-TV; Musical-TV; Documentary-TV.
Biography: Born 1948.

PARTINGTON, Joseph
ACTRA, ACCT. 3615 Haven Glenn, Mississauga, ON L4X 1X7 (416)624-1848. CBC, Box 500, Stn. A, Toronto, ON M5W 1E6 (416)975-7155.
Type of Production and Credits: TV Film-Prod; TV Video-Prod.
Genres: Drama-TV; Comedy-TV; Action-TV.
Biography: Born 1945, Toronto, Ontario. B.A.A., Radio and Television Arts, Ryerson Polytechnic Institute. Worked

as a television administrator and production unit manager, 73-76.
Selected Filmography: *High Country,* TV, 90, CDN, Pro Exec; "Material World" (7 eps), TV, 89, CDN, Prod; *Sanity Clause,* TV, 89, CDN, Co-Prod; "Coming & Going" (pilot), TV, 88, CDN, Co-Prod; *Two Men,* TV, 88, CDN, Line Prod; "Hangin' In" (111 eps) (Co-wr 3 eps), TV, 80-87, CDN, Prod/Co-Creator/Story Ed; *Momma's Going to Buy You a Mockingbird,* TV, 87, CDN, Line Prod; "Danger Bay" (6 eps), TV, 87, CDN, Pro Exec; "Flappers" (43 eps), TV, 78-80, CDN, Prod/Story cons.

PARTINGTON, Lawrence
Patterson-Partington International Television Productions, 206 Laird Dr., Suite 200, Toronto, ON M4G 3W4 (416)696-9633. FAX: 696-9640. Skytech Satellite Services Inc., 206 Laird Dr., Suite 200, Toronto, ON M4G 3W4 (416)696-9626.
Type of Production and Credits: TV Film-Prod/Dir; TV Video-Prod/Dir.
Genres: Sports-TV; Commercials-TV; Industrial-TV.
Biography: Canadian citizenship. B.A.A., Ryerson Polytechnical Institute. Has won 2 Awards of Excellence from the Canadian Public Relations Society.
Selected Filmography: "Player's GM & Formula Atlantice Car Racing Series" (41 eps), TV, 90-91, CDN, Prod; "World Cup Skiing" (4 eps), TV, 90-91, CDN, Prod/Dir; "Canadian Alpine Ski Championships Series" (9 eps), TV, 90-91, CDN, Prod/Dir; *Moscow McDonald's,* TV, 90, CDN, Prod; *World Sports Prototype Race Special,* TV, 90, CDN, Prod/Dir.

PATEL, Ishu
- see DIRECTORS

PATERSON, Iain
Agency for the Performing Arts, Inc., 9000 Sunset Blvd., Los Angeles, CA 90069 (213)273-0744. FAX: 275-9401.
Type of Production and Credits: Th Film-Prod; TV Film-Prod.
Genres: Drama-Th&TV; Comedy-Th&TV; Horror-Th&TV; Children's-Th&TV.
Biography: Started career in the film industry in Great Britain, as a film-editor on award-winning documentaries and "60 Minutes" series. In Canada, began producing TV specials and dramas, as well as becoming a segment producer and director for "Real People"series. Three award-winning "Family Playhouse" dramas for HBO. In New York, produced *High School Narc,* an "ABC After School Special"; joined the staff of "Saturday Night Live" as a film segment producer. Developed and produced "Friday the 13th: The Series", as well as an episode of *Friday the 13th: Part VII.* Winner of numerous awards.
Selected Filmography: "The Unnaturals", TV, 90-91, USA, Creator/Exec Prod/Dir/Wr; *Between Cars,* TV, 90, USA, Prod; "The Unnaturals" (2 pilots), TV, 90, USA, Creator/Exec Prod; *Ghoulies Go to College,* TV, 89, USA, Prod/2nd U Dir; *Friday the 13th: Part VII,* Th, 88, USA, Prod; "Friday the 13th: The Series", TV, 87, CDN/USA, Prod; *The Prodigious Hickey,* TV, 86, USA, Prod; *Sweet Lorraine,* Th, 86, USA, Prod; "Saturday Night Live", TV, 85, USA, Seg Prod; *High School Narc,* TV, 85, USA, Prod; *Working for Peanuts/Tucker and the Horsethief/My Father, My Rival,* "Family Playhouse" TV, 84, USA, Prod.

PATTERSON, David J.
ACCT. 65 Prince Arthur Ave., Toronto, ON M5R 1B3 (416)944-3973. Passport Productions Inc., 1240 Bay St., #701, Toronto, ON M5R 2A7 (416)944-8391. FAX: 944-8386.
Type of Production and Credits: Th Film-Prod; TV Film-Prod.
Genres: Drama-Th&TV; Action-Th&TV; Game Shows-TV; Documentary-Th&TV.
Biography: Born 1947, Montreal, Quebec. Graduate of McGill University. Following a 10-year career in advertising in Montreal and Toronto, co-founded Telescene Productions, Montreal, 77; co-founder, Filmline Productions, 81, and Filmline International, 83; joined Cineplex Odeon Corporation in 87 as Senior Vice-President, Television; Partner & President, Cinexus/Famous Players Entertainment, 89; President/co-founder, Passport Productions, 91.
Selected Filmography: "Dracula: The Series", TV, 90, CDN, Exec Prod; *Spies, Lies & Naked Thighs,* TV, 88, USA, Exec Prod; "Baloney" (game show), TV, 88, CDN, Exec Prod; "Learning the Ropes", TV, 88, CDN, Exec Prod; *Champagne Charlie* (mini-series), TV, 88, CDN, Co-Prod; *April Morning,* TV, 87, USA, Prod; *Ford: The Man and the Machine* (mini-series), TV, 87, CDN, Prod, (GEMINI 87); *Where the Dark Streets Go,* TV, 86, USA, Co-Prod; *Toby McTeague,* Th, 85, CDN, Co-Exec Prod; *Spearfield's Daughter* (mini-series), TV, 85, CDN/USA/AUS, Co-Prod; *Choices,* TV, 85, USA, Pro Spv; *Breaking All the Rules,* Th, 84, CDN, Co-Prod; *Cross Country,* Th, 82, CDN, Co-

Prod; *Heartaches*, Th, 80, CDN, Co-Prod.

PAYETTE, Jacques
AQRRCT, ACCT, SACD, FPRRTC. 751 Marie Leber, Ile des Soeurs, PQ H3E 1S8 (514)766-4213.
Types de production et générique: TV vidéo-Réal/Prod.
Types d'oeuvres: Drame-TV; Comédie-TV; Variété-TV; Musical-TV.
Curriculum vitae: Né en 1941, Granby, Québec. Langues: français et anglais. 27 ans d'expérience professionnelle en télévision. Président de l'académie du cinéma et de la télévision du Canada (Section Québec); Vice-Président National de l'ACCT. Gagnants de quatre Gémeaux en 2 ans. Réalisation du *Cirque du Soleil* gagnant d'un Emmy Award à Los Angeles, de la Rose d'Or de Montreux.
Filmographie sélective: "Scoop" (13 eps), TV, 91, CDN, Creat Prod; *Cirque du Soleil/La Nouvelle Expérience*, TV, 91, CDN, Réal; "La Misère des Riches" (30 eps), TV, 90-91, F/CDN, Réal/Ed; "Chambre en Ville" (30 eps), TV, 89, CDN, Réal; *Spécial CTF*, TV, 89, F/CDN, Prod; "Ferlan-Nadeau" (60 eps), TV, 89, CDN, Prod; *Cirque du Soleil/Le Cirque Réinventé*, TV, 88, USA/CDN, Réal,(GEMEAUX/EMMY/ROSE D'OR); "Daniel Lavoie Olympia" (2 eps), TV, 88, CDN, Réal/Prod; *Incognito*, TV, 87, CDN, Réal; *Silence ou Chante*, TV, 86, CDN, Réal; *Bye Bye 1986*, TV, 87, CDN, Réal, (GEMEAUX); "Station Soleil" (48 eps), TV, 85, CDN, Réal; "Samedi de rire" (22 eps), TV, 85, CDN, Réal; *Bye Bye 85*, TV, 85, CDN, Réal, (GEMEAUX); "Pour Une Chanson" (6 eps), TV, 84, CDN, Réal.

PAYRASTRE, George
- see CINEMATOGRAPHERS

PEARSON, Barry
WGC (ACTRA). Rosedale Film Ventures, 55 Unwin Ave., Toronto, ON M5A 1A2 (416)461-1045.
Type of Production and Credits: Th Film-Prod/Wr; TV Film-Prod/Wr; TV Video-Prod/Wr.
Genres: Drama-Th&TV; Action-Th&TV; Documentary-Th&TV; Educational-Th&TV.
Biography: Born 1936, Nipawin, Saskatchewan. Taught high school before becoming a freelance writer. Has written many television shows in addition to poetry, short stories, articles and plays. *Life and Times of Edwin Alonzo Boyd* won Best Documentary Feature, New York Film Festival; *M3 - The Gemini Strain* won several European film awards.
Selected Filmography: "Katts & Dog" (88 eps), TV, 88-91, CDN/F, Prod; "True Confessions" (25 eps), TV, 87, USA, Prod; *Covert Action*, TV, 86, CDN, Prod; *Isaac Littlefeathers*, Th, 84, CDN, Prod; *The Life and Times of Edwin Alonzo Boyd*, TV, 82, CDN, Wr/Prod; "Spirit of Adventure", TV, 80, CDN, Prod; *Crossbar*, Th, 78, CDN, Prod; *M3 - The Gemini Station*, Th, 77, CDN, Prod.

PEARSON, Peter
- see DIRECTORS

PECKMAN, Sophia
18 Squires Ave., Toronto, ON M4B 2R3 (416)285-9133.
Type of Production and Credits: TV Film-Prod/Line Prod/PM.
Genres: Drama-TV; Variety-TV; Commercials-TV; Music Video-TV.
Biography: Born Toronto, Ontario; Canadian citizenship. Extensive experience in film, television and radio broadcast production, programming and marketing with film production houses, television networks and advertising agencies. Has worked as producer on numerous commercials; clients include Labatt, Molson, Oland Brew, Schooner, Sweet Marie and Mars.
Selected Filmography: *The Meeting Place*, TV, 90, CDN, Line Prod.

PERLMUTTER, David M.
ACCT. 47 Elgin Ave., Toronto, ON M5R 1G5 (416)968-7255. Velvet Star Productions Inc., 129 Yorkville Ave., Suite 200, Toronto, ON M5R 1C4 (416)927-0016. FAX: 960-8447.
Type of Production and Credits: Th Film-Prod; TV Video-Prod; TV Film-Prod.
Genres: Drama-Th&TV; Comedy-Th.
Biography: Born 1934, Toronto, Ontario. B.Comm., University of Toronto; C.A. Producer or executive producer of several films between 72-80 including *The Neptune Factor*, *Sunday in the Country*, *Love at First Sight*, *Blood and Guts*, *Fast Company*, *Two Solitudes*. Since 80, providing financial and distribution consulting services to producers and distributors in Canadian and US film and television industries; pay-TV, standard broadcast TV productions and theatrical motion pictures. President of Velvet Star Productions Inc. since 90.
Selected Filmography: *Hidden Room*, TV, 91, CDN, Exec Prod; *The Exile*, TV, 90-91, F, Exec Prod; "The Hitchhiker", TV, 89-91, CDN/F, Exec Prod.

PERLMUTTER, Renée
Velvet Film Productions Inc., 129 York-

ville Ave. Suite 200, Toronto, ON M5R 1C4 (416)967-0016. FAX: 960-8447.
Type of Production and Credits: Th Film-Prod; TV Film-Prod; TV Video-Prod.
Genres: Drama-Th&TV; Comedy-Th&TV; Variety-TV.
Biography: Head of Production, Canada, Perlmutter/Chesler Productions.
Selected Filmography: *The Hairdressers*, TV, 83, USA, Exec Prod/Prod; *Howie Mandel Special*, TV, 83, USA, Exec Prod/Prod; *Love*, Th, 80, CDN, Exec Prod/Prod.

PERRIS, Anthony
- see DIRECTORS

PERRY, Howard
- see PRODUCTION MANAGERS

PERZEL, Anthony
Box 603, Canmore, AB T0L 0M0 (403)678-4756. FAX: 678-2694.
Type of Production and Credits: TV Film-Prod/Dir/DOP/Ed.
Genres: Documentary-TV; Educational-TV; Animation-TV.
Biography: Born 1946, Venice, Italy; Canadian citizenship. Studied Business, Ryerson Polytechnical Institute; 2-year Visual Communication Program and 3-year film apprenticeship, Banff Centre. Artistic and technical adviser, Electronic and Film Media Program, Banff Centre, 86. *Lake Louise - A Mountain Legend* won Best Film, Mountain History, Banff.
Selected Filmography: *Keeping the Circle Strong*, ED, 90, CDN, Prod/Dir/Cam/Ed; *Sniff and Huff*, ED, 89, CDN, DOP; *Sharing a Dream*, TV, 87, CDN, Ed; *Lake Louise - A Mountain Legend*, TV, 84, CDN, Prod/Dir/Cin/Co-Wr; *Sliding 29*, TV, 82, CDN, Prod/Dir/Cin/Ed; *Heritage for the Future*, TV, 80, CDN, Prod/Dir/Cin/Ed; *The Metis*, TV, 79, CDN, Assoc Prod; *Those Who Sing Together*, TV, 78, CDN, Assoc Prod/Cin/ An; *Completing Our Circle*, TV, 77, CDN, Cin/An.

PETERSEN, Curtis
- see CINEMATOGRAPHERS

PETKOVSEK, Danny S.
187 Quebec Ave., Toronto, ON M6P 2T9 (416)761-9328. City-TV, 299 Queen St. W., Toronto, ON M5W 2M1 (416)591-5757.
Type of Production and Credits: TV Film-Dir/Prod.
Genres: Documentary-TV; Experimental-TV; Current Affairs-TV; News-TV.
Biography: Born 1960, Toronto, Ontario. Diploma, Radio and TV Arts, Seneca College. Winner, Best News Documentary, Video Culture, 84; Founder's Award of Excellence, CanPro, 84; Best News Documentary, CanPro, 84; Best Local Newscast, CanPro, 87; Best 1 Hr Documentary, CanPro, 91. Producer, "City Pulse News".
Selected Filmography: "City Pulse News", TV, 85-91, CDN, Dir/Prod; "City Wide", TV, 87-88, CDN, Dir; "The Kate Wheeler Story: Diary of a Victim" (5 eps), TV, 87, CDN, Prod/Dir/Cin/Ed; *Raymond: No Fixed Address*, TV, 84, CDN, Prod/Dir/Cin/Ed.

PETRIE, Robert J.
CFTPA, ACCT, STLD. Petrivision Ltd., P.O. Box 9056, Stn. B, St. John's, NF A1A 2A3 (709)737-9502. FAX: 754-4849.
Type of Production and Credits: TV Video-Dir/Wr.
Genres: Drama-Th&TV; Comedy-Th&TV; Commercials-TV.
Biography: Born 1946, Bishop's Falls, Newfoundland. Architectural Diploma, Memorial University, 66. Technical Director, Arts and Culture Centres in Newfoundland, 67-81; President, Petrivision Ltd. since 81. *The Pilgarlic* won a Special Jury Award, Yorkton, 88.
Selected Filmography: *Bourgeois Legacy*, "Inside Stories", TV, 91, CDN, Prod; *Understnading Russ*, Th, 90, CDN, Light Dir; *No Apologies*, Th, 90, CDN, Light Dir; *Secret Nation*, Th, 90, CDN, Light Dir; *The Pilgarlic/Changing Places*, "Yarns from Pigeon Inlet", TV, 87, CDN, Dir; *Albert*, TV, 87, CDN, Light Dir; *Finding Mary March*, Th, 87, CDN, Light Dir; "On Camera" (2 eps), TV, 86, CDN, Dir; "Yarns from Pigeon Inlet" (4 eps), TV, 86, CDN, Dir; *Smoke Screen*, ED, 85, CDN, Light Dir; *Undertow*, Th, 84, CDN, Light Dir; *Lukey's Labels*, "Yarns from Pigeon Inlet", TV, 84, CDN, Wr.

PETRYSHEN, Eva
ACTRA, ACCT. 605 Ave. R. North, Saskatoon, SK S7L 2Z1 (306)382-3898. Sidelines Studio, 917 22nd St. W., Saskatoon, SK S7M 0R9 (306)244-0443.
Type of Production and Credits: TV Video-Prod/Wr.
Genres: Educational-TV; Industrial-TV.
Biography: Born in Moose Jaw, Saskatchewan. Moved to Copenhagen, Denmark; obtained Fine Arts degree at the University of Copenhagen. Resided in Europe for 7 years, returning to Canada in 1975. Obtained B.A. degree and diploma in broadcasting course. In 1980, began freelancing as a narrator/copy writer and eventually worked with Teletheatre as program buyer, promotional director and

production co-ordinator. (Teletheatre was Canada's first experimental pay-TV network.) In 1985, started Saskatchewan's first bona fide Talent agency, Sidelines Talent Agency. In Feb. 1991, expanded Sidelines into video production (industrial, educational, promotional and corporate), with partner, Angus Ouchterlony of A&A Communications Ltd.
Selected Filmography: *Rights & Obligations*, In, 91, CDN, Co Prod/Wr/Dir; *In Their Own Words*, In, 91, CDN, Co Prod/Wr/Dir; *The Way We Were*, ED, 91, CDN, Co Prod/Wr/Dir.

PETTIGREW, Jacques
APFVQ, SMPTE, ACCT. Ciné-Groupe J.P. Inc., 1151, Alexandre-de-Sève, Montréal, PQ H2L 2T7 (514)524-7567.
Types de production et générique: l métrage-Prod; c métrage-Prod; TV film-Prod; TV vidéo-Prod.
Types d'oeuvres: Action-C&TV; Documentaire-C&TV; Animation-C&TV.
Curriculum vitae: Né en 1949, Isle Verte, Québec. Langues: français et anglais. Etudes en anthropologie, Université de Montréal, 79-80. Technicien, cinéaste, caméraman pigiste, 70-74; Président et fondateur de Concept Image J.P. Inc., 74, et Ciné-Groupe J.P. Inc., 79.
Filmographie sélective: "Aventure de l'Ecriture" (112 eps), TV, 91, CDN, Prod; *Bino Fabule* (aussi 4 TV), C, 88, CDN/F/B, Prod; "Sharkey et Georges" (78 eps), TV, 88, CDN/F, Prod; "Les Oursons volants" (39 eps), TV, 88, CDN/YU, Prod; "La Bande à Ovide" (65 eps), TV, 87, CDN/B, Prod; *Les Roses de Matmata*, C, 86, CDN/B, Prod; *Du Sel sur la Peau*, C, 84, CDN/F/B, Prod; *Rien qu'un Jeu*, C, 82, CDN, Prod.

PICK, Anne
ACTRA, TWIFT. Real to Reel Productions Inc., 97 Marion St., Toronto, ON M6R 1E6 (416)531-6162. FAX: 531-6162.
Type of Production and Credits: TV Film-Prod; TV Video-Prod.
Genres: Documentary-TV; Educational-TV; Children's-TV.
Biography: Born 1950, Adelaide, South Australia; landed immigrant, Canada. Served cadetship (4 years) as reporter with several newspaper under auspices of Australian Journalists Association; 6 years experience as a general reporter, features writer and columnist. Has lived in Canada for 16 years and worked most of that time at CBC. Freelance producer, director and writer since 87. Documentaries and TV series currently in development, including *Question & Answer*, which is now going to series.
Selected Filmography: "Question & Answer" (pilot), TV, 91, CDN, Prod; *Kids Come First* (promo video), ED, 91, CDN, Prod/Dir/Co-Wr; *Breaking the Cycle* (promo mini-drama), ED, 90, CDN, Prod; "Money$worth" (26 eps), TV, 88-90, CDN, Wr/Consult; "Money$Worth Prime-Time" (3 eps), TV, 90, CDN, Prod/Wr; "Money$worth" (26 eps), TV, 88-90, CDN, Prod/Wr; "Money$worth" (26 eps), TV, 87-88, CDN, Prod; "Market Place", TV, 81-87, CDN, Prod/Dir/Wr; "Newshour", TV, 81, CDN, Prod; "Canadians" (16 eps), TV, 80, CDN, Prod; "The Week in Ontario", TV, 78-79, CDN, Prod; "Newsmakers", TV, 77-78, CDN, Story Ed; "24 Hours", TV, 75-77, CDN, Res.

PIGOTT, Susan
ACCT. (686 Boischatel), Case Postale 624, Ste-Adele, PQ J0R 1L0 (514)229-2720.
Type of Production and Credits: TV Film-Prod; TV Video-Prod.
Genres: Drama-TV; Commercials-TV; Industrial-TV; Music Video-TV.
Biography: Born in Halifax, Nova Scotia. Graduate of Ontario College of Art. Producer of over 150 commercials for a variety of clients, 80-85. Bessie Award in Food Category and TV Commercial Category.
Selected Filmography: Avon Fashion Videos, In, 87, CDN, Prod; "Johnny McLeod", MV, 85, CDN, Prod; "For the Record" (2 eps), TV, 78, CDN, Cont; "Sidestreet" (4 eps), TV, 77-78, CDN, Cont.

PIRKER, Roland K.
- see CINEMATOGRAPHERS
PODESWA, Jeremy
- see DIRECTORS
POIRIER, Anne Claire
- voir REALISATEURS
PRICE, Roger Damon
- see WRITERS
PRIETO, Claire
BFVN, CIFC, TWIFV, BFF. Prieto-McTair Productions, 133 Wilton St., #328, Toronto, ON M5A 4A4 (416)360-8829.
Type of Production and Credits: Th Short-Prod/Dir.
Genres: Documentary-TV; Educational-TV; Industrial-TV.
Biography: Born 1945, Trinidad, West Indies. B.A.A., Radio & TV Arts, Ryerson Polytechnical Institute, 77. Has been producing/directing documentary films in

Canada for 14 years; films deal with the experiences of Black people in Canada. Awards include: Red Ribbon, American Film Festival for *It's Not An Illness*; Kathleen Shannon Award, Yorkton Festival, 90 for *Black Mother, Black Daughter*; Award of Merit, City of Toronto, 91; Honourable Mention, Genie Awards, 88, for *Home to Buxton*. President and founding member, Black Film & Video Network.
Selected Filmography: *Children Are Not the Problem*, ED, 90-91, CDN, Prod; *Challenge of Diversity*, In, 89-90, CDN, Prod; *Accommodating Abilities*, In, 89-90, CDN, Prod; *Older, Stronger, Wiser*, Th, 88-89, CDN, Dir; *Black Mother, Black Daughter*, Th, 88-89, CDN, Co-Dir; *Home to Buxton*, Th, 87-88, CDN, Co-Dir/Prod; *Different Timbres*, Th, 80, CDN, Prod; *It's Not An Illness*, Th, 79, CDN, Prod.

PRINGLE, Douglas
Peak Productions International, 7 Neville Park Blvd., Toronto, ON M4E 3P5 (416)690-3478.
Type of Production and Credits: TV Video-Wr/Dir/Prod.
Genres: Musical-Th&TV; Documentary-TV.
Biography: Born 1946, Toronto, Ontario. Extensive career as composer, producer, performer of pop and contemporary music; produced Juno nominee "Romance at the Roxy," 81, for Michaele Jordana (Best New Vocalist). Staff producer at Global TV, Toronto, 81-85. *Face to Face* won Silver Medal, International Film and Television Festival, New York, 86; *The Making of the Phantom of the Opera* won Silver Eva, ITVA Awards, 90.
Selected Filmography: *The Making of the Phantom of the Opera*, ED, 89, CDN, Wr/Dir; *Moving with the Light*, TV, 88, CDN, Prod/Dir; *Face to Face*, TV, 85, CDN, Prod/Dir; "That's Life" (100 eps), TV, 82-84, CDN, Prod; *The Far Shore*, Th, 75, CDN, Comp.

PROCOPIO, Frank
101 Flushing Ave., Woodbridge, ON L4L 8H9 (416)856-1946. TMJ Productions Inc., 2065 Finch Ave. W., Ste. 206, Downsview, ON M3N 2V7 (416)749-1194.
Type of Production and Credits: Th Film-Wr; Th Short-Prod/Wr/Dir.
Genres: Drama-Th; Comedy-Th&TV.
Biography: Born in 1957 in Canada of Italian descent. Graduated honours from the University of Toronto, Faculty of Dentistry, 1981. Awarded the Albert E. Webster Award for highest achievement in Restorative Dentistry. Established stand-up comedian. Winner of the 1983 Yuk Yuk's Talent Search for Funniest Person. Club circuit followed prior to embarking on a film career.
Selected Filmography: *Last Dance*, Th, 90, CDN, Prod/Wr/Dir; *Cafe Romeo*, Th, 90, CDN, Assist Prod/Wr/Assist Dir.

PROULX, Daniel
APFTQ, OCAQ. 10 des Ardennes, La Prairie, PQ J5R 4X8 (514)659-1510. 1425 boul. René Lévesque O., 10e étage, Montréal, PQ H3G 1T7 (514)866-1761.
Types de production et générique: TV vidéo-Prod.
Types d'oeuvres: Drame-TV; Enfants-TV.
Curriculum vitae: Né en 1957 à Trois Riviéres, Québec. Citoyenneté canadienne. C.A., Bacc. en administration des affaires. Administrateur depuis 1984, successivement Trésorier, V.P. Finance, V.P. Exécutif et Producteur Exécutif chez Productions SDA Ltée. Vaste expérience dans le financement de productions télévisuelles.
Filmographie sélective: "Robin & Stella II" (30 eps), TV, 91, CDN, Prod exéc; "Robin & Stella" (111 eps), TV, 89-90, CDN, Prod Associé au financement.

PURDY, Brian E.
ACCT, BES, CBI, CFTPA, IICS, ITVA, NABET. 77 Huntley St., Suite 2522, Toronto, ON M4Y 2P3 (416)961-1776.
Type of Production and Credits: TV Film-Prod/Dir; TV Video-Prod/Dir.
Genres: Variety-TV; Musical-TV; Animation-TV; Game Shows-TV.
Biography: Born 1937, Toronto, Ontario. Attended Pickering College, Ryerson Polytechnical Institute, Royal Conservatory of Music. Has logged in excess of 2,500 hours of "live" TV programming. Has produced/directed TV variety shows, TV game shows, commercials for CFTO-TV; commercials for Baker Lovick, Ronalds Reynolds as Senior Producer. Produced/directed network programs for CBC, CTV and YTV. Negotiated first barter program with CBC, Mutual of Omaha's "Wild Kingdom." Produced first video tape animation in Canada. President, producer/director Broadcast Production Inc. since 79. Commercials have won 6 US and 1 Canadian creative awards. Recipient of 1990 Gemini for Technical Excellence - *The Building of the Skydome: 2 -1/2 Years in 2- 1/2 Minutes*
Selected Filmography: "Wild Guess" (26

eps), TV, 88, CDN, Prod/Dir; "Stress Point" (13 eps), TV, 87, CDN, Assoc Prod; *Perry Como's Bahamas Holiday*, TV, 81, USA, Assoc Prod; *The Musical Offering*, TV, 80, CDN, Exec Prod; "Country Music Hall" (39 eps), TV, 69, CDN, Dir; "It's Happening" (72 eps), TV, 67-68, CDN, Prod/Dir.

PYKE, Roger
- see DIRECTORS

RABINOVITCH, David
Moving Images, 550 Miller Ave., Box 1, Mill Valley, CA 94941 (415)383-1383. FAX: 383-1384.
Type of Production and Credits: TV Film-Prod/Dir/Wr.
Genres: Drama-Th&TV; Documentary-TV; Children's-TV; Current Affairs-TV.
Biography: Born in 1951 in Morden, Manitoba. Canadian citizen, U.S. resident alien. Freelance writer/producer/performer on CBC Radio, 66-71. Reporter, *Time* Magazine, 69-71. Producer, "Canada A.M.", 72. Producer/Director, "Take 30", "Adrienne at Large" and "Hard Times, CBC, 73-77. Emmy for magazine series "Here & Now", CBS, 78. Documentary Producer, NBC, 78-80. Emmy and Peabody Medal for *Politics of Poison*. Script Finalist, Sundance Institute, 85. Design Fellowship, National Endowment for the Arts, 86. Writer/Producer, feature films and movies-of-the-week, Los Angeles, 87-88. Numerous credits on PBS, including three episodes of "Frontline". Awards from festivals in San Francisco, Houston, Chicago, Philadelphia, Hawaii and others. Currently partner in Moving Images, production company.
Selected Filmography: *Minidragons*, TV, 91, USA/J/Aus, Dir; *Future Wave:*, TV, 90, USA/J, Exec Prod/Dir; *Vibrations*, Th, 88, USA, Prod/Dir/Co-Wr; *Captain Change*, Th, 88, USA, Dir; *Give Me That Big Time Religion*, "Frontline", TV, 84, USA, Prod/Wr; *Air Crash*, "Frontline", TV, 83, USA, Prod/Dir/Wr; *A Chinese Affair*, "Frontline", TV, 83, USA, Prod/Dir/Wr; *Slotin*, TV, 81, USA, Wr; *Shangai Shadows*, TV, 80, USA, Wr; *Politics of Poison*, TV, 79, USA, Prod/Dir/Wr, (EMMY).

RADFORD, Tom
Great North Communications Inc., 10359, 82nd Ave., Suite 300, Edmonton, AB T6E 1Z9 (403)439-1260.
Type of Production and Credits: TV Film-Prod/Dir/Wr; TV Video-Prod.
Genres: Drama-TV; Documentary-TV.
Biography: Born 1946, Edmonton, Alberta. B.A., University of Alberta. Founding member, Film Frontiers Ltd., 69; Filmwest Associates Ltd., 72; Great Plains Films Ltd., 78. Set up Northwest Atudio of NFB in Edmonton; Executive Producer, 81-86. Board member, Banff TV Festival, 82-86; Executive Director, National Screen Institute; Canada; President, Great North Communications Inc. His films have won awards at Banff, Yorkton, San Francisco, Hemisfilm and American film festivals.
Selected Filmography: *Kurt Browning: The Making of a Champion*, TV, 91, CDN, Dir; *The Alberta People Project*, TV, 91, CDN, Prod/Dir; *Doctor Anne*, TV, 91, CDN, Dir; *In Search of the Dragon*, ED, 88, CDN, Dir; *Life after Hockey*, TV, 88, CDN, Dir; *Long Lance*, TV, 86, CDN, Exec Prod; *A Change of Heart*, "For the Record", TV, 83, CDN, Exec Prod; *War Story*, TV, 82, CDN, Exec Prod; *China Mission: The Chester Ronning Story*, TV, 80, CDN, Co-Wr/Dir; *Wood Mountain Poems*, TV, 78, CDN, Prod; "The Renewable Society" (26 eps), TV, 76, CDN, Prod; *Man Chooses the Bush*, TV, 75, CDN, Dir; *Ernest Brown, Pioneer Photographer*, TV, 74, CDN, Wr/Dir; *The Country Doctor*, TV, 72, CDn, Wr/Dir.

RAFFE, Alexandra
ACCT, CFTPA, TWIFV. 151 John St., Suite 502, Toronto, ON M5V 2T2 (416)971-9401.
Type of Production and Credits: Th Film-Prod/PM; Th Short-Prod.
Genres: Drama-Th; Comedy-Th.
Biography: Born 1955, Singapore; British citizenship; landed immigrant, Canada. Ten years corporate experience internationally in a variety of capacities, Xerox; widely travelled, grew up in Far East; script editor; professional writer/editor for magazines. *I've Heard the Mermaids Singing* won 2 Genies and "Prix de la jeunesse" in Cannes, 87; *The White Room* won Prix Antenne d'Or, Avoriaz Film Festival, 91.
Selected Filmography: *Battle of the Bulge*, TV, 91, CDN, Exec Prod; *White Room/La chambre claire*, Th, 90, CDN, Prod; *I've Heard the Mermaids Singing*, Th, 86, CDN, Prod/PM/Assist Snd Ed; *Passion: A Letter in 16mm*, Th, 85, CDN, Assoc Prod/PM/Assist Snd Ed.

RAINSBERRY, Linda
115 Evans Ave., Toronto, ON M6S 3V9 TVOntario, 2200 Yonge St., Suite 303, Toronto, ON M4T 2T1 (416)484-2600.
Type of Production and Credits: TV Film-Prod; TV Video-Prod.
Genres: Drama-TV; Documentary-TV;

Educational-TV.
Biography: Born 1947, Halifax, Nova Scotia. Honours B.A., B.Ed., M.Ed. Several awards including for "Saying Goodbye" series: Gemini, 90; Best Short Dramatic Program; Panasonic Award for film to have accomplished highes overall level of quality standards, 91; finalist, NY Film Festival, 90; Bronze Award, Columbus, 90; Top Honours, Ohio State Award, 91; Silver Award, John Muir Medical Festival, San Francisco, 90.
Selected Filmography: *The First Snowfall/Thunder in My Head/A Home Alone/A Promise Broken/A Grief Shared*, "Saying Goodbye", TV, 90-91, CDN, Prod; "The Process of Reading" (6 eps), TV, CDN, Co-Wr; "Family Matters" (10 eps), TV, 87-88, CDN, Prod; "Hooked on Reading" (6 eps), TV, 86-87, CDN, Prod; "Educating the Special Child" (3 eps), TV, 85-86, CDN, Prod; "Out of the Shadows" (3 eps), TV, 84-85, CDN, Prod.

RAKOFF, Alvin
- see DIRECTORS

RANSEN, Mort
- see DIRECTORS

RASKY, Harry
- see DIRECTORS

RASTELLI, Maryse
CTPDA. 35 Moncion, Hull, PQ, J9A 1K4 (819)770-9788. Radio-Canada, B.P. 3220, Succ. A, Ottawa, ON K1E 1Y4 (613) 724-5240.
Types de production et générique: TV film-Prod; TV vidéo-Réal/Prod.
Types d'oeuvres: Drame-TV; Variété-TV; Documentaire-TV.
Curriculum vitae: Né en 1937, Longuyon, France; citoyenneté canadienne. Langues: français et anglais. Baccalauréat en Philosophie, cours à Cambridge et universités St-Paul et Ottawa, Réalisatrice à Radio-Canada depuis 74.
Filmographie sélective: "La nuit sur l'étang" (6 eps), TV, 91, CDN, Réal; "Bricomagie" (26 eps), ED, 90, CDN, Réal; *Visite au Musée des Beaux Arts du Canada*, TV, 89, CDN, Réal; *Fabienne Thibeault/Peter Pringle et Nicole Croisille*, "Les Beaux Dimanches", TV, 85, CDN, Réal; *Bal de neige*, TV, 85, CDN, Réal; "Au jour le jour" (pl seg), TV, 83-85, CDN, Réal; "La Bête...ou le caprice du temps" (2 eps), TV, 83, CDN, Réal; *Edith Butler/M.P. Belle*, "Les Beaux Dimanches", TV, 82, CDN, Réal; "Jeunes virtuoses" (3 eps), TV, 80, CDN, Réal; "Pulsion" (26 eps), TV, 76-79, CDN, Réal; "Les Beaux Dimanches" (prod dél 8 ém/réal 3 ém), TV, 77-78, CDN, Réal/Prod dél.

RATTAN, Amarjeet S.
DGC. Siren Films/Rattan Films, 827 W. Pender St., Vancouver, BC V6C 3G8 (604)662-8337.
Type of Production and Credits: Th Film-Prod/Dir; Th Short-Prod/Dir; TV Film-Prod/Dir; TV Video-Prod/Dir.
Genres: Drama-Th&TV; Documentary-TV; Commercials-TV; Industrial-TV; Current Affairs-TV.
Biography: Born 1957, Punjab, India; Canadian citizenship. Languages: Punjabi, Hindi, English. B.A., Political Science, University of British Columbia. Directed studies in film production at Simon Fraser University.
Selected Filmography: *Fire Within*, Th, 91, CDN, Prod; *Never Again?*, Th, 91, CDN, Prod; *Mexico: Pyramid of the Sun*, TV, 88, CDN, Prod/Dir; "AIDS: The New Epidemic" (2 eps)(Hindi/Punjabi series), TV, 87, Dir; *On the Fireline*, TV, 86, CDN, Prod/Dir; "Pacific Reports" (CBC), TV, 85, CDN, Prod; *Ismaili Mosque*, In, 85, CDN, Prod/Dir; *Hawaii: The Host Islands*, TV, 82, CDN, Prod/Dir; "The India Trilogy" (3 eps), TV, 82, CDN, Prod/Dir; *Lotus Shadow*, Th, 80, CDN, Wr/Ed/Dir.

RAYMOND, Bruce
ACCT, CFTPA. Bruce A. Raymond Productions Ltd., 11 Soho St., Suite 202, Toronto, ON M5T 1Z6 (416)485-3406. FAX: 340-0135.
Type of Production and Credits: TV Film-Prod; TV Video-Prod; Th Film-Prod.
Genres: Drama-TV; Documentary-TV; Educational-TV; Children's-TV; Comedy-Th.
Biography: Born 1925. Languages: English and French. B.A., McGill University. During the 50s, wrote 200 TV documentaries, film scripts and radio programs; Head, CBC Radio, 60s, then Head, CBC TV; returned to private enterprise as distributor/producer, 69. *Special People* won a Christopher Award and Silver Medal, Houston, 85. Became Life Patron, Variety Clubs International, 87.
Selected Filmography: "Connecting" (65 eps), TV, 88-89, CDN, Exec Prod; *Blue City Slammers*, Th, 87, CDN, Prod; "50 Plus" (26 eps), TV, 86, CDN, Exec Prod; "Your Health Quiz" (6 eps), TV, 85, CDN/USA, Exec Prod; "Parenting" (130 eps), TV, 84-85, CDN, Pro Exec; "Frost Over Canada" (10 eps), TV, 83, CDN, Prod; "Bingo Express" (65 eps), TV, 83,

CDN, Prod; *Special People*, TV, 83, CDN/USA, Exec Prod; *Live 'n' Kickin'*, TV, 83, CDN, Exec Prod; *Hooters*, TV, 83, CDN, Prod; *Magic of David Copperfield*, TV, 83, CDN/USA, Exec Prod; *Rich Little Lift-Off*, TV, 83, CDN, Exec Prod; "The KangaZoo Club" (26 eps), TV, 82-83, CDN, Co-Prod; *The Wreck of the Margeson*, TV, 81, CDN, Narr; "Changing Worlds" (14 eps), TV, 78, CDN, Prod.

RAYMOND, Marie-José
APFVQ, UDA, ACCT. C.P. 40, St-Paul d'Abbotsford, PQ J0E 1A0 (514)379-5304. Rose Films Inc., 86, de Brésoles, Montréal, PQ H2Y 1V5 (514)285-8901.
Types de production et générique: l métrage-Prod/Sc; TV film-Prod/Sc.
Types d'oeuvres: Drame-C&TV; Comédie-C; Documentaire-C.
Filmographie sélective: *Les Tisserands du pouvoir*(aussi série de 6 heures pour TV), C, 87, CDN/F, Prod; *Bonheur d'occasion/The Tin Flute*(aussi 5 ém TV/tourné simul fr & angl), C, 82, CDN, Prod/Co sc; *Hot Dogs*, C, 79, CDN, Prod/Co sc; *La Notte Dell'Alta Marea/The Twilight of Love*, C, 76, CDN/I, Prod exéc; *Je suis loin de toi mignonne*, C, 75, CDN, Co prod; *La Pomme, la queue...et les pépins!*, C, 74, CDN, Prod/Co sc; *Alien Thunder*, C, 72, CDN, Prod; *Les Chats bottés*, C, 71, CDN, Prod/Co sc; *Deux femmes en or*, C, 70, CDN, Co sc.

RAYMONT, Peter
- see DIRECTORS

READ, Merilyn
CFTPA. MTR Productions Limited, 17 Lambton Ave., Ottawa, ON K1M 0Z6 (613)747-9058. 233 Argyle Ave., Ottawa, ON K2P 1B8 (613)238-5867.
Type of Production and Credits: TV Film-Exec Prod/Wr; TV Video-Prod.
Genres: Children's-TV; Animation-TV; Industrial-TV; Current Affairs-TV; News-TV.
Biography: Born 1948, Bath, England. Languages: English and some French. Former journalist with CBC-TV, Maclean's and Canadian Press. *Babar & Father Christmas* won Gemini and Bronze Award, New York Film.
Selected Filmography: *Babar & Father Christmas*, TV, 86, CDN, Exec Prod/Wr, (GEMINI).

REED-OLSEN, Joan
- see DIRECTORS

REGAN, Ted
DGC. 708 Merton St., Toronto, ON M4S 1B8 Ted Regan Productions Inc., 187 King St. E., Suite 200, Toronto, ON M5A 1J5 (416)364-6636.
Type of Production and Credits: TV Video-Prod/Dir.
Genres: Documentary-TV; Children's-TV; Industrial-TV; Corporate-Th.
Biography: Born 1940, Toronto, Ontario. B.A., Sir George Williams University. Credits for more than 300 network hours. Producer/director of 9 Imax marketing videos; also produces/directs video teleconferences. Winner of several awards including Chicago and Boston.
Selected Filmography: "Geometrics" (16 eps), ED, 88, CDN, Prod/Dir; Yugo Cars, Cm, 88, CDN, Dir; "Bank Beat" (5 eps), In, 88, CDN, Dir; *Picking Winners*, TIEM, In, 87, CDN, Prod; "88 in Motion" (3 eps), In, 87, CDN, Dir; *The No Name Show*, ED, 86, CDN, Prod/Dir; *Future's Past*, Air Canada, In, 86, CDN, Prod/Dir.

REHAK, Peter
CTV - W5, P.O. Box 3000, Agincourt Postal Stn., Agincourt, ON M1S 3C6 (416)609-7314. FAX: 609-7427.
Type of Production and Credits: TV Video-Prod.
Genres: News-TV; Current Affairs-TV.
Biography: Born 1936. B.A., McGill University, Montreal. Started career in print journalism. Foreign correspondent for The Associated Press, 62-72. Bureau Chief *Time* magazine, Toronto and Ottawa, 73-76. Winner of numerous journalism awards, including George Polk Award for best reporting from overseas as well as two Gemini nominations for best information program. Senior producer, "The National" (CBC), "Newsmagazine" (CBC), 76-81. Producer/Executive Producer, "W5" (CTV), 81-91. Co-author of *Undercover Agent*, "True crime," 88.
Selected Filmography: "W5" (220 eps), TV, 81-91, CDN, Prod/Exec Prod; *A Conversation With the Prime Minister*, TV, CDN, Prod.

REICHEL, Stephane
DGC. 4620 Coolbrook, Montreal, PQ H3X 2K6 (514)481-1851. Alliance Communications, 355 Place Royale, Montreal, PQ H2Y 2V3 (514)844-3132.
Type of Production and Credits: Th Film-Prod; TV Film-Prod.
Genres: Drama-Th&TV; & Action-Th&TV.
Biography: Born 1948. Vice-President of Production, Alliance Communications; responsible for supervision of all productions.
Selcted Filmography: *Black Robe*, Th, 90, CDN/AUS, Prod; "Bordertown", TV,

88/90, CDN/F, Spv Prod; "Bordertown", TV, 89, CDN/F, Prod; *Eddie Lives*, Th, 89, CDN, Prod; *Iron Eagle II*, Th, 87, CDN/USA, Assoc Prod/PM; *Jeweller's Shop*, Th, 87, I/CDN, Prod; *The Return of Ben Casey*, TV, 87, USA/CDN, Prod Exec; *Nowhere to Hide*, Th, 86, USA, Assoc Prod/PM; *Doing Life*, TV, 86, USA, PM; *Children of a Lesser God*, Th, 85, USA, PM; *Boy in Blue*, Th, 85, CDN/USA, PM; *The Bay Boy*, Th, 84, CDN/F, PM; *Louisiana*, (mini-series), TV, 84, CDN/F, PM; *Magic Skates*, TV, 84, CDN, PM.

REID, François
voir REGISSEURS

REID, William ◊
(416)533-5790.
Type of Production and Credits: Th Film-Prod/Dir; TV Film-Prod/Dir; TV Video-Prod/Dir.
Genres: Documentary-Th&TV; Educational-TV; Current Affairs-TV.
Biography: Born 1941, Toronto, Ontario. B.A., English and Philosophy, University of Western Ontario.
Selected Filmography: *Shahira*, TV, 87, CDN, Prod; "The Space Experience" (6 eps), TV, 87, CDN, Prod; *The First Canadian Astronaut*, TV, 85, CDN, Prod/Dir; *Skating on Thin Ice*, TV, 81, CDN, Dir, (CFA); *Coming Home*, Th, 73, CDN, Dir, (CFA).

REISLER, Susan
- see WRITERS

REITMAN, Ivan
- see DIRECTORS

REITMAN, Joel ◊
MIJO Productions Ltd., 1491 Yonge St., Suite 201, Toronto, ON 416)964-7539.
Type of Production and Credits: TVFilm-Prod; TV Video-Prod.
Genres: Commercials-Th&TV.
Biography: Born 1956, Montreal, Quebec. Languages: English and French. B.Sc., Ithaca College, New York. Specializes in radio, television and theatrical commercials and trailers; also in duplication and distribution of these commercials; started company with Michael Goldberg, 78.

REMEROWSKI, Ted
ACTRA. 130 Rosewell Ave., Toronto, ON M4R 2A4 (416)487-4012. Remerowski Productions Ltd., 20 Maud St., Ste. 207, Toronto, ON M5V 2M5 (416)363-5069.
Type of Production and Credits: TV Film-Prod/Dir/Wr; TV Video-Prod/Dir/Wr.
Genres: Documentary-Th&TV; Current Affairs-TV.
Biography: Born in 1948 in Poland. Canadian citizen. Bachelor of Science (Architecture) from McGill University. Christopher awards, Columbus awards, Scales of Justice award. *Struggle for Democracy* won a Gemini for Best Documentary Series, a Gemeaux and a Columbus. *Store Wars* won an Actra award for Best Program and for Best Writer. Won a Canadian Film Award for Best Editor for *Champions*.
Selected Filmography: *The Curtain Rises*, TV, 90, USA/GB, Prod/Dir; *A Question of Leadership*, TV, 90, CDN, Exec Prod/Prod; "Struggle For Democracy", TV, 89, USA/GB, Prod; *And You Shall Be Heard*, "The Lawyers" (2 eps), TV, 86, CDN, Prod/Dir/Wr; "The Chinese" (6 eps), TV, 82, CDN, Wr/Dir; *Store Wars*, "The Canadian Establishment", TV, 80, Prod/Dir/Wr, (ACTRA); *Champions*, TV, 78, CDN, Ed.

REPKE, Ron
560 Queen St. S., Kitchener, ON N2G 1X1 (519)743-2600.
Type of Production and Credits: Th Film-Prod/PM/Wr; Th Short-Prod/PM/Wr; TV Film-Prod/PM/Dir/Wr; TV Video-Prod/PM/Dir/Wr.
Genres: Drama-Th&TV; Children's-Th&TV; Experimental-Th.
Biography: Born 1959, Kitchener, Ontario. Languages: English and German. B.A.A., Film Studies, Ryerson Polytechnical Institute; Algonquin Institute of Film, Producer/Director Course; Paul Gray Directing Seminar; "Moving the Image" Seminar. Owner of Eyelight Advertising Agency. Producer/director of numerous industrials and television commercials, 84 to present.
Selected Filmography: *Knock! Knock!*, Th, 84, CDN, Consult; *Scissere*, Th, 82, CDN, Co-Prod; *Synesthesia*, TV, 82, CDN, Co-Prod/PM; *Empty Case of Blues*, TV, 81, CDN, Co-Prod/PM.

REUSCH, Peter
- see DIRECTORS

REYNOLDS, Gene
- see DIRECTORS

REYNOLDS, Stephen P.
DGC, ACCT. 241-E Dovercourt Rd., Toronto, ON M6J 3C9 (416)534-9539. Reynolds Productions Inc., 241-E Dovercourt Rd., Toronto, ON M6J 3C9 (416)534-9539.
Type of Production and Credits: Th Film-Prod/Assist Dir; TV Film-PM/Line Prod/Assist Dir; TV Video-Prod.
Genres: Drama-Th&TV; Comedy-TV; Action-TV; Music Video-TV.

Biography: Born in 1958 in Ottawa, Ontario. Canadian citizen. B.F.A., Photography and Art History, Nova Scotia College of Art and Design, 1984. Has been involved in the production of film and television since 1981. Produced for Salter Street Films the CBC program "Codco", 1988-91. With Bill MacGillivray in 1986, produced the feature film *Life Classes*. Over the past six years, has worked with B.C. producers, Manitoba filmmakers, New York distributors, TVO, CBC, Toronto commercial/video houses and and independently produced films. Photo-graphs have been published in *On Location* magazine and been exhibited publicly including shows at the Anna Leonowens Gallery. Partner in the Nova Scotia film and TV company, Dovercourt Films. Won the 1990 Gemini award for Best Variety Series for "Codco". Won the 1986 Award of Excellence, 35mm short subject, Atlantic Festival/Atlantique. 1988 Genie nomination for Best Film, *Life Classes*
Selected Filmography: *North of Pittsburgh*, Th, 91, CDN, Assist Dir; "Codco" (27 eps), TV, 88-90, CDN, Prod; *The First Snowfall*, TV, 90, CDN, PM/Assist Dir; *A Promise Broken*, TV, 90, CDN, Assist Dir; *Cowpunk*, TV, 88, CDN, Assist Dir; *Summer Storm*, TV, 88, CDN, Assist Dir; *The Outside Chance of Maximilliam Glick*, Th, 87, CDN, Assist Dir; *Buying Time*, Th, 87, CDN, Assist Dir; *Sticky Fingers*, Th, 87, CDN, Assist Dir; *Life Classes*, Th, 86, CDN, Prod; *Windows*, TV, 82, CDN, PM.

RICHARDSON, Gillian
35 Oak Valley Drive, Novato, CA 94947 (415)892-2990.
Type of Production and Credits: Th Short-PM/Prod; TV Film-PM/Prod.
Genres: Drama-Th&TV; Action-Th&TV; Science Fiction-Th&TV; Children's-TV.
Biography: Born 1950, Jersey, Channel Islands, Great Britain; British and Canadian citizenship, American resident. Languages: English and French. Educated and trained in TV and film in Great Britain. Currently producing *The Vagrant*, a psychological thriller/black comedy (to be released fall 91/spring 92).
Selected Filmography: *The Fly II*, Th, 88, USA, Assoc Prod; *A Child's Christmas in Wales*, TV, 87, CDN/USA/GB, Prod, (GEMINI 88); *The Fly*, Th, 86, USA, Cont; *Legs of the Lame/Rebellion of Young David*, "Bell Playhouse, TV, 85, CDN, Co-Prod; *The Dream and the Triumph*, "Bell Canada Playhouse", TV, 85, CDN, Co-Prod; "Ray Bradbury Theatre" (3 eps), TV, 85, CDN, Line Prod/PM; "Bell Canada Playhouse" (7 eps), TV, 84, CDN, Line Prod/PM; *Islands*, TV, 84, CDN/USA, PM; "Sons and Daughters" (12 eps), TV, 83, CDN, Line Prod/PM; *The Dead Zone*, Th, 83, USA, Cont; *Videodrome*, Th, 81, CDN/USA, Cont; *Spasms*, Th, 81, CDN, Cont; "Kidsworld" (26 eps), TV, 80, CDN/USA, Assoc Prod/Dir; *Baker County U.S.A./The Killer Instinct*, Th, 80, CDN/USA, Cont; *Threshold*, Th, 80, CDN, Cont.

RICHER, Simon
- voir REALISATEURS

ROBBINS, Karen
Reeliable Resource, 52 Springdale Blvd., Toronto, ON M4J 1W7 (416)466-5548. Manulife Financial, Audio Visual, 200 Bloor St. E., Toronto, ON M4W 1E5 (416)926-5295.
Type of Production and Credits: Th Short-Prod/Dir/Wr; Video-Prod/Dir/Wr.
Genres: Documentary-TV; Educational-Th; Industrial-Th&TV; Current Affairs-TV.
Biography: Born 1958, Toronto, Ontario. Languages: English, working knowledge of French and Portugese. B.A.(Major in Film Studies), University of Toronto, 80; M.S., Telecommunications and Film, Syracuse University, 81; International Baccalauréat, Lester B. Pearson College of the Pacific, United World College, 77.
Selected Filmography: *Leaders of the Band, New Orleans 1991*, In, 91, CDN, Prod/ Wr; *Performax*, In, 90, CDN, Prod/Wr/ Dir; *Stranded in the Jungle*, In, 89, CDN, Prod/Wr/Dir; *Sales Concept: Ideas That Sell*, In, 89, CDN, Prod/Wr/Dir; *A Matter of Life and Health*, In, 88, CDN, Prod/ Wr/Dir; *Come Join the Group*, In, 88, CDN, Prod/Dir/Wr/Interv; *Headstart*, In, 87, CDN, Prod/Dir/Wr; *The Case for the Crown*, In, 87, CDN, Prod/Dir/Wr/ Interv; *Voices of Youth*, ED, 87, CDN, Prod/Dir/Wr/Interv; "Money Smart" (8 eps), ED, 86-87, CDN, PM/Interv/Res; "Starting a Business" (10 eps), ED, 83-84, CDN, PM/Interv/Res; *Osteoporosis: The Silent Thief*, In, 84, CDN, PM/Interv/Res; *Transitions*, ED, 84, CDN, PM/Wr/ Res/Interv.

ROBERGE, Hélène
- voir REALISATEURS

ROBERT, Nicole
APFTQ, ACCT. 865 Des Hérons, Longueuil, PQ J4G 9Z7. Lux Films inc., 640 St-Paul ouest, Bureau 605, Montréal, PQ H3C 1L9 (514)866-1888.

Types de production et générique: l métrage-Prod; TV film-Prod.
Types d'oeuvres: Drame-C&TV; Action-C&TV; Enfants-C; Animation-C&TV.
Curriculum vitae: Née à Montréal, Québec. Langues: anglais et français. Travaille à l'industrie cinématographique depuis plus de 15 ans. Débute sa carrière de cinéaste avec le film d'animation; coréalise *Québec Love* (73) qui se méritele Premier prix au Festival du film étudiant; membre fondateur, Les Films Quebec Love, 77. Crée le studio Animabec; conçoit, dessine, réalise et produit des publicités, des signatures corporatives et des indicatifs de télévision. Vice-président des Productions La Fête, 84. Produit les deux premiers longs-métrage de la série "Contes pour tous": *La Guerre des Tuques*, qui lui vaut une mise en nomination aux Prix Génie, 85 et le Prix de la Bobine d'Or, et *The Peanut Butter Solution*. Produit en Tunisie *Les Roses de Matmata* une co-production avec la Belgique, 86. Productrice déléguée pour *Kalamazoo*, 86. Ouvre sa maison de production, Lux Films, 87; elle est producteur exécutif et productrice pour *Toutes Ressemblances voulues* dont le tournage est prévu au cours de l'été 91.
Filmographie sélective: *Les naufrages du Labrador*, TV, 91, CDN, Prod; *Laura Laur*, C, 89, CDN, Prod; *Kalamazoo*, C, 86, CDN, Prod dél; *Les roses de Matmata*, C/TV, 86, CDN/B, Prod assoc; *The Peanut Butter Solution*, C, 85, CDN, Prod; *La guerre des tuques*, C, 84, CDN, Prod.

ROCHON, Gerard O.
NATPE, CANPRO. 556 Merton St., Toronto, ON M4S 1B3 (416)482-1919. CFTO-TV Ltd., Box 9, Stn. O, Toronto, ON M4A 2M9 (416)299-2171. FAX: 299-2214.
Type of Production and Credits: TV Film-Prod/Dir; TV Video-Prod.
Genres: Drama-TV; Comedy-TV; Variety-TV; Musical-TV.
Biography: Born 1934, Windsor, Ontario. Languages: English and French. B.A., Philosophy and Communications, University of Detroit, 57. "The Littlest Hobo" won Bronze, 82, Gold, 83, and Silver, 84, International Film and Television Festival of New York.
Selected Filmography: *Véronique: Wish You Were Here*, TV, 91, CDN, Exec Prod; *A Canadian in New York*, TV, 91, CDN, Exec Prod; *Nahanni and Rebekka Dawn*, TV, 89-90, CDN, Exec Prod; *Véronique: A Time to Remember*, TV, 89, CDN, Exec Prod; *Véronique Hot*, TV, 88, CDN, Prod/Exec Prod; *CTV Winter Olympics* (opening and closing ceremonies), TV, 88, CDN, Exec Prod; *Véronique Magnifique*, TV, 88, CDN, Prod/Exec Prod; "People to People" (24 eps), TV, 88, CDN, Exec Prod; "Divided Loyalties", TV, 88, CDN, Prod; "What's Cooking" (960 eps), TV, 80-88, CDN, Exec Prod; "Definition" (960 eps) (also 480 eps, 74-78), TV, 80-88, CDN, Exec Prod; "Guess What" (480 eps), TV, 84-88, CDN, Exec Prod; *Miss Canada Pageant* (also Prod 70-74), TV, 80-88, CDN, Exec Prod; *Miss Teen Canada Pageant* (also 70-74), TV, 80-88, CDN, Exec Prod; "Littlest Hobo" (72 eps), TV, 80-88, CDN, Exec Prod.

RODECK, Ken
P.O. Box 1347, Stonewall, MB R0C 2Z0 (204)467-8327. Rode Pictures Inc., 140 Bannatyne Ave., Suite 300, Winnipeg, MB R3B 3C5 (204)941-0063. FAX: 942-3568.
Type of Production and Credits: Th Film-Prod/Ed; Th Short-Ed; TV Film-Prod/Ed.
Genres: Drama-Th&TV; Documentary-TV; Educational-TV.
Biography: Born 1951, Winnipeg, Manitoba. Graduate of Banff Film & Television Production, Banff School of Fine Arts. 14 years in the film industry, first 7 with NFB. *Oceans* won Grand Prize, 3rd Film Festival Ragazzi Bellinzona, Switzerland; Best Feature Film, 9th Annual International Film Festival for Young Australians, Adelaide, Australia; Prix du President du republique, 8th Annual International Youth Film Festival, Lyon, France; Honourable Mention in the category of Best Canadian Screenplay, Vancouver International Film Festival. *Science Fair Kids* won Best Educational at Yorkton. *The Cat Came Back* and *The Big Snit* were each nominated for an Academy Award.
Selected Filmography: *The 12 Steps: Recovering from Addictions* (13 parts), TV, 90, CDN, Line Prod; *Welcome Home Hero*, "Inside Stories", TV, 90, CDN, Prod; *The Last Winter*, Th, 88, CDN, Prod; *The Cat Came Back*, Th, 88, CDN, Ed; *Science Fair Kids*, ED, 86, Assoc Prod; *The Washing Machine*, "The Way We Are", TV, 87, CDN, Assoc Prod; *The Big Snit*, Th, 85, CDN, Ed.

RODGERS, Bob
Bellair Communications Ltd., 131 Bloor St. W., #1012, Toronto, ON M5S 1R1 (416)927-1121.
Type of Production and Credits: TV Film-Dir/Prod/Wr; TV Video-Dir/Prod/Wr.

Genres: Drama-Th; Documentary-TV; Educational-TV; Industrial-TV.
Biography: Born 1933, Regina, Saskatchewan. Attended Wayne State University, B.A., University of Manitoba; M.A., University of Toronto; Research Fellow, Bodleian, Oxford. Taught English at University of Toronto and McGill, before moving into writing; then director/producer of documentary, educational films; associate producer of features, Film Consortium of Canada; President Bellair Communications Ltd. Has won IMF and AMTEC awards for several films.
Selected Filmography: *Specialists on Environment*, ED, 89-91, CDN, Prod/Dir; *Spirit of Enter Prize*, In, 89, CDN, Prod/Dir/Wr; *Les Jeunes Entrepreneurs*, ED, 89, CDN, Prod; *Behind the Scenes*, "Trade Secrets", TV, 86, CDN, Dir/Wr; *Four Seasons in a Day*, In, 85, CDN, Prod; *Cabbagetown*, "Neighbourhoods", TV, 85, CDN, Dir/Wr; *High Impact Welding*, In, 84, CDN, Dir/Wr; *Un premier prix*, ED, 84, CDN, Prod; *A Sense of Community*, In, 83, CDN, Dir; *Northrop Frye, "The Bible and Literature"*, ED, 81-83, CDN, Prod; *The Bread We Live By*, ED, 83, CDN, Prod; *Voices of Early Canada*, ED, 79-81, CDN, Prod/Dir; *China: The Cultural Revolution*, ED, 81, CDN, Prod/Dir; *Mr. Patman*, Th, 80, CDN, Assoc Prod; *Fiddlers of James Bay*, TV, 79, CDN, Co-Prod/Dir.

RODRIGUE, Michel
APFTQ, ADISQ, ACCT. 2980, Des Hopitalières, Sillery, Québec, PQ G1T 1V7 (418)650-3246. Productions de la Capitale inc., 972, St-Jean, Québec, PQ G1R 1R5 (418)694-9903.
Types de production et générique: TV vidéo-Prod.
Types d'oeuvres: Variété-TV; Enfants-TV; Vidéo clips-TV; Comédie-TV.
Curriculum vitae: Né en 1952. Citoyenneté canadienne. Langues: français et anglais. Baccalauréat en Commerce, 71, études en Marketing, 71-72, Sir George Williams University. Metteur en ondes, opérateur script, réalisateur commercial, représentant publicitaire, Entreprises Télé-Capitale Ltée., 75-81; Représentant national, producteur délégué, Pathonic Communication Ltée., 81; Vice-président, Télé-Capitale Inc., 84-85; Président, producteur, fondateur, Les Productions de la Capitale inc., depuis 85; Président, fondateur, Télévariétés inc., depuis 82. Vice-Président, ADISQ, depuis juin, 91.
Filmographie sélective: *Gala de l'ADISQ*, TV, 91, CDN, Prod; *Seulement pour toujours*, TV, 91, CDN, Co prod; *Sainte Nuit*, TV, 90, CDN, *Fais attention...les B.B. arrivent!*, TV, 90, CDN, Prod; *Au coeur de Québec*, TV, 90, CDN, Prod; *Chablcouin*, TV, 88, CDN, Prod; *L'Enfant du Cirque*, TV, 88, CDN, Prod; *Symphonique 'n' Roll*, TV, 88, CDN, Co prod; *L'Etincelle de la fête*, TV, 88, CDN, Co prod, (FELIX); *Chantez-nous la paix*, TV, 87, Prod; *33e Défilé de nuit Carnaval de Québec*, TV, 87, CDN, Prod; *Quand viendrez-vous à mon rendez-vous*, MV, 87, CDN, Prod; *Musée de la Civilisation*, In, 87, CDN, Prod; *Carnaval de Québec*, In, 87, CDN, Prod; *Patrick Sabatier au Québec*, TV, 87, CDN, Prod.

ROGAN, N. (Bert)
- see WRITERS

ROGERS, Al
- see WRITERS

ROGERS, Allen ◊
(212)772-2915.
Type of Production and Credits: Th Short-Prod/Dir; TV Film-Prod/Dir; TV Video-Prod/Dir; Video-Prod/Unit M.
Genres: Drama-TV; Comedy-TV; Documentary-Th&TV; Educational-Th&TV.
Biography: Born 1933, Toronto, Ontario; Canadian and US citizenship. M.E.S. (Environmental Studies), York University, 80.
Selected Filmography: *Modern Times* (double shot French & English), ED, 88, CDN, Prod/Dir; *Let's Get Together* (double shot French & English), ED, 86-87, CDN, Prod/Dir; "Ready, Willing and Able" (3 eps) (Prod, French adapt.), ED, 85-86, CDN, Prod/Dir; *Mr. Neverlearn Meets the Firefighter*, ED, 85, CDN, Dir; *Once in David's City*, TV, 84, CDN, Prod/Dir; *A Question of Confidence*, TV, 83, CDN, Prod/Dir; *Legacy of Time*, TV, 82, CDN, Prod/Dir; *A Fine Line*, TV, 81, CDN, Prod/Dir; *Miskito*, TV, 80, CDN, Prod/Dir; *Hospital Amazonico*, TV, 78, CDN, Prod/Dir; *Chile Nuavo*, TV, 78, CDN, Prod/Dir.

ROLAND, Herb
ATPD, ACCT. 10 Windsor Ave., Scarborough, ON M1N 1A7 (416)690-1692.
Type of Production and Credits: TV Film-Prod/Dir; TV Video-Prod/Dir.
Genres: Drama-Th&TV; Comedy-Th&TV.
Biography: Born 1926, Austria; British and Canadian citizenship. Languages: English and German. Graduate of Royal Academy of Dramatic Arts, London, England. Trained as actor and director for

theatre and TV film.
Selected Filmography: "Adrienne Clarkson Presents" (2 eps), TV, 90-91, CDN, Prod/Dir; *Three Men in Charge*, "Sunday Arts Entertainment", TV, 90-91, CDN, Prod/Dir; *Much Ado About Nothing*, TV, 87-88, CDN, Prod/Dir; *Tartuffe*, TV, 87, CDN, Prod/Dir; "Serve and Protect" (3 eps), TV, 86, CDN, Prod/Dir; "Judge" (33 eps), TV, 81-84, CDN, Prod; *Some-where the Trumpets Are Sounding*, TV, 84, CDN/USA, Dir; *As You Like It*, TV, 83, CDN, Dir; *The Tempest*, TV, 82, CDN, Dir; "A Gift to Last" (21 eps) (Dir 5 eps), TV, 77-80, CDN, Prod; *Many Faces of Love*, TV, 77, CDN/USA, Prod; *A Gift to Last*, TV, 76, CDN, Prod; *Nellie McClung*, TV, 76, CDN, Prod; "House of Pride" (52 eps), TV, 74-75, CDN, Prod/Dir; "Purple Playhouse" (3 eps), TV, 73, CDN, Dir.

ROMANOFF, Sergei
- see WRITERS

ROONEY, Edward
Stratford Children's Productions, P.O. Box 303, Stratford, ON N5A 4A0 (519)886-0612. K-W Television Productions, P.O. Box 898, Waterloo, ON N2J 4C3 (519)886-0612.
Type of Production and Credits: TV Video-Prod/Wr.
Genres: Children's-TV.
Biography: Born in Montreal, Quebec. B.A., Concordia University; B.Ed., University of Montreal; post-graduate work.
Selected Filmography: "The Treehouse Show", TV, 72-88, CDN, Prod/Wr; "Let's Go", TV, 80, CDN, Co-Prod; *The Toy Box Show*, TV, 77-78, CDN, Prod.

ROSCOE, Stephen G.
- see DIRECTORS

ROSEMOND, Perry
- see DIRECTORS

ROSEN, S. Howard
420 Leslie St., Toronto, ON M4M 3E4 Nova Motion Pictures Ltd., 275 King St. E., Ste. 204, Toronto, ON M5A 1K2 (416)466-7181.
Type of Production and Credits: Th Film-Prod; TV Video-Prod.
Genres: Drama-Th&TV; Children's-TV.
Biography: Born in Montreal, Quebec. Canadian citizen. Master of Business Administration in International Business and Finance. Has been involved in the financing and production of film and television projects for over 10 years.
Selected Filmography: "Sharon, Lois and Bram: The Elephant Show", TV, CDN, Prod; *John and the Missus*, Th, CDN, Prod; *My American Cousin*, Th, CDN, Prod; *One Magic Chirstmas*, Th, USA/CDN, Prod.

ROSS, Gerald
7661 de Fougeray, Anjou, PQ H1K 3K3 (514)356-0853. Les Productions de la Maison Rose Inc., 435 rue St-Louis, Montréal, PQ H2Y 1B1 (514)842-9678.
Types de production et générique: l métrage-Prod; TV film-Prod; TV vidéo-Prod.
Types d'oeuvres: Drame-C&TV; Variété-C&TV; Affaires Publiques-C&TV.
Curriculum vitae: Né en 1933 à Bonaventure, Québec. Citoyen canadien. Langues parlées: anglais et français. Expériences: monteur, régisseur, caméraman, réalisateur, distributeur, Vice-President Marché Français (20th Century Fox TV), producteur.
Filmographie sélective: *Justice Au Quotidien*, TV, 90, CDN, Prod; "La Cour En Direct" (105 eps), TV, 87-90, CDN, Prod; *Le Championnat Mondial de Danses Latines*, TV, 89, CDN, Prod; "Lance et Compte" (13 eps), TV, 86, CDN, Prod assoc; *Les Quacs*, TV, 85, CDN, Prod dél; *Dis-Moi si je te Dérange*, TV, 84, CDN, Prod dél; "La Cour Est Ouverte" (39 eps), TV, 64, CDN, Sup pro.

ROSS, John T.
CFTA, ACCT. 65 Heward Ave., Toronto, ON M4M 2T5 (416)594-3455.
Type of Production and Credits: Th Film-Prod; TV Film-Prod; TV Video-Prod.
Genres: Drama-Th&TV; Action-Th&TV; Science Fiction-Th&TV; Children's-Th&TV.
Biography: Born 1930, Quebec City. Attended Bishop's College School, Lennoxville; Middlebury College, Vermont. Founded Robert Lawrence Productions, 55, Eastern Sound Co., VTR Productions Ltd., Cinequip Inc., Agent for Film Finances Ltd., completion guarantors; President, ACTRA Fraternal Benefit Society; CFTA Chairman, 87-88.
Selected Filmography: "Ray Bradbury Theatre" (3 eps), TV, 85, CDN, Co-Exec Prod; "The Little Vampire" (13 eps), TV, 85, CDN/GB/D, Exec Prod; "World of Wicks" (100 eps), TV, 74, CDN, Prod; *Musicians of Bremen*, TV, 71, CDN/USA, Exec Prod; *Leaving Home*, TV, 71, CDN, Prod; *Frog Prince*, TV, 70, CDN/USA, Exec Prod; *King of Grizzlies*, Th, 70, CDN/USA, Prod; "55 North Maple" (130 eps), TV, 69, CDN, Exec Prod; *Hey! Cinderella*, TV, 69, CDN/USA, Exec Prod; "Strategy"(130

eps), TV, 68, CDN, Exec Prod; *Circlevision 360*, Th, 67, CDN/USA, Prod; "Moment of Truth" (218 eps), TV, 65, CDN/GB, Exec Prod.

ROSS, Rodger W.
SMPIA. 2633 Broder St., Regina, SK S4N 3T6 (306)789-9432. Birdsong Communications Ltd., 806 Victoria Ave., Regina, SK S4N 0R6 (306)359-3070.
Type of Production and Credits: TV Video-Prod/Dir/Ed.
Genres: Documentary-TV; Educational-TV; Industrial-TV.
Biography: Born in Regina in 1960, raised in Regina and Winnipeg; Aboriginal of Cree heritage. Has worked in the media for 10 years. Most of training achieved through various programs offered by the Association of Metis and Non-status Indians of Saskatchewan (AMNSIS); training took place with CKTV, CBC, Cable Regina and Birdsong Communications. Has acted in 2 productions, the lead role in *Story of George* and an extra in *Love and Hate*. Presently working to establish an Aboriginal filmmakers association in Saskatchewan.
Selected Filmography: *Louis*, Ed/TV, 91, CDN, Prod/Dir; *Not Bad Kids*, In/Ed/TV, 90, CDN, Prod/Dir; *No Laughing Matter*, Ed/TV, 90, CDN, Audio Rec; *Taking the Challenge*, In, 90, CDN, Audio Rec; *Steps in Time: Metis Dances*, Ed, 89, Prod/Dir; *Mary's Story*, Ed, 89, CDN, Ed.

ROTH, Stephen J.
ACCT, ACFTP, AMPAS. 330 Spadina Rd., Suite 2102, Toronto, ON M5R 2V9 (416)966-5356. Passport Productions Inc., 1240 Bay St., Suite 701, Toronto, ON M5R 2A7 (416)944-8391.
Type of Production and Credits: Th Film-Prod; TV Film-Prod.
Genres: Drama-Th&TV.
Biography: Born 1941, Montreal, Quebec. Honours B.A., English and Political Science, 63; BCL, (Law), McGill University, 66; admitted to the Bar of the Province of Quebec, 67; private practice, specializing in corporate and entertainment law, 67-77. Co-Founder, RSL Films Ltd., 75. Following RSL merger with another Canadian company to form Alliance Entertainment Corp., became President and CEO. Founded Cinexus Capital Corporation, 88. Currently, Chairman of Cinexux Capital Corporation, Passport Productions and Thoeroeg Beherr N.V., a European-based entertainment financing company. Has served as Chairman or Director of many industry associations and festivals including: ACCT, ACFTP, Banff Television Festival and the National Screen Institute. Former consultant to the federal Department of Communications and Telefilm Canada on policy. Has won many awards including, *Joshua Then and Now* won a Genie award; *In Praise of Older Women* won 4 Genies; "Best Dramatic Series" Gemini Awards for "Night Heat", 86 and 87;
Selected Filmography: *Clearcut*, Th, 90, CDN, Prod; *Bordertown Café*, Th, 90, CDN, Prod; *Beautiful Dreamers*, Th, 89, CDN, Exec Prod; "Diamonds" (65 eps), TV, 87-88, CDN, Spv Prod; "Night Heat" (96 eps), TV, 84-88, CDN, Spv Prod, (GEMINI); *Separate Vacations*, Th, 85, CDN, Exec Prod; *Heavenly Bodies*, Th, 85, CDN, Exec Prod; *Joshua Then and Now*, Th, 84, CDN, Exec Prod; *Night Magic*, Th, 84, CDN/F, Exec Prod; *Bedroom Eyes*, Th, 83, CDN, Exec Prod; *Paradise*, Th, 81, CDN, Exec Prod; *Your Ticket Is No Longer Valid*, Th, 79, CDN, Exec Prod; *Suzanne*, Th, 79, CDN, Exec Prod; *Agency*, Th, 78, CDN, Prod; *In Praise of Older Women*, Th, 77, CDN, Exec Prod.

ROWE, Peter
- see DIRECTORS

ROWLAND, Wade
ATPD. Larchwood, Mast Woods Rd., R.R. #1, Port Hope, ON L1A 3V5 (416)753-2405.
Type of Production and Credits: TV Film-Prod/Wr; TV Video-Prod/Wr.
Genres: Documentary-TV; Current Affairs-TV; News-TV.
Biography: Born 1944, Montreal, Quebec. Honours Economics, University of Manitoba. Experience as a journalist; author of several books including *Making Connections*, *Ark on the Move* (ghost-written for Gerald Durrell), *Nobody Calls Me Mr. Kirck* (co-written with Mr. Kirck). Publisher and series editor, Rowland Travel Guides; currently Director of Policy Development, CTV News, Features & Information Programming.

ROY, Robert L.M.
- see DIRECTORS

ROZEMA, Patricia
- see DIRECTORS

RUIMY, Allan
ACCT, ACTRA, DGC. Cody Films Limited, 1652 Bathurst St., Suite 304, Willowdale, ON M5P 3J9 (416)346-9387. FAX: 784-3785.
Type of Production and Credits: TV Film-Prod; Th Film-Prod; TV Video-Prod.
Genres: Drama-Th&TV; Documentary-TV; Educational-TV.

Biography: Born 1960, Paris, France; Canadian citizenship. Languages: French and English. Studied Acting for 4 years in Vancouver; studied Marketing and Public Relations, Dawson College. Has produced several music videos.
Selected Filmography: "Mystery Fare" (pilot), TV, 90, CDN, Exec Prod/Prod; "Counterstrike" (15 eps), TV, 90, CDN, Assist Loc M; "My Secret Identity" (48eps), TV, 88-90, CDN, Assist Loc M; "T and T" (16 eps), TV, 88, CDN/USA, Assist Loc M; *Parental Outreach Program*, TV, 88, CDN, Assoc Prod; *Crazy Horse*, Th, 88, CDN, Assoc Loc M.

RUSSELL, Paul
- see WRITERS

RUTHERFORD, John T.
- see WRITERS

RUVINSKY, Morrie
- see WRITERS

RYAN, John
ACTRA, ACTT, DGC, ACCT. 12 Simpson Ave., Toronto, ON M4K 1A2 (416)463-4232.
Type of Production and Credits: Th Film-Prod/PM; TV Film-Prod/PM.
Genres: Drama-Th&TV; Comedy-Th&TV; Variety-Th&TV; Action-Th&TV.
Biography: Born 1949, London, England; British and Canadian citizenship.
Selected Filmography: "T and T" (65 eps), TV, 87-90, CDN, Prod; "Nancy Drew" (2 eps), TV, 90, CDN, Prod; *Sticky Fingers*, Th, 87, USA, Line Prod; *Blue Monkey*, Th, 87, USA, PM; *Circle Man*, Th, 86, USA, Line Prod; *Walking on Air*, TV, 86, USA, Assoc Prod; *City of Shadows*, Th, 86, CDN, Line Prod; *Confidential*, Th, 85, CDN, Co-Prod; *Dancing in the Dark*, Th, 85, CDN, Co-Prod; *Intruder Within*, TV, 81, CDN, Assoc Prod; *Spring Fever*, Th, 81, CDN, PM; *The Kidnapping of the President*, Th, 79, CDN, Prod; *Christmas Lace*, TV, 78, CDN, Line Prod; *Lovey, A Circle of Children - Part II*, TV, 78, CDN, PM; *Stone Cold Dead*, Th, 78, CDN, Prod.

SADLER, Richard
APFVQ, ACCT. Les Films Stock International inc., 306, Place d'Youville, Bureau C-10, Montréal, PQ H2Y 2B6 (514)281-0134. FAX: (514)281-6584.
Types de production et générique: l métrage-Prod; c métrage-Prod; TV film-Prod/Réal; TV Vidéo-Prod.
Types d'oeuvres: Drame-C&TV; Action-C&TV; Documentaire-TV; Education-TV.
Curriculum vitae: Né en 1947, Montréal, Québec. Diplôme du Collège Sainte-Marie; études universitaires en philosophie, Université de Montréal. Au cinéma, a occupé les postes de régisseur, éclairagiste et assistant caméraman; fonde sa compagnie, Les Films Stock Ltée., 76.
Filmographie sélective: *Scream of Stone*, C, 90, Co-Prod; *Comment faire l'amour avec un nègre sans se fatiguer*, C, 88, CDN/F, Prod exéc; *Fiction accomplie*, TV, 86, CDN, Réal; *Du poil aux pattes comme les CWACs*, C, 85, CDN, Prod; *Gunrunner*, C, 83-84, USA/CDN, Prod; *Lettre morte*, ED, 83, CDN, Prod; "Discrimination" (4 eps), ED, 83, CDN, Prod; "Sur le bout de la langue" (20 eps), TV, 82, CDN, Prod.

SADR, Seyyed
- see DIRECTORS

SAGER, Ray
DGC. Simcom-Norstar Limited, 86 Bloor St. W., 5th Flr., Toronto, ON M5S 1M5 (416)961-6278.
Type of Production and Credits: Th Film-Prod; TV Film-Prod.
Genres: Drama-Th&TV; Horror-TV.
Biography: Born 1943, Chicago; landed immigrant, Canada, B.A., Goodman Theatre School of Drama. Production manager/1st assistant director in US, 70s; 1st AD on 5 features in Canada, 79. Head of Production, Simcom-Norstar Limited since 85.
Selected Filmography: *Intimate Delusions*, Th, 91, CDN, Prod; *Deliver Us From Evil - Prom Night IV*, Th, 91, CDN, Prod; *Cold Comfort*, Th, 88, CDN, Prod; *A Switch in Time*, Th, 87, CDN, Spv Prod; *Shoot Me*, Th, 87, CDN, Pro Exec; *Blindside*, Th, 87, CDN, Co-Prod; *Hello Mary Lou: Prom Night II*, Th, 86, CDN, Co-Prod; *Higher Education*, Th, 86, CDN, Co-Prod; *Bullies*, Th, 85, CDN, Pro Exec; "Mania" (4 eps), TV, 85, CDN, Co-Prod; *Flying*, Th, 84, CDN, Line Prod; *The Mark of Cain*, Th, 84, CDN, Line Prod; "Danger Bay" (5 eps), TV, 84, CDN, Line Prod; *When We First Met*, TV, 83, USA, Line Prod; *American Nightmare*, Th, 82, CDN, Prod.

SAHASRABUDHE, Deepak
Soma Film Producers, 345 Carlaw Ave., Suite 200, Toronto, ON M4M 2T1 (416)466-8022.
Type of Production and Credits: TV Film-Prod; TV Video-Prod.
Genres: Drama-Th&TV; Comedy-TV; Documentary-TV; Educational-TV.
Biography: Born 1951, Poona, India; Canadian citizenship. B.A., Sociology/Anthropology, Carleton University, 74.

Winner of several awards, including Creative Excellence, US Film and Video festival for *Inland Cruising*, "Set Your Sails," Red Ribbon, American Film and Video Festival, for *Managing Performance Problems*; Blue Ribbon, American Film and Video Festival, for *Your Will and Your Estate*, "Money Smart."
Selected Filmography: "Your Green Home" (6 eps), TV, 90-91, CDN, Co-Prod/Wr; "Personal Finance" (10 eps), TV, 89-90, CDN, Co-Prod/Wr/Co-Dir; *Walking Fit*, TV, 90, CDN, Co-Prod/Spv Wr; "Learn to Navigate" (6 eps), TV, 89, CDN, Co-Prod/Wr/Co-Host; *Overboard, In*, 88, CDN, Co-Prod/Spv Wr; "Set Your Sails" (6 eps), TV, 87, CDN, Co-Prod/Wr; "Money Smart" (13 eps), TV, 87, CDN, Co-Prod/Spv Wr; *Managing Performance Problems*, ED, 87, CDN, Co-Prod/Spv Wr; *The Termination Interview*, ED, 86, CDN, Co-Prod/Co-Wr; *Stalking the Silent Thief*, ED, 85, CDN, Co-Prod; *Transitions*, TV, 84, CDN, Co-Prod; *Bridges*, TV, 83, CDN, Co-Prod; "Starting a Business" (13 eps), TV, 82, CDN, Co-Prod; *Goodbye Mr. Dickens*, TV, 81, CDN, Co-Prod.

ST-LAURENT, François
4584 St-Michel, Montréal, PQ H1Y 3G5 (514)527-7620. Coscient Inc., 300 Léo-Parizeau, Ste. 2400, Montréal, PQ H2W 2P4 (514)284-2525.
Types de production et générique: TV film-Prod; TV vidéo-Prod.
Types d'oeuvres: Action-TV; Documentaire-TV; Affaires Publiques-TV.
Curriculum vitae: Né en 1954 à Québec. Citoyenneté canadienne. Etudes: Certificat cinéma, Certificat sociologie. Expérience en gestion et redressement d'enterprises. Direction générale de plusiers sociétés. Mise en place d'un centre de post-production vidéo.
Filmographie sélective: "Omni Science" (78 eps), TV, 88-91, CDN/F, Prod; "La Saga d'Archibald" (13 eps), TV, 91, CDN/F, Prod; "Grand Air" (60 eps), TV, 87-89, CDN, Prod; "L'Indice" (185 eps), TV, 87-88, CDN, Prod; *Vaincre les feux de forets*, TV, 86, CDN, Prod.

ST-PIERRE, Leopold
- voir SCENARISTES

SALTSMAN, Terry
- see WRITERS

SALTZMAN, Deepa Mehta
- see DIRECTORS

SALTZMAN, Paul
ACTRA, CAPAC, DGC, ACCT. Sunrise Films Limited, 160 Perth Ave., Toronto, ON M6P 3X5 (416)535-2900.
Type of Production and Credits: TV Film-Prod/Dir.
Genres: Drama-TV; Action-TV; Documentary-TV; Children's-TV.
Biography: Born 1943, Toronto, Ontario. Engineering, University of Toronto. Started at CBC as researcher, interviewer, 65-67; NFB, 67; founded Sunrise Films, 73. Directing *No Return*, a Warner Bros feature, now in production.
Selected Filmography: *Chaindance*, Th, USA, 91, Dir; "Danger Bay" (123 eps), TV, 82-91, CDN/USA, Co-Creator/Exec Prod; "My Secret Identity" (72 eps), TV, 87-91, CDN, Prod; *Sam & Me*, Th, 90, CDN, Co-Exec Prod; "Max Glick" (26 eps), TV, 89-90, CDN, Co-Exec Prod; *Martha, Ruth & Edie*, Th, 87, CDN, Exec Prod; *Hoover vs the Kennedys: The Second Civil War* (mini-series), TV, 87, CDN, Exec Prod; *Travelling Light: The Photojournalism of Dilip Mehta*, TV, 86, CDN/GB, Exec Prod; *K.Y.T.E.S. How We Dream Ourselves*, TV, 85, CDN, Exec Prod; *Valentine's Revenge*, TV, 84, USA, Dir/Pro Exec; *When We First Met*, TV, 83, USA, Prod/Dir; "Spread Your Wings" (16 eps), TV, 76-80, CDN, Co-Dir/Cin; *Dolphi George Dances*, TV, 77, CDN, Prod/Dir; *To Be A Clown*, TV, 76, CDN, Co-Prod/Dir/Co-Wr; *Indira Gandhi: The State of India*, TV, 75, CDN/USA/GB, Prod/Dir/Wr/Interv.

SANDERS, Ed
Eagle Cliff Sound & Picture, R.R. #1, J-9, Eagle Cliff Rd., Bowen Island, BC V0N 1G0 (604)947-0541. FAX: 947-0519.
Type of Production and Credits: Th Film-P Pro Spv/Prod/Dir; TV Film-P Pro Spv.
Genres: Drama-TV; Action-TV; Documentary-TV; Current Affairs-TV.
Biography: Born, England. Canadian citizenship; resident of Canada since 61. Picture and sound editor for over 500 TV documentaries; producer/writer/director for 12 one-hour documentaries; postproduction producer for 55 half-hour dramatic series episodes, including "The Beachcombers"; postproduction supervisor for 13 one-hour episodes of action series ("Fly By Night"). Winner of Gold Medal, International Film & TV Festival of New York, 83 for *The Mountain Waits*, "This Land."
Selected Filmography: "Fly By Night" (13 eps), TV, 90-91, CDN/USA/F, P Pro Spv; *Lighthouse*, TV, 91, CDN, P Pro Spv; "The Beachcombers" (55 eps), TV, 87-90, CDN, P Pro Spv; "This Land" (100 eps), TV, 70-80, CDN, Ed; "This Land" (12

eps), TV, 80-86, CDN, Prod/Dir.

SANDERSON, Deborah
ACTRA, ACCT. Phisgate Productions Inc., 3 - 225 West 16th St., North Vancouver, BC V7M 1T7 (604)984-9789. (604)671-3230.
Type of Production and Credits: TV Film-Prod; TV Video-Prod.
Genres: Drama-TV; Commercials-TV; Music Video-TV; Sports-TV.
Biography: Born 1935, Oshawa, Ontario. Languages: English and a basic knowledge of French. Studied Film, Stage, Television, Sheridan College, Toronto; Advanced TV and Radio Production, Southern Alberta Institute of Technology; AD Course, DGC.
Selected Filmography: "Kidstreet" (350 eps), TV, 87-91, CDN, Prod; *Variety Club Telethon,* TV, 90/91, CDN, Prod; *1990 CFL Season* (with TSN & CFN), TV, 90, CDN, Assist Dir; "The Last Word" (130 eps), TV, 89, CDN/USA, Prod; "Talkabout" (130 eps), TV, 88, CDN, Prod; *Peace of Mind/Backward Town,* Grapes of Wrath, MV, 87-88, CDN, Prod; *XV Olympic Winter Games,* TV, 88, CDN, Assist Dir; *Achilles Indoor Track Meet,* TV, 88, CDN, PA; "Sea Hunt" (22 eps), TV, 87, USA/CDN, Assist Prod; *I Will Be There,* Glass Tiger, MV, 87, CDN, PM; *Ocean Blue,* Tom Cochrane, MV, 87, CDN, PM; "CFL Football and Grey Cup: (7 eps), TV, 87, CDN, Coord Prod; *Schenley Awards,* TV, 87, CDN, Script; "Love Me, Love Me Not" (130 eps), TV, 86, USA Assoc Prod; "Stress Point" (13 eps), TV, 86, CDN, Assoc Prod.

SANDOR, Anna
- see WRITERS

SAROSSY, Ivan
- see CINEMATOGRAPHERS

SARRAZIN, Pierre ✧
(416)535-6740.
Type of Production and Credits: TV Film-Prod/Dir/Wr; TV Video-Prod/Dir/Wr.
Genres: Drama-TV; Comedy-TV; Variety-TV; Documentary-TV.
Biography: Born in Montreal, Quebec. Languages: English and French. B.A., Loyola College. Winner, Silver Award, NY International Film and TV Festival, for "That's Life"; *Joined at the Hip* was a finalist at CFTA awards.
Selected Filmography: "The Canadians" (2 eps), TV, 88, CDN, Dir; "Women of the World" (7 eps), TV, 85-86, CDN/USA, Prod/Dir/Wr; "The American Century" (1 eps), TV, 86, CDN, Prod; *What to Do with Mom and Dad/A Nation Divided,* "The Journal", TV, 85, CDN, Prod/dir/wr; *Joined at the Hip,* TV, 84, CDN, Prod/Co-Dir; "That's Life" (390 eps), TV, 81-84, CDN, Prod/Wr/Dir; "Chuck and Fran Show" (pilot), TV, 83, CDN, Prod/Dir; "Hour Glass" (365 eps), TV, 77, CDN, Prod/Dir; *Brethren,* Th, 75, CDN, PM.

SAVATH, Philip
- see WRITERS

SAVOIE, Elie
Four 'S' Production Consultants Ltd., 995 Ranch Park Way, Coquitlam, BC V3G 2C9 (604)941-9127. Pacific Producers Group, 207 - 1168 Hamilton, Vancouver, BC V6B 2S2 (604)683-6011.
Type of Production and Credits: TV Film-Exec Prod/Line Prod/Dir; TV Video-Prod/Dir.
Genres: Drama-TV; Variety-TV, Documentary-TV; Industrial-TV.
Biography: Born in 1935. A west coast Canadian via Ontario (Fort Frances) and Winnipeg. Started out as a stage director and actor. Began work in television at CFCR TV, Kamloops, BC in 1959 as a weather reporter, news reader, producer/director (*Kiddies Karnival, Spotlights* etc), host and general dog's body. Attended one summer at Stanford University, (Communications). Worked as studio PA and cameraman at BCTV, 1962-63. Started at CBC, Vancouver, 1964 as a co-ordinator, master control and then PA. Became a contract producer in February, 1965. In 1977 became Program Director, CBC Regina; 1979 became Director of TV, CBC Windsor; 1984, Program Director, CBC Vancouver; 1987, Director of Program Development. Retired from the CBC in 1990 to start own company, Pacific Producers Group, with 3 partners.
Selected Filmography: *The Magic Lie,* "The Infinite Worlds of Maybe" (1 eps), TV, 77, CDN, Dir; "The Beachcombers" (46 eps), TV, 75-77, CDN, Exec Prod; "The Beachcombers" (23 eps), TV, 74-75, CDN, Line Prod; "The Beachcombers" (26 eps), TV, 71-75, CDN, Dir; "The Bill Kenny Show" (7 eps), TV, 70, CDN, Prod/Dir; "The Clients" (2 eps), TV, 70-71, CDN, Prod/Dir; "Studio Pacific" (3 eps), TV, 68-69, CDN, Prod/Dir; *The Medal,* TV, 68, CDN, Prod/Dir; "20/20" (1 eps), TV, 68, CDN, Prod/Dir; "Contrast" (1 eps), TV, 68, CDN, Prod/Dir; "Hourglass" (daily), TV, 66-69, CDN, Prod; "Some of Those Days" (36 eps), TV, 65-66, CDN, Prod/Dir.

SCAINI, Stefan
- see DIRECTORS

SCHADT, Christa
- see WRITERS

SCHAFER, Joan
ACCT. Schafer/Thurling Productions, 8480 Harold Way, Los Angeles, CA 90069 (213)656-6635. FAX: 656-8993.
Type of Production and Credits: TV Film-Wr/Prod.
Genres: Drama-Th&TV; Variety-TV; Musical-TV; Documentary-TV.
Biography: Born in Switzerland; Canadian citizenship. Languages: English and some German. Attended University of Michigan and University of Toronto. Executive Producer, Producer, Director, Citytv, 72-77; Producer, CBC, 78; Vice-President, Programming, First Choice Pay TV, 81-83. Co-founder, Toronto Women in Film and Video. Feature scriptwriter, *Sweetfire* and *Tough Cookie*, 86-88. *Growing Up in America* won Silver Hugo, Chicago; *Floating Over Canada* won ACTRA and Gemini awards.
Selected Filmography: *Odyssey in Augusta*, TV, 88, CDN, Exec Prod; *Growing Up in America*, Th, 88, CDN, Prod; *Floating Over Canada*, TV, 85, CDN, Prod, (ACTRA/GEMINI); *Tough Cookie* (2 eps), TV, 84, CDN, Co-Wr; "The City Show" (52 eps), TV, 74-77, CDN, Exec Prod; "Money Game" (156 eps)(Dir 60 eps), TV, 72-74, CDN, Prod; "World of the Unexplained" (26 eps), TV, 73-74, CDN, Prod/Dir; "City Lights" (52 eps), TV, 72-73, CDN, Prod/Dir.

SCHECTER, Brian
CTPDA. Multi-Media Productions Ltd., 2329 W. 144 Ave., Vancouver, BC V6K 2W2 (604)734-1103.
Type of Production and Credits: TV Film-Prod/Dir; TV Video-Prod/Dir.
Genres: Documentary-TV; Current Affairs-TV; News-TV; Sports-TV.
Biography: Born 1950, Montreal, Quebec. Languages: English and French. M.A., Institute of Canadian Studies, Carleton University. 14 years of experience in TV, radio and print (newspaper, magazine writing).
Selected Filmography: "Baseball Allstar Game" (87-88 World Series), TV, 87-91, CDN, Prod; "Superbowl", TV, 90-91, CDN, Prod; "Canadian Masters Skiing", TV, 88-91, CDN, Prod/Dir/Wr; "NHL Breakaway" (52 eps), TV, 89-90, CDN, Prod/Dir; "Expos Baseball", TV, 85-89, CDN, Prod; *Montreal Expos - 20th Anniversary, A Look Back* (Fr & Eng), In, 88, CDN, Prod; *1988 Winter Olympics*, TV, 88, CDN, Host/Prod; *The Road to*

MMI – PRODUCT PLACEMENT INC.
TORONTO • MONTREAL • VANCOUVER

MMI loans props **free** to all films who allow **product visibility**. Work with MMI and avoid transportation costs, wasted time and money.

Recent Credits: The Mrs., FX2, The Adjuster, Bingo, This is My Life, Stepping Out, E.N.G., Katts & Dog…

20 Retainer Accounts: Budweiser, J&B Scotch, BMW, Nissan, Hostess Frito Lay, Pepsi, Quaker Oats, Polaroid, Colgate, Ray-Ban, Crayola…

"If you're not dealing with MMI you'll pay for it!"

Call Philip J. Hart
Tel: (416) 759-5000
Fax: (416) 762-8180 130 Industry St., Unit 14, Toronto, Ontario M6M 4L8

Calgary/The Road to Seoul, TV, 88, CDN, Prod; Journey Through Salt Water City, Gov't of Canada, In, 87, CDN, Prod; Pacifete 85, "A guichets fermés", TV, 85, CDN, Prod/Dir; "Hockey Night in Canada", TV, 78-85, CDN, Prod/Dir; Sea Festival Parade, TV, 79-85, CDN, Prod/Dir; Pacific Report, TV, 84-85, CDN, Prod/Dir; B.C. Lions Annual Awards Night, TV, 83-85, CDN, Prod/ Dir; "Midday" (sev seg), TV, 85, CDN, Prod/Dir.

SCHERBERGER, Aiken M.
- see DIRECTORS

SCHERER, Karl
- see CINEMATOGRAPHERS

SCHONBERG, Pasia
CFTA, ACTRA. PVS Films, 11 Austin Cres., Toronto, ON M5R 3E4 (416)535-5860. FAX: 533-8253.
Type of Production and Credits: Th Film: Prod/Dir; Th Short-Prod/Dir; TV Video-Prod/Dir.
Genres: Drama-Th; Comedy-Th; Documentary-TV; Educational-TV.
Biography: Born Tel Aviv, Israel; Canadian citizenship. President and Director, Pasia V. Schonberg Productions Inc., and PVS Films Inc. Education: New School for Social Research, Brandeis Institute, California, 64; Film, University of California, Los Angeles, 65; B.A. French and English Literature, McGill University, Montreal, 67. Diploma in Art Education for Children, Montreal Museum of Fine Arts, 69; Graduate Diploma in Child Study, Institute of Child Study, University of Toronto, 71. Master, Dept. of Early Childhood Education, George Brown College, Toronto, 71-83; director, Children's Art Programme, Georgian College of Applied Arts & Technology, 71-72. Producer, CFTA Winner, Best Canadian Feature, 87, for Taking Care.
Selected Filmography: Taking Care, Th, 87, CDN, Prod, (CFTA); "Cinema et Cinemas" (7 eps), TV, 85, CDN, Wr/Dir/Ed; Pulling Flowers, TV, 84, CDN, Assist to Dir/Dial Coach; And Time Passes in a Flash of Lightning, TV, 84, CDN, Prod/Dir; Notes on Seeing, TV, 81, CDN, Prod/Dir; A Time to Mourn, A Time to Dance, ED, 81, CDN, Wr/Dir; Maybe Yes, Maybe No, ED, 78, CDN, Wr/Dir; Curriculum Resource Films and Video Tapes (Series 1-3), ED, 77, CDN, Series Prod; And the Elephant Sneezed, Th, 65, CDN, Prod/Wr/Dir.

SCHWARTZ, Nadine
- see DIRECTORS

SCOTT, Cynthia
- see DIRECTORS

SCOTT, Michael J.F.
- see DIRECTORS

SEDAWIE, Gayle Gibson ✧
(503)496-3060.
Type of Production and Credits: TV Film-Prod/Dir/Wr; TV Video-Prod/Dir/Wr.
Genres: Comedy-TV; Variety-TV; Musical-TV; Documentary-TV.
Biography: Born 1936, Toronto, Ontario. Attended the Royal Academy of Ballet, London, England; graduated Theatre Arts, 76. Dancer, singer and actress, 53-70, then producer, director, writer. Rich Little's Christmas Carol won Best Comedy Album, Junos, 79, and Golden Rose of Montreux.
Selected Filmography: Singin' and Dancin' Tonight, TV, 84, CDN, Prod/Dir; Air Farce Live at the Bayview, TV, 84, CDN, Co-Prod/Co-Dir; Rich Little: Come Laugh With Me, TV, 84, USA, Co-Prod; Treasures, TV, 82, CDN, Co-Prod/Co-Dir/Co-Wr; Time Machine, TV, 82, CDN, Co-Prod/Co-Dir/Co-Wr; Showbiz Ballyhoo, TV, 82, CDN, Co-Prod/Co-Dir/Co-Wr; Showbiz Goes to War, TV, 80, CDN, Co-Prod/Co-Dir/Co-Wr; "Mary and Michael" (26 eps), TV, 80, CDN, Co-Prod/Co-Wr/Co-Dir; "Rich Littles Salutes" (2 eps), TV, 79, USA, Co-Prod/Co-Dir/Co-Wr; "Mixed Doubles" (26 eps), TV, 79, CDN, Co-Prod/Co-Dir/Co-Wr; "Caught in the Act" (26 eps), TV, 79, CDN, Co-Prod/Co-Dir/Co-Wr; Rich Little's Christmas Carol, TV, 78, CDN, Co-Prod, (INT'L EMMY); Tumwater Caravan, TV, 72, USA, Res; "Smothers Brothers Comedy" (3 eps), TV, 70, USA, Act; "Jackie Rae Show" (50 eps), TV, 54-55, CDN, Ch/Act; "Mr. Show Business" (36 eps), TV, 53, CDN, Act/Ch.

SEDAWIE, Norman
ACTRA, DGA, WGAw. Tel-Pro Entertainment Inc., 1436 Whistler's Lane, Roseburg, OR 97470 (503)496-3060. Tel-Pro Productions Inc., 1816 Greenview Crescent, Mississauga, ON L5L 3W1 (416)828-9575.
Type of Production and Credits: TV Film-Prod/Dir/Wr; TV Video-Prod/Dir/Wr.
Genres: Comedy-TV; Variety-TV; Musical-TV; Documentary-TV.
Biography: Born Vancouver, BC. Started as newspaper writer/columnist; television includes over 1,500 network programs as director/producer. Winner, Golden Rose of Montreux for Rich Little's Christmas Carol. Tel-Pro affiliates include: Tel-Pro Entertainment Inc. (California); Tel-Pro

Entertainment Ltd. (Vancouver); and T.A.D. Productions (Toronto).
Selected Filmography: *Canadian Museum of Civilization,* "Canada in View", TV, 90, CDN, Co-Prod/Co-Dir/Co-Wr; *Rich Little Come Laugh With Me,* TV, 85, USA, Co-Prod; *Air Farce Live at the Bayview,* TV, 84, CDN, Co-Prod/Co-Dir/Co-Wr; *Treasures,* TV, 82, CDN, Co-Prod/Co-Dir/Co-Wr; *The Time Machines,* TV, 82, CDN, Co-Prod/Co-Dir/Co-Wr; *Showbiz Ballyhoo,* TV, 82, CDN, Co-Prod/Co-Dir/Co-Wr; *Showbiz Goes to War,* TV, 80, CDN, Co-Prod/Co-Wr/Co-Dir; "Mary and Michael" (26 eps), TV, 80, CDN, Co-Prod/Co-Wr/Co-Dir; *National Sex and Marriage Test,* TV, 79, USA, Prod/Wr; "Mixed Doubles" (26 eps), TV, 79, CDN, Co-Prod/Co-Dir/Co-Wr; "Caught in the Act" (26 eps), TV, 79, CDN, Co-Prod/Co-Dir/Co-Wr; *Rich Little's Christmas Carol,* TV, 78, CDN, Co-Prod, (INT'L EMMY); *Rich Little Salutes* (2 shows), TV, 78, USA, Co-Prod/Co-Dir/Co-Wr; *The Bear Who Slept Through Christmas,* TV, 73, USA, Prod/Wr; "Organic Space Ride" (13 eps), TV, 71, USA, Prod/Dir/Wr.

SENECAL, Marguerite
ACTRA. Senecal Productions, 4 Carlton St., Suite 1717, Toronto, ON M5B 2H9 (416)340-1506.
Type of Production and Credits: TV Film-Prod/Wr; TV Video-Prod/Wr/Dir.
Genres: Documentary-TV; Educational-TV; Industrial-TV.
Biography: Born 1950, Montreal, Quebec. Languages: English and working knowledge of French. Honours B.A., English Literature, Concordia University; postgraduate English Literature, McGill University. Print and broadcast journalist for 10 years (CTV, CBC, Global, Standard Broadcasting, the "Gazette"). Freelanced for "The Journal, ", *Toronto Star, Globe and Mail, Maclean's.* Formed Senecal Productions, 84. Won Bronze, Business Category, Houston International Film Festival, 86; ITVA Award, Silver Birch Regional, 87.

SENKYIRE, Opong
CFTPA, ASIFA, LIFT. 2247 Hurontario St., Ste. 925, Mississauga, ON L5A 2G2 (416)273-7364. Kente Productions, PO Box 368, Station A, Mississauga, ON L5A 3A1 (416)273-7364.
Type of Production and Credits: Th Short-Prod/Dir; TV Video-Prod/Dir.
Genres: Educational-Th&TV; Children's-Th&TV; Animation-Th&TV; Industrial-Th&TV.
Biography: Born in 1950 in Kumasi, Ghana. Canadian citizenship. Languages: English and Twi. Diploma in Technical Animation; Certificate in Architectural Drafting and Design. Independent film/animation producer. Also experienced in script writing, illustration and video production.
Selected Filmography: *The Animation Stand,* ED, 85, CDN, Prod/Dir; *Counting One to Ten,* TV, 81, CDN, Prod/Dir.

SENS, Al
ASIFA. 2018 York Ave., Vancouver, BC V6J 1E6 (604)733-6635. Al Sens Animation Ltd., 1020 Mainland St., Vancouver, BC V6B 2T4 (604)681-9728.
Type of Production and Credits: Th Short-Dir/An; TV Film-Dir/An.
Genres: Educational-Th&TV; Experimental-Th&TV; Animation-Th&TV; Children's-Th&TV;.
Biography: Born 1933, Vancouver, BC. Attended Vancouver School of Art. *Acting Out* was a Canadian Independent Short Film Showcase winner.
Selected Filmography: *Pacific Connection,* ED, 82-83, CDN, An; *Backstage at a Nursery Rhyme,* Th, 83, CDN, Dir/An; *Acting Out,* Th, 83, CDN, Dir/An; *The Funny Cow,* Th, 81, CDN, Dir/An; *An Interview with Ivan Shusikov,* Th, 80, CDN, Dir/An; *Problems on an Imaginary Farm,* Th, 79, CDN, Dir/An; *A Hard Day at the Office,* Th, 78, CDN, Dir/An; *Physical Fitness: A New Perspective,* ED, 77, CDN, Dir/An; *La Vache Histoire,* ED, 73, CDN, An; *The Twitch,* Th, 73, CDN, Dir/An; *Dialectic Materialism,* ED, 70-71, CDN, Dir/An; *Man and Machine,* Th, 69, CDN, Dir/An; *Henry,* ED, 67-68, CDN, Dir/An; *The Brotherhood,* Th, 67, CDN, Dir/An; *The Playground,* Th, 63-74, CDN, Dir/An.

SERENY, Julia
81 Kendal Ave., Toronto, ON M5R 1L8 (416)920-7989.
Type of Production and Credits: TV Film-Prod/PM.
Genres: Drama-TV; Variety-TV; Musical-TV; Documentary-TV.
Biography: Born in 1956. Canadian citizen. Languages: English and some French, Spanish and Hungarian. Gemini award for Best Performing Arts for *Ravel.*
Selected Filmography: *America: Love It or Leave It,* TV, USA/CDN, 89, Prod Spv; *Music in the Midnight Sun,* TV, 88, CDN, Prod Cons; *Ravel,* TV, CDN/E/S, Co-Prod; *Guitar,* TV, 87, CDN, Line Prod; *Dance for Modern Times,* Th/TV, 87, CDN, PM; *All That Bach,* TV, 85, CDN, PM; *Magnificat,* TV, 85, CDN, PM; *You*

Call Me Coloured, TV, 85, CDN, Assoc Prod.

SHAVICK, James
ACCT. 7006 Babcock Ave., North Hollywood CA 91605 (818)982-6458. No. 1 Wood Ave., #605, Westmount, PQ H3Z 3C5 (514)932-7817.
Type of Production and Credits: Th Film-Prod; TV Film-Prod/Wr; TV Video-Prod/Dir/Wr.
Genres: Drama-Th&TV; Comedy-TV; Musical-TV; Documentary-TV.
Selected Filmography: *Hammer Down*, Th, 91, CDN, Dir; *It Don't Come Easy*, Th, 90, USA, Prod/Dir; *Café Romeo*, Th, 90, CDN, Prod; *Yesterday's Hero*, Th, 90, USA, Prod; *Wishful Thinking*, Th, 89, USA, Prod/Dir; "EMU T.V." (51 eps) (Prod 26 eps), TV, 88-89, CDN, Prod/Dir; *Up Your Alley*, Th, 89, USA, Exec Prod; *Contra Conspiracy*, Th, 88, USA, Exec Prod; *Payback*, Th, 88, USA, Exec Prod; *Emperor of the Bronx*, Th, 88, USA, Exec Prod; *The Connally Tarot*, TV, 87, CDN, Prod/Dir; *Elvis and Me*, TV, 87, USA, Line Prod (cdn); *Offenbach Legends of Rock*, TV, 86, CDN, Prod/Dir; *The Unknown Comic Special*, TV, 85, CDN, Prod/Dir.

SHAW, Andrea
102 Lesmount Ave., Toronto, ON M4J 3V9 (416)467-0026.
Type of Production and Credits: Th Film-Prod; TV Film-Prod; TV Video-Prod.
Genres: Drama-Th&TV; Comedy-Th&TV; Commercials-TV.
Selected Filmography: "No Place Like Home" (6 eps), TV, 91, CDN, Prod; *Thick As Thieves*, Th, 90, CDN, Prod; "Codco" (6 eps), TV, 88, CDN, Assoc Prod; "Storybook International" (5 eps), TV, 86, CDN/GB, Line Prod.

SHENKEN, Lionel
Visual Productions 80 Ltd., 101 Niagara St., Suite 2, Toronto, ON M5V 1C3 (416)868-1535.
Type of Production and Credits: TV Film-Prod/Dir; TV Video-Prod.
Genres: Drama-TV; Action-TV; Variety-TV; Musical-TV; Children's-TV; Documentary-Th&TV.
Biography: Born 1928, Glasgow, Scotland; Canadian citizenship. Languages: French and English. Diploma, Glasgow College of Art. "Niagara Repertory Company" won CanPro Award for Drama, 84.
Selected Filmography: "Brownstone Kids" (78 eps), TV, 89-91, CDN, Exec Prod; "The Best is Yet to Come" (260 eps), TV, 89-91, CDN, Exec Prod; "Showdown" (26 eps), TV, 90, CDN, Exec Prod; *Home for Christmas*, TV, 89, GB/CDN, Exec Prod; *Stranger Among Friends*, TV, 88, CDN, Exec Prod; *Come Spy With Me*, TV, 88, CDN, Exec Prod; *Diamond in the Rough*, TV, 88, CDN/ZA, Exec Prod; *Inside Split*, TV, 88, CDN, Exec Prod; *Cowboy*, TV, 88, CDN, Exec Prod; *Where's There's a Will*, TV, 88, CDN, Exec Prod; *Street Games*, TV, 88, CDN, Exec Prod; *Negative Image*, TV, 88, CDN, Exec Prod; "Let's Talk...Small Business" (13 eps), TV, 88, CDN, Exec Prod; "Let's Talk... Franchising" (26 eps), TV, 87, CDN, Exec Prod; "Challenge" (13 eps), TV, 87, CDN, Exec Prod.

SHERRIN, Robert
ACCT. 114 South Dr., Toronto, ON M4W 1R8 (416)925-8193. CBC, 790 Bay St., 5th Flr., Toronto, ON M5G 1N8 (416)975-7148.
Type of Production and Credits: TV Film-Prod/Dir; TV Video-Prod/Dir.
Genres: Drama-TV; Comedy-TV.
Biography: Born 1935, Kelowna, BC. B.Architecture, University of British Columbia; B.A., Sir George Williams (Concordia) University; graduate (Directing), National Theatre School of Canada. Fifteen years as theatre director (over 35 professional stage productions in Canada). *Sarah* was nominated for an International Emmy.
Selected Filmography: *Grand Larceny*, TV, 91, CDN, Prod; *Family Reunion*, TV, 87, CDN, Prod; *The Last Season*, TV, 86, CDN, Prod; *Showstopper*, TV, 85, CDN, Prod; *Love and Larceny*, TV, 84, CDN, Prod, (GEMINI 86); "Home Fires" (31 eps), TV, 81-83, CDN, Prod/Dir; *Population of One*, TV, 80, CDN, Dir; *Growing Up Jewish in Sault Ste. Marie* (3 parts), TV, 78-79, CDN, Prod/Dir; *The Wordsmith*, TV, 79, CDN, Prod; *Eye of the Beholder*, TV, 78, CDN, Prod; *Other People's Children*, TV, 78, CDN, Prod; *Artichoke*, TV, 77, CDN, Prod; *Sarah*, TV, 76, CDN, Prod; *Les Belles Soeurs*, TV, 76, CDN, Prod; *Bethune*, TV, 76, CDN, Prod.

SHOSTAK, Murray
ACCT. 1321 Sherbrooke St. W., #E70, Montreal, PQ H3T 1J4 (514)288-1247. Canadian International Studios Inc.,
Type of Production and Credits: Th Film-Prod; TV Film-Prod.
Genres: Drama-Th&TV; Animation-Th&TV.
Biography: Born in Montreal, Quebec. Languages: French and English.

B.Comm., McGill University; Chartered Accountant. President of Canadian International Studios Inc. since 83.
Selected Filmography: *Red Earth, White Earth*, TV, 88, CDN, Prod; *Liberace*, TV, 88, CDN/USA, Prod; *Speedzone Fever*, Th, 88, CDN/USA, Prod; *Miles to Go...*, TV, 86, CDN, Prod; *George and the Star*, TV, 85, CDN, Co-Prod; *Love Songs/Paroles et musique*, Th, 84, CDN/F, Co-Exec Prod; *Maria Chapdelaine*, Th, 82, CDN,/F, Co-Exec Prod; *Death Hunt*, Th, 80, USA, Co-Prod; *Silence of the North*, Th, 79, CDN, Co-Prod; *Child Under a Leaf*, Th, 74, CDN, Co-Prod; *The Happy Prince*, TV, 72, CDN, Prod; *The Little Mermaid*, TV, 71-72, CDN, Prod; *The Selfish Giant*, TV, 71, CDN, Prod; *Pinter People*, TV, 68, CDN, Prod.

SHRAGGE, Sherv
CTPDA, ACTRA. 1830 College, #1202, Regina, SK S4P 1C2 (306)522-0773. CBC-TV, P.O. Box 540, Regina, SK S4P 4A1 (306)347-9540.
Type of Production and Credits: TV Video-Prod/Dir/Wr/Host.
Genres: Drama-TV; Documentary-TV; Current Affairs-TV; News-TV.
Biography: Born 1936 in Regina, Saskatchewan. Languages: English and Hebrew. B.A.A., TV Studio Production, Ryerson Polytechnical Institute, 83; hons. graduate, Photojournalism, Brooks Institute, Santa Barbara. Best Drama, Saskatchewan Showcase Awards, Yorkton Film Festival, 85, for *Toyboat*. Nominee and finalist for various Actra awards.
Selected Filmography: "The Best Years" (6 eps) (Saskatchewan), TV, 86-88, CDN, Prod; *Music Lessons*, TV, 87, CDN, Prod; *Papa Goes to Town*, TV, 87, CDN, Prod/Dir; *The Salesman*, TV, 86, CDN, Prod/Dir; "Contact", TV, 85-86, CDN, Prod/Dir; "Gzowski & Co." (Saskatchewan), TV, 85-86, CDN, Prod; *The Partners*, TV, 85, CDN, Prod/Dir; *Tiger Moth*, TV, 85, CDN, Prod/Dir; *MVP*, TV, 84, CDN, Prod/Dir; *Toyboat*, TV, 84, CDN, Prod/Dir; *Any Farmers Left?*, TV, 84, CDN, Prod/Dir; "Shragge's Journal", TV, 83-84, CDN, Prod/Wr/Host, (ANIK); "Shragge's Journal", TV, 78-83, CDN, Field Prod/Wr/Host.

SHRIER, Barbara
- see PRODUCTION MANAGERS

SHUMAN, Risa
ACCT. 5460 Yonge St., Suite 1007, Willowdale, ON M2N 6K7 (416)222-6675. TVOntario, Box 200, Stn. Q, Toronto, ON M4T 2T1 (416)484-2862. FAX: 484-4519.
Type of Production and Credits: TV Video-Prod.
Genres: Educational-TV.
Biography: Born 1951, Hamilton, Ontario. Graduated York University, Honours B.F.A., 73. Employed at TVOntario since 73.
Selected Filmography: "Saturday Night at the Movies" (52 eps), TV, 89-91, CDN, Prod; "Jay Scott's Film International" (26 eps), TV, 90-91, CDN, Prod; "Jay Scott's Film International" (6 eps), TV, 88, CDN, Prod; "Saturday Night at the Movies" (26 eps), TV, 87, CDN, Exec Prod; "Magic Shadows" (90 eps), TV, 87, CDN, Co-Prod; "Saturday Night at the Movies" (26 eps), TV, 86, CDN, Prod; "Jay Scott's Film International" (6 eps), TV, 86, CDN, Prod; "Magic Shadows" (24 eps), TV, 86, CDN, Assoc Prod.

SHUMIATCHER, Cal
Acme Motion Pictures, 320 - 1140 Homer St., Vancouver, BC V6B 2X6 (604)682-5535.
Type of Production and Credits: Th Film-Prod/Snd Ed; Th Short-Prod/Snd Ed.
Genres: Drama-Th.
Biography: Born in 1957 in Calgary, Alberta. B.A. Film and Television, University of British Columbia, 1981.
Selected Filmography: *North of Pittsburgh*, Th, 91, CDN, Prod/Spv Snd Ed; *The First Season*, Th, 89, CDN, Assoc Prod/Spv Snd Ed; *Matinee*, Th, 88, CDN, Prod/Spv Snd Ed; *The Outside Chance of Maximillian Glick*, Th, 87, CDN, Spv Snd Ed; *My Kind of Town*, Th, 84, CDN, Prod/Spv Snd Ed; *My American Cousin*, Th, 84, CDN, Snd Ed; *The Little Town That Did*, TV, 84, CDN, Ed; *No Vacancy*, Th, 83, CDN, Prod/Spv Snd Ed; *Tiers, A Story of the Penitentiary*, TV, 82, CDN, Ed.

SIEGEL, Lionel E.
- see WRITERS

SILVER, Jonny
- see DIRECTORS

SILVER, Malcolm
CFTA, ACCT. 390 Cortleigh Blvd., Toronto, ON M5N 1R4 (416)256-7234. Malcolm Silver Co. Ltd., 102 Peter St., Ste. 201, Toronto, ON M5V 2G8 (416)340-2375.
Type of Production and Credits: TV Video-Prod.
Genres: Drama-TV.
Biography: Born 1946, Northern Ireland; Canadian citizenship. Languages: English and French. C.A.; M.B.A., INSEAD, Fontainebleau, France. Principally

involved in production financing.
Selected Filmography: *The Country Wife*, TV, 84, CDN, Exec Prod.
SIMANDL, Lloyd ◊
(604)421-1475.
Type of Production and Credits: Th Film-Prod/Dir/Wr.
Genres: Drama-Th; Action-Th; Horror-TV.
Biography: Born 1948, Czechoslovakia; Canadian citizenship. Attended Academy of Fine Arts, Prague; founded North American Pictures Ltd., 77; produced over 30 TV commercials and sponsored films; exclusively feature films since 79; shareholder, co-founder and member of the board of directors of world-wide distribution company, North American Releasing Inc.
Selected Filmography: *Empire of Ash III*, Th, 88, CDN, Prod/Dir/Wr; *Empire of Ash II*, Th, 87, CDN, Prod/Dir/Co-Wr; *Possession*, Th, 86, CDN, Prod/Dir/Co-Wr; *Ladies of the Lotus*, Th, 85, CDN.

SIMARD, Alain
ADISQ, APFVQ. Spectel Vidéo Inc., 355 Ste. Catherine ouest, Ste. 700, Montréal, PQ H3B 1A5
Types de production et générique: TV vidéo-Prod.
Types d'oeuvres: Comédie-TV; Variété-TV; Enfants-TV; Vidéo-Clips-TV.
Curriculum vitae: Né en 1950.
Filmographie sélective: "Rock et Belles Oreilles" (40 eps), TV, 88-90, CDN, Prod, (GEMEAUX/FELIX); "Festival International de Jazz de Montréal" (60 eps), TV, 80-90, CDN, Prod; "Les Franco Folies de Montréal" (22 eps), TV, 89-90, CDN, Prod.

SIMMONDS, Alan Francis
- see DIRECTORS

SIMPSON, Dee E.
ACCT, ACFTP, CIFC. Forevergreen Television & Film Productions, Inc., 181 Carlaw Ave., #230, Toronto, ON M4M 1S2 (416)778-9944.
Type of Production and Credits: TV Film-Prod/Dir; TV Video-Prod/Dir/PM.
Genres: Action-TV; Documentary-TV; Educational-TV.
Biography: Born in 1943 in London, England. Canadian citizen. Bilingual. B.Sc., Medical Illustration, University of London. M.A. in Film and Television. Medical illustrator and university lecturer in South Africa, 1968-73. Producer, production manager and researcher for the Independent Television Network in England, 1974-79. Freelance producer/director in Canada 1980-87. Outdoor recreation councillor in Northern Ontario, 1988-89. Executive producer/partner in Forevergreen Productions which was founded to produce positive impact programming, 1989 to date. *Flight for Freedom* winner of the Gold, TV Special, Houston International Film Festival and Honourable Mention, American Film and Video Association, 90. *Hidden Heritage* won a Gold, Houston International Film Festival and Honourable Mention, Columbus International Film Festival.
Selected Filmography: *Flight for Freedom*, TV, 90, Exec Prod/Prod/Dir; *L'Envol vers la Liberté*, TV, 90, Exec Prod/Assoc Prod; *All In A Day's Work*, Un, 90, CDN, Prod; *Dollars & Sense*, ED, 89, CDN, Prod/Dir; *Hidden Heritage*, ED, 89, CDN, Prod/Dir; *Justice In Either Language*, In, 88, CDN, Prod; *Life After Eight*, ED, 87, CDN, Prod; "Assignment Adventure" (13 eps), TV, 86, GB, Prod; *Against All Odds*, TV, 84, GB, PM; *Communications on the Move*, ED, 83, CDN, Prod; *Just For Me*, ED, 82, CDN, Prod.

SIMPSON, Peter R.
ACCT. Norstar Entertainment Inc., 86 Bloor St. W., 5th Flr., Toronto, ON M5S 1M5 (416)961-6278. FAX: 961-5608.
Type of Production and Credits: Th Film-Prod; TV Film-Prod.
Genres: Drama-Th&TV; Comedy-Th; Action-Th; Horror-Th.
Biography: Born 1943. Created Simcom Limited, 71, corporate name change, 87, to Norstar Entertainment Inc., now Chairman and C.E.O.; Chairman, Norstar Releasing Inc., Norstar Home Video, and Media Canada Inc.
Selected Filmography: *Intimate Delusions*, Th, 91, CDN, Exec Prod; *Deliver Us From Evil - Prom Night IV*, Th, 91, CDN, Exec Prod; *The Last Kiss: Prom Night III*, 90, CDN, Exec Prod; *Cold Comfort*, Th, 88, CDN, Exec Prod; *Blindside*, Th, 87, CDN, Exec Prod; *Hello Mary Lou: Prom Night II*, Th, 86, CDN, Exec Prod; *Higher Education*, Th, 86, CDN, Exec Prod; *Bullies*, Th, 85, CDN, Exec Prod; *High Stakes*, Th, 85, CDN, Exec Prod; "Mania" (4 eps), TV, 85, CDN, Exec Prod; *Hank Williams: "The Show He Never Gave"*, Th, 81, CDN, Co-Exec Prod; *Melanie*, Th, 80, CDN, Exec Prod; *Curtains*, Th, 80, CDN, Exec Prod; *Prom Night*, Th, 79, CDN, Prod; *The Sea Gypsies*, Th, 78, CDN, Exec Prod.

SINGER, Gail
- see DIRECTORS
SINGER, Sharon
- see PUBLICISTS

SIRETEANU, Ion-Dragos
CSC, IATSE 667. 2770 Yonge St., #201, Toronto, ON M4N 2J3 (416)486-3127. (416)482-0629.
Type of Production and Credits: Th Film-DOP; Th Short-DOP; TV Film-Prod/Dir/DOP; TV Video-Prod/Dir/DOP.
Genres: Drama-Th&TV; Industrial-TV; Documentary-Th&TV; Commercials-Th&TV;
Biography: Born in 1958 in Bucharest, Romania. Romanian citizen and Canadian resident. Master degree in Arts of Movie and TV. Speaks English, Romanian, French and Italian. Also a painter with exhibitions in Canada and Europe. Film festivals: 1st Lylle, France; 1st Moscow, USSR; 1st Baia Mare, Romania.
Selected Filmography: *Obscure Alternatives*, TV, 90, CDN, Prod/Wr/Dir; *Helena - The Blues*, TV, 90, CDN, Co Prod/Wr/Dir/DOP; *Folcloric Art of North Carpatians*, TV, 90, CDN, Prod; *Romanian Segment*, "Trilogy of Sports", TV, 90, CDN, DOP; *Trans-Alta*, TV, 89, CDN, DOP.

SKY, Laura
- see DIRECTORS

SKERRETT, Bill
46 Swanton Dr., Dartmouth, NS B2W 2C5 (902)434-3187. SCL Media, 165 Portland Street, Dartmouth, NS B2Y 1N2 (902)463-8822.
Type of Production and Credits: TV Video-Prod/Dir.
Genres: Documentry-Th&TV; Industrial-Th&TV; Commercials-Th&TV; Educational-Th&TV.
Biography: Over 20 years experience as a film and video producer; originally with the CBC; independent for the last 18 years. Produced television specials, live shows, film commercials, multi AV events, documentary series, and corporate and training videos. Researches, writes, directs, and supervises the total film or video project and implements the distribution of the product. Company is also involved in the development of television specials such as the Global Project, a 13-part science video series for worldwide disrtribution. Has produced films and videos throughout Canada, Europe, and Scandinavia. Film and video products, which now number over 500, are seen throughout the world.
Selected Filmography: *Celebration Of Excellence*, TV, 91, CDN, Dir/Prod; *The Recent Ice Age*, TV, 90, CDN, Dir/Prod; *So Much To Sea*, In, 90, CDN, Dir/Prod; *Can Fishing Be Safe*, In, 90, CDN, Dir/Prod; *Learn The Right Way*, In, 90, CDN, Dir/Prod; *Agrifood News*, In, 90, CDN, Dir/Prod; *Sunshine Vacation*, Cm, 90, CDN, Dir/Prod; *Convervation*, Cm, 90, Dir/Prod; *The Appalachian Story*, TV, 89, CDN, Dir/Prod; *Mineral Wealth Of Atlantic Canada*, In, 89, CDN, Dir/Prod; *George Bank Studies*, In, 89, CDN, Dir/Prod; *Black Jack*, Cm, 89, CDN, Dir/Prod; *Arms Drill*, In, 89, CDN, Dir/Prod.

SLAN, Jon
3442 Caribeth Dr., Encino, CA 91436 Paragon Entertainment Corporation, 119 Spadina Ave., #900, Toronto, ON M5V 2L1 (416)977-2929. Paragon Entertainment Corporation, 2211 Corinth Ave., #305, Los Angeles, CA 90212 (213)478-7272.
Type of Production and Credits: Th Film-Prod; TV Film-Prod.
Genres: Drama-Th&TV; Comedy-Th&TV.
Biography: Born 1946, Toronto, Ontario. B.A., York Univ.; M.A., Columbia Univ.; Ph.D., Univ. of Toronto. Lecturer, Univ. of Toronto and Univ. of Western Ontario. Chairman of Superchannel from 82 until its merger with First Choice, 85. Currently CEO and Chairman of the Board, Paragon Entertainment. *Day One* won Emmy, Most Outstanding Drama Special; "Alfred Hitchcock Presents" won Ace, Best Dramatic Series; recognized for Outstanding Achievement in Cinema and Television, International Film & Television Festival of New York, for *Taking Care of Terrific*.
Selected Filmography: "Power Pack", TV, 90, USA, Exec Prod; "Dog House" (26 eps), TV, 90, USA, Exec Prod; *Held Hostage: The Sis and Jerry Levin Story*, TV, 90, USA, Exec Prod; *Anything to Survive*, TV, 90, USA, Exec Prod; *Day One*, TV, 89, USA, Exec Prod; "Alfred Hitchcock Presents" (54 eps), TV, 88, CDN/USA, Exec Prod; *Taking Care of Terrific*, TV, 87, CDN/USA, Exec Prod; "Philip Marlowe, Private Eye" (6 eps), TV, 85, CDN, Prod; *Threshold*, Th, 81, CDN, Prod; *American Christmas Carol*, TV, 80, USA, Prod; *Improper Channels*, Th, 79, CDN, Exec Prod; *Fishawk*, Th, 79, CDN, Prod; *Kavik the Wolfdog*, TV, 78, CDN, Prod; *Highballin'*, Th, 77, CDN, Prod.

SLIPP, Marke
- see EDITORS

SMALE, Joanne Muroff
- see PUBLICISTS

SMALLEY, Katherine
- see DIRECTORS

SMILSKY, Peter
- see DIRECTORS

SMITH, Arthur
ATPD, ACCT. 3938 Witzel Dr., Sherman Oaks, CA 91423 (818)995-0631. Dick Clark Productions, 3003 W. Olive, Burbank, CA 91510 USA. (818)841-3003.
Type of Production and Credits: TV Film-Prod/Dir; TV Video-Prod/Dir.
Genres: Comedy-TV; Variety-TV; Sports-TV.
Biography: Born 1959, Montreal, Quebec. Languages: English and French. B.A.A., (first in class), Radio and TV Arts, Ryerson Polytechnical Institute, 82. Background in performing, TV and features, announcing. Winner of 2 Gemini awards for producing 1988 Summer Olympics. Head of CBC-TV network sports, 88-90; currently Vice-President, Dick Clark Productions.
Selected Filmography: *CRASH-TV*, TV, 90, USA, Prod; *Matchmaker*, TV, 90, USA, Prod; "1988 Calgary Winter Olympics" (17 eps), TV, 88, CDN, Sr Prod; "1988 Seoul Summer Olympics" (17 eps), TV, 88, CDN, Sr Prod, (2 GEMINIS); "CFL on CBC" (25 eps), TV, 87-88, CDN, Exec Prod; *1987 Grey Cup*, TV, 87, CDN, Exec Prod; "1986 Edinburgh Commonwealth Games" (12 eps), TV, 86, CDN, Sr Prod; "World Junior Hockey Championships" (10 eps), TV, 85-87, CDN, Prod; "World Cup Downhill Skiing" (17 eps), TV, 85-87, CDN, Prod/Dir; *Rothmans' International Horse Race*, TV, 85, CDN, Prod; "National Hockey League Draft" (2 eps), TV, 84-85, CDN, Prod; "Calgary Stampede" (3 eps), TV, 85, CDN, Prod; "1984 Los Angeles Summer Olympics" (17 eps), TV, 84, CDN, Prod; "World University Games" (15 eps), TV, 83, CDN, Prod/Dir; "Hockey Night in Canada" (35 eps), TV, 83, CDN, Dir.

SMITH, Clive A.
ACTRA, DGC, ACCT. Nelvana Ltd., 32 Atlantic Ave., Toronto, ON M6K 1X8 (416)588-5571.
Type of Production and Credits: Th Film-Dir/Prod; TV Film-Dir/Prod; TV Video-Dir/Prod.
Genres: Drama-Th&TV; Comedy-Th&TV; Children's-Th&TV; Animation-Th&TV.
Biography: Born in England; immigrated to Canada, 67. Worked on TV commercials; graphic arts. Co-founder, Vice-President of Nelvana Ltd. Recipient of many awards including Graphica, US Industrial Film Festival, Wilderness, Chris and a Special Award at Canadian Film Awards, 78. *The Care Bears Movie* won the Golden Reel Award, 86; "Babar" won Geminis, 89 and 90, for Best Animated Program or Series; *Babar, The Movie*, won, Gold Award, Houston International Film Festival; "Beetlejuice" won Emmy, 90, for Best Animated Program.
Selected Filmography: "Beetlejuice" (86 eps), TV, 89-91, CDN, Prod, (EMMY); "Babar" (Series I, II, III)(65 eps), TV, 89-91, CDN/F, Exec Prod; *Babar, The Movie*, Th, 89, CDN/F, Prod; "T and T" (26 eps), TV, 87-88, CDN, Exec Prod; "The Edison Twins" (39 eps)(Dir 2 eps), TV, 83-86, CDN, Exec Prod; "The Care Bears" (13 eps), TV, 86, CDN, Co-Prod; *The Care Bears Movie II*, Th, 86, CDN, Co-Prod; "My Pet Monster", TV, 86, CDN, Co-Prod; *Mad Balls*, TV, 86, CDN, Co-Prod; *The Care Bears Movie*, Th, 85, CDN, Co-Prod; *The Great Heep*, TV, 85, CDN, Dir/Co-Prod; *The Ewok-Droids Adventure Hour*, TV, 85, CDN, Dir/Co-Prod; "Ewoks" (13 eps), TV, 85, CDN, Co-Prod; *Strawberry Shortcake Meets the Berrykins*, TV, 84, CDN, Co-Prod; *The Get Along Gang*, TV, 84, CDN, Co-Prod.

SMITH, John N.
- see DIRECTORS

SMITH, Morag ✧
(416)574-5570.
Type of Production and Credits: TV Film-Prod/Wr; TV Video-Prod/Wr.
Genres: Comedy-TV; Variety-TV; Musical-TV; Music Video-TV.
Biography: Born in Scotland; Canadian citizenship. CanPro Gold award, 84, and Iris award, 85, for "Smith & Smith".
Selected Filmography: "Smith & Smith's Comedy Mill" (48 eps), TV, 88, CDN, Co-Prod/Co-Wr; "Me & Max" (26 eps), TV, 86, CDN, Co-Prod/Co-Wr; "Laughing Matters" (13 eps), TV, 85, CDN, Co-Wr; "Smith & Smith" (195 eps), TV, 78-85, CDN, Co-Prod/Co-Wr; "Out of Our Minds" (pilot), TV, USA, Co-Wr.

SMITH, Robert F.
ATPD. Rob Francis Productions, 80 Summerhill Gardens, Toronto, ON M4T 1B4 (416)968-0186.
Type of Production and Credits: TV Film-Prod/Dir; TV Video-Prod/Dir.
Genres: Variety-TV; Documentary-TV; Commercials-TV; Educational-TV; Corporate-Th; Sports-TV.
Biography: Born 1940, Halifax, Nova Scotia. B.A.A., Radio and TV Arts,

Ryerson Polytechnical Institute; Landscape Architecture Certificate, Ryerson Polytechnical Institute. Worked extensively for the networks in entertainment, sports and special events coverage, as well as in documentary. Own production company, Rob Francis Productions, specializes in marketing communications for the horticultural and sports industries; work includes TV commercials, marketing videos, profiles and documentaries.
Selected Filmography: "The Hobby Garden" (26 eps), TV, 90-91, CDN, Prod/Dir; *Top Dresser*, Hillview Farms, Cm, 91, CDN, Prod/Dir; *Triple Mix*, Hillview Farms, Cm, 91, CDN, Prod/Dir; *Clay Breaker*, Hillview Farms, Cm, 91, CDN, Prod/Dir; *Peat Moss*, Premier, Cm, 91, CDN, Prod/Dir; *Calgary Olympics*, TV, 88, CDN, Prod/Dir; "Front Page Challenge" (132 eps), TV, 81-85, CDN, Dir; *The Papal Visit*, TV, 84, CDN, Prod/Dir; *Jazz Alive*, "Super Special", TV, 84, CDN, Prod; *From Our Family to Yours*, "Super Special", TV, 83, CDN, Prod; *New Year's Eve Live*, "Super Special", TV, 82, CDN, Prod; "Hockey Night in Canada" (120 eps), TV, 76-79, CDN, Prod/Dir; "Expos Baseball" (150 eps), TV, 74-79, CDN, Prod/Dir; "Sports of the XXI Olympiad" (28 eps), TV, 75-76, CDN, Prod/Dir; "Basketball Coverage, Montreal Olympics", TV, 76, CDN, Prod/Dir.

SMITH, Steve ◊
(416)574-5570.
Type of Production and Credits: TV Film-Prod/Wr; TV Video-Prod/Wr.
Genres: Comedy-Th&TV; Variety-Th&TV; Musical-Th&TV; Music Video-TV.
Biography: Born in Toronto, Ontario.
Selected Filmography: "Smith & Smith's Comedy Mill" (48 eps), TV, 88, CDN, Co-Prod/Co-Wr; "Me & Max" (26 eps), TV, 86, CDN, Co-Prod/Co-Wr; "Laughing Matters" (13 eps), TV, 85, CDN, Co-Wr; "Smith & Smith" (195 eps), TV, 78-85, CDN, Co-Prod/Co-Wr; "Out of Our Minds" (pilot), TV, 83, USA, Co-Wr.

SOBELMAN, David
- see WRITERS

SOLNICKI, Victor
53 Hillholm Rd., Toronto, ON M5P 1M4 (416)486-5498. FAX: 486-6433.
Type of Production and Credits: Th Film-Prod; TV Video-Prod.
Genres: Drama-Th&TV; Comedy-Th&TV; Horror-Th; Documentary-TV.
Biography: Born 1938, Paris, France; Canadian citizenship. Languages: English and French. B.A., LL.B., University of Toronto. Executive producer and entertainment lawyer.
Selected Filmography: "Starting from Scratch" (13 eps), TV, 88, CDN, Co-Exec Prod; "The Originals" (26 eps), TV, 88, CDN, Co-Exec Prod; "Peter Ustinov's Russia" (6 eps), TV, 85-86, CDN, Co-Exec Prod; *Videodrome*, Th, 81, CDN/USA, Co-Exec Prod; *Gas*, Th, 80, CDN, Exec Prod; *Visting Hours*, Th, 80, CDN, Co-Exec Prod; *The Funny Farm*, Th, 80, CDN, Co-Exec Prod; *Dirty Tricks*, Th, 79, CDN, Co-Exec Prod; *Hog Wild*, Th, 79, CDN, Co-Exec Prod; *Scanners*, Th, 79, CDN, Co-Exec Prod; *The Brood*, Th, 78, CDN, Co-Exec Prod.

SOMMERS, Frank G.
Pathway Productions Inc., 360 Bloor St. W., #406, Toronto, ON M5S 1X1 (416)922-4506. FAX: 922-7335.
Type of Production and Credits: Th Short-Prod/Dir; TV Video-Prod/Dir.
Genres: Documentary-TV; Educational-TV; Children's-TV.
Biography: Born 1943, Budapest, Hungary; arrived in Canada, 57; Canadian citizenship. M.D., University of Toronto. Now lecturer at U.of T. Medical School; psychiatrist iwth special interest in sexual and marital therapy; founding President of Physicians for Social Responsibility/Canada; co-author of *Curing Nuclear Madness*; President, Pathway Productions Inc.; producer of films on human sexuality, including American Film Festival finalist, *Taking Time to Feel*.
Selected Filmography: *Great Sex Video Series*, ED, 90, CDN, Prod/Dir; *Mutuality* (parts 1,2,3), ED, 84, CDN, Prod/Dir; *Taking Time to Feel* (parts 1,2,3), ED, 78, CDN, Prod/Dir.

SPENCER, Michael
ACTRA, CFTA, APFVQ, ACFTP, ACCT, OC. 1321 Sherbrooke St. W., #D-31, Montreal, PQ H3G 1J4 (514)288-7589. Film Finances Canada, 1001 de Maisonneuve W., #910, Montreal, PQ H3A 3C8 (514)288-6763.
Type of Production and Credits: Th Film-Prod; Th Short-Prod.
Genres: Drama-Th; Documentary-Th.
Biography: Born in London, England; Canadian citizenship. Languages: English and French. Attended Rugby School and Oxford University. Cameraman and director, Canadian Army Film and Photo Unit, 41-46; producer, NFB, 46-56; Head of NFB Ottawa office, 56-60; Director of Planning, NFB, 60-68; Executive Director,

Canadian Film Development Corporation, 68-78; Producer, Lamy, Spencer Inc., 79-81; Filmline, 81-84; President, Film Finances Canada since 84; President, AOFVA, 81; member of the jury, Cannes Film Festival, 80; consultant, Department of Communications, Applebaum-Hébert, CFDC, Telefilm Canada since 79. Films have won awards at national and international film festivals, including Silver Statuette (Rome), Silver Medal (Uruguay). Member, Order of Canada, 89.
Selected Filmography: *Point Pelee Nature Sanctuary*, ED, 58, CDN, Prod; *World in a Marsh*, ED, 56, CDN, Prod; *The Son*, Th, 56, CDN, Prod; *Western Wheat*, Th, 55, CDN, Prod; *Land of the Long Day*, Th, 53, CDN, Prod; *Angotee*, Th, 53, CDN, Prod; *Birds of Canada*, ED, 50, CDN, Prod.

SPICKLER, Bernard
5627, Wilderton, Montréal, PQ H3T 1S1 (514)737-6357.
Types de production et générique: TV film-Prod dél/Dir prod; TV vidéo-Prod dél/Dir prod.
Types d'oeuvres: Drame-C&TV; Comédie-C&TV; Variété-C&TV; Comédie musicale-C&TV.
Curriculum vitae: Né en 1948, Montréal, Québec. Langues: français et anglais. Travaille dans le domaine de la production depuis 69; directeur de production en télévision pour des producteurs privés depuis 74.
Filmographie sélective: "Samedi PM" (32 eps), TV, 89-90, CDN, Prod dél; *Groupe Sanguin/Prise II*, TV, 90, CDN, Prod dél; *Nelligan/An Opera Romantique*, TV, 90, CDN, Prod; *20e Anniversaire de Loto Québec*, TV, 90, CDN, Prod dél; *Rendez-vous doux*, TV, 89, CDN, Dir pro; *Fiesta des sol*, TV, 89, CDN, Prod dél; *Le cirque réinventé*, TV, 89, CDN, Dir pro; "L'univers est dans la pomme" (2 eps), TV, 89, CDN, Dir pro; *Napoleon/Lama*, TV, 89, CDN/F, Dir pro; "Samedi de rire" (80 eps), TV, 85-88, CDN, Dir pro; *Les obsedes corporels*, TV, 88, CDN, Dir pro; *Mon royaume pour un bleuet*, TV, 88, CDN, Dir pro; "Vie de famille" (2 eps), TV, 87, CDN/F, Dir pro; *Extra extra*, TV, 83, CDN, Dir pro; *Deschamps vs Deschamps*, TV, 83, CDN, Dir pro.

SPRINGBETT, David
- see DIRECTORS

SPRY, Robin
ACTRA, APFVQ, ARRFQ, DGA, DGC. 5330 Durocher, Montreal, PQ H2V 2Y1 (514)277-1503. Telescene Film Group Inc., 5510 Ferrier St., Montreal, PQ H4P 1M2 (514)737-5512. FAX: 737-7945.
Type of Production and Credits: Th Film-Dir/Prod/Wr; TV Film-Dir/Prod/Wr; TV Video-Prod/Dir/Wr.
Genres: Drama-Th&TV; Comedy-Th&TV; Action-Th&TV; Documentary-Th&TV; Educational-Th&TV; Commercials-TV; Industrial-TV.
Biography: Born 1939, Toronto, Ontario. Languages: English and French. M.A., Oxford University; M.Sc., London School of Economics. Joined NFB, 65; directed first feature, 68-69; has directed numerous commercials in both French and English. Recipient of many awards for his film work, including Chicago, Sri Lanka, Yugoslavia, Great Britain. *Une Histoire Inventée* was Canada's selection to the Academy Awards for Best Foreign Language Film; was Directors Fortnight selection for Cannes, 91; winner of Most Popular Film and Best Canadian Film, Montreal Film Festival, 90. Currently President, Telescene Film Group Inc.
Selected Filmography: "Urban Angel" (6 eps, Dir eps I&II), TV, 90-91, CDN, Exec Prod; *Une Histoire Inventée*, Th, 89-90, CDN, Prod; *Malarek*, Th, 88, CDN, Prod; *A corps perdu*, Th, 87, CDN/CH, Co-Prod; *Obsessed/Hitting Home*, Th, 86, CDN, Co-Prod/Dir/Co-Wr; *Keeping Track*, Th, 85, CDN, Dir/Co-Prod/Co-Wr; *Stress and Emotion*, "The Brain", TV, 83-84, CDN, Dir/Wr/Prod; "The Journal" (sev seg), TV, 82-83, CDN, Dir/Prod; *To Serve the Coming Age*, ED, 83, CDN, Dir/Wr; *Winnie*, TV, 81, CDN, Dir; *Suzanne*, Th, 79, CDN, Dir; *Don't Forget - Je me souviens/Drying Up the Streets*, "For the Record", TV, 78-79, CDN, Dir; *One Man*, Th, 76, CDN, Dir/Co-Wr, (CFA); *Face*, Th, 75, CDN, Co-Prod/Ed/Dir, (CFA); *Prologue*, Th, 68, CDN, Dir.

STAMPE, Bill
- see DIRECTORS

STANKE, Alain
SARDEC, UDA. Productions Audio-visuelles Stanké, 1212 St-Mathieu, Montréal, PQ H3H 2H7 (514)931-0124.
Types de production et générique: TV film-Sc/Prod; TV vidéo-Sc.
Types d'oeuvres: Documentaire-TV; Variété-TV.
Curriculum vitae: Né en 1934, Kaunas, Lithuanie; citoyenneté canadienne. Langues: français, anglais, russe, polonais, allemand, lithuanien. Producteur: Les Productions Stanké Inc. et Les Productions Audio-Visuelles Stanké; éditeur: Les Editions internationales Alain Stanké Ltée. *Cent ans déjà* remporte le Prix Wilderness,

67; Communicateur et chef de file de l'année, 83.
Filmographie sélective: "Par lui-même" (26 eps), TV, 90-91, CDN, Prod; *Bla, Bla de Robert Lapalme*, TV, 91, CDN, Interv/Prod; *Premier Amour*, TV, 90, CDN, Prod/Interv; "Les Insolences d'une caméra" (39 eps), TV, 87-88, CDN, Prod; *Les Ecrivains*, TV, 88, CDN, Prod; *St-Barthélémy*, MV, 88, F, Prod; *Soins palliatifs*, ED, 87, CDN, Prod; *Auto Mag*, TV, 87, CDN, Prod; *Carré blanc*, C, 85, F, Com/Interv; "Venez donc chez moi" (72 eps), TV, 81-82, CDN, Conc/Interv; *Jean-Paul Lemieux* (versions française et anglaise), TV, 81, CDN, Sc/Interv; *Richard Nixon*, TV, 78, CDN//F, Prod; *Pierre E. Trudeau: portrait intime*, TV, 77, CDN, Conc/Interv; *Cents ans déjà*, TV, 67, CDN, Interv; "Les Insolences d'une caméra" (180 eps), TV, 62-67, CDN, Sc/Anim.

STANKOVA, Maruska
ACTRA, UDA, CAEA. 50 Prince Arthur Ave., Ste. 1407, Toronto, ON M5R 1B5 (416)922-5378.
Type of Production and Credits: Th Short-Prod; TV Video-Prod.
Genres: Drama-Th&TV; Comedy-Th&TV; Educational-Th&TV; Commercials-Th&TV.
Biography: Born in Czechoslovakia. Canadian citizen. Languages: English, French, Czech, Russian and German. Leading performer of Laterna Magika, acting in seven European countries. Genie nomination for Best Supporting Actress in 1988. Has taught at Concordia University, the University of Alberta, Loyola College and Queen's University. Workshops for directors given in Toronto, Edmonton and Halifax for organizations such as Women in Film and Television and the Canadian Centre for Advanced Studies. Founder and Artistic Director of "Directing, Acting and Writing for Camera" workshop. Produced sixty short original dramas since 1982.
Selected Filmography: *Nothing Personal*, Th, 91, CDN, Prod; *The Vigil*, Th, 90, CDN, Prod; *Sweet Dreams*, Th, 89, CDN, Prod; *Rinse Cycle*, Th, 88, CDN, Prod; *Princess Margaret*, Th, 88, CDN, Prod; *Dreams Beyond Memory*, Th, 88, CDN, Act; *I Wake Up Married*, Th, 87, CDN, Prod; *SPAT*, Th, 84, CDN, Prod.

STANSFIELD, David
- see WRITERS

STAROWICZ, Mark
ATPD, ACCT. CBC, Box 14,000, Stn. A, Toronto, ON M5W 1A0 (416)975-7901.
Type of Production and Credits: TV Video-Prod.
Genres: News-TV.
Biography: Born 1946, Nottinghamshire, England; immigrated to Canada, 53. B.A., Europena Diplomatic History, Chinese History, McGill University, 68. Executive Producer, CBC Radio "Five Nights", "Commentary", "As it Happens", "Sunday Morning", which won an ACTRA Award (Best Radio Program, 76). As a journalist, has won many awards, including the Ohio State Award for radio documentary (73), Canadian Broadcasting League's Award (73); first recipient, CBC President's Award; Radio and Television News Directors Association of Canada President's Award (88). Also, TV Guide Award, 89, for "The Journal".
Selected Filmography: "The Journal", TV, 82-91, CDN, Exec Prod, (ANIK 85, 87/GEMINI 87, 89, 90), "Midday", TV, 85-91, CDN, Exec Prod.

STARR, Peter G.
87 Stonegate Dr., Kitchener, ON N2A 2Y8 (519)893-1097. National Film Board, 150 John St., Toronto, ON M5V 3C3 (416)973-9095.
Type of Production and Credits: TV Film-Prod; TV Video-Prod.
Genres: Drama-TV; Documentary-TV; Children's-TV.
Biography: Born in 1951. Canadian citizen. Film editor and producer.
Selected Filmography: "Creative Eye" (6 eps), TV, 91, CDN/USA, Prod.

START, Wally
SMPIA. 604 Walmer Rd., Saskatoon, SJ S7K 0E2 (306)665-9114. Cinepost Productions, 1937 Ontario Ave., Saskatoon, SK S7K 1T5 (306)244-7788.
Type of Production and Credits: Th Short-Prod; TV Film-Prod; TV Video-Prod.
Genres: Drama-TV; Documentary-TV; Commercials-TV; Industrial-TV.
Biography: Born 1955, Saskatoon, Saskatchewan; Canadian citizenship. Bachelor of Commerce. Has produced over 100 television commercials, corporate videos; also producing television drama and documentary. Projects have won awards including Showcase and Bessie.
Selected Filmography: *Winter Seasoned*, TV, 90-91, CDN, Prod; *Knowing Each Other*, TV, 90-91, CDN, Prod; *In Perfect Harmony*, TV, 90, CDN, Prod; *Take a Vacation in Your Own Back Yard* (tourism vignettes), TV, 91, CDN, Prod; *Lightbridge*, In, 91, CDN, Prod; *New Kids on the Farm*, In, 91, CDN, Prod;

Community Bonds (12 spots), Cm, 90-91, CDN, Prod; United Way (3 spots), Cm, 90-91, CDN, Prod.

STAVRIDES, Stavros
- see DIRECTORS

STEELE, Fraser
- see DIRECTORS

STEELE, Michael
ACCT. 207 Erskine Ave., Toronto, ON M4P 1Z5 (416)482-2867. FAX: 482-8298.
Type of Production and Credits: Th Film-Prod/Wr/Dir; TV Video-Prod/Wr/Dir.
Genres: Drama-Th; Comedy-TV; Variety-TV; Musical-TV.
Biography: Born 1944, Montreal, Quebec. 2 years of college; studied music for 6 years at the Royal Conservatory of Music in Toronto. Has produced, directed and/or written over 680 television shows and films including specials, series, documentaries and commercials.
Selected Filmography: *The Ice Star's Hollywood Revue*, TV, 89, USA, Prod/Dir/Wr; "Variety Tonight" (26 eps), TV, 86-87, CDN, Prod/Dir/Wr; *Rich Little & Friends in New Orleans*, TV, 85, CDN/USA, Prod/Dir/Wr; *Mutual of Omaha*, Cm, 86, CDN/USA, Prod/Dir/Wr; *The Hair Cutting Place*, Cm, 85, CDN, Prod/Dir/Wr; *Western Canada's 10th Anniversary Gala*, TV, 85, CDN, Dir; *Live from Harrah's*, TV, 85, USA, Dir; "Stars on Ice" (130 eps), TV, 77-83, USA, Prod/Dir/Wr; *Ginger Rogers at Radio City Music Hall*, TV, 83, USA, Dir; *A Spectacular Evening in Cairo*, TV, 82, USA, Co-Prod/Dir; "Miss Canada Pageant" (annual), TV, 72-81, CDN, Prod/Dir/Wr; "Miss Teen Canada Pageant" (annual), TV, 72-80, CDN, Prod/Dir/Wr; *Harry Belafonte Sings*, TV, 80, CDN/USA, Co-Prod/Dir; *John Curry Ice Dancing*, TV, 80, USA, Co-Prod/Dir; "The Ian Tyson Show" (150 eps), TV, 73-77, CDN, Prod/Dir/Wr.

STEER, Kim
ACCT. 1934 William St., #1, Vancouver, BC V5L 2R8 (604)245-2863. 320 - 1140 Homer St., Vancouver, BC V6B 2X6 (604)682-5599. FAX: 682-6333.
Type of Production and Credits: Th Film-Art Dir.
Genres: Drama-Th; Action-Th.
Biography: Born 1953, Vancouver, BC. Worked as graphic artist after graduating from Capilano College.
Selected Filmography: *North of Pittsburgh*, Th, 91, CDN, Prod; *Matinee*, Th, 89, CDN, Prod/Art Dir; *The Outside Chance of Maximilian Glick*, Th, 87, CDN, Art Dir; *Samuel Lount*, Th, 84, CDN, Art Dir.

STEIN, Allan
- see WRITERS

STEINMETZ, Peter E.
ACCT. 1 Aberfoyle Cres., Suite 2304, Toronto, ON M8X 2X8 (416)239-1825. FAX: 360-8877. Cassels, Brock & Blackwell, 40 King St. W., Suite 2100, Toronto, ON M5N 1B5 (416)869-5725.
Type of Production and Credits: TV Video-Prod.
Genres: Variety-TV; Musical-TV.
Biography: Born 1941, Toronto, Ontario. B.A., University of Western Ontario, 63; LL.B., University of Toronto, 67; called to the Bar of Ontario, 70; appointed Queen's Counsel, 83. Joined law firm of Cassels, Brock & Blackwell, 70; became a partner, 74, practising entertainment law. Director, President, Canadian Academy of Recording Arts and Sciences; counsel to the Canadian Recording Industry Association and represents numerous independent film, TV and record production companies as well as performing artists and creative talent.
Selected Filmography: *Juno Awards* (7 shows), TV, 84-91, CDN, Exec Prod.

STEPHENS, Paul
CFTA, ACCT. 5 Willow Ave., Ward's Island, Toronto, ON M5J 1Y1 (416)368-9785. The Film Works Ltd., 194 Sherbourne St. E., Suite 1, Toronto, ON M5A 2R7 (416)360-7968. FAX: 360-8569.
Type of Production and Credits: Th Film-Prod; TV Film-Prod; TV Video-Prod.
Genres: Drama-TV; Documentary-TV; Educational-TV; Children's-TV.
Biography: Born Toronto, Ontario. Honours B.A., Glendon College, York University. Taught high school in Jamaica. Joined forces in 75 with Eric Jordan to form The Film Works Ltd. *Where the Spirit Lives* won Gemini, 90, as well as 21 international awards; "African Journey" won Chris Award.
Selected Filmography: *Ganesh*, Th, 91, CDN, Exec Prod; "Journey to Understanding" (6 eps), TV, 90, CDN, Prod; "African Journey" (6 eps), TV, 89, Prod; *Where the Spirit Lives*, TV, 88, CDN, Exec Prod; "Spirit Bay" (13 eps), TV, 84-87, CDN, Prod/Dir/Wr; "Pictures of Health" (10 eps), TV, 87, CDN, Prod/Dir/Wr.

STERN, Steven
- see DIRECTORS

STEWART, Gordon
BUPD, ACCT. 31 Bernard Ave., Toronto, ON M5R 1R3 (416)924-4635. CBC, Box 500, Stn. A, Toronto, ON M5W 1E6 (416)975-6869.
Type of Production and Credits: TV Film-Dir/Prod/Wr; TV Video-Prod.
Genres: Documentary-TV.
Biography: Born 1940, London, England; Canadian citizenship. Founding producer of "the fifth estate," 75-89; former newspaper, television and radio reporter in Canada, Africa, the Middle East and Europe. Currently senior producer of "Adrienne Clarkson Presents."
Selected Filmography: *The World of Janina Fialkowska*, TV, 91, CDN, Prod/Dir/Wr; *Mastersinger Paul Frey*, TV, 91, CDN, Prod/Dir/Wr; *The Mystery of Van Gogh*, TV, 90, CDN, Prod/Dir/Wr; *Pinteresque*, TV, 90, CDN, Prod/Dir/Wr; *A Passion for Peru*, TV, 89, CDN, Prod/Dir/Wr; "the fifth estate" (sev seg), TV, 75-89, CDN, Prod/Dir/Wr.

STEWART, Sandy
ATPD, ACCT. 272 Major St., Toronto, ON M5S 2L6 (416)927-7923.
Type of Production and Credits: TV Film-Prod/Dir; TV Video-Prod/Dir.
Genres: Drama-TV; Documentary-TV; Educational-TV; Children's-TV.
Biography: Born 1930, Calgary, Alberta. Started as radio technician at CFPL, London, 48; CBC Radio producer, 52; CBC TV producer, 61; executive producer, 66. Author of two histories of broadcasting; President of Canadian Science Writers Association, 86; media adviser to City of Toronto Board of Health.
Selected Filmography: "Reach for the Top" (Dir sev eps), TV, 63-88, CDN, Exec Prod; *International Reach for the Top*, TV, 88, CDN/USA, Exec Prod; "The Winners" (3 eps), TV, 80-81, CDN, Exec Prod; "Canadian Short Stories" (8 eps), TV, 67-70, CDN, Prod/Dir; *Through the Eyes of Tomorrow Indians*, TV, 68, CDN, Dir.

STILIADIS, Nicolas
ACCT. SC Entertainment International Incorporated, 434 Queen St. E., Toronto, ON M5A 1T5 (416)363-6060. FAX: 363-2305.
Type of Production and Credits: Th Film-Prod.
Genres: Drama-Th.
Biography: Born 1955, Florina, Greece; Canadian citizenship. B.A.A., Motion Picture Studies, Ryerson Polytechnical Institute. Projects now in development include *Red Hot*, *In the Blood*, and *In Search of Alexander*.
Selected Filmography: *Stepping Razor*, Th, 91, CDN, Exec Prod; *Red Blooded American Girl*, Th, 90, CDN, Prod; *The Big Slice*, Th, 90, CDN, Prod; *Pump Up the Volume*, Th, 90, USA, Exec Prod; *Blood Relations*, Th, 88, CDN, Prod; *Friends, Lovers & Lunatics*, Th, 88, CDN, Prod; *One Man Out*, Th, 88, CDN, Prod; *Hostile Takeover*, Th, 88, CDN, Exec Prod; *Murder One*, Th, 87, CDN, Prod; *Caribe*, Th, 87, CDN, Prod; *Into the Fire*, Th, 86, CDN, Prod; *The Pink Chiquitas*, Th, 85, CDN, Prod.

STILMAN, Philip Samuel
- see EDITORS

STINSON, Fred T.
62 Wellesley St. W., Toronto, ON M5S 2X3 (416)483-3551. AD Films Limited, 250 Merton St., Toronto, ON M4S 1B1
Type of Production and Credits: Th Film-Prod/Dir.
Genres: Commercials-Th&TV; Industrials-Th.
Biography: Born 1920, Lindsay, Ontario. Attended University of Toronto and King's College, Naval Officers' Training School, Dalhousie University. Lieutenant/Commander RCN (Reserve). Founded AD Films Limited, 53. Distributor and placement specialists for advertising on cinema and drive-in theatre screens in English and French. Represents Cannes International Advertising Film Festival in Canada and produces annual feature made up of prize-winning commercials distributed by AD Films in Canada and USA. Long-term member (Barker) of Variety Club of Ontario, Tent 28. Trustee, Metropolitan United Church, Toronto; Member, Naval Officers Association, Toronto Branch, and Naval Club of England.
Selected Filmography: *La Publicité 87: ça change le monde ou presque*, Th, 87, CDN, Prod/Dir.

STIRLING, Michelle G.
1725 - 10 Ave. S.W., 2nd Flr., Calgary, AB T3C 0K1 (403)245-5558. Jared Levine, One Century Plaza, 2029 Century Park E., Suite 3250, Los Angeles, CA USA. (213)553-6900.
Type of Production and Credits: Th Film-Wr/Ed; TV Film-Prod/Dir/Wr; TV Video-Prod/Dir/Wr.
Genres: Drama-Th&TV; Comedy-Th; Documentary-Th&TV; Educational-Th&TV.
Biography: Born 1954, Calgary, Alberta. Languages: English and French. Special-

izes in Canadian history, historical drama, literary translations to film/video. Winner of several AMPIA awards and at Yorkton.

STOHN, J. Stephen
ACCT. 86 Balmoral Ave., Toronto, ON M4V 1J4 (416)924-3118. McCarthy Tétrault, Suite 4700, T-D Bank Tower, T-D Centre, Toronto, ON M5K 1E6 (416)362-1812.
Type of Production and Credits: Th Film-Prod.
Genres: Drama-Th.
Biography: Born 1948. Practising law in Toronto.
Selected Filmography: *The Clown Murders*, Th, 75, CDN, Exec Prod; *Me*, Th, 74, CDN, Exec Prod.

STOLLER, Bryan M.
- see DIRECTORS

STONEMAN, John
- see CINEMATOGRAPHERS

STORRING, Virginia
ACTRA, ACCT. 49 Cavell Ave., Toronto, ON M4J 1H5 (416)466-8202.
Type of Production and Credits: TV Film-Prod.
Genres: Variety-Th&TV; Documentary-Th&TV; Current Affairs-TV.
Biography: Born 1953, Kirkland Lake, Ontario. Languages: English and French. N.D.S.S. Institut du Villefrance-Sur-Mer, France. Production assistant CBC, 74-83; researcher for Current Affairs, freelance research for TV Dramas; independent documentary producer, K.A., Productions Inc., 83-present. Winner of ACE (Award for Cable Excellence); Prix Anik; Blue Ribbon, American Film Festival; *Born in Africa*, produced for PBS "Frontline," won Robert F. Kennedy Journalism Award.
Selected Filmography: "Frontline" (6 eps), TV, 88-91, USA, Prod; *Broken Promises*, TV, 88, CDN, Prod; *The Real Stuff*, TV, 87, CDN, Prod; *Rapists - Can They Be Stopped? "Undercover America"*, TV, 86, CDN/USA, Assoc Prod; *Bjor Borg*, "The Champions", TV, 86, CDN, Res; *Tears Are Not Enough*, TV, 85, CDN, Assoc Prod; *I'll Get There Somehow*, TV, 84, CDN, Assoc Prod, (ANIK).

STRAYER, Colin J.
P.O. Box 549, Adelaide Stn., Toronto, ON M5C 2J6 (416)591-7766.
Type of Production and Credits: Th Film-Prod/Dir/Wr; Th Short-Prod/Dir; TV Film-Prod/Dir/Wr.
Genres: Drama-Th&TV; Comedy-Th&TV; Documentary-Th&TV; Commercials-TV; Music Video-Th&TV.
Biography: Born 1960, Boston, Massachusetts; Canadian and US citizenship. President, Northland Pictures. Formed Northland Home Video which offers over 35 video titles, dealing primarily with the evolution of planes, trains and automobiles in North America. *Red Rocket* and *The Big Adventure* were invited to Krakow Short Film Festival, 86-87; *Red* won Golden Sheaf, Best Sound, 85; also nominated for CFTA Award and finalist in Academy Awards, 87. *Big* was nominated for Golden Sheaf, 86; Budge Crawley Award for excellence in film-making, 80; r1989 Director-Observer scholarhsip for *Joe Versus the Volcano* (Warner Bros.).
Selected Filmography: *Flight 143*, Th, 91, CDN, Prod/Dir/Wr; *American Diner* (documentary), Th, 91, CDN, Prod/Dir/Wr; *Iskowitz* (documentary), TV, 91, CDN, Prod/Dir/Ed; *Joe Versus the Volcano*, Th, 89-90, USA, Dir-Assist; *Jimmy Durante*, TV, 89, CDN, Dir; *Scotia Plaza*, In, 88, CDN, Assoc Prod/Co-Dir; *DC 3 Reunion*, TV, 87, CDN, Prod/Dir/Wr; "Happy Now I Know", MV, 86, CDN, Prod/Dir; *The Big Adventure*, Th, 86, CDN, Prod/Dir; "This Time Tomorrow", MV, 86, CDN, Prod/Dir; *Red Rocket*, Th, 85, CDN, Prod/Dri; *Living Longer*, "The Journal", TV, 84, CDN, Story cons; *Running Gag*, TV, 84, CDN, Prod/Dir; *Eye Openers*, "the fifth estate", TV, 82, CDN, Assoc Prod; *The Road to Patriation*, TV, 81-82, CDN, Assoc Prod.

STRINGER, Richard A.
- see CINEMATOGRAPHERS

STROMBERG, Jeanne
CFTPA. Strømhaus Productions, 1182 Gerrard St. E., Toronto, ON M4L 1Y4 (416)466-5460.
Type of Production and Credits: TV Film-Assoc Prod; TV Video-Prod.
Genres: Drama-TV; Documentary-TV.
Biography: Born in 1954 in Copenhagen, Denmark. Languages: English, Danish. Honours B.A., Fine Arts, York University.
Selected Filmography: *Behind the Mask: The Making of the Phantom of the Opera*, TV, 89, CDN, Prod; "Not My Department" (12 eps), TV, 87, CDN, Assoc Prod; *Island Love Song*, TV, 86, CDN, Assoc Prod; "Seeing Things" (4 eps), TV, 86, CDN, Assoc Prod; *One For The Pot*, TV, 85, CDN, Assoc Prod; *Twelfth Night*, TV, 85, CDN, Assoc Prod; *Home Free*, TV, 85, CDN, Assoc Prod; *Friends of a Feather/Celimare*, TV, 84, CDN, Assoc Prod.

SUISSA, Danièle J.
- see DIRECTORS

SULLIVAN, Kevin R.
ACTRA, DGC, ACCT. Sullivan Films,

16 Clarence Square, Toronto, ON M5V 1H1 (416)597-0029.
Type of Production and Credits: TV Film-Dir/Exec Prod/Prod/Wr.
Genres: Drama-TV.
Biography: Born 1955, Toronto, Ontario. Languages: English and French. Established Sullivan Films, 79 and produced several half-hour specials, coporate films and documentaries. Produced award-winning *Megan Carey* and *Krieghoff*; directed and produced the first feature film made for Canadian Pay TV, *The Wild Pony*. *Anne of Green Gables* won over 31 international awards including the Peabody and Prix Jeunesse Awards, and 10 Gemini Awards, a 1986 Emmy Award for Best Children's Television Program. *Anne of Green Gables-The Sequel* won American TV Guide's Best Family Series Award and 2 ACE Awards. *Looking for Miracles*, produced with long-time partner Trudy Grant, was nominated for seven 1990 Gemini awards, including Best Director, and won Daytime Emmy Award. "Road to Avonlea" won 4 Gemini awards and John Labatt Classic Award
Selected Filmography: "Road to Avonlea" (26 eps), TV, 90-91, CDN/USA, Exec Prod, (4 GEMINIS); *Lantern Hill*, TV, 90, USA/CDN, Dir/Prod/Wr, (ACE); *Looking for Miracles*, TV, 89, USA/CDN, Dir/Prod/Wr; *Anne of Green Gables - The Sequel* (mini-series), TV, 87, CDN/USA, Dir/Prod/Wr, (ACE); *Anne of Green Gables* (mini-series), TV, 85, CDN/UA, Dir/Prod/Wr, (EMMY/2 GEMINIS 86); *The Wild Pony*, TV, 82, CDN, Dir/Prod/; *The Fir Tree*, TV, 79, CDN, Wr/Prod.

SULYMA, Michael H.
Sulyma Productions Inc., 6620 - 124 St., Edmonton, AB T6H 3V3 (403)438-8316.
Type of Production and Credits: Th Short-Prod; TV Film-PM; TV Video-Prod/Dir.
Genres: Drama-TV; Musical-Th&TV; Science Fiction-TV; Documentary-TV.
Biography: Producer/Director, comes to the industry with a diverse background. Many years with a C.A. firm, providing a strong financial background; over 20 years in the live theatre as both administrator and dancer/actor; producing and directing, for the last 4 years, using experience to provide creative and effective services.
Selected Filmography: *Return of the Whirlwind*, TV, 90, CDN/USR, Prod/Dir; "Ray Bradbury Theatre" (4 eps), TV, 89, CDN/USA/NZ, PM; *Down Came the Rain*, TV, 89, CDN, PM; *AMPIA Awards*, TV, 89, CDN, Assoc Prod; *Is Everyone Here Crazy?/Without Work*, Th, 88, CDN, Prod; *CANADArts*, In, 88, CDN, Assoc Prod; *Rattle of a Simple Man*, TV, 87, CDN, Prod/Dir.

SUSSMAN, Peter
ACCT. Atlantis Films Limited, 65 Heward Ave., Toronto, ON M4M 2T5 (416)462-0246.
Type of Production and Credits: Th Film-Prod; TV Film-Prod; TV Video-Prod.
Genres: Drama-Th&TV; Comedy-Th&TV; Action-Th&TV; Science Fiction-Th&TV.
Biography: Born 1958, Toronto, Ontario. Executive Producer and partner, Atlantis Films Limited; company's productions have won over 75 international awards, including an Academy Award; *Pray for Me Paul Henderson* won Canadian Children's Broadcast Institute Awards; "Ray Bradbury Theatre" won 10 ACE awards 86-90 and Silver Hugo 88.
Selected Filmography: "Maniac Mansion" (44 eps), TV, 90-91, CDN/USA, Co-Exec Prod; *Journey Into Darkness: The Bruce Curtis Story*, TV, 90, CDN, Co-Exec Prod; *The Quarrel*, Th, 90, IL, Co-Exec Prod; *Rookies*, "Magic Hour", TV, 90, CDN, Co-Exec Prod; *The Prom*, "Magic Hour", TV, 90, CDN, Co-Exec Prod; "Ray Bradbury Theatre" (42 eps), TV, 87-90, F/GB/USA, Co-Exec Prod; *Dark Horse*, "Magic Hour", TV, 89, CDN, Co-Exec Prod; *The Fighter*, "Magic Hour", TV, 89, CDN, Co-Exec Prod; *Tom Alone*, "Magic Hour", TV, 89, CDN, Co-Exec Prod; *Pray for Me Paul Henderson*, "Magic Hour", TV, 89, CDN, Co-Exec Prod; *100 Lombard*, TV, 87-88, USA, Spv Prod; *Cowboys Don't Cry*, Th, 87, CDN, Exec Prod.

SUTHERLAND, Neil
ACTRA, CTPDA, ACCT. Angles Productions, 1027 Clyde Ave., West Vancouver, BC (604)922-6053.
Type of Production and Credits: TV Film-Prod/Dir/Wr; TV Video-Prod/Dir/Wr.
Genres: Drama-TV; Documentary-TV; Variety-TV; .
Biography: Born 1931, Britain; Canadian citizenship. B.Mus.; M.A.
Selected Filmography: *Bluegrass: The People and the Music*, TV, 91, CDN, Prod/Dir; "Winners", TV, 90, CDN, Dir; "Red Serge" (12 eps)(Dir 8 eps), TV, 85-86, CDN, Exec Prod/Wr; *Trials of Lord Selkirk*, TV, 83, CDN, Prod/Dir/Wr; *Mackenzie/Captain Vancouver/Captain*

Cook, "As Far as Man Could Go", TV, 79-82, CDN, Prod/Dir/Wr; *The World of Emmelich Kalman*, TV, 82, CDN, Prod/Dir/Wr; *The Look of Music*, TV, 80, CDN, Prod/Dir/Wr; *Gershwin and Porgy*, TV, 79, CDN, Prod/Dir/Wr; *Schubert Remembered*, TV, 78, CDN, Prod/Dir/Wr; *The World of Noel Coward*, TV, 77, CDN, Prod/Dir; *They All Play Ragtime*, TV, 76, CDN, Prod/Dir/Wr; *The World of Ivor Novello*, TV, 75, CDN, Prod/Dir; *The World of Jacques Offenbach*, TV, 72, CDN, Prod/Dir/Wr; *The World of Franz Lehar*, TV, 70, CDN, Prod/Dir.

SUTHERLAND, Paul
- see DIRECTORS

SWAN, James
- see DIRECTORS

SWEENEY, Irene M.
The Sweeney Production Agency, 99 Harbour Square, Suite 2407, Toronto, ON M5J 2H2 (416)947-0020.
Type of Production and Credits: TV Film-Prod; TV Video-Prod.
Genres: Commercials-TV; Industrial-TV; Music Video-TV.
Biography: Born 1949, Heidelberg, West Germany; Canadian citizenship. Studied Social Sciences, Business, Finance, Economics. Certificates: Investment Dealers/Canadian Securities Course, and Interior Design. Commercial broadcast producer since 75; freelance producer, since 83. Has won several Rac and Sam awards, and Bessies.
Selected Filmography: *Letter X, NDP National Election Campaign*, TV, 90, CDN, Prod; *Dungeon*, Canadian Arthritis Foundation, TV, 90, CDN, Prod.

SWEETMAN, Bill
Alligator Films, 99 Fermanagh Ave., Toronto, ON M6R 1M1 (416)534-7320.
Type of Production and Credits: Th Short-Prod/Dir; TV Video-Prod/Dir.
Genres: Drama-Th&TV; Documentary-Th&TV; Commercials-TV.
Biography: Born 1965, Brighton, England; Canadian citizenship. B.A.A., Ryerson Polytechnial Institute. Worked at Centre for Advanced Film Studies, 88. Winner of 1988 National Screen Apprentice Award. *Jennifer Dickson's Bianca* was invited to the ARCO Film Festival, Madrid. Assistant Producer, Katherine Smalley Productions, 89. Developed Citytv's weekly show *Speakers Corner*, 90.
Selected Filmography: *Alien Garden*, Th, 91, CDN, Dir/Prod; "Speakers Corner" (pilot & 27 eps), TV, 90-91, CDN, Assoc Prod/Ed; "MuchMusic", TV, 90, CDN, Prod; "Speaking Parts", Th, 89, CDN, Prod Coord; *At the Sound of the Tone*, Th, 88, CDN, Dir/Prod/Wr; *Jennifer Dickson's Bianca*, Th, 87, CDN, Dir/Prod; *Rio Painted Blue*, Th, 87, CDN, Co-Prod.

SWERHONE, Elise
- see DIRECTORS

SYMANSKY, Adam
SGCT, ACCT. 63 Chesterfield Ave., Westmount, PQ H3Y 2M4 (514)489-3582. NFB, Box 6100, Montreal, PQ H3C 3H5 (514)283-9555.
Type of Production and Credits: Th Film-Prod; Th Short-Prod; TV Film-Prod; TV Video-Prod.
Genres: Drama-TV; Documentary-Th&TV; Educational-Th&TV.
Biography: Born 1944. Has won awards at several international film festivals, including Chicago, San Francisco, Melbourne, Los Angeles, New York, Salerno, Columbus.

TADMAN, Aubrey
- see WRITERS

TAKACS, Tibor
- see DIRECTORS

TAYLOR, Rick
- see DIRECTORS

TAYLOR, Robin
ATPD, ACCT. 964 Avenue Rd., #1, Toronto, ON M5P 2K8 (416)481-2657. CBC, the fifth estate, Box 500, Stn. A, Toronto, ON M5W 1E6 (416)975-6647.
Type of Production and Credits: TV Film-Prod; TV Video-Prod.
Genres: Documentary-TV; Current Affairs-TV.
Biography: Born 1932, South Shields, England; Canadian citizenship. B.A., Modern History, University of British Columbia; M.A., Stanford University. Arrived in Canada, 56; worked on survey crews in Alberta and B.C.; bookstore clerk in Ottawa; reporter with *Winnipeg Free Press*, *Winnipeg Tribune* and *Vancouver Sun*; radio producer with CBC Winnipeg; TV producer and executive producer with CBC Edmonton, St. John's and Toronto; TV Area Head, CBC Current Affairs, 77-80.
Selected Filmography: "the fifth estate", TV, 81-88, CDN, Exec Prod, (GEMINI 86)

TERRY, Christopher
- see DIRECTORS

TESTAR, Coralee Elliott
- see WRITERS

TESTAR, Gerald
643 Plymouth Dr., North Vancouver, BC V7H 2H5 (604)929-7769.
Type of Production and Credits: Th Film-Prod/Dir; TV Film-Prod/Dir; TV

Video-Prod/Dir.
Genres: Drama-TV; Educational-TV.
Biography: Born Vancouver, B.C. Attended University of British Columbia; M.F.A., Theatre, Pacific University, Oregon; Diploma, BBC Producers Training Program, London. Story editor, CBC Drama; educator, Mohawk College, University of Victoria; independent producer of educational/industrial productions. Most recently, devloped and co-produced *The Little Kidnappers*.

TÉTREAULT, Louis-Georges
APFVQ, CFTA, ACCT. 1425 René Lévesque ouest, Montréal, PQ H3G 1T7 (514)866-1761.
Types de production et générique: c métrage-Prod; TV film-Prod; TV vidéo-Prod.
Types d'oeuvres: Drame-C&TV; Documentaire-C&TV; Education-C&TV; Enfants-TV.
Curriculum vitae: Né en 1954. Langues: français et anglais. Baccalauréat en Communications, Université Concordia. Décorateur théâtral, danseur, jazz et classique. Se joint à SDA Productions, 80; présentement Vice-président et producteur, SDA Productions Ltd.
Filmographie sélective: *Pédibus*, ED, 90-91, CDN, Prod; *Les Cadets* (3 eps), ED, 91, CDN, Prod; "Salut Martin" (39 eps), TV, 91, CDN, Prod; *Where Your Tax Dollars Go*, TV, 90, CDN, Prod; "Vos droits en matière de langues officielles" (2 eps), TV, 90, CDN, Prod; "Vidéo-Théâtre" (13 eps), TV, 90, CDN, Prod; *Bubusse en Autobus*, TV, 89, CDN, Prod; "Impot 88 - Impot 89" (4 eps), TV, 88-89, CDN, Prod; "AZ" (26 eps), TV, 88, CDN, Prod; *Pluie d'ete*, TV, 85, CDN, Prod; "Francomer I et II" (2 eps), TV, 84, CDN, Prod; *Quebec +*, TV, 83, CDN, Prod; *Poissons et Pecheries*, TV, 83, CDN, Prod; *Touchons du Bois*, TV, 83, CDN, Prod.

THICKE, Alan
ACTRA, AFTRA, SAG, WGAw. Fred Lawrence, ICM, 1888 Century Pk. E., #622, Los Angeles, CA 90067 USA. (213)478-6100.
Type of Production and Credits: TV Film-Prod/Wr/Act; TV Video-Prod/Wr/Act.
Genres: Drama-TV; Comedy-TV;Variety-TV.
Biography: Born in Kirkland Lake, Ontario. B.A., University of Western Ontario. Moved to Los Angeles, 70; has received 4 Emmy nominations.
Selected Filmography: "Growing Pains", TV, 85-91, USA, Act; *The Case of the Shooting Star*, TV, 86, USA, Act; *Who Killed Martin Hastings?*, TV, 86, USA, Act; *Anne Murray Specials*, TV, 77-85, USA, Prod/Co-Wr; *The Calendar Girl Murders*, TV, 84, USA, Act; "Thicke of the Night", TV, 84, USA, Host; "Alan Thicke Show", TV, 80-83, USA, Host; *Olivia Newton John Specials*, TV, 81-82, USA, Prod/Wr; *Bill Cosby*, TV, 82, USA, Prod/Wr; *Richard Prior Special*, TV, 80, USA, Prod/Co-Wr, (WGA); "Fernwood Tonight", TV, 78-79, USA, Prod/Co-Wr.

THOMAS, Dave
- see DIRECTORS

THOMAS, Stan
ACCT, BCMPA, CFTA. #136 - 28 Richmond St., New Westminster, BC V3L 5P4 (604)522-9914. CanWest Broadcasting, c/o UTV/CKVU, 180 West 2nd Ave., Vancouver, BC V5Y 3T9 (604)876-1344.
Type of Production and Credits: TV Film-Prod; TV Video-Prod.
Genres: Drama-TV; Documentary-TV; Educational-TV; Children's-TV.
Biography: Born 1933, Saskatoon, Saskatchewan. B.A., B.Ed., University of Saskatchewan. Vice-President of Programming, CanWest Broadcasting; Board of Directors, Banff Television Festival; Board of Directors, F.U.N.D. Past President of Manitoba Association of Broadcasters; past Director of Western Association of Broadcasters; past Director of National Screen Institute. Numerous awards including Columbus, Ohio, Yorkton, CanPro, Iris, ACTRA, Banff, CFTA, Chicago, Houston, San Francisco, Gabriel and Gemini nominations.
Selected Filmography: *Canada's Magnificent Snowbirds - The First Twenty Years*, TV, 91, CDN, Assoc Prod; *Raider of the South Seas*, TV, 90, CDN/NZ, Act; *Daughters of the Country*, TV, 87, CDN, Act; *Tramp at the Door*, TV, 85, CDN, PProd/Act; *The Prodigal*, TV, 84, CDN, Prod; *Hunting Season*, TV, 83, CDN, Prod; *Reunion*, TV, 83, CDN, Prod; *In the Fall*, TV, 83, CDN, Prod/Act; "Size Small" (65 eps), TV, 83, CDN, Exec Prod; "Size Small Island" (55 eps), TV, 83, CDN, Exec Prod; *The Catch*, TV, 82, CDN, Prod.

THOMPSON, Peggy
- see WRITERS

THOMSON, Andy
CFTA, AMPIA. Great North Communications Inc., 10359 - 82 Ave., Suite 300, Edmonton, AB T6E 1Z9 (403)439-1260.
Type of Production and Credits: Th

Film-Prod; Th Short-Dir; TV Film-Dir/Prod.
Genres: Drama-Th&TV; Documentary-TV; Educational-TV.
Biography: Born 1946, Montreal, Quebec. Honours B.A., Acadia University. Joined NFB, 68, as trainee director; director, 69; producer, 76; executive producer, 83. Left NFB, 86, to become President of Norwolf Film Corporation. Produced and directed *The New North*, 86, a 2-hour documentary with Farley Mowat; began Great North Communications Inc., 87, in partnership with Tom Radford in Edmonton, to produce television documentaries, dramatic series, feature films and Imax films. *Blackwood* and *The Painted Door* were each nominated for an Oscar. *In Search of Farley Mowat* won a Chris Plaque, Columbus; *High Country* won Best Drama under 60 mins. at Alberta Film Awards; *Life After Hockey* won six awards including Best of Festival at Alberta; *The New North* won Gemini for Best Documentary Script; *A Good Tree* won ACTRA for Best Children's Program; *Canada's Sweetheart: The Saga of Hal C. Banks* won numerous ACTRA awards.
Selected Filmography: *In Search of the Dragon*, TV, 91, CDN, Prod/Co-Dir; "My Partners, My People" (13 eps), TV, 91, CDN, Prod/Exec Prod; *High Country*, "Family Hour", TV, 91, CDN, Prod; *Tom Alone/Last Train Home*, "Family Hour", TV, 90, CDN, Prod; *Life After Hockey*, TV, 89, CDN, Prod; *The New North*, TV, 87, CDN, Dir/Co-Prod, (GEMINI); *The Painted Door*, "Bell Canada Playhouse" (26 eps), TV, 85, CDN, Prod; *A Good Tree*, "Bell Canada Playhouse", TV, 85, CDN, Prod, (ACTRA); *90 Days*, Th, 85, CDN, Exec Prod; *Canada's Sweetheart: The Saga of Hal C. Banks*, TV, 85, CDN, Exec Prod, (ACTRAs); *Bayo*, Th, 85, CDN, Exec Prod; *River Journey*, Th, 84, CDN, Prod; *Incident at Restigouche*, TV, 84, CDN, Prod; *In Search of Farley Mowat*, TV, 81, CDN, Dir/Co-Prod; *Blackwood*, Th, 76, CDN, Dir.

THOMSON, Lorraine
ACTRA. 66 Collier St., #6A, Toronto, ON M4W 1L9 (416)964-9579.
Type of Production and Credits: TV Film-Prod/Host; TV Video-Prod/Wr.
Genres: Variety-TV; Musical-TV; Documentary-TV.
Biography: Born 1934; originally a dancer and choreographer; switched to hosting and interviewing. Fifteen seasons as program co-ordinator for "Front Page Challenge"; producer and writer of industrials.
Selected Filmography: *Gordon Pinsent Sings Those Hollywood Songs*, TV, 88, CDN, Prod/Wr; *Profile of Celia Franca*, TV, 83, CDN, Co-Prod/Host; *Gordon Sinclair Gala*, TV, 82, CDN, Prod; *Profile of Ludmilla Chiarieff*, TV, 82, CDN, Co-Prod/Host; *Juliette's Return Engagement*, TV, 81, CDN, Head Wr; *Profile of Gweneth Lloyd*, TV, 81, CDN, Co-Prod/Host; *ACTRA Awards*, TV, 80, CDN, Prod; *Juliette's Favourite Things*, TV, 77, CDN, Prod.

TICHENOR, Harold
Crescent Entertainment, #2 - 1163 Commercial Dr., Vancouver, BC V5L 3X3 (604)255-6488. FAX: 255-6465.
Type of Production and Credits: Th Film-Prod/PM; TV Film-Dir/Prod/PM/Ed; TV Video-Dir/Prod/PM.
Genres: Drama-Th&TV; Documentary-TV; Educational-TV; Children's-TV.
Biography: Born 1946, Philadelphia, Pennsylvania; Canadian citizenship. Received original training for career in music; studied Biological Sciences, University of Alaska, 63-66. Produced anthropological-science films until 66; freelance cameraman, Vancouver, 67; media producer for University of Lethbridge, 67-72; formed own company: independent production since 72. Over 160 directing, editing credits; 28 film festival awards.
Selected Filmography: "Kurt Vonnegut's Monkey House" (3 eps), TV, 91, CDN, Exec Prod; *Kootenai Brown*, Th, 90, CDN, Spv Prod; *Neverending Story II*, Th, 89, D, Cons Prod; "Danger Bay" (44 eps), TV, 88-89, CDN/USA, Spv Prod; *The Penthouse*, TV, 89, CDN, Prod; "Danger Bay" (66 eps), TV, 85-87, CDN, PM; *After the Promise*, TV, 87, USA, Spv Prod; *Vanishing Act*, TV, 86, CDN, PM; *Home Is Where the Hart Is*, Th, 86, CDN, PM; *The Neverending Story*, Th, 83, D, PM; *Inupiatun*, TV, 81, CDN, Prod/Dir; *Latitude 55*, Th, 80, CDN, PM; *The Snow War*, ED, 80, CDN, Prod/Dir; *Katei Seikatsu*, ED, 78, CDN, Prod/Dir.

TKACH, Alex
AMPIA, AAMP. Northwest Imaging & FX, 100 - 2339 Columbia St., Vancouver BC V5Y 3Y3 (604)873-9330.
Type of Production and Credits: TV Video-Prod/Dir/Ed.
Genres: Comedy-TV; Variety-TV; Musical-TV; Commercials-TV.
Biography: Born in 1955 in Wildwood, Alberta. Videotape Operator, ITV, 1977-

80; Editor/Editor Supervisor, ITV, 1980-81; ITV Program Director, 1981-83; Post Production Consultant/Animation Director, ITV/Firehall Production, 1982; Producer/Director, C.I.T.V., 1982-83; General Manager, Video Pack, 1983-86; Sales Manager, Studio Post and Transfer, 1986 to date. Nominated for an Emmy, SCTV series III (NBC Network), 90 minute program.
Selected Filmography: *Secrets of Magic,* TV, 91, CDN, Prod/Dir; *Breakin' Tough Rodeo,* TV, 91, CDN, Prod/Dir; "The Barbara Kelly Show" (200 eps), TV, 83, CDN, Prod/Dir; "SCTV" (26 eps), TV, 81-82, CDN, Postprod Cons; "SCTV" (26 eps), TV, 79-80, CDN, Ed.

TODD, Kim
DGC, TWIFT. 103 Wheeler Ave., Toronto, ON M4L 3V3 (416)690-2001. Atlantis Films Ltd., 65 Heward Ave., Toronto, ON M4M 2T5 (416)462-0246. Nighlight Films Inc, 103 Wheeler Ave., Toronto, ON M4L 3V3 (416)690-2001.
Type of Production and Credits: Th Film-Prod; TV Film-Prod; TV Video-Prod/Dir.
Genres: Drama-Th&TV; Comedy-TV; Children's-TV; Current Affairs-TV.
Biography Born 1955, Hamilton, Ontario. Canadian citizen. B.A. (English Literature and Creative Writing), York University, 1977. Editor of Canadian poetry, fiction and non-fiction at Press Porcepic in Erin, Ontario. Co-founder of YYZ Artists' Outlet in Toronto. Began work in the film and television industry as a production assistant. Assistant director on many industrials, commercials and rock videos. Awards: *Pray For Me Paul Henderson* nominated for a Genie for Best Short Drama. "Ramona" won a Genie for Best Children's Series,
Selected Filmography: *The Quarrel,* Th, 90, CDN, Prod; *The Prom,* TV, 90, CDN, Prod; *Pray For Me Paul Henderson,* TV, 89, CDN, Prod; "Men" (8 eps), TV, 88-89, CDN, Prod; *Almost Grown,* TV, 88, CDN, Prod; "Ramona" (10 eps), TV, 88, CDN, Prod; "Airwaves II" (13 eps), TV, 87, CDN, Line Prod; "Airwaves I" (13 eps), TV, 85-86, CDN, PM; *The Truth About Alex,* TV, 86, CDN/USA, PM; "Bell Canada Playhouse" (3 eps), TV, 85, CDN, PM; "The Journal", TV, 83-84, CDN, Prod/Dir; "Comedy Tonight", TV, 83, CDN, Ed.

TOVELL, Vincent
- see DIRECTORS
TOWSTEGO, Tony
SMPIA, ACCT. 58 Middleton Cres., Saskatoon, SK S7J 2W4 (306)492-4783. Tri-Media Productions, 1105 - 8th St. E., Saskatoon, SK S7H 0S3 (306)373-3765.
Type of Production and Credits: TV Video-Prod.
Genres: Drama-TV; Comedy-TV; Documentary-TV; Commercials-TV; Industrial-TV.
Biography: Born in 1960 in Saskatoon, Saskatchewan. Canadian citizen. As President of Tri-Media Productions, has experience in the production of corporate, industrial videos, TV commercials, training videos and, most recently, drama productions. Currently serving on the Finance Committee for SMPIA; Saskatchewan, ad hoc member of ACCT.
Selected Filmography: *Bami, Zoomer for Kids,* Cm, 91, CDN, Co Prod; *Harbor Golf,* Cm, 91, CDN, Prod; *Cairns Homes* (3 spots), Cm, 91, CDN, Prod; *House That Love Built,* Ronald McDonald House, Cm, 90, CDN, Prod; *Feel the Heat,* Cm, 90, CDN, Prod; *Dent Repair,* Canadian Tire, Cm/ED, 90, CDN, Co-Prod; *Air-Threat,* In, 90, CDN, Prod; *Shur-Shot at Winning,* ED, 90, CDN, Prod; *A Viking's Carol,* TV, 89, CDN, Prod; *Shur-Shot,* TV, 84, CDN, Prod.

TRAEGER, Tracy
202 Morley Ave., Winnipeg, MB R3L 0Y3 (204)453-7917. The Greg & Tracy Film Ministry Inc., 175 McDermot Ave., 3rd Flr., Winnipeg, MB R3B 0S1 (204)943-5410. FAX: 947-0197.
Type of Production and Credits: Th Film-Prod/PM; Th Short-Wr/Prod/Dir.
Genres: Drama-Th; Comedy-Th; Music Video-Th&TV.
Biography: Producer of *The Monster in the Coal Bin,* nominated for a Genie for Best Live Action Short Drama, 1990.
Selected Filmography: *Smoked Lizard Lips,* Th, 90, Prod; *We're Talking Vulva,* MV, 90, Prod/Dir/Ed; "Night Visions" (13 eps), TV, 90, Assoc Prod/PM/Ed; "The 12 Steps" (13 eps), TV, 90, PM; *Archangel,* Th, 89, PM; *The Will To Win,* TV, 89, Assist Ed; *The Monster in the Coal Bin,* Th, 89, Prod/PM/Assist Ed/Cont; *See What I Mean,* ED, 89, Line Prod; *Festival Theatre Japanese,* ED, 89, Line Prod; *Mike,* Th, 88, Art Dir/Cont; *Rape Fantasies,* Th, 86, Prod/Wr/Dir; *The Celestial Matter,* Th, 85, Assist PM.

TRANTER, Barbara ◆
(416)595-9663.
Type of Production and Credits: Th Film-Art Dir; Th Short-Wr/Dir; TV Film-Prod; TV Video-Prod.
Genres: Drama-Th&TV; Comedy-

Th&TV; Variety-TV; Documentary-Th.
Biography: Born in Niagara-on-the-Lake, Ontario. Fine Arts, York University, 72; Film Study, Simon Fraser University, 76-78; 1 year of graduate study, University of California at Los Angeles, 78-79. *Artist on Fire: The Work of Joyce Wieland* won Best Canadian Documentary, Festival of Festivals, 87.
Selected Filmography: *Artist on Fire: The Work of Joyce Wieland*, Th, 87, CDN, Prod; *The Canadian Conspiracy*, TV, 85, CDN/USA, Co-Prod, (GEMINI 86); *Passion: A Letter in 16mm*, Th, 85, CDN, Art Dir; "OWL-TV" (pilot), TV, 84, CDN, Wr/Dir; *Unfinished Business*, Th, 83, CDN, Co-Art Dir; *Hello Goodbye*, TV, 82, CDN, Prod; *Porky's*, Th, CDN, Assist Art Dir; *Love*, Th, 80, CDN, Assist Art Dir; *Circle of Two*, Th, 79, CDN, Assist Art Dir; *She's a Railroader*, Th, 78, CDN, Wr/Dir; *Ernie*, Th, 77, CDN, Wr/Dir.

TREMBLAY, Robert
- voir REALISATEURS

TROFYMOW, L.A.
- see WRITERS

TROSTER, David
- see DIRECTORS

TUNNICLIFFE, Jack
see DIRECTORS

TURL, Jeff
ACCT. 13 Birch St., North Bay, ON P1A 1R7 (705)474-6510. Mid Canada Television, 245 Oak St. E., North Bay, ON P1B 8P8 (705)476-3111.
Type of Production and Credits: TV video-Prod/Wr.
Genres: Variety-TV; Commercials-TV; Current Affairs-TV; News-TV.
Biography: Born 1949, London, England; Canadian citizenship. College Diploma in Radio and Television. Former news and sports reporter and television anchorman; former news and program director. Currently Station Operations Managers for television. Has written and narrated numerous commercials and industrial videos. Produces and hosts weekly TV talk show. Executive Producer of sports and telethon specials.

TURNER, Timothy
Circle Productions Limited, 174 Bedford Rd., Toronto, ON M5R 2K9 (416)922-9900.
Type of Production and Credits: TV Film-Prod.
Genres: Commercials-TV.
Biography: Born in Vancouver, BC. Producer of numerous television commercials. Awards include Silver Bessie, 88;

DON'T SHOOT
Until you see the dots on the i's

Before you begin any film or television project, you need complete insurance protection in place to safeguard your investment and your peace of mind.

At Ruben-Winkler, our entertainment insurance specialists are available around the world to help you arrange solid, cost effective insurance coverage *before* you shoot.

When you're planning your next project, give us a call. We'll make sure your i's are dotted and we'll cross the t's while we're at it.

RUBEN-WINKLER
ENTERTAINMENT INSURANCE LIMITED

20 Bay Street Toronto, Ontario M5J 2N8
Tel: (416) 868-2442   Fax: (416) 868-2443
Contact: Arthur Winkler, President

Associated Offices:
Montreal • Vancouver • Beverly Hills • New York • London • Paris • Rome • Munich
Tel Aviv • Mexico City • Manila • Auckland • Sydney • Bangkok • Tokyo

Judges' Choice Marketing Awards, 87; Gold Bessie, 86; Producer of the Year, *Playback* magazine, 88/89, Canada. Appointed Executive Producer & General Manager of Circle Productions, 89.

TUSTIAN, Jim
CSC. Tustian Film Productions, 10245 - 116 St., #18, Edmonton, AB T5K 1W3 (403)488-8932.
Type of Production and Credits: TV Film-DOP/Dir/Ed; TV Video-DOP/Dir/Ed.
Genres: Educational-TV; Commercials-TV; Industrial-TV; News-TV.
Biography: Born 1939, Pincher Creek, Alberta. Certificate, Basic Motion Picture Camera, Southern Alberta Institute of Technology; projection and exhibition training and apprenticeship. Has taught Radio and Television Production; more than 30 years experience in film and TV; established own film production company, 66. Many awards for films and commercials. Recent work has involved increased activity in free-lance directing for other producers of industrial/promotional video productions; transfer of capabilities from total film to video editing and shooting. Latest production credits include aerospace promotional productions for Northwest Industries Limited and various provincial agencies; have utilized some modified editing processes in the use of both film and tape (creating a kine with time-code burn for editing film, with on-line being done from film on-screen time codes.
Selected Filmography: *Aerospace Association Alberta*, In, CDN, Dir/DOP/Ed; *Rx - Burn*, ED, 87, CDN, Dir/DOP/Ed; *Native Journey*, ED, 87, CDN, Prod/Dir/DOP/Ed; *Repairedness*, Northwest Industries, In, 86, CDN, Dir/DOP/Ed; *Lethbridge Story*, In, 86, CDN, Dir/DOP/Ed; *Centre Site*, In, 86, CDN, Dir/DOP/Ed; *A Place to Grow*, In, 86, CDN, Dir/DOP/Ed; *Options*, In, 86, CDN, Cin/Ed; *Buck Stops Here*, In, 86, CDN, Dir/DOP/Ed; *New Breed*, In, 85, CDN, Dir/DOP/Ed; *Oh, Gulley*, In, 85, CDN, Dir/DOP/Ed; *Forests for the Future*, In, 83, CDN, Dir/DOP/Ed.

VADNAIS, Yvon G.
AR. Le Réseau des Sports, 1755, boul. René-Lévesque Est, Bureau 300, Montréal, PQ H2K 4P6 (514)599-2244. FAX: 599-2299.
Types de production et générique: TV film-Prod/Réal.
Types d'oeuvres: Documentaire-TV; Affaires publiques-TV; Nouvelles-TV.
Curriculum vitae: Né en 1946; citoyenneté canadienne, Diplôme du Collège Canada. Journaliste (Rédacteur/ reporter), CFCF Radio-TV; reporter radio-TV, CBC/Radio Canada; maintenant, producteur délégué à l'information, Le Réseau des Sports.
Filmographie sélective: *Tel quel*, TV, 86, CDN, Réal; *Newswatch*, TV, 82-85, CDN, Prod exéc; *Decision/Referendum Quebec*, TV, 79, CDN, Réal; *Referendum Question*, TV, 79, CDN, Prod/Réal; *Lapierre"* (45 eps), TV, 76, CDN, Prod/Réal; *Two Years to Go/One Year to Go*, "Olympic Countdown", TV, 74-75, CDN, Journ; *Weekend Rouge/Firemen's Strike*, TV, 75, CDN, Prod.

VAITIEKUNAS, Vincent
- see DIRECTORS

VALCOUR, Nicolas M.
APFVQ, ADISQ. Publicité Club, 367 est, boul. St-Joseph, Montréal, PQ H2T 1J5 (514)848-6099. Les Productions Quai 32 inc., 1600, de Lorimier, Montréal, PQ H2K 3W5 (514)521-1984. FAX: 521-7081.
Types de production et générique: l métrage-Prod; TV film-Prod; TV vidéo-Prod.
Types d'oeuvres: Documentaire-C&TV; Animation-C&TV; Annonces-TV; Vidéo clips-TV.
Curriculum vitae: Né en 1960, Montréal, Québec. Langues: français et anglais. DEC, Science de la Santé; HEC, Gestion d'entreprise. Clef de sol a gagné Coq de Bronze au PCM; Hélène, Clip de l'année, Catégorie popularité, MusiquePlus.
Filmographie sélective: *Hong Kong - Macao* (5 eps), TV, 92, CDN, Prod; *Archéologie* (13 eps), TV, 91-92, CDN, Prod; *Darlin*, MV, 91, CDN, Prod; *America #3*, Cm, 90, CDN, Prod; *Clef de sol*, Cm, 89, CDN, Prod; *Hélène*, MV, 89, CDN, Prod; *Une dernière fois*, MV, 90, CDN, Prod; "Par les chemins d'Ambroise" (13 eps), TV, 85-86, CDN, Dir pro; "Les décennies 29 à 69" (7 eps), TV, 79-82, CDN, Dir pro; "Les intrépides là 6" (6 eps), TV, 82, CDN, Dir pro.

VALCOUR, Pierre
APFTQ, ACCT. 1600, av. de Lorimier, Montréal, PQ H2K 3W5 (514)521-1984.
Types de production et générique: l métrage-Réal/Prod; c métrage-Sc; TV film-Réal/Prod.
Types d'oeuvres: Drame-C&TV; Documentaire-C&TV; Expérimental-C&TV.
Curriculum vitae: Fondateur et Directeur-général de la Maison Premier Plan; Président de Ciné-Mundo Inc.

Officier de l'Ordre de la Paix, Consul Général de la République du Rwanda.
Filmographie sélective: *Les gorilles des Volcans*, TV, 90, CDN, Prod; "Le monde des sens" (2 eps), TV, 89, CDN, Prod; *Rwanda Sauvage*, TV, 88, CDN, Prod; *Rwanda, les collines de l'effort*, TV, 87, CDN, Prod/Réal; *Boogie Woogie Duke*, TV, 87, CDN, Prod; *Irak et les Emirats du Golfe*, TV, 87, CDN, Prod; *Au nord du Nord Akpatok*, TV, 87, CDN, Prod/Réal; *Le Monde des odeurs*, TV, 86, CDN, Prod; *Les Pharaons*, TV, 86, CDN, Prod/Réal; *Le Frère André*, C, 86, CDN, Prod; *Jeunesse Canada Monde*, TV, 85, CDN, Prod; *Georges Henri Lévesque/Marie Victorin*, TV, 84, CDN, Prod; "Par les chemins" (13 eps), TV, 83, CDN, Prod/Réal; "Les Intrépides" (6 eps), TV, 82, CDN, Prod; "Histoire des décennies - 49-59/69-79" (6 eps), TV, 78-81, CDN, Prod/Réal.

VALLEE, Jacques
CQ. 22, chemin du Fleuve, Côteau du Lac, PQ J0P 1B0 (514)267-0452. ONF, 3155, Côte-de-Liesse, Montréal, PQ H4N 2N4 (514)283-9325.
Types de production et générique: l métrage-Prod; c métrage-Prod; TV film-Prod; TV vidéo-Prod.
Types d'oeuvres: Documentaire-C&TV; Education-C&TV; Animation-C&TV; Expérimental-C&TV.
Curriculum vitae: Né en 1941, Montréal, Québec. Licencié en Sciences de l'Education; Baccalauréat en pédagogie, Université de Montréal. Travaille à l'ONF, 67-72; scénarisation/réalisation; Productions Carle-Lamy, 72-76; cinéaste conseil pour l'Agence canadienne de développement international, 76-78; membre de la délégation canadienne à la conférence des Nations Unies, 82; producteur exécutif, production française, ONF depuis 80-86; producteur, TVO, la châine française, depuis 2 ans.
Filmographie sélective: *Cinq siècles après*, C, 90-91, CDN, Prod; *La Débâcle*, C, 89-90, CDN, Prod; *Les silences de Bolsant*, C, 88-89, CDN, Prod; "La Châine d'eux" (10 eps), TV, 88-89, CDN, Prod; "Cinéma Cinéma" (49 eps), TV, 87-88, CDN, Prod; "Qu'ont-ils en commun?" (13 eps), TV, 87, CDN, Prod; *Prison en moi-même*, TV, 87, CDN, Prod; *O Picasso - tableaux d'une surexposition*, C, 85, CDN, Prod exéc; "Trois milliards" (7 eps), TV, 85, CDN, Prod; *Passiflora*, C, 85, CDN, Prod exéc/Prod; *L'Emotion dissonante*, C, 84, CDN, Prod; *La Grande Allure*, C, 84, CDN, Co prod; *Le Travail piège*, C, 83-84, CDN, Prod; *Carnets du Maroc: mémoire à rebours*, TV, 83-84, CDN, Prod exéc; *Mémoires d'une enfant des Andes*, C, 83-84, CDN, Prod exéc.

VAN DE WATER, Anton
533 ch. de la Montagne, Mont St. Hilaire, PQ J3G 4S6 (514)467-4708.
Type of Production and Credits: Th Film-Wr/Dir/Prod; Th Short-Wr/Dir/Prod; TV Film-Wr/Dir/Prod; TV Video-Wr/Dir/Prod.
Genres: Variety-Th&TV; Musical-Th&TV; Action-Th&TV; Children's-Th&TV.
Biography: Born 1923, The Netherlands; moved to Montreal, 49; Canadian citizenship. Languages: English, Dutch, French and German. M.A., Literature, University of Utrecht. During WWII worked with Dutch Underground making films; continued in this field in which he has worked for 35 years; has designed production and post-production studios; has freelanced for CBC, NFB and private enterprise; photographer and editor of book *Sous le ciel de Québec*; writer of feature film scripts *The Right to Kill*, *The Cup of Youth*. Winner of several awards. Now in production - *Hiryu...La Fabuleuse*, a series of 13 animated films of 25 minutes each; in pre-production, *The Magic Balloon with Cyrus and Snorky*, also a series of 13 animated films of 25 minutes each.
Selected Filmography: *Chansons*, TV, CDN, Prod/Dir/DOP; "The Magic Balloon" (26 eps), ED, 87-89, CDN, Prod/Dir; *Sous le ciel de Québec*, ED, 87, CDN, Cin/Ed; *Heidi and the Gorilla*, TV, 85-86, CDN, Prod; *Airports of Canada*, ED, 78, CDN, Prod/Dir; *La Maîtrisse/And I Love You Dearly*, Th, 72, CDN, Prod/Dir; *Health Insurance*, TV, 70-71, CDN, Prod/Dir/DOP; *Health Insurance*, In, 71, CDN, Prod/Dir/DOP; "Chansons" (39 eps), TV, 66-68, CDN, Prod/Dir/DOP; *First Canadian Winter Games*, TV, 67, CDN, Prod/Dir/DOP; *Mon Pays mes chansons*, TV, 65-66, CDN, Prod/Dir/DOP; *Montreal, Where Two Cultures Meet*, TV, 64, CDN, Prod/Dir/DOP.

VAN DER KOLK, Henk
21, Communication Arts Consortium, Inc., 185 Carlton St., Toronto, ON M5A 2K7 (416)966-2121. FAX: 966-1299.
Type of Production and Credits: Th Film-Prod.
Genres: Drama-Th; Documentary-Th; Industrial-Th.
Biography: Born in The Netherlands; landed immigrant, Canada. Has been producing films for 21 years.
Selected Filmography: *Hank Williams -*

"The Show He Never Gave", Th, 81, CDN, Co-Prod; *Mr. Patman*, Th, 80, CDN, Exec Prod; *Circle of Two*, Th, 79, CDN, Prod; *Wild Horse Hank*, Th, 78, CDN, Co-Prod; *Outrageous!*, Th, 77, CDN, Co-Prod.

VAN DER VEEN, Milton
- see DIRECTORS

VANDERBURGH, Clive
ACTRA, AFM, ACCT. Ryerson Polytechnical Institute, School of Radio & Television Arts, 350 Victoria St., Toronto, ON M5B 2K3 (416)979-5107.
Type of Production and Credits: TV Film-Prod/Dir; TV Video-Prod/Dir.
Genres: Drama-TV; Variety-TV; Musical-TV; Educational-TV.
Biography: Born 1949, Stratford, Ontario. B.A., English, University of Toronto; M.Sc., Syracuse University.
Selected Filmography: *Bookmice*, TV, 91, CDN, Dir; *Transformations*, TV, 91, CDN, Prod/Dir/Comp; *Roots and Wings*, ED, 88, CDN, Prod/Dir/Comp; "Today's Special" (121 eps), TV, 80-87, CDN, Prod/Dir/Comp; *Music Inc.*, ED, 79, CDN, Prod/Dir/Comp; "Mathmakers" (20 eps), TV, 76-78, CDN, Prod/Dir/Comp; "Math Patrol" (20 eps), ED, 74-76, CDN, Prod/Dir/Comp.

VEILLEUX, Lucille
2150, St-Timothée, Montréal, PQ H2L 3P6 (514)521-4085.
Types de production et générique: l métrage-Prod; c métrage-Prod.
Types d'oeuvres: Drame-C; Documentaire-C&TV; Expérimental-C.
Curriculum vitae: Née en 1953. Licence en Droit, Université Laval; avocate depuis 79. Vice-présidente et administratrice des Productions Vent d'Est, de 76 à 87. *La Turlute des années dures* remporte le prix Ouimet Molson pour le meilleur long métrage québécois (83) et 2 prix au Festival de Nyon en Suisse; *La Guerre oubliée* remporte le prix Québec Alberta Innovation (88). Directrice-adjointe du Programme français de l'Office national du film depuis 87.
Filmographie sélective: *Du jour au lendemain*, C, 85, CDN, Prod; *Le Rêve de voler*, C, 85, CDN, Prod; *La Fuite*, C, 85, CDN, Prod; *L'Objet*, C, 84, CDN, Prod, (GEMEAUX 86); *La Turlute des années dures*, C, 83, CDN, Prod; *La Guerre oubliée*, C, 88, CDN, Prod; *Chroniques d'un temps flou*, C, 88, CDN, Prod.

VERRIER, Hélène
4001, Hingston, Montréal, PQ H4A 2J6 (514)486-2077. 335 est, de Maisonneuve, Montréal, PQ (514)844-1954.

Types de production et générique: l métrage-Prod; c métrage-Prod; TV film-Prod; TV vidéo-Prod.
Types d'oeuvres: Drame-C&TV; Comédie-C&TV; Enfants-C&TV; Animation-C&TV.
Curriculum vitae: Née en 1948. Langues: français et anglais. Productrice d'agence sur plus de 350 annonces, 73-77. *Jouer sa vie* remporte de nombreux prix dont le Prix de la Presse Internationale et le Film de l'Année, London Film Festival; *Une Guerre dans mon jardin* remporte le Prix de la Critique québécoise.
Filmographie sélective: *Clair Obscure*, Th, 88, CDN, Prod; *Une guerre dans mon jardin*, TV, 85, CDN, Prod; *La Grande Allure*, C, 84, CDN, Co prod; *Mario*, C, 83, CDN, Co prod; *La Plante*, C, 83, CDN, Prod; *Jouer sa vie*, TV, 82, CDN, Prod; *Le Jongleur*, C, 81, CDN, Prod; *St-Malo*, TV, 81, CDN/F, Prod; *Passe-Partout*, TV, 79, CDN, Prod assoc.

VEVERKA, Jana
ACTRA, ACCT. 6044 Gleneagles Dr., West Vancouver, BC V7W 1W2 (604)921-7653.
Type of Production and Credits: TV Film-Prod/Wr; Th Film-Prod/Wr.
Genres: Drama-Th&TV; Action-Th&TV; Children's-TV.
Biography: Born 1946, Marienbad, Czechoslovakia; Canadian citizenship. Languages: English, French and Czech. Honours B.A., English, Bishop's University, 68; M.A., Theatre (directing), University of British Columbia, 70. Many years experience directing theatre, some television; story editing, script consulting; taught theatre and film at Queen's University. Winner of several awards.
Selected Filmography: *Bordertown*, Th, 91, CDN/USA, Prod/Wr; "Bordertown" (52 eps), TV, 89-91, CDN/USA/F, Prod/Wr; "Bordertown" (26 eps), TV, 88-89, CDN/USA/F, Wr/Script Cons; "Family Pictures" (18 eps), TV, 88, CDN, Script Cons; "Airwolf" (24 eps), TV, 87, CDN/USA, Co-Prod/Script Cons/Wr; "Danger Bay" (44 eps), TV, 86-88, CDN/USA, Exec Script Cons/Wr; "The Campbells" (12 eps), TV, 85, CDN/USA/ GB, Exec Script Cons; "The Beachcombers" (95 eps), TV, 81-85, CDN, Exec Story Cons.

VIAU, Catherine
APFVQ, ACCT. Vie le Monde, 326 rue St-Paul Ouest, Montréal, PQ H2Y 2A3 (514)285-1658. FAX: 285-1970.
Types de production et générique: c métrage-Prod; TV film-Prod; TV vidéo-Prod.

Types d'oeuvres: Documentaire-TV; Drame-TV.
Curriculum vitae: Née en 1960, Montréal, Québec. Langues: français et anglais. Maîtrise en histoire de l'art. Université de Montréal. A travaillé au secteur des émissions dramatiques à Radio-Canada; a dirigé l'APFVQ, 83; entrée à Via le Monde, 83; Vice-présidente, depuis 84; supervise les productions, orchestre les distributions internationales; a développé le secteur de l'animation.
Filmographie sélective: "Vie Privée" (22 eps), TV, 90-91, CDN, Prod/Co sc; "Journal de l'Histoire"/"Stopwatch" (65 eps), TV, 89-91, CDN/F, Co prod/Sc; "Fortunes d'ici et d'ailleurs" (8 eps), TV, 89-90, CDN, Co prod; "Bien dans sa Peau" (26 eps), TV, 89-90, CDN, Prod; "Education: Option 2000" (2 eps), TV, 89-90, CDN, Prod; "Services secrets" (6 eps), TV, 88, CDN, Co prod; "Cinq Défis pour le Président" (5 eps), TV, 88, CDN, Co prod; "Santé du monde" (10 eps), TV, 88, CDN, Co prod; "Traquenards" (13 eps), TV, 87, CDN, Co prod; "Points chauds" (6 eps), TV, 87, CDN, Co prod; "Le Défi mondial" (6 eps), TV, 86, CDN, Co prod, (GEMEAUX 86); "Légendes du monde" (40 eps), TV, 85-86, CDN, Co prod.

VICKERY, Dorothy
705 - 2020 Haro St., Vancouver, BC V6G 1J3 (604)681-0760.
Type of Production and Credits: TV Video-Prod.
Genres: Musical-TV; Documentary-TV; Educational-TV; Children's-TV.
Biography: Born Saskatoon, Saskatchewan. Studied singing, piano, using the Toronto Conservatory of Music curriculum. Began career with CJNB Radio, North Battleford, Sask., then CHAB Radio, Moose Jaw, Sask. Entered Canadian television industry at CHCH-TV Hamilton, Ont. Joined KCOP-TV in Hollywood. Returned to Canada and joined the CBC, Television Production Division. Now an independent producer.
Selected Filmography: *A Future - The Right of the Child*, TV, 90-91, CDN, Prod; *Audrey Hepburn - A Gift of Music*, TV, 88-89, CDN, Prod; *The Sinterklaas Fantasy*, TV, 86-87, CDN, Prod; *People & Profit*, In, 87, CDN, Prod; *Enjoy Your Flight*, In, 86, CDN, Prod; *You Have to Know The Game To Be A Winner*, In, 81, CDN, Prod; *Michelangelo and the Shoemaker*, TV, 80, CDN, Prod; *Anna in Graz*, TV, 79, CDN, Prod; *Prince Charles at Pearson College*, TV, 72-73, CDN, Prod; *Cardiac Arrest*, In, 68, CDN, Prod; *It Takes All Types*, In, 66, CDN, Prod.

VINET, Paul
On/Q Corporation, 1405 Bishop St., Suite 101, Montreal, PQ H3G 2E4 (514)842-1183.
Type of Production and Credits: TV Video-Prod; Interact V-Prod.
Genres: Industrial-TV.
Biography: Born in Montreal, Quebec. Languages: English and French. M.A., Educational Technology, Concordia University. Winner of several awards, including Gold Cindy for Best Level 3 Interactive Video Training Program and Best of Show Cindy, Outstanding Production for *Interact: Meridian Business Services*, 87; Best Industrial/Military Training Achievement, Nebraska Video Disc Awards for *PIVOT-1*, 86.
Selected Filmography: *Call Management Services*, In, 90, CDN, Prod/Wr; *Custom Calling Services*, In, 88, CDN, Co-Prod; *Interact*, Meridian Business Services, In, 87, CDN, Co-Prod; *Talking P.C. Data Demo*, Northern Telecom, In, 87, CDN, Co-Prod; *PIVOT-1*, In, 86, CDN, Co-Prod.

VOLKMER, Werner
- see WRITERS

VON HELMOLT, Vonnie
- see PRODUCTION MANAGERS

WACHNIUC, Michel
- see DIRECTORS

WALKER, Giles
- see DIRECTORS

WALKER, Joel ◆
(416)961-6426.
Type of Production and Credits: TV Video-Prod/Host.
Genres: Documentary-TV.
Biography: Born 1942, Toronto, Ontario. M.D., Fellow of the Royal College of Physicians, Psychiatrist.
Selected Filmography: "Second Chance" (13 eps), TV, 88, CDN, Co-Host/Exec Prod/Stills.

WALKER, John
- see DIRECTORS

WALLACE, Ratch
WGC (ACTRA),WGAw. 50 Hillsboro Ave., #301, Toronto, ON M5R 1S7 (416)922-0186. The Core Group, 489 College St., Toronto, ON M6G 1A5 (416)944-0193.
Type of Production and Credits: Th Film-Wr/Prod; Th Short-Wr/Prod; TV Film-Wr; TV Video-Wr.
Genres: Drama-Th&TV; Comedy-Th&TV.
Biography: Born 1944, Toronto, Ontario.

Languages: English and French. B.A.A., Cinematography, Ryerson Polytechnical Institute; Film History, UCLA. Master of steamship licence (MPT Canada). Co-owner of Movie Marine and Sons, service business to assist water filming; owner of Lakefield Film Productions Inc. Principal actor in 10 feature films and many TV productions.
Selected Filmography: "Seeing Things" (23 eps), TV, 80-86, CDN, Act; *The Unexpected*, "Jack London's Tales of the Klondike", TV, 81, CDN, Co-Wr; *Poetry in Motion*, Th, 81, CDN, PM/1st AD; *Ragtime Summer*, Th, 76, CDN/GB, Wr; *The Tree Has Grown*, In, 75, CDN, Wr; *The Hard Part Begins*, Th, 73, CDN, Exec Prod; *The Match*, Th, 72, CDN, Prod/Wr/Dir.

WALTON, Lloyd A.
CSC. 7 Harding Blvd., Scarborough, ON M1N 3C8 (416)690-3445.
Type of Production and Credits: Th Short-Dir/DOP; TV Film-Dir/Prod; TV Video-Dir/Prod.
Genres: Drama-Th&TV; Comedy-Th&TV; Documentary-Th&TV; Educational-Th&TV.
Biography: Born 1946, Sault Ste. Marie, Ontario. Graduate of Ontario College of Art. Has won 5 First Place Gold Camera Awards, Chicago; Silver Screen Award, Chicago; Bijou Award, Best Promotional Film, 81; Best Live Action Short Subject, American Indian Film Festival, San Francisco, 87.
Selected Filmography: *Gone Forest Fire Fighting*, ED, 91, CDN, Dir/Cin; *The Sustaining Forest*, ED, 90, CDN, Prod/Dir; *At the Airshow*, TV, 89, CDN, Dir/Cin; *The Teaching Rocks*, Th, 87, CDN, Dir/Prod/Cin; *The Winter Camp*, Th, 86, CDN, Prod/Dir/Cin; *Beyond the Polar Bear Express*, Th, 85, CDN, Prod/Dir/Cin; *Futures in Water*, TV, 84, CDN, Exec Prod; *Of Moose and Man*, Th, 84, CDN, Prod/Cin; *Peregrine 1P9*, Th, 83, CDN, Prod/Dir/Cin; *Snow*, ED, 81, CDN, Prod/Dir/Cin, (BIJOU); *Natural Journey*, Th, 80, CDN, Prod/Dir/Cin; *In Search of the Perfect Campsite*, Th, 79, CDN, Prod/Dir/Cin; *Crickets Make Me Nervous*, Th, 78, CDN, Prod/Dir/Cin.

WATSON, Patrick
OC, ACCT. Michael Levine, Goodman & Goodman, 20 Queen St. W., Suite 3000, Toronto, ON M5H 1V5 (416)979-2211.
Type of Production and Credits: TV Film-Prod/Wr/Host; TV Video-Prod/Wr/Host.
Genres: Variety-TV; Documentary-TV; Educational-TV.
Biography: First North American filmmaker to film in People's Republic of China. Founded Patrick Watson Enterprises Ltd., 66; co-founded Immedia Inc., Ottawa, 67; anchorman, editor on "The Fifty-first State," New York, 77; host, CBS Cable Service, NY, 81. Author of 5 books, 2 of which were Book of the Month Club selections. Officer of the Order of Canada. Chairman of CBC since 89.
Selected Filmography: "The Struggle for Democracy" (10 eps), TV, 88, CDN/GB, Exec Ed/Wr/Host; "Live from Lincoln Center", TV, 83-86, USA, Host; "Lawyers" (8 eps), TV, 85, CDN, Host; *Countdown to Looking Glass*, TV, 84, CDN/USA, Act; *The Terry Fox Story*, Th, 82, CDN, Act; "The Watson Report" (135 eps), TV, 75-81, CDN, Interv, (ACTRA); "Titans" (13 eps), TV, 81, CDN, Interv/Wr; "The Chinese" (6 eps), TV, 81, CDN, Contr Wr/Host/Narr; "The Canadian Establishment" (7 eps), TV, 80, CDN, Contr Wr/Host, (ACTRA); "Flight: The Passionate Affair" (4 eps), TV, 78, CDN, Host/Wr; "Witness to Yesterday" (36 eps) (Wr 6 eps), TV, 74-76, CDN, Interv; "This Hour Has Seven Days" (35 eps) (Co-host 35 eps), TV, 64-66, CDN, Exec Prod; "Inquiry" (120 eps), TV, 60-64, CDN, Prod/Dir; *The 700 Million*, TV, 64, CDN, Prod/Dir.

WAXMAN, Martin
- see WRITERS

WEINBERG, Ronald A.
ACCT. 734 Landsdowne, Montreal, PQ H3Y 1J7 (514)484-7469. CINAR, 1207 rue St-André, Montreal, PQ H2L 3S8 (514)843-7070. FAX: 843-7080.
Type of Production and Credits: Th Film-Prod; TV Film-Prod; TV Video-Prod.
Genres: Variety-TV; Children's-Th&TV.
Biography: Born 1951, California, USA; landed immigrant Canada. Graduate of School of Engineering, Tulane University, New Orleans. Executive Vice-President, CINAR, co-founding the company with Micheline Charest, 76. Past chairman, Tulane Film Society; active in organizing several international film festivals in New Orleans in mid-70s culminating in the first International Women's Film Festival in 76. Current responsibilities include CINAR Studios and Crayon Animation. Now in development are 2 series of animated specials - "A Bunch of Munsch" and "White Fang."
Selected Filmography: "The Real

Story"/"Favourite Songs" (13 eps), TV, 91, CDN/F, Exec Prod/Prod; "C.L.Y.D.E." (26 eps), TV, 91, CDN/F, Exec Prod/Prod; "Madeline" (13 eps), TV, 91, CDN/F, Exec Prod/Prod; "Young Robin Hood", TV, 91, CDN/F, Exec Prod/Prod; "Les Intrépides" (26 eps), TV, 91, CDN/F, Exec Prod/Prod; "Happy Castle"/"Château du Bonheur" (13 eps), TV, 90, CDN, Exec Prod/Prod; "Stand In For Danger"/"Festival International des Cascadeurs, TV, 90, CDN, Exec Prod/Prod; "Smoggies!"/"Touftoufs et Polluards" (52 eps), TV, 89, CDN/F, Exec Prod/Prod; "The Wonderful Wizard of Oz"/"Le Magicien d'Oz" (52 eps), TV, 87, CDN, Exec Prod/Prod.

WEINSTEIN, Larry
- see DIRECTORS

WEINSTEIN, Les
ACCT. Salish Park Productions Inc., A Division of Madison Park Inc., 747 Cardero St., Vancouver, BC V6G 2G3 (604)681-8311.
Type of Production and Credits: TV Film-Prod.
Genres: Drama-TV; Variety-TV; Documentary-TV; Children's-TV.
Biography: Born 1933, Montreal, Quebec. Seven years at Columbia Pictures in distribution; personal manager for The Irish Rovers for 27 years; President, Salish Park Productions Inc., A Division of Madison Park Inc.
Selected Filmography: *Irish Rovers Silver Anniversary*, TV, 89, CDN, Exec Prod; "Party with the Rovers" (36 eps), TV, 83-85, CDN, Exec Prod; *Harvest Moon with Frank Mills*, TV, 85, CDN, Exec Prod; *Rocky Mountain Christmas with Frank Mills*, TV, 84, CDN, Exec Prod; "Kid-TV" (pilot), TV, 83, CDN, Exec Prod; *Magical Halloween Party*, TV, 82, CDN, Exec Prod; *Children of the Gale*, TV, 80, CDN, Exec Prod; *Brendon Behan Holding Forth*, TV, 78, CDN, Exec Prod; *Second Wind*, Th, 75, CDN, Exec Prod.

WEINZWEIG, Daniel
10 Olive Ave, Toronto, ON M6G 1T8 (416)535-9614. Cinephile Limited, 388 King St. West,, Suite 211, Toronto, ON M5V 1K2 (416)581-1251.
Type of Production and Credits: Th Film-Prod.
Genres: Drama-Th; Comedy-Th.
Biography: Born in 1947. Chairman, Cinephile Ltd., 89; Producer Advisor to the Canadian Centre for Advanced Film Studies Inc., 89-90; appointed by Federal Minister of Communications (Marcel Masse), Industry Task Force, 86; President, Norstar Releasing Inc., 84 (co-founded and developed Norstar as Canada's premier theatrical television and video distribution company). Appointed Senior Vice-President, Cineplex Corp., 83; Chief Buyer & Booker for the Cineplex Corp. 80-83; Executive Producer, *Pinball Summer*, 79; President, Danton Films Ltd., 69-80; Sales Manager, Astral Films, 68-69; Head Booker, International Film Dist., 64-67. Co-Chairman of the National Association of Canadian Film & Video Dist., 86-91; member, Board of Directors, Canadian Film Institute, Academy of Canadian Cinema, 82; Member, Canadian Association of Motion Picture Producers, 79-81; founding member and Secretary of the Motion Picture Institute of Canada, 78-80; founding member and President of the Association of Independent and Canadian Owned Motion Picture Distributors, 77-80.
Selected Filmography: *Pinball Summer*, Th, 78, CDN, Exce Prod; *Smoked Lizard Lips*, Th, 90, CDN, Assoc Prod; *Careful*, Th, 91, CDN, Exec Prod.

WERTHEIMER, Bob
DGC, CFTPA. 25 Riverdale Ave., Toronto, ON M4K 1C2 (416)463-2123. 565-5911.
Type of Production and Credits: Th Film-Prod/PM; TV Film-Prod/PM; TV Video-Prod/PM.
Genres: Drama-Th&TV; Comedy-Th&TV; Action-Th&TV; Science Fiction-Th&TV; Horror-Th&TV.
Biography: Born in 1955. Former board member of The Academy of Canadian Cinema and Television. Founding member of ETAC and OPIC.
Selected Filmography: *Psychic*, Th, 90, CDN, Dist Rep; *Sam & Me*, Th, 90, CDN, Prod/Unit PM; *Shadow Dancing*, Th, 87-88, CDN, Line Prod; *Martha, Ruth & Edie*, Th, 88, CDN, Line Prod/Unit PM; "Friday The 13th - The Series", TV, 87, USA/CDN, Line Prod/Unit PM; *Normanicus*, TV, 87, CDN, Dist Rep; *Blindside*, Th, 86, CDN, Unit PM; *Hello Mary Lou - Prom Night II*, Th, 86, CDN, Unit PM; *The Gate*, Th, 86, CDN, Unit PM.

WEYMAN, Peter (Bay)
ATPD, CIFC. 36 Springhurst Ave., Toronto, ON M6K 1B6 (416)534-7114. Close Up Films, 345 Adelaide St. W., Suite 607, Toronto, ON M5V 1R5 (416)597-2211.
Type of Production and Credits: TV Film-Dir/Prod/Wr/Ed; TV Video-Dir/Prod/Wr/Ed.

Genres: Musical-TV; Documentary-TV.
Biography: Born 1954, Toronto, Ontario. M.F.A., Film Production, York University; Honours B.A. in Cultural Studies/Comparative Development Studies, Trent University; awarded Special M.A. Scholarship, Social Sciences & Humanities Research Council of Canada; Film awards include Gemini nomination for Best Direction, 90; Special Heritage Award, Yorkton, 86; Student Oscar, Los Angeles, 85.
Selected Filmography: *Mariposa: Special at Thirty/Mariposa: Under a Stormy Sky*, TV, 91, CDN, Co-Prod/Co-Dir/Wr; *Oyster Country*, "Adrienne Clarkson Presents", TV, 91, CDN, Prod/Dir; *Bearing Straight: A Portrait of Don Ross*, "Adrienne Clarkson Presents", TV, 90, CDN, Prod/Dir; *Diva on Queen*, "Adrienne Clarkson Presents", TV, 90, CDN, Prod/Dir; *Fiddleville*, TV, 89, CDN, Prod/Dir; *Against Reason: A Portrait of Jack McClelland*, TV, 86, CDN, Co-Prod/Co-Dir/Ed; *The Leahys: Music Most of All*, TV, 83, CDN, Prod/Dir/ Wr/Co-Ed.

WHALEY, Ronald T. ✧
(403)521-6000.
Type of Production and Credits: TV Film-Prod/Dir/Wr; TV Video-Prod/Dir/Wr;.
Genres: Variety-TV; Educational-Th&TV; Children's-TV; Commercials-Th&TV.
Biography: Born 1956, Regina, Saskatchewan. Winner of several awards for commercials production and many nominations for children's programming. Awards include 2 TVB Top Ten in Canada and several local and provincial awards of excellence.
Selected Filmography: "Switchback" (30 eps), TV, 87-88, CDN, Prod/Dir; "Olympic Night Live" (13 eps), TV, 88, CDN, Field Prod; *Easter Seal Telethon*, TV, 88, CDN, Dir; "Hockey Night in Canada" (30 eps) (Presentation), TV, 86-88, CDN, Prod; "Meeting Place" (3 eps), TV, 87-88, CDN, Prod/Dir; *Best on the Box*, CBC, (20 eps), Cm, 87-88, CDN, Prod/Dir.

WHEELER, Anne
- see DIRECTORS

WHITE, Helene B.
- see DIRECTORS

WHITING, Glynis
WGC (ACTRA), CFTPA, ACCT. 9839 - 91 Ave., Edmonton, AB T6E 2T5 (403)439-3560. 10022 - 103 St., 2nd Flr., Edmonton, AB T5J 0X2 (403)428-1943.
Type of Production and Credits: Th Film-Prod/Wr; TV Video-Prod/Wr.
Genres: Drama-Th&TV; Educational-TV; Children's-TV.
Biography: Born in 1955.
Selected Filmography: *Blood Clan*, Th, 90, CDN, Prod/Wr; *Baba's House*, TV, 90, CDN, Prod/Wr.

WIENER, Martin
ACCT. High Horse Productions, 44 Charles St. W., #2308, Toronto, ON M4Y 1R7 (416)920-3116.
Type of Production and Credits: TV Film-Prod.
Genres: Drama-TV; Comedy-TV; Action-TV.
Biography: Born 1943, Winnipeg, Manitoba. Studied Architecture, University of Manitoba. Graduate, Radio and TV Arts, Ryerson Polytechnical Institute, 67. Worked as theatrical stage manager, publicist (2 years, Stratford Festival) and administrator (2 years, Studio Lab Theatre; 7 years, Toronto Arts Production), now Canadian Stage Company.
Selected Filmography: *Breaking All the Rules*, TV, 87, CDN, Co-Prod; "Seeing Things"(Co-Prod 16 eps/Assoc Prod 24 eps/Unit M 2 eps), TV, 81-86, CDN, Co-Prod/Assoc Prod/Unit M (2 GEMINIS 87/GEMINI 86); *I Married the Klondike* (3 eps), TV, 81, CDN, Unit M.

WILDEBLOOD, Peter
ACTRA, ACCT. 526 Toronto St., Victoria, BC V8V 1N9 (604)381-0788. FAX: 381-0441. Douglas Rae Management Ltd., 28 Charing Cross Rd., London, GB WC2HODB England. (01)836-3903.
Type of Production and Credits: TV Film-Prod/Wr; TV Video-Prod/Wr.
Genres: Drama-Th&TV; Musical-TV.
Biography: Born in Alassio, Italy; British and Canadian citizenship. Radley College, Trinity College, Oxford. Languages: English, French, Spanish and some Arabic. Author of 4 books, including *Against the Law*; wrote book and lyrics for musicals including *The Crooked Mile* (Ivor Novello Award for Light Music, GB, 59); under contract to Granada TV, 58-70, as producer, screenwriter; Executive Producer (plays), London Weekend TV till 72; Executive-in-Charge (independent production), CBC drama, Toronto, 86; V.P., Creative Affairs, Wacko Entertainment Ltd., 88.
Selected Filmography: "Backstretch" (12 eps)(Wr 5 eps), TV, 82-84, CDN, Prod, (ANIK); *I Married the Klondike* (3 parts),

TV, 83, CDN, Wr; "The Great Detective" (35 eps)(Wr 5 eps), TV, 78-82, CDN, Prod; *Ladies Choice*, TV, 82, CDN, Prod; "A Gift to Last" (25 eps)(Wr 5 eps), TV, 77-79, CDN, Story Ed; "Father Brown" (4 eps), TV, 76, GB, T'play; "Upstairs Downstairs", TV, 74, GB, Wr; *Ten from the Twenties*, TV, 74, GB, T'play; *Crime of Passion*, TV, 73, GB, Wr; *Parables*, TV, 73, GB, Wr; *Crown Court*, TV, 72, GB, Prod/Wr; "Big Brother" (13 eps), TV, 71, GB, Prod; "Adventures of Don Quick" (6 eps), TV, 70, GB, Prod; *Testament of François Villon*, TV, 70, GB, Wr/Prod; *The People's Jack*, TV, 69, GB, Prod/Wr.

WILKINSON, Douglas
SMPTE. 68 Tranby Ave., #4, Toronto, ON M5R 1N5 (416)963-8486. CBC, Street Legal, 420 Dupont St., Toronto, ON M5R 3P3 (416)588-4200.
Type of Production and Credits: TV Film-Prod (Post)/Post Spv.
Genres: Drama-TV; Comedy-TV; Science Fiction-TV.
Biography: Born in 1964. Canadian citizen. Education: B.A.A., Radio & Television Arts, Ryerson Polytechnical Institute; M.S., Television/Film, Syracuse University. Special skills: visual effects - blue screen/matting, electronic animation and computer graphics. Effect design and implementation on weekly TV series "My Secret Identity". Preparation of post production budgets & schedules for series, TV movies, etc.
Selected Filmography: "Street Legal" (30 eps), TV, 90-91, CDN, Prod (Post); "My Secret Identity" (42 eps), TV, 88-89, USA/CDN, Postprod Spv.

WILKS, Wendell G.
668 Woodpark Blvd. S.W., Calgary, AB T2W 3R7 (403)238-351. Alberta Television Network Inc., 803 - 24 Ave. S.E., Calgary, AB T2G 1P5 (403)266-8777.
Type of Production and Credits: Th Film-Wr; TV Video-Prod.
Genres: Drama-TV; Comedy-TV; Variety-TV; Musical-TV.
Biography: Born in 1941. Broadcast executive. Founding CEO of CITV, Edmonton.
Selected Filmography: *Confessions of an Undertaker*, Th, 91, CDN, Wr; *Something's Gotta Give*, Th, 90, CDN, Wr; "Palace" (26 eps), TV, 80-87, CDN, Prod; "Live at the Forum" (78 Eps), TV, 78-82, CDN, Prod; "The Baxters" (52 eps), TV, 81, CDN, Prod; *Astonishing Odyssey*, Th, 80, CDN, Prod; *Soiree Canadienne de Paris*, Th, 78, F/CDA, Prod/Wr; "Michel Legrand" (8 eps), TV, 78, CDN, Prod; "Celebrity Revue" (130 eps), TV, 77, CDN, Prod; "Celebrity Concerts" (36 eps), TV, 74-76, CDN, Exec Prod.

WILLIAMS, Don S.
- see DIRECTORS

WILLIAMS, Douglas
- see DIRECTORS

WILLIAMS, Roger
- see CINEMATOGRAPHERS

WINEMAKER, Mark Joesph
187 Hastings Ave., Toronto, ON M4L 2L6 (416)466-5691. Winemaker Productions Inc., 187 Hastings Ave., Toronto, ON M4L 2L6 (416)466-5691.
Type of Production and Credits: Th Film-Prod/Dir/Wr/Ed; TV Film-Prod/Dir/Wr/Ed; TV Video-Prod/Dir/Wr/Ed.
Genres: Drama-Th&TV; Documentary-TV; Educational-TV; Children's-TV.
Selected Filmography: *Building Communities*, In, 91, CDN, Wr/Dir; "Journey To Understanding", ED, 90-91, CDN, Dir/Wr; *Testimonials/A New Beginning*, In, 90, CDN, Prod/Wr; "African Journey", TV, 88-90, CDN/NZ, Prod/2nd Unit Dir; *The Big Break*, Ed, 89, CDN/USA, Wr; *Super Circus '89*, Cm, 89, CDN, Prod/Dir; *Going Back to the Blanket*, TV, 89, CDN, Ed; *Your Child In Sport*, In, 88, CDN, Prod/Dir/Wr; *Just Like You*, TV, 88, CDN, Ed; "Role Models", ED, 88, CDN, Ed; *Investing In Children*, In, 87, CDN, Line Prod/Ed; "Solve It", ED, 87, CDN/USA, Dir/Ed; *Home Sounds*, TV, 87, CDN, Prod/Dir.

WINKLER, Meita
- see DIRECTORS

WINNING, David
- see DIRECTORS

WINTONICK, Peter
- see EDITORS

WISEMAN, Sheldon
ACCT. 17 Lacewood Court, Nepean, ON K2E 7E2 (613)226-5112. Lacewood Productions Inc., 400 McLaren St., Ottawa, ON K2P 0M8 (613)238-4455.
Type of Production and Credits: Th Film-Exec Prod; TV Video-Exec Prod.
Genres: Children's-Th&TV; Animation-Th&TV.
Biography: Born 1941, Smiths Falls, Ontario. B.A., Queen's University; LL.B., University of Toronto, 66; called to the Bar of Ontario, 68; legal practice is primarily entertainment related. Executive Producer of numerous television television specials and series; President: Evergreen Raccoons Television Productions Inc.; Lacewood Studios Inc., Lacewood

Productions Inc.; Chairman, Ottawa International Animation Festival. Director, CFTPA.
Selected Filmography: "The Raccoons" (Series I-V) (60 eps), TV, 84-91, CDN, Exec Prod; *The Raccoons and the Lost Star*, TV, 83, CDN, Exec Prod; *The Raccoons on Ice*, TV, 81, CDN, Exec Prod; *The Christmas Raccoons*, TV, 80, CDN, Exec Prod.

WINKLER, Meita
- see DIRECTORS

WODOSLAWSKY, Stefan ◊
(514)283-9535.
Type of Production and Credits: Th Film-Prod/Wr/Act; Th Short-Prod/1st AD; TV Video-Dir.
Genres: Drama-Th&TV; Documentary-TV; Children's-TV.
Biography: Born 1952, Sydney, Nova Scotia; US resident alien. Honours B.A., Theatre, Dalhousie University. Producer at NFB for 10 years. Nominated for Oscar, 80, Best Dramatic Short Subject, for *Bravery in the Field*.
Selected Filmography: *Give Me Your Answer True*, TV, 88, CDN, Prod/Dir; *Something about Love*, Th, 87, CDN, Prod/Co-Wr/Act; *The Last Straw*, Th, 86, CDN, Act; *Crazy Moon*, Th, 85, CDN, Pord/Co-Wr; *90 Days*, Th, 85, CDN, Act; *Blueline*, TV, 85, CDN, Prod/Wr; "Empire Inc." (6 eps), TV, 84-85, CDN, Assoc Prod; *The Masculine Mystique*, Th, 83, CDN, Act; *The Wars*, Th, 81, CDN/D, Co-Prod; *Bravery in the Field*, TV, 80, CDN, Co-Prod; *Gopher Broke*, TV, 79, CDN, Co-Prod; *Breakdown*, TV, 77, CDN, Co-Prod.

WOLFSON, Steve
ACTRA, CFTPA. Wolf Sun Productions Ltd., 4 - 1953 Garnet St., Regina, SK S4T 2Z5 (306)352-1976.
Type of Production and Credits: TV Film-Prod; TV Video-Prod/DOP.
Genres: Drama-Th&TV.
Biography: Born 1948, Omaha, Nebraska; Canadian resident since 75; landed immigrant. Also writes children's books and is a public health consultant. Winner of award for Best Promotional Production, Saskatchewan Film and Video Showcase, for *Yesterday's Farmer*.
Selected Filmography: *Mozambique: Building a Future*, ED, 87, CDN, Prod; *Yesterday's Farmer*, MV, 87, CDN, Prod/Dir.

WOLOSCHUK, Walter
IATSE 873. Walleye Productions Inc./Rock 'n' Reel Motion Pictures Inc., 14 Bulwer St., Toronto, ON M5T 2V3 (416)598-5382/597-0404. FAX: 596-7087.

SERVING THE INDUSTRY WITH THE BOOKS YOU NEED

THEATREBOOKS

FOR A GREAT SELECTION OF BOOKS ON FILM AND FILMMAKING.
FREE CATALOGUES • MAIL ORDERS
25 BLOOR STREET WEST, TORONTO M4W 1A3 922-7175

Type of Production and Credits: Th Film-Prod; TV Video-Prod/Dir.
Genres: Drama-Th; Educational-TV; Commercials-Th&TV; Music Video-Th&TV.
Biography: Born in 1954 in Sudbury, Ontario. Languages: English, French, Ukrainian. Media Arts Film and Television diploma. Director and producer of music videos, commercials, educational, industrial and 3-D theatrical (65mm film). Film instructor at the Harris Institute. Interests: directing, producing. Wide knowledge of motion picture and video production. Juno award winner.
Selected Filmography: *Animal Heat,* Glass Tiger, MV, 91, CDN/USA, Prod; *Articulation,* ED, 90-91, CDN, Dir/Prod; *Can't Repress The Cause,* various artists, MV, 91, CDN, Dir/Prod; *Hole in my Heart,* Cyndi Lauper, MV, 91, USA, Line Prod; *Dream Big,* MV, 90, CDN, Prod/Dir; *Brain Show,* ED/Th, 90, CDN, Line Prod; *Shooting Star/Special Place Special Time,* Th, 90, CDN, Prod; *Boomtown,* Andrew Cash, MV, 89, CDN, Prod; *Black Velvet,* Alannah Myles, MV, 89, CDN/USA, Line Prod; *Gulf Oil* (3 spots), Cm, 88, USA, Prod; Silkience, Cm, 88, USA, Prod; *Confidence Man,* The Jeff Healey Band, MV, 88, USA, Prod; *Bailey's Irish Cream* (2 spots), Cm, 87, F, Prod.

WOLSZTEJN, Jean-Victor
Toronto, ON (416)362-0286.
Type of Production and Credits: Th Short-Prod/D.O.P.
Genres: Documentry-TV&Th; Industrial-TV; Music Video-TV.
Biography: Born 1962 in Paris, France. Languages: English, French, German, Hebrew, Yiddish. Affiliate member, CSC. Special skills: fine arts, interior design, prof. photography; all formats. 1989 sponsored by the National Film Board of Canada to represent the film students in Canada at the 17th International UNIATEC Congress.
Selected Filmography: *David Kibuka,* ED, 91, CDN, Dir Prod/DOP; *PSI,* In/ED,91, CDN, Prod/Dir; *Blind Betray,* Th, 90, CDN, Prod/DOP; *Don't Make Me Mad Son/Top Secret,* MV, 90, CDN, Prod/DOP; *Without A Single Word,* Th, 88, CDN, Prod/Dir.

WRIGHT, Charles R.D.
3569 West 3rd Ave., Vancouver, BC V6R 118 (604)737-6898. British Columbia Telephone Company, 3777 Kingsway, Burnaby, BC V5H 3Z7 (604)432-2939.
Type of Production and Credits: TV Video-Dir/Prod/Wr.
Genres: Corporate-Th&TV; Commercials-TV; Variety-TV; Musical-TV; Documentary-Th&TV.
Biography: Born 1961 in Hamilton, Ontario. 15 years in broadcasting, corporate and commercial production, including 2 years in Australian television.
Selected Filmography: "KidZone", TV, 90, CDN, Dir; "Vancouver Live", TV, 84-86, CDN, Dir, (CanPro); Pirate TV, TV, 86, CDN, Dir; "TeleClub", TV, 81-82, AUS, Prod/Dir/Wr.

WRIGHT, Richard
ATPD, ACTRA. 287 Crawford St., Toronto, ON M6J 2V7 (416)537-0484.
Type of Production and Credits: TV Video-Prod.
Genres: Current Affairs-TV; News-TV; Arts Features-TV.
Biography: Canadian citizen. Languages: English and some French. Producer of current affairs and arts short features and documentaries. Also a magazine feature writer.
Selected Filmography: *When The Wind Blows/Joe Machado: Folk Artist,* TV, 91, CDN, Prod; *Mas'/Carnival Art,* TV, 91, CDN, Prod; *Moveable Feast/Via Rail's Traveling Gallery,* TV, 91, CDN, Prod; *Colour Me Blue/The Meaning of Colour,* TV, 91, CDN, Prod; "CBC Market Place", TV, 88-91, CDN, Prod.

WRIGHT, Paul
ATPD. 475 Prince Albert, Westmount, PQ H3Y 2P7 (416)967-0345. CBC, Box 500, Stn. A, Toronto, ON M5W 1E6 (416)975-6644.
Type of Production and Credits: TV Film-Prod/Wr.
Genres: Documentary-TV.
Biography: Born 1924, Winnipeg, Manitoba. Joined CBC, 55. Worked in Winnipeg, Toronto, London (England), Montreal; 10 years as executive producer, documentary specials.
Selected Filmography: "Defence of Canada" (3 eps), TV, 86, CDN, Exec Prod; *Canada's Sweetheart: The Saga of Hal C. Banks,* TV, 85, CDN, Co-Exec Prod; *For All Good Intentions,* TV, 85, CDN, Exec Prod; *All Things Bright and Beautiful,* TV, 85, CDN, Exec Prod; *The Lifer and the Lady,* TV, 85, CDN, Exec Prod; *20th Century Disease,* TV, 83, CDN, Exec Prod; *On Guard for Thee* (3 parts), TV, 81, CDN, Exec Prod; *The Dionne Quintuplets,* TV, 79, CDN, Exec Prod; *Tanker Bomber,* TV, 78, CDN, Exec Prod, (ANIK); *The Champions* (parts I & II), Th, 77, CDN, Co-Exec Prod; *Henry Ford's America,* TV, 76, CDN, Exec Prod, (EMMY).

WRONSKI, Peter
- see DIRECTORS

YATES, Rebecca ✧
(416)531-2612.
Type of Production and Credits: TV Film-Prod/Dir.
Genres: Drama-TV; Children's-TV.
Biography: Born 1950, London, England; Canadian citizenship. Honours B.F.A., York University, 74. Has produced/directed original TV drama in partnership with Glen Salzman since 76. Has won awards from American, Yorkton, Chicago and Tehran Film Festivals.
Selected Filmography: *Milk and Honey*, Th, 87, CDN, Co-Prod/Co-Dir; *Jen's Place*, TV, 82, CDN, Co-Prod; *Introducing...Janet*, TV, 81, CDN, Co-Prod/Co-Dir, (CFTA); *Reaching Out*, TV, 80, CDN, Co-Prod/Co-Dir; *Corletto & Son*, TV, 80, CDN, Co-Prod/Co-Dir; *Nikkolina*, TV, 78, CDN, Co-Prod/Co-Dir; *Another Kind of Music*, TV, 77, CDN, Co-Prod/Co-Dir; *Home Free*, TV, 76, CDN, Co-Prod/Co-Dir.

YOLLES, Edie
- see DIRECTORS

YOSHIHARA, Mark R. G.
605 - 1399 Fountain Way, Vancouver, BC V6H 3T3 (604)731-2862. Plasma Films Inc., 310 - 1510 Nelson St., Vancouver, BC V6G 1M1 (604)682-7319.
Type of Production and Credits: Th Film-Prod; TV Video-Prod.
Genres: Science Fiction-Th; Horror-Th; Music Video-Th&TV.
Biography: Born in 1961 in Vancouver, British Columbia. Chartered accountant designation. Instrumental in most successful private film investment offering in B.C. - Excalibur (VCC) offering 89/90. Also a freelance financial consultant in the film and music industry. Latest music video production was nominated at the 1991 Yorkton Short Film Festival.
Selected Filmography: *Spasmolytic*, MV, 91, CDN, Co-Prod; *Too Dark Park*, Th, 91, CDN, Co-Prod.

YOSHIMURA-GAGNON, Yuri
APFVQ, ACCT. 824, des Colibris, Longueuil, PQ J4G 2C1 Aska Film International Inc., 1600, av. de Lorimier, #211, Montréal, PQ H2K 3W5 (514)521-7103. FAX: 521-6174.
Types de production et générique: l métrage-Prod; c métrage-Prod; TV film-Prod.
Types d'oeuvres: Drame-C; Comédie-C; Documentaire-C; Enfants-C.
Curriculum vitae: Née en 1948, Japon; citoyenneté japonaise; immigrante reçue. Langues: japonais, anglais, français. Produit tous les films de Claude Gagnon; s'occupe activement d'exportation de films à l'étranger dont entre autres la promotion du cinéma canadien au Japon et s'implique dans le dossier de co-production Canada-Japon. Ses films ont gagné de nombreux prix internationaux dont 2 prix au Japon; le Prix de la Presse internationale, 85, et le Grand Prix des Amériques, 87, au Festival de Films du Monde, Montréal; 2 prix au Festival de Berlin, 88.
Filmographie sélective: *The Pianiste*, C, 91, CDN/J, Prod; *Rafales*, C, 90, CDN, Prod; *The Kid Brother*, C, 86, CDN/USA/J, Sup pro; *Visage pâle*, C, 85, CDN/J, Prod; *Larose, Pierrot et la Luce*, C, 81, CDN, Prod; *L'Homme d'ailleurs*, C, 79, J, Co prod; *Keiko*, C, 78, J, Prod; *Yui to hi*, C, 77, J, Co prod; *Geninin*, C, 75, J, Prod; *Essai filmique sur musique japonaise*, C, 74, J, Prod.

YOST, Elwy
ACTRA. 6237 St. George's Cres., West Vancouver, BC V7W 1Z3 (604)921-6752.
Type of Production and Credits: Th Film-Act/Wr; Th Short-Act/Wr; TV Film-Act/Wr; TV Video-Prod/Host/Wr.
Genres: Variety-TV; Educational-Th&TV; Commercials-TV.
Biography: Born 1925, Weston, Ontario. Honours B.A., Sociology, University of Toronto, 48. Active service, Canadian Army, 44-45; worked at the *Toronto Star*, 48-52; stage actor, 45-53; AVRO Aircraft, 53-59; CBC-TV panel shows, 59-68; high school English, History, Geography teacher, 59-64; producer and Executive Director, Metropolitan Educational Television Association of Toronto, 64-70; regional executive, TVOntario, 70-73; executive producer, host, writer of "Saturday Night at the Movies," TVO, and host, "Magic Shadows," 73-present. Nominated for Best Host, ACTRA Awards, 82 and 84, for "Saturday Night at the Movies." Retired from TVOntario, 87.
Selected Filmography: "Saturday Night at the Movies" (377 eps), TV, 74-91, CDN, Wr/Host (Exec Prod/Wr/Host 74-87); "Talking Film" (80 eps), TV, 75-87, CDN, Exec Prod/Host; "Film International" (130 eps), TV, 82-87, CDN, Exec Prod; "The Movie Show" (52 eps), TV, 83-85, CDN, Exec Prod; "Rough Cuts" (130 eps), TV, 78-83, CDN, Exec Prod; *The National Scream*, ED, CDN, Host; "Magic Shadows" (1500 eps), TV, 74-87, CDN, Exec Prod/Host; "Flashback" (4 years), TV, 64-68, CDN, Panel;

"Passport to Adventure" (2 years), TV, 65-67, CDN, Host; "Live a Borrowed Life" (3 years), TV, 59-62, CDN, Panel; "The Superior Sex" (1 year), TV, 61, CDN, Host; *Moulin Rouge*, Th, 52, USA/GB, Act; *In Between*, Th, 47-48, CDN, Wr/Dir/Prod/Act.

YOUNG LECKIE, Mary
DGC, ACCT. Perth Avenue Productions, 194 Sherbourne St., Suite 3, Toronto, ON M5A 2R7 (416)360-7968.
Type of Production and Credits: Th Film-Prod; TV Film-Prod.
Genres: Drama-Th&TV; Children's-TV; Industrial-TV.
Biography: Born 1955, Toronto, Ontario. B.F.A., York University.
Selected Filmography: *Where the Spirit Lives*, TV, 88, CDN, Prod; "The Prodigious Hickey" (2 eps)(Parts I & II), TV, 87, CDN/USA, PM; "Spirit Bay" (13 eps), TV, 84-86, CDN, PM.

ZACK, Lawrence
CFTPA, ACTRA, ACCT. Metaphor Productions Inc., 788 King St. W., Toronto, ON M5V 1N6 (416)336-3887. 925 14th St., Suite 28, Santa Monica, CA 90403 USA. (213)451-9277. FAX: 451-9277.
Type of Production and Credits: Th Film-Prod; TV Film-Prod; TV Video-Prod.
Genres: Drama-Th&TV; Comedy-Th&TV.
Selected Filmography: *Smokescreen*, Th, 91, CDN, Exec Prod/Prod; *Palais Royale*, Th, 89, CDN, Exec Prod/Prod.

ZALOUM, Jean
APFVQ, ADFVQ, ACCT. 4599 ave Montclair, Montreal, PQ H4B 2J8 (514)481-9371. les Productions Optima Inc., 1253 McGill College, #452, Montreal, PQ H3B 2Y5 (514)397-9988. FAX: 954-1237.
Type of Production and Credits: Th Film-Prod/Dist; TV Film-Dist.
Genres: Drama-Th&TV; Comedy-Th&TV; Action-Th&TV; Commercials-Th&TV.
Biography: Born in Egypt. Canadian citizen. Languages: English, French and Arabic. President of les Productions Optima Inc., a film production and distribution company, 1971 to date; President, Publicité Jean Zaloum, a public relations and publicity firm, 1969-71; Publicity Manager, Cine-Art Films, 1965-69; Booker, Paramount pictures, 1966-65. Member of Pionniers du cinéma and cinémathèque Québécoise.
Selected Filmography: *Canvas*, Th, 91, CDN, Prod; *Baxter*, Th, 89, F, Dist; *Thank You Satan!Oh!Oh!Satan*, Th, 88, F, Co Prod; *Ange Gardien/Guardian Angel*, Th, 88, YU, Dist; *Lieu du Crime*, Th, 88, F, Dist; *Jean de Florette*, Th, 87, F, Dist; *Manon des Sources*, Th, 87, F, Dist; *American Way*, Th, 86, GB, Dist; *le Sacrifice*, Th, 86, S, Dist; *La Guêpe*, Th, 86, CDN, Assoc Prod; *Bateau Phare/Lightship*, Th, 85, USA, Dist; *La Femme Publique/Public Woman*, Th, 84, F, Dist; *1984*, Th, 84, GB, Dist; *Les Beaux Dimanches*, Th, 74, CDN, Assoc Prod; *Après Ski/Winter Games*, Th, 71, CDN, Prod.

ZAMARIA, Charles
- see PRODUCTION MANAGERS

ZARITSKY, John
- see DIRECTORS

ZBOROWSKY, William
- see PRODUCTION MANAGERS

ZELDIN, Toby
- see WRITERS

ZIELINSKA, Ida Eva
- see WRITERS

ZIPURSKY, Arnie
CFTA, ACCT. 163 Armour Blvd., Toronto, ON M3H 1M1 (416)630-9860. Cambium Productions, 141 Gerrard St. E., Toronto, ON M5A 2E3 (416)964-8750.
Type of Production and Credits: TV Film-Ed/Prod; TV Video-Ed/Prod.
Genres: Drama-TV; Variety-TV; Musical-TV; Children's-TV.
Biography: Born 1955, Winnipeg, Manitoba. Diploma, Applied Arts and Science, Capilano College, Vancouver, 75; Honours B.F.A., York University, 78; received Maple Leaf Award for Excellence in Film Studies, 78. Video switcher, CBC Winnipeg, 74-77; editor, CTV Vancouver, 78. Awards include: CBI Award for "Eric's World", 90; US Parents' Choice Award, 86/87 and NY Festival Silver Medal, 87, for "Elephant Show"; *Jane Siberry: One More Colour* won Gold Medal, NY; *Jane Siberry: I Muse Aloud* won Gold Hugo Chicago; *Luba, Between the Earth & Sky* won Bronze Award at Houston; *Einstein Tonight* was a finalist at American Film Festival and 88 Gemini Awards; won Bronze, Barcelona International Science Festival.
Selected Filmography: "Eric's World" (13 eps), TV, 90, CDN, Prod; *Eric Nagler Family Special*, TV, 89, CDN, Prod; "Sharon, Lois & Bram's Elephant Show" (65 eps), TV, 84-88, CDN, Prod; *Einstein Tonight*, TV, 88, CDN, Dir/Prod; *Luba: Between the Earth and Sky*, TV, 88, CDN,

Prod; *Jane Siberry: One More Colour*, TV, 87, CDN, Prod; *Jane Siberry: I Muse Aloud*, TV, 87, CDN, Prod; *Sharon, Lois & Bram at Young People's Theatre*, TV, 83, CDN, Dir/Prod/Ed; *For Paul*, TV, 83, CDN, Ed/Comp; *Michael: A Gay Son*, TV, 82, CDN, Ed; *Contact*, TV, 80, CDN, Prod/Dir/Ed.

ZLATARITS, Harvey
- see EDITORS

ZNAIMER, Moses
ACCT. Citytv, 299 Queen St. W., Toronto, ON M5V 1Z9 (416)591-5757.
Type of Production and Credits: TV Film-Prod; TV Video-Prod.
Genres: Musical-TV; News-TV.
Biography: Born in Kulab, Tajikistan; grew up in Montreal. Honours B.A., Philosophy & Politics, McGill University M.A., Government, Harvard University. Co-founder, President, Chief Executive Officer and Executive Producer of Citytv, 72, MuchMusic, 84, and MusiquePlus, 86; worked for CBC Radio and TV, 65-69, as producer/director/host of several shows, including "Cross-Country Checkup," "Twenty Million Questions," "The Way It Is," "Revolution Plus Fifty." Vice-President, Helix Investments and T'ang Management Ltd., 69-71; theatrical producer: *Miss Margarita, Travesties*, and *Tamara*.
Selected Filmography: "MuchMusic", TV, 84-91, CDN, Exec Prod; "MusiquePlus", TV, 86-91, CDN, Exec Prod; "Move Television", TV, 89-91, CDN, Exec Prod.

ZOLF, Janice
975 Wellington St., London, ON N6A 3T3 (519)672-8648. CFPL Television, #1 Communications Rd., London, ON (519)686-8841.
Type of Production and Credits: TV Video-Prod.
Genres: Documentary-TV; Current Affairs-TV; News-TV.
Biography: Born in 1954 in Edmonton, Alberta. English. Honours degree, English Literature.
Selected Filmography: "Encore '89/'90", TV, 89-90, CDN, Prod/Host; "Big Screen", TV, 89, CDN, Prod/Wr/Host.

ZOLF, Larry
WGC (ACTRA), WUC, BUPD. 217 Lippincott St., Toronto, ON M5S 2P4 (416)532-3920. CBC, 790 Bay St., 3rd Flr., Toronto, ON M5G 1N8 (416)975-6641. Robin Mackenzie, 88 Erskine Ave., Suite 2208, Toronto, ON M4P 1Y3 (416)440-1790.
Type of Production and Credits: TV Film-Prod; TV Video-Prod.
Genres: Drama-TV; Comedy-TV; Documentary-TV; Current Affairs-TV.
Biography: Born 1934, Winnipeg, Manitoba. Languages: English, German. One year Law; M.A., History, University of Toronto. Producer/director of numerous documentary items for CBC TV; produced propaganda for US Democratic Party gubernatorial race, Pennsylvania, 66; has done politics column for "Metro Morning," CBC, since 81; author of 3 books: *Dance of the Dialectic, Just Watch Me, Survival of the Fattest: An Irreverent View of the Senate*; Wilderness Award, Best TV Journalism, for *Strike: Men against Computers* which also won a Prize at the International Labour and Industrial Film Festival, Brussels; *A Question of Leadership*, 4 one-hour specials was nominated for a Gemini, 90. Awarded the Isbister, Principal Sparling, Marcus Hyman and A.A. Baird scholarships.
Selected Filmography: *Grits for the Killing*, TV, CDN, Wr/Dir/Prod; *The Moveable Feast*, TV, CDN, Wr/Dir/Prod; *A Question of Leadership* (4 specials), TV, CDN, Wr/Sr Prod; *The GST and You*, TV, CDN, Politics Advisor; "the fifth estate", TV, CDN, Story Cons; *Come to Us*, TV, 75, CDN, Prod/Wr; *Strike: Men Against Computers*, TV, 66, CDN, Dir/Wr.

ZOLLER, Stephen
- see WRITERS

Production Managers
Régisseurs

ALEXANDER, Vince
- see PRODUCERS

ALEXANDRA, Christopher P.
- see COMPOSERS

ALVAREZ, Paco
- see PRODUCERS

ANDERSON, G. Bruce
G.B.A. Productions, 70 Hollis St., Scarborough, ON M1N 2C5 (416)699-3394.
Type of Production and Credits: TV Film-Snd; TV Video-PM.
Genres: Variety-Th&TV; Commercials-TV; Industrial-TV; Music Video-Th&TV.
Biography: Born in 1958.
Selected Filmography: "Power Pack" (pilot), TV, 90, CDN/USA, Snd; "Incontri" (weekly), TV, 90, CDN, PM.

ANDREWS, Neil
- see PRODUCERS

ARBEID, Gerry
ACTT, DGA, DGC. 95 Pears Ave., Toronto, ON M5R 1S9 (416)960-8007.
Type of Production and Credits: Th Film-PM/1st AD; Th Short-PM/1st AD; TV Film-PM/1st AD; TV Video-PM/1st AD.
Genres: Drama-Th&TV; Comedy-Th&TV; Science Fiction-Th&TV; Horror-Th&TV.
Biography: Born 1934, London, England; Canadian citizenship. Entered film industry, 53; has worked in various capacities on over 70 feature films; also 8 years of film editing experience; consultant to completion bond companies, 86-88.
Selected Filmography: *The Vatican*, TV, 90, I, Line Prod; *Dracula*, TV, 89, H/CDN, Line Prod; *Alter Ego*, TV, 85,

USA, Assist Dir; *Mystery Haunted Castle*, Th, 84, USA, Assist Dir; *Bedroom Eyes*, Th, 83, CDN, PM; *Heavenly Bodies*, Th, 83, CDN, PM; *Overdrawn at the Memory Bank*, TV, 83, CDN/USA, PM; *Between Friends*, TV, 83, CDN, PM; *Hank Williams: The Show He Never Gave*, Th, 81, CDN, Post PM; *Melanie*, Th, 80, CDN, PM; *Tribute*, Th, 80, CDN, PM; *Curtains*, Th, 80, CDN, PM; *The Kidnapping of the President*, Th, 79, CDN, PM; *An American Christmas Carol*, TV, 79, USA, PM; *Yesterday*, TV, 79, CDN, Line Prod.

BARKER, Nicholas
STCQ. 1469 ave. Van Horne, #2, Outremont, PQ H2V 1L3 (514)279-5855.
Types de production et générique: TV vidéo-Dir prod/Prod; TV film-Dir prod/Prod;
Types d'oeuvres: Documentaire-TV; Education-TV; Annonces-TV.
Curriculum vitae: Né en 1948, Angleterre; citoyenneté canadienne. Producteur d'agence pour annonces, TV et radio; rédacteur (scénarios) et concepteur; régisseur/directeur de production sur maintes annonces, documentaires et films éducatifs.

BENOIT, Ted
- see PRODUCERS
BERGERON, Guy
- voir PRODUCTEURS
BERMAN, Jeffrey
ACCT. Teleview Productions Limited, 104 Browning Ave., Toronto, ON M4K 1V9 (416)466-8042.
Type of Production and Credits: TV Video-PM.
Genres: Drama-TV; Comedy-TV; Variety-TV; Musical-TV.
Biography: Born in 1957 in Toronto, Ontario. Canadian citizen. Hon. B.A. (political science), University of Western Ontario. M.A. (journalism), University of Western Ontario.
Selected Filmography: "The Kids in the Hall" (20 eps), TV, 90, CDN, Line Prod; "The Kids in the Hall" (22 eps), TV, 89, CDN, Assoc Prod; *Andrea Martin - Together Again*, TV, 89, CDN, Line Prod; "The Super Dave Osborne Show" (24 eps), TV, 88, CDN, PM; "Mosquito Lake" (pilot), TV, 88, CDN, Assoc Prod; "In Opposition" (pilot), TV, 88, CDN, Assoc Prod; *The 1988 NHL Awards*, TV, 88, CDN, Assoc Prod; *The 1987 Gemini Awards*, TV, 87, CDN, Assoc Prod; "It's Only Rock 'N' Roll" (13 eps), TV, 87, CDN, Assoc Prod; *The 1987 Genie Awards*, TV, 87, CDN, Assoc Prod; "Sexton and Malone Comic Book" (3 eps), TV, 87, CDN, Assoc Prod; *The 1986 Juno Awards*, TV, 86, CDN, Prod Coord; *Turkey Television*, TV, 85, CDN, Assoc Coord; "Bizarre" (48 eps), TV, 84-85, CDN, Prod Assoc.

BIENSTOCK, Ric Esther
- see PRODUCERS
BIRD, Christopher
DGC. Seabird Productions Ltd., 2559 Bloor St. W., Suite 1, Toronto, ON M6S 1S2 (416)767-7412.
Type of Production and Credits: TV Film-PM/1st AD; TV Video-PM/1st AD.
Genres: Musical-TV; Documentary-TV; Children's-TV.
Biography: Born 1942, London, England; British and Canadian citizenship. Stage manager, Canadian Equity; musician/artist; production manager/1st assistant director on numerous commercials and industrial films, 79-86.
Selected Filmography: "Two for Joy" (pilot), TV, 90-91, CDN, PM; *Life of the Party*, ED, 90, CDN, Prod; *Lindsay's Story*, ED, 89, CDN, Line Prod/PM; "The Campbells", TV, 89, CDN/GB/USA, 1st AD; *Brown Bread Sandwiches*, Th, 89, CDN, Assoc Prod/PM; *Dreams Beyond Memory*, Th, 87, CDN, PM; "T and T" (5 eps), TV, 87, CDN, PM; *Concrete Angel*, Th, 86, CDN, PM; *The Chimney Sweep*, TV, 85, CDN, PM/1st AD; "Vid Kids" (13 eps), TV, 85, CDN, PM/1st AD; *Morgentaler: In Conversation*, TV, 85, CND, PM/1st AD; *Ronnie Hawkins Special*, TV, 80, CDN, PM/1st AD; *Gino Vanelli in Concert*, TV, 79, CDN, PM/1st AD.

BRAIDWOOD, Tom◆
DGC. (604)463-9650.
Type of Production and Credits: Th Film-PM; Th Short-PM; TV Film-PM; TV Video-PM.
Genres: Drama-Th; Documentary-Th&TV; Educational-Th&TV; Experimental-Th&TV.
Biography: Born 1948, Vancouver, British Columbia. B.A., Theatre, University of British Columbia, 71; M.A., Film Studies, U.B.C., 75. Resident actor/writer/director, Tamahnous Theatre Co., 72-78; author; film lecturer, Simon Fraser University. Executive Director, Pacific Cinematheque, 82-85.
Selected Filmography: *And after Tomorrow...*, Th, 86, CDN, PM; *Emma*, ED, 85, CDN, PM; "Danger Bay" (1 eps), TV, 85, CDN, 1st Assist Dir; *Seed*, Th, 85, CDN, PM; *My American Cousin*, Th,

84, CDN, PM; *Walls*, Th, 84, CDN, Assoc Prod/PM; *Low Visibility*, Th, 84, CDN, Assoc Prod/PM; *Deserters*, Th, 82, CDN, Assoc Prod/PM; *Marathon*, Th, 81, CDN, PM; *Tapestry Artist*, ED, 81, CDN, Prod/Dir; *Right to Fight*, ED, 81, CDN, Dir; *Limited Engagement*, Th, 76, CDN, Dir; *Skin Tracer*, Th, 76, CDN, 1st Assist Dir; *Inside the Reflection*, Th, 74, CDN, Dir; *Wind From the West*, Th, 73, CDN, Prod/Dir.

BUCHSBAUM, Don
834 - 4th St., Santa Monica, CA 90403 USA (213)394-3494.
Type of Production and Credits: Th Film-PM/1st AD; TV Film-PM/1st AD.
Genres: Drama-Th&TV; Comedy-Th; Action-Th&TV.
Biography: Born 1934, New York City; landed immigrant, Canada. In charge of production, Introvision, Los Angeles, 86.
Selected Filmography: *Fatal Judgement*, TV, 88, USA, PM; "Captain Power and the Soldiers of the Future", TV, 87, CDN, PM; *Mafia Princess*, TV, 85, USA, 1st AD; *Blackout*, TV, 84, USA, 1st AD; *Running Brave*, Th, 83, CDN/USA, PM; *Spring Fever*, Th, 81, CDN, PM; *Heartaches*, Th, 80, CDN, PM/1st AD; *Hog Wild*, Th, 79, CDN, PM; *Yesterday*, Th, 79, CDN, PM; *Scanners*, Th, 79, CDN, PM; *Who Has Seen Our Children?*, TV, 78, USA, PM; *Just Jessie*, Th, 78, CDN, Assoc Prod; *Fighting Men*, "For the Record", TV, 77, CDN, 1st AD; "The New Avengers" (4 eps), TV, 77, CDN/GB/F, PM; *Maria*, TV, 75, CDN, Assoc Prod.

BUJOLD, Paul
DGC. 964 - 44 Ave., Laval, PQ H7R 5A3 (514)962-1073.
Type of Production and Credits: Th Film-PM; TV Film-PM.
Genres: Drama-Th&TV; Comedy-Th&TV; Variety-Th&TV; Action-Th&TV.
Selected Filmography: "First Circle/Premier Cercle" (4 eps), TV, 90, CDN/F, PM; *Scanners III*, Th, 90, CDN, PM; *Falling Over Backwards*, Th, 89, CDN, PM; *Princes in Exile*, TV, 89, CDN, PM; *Snakeeater*, Th, 89, CDN, PM.

BURTON, Robert H.
- see PRODUCERS

CAMPEAU, Luc◇
(514)282-0834.
Type of Production and Credits: Th Film-PM; TV Film-PM/1st AD.
Genres: Drama-Th&TV; Action-Th&TV; Commercials-TV.
Biography: Born in 1956 in Montreal, Quebec. Languages: English and French. B.A., Film, Concordia Univ. Extensive experience in feature film budgeting and film shoots in foreign countries.
Selected Filmography: *Chrysler*, Cm, 88, CDN, Assist Dir; *Pontiac*, Cm, 88, CDN, Assist Dir/PM; *O'Keefe*, Cm, 88, CDN, PM/Assist Dir; *Gaspard et Fils*, Th, 87, CDN, PM; *Adramélech*, Th, 86, CDN, PM/Assoc Prod; *The Blue Man*, Th, 85, CDN, PM; *The King's People*, ED, CDN, PM/Assoc Prod; *Direction, l'an 2000*, ED, 84, CDN, PM.

CARR, Warren H.
- see PRODUCERS

CAYWOOD, Bill
DGC. 479 Shannon Way, Delta, BC V4M 2W6 (416)943-2332.
Type of Production and Credits: Th Film-PM; TV Film-Unit M/PM.
Genres: Drama-Th&TV; Documentary-TV; Educational-TV; Children's-TV.
Biography: Born in 1953 in Edmonton, Alberta. Canadian citizen. Graduate of Ryerson Polytechnical Institute, Toronto with a BAA in Film. Producer/Director of the documentary *Drink No Longer Water* which was a Finalist at the American Film Festival, screening at the Museum of Modern Art, NYC and won 2nd Place, Documentary Feature, CBC Telefest.
Selected Filmography: "Wiseguy" (2 eps), TV, 90, USA, Unit M; "21 Jump Street" (20 eps), TV, 90, USA, Unit M; *Discover the Sea*, TV, 89, CDN, Prod; "My Secret Identity" (10 eps), TV, 88, CDN/USA, PM; *Cold Comfort*, Th, 88, CDN, PM; *Higher Education*, Th, 86, CDN, PM; *Hello Mary Lou - Prom Night II*, Th, 86, CDN, Loc M; *Bullies*, Th, 85, CDN, Unit M/Loc M; *Mark of Cain*, Th, 84, CDN, PM; *Drifting On The Wind*, In, 84, CDN, Prod; *Drink No Longer Water*, ED, 83, CDN, Prod/Dir.

CHAPMAN, Dennis◇
DGC. (416)461-8718.
Type of Production and Credits: Th Film-PM; TV Film-PM/1st AD.
Genres: Drama-Th&TV; Commercials-TV; Documentary-Th&TV; Action-Th&TV;
Biography: Born 1948, Sault Ste. Marie, Ontario. B.A., Film and Sociology, Queen's University.
Selected Filmography: *Mad Avenue*, TV, 88, USA, 1st Assist Dir; *St. Nicholas and the Children*, TV, 88, CDN, PM; *Criminal Law*, Th, 87, USA, PM; *Bluffing It*, TV, 87, USA, PM; *Street Justice*, Th, 87, USA, PM; *Calhoun/Night Stick*, Th, 86, USA, PM; "Hot Shots" (7 eps), TV, 86, CDN, 1st Assist Dir; *Oklahoma Smugglers*, Th,

86, USA, 1st Assist Dir; "The Edison Twins" (41 eps), TV, 84-85, CDN, 1st Assist Dir; *Alligator Shoes*, Th, 80, CDN, 1st Assist Dir.

CHERCOVER, Murray
- see PRODUCERS

CLACKSON, Brent-Karl
DGC. 1518 Lighthall Court, North Vancouver, BC V7G 2H5 (604)929-9558.
Type of Production and Credits: TV Film-PM.
Genres: Drama-TV; Comedy-TV; Action-TV; Children's-TV.
Biography: Born 1952, Duncan, BC. Diploma, Film and Televison Production, Humber College. Worked freelance as production assistant, AD, assistant location manager, location manager; worked 2 years as production /location consultant at BC Film; presently Production Manager at Canell Films of Canada.
Selected Filmography: "Palace Guard", TV, 91, USA, PM; *My Son Johnny*, TV, 91, USA, PM; "Saturday's" (pilot), TV, 91, USA, PM; "Crow's Nest" (pilot), TV, 91, USA, PM; "Jumpin' Joe" (pilot), TV, 91, USA, PM; "Broken Badges", TV, 90, USA, PM; "Wiseguy", TV, 87-90, USA, PM; *The Lame Duck*, TV, 88, USA, PM; "J.J. Starbuck", TV, 87, USA, PM.

CLARK, Louise
- see PRODUCERS

COATSWORTH, David
DGC, DGA. 177 Snowdon Avenue, Toronto, ON M4N 2B1 (416)485-2884.
Type of Production and Credits: Th Film-PM; TV Film-PM/Line Pro.
Genres: Drama-Th&TV; Comedy-Th&TV; Musical-TV; Action-Th&TV.
Biography: Born 1951, Toronto, Ontario. B.A., University of Toronto. Twelve years experience as line producer, production manager and assistant director throughout North America.
Selected Filmography: *The Mrs.*, Th, 91, USA, PM; *If Looks Could Kill*, Th, 90, USA, Line Pro/PM; *Lady on a Corner*, Th/TV, 89, USA, PM; *Stella*, Th, 89, USA, Assoc Prod/PM; *The Good Mother*, Th, 88, USA, PM; *Cocktail*, Th, 87, USA, PM; *Adventures in Babysitting*, Th, 87, USA, PM; *Hostage*, Th, 87, USA, PM; *Hot Paint*, Th, 87, USA, PM; *The Believers*, Th, 86, USA, PM; *The Fly*, Th, 86, USA, PM; *One Magic Christmas*, Th, 85, CDN/USA, PM; *Act of Vengeance*, Th, 85, USA, PM; *King of Friday Night*, Th, 84, CDN, PM/Assoc Prod; *Star-Crossed*, Th, 84, USA, PM.

COLEMAN, Rob
ACCT, ASIFA. 163 Marlborough Place, Toronto, ON M5R 3J5 (416)960-1567.
Type of Production and Credits: TV Film-PM; TV Video-PM.
Genres: Science Fiction-TV; Children's-Th&TV; Animation-Th&TV.
Biography: Born 1964, Toronto, Ontario. B.F.A. (Animation), Concordia University, 1987. Member of the computer animation team awarded the Gemini, Best Technical Achievement, 1988 for the combination of animation and live action in "Captain Power".
Selected Filmography: *Johann's Gift to Christmas*, TV, 91, CDN, Line Prod/SFX Des; *Karate Kids*, ED/TV, 89, CDN, PM; "Captain Power and the Soldiers of the Future" (22 eps), TV, 87, CDN, An PM/SFX Spv.

COLVIN, Suzanne
DGC. Suzanne Colvin Productions Inc., 77 Hanson St., Toronto, ON M4C 5P3 (416)694-2247.
Type of Production and Credits: Th Film-PM; TV Film-PM.
Genres: Drama-Th&TV; Action-Th; Horror-Th; Children's-Th.
Biography: Born in Toronto in 1962. Canadian and British citizen. University degree in mass communication and sociology.
Selected Filmography: *On My Own*, Th, 90-91, CDN/I/AUS, PM; *Journey Into Darkness: The Bruce Curtis Story*, TV, 90, CDN, PM; *Defy Gravity*, Th, 89, CDN, PM; *Cold Comfort*, Th, 88-89, CDN, PM/Pro Spv; *George's Island*, Th, 88, CDN, PM; *An Act of God*, Th, 88, CDN, PM; *A Switch in Time/Norman's Excellent Adventure/Normanicus*, Th, 87, CDN/RA, P Pro Spv; *Higher Education*, Th, 86/87, CDN, P Pro Spv/Assist PM; *Hello Mary Lou - Prom Night II*, Th, 86/87, CDN, P Pro Spv; *Blindside*, Th, 86/87, CDN, P Pro Spv.

COPELAND, Greg
- see PRODUCERS

CUDDY, Janet
DGC. 44 Grace St., Toronto, ON M6J 2S2 (416)530-0409.
Type of Production and Credits: Th Film-PM; TV Film-PM.
Genres: Drama-Th&TV.
Biography: Born in 1958 in Ottawa, Ontario. Languages: French, English and Italian. Attended Queen's University and Concordia University. Currently works as Risk Manager with Motion Picture Bond Co., a film guarantor.
Selected Filmography: *F/X 2*, Th, 90, US, PM; "African Journey" (6 eps), TV, 89, CDN/NZ, PM; *Beautiful Dreamers*, Th,

89, CDN, PM; "My Secret Identity", TV, 88-89, CDN/US, PM.

D'AGOSTINO, Len
DGC. 433 Sackville St., Toronto, ON (416)925-0188.
Type of Production and Credits: TV Film-PM; TV Video-PM.
Genres: Drama-TV; Variety-TV; Action-TV; Documentary-TV.
Biography: Born 1929, Edinburgh, Scotland; Canadian citizenship. Radio and Television Arts, Ryerson Polytechnical Institute. Worked on numerous variety specials, current affairs and religious documentaries, 61-72.
Selected Filmography: *On Thin Ice*, TV, 90, USA, PM; "Road to Avonlea" (13 eps), TV, 89-90, CDN, Line Prod; "Alfred Hitchcock Presents" (27 eps), TV, 88, USA, PM; "Ray Bradbury Theatre" (4 eps), TV, 87, CDN, PM; *Drop-Out Mother*, TV, 87, USA, PM; *The Prodigious Hickey II*, TV, 86, CDN/USA, PM; *Heaven on Earth*, TV, 86, CDN/GB, PM; *Onegin*, TV, 85, CDN, PM; *Papal Visit*, TV, 84, CDN, PM; "A Planet for the Taking" (10 eps), TV, 83, CDN, PM; *The Songs of Leonard Cohen*, TV, 81, CDN, PM; *The Golden Mountain*, TV, 81, CDN, PM; *Songs of a Sourdough*, TV, 80, CDN/GB, Assoc Prod; "Dieppe 1942" (2 eps), TV, 79, CDN, PM; *Fields of Endless Day*, TV, 77, CDN, PM.

DALEN, Laara
- see PRODUCERS

DANYLKIW, John
- see PRODUCERS

DARLING, Gillian
- see PRODUCERS

DAVIS, Richard
- see PRODUCERS

DAY, Deborah
- see PRODUCERS

DE GRANDPRE, Sylvie
564, Birch, St-Lambert, PQ J4P 2N1 (514)672-6837. 86, De Brésoles, Montréal, PQ H2Y 1V5 (514)285-8901. FAX: 285-8936.
Types de production et générique: l métrage-Dir prod; TV film-Dir prod; TV vidéo-Dir prod.
Types d'oeuvres: Drame-C&TV; Comédie-TV.
Curriculum vitae: Née en 1950. Langues: français et anglais. A travaillé comme assistante et directrice de production pour diverses compagnies: cinéma, télévision et annonces publicitaires.
Filmographie sélective: *Les Tisserands du pouvoir* (I et II), C, 87, CDN/F, Dir pro; *Un Ordinateur au coeur*, "Page trois" (pilote), TV, 85, CDN, Dir pro; *Bonheur d'occasion/The Tin Flute* (aussi 5 ém-tv/tournées simultanément fr. et angl.) C, 82, CDN, Dir pro; *Black Mirror*, C, 80, CDN/F, Dir pro; *Une journée particulière/Una gironata particolara/A Special Day* C, 77, CDN/I, Dir pro; *La Notte Dell'Alta Marea/The Twilight of Love*, C, 76, CDN/I, Ass pro; *Je suis loin de toi mignonne*, C, 75, CDN, Ass pro.

DIEHL, Barrie
- see PRODUCERS

DUFRESNE, Hélène
- voir PRODUCTEURS

DURBAN, Jan
DGC. 2965 Allan Rd., North Vancouver, BC V7J 3P4 (604)987-1652.
Type of Production and Credits: TV Film-PM; TV Video-PM.
Genres: Drama-TV; Comedy-TV; Documentary-TV; Children's-TV.
Biography: Born, 1949, Hamilton, Ontario. Has worked in B.C. since 1974, primarily at the CBC but now freelance. Specializing in location filming in small-town, B.C.
Selected Filmography: "The Beachcombers" (86 eps), TV, 86-90, CDN, PM; "Lies From Lotus Land" (6 eps), TV, 86-87, CDN, PM.

EL-SISSI, Azza
- see PRODUCERS

FERSTMAN, Brian
DGC. Indigo Films Inc., 464 Oakwood Ave., Toronto, ON M6E 2W6 (416)652-6770. FAX: 651-7191.
Type of Production and Credits: TV Film-Prod/PM; TV Film-Prod/PM.
Genres: Drama-Th&TV; Comedy-Th&TV; Action-Th&TV.
Biography: Born in 1951 in Montreal, Quebec. Languages: English and French. D.E.C., (English and Psychology), Concordia University, 72; B.A., Political Science, 77; LL.B., University of British Columbia, 81; practised law, Vancouver, 82-83; Film Production Diploma Program, University of British Columbia, 83-84. Production Manager/Assistant Director on over 50 commercials, music videos & corporate films, 85-88. Founded Indigo Films Inc., 87; currently independent producer and freelance Production Manager.
Selected Filmography: *Baby Pinsky*, TV, 90, CDN, Spv Prod; *Love 40*, Th, 89, CDN, Assoc Prod; *A Different Dance*, TV, 88, CDN, Line Prod/PM; *Paper Route*, TV, 88, CDN, PM; *Brothers by Choice*, TV, 85, CDN, Loc M; "Danger Bay", TV, 85, CDN, Spec Coord; *Journey of Natty*

Gann, Th, 85, USA, Assist Loc M.
FLEMING, Susan K.
- see DIRECTORS
FORD-BAKER, Heather
124 Burrows Hall Blvd., Scarborough, ON M1B 1M6 (416)293-0443.
Type of Production and Credits: TV Video-PM.
Genres: Drama-TV; Action-TV; Educational-TV; Children's-TV.
Biography: Born in 1964 in Ottawa, Ontario. Bachelor of Applied Arts in Radio and Television Arts.
Selected Filmography: *1990 Gemini Awards*, TV, 90, CDN, PM; "The Judge" (175 eps), TV, 89-90, CDN/USA, PM; "Kingdom Adventure" (23 eps), TV, 89-90, CDN, PM; *Final Approach*, TV, 89, CDN, Prod Coord; *Parlons de la Sexualité*, TV, 88, CDN, Prod Coord.
GERRETSEN, Patricia
- see PRODUCERS
GILL, Shirley J.
DGC. 805 - 3740 Albert St., Burnaby, BC V5C 5Y7 (604)293-0333.
Type of Production and Credits: Th Film-PM; TV Film-PM; TV Video-PM.
Genres: Drama-Th&TV.
Biography: Born in 1938 in Brantford, Ontario. Canadian citizen, also holds British passport. Secondary school diploma (grade 12).
Selected Filmography: *Bitter Creek/ Nightmare at Bitter Creek*, TV, 87, USA, PM; *Gunsmoke/Gunsmoke: Return to Dodge City*, TV, 87, USA, PM; "Wiseguy" (pilot), TV, 87, USA, PM; *Paper Marriage*, Th, 86, HK/CDN, PM; "The Hitchhiker Trilogy" (pilot), TV, 83, CDN/USA, PM; *The Life and Times of Edwin Alonzo Boyd*, TV, 82, CDN, Assoc Prod/PM.
GILROY, Grace◊
DGC. (403)426-6441
Type of Production and Credits: Th Film-PM; TV Film-PM.
Genres: Drama-Th&TV; Action-Th&TV; Horror-Th.
Biography: Born in Edmonton, Alberta. Partner in Kicking Horse Prod. Ltd., 77.
Selected Filmography: *I'll Take Manhattan* (mini-series), TV, 86, USA, Pro Spv: *The Case of the Notorious Nun*, TV, 86, USA, PM; *Kane & Abel* (mini-series), TV, 84-85, USA, PM; *A Nice, Pleasant, Deadly Weekend*, TV, 85, USA, PM; *A Letter to Three Wives*, TV, 85, USA, PM; *Loyalties*, Th, 85, CDN/GB, PM; *Evergreen* (mini-series), TV, 84, USA, PM; *Killer Party*, Th, 84, USA, PM.
GORD, Ken
- see PRODUCERS

GRAY, Nicholas J.
DGC. 147 Gough Ave., Toronto, ON M4K 3N9 (416)465-9155. FAX: 465-7826.
Type of Production and Credits: Th Film-PM/Prod; TV Film-PM/Prod.
Genres: Children's-Th&TV; Drama-Th; Action-TV.
Biography: Born 1955, Toronto, Ontario. B.A., Film, Queen's University.
Selected Filmography: *Rolling Stones*, Th (Imax), 91, Assoc Prod; *Hitler's Daughter*, TV, 90, USA, Assoc Prod/PM; *Kissing Place*, TV, 89, USA, Assoc Prod/PM; *Termini Station*, Th, 88, Assoc Prod/PM; *Almost Grown*, TV, 88, Line Prod/PM; *Niagara: Miracles, Myths & Magic*, Th, 86, Prod; *The Dream Team*, Th, 88, PM; "Philip Marlowe Private Eye" (6 eps), TV, 86, CDN, PM; *Anne of Green Gables* (mini-series), TV, 85, CDN, PM; *Tucker and the Horse Thief/Workin' for Peanuts/My Father, My Rival*, "Family Playhouse"", TV, 84, CDN, Co-Prod/PM; *Humongous*, Th, 81, CDN, PM; *Alligator Shoes*, Th, 80, CDN, Line Prod/PM.
GREAN, Wendy
- see PRODUCERS
GREENLAW, Terry
- see PRODUCERS
HACKETT, Jonathan
- see PRODUCERS
HAIGHT, Adam
DGC. 1382 Avenue Rd., Toronto, ON M5N 2H4 (416)482-8179. Cinegramme IV Inc., 920 Yonge St., Suite 400, Toronto, ON M4W 3C7
Type of Production and Credits: TV Film-PM; TV Video-PM.
Genres: Drama-TV; Variety-TV; Action-TV; Commercials-TV.
Biography: Born 1959, Toronto, Ontario. B.A., University of Waterloo, 81. Staff Production Manager, CFTO-TV, 81-86. Freelance Production Manager, 86-90.
Selected Filmography: "Counterstrike" (22 eps), TV, 90, CDN/F, Prod; "T and T" (21 eps), TV, 89, CDN, PM; "Diamonds" (10 eps), TV, 88-89, CDN/F, PM; "Night Heat" (57 eps), TV, 86-88, CDN/USA, PM; various commercials (over 100, incl. G.W.), TV, 85-86, CDN, Prod; "Littlest Hobo" (56 eps), TV, 82-84, CDN, PM.
HAMILTON, Elizabeth
217 Erskine Ave., Toronto, ON M4P 1Z5 (416)483-3241.
Type of Production and Credits: Th Film-PM; TV Film-PM; Video-PM.
Genres: Variety-TV; Musical-TV; Documentary-TV; Industrial-TV.

Biography: Born 1956, Toronto, Ontario.
Languages: English, French. B.A., Queen's University.
Selected Filmography: *Here We Go*, TV, 88, CDN, PM; *A Moving Picture*, TV, 87, CDN, Prod coord; *Whalesong*, TV, 86, CDN, Prod coord; *Lumière*, Th, 86, CDN, PM; *Eternal Earth*, TV, 86, CDN, PM; "Gzowski & Co.", TV, 86, CDN, PM; *Musical Connection*, TV, 86, CDN, PM; *TSO Promo*, In, 86, CDN, PM.

HARRISON, Jane
24 Breda Court, Richmond Hill, ON L4C 6E1 (416)886-1659. Global Television Network, 81 Barber Greene Rd., Don Mills, ON M3C 2A2 (416)446-5311.
Type of Production and Credits: TV Video-PM/Assoc Prod.
Genres: Documentary-TV; Industrial-TV; Current Affairs-TV; Game Shows-TV.
Biography: Born, 1960, North Shields, Great Britain.
Selected Filmography: "Jackpot" (390 eps), TV, 87-90, CDN/USA, Assoc Prod; "Bumper Stumpers" (385 eps), TV, 86-89, CDN/USA, Assoc Prod; "Hanes Report" (4 eps), TV, 89, CDN, Unit Mgr; "Pizzazz" (130 eps), TV, 86, CDN, Unit Mgr; "That's Life" (520 eps), TV, 82-86, CDN, PM.

HAUKA, David
- see DIRECTORS

HENDERS, Karen P.
416 - 18th Ave., Regina, SK S4N 1G1 (306)359-7236.
Type of Production and Credits: TV Film-PM; TV Video-PM.
Genres: Drama-TV; Documentary-Th&TV; Commercials-TV;Educational-Th&TV;
Biography: Born and raised in the province of Saskatchewan. B.A. in history from the University of Saskatchewan. B.F.A. in film and video from the University of Regina. Academy of Canadian Cinema and Television apprentice/trainee in 1989. Range of experience from nature documentaries to television dramas.
Selected Filmography: "It Starts At Home" (7 eps), ED/TV, 91, CDN, 1st Assist Dir; "Get Smart" (4 spots), Cm, 91, CDN, 1st Assist Dir; *A Dance to Remember*, TV, 91, CDN, 2nd Assist Dir; *Home on the Range*, TV, 91, CDN, 2nd Assist Dir; *The Garden*, TV, 91, CDN, 2nd Assist Dir; *There's More to a Marsh*, ED/TV, 91, CDN, PM, Res; *Reflections on a Prairie Slough*, ED/TV, 91, CDN, 1st Assist Dir/PM; *Arts Education - Dance*, ED/TV, 91, CDN, 1st Assist Dir/PM; *Forestry*, ED/TV, 91, CDN, 1st Assist Dir/PM; *Heart of Christmas*, TV, 90, CDN, 2nd Assist Dir; *Sylvan Lake Summer*, TV, 90, CDN, 3rd Assist Dir; *The Challengers*, TV, 89, CDN, 3rd Assist Dir/Dir Trainee; *Final Notice*, TV, 89, CDN/USA, Training Assist Dir; *The Great Electrical Revolution*, TV, 89, CDN, 2nd Assist Dir.

HENSHAW, Helen
- see PRODUCERS

HÉROUX, Roger
- voir PRODUCTEURS

HOOD, David
DGC. 1252 King St. W., #10, Toronto, ON M6K 1G5 (416)538-9310.
Type of Production and Credits: Th Film-PM; TV Film-PM;.
Genres: Drama-Th&TV; Comedy-Th&TV; Action-Th&TV.
Biography: Born in Paris, France. Fluent in French. Experienced in Canada-France co-productions
Selected Filmography: "The Hitchhiker" (41 eps), TV, 89-90, CDN/F, PM.

HOWARD, Dan
- see PRODUCERS

HUTTON, Howard
DGC. #1 Lawrence Ave. W., Toronto ON M5M 1A3 (416)322-7090. Rudy Inc., 40 Glengarry Ave., Toronto, ON M5M 1C9 (416)489-7115.
Type of Production and Credits: Th Short-PM; TV Film-PM.
Genres: ; Children's-TV; Commercials-TV; Documentary-Th&TV; Industrial-Th&TV.
Biography: Born in 1951 in Montreal, Quebec. Interests: large-format theatrical production, 65mm, 3-D, multi-screen, Imax; interactive, laser disc production; children's television; documentary. *Let's Get a Move On* won a Red Ribbon, American Film Festival and a Chris award, Columbus Film Festival.
Selected Filmography: *Shooting Star*, Th, 91, CDN, PM; "The Spacewatch Club" (4 eps), TV, 91, USA/CDN, PM; *Alan Bran/Art Off This Earth*, TV, 90, CDN, PM; *Gulf of Oil* (3 spots), Cm, 88, USA, PM; *Emergency Response*, In, 88, CDN, PM; *Space Pioneers of Canada*, TV, 88, CDN, PM; *Building on Strength*, In, 87, CDN, PM; *Walter's Mystery* (pilot), "The Spacewatch Club", TV, 87, USA/CDN, PM; *Bartlett's*, ED, CDN, PM; "The Elephant Show" (13 eps), TV, 85, CDN, Unit Mgr/Loc Mgr; *Tourism Canada*, Cm, 85, CDN, Loc Mgr; *Inward Passage*, Th, 83, CDN, PM; *Stop..Look..Listen*, ED, 77, CDN, Prod; *Let's Get a Move On*, ED,

76, CDN, Prod; *A Matter of Choice*, ED, 76, CDN, PM.

IVESON, Gwen
DGC. 64 Langley Ave., Toronto, ON M4K 1B5 (416)466-9436. Primedia Productions Ltd., 219 Front St. E., Toronto, ON M5A 2E8 (416)361-0306.
Type of Production and Credits: Th Film-PM/Prod; TV Film-PM/Prod.
Genres: Drama-Th&TV; Science Fiction-Th; Documentary-Th&TV; Current Affairs-TV.
Biography: Born in 1937 in Victoria, British Columbia. Manager, Business Affairs-Toronto, Telefilm Canada, 83-86; Vice-President, Production and Business Affairs, Primedia Productions Ltd., since 86.
Selected Filmography: *Dinosaur!* (4 eps), TV, 90-91, CDN/GB, Pro Exec; *Stage on Screen* (8 eps), TV, 90-91, CDN, Pro Spv; *Young Catherine* (mini-series), TV, 90, CDN/GB, Pro Exec; *Born Talking* (4 eps), TV, 90, CDN, Pro Spv; *Passion & Paradise* (mini-series), TV, 89, CDN/GB, Pro Spv; *Bloodsport*, "Dick Francis Mysteries" (3 eps), TV, 89, CDN/IRL, Pro Spv; *The Big Top*, TV, 88, CDN, Pro Spv; *Merry Widow*, TV, 87, CDN, Pro Spv; *Glory Enough for All* (mini-series), TV, 87, CDN/GB, Pro Spv; *A Matter of Sex*, TV, 83, CDN/USA, Co-Prod/PM; *Will There Really Be a Morning?*, TV, 82, USA, PM; *Videodrome*, Th, 81, CDN/USA, PM; *Silence of the North*, Th, 79, CDN, PM; *Who Has Seen the Wind*, Th, 76, CDN, Assoc Prod; *A Married Couple*, Th, 68, CDN, Assoc Prod.

IVESON, Rob
- see PRODUCERS

JEPHCOTT, Samuel C.
- see PRODUCERS

JONES, Dennis
- see PRODUCERS

KAHN, Mary
- see PRODUCERS

KELLY, Barbara
DGC. 63 West Ave., Toronto, ON M4M 2L7 (416)466-5775. Screen Mgmt. Services Inc., 32 Barton Ave., Toronto, ON M6G 1P1 (416)535-4104.
Type of Production and Credits: Th Film-PM; TV Film-PM.
Genres: Comedy-Th&TV; Drama-Th&TV.
Selected Filmography: "Max Glick" (26 eps), TV, 90-91, CDN, Spv Prod; *This Is My Life*, Th, 91, USA, PM; *Perfectly Normal*, Th, 90, CDN, Assoc Prod; *High Flying Mermaid*, Th, 89, DK, Assoc Prod; "Knightwatch" (9 eps), TV, 88, USA, Co-Prod; *Sea of Love*, Th, 88, USA, PM; *Hoover vs the Kennedys: The Second Civil War* (mini-series), TV, 87, USA/CDN, Assoc Prod; *A New Life*, Th, 87, USA, Assoc Prod; *Amerika* (mini-series), TV, 86, USA, PM; *Deadly Business*, TV, 85, USA, PM; *Mafia Princess*, TV, 85, USA, OPM; *Perry Mason Returns*, TV, 85, USA, PM; *Eleni*, Th, 85, USA/GB, PM (in Canada); *Davies and Hearst*, TV, 84, USA, PM; *Heartsounds*, TV, 84, USA, U Loc M; "SCTV" (16 eps), TV, 83-84, CDN, Loc M.

KIMBER, Les
ACTRA, DGC, IATSE. R.R. #4, Calgary, AB T2M 4L4 (403)239-1060.
Type of Production and Credits: Th Film-PM; TV Film-PM; TV Video-PM.
Genres: Drama-Th&TV; Comedy-Th; Action-Th; Horror-Th&TV.
Biography: Born 1942, Calgary, Alberta.
Selected Filmography: *Killer Image*, Th, 90, USA, Line Prod/PM; *The Reflecting Skin*, Th, 89, CDN/GB/USA, Line Prod/PM; *Who's Harry Crumb?*, Th, 88, USA, PM; "Airwolf" (20 eps), TV, 86-87, USA, Line Prod; "The Hitchhiker" (13 eps), TV, 85, USA, PM; *The Journey of Natty Gann*, Th, 84, USA, Assoc Prod; *Finders, Keepers*, Th, 84, USA, PM; *Superman III* (in Canada), Th, 83, USA/GB, PM; *Motherlode*, Th, 80, USA, PM/Assoc Prod; *Death Hunt*, Th, 80, USA, PM; *Ski Lift to Death*, TV, 79, USA, PM; *Touched by Love*, TV, 78, USA, PM; *Amber Waves*, TV, 78, USA, PM; *Superman*, Th, 78, USA/GB, Unit PM; *Orca*, Th, 75, USA, Unit PM.

KING, Jeff
- see PRODUCERS

KLINCK, Elizabeth
- see PRODUCERS

KORNYLO, Lacia
DGC. 317 Warren Rd., Toronto, ON M5P 2M7 (416)484-6754.
Type of Production and Credits: Th Film-PM.
Genres: Drama-Th&TV; Comedy-Th&TV.
Selected Filmography: "Sweating Bullets" (22 eps), TV, 91, CDN/USA/MEX, Assoc Prod; *Storm & Sorrow*, MV, 90, USA, Prod Spv; *The Freshman*, Th, 89, USA, PM; *Stanley & Iris*, Th, 88, USA, Prod Compt; *The January Man*, Th, 88, USA, Prod Compt; *Short Circuit II*, Th, 87, USA, PM.

LABERGE, Pierre
- voir PRODUCTEURS

LAFONTAINE, Lyse
DGC. 665, Stuart, Outremont, PQ H2V

2H2 (514)273-6018.
Types de production et générique: l métrage-Dir prod.
Types d'oeuvres: Drame-C; Comédie-C; Action-C; Annonces-C&TV.
Curriculum vitae: Née en 1942, Montréal, Québec. Langues: français, anglais and espagnol. Maîtrise en traduction, Université de Montréal.
Filmographie sélective: "D'amour & d'amitié" (30 eps), TV, 90-91, CDN, Prod; *Les heures précieuse,* TV, 89, CDN, Prod dél; *Jésus de Montréal,* C, 88, CDN, Dir pro; *Les Portes tournantes,* C, 87, CDN/F, Prod dél; *Wild Thing,* C, 86, CDN/USA, Dir pro; *Le Lys Cassé,* TV, 86, CDN, Dir pro; *Le Déclin de l'Empire américain,* C, 85, CDN, Dir pro; *The Peanut Butter Solution,* C, 85, CDN, Dir pro; *Race to the Pole,* C, 84, USA, Dir pro; *Breaking All the Rules,* C, 84, CDN, Dir pro; *Your Ticket Is No Longer Valid,* C, 79, CDN, Dir pro.

LALONDE, Richard
6250 Deacon, Montréal, PQ H3S 2P5 (514)733-5053.
Types de production et générique: l métrage-Dir pro; TV film-Dir pro.
Filmographie sélective: *L'Enfant Sur Le Lac,* C, 91, CDN, Dir pro; *Ding et Dong, Le Film,* C, 90, CDN, Dir pro; *Moody Beault,* C, 89, CDN, Dir pro; *Un Autre Homme,* C, 89, CDN, Dir pro.

LANSING, Floyd
- see DIRECTORS

LAURENDEAU, Jean Pierre✧
6877, de la Roche, Montréal, PQ H2S 2E5 (514)274-5175.
Types de production et générique: c métrage-Dir prod/Rég/Réal/Cam; TV vidéo-Dir prod/Rég/Prod/Réal.
Types d'oeuvres: Drame-C&TV; Documentaire-C&TV; Annonces-TV; Industriel-TV.
Curriculum vitae: Né en 1954; citoyenneté canadienne. Langues: français et anglais. Baccalauréat, Histoire de l'art, Université de Montréal, 78; DEC, Sciences humaines, Collège Bois-de-Boulogne, 74. Expérience dans tous les domaines de production; producteur, directeur de production, Les Productions Prisma, 87-88; réalisateur, chroniqueur, Télé-Métropole inc., 87-88; réalisateur, coordonnateur, agent administratif, JPL Productions inc., 85-87; coord., Alliance du Cinéma Indépendant, 84-85; analyste de scénario/ consultant pigiste, Téléfilm Canada et Conseil des Arts du Canada, 84-87.
Filmographie sélective: "Garderie des amis" (26 eps), TV, 88, CDN, Prod dél; *La Rivière,* TV, 87, CDN, Dir pro; "La Quotidienne", TV, 86, CDN, Réal; Céline Dion, MV, 86, CDN, Dir pro; "Tirages Loto-Québec", TV, 85-86, CDN, Dir pro; *Pour l'amour du monde,* TV, 85, CDN, Dir pro; "Cousin Cuisine des Amériques" (13 eps), TV, 85, CDN, Dir pro; *Le Cahier noir,* TV, 82, CDN, Assist rég; *Réveillon,* C, 82, CDN, Ass pro; *Lucien Brouillard,* C, 82, CDN, Ass prod; *The Summit,* C, 81, CDN, Co prod; *The Referendum,* C, 80, CDN, Co prod; *Cross Country,* C, 82, CDN, Ass pro.

LEVINE, Allan
DGC, ACTRA, EQUITY. 922 Bathurst St., #18, Toronto, ON M5R 3G5 (416)534-5210.
Type of Production and Credits: Th Film-PM; TV Film-PM; TV Video-Dir.
Genres: Drama-Th&TV; Comedy-Th&TV; Action-Th&TV; Science Fiction-TV; Horror-Th&TV; Commercials-Th&TV; Industrial-Th&TV; Music Video-Th&TV.
Biography: Born in 1956 in Hamilton, Ontario. Speaks English and partial French, Hebrew, Malay/Indonesian. B.A. from the University of Guelph; B.Ed., University of Toronto. Winner of the CanPro award, 1983 for Best Drama. All budgets and cash-flows done on MacIntosh disk. Experience in production overseas, crewing a specialty.
Selected Filmography: *Hurt Penguins,* Th, 91, CDN, Line Prod; *Murder Blues/New Souls,* Th, 90, I, PM; *My Happy Days In Hell,* TV, 90, CDN, PM; *Home for Christmas,* TV, 90, CDN, PM; *Johnny Shortwave,* Th, 89, CDN, Prod Spv; *Whispers,* TV, 89, CDN, Assoc Prod; *Graveyard Shift III/Love and Die/To Die For,* Th, 88, CDN, PM; *Harbord Tigers in Europe,* TV, 88, CDN, PM; *Black Roses,* Th, 87, CDN, 1st Assist Dir; *Skull, Night of Terror/Night of Retribution/Assault,* Th, 87, CDN, Assoc Prod; *Splatter, The Architects of Fear,* TV, 86, CDN, 1st Assist Dir; *Graveyard Shift,* Th, 85, CDN, 1st Assist Dir; *Fear Stalker/Panic in the City,* Th, 86, CDN, 1st Assist Dir; *Sword of the Prophet,* TV, 83, CDN, Dir; *The Dude Ranch,* "Brooker & Son" (2 eps), TV, 82, CDN, PM.

LINDSAY, Gillian
-see PRODUCERS

LITINSKY, Irene
DGC. 119 Wallenberg, Dollard des Ormeaux, PQ H9A 3G2 (514)696-5477. (514)944-4765.
Type of Production and Credits: Th

Film-PM.
Genres: Drama-Th; Comedy-Th; Action-Th; Horror-Th.
Biography: Born in 1952 in Montreal, Quebec. Canadian citizen. Fluent in French and English. In-House, Cinepix, 1973-82.
Selected Filmography: *Map of the Human Heart*, Th, 91, CDN/GB/F/AUS, PM; *Scanners III*, Th, 90, CDN, Line Prod; *Money*, Th, 90, I/F/CDN, PM; *Whispers*, Th, 89, CDN, Line Prod; *Princes in Exile*, TV, 89, CDN, Line Prod; *Jackknife*, Th, 88, USA, PM.

LOSIER, Aurel◊
(514)737-4204.
Types de production et générique: TV vidéo-Dir pro/Réal; Vidéo-Dir pro.
Types d'oeuvres: Industriel-TV.
Curriculum vitae: Né en 1944, Acadie. Baccalauréat en Communications, Université du Québec à Montréal, 74; cours chez Parlimage. Assistant réalisateur, 74-84; réalisateur, Radio-Québec, 85-86; Directeur de production, Lambert Multimédia, 86-88; Directeur de production, relations publiques, marketing, Vidéo-trame inc., juillet 88; assistant réalisateur, Radio-Québec, août, 88.
Filmographie sélective: *Le Québec, un mode en action*, In, 87-88, CDN, Dir pro; Groupe la Laurentienne, In, 87-88, CDN, Dir pro; Les Caisses Populaires Desjardins, In, 87-88, CDN, Dir pro; La Banque canadienne nationale, In, 87-88, CDN, Dir pro; Pétro-Canada, In, 87-88, CDN, Dir pro; Bell Canada, In, 87-88, CDN, Dir pro; "Prise de vue" (13 eps), TV, 87-88, CDN, Dir pro; Northern Telecom, ED, 87-88, CDN, Dir pro; Institut Teccart, In, 87-88, CDN, Dir pro; Ultramar, In, 87-88, CDN, Dir pro; *Conférence mondiale sur l'énergie* Vidéo-trame inc., In, 88, CDN, Dir pro; CNC Construction, In, 86-87, CDN, Dir pro; Le Groupe Jean-Coutu, In, 86-87, CDN, Dir pro; Collège Regina Assumpta, In, 86-87, CDN, Dir pro; Ralston Purina, In 86-87, CDN, Dir Pro.

MacDONALD, Michael
DGC. 10A Pretoria Avenue, Toronto, ON M4K 1T1 (416)461-8508. FAX: 461-1226.
Type of Production and Credits: Th Film-PM/Loc M/Unit M; TV Film-PM/Loc M/Unit M.
Genres: Drama-Th&TV; Science Fiction-Th&TV; Comedy-Th&TV; Action-Th&TV.
Biography: Born 1949, Toronto, Ontario. Canadian citizenship; landed alien resident, USA. In addition to work in features, 6 years experience as freelance and staff animation cameraman: 5 features - 3 Cannes Film Festival Awards. Over 200 1/2 hour episodes of various series. 500 commercials for companies such as Al Guest Animation, Film Effects, E.T.V., Video Art, Trickett Prods, Rainbow Films, Carlos Marchiori Prods, Sesame Street and the CBC. Produced numerous sports instructional films for the Youth and Recreation Br. of the Ont. Dept. of Ed.
Selected Filmography: (untitled), Th, 90-91, USA, Prod/PM; *Diplomatic Immunity*, Th, 90, CDN, Co-Prod/PM; *The Freshman*, Th, 89, USA, Line Prod; *Stanley & Iris*, Th, 88, USA, PM; *January Man*, Th, 88, USA, Pro Exec/PM; *Short Circuit II*, Th, 87, USA, PM; *Suspect*, Th, 87, USA, PM; "Alfred Hitchcock Presents" (5 eps), TV, 86, USA, PM; *Perry Mason: The Case of the Shooting Star*, TV, 86, USA, PM; *Dead of Winter*, Th, 86, USA, Assoc Prod/2nd U Dir/PM; *One Magic Christmas*, Th, 85, USA/CDN, Assoc Prod/2nd U Dir; "The Edison Twins" (Cycle III), TV, 84, CDN/USA, PM; *Youngblood*, Th, 84, USA, PM (CDN); "The Edison Twins" (Cycle I), TV, 83, CDN/USA, Loc M/Assist PM; *Mrs. Soffel*, Th, 83, USA, U Loc M.

MACFARLANE, Douglas
57 Bellevue Ave., Toronto, ON M5T 2N5 (416)595-5786.
Type of Production and Credits: Th Film-Prod Exec; TV Film-Prod/Prod Exec; TV Video-PM.
Genres: Drama-Th&TV; Documentary-Th.
Biography: Born in 1962. Production Manager of Primedia's Stage On Screen, eight 120 minute dramas. Head of Production/Production Executive at Lauron Productions from 1988 to 1990. Broad range of experience in both film and tape, single or multicamera, drama or documentary. Graduated from Queen's University in 1985 (BAH).
Selected Filmography: "Stage On Screen" (8 eps), TV, 90-91, CDN, PM; *Ustinov in the Eighties*, TV, 89, CDN, Prod Exec; *The Challenge*, TV, 89, CDN, Prod Exec; *Something To Talk About*, ED, 89, CDN, Prod; *The Inside Story*, Th, 88, CDN, PM; *A Winter To Remember*, TV, 88, CDN, Prod/Co Dir; *Dreams of Glory*, TV, 87, CDN, PM; *On The Way To The Olympics*, TV, 87, CDN, PM; *Share The Flame*, TV, 87, CDN, PM.

MACKAY, Margaux◊
DGC, DGA. (212)684-0830.

Type of Production and Credits: Th Film-1st AD; TV Film-1st AD/Prod; TV Video-PM/Prod.
Genres: Drama-Th&TV; Children's-TV; Documentary-Th; Commercials-Th&TV.
Biography: Born 1952, Rothesay, New Brunswick. Specializes in location shoots; world-wide location experience; has been working out of Los Angeles and New York for past 10 years; producer of big-budget commercials; 1st AD in film and TV drama; PM for TV series
Selected Filmography:: "Sharon, Lois and Bram's Elephant Show" (13 eps), TV, 88, CDN, PM; *Gotham*, TV, 87, CDN, 1st AD; *Coke*, Cm, 86, CDN, Prod; "American Playhouse" (1 eps), TV, 85, USA, 1st AD; *The Rebel*, Th, 84, USA, PM/1st AD; *Children of the Third World*, ED, 83, GB, PM/1st AD; *Jack Dempsey Story*, TV, 82, USA, 1st AD; *The Children*, Th, 82, USA, 1st AD.

MACKENZIE, Scott
- see PRODUCERS

MACNEE, Rupert
- see PRODUCERS

MAITLAND, Scott
IATSE 44, IATSE 156, IATSE 873, ACTRA, DGA, DGC, SAG. P.O. Box 1079, Murphy's, CA 95247 (209)728-2731.
Type of Production and Credits: Th Film-PM/1st AD; TV Film-PM/1st AD.
Genres: Drama-Th&TV; Comedy-Th; Action-Th&TV; Horror-Th.
Biography: Born in Sudbury, Ontario; US resident alien. Languages: English and French. Specializes in distant locations.
Selected Filmography: *Eye for an Eye*, TV, 91, USA, Co-Prod/Unit PM; *Lights Out*, TV, 90, USA, Co-Prod/Unit PM; *Dangerous Passion*, TV, 89, USA, Unit PM; *The Preppy Murder*, TV, 89, USA, Unit PM/Assist Dir; *Next of Kin*, Th, 87, USA, Unit PM; "Once a Hero" (6 eps), TV, 88, USA, Unit PM; *The Stepford Children*, Th, 86, USA, Unit PM; *Jaws 3D*, Th, 83, USA, 1st AD; *Thief*, Th, 81, CDN, 1st AD; *Harry Tracy*, Th, 80, CDN, 1st AD; *Never Cry Wolf*, Th, 80, CDN, 1st AD; *Raging Bull*, Th, 80, USA, 1st AD; *King of Comedy*, Th, 79, USA, 1st AD; *Jaws 2*, Th, 77, USA, 1st AD; *MacArthur*, Th, 76, USA, 1st AD.

MARCIL, Michelle
4241 Brébeuf, Montréal, PQ H2J 3K6 (514)598-7811.
Types de production et générique: l métrage-Rég; c métrage-Rég; TV film-Rég; TV vidéo-Rég.
Types d'oeuvres: Drame-C; Comédie-C; Documentaire-C&TV; Education-TV; Enfants-C&TV.
Curriculum vitae: Née en 1948 à Rawdon, Québec. Citoyenneté canadienne. Langues: français et anglais. Expérience professionnelle: scripte assistante, 1977-82; direction de post-production, 1990-91; direction de production, 1982-91.
Filmographie sélective: *Le fabuleux Voyage de l'Ange*, C, 90-91, CDN, Dir pro; "On the 8th Day" (2 eps), TV, 91, CDN, Dir pro; *Vincent and Me*, C, 89, CDN/F, PM; *Cruising Bar*, C, 88, CDN, Dir pro; *Coeur de Nylon*, TV, 88, CDN, Dir pro; *Salut Victor*, TV, 88, CDN, Dir pro; *T'es belle, Jeanne*, C/TV, 87, CDN, Dir pro; *Danny*, TV, 87, CDN, Dir pro; "17 rue Laurier" (13 eps), TV, 87, CDN, Dir pro; "20 ans Express" (13 eps), TV, 86-87, CDN, Dir pro; "Super Clique" (20 eps), TV, 86-87, CDN, Dir pro; "C'est Chouette" (26 eps), TV, 86-87, CDN, Dir pro; "Ani-maths" (39 eps), TV, 84, CDN, Dir pro.

MARGELLOS, James
- see PRODUCERS

MARK, Gordon
- see PRODUCERS

MARTIN, James G.
DGC. Quixote Film Corporation, 7726A Carrington St., Vancouver, BC V6N 1T9 (604)263-4619.
Type of Production and Credits: Th Film-PM; Th Short Prod Spv; TV Film-PM/Assist Dir.
Genres: Drama-Th&TV; Comedy-Th; Action-Th&TV; Science Fiction-TV; Horror-TV; Documentary-Th; Educational-Th; Commercials-Th&TV; Music Video-TV; Sports-TV.
Biography: Born in 1952 in Dublin, Ireland. Canadian citizen. English, some Spanish. Two years film course, Sheridan College. Two years Humanities, McMaster University. Computer literate in budgeting, scheduling, windows, etc. Interests: action, SPFX, photography and production management, 65mm, Imax, 3-D motion pictures. Has worked on over 400 commercials since 1982.
Selected Filmography: *Shooting Star/ Special Time, Special Place*, Th, 91, CDN, Prod Spv; "Black Stallion" (12 eps), TV, 90, CDN/F, Assist Dir; *Molson Indy - Vancouver*, TV, 90, CDN, PM; "Booker" (10 eps), TV, 89, CDN/USA, Assist Dir; *Canada Tourism*, Cm, 89, CDN, PM/ Assist Dir; *Friday the 13th, Part VIII*, Th, 89, USA/CDN, Assist Dir; *Jane of Lantern Hill*, TV, 88, USA/CDN, PM; *Looking*

For Miracles, TV, 88, USA/CDN, PM; "Captain Power" (22 eps), TV, 87, USA, Assist Dir; U.S. Pontiac campaign (10 spots), Cm, 87, USA, PM; *Niagara: Miracles,* Imax, Th, 86, CDN/USA, Unit Mgr/Loc Mgr; *Rites of Summer,* Th, 86, USA, Assist Dir; *Journey of Discovery,* IMAX, Th, 84, CDN, PM

McLEAN, Andrew R.
DGC. Parallel Films Inc., 7677 French St., Vancouver, BC V6P 4V5 (604)263-6729.
Type of Production and Credits: Th Film-PM; Th Short-PM; TV Film-PM.
Genres: Drama-Th&TV; Comedy-Th&TV; Action-Th&TV; Commercials-TV.
Biography: Born in 1951 in Saint John, New Brunswick. After high school, worked as an Ordinary Seaman aboard foreign-going tankers plying eastern North America and northern South America for 1 year. Acquired B.Sc. in Biology and Biochemistry in 1974 from Acadia University, Nova Scotia. Travelled extensively in Western Europe for 1 year. Speaks reasonable French, worked many biological research contracts, worked a photo retail/studio/lab business then freelance jobs with the NFB and CBC Halifax. Extensive travel in Mexico, Central and South American for 1 year. Arrived in Vancouver in 1979 and worked hundreds of commercials, documentaries, industrials, etc., doing everything from sound recording, lighting, gripping, set design and construction, etc. Joined DGC in 198;, did 4-1/2 years as Location Manager, now 2-1/2 years as PM. Married with 4 children.
Selected Filmography: *And The Sea Will Tell,* TV, 90, USA, PM; *Deadly Intentions ...Again,* TV, 90, USA, PM; "Neon Rider" (24 eps), TV, 89-90, CDN/USA, PM; *The Lady Forgets,* TV, 89, USA, Unit M; "Murphy's Law" (6 eps), TV, 89, USA, PM; *Look Who's Talking,* Th, 88, USA, Loc M; "Whattley By The Bay" (pilot), TV, 88, USA, Loc M; *Laura Lansing Slept Here,* TV, 87, USA, Loc M; *Assault & Matrimony,* TV, 87, USA, Loc M; *Sworn to Silence,* TV, 87, USA, Loc M; *Backfire,* Th, 86, USA, Loc M; *Firefighter,* TV, 86, USA, Loc M; *Nobody's Child,* TV, 85, USA, Loc M; *Love is Never Silent,* TV, 85, USA, Loc M; "Danger Bay", TV, 85, CDN, Loc M.

MILINKOVIC, Gerry
- see DIRECTORS

MORAIS, Robert D.
6 West 38th Ave., Vancouver, BC V5Y 2N4 (604)327-0210.
Type of Production and Credits: Th Film-PM; Th Short-Prod/PM.
Genres: Drama-TV; Comedy-Th; Science Fiction-Th; Horror-Th.
Biography: Born in 1955 in Montreal, Quebec. Fluent in French and English with basic knowledge of Spanish, German and Japanese. Studied computer management and stage management. Dancer since 1967 with ample experience in entertainment management.
Selected Filmography: *Scanners II - The New Order,* Th, 90, CDN/USA, PM; *Voisins Ombrageux...,* Th, 90, CDN, Prod; *Backstab,* Th, 89, CDN/USA, PM; *Appel Longue Distance,* Th, 89, CDN, PM; *El Vidente Ciego,* Th, 89, CDN, Wr/Actor; *Amityville - The Final Curse,* Th, 88, CDN/USA, Unit Mgr; *Les Noces de Papier,* TV, 88, CDN, Prod Assist.

MORGAN, June
SMPIA. 114 Acadia Dr., #19, Saskatoon, SK S7H 4T8 (306)373-8745. Cinepost Productions, 1937 Ontario Avenue., Saskatoon SK S7H 1T5, (306)244-7788.
Type of Production and Credits: Th Short-Assist Ed; TV Film-PM; TV Video-PM/Assist Ed.
Genres: Documentary-TV; Industrial-TV.
Biography: Born 1958, Saskatoon, Saskatchewan. Canadian citizen. Graduate of the Film Production program, Ryerson Polytechnical Institute, Toronto. Active in the film business since 1985. Has been involved in several award-winning productions.
Selected Filmography: *Junior Citizens' Awards,* TV, 91, CDN, PM; *Winter Seasoned,* TV, 90-91, CDN, PM; *Knowing Each Other,* TV, 90-91, CDN, Script Ed; *Take a Vacation in Your Own Backyard* (11 spots), TV, 91, CDN, PM; *Community Bonds* (12 spots), Cm, 90-91, CDN, PM; "Second Chance" (26 eps), TV, 89/90, CDN, Assist Ed; *Watershed,* TV, 89, CDN, Assist Ed; *Shooting Images,* Th, 88, CDN, Prod Coord.

MURDOCH, Susan
DGC. 620 Jarvis St., Ste. 907, Toronto, ON M4Y 2R8 (416)928-0576.
Type of Production and Credits: Th Film-PM; TV Film-PM.
Genres: Drama-Th&TV; Comedy-Th&TV; Action-Th&TV; Science Fiction-TV.
Selected Filmography: *The Cutting Edge,* Th, 91, USA, PM; *Black Robe,* Th, 90, CDN/AUS, PM; "War of the Worlds" (44 eps), TV, 88-90, USA/CDN, PM; "Adderly" (44 eps), TV, 86-88, USA/CDN, PM; "Vid Kids" (13 eps), TV, 86, CDN, PM.

NELSON, Keri
5544 Woodchuck Place, North Vancouver, BC V7R 4P1 (604)986-1292. Select Canada, 5544 Woodchuck Place, North Vancouver, BC V7R 4P1 (602)986-0252.
Type of Production and Credits: Th Film-PM; TV Video-Assoc Prod.
Genres: Documentary-TV; Comedy-TV Musical-TV; Science Fiction -Th
Biography: Born in 1959 in Edmonton, Alberta. Fluent in German.
Selected Filmography: "Airborne", TV, 91, CDN, Assoc Prod; *Seeds of Time A Long Time Ago*, MV, 91, CDN, Assoc Prod; "Rock Classics" (2 eps), TV, 90, CDN, Assoc Prod; *Husky World Cup Bobsleigh Championship*, TV, 90, CDN, PM; *Molson World Cup Luge Championship*, TV, 90, CDN, PM; *FleshGordon II*, Th, 90, CDN, Pro Acc't/Asst to Prod.

NYSTEDT, Colleen
- see PRODUCERS

PECKAN, Sophia
- see PRODUCERS

PERRY, Howard
DGC. R.R. #5, Alexandria, ON K0C 1A0 (613)594-9310. FAX: 230-6004.
Type of Production and Credits: Th Film-1st AD/PM; Th Short-PM; TV Film-PM.
Genres: Drama-Th&TV; Variety-TV; Documentary-Th&TV; Commercials-TV.
Biography: Born 1939, Ottawa, Ontario. Languages: French and English. Several multi-screen and Circlevision films for Walt Disney. Latest feature, *Cool and Free*, is in development (Assoc. Producer). Postproduction expert.
Selected Filmography: *Hoax*, Th, 91, CDN, Co-Prod; *Silent Conversations*, Th, 91, CDN, Prod.

PHILLIPS, Jim
- see ART DIRECTORS

RACINE, Pierre
- voir DIRECTEURS-PHOTO

RAFFE, Alexandra
- see PRODUCERS

REICHEL, Stéphane
- see PRODUCERS

REID, François
3570 Ridgewood, #106, Montreal, PQ H3V 1C2 (514)733-5215. Ideacom, 5225 rue Berri, #300, Montréal, PQ H2J 2S4 (514)274-6538.
Types de production et générique: l métrage-Dir prod; c métrage-Dir prod; TV film-Dir prod/Prod dél; TV vidéo-Dir prod.
Types d'oeuvres: Drame-C&TV; Affaires publiques-TV; Variété-TV; Documentaire-Th.
Curriculum vitae: Né en 1956, Montréal, Québec. Langues: français et anglais. Baccalauréat en Comm., Université du Québec à Montréal. Expérience en informatique, réalisation de documentaires industriels; producteur délégué pour une série de vidéo-clips, 86-87; directeur de production et producteur délégué pigiste, plusieurs messages publicitaires, 84-85.
Filmographie sélective: *Ruses et Vengeances*, C, 91, CDN, Dir pro; *Nenette*, C, 90, CDN, Dir pro; "Comment ça va?" (26 eps), TV, 88, CDN, Dir pro; *Le Rêve accompli*, In, 88, CDN, Prod dél; *Les Bleus au coeur*, C, 87, CDN, Ass prod; *Les Enfants de la rue*, TV, 86-87, CDN, Ass prod; "A première vue", TV, 86-87, CDN, Dir pro; "Enquête sur les enfants mal-aimés" (12 eps), TV, 85-86, CDN, Dir pro.

REPKE, Ron
- see PRODUCERS

REYNOLDS, Stephen P.
- see PRODUCERS

RICHARDSON, Gillian
- see PRODUCERS

ROBINSON, Gord◊
DGC. (416)485-6098.
Type of Production and Credits: Th Film-PM/1st AD; TV Film-PM/1st AD.
Genres: Drama-Th&TV; Comedy-Th; Action-Th; Horror-Th.
Selected Filmography: *Christmas Show*, TV, 87, USA, 1st Assist Dir; "Night Heat" (2 eps), TV, 85, CDN/USA, PM; *Killer Party*, Th, 84, USA, 1st Assist Dir; *Reckless Disregard*, TV, 84, CDN/USA, PM; *Full Circle Again*, TV, 84, CDN, PM; *Cougar*, TV, 83, USA, PM/1st Assist Dir; *Shocktrauma*, TV, 83, CDN, PM, 1st Assist Dir; *Frank and Fearless*, TV, 82, USA, PM/1st Assist Dir; *Spasms*, Th, 81, CDN, Co-Prod/PM; *Magic Show*, TV, 81, CDN, PM; *An American Christmas Carol*, TV, 79, USA, U Loc M; "Matt and Jenny" (26 eps), TV, 79, CDN/GB/D, PM.

RODGERS, Bob
- see PRODUCERS

ROMANOFF, Sergei
- see WRITERS

ROSS, Brian◊
DGC. (416)785-9599.
Type of Production and Credits: Th Film-PM/1st AD; TV Film-PM/1st AD; TV Video-PM/1st AD.
Genres: Drama-Th&TV; Comedy-Th&TV; Action-Th; Horror-Th.
Biography: Over twenty years experience in film and videotape; production

supervisor for more than 2,000 commercials world-wide; producer of short films in the Arctic and South Seas; extensive travel; experienced as PM, unit location manager and 1st AD, theatrical, made-for-TV movies and commercials; floor director for satellite programming; Special Effects Supervisor and PM at Light and Motion Inc.

ROSSNER, Danny
DGC, STCQ. 5601 Parkhaven, Côte St. Luc, PQ H4W 1X2 (514)481-3676. (514)481-5533.
Type of Production and Credits: Th Film-PM/Line Prod; TV Film-PM; TV Video-PM.
Genres: Drama-Th&TV; Action-Th& TV; Horror-Th&TV; Industrial-Th&TV.
Biography: Born 1950, Deauville, France; Canadian citizenship. Languages: French, English, working knowledge of Hebrew and Hungarian. B.A., Cinema and Social Sciences, 75, and M.B.A., 86, McGill University.
Selected Filmography: *I Won't Dance*, Th, 91, CDN, Prod Cons; "Urban Angel" (6 eps), TV, 90, CDN, PM/Prod Cons; "Three Themes Suspense" (5 eps), Th/TV, 89, CDN/F, Unit PM; *Thank You Satan/Oh Oh Satan*, Th, 88, F/CDN, Co-Prod; *The Jeweller's Shop*, Th, 87, I/F/CDN, PM (Cdn); "War and Remembrance" (30 eps), TV, 86-87, USA, PM (Cdn); *13*, Th, 88, F/GB, PM; *Miles to Go*, TV, 86, CDN, Unit PM; *Taming of the Demons*, Th, 85, CDN, PM; *Joshua Then and Now*, Th, 84, CDN, Unit M; *Candy the Stripper*, TV, 83, PMA/PM; *A Matter of Cunning*, TV, 83, CDN, PM; *FLTRR*, TV, 82, CDN, PM; *Till Death Do Us Part*, Th, 81, CDN, PM; *My Bloody Valentine*, Th, 80, CDN, PM.

ROUSE, Ted
DGC, ACCT. 129 Valecrest Dr., Etobicoke, ON M9A 4P7 (416)233-0213. Mobile Image of Canada Ltd., 26 Soho St., Toronto, ON M5T 1Z7 (416)591-1400.
Type of Production and Credits: Th Film-PM/Loc M/Unit M; TV Film-PM/Loc M/Unit M.
Genres: Drama-Th&TV; Documentary-TV; Commercials-TV.
Biography: Born 1943, Calgary, Alberta. B.A., University of Saskatchewan, 65. Worked at local western television Stations - CHAB, CFCN, CFQC; began at RPL Productions, 65; moved to Rabko, 69; Toronto Projects Co-ordinator, CFDC (Telefilm Canada), 72-77; consulting practice and PM, 77-81; joined Mobile Image, Vice-President, 82; joined Pathe Sound, 88, Vice-President and General Manager; joined Astral Film Enterprises, 90, Director of Business Development. Independent Production Executive, Cinexus and Passport Productions '91.
Selected Filmography: "Cagney and Lacey" (pilot), TV, 81, USA, Loc M; *Heartaches*, Th, 80, CDN, Unit M; *Murder by Decree*, Th, 78, CDN/GB, PM.

ROY-DECARIE, Matthieu
- voir MONTEURS SON

RYAN, John
- see PRODUCERS

ST-ARNAUD, Michèle
STCQ. 4589, rue de la Roche, Montréal, PQ H2J 3J5 (514)527-3082. (514)523-3600.
Types de production et générique: l métrage-Dir prod/Rég/Ass réal; TV film-Dir prod/Rég.
Types d'oeuvres: Drame-C; Documentaire-C; Industriel-C&TV.
Curriculum vitae: Née en 1954, Ste-Foy, Québec. Langues: français et anglais. Etudes en administration, Université du Québec à Montréal. Longs séjours à l'étranger: 2 ans en Afrique; 4 ans en Europe.
Filmographie sélective: *L'Automne Sauvage*, C, 91, CDN, Rég ext; *Descending Angel*, C, 90, USA, Rég ext; *Une Histoire Inventée*, C, 90, CDN, Rég ext; *Vincent & Me*, C, 89, CDN, Rég ext; *Le Party*, C, 89, CDN, Rég; *Laura Laur*, C, 88, CDN, Rég ext; *Le Chemin de damas*, TV, 88, CDN, Rég ext; *Onzième spéciale*, C, 88, CDN, Rég ext; *Bethune* (Montréal), C, 88, CDN/RC/F, Ass décor; *Gaspard et Fils*, C, 87, CDN, Rég ext; *La Peau sur les os*, C, 87, CDN, Dir pro/1er ass réal; *L'Homme de papier*, C, 87, CDN, Chef rég; *Kalamazoo*, C, 86, CDN, Chef rég; *Un zoo la nuit*, C, 86, CDN, Rég ext; *Pouvoir intime*, C, 85, CDN, Chef rég.

SERENY, Julia
- see PRODUCERS

SHRIER, Barbara
812 Gilford, Montreal, PQ H2J 1N9 (514)526-4766. FAX: 526-3517.
Type of Production and Credits: Th Film-PM/Loc M; Th Short-Prod; TV Film-Prod/PM.
Genres: Drama-Th&TV; Action-Th& TV; Documentary-TV; Children's-Th&TV.
Biography: Born in 1955 in Montreal, Quebec. Languages: French, English, Mandarin and Hebrew. B.A., Comm., McGill Univ. Extensive travel through Southeast Asia, Middle East, Australia, Europe, Caribbean, US and Canada.

Selected Filmography: *L'Automne Sauvage*, Th, 91, CDN, PM; "The Hitchhiker" (11 eps), TV, 90, CDN/F, Prod; *Descending Angel*, TV, 90, USA, Line Prod; *Cargo*, Th, 89, CDN, PM; "The Hitchhiker" (15 eps), TV, 89, CDN/F, Line Prod; *Comment faire l'amour avec un nègre sans se fatiguer*, Th, 88, CDN/F, PM; *The Moderns*, Th, 87, CDN, PM; *Pin*, Th, 87, CDN, PM; "William Tell" (6 eps), TV, 86, USA/F, Line Prod; *Obsessed*, Th, 86, CDN, Loc M; *Choices*, TV, 85, USA/F, Loc M; *Spearfield's Daughter* (mini-series), TV, 85, CDN/USA/AUS, Loc M; *The Boy in Blue*, Th, 84, CDN/USA, Art Dept Coord; *Quest for Fire*, Th, 81, CDN/F, Pro Coord; *Atlantic City*, Th, 79, CDN/F, Pro Coord.

SIMPSON, Dee E.
- see PRODUCERS

SORA, Bob
Bob Sora Production Services, 93 Drayton Ave., Toronto, ON M4C 3L8 (416)694-4847.
Type of Production and Credits: TV Film-PM/Assist Dir/Prod; TV Video-PM/Assist Dir/Prod.
Genres: Commercials-Th&TV; Industrial-TV; Music Video-TV.
Biography: Born,Toronto, 1961. Studied Film Production and English Lit. at York Univ. Worked on over 500 commercials, music videos and industrials as PM, AD or line producer. Throws right, bats right and can hit the jump shot from outside.
Selected Filmography: *Gothic*, Black Label, Cm, 91, CDN, PM; *Dreamscape*, Black Label, Cm, 91, CDN, PM; *Barbados Tourism*, Cm, 89, CDN, PM/Assist Dir.

SPICKLER, Bernard
- voir PRODUCTEURS

STONEHOUSE, Marilyn◊
(416)920-1532
Type of Production and Credits: Th Film-PM; TV Film-PM; TV Video-PM.
Genres: Drama-Th&TV; Comedy-Th&TV; Action-Th&TV.
Selected Filmography: *The Von Metz Incident*, Th, 88, USA, PM; *Noble House* (4 eps)(mini-series), TV, 87, USA, PM; *Collision Course*, Th, 87, USA, PM; *From the Hip*, Th, 86, USA, PM; *Maximum Overdrive*, Th, 85, USA, PM; *Letting Go*, TV, 85, USA, PM; *Into the Looking Glass Darkly*, TV, 84, CDN/USA, PM; *Head Office*, Th, 84, USA, PM; *Martin's Day*, Th, 83, CDN/GB, PM; *Follow the Parade*, TV, 83, CDN, PM; *Quebec/Canada 1995*, TV, 83, CDN, PM; *A Christmas Story*, Th, 83, CDN, PM; *When Angels Fly*, TV, 82, CDN/USA, PM; *Strange Invaders*, Th, 82, USA, PM; *Class of 1984*, Th, 81, CDN, PM; *The Amateur*, Th, 81, CDN, PM.

SULYMA, Michael H.
- see PRODUCERS

THATCHER, Tony
DGC. 1970 Woodview Ave., Pickering, ON L1V 1L6 (416)286-2065.
Type of Production and Credits: Th Film-PM/1st AD; TV Film-PM/1st AD.
Genres: Drama-Th&TV; Comedy-Th&TV; Action-Th&TV; Horror-Th&TV.
Biography: Born 1943, Oxford, England; British citizenship; landed immigrant, Canada, 68.
Selected Filmography: "Counterstrike" (30 eps), TV, 90-91, CDN, PM; *Last Best Year of My Life*, Th, 90, USA, 1st AD; "Diamonds" (9 eps), TV, 89, CDN, PM; "E.N.G." (3 eps), TV, 89, CDN, 1st AD; "T and T" (10 eps), TV, 88-89, CDN, 1st AD; *Bridge to Silence*, Th, 88, USA, 1st AD; *God Bless the Child*, TV, 87, USA, 1st AD; *Glory Enough for All*, TV, 87, CDN, 1st AD; *Dead of Winter*, Th, 86, USA, 1st AD; *Deadly Business*, TV, 85, USA, 1st AD; *In Defense of Kids*, Th, 82, USA, PM; *The Kidnapping of the President*, Th, 80, CDN, PM; *Full Circle*, Th, 80, GB, 1st AD; *Disappearance*, Th, 77, GB, 1st AD; *Black Christmas*, Th, 74, CDN, 1st AD.

TRAEGER, Tracy
- see PRODUCERS

VALCOUR, NICHOLAS
- voir PRODUCTEURS

VAN LAMBALGEN, Monzine
SMPIA. 1550 McKercher Dr., Saskatoon, SK S7H 5E1 (306)477-1616. Cinepost Productions, 1937 Ontario Avenue, Saskatoon, SK S7K 1T5 (306)244-7788.
Type of Production and Credits: Th Short-PM; TV Film-PM; TV Video-PM.
Genres: Documentary-Th&TV; Industrial-Th&TV;
Biography: Born in 1962 in Wynyard, Saskatchewan. Canadian citizen. Fluent in English and Chinese. Certified make-up artist for film, video, theatre and stills. Broadcast training at BCIT and the University of Saskatchewan. Active in the film and television industry for eight years. Has been involved in several award-winning productions.
Selected Filmography: *Knowing Each Other*, TV, 90-91, CDN, PM; *New Kids on the Farm*, In, 91, CDN, PM/Make-up; *Lightbridge*, In, 91, CDN, PM; *Tux & Tails*, Cm, 90, CDN, PM/Make-up; *In Perfect Harmony*, TV, 90, CDN, PM; *White Orchid Wedding*, Cm, 90, CDN, PM/Make-up; *United Way* (3 spots), Cm,

90, CDN, PM/Make-up; *Junior Citizens Awards*, TV, 90, CDN, PM/Make-up.

VON HELMOLT, Vonnie
ACCT, MMPIA. 225 Symington Rd., Winnipeg, MB R2C 2Z3 (204)222-6153.
Type of Production and Credits: Th Film-PM/Loc M; Th Short-Prod/Dir; TV Film-PM/Prod/Dir/Art Dir; TV Video-PM/1st AD/Art Dir.
Genres: Drama-Th&TV; Comedy-Th&TV; Commercials-TV; Animation-Th&TV.
Biography: Born Winnipeg, Manitoba. Lives in Los Angeles and northern Ontario. Began film career as writer/researcher for weekly CBC entertainment and arts half hour, and site co-ordinator for rock concerts including the Eagles tour, 78.
Selected Filmography: *True Confections*, Th, 90, CDN, Co-Prod; *Lost in the Barrens*, "Magic Hour" (2 eps), TV, 90, CDN, PM; *Smoked Lizard Lips*, Th, 90, CDN, Cons Line Prod; *Welcome Home Hero*, TV, 90, CDN, PM; *Turn in the Road*, TV, 89, CDN, PM; *Mob Story*, Th, 88, CDN, Assoc Prod; *Adam's Dream*, Th, 88, CDN, Prod; *Miss Manitoba*, TV, 88, CDN, PM; *The Outside Chance of Maximilian Glick*, Th, 87, CDN, PM; *Carried Away*, Th, 85, CDN, Prod/Dir; *Tramp at the Door*, TV, 84, CDN, Assoc Prod/Art Dir; *The Prodigal*, TV, 83, CDN, Assoc Prod/Art Dir/Assist Dir; *The Pedlar*, Th/TV, 83, CDN, PM; *Daydream*, Th, 78, CDN, Prod; *Silence of the North*, Th, 79, CDN/USA, Asst Loc M.

WERTHEIMER, Bob
- see PRODUCERS

WINKLER, Meita
- see DIRECTORS

WINTONICK, Peter
- see EDITORS

ZAMARIA, Charles
DGC, ACCT. Zamaria Productions, 61 Rainsford Rd., Toronto, ON M4L 3N7 (416)694-5252.
Type of Production and Credits: Th Film-PM; TV Film-PM; TV Video-Prod/PM/Ed.
Genres: Drama-Th&TV; Variety-TV; Documentary-TV; Children's-Th&TV.
Biography: Born in 1957 in Toronto, Ontario. University of Windsor, (Master of Arts - Communications Studies); York University, (Bachelor of Fine Arts - Honours); Pearson College, Victoria (International Baccalaureate). Presently Manager of Production at YTV Canada Inc. Twelve years experience as line producer, PM, producer, production accountant and editor. Has worked with CBC and CTV as PM and film/video editor and as Assistant Manager, Business Affairs for Telefilm Canada. Experienced in several craft areas: production accountant, editor, sound recordist, 1st AD. Teaching experience at Seneca College and the University of Windsor. Staff film editor with CBC for 5 years (1979-84). Worked as a sound recordist for CBC's "Venture". Freelance consultant on production and business aspects of film and television production.
Selected Filmography: "Sweating Bullets" (13 eps), TV, 90-91, USA/CDN/MEX, Pro Acc't; *Welcome Home*, TV, 89, CDN, Exec Prod/Pro Acc't; *The Last Winter*, TV, 89, CDN, Line Prod/PM; *Eric Nagler: A Special for all Seasons*, TV, 88, CDN, Assoc Prod; *Einstein Tonight*, TV, 88, CDN, Assoc Prod/Pro Acc't; *Luba - Between the Earth and the Sky*, TV, 88, CDN, Assoc Prod/PM/Pro Acc't; *Sharon, Lois and Bram's The Elephant Show* (13 eps), TV, 88, CDN, Assoc Prod; *Sharon Lois and Bram's The Elephant Show* (52 eps), TV, 84-87, CDN, Assoc Prod/PM/Pro Acc't/Ed; *Jane Siberry - One More Colour*, TV, 87, CDN, Assoc Prod/PM/Pro Acc't; *Jane Siberry - I Muse Aloud*, TV, 87, CDN, Assoc Prod/PM/Pro Acc't; *Jade*, MV, 85, CDN, PM; *Sharon, Lois and Bram at The Young People's Theatre*, TV, 84, CDN, PM/1st Assist Dir; *Seeing It Our Way: Mary Celestino*, TV, 82, CDN, Ed/Co Dir; *Seeing It Our Way: Adele Duck*, TV, 81, CDN, Ed/Co Dir; *Islanders*, TV, 78, CDN, Ed/Dir.

ZBOROWSKY, William
DGC. Z.I.P. Inc., PH3, 330 Spadina Rd., Toronto, ON M5R 2V9 (416)920-3553.
Type of Production and Credits: Th Film-PM/Line Prod; TV Film-PM/Prod; TV Video-PM/Prod.
Genres: Drama-Th&TV; Action-Th&TV; Comedy-Th&TV; Science Fiction-Th&TV.
Biography: Entered industry, 59; CBC Winnipeg 6 years; CBC Toronto 6 years; freelance since 71; has filmed throughout Canada, USA, Europe, Africa, Bahamas and Caribbean islands; specializes in distant locations; trouble shooter; expert near, on or under water; over a dozen stage productions (stage manager/assistant director); more than 350 documentaries (Prod/Wr/PM/1st AD/Dir); 20 features (PM/1st AD/Line Prod/Pro Spv); over 100 TV dramas and specials (Prod/PM/1st AD/2nd U Dir/Dir/Co-Wr). Awards for producing, directing and writing.

Selected Filmography: *Payoff,* Th, 90, USA, Pro Spv; *Uncut Gem,* Th, 88/90, CDN, Line Prod; *Betrayed,* Th, 87, USA, PM; *The Liberators,* TV, 86, USA, PM; *High Price of Passion,* TV, 86, USA, Pro Spv; *Meatballs III,* Th, 84, CDN, PM; *Spacehunters: Adventures in the Forbidden Zone,* Th, 83-84, USA, PM; *Family Man,* TV, 82, USA, U Loc M; *Mazes and Monsters,* TV, 81, USA, U Loc M; *Love,* Th, 80, CDN, PM; *Terror Train,* Th, 79, CDN/USA, PM; *Stampede,* Th, 77, CDN, PM; *Only God Knows,* Th, 73, CDN, 1st AD; *The Neptune Factor,* Th, 72, CDN, Assist PM.

Production Sound Mixers
Mixeurs son production

AIKENHEAD, Chris◆
(604)299-7726.
Type of Production and Credits: Th Film-Snd Rec/Ed/Wr/Dir; Th Short-Snd Rec.
Genres: Drama-Th&TV; Documentary-Th&TV; Educational-Th&TV; Commercials-Th&TV; Industrial-Th.
Biography: Born 1952, Brantford, Ontario. B.A., English, Simon Fraser University. Over 15 years production experience on documentaries, dramas, industrials, educational films, corporate videos and commercials; complete location sound recording package. Awards include the Norman McLaren Grand Prix at Fifth Canadian Student Film Festival; Silver Screen Award at the US Industrial Film Festival; Cambridge Film Forum.
Selected Filmography: *Living the Difference*, Th, 88, CDN, Snd Rec/Ed; *First Harvest*, Th, 88, CDN, Ed/Wr; *Aga Kahn Health Services*, Th, 87, CDN, Wr/Ed; *Common Ground*, Th, 87, CDN, Snd Rec/Wr; *And After Tomorrow...*, Th, 86, CDN, Ed; *Camp Goodtimes*, Th, 85, CDN, Dir/Ed; *Nuclear Follies*, Th, 85, CDN, Ed; *Kangaroos Under Fire*, Th, 85, CDN, Wr/Ed; *The Nuclear Path*, Th, 85, CDN, Dr/Wr/Ed; "The Way of the Dream" (20 eps), TV, 85, CDN, Wr/Ed/Snd Rec; *Ecology in Action*, Th, 85, CDN, Wr/Ed; *New Light on Cancer*, Th, 85, CDN, Dir/Snd Rec/Ed; *Growth Dilemma*, Th, 85, CDN, Dir/Snd Rec/Ed; *Greenpeace: Voyages to Save the Whales*, Th, 85, CDN, Wr/Snd Rec.

ARCHER, Tim
6906 Montevideo Rd., Mississauga, ON

L5N 1A4 (416)542-3596. Masters Workshop, 306 Rexdale Blvd., Unit #1, Rexdale, ON M9W 1R6 (416)741-1312.
Type of Production and Credits: Th Film-Re-record Mix; Th Short-Re-record Mix; TV Film-Re-record Mix; TV Video-Re-record Mix; Imax-Re-record Mix.
Genres: Drama-Th&TV; Variety-Th& TV; Action-Th&TV; Horror-Th&TV.
Biography: Born in 1961 in Walford, England. British and Canadian citizenship. Worked for 3 years in British Columbia and Alberta as a location sound recordist. Moved to Toronto in 1986 to work at Masters Workshop. Worked on 3 MPSA-Golden Reel Award winners, "The Hitchhiker", "Friday The 13th - The Series" and *Ford: The Man and the Machine*.
Selected Filmography: *Scanners III - The Takeover*, Th, 91, CDN, Re-record Mix; *Psychic*, Th, 91, CDN, Re-record Mix; *Switzerland*, Th, 91, CH, Re-record Mix; *Deadly Surveillance*, Th, 91, CDN, Re-record Mix; "The Hitchhiker" (52 eps), TV, 89-91, CDN/USA/F, Re-record Mix; *Scanners II - The New Order*, Th, 90, CDN, Re-record Mix; *The Last Elephants/ Ivory Hunters*, Th, 90, USA, Re-record Mix; *Simon Les Nuages*, Th, 90, CDN, Re-record Mix; *The Bruce Curtis Story*, TV, 90, CDN, Re-record Mix; "Friday The 13th - The Series" (45 eps), TV, 88-90, CDN/USA, Re-record Mix; "War of the Worlds" (26 eps), TV, 89-90, CDN/USA, Re-record Mix; *Small Sacrifices*, TV, 89, USA/CDN, Re-record Mix; "The Campbells" (74 eps), TV, 86-89, CDN, Foley Rec/Re-record Mix; "Nightheat" (82 eps), TV, 86-88, CDN, Foley Rec/Re-record Mix; *Ford:The Man and the Machine*, TV, 87, CDN/USA, Foley Rec.

BEAUCHEMIN, Claude✧
(514)449-0744.
Types de production et générique: c métrage-Pren son; TV film-Pren son; TV vidéo-Pren son.
Types d'oeuvres: Documentaire-C&TV; Annonces-TV; Industriel-TV; Affaires publiques-TV.
Curriculum vitae: Né en 1942, Montréal, Québec. Langues: français et anglais. Preneur de son, Radio-Canada, 15 en portatif, 5 ans en studio. A travaillé comme pigiste en film et vidéo pour l'ONF, l'industrie privée, Radio-Canada et CBC-TV depuis 87.
Filmographie sélective: *Le Jazz, un vaste complot*, C, 87, CDN, Pren son; *Québec une ville*, C, 87, CDN, Pren son; *Ontario Pop*, TV, 86, CDN, Pren son; "Country Report" (5 eps), TV, 85-86, CDN, Pren son; *Cosmique spéciale*, TV, 85, CDN, Pren son; *Getaway Special*, TV, 85, CDN, Pren son; "La semaine verte" (100 eps), TV, 74-82, CDN, Pren son; "La Femme d'aujourd'hui" (1 eps), TV, 79, CDN, Pren son; *Réunion des chefs des gouvernements du Commonwealth en Angleterre*, TV, 77, CDN, Pren son; "La Femme d'aujourd'hui" (1 eps), TV, 77, CDN, Pren son; *Réunion des chefs des gouvernements du Commonwealth en Jamaïque*, TV, 75, CDN, Pren son; *Cour Suprême du Canada*, TV, 75, CDN, Pren son; "La Femme d'aujourd'hui" (3 eps), TV, 75, CDN, Pren son; *Réunion des chefs des gouvernements du Commonwealth au Canada*, TV, 73, CDN, Pren son.

BEAUCHEMIN, Serge
STCQ, ACCT. 650, de lEpée, Outremont, PQ H2V 3T8 (514)276-5126.
Types de production et générique: l métrage-Pren son; c métrage-Pren son; TV film-Pren son; TV vidéo-Pren son.
Types d'oeuvres: Drame-C; Comédie-C&TV; Documentaire-C; Enfants-C&TV.
Curriculum vitae: Né en 1942, Montréal, Québec. Langues: français et anglais. Baccalauréat en Pédagogie et Brevet d'enseignement, Université de Montréal, 65. Prix pour Meilleur Son et Montage Son, Palmarès du Film canadien, *Le Règne du jour*, 68, *Les Philarmonistes*, 71, *L'Age de la machine*, 78; nomination au Génie, Meilleur Son, *La Guerre des tuques*, 85.
Filmographie sélective: *King's Ransom*, TV, 91, CDN, Op son; *Montréal OFF*, C, 91, CDN, Op son; *Une Nuit a l'Ecole*, TV, 91, CDN, Op son; *L'Ange Noir (Nelligan)*, C, 90, CDN, Op son; *Vaclav Havel*, TV, 90, CDN, Op son; *Amoureux Fou*, C, 90, CDN, Op son; *Une Histoire Inventée*, C, 90, CDN, Op son; *Rafales*, C, 90, CDN, Op son; *Le Party*, C, 89, CDN, Op son/Conc son; *Comment faire l'amour avec un nègre sans se fatiguer*, C, 88, CDN, Op son/Conc son; *The Dumb Waiter*, C, 88, CDN, Op son/Conc son; *La guerre des tuques*, C, 85, CDN, Op son/Conc son; *Le confort et l'indifférence*, C, 81, CDN, Op son/Conc son; *L'Age de la machine*, C, 78, CDN, Op son/Conc son; *Film Olympique*, C, 76, CDN, Op son/Conc son.

BOOK, Don
550 Jarvis St., #123, Toronto, ON M4Y 1N6 (416)922-2034.
Type of Production and Credits: Th Film-Snd Mix/Snd Rec; Th Short-Snd Mix/Snd Rec; TV Film-Snd Mix/Snd Rec;

TV Video-Snd Mix/Snd Rec.
Genres: Drama-Th&TV; Documentary-Th&TV; Commercials-Th&TV; Industrial-Th&TV.
Biography: Born 1950, North Bay, Ontario. Freelance audio recording and mixing since 1973.
Selected Filmography: Toyota, Cm, 91, CDN, Snd Mix/Snd Rec; Chrysler, Cm, 91, CDN, Snd Mix/Snd Rec; Honda, Cm, 91, CDN, Snd Mix/Snd Rec; Bank of Montreal, Cm, 91, CDN, Snd Mix/Snd Rec; The Toronto-Dominion Bank, Cm, 91, CDN, Snd Mix/Snd Rec; United Financial Services, Cm, 91, CDN, Snd Mix/Snd Rec; Toronto Hospital, Cm, 91, CDN, Snd Mix/Snd Rec; Motorola, Cm, 91, CDN, Snd Mix/Snd Rec; Toronto Symphony, Cm, 91, CDN, Snd Mix/Snd Rec; "The Bo" - Giles Blunt, Cm, 91, CDN, Snd Mix/Snd Rec; Chrysler Dealers, Cm, 88, CDN, Snd Mix/Snd Rec; Investors Group (2 cms), Cm, 88, CDN, Snd Mix/Snd Rec; *Margaret Atwood*, "Realities", TV, 88, CDN, Snd Mix/Snd Rec; "Consumers Gas" (3 eps), In, 88, CDN, Snd Mix/Snd Rec; "Bank of Montreal" (2 eps), In, 88, CDN, Snd Mix/Snd Rec.

BUCHANAN, Jack
Wiarton, ON N0H 2T0 (519)534-4628.
Type of Production and Credits: Th Film-Snd Mix; Th Short-Snd Rec; TV Film-Snd Rec Wiarton, ON N0H 2T0 (519)534-4628.
Genres: Drama-Th&TV; Musical-Th&TV; Children's-TV; Experimental-Th.
Biography: Born in 1957; Canadian citizenship. Trained and worked as camera repair mechanic; stage musician; road manager.
Selected Filmography: *Stepping Razor* (Bush Doctor, Peter Tosh), Th, 91, CDN, Snd Rec; *The Big Slice*, Th, 90, CDN, Snd Rec; *Thick as Thieves*, Th, 89, CDN, Snd Rec; *Beautiful Dreamers*, Th, 89, CDN, Boom; *Blind Fear*, Th, 88, CDN, Snd Rec; *Crazy Horse*, Th, 88, CDN, Snd Rec; "The Return of Hickey", TV, 87, CDN/USA, Snd Rec; *A Child's Christmas in Wales*, TV, 87, CDN/USA/GB, Boom; *Milk and Honey*, Th, 87, CDN, Snd Rec/Boom; *Blindside*, Th, 87, CDN, Boom; "Really Weird Tales" (3 eps), TV, 86, CDN/USA, Boom; *Legs of the Lame*, TV, 86, CDN, Boom; "Ray Bradbury Theatre" (4 eps), TV, 84-85, CDN, Boom; *Miracle at Moreaux*, TV, 85, CDN, Boom; "Sharon, Lois and Bram's Elephant Show" (26 eps), TV, 84-85, CDN, Boom.

BURKE, Dennis
- see COMPOSERS

CARWARDINE, D. Bruce
IATSE 873. 90 Balsam Ave., Toronto, ON M4E 3B7 (416)690-4755. Cairn Sound Inc., 90 Balsam Ave., Toronto, ON M4E 3B7 (416)690-4755.
Type of Production and Credits: Th Film-Prod Snd Mix; TV Film-Prod Snd Mix.
Genres: Drama-Th&TV; Comedy-Th&TV; Musical-Th&TV; Action-Th&TV.
Biography: Born in Ottawa in 1954. Canadian citizen. Nominated for a Genie for *Ticket To Heaven*. Winner of a Genie for *One Magic Christmas* and *The Terry Fox Story*.
Selected Filmography: *Body Parts*, Th, 91, USA, Snd Mix; *Stepping Out*, Th, 90, USA/GB, Snd Mix; *FX 2*, Th, 90, USA, Snd Mix; *Stella*, Th, 89, USA, Snd Mix; *Immediate Family*, Th, 89, USA, Snd Mix; *Dream Team*, Th, 88, USA, Snd Mix; *January Man*, Th, 88, USA, Snd Mix; *A New Life*, Th, 87, USA, Snd Mix; *Dead of Winter*, Th, 86, USA, Snd Mix; *One Magic Christmas*, Th, 85, CDN/USA, Snd Mix, (GENIE); *Terry Fox Story*, Th, 82, CDN, Snd Mix, (GENIE); *Ticket To Heaven*, Th, 81, CDN, Snd Mix/Snd Ed.

CLARK, Alison
- see SOUND EDITORS

CLEMENTS, Peter
ACFC, NABET 700. 27 Elmer Ave., Toronto, ON M4L 3R6 (416)690-2656.
Type of Production and Credits: Th Film-Prod Snd Mix; Th Short-Prod Snd Mix; TV Film-Prod Snd Mix; TV Video-Prod Snd Mix.
Genres: Drama-Th&TV; Comedy-Th&TV; Action-Th; Documentary-TV; Music Video-Th&TV.
Biography: Worked as the Production Sound Mixer for *Abducted* which was nominated for a Genie for Best Sound.
Selected Filmography: *The Events Leading Up To My Death*, Th, 90, CDN, Prod Snd Mix; "Chemical Solutions" (2 eps), TV, 90, CDN, Prod Snd Mix; "Top Cops" (1 eps), TV, 90, CDN/USA, Prod Snd Mix; *Hot Licks*, TV, 90, CDN, Prod Snd Mix; "Saying Goodbye" (4 eps), TV, 89-90, CDN, Prod Snd Mix; *Destiny To Order*, Th, 88, CDN, Prod Snd Mix; *Skin*, TV, 88, CDN, Prod Snd Mix; *Rock Around the Clock*, TV, 88, CDN, Prod Snd Mix; "War of the Worlds" (5 eps), TV, 88-89, CDN/USA, Prod Snd Mix; "Les Ambassadeurs" (12 eps), TV, 86, CDN, Prod Snd Mix; *Babar and Father Christmas*, TV, 86, CDN, Re-record Mix; *Abducted*, Th, 86,

CDN, Prod Snd Mix; "W5" (40 eps), TV, 83-84, CDN, Snd Rec.

CLYNE, Dale
- see POSTPRODUCTION SOUND MIXERS

COHEN, Donald
STCVQ, ACFC. 76 Somerville, Westmount, PQ H3Z 1J5 (514)489-4064.
Type of Production and Credits: Th Film-Snd Rec; Th Short-Snd Rec; TV Film-Snd Rec; TV Video-Snd Rec.
Genres: Drama-Th&TV; Comedy-Th&TV; Action-Th&TV; Horror-Th&TV.
Biography: Born in 1951 in Montreal, Quebec. Canadian citizen. Languages: English and French. BFA, Concordia University, 1977. Professional notes: Picture and sound editing, sound mixes, transfers, projection 16/35mm, audio visual.
Selected Filmography: "Urban Angel", TV, 90, CDN, Snd Rec; *The Quarrel*, Th, 90, CDN, Snd Rec; *If Looks Could Kill*, Th, 90, USA, Snd Rec; *White Gold*, TV, 90, USA, Snd Rec; *The Road to New Hope*, TV, 89, CDN, Snd Rec; *Pour Cent Million*, TV, 89, CDN, Snd Rec; *Justice Express*, TV, 89, CDN, Snd Rec; *The Thriller*, TV, 89, CDN, Snd Rec; *The Phone Call*, TV, 89, CDN, Snd Rec; *Enemies: A Love Story*, Th, 89, USA, Snd Rec; *Eddie & The Cruisers*, Th, 89, USA, Snd Rec; *Mindfield*, Th, 89, CDN, Snd Rec; *Cannonball 3*, Th, 88, USA, Snd Rec; *Day One*, TV, 88, USA, Snd Rec; *Spies, Lies & Naked Thighs*, TV, 88, USA, Snd Rec.

FRENCH, Stuart
ACFC, NABET. 298 Riverside Dr., Toronto, ON M6S 4B2 (416)766-6177.
Type of Production and Credits: Th Film-Snd Mix/Snd Rec; Th Short-Snd Mix/Snd Rec; TV Film-Snd Mix/Snd Rec; TV Video-Snd Mix/Snd Rec.
Genres: Drama-Th&TV; Documentary-TV; Industrial-TV; Current Affairs-TV.
Biography: Born in 1944 in England; Canadian and British citizenship. Languages: English, some French and German. Graduate of London Film School, England. Extensive list of credits includes work on documentaries, public affairs TV.
Selected Filmography: *Tribal Wisdom & the Modern World*, "Millennium" (10 eps), TV, 89-91, GB/CDN/US, Snd Rec; *Where the Spirit Lives*, Th&TV, 88, GB/CDN, Snd Mix; *By the Seat of Their Pants - Flying in Canada's North*, TV, 88, CDN/GB, Snd Rec; *Vista - Electronic Jam*, TV, 88, CDN, Snd Rec; *Flying On Her Own*, TV, 88, CDN, Snd Rec; *Anne of Green Gables - The Sequel*, TV, 87, CDN/GB/D, Snd Mix; *The Making of an Opera*, TV, 87, CDN, Snd Rec; "The Canadians" (2 eps), TV, 87, CND, Snd Rec; *Anne of Green Gables*, TV, 87, CDN/GB/D, Snd Mix; "Ray Bradbury Theatre" (3 eps), TV, 86, CDN, Snd Mix; "Spirit Bay" (8 eps), TV, 85-86, CDN, Snd Mix; "Phillip Marlowe, Private Eye" (4 eps), TV, 85, CDN, Snd Mix; "Night Heat" (6 eps), TV, 85, CDN, Snd Mix; "Tales of the Klondike" (6 eps), TV, 84, CDN/GB/D, Snd Mix; *John Huston's Dublin*, "Cities", TV, 84, CDN, Snd Rec.

FRICKER, Brock
AES. Brock Sound Productions, 576 Manning Avenue, Toronto, ON M6G 2V9 (416)534-7464.
Type of Production and Credits: Th Film-Snd Rec/Snd Ed/Comp; TV Film-Snd Rec/Comp; TV Video-Snd Rec/Comp.
Genres: Drama-Th&TV; Science Fiction-Th&TV; Horror-Th&TV; Industrial-Th.
Biography: Born in 1952 in Chatham, Ontario. Sixteen years audio engineering and production experience; seminar coordinator for Toronto Recording Association for 5 years; numerous film and album credits; has worked extensively on commercials.
Selected Filmography: *Shuttle Command*, TV, 88, CDN, Comp/Co-Snd Rec; *Don't Look Cow*, TV, 88, CDN, Comp/Co-Snd Rec; *Perfectly Sane*, TV, 88, CDN, Comp/Co-Snd Rec; *Xerox*, In, 88, CDN, Comp/Co-Snd Rec; *Chambers of Terror*, Th, 87, CDN, Comp/Co-Snd Rec; *Fight Back*, TV, 87, CDN, Comp/Co-Snd Rec; *The Visitor*, TV, 87, CDN, Comp/Co-Snd Rec; *American Express*, In, 87, CDN, Comp/Co-Snd Rec; *R.T. Kelly*, In, 87, CDN, Comp-Co-Snd Rec; *Bell Cellular*, In, 86, CDN, Comp/Co-Snd Rec; *Transamerica Life*, In, 86, CDN, Comp/Co-Snd Rec; *Psychodrama*, ED, 85, CDN, Comp/Co-Snd Rec; *General Foods*, In, 85, CDN, Comp/Co-Snd Rec; *The Simulator Challenge*, In, 84, CDN, Comp/Co-Snd Rec; *IBM Corporation*, In, 84, CDN, Comp/Co-Snd Rec.

GAMBLE, Victor
ACFC. The Gamble Group, P.O. Box 928, Stn. F, Toronto, ON M4Y 2N9 (416)423-8899.
Type of Production and Credits: Th Short-Snd Rec; TV Film-Snd Rec; TV Video-Snd Rec.
Genres: Drama-TV; Documentary-TV; Educational-TV; Children's-TV.

Biography: Born 1947, Halifax, Nova Scotia; Canadian and British citizenship. Diploma, Film Production, Conestoga College, 73; Diploma, Advertising and Promotion, Algonquin College, 71. Experienced in all areas of production, including Production assistant, story ideas for "Behind the Scenes," co-producer of radio spots for Words and Music Organization; sound recordist for public affairs programs, 73-88, "W5," "Maclear," "the fifth estate," and for many educational and special features, 78-81; recordist and postproduction effects for TV commercials, including Yardley, Toyota, since 76; specializes in travel documentary and has worked as sound recordist in many locations including Haiti, India, Ghana, Mali, Philippines, China, Ecuador and Chile. Received Best Sound awards for *Imperial Oil Explorations* and *David Milne: A Path of His Own*.
Selected Filmography: *Scotia Plaza*, In, 87-88, CDN, Snd Rec; "Museum Heroes" (pilot), TV, 88, CDN, Snd Rec; *Those Roos Boys*, TV, 87, CDN, Snd Rec; "Owl TV" (3 eps)(loc drama, studio video, loc travel), TV, 85-87, CDN, Snd Rec; *Immigration Hong Kong*, Th, 87, CDN, Snd Rec; *The Joy of Stress*, In, 86, CDN, Snd Rec; *Stand Up for Ontario*, In, 86, CDN, Snd Rec; *Toronto Ethnic Neighbourhoods*, TV, 84, GB, Snd Rec; "The Kids of Degrassi Street" (17 eps), TV, 82-83, CDN, Snd Rec; *Famous People Players in China*, TV, 82, CDN, Snd Rec; *Jimmy and Luke*, TV, 82, CDN, Snd Rec; *The World According to Nicholas*, TV, 81, CDN, Snd Rec; "Live It Up", TV, 79-81, CDN, Snd Rec; "Morocco", TV, 80, CDN, Snd Rec; *Dar Robinson, CN Tower Jump*, TV, 80, USA, Snd Rec.

GANDOL, Pedro B.
- see DIRECTORS

GANTON, Douglas
IATSE. 5 Third St., Wards Island, Toronto, ON M5J 2B1 (416)368-0847. Pinedene Pictures Inc., 52 Stewart St., Toronto, ON M5V 1H6 (416)861-0866. Julie Ganton, 52 Stewart St., Toronto, ON M5V 1H6 (416)861-0866.
Type of Production and Credits: Th Film-Snd Mix; Th Short-Snd Mix; TV Film-Snd Mix; TV Video-Snd Mix.
Genres: Drama-Th&TV.
Biography: Born in 1944 in London, England. Canadian citizen and has Canadian and British passports. Has state-of-the-art sound recording equipment. Genie nomination for Best Sound for *Millenium*. Genie Award for Best Sound in a Dramatic Program or Series for *Hoover vs. The Kennedys*
Selected Filmography: *This is My Life*, Th, 91, USA, Snd Mix; *Married To It*, Th, 90, USA, Snd Mix; *Queen of Mean: The Story of Leona Helmsley*, TV, 90, USA, Snd Mix; *The Phoenix*, Th, 90, USA, Snd Mix; *End Run*, Th, 90, USA, Snd Mix; *Perfectly Normal*, Th, 89, USA, Snd Mix; *Kissing Place*, Th, 89, USA, Snd Mix; *Lady in a Corner*, Th, 89, USA, Snd Mix; *Perfect Witness*, Th, 89, USA, Snd Mix; *The Fourth War*, Th, 89, USA, Snd Mix; *Millenium*, Th, 88, USA, Snd Mix; *Short Circuit II*, Th, 87, USA, Snd Mix; *Hoover vs. The Kennedys*, TV, 87, USA, Snd Mix, (GENIE); *Hot Shots*, Th, 87, USA, Snd Mix; *Doing Life*, Th, 87, USA, Snd Mix.

GELDART, Alan
- see SOUND EDITORS

GORBACHOW, Yuri
MPSE, ITS. 109 Mercury Rd., Rexdale, ON M9W 3H7. Masters Workshop Corp., 306 Rexdale Blvd., #7, Rexdale, ON M9W 1R6 (416)741-1312.
Type of Production and Credits: Th Film-Snd Mix/Mus Ed; TV Film-Snd Mix/Mus Ed; TV Video-Snd Mix/Mus Ed/Snd FX Ed.
Genres: Drama-Th&TV; Comedy-TV; Action-TV; Science Fiction-TV.
Biography: Born in 1962 in Ottawa, Ontario. A graduate of Fanshawe College, recording engineering, as well as a graduate in recorded music production (also from Fanshawe). Attended the University of Western Ontario for acoustics. M.I.D.I. programmer and keyboard player. Designer of the "S.D. System" at Masters Workshop (disk-based SFX editing and A.D.R. fitting). Member of the Audio Engineering Society (AES). Post Audio Instructor at the Harris Institute for the Arts. Remote music engineer for the Discovery Mobile. Recipient of Golden Reel awards for Best Sound Editing and Sound Design (1988 and 1989).
Selected Filmography: *Bethune - The Miniseries*, TV, 91, CDN/RC, Snd Mix; "The Simpsons" (8 eps), TV, 91, USA, Dial Rec; *Mountain Gorilla*, Imax Th, 91, CDN, Snd Mix; "My Secret Identity" (26 eps), TV, 91, CDN/USA, Snd Mix; *Switzerland*, Imax, Th, 91, CDN/CH, Snd Mix; "Dog House" (26 eps), TV, 91, CDN/USA, Snd Mix; "Profiles of Nature" (12 eps), TV, 87-91, CDN, Mus Mix; *Echoes of the Sun*, Imax, Th, 90, CDN/J, Snd Mix; "War of the Worlds" (8 eps), TV, 90, CDN/USA, Snd Mix; *The Last Buffalo*, Imax Th, 90, CDN/J, Snd Mix;

Day One, TV, 89, CDN/USA, Snd FX Ed; "Captain Power and the Soldiers of the Future" (26 eps), TV, 88, CDN/USA, SFX/Mus Ed; *Glory! Glory!*, TV, 88, CDN/USA, Mus Ed; *Glory Enough For All*, TV, 88, CDN, Mus Ed; "The Campbells" (46 eps), TV, 87, CDN/GB, Mus Ed.

GORDICA, Terry
- see POSTPRODUCTION SOUND MIXERS

HALISKIE, Brent
CFSS, ACCT. 33 Rivercourt Blvd., Toronto, ON M4J 3A3 (416)422-1367.
Type of Production and Credits: Th Short-Snd Rec; TV Film-Snd Rec; TV Video-Snd Rec.
Genres: Documentary-Th&TV; Educational-TV; Industrial-TV; Current Affairs-Th&TV.
Biography: Born 1953, Edmonton, Alberta. Graduate of Film program, Conestoga College.
Selected Filmography: "W5", TV, 78-91, CDN, Snd Rec; *Organ Donations*, ED, 87, CDN, Snd Rec; *Rapists - Can They Be Stopped?*, "America Undercover", TV, 85, CDN/USA, Snd Rec; *The First Canadian Astronaut*, TV, 84, CDN, Snd Rec.

HERMANT, Andrew S.
AFM, ACCT. 185 Frederick St., Toronto, ON M5A 4L4 (416)868-6836.
Type of Production and Credits: Th Film-Snd Rec; TV Film-Snd Rec.
Genres: Drama-Th&TV.
Biography: Born 1948, Toronto, Ontario. Attended Royal Conservatory of Music.
Selected Filmography: *Moonstruck*, Th, 87, USA, Snd Rec; *Sword of Gideon*, TV, 86, CDN, Snd Rec; *Hoax*, TV, 86, CDN, Snd Rec; *The Dream Is Alive*, Th, 85, CDN, Snd Rec; *Murder in Space*, TV, 85, CDN/USA, Snd Rec; *Hail Columbia*, Th, 82, CDN, Snd Rec; *Threshold*, Th, 80, CDN, Snd Rec; *Ticket to Heaven*, Th, 80, CDN, Snd Rec.

HIDDERLEY, Tom
ACFC, NABET, ACCT. Soundteck Productions Inc., 39 Gloucester Grove, Toronto, ON M6C 2A2 (416)787-0090.
Type of Production and Credits: Th Film-Snd Rec; TV Film-Snd Rec; TV Video-Snd Mix.
Genres: Drama-Th&TV; Documentary-Th&TV; Commercials-TV; Current Affairs-TV.
Biography: Born 1946, Cheadle, England. Spent 7 years at BBC London, including training period; 4 years in Africa with Anglo-American Corporation film unit; trained NASA astronauts in sound equipment on board shuttle for Imax film *The Dream is Alive*. Nominated for Geminis for Best Sound "The Hitchhiker" (90); *Glory !Glory!* (89); "Ustinov's Russia" (86).
Selected Filmography: "Hidden Rooms" (13 eps), TV, 91, USA/CDN, Snd Rec; "Counterstrike" (17 eps), TV, 90, USA/F/CDN, Snd Rec; "The Hitchhiker" (32 eps), TV, 89-91, USA/F/CDN, Snd Rec; *Glory! Glory!*, Th, 89, USA/CDN, Snd Rec; "Diamonds" (22 eps), TV, 87-88, USA/F/CDN, Snd Rec; *Bay Coven*, TV, 87, USA/CDN, Snd Rec; "Mariah" (7 eps), TV, 87, USA/CDN, Snd Rec; "Night Heat" (55 eps), TV, 85-86, USA/CDN, Snd Rec; "Ustinov's Russia" (6 eps), TV, 85, CDN, Snd Rec; *Heavenly Bodies*, Th, 83, CDN, Snd Rec; *Overdrawn at the Memory Bank*, Th, 83, USA/CDN, Snd Rec; *The Dream Is Alive*, Th, 85-86, USA/CDN, Snd Rec; *Hail Columbia*, Th, 82, CDN, Snd Rec; *Waiting for the Parade*, TV, 83, CDN, Snd Rec; *Improper Channels*, Th, 79, CDN, Snd Rec.

HONE, Louis
- voir MIXEURS SON POSTPRODUCTION

JOUTEL, Jean-Pierre
SONIC, ACCT. 3538 ave Prud'Homme #3, Montréal, PQ H4A 3H4 (514)486-4562. Office National Du Film, (514)283-9223.
Types de production et générique: l métrage-Mixeur/Mont son; c métrage-Mixeur/Mont son; TV film-Mixeur/Mont son.
Types d'oeuvres: Drame-C&TV; Action-C&TV; Documentaire-C&TV; Animation-C&TV.
Curriculum vitae: Né en France à Pontoise en 1940. Citoyen canadien. Langues: français et anglais. A commencé à travailler a L'O.N.F. en 1958 comme monteur sonore. Montage sonore et mixage de Labyrinth Expo '67. A mixé les films Imax *Circus World*, *The Storm*, *Transition* (3D), *Urgence*, *Benthos*, *Premier Empereur*. Aime la course automoblie, ordinateurs, musique.
Filmographie sélective: *Une Histoire Inventée*, C, 90, CDN, Mixeur; *Beautiful Dreams*, C, 90, CDN, Mixeur; *Le Déclin de l'empire américain*, C, 86, CDN, Mixeur, (GENIE); *Les Beaux Souvenirs*, C, 79, CDN, Mixeur; *The Champions*, TV, 78, CDN, Mixeur, (ETROG); *J.A. Martin, Photographe*, C, 76, CDN, Mixeur, (ETROG); *Whistling Smith*, TV, 75, CDN, Mixeur, (ETROG); *Les Males*, C, 71, CDN, Mixeur; *Deux Femmes en Or*,

C, 70, CDN, Mixeur; *Act Of The Heart*, C, 70, CDN, Mont Son, (ETROG); *Entre la mer et l'eau douce*, C, 64, CDN, Mont Son; *Yul 871*, C, 65, CDN, Mixeur; *La Corde Au Cou*, C, 64, CDN, Mont Son; *Canada At War*, TV, 61-62, CDN, Mont Son; *Nobody Waved Goodbye*, C, 62m CDN, Mont Son.

LATOUR, Daniel
ACFC, NABET 700, ACCT. Soundspeed Inc., 9 Fiesta Lane, Toronto, ON M8Y 1V3 (416)253-9997.
Type of Production and Credits: Th Film-Snd Rec; TV Film-Snd Rec.
Genres: Drama-Th&TV; Musical-Th&TV; Documentary-TV.
Biography: Born in 1949 in Montreal, Quebec. Languages: French and English. Nominated for Genies, 86 and 87, for Best Overall Sound.
Selected Filmography: "E.N.G." (pilot & 44 eps), TV, 89-91, CDN, Prod Snd; *Drop Dead Gorgeous*, TV, 91, CDN, Prod Snd; *Paroles D'Echanges*, TV, 90, CDN, Prod Snd; "My Secret Identity" (5 eps), TV, 88, CDN, Prod Snd; "Night Heat" (53 eps), TV, 87-88, CDN/USA, Prod Snd; *Too Outrageous*, Th, 87, CDN, Prod Snd; *Heaven on Earth*, TV, 86, CDN/GB, Prod Snd; *Pretty Kill*, Th, 86, USA, Prod Snd; "Ray Bradbury Theatre" (2 eps), TV, 85, CND/USA, Prod Snd; *Mafia Princess*, TV, 85, USA, Prod Snd; *The House of Dies Drear*, TV, 84, USA, Prod Snd; *The Boy in Blue*, Th, 84, CDN, Prod Snd; *When We First Met*, TV, 83, CDN, Prod Snd.

LIVINGSTON, Neal
- see DIRECTORS

LOO, Ao
AES, SMPTE. Kinovox Inc., 167 Boulton Avenue., Toronto, ON M4M 2J8 (416)465-2612.
Type of Production and Credits: TV Film-Snd Rec; TV Video-Snd Rec.
Genres: Drama-TV; Documentary-TV; Current Affairs-TV.
Biography: Born 1954, Toronto, Ontario. B.A.A., Radio and Television Arts, Ryerson Polytechnical Institute, 76. Extensive equipment package, including digital recording and signal processing, Nagra Analog Timecode Recorder, Neumann microphones and 5 channels of Micron wireless.
Selected Filmography: "Katts & Dog" (54 eps), TV, 89-91, CDN/F/USA, Prod Snd Mix; *Psychic*, Th, 90, CDN/USA, Prod Snd Mix; "Born Talking" (4 eps), TV, 90, CDN/GB, Prod Snd Mix; *Road to Kolyma*, "Hand of Stalin", TV, 90, CDN/USA/GB, Prod Snd Mix; "Friday the 13th, The Series" (28 eps), TV, 88-89, CDN/USA/GB, Prod Snd Mix; *Blood Relations*, Th, 88, CDN, Prod Snd Mix; "Return Journey" (3 eps), TV, 87-88, CDN/GB/NZ, Prod Snd Mix; "Aviation in the North" (2 eps), TV, 88, CDN/GB, Prod Snd Mix; *Juju Music*, TV, 87, CDN, Snd Mix; "Small Miracles" (4 eps), TV, 87, CDN, Prod Snd Mix; "W5", TV, 80-87, CDN, Prod Snd Mix; *Strangers in a Strange Land*, Th, 87, CDN, Prod Snd Mix; "Durrell's Russia" (6 eps), TV, 85, CDN/GB, Prod Snd Mix; *Marshall McLuhan*, TV, 83, CDN, Prod Snd Mix; *The Olden Days Coat*, TV, 81, CDN, Prod Snd Mix.

MARTIN, John
ACFC, CIFC. 56 King St., Elmira, ON N3B 2R9 (519)669-2661.
Type of Production and Credits: Th Film-Snd Rec; Th Short-Snd Rec; TV Film-Snd Rec; TV Video-Snd Rec.
Genres: Drama-Th&TV; Documentary-Th&TV; Educational-Th&TV; Industrial-Th&TV; Music Video-TV; Current Affairs-TV.
Biography: Born 1952, Charlottetown, PEI; Canadian and British citizenship. Languages: English and conversational French. B.A. (Dean's List), University of Waterloo, 75. Gemini, 90 - Best Sound in a Comedy, Variety or Performing Arts Program or Series for *Carnival of Shadows*, and 89 for *Ravel*; Gemini, 88 - Best Sound in an Information Documentary Program or Series for *North to Nowhere - Quest for the Pole*; Award of Merit for Sound Recording, Atlantic Film Festival, 89 for *Pelts: The Politics of the Fur Trade*. Also 3 additional Gemini nominations and 1 Gemeaux nomination.
Selected Filmography: *South of Wawa*, Th, 91, CDN, Loc Snd Mix; *The Hand of Stalin* (2 eps), TV, 90, CDN/GB, Loc Snd Mix; *Carnival of Shadows*, TV, 89, CDN, Loc Snd Mix; *For the Whales*, TV, 89, CDN, Loc Snd Mix; *The Radical Romantic*, TV, 89, CND, Loc Snd Mix; *Ravel*, TV, 88, CDN/F/D/E, Loc Snd Mix; *Music in the Midnight Sun*, TV, 88, CDN, Loc Snd Mix; *The Top of His Head*, Th, 88, CDN, Loc Snd Mix; *North to Nowhere*, TV, 87, CDN, Loc Snd Mix; *Fanfares*, TV, 87, CDN, Loc Snd Mix; *Spacewatch*, TV, 87, CDN, Loc Snd Mix; *Masterclass with Menuhin*, TV, 87, CDN, Loc Snd Mix; *Pelts*, TV, 88, CDN, Loc Snd Mix; *World Drums*, TV, 86, CDN, Loc Snd Mix.

MATHER, Tom
ACFC, ACCT. Xanadu Sound Services

Inc., 37 Cavell Avenue., Toronto, ON M4K 1L5 (416)463-9825.
Type of Production and Credits: Th Film-Snd Rec; Th Short-Snd Rec; TV Film-Snd Rec; TV Video-Snd Rec.
Genres: Drama-Th&TV; Comedy-Th&TV; Documentary-Th&TV; Current Affairs-TV.
Biography: Born 1955, North Bay, Ontario. Studied at University of Western Ontario; left to work in film business; was employed in various capacities including propsman, production assistant and assistant director. Interest in sound led to work as a boom operator for 2 years. Has worked as freelance and contract sound mixer since 78; incorporated as Xanadu Sound Services in 81.
Selected Filmography: "Manic Mansion" (22 eps), TV, 90-91, USA, Loc Snd Mix; "War of the Worlds", TV, 89, CDN/USA, Loc Snd Mix; "The Twilight Zone" (30 eps), TV, 88, CDN/USA, Loc Snd Mix; *On Tidy Endings*, TV, 88, CDN/USA, Loc Snd Mix; "Adderly" (44 eps), TV, 86-87, CDN, Loc Snd Mix; *Covert Action*, TV, 86, CDN, Loc Snd Mix; *As Is*, TV, 86, CDN, Loc Snd Mix; *The Incredible Time Travels*, TV, 85-86, CDN/USA, Loc Snd Mix; *Letting Go*, TV, 85, USA, Loc Snd Mix; *The Mark of Cain*; *By Our Own Hands*, TV, 85, CDN, Loc Snd Mix; "The Frantics" (13 eps), TV, 85, CDN, Loc Snd Mix; *Starcrossed*, TV, 84, USA, Loc Snd Mix; *The Last Polka*, TV, 84, USA, Loc Snd Mix; *Youngblood*, Th, 84, USA, Loc Snd Mix.

McCLEMENT, Doug
AES. 787 Adelaide St. W., Toronto, ON M6J 1B3 (416)868-0713. Comfort Sound, 26 Soho St., Suite 309, Toronto, ON M5T 1Z9 (416)593-7992.
Type of Production and Credits: Th Film-Snd Rec; TV Film-Snd Mix; TV Video-Snd Mix.
Genres: Variety-Th&TV; Musical-Th&TV; Children's-Th&TV; Music Video-Th&TV.
Biography: Born in1953 in Kingston, Ontario. Honours B.Comm., Queen's University, 1975. Established Comfort Sound, a 24-track audio post production facility. Operates a 24-track audio mobile for concert and television specials recording. Has over 900 location recordings to his credit including radio and television specials, film soundtracks, telethons, awards shows and live broadcasts. Has built temporary sound studios across Canada, on a moving train, and in Nigeria to record television specials.
Selected Filmography: "Big Ticket Special" (60 eps), TV, 81-91, CDN, Prod Snd/Mus Ed; *Easter Seals Superthon*, TV, 86/87/91, CDN, Prod Snd; "The 12 Steps" (13 eps), TV, 91, CDN, Prod Snd Ed; "The Super Dave Osborne Show" (13 eps), TV, 90-91, USA, Prod Snd; "Sharon, Lois & Bram's Elephant Show" (52 eps), TV, 87-91, CDN/USA, Prod Snd; *Genie Awards*, TV, 84/90, CDN, Prod Snd; *Gemini Awards*, TV, 87/88/90, CDN, Prod Snd; *Canadian Music Video Awards*, TV, 89/90, CDN, Prod Snd; *Mariposa 90*, TV, 90, USA, Prod Snd; "La nuit sur l'Etang" (26 eps), TV, 87-90, CDN, Prod Snd; *Raffi In Concert*, TV, 89, USA, Prod Snd; *Juju Music*, Th, 87, CDN, Prod Snd/Mus Ed; *Martin Short's Concerts for the Americas*, TV, 87, USA, Prod Snd; *Variety Club Telethon*, TV, CDN, Prod Snd; "In Session" (26 eps), TV, CDN, Prod Snd.

McKAY, Arthur C.
ACFC. 1555 Lemarchont St., Halifax, NS B3H 3R2 (902)429-6921
Type of Production and Credits: Th Film-Boom; Th Short-Snd Mix; TV Film-Snd Mix; TV Video-Snd Mix/Boom.
Genres: Drama-TV; Documentary-TV; Commercials-TV; Industrial-TV.
Biography: Born 1952, Nova Scotia. B.A., Sociology and English, Dalhousie University. Founding member of Atlantic Filmmakers' Co-op, N.S. Photo Co-op. Freelancing for NFB since 74. Has been involved in all sizes of video production, location sound recording, booming, lighting for all types of shoots; also, research, post-sync effects, Foley and theatre control room acoustics. Won award for Best Sound Recording for *Pelts, Politics and the Fur Trade*, Atlantic Film Festival, 1989. *Room at the Back* won Best Short Drama, Atlantic Film Fesitval, 1990.
Selected Filmography: *Kwa'nu'te' - Micmac and Maliseet Artists*, TV, 91, CDN, Snd Mix; *Children's Rainforest of Costa Rica*, TV, 90, CDN, Snd Mix; *Room at the Back*, TV, 90, CDN, Snd Mix; *Trick or Treasure*, TV, 90, CDN, Boom; *Pelts, Politics and the Fur Trade*, TV, 89, CDN, Snd Mix; "Family Matters" (1 eps), TV, 88, CDN, Snd Rec; *Integrating Nicholas*, ED, 88, CDN, Snd Rec; *The Church and the Hearth*, ED, 87, CDN, Snd Rec; *The Ballad of South Mountain*, ED, 86, CDN, Snd Rec; *Enterprising Women*, ED, 86, CDN, Snd Rec; *Reference Checking/Interviewing*, In, 85, CDN, Snd Rec; *The Last Log Drive*, ED, 85, CDN, Boom; *Seeing Ourselves*, TV, 84, CDN,

Snd Rec; *In Love and Anger, Milton Acorn Poet*, ED, 84, CDN, Snd Rec; *Labour of Love*, TV, 84, CDN, Boom; *Alden Nowlan, Port*, ED, 83, CDN, Snd Rec.

McKEOWN, Terence
- see COMPOSERS

MEGILL, John Peter
ACFC, ACCT. 87 Wroxeter Ave., Toronto, ON M4J 1E7 (416)465-2932. FAX: 465-2932.
Type of Production and Credits: Th Film-Snd Mix/Snd Rec; Th Short-Snd Mix/Snd Rec; TV Film-Snd Mix/Snd Rec; TV Video-Snd Mix/Snd Rec.
Genres: Drama-Th&TV; Documentary-Th&TV; Commercials-Th&TV; Industrial-Th&TV.
Biography: Born in 1945 in Northern Ontario. B.A.A., Photographic Arts (Motion Picture major), Ryerson Polytechnical Institute, 67. Photographer and sound technician, McLaughlin Planetarium, 69-70; Toronto Film Lab sound technician, mixing news specials and sound transfers, 68-70; freelance sound recordist since 71. *Glory Enough for All* and *The Playground* each won a Gemini for Best Sound in a Drama.
Selected Filmography: *Ice Princess*, Th, 90, CDN/USA, Snd Mix; *Sam & Me/Waiting for Baldev*, Th, 90, CDN, Snd Mix; *Deep Sleep*, Th, 90, CDN, Snd Mix; *Beautiful Dreamers*, Th, 89, CDN, Snd Mix; *Cold Comfort*, Th, 88-89, CDN, Snd Mix; *Glory Enough for All* (mini-series), TV, 87, CDN, Snd Mix; *The Truth About Alex*, TV, 86, USA, Snd Mix; *The Playground*, "Ray Bradbury Theatre", TV, 85, USA/CDN, Snd Mix.

MITCHELL, Brian
- see POSTPRODUCTION SOUND MIXERS

MONK, Roger J.
- see SOUND EDITORS

MORRONE, Frank
45 Sellmar Rd., Etobicoke, ON M9P 3E7 (416)242-3701. Master's Workshop Corp., 306 Rexdale Blvd., Rexdale, ON M9W 1R6 (416)741-1312.
Type of Production and Credits: Th Film-Snd Mix; TV Film-Snd Mix; Th Short-Snd Mix; TV Video-Snd Mix.
Genres: Drama-Th&TV; Action-Th&TV; Documentary-Th&TV; Music Video-Th&TV.
Biography: Born 1955, Toronto, Ontario. Graduate of DeVry Institute of Technology, 76. Started as music engineer, recording music for several film scores including *Murder by Decree, Prom Night, Melanie* and *Porky's*. Experienced in post production sound mixing. Awards include Golden Reel, 90 from the Motion Picture Sound Editors, Hollywood for "My Secret Identity", Gemini, 89 for *Glory Enough for All*; Gemini nomination, 87 and Golden Reel, 87 for *Ford: The Man and the Machine*; Golden Reel, 87 for "Captain Power and the Soldiers of Fortune"; Silver Award, 84 (New York Film Festival), *Profiles of Nature*. Currently senior re-recording mixer at Master's Workshop in Toronto.
Selected Filmography: *Bethune*, Th, 91, CDN/RC, Re-record Mix; *Black Robe*, Th, 91, AUS, ADR Rec; "My Secret Identity" (26 eps), TV, 91, CDN/USA, Re-record Mix; "Dracula, The Series" (26 eps), TV, 90, USA, Re-record Mix; "War of the Worlds" (22 eps), TV, 90, USA, Re-record Mix; *Glory Enough for All* (mini-series), TV, 89, CDN, Re-record Mix; "Chasing Rainbows" (14 eps), TV, 87-88, CDN, Re-record Mix; "Captain Power and the Soldiers of Fortune" (13 eps), TV, 87, USA, Re-record Mix; *Ford: The Man and the Machine* (mini-series), TV, 87, CDN, Re-record Mix/Dial Engin; *Jim Henson Muppet Family Christmas*, TV, 87, USA, Re-record Mix; "Woman of the World" (14 eps), TV, 87, USA, Re-record Mix/Mus Ed/Dial Ed; *Muppets - A Christmas Toy*, TV, 86, USA, Re-record Mix; *Tears Are Not Enough*, Th, 85, CDN, Mus Ed; "The Campbells" (100 eps), 83-85, CDN/GB/USA, Re-record Mix; *Murder by Decree*, Th, 79, CDN, Mus Engin.

PELLERIN, Daniel
- see POSTPRODUCTION SOUND MIXERS

ROUARD, Jean-Michel
STCQ. 564 rue Birch, St-Lambert, PQ J4P 2N1 (514)672-6837.
Types de production et générique: l métrage-Mix Son; C métrage-Mix Son; TV film-Mix Son.
Types d'oeuvres: Drame-C&TV; Documentaire-C&TV; Annonces-C&TV; Industriel-C&TV.
Curriculum vitae: Né en 1946 à Paris, France. Langue: français. Ecole de cinéma, Paris. Ingénieur du son, mixeur pour drames, documentaires, annonces et films industriels en film et vidéo.
Filmographie sélective: *Blake*, C, 89, CDN, Ing son; *Gilles Villeneuve*, C, 85, CDN, Ing son; *Arabie Saoudite*, C, 82, CDN, Ing son; *Black Mirror*, C, 80, CDN/F, Ing son; *Une journée particulière*, C, 77, CDN/I, Ing son; *La nuit de la marée haute/La Notte Dell'Alta Marea*, C, 76,

CDN/I, Ing son; *Y'a plus de trous à percer*, C, 69, CDN, Ing son.

ROWAN, Patrick
- see ART DIRECTORS

SCHERER, Karl
- see CINEMATOGRAPHERS

SENGMUELLER, Fred
NABET. R.R. #1, Sharon, ON L0G 1V0 (416)478-2218.
Type of Production and Credits: Th Film-Snd Rec; TV Film-Snd Mix.
Genres: Drama-Th&TV; Documentary-Th&TV; Educational-Th&TV; Commercials-Th.
Biography: Born 1927, Austria; Canadian citizenship. Languages: German, French and English. Electronic engineer, studio mixer, location recording engineer, directed laser-videodisc productions for General Motors on technical subjects; on-air mixing for CTV at Sarajevo, Lake Placid, Montreal; location recording for features, docudramas and commercials in 16 and 35 mm film and on video.

SEREDA, John
- see COMPOSERS

SHEWCHUK, Peter
IATSE 873, ACCT. P.O. Box 70, Bethany, ON L0A 1A0 (705)277-2474.
Type of Production and Credits: Th Film-Snd Mix/Snd Rec; TV Film-Snd Mix/Snd Rec.
Genres: Drama-Th&TV; Commercials-TV; Music Video-TV.
Biography: Born 1939, Kenora, Ontario. Studied Electronics, DeVry Institute, Toronto. Worked for many years at CBC; now freelance. *Termini Station* was nominated for Genie, Best Sound.
Selected Filmography: "Sweating Bullets" (22 eps), TV, 90-91, CDN/USA/MEX, Snd Mix; *Car 54, Where Are You?*, TV, 90, USA, Snd Mix; *Anne of Green Gables* (mini-series), TV, 89, CDN, Snd Mix; *Welcome Home*, Th, 88, USA, Snd Mix; *Termini Station*, Th, 88, CDN, Snd Mix; *Criminal Law*, Th, 87, USA, Snd Mix; "Force III" (pilot), TV, 86, USA, Snd Mix; *The Liberators*, Th, 86, USA, Snd Mix; *Burnin' Love*, Th, 86, USA, Snd Mix; *Many Happy Returns*, TV, 86, USA, Snd Mix; *Apology*, TV, 85, USA, Snd Mix; *Killer Party*, Th, 84, USA, Snd Mix; *Head Office*, Th, 84, USA, Snd Mix; *Terminal Choice*, Th, 82, CDN, Snd Mix; *Class of 84*, Th, 81, CDN, Snd Mix.

STEWART, Douglas Thane
IATSE 873. 526 Westwood Dr., Cobourg, ON K9A 4P7 (416)399-1315.
Type of Production and Credits: Th Film-Snd Mix; TV Film-Snd Mix; TV Video-Snd Mix/Boom.
Genres: Drama-Th&TV; Comedy-Th&TV; Variety-Th&TV.
Biography: Born 1943; Canadian citizen. Twenty years in the industry: sound/audio/boom operator in film and tape for numerous commercials; boom operator, "SCTV," several years; time code experience.
Selected Filmography: *Love and Murder*, Th, 88, CDN, Prod Snd; *Knightwatch*, TV, 88, CDN, 2nd Unit Prod Snd; *Sing*, Th, 88, CDN, 2nd Unit Prod Snd; *The Ann Jillian Story*, TV, 87, USA, Prod Snd; *PArents*, Th, 87, CDN, Prod Snd; *Haunted by Her Past*, Th, 87, USA, Prod Snd; *Fight for Life*, TV, 87, USA, Prod Snd; *Police Academy IV*, Th, 86, USA, 2nd Unit Prod Snd.

SVAB, Peter
- see EDITORS

THOMSON, John J.
ACFC. 31 Hampton Ave., Toronto, ON M4K 2Y5 (416)465-9752.
Type of Production and Credits: Th Film-Snd Mix/Snd Rec; Th Short-Snd Mix/Snd Rec; TV Film-Snd Mix/Snd Rec; TV Video-Snd Mix/Snd Rec.
Genres: Drama-Th&TV; Comedy-TV; Documentary-TV; Children's-TV.
Biography: Born 1950, Winnipeg, Manitoba. B.A., University of Toronto; Theatre Technology, McMillan Theatre, University of Toronto; Josef Svoboda Scenography Master Classes, Banff School of Fine Arts; RIA Recording Techniques course, Phase One Recording Studio. Eight years experience in all forms of theatrical stage production.
Selected Filmography: "Top Cops" (23 eps), TV, 90-91, CDN/USA, Snd Mix; "Magic Hour" (9 eps), TV, 89-90, CDN, Snd Mix; *The Last Winter*, Th, 89, CDN, Snd Mix; "Men" (7 eps), TV, 88-89, CDN/USA, Snd Mix; "War of the Worlds" (11 eps), TV, 88, CDN/USA, Snd Mix; *Palais Royale*, Th, 87, CDN, Snd Mix; "Sharon, Lois & Bram's Elephant Show" (40 eps), TV, 84-87, CDN, Snd Mix; "Ramona" (13 eps), TV, 87, CDN/USA, Snd Mix; *Niagara - Miracles, Myths and Magic* (Imax), Th, 86, CDN/USA, Snd Mix; *Passion*, TV, 86, CDN, Snd Mix; "SCTV" (53 eps), TV, 84-86, CDN/USA, Snd Mix; "Frontiers" (4 eps), TV, 85, CDN/GB/F, Snd Mix; *The Kidnapping of Baby John Doe*, Th, 85, CDN, Snd Mix; *Skullduggery*, Th, 84, CDN/USA, Snd Mix; *The War Boy*, Th, 84, CDN/YU, Snd Mix.

VADNAY, Gabor

ACCT, ACFC, STCQ. 155 - 52nd Ave., Lachine, PQ H8T 2X1 (514)639-1079.
Type of Production and Credits: Th Film-Snd Rec/Snd Mix; TV Film-Snd Rec/Snd Mix.
Genres: Drama-Th&TV; Horror-Th&TV; Documentary-Th&TV; Commercials-TV.
Biography: Born in 1953 in Budapest, Hungary; Canadian citizen. Languages: English, French and Hungarian. B.A., Concordia University, 77. Has taught part-time for 6 years at Concordia University (technical course on sound recording for 2nd-year Cinema program).
Selected Filmography: *The Takeover - Scanners III*, Th, 90, CDN, Prod Snd Mix; "Dracula - The Series" (20 eps), TV, 90, CDN/USA/L, Prod Snd Mix; *Whispers*, Th, 89, CDN, Prod Snd Mix; *Princes in Exile*, Th, 89, CDN, Prod Snd Mix; *Le Marche du Couple*, TV, 89, CDN, Prod Snd Mix; *L'abime du rêve*, TV, 89, CDN, Prod Snd Mix; *Dracula - Live from Transylvania*, TV, 89, CDN/USA, Prod Snd Mix; *Dead Man Out*, Th, 88, CDN/USA, Loc Snd Mix; "Friday the 13th, The Series" (26 eps), TV, 87-88, CDN/USA, Loc Snd Mix; "War and Remembrance" (Cdn seg), TV, 87, CDN/USA, Loc Snd Mix; "Women of the World" (7 eps), TV, 87, CDN/USA, Loc Snd Mix; *Shahira*, TV, 87, CDN, Loc Snd Mix; *Obsessed/Hitting Home*, Th, 86, CDN, Loc Snd Mix; *The Blue Man*, Th, 85, CDN, Loc Snd Mix.

VERMETTE, Robert
SERT. 5934 2e Ave., Montréal, PQ H1Y 2Y9 (514)728-1588. Radio-Québec, 1000 Fullum, Montréal, PQ (514)521-2424.
Types de production et générique: TV film-Pren son.
Types d'oeuvres: Drame-TV; Comédie-TV; Variété-TV.
Curriculum vitae: Né à Montréal. Citoyen canadien. Parle français. D.E.C. en électronique. 13 ans d'expérience en télévision, 10 ans en son. En nomination pour un prix Gémeaux en 1989, et prix Gémeaux en 1990, meilleur son d'ensemble émission de variétés. ("Beau et Chaud", 1990).
Filmographie sélective: *Le Fantôme de L'Opera*, TV, 91, CDN, Pren son; "Beau et Chaud", TV, 88-90, CDN, Pren son; "Station Soleil", TV, 86-87, CDN, Pren son; 'Les travaillants", TV, 85, CDN, Pren son.

WHITE, Don
ACCT. 4388 Beacon Lane, Mississauga, ON L5C 4J7 (416)848-2158. The Film House Group Inc., 424 Adelaide St. E., Toronto, ON M5A 1N4 (416)364-4321.
Type of Production and Credits: Th Film-Snd Mix; Th Short-Snd Mix; TV Film-Snd Mix; TV Video-Snd Mix.
Genres: Drama-Th&TV; Comedy-Th&TV; Science Fiction-Th&TV; Action-Th&TV; .
Biography: Born Bowmanville, Ontario. Diploma, Media Arts, Sheridan College, 73. 14 years as rerecording mixer; has worked on over 140 motion pictures. Also worked on many series and documentaries. Several nominations and awards for sound work.
Selected Filmography: *Other Peoples' Money*, Th, 91, USA, Re-record Mix; *The Naked Lunch*, Th, 91, CDN, Re-record Mix; *Perfectly Normal*, Th, 91, CDN, Re-record Mix; *Blue Planet*, Th, 90, CDN, Re-record Mix; *The Long Walk Home*, Th, 90, CDN, Re-record Mix; *Prancer*, Th, 90, USA, Re-record Mix; *In Country*, Th, 89, USA, Re-record Mix; *Dead Ringers*, Th, 88, CDN, Re-record Mix, (GENIE); *A Winter Tan*, Th, 87, CDN, Re-record Mix; *Moonstruck*, Th, 87, USA, Re-record Mix; *One Magic Christmas*, Th, 85, CDN, Re-record Mix, (GENIE); *Agnes of God*, Th, 85, USA, Re-record Mix; *Quest for Fire*, Th, 81, CDN/F, Re-record Mix, (GENIE); "Alfred Hitchcock Presents" (21 eps), TV, 88, CDN/USA, Re-record Mix; "Twilight Zone - The Series" (11 eps), TV, 88, CDN, Re-record Mix.

Publicists
Publicistes

ALEXANDER, Kelley
23 Palmerston Ave., Toronto, ON M6J 2H9 (416)941-9150. Cinephile Limited, 388 King St. W., Ste. 211, Toronto, ON M5V 1K2 (416)581-1251.
Type of Production and Credits: Th Film-Pub; Th Short-Pub; TV Film-Pub; TV Video-Prod Coord.
Genres: Drama-Th&TV; Comedy-Th&TV; Documentary-Th&TV; Animation-Th&TV.
Biography: Born in 1961 in Toronto, Ontario. Canadian citizen. B.A. from the University of Western Ontario. Has set design experience in theatre and television.
Selected Filmography: *Highway 61*, Th, 91, CDN, Pub; *Secret Nation*, Th, 91, CDN, Pub; *Masala*, Th, 91, CDN, Pub; *Smoked Lizard Lips*, Th, 90, CDN, Pub; *Swan Lake - The Zone*, Th, 90, CDN, Pub; *Eating*, Th, 90, USA, Pub; *Archangel*, Th, 90, CDN, Pub; *To Sleep With Anger*, Th, 90, USA, Pub; *Metropolitan*, Th, 90, USA, Pub; *Paris Is Burning*, Th, 90, USA, Pub; *The Killer*, Th, 89, HK, Pub; *Interrogation*, Th, 86, PL, Pub.

BAILIE, Barbara
Family Channel, 3 Mutual St., Toronto, ON M5B 2A7 (416)867-8866.
Type of Production and Credits: TV Film-Pub.
Genres: Drama-TV; Documentary-TV; Children's-TV; Animation-TV.
Biography: Born in 1951. Responsible for all Family Channel publicity since October, 1988.
Selected Filmography: *Girl From Mars*, TV, 91, CDN, Pub; "Judy Garland: The Television Classics, 1962", TV, 91, USA,

Pub; *Polar Bridge*, TV, 90, CDN, Pub; "Eric's World", TV, 90, CDN, Pub.

CUTAJAR, Susan
6 Beckwith Rd., Etobicoke, ON M9C 3X9 (416)621-5099. CTV Television Network, 42 Charles St. E., Toronto, ON M4Y 1T5 (416)928-6047.
Type of Production and Credits: TV Video-Pub.
Genres: Drama-TV; Comedy-TV; Sports-TV.
Biography: Born in Toronto, Ontario. Canadian citizen. Languages: English and French.
Selected Filmography: "Wide World of Sports", TV, 89-91, CDN, Pub; "Blue Jays Baseball", TV, 89-91, CDN, Pub; "Canadian Open Golf", TV, 89-91, CDN, Pub.

DODD, Marian
- see PRODUCERS

EASTWOOD, Janet
65 Talara Dr., #5, North York, ON M2K 1A3 (416)229-0906. CTV Television Network, 42 Charles St. E., Toronto, ON M4Y 1T5 (416)928-6033.
Type of Production and Credits: TV Video-Pub.
Genres: News-TV; Current Affairs-TV; Documentary-TV; Drama-TV.
Biography: Born in 1965 in Toronto, Ontario. Canadian citizen. B.A.A., Radio & Television Arts, Ryerson. Manager, Client Services, Columbia Pictures Television, 1987-88. News Publicist, CTV Television Network, 1989 to date.
Selected Filmography: "W5" (26 eps), TV, 89-91, CDN, Pub; "CTV News" (nightly), TV, 89-91, CDN, Pub; "Canada A.M." (daily), TV, 89-91, CDN, Pub; "Question Period" (52 eps), TV, 89-91, CDN, Pub.

EKMAN, Brian
CUPE. 40 Pleasant Blvd., Apt. 1007, Toronto, ON M4T 1J9 (416)925-0447. CBC National TV News, 354 Jarvis St., 5th Floor, TV Building, Toronto, ON M4Y 2H3 (416)975-7831.
Type of Production and Credits: TV Video-Pub.
Genres: Current Affairs-TV; News-TV.
Biography: Born in 1958 in Toronto, Ontario. Bachelor of Arts in Radio and Television Arts from Ryerson Polytechnical Institute, Toronto. Publicist for CBC National News since September 1989, representing "The National", "CBC Morning News", "Sunday Report", "Midday News" and news specials. Worked for CBC National TV News from 1981-89 as a writer/editor, assignment editor, researcher and editorial assistant.

ELLIS, Kathryn
Kathryn Ellis Associates, 65 Heward Ave., #702, Toronto, ON M4M 2T5 (416) 778-4985.
Type of Production and Credits: TV Video-Pub/Wr.
Genres: Drama-TV; Comedy-TV; Documentary-TV; Children's-TV.
Biography: Born 1955, Canada. B.A. (Hons.), Queen's University.
Selected Filmography: "Degrassi High" (28 eps), TV, 89-90, CDN/USA, Pub; "Mom P.I." (13 eps), TV, 90, CDN, Pub; *The All-nighter*, "Degrassi High", TV, 90, CDN/USA, Wr; *Just Friends*, "Degrassi High", TV, 89, CDN/USA, Wr; *The Degrassi Kids Rap on Rights*, ED, 89, CDN, Co-Wr; "Degrassi Junior High" (42 eps), TV, CDN/USA, Pub; *Twenty Bucks*, "Degrassi Junior High", TV, 88, CDN/USA, Wr; *Censored*, "Degrassi Junior High", TV, 87, CDN/USA, Wr; "Set Your Sails" (6 eps), TV, 86, CDN, Pub; *Smokescreen*, "Degrassi Junior High", TV, 86, CDN/USA, Wr; *CFTA Award-Winners*, In, 86, CDN, Wr; "Kids of Degrassi St." (11 eps), TV, 84-85, CDN, Pub.

EMERY, Prudence
Prudence Emery Publicity (PEPI) Inc., 161 Gough Ave., Toronto, ON M4K 3N9 (416)463-3105.
Type of Production and Credits: Th Film-Unit Pub; TV Film-Unit Pub.
Genres: Drama-Th&TV; Comedy-Th&TV; Musical-Th&TV; Action-Th&TV; Science Fiction-Th&TV; Horror-Th&TV.
Biography: Born in Nanaimo, B.C. Attended the University of British Columbia for two years, and the Chelsea School of Art in London, England for one year. Worked in public relations at Expo 67; was PR for the Savoy Hotel Group in London, England for five years; launched Global TV Network, the Metro Toronto Zoo and became a unit publicist in 1974. Since then has worked on nearly 60 feature films. Has also done freelance publicity in other areas such as fashion and special events.
Selected Filmography: *Naked Lunch*, Th, 91, CDN/GB, Unit Pub; *Married To It*, Th, 90, USA, Unit Pub; *If Looks Could Kill*, Th, 90, USA, Unit Pub; *South of Wawa*, Th, 90, CDN, Unit Pub; "Sweating Bullets", TV, 90, CDN/ MEX/ USA, Unit Pub; *Stella*, Th, 89, USA, Unit Pub; *Beautiful Dreamers*, Th, 89, CDN, Unit Pub; *Renegades*, Th, 88, USA, Unit Pub; *Murderers Among Us: The Simon*

Wiesenthal Story, Th, 88, US/GB/H, Unit Pub; *Dead Ringers*, Th, 88, USA, Unit Pub; *Termini Station*, Th, 88, CDN, Unit Pub; *Short Circuit II*, Th, 87, USA, Unit Pub; *Adventures in Babysitting*, Th, 87, USA, Unit Pub; *The Fly*, Th, 86, USA, Unit Pub; *Street Smart*, Th, 86, USA, Unit Pub.

EMPRY, Gino
130 Carlton St., #1508, Toronto, ON M5A 4K3 (416)977-2429. Gino Empry Public Relations, 25 Wood St., Ste. 104, Toronto, ON M4Y 2P9.
Type of Production and Credits: Th Film-Pub; TV Film-Pub; TV Video-Pub.
Genres: Drama-Th&TV; Comedy-Th&TV; Variety-TV; Musical-TV.
Biography: Born in 1949 and raised in Toronto. Graduated from St. Michael's College in 1961. In 1963, founded his public relations agency and signed his first client, the Royal Alexandra Theatre, commencing a career-long relationship with Ed Mirvish. In 1968, he became Entertainment Director/Public Relations Entertainment Consultant for the Imperial Room in the Royal York Hotel. He was Tony Bennett's manager for 10 years and currently he represents such artists as Peggy Lee, Patrick Macnee, Roger Whittaker, William Hutt, Karen Kain, André-Philippe Gagnon and Roch Voisine to name a few. His show business corporate accounts include Norman Jewison's *Moonstruck*, CPI, Famous People Players and John Lombardi, President of CHIN Radio/TV. He is a member of CPRS, ATPAM, CARAS, Toronto Theatre Alliance, American Federation of Musicians, ACCT, Stratford Shakespearean Foundation of Canada, PAPA and Variety Club of Ontario.
Selected Filmography: *Stage by Stage*, TV, 89, GB, Pub; *Moonstruck*, Th, 89, USA, Pub; *Ian and Sylvia Reunion*, TV, 88, CDN, Pub; *Case of the Shooting Stars*, TV, 88, USA, Pub; *Too Outrageous*, Th, 87, CDN, Pub; *Surfacing*, Th, 80, CDN, Pub; *Second Wind*, Th, 76, CDA, Pub.

FARB, Robin
530 Russell Hill Rd., Toronto, ON M5P 2T3 (416)483-3677. FAX: 322-7234.
Type of Production and Credits: Th Film-Pub.
Genres: Drama-Th; Comedy-Th; Variety-Th; Musical-Th; Action-Th; Science Fiction-Th; Horror-Th; Children's-Th; Animation-Th; Experimental-Th.
Biography: Born in 1956. Graduated from York University in 1979, then completed an intensive summer program in Book and Magazine Publishing at Sarah Lawrence College in New York. Background also includes: a teaching degree; 3 years in bookstore sales (during university); a stint in marketing for a book publishing company; and guest relations work at the Festival of Festivals in 1979. Natational Manager of Publicity & Promotion at Paramount Pictures Canada/Walt Disney Pictures for 6 years. VP of Publicity & Promotion for 4 years in the film distribution division of Cineplex Odeon Corp.oration. In 1989, opened her own marketing and communications company Robin Farb Promotes!
Selected Filmography: *The Last Temptation of Christ*, Th, 88, USA, Dist Pub; *The Glass Menagerie*, Th, 87, USA, Dist Pub.

FERNANDES, Eliza
18 Tangle Briarway, Willowdale, ON M2J 2M4. Columbia Tri-Star Films of Canada, 1300 Yonge St., Ste. 606, Toronto, ON M4T 2W3 (416)922-5740.
Type of Production and Credits: Th Film-Pub.
Genres: Drama-Th; Comedy-Th; Action-Th.
Biography: Manager of Publicity and Promotions for Columbia Tri-Star Films of Canada.
Selected Filmography: *Terminator 2 - Judgment Day*, Th, 91, USA, Dist Pub; *Boyz N the Hood*, Th, 91, USA, Dist Pub.

FLAHIVE, Gerry
234 Manor Rd. E., Toronto, ON M4S 1R8 (416)483-5339. National Film Board of Canada, 150 John St., Toronto, ON M5V 3C3 (416)973-9640.
Type of Production and Credits: Th Film-Pub; Th Short-Pub; TV Film-Pub.
Genres: Documentary-Th&TV; Educational-Th&TV; Children's-Th&TV; Animation-Th&TV.
Biography: Born in 1956. Graduate of York University, 1978. Film programmer and critic, 1979-81. Joined NFB in 1981 as a marketing officer. Named Ontario Publicity Co-ordinator, 1986. Publicist on dozens of launches, festival screenings and telecasts of NFB productions. Senior Communications Manager, 1990 to date.
Selected Filmography: *Karate Kids*, ED/TV, 90, CDN, Pub; *The Falls*, Th, 90, CDN, Pub.

HOLM, Judy
C/FP Distribution, 146 Bloor St. W., Stuie. 204, Toronto, ON M5S 1P3 (416) 944-0104.
Type of Production and Credits: Th Film-Dist Pub.

Genres: Drama-Th; Comedy-Th; Action-Th; Science Fiction-Th.
Biography: Canadian citizen. English with some French.
Selected Filmography: *Cyrano de Bergerac*, Th, 90, F, Dist Pub; *Lionheart*, Th, 90, USA, Dist Pub; *Beautiful Dreamers*, Th, 90, CDN, Dist Pub; *Taxi Blues*, Th, 90, F/USR, Dist Pub; *The Icicle Thief*, Th, 89, I, Dist Pub; *Trop Belle Pour Toi*, Th, 89, F, Dist Pub; *Palais Royale*, Th, 88, CDN, Pub.

JAMISON, Lorraine
Communications Encouleur Jamison Inc., 364 Parc Cartier, Montreal, PQ H4C 3A2 (514)931-6263.
Type of Production and Credits: Th Film-Pub; TV Film-Pub; TV Video-Pub.
Genres: Drama-Th; Comedy-Th; Documentary-TV; Animation-Th&TV.
Biography: Born in 1960 in Montreal, Quebec. Canadian citizen. Fluent in English and French. A graduate of Concordia University's Fine Arts program, majoring in Creative Writing, Drawing and Art History ("a cocktail party education"). Career began in 1985 with David Novek. In 1990, opened own firm, Jamison Incolour Communications Inc. Best known for her work with the Montreal World Film Festival. Began as press conference coordinator, 1986; Press Office Director, 1989; Director of Communications, 1990. Also managed press offices for the Ottawa International Animation Festival and Cités-Cinés at the Palais de la civilisation.
Selected Filmography: *After the Montreal Massacre*, "Man Alive", TV, 90, CDN, Unit Pub; *The Last Train Across Canada/Making Tracks*, "Travels", TV, 90, CDN/USA/GB, Pub; "Favorite Songs" (3 eps), TV, 90, CDN, Pub; *Falling Over Backwards*, Th, 89, CDN, Unit Pub; *Bethune: The Making of a Hero*, Th, 89, CDN/RC/F, Unit Pub; "Smoggies!" (26 eps), TV, 89, CDN/F, Pub; *Malarek: A Street Kid Who Made It*, Th, 88, CDN, Unit Pub; *Mario, Mike and Mr. Greatness*, TV, 88, CDN, Pub.

KATZ, Jeremy
867 Bathurst St., Toronto, ON M5R 3G2 (416)588-6713. Atlantis Films Limited, 65 Heward Ave., Toronto, ON M4M 2T5 (416)462-0246.
Type of Production and Credits: Th Film-Pub; TV Film-Pub.
Genres: Drama-Th&TV; Comedy-Th&TV; Children's-Th&TV; Educational-Th&TV; .
Biography: Born in 1950 in Toronto, Ontario. Canadian citizen. Graduate of University of Toronto, Arts & Literature. Publicist for NFB, Toronto, 1980-85. Publicist for all Atlantis Films Limited productions (and corporate publicity), 1985 to date.
Selected Filmography: *Kurt Vonnegut's Monkey House*, TV, 91, CDN/USA, Pub; "Maniac Mansion" (44 eps), TV, 90-91, CDN/USA, Pub; "Neon Rider" (38 eps), TV, 89-91, CDN, Pub; "Mom P.I." (25 eps), TV, 90-91, CDN, Pub; "The Ray Bradbury Theater" (65 eps), TV, 85-91, CDN/USA/NZ, Pub; *Talkin' About AIDS*, TV, 90, CDN, Pub; *Journey Into Darkness: The Bruce Curtis Story*, TV, 90, CDN, Pub; *Lost in the Barrens*, TV, 89, CDN, Pub; "The Twilight Zone" (30 eps), TV, 88, CDN/USA, Pub; *Cowboys Don't Cry*, Th/TV, 87, CDN, Pub; "Ramona" (10 eps), TV, 87, CDN/USA, Pub; *A Child's Christmas in Wales*, TV, 87, CDN/USA/GB, Pub; *90 Days*, Th, CDN, Pub; *If You Love This Planet*, ED/TV, CDN, Pub; *Not a Love Story*, ED/Th, CDN, Pub.

KAYE, Janice
RR #2, Marlbank, ON K0K 2L0 (613)478-5858.
Type of Production and Credits: Th Film-Unit Pub; TV Film-Pub; TV Video-Pub.
Genres: Drama-Th&TV; Variety-TV; Documentary-TV; Children's Th&TV.
Biography: Born in 1950 in Toronto, Ontario. Canadian citizen, also holds a British passport. Hon. Degree in Art History, University of Toronto, 1972; Hon. Degree in Film Studies, Queen's University, 1992. Has worked as an advertising copywriter. Wrote articles on TV for the national TV publication, "TV Times". Wrote the Press Book for CBC TV Fall Launch. Took 3 screenwriting courses outside formal film education. Has worked as a publicist for the Festival of Festivals.
Selected Filmography: *FX II*, Th, 90, USA, Unit Pub; *Millennium*, Th, 88, USA, Unit Pub; *Gate II*, Th, 88, USA, Unit Pub; "Alfred Hitchcock Presents" (41 eps), TV, 88, CDN/USA, Unit Pub; *Milk & Honey*, Th, 87, CDN, Unit Pub; *The Gate*, Th, 86, USA, Unit Pub; "Anne of Green Gables", TV, 84, CDN, Unit Pub; *Reckless Disregard*, TV, 84, USA, Unit Pub; "Fraggle Rock", TV, 84, CDN, Unit Pub; "The Kids of Degrassi Street", TV, 84, CDN, Unit Pub; "Wayne & Shuster International", TV, 84, CDN, Unit Pub; *A Christmas Story*, Th, 83, USA, Unit Pub; *Heartaches*, Th, 82, CDN, Rel Pub;

Meatballs, Th, 79, CDN/USA, Rel Pub; *The Silent Partner*, Th, 79, CDN, Rel Pub.

KIERANS, Genevieve
ACCT, TWIFV. 5 Geneva Ave., Toronto, ON M5A 2J9. The Publicity Company, 387 Bloor St. E., 5th Floor, Toronto, ON M4W 1H7 (416)323-1500. FAX: 323-9520. Vancouver Office: Carol Marks-George, 1771 Nelson St., Ste. 202, Vancouver, BC V6G 1M6
Type of Production and Credits: Th Film-Pub; Th Short-Pub; TV Film-Pub; TV Video-Pub.
Genres: Drama-Th&TV; Comedy-Th&TV; Variety-TV; Musical-Th&TV; Action-Th&TV; Documentary-Th&TV; Children's-TV; Experimental-Th&TV; Music Video-TV.
Biography: Born in 1959. Bilingual English/French, competent Spanish. Top graduate Marianopolis College, Montreal, Lit., Lang. & Theatre; scholarship Queen's University, Lit. & Theatre; Journalism at Ryerson. Former prof. actor. 12 years contributing journalist. Ex-officio Board of Directors, Toronto Drama Bench; Toronto Theatre Alliance & TWIFV. 8 yrs professional publicist & mktg. consultant for film, TV etc. Specialty writing.
Selected Filmography: "Road to Avonlea" (26 eps), TV, 89-91, CDN, Unit Pub/Broad Pub; *Lantern Hill*, TV, 90, CDN, Broad Pub; "Kids in the Hall", TV, 90-92, CDN, Unit Pub/Broad Pub; "Urban Angel", TV, 90-92, Unit Pub/Broad Pub; *Cross My Heart/La Fracture du Myocarde*, Th, 91, Rel Pub; *Mr. Johnson*, Th, 90, Fest Pub; *The Field*, Th, 90, Fest Pub; *After Dark, My Sweet*, Th, 90, Fest Pub; *Buster*, Th, 88, Rel Pub; *Un zoo, la nuit*, Th, 88, Fest Pub; *The Decline of the American Empire*, Th, 86, Fest Pub; *C.D. Howe: Minister of Everything*, TV, 91, Broad Pub; *The Last Winter*, Th, 90, Rel Pub; *No Blame*, Th/TV, 88, Unit Pub; *The Conserving Kingdom*, TV, 87, Broad Pub.

KONOPACKI, Margaret
20 First Ave., Toronto, ON M4M 1W7. CTV Television Network, 42 Charles St. E., Toronto, ON M4Y 1T5 (416)928-6035.
Type of Production and Credits: TV Film-Pub; TV Video-Pub.
Genres: Drama-TV; Variety-TV; Musical-TV; Documentary-TV.
Biography: Born in 1958 in Toronto, Ontario. Canadian citizen. Speaks English and Polish. B.A. from Carleton University, Ottawa. 2 years Film & Television Broadcasting Diploma from Loyalist College in Belleville, Ontario.

Selected Filmography: "Counterstrike", TV, 90-91, CDN/USA/F, Pub; *To Catch a Killer*, TV, 91, CDN, Pub; "E.N.G." (43 eps), TV, 89-91, CDN, Pub; "Neon Rider" (23 eps), TV, 90-91, CDN/USA, Pub; "My Secret Identity" (44 eps), TV, 89-91, CDN/USA, Pub; "Katts and Dog" (44 eps), TV, 89-91, CDN, Pub; *Young Catherine*, TV, 89-90, CDN/USA/USR/GB, Pub; "Shirley" (149 eps), TV, 89-90, CDN, Pub; *Canadian Country Music Awards*, TV, 90, CDN, Pub; *Flying On Her Own*, Rita MacNeil Special, TV, 90, CDN, Pub; *All The Bells Ring*, TV, 90, CDN, Pub; *French Revolution*, TV, 89-90, CDN/F/D/GB/I, Pub; *I Am a Hotel*, TV, 82, CDN, PA.

MANGONE, Rose
ACCT. 2058 Grosvenor St., Oakville, ON L6H 2Z1 (416)338-3660. National Film Board, 150 John St., National Publicity Department, Toronto, ON M5V 3C3 (416)973-9094.
Type of Production and Credits: Th Short-Pub; TV Film-Pub; TV Video-Pub.
Genres: Drama-TV; Documentary-TV; Educational-TV; Animation-Th&TV.
Biography: Born in 1946 in Frosinone, Italy. Holds both Canadian and Italian citizenship. Has extensive experience as a film marketing administrator prior to publicity. Assists regularly with the Toronto Women in Film activities. Has been assigned to Toronto Festival of Festivals Press Office for 2 years now. Consults regularly (gratis) with independent filmmakers re publicity. This is part of the NFB's ongoing assistance to the film community in Ontario and elsewhere in Canada. Is a member of CAJ, the Canadian Association of Journalists. Is also a member of Ontario Cinematique and is a Friend of the Festival (Toronto Festival of Festivals).
Selected Filmography: "Feminization of Poverty", Unit Pub.

MARGINSON, Karen
ACTRA. 2485 St. Patrick St., #113, Montreal, PQ H3K 3H7 (514)989-7769. National Film Board of Canada, P.O. Box 6100, Stn. A, Montreal, PQ H3C 3H5 (514)283-9410.
Types of Production and Credits: Th Film-Pub; Th Short-Pub; TV Film-Pub; TV Video-Pub.
Genres: Drama-Th&TV; Documentary-Th&TV; Children's-Th&TV: Educational-Th&TV; Animation-Th&TV; Experimental-Th&TV.
Biography: Born in 1952 in Nova Scotia. Canadian citizen. Languages: English and

French. Honours B.A., Theatre and English Lit., Dalhousie University, 1972-82. Acted professionally at Neptune Theatre, Pier One, Confederation Centre etc., as well as on film, TV and radio (in the Maritimes). Since 1982, National Publicity Coordinator for NFB on hundreds of documentaries, features, animation, etc. Recently complered unit publicity on Bruce Beresford's *Black Robe* (Alliance Feature Film).
Selected Filmography: *Black Robe*, Th, 90-91, CDN/AUS, Unit Pub; *The Company of Strangers*, Th, 90, CDN, Pub; *Justice Denied*, TV, 89, CDN, Pub; *To A Safer Place*, TV, 89, CDN, Pub; "The King Chronicles" (3 eps), TV, 89, CDN, Pub; "Canada: True North" (4 eps), TV, 89, CDN/USA, Pub; *Train of Dreams*, Th, 88, CDN, Pub; *Sitting in Limbo*, Th, 87, CDN, Pub; *Behind the Veil: Nuns*, ED/TV, 87, CDN, Pub; *Flamenco at 5:15*, Th/TV, 86, CDN, Pub; *90 Days*, Th, 85, CDN, Pub; *If You Love This Planet*, TV, 85, CDN, Pub; *The Kid Who Couldn't Miss*, TV, 84, CDN, Pub; "War" (7 eps), TV, 83, CDN, Pub; *Not a Love Story*, Th, 82, CDN, Pub.

MURPHY, Gaye
79 Allen Ave., Toronto, ON M4M 1T5 (416)461-8291. Business (416)690-0775 or 690-0667.
Type of Production and Credits: Th Film-Pub; Th Short-Pub; TV Film-Pub.
Genres: Drama-Th; Documentary-Th&TV; Animation-Th&TV.
Biography: Born in 1956, Toronto, Ontario. English speaking. Graduate of York University, Humanities. Freelance film publicist. Clients include Festival Cinemas of Toronto (exhibitors of films) and Creative Exposure (Canadian distributors of art and commercial films). Has been working for the past three years for the Festival of Animation, San Diego, CA. and also for Expanded Entertainment of L.A.

ODDIE, Jan
256 Jarvis St., Apt. 7D, Toronto, ON M5B 2J4 (416)599-6517. CBC Television, Box 500, Station A, Toronto, ON M5W 1E6 (416)975-6772.
Type of Production and Credits: TV Film-Pub; TV Video-Pub.
Genres: Drama-TV; Variety-TV; Musical-TV; Children's-TV.
Biography: Born, 1951, Campbellford, Ontario. Canadian citizen. English speaking with an understanding of written/oral French. Graduate of Victoria College, University of Toronto with Hons. in English, French and Communications. Excellent writer; certificate in photography from the Ontario College of Art. Advertising copy and layout experience. 16 years of experience in CBC radio and television as producer, editor and publicist.
Selected Filmography: "Northwood" (22 eps), TV, 90-91, CDN, Pub; "Canadian Sesame Street" (26 eps/yr), TV, 87-91, USA/CDN, Pub; *Talkin' About AIDS*, ED/TV, 90, CDN, Pub; "Degrassi High" (28 eps), TV, 89-90, CDN/USA, Pub; "Street Legal" (13 eps), TV, 86, CDN, Pub; "Sunday Arts" (28 eps), TV, 84-86, CDN/USA/GB, Pub; various Harry Rasky films, TV, 80-85, CDN, Pub; *Indigo*, TV, 81, CDN, Pub.

OLIVERIO, Edmund A.
AMPIA, SMPIA, PAPA, CPRS. EAO Communications Inc., P.O. Box 1240, Stn. M, Calgary, AB T2P 2L2 (403)228-9388. FAX: 229-3598.
Type of Production and Credits: Th Film-Pub; Th Short-Pub; TV Video-Pub.
Genres: Drama-Th&TV; Comedy-Th&TV; Action-Th&TV; Documentary-Th&TV.
Biography: Born in 1946. Western Canada's premier publicist for over 25 years. Executive Director, Canadian Film Celebration. Chairman of PAPA/Calgary, 1988-92.
Selected Filmography: *The Perfect Modern Romance*, Th, 91, CDN, Pub; *Pathfinders*, TV, 91, CDN, Pub; *A Bit of Heaven*, Th, 90, CDN, Pub; "Connecting", TV, 90, CDN, Pub; "One Night Stand", TV, 89-90, CDN, Pub; *He-Man and She-Ra & The Masters of the Universe*, Th, 88, USA, Pub.

PIDGURSKI, Karen
107 Kenilworth Ave., Toronto, ON M4L 3S4 (416)699-1047.
Type of Production and Credits: Th Film-Pub; TV Film-Pub.
Genres: Drama-Th&TV; Comedy-Th&TV; Action-Th&TV; Children's-Th&TV.
Biography: Born in 1957 in Saskatoon, Saskatchewan. Graduated Film and Photography dept., Ryerson Polytechnical Institute, 1979. Director of Communications for Alliance Entertainment Corporation, 1986-87. Director of Communications for Sunrise Films Limited, 1987-91.
Selected Filmography: "My Secret Identity" (72 eps), TV, 87-91, CDN/USA, Pub; *Sam & Me*, Th, 90, CDN, Pub; "Max Glick" (13 eps), TV, 90, CDN, Pub; "Danger Bay" (66 eps), TV, 87-89, CDN, Pub; *Shadow Dancing*, Th, 88, CDN, Pub;

Hoover Vs. The Kennedys, TV, 87, CDN/USA, Pub; "Night Heat" (13 eps), TV, 87, CDN/USA, Pub; "Mount Royal" (2 eps), TV, 87, CDN/F, Pub; "Diamonds" (6 eps), TV, 87, CDN/USA/F, Pub; *The Gunfighters*, TV, 87, CDN/USA, Pub; *The Jeweller's Shop*, TV, 87, CDN/I, Pub; "Mariah" (6 eps), TV, 87, CDN/USA, Pub; *Blindside*, Th, 86, CDN, Pub; *Hello Mary Lou - Prom Night II*, Th, 86, CDN, Pub; *Strikers Mountain*, TV, 85, CDN, Pub.

PODESWA, Jeremy
- see DIRECTORS

SCHAEFFER, Shelley
144 Cactus Ave., Willowdale, ON M2R 2V2 (416)226-1416.
Type of Production and Credits: Th Film-Pub/Dist; Th Short-Pub/Dist.
Genres: Drama-Th; Comedy-Th; Action-Th; Horror-Th; Children's-Th; Commercials-Th; Home Video-TV/Cassette.
Biography: Born in 1955 in Toronto, Ontario. Canadian citizen. Bachelor of Arts (Radio and Television) from Ryerson Polytechnical Institute, Toronto, Ont.. Responsible for release marketing campaigns for Golden Reel Award Winners, (highest-grossing Canadian feature film) *Porky's*, 1982 and *The Care Bears Movie*, 1985. Extensive experience in domestic release marketing; strategic planning of media campaigns, publicity tours and promotions for theatrical film and home video programming. American and foreign film and video credits include *Hallowe'en*, *Nightmare on Elm Street 3*, *Drugstore Cowboy*, *Pascali's Island*, *Gregory's Girl* and *Distant Voices, Still Lives*. Intensive marketing experience with the Montreal, Toronto and Vancouver Film Festivals.
Selected Filmography: *Une histoire inventée*, Th, 90, Pub/Dist; *Babar: The Movie*, Th, 89, Pub/Dist; *Termini Station*, Th, 89, Pub/Dist; *Dead Ringers*, Th, 88, Pub/Dist; *The Kiss*, Th, 88, Pub/Dist; "Shades of Love" (16 eps), TV, 87-88, Pub/Dist; *Sitting In Limbo*, Th, 86, Pub/Dist; *The Care Bears Movie*, Th, 85, Pub/Dist; "The Bradbury Trilogy" (6 eps), TV, 85, Pub/Dist; *Les Canadiens*, TV, 85, Pub/Dist; *Maria Chapdelaine*, Th, 83, Pub/Dist; *Porky's*, Th, 82, Pub/Dist; *By Design*, Th, 82, Pub/Dist; *In Praise of Older Women*, Th, 78, Pub/Dist; *Who Has Seen The Wind*, Th, 77, Pub/Dist.

SCHWARZ, Alan J.
50 Rosehill, #406, Toronto, ON M4T 1G6 (416)925-7884. Wafwot Communications Corp., 23 Brentcliffe Rd., Ste. 325, Toronto, ON M4G 4B7 (416)467-9444.
Type of Production and Credits: TV Video-Pub.
Genres: Commercials-TV; Current Affairs-TV.
Biography: Born in 1960 in Oshawa, Ontario. Member of the International Radio & Television Society. Has a degree in Mass Communications from Carleton University. Has an excellent relationship with 3rd language media stemming from time spent as the Director, Public Relations, Channel 47, MTV. Experienced in promotion of celebrities, re setting up media tours, etc. Responsible for media, public relations for the Life Channel from its inception. Founder and President of Wafwot Communications Corp.
Selected Filmography: "Bubbie Break" (13 eps), TV, 90-91, CDN, Pub; Jayson Schwarz, Cm, 91, CDN, Prod; "Hanes Report" (26 eps), TV, 89, CDN, Pub; "Hobby Garden" (13 eps), TV, 89, CDN, Pub.

SINGER, Sharon
117 Orchard View Blvd., Toronto, ON M4R 1C1 (416)488-2832. First Canadian Artists Inc., 181 Carlaw Ave., Suite 226-228, Toronto, ON M4M 2S1 (416)778-7411. FAX: 778-7772.
Type of Production and Credits: Th Short-Prod; TV Video-Prod.
Genres: Drama-Th; Comedy-Th&TV; Action-Th; Educational-Th&TV.
Biography: Born in Toronto, Ontario. Honours B.A., University of Toronto; studied Film in New York and London; Certificate, London Film School. Worked in film distribution in Canada for several years before forming own distribution company, Dabara Films. Distributing quality feature films including *Madame Rosa*, *Dona Flor and Her Two Husbands*, George Romero's *Martin*, and *It's Alive*. Currently produces electronic press kits for feature films, TV series and mini-series; does unit publicity and consults on marketing and advertising campaigns.
Selected Filmography: *To Catch a Killer* (mini-series), TV, 91, CDN, Unit Pub; *Clearcut*, Th, 90, CDN, Unit Pub; *Bordertown Cafe*, Th, 90, CDN, Unit Pub; *Betrayal of Silence/Cardinal Sins*, TV, 90, CDN, Unit Pub; *The Last Winter*, Th, 89, CDN, Unit Pub; *Mob Story*, Th, 89, CDN, Unit Pub; *Murder by Night*, TV, 89, CDN/USA, Unit Pub; *Final Notice*, TV, 89, CDN/USA, Unit Pub; *Love and Murder*, Th, 88, CDN, Unit Pub; *The Outside Chance of Maximilian Glick*, Th,

87, CDN, Unit Pub; *Blue City Slammers*, Th, 87, CDN, Unit Pub; "Comedy Tonight" (13 eps), TV, 83-84, CDN, Assoc Prod; *Not by Design Alone*, In, 76, CDN, Prod; *Les Fables de Lafontaine*, Conversational French, ED, 75, CDN, Prod; *Economics*, Th, 73, CDN, Prod.

SMALE, Joanne Muroff
Joanne Smale Productions Ltd., 686 Richmond St. W., Main Floor, Toronto, ON M6J 1C3 (416)363-4051. FAX: 363-6986.
Type of Production and Credits: TV Video-Pub/Prod.
Genres: Documentary-Th&TV.
Biography: Born in 1949 in Brooklyn, New York. Landed immigrant. Graduated from the University of Miami. Has represented many of Canada's foremost performers, acting variously as booking agent, business manager and publicist for such artists as Murray McLauchlan, Bruce Cockburn, Lorraine Segato, Leroy Sibbles, Rough Trade, Sam Sniderman, Gordon Lightfoot and Mark Breslin, among others. Has also represented many high-profile national and local events. Currently co-producing a national environmental project, ECOFEST. Sits on the boards for VideoFact, CIRPA, and Toronto Women in Film and Television .
Selected Filmography: *Mondo Moscow*, TV, 90, CDN/I, Co Prod/Pub; *Calling the Shots*, Th, 90, CDN, Pub.

VALCOUR, Nicolas M.
- voir PRODUCTEURS

VILLENEUVE, Suzanne
Suzanne Villeneuve & Associés Inc., 445, St-François-Xavier, bur.12, Montréal, PQ H2Y 2T1 (514)842-9964.
Types de production et générique: l métrage-Rel.
Types d'oeuvres: Drame-C&TV; Comédie-C&TV; Science-Fiction-C&TV; Documentaire-C&TV.
Curriculum vitae: Née en 1950, Maniwaki, Québec. Citoyenneté canadienne. Langues: anglais, français. Specialisée en lancements de films en salle et création d'événements cinématographiques (festivals, rétrospectives). Représentante de la 20th Century Fox à Montréal depuis 1983. Co-fondatrice et VP du "Répertoire Photos Gros Plan sur les comédiens et comédiennes québécois".
Filmographie sélective: *King's Ransom*, "Love & Adventure", TV, 91, CDN, Rel; *Shadows of the Past*, "Love & Adventure", TV, 90, CDN, Rel; *Une histoire inventée*, C, 89, CDN, Rel; *Cargo*, C, 89, CDN, Rel; *The Phone Call*, TV, 88-89, CDN, Rel; *The Thriller*, TV, 88-89, CDN, Rel; *Justice Express*, TV, 88-89, CDN, Rel; *Pour 100 millions*, TV, 88-89, CDN, Rel; *The Road to New Hope*, TV, 888-89, CDN, Rel; *Babylone*, C, 88, CDN, Rel; *A corps perdu*, C, 88, CDN, Rel; *Laura Laur*, C, 89, CDN, Rel; *Exit*, C, 86, CDN, Rel; "Mont-Royal", TV, 87, CDN, Rel.

WILLIAMS, Karen
Artist Representation/Public Relations, 268 Poplar Plains Rd., Ste. 901, Toronto, ON M4V 2P2 Phone and FAX number, (416)960-8376.
Type of Production and Credits: Th Film-Pub; TV Film-Pub; TV Video-Pub.
Biography: Born in England in 1950. Moved to Canada in 1957. Works on contract or retainer basis as a publicist, agent and manager, specializing in individual artist representation. Special events, film, television, theatrical launches and publicity tours also handled, as well as publicity and promotion of music events and artist performances. Clients have included Megan Follows, Gordon Clapp, Gabrielle Rose, Greg Spottiswood, Manteca, Brian Hughes, Beaches Jazz Festival, Mel Lastman Square Summer /Winter concert series, Andrew Bednarski, Kirk McMahon, Mump & Smoot, Reggae Sunsplash, *Termini Station*, Allan King, "Material World".
Selected Filmography: *Bodyguard*, TV, CDN, Pub; "Material World", TV, 90-91, CDN, Pub; *Termini Station*, Th, 90, CDN, Pub.

WINEBERG, Tami
30 Thelma Ave., #204, Toronto, ON M4V 1X9 (416)488-5287. MGM/UA Distribution of Canada, 720 King St. W., Suite 611, Toronto, ON M5V 2T3 (416)865-9579.
Type of Production and Credits: Th Film-Dist Pub.
Genres: Drama-Th; Comedy-Th; Action-Th; Science Fiction-Th; Amination-Th.
Biography: Born in 1958 in Toronto, Ontario. B.F.A., Film Production, York University. Currently Director of Publicity and Promotion at MGM/UA Distribution of Canada.
Selected Filmography: *Thelma & Louise*, Th, 91, USA, Dist Pub; *Not Without My Daughter*, Th, 91, USA, Dist Pub; *Russia House*, Th, 90, USA, Dist Pub; *Rocky V*, Th, 90, USA, Dist Pub; *Stanley & Iris*, Th, 90, USA, Dist Pub; *All Dogs Go To Heaven*, Th, 89, USA, Dist Pub; *A Dry White Season*, Th, 89, USA, Dist Pub; *Licence To Kill*, Th, 89, USA/GB, Dist Pub; *Road House*, Th, 89, USA, Dist Pub;

The January Man, Th, 89, USA, Dist Pub; *Rain Man*, Th, 88, USA, Dist Pub; *Willow*, Th, 88, USA, Dist Pub; *A Fish Called Wanda*, Th, 88, USA/GB, Dist Pub; *Betrayed*, Th, 88, USA, Dist Pub; *Moonstruck*, Th, 87, USA, Dist Pub.

Sound Editors
Monteurs son

ADAMS, Ellen
DGC. R.R. #2, Ayton, ON N0G 1C0 (519)665-2245.
Type of Production and Credits: Th Film-Snd Ed; TV Film-Snd Ed.
Genres: Drama-Th&TV; Comedy-Th; Action-Th&TV; Horror-Th.
Biography: Born 1941, Toronto, Ontario. B.Sc., Honours, Zoology, University of British Columbia; M.A., Zoology, University of British Columbia; A.O.C.A., Design, Ontario College of Art.
Selected Filmography: *Beautiful Dreamers*, Th, 89, CDN, Dial Ed; *Iron Eagle II*, Th, 88, CDN/IL, Dial Ed; *Murderers Among Us*, TV, 88, GB, Dial Ed; "Race for the Bomb" (3 eps), TV, 86, CDN/F, Dial Ed; *Follow That Bird*, Th, 85, USA, Dial Ed; *Little Gloria...Happy at Last*, TV, 82, CDN/USA, Dial Ed; *Mary and Joseph*, TV, 82, CDN, Dial Ed; *Death by Phone*, Th, 81, CDN, Dial Ed; *Spasms*, Th, 81, CDN, Dial Ed; *Best Revenge*, Th, 80, CDN, Dial Ed; *Crunch*, Th, 79, CDN/USA, Dial Ed; *Klondike Fever*, Th, 79, CDN, Dial Ed; *The Intruder*, Th, 79, CDN, Dial Ed; *Terror Train*, Th, 79, CDN/USA, Dial Ed; *A Man Called Intrepid*, TV, 78, CDN/GB, Dial Ed.

BALL, Christopher
- see DIRECTORS

BELANGER, Fernand
- voir REALISATEURS

BOCKING, Robert V.
- see CINEMATOGRAPHERS

BOISVERT, Dominique
- see EDITORS

BOND, Richard
- see EDITORS

BRENNAN, Fred
DGC. 350 Sorauren Ave., Apt. 205, Toronto, ON M6R 2G8 (416)532-3865.
Type of Production and Credits: Th Film-Spv Snd Ed; TV Film-Spv Snd Ed; TV Video-Spv Snd Ed.
Genres: Drama-Th&TV; Comedy-Th&TV; Action-Th&TV; Horror-Th&TV.
Biography: Born in 1950 in Winnipeg, Manitoba. Graduated from Red River College, 1973. Trained as a writer, specializing in TV advertising. Became interested in filmmaking while writing and producing ads for a local TV station which led to an interest in film editing. Came to Toronto in the late seventies. Concentrated on sound editing, sound effects editing and dialogue editing. Has also supervised the editing and mixing of several TV series and features. Has been nominated for sound awards.
Selected Filmography: *Clear Cut*, Th, 91, CDN, Dial Ed; *Sam and Me*, Th, 90, CDN, Dial Ed; "Magic Hour" (8 eps), TV, 90, CDN, Dial Ed; *Speed Zone*, Th, 89, USA, Snd FX Ed; *Champagne Charlie*, TV, 88, CDN/F, Spv Snd Ed; "Danger Bay" (79 eps), TV, 87, CDN, Spv Snd Ed; *Home is Where the Heart Is*, Th, 87, CDN, Spv Snd Ed; *Joshua, Then and Now*, Th, 86, CDN, Post Sync Ed; *Expo 86, Ontario*, Th, 86, CDN, Spv Snd Ed; "Littlest Hobo" (91 eps), TV, 83, CDN, Snd Ed; *Hank Williams: The Show He Never Gave*, TV, 81, CDN, Snd/Mus Ed; *Terror Train*, Th, 80, CDN, Snd FX Ed; *Crunch*, Th, 80, CDN, Snd FX Ed; *I Miss You Hugs & Kisses*, Th, 78, CDN, Snd Ed.

CEREGHETTI, Jean-Pierre
- voir MONTEURS

CLARK, Alison◇
DGC, ACCT. (416)653-0456.
Type of Production and Credits: Th Film-Snd Ed/Snd Rec; TV Film-Snd Ed/Snd Rec/Ed.
Genres: Drama-Th&TV; Comedy-Th; Documentary-Th&TV; Commercials-TV.
Biography: Born in 1956 in Pembroke, Ontario. Fine Arts graduate, Film major, Fanshawe College, 79. Nominated for several Genies for sound editing; winning in 86.
Selected Filmography: *Milk and Honey*, Th, 87, CDN, Snd Ed; *A Winter Tan*, Th, 87, CDN, Snd FX Ed; *Moonstruck*, Th, 87, USA, Snd FX Ed; *The Big Town*, Th, 87, USA, Snd FX Ed; *The Prodigious Hickey*, TV, 86, CDN/USA, Snd Ed; *The Truth about Alex*, TV, 86, CDN, Snd Ed; *One Magic Christmas*, Th, 85, CDN/USA, Snd Fx Ed, (GENIE); *Agnes of God*, Th, 85, USA, Snd FX Ed; *The Pink Chiquitas*, Th, 85, CDN, Snd FX Ed; *Zargon*, Th, 85, CDN, Snd FX Ed; *My American Cousin*, Th, 84, CDN, Snd FX Ed; *Skyward*, Th, 84, CDN/J, Snd FX Ed; *The National Safety Drill*, TV, 83, CDN, Snd Ed/Ed; *Split Seconds*, TV, 83, CDN, Snd Ed.

CLYNE, Dale
- see POSTPRODUCTION SOUND MIXERS

COLE, Steven
- see POSTPRODUCTION SOUND MIXERS

CORNFORD, Darryl
- see EDITORS

CURRIE, Anthony
DGC, ACTRA, ACCT. 101 Glen Manor Dr., Apt. 5, Toronto, ON M4E 3V3 (416)690-5915.
Type of Production and Credits: Th Film-Snd Ed/Dir/Wr; Th Short-Dir/Wr; TV Film-Snd Ed.
Genres: Drama-Th; Comedy-Th.
Biography: Born 1956, Toronto, Ontario. B.A.A., Photographic Arts, Ryerson Polytechnical Institute. Winner of awards at Houston, Chicago; nominated for Genie in Sound Editing for *The Grey Fox*, *My American Cousin*, *Threshold* and *Buying Time*. Nominated for a Genie in Directing in Theatrical Short for *Productivity and Performace by Alex K*.
Selected Filmography: *The Naked Lunch*, Th, 91, CDN, Snd Ed; *The Hit Man*, Th, 91, CDN, Snd Ed; *Highway 61*, Th, 91, CDN, Snd Ed; *South of Wawa*, Th, 91, CDN, Snd Ed; *The Quarrel*, Th, 90, CDN, Snd Ed; *Perfectly Normal*, Th, 90, CDN, Snd Ed; *The Little Kidnappers*, TV, 90, CDN, Snd Ed; *Beautiful Dreamers*, Th, 89, CDN, Snd Ed; *Loose Cannons*, Th, 89, USA, Snd Ed.

DANDY, Michael◇
(416)920-664
Type of Production and Credits: Th Short-Ed/Snd Ed; TV Film-Ed/Snd Ed.
Genres: Drama-TV; Musical-TV; Documentary-Th&TV; Educational-TV.
Biography: Born 1955, Toronto, Ontario. Edited the *Tribute to Martin Scorsese* for the Festival of Festivals, 82.
Selected Filmography: "T and T" (24 eps), TV, 88, CDN/USA, Snd Ed; *Shadow Dancing*, Th, 88, CDN, Snd Ed; *The Boys on the Bus*, TV, 87, CDN, Snd Ed/Ed; "the fifth estate" (8 eps), TV, 83-86, CDN, Ed; *Roots Athletics*, Cm, 85-86, CDN, Ed; *Les Canadiens, Minomen Harvest*, Th, 85, CDN, Ed/Snd Ed;

Cleared for Take-Off, In, 83-85, CDN, Ed/Snd Ed/Snd Rec.

EVANS, David
DGC. 8 Bingham Ave., Toronto, ON M4E 3P9 (416)694-7952. Casablanca Sound Services, 181 Carlaw Ave., Suite 301, Toronto, ON M4M 2S1 (416)465-6387. FAX: 465-8232.
Type of Production and Credits: Th Film-Snd Ed; Th Short-Snd Ed; TV Film-Snd Ed; TV Video-Snd Ed.
Genres: Drama-Th&TV; Comedy-Th&TV; Action-Th&TV; Documentary-Th.
Biography: Born in 1950 in Thunder Bay, Ontario. Co-owner, Casablanca Sound Services: 35 and 16 mm cutting room; digital and analogue working formats; tape-to-video lock; full service postproduction facility. *Divided Loyalties* won Gemini, 90 and *Dead Ringers* won Genie, 89. "Maniac Mansion" was nominated for an Emmy.
Selected Filmography: *Naked Lunch,* Th, 91, CDN, Spv Snd Ed; "Maniac Mansion" (22 eps), TV, 90-91, CDN, Spv Snd Ed; *Scales of Justice,* TV, 90-91, CDN, Spv Snd Ed; *Perfectly Normal,* Th, 90, CDN, Spv Snd Ed; *Divided Loyalties,* TV, 89-90, CDN, Spv Snd Ed; *Dead Ringers,* Th, 88, CDN, Spv Snd Ed; *Switching Channels,* Th, 87, CDN, Co-Snd Ed; *A Child's Christmas in Wales,* TV, 87, CDN/USA/GB, Co-Snd Ed; *The Gate,* Th, 86, CDN, Co-Snd Ed; *Nowhere to Hide,* Th, 86, CDN, Co-Snd Ed; *The Fly,* Th, 86, USA, Co-Snd Ed; *Joshua Then and Now,* Th, 84, CDN, Snd Ed; *A Christmas Story,* Th, 83, CDN, Snd Ed; *Hail Columbia* (Imax), Th, 82, CDN, Snd Ed; *Porky's II,* Th, 82, CDN, Snd Ed.

FRICKER, Brock
- see PRODUCTION SOUND MIXERS

GELDART, Alan◊
DGC, ACCT. (416)925-5008.
Type of Production and Credits: Th Film-Snd Ed/Snd Rec; TV Film-Snd Ed/Snd Mix.
Genres: Drama-Th&TV; Horror-Th; Documentary-Th&TV; Current Affairs-TV.
Biography: Born 1957, Ottawa, Ontario. Languages: English, French and Spanish. Began in film business at 19; considerable experience in a variety of film formats including Imax; specializes in FX recording/editing and special-event location mixing; expert in digital recording, location dialogue mixing on DAT.
Selected Filmography: "Ghostbusters"/"Alf" (6 eps), TV, 87, USA, Anim/Overseas Ed; *Beavers* (Imax), Th, 87, CDN, Snd Fx Ed; "Street Legal" (4 eps), TV, 87, CDN, Snd FX Ed; "Shades of Love" (3 eps), TV, 87, CDN, Snd FX Ed; *Smoke,* Th, 87, USA, Snd Rec/Snd FX Ed; *The Kiss,* Th, 87, CDN, Snd FX Ed; "Race for the Bomb", TV, 86, CDN/F, Snd FX Ed; *Discovery* (Expo 86), Th, 86, CDN, Snd FX Ed; *Rolling Vengeance,* Th, 86, USA, Snd FX Ed/Snd Rec; *One Magic Christmas,* Th, 85, CDN/USA, Snd FX Ed, (GENIE); *Samuel Lount,* Th, 84, CDN, Snd Rec/Snd FX Ed; *Waterwalker,* Th, 84, CDN, Snd FX Ed/Snd Rec/Mus Ed; *The Land That Devours Ships,* TV, 84, CDN/USA, Snd Rec/Snd Rd; *Hands That Heal,* TV, 83, CDN, Snd Rec/Snd Mix; "The Myth" (4 eps), TV, 83, CDN, Snd Rec/Snd Mix.

GEROFSKY, Susan
DGC. 87 Hepbourne St., Toronto, ON M6H 1K6 (416)532-7493.
Type of Production and Credits: Th Film-Ed; TV Film-Snd Ed/Ed.
Genres: Drama-Th&TV; Documentary-TV; Children's-TV; Animation-Th.
Biography: Born in 1955 in Hamilton, Ontario; Canadian and US citizenship. Languages: English, French, Portuguese and Mandarin Chinese. Honours B.A., Chinese Language, University of Toronto, 77; M.A., Applied Linguistics, University of Durham, England, 90. Has been director and interviewer for CBC Radio. Teaches English as a Second Language. Also supervises postproduction budgets for TV series and features.
Selected Filmography: "Ray Bradbury Theatre" (24 eps), TV, 86-88, CDN/USA/GB/F, P Pro Spv; "Airwaves" (26 eps), TV, 88, CDN, P Pro Spv; *Cowboys Don't Cry,* Th, 87, CDN, P Pro Spv; *The New North,* TV, 87, CDN, P Pro Spv; "Brothers by Choice" (6 eps), TV, 86, CDN, P Pro Spv; "Really Weird Tales" (3 eps), TV, 86, CDN/USA, P Pro Spv; *A Time for Miracles/Islands,* "PBS Wonderworks", TV, 84-85, CDN, P Pro Coord; "Global Playhouse" (4 eps), TV, 85, CDN, P Pro Spv; *Oh So Programmable Computers,* In, 84, CDN, Prod/Dir; *Miracle at Moreaux,* TV, 84, CDN, P Pro Spv; "The Edison Twins" (6 eps), TV, 83, CDN, Snd Ed/Assist Ed; "The Chinese" (6 eps), TV, 81-82, CDN/RC, Snd Ed/Assist Ed; *Harry Tracy,* Th, 80, CDN, Assist Ed; *Baker County U.S.A.,* Th, 80, CDN/USA, Assist Ed.

GILLSON, Malca
- see DIRECTORS

GORDICA, Terry
- see POSTPRODUCTION SOUND MIXERS

GRACE, Alison◊
DGC. (416)921-9272.
Type of Production and Credits: Th Film-Snd Ed; TV Film-Snd Ed.
Genres: Drama-Th&TV; Comedy-Th&TV.
Biography: Born in 1959 in Nipawin, Saskatchewan. B.A., University of British Columbia, 81.
Selected Filmography: "The Twilight Zone" (6 eps), TV, 88, CDN/USA, Dial Ed; *The Kiss*, Th, 87, CDN, Dial Ed; "Ray Bradbury Theatre" (1 eps), TV, 87, CDN/NZ, Dial Ed; *A Winter Tan*, Th, 87, CDN, Spv Dial Ed; *Moonstruck*, Th, 87, USA, Dial Ed; *The Big Town*, Th, 87, USA, Dial Ed; *Smoke*, Th, 87, USA, Dial Ed; *From the Hip*, Th, 86, USA, ADR Ed; *The Last Season*, TV, 86, CDN, Dial Ed; "Philip Marlowe Private Eye" (6 eps), TV, 86, CDN, Assist ADR Ed; "Airwaves" (13 eps), TV, 86, CDN, Assist ADR Ed; *Overnight*, Th, 85, CDN, Snd Ed/Assist Ed; *Agnes of God*, Th, 85, CDN, Assist ADR Ed; *The Pink Chiquitas*, Th, 85, CDN, ADR Ed; *Samuel Lount*, Th, 84, CDN, Assist Dial Ed.

GRIFFIN, Wayne
DGC. 73 Willowbank Boulevard., Toronto, ON M5N 1G7 (416)486-0292. Casablanca Sound Services, 181 Carlaw Ave., Suite 301, Toronto, ON M4M 2S1 (416)465-6387. FAX: 465-8232.
Type of Production and Credits: Th Film-Snd Ed; Th Short-Snd Ed; TV Film-Snd Ed; TV Video-Snd Ed.
Genres: Drama-Th&TV; Comedy-Th&TV; Action-Th; Horror-Th; Documentary-Th.
Biography: Born 1946, Bobcaygeon, Ontario. Also works as sound editor for Imax. "Maniac Mansion" received an Emmy nomination; *Divided Loyalties* won Gemini, 90 and *Dead Ringers* won Genie, 89.
Selected Filmography: *Robin Hood, Prince of Thieves*, Th, 91, USA, Snd Ed; *Boys on the Hood*, Th, 91, USA, Snd Ed; *Naked Lunch*, Th, 91, CDN, Spv Snd Ed; "Maniac Mansion" (22 eps), TV, 90-91, CDN, Spv Snd Ed; *Perfectly Normal*, Th, 90, CDN, Spv Snd Ed; *Scales of Justice*, TV, 90, CDN, Spv Snd Ed; *Divided Loyalties*, TV, 89-90, CDN, Spv Snd Ed; *Breaking In*, Th, 88-89, CDN, Spv Snd Ed; *Dead Ringers*, Th, 88, CDN, Spv Snd Ed; *Switching Channels*, Th, 87, USA, Co-Snd Ed; *A Child's Christmas in Wales*, TV, 87, CDN/USA/GB, Co-Snd Ed; *Nowhere to Hide*, Th, 86, CDN, Co-Snd Ed; *The Gate*, Th, 86, CDN, Co-Snd Ed; *The Fly*, Th, 86, USA, Co-Snd Ed; *Joshua Then and Now*, Th, 84, CDN, Co-Snd Ed.

HALL, Grant
- see POSTPRODUCTION SOUND MIXERS

HALLIS, Ophera
- see EDITORS

HANNIGAN, Teresa
- see EDITORS

HARDIMAN, Alan
DGC, NABET. 79 Allen Ave., Toronto, ON M4M 1T5 (416)461-8291.
Type of Production and Credits: Th Film-Snd Ed; TV Film-Snd Ed; TV Video-Snd Ed/Re-record Mix.
Genres: Drama-Th&TV; Musical-TV; Science Fiction-Th&TV; Educational-TV.
Biography: Born in 1951 in London, England. English and French spoken. B.Sc., M.A. degrees from McGill University. Genie nominations for Best Sound Editing for *Millennium* and *American Boyfriends*.
Selected Filmography: "A la Claire Fontaine" (13 eps), TV, 91, CDN, Snd Ed/Snd Mix; "Material World" (6 eps), TV, 91, CDN, Snd Ed; "A Sense of Design" (7 eps), TV, 91, CDN, Re-record; *The Little Kidnappers*, TV, 90, CDN/USA, Snd Ed; *I Can't Remember*, "Vital Signs", TV, 90, CDN, Mix; *Sun City*, "Vital Signs", TV, 90, CDN, Mix; "La nuit sur l'etang" (6 eps), TV, 90, CDN, Co-Mix; "Street Legal" (15 eps), TV, 88-89, CDN, Snd Ed; *American Boyfriends*, Th, 89, CDN, Snd Ed; *One Warm Line: The Legacy of Stan Rogers*, TV, 89, CDN, Snd Ed; *The Penthouse*, TV, 89, CDN/USA, Snd Ed; *Millennium*, Th, 88, CDN/USA, Snd Ed.

HAWKES, Kirk
- see EDITORS

HECTOR, Nick
- see EDITORS

HUNT, Catherine
- see POSTPRODUCTION SOUND MIXERS

JOUTEL, Jean-Pierre
- voir MIXEURS SON PRODUCTION

KLIS, Danuta
SGCT. 261 Jeannette, Fabreville, Laval, PQ H7P 5C5 (514)622-5323. National Film Board of Canada, 3155 Côte de Liesse, Montreal, PQ H4N 2N4 (514)283-9596.
Genres: Drama-Th&TV; Documentary-Th&TV; Educational-Th&TV; Animation-Th&TV.

Biography: Born in 1958 in Montreal, Quebec. Canadian citizen. Speaks English, French and Polish. Has a Bachelor in Music from McGill University. Presently working on a long-term contract at the N.F.B. which ends July 91. Would like to specialize not only in sound editing, but also in music editing. Worked as Co Sound Editor on the award-winning film *Company of Strangers*.
Selected Filmography: *Mother Earth*, ED, 91, CDN, Mus Ed; *Building Bridges*, ED/TV, 91, CDN, Snd Ed/Mus Ed; *When The Day Comes*, ED, 90, CDN, Snd Ed; *Company of Strangers*, Th, 90, CDN, Co Snd Ed; *Half the Kingdom*, ED, 89, CDN, Snd Ed; *First Emperor of China*, ED, 89, CDN, Snd Ed; *To A Safer Place*, ED, 88, CDN, Co Snd Ed; *Train of Dreams*, TV, 88, CDN, Snd Ed; *Morning Man*, Th, 86, CDN, Snd Ed; *Image par Image*, TV, 86, CDN, Snd Ed; *Le Vieillard et l'Enfant*, Th, 85, CDN, Snd Ed; *Toby McTeague*, Th, 85, CDN, Snd Ed; "Tin Flute Series" (5 eps), Th, 84, CDN, Co Snd Ed; *Bayo*, Th, 84, CDN, Snd Ed; *Latitude SS*, Th, 82, CDN, Snd Ed.

LACKIE, Sharon
DGC, ACCT. 18 Sydenham St., Toronto, ON M5A 4H6 (416)941-1636. 1456 Shenandoah St., #302, Los Angeles, CA 90035 (213)657-9563. (213)286-2999.
Type of Production and Credits: Th Film-Snd Ed; TV Film-Snd Ed.
Genres: Drama-Th&TV; Comedy-Th&TV; Action-Th; Horror-Th.
Selected Filmography: *Other People's Money*, Th, 91, USA, Spv Snd Ed; *The Linguine Incident*, Th, 91, USA, Spv Snd Ed; *In Country*, Th, 89, USA, Spv Snd Ed; *The January Man*, Th, 88, USA, Spv Snd Ed; *Physical Evidence*, Th, 88, USA, Spv Snd Ed; *Cowboys Don'y Cry*, Th, 87, CDN, Snd Ed; *Moonstruck*, Th, 87, USA, Spv Snd Ed; *Smoke*, Th, 87, USA, Spv Snd Ed; *From the Hip*, Th, 86, USA, Spv Snd Ed; "Philip Marlowe Private Eye" (6 eps), TV, 86, CDN, ADR Ed; *The Big Town*, Th, 86, USA, Spv Snd Ed; *Loyalties*, Th, 85, CDN/GB, Snd Ed; *Anne of Green Gables* (mini-series), TV, 85, CDN, Spv Dial Ed; *Agnes of God*, Th, 85, CDN, Snd Ed; *The Wars*, Th, 81, CDN/D, Dial Ed, (GENIE).

LANCETT, Anthony J. R.
2373 Bloor St. W., Toronto, ON M6S 1P6 (416)769-5393.
Type of Production and Credits: TV Film-Snd Ed/Comp.
Genres: Drama-Th&TV; Action-Th& TV; Documentary-TV.
Biography: Born in 1948 in Glasgow. Citizenship: British and Canadian (pending). Languages: English and French. Fully conversant with electronic sound editing. Extensive library of digitally-recorded sound effects and re-recorded effects. Sound effects location recording services. M.P.S.E. Golden Reel Award, Best Sound, TV Series for "The Equalizer", 1989 and "Captain Power", 1988.
Selected Filmography: "The Hitchhiker" (52 eps), TV, 89-91, CDN/USA, Snd Ed/Comp; *Deadly Surveillance*, Th, 91, CDN, Snd Ed; *Psychic*, Th, 91, CDN, Snd Ed; "The Equalizer" (26 eps), TV, 89-90, CDN/USA, Snd Ed; "War of the Worlds" (26 eps), TV, 89-90, CDN/USA, Snd Ed; *Captain Power - The Movie*, Th/TV, 90, CDN, Snd Des/Snd Ed; *Whalesong*, TV, 89, CDN, Snd Ed, (GEMINI); "Captain Power" (26 eps), TV, 88-89, CDN/USA, Snd Des/Snd Ed; *All That Bach*, TV, 88, CDN, Snd Ed, (GEMINI); *Chasing Rainbows*, TV, 87-88, CDN, Snd Ed; "The Nature of Things" (40 eps), TV, 83-87, CDN, Snd Ed, (ANIK).

LAWRENCE, Stephen
- see EDITORS

MacLAVERTY, Michael
- see EDITORS

MITCHELL, Steven R.
DGC. 345 Dufferin St., Ste. 825, Toronto, ON M6K 3G1 (416)537-0512. Visual Fixations Inc., 345 Dufferin St., Ste. 825, Toronto, ON M6K 3G1 (416)537-0512.
Type of Production and Credits: Th Film-Snd FX Ed/Mus Ed; TV Film-Spv Snd Ed/Mus Ed; TV Video-Spv Snd Ed/Mus Ed.
Genres: Drama-Th&TV; Action-TV; Documentary-TV; Animation-Th&TV.
Biography: Born in 1957 in Toronto, Ontario. Graduate of Humber College's Cinematography program, 1982. Studied picture editing with Ralph Rosenblum at the International Film Workshops, 1983. Completed the Full Sail Synclavier 9600 digital audio editing course, 1989. Completed the Business of Film I & II courses at Ryerson Polytechnical Institute, 1991. Canadian citizen. Some command of the Swedish language. Won the Golden Reel Award for Best ADR in a 1/2 hr. TV series for "My Secret Identity".
Selected Filmography: "My Secret Identity" (24 eps), TV, 90-91, CDN/USA, Spv Snd Ed; "Danger Bay" (44 eps), TV, 88-90, CDN/USA, Spv Snd Ed; *The Midday Sun*, Th, 89, CDN, Snd Ed; *Dog*

City, "The Jim Henson Hour", TV, 89, USA, Mus Ed/Mus Re-record; *And Then You Die*, TV, 88, CDN, Mus Ed; *The Twin*, "Inside Stories", TV, 88, CDN, Mus Ed; "T and T" (24 eps), TV, 87, CDN/USA, Mus Ed; *Into The Fire*, Th, 87, CDN, 1st Assist Ed/Mus Ed; "Lorne Greene's New Wilderness" (78 eps), TV, 83-86, CDN, Mus Ed/Mus Re-record; *The Care Bear Movie*, Th, 85, CDN, Mus Ed; "Wheeled Warriors" (36 eps), TV, 85, USA, Mus Ed; "Mask" (16 eps), TV, 85, USA, Mus Ed; "Robotman & Friends" (3 eps), TV, 85, USA, Mus Ed; "Heathcliffe" (7 eps), TV, 84, USA, Mus Ed.

MONK, Roger J.
CAS. Dick & Roger's Sound Studio Limited, 2339 Columbia St., 3rd Flr., Vancouver, BC V5Y 3Y3 (604)873-5777. FAX: 872-1356.
Type of Production and Credits: Th Film-Snd Mix; TV Film-Snd Mix; TV Video-Snd Mix.
Genres: Drama-Th; Comedy-Th; Action-Th; Science Fiction-Th.
Biography: Born in London, England; Canadian citizenship. Started recording music in 71. Scoring mixer on the Best Sound Oscar winner, *Platoon*, 87.
Selected Filmography: "Hot Wheel Heroes" (sev eps), TV, 91, USA, Snd Ed/Post Mix; *Molson Hot Licks*, TV, 90, CDN, Snd Ed/Post Mix; *Molson Comedy Relief*, TV, 89, CDN, Snd Ed/Post Mix; *Dirty Dozen*(part V), TV, 88, USA, Score Mix; *My Father, My Son*, TV, 88, USA, Score Mix; *Red River*, TV, 88, USA, Score Mix; *Dirty Dozen*(part IV), TV, 88, USA, Score Mix; *Promise a Miracle*, Th, 88, USA, Score Mix; *The Unholy*, Th, 87, USA, Score Mix; *Mortuary Academy*, Th, 87, USA, Score Mix; *The Alamo*, TV, 87, USA, Score Mix; *Platoon*, Th, 86, USA, Score Mix; *Salvador*, Th, 85, USA, Scoer Mix; *Our British Columbia*, Th, 85, CDN/USA, Score Mix; *Day in the Life of Canada*, Th, 85, CDN, Score Mix.

MOORE, James
- see EDITORS

NEWELL, Jacqueline
SGCT, ACCT. 3538 Prud'homme, Montreal, PQ (514)486-4562. NFB, 3155 Côte de Liesse, Montreal, PQ (514)283-9586.
Type of Production and Credits: Th Film-Snd Ed; Th Short-Snd Ed; TV Film-Snd Ed.
Genres: Drama-TV; Documentary-Th& TV; Educational-Th&TV; Animation-Th.
Biography: Born 1946, Ottawa, Ontario. B.A., English, McGill University; M.Sc., Radio and TV, Syracuse University. Freelancing as location manager and sound editor, 68-78; sound editor at NFB, 78 to present. Recipient of Golden Sheaf, Yorkton; sound editor on many award-winning films.
Selected Filmography: *Wisecracks*, Th/TV, 91, CDN, Snd Ed; *Burning Times*, Th/TV, 90, CDN, Snd Ed; *Russian Diary*, Th/TV, 89, CDN, Snd Ed; *Goddess Remembered*, Th/TV, 89, CDN, Snd Ed; *The Defender*, TV, 88, CDN, Snd Ed; "At the Wheel" (2 eps), TV, 86, CDN/USA, Snd Ed; *Speaking Our Peace*, Th, 86, CDN, Snd Ed; *Abortion: Stories from North and South*, TV, 84, CDN, Snd Ed; *Behind the Veil* (2 films), Th, 84, CDN, Snd Ed; *The Kid Who Couldn't Miss*, Th, 83, CDN, Snd Ed; *If You Love This Planet*, TV, 81, CDN, Snd Ed; *Not a Love Story*, Th, 80, CDN, Snd Ed; *Why Me?*, Th, 78, CDN, Snd Ed; *The Rubber Gun*, Th, 75, CDN, Snd Ed; *Circus World* (Imax), Th, 72, CDN, Snd Ed.

NYZNIK, Bruce
- see POSTPRODUCTION SOUND MIXERS

O'FARRELL, Michael✧
DGC, ACCT. (416)368-0612.
Type of Production and Credits: Th Film-Snd Ed; TV Film-Snd Ed; TV Video-Snd Ed.
Genres: Drama-Th&TV; Comedy-Th&TV; Science Fiction-Th&TV; Animation-Th&TV.
Biography: Born 1954, Ottawa, Ontario.
Selected Filmography: *The January Man*, Th, 88, USA, Spv Snd Ed; *Physical Evidence*, Th, 88, USA, Spv Snd Ed; *Moonstruck*, Th, 87, USA, Spv Snd Ed; *Smoke*, Th, 87, USA, Spv Snd Ed; *The Kiss*, Th, 87, CDN, Snd Ed; *From the Hip*, Th, 86, USA, Spv Snd Ed; *The Big Town*, Th, 86, USA, Spv Snd Ed; *One Magic Christmas*, Th, 85, CDN/USA, SFX Ed (GENIE); *Agnes of God*, Th, 85, CDN, SFX Ed; *The Pink Chiquitas*, Th, 85, CDN, Spv Snd Ed; *Samuel Lount*, Th, 84, CDN, Spv Snd Ed; *Isaac Littlefeathers*, Th, 84, CDN, SFX Ed; *Losin' It*, Th, 82, USA, SFX Ed; *The Amateur*, Th, 81, CDN, SFX Ed; *Terror Train*, Th, 79, CDN/USA, SFX Ed.

PINDER, Chris
- see EDITORS

POTHIER, Marcel
- voir MONTEURS

RAVOK, Brian
- see EDITORS

REED, Tony
- see EDITORS

REIART, Arvo
- see EDITORS

ROBERTS, Tim N.
DGC. 33 McCord Rd., Toronto, ON M4S 2T7 (416)482-6396.
Type of Production and Credits: Th Film-Snd Ed; TV Film-Snd Ed; TV Video-Snd Ed.
Genres: Drama-Th&TV; Action-Th& TV; Horror-TV; Animation-Th&TV.
Biography: Born in the UK in 1955. British and Canadian citizen.
Selected Filmography: "Sweating Bullets" (13 eps), TV, 91, USA/CDN/MEX, Snd FX Ed; "Road to Avonlea" (26 eps), TV, 89-91, CDN, Dial Ed ADR; *Love & Hate*, TV, 89, CDN, Dial Ed; *Jane of Lantern Hill*, TV, 88-89, Dial Ed; "Street Legal" (7 eps), TV, 88, CDN, Dial Ed; *Murder One*, Th, 88, CDN, Snd FX; *Blood Relations*, Th, 88, CDN, Snd FX; *Champagne Charlie*, TV, 88, CDN, Dial Ed; *Rainbow Bright*, Th, 86, CDN, P Prod Snd Spv; *Care Bears*, Th, 86, CDN, Snd Spv; *Incubus*, Th, 83, CDN, Dial Ed; *Harry Tracy, The Last Desperado*, Th, 83, CDN, Dial Ed.

ROMANOVICH, Cindy◇
(416)463-6918.
Type of Production and Credits: Th Film-Snd Ed; TV Video-Snd Ed; TV Film-Snd Ed.
Genres: Drama-TV; Action-TV; Children's-TV; Animation-Th&TV.
Biography: Born 1961, Niagara Falls, Ontario. Diploma, Media Arts, Sheridan College. Experienced in Soundmaster tape lock editing.
Selected Filmography: "Alfred Hitchcock Presents" TV, 88, CDN/USA, SFX Ed; *The Return of Ben Casey*, TV, 87, USA, SFX Ed; *The Gunfighters*, TV, 87, CDN, SFX Ed; *Ford: The Man and the Machine* (mini-series)(4 eps), TV, 87, CDN, SFX Ed; *Chasing Rainbows* (mini-series)(3 eps), TV, 87, CDN, Assist Snd Ed; *Stone Fox*, TV, 87, CDN, Assist Dial Ed; *Jim Henson's Christmas Toy*, TV, 86, SFX Ed; "Sword of Gideon", TV, 86, CDN, SFX Ed; *The Care Bears Movie II*, Th, 86, CDN, SFX Ed; *The Great Heep*, TV, 85, CDN, SFX Ed; "Droids: The Adventures of R2D2 and C3P0" (13 eps), TV, 85, SFX Ed; *The Care Bears Movie*, Th, 85, CDN, Assist Snd FX Ed.

ROTUNDO, Nick
- see EDITORS

ROY-DECARIE, Matthieu
STCQ. Matthieu Roy-Décarie enr., 6581, St-Denis, #1, Montréal, PQ H2S 2S1 (514)272-6205.
Types de production et générique: l métrage-Mont son; TV film-Mont son; TV vidéo-Mont son.
Types d'oeuvres: Fiction-C&TV; Vidéo-clips-C&TV; Enfants-C&TV.
Curriculum vitae: Né en 1960, Montréal, Québec. Langues: français et anglais. D.E.C. en communications, Collège Jean-de-Brébeuf. Chef monteur, Bellvue-Pathé inc. (Québec), la section doublage, 78-84; monteur sonore pigiste depuis 85; directeur de postproduction depuis 86, en film et en vidéo; scénariste depuis 89; réalisateur depuis 90.
Filmographie sélective: *Scream of Stone/Cerro Torre*, C, 91, CDN/D/F, Dir post-synchro/ADR; *He Wants More*, Albert E., MV, 91, CDN, Mont/Réal/Sc; *Speed of Light*, Albert E., MV, 90, CDN, Mont/Réal/Sc; *Teenage Mutant Ninja Turtles II, The Secret of Ooze* (3 cm), Cm, 90, CDN, Mont; *Y'a pas que les loups*, TV, 90, CDN, Sc/Act; *Vincent and Me*, C, 90, CDN, Dir/Mont post-synchro/ADR; "Ray Bradbury Theatre" (13 eps)(version française), TV, 90, CDN, Dir; *Jésus de Montréal*, C, 89, CDN/F, Mont post-synchro/ADR; *Dans le ventre du dragon*, C, 89, CDN, Mont post-synchro/ADR; "The Northern Lights" (15 eps)(version française), TV, 89, CDN, Dir; *Journey of Tears*, C, 88, CDN/F/RC, Mont post-synchro/ADR; *Les Portes Tournantes*, C, 87, CDN/F, Mont post-synchro/ADR; *La Grenouille et la Baleine*, C, 87, CDN, Dir/Mont post-synchro/ADR; "La Bande à Ovide" (65 eps), TV, 86-87, CDN/B, Dir p pro; *La guerre des Tuques*, C, 84, CDN, Mont dial.

SANDERS, Ronald
- see EDITORS

SAUNDERS, Peter
- see EDITORS

SAUVE, Alain
SGCT. 11495, Gariépy, Montréal-Nord, PQ H1H 4E2 (514)322-6883. ONF, 3155, Côte de Liesse, Montréal, PQ H4N 2N4 (514)283-9366.
Types de production et générique: c métrage-Réal/Sc/Mont/Mont son; TV film-Mont/Mont son; TV vidéo-Mont/Mont son.
Types d'oeuvres: Drame-C&TV; Documentaire-C&TV; Education-TV; Enfants-C&TV.
Curriculum vitae: Né en 1947, Montréal, Québec. Baccalauréat en Sciences, Collège du Mont St-Louis; comptabilité, administration, Ecole des Hautes Etudes Commerciales. Administrateur de production, ONF, 68-71; cinéaste pigiste, 71-

79; monteur, réalisateur, ONF, 79-91.
Filmographie sélective: *Jean-Yves Thériault, l'ultime combat,* C, 91, CDN, Mont son; *Le Marché du couple,* C, 89, CDN, Mont; *Visiteur d'un soir,* C, 89, CDN, Mont/Mont son; *Rendez-vous 10h.30,* C, 85, CDN, Sup mont/Mont son/Réal; *Cinéma, Cinéma,* C, 85, CDN, Mont son; *Le Vieillard et l'Enfant,* C, 85, CDN, Mont son; *L'Emotion Dissonante,* C, 84, CDN, Mont son; *La Plante,* C, 82, CDN, Mont son; *La Quarantaine,* C, 82, CDN, Mont son; *Le Jongleur,* C, 81, CDN, Mont son; *Des Astres et Désastres,* C, 78, CDN, Mont/Mont son/Réal/Sc; *Vingt-six fois de suite,* C, 78, CDN, Mont/Réal; *Chronique de la Vie Quotidienne* (8 eps), C, 77, CDN, Mont/Mont son; *Jeux de la XXIe Olympiade,* C, 76, CDN, Mont; *La Gammick,* C, 74, CDN, Ass mont/Mont son.

SEREDA, John
- see COMPOSERS

SHUMIATCHER, Cal
- see PRODUCERS

STILMAN, Philip Samuel
- see EDITORS

TATTERSALL, Jane
DGC, ACCT. T Productions, 184 Madison Ave., Toronto, ON M5R 2S5 (416)923-0888.
Type of Production and Credits: Th Film-Snd Ed; TV Film-Snd Ed; Th Short-Snd Ed; TV Video-Snd Ed.
Genres: Drama-Th&TV.
Biography: Born 1957, England; Canadian citizenship. B.A., Philosophy, Queen's Univ. Gemini for *Carnival of Shadows*; Golden Reel and Golden Scissors awards for *Murderers Among Us*; Genie nominations, *Buying Time* and *The Climb*; Golden Reel nomination for *The Fly*.
Selected Filmography: *South of Wawa,* Th, 91, CDN, Spv Snd Ed; *Diplomatic Immunity,* Th, 91, CDN, Spv Snd Ed; *White Room,* Th, 90, CDN, Spv Snd Ed; *Welcome Home,* Th, 90, CDN/USA, Spv Snd Ed; *Breaking In,* Th, 89, CDN/USA, Snd FX Ed; *Carnival of Shadows,* TV, 90, CDN, Snd FX Ed, (GEMINI); *Iron Eagle II,* Th, 89, CDN/USA, Snd FX Ed; *Murderers Among Us,* TV, 89, CDN/GB, Snd FX Ed; *Buying Time,* Th, 89, CDN, Snd FX Ed; *Switching Channels,* Th, 88, CDN/USA, Snd FX Ed; *Nowhere to Hide,* Th, 87, CDN/USA, Snd FX Ed; *The Gate,* Th, 86, CDN, Snd FX Ed; *The Fly,* Th, 86, CDN, Snd FX Ed; *The Climb,* Th, 85, CDN, Snd FX Ed; *A Child's Christmas in Wales,* TV, 87, CDN/GB, Snd FX Ed.

THILLAYE, Peter◊
DGC. (416)690-9556.
Type of Production and Credits: Th Film-Snd Ed; TV Film-Snd Ed.
Genres: Drama-Th&TV; Comedy-Th; Animation-Th&TV; Documentary-Th&TV.
Biography: Born 1952, Halifax, Nova Scotia. Languages: English and French.
Selected Filmography: *The January Man,* Th, 88, USA, Snd FX Ed; *The Cry of Reason,* TV, 87, USA, Snd Ed; *Heartland* (Imax), Th, 87, CDN, Spv Snd Ed;*The Big Town,* Th, 87, USA, Snd Ed; *The Kiss,* Th, 87, CDN, Snd Ed; *Another Government Film* (Expo 86), Th, 86, CDN, SPv Snd Ed; *Hello Mary Lou - Prom Night II,* Th, 86, CDN, Snd Ed; *The Prodigiuos Hickey,* TV, 86, CDN/USA, Snd Ed; *John and the Missus,* Th, 86, CDN, Snd Ed; "Ray Bradbury Theatre II" (1 eps), TV, 86, CDN/NZ, Snd Ed; *Loyalties,* Th, 85, CDN/GB, Snd Ed; *One Magic Christmas,* Th, 85, CDN/USA, Snd Ed, (GENIE); *Agnes of God,* Th, 85, USA, Snd Ed; *Heavy Metal,* Th, 81, CDN, Snd Ed, (GENIE); *The Silent Partner,* Th, 77, CDN, Snd Ed, (CFA);

TINGLEY, Cameron
- see EDITOR

TREMBLAY, Robert
- voir REALISATEURS

WERTH, Michael
DGC, LIFT. 1660 Bathurst St., Apt. 40, Toronto, ON M5P 3K1 (416)781-5416.
Type of Production and Credits: Th Film-Snd Ed/Ed; Th Short-Snd Ed/Ed.
Genres: Drama-Th&TV; Documentary-Th&TV; Educational-TV; Experimental-Th.
Biography: Film/Television Program, UBC, 1979-85. Also studied Technical theatre, educational media design, scored high in technical courses. Studied computer programming and still do it in film related applications. Sound engineering course in 1987. Does a lot of work with and for beginning filmmakers, as a sound recordist, editor, consultant and technical workshop leader. Currently doing a lot of optical printing at L.I.F.T. (Liaison of Independent Filmmakers of Toronto) facilities. Working knowledge of German.
Selected Filmography: *Adjuster,* Th, 91, CDN, Ed; *Highway 61,* Th, 90/91, CDN, Snd Rec/Dial Ed; *The Year the River Caught Fire,* Th, 90, CDN, Snd Rec/Ed; *Home for Christmas,* TV, 89-90, CDN, Snd Rec; *Stealing Images,* Th, 89, CDN, Snd Ed/Ed; *Speaking Parts,* Th, 89, CDN, Dial Ed; *Still Life,* Th, 89, CDN, Snd FX

Ed; *No. 5 Reversal*, Th, 89, CDN, Cam Assist; *Harriet Loves*, Th, 88, CDN, Snd Ed; *Friend, Go Up Higher*, Th, 88, CDN, Snd Ed; *Friends, Lovers, Lunatics*, Th, 88, CDN, Dial Ed; *Northbound Cairo*, Th, 88, CDN, Snd Ed; *World Drums*, TV, 88, CDN, Snd Ed; *Inside Out*, Th, 88, CDN, Assist Ed; *I've Heard the Mermaids Singing*, Th, 87, CDN, Assist Ed.

Writers
Scenaristes

A'COURT, Susan
ACCT. 167 Boulton Ave., Toronto, ON M4M 2J8 (416)465-4874. FAX: 465-7760.
Type of Production and Credits: TV Film-Wr/Prod.
Genres: Documentary-TV; Drama-TV; Educational-TV; Children's TV.
Biography: Born 1952, Toronto, Ontario. B.Sc.N., University of Toronto. *Red Shoes* won Bronze, Columbus Film Festival, 86 and earned an honourable mention, Chicago International Festival of Children's Films, 86; Award of Excellence, Children's Broadcast Institute for "Kids of Degrassi Street."
Selected Filmography: *The Path Ahead*, ED, 89-90, CDN, Wr/Assoc Prod; "School Works" (4 eps), ED, 89-90, CDN, Wr/Assoc Prod; *Being Canadian*, TV, 87-88, CDN, Wr; *Hell & High Water*, "Assignment Adventure", TV, 85-86, CDN/GB, Wr; *Red Shoes*, "Bell Canada Playhouse", TV, 85-86, CDN, Prod; *Hotwalker*, "Bell Canada Playhouse", TV, 85-86, CDN, Prod; *Esso*, "Bell Canada Playhouse", TV, 85-86, CDN, CDN, Prod; *Going to War*, "Bell Canada Playhouse", TV, 85-86, CDN, Prod; *Women's Work*, "The Campbells", TV, 86, CDN/USA/GB, Wr; Air Canada: *Sun Destinations*, Cm, 84-85, CDN, Wr/Field Prod; "Kids of Degrassi Street" 4 eps), TV, 81-84, CDN, Wr; "Kids of Degrassi Street" (6 eps), TV, 82-83, CDN, PM.

ABBOTT, Roger
ACTRA, WGA. Abbott/Ferguson Productions Ltd., 66 Gerrard Street East, Toronto, ON M5B 1G3 (416)977-6222.

FAX: 977-3759.
Type of Production and Credits: TV Film-Wr; TV Video-Wr.
Genres: Comedy-TV; Variety-TV.
Biography: Born 1946, Birkenhead, England; landed immigrant, Canada. Radio station promotion director, programming, operations manager, 65-70. Comedy and variety writer, performer, director, producer (TV, radio, stage), 71-present, notably with "Royal Canadian Air Farce" series. Awards: 3 ACTRA Awards for TV variety writing, 5 for radio variety writing, 5 for performing; Juno for Air Farce comedy album.
Selected Filmography: *Gemini Awards, 1990*, TV, 90, CDN, Co-Wr; "Royal Canadian Air Farce Specials" (4 eps), TV, 80-84, CDN, Co-Wr/Act; "Royal Canadian Air Farce" (10 eps), TV, 81, CDN, Co-Wr/Act; "Mary and Michael" (26 eps), TV, 77, CDN, Head Wr/Pro Spv; "Mixed Doubles" (13 eps), TV, 76, CDN, Story Ed/Pro Spv; "Caught in the Act" (13 eps), TV, 76, CDN, Story Ed/Pro Spv.

ADAMAKOS, Peter
- see PRODUCERS

ADETUYI, Robert
WGC (ACTRA). 406 - 2261 Lake Shore Blvd. W., Toronto, ON M8V 3X1 (416)503-2729. Lynne Kinney, Credentials, 387 Bloor St. E., Toronto, ON (416)926-1507.
Type of Production and Credits: Th Film-Wr; Th Short-Dir; TV Video-Dir.
Genres: Drama-Th&TV; Comedy-Th&TV.
Biography: Born in 1959 in Sudbury, Ontario. Honours B.A. in Mass Communications and Film, York University, 1986. Co-founder of Telelight Entertainment, acting as producer/writer from 1983-87. Co-founder/partner of Inner City Films from 1987. Established Ade Films in 1990 to produce theatrical films that explore themes of race, social class and contemporary values. Selected for the Canadian Centre for Advanced Film Studies, Summer 1991 Lab, as director of his feature screenplay, *Dancing with the Devil.*
Selected Filmography: *Hey, I've Got Rights!*, ED, 91, CDN, Co-Wr/Dir/Co-Prod; *A Place for Everyone*, In, 87, CDN, Prod; *Lawyers' Suite*, TV, 86, CDN, Wr/Prod; *Enough is Enough*, TV, 81, CDN, Prod/Wr/Dir.

AIKENHEAD, Chris
- see PRODUCTION SOUND MIXERS

ALEXANDRA, Christopher P.
- see COMPOSERS

ALIANAK, Hrant
- see DIRECTORS

ALIX, Stephen
ACTRA. 105 Alcina Ave., Toronto, ON M6G 2E7 (416)653-6611. FAX: 653-6611.
Type of Production and Credits: Th Film-Wr/Prod; TV Film-Wr.
Genres: Drama-Th&TV; Action-Th&TV; Children's-Th&TV.
Selected Filmography: "Counterstrike" (1 eps), TV, 91, USA, Wr; *Clearcut*, Th, 90, CDN, Exec Prod; *Royal Wedding*, "Mount Royal", TV, 88, CDN/F, Wr; *Rebel High*, Th, 84, CDN, Wr.

ALLAN, Sean
- see PRODUCERS

ALLAN, Ted
ACTRA, WGAw. Linda Butler, Butler Ruston Bell Assoc., 501 Yonge St., Suite 301, Toronto, ON M4Y 1Y4 (416)964-6660. Mike Zimring Agency, 1387 Doheny Dr., Los Angeles, CA 90069 USA (213)278-8240.
Type of Production and Credits: Th Film-Wr; TV Film-Wr.
Genres: Drama-Th&TV; Comedy-Th&TV.
Biography: Born Montreal, Quebec. Feature films: *Bethune: The Making of a Hero; Love Streams; Lies My Father Told Me.* Berlin Golden Bear for *Love Streams* with John Cassavetes. Oscar nomination for *Lies My Father Told Me* which also won a Golden Globe Award, ACTRA, Genie and Virgin Island Film Festival Award for best original screenplay. Stage Plays: *The Money Makers; Legend of Paradiso; Oh, What a Lovely War.* Stage treatment: *Double Image; Gog and Magog* (with R. MacDougal); *Chu Chem, A Zen Buddhist-Hebrew Musical; Love Streams; Lies My Father Told Me; I've Seen You Cut Lemons.* Books: *The Scalpel, The Sword, The Story of Dr. Bethune* (with S. Gordon); *Willie The Squows; Love Is A Long Shot; Don't You Know Anybody Else?; This Time, a Better Earth.* Many radio and television plays for CBC, BBC, ITV. Actor in television and films.
Selected Filmography: *Bethune: The Making of a Hero*, Th, 90, CDN, Scr; *Love Streams*, Th, 83, CDN, Co-Scr; *Lies My Father Told Me*, Th, 75, CDN, Scr, (CFA).

ALMOND, Paul
- see DIRECTORS

AMITAY, Jonathan
- see PRODUCERS

ANDERSON, Jon C.
- see PRODUCERS

ANDREWS, Neil
- see PRODUCERS

ARCAND, Denys
- voir REALISATEURS

ARNOTT, Duane S.
42 Servington Cres., #1, Toronto, ON M4S 2J4 (416)483-5596.
Type of Production and Credits: Th Film-Wr.
Genres: Drama-Th; Comedy-Th&TV; Action-Th; Science Fiction-Th; Documentary-TV; Commercials-Th; Adventure-Th; Martial Arts-Th.
Biography: Canadian citizen. Born in Regina in 1955. Got involved in film originally with the Saskatchewan Filmpool. Diploma of Associate in Arts, University of Regina, 1975. Karate club member, 1973-75. Algonquin Summer Institute, 90/91. Courses included Danny Simon's comedy writing, Robert McKee's story structure and Robert Bordiga's Film & TV. President, Intermission International Productions Inc., producing ads for drive-ins. As a freelance writer, articles have appeared in *Starlog*, *You*, *Comics Scene* and *Inside King Fu*, as well as numerous stories in local papers and magazines. Has written a biography of Bruce Lee, *Bruce Lee - The Life Not the Legend*, which is slated for a 1992 release.
Selected Filmography: *Tiger Claus*, Th, 91, CDN, Unit Pub; *It's Intermission Time*, the trailer, Th/Cm, 88, CDN, Prod/Wr; *Looking Back*, Th, 80, CDN, Unit Pub; *Folks Call Me Tommy*, Th, 80, Assoc Prod; *So You Think You're the Toughest Guy in Town?/The Fight*, Th, 79, CDN, Prod.

ARSENAULT, Yvon
- voir REALISATEURS

ARSENEAU, Joanne◇
SARDEC. (514)274-2906.
Types de production et générique: TV vidéo-Sc.
Types d'oeuvres: Drame-TV; Comédie-TV; Enfants-TV.
Curriculum vitae: Née en 1953, Montréal, Québec. Langues: français et anglais. Maitrise en psychologie, scolarité de doctorat.
Filmographie sélective: "A plein temps" (30 eps), TV, 84-86, CDN, Aut; "Samedi de rire" (5 eps), TV, 84-86, CDN, Co-Aut; "Court Circuit" (6 eps), TV, 85, CDN, Aut; "Pop Citrouille" (20 eps), TV, 80-83, CDN, Co aut; "Bof et Cie" (5 eps), TV, 83, CDN, Aut.

AUDY, Michel
- voir REALISATEURS

AYLWARD, Alan W.
- see DIRECTORS

AZZOPARDI, Anthony
- see DIRECTORS

BALCER, Rene C.
ACTRA, WGA. 2585 N. Beachwood Dr., Los Angeles, CA 90068 (213)469-6081. David Lonner/Richard Feldman, I.C.M., 8899 Beverly Blvd., Los Angeles, CA 90048 USA. (213)550-4000.
Type of Production and Credits: Th Film-Wr; Th Short-Wr/Dir/Ed; TV Film-Wr.
Genres: Drama-Th&TV; Action-Th&TV; Science Fiction-Th&TV; Documentary-Th&TV; Experimental-Th&TV.
Biography: Born in 1954 in Montreal, Quebec. Canadian citizen, U.S. resident. Languages: English and French. Concordia University. National Psychology Award for Excellence in the media; Lillian Gish Award for Best MOW. Photojournalist, reporter, magazine editor. Has travelled throughout North America, Europe, the Middle East and Africa. Many features in development at various majors.
Selected Filmography: "Law & Order" (6 eps), TV, 90-91, USA, Wr; *A Son's Memories*, TV, 91, USA, Wr; "Nasty Boys" (4 eps), TV, 90, USA, Wr/Story Ed; *Out on the Edge/Au bord de L'Abyme*, TV, 89, USA, Wr.

BANNING, Everett
- see PRODUCERS

BARBEAU, Manon
760, Champagneur, Outremont, PQ H2V 3P8 (514)276-5728. Radio-Québec, 1000, rue Fullum, Montréal, PQ H2K 3L7 (514)521-2424.
Types de production et générique: c métrage-Sc; TV film-Sc; TV vidéo-Sc.
Types d'oeuvres: Drame-C&TV; Comédie-C&TV; Comédie musicale-C&TV; Documentaire-C&TV.
Curriculum vitae: Neé en 1949, Montréal, Québec. Langues: français et anglais. Baccalauréat spécialisé en communications.
Filmographie sélective: "Tristan et Juliette"/"L'amour en l'an 2000" (5 eps), TV, 91, CDN, Sc; *Pour faire une histoire courte*, C, 91, CDN, Sc; "Les Club des 100 watts" (30 eps), TV, 90, CDN, Sc, (GEMEAUX); "Les Club de 100 watts" (hebdo), TV, 88, CDN, Co aut; "Adèle Comeau mène l'enquête" (6 eps), TV, 86, CDN, Sc/Dial; *Agora: Stéphane Tremblay, paroles et musique*, TV, 85, CDN, Sc; *Les Chérubins*, TV, 85, CDN, Sc; *Tilt*, TV, 84, CDN, Sc; *T'as bien changé, Marie*, TV, 83, CDN, Sc; *Paysages sonores*, TV, 82, CDN, Sc; "Bozéjeunnes" (5 eps), TV, 81,

CDN, Sc; *Nous sommes plusieurs beaucoup de monde*, TV, 80, CDN, Réal; *L'Attente*, "Contrejour", TV, 79, CDN, Sc; "Visages" (2 eps), TV, 78, CDN, Sc; *Les Arpenteurs de Karnak*, C, 77, F, Sc.

BARLOW, David
- see PRODUCERS

BARNEY, Bryan
ACTRA. 19 Portneuf Court, Toronto, ON M5A 4E4 (416)368-3578.
Type of Production and Credits: Th Film-Wr; TV Film-Wr; TV Video-Wr.
Genres: Drama-Th&TV; Comedy-TV; Action-TV.
Biography: Born 1930, Reading, England; Canadian citizenship. Worked as magazine editor and journalist.
Selected Filmography: "The Phoenix Team" (2 eps), TV, 80, CDN, Wr; "The Great Detective" (1 eps), TV, 78, CDN, Wr; "Flappers" (1 eps), TV, 78, CDN, Wr; "High Hopes" (32 eps), TV, 78, CDN/USA, Dial; *Delilah*, "To See Ourselves", TV, 76, CDN, Wr; *The Far Shore*, Th, 75, CDN, Scr; "Police Surgeon" (1 eps), TV, 74, CDN/USA, Story; *Close Call*, TV, 74, CDN, Wr; *Some Are So Lucky/Rigmarole*, "Canadian Short Stories", TV, 70, CDN, T'play; *The Fur Coat/Fringe Benefits*, "Anthology", TV, 69-70, CDN, Wr; "McQueen" (3 eps), TV, 69, CDN, Wr; *Trophy Room*, TV, 67, CDN, Wr.

BARRA, Gemma
SARDEC. Les Editions Vient de la Mer, 400, boul. Père Levièvre, Québec, PQ G1M 1N1 (418)527-5167.
Types de production et générique: 1 métrage-Sc/Réal.
Types d'oeuvres: Drame-C; Documentaire-C; Education-TV; Enfants-C.
Curriculum vitae: Née en 1939, Vanier, Québec. Comédienne, scénariste, écrivain, auteur-compositeur de plus de 300 chansons, pionière de la chanson québécoise; animatrice de radio, "Mes Chansons" et "Créations du Québec", 56-66; animatrice de TV, "Mon pays, mes chansons," 67-68. Publications: *Sous le ciel de Québec*, 87, *Père Noël te raconte ses histoires*, 88, et *Le Lutin, le Géant et le Nain*, 88.
Filmographie sélective: *Une Grande Fille toute simple*, ED, 91, CDN, Aut/Comp/Sc; *Hirsy*, ED, 88, CDN, Aut; *Monsieur Document*, In, 75, CDN, Aut/Réal; *La Maîtrise*, C, 72, CDN, Co sc; *Le Ski à la façon des Autrichiens*, C, 70, CDN/A, Sc; *L'Assurance Maladie*, In, 70, CDN, Sc/Rech/Dir pro; *Transport Canada*, In, CDN, Rech/Co sc.

BARRIE, Scott
ACTRA, DGC, ACCT. 31 Northcliffe Blvd., Toronto, ON M6H 3G9 (416)652-2232.
Type of Production and Credits: Th Short-Dir/Prod/Wr; TV Film-Dir/Wr/Ed.
Genres: Drama-TV; Documentary-Th&TV; Children's-TV.
Biography: Born 1951, Collingwood, Ontario. Social Sciences, McMaster University, Hamilton Teachers' College. Taught children with learning disabilities. Film Production, Conestoga College. His films have won numerous awards at Houston, Yorkton, NY, Chicago; *In Search of the Edge* won a Worldfest Silver Award at Houston and a Silver Hugo in Chicago; twice winner of Canadian Independent Short Film Showcase for *I Think of You Often* and *Footsteps*; 2 Genie nominations, theatrical short films.
Selected Filmography: "Two for Joy" (pilot), TV, 91, CDN, Assoc Prod/Co-Wr; *In Search of the Edge*, ED, 90, CDN, Prod/Wr/Dir; "My Secret Identity" (2 eps), TV, 89-90, CDN, Wr; *Stay Alert...Stay Safe*, ED, 90, CDN, Wr; "The Campbells" (22 eps)(Wr 6 eps), TV, 87-88, CDN/USA/GB, Ed/Wr; "Blizzard Island" (1 eps), TV, 88, CDN, Wr; "OWL-TV" (12 seg), TV, 86-87, CDN, Dir; *Home Alone*, Th, 86, USA, Dir; "The Edison Twins" (Dir 3 eps/Wr 5 eps/Ed 10 eps), TV, 83-85, CDN, Dir/Wr/Ed; *I Think of You Often*, Th, 83, CDN, Wr/Dir/Prod; *Bookwright*, TV, 83, CDN, Dir/Prod/Cin; *Newfoundland Sketchbook*, TV, 83, CDN, Dir/Prod/Cin; *K.C.I. Beyond the Three R's*, TV, 82, CDN, Dir; *American Nightmare*, Th, 82, CDN, 1st Assist Cam; *Footsteps*, Th, 79, CDN, Dir/Wr/Ed.

BARRIS, Alex
ACTRA, WGAw. 6 Malamute Cr., Agincourt, ON M1T 2C7 (416)292-7488.
Type of Production and Credits: TV Film-Wr; TV Video-Wr.
Genres: Drama-TV; Comedy-TV; Variety-TV; Documentary-TV.
Biography: Born 1922, US; Canadian citizenship since 65. Has written many TV shows in Canada, 56-68; Los Angeles, 69-76; returned to Canada, 77. *A Funny Thing Happened on the Way to the Symphony* won Best Musical Variety, AMPIA, 1986; Nominated for an Emmy for the *Doris Day Special*.
Selected Filmography: *Gordon Pinsent Sings Those Hollywood Songs*, TV, 87, CDN, Co-Wr/Co-Prod; *Lorne Greene Remembered*, TV, 87, CDN, Wr; "Rear

View Mirror" (30 eps), TV, 81-85, CDN, Wr; *A Funny Thing Happened on the Way to the Symphony*, TV, 84, CDN, Wr; *Jazz Alive*, TV, 83, CDN, Wr; "The Palace" (26 eps), TV, 79-80, CDN/USA, Head Wr; *ACTRA Awards* (2 shows), TV, 78-79, CDN, Wr; *Irish Rovers' Celebration*, TV, 78, CDN, Wr; "King of Kensington" (7 eps), TV, 78, CDN, Wr; *A Little Part of Canada*, TV, 78, CDN, Wr; "So the Story Goes" (16 eps), TV, 77, CDN, Story Ed; *Juliette Special*, TV, 77, CDN, Wr; "Celebrity Revue" (120 eps), TV, 76, CDN/USA, Head Wr; "Entertainment Hall of Fame" (2 eps), TV, 75-76, USA, Co-Wr; "Wizard of Odds" (65 eps), TV, 74, USA, Co-Wr.

BARRIS, Kate
ACTRA. 192 Gillard Ave., Toronto ON M4J 4N8 (416)778-0241 FAX: 778-8476.
Type of Production and Credits: TV Film-Wr; TV Video-Wr; Industrial Video-Wr.
Genres: Comedy-TV; Musical-TV; Variety-TV; Children's-TV.
Biography: Born 1953, Toronto, Ontario. B.A.A., Radio & TV Arts, Ryerson Polytechnical Institute. Freelance writer in TV as well as advertising, for which she has won Canadian and international awards.
Selected Filmography: *Miss Teen Canada Pageant* (4 shows), TV, 85-88, CDN, Co-Wr; *Hospital for Sick Children Telethon* (4 shows), TV, 85-88, CDN, Co-Wr; "Check It Out!" (1 eps), TV, 88, CDN/USA, Wr; "The Riddle of Wizard's Oak" (3 eps), TV, 88, CDN, Wr; "Sesame Street" (numerous sketches), TV, 87-88, CDN, Wr; *Miss Canada Pageant* (4 shows), TV, 84-87, CDN, Co-Wr; *Santa Claus Parade* (3 shows), TV, 85-87, CDN, Wr; *ACTRA Awards* (4 shows), TV, 83-86, CDN, Co-Wr; "Today's Special" (15 eps), TV, 81-86, CDN, Wr; "Mr. Dressup" (30 eps), TV, 83-86, CDN, Wr; CFTO *Celebrates 25 Sensational Years*, TV, 85, CDN, Wr; "Laughing Matters" (13 eps), TV, 85, CDN, Contr Wr; "Welcome Home" (pilot), TV, 85, CDN, Co-Wr; "Just Kidding" (22 eps), TV, 84-85, CDN, Co-Wr; "Gallager Gardens" (pilot), TV, 85, CDN, Co-Wr.

BASEN, Leila
ACTRA. 5180 Côte St-Antoine, Montreal, PQ H4A 1N8 (514)485-1174. FAX: 485-1174. The Jennifer Hollyer Agency, 112 Westmount Ave., #4, Toronto, ON M6H 3K4 (416)651-8246.
Type of Production and Credits: Th Film-Wr; Th Short-Wr; TV Film-Wr.
Genres: Drama-Th&TV; Comedy-Th&TV; Variety-TV; Educational-Th&TV.
Biography: Born in 1955 in Toronto, Ontario. Honours B.A., Film, York University.
Selected Filmography: *Weep No More My Lady*, "Mary Higgins Clark Series", TV, 91, CDN/F/GB, Wr; *Too Many Cooks*, "Street Legal", TV, 91, CDN, Wr; *The Divine Comedian*, "Max Glick", TV, 90, CDN, Wr; *Queen for a Day*, "Max Glick", TV, 90, CDN, Wr; *Love's Labours*, "Max Glick", TV, 90, CDN, Wr; *Postcards from the Past*, "Urban Angel", TV, 90, CDN, Wr; *Equal Partners*, "Street Legal", TV, 88, CDN, Wr; "Rockit Records" (pilot), TV, 85, CDN, Wr; *If You Want a Girl Like Me*, "Bioethics", ED, 85, CDN, Wr; *My Own Way to Rock/Burton Cummings Variety Special*, TV, 83, CDN, Wr; *Killing 'em Softly*, Th, 82, CDN, Co-Wr; "Hangin' In" (4 eps), TV, 82, CDN, Wr; "Flappers" (2 eps), TV, 81, CDN, Wr; *Your Ticket Is No Longer Valid*, Th, 79, CDN, Co-Wr.

BATTLE, Murray
- see DIRECTORS

BAUMAN, Larry
- see DIRECTORS

BEARDE, Chris
- see PRODUCERS

BEAUBIEN, Conrad
- see PRODUCERS

BEAUCHEMIN, Yves
SARDEC. 247, St-Jacques, Longueuil, PQ J4H 3B8 (514)670-4919. Jacques Fortin, Editions Québec/Amérique, 425, rue Saint-Jean Baptiste, Montréal, PQ H2Y 2Z7 (514)393-1450.
Types de production et générique: c métrage-Sc.
Types d'oeuvres: Comédie-C.
Curriculum vitae: Né en 1941, Noranda, Québec. Licence ès Lettres (français, littérature, histoire de l'art), Université de Montreal, 65. Editeur, professeur, recherchiste; écrivain: *l'Enfirouapé*, *Le Matou*, 81, *Du sommet d'un arbre*, 87, *Juliette Pomerleau*, 89. Récipiendaire du prix France-Québec décerné par l'Association des écrivains de langue français pour *Enfirouapé*. Autres prix: Prix du Roman de l'été (France) et Prix de la Communauté urbaine de Montréal pour *Le Matou*; Prix Jean Giono, (France) et Prix des Lectrices de Elle (France) pour *Juliette Pomerleau*.
Filmographie sélective: *Burlex*, C, 70, CDN, Réal/Sc/Com.

BEAUDRY, Jean
- voir REALISATEURS

BEAUDRY, Michel
- voir REALISATEURS

BECKMAN, Henry
AFTRA, SAG, WGA, WGC, DGC. 3906 Nelson Rd., Deming, WA 98244 (206)592-2618. FAX: 592-2618. Gayle Abrams, 59 Berkeley St., Toronto, ON (416)860-1790.
Type of Production and Credits: TV Video-Wr/Prod/Dir.
Genres: Drama-Th&TV; Comedy-Th&TV; Musical-Th; Horror-Th&TV.
Biography: Actor, writer, producer, director. Born in 1921. Twice awarded a Genie for acting. Has performed in over 800 TV shows and 8 series (featured and co-starred). Featured player in *Stuck With Each Other*, *I Love You To Death*, *Blood River*, *Garwood*, *The Last P.O.W.* "MacGyver" and "Street Legal". Dubbed Chevalier (Sir) Henry, Sovereign Order of St. John of Jerusalem, Knights of Malta, Sept. 1990. Writer/producer/director/editor/Music/D.O.P./lighting director/props/actor of *The Screen Test*, the definitive "auteur" film, (in short, Beckman makes a movie all by himself). Founder and Exec. Dir. of the Canadian Film-Stars Hall of Fame. Awarded the Queen Elizabeth Jubilee Medal, 1977, for contributions to Canadian culture. Has received many other awards.
Selected Filmography: "Juvenile Court", TV, 91, USA, Wr/Prod/Dir; *The Screen Test*, Wr/Prod/Dir/Ed.

BELANGER, Fernand
- voir REALISATEURS

BELL, John G.
- see DIRECTORS

BENEDIKT, Bozidar
DGC, ACCT. 1521 Indian Grove, Mississauga, ON L5H 2S5 (416)274-0879.
Type of Production and Credits: Th Film-Wr/Dir.
Genres: Drama-Th.
Biography: Born in 1938 in Yuoslavia. Produced, wrote and directed 16 short and animated films. Worked in Italy, Germany and Hollywood. From 1988, has worked only on television and theatrical features, specializing in mystery suspense. Has published 36 books, both in Slavic and English. Married with 2 children. Won a Golden Screen Award for his work on the Yugoslavian film *Higija*, 1966.
Selected Filmography: *Graveyard Story*, Th, 90, CDN, Wr/Dir; *Brooklyn Nights*, TV, 88, CDN, Co-Wr/Dir; *Beyond the 7th Door*, TV, 86, CDN, Wr/Dir; *Higija*, 66, YU, Wr/Dir.

BENOIT, Denyse
- voir REALISATEURS

BENOIT, Jacques
SARDEC. 4139, av. Old Orchard, Montréal, PQ H4A 3B3 (514)484-3952. La Presse, 7 ouest, rue St-Jacques, Montréal, PQ (514)285-7070.
Types de production et générique: 1 métrage-Sc; TV vidéo-Sc.
Types d'oeuvres: Drame-C&TV; Action-C.
Curriculum vitae: Né en 1941. Remporte le Prix du Québec pour son roman *Jos Carbone*, 69; Prix Judith Jasmin (journalisme), 76. Chroniqueur viticole pour *La Presse* depuis 82.
Filmographie sélective: "Empire Inc." (1 eps), TV, 81, CDN, Co sc; *L'Affaire Coffin*, C, 79, CDN, Sc; *Réjeanne Padovani*, C, 72, CDN, Co sc, (CFA); *La Maudite Galette*, C, 71, CDN, Sc.

BERGMAN, Robert
- see DIRECTORS

BERTON, Pierre
OC. R.R. #1, Kleinburg, ON L0J 1C0 (416)893-1103. My Country Productions, 21 Sackville St., Toronto, ON M5A 3E1 (416)864-9753.
Type of Production and Credits: Th Short-Wr; TV Film-Wr; TV Video-Wr.
Genres: Documentary-Th&TV; Educational TV.
Biography: Born 1920; raised in the Yukon. Has 11 honorary degrees. Managing Editor of *Maclean's*, 1947; editor, columnist, *Toronto Star*, 1958-62; host of "The Pierre Berton Show", 1972-73. Has written revue sketches, musical comedy for the stage; plays and documentaries for radio, film and TV, a daily newspaper column and 36 books; is seen weekly on CBC's "Front Page Challenge". Has won 3 Governor General's Awards for Creative Non-fiction: *The Mysterious North*, *Klondike*, *The Last Spike*; 2 National Newspaper Awards, 2 ACTRA Awards for broadcasting; Companion of the Order of Canada; member, Canadian News Hall of Fame; Entertainment Columnist, *Toronto Star*, "Weekend."
Selected Filmography: "The Secret of My Success" (20 eps), TV, 88, CDN, Wr/Interv; "Heritage Theatre" (26 eps), TV, 84-85, CDN, Story Ed/Host; *Spirit of Batoche*, TV, 85, CDN, Wr/Narr; *The Dionne Quintuplets*, TV, 79, CDN, Wr/Narr; *Grenfell*, TV, 76, CDN, Wr/Narr; "The National Dream" (8 eps), TV, 74, CDN, Narr; *City of Gold*, Th, 58, CDN, Wr/Narr.

BESSADA, Milad
- see PRODUCERS

BINGEMAN, Alison
ACTRA. Jerry Adler/The Adler Agency, 12725 Venture Blvd., Ste. B, Studio City, CA 91604 USA (818)761-9850.
Type of Production and Credits: TV Film-Wr; TV Video-Wr.
Genres: Drama-Th&TV; Science Fiction-TV; Horror-TV; Children's-TV.
Biography: Born in Wilmington, Delaware. Canadian citizen. Attended Université de la France-Compte, Besançon France; McGill University (B.A., Joint Honours, English and French); Concordia University (Diploma, Communication Studies). Fluent in English and French.
Selected Filmography: *To The Orchards*, "The Hidden Room", TV, 91, USA/CDN, Wr; *Little Nightmares, Little Dreams*, "The Hidden Room", TV, 91, USA/CDN, Wr; *Pawns*, "The Hitchhiker", TV, 89, USA/CDN/F, Wr; *Paddington Meets the Queen*, "Paddington Bear", TV, 89, USA/GB, Wr; *In Shadows Find Me*, "Captain Power", TV, 88, USA/CDN, Wr.

BLAIS, Marc
- voir REALISATEURS

BJORNSON, Michelle
3216 West Second Ave., Vancouver, BC V6K 1K8 (604)733-3645. Point of View Film, 3216 West Second Ave., Vancouver, BC V6K 1K8 (604)734-5035.
Type of Production and Credits: Th Short-Wr/Dir/Ed/Prod; TV Film-Wr/Dir/Ed/Prod.
Genres: Drama-Th&TV; Documentary-Th&TV; Educational-Th&TV; Commercials-TV; Promotional-Th&TV.
Biography: Born in 1945 in Toronto, Ontario. Canadian citizen. English first language, some French and Spanish. B.A. (History), University of Toronto; M.A. (Theatre), University of B.C.; Diploma, Film & TV Arts, University of B.C.; B.C. Arts Award (screenwriting professional development); Banff Television Festival Fellowship; Association Tele-Education Canada Fellowship. *The Mailboat Doesn't Stop Here Anymore* awarded HIFF World Fest Finalist Award. Extra skills in stage design.
Selected Filmography: *The Mailboat Doesn't Stop Here Any More*, Th/TV, 90, CDN, Wr/Dir/Ed/Prod; *UBC 75th Anniversary Campaign*, In, 89, CDN, Wr/Dir/Ed; *C.K.N.W. Children's Fund "Thank You"* (3 cm), Cm, 88, CDN, Wr/Dir/Ed; *End of the Game*, Th/TV, 87, CDN, Wr/Dir/Ed/Prod.

BLANCHARD, André
ARRFQ, SARDEC. 4443, de Bordeaux, Montréal, PQ H2H 1Z6 (514)524-5149.
Types de production et générique: l métrage-Sc/Prod/Réal; TV film-Sc/Réal; TV vidéo-Sc/Réal.
Types d'oeuvres: Drame-C&TV; Comédie-C&TV; Documentaire-C&TV.
Curriculum vitae: Né en 1951, Laval, Québec. Docteur en cinéma, télévision et audio-visuel (Sorbonne). Direction de photographie, Institut des Arts de Diffusion, Bruxelles, 70-73. Multi-Média et Noranda, 75-76; Radio-Québec, 79. Scénariste de 3 longs métrages, 86-88. *L'Hiver bleu* remporte Ducat d'Or, Mannheim et le Prix de la Critique québécoise.
Filmographie sélective: *Alisée*, C, 91, CDN/F, Réal/Sc; émissions pour Radio-Québec (10), TV, 79-83, CDN, Réal/Sc; *L'Hiver bleu*, C, 79, CDN, Réal/Sc; "Le fond de l'affaire" (20 eps), TV, 77-79, CDN, Réal/Sc; *Beat*, C, 76, CDN, Réal/Sc.

BLICKER, Seymour
WGC (ACTRA), WGA. 4324 Sherbrooke St. W., #43, Westmount, PQ H3Z 1E1 (514)937-0405.
Type of Production and Credits: Th Film-Wr; TV Film-Wr; TV Video-Wr.
Genres: Drama-Th&TV; Comedy-Th&TV; Action-Th&TV.
Biography: Born in Montreal, Quebec. Canadian citizen. Graduate of Loyola College (B.A.), 1962. Speaks English and French. Also a novelist and playwright. Novels, *Blues Chased a Rabbit*, 1969; *Shmucks*, 1972; *The Last Collection*, 1976. Plays produced in Canada, U.S. and Europe, *Up Your Alley*, 1987; *Never Judge a Book By It's Cover*, 1987. Was Special Lecturer in Creative Writing at Concordia University, Montreal, from 1978-90. Also a script consultant. Awards include Senior Fellowship from the Canada Council, 1974, for writing and the Ontario Arts Council Award for Fiction, 1977.
Selected Filmography: *Old Boys*, "Urban Angel", TV, 90, CDN, Wr; *'N Hoofdstuk Apart/Another Story*, TV, 88, NL, Wr; *Big Brother*, "Sidestreet", TV, 78, CDN, Wr; *Werewolf*, "Barney Miller", TV, 76, USA, Wr.

BLOW, Peter
ACTRA, ACTT. 67 Marjory Ave., Toronto, ON M4M 2Y2 (416)461-2305. Charles Northcote, Core Group Talent Agency, 489 College St., #501, Toronto, ON M6G 1A5 (416)944-0193.
Type of Production and Credits: Th

Film-Wr; TV Film-Wr/Dir.
Genres: Drama-Th&TV; Documentary-Th&TV; Educational-TV; Children's-Th&TV.
Biography: Born in 1952 in Lincoln, England. In Canada since 1978. Educated at the London School of Film Technique, under tutelage of film veteran Charles Crichton. Student Documentary, *Pigdom* gathered multiple awards. Worked as a stage manager in a small London West-End theatre. Worked in various departments at Studio Film Labs, London (rostrum cameraman, etc.). Was Assistant Technical Manager on Oscar-nominated documentary *Mysterious Castles of Clay* and 50 additional half hours for Anglia TV's "World of Survival" Emmy-award-winning wildlife series. Canadian documentary *Harvest of Despair* has won the Gold Medal and Grand Award, International Film & Television Festival, New York and first prizes at Houston, Columbus and Yorkton; *Borrowed Time* won honourable mention at Yorkton and Columbus; *Fast and the Furious* won the Silver Medal, International Sports Festival and the Red Ribbon, American Film Festival. Was nominated for a Genie for *Dream Never Dies* which also won the Grand Award, Houston.
Selected Filmography: *Borrowed Time*, "Human Edge", TV, 90, CDN/GB, Wr/Dir; *Secret of the Phantom of the Opera*, TV, 89, CDN/USA, Wr; *National Drug Test*, TV, 89, CDN, Co-Wr; *Omar Sharif's Egypt*, "Return Journey", TV, 88, CDN/GB, Story Cons; *Toronto*, "Cities Fit To Live In", TV, 87, CDN/GB, Wr; *Big Horns*, "Danger Bay", TV, 87, CDN/USA, Co-Wr; *People United*, "Canadian Reflections", TV, 86, CDN, Wr/Dir; *Harvest of Despair*, Th, 85, CDN, Wr/Pict Cons/Res; *Fast and the Furious*, TV, 83, CDN, Wr/Pict Cons; *Those Flying Canucks*, TV, 82, CDN, Wr/Pict Cons; *Dream Never Dies*, Th, 81, CDN, Wr/Story Cons.

BLUM, Jack
WGC (ACTRA). 10 Sackville Pl., Toronto, ON M4X 1A4 (416)923-3357.
Type of Production and Credits: TV Film-Wr; TV Video-Wr.
Genres: Drama-TV; Comedy-TV; Children's-TV.
Biography: Born in 1956 in Toronto, Ontario; Canadian and US citizenship. Graduate, National Theatre School (acting, directing). Has written and directed for the stage in Canada and US; associate artistic director, LaJolla Playhouse, California, 83. Won the Dora Mavor Moore Award for *Getting Out*, 83. *Hockey Night* won a CFTA. Created the series "On Our Own" and supervised development of 13 episodes, wrote 4 scripts and was executive story editor for 9 others. Children's audio cassette, *What it Means to be Jewish* won INDIE Award for Best Spoken Word Recording, 86.
Selected Filmography: *My Girlfriend's Back*, "Dracula: The Series", TV, 90, CDN/USA/L, Co-Wr; *Black Jellybeans*, "On Our Own" (pilot), TV, 90, CDN, Prod/Wr; *Otis the Amazing*, "The Twilight Zone" (1 eps), TV, 89, USA/CDN, Co-Wr; *Mirror Mirror*, "Alfred Hitchcock Presents" (1 eps), TV, 88, CDN/USA, Co-Wr; "Street Legal" (6 eps), TV, 86, CDN, Story Ed; *Jack of Hearts*, "Bell Canada Playhouse", TV, 85, CDN, T'play; *The Hospital*, "Home Movies", TV, 85, CDN, Wr; *Hockey Night*, TV, 84, CDN, Co-Wr; *The Umpire*, "Home Movies", TV, 84, CDN, Co-Wr; "The Edison Twins" (2 eps), TV, 83, CDN, Co-Wr; *R.W.*, "Sons and Daughters", TV, 82, CDN, Co-Wr.

BLUM, Len
ACTRA. Robert Bookman/C.A.A., 9830 Wilshire Blvd., Beverly Hills, CA 90212-1825 (213)288-4800.
Type of Production and Credits: Th Film-Wr/Prod.
Genres: Comedy-Th.
Biography: Born 1951, Toronto, Ontario; US resident alien. From 0-13: chess, ping-pong, schoolwork; 13-28: rock-and-roll musician, studio musician; 28-present: film writer and producer.
Selected Filmography: *Feds*, Th, 87, USA, Wr/Prod; *Spacehunter*, Th, 83, CDN, Co-Wr; *Stripes*, Th, 81, USA, Wr; *Heavy Metal*, Th, 81, CDN, Co-Wr; *Meatballs*, Th, 78, CDN, Co-Wr, (GENIE).

BLYE, Garry
- see PRODUCERS

BOBET, Jacques
- voir PRODUCTEURS

BOCKING, Richard C.
- see PRODUCERS

BODOLAI, Joe
WGC (ACTRA). Quality Shows, Inc., 489 Ontario St., Toronto, ON, M4X 1M8 (416) 928-0221 (W), 922-4050 (H).
Type of Production and Credits: Th Film-Wr/Prod/Dir; TV Film-Wr/Prod/Dir.
Genres: Drama-Th&TV; Comedy-Th&TV.
Biography: Born in 1948 in Youngstown, Ohio. US citizen, Canadian landed immigrant. Education: B.A. History, Phu

Beta Kappa, Allegheny College, Meadville, Pennsylvania; King's College, University of Cambridge, England; University of Manchester, England. Video artist, 1969-75. Works exhibited at "A" Space; Art Gallery of Ontario, Canada; Musée d'Art Contemporain, Paris. Producer and writer on "It's Only Rock 'n' Roll", which won a Gemini for Best Variety Series, 1987.
Selected Filmography: *Wayne's World: The Movie*, Th, 91, USA, Co-Wr; "Three Dead Trolls in a Baggie" (5 eps), TV, 91, CDN, Prod; "Kids in the Hall", TV, 90, CDN/USA, Spv Prod; *A David Foster Christmas Card*, TV, 89, CDN, Wr; "Just For Laughs" (6 eps), TV, 89, CDN, Head Wr; *The 1988 Gemini Awards*, TV, 88, CDN, Wr; "It's Only Rock 'n' Roll" (14 eps), TV, 87, CDN, Prod/Wr; *Rockit Records*, TV, 87, CDN, Wr; *The Singing Nun*, Th, 87, CDN, Dr/Wr; *Live From Planet Earth*, TV, 84, USA, Wr; "Saturday Night Live" (39 eps), TV, 81-82, USA, Wr.

BOITEAU, Denise
ACTRA, WGA. 7105 Fernhill Dr., Malibu, CA 90265 (213)457-7500. Glenhill Productions Ltd., 41 Peter St., Toronto, ON M5V 2C2 (416)971-6667. FAX: 971-6565.
Type of Production and Credits: Th Film-Wr; TV Film-Wr/Prod.
Genres: Documentary-Th&TV; Educational-Th&TV; Children's-Th&TV; Animation-Th&TV.
Biography: Has won over 40 international film and television awards. Canadian citizen.
Selected Filmography: "The Earth Revealed" (26 eps), ED/TV, 91, USA, Wr; "The Power of Algebra" (10 eps), ED/TV, 90, USA, Wr; "How Do You Do?" (24 eps), ED/TV, 90, CDN, Wr/Prod; "Straight Up" (3 eps), ED/TV, 89, USA, Wr/Prod; "Origins: A History of Canada" (16 eps), ED/TV, 89, CDN, Wr/Prod; "The Middle East" (14 eps), ED/TV, 87, CDN/USA, Wr/Prod; "Bits and Bytes" (12 eps), ED/TV, 83, CDN/USA, Wr/Prod; "It Figures" (25 eps), ED/TV, 80, USA, Wr/Prod; "Eureka!" (30 eps), ED/TV, 78, CDN, Wr/Prod; "Parlez-Moi" (90 eps), ED/TV, 77, CDN, Wr/Prod; "Mathworks" (25 eps), ED/TV, 77, USA, Wr/Prod; "Report French" (25 eps), ED/TV, 75, CDN, Wr/Prod; "The French Show" (13 eps), ED/TV, 76, CDN, Wr/Prod.

BOLEN, Norm
- see PRODUCERS

BOMPHRAY, Clinton◊
ACTRA. (416)463-6717.
Type of Production and Credits: Th Short-Wr; TV Film-Wr/Dir; TV Video-DOP/Dir/Prod.
Genres: Drama-TV; Action-TV; Documentary-TV.
Biography: Born 1943, Regina, Saskatchewan. Studied English Literature, History and Psychology, University of Saskatchewan. Has worked as writer, director, grip, props, DOP. Received 3 Ontario Arts Council Screenwriting grants. *October Stranger* was named Best Short Film, American Film Festival, 85.
Selected Filmography: *Yad*, TV, 86, CDN, Prod/Dir/DOP; *October Stranger*, Th, 84, CDN, Co-Wr; "The Great Detective" (2 eps), TV, 82-83, CDN, Wr; *Talkin' Union*, TV, 78, CDN, Dir.

BOND, Timothy
- see DIRECTORS
BONNER, Michael
- see DIRECTORS
BORRIS, Clay
- see DIRECTORS

BOUCHARD, Louise-Anne
SARDEC. 229, Demers, Montréal, PQ H2T 1K6 (514)286-0295.
Types de production et générique: c métrage-Sc; l métrage-Sc; TV vidéo-Sc.
Types d'oeuvres: Drame-C&TV; Comédie-C&TV.
Curriculum vitae: Née en 1955, Montréal, Québec. Langues: français et anglais. D.E.C. en photo. Bacc. en littérature, Univ. du Québec à Montréal. Enseigne la photo au Cégep André Laurendeau; a publié le roman *Sept fois, Jeanne*, VLB éditeur. *Alice au pays des Merguez* a gagné un concours de fiction organisé à l'interieur du cadre de Radio-Québec.
Filmographie sélective: *Coyote*, C, 90-91, CDN/F, Sc; *Thomas*, C, 90, CDN, Sc; *Alice au Pays des Merguez*, TV, 90, CDN, Sc; *Double Jeu*, C, 89, CDN, Sc; *Le ciel à la carte*, TV, 89, CDN, Sc; *L'infirmière à domicile*, TV, 89, CDN, Sc; *Larue Landreville*, TV, 89, CDN, Sc; *L'ordinateur qui tue!*, TV, 89, CDN, Sc; *Nathalie*, TV, 88, CDN, Sc; *Geneviève*, TV, 88, CDN, Sc; *J'ai blessé un ami en jouant*, TV, 88, CDN, Sc; *J'aime pas Marcel*, TV, 88, CDN, Sc; *La source du mal*, "Les Traquenards", TV, 87, CDN, Sc.

BOUCHARD, Michel
- voir REALISATEURS

BOURGET, Elizabeth
SARDEC. 1022, Marie-Anne, Montréal, PQ H2J 2B4 (514)522-4467.

Types de production et générique: TV vidéo-Sc.
Types d'oeuvres: Comédie-TV; Education-TV.
Curriculum vitae: Née en 1953, Montréal, Québec. Diplôme en écriture dramatique, Ecole nationale de théâtre, 78. Ecrit aussi pour le théâtre, 9 pièces jouées et 3 pièces publiées chez VLB éditeur. *Bonne Fête, Maman* représentait Radio-Canada au Festival de Monaco, 84.
Filmographie sélective: "A plein temps" (17 eps), TV, 84-88, CDN, Sc; *Bonne Fête, Maman,* TV, 84, CDN, Aut.

BOURNE, Lindsay
UBCP, ACTRA. 2137 W. 1st Ave., #8, Vancouver, BC V6K 1E7 (604)732-7135. Stellar Production Services Inc., L330 - 560 Beatty St., Vancouver, BC V6B 2L3. Characters Talent Agency, 1505 W. 2nd Ave., Suite 200, Vancouver, BC (604) 733-9800.
Type of Production and Credits: Th Film-Wr/Act; TV Film-Act/Prod/Wr; TV Video-Act/Prod.
Genres: Drama-Th&TV; Comedy-Th&TV; Action-Th&TV; Science Fiction-Th&TV.
Biography: Born in 1948 in Barbados; Canadian citizenship. B.A., Theatre, University of Guelph. Producer of numerous commercials including United Way; Eyemasters and the Provincial Lottery. Producer/Director of numerous special events including: Opening Ceremony for the Canadian Special Olympics; Opening Ceremony for Pacific International Festival of Male Choirs; and 1990 CFL Most Outstanding Player Awards.
Selected Filmography: "Fly By Night" (1 eps), TV, 91, USA, Act; *And the Sea Will Tell,* TV, 90, CDN/USA, Act; *Beneath the Pacific,* "Mom P.I.", TV, 90, CDN, Act; *Deadly Intentions Again,* TV, 90, USA/CDN, Act; *Death of the Incredible Hulk,* TV, 90, USA, Act; "Bordertown" (2 eps), TV, 90, CDN/F, Act; *1990 CFL Most Outstanding Player Awards,* TV, 90, CDN, Wr/Dir; *Narrow Margin,* Th, 89, USA, Act; *Bird on a Wire,* Th, 89, USA, Act; "The Beachcombers" (2 eps), TV, 89, CDN, Act; "Wiseguy" (4 eps), TV, 89, USA, Act; *Share the Dream: A Tribute to Rick Hansen,* TV, 87, CDN, Wr/Dir; *Abducted,* Th, 85, CDN, Wr.

BOWIE, Douglas
ACTRA, ACCT. 414 Albert St., Kingston, ON K7L 3W3 (613)544-9596.
Type of Production and Credits: Th Film-Wr; TV Film-Wr.
Genres: Drama-Th&TV; Comedy-Th&TV.
Biography: Canadian citizen. B.Sc., Carleton University, Ottawa. Films have won CFTA, American Film Festival Awards; received the CBC Centennial Playwriting Prize, 67; *Love and Larceny* won a Gemini for Best TV Movie, 86; *Obsessed* won O'Keefe Award for Best Canadian Film, Montreal Film Festival, 88. Author of the stage play, *The Noble Pursuit.*
Selected Filmography: *Grand Larceny,* TV, 91, CDN, Wr; "Chasing Rainbows" (7 eps), TV, 88, CDN, Wr; *Obsessed/Hitting Home,* Th, 86, CDN, Wr; *The Boy in Blue,* Th, 84, CDN/USA, Wr; *Love and Larceny,* TV, 84, CDN, Wr; "Empire Inc." (6 eps), TV, 82, CDN, Wr, (ACTRA); "The Newcomers" (1 eps), TV, 78, CDN, Wr; *The War Is Over,* TV, 77, CDN, Wr; *Shantymen of Cache Lake/No Way of Telling,* "The Magic Lie", TV, 76-77, CDN, T'play; *Scoop,* "For the Record", TV, 77, CDN, Wr; *Breakdown,* TV, 77, CDN, Wr; *A Gun, a Grand, a Girl/The Man Who Wanted to Be Happy,* TV, 75, CDN, T'play; *Bargain Basement,* TV, 74, CDN, Wr; *U-Turn,* Th, 72, CDN, Wr; *Gunplay,* TV, 71, CDN, Wr.

BOYDEN, Barbara
- see PRODUCERS

BRADSHAW, John R.
- see DIRECTORS

BRAITHWAITE, Diana
ACTRA. 389 Church St., PO Box 405C, Toronto, ON M5B 2A1 (416)596-0994.
Type of Production and Credits: TV Film-Wr.
Genres: Drama-Th&TV; Musical-Th&TV; Children's-Th&TV.
Biography: Born in 1957 in Toronto, Ontario. Canadian citizen. Studied at San Jose State University. Course work included: Afro-American History; Sociology. Special skills: Black history background and writing and performing music. Also writes for children and adults. Wrote the teleplay and music for *Gracie,* which won the 1989 Gemini for Best Short Drama, the Golden Sheaf Award for Best Short Drama, and the award for Best Musical Score at the Yorkton Short Film & Video Festival.
Selected Filmography: *Gracie,* TV, 89, CDN, Wr, (GEMINI).

BRANDES, David◆
ACTRA. (213)399-8901.
Type of Production and Credits: Th Film-Wr; TV Video-Wr.
Genres: Drama-Th; Horror-Th; Docu

mentary-TV; Children's-TV.
Biography: Born 1944, Kemptville, Ontario. M.F.A., Film Production, UCLA. Has received a Canada Council grant, 2 Ontario Arts Council Grants. Worked for CBC-TV and CJOH as news reporter, interviewer.
Selected Filmography: *The Dirt Bike Kid*, Th, 85, USA, Wr; "Fraggle Rock" (1 eps), TV, 83, CDN, Wr; *Blood Root*, Th, 83, CDN, Wr; *My Mother's House*, Th, 78, USA, Wr/Dir.

BRESLIN, Mark
ACTRA. 26 Bellair St., Toronto, ON M5R 2C7 (416)923-9124. Yuk-Yuk's Inc., 1280 Bay St., Toronto, ON M5R 3L1 (416)967-6431. Larry Goldhar, Characters, 150 Carlton St., Toronto, ON M5A 2K1 (416)964-8522.
Type of Production and Credits: Th Film-Wr; TV Video-Wr.
Genres: Comedy-Th&TV; Variety-TV.
Biography: Born in 1952; Canadian citizen. Founder of Yuk-Yuk's Komedy Kabaret and Funny Business Inc.
Selected Filmography: "Yuk-Yuk's - The TV Show" (13 eps), TV, 90, CDN, Exec Prod/Perf; "The Late Show", TV, 88, USA, Prod; *The Journal* (4 segs), TV, 84-86, CDN, Wr/Act; *Take My Husband and Leave*, TV, 85, CDN, Wr; *Mr. Nice Guy*, Th, 85, CDN, Wr; *Yuk-Yuk's Global Pilot*, TV, 82, CDN, Prod.

BROADFOOT, Dave
OC. ACTRA. Dave Broadfoot Productions Inc., 7 Hillholm Rd., Toronto, ON M5P 1M1 (416)487-9259. Rhonda Cooper, Character Talent Agency, 150 Carlton St., Toronto, ON M5A 2K1 (416)964-8522.
Type of Production and Credits: TV Film-Wr/Act.
Genres: Drama-TV; Comedy-TV; Documentary-TV.
Biography: Born 1925, North Vancouver, BC. Has appeared in over 30 stage reviews and produced 8; appeared in 4 feature films. Has been with "Royal Canadian Air Farce" for 18 years. Won 13 ACTRA Awards for writing and performing comedy on TV and radio; Juno Award for comedy recording; CSP (US) Award; Queen's Silver Jubilee Medal; Officer, Order of Canada. Honourary Doctorate, Athabasca University. Honorary Staff Sergeant, RCMP. Presently in third year touring his theatrical production, *Dave Broadfoot's Comedy Crusade*. Member of Canadian Actors Equity.

BROCHU, Pierre
ACCT, ADISQ, SARDEC. 522 Wickham, Saint Lambert, PQ J4R 2B7 (514)465-2467. Poly-Productions, 1583 Blvd. Saint-Laurent, Montréal, PQ H2X 2S9 (514)288-4023.
Types de production et générique: TV-film, Sc, Réal, Prod.
Types d'oeuvres: Variété-TV; Documentaire-Th&TV; Education-Th&TV; Affaires Publiques-Th&TV.
Curriculum vitae: Né au Québec. Directeur-général Imageries ltée Sherbrooke; Université de Sherbrooke, Faculté des Arts; Réalisateur/Scénariste, Radio-Canada; écrit, produit de documents imprimés ou audio-visuels; brochures, affiches, dépliants, films, vidéos, diaporamas; créations institutionnelles, éducatives ou documentaires produites pour: Radio-Québec, Union des producteurs agricoles, Générale Electrique, Bombardier, Ministère de L'Education du Québec, Office National du Film, Radio-Canada, Ministère de L'Environnement du Canada.
Filmographie sélective: *Le Monde Selon Clémence*, TV, 90, CDN, Prod/Sc/Réal; *Tête à Tête Avec J.G. Moreau*, TV, 90, CDN, Prod/Sc/Réal.

BROMFIELD, Rex
DGC, ACCT. 1034 Princess Ave., Victoria, BC V8T 1L1 (604)383-9583. Brom Films Productions 1988 Inc., 6395 Chatham St., West Vancouver, BC V7W 2E1 (604)921-9394. FAX: 921-9393.
Type of Production and Credits: Th Film-Wr/Dir; TV Film-Dir.
Genres: Drama-Th; Comedy-Th.
Biography: Born in 1946 in Toronto, Ontario. Canadian citizen.
Selected Filmography: *Café Romeo*, Th, 90, CDN, Dir/Script Ed; "The Beachcombers" (5 eps), TV, 85-88, CDN, Dir; "Danger Bay" (4 eps), TV, 86-88, CDN, Dir; *Home Is Where The Heart Is*, Th, 87, CDN, Wr/Dir; *Melanie*, Th, 81, CDN, Dir; *Love At First Sight*, Th, 76, CDN, Wr/Dir.

BROWN, Barbara
WGC. 14864 - 17 Ave., White Rock, BC V4A 6V4 (604)536-0526. FAX: 536-0526.
Type of Production and Credits: TV Film-Wr; TV Video-Wr.
Genres: Drama-TV; Documentary-TV; Educational-TV; Children's-TV.
Biography: Born in Edmonton, Alberta. B.A., Journalism, University of Western Ontario. Journalist, radio commentator, writer of documentaries (educational TV), and TV series; film writer, series developer and story editor.

Selected Filmography: "The Adventures of the Black Stallion" (3 eps), TV, 90-91, CDN/USA/F, Co-Wr; "Bordertown" (1 eps), TV, 89, CDN/USA/F; *Getting Married in Buffalo Jump*, TV, 89, CDN, Co-Wr (story); "The Beachcombers" (13 eps), TV, 81-88, CDN, Wr/Co-Wr; "Airwolf II" (2 eps), TV, 87, CDN/USA, Co-Wr; "The Campbells" (1 eps), TV, 86, CDN/USA/GB, Co-Wr; *Chung Chuck*, TV, 85, CDN, Co-Wr; "Legend of the Silver Raven" (pilot), TV, 82, CDN, Co-Wr; "Ritter's Cove" (19 eps), TV, 79-80, CDN/D/GB, Co-Creator/Co-Wr.

BROWN, Jamie
- see PRODUCERS

BROWN, Lyal D.
WGC (ACTRA), CTPDA. 14864 - 17 Ave., White Rock, BC V4A 6V4 (604) 536-0526. FAX: 536-0526.
Type of Production and Credits: TV Film-Wr/Dir/Prod; TV Video-Wr.
Genres: Drama-TV; Action-TV; Documentary-TV; Children's TV.
Biography: Born Medicine Hat, Alberta. Studied Journalism, Montana State University; Political Science, History, University of British Columbia. Worked in radio as continuity writer, announcer; writer for *CBC Times*, 52; after 8 years at CBC as Director of Information Services, Executive Assistant to General Manager, English Network, began freelancing as writer, broadcaster; has written more than 70 teleplays; story editor on "The Beachcombers", 86 and "Ritter's Cove", 78-79.
Selected Filmography: "Adventures of the Black Stallion" (3 eps), TV, 90-91, CDN/USA/F, Co-Wr; "Bordertown" (1 eps), TV, 89, CDN/USA/F; *Getting Married in Buffalo Jump*, TV, 89, CDN, Co-Wr (story); "The Beachcombers" (16 eps), 74-88, CDN, Wr/Co-Wr; "Airwolf II" (2 eps), TV, 87, CDN/USA, Co-Wr; "The Campbells" (1 eps), TV, 86, CDN/USA/GB, Co-Wr; *Chung Chuck*, TV, 85, CDN, Co-Wr; "Constable, Constable" (pilot), TV, 85, CDN, Wr; "Home Fires" (3 eps), TV, 83, CDN, Wr; "Legend of the Silver Raven" (pilot), TV, 82, CDN, Co-Wr; "Ritter's Cove" (19 eps), TV, 79-80, CDN/D, Co-Creator/Co-Wr; "The Albertans" (trilogy), TV, 79, CDN, Wr; "Sidestreet" (3 eps), TV, 76-77, CDN, Wr; "Collaborators" (4 eps), TV, 73-74, CDN, Wr; *An Angel Against the Night*, "Performance", TV, 69, CDN, Wr.

BROWNE, Colin
- see DIRECTORS

BRULOTTE, Gaétan
SARDEC. 82, rue des Casernes, Trois-Rivières, PQ G9A 1X2 (819)379-6347. University of South Florida, Division of Languages, Tampa, FL 33620 (813)974-2547. Loise Myette, 3707, Aylmer, Montréal, PQ (514)844-9009.
Types de production et générique: l métrage-Sc; TV film-Sc.
Types d'oeuvres: Drame-C&TV.
Curriculum vitae: Né en 1945, Lauzon, Québec. Etudes à l'Université Laval et à Paris; détient un doctorat en sémiologie. A publié plusieurs livres et des centaines d'articles; a reçu 8 prix littéraires dont le Prix Robert Cliche pour *L'Emprise*, Prix Adrienne-Choquette et Prix France-Québec pour *Le Surveillant*. Fellow, World Literary Academy, Cambridge, Angleterre. A réalisé 31 émissions de radio; invité aux Etats-Unis depuis 81. A écrit un film pour TVO intitulé *La mort d'un chauffeur de taxi*.
Filmographie sélective: *L'Emprise*, C, 81 CDN, Co sc; *L'Emprise*, "Les Chemins de l'imaginaire", TV, 80, CDN, Aut.

BRUNELLE, Wendy A.
705 - 360 Bloor St. E., Toronto, ON M4W 3M3.
Type of Production and Credits: TV Film-Wr/Dir; TV Video-Wr/Dir/Prod.
Genres: Documentary-TV; Current Affairs-TV.
Biography: Born in Regina, Saskatchewan. B.A., B.L.S. (cum laude), M.L.S. (cum laude). Consulting editor of *Interface: The West's View of the Arts & Entertainment*. Editor of *Pacific Report* and a writer for *Burnaby Now*. Alberta Psychic Society Award for Journalistic Investigation; Expo 86 Award of Achievement.
Selected Filmography: "Dayscene" (360 eps), TV, 89-91, CDN, Host/Assoc Prod; "Expo Update" (30 eps), TV, 85-86, CDN, Prod/Dir/Host; "People Coping with Cancer" (7 eps), TV, 84, CDN, Host/Prod; *New Light on Cancer*, ED, 84, CDN, Prod; "Technology West" (30 eps), TV, 83-84, CDN, Host; "Super Program About Art, Culture & All That Stuff" - SPAACAAT (weekly), TV, 79-83, CDN, Host/Assoc Prod; "CFRN-TV Morning Magazine" (daily), TV, 79-83, CDN, Host/Assoc Prod; *A Contrast of Visions*, ED, 78-79, CDN, Wr/Dir/Prod; "Only Yesterday" (26 eps), TV, 78-79, CDN, Host/Wr/Res; "Artists in Depth" (13 eps), TV, 78, CDN, Host/Res; *Sculptor in Paradise*, ED, 77-78, CDN, Wr/Prod/Dir.

BRUYERE, Christian◆
ACTRA, WGw, ACCT. Vancouver, B.C.

9983.
Type of Production and Credits: Th Film-Wr/Dir/Prod; TV Film-Wr/Dir/Prod; TV Video-Ed/Prod/Wr/Dir.
Genres: Drama-Th&TV; Variety-TV; Documentary-TV; Educational-TV.
Biography: Born 1944, Paris, France; raised in Chicago and Los Angeles. Graduate Film School, scriptwriting, USC. Teaches scriptwriting at University of British Columbia. *Dads and Kids* won Golden Sheaf, Yorkton, 85, and Genie for Best Documentary, 88; *Rape: Face to Face* won the Dupont-Columbia Award, 83, Corporation for Public Broadcasting Award and a Blue Ribbon, American Film Festival.
Selected Filmography: *Shelley*, TV, 86, CDN, Wr/Dir/Prod; *B.C. Lions: Then and Now*, TV, 86, CDN, WR/Dir/Prod; *Dads and Kids*, ED, 85, CDN, Wr/Dir/Prod, (GENIE 88); "Who Am I?" (2 eps), ED, 85, CDN, Dir/ED; "Danger Bay" (1 eps), TV, 85, CDN, Wr; "The Beachcombers" (2 eps), TV, 84, CDN, Wr; "Sex Offender Treatment" (7 eps), Ed, 84, CDN, Wr/Prod; *Walls*, Th, 84, CDN, Co-Prod/Wr; *UNICEF Halloween Special*, TV, 83, CDN, Wr; *Rape: Face to Face*, TV, 83, CDN/USA, Co-Wr/Co-Dir/Co-Prod.

BRYANT, Chris
WGA, WGGB, ACTRA, ACTT, ACCT. Broughton Hall, Near Lechlade, Glos., GB GL7 3JH TEL: 011-44-367860-363 FAX: 011-44-367860-677. Lake & Douroux, #310-445 South Beverly Drive, Beverly Hills, CA 90212 USA. (213)557-0700.
Type of Production and Credits: Th Film-Wr; TV Film-Wr.
Genres: Drama-Th&TV; Comedy-Th; Action-Th.
Biography: Born 1936, Bolton, England; Canadian citizenship; U.S. resident alien. M.A., Cambridge; M.C.L., McGill University. Legal journalistic and political background before starting to write. Has written some 90 screenplays, mainly for US major studios and companies. Various awards.
Selected Filmography: *Young Catherine* (mini-series), TV, 90, USR/GB/ CDN/ USA, Wr/Co-Prod; *Stealing Heaven*, Th, 88, USA, Wr; *Sword of Gideon*, TV, 86, CDN, Wr; *Joseph Andrews*, Th, 77, USA/GB, Wr; *The Girl from Petrovka*, Th, 76, USA, Wr; *Don't Look Now*, Th, 75, USA, Wr.

BRYDON, Loyd
- see PRODUCERS
BUGAJSKI, Richard
- see DIRECTORS
BURKE, Martyn
- see DIRECTORS
BURMAN, Tony
- see PRODUCERS

BURT, Jim
ACTRA, ACCT. 169 Harbord St., Toronto, ON M5S 1H3 (416)537-6216. CBC, Box 500, Stn. A, Toronto, ON M5W 1E6 (416)977-7156. Ralph Zimmerman, Great North Artists Mgmt., 350 Dupont St., Toronto, ON M5R 2V9 (416)925-2051.
Type of Production and Credits: TV Video-Wr.
Genres: Drama-TV; Variety-TV.
Biography: Born 1947, Providence, Rhode Island; landed immigrant Canada. B.A., Harvard University, 69; M.F.A., Yale School of Drama, program in directing, 69-70. Background in stage directing, acting, teaching; Director, New School of Theatre and Pears Cabaret, Toronto. Supervisor of Script Development, CBC Independent Drama, 84-87; Script Development Executive, CBC Movies and Mini-series, 88; Creative Head, CBC Movies and Mini-series, 89 to present.
Selected Filmography: *And Miles to Go*, TV, 85, CDN, Story Ed; *Sam Hughes's War*, "Some Honourable Gentlemen", TV, 84, CDN, Wr; *Artichoke*, TV, 77, CDN, Story Ed.

BURT, Montgomery
NABET, BCMPA. 107 West 15th Ave., Vancouver, BC V5Y 1X8 (604)875-0660. FAX: 876-6282. Michael Stipanich, Writers and Artists Agency, 11726 San Vincente Blvd., Suite 300, Los Angeles, CA 90049 USA (213)820-2240. FAX: 207-3781.
Type of Production and Credits: TV Film-Wr.
Genres: Film Noir-TV; Suspense/Thriller-TV; Science Fiction-TV.
Biography: Born 1959, Saskatchewan. Radio and TV Broadcasting, Mount Royal College, Calgary, 77-78. Employed at CBC Calgary as news-tape editor, ITV Edmonton as news cameraman, and presently at BCTV Vancouver as news-tape editor. Writer/director of "Blooper" tapes, some portions of which appeared on syndicated TV series "Foul Ups, Bloops and Blunders." "Twilight Zone" script *Borrowed Time* won second prize in the 1987 *Writer's Digest* Writing Competition, Scripts Division. Story editor for screenplay *The Boiler Room* by Jim Hamm. Co-founder of Upwords Writers' Group. Participated in Praxis Screenwriting Workshop in autumn of 1990 with script

Outskirts of Paradise.
Selected Filmography: *Career Move,* "Alfred Hitchcock Presents" (1 eps), TV, 88, CDN/USA, Story/Co-Wr.
BURTON, Robert H.
- see PRODUCERS
BUSATO, Paul
531 Wallenberg Cres., Mississauga, ON L5B 3L8 (416)897-7199. Palner Productions, 363 Hillmount Ave., Toronto, ON M6B 1Y9 (416)782-3309.
Type of Production and Credits: TV Video-Wr/Prod.
Genres: Musical-Th&TV; Educational-Th&TV; Children's-Th&TV; Commercials-TV.
Biography: Born in 1957 in Toronto, Ontario. Languages: English, French and Italian. Studied music and direction in Paris, France. Concert organist, pianist, conductor. Writer and producer of children's videos and cassettes. Song writer, singer, producer for Clara Records.
Selected Filmography: *Let's All Sing,* MV, 91, CDN/GB, Wr/Prod; "Columbus Centre Spotlight" (15 eps), TV, 87, CDN, Wr/Prod.
BUTLER, Rick
ACTRA, WGAw. 939 Nowita Place, Venice, CA 90291 (213)301-1041. (213)301-8170. Robert Marshall, Greenberg/Glusker, 1900 Avenue of the Stars, Suite 2000, Los Angeles, CA 90068 USA (213)201-7448.
Type of Production and Credits: Th Film-Wr.
Genres: Drama-Th&TV; Comedy-Th; Animation-Th.
Biography: Born 1949, raised in Truro, Nova Scotia. B.A., Carleton University; M.A., University of Sussex, England. University professor prior to becoming a full-time writer/producer. Author of 3 books: *Quebec: The People Speak, The Trudeau Decade, Vanishing Canada.* Producer of 10 RCA record albums; 2 TV movies nominated as Best Drama of the Year, ACTRA; studio-approved writer in Los Angeles.
Selected Filmography: "Friday the 13th: The Series" (1 eps), TV, 88, CDN/USA, Wr; "Bordertown" (1 eps), TV, 88, CDN/USA/F, Wr; *Maggie and Pierre,* TV, 84, CDN, Prod; *Balconville,* TV, 83, CDN, Prod; *The Magic of Animation,* TV, 77, CDN, Prod/Wr.
BUTTIGNOL, Rudy
- see PRODUCERS
BUXTON, Bonnie◊
ACTRA. (416)694-2480.
Type of Production and Credits: TV Film-Wr; TV Video-Wr.
Genres: Drama-TV; Comedy-TV; Documentary-TV; Current Affairs-TV.
Biography: Born and educated in Alberta. Studied at Stanford University, California. Has worked in various media; newspaper reporter, award-winning copywriter, magazine journalist and travel editor; book author, editor and publisher; TV public affairs story editor; began screenwriting, 86. Awarded second prize in NFB's Writers' Call Competition, 78.
Selected Filmography: "The Campbells" (2 eps), TV, 86, CDN/US/GB, Wr.
CACOPARDO, Max
- voir REALISATEURS
CAHILL, T.J.
ACTRA. 39 Quidi Vidi Village Rd., St. John's, NF A1A 1E9 (709)576-0547.
Type of Production and Credits: TV Film-Wr/Prod; TV Video-Wr/Prod.
Genres: Drama-TV; Documentary-TV.
Biography: Born 1929, St. John's, Newfoundland; B.A., Memorial University, 53. Writer, stage plays and radio. Winner: Golden Sheaf Special Jury Award, Short TV Drama, Yorkton, 88; CBC President's Award, Regional Drama Production, 85; ACTRA Award, Best Canadian TV Production for *The Undaunted,* 83; Anik Special Jury Award for TV adaptation of own stage play, *As Loved Our Fathers,* 76.
Selected Filmography: "Yarns from Pigeon Inlet" (17 eps), TV, 80-89, CDN, Wr/Prod; *The Undaunted,* TV, 83, CDN, Wr/Prod, (ACTRA); "Yesterday's Heroes" (12 eps), TV 78-79, CDN, Wr/Dir/Prod; "Where Once They Stood" (18 eps), TV, 75-77, CDN, Wr/Prod/Dir; *As Loved Our Fathers,* TV, 76, CDN, Wr/Prod (ANIK).
CAILHIER, Diane
SARDEC, SACD. 205 Ch, North-Hatley, Katevale, PQ J0B 1W0 (819)843-1944. Suzanne Vachon, 305 ave, Elm, Westmount, PQ H3Z 1Z4 (514)937-1057.
Types de production et générique: long métrage-Sc; court métrage-Sc; TV Film-Sc.
Types d'oeuvres: Drame-Th&TV; Comédie-Th&TV; Documentaire-C; Enfants-C.
Curriculum vitae: Née à Valleyfield en 1947. Langue: français. Maîtrise es Lettres, Université de Montréal. Lauréat en Piano, Ecole Vincent D'Indy. *Des Amis pour la Vie,* nominé pour Meilleur Texte - Prix Gémeaux; *L'Etau Bus* remporte Prix Anik, Prix du Public Clermont Ferand et Prix du Public Belfort.
Filmographie sélective: *Une nuit à l'école,*

C, 91, CDN, Sc; *Un Homme de Parole*, ED, 90, CDN, Sc/Comm; *Des Amis pour la Vie*, C, 88, CDN, Sc; *Terre et Mémoire*, ED, 83, CDN, Sc/Comm; *L'Etau Bus*, C, 82, CDN, Co sc; *L'Estrie en Musique*, ED, 81, CDN, Rech/Sc; *Les Douces*, ED, 80, CDN, Rech/Sc/Comm; *Images de l'Estrie*, ED, 80, CDN, Rech/Sc; *La Piastre*, C, 75, CDN, Sc.

CAILLOUX, Michel
CAPAC, SARDEC, UDA. 3562, Abbé-Desrosiers, Laval PQ, H7E 2K5, (514)661-7624.
Types de production et générique: TV vidéo-Sc.
Types d'oeuvres: Comédie-TV; Variété-TV; Education-TV; Enfants-TV.
Curriculum vitae: Né en 1931, Issoudun, France; au Canada depuis 55; citoyenneté canadienne. Auteur d'émissions TV pour enfants depuis 56. Récipiendaire du Grand Prix du Children's Broadcast Institute pour "Nic et Pic"; a reçu un trophée Caméreo pour les textes "Bobino", Carrousel du film de Rimouski, 87; le prix d'honneur, l'Alliance des professeurs et professeures de Montréal, pour 30 ans de pédagogie en tant qu'auteur à la télévision. Prix des communications et Médias, Ministère des Communications du Québec, 1989; Prix d'Honneur du Children's Broadcast Institute, 1989 pour l'ensemble de son oeuvre.
Filmographie sélective: "Alphabus" (39 eps), TV, 90-91, CDN, Aut/Com; "Bobino" (5150 ém), TV, 59-85, CDN, Aut; "Nic et Pic" (72 eps), TV, 70-77, CDN, Sc/Dial; *Michel-le-Magicien*, "La Boîte à surprise" (480 eps), TV, 56-68, CDN, Aut/Com; *Picolo*, "La Boîte à surprise" (40 eps), TV, 66-68, CDN, Co aut; *Il faut marier Colombe*, TV, 58, CDN, Aut; *Les Hutto, père et fils*, TV, 57, CDN, Aut.

CALLAGHAN, Barry◊
ACTRA. (416)977-7937.
Type of Production and Credits: TV Film-Wr/Prod; TV Video-Wr/Prod.
Genres: Drama-TV; Variety-TV; Documentary-TV; Educational-TV.
Biography: Born 1937, Toronto, Ontario. Professor, York University, for 21 years; literary critic and editor, *Toronto Telegram*, 66-71; host and filmmaker for CBC-TV, 68-71; co-writer, producer, documentaries, Vilions Films, 74-77; weekly commentator, "Canada AM," (CTV), 76-82; host, "Enterprise" (Citytv), 84; 30 appearances, "Fighting Words" (CHCH-TV), 82-83; founder, editor of *Exile: A Literary Quarterly* 72, and Exile Editions, 76; magazine journalist; poet; translator; fiction writer. Winner of 6 National Magazine Awards; Canadian Periodical Publication Award for Fiction, 85.
Selected Filmography: *Love*, "Enterprise", TV, 85, CDN, Host; *Gambling*, "Enterprise", TV, 84, CDN, Host, (ACTRA); *The White Lager*, TV, 77, CDN/USA/J/S, Host/Wr/Interv; *Counterpoint*, TV, 75, CDN/USA/J/S, Host; *Canada: Quebec*, TV, 74, CDN, Wr; *The Tin Canoe*, TV, 73, CDN, Wr; *Mary Queen of Scots/Louis Riel*, "Man Alive", TV, 72, CDN, Wr; *Golda Meir/Drugs/Angela Davis in Prison*, "Weekend", TV, 70-71, CDN, Wr/Prod/Interv; *My Lai/Vietnam Veterans/Knapp Commission(NY Crime)* "Weekend", TV, 71, CDN, Wr/Prod; *Arabs-Israeli/Speed City (Drugs)/Black Panther/Jurisprudence*, TV, 69-70, CDN, Wr Prod/Interv; *Six Days in Amwan (Black Sept. war)/Egypt/Middle East, (Palestinians)*, "Weekend", TV, 70, CDN,Wr/Prod/Interv.

CAMERON, B.A. (Anne)
ACCT. 350 Taku St., Powell River, BC (604)483-9849.
Type of Production and Credits: Th Film-Wr; TV Film-Wr.
Genres: Drama-Th&TV; Comedy-TV; Action-Th.
Biography: Born 1938, Nanaimo, British Columbia. Several poems and short stories published in anthologies; novels in Canada, USA. Has won poetry, film and literary awards. Writer-in-residence, Simon Fraser University; teaches creative writing and screenwriting.
Selected Filmography: *Madeleine*, "Daughters of the Country", TV, 86, CDN, Co-Wr; *California Aunts*, "Pov", TV, 86, CDN, Wr; "The Tin Flute"/ "Bonheur d'occasion" (5 eps), TV, 82, CDN, Co-T'Play (Fr/Eng shot simultaneously); *Ticket to Heaven*, Th, 80, CDN, Co-Scr; "For the Record" (3 eps), TV, 77-79, CDN, Wr; *Coal Tyee*, TV, 77, CDN, Wr; *Bomb Squad*, TV, 77, CDN, Wr; *Dreamspeaker*, "For the Record", TV, 76, CDN, Wr, (CFA).

CAMERON, Silver Donald
ACTRA. 6243 Lawrence St., Halifax, NS B3L 1J8 (902)420-1395.
Type of Production and Credits: TV Film-Wr; TV Video-Wr.
Genres: Drama-TV; Documentary-TV.
Biography: Born 1937. B.A., University of British Columbia; M.A., University of California; Ph.D., University of London. Has taught English Language and Literature at Dalhousie University,

University of British Columbia and University of New Brunswick. Since 71, has been a full-time writer for film, TV and radio; has written for many magazines including *Saturday Night*, *Maclean's*, *The Financial Post*; Contributing Editor of *Weekend*, 74-76; has received National Magazine Awards. Television credits include *That Old Buccaneering Spirit*, *The Atlantic Provinces* and *A Gift of River*. *Peggy* won Best Short Film at the Canadian Film Celebration, 1991. Writer-in-residence, University College of Cape Breton, 77-79; University of Prince Edward Island, 85-86; Nova Scotia College of Art and Design, 87-89. Has had 10 books published, most recently, *Wind, Whales and Whisky: A Cape Breton Voyage*.

CAMPBELL, Peg
- see DIRECTORS

CAMPBELL, Robin
- see DIRECTORS

CAPISTRAN, Michel◆
SARDEC, UDA. (514)340-1770.
Types de production et générique: l métrage-Sc; TV film-Sc.
Types d'oeuvres: Drame-C; Documentaire-TV.
Curriculum vitae: Né en 1946, Montréal, Québec. Etudes universitaires en sociologie et psycho-pédagogie. Huit ans à Radio-Canada comme scénariste; cinéma; courts et longs métrages. Consultant en communications et stratégie politique à National inc.
Filmographie sélective: *Bingo*, C, 73, CDN, Co sc/Ass réal; "Si tous les gens du monde" (13 eps), TV, 71, CDN, Sc.

CARLE, Gilles
- voir REALISATEURS

CARLSON, Elaine◆
ACTRA. (306)781-2286.
Type of Production and Credits: Th Short-Wr; TV Film-Wr; TV Video-Wr.
Genres: Documentary-TV; Educational-Th; Commercials-TV; Industrial-TV.
Biography: Born 1946, Candra, Saskatchewan. Studied Journalism, Carleton University. Full-time freelance writer. Numerous awards for excellence in commercial production (print, radio and TV), Vancouver Creative Club Silver Award; Sam Award (print); Toronto Art Directors' Club, Honourable Mention; sector-specialized competitions, including best overall traffic safety promotion (all media) in North America.
Selected Filmography: *The Saskatchewan Pension Plan*, Cm, 88, CDN, Wr; *Saskatchewan Pension Plan*, ED, 87-88, CDN, Wr/Narr; *Saskatchewan Pension Plan* (13 mini videos), ED, 88, CDN, Wr/Narr; *Powers of Arrest* (Saskatchewan Police College), ED, 86-87, CDN, Wr; *Welcome to the Public Service* (Saskatchewan Public Service), ED, 87, CDN, Wr; *Young Offenders' Act* (Saskatchewan Police College), ED, 86-87, CDN, Wr; *Wise Use of Credit* (Saskatchewan Consumer Affairs), ED, 83-84, CDN, Wr/Res; *Supermarket Survival Skills* (Saskatchewan Consumer Affairs), ED, 83, Cdn, Wr/Res; *Bridging the Gap*, ED, 83, CDN, Wr/Interv/Res; *Community Schools* (Dept. of Education), ED, 82-83, CDN, Wr/Res; *Saskatchewan Inventions*, ED, 81-82, CDN, Wr/Res; *Dear Norman*, TV, 81-82, CDN, Wr; "It's All Here", TV, 81-82, CDN, Wr/Res/Interv.

CARMODY, Don
- see PRODUCERS

CARON, Louis◆
SACD, SARDEC.(514)463-1183.
Types de production et générique: TV film-Sc.
Types d'oeuvres: Drame-TV, Education-TV.
Curriculum vitae: Né en 1942. Ecrivain: *La Vie d'artist*, Boréal, 87.
Filmographie sélective: "Lance et compte" (13 eps), TV, 88, CDN, Co sc; "Bulletin Spécial" (2 eps), TV, 88, CDN, Sc; "Louis-Joseph Papineau" (6 eps), TV, 88, CDN, Sc; "Les Racontages de Louis Caron" (12 eps), TV, 82, CDN, Sc; "Les Fils de la liberté" (6 eps), TV, 81, CDN/F, Sc; *Regarde Papa!*, TV, 79, CDN, Sc.

CARTMER, Debbie
- see DIRECTORS

CASTRAVELLI, Claudio
- see DIRECTORS

CHAREST, Gaétan
- voir PRODUCTEURS

CHATO, Paul◆
ACTRA. (416)923-9844.
Type of Production and Credits: TV Video-Wr/Act.
Genres: Comedy-TV.
Biography: Born in 1954 in Canada. Languages: English and Hungarian. B.A.A., Radio and TV Arts, Ryerson Polytechnical Institute. Received the Don Hudson Award. Has been a graphic designer and advertising manager.
Selected Filmography: "4 on the Floor" (13 eps), TV, 85, CDN, Co-Wr/Act.

CHERNIACK, David
- see DIRECTORS

CHETWYND, Lionel◆
ACTRA, WGGB, WGAw. (213)285-6752.
Type of Production and Credits: Th

Film-Wr/Dir/Prod; TV Video-Wr/Dir.
Genres: Drama-Th&TV; Comedy-Th&TV; Variety-TV; Documentary-TV.
Biography: Born 1940, London, England; Canadian citizenship, 64. Honours B.A., Philosophy, Economics, Sir George Williams (Concordia) Univ., 63; Bachelor of Civil Law, McGill Univ., 67. Assistant managing director, Columbia Pictures, 68-72; freelance writer, film, TV, essays, articles for *Punch*, *Encounter*, *L'Express*. *Miracle on Ice* won a Chris Award, Columbus; *The Apprenticeship of Duddy Kravitz* won the Silver Bear, Berlin, an Oscar nomination (Best Screenplay Adaptation); *Two Solitudes* won the Silver Laurel, Salonika.
Selected Filmography: *Children in the Crossfire*, TV, 84, USA/IRL, Wr; *Sadat*, TV, 82, USA, Wr; *The Hot Touch/French Kiss*, Th, 82, CDN, Scr; *Miracle on Ice*, TV, 81, USA, Wr; *Escape from Iran: The Canadian Caper*, TV, 80, CDN, Wr; *A Whale for the Killing*, TV, 80, CDN/USA, T'play; *Two Solitudes*, Th, 77, CDN, Scr/Dir; *It Happened One Christmas*, TV, 77, USA, T'play; *Quintet*, Th, 77, USA, Story; *The Adams Chronicles*, "Bicentennial Series"(2 eps), TV, 76, USA, Wr; *The American 1776*, Th, 76, USA, Wr; *Goldenrod*, Th, 76, CDN, Scr/Co-Prod; *Johnny We Hardly Knew Ya*, TV, 75, USA, Scr/Prod; *The Guest Room*, "Playhouse 90", TV, 73, USA, Wr; *The Apprenticeship of Duddy Kravitz*, Th, 73, CDN, Scr, Adapt, (WGA).

CHILCO, Joe✥
ACTRA. (818)880-5697.
Type of Production and Credits: TV Film-Wr/Act; TV Video-Wr/Act.
Genres: Drama-TV; Comedy-TV; Industrial-Th.
Biography: Born 1953, Toronto, Ontario. Bachelor of Arts, York University. Winner of a Graham Award for Cable TV Production. Nominated for a Dora Award, 83.
Selected Filmography: "Starting from Scratch" (1 eps), TV, 88, CDN, Wr; "Comedy Mill" (6 eps), TV, 88, CDN, Contr Wr; "Semi-detached" (pilot), TV, 88, CDN, Co-Creator/Wr; "Check It Out!" (22 eps), TV, 87, CDN/USA, Story Ed; "Pet Peeves" (22 eps), TV, 86, CDN, Wr; "Lifestyle Workout" (pilot), TV, 85, CDN, Act/Co-Wr; "Hangin' In" (1 eps), TV, 85, CDN, Act; "Laughing Matters" (13 eps), TV, 85, CDN, Contr Wr; *Society Centran/Brewer's Retail*, In, 85, CDN, Act; "Snowjob" (1 eps), TV, 84, CDN, Act; "Hangin' In" (1 eps), TV, 84, CDN, Wr.

CHRISTIE, Keith
- see DIRECTORS

CICCORITTI, Gerard
- see DIRECTORS

CLARK, Barry
- see PRODUCERS

CLARK, Ron
WGA, AMTDG. 325 N. Barrington Avenue, Los Angeles, CA 90049 (213)827-1717. Augustus Productions, 315 S. Beverly Drive, #412, Beverly Hills, CA 90212 USA (213)553-0171. David Shapira & Associates, 15301 Ventura Boulevard., Sherman Oaks, CA 91403 (818)906-0322.
Type of Production and Credits: Th Film-Wr; TV Film-Wr; TV Video-Wr/Prod.
Genres: Drama-TV; Comedy-Th&TV; Variety-TV; Musical-TV.
Biography: Born in 1933 in Montreal, Quebec. Canadian citizen living in USA. Bilingual. Educated at McGill University. Author of 4 Broadway plays, *Norman, Is That You?*, *No Hard Feelings*, *Murder at the Howard Johnson's*, *Wally's Café*. Conceived and staged *The World According to Me*, starring Jackie Mason. Directed the Canadian film *The Funny Farm*. Directs plays as well as writing music and lyrics. Film writing credits include Mel Brooks' *Life Stinks*, *Silent Movie* and *High Anxiety*. Also *Revenge of the Pink Panther*, *Norman, Is That You?* and *The Funny Farm*.
Selected Filmography: "The Ray Sharkey Show"/"The Man in the House" (7 eps), TV, 91, USA, Spv Prod; "Baby Talk" (13 eps), TV, 91, USA, Co-Exec Prod; *Life Stinks*, Th, 91, USA, Wr; "Oh Henry" (pilot), TV, 90, USA, Exec Prod; "The Van Dyke Show" (13 eps), TV, 89, USA, Wr/Exec Prod; "Moonlighting" (5 eps), TV, 89, USA, Wr/Creat Cons; "Glory Days" (pilot), TV, 87, USA, Co-Exec Prod; "Silver Spoons" (22 eps), TV, 86, USA, Wr/Creat Cons; "E/R" (12 eps), TV, 85, USA, Wr/Creat Cons; *Bloomies*, Th, 84, USA, Wr; *Hardware*, Th, 83, USA, Wr; *The Funny Farm*, Th, 82, USA/CDN, Wr; "Ace Crawford, Private Eye" (7 eps), TV, 81, USA, Wr/Exec Prod.

CLARKSON, Adrienne
- see PRODUCERS

COACH, Ken
- see PRODUCERS

COCHRAN, Andrew
- see PRODUCERS

COCK, Peter J.
- see DIRECTORS

COHEN, Annette
- see PRODUCERS

COHEN, Jeffrey
WGC (ACTRA). 2435 West 7th Ave., Vancouver, BC V6K 1Y6 (604)737-1282. Crescent Entertainment, 2 - 1163 Commercial Dr., Vancouver, BC V5L 3X3 (604)255-6488. Suzanne Depoe, 483 Euclid Ave., Toronto ON M6G 2T1 (416)924-0341.
Type of Production and Credits: Th Film-Wr/Story Ed; TV Film-Wr/Story Ed.
Genres: Drama-Th&TV; Comedy-Th&TV; Action-Th&TV; Children's-TV.
Biography: Born in 1952. Honours B.A. from York University, Toronto. Has worked as an actor on stage, film and in television. Co-founder and first Artistic Director of Skylight Theatre, Canada's only professional open air theatre, 1979. Has been resident story editor for "Danger Bay" and "Mom P.I.". For his own company, Crescent Entertainment Ltd., served as the story editor and pilot writer for *Kurt Vonnegut's Welcome to the Monkey House*. The teleplay, *Clown White*, was a Finalist at the American Festival, 1982 and the winner of a Special Jury Award, Mifed, Children In Our Time Film Festival, 1981. *Miracle At Moreaux* won the President's Chris Award, Columbus International Film Festival, 1986; a Gold Award from the Houston International Television Festival, 1986; and a Gold Award and Grand Award, International Film and Television Festival, New York, 1986.
Selected Filmography: *The Euphio Question - Kurt Vonnegut's Monkey House*, TV, 90, CDN/USA, Wr; *Looking For A Living*, "Mom P.I.", TV, 90, CDN, Wr; *Rookies*, TV, 90, CDN, Co-Wr; *Lifeline*, "Danger Bay", TV, 89, CDN, Wr; *Listening In*, "Danger Bay", TV, 89, CDN, Wr; *Miracle at Moreaux*, "Wonderworks", TV, 85, CDN/USA, Co-Wr; *Clown White*, TV, 80, CDN, Co-Wr.

COHEN, M. Charles
ACTRA, WGAw. 2045 Grey Ave., Montreal, PQ H4A 3N3 (514)488-5476. Shelly Wile, Wile Enterprises, 2730 Wilshire Blvd., Suite 500, Santa Monica, CA 90403 (213)828-9768.
Type of Production and Credits: Th Film-Wr; Th Short-Wr; TV Film-Wr; TV Video-Wr.
Genres: Drama-Th&TV; Comedy-Th&TV.
Biography: Born 1926, Warner, Alberta. B.A., B.S.W., University of Manitoba; M.S.W., University of Toronto. Thirty years of experience as freelance writer in Canada for CBC and NFB, in US for 3 major networks. Western Heritage Award for *Age of the Buffalo*, NFB; Humanitas Award, 75, for "Sunshine" series; Emmy nomination for *Roots* mini-series; winner of Margaret Collier Award, Gemini Awards 88, for an Outstanding Body of Work by a Television Writer.
Selected Filmography: *The First Circle* (mini-series), TV, 90-91, CDN/F, Scr.

COLE, Janis
- see PRODUCERS

COLLEY, Peter
ACTRA, WGAw, ACCT. 238 Davenport Rd., Suite 100, Toronto, ON M5R 1J6. 3960 Laurel Canyon Blvd., #259, Studio City, CA 91604 (818)704-7720. Charles Northcote, The Core Group, 489 College St., Suite 501, Toronto, ON M6G 1A5 (416)944-0193.
Type of Production and Credits: Th Film-Wr.
Genres: Drama-Th.
Biography: Born 1949, Great Britain. B.A., Honours, Sheffield University. Resident playwright, Grand Theatre, London, Ontario; author of 8 stage plays with over 300 productions in 11 countries including *I'll Be Back Before Midnight*. President, Buckingham International Productions. Now working on *Before Midnight* (91); associate producer on US film.
Selected Filmography: *The Mark of Cain*, Th, 85, CDN, Co-Scr.

COLLINS, Neil
SWG, SMPA. Project Productions, #6, 212 Saskatchewan Cres. E., Saskatoon, SK S7N 0K6 (306)244-7758.
Type of Production and Credits: TV Film-Wr/Prod/Dir; TV Video-Wr/Prod/Dir.
Genres: Documentary-TV; Industrial-TV; Music Video-Th&TV; Sports-TV.
Biography: Born in 1953 in Toronto, Ontario. Canadian citizen. English speaking. Mount Royal College, Calgary, Alberta. Saskatchewan Story, Drama Writers' Workshop: photography, television production, commercial writing. Nominated for a Golden Sheaf award for the documentary *Getting There*. Winner of the Canadian Cable Television Association C.C.T.A. award, Mid-West Region, for *New Beginnings*, 1989 and again, 1990.
Selected Filmography: *Canadian Cattle, Moving Out*, In, 91, CDN, Wr/Prod/Dir; *Regional Processing in Saskatchewan*, In, 90, CDN, Wr/Prod/Dir; *Micropropagation - A Growth Industry*, In/ED, 90, CDN, Wr/Prod/Dir; *Killer 50*, MV, 90, CDN, Wr/Prod; *Cowboys & Outlaws*, TV, 89,

CDN, Dir; *Getting There*, TV, 89-90, CDN, Wr/Prod/Dir; *N.R.T. Rolling North*, In, 89, CDN, Wr; *A Creek Forming A Valley*, ED, 88, CDN, Wr; *New Beginnings*, TV, 88, CDN, Wr/Prod/Dir.

COMEAU, Phil
- see DIRECTORS

CONNOLLY, Bea Broda
- see PRODUCERS

CONNOLLY, Phillip J.
- see DIRECTORS

COOK, Heather
- see PRODUCERS

COOKE, Lindsay Ann
- see PRODUCERS

COOPER, Richard◊
ACTRA, ACCT. (613)729-2539.
Type of Production and Credits: Th Film-Comp; TV Film-Dir/Wr; TV Video-Prod/Dir/Wr/Comp.
Genres: Drama-TV; Comedy-TV; Children's-TV.
Biography: Born 1948, Ottawa, Ontario. Literature degree from Ottawa University. Spent 15 years in the music business as founding member of the Cooper Brothers; recorded 4 albums; has done extensive scoring for documentary films. Won a ASCAP for composing "The Dream Never Dies", which was subsequently recorded by several other artists including Juice Newton and Bill Anderson.
Selected Filmography: "C.O.P.S." (2 eps), TV, 88, CDN/USA, Co-Wr; "Denim Blues" (13 eps), TV, 88, CDN, Wr/Dir/Comp; "High School Confidential" (13 eps), TV, 86-87, CDN, Wr/Dir/Comp/Prod; *Body Electric*, TV, 86, CDN, Co-Wr; "You Can't Do That on Television" (10 eps), TV, 85, CDN/USA; "Turkey Television" (pilot), TV, 85, CDN/USA, Co-Wr.

CORDER, Sharon
WGC (ACTRA). 10 Sackville Place, Toronto, ON M4X 1A4 (416)923-3357.
Type of Production and Credits: TV Film-Wr/Prod; TV Video-Wr.
Genres: Drama-TV; Comedy-TV; Children's-TV.
Biography: Born in the United States. Holds dual citizenship. Trained in theatre at the University of California at Davis. Has produced, written and acted for the stage. Won a Dora Mavor Moore Award for *Getting Out*, 1983. Created the series "On Our Own" and supervised development of 13 episodes, wrote 4 scripts and was executive story editor for 9 others. Wrote the children's audio cassette *A Child's Look at...Mozart*
Selected Filmography: *My Girlfriend's Back..*, "Dracula: The Series", TV, 90, CDN/USA/L, Co-Wr; *Black Jellybeans*, "On Our Own", (pilot), TV, 90, CDN, Prod/Wr; *Otis the Amazing*, "The Twilight Zone", TV, 89, CDN/USA, Co-Wr; *Mirror Mirror*, "Alfred Hitchcock Presents", TV, 88, CDN/USA, Co-Wr; *The Letter, the Witch & the Ring*, TV, 88, CDN/GB, Co-Wr; *Jack of Hearts*, "Bell Canada Playhouse", TV, 86, CDN, Co-Wr; *The Hospital*, "Home Movies", Th, 85, CDN, Co-Wr.

COUTURE, Jacques
SARDEC. 979, rue Napoléon, Montréal, PQ H2L 1C6 (514)523-5576.
Types de production et générique: TV film-Sc; TV vidéo-Sc.
Types d'oeuvres: Variété-TV; Comédie-TV; Documentaire-Th&TV; Industriel-Th&TV.
Curriculum vitae: Né en 1950, Sherbrooke, Québec. Maîtrise en études littéraires, Université de Sherbrooke; 12 années de théâtre avant de se consacrer à la production audio-visuelle. Scénariste ayant travaillé pour des compagnies privées autant que pour le gouvernement.
Filmographie sélective: "100 Limite" (225 eps), TV, 89-91, CDN, Rech/Scripte; "Surprise sur prise" (12 eps), TV, 90-91, CDN, Rech; "Jasmine Centre-Ville" (217 eps), TV, 87-88, CDN, Rech; "Carte d'identité" (215 eps), TV, 86-87, CDN, Textes/Rech; "Premières" (20 eps), TV, 87, CDN, Rech; "Le Train de 5 heures" (210 eps), TV, 85-86, CDN, Textes/Rech; "Comment va la santé?" (5 eps), TV, 84, CDN, Textes/Rech/Anim; "Visite de Jean-Paul II au Canada" (12 eps), TV, 84, CDN, Textes; "Galt et Cie" (2 eps), TV, 82, CDN, Textes/Rech.

COUTURE, Suzette
WGC (ACTRA), WGA. Pierre Sarrazin Productions, 42 Bernard Ave., Toronto, ON M5R 1R2 (416)530-4437. Ken Neisser, Triad Artists, 10100 Santa Monica Blvd., 16th Flr., Los Angeles, CA 90067 (213)556-2727.
Type of Production and Credits: TV Film-Wr/Prod.
Genres: Drama-TV; Comedy-TV.
Biography: Born Ottawa, Ontario. Languages: English and French. B.A., Carleton University. Began career as journalist; trained as an actor with the Yale School of Drama. Performed extensively in theatre and was a comedy writer/performer touring comedy clubs.
Selected Filmography: *Conspiracy of Silence* (mini-series), TV, 91, CDN, Wr; "Road to Avonlea" (4 eps), TV, 89-90,

CDN/USA, Wr; *Love and Hate* (mini-series), TV, 89, CDN, Wr (GEMINI 90); *Skate*, TV, 87, CDN, Wr (GEMINI 88); *Joined at the Hip*, TV, 85, CDN, Wr.

COWLING, Barry
- see PRODUCERS

CRONENBERG, David
- see DIRECTORS

CROSSLAND, Harvey James
- see DIRECTORS

CURRIE, Anthony
- see SOUND EDITORS

CURTIS, Dan
- see DIRECTORS

CUTHAND, Doug
- see PRODUCERS

CUTLER, Keith
- see PRODUCERS

CYNAMON, Helena
- see PRODUCERS

D'AIX, Alain
- voir REALISATEURS

DALEN, Zale R.
- see DIRECTORS

DAMBERGER, Francis
ACTRA. 9120 - 80 Ave., Edmonton, AB T6C 0T8 (403)466-4259. Damberger Film & Cattle Co., 9120 - 80 Ave., Edmonton, AB T6C 0T8 (403)466-4259.
Type of Production and Credits: Th Film-Wr/Dir/Prod; Th Short-Wr/Dir/Prod; TV Film-Wr/Dir/Prod.
Genres: Drama-Th; Comedy-TV; Documentary-Th&TV; Educational-Th&TV.
Biography: Born 1957, Tofield, Alberta. B.F.A., Acting, University of Alberta, 81. Has worked as an actor in theatre and film, most recently in *Bye Bye Blues*. First film as writer/director, *On the Edge*, won 6 international awards: Silver Plaque and Certificate of Merit, (Chicago); Silver Apple, National Educational Film Festival; Silver Plaque, Intercom Festival; Certificate of Merit, Columbia International Film Festival; and finalist, American Film & Video Festival. Documentary awards - Best Film and Best Director - for *U of Agers*, a film on senior fitness for the NFB; *Gagmen* won Best Variety Special and Award of Merit, 85 CanPro Awards; has also won an AMPIA for his work as an actor; *Ordinary Man* was a Juno nominee, 87.
Selected Filmography: *Solitaire*, Th, 91, CDN, Prod/Wr/Dir; *U of Agers*, Th/TV, 90, CDN, Wr/Dir; *Ordinary Man*, MV, 87, CDN, Dir; *Road to Yorkton*, Th/TV, 86, CDN, Prod/Wr/Dir; *Gagmen*, TV, 85, CDN, Wr; *On the Edge*, Th/TV, 85, CDN, Prod/Wr/Dir.

DAMUDE, D. Brian
ACCT, ACTRA, DGC. Brian Damude Productions Inc., 366 Brunswick Avenue, Toronto, ON M5R 2Y9 (416)961-9950.
Type of Production and Credits: Th Film-Dir/Wr; TV Film-Dir/Prod/Wr/Ed; TV Video-Dir/Prod/Wr/Ed.
Genres: Drama-Th&TV; Action-Th&TV; Documentary-Th&TV; Industrial-Th&TV.
Biography: Born 1945, Fredericton, New Brunswick. Languages: English, French, Portuguese, Spanish. B.A., McGill University; M.F.A., Graduate Institute of Film and Television, New York University; studied History of Still Photography, 1 year, Museum of Modern Art; studied still photography with Paul Coponegro, 1 year; studied acting and directing actors, Scholarship Workshop Program, National Film Board of Canada. Ten years as full-time lecturer and instructor in Motion Picture and Video Production Theory, Acting and History, Department of Film and Photography, Ryerson Polytechnical Institute. Experience as editor of film and video, producer, cameraman and actor. Worked as consultant to Beijing Film Academy, P.R. of China, 86. Nominated for CFTA award for *Trenton Works*, 82; in 3 categories for *Ocean Heritage*, 75. *Sudden Fury*, 74, was nominated for 5 Canadian Film Awards and won Canadian Film Editors' Guild award for best picture; screenplay for feature, *Deadly Prey*, sold to Leone Int'l (US); currently teaching, Film Department, Ryerson.
Selected Filmography: *Strange Noises*, TV, 87, CDN, Wr/Dir; *Covert Action*, TV, 86, CDN, Prod; "Last Frontier" (4 eps), TV, 85, CDN, Res/Wr; *Out of the Blue*, ED, 85, CDN, Wr/Dir/Ed; *Trenton Works*, In, 82, CDN, Wr/Dir/Ed; *Bi-level Commuter Cars*, In, 81, CDN, Wr/Ed; *Courting*, TV, 80, CDN, Wr/Dir; *I, Maureen*, Th, 78, CDN, Act; *Ocean Heritage*, TV, 75, CDN, Wr/Dir/Ed; *Ghost of a Chance*, Th, 75, CDN, Wr/Dir/Ed; *Sudden Fury*, Th, 74, CDN, Dir/Wr; *Nightmare*, TV, 74, CDN, Wr/Dir/Ed; *Come by Chance*, In, 74, CDN, Wr/Dir/Ed; *Where It's At*, ED, 74, CDN, Wr/Dir/Ed; *Beginning Driving*, ED, 74, CDN, Wr/Dir/Ed.

DANSEREAU, Mireille
- voir REALISATEURS

DARCUS, Jack
- see DIRECTORS

DARK, Randall Paris
- see PRODUCERS

DARLING, Gillian
- see PRODUCERS

DAY, Deborah
- see PRODUCERS

DE ROCHEMONT, Nicole
- voir PRODUCTEURS

DEFELICE, James
ACTRA. 5611 - 109 St., Edmonton, AB T6H 3A7 (403)434-9702.
Type of Production and Credits: Th Film-Wr; Th Short-Wr; TV Film-Wr; TV Video-Wr.
Genres: Drama-Th&TV; Comedy-Th& TV; Children's Th&TV.
Biography: Has lived and worked in Edmonton since 1969. Experience as a screenwriter, teacher, professional director and actor. Has written twenty plays that have been produced in Canada and US and has written and acted for film television and radio. Story editor and story consultant on numerous films. Canadian Film Award for best screenplay (adapted) for *Why Shoot the Teacher?*. Wrote script for *Letting Go*, which received Golden Gate Award for Best Local Station Entertainment at 1986 San Francisco Film Festival.
Selected Filmography: *Angel Square*, Th, 90, CDN, Co-Wr; *Cowboys Don't Cry*, Th, 87, CDN, Act; *The Gunfighters*, TV, 87, CDN, Act; *Hotwalker*, "Bell Canada Playhouse", TV, 85, CDN, Wr; *Letting Go*, TV, 85, USA, Wr; *The Mortal Coil*, "Stony Plain", TV, 83, CDN, Wr; *Draw!*, TV, 83, CDN/USA, Act; "Nuggets" (1 eps), TV, 82, CDN, Wr; *Harry Tracy*, Th, 80, CDN, Act; *Prisoners in the Snow*, "The Magic Lie", TV, 79, CDN, Wr; *Why Shoot the Teacher?*, Th, 76, CDN, Scr, (CFA); *Wings of Time*, Th, 76, CDN, Wr/Act.

DEMEULE, Nadine
- voir REALISATEURS

DENIKE, Brian
- see PRODUCERS

DENSHAM, Pen
- see PRODUCERS

DESCHAMPS, Yvon
- voir PRODUCTEURS

DESCHENES, Clément
ARRQ. B.P. 40, Cascapedia, Co. Bonaventure, PQ G0C 1T0 (418)759-3514.
Types de production et générique: TV vidéo-Réal/Sc.
Types d'oeuvres: Documentaire-TV.
Curriculum vitae: Né en 1947, St-Jean Port-Joli, Québec. Bac. en Anthropologie et formation en journalisme.
Filmographie sélective: *La peche au Québec; l'Industrie de transformation en 1991*, "Première Ligne", TV, 90-91, CDN, Réal; "Voyage en Nunavik" (6 eps), TV, 90, CDN, Rech; *Homosexualité*, "Première Ligne", TV, 90, CDN, Réal; *La fin/The End: Le français écrit*, "Première Ligne", TV, 89, CDN, Réal; "Route des vacances" (10 eps), TV, 89-90, CDN, Réal.

DESJARDINS, Jacques
SARDEC. 622, Moffat, Verdun, PQ H4H 1Y8 (514)767-2643. Via Le Monde, 326 ouest, St-Paul, Montréal, PQ (514)285-1658.
Types de production et générique: l métrage-Sc; TV film-Mont.
Types d'oeuvres: Drame-C&TV; Documentaire-TV.
Curriculum vitae: Né en 1955, Montréal, Québec. Langues: français et anglais. Monteur: Montage Eclair, 79-86; Les Productions Via le Monde (Daniel Bertolino), 86-89; Les Productions Via le Monde (François Floquet), 89-91. Scénariste, Les Productions la Fête, 90-91.
Filmographie sélective: *Tire Lire, combines et cie*, C, 91, CDN, Sc; *Les Naufragés du Labrador*, TV, 91, CDN, Mont; *Philippines: Les nomades de la mer*, TV, 89, CDN/F, Mont; "Les Légendes du monde", TV, 87-88, CDN, Mont; "Traquenards", TV, 88, CDN, Mont; "Point Chaud", TV, 87-88, CDN, Mont vidéo off-line; *Les Services secrets*, TV, 88, CDN, Mont vidéo off-line; *Le Défi algérien*, TV, 88, CDN, Mont vidéo off-line/Ass réal; *On peut se débrouiller seul*, TV, 79, CDN, Mont/Sc/Réal/Prod; *Bétonville*, C, 76-77, CDN, Mont/Sc/Réal/Prod.

DESJARDINS, Normand
SARDEC. 517 rue Ash, Montréal, PQ H3K 2R5 (514)989-8808.
Types de production et générique: c métrage-Sc.
Types d'oeuvres: Drame-C; Enfants-C.
Curriculum vitae: Né en 1950, St-Antoine des Laurentides, Québec. Langues: français et anglais. Rédacteur de romans, contes et pièces de théâtre; scénariste, traducteur, auteur, journaliste pigiste auprès de divers magazines. "Mémoire Vive" mise en nomination prix Gémeaux, 89, Meilleur texte série dramatique; *Cher monsieur l'aviateur*, 1er premio de argumento Mursia et Alicante, Espagne.
Filmographie sélective: *Le fabuleux voyage de l'ange*, C, 91, CDN, Conc/1er Sc; *Bonjour! Shalom!*, TV, 91, CDN, Trad/Adapt; *Eaux Profondes*, ED, 89, CDN, Sc; "Mémoire Vive" (6 eps), TV, 88, CDN, Sc; "Vidéotour" (14 eps), TV, 87-89, CDN, Sc; *Pour bien se comprendre* (en public, au téléphone), ED, 88, CDN, Sc; *L'orphelin et la lune*, TV, 86, CDN, Sc;

Cher monsieur l'aviateur, C, 85, CDN, Conc/Sc.
DEVERELL, Rex
ACTRA. 36 Dentonia Park Ave., Toronto, ON M4C 1W7 (416)690-3190.
Type of Production and Credits: TV Film-Wr; TV Video-Wr.
Genres: Drama-TV; Documentary-Th&TV; Educational-TV; Children's-TV.
Biography: Born 1941, Toronto, Ontario. B.A., B.D., McMaster University; S.T.M., Theatre and Theology, Union Theological Seminary, New York, 67. Resident playwright, Globe Theatre 75-90. Winner, Canadian Authors' Award, 78; author of a number of stage and radio plays.
Selected Filmography: *Oh, For a Thousand Tongues,* ED, 91, CDN, Wr; *Paper Tiger,* TV, 90, CDN, Wr; *Voyage-voyageur,* TV, 84, CDN, Wr; *Battleford,* TV, 79, CDN, Wr; *What's a Moose Jaw,* TV, 78, CDN, Wr; *Welcome with Joy,* ED, 74, CDN, Wr; *Verse and Worse,* "Hi Diddle Day", TV, 74, CDN, Wr.
DEVERELL, William H.
ACTRA. Razor Point Rd., North Pender Island, BC V0N 2M0 (604)629-6622.
Type of Production and Credits: TV Film-Wr.
Genres: Drama-TV.
Biography: Born in Regina, Saskatchewan. Education: B.A. and LL.B. Has written 5 CBC radio scripts and 5 screenplays. Novels: *Needles* (also wrote screenplay), *High Crimes, Mecca, The Dance of Shiva, Platinum Blues.* Created concept for "Street Legal" series.
Selected Filmography: *Mindfield,* Th, 88-89, CDN, Wr; "Street Legal" (2 eps), TV, 86, CDN, Wr; "Shell Game" (pilot), TV, 85, CDN, Wr.
DEVINE, David
- see PRODUCERS
DEWAR, Stephen W.
- see PRODUCERS
DEY, Wendy E.
- see PRODUCERS
DIMARCO, Steve
- see DIRECTORS
DINEL, Pierre
ARRQ, ARRFQ. Radio-Canada, 516 Rivière Nord, St-Roch de l'Achigan, PQ J0K 3H0 (514)588-6047. Radio-Canada - Montréal, Service du Nord, (514)597-4372. FAX: 597-4501.
Types de production et générique: c métrage-Réal/Sc; TV film-Réal/Prod/Sc; TV vidéo-Réal/Sc.
Types d'oeuvres: Documentaire-C&TV; Education-C&TV.
Curriculum vitae: Né en 1952, Montréal, Québec. Langues: français et anglais.
Filmographie sélective: "Maamuitaau" (65 eps), TV, 89-91, CDN, Réal; "Première Ligne" (32 eps), TV, 88-89, CDN, Réal; *La Route des vacances,* TV, 88, CDN, Réal; "Le Magazine" (22 eps), TV, 87-88, CDN, Réal; "Sur la piste" (1 eps), TV, 87, CDN, Réal/Sc; *Safari-Zoopsi,* MV, 86, CDN, Réal; *Hors-Mouane,* ED, 86, CDN, Réal; "L'Univers d'André Michel" (1 eps), TV, 86, CDN, Réal; "Une minute, un artiste" (120 eps), TV, 86, CDN, Sc; "Cité des jeunes" (1 eps), TV, 85, CDN, Réal; *Terre des poissons blancs,* C, 85, CDN, Sc; *La Raquette montagnaise,* "Métiers traditionnels", TV, 84, CDN, Prod dél; "Les Six Saisons des Attikamek" (6 eps), TV, 82-83, CDN, Prod/Réal/Sc; *La Trappe,* ED, 83, CDN, Réal; "Connaissance du milieu" (5 eps), TV, 80, CDN, Ass réal.
DION, Yves
- voir REALISATEURS
DIXON, Will
- see DIRECTORS
DODD, Marian
- see PRODUCERS
DONLON, Denise
- see PRODUCERS
DONOVAN, Michael Leo
ACTRA. 4143 Delaney St., Pierrefonds, PQ H8Y 3L8 (514)685-3789. Mary Rader/Ben Conway & Associates, c/o South Maple Rd., Beverly Hills, CA 90212 USA (213)273-1635. Jane Butler, Shadowcast Management, 4143 Delaney St., Pierrefonds, PQ H8Y 3L8 (514)685-3789.
Type of Production and Credits: TV Film-Wr; TV Video-Wr.
Genres: Drama-Th&TV; Comedy-Th&TV; Action-Th&TV; Horror-Th&TV.
Biography: Born in 1956 in Montreal, Quebec. University of Southern California, Master of Professional Writing. 2 awards at USC, the Phi Kappa Phi award for Original Work, Graduate Level (for a script called *Roses of Shadow*), and the Journalism award for founding *The Southern California Anthology.* As a songwriter, released two singles, 'More Than Love' and 'Coming Apart at the Dreams'. One feature film script optioned by Astral Films and one M.O.W. developed by CBC.
Selected Filmography: "Top Cops" (1 eps), TV, 91, CDN/USA, Wr; "Counterstrike" (3 eps), TV, 91, CDN/ USA/F, Story Ed; "Counterstrike" (2 eps), TV, 91, CDN/USA/F, Wr; "Urban Angel" (1 eps), TV, 90, CDN, Story Ed; "Street Legal" (1

eps), TV, 89, CDN, Wr; *The African Journey*, TV, 88, CDN/(6 European Countries), Co-Wr; "Diamonds" (2 eps), TV, 88, CDN/USA/ F, Wr; "Night Heat" (1 eps), TV, 87, CDN/USA, Wr; "Hot Shots" (2 eps), TV, 86-87, CDN/USA, Wr.

DONOVAN, Paul
- see DIRECTORS

DORN, Rudi
- see ART DIRECTORS

DOUGLAS, Michael
- see DIRECTORS

DRAKE, Sally
ACTRA. Project Hill Productions, 434 E. 20th Ave., Vancouver, BC V5V 1M5 (604)874-8005. FAX: 875-9494. The Hamilburg Agency (U.S. only), 292 La Cienga Blvd., #312, Los Angeles, CA 90211 USA (213)657-1501.
Type of Production and Credits: TV Film-Wr; TV Video-Wr.
Genres: Drama-TV.
Biography: Raised in Southern California. Worked from age 13 as an actress and danced on stage and TV until immigration to Canada in 1971. Starred opposite Christopher Lee in the Canadian feature *The Keeper* in 1976. Began writing full time in 1980. Has three grown sons, all of them working successfully in the industry.
Selected Filmography: *King of the Cowboys*, "The Black Stallion", TV, 90, CDN/F, Wr; *Wild Horses*, "Bordertown", TV, 90, CDN/F, Wr; *Over The Line*, "Neon Rider", TV, 90, CDN, Wr; *The Ten Percent Solution*, "MacGyver", TV, 89, USA, Wr; *Letter of the Law*, "Bordertown", TV, 89, CDN/F, Wr; *Hamilton's Quest* (mini-series), TV, 86-87, CDN, Creat/Prod/Wr/Exec Story Cons.

DRAKE, Tom
ACTRA, WGA. Project Hill Productions, 434 E. 20 Ave., Vancouver, BC V5V 1M5 (604)874-8005. FAX: 875-9494. The Hamilburg Agency (U.S. only), 292 S. La Cienga Blvd., #212, Los Angeles, CA (213)657-1501.
Type of Production and Credits: Th Film-Wr/Dir; TV Film-Wr/Prod; TV Video-Wr/Dir.
Genres: Drama-Th&TV; Comedy-Th&TV; Action-Th&TV; Horror-Th&TV.
Biography: Born in 1936 in Vancouver, British Columbia. Worked as a child actor on CBC radio. U.S. resident from 1947-71. Dual Canadian/U.S. citizenship. Winner of the WGAw award for Best Episodic TV Drama in 1971. Currently President of the B.C. Writers' Branch of ACTRA.
Selected Filmography: *King of the Cowboys*, "The Black Stallion", TV, 90, CDN/F, Wr; *Wild Horses*, "Bordertown", TV, 90, CDN/F, Wr; *Over the Line*, "Neon Rider", TV, 90, CDN, Wr; *The Ten Percent Solution*, "MacGyver", TV, 89, USA, Wr; *Letter of the Law*, "Bordertown", TV, 89, CDN/F, Wr; *Hamilton's Quest* (mini-series), TV, 86-87, CDN, Creat/Prod/Wr/Exec Story Cons; *Terror Train*, Th, 80, CDN/USA, Wr; *The Keeper*, Th, 76, CDN, Wr/Dir; *Par for the Course*, "The Psychiatrist", TV, 71, USA, Wr; "Then Came Bronson" (4 eps), TV, 70, USA, Wr; "Then Came Bronson" (6 eps), TV, 70, USA, Story Cons.

DREW, Rick
ACTRA, WGA. 7037 Canada Way, Burnaby, BC V5E 3R7 (604)526-5012. FAX: 526-4850. Bernie Weintraub/Robinson Weintraub, Gross & Assoc., 8428 Melrose Place, Los Angeles, CA 90069 USA (213)653-5802.
Type of Production and Credits: TV Film-Wr; TV Video-Wr.
Genres: Drama-TV; Comedy-TV; Variety-TV.
Biography: Born in 1956 in Calgary, Alberta. Attended the American Film Institute. An ACTRA award nominee. Former feature film assistant director. Has written all forms of TV, sitcom, drama, gameshows, current affairs, variety, etc.
Selected Filmography: "Northwood" (2 eps), TV, 90-91, CDN, Wr/Ed; "Neon Rider" (1 eps), TV, 91, CDN, Wr; "The Black Stallion" (2 eps), TV, 90, CDN/F, Wr; "MacGyver" (7 eps), TV, 88-90, USA/Wr/Exec Story Cons; "Mom P.I." (1 eps), TV, 90, CDN, Wr; "Max Glick" (2 eps), TV, 90, CDN, Wr; "Danger Bay" (11 eps), TV, 84-88, CDN/USA, Wr; "The Beachcombers" (7 eps), TV, 80-88, CDN, Wr; "Airwolf II" (3 eps), TV, 86-87, USA, Wr/Story Ed; "The Twilight Zone" (1 eps), TV, 86, CDN/USA, Wr; "The Paul Anka Show" (26 eps), TV, 82-83, CDN, Wr.

DROUIN, Dominique
SARDEC. 16, St-Joseph, Ste-Rose de Laval, PQ H71 1H9 (514)625-4624.
Types de production et générique: TV film-Sc; TV vidéo-Sc.
Types d'oeuvres: Drame-TV; Education-TV.
Curriculum vitae: Née en 1958, Montréal, Québec. Langues: français et anglais. Baccalauréat ès sciences et maîtrise ès sciences de la communication, Université de Montréal, 78-85. Auteure du roman *Tableau de jeunesse*, Editions

Pierre Tisseyre, 87.
Filmographie sélective: "L'Addition S.V.P." (6 eps), TV/ED, 91, CDN, Sc; "Deux pour Un" (4 eps de développement), TV, 91, CDN, Sc; "Le Grand Remous" (105 eps), TV, 88-91, CDN, Sc/Dial; *Une Histoire de Coeur*, ED, 90, CDN, Sc; "Terre Humaine" (117 eps), TV, 81-84, CDN, Sc/Dial; *L'Enseignement à la maternelle*, ED, 82, CDN, Sc; *La Musique au secondaire*, ED, 82, CDN, Sc; "La Déficience auditive" (13 eps), ED, 81, CDN, Sc/Anim.

DRYSDALE, Alyson
- see PRODUCERS

DUBRO, James R.
Beacon Hill Prod. Inc., 86 Gloucester St., #402, Toronto, ON M4Y 2S2 (416)922-8706. Jan Whitford, Lucinda Vardey Agency, 297 Seaton St., Toronto, ON M5A 2T6 (416)922-0250. FAX: 925-4943.
Type of Production and Credits: TV Film-Prod; TV Film-Wr; TV Video-Prod; TV Video-Wr.
Genres: Documentary-TV.
Biography: Born in 1946 in Boston, Massachusetts; Canadian and US citizenship. M.A. with high honours, Columbia University; member, Phi Beta Kappa; teaching fellowship, University of Toronto, Victoria College, 70-72. Author, *Mob Rule: Inside the Canadian Mafia*, 85; *Mob Mistress: How A Canadian Housewife Became a Mafia Playgirl*, 88; *Undercover for the Mounted Police*, 91. Co-author, *King of the Mob: Rocco Perri and the Women Who Ran His Rackets*, 87; *King of the Bootleggers*, CBC "Morningside" radio drama, 86-87.
Selected Filmography: "The Mob in Metro" (10 eps news serial), TV, 91, CDN, Prod/Wr; "Shattered Dream"/ "Inside Cuba Today" (4 eps), TV, 90, CDN/USA, Dir/Wr; *Inside Cuba*, "Soviets at the Crossroads", TV, 88, USA, Dir/Wr; *The Informer/Bounty Hunter/Traitor in the Mounties*, TV, 82-84, CDN, Assoc Prod; *Agents of Deception*, TV, 84, CDN, Co-Wr/Co-Dir; *Chinese Gangs and Murders*, "the fifth estate", TV, 81-83, CDN, Assoc Prod; *The KGB Connections*, TV, 81, CDN, Co-Prod; *Connections: A Further Investigation into Organized Crime*, TV, 79, CDN, Assoc Prod/Res; *Connections: An Investigation into Organized Crime in Canada*, TV, 77, CDN, Assoc Prod/Res, (ANIK); *The Espionage Establishment*, "the fifth estate", TV, 74, CDN, Res.

DUCHESNE, Christiane
SARDEC, SACD. 4426, Boyer, Montréal, PQ H2J 3E7 (514)522-4854.
Types de production et générique: c métrage-Sc; TV film-Sc.
Types d'oeuvres: Education-TV; Enfants-C&TV.
Curriculum vitae: Née en 1949, Montréal, Québec. Ecrit pour les enfants depuis 72 (scénarios pour TV et livres); 7 livres qu'elle a elle-même illustrés. *Matilde ou les ballots de foin* remporte le 1er Prix du Concours des Dramatiques de Radio-Canada et le 1er Prix Court-métrage à Bruxelles. Prix du Gouverneur Général 1990 avec *La vraie histoire du chien de Clara Vic.*
Filmographie sélective: "Michou et Pilo" (7 eps), TV, 84-85, CDN, Sc; *Victor, la terre est plate?*, C, 83, CDN, Sc; "Salut santé" (26 eps), TV, 81-82, CDN, Sc/Rech; "Bonjour, comment mangez-vous?" (13 eps), TV, 77, CDN, Sc/Rech; "Surville" (3 eps), TV, 77, CDN, Sc.

DUFRESNE, Guy
SARDEC, SACD. 1, ch. Abbott's Corner, Frelighsburg, PQ J0J 1C0 (514)298-5174. 3555, rue Berri, #413, Montreal, PQ H2L 4G4 (514)844-1268.
Types de production et générique: TV film-Sc; TV vidéo-Sc.
Types d'oeuvres: Drame-TV; Comédie-TV; Documentaire-TV; Enfants-TV.
Curriculum vitae: Né en 1915, Montréal, Québec. Cours classique. Scénariste à la radio, 45-55; télévision, 55-75; théâtre, 59-67. "Cap-aux-Sorciers" fut proclamée émission de l'année, 56-57; *Des souris et des hommes*, meilleur télé-théâtre de l'année, 73.
Filmographie sélective: *Le Frère André*, C, 86, CDN, Sc; *L'Enigme Louis Riel*, TV, 85, CDN, Sc; *Les Pluies acides au Québec*, TV, 85, CDN, Sc; *France Lafontaine Propiétaire*, TV, 85, CDN, Co sc; *Norman Bethune*, TV, 84, CDN, Sc; "Propos d'écologie" (12 eps), TV, 78-81, CDN, Sc; *C'est pour Mathieu*, TV, 81, CDN, Sc; *Ces dames de l'Estuaire*, TV, 79, CDN, Adapt/Trad; *Décembre*, TV, 78, CDN, Sc; *Johanne et ses vieux*, TV, 76, CDN, Sc, (ANIK); "Les Forces de Saint-Maurice (114 eps), TV, 72-75, CDN, Sc; *Des souris et des hommes*, TV, 73, CDN, Adapt; *Les Ordres*, Th, 73, CDN, Dial; *Les Trois Souers*, TV, 69, CDN, Aut; "Septième-Nord" (169 eps), TV, 63-67, CDN, Aut.

DUMOULIN-TESSIER, Françoise
SARDEC. 1075, Jean-Dumetz, Ste-Foy, PQ G1W 4K6 (418)653-8862.
Types de production et générique: TV film-Sc.
Types d'oeuvres: Drame-TV; Comédie-TV.

Curriculum vitae: Née en 1939, Québec. Langues: français et anglais. Doctorat en littérature; recherche post doctorale en dialogue cinéma et TV. Documentaliste, critique littéraire, enseignement (spécialiste en français); remplaçante en Afrique du Sud, ecole de métis; publie depuis 80; donne des ateliers en création litéraire. Gagne le Prix littéraire Esso du Cercle du livre pour *Le Salon vert*, 80; *Quatre Jours, pas plus*, 81, mis en nomination pour le Prix France-Québec. *Antoine et Sébastien* est présenté au Festival des télévisions à Prague.
Filmographie sélective: *Antoine et Sébastien*, "Les Beux Dimanches", TV, 80, CDN, Aut; *Antoine et Sébastien/Elise ou le temps d'aimer*, "Premier Plan", TV, 76-77, CDN, Aut.

DUNCAN, Bob◇
ACTRA. (514)937-0959.
Type of Production and Credits: Th Film-Wr/Prod; TV Film-Wr/Dir/Prod; TV Video-Wr/Dir/Prod.
Genres: Drama-TV; Comedy-Th&TV; Documentary-Th&TV; Industrial-Th&TV.
Biography: Born 1947, Scotland; landed immigrant Canada, 67. Worked as a journalist on the *Montreal Gazette*; to CBC, 69 (radio and television variety and documentary); to NFB as co-producer of the Oscar-nominated film on Malcolm Lowry, 75. Has won numerous awards (Chicago, New York, Los Angeles); in 84 became independent writer/director/producer.
Selected Filmography: *Yesterday's Heroes*, TV, 87, CDN, Wr/Dir/Prod; *The Cap*, TV, 85, CDN, Wr/Dir; *Cages*, TV, 85, CDN, Wr; *Hugh MacLennan: A Portrait*, TV, 83, CDN, Wr/Dir/Prod; *The Road to Patriation*, TV, 82, CDN, Wr/Dir/Prod; *A Choice of Two*, TV, 81, CDN, Wr; *In Search of Farley Mowat*, TV, 81, CDN, Wr/Co-Prod; *The Stongest Man in the World*, Th, 80, CDN, Wr; *W.O. Mitchell: Novelist in Hiding*, TV, 80, CDN, Wr/Dir/Co-Prod; *Bravery in the Field*, TV, 79, CDN, Co-Wr; *Margaret Laurence: First Lady of Manawaka*, TV, 78, CDN, Wr/Dir; *The Agony of Jimmy Quinlan*, Th, 78, CDN, Wr/Co-Prod; *Volcano: An Inquiry into the Life and Death of Malcom Lowry*, Th, 75, CDN, Co-Prod.

DUNNING, John
- see PRODUCERS

DUNPHY, Timothy
ACTRA, DGC. 100 Gloucester St., #1003, Toronto, ON M4Y 1M1 (416) 968-2225.
Type of Production and Credits: Th Film-Wr; TV Film-Wr; TV Video-Wr.
Genres: Drama-TV; Comedy-Th&TV; Action-TV.
Biography: Born 1954, New York City; US and Canadian citizenship.
Selected Filmography: "Counterstrike" (1 eps), TV, 90, CDN/USA/F, Wr; "Night Heat" (7 eps)(Wr 1eps/Co-Wr 6 eps), TV, 85-87, CDN, Wr, (GEMINI 88); "Hot Shots" (3 eps), TV, 86-87, CDN, Wr; *Big Deal*, Th, 85, CDN, Co-Wr.

DYS, Hans J.
11314 - 33A Ave., Edmonton, AB (403)437-7690. Allarcom Limited, 5325 - 105 St., Edmonton, AB (403)436-1250.
Type of Production and Credits: TV Film-Prod/Wr; TV Video-Prod/Wr.
Genres: Drama-Th&TV; Documentary-Th&TV; Commercials-Th&TV; Industrial-Th&TV.
Biography: Born 1949, Baarn, The Netherlands; Canadian citizenship. Studied Radio and Television, Mount Royal College. Has worked 20 years in television production and 1 year in radio as a writer, producer and director; has written for live television and several feature film scripts.
Selected Filmography: *Jewel on the Hill*, TV, 91, CDN, Wr/Prod; "Adventures Down Under" (13 eps), TV, 87, CDN, Exec Prod; "Stony Plain" (13 eps), TV, 81, CDN, Exec Prod; *Big Deal*, "Stony Plain", TV, 81, CDN, Wr.

EAMES, David
ACTRA. 524 - 133 Wilton St., Toronto, ON M5A 4A4 (416)368-8787.
Type of Production and Credits: Th Film-Wr; TV Film-Wr; TV Video-Wr.
Genres: Drama-Th&TV; Comedy-Th&TV; Children's-Th&TV.
Biography: Born 1950, Toronto, Ontario. B.A., Dramatic Literature, McGill University, 72. Story Editor, Telefilm Canada, 78-86.
Selected Filmography: "Max Haines Crime Flashback", TV, 91, CDN/F/IRL, Exec Story Ed; *The Butter Box Babies*, Th, 91, CDN, Scr; *Judi Loves Elvis*, Th, 91, CDN, Scr; "Neon Rider" (3 eps), TV, 90, CDN, Wr; "African Journey" (6 eps), TV, 90, CDN/USA/AUS, Wr/Story Ed; "Danger Bay" (3 eps), TV, 86-88, CDN, Wr/Script; *This Side of Heaven: The Guy Lombardo Story*, TV, 88, CDN, Wr; *Deadly Companions: The Bruce Curtis Story*, TV, 88, CDN, Wr; *My Sister's Keeper*, TV, 87, CDN, Wr; *Wilder Point*, TV, 86, CDN, Story Ed; *Café Romeo*, Th, 86, CDN, Story Ed; "The Edison Twins" (1

eps), TV, 85, CDN, Wr; *Musclebound/Being Dead/The Cupid Game*, "Windows", TV, 85, CDN, Wr; *Animal Fever*, "Parents and Reading", TV, 85, CDN, Wr; 'The Edison Twins" (12 eps), TV, 85, CDN, Story Ed.

EARL, Morgan
- see PRODUCERS

EDMONDS, Alan
- see PRODUCERS

EDWARDS, Cash
WGAw, ACCT. 4672 Quebec St., Vancouver, BC V5V 3M1 (606)876-0156. Samurai Productions Ltd., 1138 Homer St., Vancouver, BC V6B 2X6 (604)689-8807. Corby Coffin, Characters, (604) 733-9800.
Type of Production and Credits: Th Film-Wr; Th Short-Wr/Prod/Dir; TV Video-Wr/Prod/Dir.
Genres: Comedy-Th&TV; Variety-TV; Documentary-TV; Industrial-TV.
Biography: Born 1949, Santa Monica, California; landed immigrant Canada. Studied History and Film, UCLA. Member, Hole in the Wall Gang (western preservation society). President, Zorah Productions, 87-89; President, Samurai Productions, 86-present. "Vancouver Live" won CanPro Gold for Best Continuing Variety Show.
Selected Filmography: *Cowboy Heart*, Th, 91, CDN, Prod/Wr/Dir; "Extraordinary Customer Relations" (2 eps), ED, 90-91, USA/CDN, Prod; *Rules of the Road*, In, 90, CDN, Prod/Dir; "Kidzone" (6 eps), TV, 89-90, CDN, Dir/Wr; *Dayglow Warrior*, TV, 90, CDN, Wr; *You Can Run*, "Neon Rider", TV, 90, CDN, Wr; *The Prophet*, "War of the Worlds", TV, 88, CDN/USA, Wr; "Spirit People" (3 eps), TV, 88, CDN, Prod/Dir; *The Number 1 Killer*, "Doctor, Doctor", TV, 88, CDN, Prod/Wr; *Beyond the Line*, TV, 88, USA/CDN, Prod; *The Renegade*, "Star Trek, The Next Generation", TV, 87, USA, Wr; "Newsmakers" (12 eps), TV, 86, CDN, Prod/Wr; "Press Conference" (12 eps), TV, 86, CDN, Prod/Wr; "Vancouver Live" (288 eps), TV, 85-86, CDN, Sr Prod/Head Wr; *Torc: Legend of Kahulin*, Th, 83, USA/IRL, Wr.

EGOYAN, Atom
- see DIRECTORS

EL-SISSI, Azza
- see PRODUCERS

ELLIS, Kathryn
- see PUBLICISTS

ENDERSBY, Clive
ACTRA, ACCT, WGAw. 834A Westmount Dr., West Hollywood, CA 90069 (213)652-3345.
Type of Production and Credits: TV Film-Wr; TV Video-Wr.
Genres: Drama-TV; Documentary-TV; Educational-TV; Children's-TV.
Biography: Born Edinburgh, Scotland; Canadian citizenship. Child actor, 150 productions; won scholarship to acting school, England and appeared in numerous stage, TV and film productions. During 70s, returned to Canada as a writer; 200 TV scripts produced, TVOntario; 5 children's plays; 2 published noves, *Read All About It* and *Journey through the Stars*; has written lyrics to 150 songs. His educational series have won Silver and Bronze, New York Film Festival; has won 2 ACT awards and the International Reading Association Award of Merit.
Selected Filmography: *Alligator Pie*, TV, 91, CDN, Wr; The Adventures of the Black Stallion" (26 eps), TV, 90, CDN, Exec Story Ed/Wr; "The Challengers", TV, 88, CDN, Wr; "Night Heat" (2 eps), TV, 88, CDN, Wr; "Today's Special" (41 eps), TV, 81-86, CDN, Wr; "Dear Aunt Agnes" (11 eps), TV, 84-86, CDN, Wr; "Polka Dot Door" (30 eps), TV, 75-85, CDN, Wr; "Artscape" (8 eps), TV, 81-82, CDN, Wr; "It's Mainly Music" (6 eps), TV, 82, CDN, Wr; "Canada - The Great Experiment" (14 eps), TV, 79-81, CDN, Wr; "Read all About It" (40 eps), TV, 76-80, CDN, Wr; "Music Box" (2 eps), TV, 79, CDN, Wr; "Like No Other Place" (2 eps), TV, 78, CDN, Wr; "One World" (13 eps), TV, 77-78, CDN, Wr; "Person to Person" (7 eps), TV, 77, CDN, Wr; *Knowledge is Understanding*, TV, 76, CDN, Wr; "Our Heritage" (3 eps), TV, 75, CDN, Wr.

ENGEL, Howard
ACTRA, ACCT. 281 Major St., Toronto, ON M5S 2L5 (416)960-3829. Beverley Slopen, 131 Bloor St. W., #711, Toronto, ON M5S 1S3 (416)964-9598.
Type of Production and Credits: TV Film-Wr; TV Video-Wr.
Genres: Drama-TV; Comedy-TV; Action-TV.
Biography: Born 1931, Toronto, Ontario. B.A., McMaster University, 54. Freelance writer/producer, CBC radio (wrote thousands of radio programs, 55-85); freelanced in U.K., France, Cyprus, 60-64. Did literary and political interviews for documentaries (Alice B. Toklas, Sylvia Beach, Archbishop Makarios); CBC staff producer, 68-85. Published 7 books beginning with *The Suicide Murders*, 80, and most recently *Dead and Buried*, 90.

Became full-time writer, 85. Screenplay for Harvey Hart, *Call Me Sammy*, a biography of prize-fighter Sammy Luftspring, was in progress at the time of Hart's death; currently developing outline for "Cat and Mouse" for CBC-TV. Received Habourfront Festival Prize, 90, for Contributions to Writing.
Selected Filmography: *Murder Sees the Light*, TV, 86, CDN, T'play; *The Suicide Murders*, TV, 85, CDN, T'play/Act; *The Observer*, TV, 64-65, CDN, Story Ed/Wr.

ERNE, Andreas
- see PRODUCERS

EVANS, Margaret◇
(604)533-1970
Type of Production and Credits: TV Film-Wr/Prod; TV Video-Wr/Prod.
Genres: Drama-TV; Documentary-TV; Educational-TV; Children's-TV.
Biography: Born 1944, England; Canadian citizenship. Writer of children's materials since 71 in all media; many documentary films and radio plays, numerous print pieces; 4 TV series, 72-79, on nature and environmental themes, one of which was a CanPro winner; syndicated journalist with extensive experience interviewing and writing about film and TV personalities and on general movie industry subjects; author of 2 books.
Selected Filmography: "Serendipity" (13 eps), TV, 88, CDN, Wr/Prod; *Delay of the Sockeye*, ED, 82, CDN, Wr/Spv; "Creatures Beyond" (39 eps), TV, 78-79, CDN, Wr/Res; "Canada's Wildlife" (13 eps), TV, 75, CDN, Wr/Res; "Noah's Endangered Ark" (26 eps), TV, 73-74, CDN, Wr.

FAIRE, Sandra
- see PRODUCERS

FARR, Gordon
- see PRODUCERS

FAVREAU, Robert
- voir REALISATEURS

FEINGOLD, Stan
335 E. St. James Rd., North Vancouver, BC V7N 1L3 (604)986-1407. The Eyes Multi Media Productions, 223 W. 2nd Ave., Vancouver, BC V5Y 1C7 (604)876-3937.
Type of Production and Credits: TV Film-Wr/Dir/Prod/Comp; TV Video-Wr/Dir/Prod.
Genres: Documentary-TV; Educational-TV; Commercials-TV; Industrial-TV.
Biography: Born, 1952, and raised in Los Angeles, California. Has been working professionally in film, theatre, television and corporate communications since 1974. B.A. (Honours), English Literature, Simon Fraser University, 1977. Professional musician; taught Songwriting and History of Popular Music, Commercial Music Program, Capilano College, 1979-86. Was Senior Writer/ Producer, Vancouver Community College, 1979-83. Creative Director, Changing Images Productions, 1983-89. Since July, 1989, has been Creative Director for The Eyes Multi-Media Productions Inc. Recipient of over three dozen national and international awards.
Selected Filmography: *K2: The Making of the Movie*, TV, 91, CDN/USA/GB, Comp; *Beyond the Barriers*, In/TV, 91, CDN, Wr/Prod/Dir; *Hawaiian Sun*, Cm, 91, CDN, Prod/Dir; "Entertainment Tonight", TV, 90-91, USA, Prod; "America's Most Wanted", TV, 91, USA, Prod; "Preview", TV, 91, CDN/USA, Prod; *B.C. Tel: New Frontiers*, In, 90, CDN, Wr/Prod/Dir; *Don't Take the Keys*, Cm, 89, CDN, Wr/Prod/Dir.

FERGUSON, Don
ACTRA, WGAw. Air Farce Productions, 66 Gerrard St. E., Toronto, ON M5B 1G3 (416)977-6222.
Type of Production and Credits: Th Film-Wr; TV Video-Wr.
Genres: Drama-Th&TV; Comedy-Th&TV.
Biography: Born 1948, Montreal, Quebec. Languages: English, Italian. Honours B.A., Loyola University, Montreal. Won Juno Award, Best Comedy Album, 79; 8 ACTRA Awards for "Royal Canadian Air Farce," radio.
Selected Filmography: *Air Farce Live at the Bayview*, TV, 84, CDN, Co-Wr/Act; *Air Farce Enquirer*, TV, 82, CDN, Co-Wr/Act; *Air Farce Factory Comedy Outlet*, TV, 81, CDN, Co-Wr/Act, (ACTRA); "Air Farce" (10 eps), TV, 81, CDN, Co-Wr/Act, (ACTRA); *Air Farce*, TV, 80, CDN, Co-Wr/Act; *Highpoint*, Th, 79, CDN, Uncr Rewr; *Improper Channels*, Th, 79, CDN, Uncr Rewr; "Mary and Michael" (26 eps) (Wr 8 eps/Dir 1 eps), TV, 78, CDN, Pro Coord; "Money Makers" (4 eps), TV, 75-76, CDN, Dir; *Our Costly Clean-Up*, TV, 75, CDN, Dir; "The Plane Game" (4 eps), TV, 73-74, CDN, Wr.

FERNS, W. Paterson
- see PRODUCERS

FERRAGNE, Marielle
SARDEC, ACCT. 6535, Molson, Montréal, PQ H1Y 3C4 (514)376-0456.
Types de production et générique: TV vidéo-Sc.
Types d'oeuvres: Education-TV; Enfants-

TV; Animation-TV; Comédie-TV.
Curriculum vitae: Née en 1954, Grand Mère, Québec. Bac. en animation et recherche culturelle. Intérêts particuliers: la réalité interculturelle, les publics enfant et adolescent.
Filmographie sélective: "Pacha et les chats" (3 eps), TV, 91, CDN, Sc; "A la claire fontaine" (2 eps), TV/ED, 90, CDN, Sc; "Picoli et Lirabo" (7 eps), TV/ED, 89, CDN, Sc; "Dis-moi Lou" (21 eps), TV, 89, CDN, Sc; "Brico-Magie" (6 eps), TV, 89, CDN, Sc; "Science-Mag" (2 eps), TV/ED, 89, CDN, Sc; "Ritournelle" (7 eps), TV/ED, 89, CDN, Sc; "Les oursons volant" (12 eps), TV, 88, CDN/YU, Co sc; "17 rue Laurier" (6 eps), TV/ED, 88, CDN, Sc; "Passe-Partout" (20 eps), TV, 87, CDN, Sc; "Court Circuit" (2 eps), TV, 84, CDN, Sc.

FERRETTI, NINA
- see PRODUCERS

FIELDING, Joy
ACTRA. Owen Laster, William Morris Agency, 1350 Ave. of the Americas, New York, NY 10019 (212)586-5100.
Type of Production and Credits: Th Film-Wr; TV Film-Wr.
Genres: Drama-Th&TV; Comedy-Th&TV.
Biography: Born 1945, Canada. B.A., University of Toronto. Known primarily as an author; has 9 books published: *The Best of Friends, The Transformation, Trance, The Other Woman, Life Penalty, The Deep End, Kiss Mommy Goodbye,* (Book-of-the-Year Award, Canadian Periodical Society), *Good Intentions* and, most recent novel, *See Jane Run*. Has written for TV, "Program X"; several film scripts; writes book reviews for the *Globe & Mail*, and CBC radio.

FINDLEY, Timothy
OC, O.Ont. ACTRA. Janet Turnbull, P.O. Box 757, Dorset, NT 05251 USA (416)923-9111.
Type of Production and Credits: Th Film-Wr; TV Film-Wr; TV Video-Wr.
Genres: Drama-Th&TV; Comedy-TV; Variety-TV; Documentary-TV.
Biography: Born 1930, Toronto, Ontario. Education in Drama and Speech in Toronto and London, England; career as actor, 48-62. Full-time writer since 62: novels, short fiction, plays, films and television drama and documentaries. Awards include Governor-General's Award for Fiction, 77; Author of the Year, Canadian Booksellers' Association, 84; Canadian Authors' Association Award for Fiction, 85; CNIB Talking Book of the Year Award, 86; Periodical Marketers of Canada, Best Paperback Fiction, 87; Western Magazine Award for Fiction, 88; Periodical Marketers of Canada, Best Magazine Fiction, 88; Government of Ontario Trillium Award, 89; Mystery Writers of America ("Edgar"), Best Original Paperback, 89; National Radio Award, 89, 90; Canadian Authors' Association, Non-Fiction, 91. Hon. D.Litt., Trent University, 82, University of Guelph, 84, York University, 89; Officer of the Order of Canada, 86; Order of Ontario, 91.
Selected Filmography: "Belafonte Sings" (2 eps), TV, 83, CDN, Co-Wr; *The Wars*, Th, 81, CDN/D, Wr; *Other People's Children*, TV, 81, CDN, Wr; "Dieppe 1942" (2 eps), TV, 79, CDN, Co-Wr; "The Newcomers" (2 eps), TV, 78, CDN, Wr; *The Garden and the Cage*, TV, 77, CDN, Co-Wr; "The National Dream" (8 eps), TV, 72-74, CDN, Wr; "The Whiteoaks of Jalna" (6 eps), TV, 71-72, CDN, Wr; *Don't Let the Angels Fall*, Th, 68, CDN, Wr; *The Paper People*, TV, 67, CDN, Wr; *Who Crucified Christ?*, TV, 66, CDN, Wr.

FINE, David
- see DIRECTORS

FINNIGAN, Joan
Chalmers Adams, 1255 Yonge St., Toronto, ON M4T 1W6 (416)929-7232.
Type of Production and Credits: TV Film-Wr.
Genres: Drama-TV.
Biography: Born 1925, Ottawa, Ontario. B.A., English, History, Economics, Queen's University. Has written many radio scripts; published 21 books, including *Entrance to the Greenhouse*, 68 (Centennial Award for Poetry), *I Come from the Valley, Some of the Stories I Told You Were True*, 81, *Legacies, Legends and Lies*, 85.
Selected Filmography: *Celebrate This City*, TV, 73, CDN, Wr; *Home*, "This Land", TV, 72, CDN, Wr; *They're Putting Us Off the Map*, TV, 70, CDN, Wr; *The Best Damn Fiddler from Calabogie to Kaladar*, TV, 69, CDN, Wr, (CFA).

FIRUS, Karen
- see DIRECTORS

FLAHERTY, David◇
ACTRA, WGA. (416)628-3164.
Type of Production and Credits: TV Film-Wr; TV Video-Wr.
Genres: Comedy-Th&TV; Variety-TV.
Biography: Born 1948, Pittsburgh, Pennsylvania; landed immigrant Canada, 73. Attended University of Pittsburgh. Has writing, directing, editing experience

in film; copy writer J. Walter Thompson, Cockfield Brown, Raymond Lee & Associates.
Selected Filmography: *Mob Story*, Th, 89, CDN, Co-Wr; "Friday the 13th: The Series" (1 eps), TV, 88, CDN/USA, Wr; *Gemini Awards*, TV, 88, CDN, Wr; *Best of SCTV*, TV, 88, CDN/USA, Wr; "Really Weird Tales" (5 eps), TV, 86-87, CDN/USA; *Dynaman*, TV, 87, USA, Co-Head Wr; "SCTV" (18 eps), TV, 84, CDN, Co-Wr.

FOLDY, Peter
ACTRA, SAG, AFM. 6252 Colgate Ave., Los Angeles, CA 90036 USA. Media Artist Group, 6255 Sunset Blvd., Hollywood, CA 90028 (213)463-5610.
Type of Production and Credits: Th Film-Wr/Prod; Th Short-Prod; TV Video-Wr.
Genres: Drama-Th; Comedy-Th; Action-Th; Horror-Th; Educational-Th; Current Affairs-TV.
Biography: Born in Hungary. Canadian citizen. Lived for 10 years in Australia. Studied Film at York University, Toronto. Canadian recording artist with a 1973 #1 hit, 'Bondi Junction', several Top 10 recordings. 2 Juno award nominations and a 2-time BMI award winner. Speaks fluent Hungarian. Is an exhibited photographer. *Who Do You Listen To?* won the Golden Eagle (Cine 1989).
Selected Filmography: *Homeboys*, Th, 91, USA, Wr/Co-Prod; *It Happened To Me*, Th, 90, USA, Co-Prod; "The Prestons" (3 eps), TV, 90, USA, Wr; *Who Do You Listen To?*, Th, 89, USA, Co-Prod; *Hot-Moves*, Th, 85, USA, Co-Wr/Assoc Prod.

FORTIER, Josée
ACCT, SARDEQ. Productions Olive Inc., 14 Parkside Place, Montréal, PQ H3H 1A8 (514)935-5104.
Types de production et générique: TV vidéo-Sc.
Types d'oeuvres: Comédie-TV; Variété-TV; Publicité-C&TV.
Curriculum vitae: Née en 1954. Langues: français. UQAM, Communications. 7 ans avec publicité, Cosette. 8 ans avec télévision. Felix - Meilleure Special Variétés "Mon Royaume Pour Un Bleuet". Concepteur de plus 40 commerciaux (Renault 5, Radio-Québec, Caisse Populaires, Provigo), 1977-85.
Filmographie sélective: "Samedi P.M." (24 eps), TV, 90-91, CDN, Sc/Script éd; "Samedi De Rire", TV, 85-89, CDN, Sc/Script éd; *Juste Pour Rire*, TV, 89, CDN, Sc; *Mon Royaume Pour Un Bleuet*, TV, 88, CDN, Sc; *C'est Dans La Tête*, TV, 87, CDN, Sc; *Rendez-Vous '87*, TV, 87, CDN, Sc.

FORTIN, Dominique
- voir MONTEURS

FOSTER, Christine
WGC (ACTRA). 46 Chine Dr., Scarborough, ON M1M 2K7 (416)264-4081. Charles Northcote, The Core Group, 489 College St., Ste. 501, Toronto, ON M6G 1A5 (416)944-0193.
Type of Production and Credits: Th Film-Wr; TV Film-Wr; TV Video-Wr.
Genres: Drama-Th&TV; Comedy-TV; Action-Th&TV; Horror-Th.
Biography: Born in England in 1950. Member of the Stratford Festival, Canada, 1971-73. Has worked as an actress, journalist and associate casting director. Honours B.A., Archaeology, University of Toronto; won the Victoria College Governor General's Gold Medal for Academic Achievement, 1990. Member of the Canadian Guild of Musical Theare Writers. Has written the book and lyrics for 5 adult and children's musicals produced in Canada and Denmark. Is also a professionally produced playwright and member of the Playwrights' Union of Canada (PUC). Script editor on "Littlest Hobo" for 3 years and executive story editor for 1 year. Wrote the episode *The Imaginative Invalid* which won the Silver Medal at the 1983 International Film and Television Festival in New York.
Selected Filmography: "Top Cops" (1 eps), TV, 91, USA/CDN, Wr; "Bordertown" (1 eps), TV, 90, CDN, Wr; "Friday The 13th - The Series" (1 eps), TV, 90, USA/CDN, Wr; *Shadow Dancing*, Th, 89, CDN, Wr; "The Campbells" (3 eps), TV, 87, CDN, Wr; "Littlest Hobo" (96 eps), TV, 80-84, CDN, Script Ed; "Littlest Hobo" (20 eps), TV, 80-84, CDN, Wr; "Judge" (1 eps), TV, 83, CDN, Wr; "Mary & Michael" (2 eps), TV, 78, CDN, Wr; "King of Kensington" (1 eps), TV, 76, CDN, Wr.

FOSTER, John C.
- see PRODUCERS

FOURNIER, Claude
- voir REALISATEURS

FOURNIER, Roger◊
AR, SARDEC.(514)937-1900.
Types de production et générique: l métrage-Sc/Réal; TV video-Réal.
Types d'oeuvres: Drame-C&TV; Comédie-C&TV.
Curriculum vitae: Né en 1929, St-Anaclet, Québec. Licencié en lettres, Université Laval. Réalisateur TV depuis 30 ans, Radio-Canada (Montréal); auteur

de 13 livres, romans pour la plupart. Récipi-endaire du Prix du Gouverneur Général du Canada en 82 et France-Canada, 76; Prix Louis Barthou de l'Académie Française.
Filmographie sélective: "Pour l'amour de Sawine" (6 eps), TV, 89, CDN/F/B, Sc; *Une journée en taxi*, C, 80, CDN/F, Sc; *Au revoir ... à lundi*, C, 79, CDN/F, Co sc; *Les Aventures d'une jeune veuve*, C, 74, CDN, Real/Co sc.

FRASER, Fil
ACTRA, ACCT. 9027 - 145 St., Edmonton, AB T5R 0V1 (403)483-6381.
Type of Production and Credits: Th Film-Prod; TV Film-Prod; TV Video-Prod.
Genres: Drama-Th&TV; Documentary-TV; Educational-TV.
Biography: Born in 1932 in Montreal, Quebec. Languages: English and French. Broad-caster in radio and TV, on air and in production since 1951; founder, Banff TV Festival, Alberta Film Festival, Commonwealth Games Film Festival, 1978. Member, Alberta Film Industry Task Force, 1978; past Director, National Film Institute, Motion Picture Institute of Canada. Producer of the Year, Alberta Motion Picture Distributors, 76; 2 Best Film Awards, Alberta.
Selected Filmography: *The Hounds of Notre Dame*, Th, 80, CDN, Prod; *Latitude 55*, Th, 80, CDN, Exec Prod; "Marie Anne" (pilot), TV, 79, CDN, Prod; *Marie Anne*, Th, 77, CDN, Prod; *Why Shoot the Teacher*, Th, 76, CDN, Exec Prod.

FREEMAN, Jean
ACTRA, SMPIA. 843 Morris Cr. N., Regina, SK S4X 2L6 (306)777-2858.
Type of Production and Credits: TV Film-Wr; TV Video-Wr.
Genres: Comedy-TV; Variety-TV; Documentary-TV; Children's-TV.
Biography: Born 1934, Saskatchewan. Worked as retail advertising writer, commercial radio writer, editor, performer; CBC radio writer, contract performer; live stage performer, speaker and lecturer. Ohio State Award for TV Writing, two Media Club Writer/Performer Awards; YWCA Woman of the Year; Toastmasters' Communicator of the Year; Award for Educational Television Writing; Shield of Services from Canadian Public Relations Society.
Selected Filmography:
If You Were in My Schoes/Cancelled Christmas, "Puttnam's Prairie Emporium", TV, 88, CDN, Wr; *Money, Money/Being Wrong's Allright*, "Puttnam's Prairie Emporium" TV, 88, CDN, Wr; *Black and White and Read All Over*, "Puttnam's Prairie Emporium", TV, 87, CDN, Wr; *The Partners*, "The Way We Are", TV, 86, CDN, WR.

FREWER, Terry
- see COMPOSERS

FRIZZELL, John◊
ACTRA, ACCT. (416)941-9570.
Type of Production and Credits: Th Film-Wr/Dir; TV Film-Wr/Dir.
Genres: Drama-Th&TV; Comedy-TV; Documentary-TV; Educational-TV.
Biography: Born in Kingston, Ontario. B.A., Queen's University, 80. Member, Ontario Film and Video Appreciation Society.
Selected Filmography: "Airwaves" (26 eps) (Wr 8 eps), TV, 85-86, CDN, Head Wr; *Neon: An Electric Memoir*, TV, 84, CDN, Wr; *I Love a Man in a Uniform*, "For the Record", TV, 83, CDN, Wr; *An Ounce of Cure*, "Sons and Daughters", TV, 82, CDN, T'play; *White Lies*, "Sons and Daughters", TV, 82, CDN, Wr; *Ricky Goes to Camp*, TV, 82, CDN, Dir; *Uprooted*, TV, 82, CDN, Dir.

FROST, F. Harvey
- see DIRECTORS

FRUET, William
- see DIRECTORS

FURIE, Sidney J.
- see DIRECTORS

FUSCA, Martha
- see PRODUCERS

GABOURIE, Richard
- see PRODUCERS

GAGLIARDI, Laurent
- voir REALISATEURS

GAGNON, Claude
- voir REALISATEURS

GAUVREAU, Gil
- see DIRECTORS

GELINAS, Gratien◊
OC. UDA, ACTRA.. (514)479-8796.
Types de production et générique: l métrage-Sc/Prod/Com; TV film-Sc/Com.
Types d'oeuvres: Drame-C&TV; Comédie-C&TV.
Curriculum vitae: Né en 1909. A reçu des doctorats honorifiques des universités de Toronto, Nouveau-Brunswick, McGill, Trent, Saskatchewan, Mount Allison. Devient membre de la Société Royale du Canada, 58; reçoit la médaille de l'Ordre du Canada, 67. Comédien et auteur à la radio et au théâtre; fonde la Comédie-Canadienne, 57; membre fondateur de l'Ecole nationale de théâtre du Canada, 60; Président, Société de développement de l'industrie cinématographique canadienne,

69-78; Chef de la délégation du Canada, Festival du Film de Cannes, 72-75; Vice-President, Union des Artistes, 84-85; auteur de la pièce *La Passion de Narcisse Mondoux*, 86.
Filmographie sélective: *Agnes of God*, C, 85, CDN, Com; *Tit-Coq*, TV, 84, CDN, Sc/Prod/Com; *Bonheur d'occasion/The Tin Flute* (aussi TV/tourné simultanément fr. et angl.)C, 82, CDN, Com; *Yesterday the Children Were Dancing*, TV, 67, CDN, Sc/Com; *Bousille et les Justes*, TV,, 62, CDN, Sc/Com; *Tit-Coq*, C, 52, CDN, Sc/Com/Prod, (CFA); *La Dame aux camélias, la vraie*, C, 43, CDN, Sc/Prod/Com/Real.

GELINAS, Josée P.✧
SARDEC, UDA. 495 de la Colline, C.P. 1757, Ste-Adèle, PQ J0R 1L0 (514)229-6707.
Types de production et générique: TV vidéo-Sc.
Types d'oeuvres: Variété-TV; Enfants-TV.
Curriculum vitae: Neé en 1949, Montréal, Québec
Filmographie sélective: "Traboulidon" (5 eps), TV, 84-85, CDN, Co aut; "Bravo" (65 eps), TV, 81, CDN, Co conc/Co aut.

GELINAS, Marc
- voir COMPOSITEURS

GELINAS, Marc F.
SARDEC. 5355, Durocher, Outremont, PQ H2V 3X9 (514)279-9485.
Types de production et générique: c métrage-Sc; TV film-Sc; TV vidéo-Sc.
Types d'oeuvres: Drame-TV; Comédie-TV; Documentaire-C&TV; Enfants-TV.
Curriculum vitae: Né en 1937. Auteur pigiste; enseigne à temps partiel à l'Université de Montréal; membre de l'Ordre des Ingénieurs du Québec.
Filmographie sélective: *Expérience pilote sur l'exportation des BPC*, In, 88, CDN, Sc/Rech; *Sun in Autumn*, TV, 88, CDN, Aut; "Moi aussi j'écrase" (3 eps), TV, 83, CDN, Conc/Co sc; *Cap au Nord/Northward Bound*, TV, 83, CDN, Conc/Sc; *La Qualité, la clé du succès/Quality Starts at the Top*, In, 81, CDN, Sc; "Chère Isabelle" (39 eps), TV, 76, CDN, Partic sc; *Margo*, TV, 74, CDN, Aut.

GEOFFRION, Robert
ACTRA, SACD. 25 Nelson St., Montreal West, PQ H4X 1G2 (514)486-8735. Stephan Gray, Gray-Goodman, 211 S. Beverly Dr., Ste. 100, Beverly Hills, CA 90212 (213)276-7070.
Types de production et générique: l métrage-Sc; TV film-Sc.
Types d'oeuvres: Drame-C; Comédie-C; Action-C; Horreur-C.
Curriculum vitae: Né en 1949.
Filmographie sélective: *The Hitman*, C, 91, USA/CDN, Co sc; *Scream of Stone*, C, 90, D/CDN, Co sc; *Double Identity*, TV, 89, CDN/F, Sc; *Frame-Up Blues*, TV, 89, F/CDN, Co sc; *Champagne Charlie*, TV, 88, F/CDN, Co sc; "Formule I" (13 eps), TV, 87, CDN/F, Prod; *Les Bottes*, TV, 86, CDN, Sc; *The Temptations of Big Bear*, C, 86, CDN, Sc; *Eternal Evil/The Blue Man*, C, 85, CDN, Sc; *Deep Sea Conspiracy*, C, 85, CDN, Co sc; *Lune de Miel* (adaptation ang.), C, 85, CDN/F, Sc; "La Police d l'art" (6 eps, TV, 85, CDN/F, Co sc; *A Fighting Chance*, ED, 84, CDN, Sc/Real; *Blipss*, ED, 84, CDN, Sc/Real; *L'Entrevue formelle*, ED, 84, CDN, Réal; *L'Officierd'information*, ED, 84, CDN, Sc/Réal; *The Surrogate*, C, 82, CDN, Sc; *Joy* (tourné simultanément fr/ang), C, 83, CDN, Sc; *Scandale*, C, 82, CDN, Sc; *Le Rôle clé des surveillants*, TV, 82, CDN, Sc/Réal.

GERBER, Sig
- see PRODUCERS

GERRETSEN, Peter
- see DIRECTORS

GILBERT, Tony
- see PRODUCERS

GILDAY, Katherine
ACTRA, TWIFT, CIFC. Kandor Productions Ltd., 76 Marion St., Toronto, ON M6R 1E7 (416)588-0239. FAX: 588-0239.
Type of Production and Credits: TV Film-Dir/Prod/Wr.
Genres: Documentary-TV; Educational-TV.
Biography: Born in Budapest; has lived in Canada since early childhood. Studied and taught English Literature at the University of Toronto for several years before becoming a freelance journalist, and for a period, a staff entertainment writer for *The Globe and Mail*. Since 1981, has been working as a freelance writer and researcher in the documentary field. Has been a regular contributor to the CBC's "The Nature of Things" and has also worked for TVOntario, in particular the science series, "Vista", as well as for the National Film Board on its series "The Feminization of Poverty". *The Famine Within* is her first solo project as producer, director and writer.
Selected Filmography: *The Famine Within*, Th/TV, 90, CDN, Prod/Wr/Dir; *For Richer or Poorer*, "The Feminization of Poverty", Th, 88, CDN, Wr; "The Nature of Things" (8 eps), TV, 81-89, CDN, Wr;

Coming to Grips with the Grippe, "The Nature of Things", TV, 88, CDN, Wr; *Euthanasia*, "The Nature of Things", TV, 87, CDN, Wr; *Pebbles to Computers*, "Vista", TV, 87, CDN, Wr; *More Than Meets The Eye*, "Vista", TV, 86, CDN, Wr/Assoc Prod; "Search for an Answer" (2 eps), TV, 84-85, CDN, Wr.

GILLARD, Stuart
- see DIRECTORS

GILLIS, Kevin
- see PRODUCERS

GIRALDEAU, Jacques
- voir REALISATEURS

GJERSTAD, Ole
- see PRODUCERS

GLASSBOURG, Michael
WGC (ACTRA). 135 Bleecker St., #102, Toronto, ON M4X 1X2 (416)921-8103. 376 College St., 2nd Floor, Toronto, ON M5T 1S6 (416)967-3446. Charles Northcote, The Core Group, 489 College St., Ste. 501, Toronto, ON M6G 1A5 (416)944-1093.
Type of Production and Credits: Th Film-Wr; TV Film-Wr/Prod; ED Video-Wr/Prod.
Genres: Drama-Th&TV; Comedy-TV; Educational-TV; Children's-Th&TV.
Biography: Born in 1951 in Montreal, Quebec. Began his career in theatre, first acting, then writing and directing. Has had six plays produced. *Bad Apples* was called the "year's best musical" by CHUM-FM. Wrote *Thundering Herds: The Music of Woody Herman* and *Scandalize My Name: The Life and Music of Paul Robeson* for CBC Radio. Has given public readings of his work (prose & poetry), worked as a story editor, an acting coach and as an assistant director. Has written music and lyrics for various shows. Won the Information Film Producers of America Special Award for Screenwriting for *Introducing...Janet*.
Selected Filmography: *Boys Will Be...*, ED, 90, CDN, Wr/Prod; *The Conserving Kingdom*, TV, 87, CDN, Wr; *The Juggler*, TV, 86, CDN, Wr/Assoc Prod; *Jen's Place*, TV, 84, CDN, Wr; *Introducing...Janet*, TV, 83, CDN, Wr.

GOLDMAN, Alvin
ACTRA, WGAe, ACCT. 208 Dufferin Rd., Hampstead, PQ H3X 2Y1 (514)483-3371.
Type of Production and Credits: Th Film-Wr; Th Short-Wr; TV Film-Wr; TV Video-Wr.
Genres: Drama-Th&TV; Documentary-Th&TV.
Biography: Born 1927, Winnipeg, Manitoba. Chancellor's Prize in Literature, University of Manitoba, 48; postgraduate work in French Literature, Sorbonne, Paris, 50-51. Writer and filmmaker, NFB, 51-58; freelance writer, 58-84; freelance writer, script editor and script consultant since 85; also translator (from French).
Selected Filmography: *Night Flight*, TV, 78, CDN, T'play; "Salty" (2 eps), TV, 74, CDN, Co-Wr; *The Sloane Affair*, TV, 73, CDN, Co-Wr; *The Painted Door*, "Festival", TV, 67, CDN, T'play; *Yerma*, "Festival", TV, 67, CDN, T'play; *The Betrayal*, "Show of the Week", TV, 66, CDN, T'play; *A Cheap Bunch of Nice Flowers*, "Festival", TV, 65, CDN, T'play; *The Magician of Lublin*, "Festival", TV, 64, CDN, T'play; *The Private Memoirs and Confessions of a Justified Sinner*, TV, 64, CDN, T'play; *The Endless Echo*, "Festival", TV, 63, CDN, T'play; *The Wild Duck*, "Festival", TV, 63, CDN, T'play; *The Gambler*, "Festival", TV, 62, CDN, T'play; *The Queen and the Rebels*, "Festival", TV, 62, CDN, T'play; *Quebec Separatism*, "Inquiry" (2 parts), TV, 61, CDN, Wr/Dir; *Bar Mitzvah*, Th, 57, CDN, Wr/Dir.

GOLICK, Jill
WGC. 41 Silas Hill Dr., Willowdale, ON M2J 2X8 (416)756-0721. Krisztina Bevilacqua, 85 Roosevelt Rd., Toronto, ON M4J 4T8 (416)463-7009.
Type of Production and Credits: TV Film-Wr; TV Video-Wr.
Genres: Comedy-TV; Educational-TV; Animation-TV.
Biography: Has written on subjects ranging from AIDS to zed and for media as diverse as Saturday morning cartoons and high school science texts. Author of 5 nonfiction books and several magazine and newspaper articles, Has designed and implemented 7 multimedia kits for use in classrooms and 9 computer software games, including a Parents' Choice Award winner. Has written lyrics for dozens of songs, many of which can be heard on Canadian Sesame Street and one of which formed the basis for a Clio Award finalist in the public service/radio category. Has edited 3 newsletters and 2 books. Born in Montreal; graduate of Brown Univ. Dir., Children's Broadcast Institute; former VP, ACTRA Writers' Guild, Toronto Branch Council; member of CANSCAIP.
Selected Filmography: "Shining Time Station" (4 eps), TV, 91, USA, Wr; "Eric's World" (1 eps), TV, 90, CDN, Wr; *Lee's Forest*, "NFB Environment Series", ED,

90, CDN, Wr; "Sesame Street", TV, 78-90, CDN, Wr; "Smoggies" (3 eps), TV, 89, CDN/F, Wr; "Happy Castle" (6 eps), TV, 88, CDN, Wr; *A Room Full of Energy*, ED, 83, CDN, Story Ed; *Four Summers*, TV, 78, CDN, Wr/Res.

GOODMAN, Paul W.
- see PRODUCERS

GOOREVITCH, David S.
- see EDITORS

GORDON, Ben
ACTRA, SAG, WGAw, ACCT. 21 Relmar Rd., Toronto, ON M5P 2Y4 (416)488-9515. Ben Gordon Enterprises Inc., 12 Upjohn Rd., Don Mills, ON M3B 2V9 (416)444-5004.
Type of Production and Credits: Th Film-Wr/Act; TV Film-Wr/Act; TV Video-Wr/Prod/Act.
Genres: Drama-Th&TV; Comedy-Th&TV; Variety-TV.
Biography: Born 1951, Toronto, Ontario. Graduate of Boston University, 73. Experience with all major American and Canadian TV networks. Numerous American and Canadian awards and nominations, including Best TV Program of the Year (ACTRA), Best Comedy Writing (ACE), and Best Variety Performer (ACTRA); Clio and IBA awards for humour/performing in advertising. Writer/Actor, Juno and Gemini Award Shows, 85-89; Director of Development, Sunrise Films, 90-91.
Selected Filmography: "Check It Out!", TV, 85-87, CDN/USA, Prod/Story Ed; "CBC Late Night", TV, 85-86, CDN, Host/Comm; *Club Sandwich*, Th, 86, USA, Wr; "Laughing Matters", TV, 85, CDN, Wr/Act; *Genie Awards*, TV, 85, CDN, Co-Wr; *Lost Satellite Network* (2 Shows), TV, 83, CDN/USA, Prod/Wr/Act.

GOTTLIEB, Paul
ACTRA, WGAe, ACCT. 149 Lytton Blvd., Toronto, ON M4R 1L6 (416)486-7970. Sheridan College, Media Writing, Oakville, ON L6H 2L1 (416)845-9430.
Type of Production and Credits: Th Film-Wr; TV Film-Wr.
Genres: Drama-Th&TV; Comedy-Th&TV; Documentary-Th&TV; Commercials-TV.
Biography: Born 1936, Hungary; in Canada since 57; Canadian citizenship. Languages: English, Hungarian, French and German. M.A. Concordia University, Montreal, Quebec. Lecturer, screenwriting, Ryerson Polytechnical Institute, Toronto, Ontario Novelist, *Agency*, filmed 80; freelance screenwriter and script doctor. Reviewer and journalist with contributions to *Maclean's*, *Toronto Life*, *Marketing*. Banff Screenwriters' Workshop, 90; Hungary Media, Project Consultant, 91. Currently Head of Media Writing, Sheridan College. Winner of over 30 awards for commercials.
Selected Filmography: *Black and Decker* (Corporate Video), In, 91, CDN, Wr; *The Avinda Report* (Corporate Video), In, 86, CDN, Wr; *The Good News in Printing*, In, 85, CDN, Wr; *In Praise of Older Women*, Th, 77, CDN, Scr.

GOUGH, William
- see PRODUCERS

GOULET, Stella
- voir REALISATEURS

GRAY, John H.
ACTRA. 3392 W. 37 Ave., Vancouver, BC V6N 2V6 (604)266-7031.
Type of Production and Credits: TV Video-Comp/Wr.
Genres: Drama-TV; Comedy-TV; Musical-TV.
Biography: Born in 1946 in Ottawa, Ontario. Honorary Doctorate, LL.D., Mount Allison University, 89; M.A., Theatre (Directing), University of British Columbia. Writer/Composer of musicals for the stage: *Billy Bishop Goes to War*, *18 Wheels*, *Rock and Roll*, *Don Messer's Jubilee*, *Health*, *Balthazaar*, *Bongo from the Congo*. Regular contributor to CBC's "The Journal." Many awards including the Governor General's, Los Angeles Drama Critics', Golden Globe Awards (Boston); *Billy Bishop Goes to War* won ACTRA Award; *King of Friday Night* won a Gold Medal (New York), two CFTA awards, Silver Hugo (Chicago) and a Rocky at Banff.
Selected Filmography: *Kootenai Brown*, Th, 90, CDN, Wr; *King of Friday Night*, TV, 84, CDN, Wr/Comp/Co-Dir; *Billy Bishop Goes to War*, TV, 82, CDN/GB, Wr/Comp.

GRAY, William
ACTRA, WGAw. Barry Perelman Agency, 9200 Sunset Blvd, Suite 531, Los Angeles, CA 90069 USA (213)274-5999.
Type of Production and Credits: Th Film-Wr; TV Film-Wr/Prod.
Genres: Drama-Th&TV; Action-Th&TV; Science Fiction-Th&TV; Horror-Th&TV.
Biography: Born in Toronto, Ontario.
Selected Filmography: "Dark Shadows" (6 eps)(2 Wr/4 Prod), TV, 90, USA, Wr/Prod; "The Hitchhiker" (2 eps), TV, 89, USA/CDN, Wr; "In the Heat of the Night" (2 eps), TV, 88, USA, Scr; *The*

Abduction of Carrie Swenson, TV, 87, USA, Scr; *Black Moon Rising*, Th, 85, USA, Co-Scr; *The Philadelphia Experiment*, Th, 84, USA, Co-Scr; *Cross Country*, Th, 82, CDN, Co-Scr; *An Eye for an Eye*, Th, 81, USA, Co-Scr; *Prom Night*, Th, 79, CDN, Co-Scr; *The Changeling*, Th, 79, CDN, Co-Scr, (GENIE); *Blood & Guts*, Th, 77, CDN/USA, Co-Scr/Ed.

GREEN, Howard
- see PRODUCERS

GREENE, Charles J.
- see PRODUCERS

GREENWALD, Barry
- see DIRECTORS

GRIGSBY, Wayne
ACTRA, ACCT. 6 Dunwatson Dr., Scarborough, ON M1C 3M2.
Type of Production and Credits: TV Film-Wr; TV Video-Wr.
Genres: Drama-TV; Variety-TV; Documentary-TV; Current Affairs-TV.
Biography: Born in 1947 in Calgary, Alberta; raised in Montreal. Languages: French and English. Bachelor of Arts, Concordia University. Journalist, 1972-86, both electronic and print; contributions to most major national media. "E.N.G." won Gemini 90, for Best Series, and received nomination for writing; *And Then You Die* received Gemini nomination for script; Anik for *Stepping Out*
Selected Filmography: "E.N.G." (44 eps), TV, 89-91, CDN, Exec Story Ed; "E.N.G." (10 eps), TV, 89-91, CDN, Wr; "L'or et le papier" (26 eps), TV, 88-89, CDN/F, Co-Aut; "Mount Royal" (15 eps), TV, 87-88, CDN/F, Exec Story Ed; *And Then You Die*, TV, 86, CDN, Co-Scr; "Stepping Out" (over 100 eps), TV, 82-86, CDN, Host, (ANIK); "Newswatch" (over 1000 eps), TV, 73-85, CDN, Ed (entertainment).

GROBERMAN, Jeffrey
WGC (ACTRA). 5220 Cranbrook St., Richmond, BC V7C 4K9 (604)274-5532. Prime Time Productions Inc., #303 - 990 Homer St., Vancouver, BC V6B 2W7 (604)687-1271. FAX: 682-3527.
Type of Production and Credits: TV Video-Wr/Prod.
Genres: Comedy-TV; Variety-TV; Animation-TV; Industrial-TV.
Biography: Born and raised in Vancouver, BC. B.Sc., Geophysics; additional graduate work in Business Administration and English. Co-originator of "Dr. Bundolo's Pandemonium Medicine Show"; writer for same for 6 years; produced show on CBC-TV. Has written and produced drama, variety, educational and game shows. Presently owns production companies which have co-produced two major comedy series with CBC over the last 3 years.
Selected Filmography: *Three Dead Trolls in a Baggie*, "The Trolls" (5 eps), TV, 91, CDN, Prod; Infomercials (6), ED, 91, CDN, Prod; *Hot Property*, Cm, 91, CDN, Prod; *Living Together*, TV, 90, CDN, Wr; *B.C.: Best of Both Worlds*, In, 89, CDN, Prod; "New Opportunities" (9 eps), ED, 89, CDN, Prod; "Comedy College" (16 eps), TV, 89, CDN, Prod; "Second Honeymoon" (52 eps), TV, 87, USA, Wr; "The Botts" (6 eps), TV, 86, USA, Wr; "Airwolf" (1 eps), TV, 86, USA, Wr; *Our Time to Shine*, TV, 86, CDN, Wr; "The Paul Anka Show" (26 eps), TV, 82, USA, Prod.

GRUBEN, Patricia
- see DIRECTORS

GUENETTE, Pierre
CAPAC, SARDEC. 4062, rue St-Hubert, Montréal, PQ H2L 4A8 (514)527-8149.
Types de production et générique: TV vidéo-Sc.
Types d'oeuvres: Documentaire-TV; Enfants-TV.
Curriculum vitae: Né en 1947, Mont Rolland, Québec. Etudes en pédagogie; auteur de 4 pièces de théâtre; auteur conseil pour une maison d'éditions; auteur d'un roman pour enfants publié aux éditions Québec-Amérique.
Filmographie sélective: *Visages d'église*, ED, 91, CDN, Sc; *Marguerite*, ED, 90, CDN, Sc; *Le Bon Dieu?*, ED, 88, CDN, Sc; *Le Bon Berger*, ED, 86-87, CDN, Sc; *Allumer un soleil*, ED, 86-87, CDN, Sc; *Les Sans-Abris*, TV, 86, CDN, Sc; *Elizabeth Bégeon/Pamphile Lemay/Albert Lozeau/Laure Conan*, "Manuscrits", TV, 81-84, CDN, Aut; "Place du fondateur" (35 eps), TV, 79-81, CDN, Aut; "Télé-Ressources" (25 eps), TV, 78, CDN, Aut; "Le Grenier" (89 eps), TV, 75-79, CDN, Aut.

GUNN, John
- see DIRECTORS

HALL, Mark
- see DIRECTORS

HALLÉ, Roland
- see DIRECTORS

HALLER, Ty
2250 Trimble St., Vancouver, BC V6R 3Z6 (604)224-2666. Vancouver Film School Ltd., 400 - 1168 Hamilton St., Vancouver, BC V6B 2S2 (604)685-5808. FAX: 685-5830. 21st Century Artists Inc., 201 - 1224 Hamilton St., Vancouver, BC (604)669-7486.
Type of Production and Credits: TV

Film-Wr; TV Video-Wr.
Genres: Drama-TV; Comedy-TV; Action-TV.
Biography: Born 1942. Currently Program Director, Vancouver Film School.
Selected Filmography: *Kingsgate*, Th, 88, CDN, 1st AD; *American Gothic*, Th, 86, GB, 2nd AD; *Lost!*, Th, 85, CDN, 1st AD; *Overnight*, Th, 85, CDN, 2nd AD; *For the Whales*, "Centre Play Theatre", TV, 78, GB, Wr; *Boy on Defence*, "Magic Lie", TV, 76, CDN, Wr; "Sidestreet" (1 eps), TV, 75, CDN, Wr; *The Victim*, "Peep Show", TV, 75, CDN, Wr; *Wolfpen Principle*, Th, 73, CDN, 1st AD.

HALLIS, Ron
- see DIRECTORS

HAMORI, Andras
- see PRODUCERS

HANDEL, Alan
- see DIRECTORS

HARBURY, Martin
- see PRODUCERS

HARRIS, Alfred
ACTRA, WGA. 29377 Quail Run Drive, Agoura Hills, CA 91301 (818)889-8238. Ms. Sylvia Hersch/Preferred Artists, 16633 Venture Blvd., Ste. 1421, Encino, CA 91436 USA (818)990-0305.
Type of Production and Credits: Th Film-Wr; TV Film-Wr.
Genres: Drama-Th&TV; Comedy-Th&TV; Action-Th&TV; Science Fiction-Th&TV.
Biography: Born in 1928 in Toronto, Ontario. Canadian citizen. English only.
Selected Filmography: "Adderly" (1 eps), TV, 89, CDN/USA, Wr; "Danger Bay" (2 eps), TV, 88, CDN, Wr; "Huckleberry Finn" (5 eps), TV, 85, CDN, Wr; "Jason of Star Command" (2 eps), TV, 83, USA, Wr; "Dan'l Boone" (1 eps), TV, 82, USA, Wr; "Mulligan Stew" (1 eps), TV, 82, USA, Wr; "Barnaby Jones" (3 eps), TV, 75, USA, Wr; "The Bionic Woman" (1 eps), TV, 74, USA, Wr; "Starlost" (1 eps), TV, 70, CDN, Wr; "Daktari" (4 eps), TV, 69, USA, Wr; "Adam-12" (2 eps), TV, 69, USA, Wr; "Bonanza" (2 eps), TV, 69, USA, Wr; "Mission Impossible", TV, 69, USA, Wr; "Dragnet" (7 eps), TV, 67-68, USA, Wr.

HARRON, Don ◇
OC, ACTRA, AFTRA, SAG, WGAE. (416)920-1500.
Type of Production and Credits: Th Short-Wr; TV Film-Wr.
Genres: Comedy-TV; Variety-TV; Musical-TV; Documentary-Th.
Biography: Born 1924, Toronto, Ontario. Television writer since 53; worked for BBC (London), 50-51; Los Angeles and New York, 54-66; writes for radio and stage: 3 musicals including "Anne of Green Gables"; stand-up comic; author of 6 books. Officer, Order of Canada, 80. Won an ACTRA award, Best Radio Host, for "Morningside", 82.
Selected Filmography: "Really Weird Tales" (1 eps), TV, 86, CDN/USA, Act; "The Don Harron Show" (daily), TV, 83-84, CDN, Host; "Shh...it's the News" (52 eps), TV, 74-75, CDN, Prod/Head Wr; *Snow Job*, Th, 74, CDN, Wr; *Hospital*, Th, 71, USA, Act; *The Wonder of It All*, TV, 70, CDN, Wr; *The Best of Everything*, Th, 59, USA, Act.

HAWLEY, Gay
Wild Ginger Productions Inc., 1204 Lakewood Dr., Vancouver, BC V5L 4M4 (604)254-8998.
Type of Production and Credits: Educational-Wr/Prod.
Genres: Documentary-TV; Educational-TV; Children's-TV.
Biography: Born in Victoria, British Columbia. Graduate B.A. Communications (and Film Workshop), Simon Fraser University, Burnaby, B.C.
Selected Filmography: *Working With Knives*, In/ED, 91, CDN, Prod/Dir; *Needles*, "Youth & AIDS", ED, 91, CDN, Ed; *Safer Sex*, "Youth & AIDS", ED, 91, CDN, Ed; *Eric's Video*, ED, 91, CDN, Prod/Ed; *Too Close...For Comfort*, ED, 90, CDN, Wr/Prod.

HAZZAN, Ray
- see PRODUCERS

HEINEMANN, Michelle
ACTRA, SWG. Box 1409, Iqaluit, NT X0A 0H0 (819)979-0804. FAX: 979-6493.
Type of Production and Credits: TV Video-Wr/Dir/Prod.
Genres: Documentary-TV; Educational-TV.
Biography: Born in 1956 in Regina, Saskatchewan. B.A., Sociology, University of Regina; postgraduate diploma, Continuing/Adult Education, University of Saskatchewan; M.A., Creative Writing, University of East Anglia; Arts Journalism and Publishing Workshop, Banff School of Fine Arts; various fiction-writing workshops in Canada. Freelance writer since 79, specializing in magazines, TV and fiction. Member, Saskatchewan Writers' Guild and ACTRA. Recipient of writing grants from Saskatchewan Arts Board, Alberta Foundation for the Literary Arts, Canada Council Explorations. Recipient of CTV Fellowship, Banff TV Festival, 89.

Selected Filmography: *Putting the Pieces Together*, TV, 91, CDN, Wr/Dir/Prod; "Through the Eyes of a Writer" (5 parts), TV, 90, CDN, Wr/Narr/Co-Prod; *Healing*, Th, 87, CDN, Assist Dir; *The Cooperative Connection*, ED, 86, CDN, Wr/Dir/Prod/Narr.

HELLIKER, John
- see DIRECTORS

HELWIG, David
ACTRA. 106 Montreal St., Kingston, ON K7K 3E8 (613)542-8667.
Type of Production and Credits: TV Film-Wr; TV Video-Wr.
Genres: Drama-TV.
Biography: Born 1938, Toronto, Ontario. B.A., University of Toronto; M.A., Liverpool. Author of 16 books; editor of many others; literary manager, CBC-TV drama, 74-76; extensive magazine journalism and radio drama.
Selected Filmography: *Backstretch* (Wr 2 eps/Co-Wr 2 eps), TV, 82-83, CDN, Creator; "The Great Detective" (1 eps), TV, 78, CDN, Wr; "Sidestreet" (1 eps), TV, 77, CDN, Wr.

HENLEY, Gail
WGC. Renfrew County Films Ltd., 180 Cottingham St., Toronto, ON M4V 1C5 (416)967-7740.
Type of Production and Credits: Th Film-Wr; Th Short-Prod.
Genres: Drama-Th&TV; Comedy-Th&TV; Documentary-Th&TV; Educational-Th&TV.
Biography: An entertainment and communications lawyer, in private practice. Executive producer for all types of films. Awarded KIK Insignia for best novel published in Eastern Europe in 1985. *Where the Cherries End Up*, a novel, published in 4 editions (hardcover and paperback). National Screen Institute award for most oustanding film, Yorkton Festival, 1989.
Selected Filmography: *The Parable of Leaven*, Th, 88, CDN, Prod/Dir/Wr; *Where the Cherries End Up*, TV, 85, CDN, Wr; *Odyssey of the Children*, TV, 79, CDN, Wr.

HENSHAW, Jim
ACTRA, ACCT, WGA. 75 Walmer Rd,, Toronto, ON M5R 2X6 (416)925-0428. Ralph Zimmerman, Great North Artists Management, 350 Dupont St., Toronto, ON M5R 1V9 (416)925-2051.
Type of Production and Credits: Th Film-Wr/Act; Th Short-Wr/Act; TV Film-Wr/Act; TV Video-Wr/Act.
Genres: Drama-Th&TV; Comedy-Th& TV; Action-Th&TV; Children's-TV.

Biography: Born 1949, Bassano, Alberta. B.F.A., University of Saskatchewan, 70. Professional actor, theatre, film and TV; several foreign tours with Canadian theatre; first screenplay produced, 75. Writer resident in L.A., 70-80. Winner, Crystal Cube (ACTRA Writers' Guild), 80; founding member, Academy of Canadian Cinema; member, National Writers' Council, ACTRA, 83-87.
Selected Filmography: *A Perfect .38/Mafia Mistress*, "Sweating Bullets", TV, 91, CDN/USA/MEX, Wr; *Moment of Truth*, TV, 91, CDN/USA, Wr/Exec Story Cons; "Top Cops" (27 eps), TV, 90-91, CDN/USA, Wr/Exec Story Cons; "Friday the 13th - The Series" (48 eps)(Wr 9 eps), TV, 88-90, CDN/USA, Wr/Exec Story Cons; *The True Believer*, "War of the Worlds", TV, 90, CDN/USA, Wr; *The Juggler*, "She-Wolf", TV, 90, USA, Wr; *For Art's Sake*, "Counterstrike", TV, 90, CDN/USA; "Adderly" (44 eps) (Wr 7 eps), TV, 86-88, CDN, Story Ed; *You're No Bunny Till Some Bunny Loves You*, TV, 88, CDN, Wr; "Family Matters", TV, 87, CDN, Wr; *One Enchanted Evening*, TV, 87, CDN, Wr; *The Spirit of Christmas*, TV, 85, CDN, Wr; *Invisible Burden/Tigers in a Cage*, "Educating the Special Child", TV, 84, CDN, Wr; *The Christine Jessop Story*, TV, 84, CDN, Wr; "Pizzazz" (130 eps), TV, 84, CDN, Co-Wr/Host.

HILL, Don
ACTRA, AMPIA. Don Hill Productions, Box 1647, Canmore, AB T0L 0M0 (403)678-5352. FAX: 678-5275.
Type of Production and Credits: Th Film-Wr; TV Film-Wr/Prod; TV Video-Wr/Prod.
Genres: Comedy-TV; Variety-TV; Musical-TV; Documentary-TV.
Biography: Born in 1954. Strong background in current affairs and documentary production. As a writer, twice nominated for an ACTRA award, Best Writer, Documentary and Public Affairs. Recent credits include writer, producer of variety/awards specials (last effort awarded by the Canadian Conference of the Arts). Telethons; live music specials and remote pickups are among areas of expertise.
Selected Filmography: *Necessary Angel*, Th, 90-91, CDN, Wr; *Bravo Alberta*, TV, 90, CDN, Prod/Wr; *For Art's Sake*, TV, 90, CDN, Prod/Wr; "Microcomputers for Learners" (13 eps), ED, 88, CDN, Wr; *The Endless Journey*, ED, 88, CDN, Prod/Wr; "Learning for Life" (26 eps), ED, 86-87, CDN, Prod/Wr.

HODGINS, Barbara L.
- see PRODUCERS

HOFFMAN, KITTY
- see PRODUCERS

HOLE, Jeremy
ACTRA, ACCT. 18 Wychwood Park, Toronto, ON M6G 2Y5 (416)657-1632. Pamela Paul, 14 - 1778 Bloor St. W., Toronto, ON M6P 3K4 (416)769-0540.
Type of Production and Credits: TV Film-Wr.
Genres: Drama-Th&TV; Comedy-TV; Action-TV; Science Fiction-Th&TV.
Biography: Canadian and British citizenship.
Selected Filmography: *Next Door*, "Kurt Vonnegut's Welcome to the Monkey House", TV, 91, CDN/USA, Wr; *Firing Squad*, Th/TV, 90, CDN/F, Wr; "War of the Worlds" (12 eps) (Wr 1 eps), TV, CDN/USA, Exec Story Ed; "Night Heat" (16 eps)(Wr 3 eps), TV, 88, CDN, Story Ed; "Diamonds" (8 eps)(Wr 1 eps), TV, 88, CDN, Story Ed; "Alfred Hitchcock Presents" (14 eps)(Wr 1 eps), TV, 87, CDN/USA, Story Ed; "Mount Royal" (1 eps), TV, 87, CDN/F, Wr; *The Cask of Amontillado*, TV, 86, USA, T'play; *Control*, Th, 86, CDN/F/I, Co-Wr; "Philip Marlowe Private Eye" (5 eps)(Wr 2 eps, Co-Wr 3 eps), TV, 85, CDN, Wr.

HOMBERT, Madeline
- see PRODUCERS

HOPE, Kathryn Ruth
- see PRODUCERS

HORNE, Jerry
- see PRODUCERS

HORNE, Tina
- see DIRECTORS

HOWARD, Christopher
- see PRODUCERS

HUG-VALERIOTE, Joan F.
IATSE 873, TWIFT. 170 Wolverleigh Blvd., Toronto, ON M4C 1S2 (416)466-3831.
Type of Production and Credits: Th Film-Wr/Dir; Th Short-Wr/Dir; TV Film-Wr/Dir; TV Video-Wr/Dir.
Genres: Drama-Th&TV; Variety-ThTV; Documentary-Th&TV; Educational-Th&TV; Children's-Th&TV; Commercials-Th&TV.
Biography: Born, 1948, Guelph, Ontario; Swiss and Canadian citizenship. Languages: English, French, German, Spanish and Italian. B.A.(French), B.Ed., Univ. of Toronto; Diploma, Continuity and AD, Conservatoire Indépendant du Cinéma Français, Paris. Extensive experience in continuity for commercials and features. Leads French and English workshops in film animation and continuity.
Selected Filmography: *Pippi Longstocking*, "ABC Children's Classics" (2 eps), TV, 85, CDN/USA, Cont; *Beach Arts Centre*, TV, 84, CDN, Wr/Dir; *Earl Beatty Swim Show*, TV, 82, CDN, Wr/Dir; *Swiss Carnival in Toronto*, TV, 82, CDN, Wr/Dir/Prod; *The Magic Show*, TV, 80, CDN, Cont; *Lions for Breakfast*, Th, 74, CDN, Cont; *Recommendation for Mercy*, Th, 74, CDN, Cont.

HUNT, Graham
- see DIRECTORS

HUNT, Krystyna
TWIFT. 165 Brookside Dr., Toronto, ON M4E 2M5 (416)698-8283.
Type of Production and Credits: TV Video-Wr.
Genres: Drama-TV; Documentary-TV; Educational-TV; Current Affairs-TV.
Biography: Born in a refugee camp for Ukrainian displaced persons just outside of Goettingen, Germany after the Second World War. Came to Canada at age 4 and is a naturalized Canadian citizen. Speaks English and Ukrainian. Degree from the University of Manitoba in History, English and Sociology. Has worked as an actress, production coordinator for TV and radio commercials and journalist for such publications as the *Toronto Star*, *Flare* and *Cinema Canada*. Has also worked as a story researcher, developer and script analyst for the motion picture and TV industry.
Selected Filmography: "Time of Your Life" (3 eps), TV, 91, CDN, Story Ed; *A Survivor's Guide to the 90s/A Scrooge's Guide to Christmas/A Cheapskate's Guide to the Best of Everything/A Romantic's Guide to Sex Appeal*, "Live It Up", TV, 90, CDN, Res; *Martyn Godfrey*, ED, 90, CDN, Wr.

HUNTER, John
ACTRA, WGAw. Centaur Productions Ltd., 25 St. Mary St., #2410, Toronto, ON M4Y 1R2 (416)967-9180. Michael Carlisle, William Morris Agency, 1350 Avenue of the Americas, New York, NY USA (213)903-1461.
Type of Production and Credits: Th Film-Wr/Prod; TV Film-Wr/Dir; TV Video-Wr.
Genres: Drama-Th&TV; Action-Th&TV; Horror-Th.
Biography: Born 1941, Winnipeg, Manitoba. B.Comm., UBC.
Selected Filmography: *The Midday Sun*, Th, 88, CDN, Co-Prod; *John and the Missus*, Th, 86, CDN, Co-Prod; *The Boy Next Door*, "For the Record", TV, 84, CDN, Dir/Wr; "Vanderberg" (eps 4&5), TV, 83, CDN, Wr; *Class of 1984*, Th, 81,

CDN, Uncr Rewr; *The Grey Fox*, Th, 80, CDN, Wr, (GENIE); *Prom Night*, Th, 79, CDN, Uncr Rewr; *Blood & Guts*, Th, 77, CDN/USA, Co-Wr/Co-Prod; "Sidestreet" (4 eps), TV, 75-77, CDN, Wr; *Sweeter Song*, Th, 75, CDN, Prod; *The Kill*, "Peep Show", TV, 75, CDN, Wr; *The Hard Part Begins*, Th, 73, CDN, Wr/Prod; *Banana Peel*, "Program X", TV, 71, CDN, Wr; *Black Phoenix*, "Sunday at Nine", TV, 69, CDN, Co-Wr.

HURST, Bill
ACTRA. 1749 Collingwood St., Vancouver, BC V6R 3K2 (604)732-6684. Jennifer Hollyer, 112 Westmount Ave., #4, Toronto, ON M6H 3K4 (416)651-8246.
Type of Production and Credits: TV Film-Wr/Story Ed; TV Video-Wr/Story Ed.
Genres: Drama-TV; Comedy-TV; Action-TV; Animation-TV.
Biography: Born in 1951 in England. Canadian citizen. MFA in Creative Writing. Special skills in comedy. Has also written novels and short fiction.
Selected Filmography: *First Among Equals*, "The Black Stallion", TV, 90, CDN/F, Wr; *Mutiny*, "The Beachcombers", TV, 90, CDN, Wr; *Insecurity System*, "Babar", TV, 90, CDN/F, Co-Wr; *Not For Sale*, "The Beachcombers", TV, 89, CDN, Wr; *Club Laundromat*, "The Beachcombers", TV, 89, Co-Wr; *Second Growth*, "The Beachcombers", TV, 89, CDN, Co-Wr; *Anniversary*, "Family Pictures", TV, 89, CDN, Wr; *Give 'Em Enough Rope*, "Family Pictures", TV, 89, CDN, Wr; *Gnome, Sweet, Gnome*, "The Way We Are", TV, 88, CDN, Wr; *Something Old..*, "The Way We Are", TV, 88, CDN, Wr.

HYDE, Steve
ACTRA, CUPE, ACCT. 25 St. Mary St., #1901, Toronto, ON M4Y 1R2 (416)964-1048. CBC, Box 500, Stn. A, Toronto, ON M5W 1A6 (416)975-7417.
Type of Production and Credits: Th Film-1st AD; TV Film-Wr/Dir; TV Video-Wr/Dir/PM.
Genres: Comedy-Th&TV; Variety-Th&TV; Musical-Th&TV; Documentary-Th&TV.
Biography: Born 1935, Melborne, Australia; moved to England, 40, and at age 5 joined family act, Jan and Maurice, and toured through the war with Ensa shows. After stint in Royal Navy went back on variety tours, comedy, acrobatic dancing, then joined stunt team at J. Arthur Rank Studios; moved into writing and 1st AD. Came to Canada and joined CBC, 68. Canadian citizen, 73. Also does cartoons and writes lyrics. Received awards for films and 4 awards for newspaper articles, 2 special awards for services to Canadian music and a special country music award.
Selected Filmography: *Agribition Rode*, "Labatt's Rodeo Series" (1 eps), TV, 81, CDN, Wr/Dir; "Behind the Scenes" (1 eps), TV, 77, CDN, Wr/Dir; *Weekend Cowboy*, TV, 73, CDN, Wr/Dir; "Hart & Lorne Show" (1 eps), TV, 71, CDN, Co-Wr; "The Good Company" (13 eps), TV, 68, CDN, Co-Wr; "Mike & Bernie Winters Show" (13 eps), TV, 66, GB, Co-Wr; "Dick Emery Show" (13 eps), TV, 65, GB, Co-Wr; "Val Doonican Show" (3 eps), TV, 64, GB, Co-Wr; "Vision On" (13 eps), TV, 63, GB, Wr/Act.

ISRAEL, Charles E.
ACTRA, WGAw, ACCT. 21 Dale Ave., #647, Toronto, ON M4W 1K3 (416)924-7174.
Type of Production and Credits: Th Film-Wr; TV Film-Wr; TV Video-Wr.
Genres: Drama-Th&TV; Action-Th&TV; Documentary-Th&TV.
Biography: Born 1920, Indiana, USA; Canadian citizenship. B.A. and B.H.L. degrees. Has had 2 novels and 2 biographies published, including *Rispah* (Literary Guild Main Selection) and *The Mark* (made into a movie). *The Veteran and the Lady* won Best Screenplay, Yorkton Festival. *The Open Grave* won the Prix Italia and Best Scenario, Prague Festival. Head, Screenwriters' Workshop, Banff School of Fine Arts, sicne 86. Winner of Margaret Collier Award, Geminis 86, for Outstanding Body of Work by a Television Writer.
Selected Filmography: *Mayflower Madam*, TV, 87, USA, Wr; *Arch of Triumph*, TV, 84, USA/GB, T'play; *Louisiana* (also 6 eps, TV), Th, 83, CDN/F, Co-T'play; "Harvest Home" (3 eps), TV, 77, USA, T'play; "The Newcomers" (wr, 1 eps/co-wr, 1 eps), TV, 76-77, CDN, Wr; *The Veteran and the Lady*, TV, 72, CDN, Wr; "Marcus Welby, M.D." (1 eps), TV, 69, USA, Wr; *Let Me Count the Ways*, TV, 66, CDN, Wr; *The Labyrinth*, TV, 65, CDN, Wr; *The Open Grave*, TV, 64, CDN, Wr.

IVESON, Rob
- see PRODUCERS

JACKSON, Doug
- see DIRECTORS

JACOBOVICI, Simcha
- see DIRECTORS

JACOBSON, Avrum
ACTRA, ACCT. 111 Jackman Ave., Toronto, ON M4K 2X8 (416)469-1559.
Type of Production and Credits: Th Film-Wr; TV Film-Wr.
Genres: Drama-Th&TV; Comedy-Th&TV.
Biography: Born 1955, Montreal, Quebec. B.A., Psychology, Brandeis University. As Executive Story Editor on "Katts & Dog" co-wrote stories for 22 episodes. Co-developed the characters, format and stories for the premiere season of "Degrassi Junior High." *Malarek* became the basis of the CBC series "Urban Angel." Humour published in *Playboy* and other magazines. Prior to writing, worked as film editor.
Selected Filmography: "Katts & Dog" (13 eps Wr/22 eps Exec Story Ed), TV, 88-91, CDN/USA/F, Exec Story Ed/Wr; "E.N.G." (1 eps), TV, 89, CDN, Wr; *Malarek*, Th, 88, CDN, Wr; *Family Reunion*, TV, 87, CDN, Wr, (GEMINI 88); "Degrassi Junior High" (2 eps), TV, 86, CDN, Wr.

JAY, Paul
- see DIRECTORS

JEFFREY, Robert
- see PRODUCERS

JOBIN, Peter
ACTRA, WGAe. 172 Crawford St., Toronto, ON M6J 2V4 (416)532-6981.
Type of Production and Credits: Th Film-Wr/Prod/Act; TV Film-Wr/Act; TV Video-Wr/Act.
Genres: Drama-Th&TV; Comedy-Th&TV; Action-Th&TV; Horror-Th&TV.
Biography: Born 1944, Montreal, Quebec. Languages: French and English
Selected Filmography: "African Journey" (1 eps), TV, 91, CDN/US, Wr; *Divided Loyalties*, TV, 90, CDN, Wr; "Friday the 13th - The Series" (1 eps), TV, 89, CDN/USA, Co-Wr; "The Campbells" (3 eps), TV, 87-88, CDN/USA/GB, Wr; "Night Heat" (1 eps), TV, 87, CDN, Wr; *You Gotta Come Back a Star*, Th, 86, CDN, Wr/Co-Prod; *Oakmount High*, TV, 85, CDN, Co-Wr; *Till Death Do Us Part*, Th, 81, CDN, Co-Wr; *Happy Birthday to Me*, Th, 80, CDN, Co-Scr; *She Cried Murder*, TV, 74, CDN/USA, Co-Story.

JOHNSON, John A.
- see DIRECTORS

JOHNSON, Nancy
- see PRODUCERS

JONES, Cliff
- see PRODUCERS

JUDGE, Maureen
- see DIRECTORS

KABELIK, Vladimir
- see PRODUCERS

KANDALAFT, Cécile Gédéon◊
(514)733-0750.
Types de production et générique: c métrage-Sc/Prod; TV film-Sc/Prod; TV vidéo-Sc/Prod.
Types d'oeuvres: Drame-C&TV; Documentaire-C&TV; Enfants-C&TV.
Curriculum vitae: Née en 1937; citoyenneté canadienne. Etudes universitaires en lettres françaises, Beyrouth, Liban; art dramatique, Académie Libanaise des Beaux Arts. A travaillé dans le domaine du théâtre au Liban; radio, ORTF, Liban, productrice, réalisatrice, animatrice; TV comédienne, animatrice et productrice, Liban, 59-68. Directrice, rédactrice, *Châtelaine*, Quebec, 74-76; adaptrice et traductrice de livres, 76-79; reporter pigiste, magazines libanais et québécois, 59-85; crée et rédige plusieurs scénarios de documentaires et documentaires-fiction dont *Ramses II, la Princesse lointaine, Ophelie, A Boy from Saudi Arabia, 15 Circle Road, Des jeux et des formes*.

KARDASH, Virlana
1405-1/2 Scott Ave., Los Angeles, CA 90026 (213)481-2427.
Type of Production and Credits: Th Film-Wr/Dr/Ed; Th Short-Dir/Ed/Wr; TV Film-Ed.
Genres: Drama-Th; Documentary-TV; Educational-TV.
Biography: Born 1959, Winnipeg, Manitoba. Languages: English, French, Ukrainian and Spanish. Attended General Arts program, University of Toronto; London International Film School, England.
Selected Filmography: *Guadalajara Express*, Th, 91, USA, Scr; *The Ace of Spades*, Th, 90, USA, Scr; *Oh God, Are You Satisfied*, Th, 88, USA, Scr; *Curfew*, Th, 88, USA, 2nd AD; *A Day in the Life of America*, TV, 86, USA, Pro Coord; "Planet Earth" (3 eps), TV, 85, USA, Assist Ed; *San Francisco Mime Troupe*, TV, 84, USA, Assist Ed; *The Making of Lady Hawke*, TV, 84, USA, Assist Ed; *Jimmy*, Th, 84, USA, Dir/Ed; *First Fashion Show*, Th, 83, GB, 2nd AD; *Fragments of Tenderness*, Th, 83, GB, 1st AD; *Hospice*, TV, 83, GB, Ed; *A Day to Remember*, Th, 82, GB, Assist Ed; *Grace*, Th, 82, GB, Dir/Ed; *The Lost Maya*, TV, 82, GB, Assist Ed.

KATZ, John Stuart
ACTRA, ACCT. 59 Bowden St., Toronto, ON M4K 2X3 (416)462-1820. Film Dept., York University, 4700 Keele

St., Downsview, ON (416)736-5149.
Type of Production and Credits: Th Film-Wr; TV Film-Wr.
Genres: Drama-Th&TV; Documentary-TV; Educational-TV.
Biography: Born 1938, Cincinnati, Ohio. Landed immigrant, Canada. M.A., English Literature, Columbia University; Ph.D., Harvard University, 67. Has taught at University of Toronto and York University for past 20 years; has written and edited 6 books on film (most recent book, "Image Ethics", published by Oxford University Press, 88); has reviewed films on CBC Radio and TV; former programmer for Festival of Festivals; founded and ran distribution company, Beacon Films.
Selected Filmography: *Isaac Littlefeathers*, Th, 84, CDN, Co-Wr; *Rubin*, ED, 74, CDN, Prod/Wr/Dir; *Alphaville Study*, ED, 72, CDN, Co-Dir/Wr; *Document*, ED, 71, CDN, Co-Dir/Wr.

KAUFMAN, David
- see PRODUCERS

KAUFMAN, James T.
- see DIRECTORS

KEATING, Lulu
- see DIRECTORS

KENDALL, Nicholas
- see DIRECTORS

KENNEDY, Michael
- see DIRECTORS

KEUSCH, Michael
- see DIRECTORS

KING, Durnford◊
DGA, DGC, WGAw. (213)394-0877
Type of Production and Credits: TV Film-Wr; TV Video-Dir/Prod.
Genres: Drama-Th&TV.
Biography: Born 1939, Toronto, Ontario. B.A.A., Communication Arts, Ryerson Polytechnical Institute, Toronto. Worked in Toronto, Los Angeles, Tokyo as producer/director music videos, specials; Senior Vice President of Creative Affairs, Discovery International; has won numerous advertising awards in New York, Hollywood, Toronto. *Something Else* was Cannes TV Festival Winner; "Peterson's Canadiana Suite" received Emmy nomination for Best Music Series.
Selected Filmography: "Friday the 13th: The Series" (3 eps), TV, 87, CDN/USA, Wr; "Gummy Bears" (1 eps), TV, 86, USA, Wr; "The Real Ghostbusters" (1 eps), TV, 86, USA, Wr; "Heathcliff" (2 eps), TV, 86, USA, Wr; "She-ra, Princess of Power" (3 eps), TV, 85, USA, Wr; "Ghostbusters" (4 eps, animation), TV, 85, USA, Wr; "Evening at the Improv" (pilot), TV, 81, USA, Wr; *Oscar Peterson's Canadiana Suite*, TV, 79, CDN, Prod/Dir; *Superstunt*, TV, 79, USA, Co-Wr; *Something Else*, TV, 78, USA, Dir; *Preacher and the Rabbi*, TV, 77, USA, Dir; *Greasy Heart*, MV, 76, USA, Dir; *True North*, TV, 76, CDN, Dir/Co-Wr.

KING, Robert
33 Angus Cres., Regina, SK S4T 6N1 (306)757-3604. Mind's Eye Pictures, 1212A Winnipeg St., Regina, SK S4R 1J6 (306)359-7618.
Type of Production and Credits: TV Video-Wr/Dir.
Genres: Documentary-TV; Educational-TV; Commercials-TV; Industrial-TV; Drama-TV.
Biography: Born, 1959, Saginaw, Michigan; has lived in Saskatchewan for most of his life. B.A., English and Psychology; is one thesis short of M.A. in Psychology. Has also worked as a labourer, waiter, cook, social worker, teacher, bartender; now Partner and Creative Director for Mind's Eye Pictures in Regina, a film and video production house. Has written and directed hundreds of productions, including documentary, corporate, commercial, drama. Published fiction writer and member of the Saskatchewan Writers' Guild. *Denro* won a Canadian Public Relations Society (CPRS) Saskatchewan Regional Award.
Selected Filmography: "It Starts at Home" (7 eps), TV, 90-91, CDN, Dir; *See What You Wanna See*, ED/TV, 91, CDN, Wr/Dir; *It's Your Right*, ED/TV, 90, CDN, Co-Wr; *Make the Right Choice*, Cm, 90, CDN, Dir; *Survival in the High Arctic*, ED, 90, CDN, Story Ed; *Denro*, In, 89, CDN, Wr.

KLENMAN, Norman
ACTRA, WGAw. R.R. #2, 130 Bittancourt Rd., Ganges, BC V0S 1E0 (604)537-4802. FAX: 537-4803. MGA Agency, 10 St. Mary St., Toronto, ON M4Y 1P9 (416)964-3302.
Type of Production and Credits: Th Film-Wr/Prod; TV Film-Wr/Prod.
Genres: Drama-Th&TV; Comedy-Th&TV; Action-Th&TV; Science Fiction-Th&TV.
Biography: Born 1923, Brandon, Manitoba. Served 3 years with RCAF. B.A., University of British Columbia, 48. Formerly a journalist, *Vancouver Sun* and *Province*, Reuters, London, England; television and film writer in Canada, England and USA since 50; worked in TV drama, BBC; NFB; public affairs, features and drama, CBC; worked in Los Angeles,

Twentieth Century-Fox, Columbia, MGM and Warner Bros., 65-74; feature films for Klenman-Davidson, Toronto, and freelance screenwriter in Hollywood; one of the founders of Citytv Toronto, and CKVU-TV, Vancouver.
Selected Filmography: "Vancouver" (daily), TV, 81-86, CDN, Co-Exec Prod; *HR*, "The Winners", TV, 80, CDN, Wr; *The Swiss Conspiracy*, Th, 77, USA, Wr; *Flint: Dead On Target*, Th, 76, USA, Wr; *Six War Years*, TV, 75, CDN, T'play/Creator; "The Starlost" (16 eps), TV, 74, CDN/USA, Story Ed; *An Enemy of the People*, TV, 73, CDN, T'play; "Felony Squad", TV, 66-69, USA, Wr; *The Survivors* (mini-series), TV, 69, USA, Staff Wr; "Les Crane Show" (125 eps), TV, 64-65, USA, Head Wr; "On the Same Scene" (250 eps), TV, 60-64, CDN, Wr; "Steve Allen Show" (45 eps), TV, 64, USA, Head Wr; "Quest" (12 eps), TV, 60-61, CDN, Wr; *Now That April's Here*, Th, 58, CDN, Scr/Co-Prod; *Ivy League Killers*, Th, 58, CDN, Wr/Co-Prod.

KOLBER, Sandra
CAPAC, ACCT. 100 Summit Circle, Westmount, PQ H3Y 1N8 (514)482-5871. Claridge Inc., 1170 Peel, 8th Floor, Montreal, PQ H3B 4P2 (514)878-5245.
Type of Production and Credits: Th Film-Wr.
Genres: Drama-Th; Comedy-Th; Animation-TV.
Biography: Born 1934; Canadian citizenship. Languages: English, French, Hebrew and Spanish. B.A., McGill Univ. Two books of poetry published: *Bitter Sweet Lemons & Love*, 67, *All There Is of Love*, 69; worked for many years as a journalist; story editor for Sagittarius Productions Ltd., New York, 70; one of the first readers for CFDC; later became Director of Creative Development, Astral Film Productions; founder and, until 85, partner in Canadian International Studios Inc.; Director, Cineplex Odeon Corp., 84-90. Vice-President, Member of Executive Committee, Co-President of Honorary Council, Orchestre symphonique de Montréal. Appointed to Board of Canadian Broadcasting Corporation/Société Radio-Canada by Canadian Government Order-in-Council, June 90.
Selected Filmography: *George and the Star*, TV, 84, CDN, Co-Prod; *Tell Me that You Love Me*, Th, 82, CDN/IL, Co-Wr.

KOOL, Allen
- see PRODUCERS
KOTTLER, Les
- see PRODUCERS
KREPAKEVICH, Jerry
- see PRODUCERS
KROEKER, Allan
- see DIRECTORS
KUPER, Jack
- see DIRECTORS

L'HERBIER, Benoit
UDA. 1061, Jean XXIII, Laval, PQ (514)661-7297. FAX: 661-4014.
Types de production et générique: TV vidéo-Sc/Réal.
Types d'oeuvres: Variété-TV; Annonces-TV.
Curriculum vitae: Né en 1952, Montréal, Québec. Journaliste, recherchiste, scripteur, concepteur, rédacteur publicitaire.
Filmographie sélective: "Zizanie" (130 eps), TV, 90-91, CDN, Scripte; *Grand Prix* (spectacle), TV, 91, CDN, Conc; "Action Réaction" (445 eps)(écr des jeux), TV, 86-88, CDN; *Entrepôt IGA*, In, 87, CDN, Sc; *Juste pour rire*, TV, 87, CDN, Réal; "Made in Quebec" (9 eps), TV, 85, CDN, Rech.

LABROSSE, Sylvain
- voir DIRECTEURS-PHOTO
LAFOND, Jean-Daniel
- voir REALISATEURS
LAFORÊT, Megan
- see PRODUCERS

LAGER, Martin
ACTRA. 360 Bloor St. E., Suite 403, Toronto, ON M4W 3M3 (416)961-3923. FAX: 323-3983.
Type of Production and Credits: Th Film-Wr; TV Film-Wr/Prod; TV Video-Wr.
Genres: Drama-Th&TV; Comedy-Th&TV; Action-Th&TV; Science Fiction-Th&TV.
Biography: Born 1936, Toronto, Ontario. Former professional actor, musician; playwright: 15 produced plays; *A Time to Reap* won Best Canadian Play Award, EODL Festival, 73. Awarded 2 Canada Council grants, 4 Ontario Arts Council grants; taught creative writing, Sir Sanford Fleming College, 73-79; Executive Producer, CTV Television, 85-90, supervising all drama production and co-production, including such series as "Night Heat," "E.N.G.," "Neon Rider," "Katts & Dog", "Bordertown."
Selected Filmography: "Top Cops" (3 eps), TV, 90-91, CDN/USA, Wr; "Katts & Dog" (5 eps), TV, 90-91, CDN/USA/F, Wr; "My Secret Identity" (1 eps), TV, 90, CDN/USA, Wr; "The Campbells" (90 eps), TV, 85-88, CDN/USA/GB, Exec Prod; "Profiles of Nature" (6 eps), TV, 84-85, CDN, Wr; *Slim Obsession/Out of Sight*,

Out of Mind, "For the Record", TV, 82-83, CDN, Wr; "Citizen's Alert" (2 eps), TV, 81-82, CDN, Wr; "Littlest Hobo" (22 eps) (Wr 11 eps), TV, 80-81, CDN, Exec Story Ed; "Stony Plain" (2 eps), TV, 81, CDN, Wr; "Matt and Jenny" (26 eps) (Wr 11 eps), TV, 79, CDN/GB/D, Exec Story Ed; *Klondike Fever*, Th, 79, CDN, Co-Scr; *The Shape of Things to Come*, Th, 78, CDN, Scr; "Sidestreet" (1 eps), TV, 77, CDN, Wr; *Deadly Harvest*, Th, 76, CDN, Wr; *Wings in the Wilderness*, Th, 74, CDN, Wr.

LAMBERT, Andrée
SARDEC. 1740 Côte De L'Eglise, Sillery, PQ G1T 2A7 (418)527-2862. Scénariste Pigiste, 707, rue de la Salle, Bureau #105, Québec, PQ G1K 2V6 (418)529-9726.
Types de production et générique: TV vidéo-Sc.
Types d'oeuvres: Comédie-TV; Education-TV; Industriel-TV; Jeunes-TV.
Curriculum vitae: Née en 1954. Traduction anglais-français. Formation en linguistique. Aptitude en vulgarisation scientifique ou technique. Intérêt pour le public jeune.
Filmographie sélective: "Comment ça va?" (en cours), TV, 91, CDN, Sc; "Comment ça-va?" (3eps), TV, 90, CDN, Sc; *Ma Douce Moitié*, In, 89, CDN, Sc; "17, rue Laurier" (33 eps), TV/ED, 86-88, CDN, Sc; "La Santé Contagieuse" (13 deps), TV/ED, 86, CDN, Sc; "Octogiciel" (12eps), TV/ED, 84-85, CDN, Sc; "Court Circuit" (6 eps), TV, 83-35, CDN, Sc.

LAMOTHE, Arthur
- voir REALISATEURS

LANCTOT, Micheline
- voir REALISATEURS

LANSING, Floyd
- see DIRECTORS

LAPOINTE, Yves
- voir REALISATEURS

LAURIER, Nicole
- voir PRODUCTEURS

LAVOIE, PATRICIA
- see PRODUCERS

LAZER, Charles
WGC (ACTRA), ACCT. Lazer Media, 73 Beaconsfield Ave., Toronto, ON M6J 3J1 (416)530-4767. FAX: 530-4507. Lynn Kinney, Credentials, 387 Bloor Street E., 5th Floor., Toronto, ON (416)926-1507. FAX: 926-0372.
Type of Production and Credits: Th Film-Wr; Th Short-Wr; TV Video-Wr.
Genres: Drama-Th&TV; Comedy-Th&TV; Action-Th&TV; Industrial-Th&TV.
Biography: Born 1946, Saskatchewan.

A.B., Princeton; Ph.D., Mathematical Sociology, Michigan State. Published in scientific journals. Many awards for government and corporate productions, including Golds at NY, Houston and the American International Film & TV Festival; 2 Silver Hugos (Chicago) for 1/2-hour educational dramas. Gemini/York Trillium Award, Most Promising Writer, TV, 89.
Selected Filmography: "Max Glick" (13 eps)(4 Wr/2 Co-Wr/4 Story Ed), TV, 90-91, CDN, Wr/Story Ed; "Road to Avonlea" (1 eps), TV, 91, CDN/USA, Wr; "Top Cops" (3 eps), TV, 90-91, CDN/USA, Wr; "The Black Stallion" (1 eps), TV, 91, CDN/F/USA, Wr; "Katts & Dog" (1 eps), TV, 90, CDN, CDN/F/GB, Wr; "Danger Bay" (3 eps), TV, 88-89, CDN, Wr; "Neon Rider" (1 eps), TV, 89, CDN, Wr; *Doctors in Uniform*, In, 89, CDN, Wr; *The Breakfast Club*, In, 89, CDN, Wr; "Diamonds" (3 eps), TV, 88, CDN/USA, Story Ed; *Genie Awards*, TV, 88, CDN/USA, Story Ed; "The Campbells" (2 eps) (1 Wr/1 Co-Wr), TV, 85-86, CDN/USA/GB, Wr; "Thrill of a Lifetime" (40 eps), TV, 81-83, CDN, Prod/Wr; *The Devil at Your Heels*, Th, 80, CDN, Wr.

LAZURE, Jacques
SARDEC. 47, rue St-Joseph, Ste-Martine, PQ J0S 1V0 (514)427-2208.
Types de production et générique: TV film-Sc; TV vidéo-Sc.
Types d'oeuvres: Drame-TV; Comédie-TV; Comédie musicale-TV; Action-TV.
Curriculum vitae: Né en 1956. Baccalauréat en Communications. Auteur de nombreux textes pour enfants. Publications: *La Valise rouge*, 87; *Le Domaine des sans Yeux*, 89. Prix des jeunes scénaristes, Radio-Québec, 83 et 84; deuxième prix au concours "La Relève du Roman québécois," 85; finaliste au Prix du Conseil des Arts, 90.
Filmographie sélective: "Les Atomes crochus" (26 eps), TV, 90, CDN, Sc; "Zig-Zag" (26 eps), TV, 89, CDN, Sc; "Flanelle et Majuscule" (26 eps), TV, 89, CDN, Sc; *Les Somnambules*, TV, 85, CDN, Sc; *Le Commando des sans-soleil*, TV, 84, CDN, Sc.

LE BOURHIS, Dominique
SARDEC. 785 ave. Querbes, Outremont, PQ H2V 3W6 (514)271-2136. FAX: 271-2151.
Types de production et générique: c métrage-Sc/Réal; TV film-Sc/Réal; TV vidéo-Sc/Réal.
Types d'oeuvres: Drame-C&TV; Com

édie-C&TV; Education-TV; Vidéo-Clips-C&TV.
Curriculum vitae: Né en 1950, France; citoyenneté canadienne. Langues: français et anglais.
Filmographie sélective: *Terre en Friche*, TV, 91, CDN, Sc; "Pacha & les chats" (196 eps), TV, 91, CDN, Dial; *Choisis ton monde*, ED, 91, CDN, Sc; "Les championats du monde d'orthographe" (2 eps), TV, 90, CDN, Sc; "Flash-maths" (13 eps), ED, 90, CDN, Sc; *Juste pour lire*, ED, 90, CDN, Sc; "Samedi P.M." (24 eps), TV, 90, CDN, Aut; "Samedi de rire" (96 eps), TV, 87-89, CDN, Sc; "C'est ton droit" (13 eps), TV, 88, CDN, Sc; "Super-clique" (26 eps), TV, 87, CDN, Conc/Sc; "Badaboks" (13 eps), TV, 87, CDN/F, Sc; *Misinterprétation*, MV, 87, CDN, Conc/Réal.

LE BOUTILLIER, Geoff
ACTRA, CFTPA, ACCT. 10609 - 127 St., Edmonton, AB T5N 1W2 (403)451-0462. Tohaventa Holdings, 10022 - 103 St., Edmonton, AB T5J 0X2 (403)426-2564. FAX: 426-1049.
Type of Production and Credits: Th Film-Prod; TV Film-Wr/Prod; TV Video-Wr/Prod.
Genres: Drama-Th&TV; Comedy-Th&TV; Documentary-TV; Children's-TV.
Biography: Born 1947, Baltimore, Maryland; immigrated to Canada, 67; Canadian citizen, 72. Honours B.A., English, Harvard University, 69. Canadian professional theatre, 68-78; writer/producer, television & film, 78 to present.
Selected Filmography: "Chatterbox" (pilot), ED, 91, CDN, Prod; *Day One-Won*, In, 91, CDN, Prod/Wr/Dir; *Tic Tactics*, In, 91, CDN, Prod/Wr/Dir; *Bigger Than a Basket*, ED, 90, CDN, Wr; *The Anti-Elope Play*, "Family Pictures", TV, 89, CDN, Wr/Prod; *Bordertown Café*, "Family Pictures", TV, 88, CDN, Prod; *Miss Manitoba*, "Family Pictures", TV, 88, CDN, Wr.

LE GRAND, Eva
SARDEC. 341, Bloomfield, Outremont, PQ H2V 3R7 (514)277-7622.
Types de production et générique: c métrage-Sc; TV vidéo-Sc; TV film-Sc.
Types d'oeuvres: Drame-C&TV; Documentaire-C&TV; Education-TV; Enfants-TV.
Curriculum vitae: Née en 1945, Tchécoslovaquie; citoyenneté canadienne. Langues: français, tchèque, russe, compréhension de l'anglais. Doctorat en littérature comparée, Université de Montréal. Professeur de littérature à l'Université du Québec à Montréal, Département d'Etudes littéraires. Professeur, scénariste, auteur, dialoguiste et parolière.
Filmographie sélective: "Milena Nova Tremblay" (6 eps), TV, 86-87, CDN, Sc/Dial; "Les Nouveaux Mondes" (8 eps), TV, 86, CDN, Co sc/Rech/Parol; *Bien dans ma peau*, MV, 86, CDN, Parol; "Assez!", MV, 86, CDN, Parol; *Explorons de nouveaux espaces*, ED, 85, CDN, Sc; *Pologne à travers sa poésie*, "Planète", TV, 80, CDN, Rech; *Femmes slaves/Tchèques au Québec/Mosaïque slave*, "Planète", TV, 79-80, CDN, Rech.

LEACH, David
- see EDITORS

LEANEY, Cindy
- see PRODUCERS

LECKIE, Keith Ross
ACTRA, ACCT. Perth Avenue Productions, 213 Perth Ave., Toronto, ON M6P 3X7 (416)536-5255.
Type of Production and Credits: TV Film-Dir/Wr.
Genres: Drama-TV; Action-TV; Documentary-TV.
Biography: Born in 1952 in Toronto, Ontario. B.A.A., Motion Picture, Ryerson Polytechnic Institute. Has worked in film as AD, prop specialist, set designer, loc. mgr.; also instructor for secondary school filmmaking courses; novelist; journalist. Has won Golden Gate, San Francisco, 87; Chris Award, Columbus, 87; and Blue Ribbon, New York, 88 for *Words on a Page*, "Spirit Bay"; Gemini award, Best Canadian Television Feature for *Where the Spirit Lives*; nominated for Emmy award, Family Drama, for *Lost in the Barrens*, 90.
Selected Filmography: *Journey Into Darkness - The Bruce Curtis Story*, TV, 90, CDN, Wr; *Where the Spirit Lives*, TV, 88, CDN, Wr; *A House Divided*, "The Beachcombers", TV, 87, CDN, Dir; "Spirit Bay" (4 eps), TV, 84-86, CDN, Wr; "Danger Bay" (2 eps), TV, 86, CDN, Wrr; *Words on a Page*, "Spirit Bay", TV, 86, CDN, Dir; *Special Delivery*, TV, 85, CDN, Wr; *Crossbar*, "Anthology", TV, 80, CDN, Wr.

LEDOUX, Paul
ACTRA. 41 Cowan Ave., Toronto, ON M6K 2N1 (416)538-2266. FAX: 538-2266.
Type of Production and Credits: TV Film-Wr; TV Video-Wr.
Genres: Drama-TV; Comedy-TV; Musical-TV; Children's-TV.
Biography: Born 1949, Halifax, Nova

Scotia. Bachelor of Arts, Dalhousie University; Nova Scotia College of Art and Design (video and performance). Past Chairman, Playwrights' Union of Canada. 27 produced plays. Winner, Dora Mavor Moore and Chalmer's Awards.
Selected Filmography: *Johann's Gift to Christmas*, TV, 91, CDN, Wr; *Trick of Treasure*, TV, 90, CDN, Wr; "Bordertown" (1 eps), TV, 90, CDN, Wr; *St. Nicholas and the Children*, TV, 88, CDN, Wr; "The Campbells", TV, 87-88, CDN/USA/GB, Wr; "Blizzard Island" (1 eps), TV, 88, CDN, Wr; "Danger Bay" (1 eps), TV, 87, CDN, Wr; "Edison Twins" (11 eps), TV, 83-85, CDN, Wr; *Star Reporter*, MV, 83, CDN, Co-Wr; "Looks at Books" (5 eps), TV, 81, CDN, Wr/Ed; "Forceful Follies" (5 eps), TV, 80, CDN, Wr/Ed; "Dr. Muszoski" (10 eps), TV, 79, CDN, Wr/Ed.

LEFEBVRE, Jean Pierre
- voir REALISATEURS

LEIS, Hank
- see PRODUCERS

LEMAY-ROUSSEAU, Lise
SACD. 249, Simon Saladim, Boucherville, PQ J4B 1L5 (514)655-5936. Radio-Québec, 100, rue Fullum, Montréal, PQ H2K 3L7 (514)521-2424.
Types de production et générique: l métrage-Sc; TV film-Sc; TV vidéo-Sc.
Types d'oeuvres: Drame-C&TV; Comédie-C; Education-TV; Enfants-TV.
Curriculum vitae: Née en 1937, Frontierville, Québec. Baccalauréat, maîtrise. *Le Matou* remporte le Prix du public au Festival du film du Québec et au Festival des Films du monde Montréal (ainsi que le Prix du jury).
Filmographie sélective: *Love-Moi*, C, 90, CDN, Co-Sc; "Retraite-Action" (20 eps), TV, 83-85, CDN, Sc; *Le Matou*, C, 85, CDN/F/I, Sc; "Agora" (3 eps), TV, 83-84, CDN/F/CH, Sc; "Ecoute-moi donc quand je te parle" (26 eps), TV, 80, CDN, Sc; "Les Oraliens" (125 eps), TV, 69-70, CDN, Sc; "Aux yeux du présent" (2 eps), TV, 69-70, CDN, Sc; "Moi..." (17 eps), TV, 78-79, CDN, Sc.

LENNICK, Michael
54 Scarborough Beach Blvd., Toronto, ON M4E 2X1 (416)969-3341. Charles Northcote, The Core Group, (416)944-0193. FAX: 944-0446.
Type of Production and Credits: Th Short-Dir/Wr; TV Film-Dir/Prod/Wr; TV Video-Dir/Prod/Wr.
Genres: Comedy-Th&TV; Science Fiction-Th&TV; Documentary-TV; Children's-TV.
Biography: Born 1952. Visual effects supervisor on many films. *Space Movie* won First Prize, Cinemagic, and Top Prize, First Choice-Great Canadian Shorts Competition, 86.
Selected Filmography: *Eye Candy*, Th, 91, CDN, Wr/Dir; "OWL-TV" (20 eps), TV, 91, CDN/GB, Wr/Dir; *Pat Travers in Concert*, TV, 90, CDN, Dir; "War of the Worlds", TV, 88, USA, VFX Des/VFX Co-Spv; *Wonderstruck*, TV, 88, CDN, Wr/Dir; "Friday the 13th: The Series" (6 eps), TV, 87, CDN/USA, VFX Des/VFX 2nd Spv; *Different Worlds* (Expo 86), Th, 86, CDN, Wr; *The New Magicians*, "Vista", TV, 85, CDN, Dir/Wr/Prod; *Space Movie*, TV, 83, CDN, Dir/Wr/Prod/VFX Des; "Film Magic" (22 seg), TV, 83, CDN, Dir/Wr/Prod; *The Dead Zone*, Th, 83, CDN, VFX Des; "Kidbits" (6 eps), TV, 82, CDN, Dir; "The All Night Show" (302 eps), TV, 80-81, CDN, Dir; *Videodrome*, Th, 81, CDN/USA, VFX Des; *Comicon*, TV, 76, CDN/USA, Dir/Wr.

LENNON, Randy
- see PRODUCERS

LENNON, Rob◊
(604)732-4827.
Type of Production and Credits: TV Video-Wr/Act.
Genres: Comedy-TV; Variety-TV; Commercials-TV.
Biography: Born 1961, Edmonton, Alberta. Performing musician (guitar/vocals), comedic actor, broadcaster, announcer, writer and impressionist.
Selected Filmography: *Smarty Mart* (Vegas), Cm, 88, CDN, Wr/Act; *Gasland Pump Jockey*, Cm, 87, CDN, Wr; "Midnight with Randy Lennon" (33 eps), TV, 86-87, CDN, Wr/Act; *Smarty Mart*, Cm, 86, CDN, Wr/Act; "Edmonton Alive" (13 eps), TV, 85-86, CDN, Wr; "Sidetrack Summernights" (13 eps), TV, 86, CDN, Wr/Annoc/Act; "Spruce Grove Alive" (9 eps), TV, 85, CDN, Wr/Annoc/Act.

LEPAGE, Marquise
- voir REALISATEURS

LEROUX, Yvon
UDA, ACTRA, SARDEC. 81, Jean de Lafond, Boucherville, PQ J4B 2B6 (514)655-0244.
Types de production et générique: l métrage-Com; TV film-Sc/Com; TV vidéo-Sc/Com.
Types d'oeuvres: Drame-C&TV; Comédie-C&TV; Documentaire-C&TV; Annonces-TV.
Curriculum vitae: Né en 1929, Saint-

Eustache, Québec. Langues: français et anglais. Formation dramatique avec Sita Riddez, du Conservatoire de Paris, et avec Jean Valcourt, de la Comédie Française. Comédien et metteur en scène au théâtre depuis 48; à la radio et à la télévision depuis 52; auteur à la radio et à la télévision depuis 55; signe des textes depuis 54.
Filmographie sélective: "La Maison Deschênes" (225 eps), TV, 87-88, CDN, Com; *Faut divorcer*, TV, 87, CDN, Adapt/Com; "Erreur sur la personne" (4 eps), TV, 87, CDN, Com; "La Clé des champs" (22 eps), TV, 86-87, CDN, Com; "Pensez vite" (3 ém/semaine), TV, 71-72, CDN, Aut; "Oui ou Non" (2 ém/semaine), TV, 70-71, CDN, Aut; "Pierre, Jean Jacques" (hebdo), TV, 70-71, CDN, Aut; "Ni oui, ni non", TV, 70, CDN, Aut; "Les Arts Plastiques" (3 eps), TV, 68, CDN, Aut; *Une incroyable Histoire*, TV, 67, CDN, Adapt; *Monserrat*, TV, 66, CDN, Adapt; "Jeunesse doré" (quot), TV, 66, CDN, Aut; *Père*, TV, 64, CDN, Adapt; "Défi aux chansonniers" (hebdo), TV, 62, CDN, Textes; "Où sont-ils donc?" (hebdo), TV, 61, CDN, Textes.

LETOURNEAU, Diane
- voir REALISATEURS

LEVY, Joanne T.
ACTRA. Scorpio Productions Inc., 4328 Brisebois Dr. N.W., Calgary, AB T2L 2G2
Type of Production and Credits: TV Film-Wr/Prod/Dir; TV Video-Wr/Prod/Dir.
Genres: Documentary-TV; Educational-TV; Industrial-TV; Current Affairs-TV.
Biography: Born in 1950 in Radisson, Saskatchewan. B.A. (Hon) Pol.Sc., University of Saskatchewan. 15 years experience in broadcast journalism as a reporter and writer/broadcaster, primarily for CBC news in Calgary. 3 years experience as an independent writer, producer and director. Specialty is one-camera production - managing budgets, coordinating projects, directing field production and editing. Professional development: CBC Current Affairs Producers' Course; First Draft Workshop (Drama). Other experience: Trainer with the CBC Training Department; Lecturer in TV Journalism.
Selected Filmography: "Talk Calgary" (23 eps), TV, 90-91, CDN, Prod; *A Flash of the Past*, In/ED, 91, CDN, Wr; *Plant Tour*, Chem-Security Ltd., In, 91, CDN, Wr/Prod/Dir; *Re-Discovering Fire*, Trans-Alta Utilities Corp., In, 91, CDN, Prod/Dir; *Jack & Roll Method*, Premay Equipment Ltd., In, 90, CDN, Wr/Prod; *Game's End*, ED/TV, 90, CDN, Wr/Prod/Dir; *Smoky River Coal*, In, 90, CDN, Wr/Prod; *Westcoast Petroleum Ltd.*, In, 90, CDN, Wr.

LEWIS, Jefferson
ACCT, SARDEC. Evelyne St.-Pierre, 3575 boul. St. Laurent, Montreal, PQ H2X 2T7 (514)848-9059.
Type of Production and Credits: Th Film-Wr; TV Film-Wr.
Genres: Drama-Th&TV; Comedy-Th&TV; Musical-Th&TV.
Biography: Born in Montreal. Languages: French and English. Educated in Europe and USA. Graduated in Film Studies from Queen's University in 1972. Journalist for Ottawa Citizen, Southam News Service, CBC Radio. Author of *Something Hidden: A Biography of Wilder Penfield*. Directed and wrote documentaries and short dramas. Presently writing features and TV films. Prix Futura (Berlin) for *Democracy on Trial: The Morgentaler Affair*. Gémeaux for *Les Noces de Papier*.
Selected Filmography: *The Lonely Wolf*, TV, 89, CDN/USA, Wr; *Les Noces de Papier*, TV, 88, CDN, Wr; *A Question of Honour*, "Mount Royal", TV, 87, CDN/F, Wr; *Table For Two*, "Mount Royal", TV, 87, CDN/F, Wr; *Death Of The Working Class*, TV, 86, CDN, Wr/Dir; *Who Decides?*, "Bioethics" (NFB), ED, 85, CDN, Wr; *Happy Birthday*, "Bioethics" (NFB), ED, 84, CDN, Wr/Dir.

LICCIONI, Jean-Pierre
SARDEC. 109, MacAulay, St-Lambert, PQ J4R 2G8 (514)671-6980.
Types de production et générique: c métrage-Sc/Réal; TV film-Sc; TV vidéo-Sc/Réal.
Types d'oeuvres: Comédie-C&TV; Education-TV; Enfants-TV; Animation-TV.
Curriculum vitae: Né en 1942; citoyenneté canadienne et française. Dix ans de réalisation (60 vidéos et courts métrages) et 15 ans de scénarisation (plus de 150 scénarios). *Qu'est-ce qui m'arrive?* remporte le Prix du meilleur scénario de court métrage, Yorkton, 83.
Filmographie sélective: "Tes Choix, ta Santé" (10 eps), TV, 90-91, CDN, Sc; "Les Oursons volants" (39 eps), TV, 88-90, CDN/YU, Sc; "Semi-détaché" (32 eps), TV, 88, CDN, Co sc; *Bino Fabule*, C, 88, CDN/B/F, Co sc; "La Bande à Ovide" (65 eps), TV, 87, CDN/B, Sc; "Passe-Partout II" (50 eps), TV, 83-84, CDN, Sc; *La Satanée Question*, C, 82-83, CDN, Sc; *Que la fête continue*, TV, 82-83,

CDN, Sc; *Qu'est-ce qui m'arrive?*, C, 83, CDN, Sc; "Faut voir à son affaire" (13 eps), TV, 80-81, CDN, Réal/Sc; "Sur le bout de la langue" (20 eps), TV, 80-81, CDN, Sc; "Manger comme du monde" (13 eps), TV, 78-79, CDN, Sc; *Bye Bye 79*, TV, 79, CDN, Co sc; "Passe-Partout I" (125 eps), TV, 77-79, CDN, Réal.

LISHMAN, Eda Lever
- see PRODUCERS

LIU, Harrison
- see DIRECTORS

LIVESLEY, Jack
101 - 530 Scarlett Rd., Etobicoke, ON M9P 2S3 (416)248-1384.
Type of Production and Credits: TV Film-Wr/Host; TV Video-Wr/Host.
Genres: Documentary-TV; Educational-TV; Children's-TV.
Biography: Born in Brantford, Ontario. B.A., McMaster Univ. Wrote, designed, hosted or assisted with 200 television productions; freelance writer, 86; Author, *Media Scenes and Class Acts*, 87; co-author, *Meet the Media*, 90. *The No Name Show* won a Silver Hugo, Chicago Film Festival.
Selected Filmography: "Questions of Choice" (6 eps), TV, 86, CDN, Wr/Host; "The Academy" (31 eps), TV, 82-86, CDN, Wr/Host/Interv; "The No Name Show" (pilot), TV, 84, CDN, Assoc Prod; *Playing Shakespeare*, TV, 84, CDN, Host/Interv.

LOBLAW, D. Bob
ACTRA, SMPIA. 18 - 2104 14th Ave., Regina, SK S4P 0X6 (306)569-2820. Pig E. Wiggy Productions, 18 - 2104 14th Ave., Regina, SK S4P 0X6
Type of Production and Credits: TV Video-Wr.
Genres: Drama-TV; Comedy-TV; Children's-TV; Music Video-TV.
Biography: Physically-fit fatherless white university-educated apartment-dwelling cynical curly-haired heterosexual unilingual English writer in his early-thirties barely eking out a living on the bleak Saskatchewan prairies with excellent teeth, a fear of birds, and no facial hair. Until recently, his favourite colour was aqua.
Selected Filmography: "Puttnam's Prairie Emporium" (5 eps), TV, 88-89, CDN, Wr.

LOCK, Keith
- see DIRECTORS

LOCKE, Jeannine
- see PRODUCERS

LORD, Jean-Claude
- voir REALISATEURS

LOWER, Peter
- see PRODUCERS

LOWER, Robert
- see EDITORS

LUCAS, Steve
ACCT, ACTRA. 577 Church St., 2nd Flr., Toronto, ON M4Y 2E4 (416)964-6219. Suzanne Depoe, Creative Technique, Box 311, Stn. F, Toronto, ON M4Y 2L7 (416)466-4173.
Type of Production and Credits: TV Film-Wr/Prod.
Genres: Drama-Th&TV; Documentary-Th&TV; Educational-TV; Industrial-TV.
Biography: Born 1952, Vancouver, BC. Bachelor of Arts, English, University of Toronto. Nominated for an Oscar, 83, for his first film *After the Axe*, which won awards at Yorkton, New York and Chicago. Has written, produced and story-edited numerous other documentaries and dramas. *The Truesteel Affair* won a Gold Camera (Best Film) at the U.S. Industrial Film Festival, 86, and a Chris at Columbus Int'l Film Festival. The immigration docu-mentary *Who Gets In?* was nominated for a Genie, 90. His first theatrical feature, *Diplomatic Immunity*, is scheduled for release in the Fall, 91.
Selected Filmography: *Diplomatic Immunity*, Th, 91, CDN/GB, Wr/Prod; *Distress Signals*, TV, 91, CDN/GB, Wr; *Transplant, The Breath of Life*, TV, 90, CDN, Wr; "My Secret Identity" (1 eps), TV, 90, CDN/USA, Wr; *Who Gets In?*, TV, 89, CDN, Wr; *A Man of Means*, "The Campbells", TV, 88, CDN/USA/GB, Wr; "Hot Shots" (1 eps), TV, 86, CDN, Wr; "Airwaves" (1 eps)(Uncredited by request), TV, 85, CDN; *All the Years*, "Bell Canada Playhouse", TV, 84, CDN, T'play; *Pitchmen*, TV, 84, CDN, Wr/Co-Prod; *Jamini, Cm*, 84, CDN, Wr; *The Truesteel Affair*, TV, 83, CDN, Wr; *Fired*, "Enterprise", TV, 82, USA, Wr; *Ridley: A Secret Garden*, TV, 81, CDN, Wr; *After the Axe*, Th, 81, CDN, Wr/Co-Prod.

LYNN, William◆
ACTRA, WGAe. (416)920-0649.
Type of Production and Credits: TV Film-Wr/Prod; TV Video-Wr/Prod.
Genres: Drama-TV; Comedy-TV; Variety-TV; Musical-TV.
Biography: Born 1938, Toronto, Ontario. Honours B.A., English, McGill University, 60; Gold Medal (Speech), London Academy of Music and Dramatic Art, England, 63. Professor of drama: RADA, Guildhall, Webber Douglas, London, England, 65-67. Gemini nomination, Best Comedy Writing for "Seeing Things", 86, 87. Wrote and produced pilot of "For

Heaven's Sake", 88.
Selected Filmography: "Seeing Things" (4 eps), TV, 85-86, CDN, Co-Wr; "Honky Tonk" (pilot), TV, 84, CDN, Co-Wr; "Julie Amato Show" (50 eps), TV, 80-82, CDN, Co-Wr; "Nellie, Daniel, Emma and Ben" (13 eps), TV, 78, CDN, Co-Wr/Co-Prod; "Mary and Michael" (26 eps), TV, 77-78, CDN, Co-Wr; *Northeast Passage*, TV, 77, CDN, Wr/Prod/Dir; "Tommy Hunter Show" (156 eps), TV, 70-76, CDN, Co-Wr/Prod; *Fit to Print*, TV, 76, CDN, Wr/Prod; "Mixed Doubles" (26 eps), TV, 76, CDN, Co-Wr; "Frankie Howerd Show" (13 eps), TV, 75, CDN, Co-Wr/Prod; "Ronnie Prophet Show" (20 eps), TV, 74-75, CDN, Co-Wr/Prod; "Wayne & Shuster" (10 eps), TV, 70-71, CDN, Contr Wr; "Ed Sullivan Show" (30 eps), TV, 69-70, USA, Co-Wr; "That Girl" (1 eps), TV, 69, USA, Co-Wr; "Dean Martin Presents Marty Feldman" (13 eps), TV, 68, USA/GB, Co-Wr.

MacADAM, William I.
- see PRODUCERS

MacDONALD, Ramuna
- see DIRECTORS

MacGILLIVRAY, William D.
- see DIRECTORS

MacGREGOR, Roy
ACTRA. 22 Banting Cres., Kanata, ON K2K 1P4 (613)592-0982. The Ottawa Citizen, Baxter Rd., Ottawa, ON (613) 596-3664. FAX: 232-2620. Lucinda Vardey Agency, 297 Seaton St., Toronto, ON M5A 2T6 (416)922-0250. FAX: 925-4943.
Type of Production and Credits: TV Film-Wr; TV Video-Wr.
Genres: Drama-TV.
Biography: Born 1948, Whitney, Ontario. Educated at Laurentian University; University of Western Ontario. Has received 4 National Magazine Awards; National Newspaper Award; *Tyler* won the Grand Prix de la Presse, Montreal World Festival, 79; *Ready for Slaughter* won Best TV Drama, Banff Film Festival, 83.
Selected Filmography: *The Last Season*, TV, 87, CDN, Wr; *Ready for Slaughter*, "For the Record", TV, 83, CDN, Wr; *An Honourable Member*, TV, 82, CDN, Wr; *Every Person Is Guilty*, "For the Record", TV, 80, CDN, Co-Wr, (ACTRA); *Cement Head*, "For the Record", TV, 80, CDN, Co-Wr; *Tyler*, TV, 79, CDN, Wr, (ACTRA).

MacINTYRE, Rod
ACTRA. 57 McLellan Ave., Saskatoon, SK S7H 3K7 (306)955-4343.
Type of Production and Credits: TV Video-Wr.
Genres: Drama-Th&TV; Comedy-Th&TV; Variety-TV; Educational-TV.
Biography: Born 1946, Saskatoon, Saskatchewan. B.A., English and Drama, University of Saskatchewan. Primarily a scriptwriter for television and stage, specializing in social issue documentary and young adult drama writing. *Toy Boat* won Best Drama at Yorkton, 85.
Selected Filmography: *Winter Seasoned*, ED, 91, CDN, Wr/Ed; *A Room Full of Men*, Cm, 90-91, CDN, Wr/Ed; *In Perfect Harmony*, Cm, 90, CDN, Wr; *Prairie Confidential*, TV, 87, CDN, Wr; *Seeing Your Lawyer*, ED, 86, CDN, Wr; *Toy Boat*, TV, 85, CDN, Wr.

MACKAY, Bruce
- see DIRECTORS

MacKAY, Jed◇
ACTRA.
Type of Production and Credits: TV Video-Wr/Prod.
Genres: Comedy-TV; Educational-TV; Children's-TV.
Biography: Born Vancouver, BC. Honours B.A., Modern Languages, University of Toronto. Also a composer, lyricist. Won National Educational Film Festival Silver for "Today's Special", *Bliss Symbols*; Ohio State Award for *Phil's Visit* and "Today's Special".
Selected Filmography: "Polka Dot Door" (60 eps) (Wr 13 eps), TV, 86-88, CDN, Prod; "Today's Special" (19 eps), TV, 84-87, CDN, Wr; "Téléfrançais" (30 eps), TV, 85-86, CDN, Lyrics; "Storylords" (12 eps), TV, 84-85, USA, Wr.

MACKEY, Clarke
- see DIRECTORS

MacLEAN, Janet
ACTRA, WGA. 18 Wychwood Park, Toronto, ON M6G 2Y5 (416)657-1632. Pamela Paul, 14 - 1778 Bloor St. W., Toronto, ON M6P 3K4 (416)769-0540.
Type of Production and Credits: Th Film-Wr; TV Film-Wr; TV Video-Wr.
Genres: Drama-Th&TV; Comedy-Th&TV; Action-TV; Horror-Th&TV.
Biography: Winner of York-Trillium Award as Most Promising Writer in Film - 90, for screenplay of *Almost Japanese*.
Selected Filmography: *The Dark Horse*, Th, 91, USA, Wr; *The Sea-Ghost*, "Road to Avonlea", TV, 90, CDN, Wr; *All That Glitters*, "Road to Avonlea", TV, 90, CDN, Wr; *Quilt of Hathor*, "Friday the 13th, The Series", TV, 89, CDN/USA, Wr; "War of the Worlds" (1 eps), TV, 89, CDN/USA, Wr; *Katie-Girl*, "Inside Stories", TV, 88, CDN, Wr; *Martha, Ruth*

and *Edie*, Th, 88, CDN, Co-Wr; "Danger Bay" (8 eps), TV, 86-88, CDN/USA, Wr.

MACLEAR, Michael
- see PRODUCERS

MacNAUGHTON, Ann M.
ACTRA, ACCT. 317 Seaton St., Toronto, ON M5A 2T6 (416)964-6238. FAX: 925-4075.
Type of Production and Credits: TV Film-Wr; TV Video-Wr.
Genres: Drama-TV; Comedy-TV.
Selected Filmography: "African Journey" (eps #3), TV, 89, CDN, Wr; *Flying Blind*, "Danger Bay", TV, 89, CDN, Wr; "Danger Bay" (22 eps), TV, 88, CDN, Exec Story Ed; "Friday the 13th - The Series" (10 eps), TV, 87, CDN/USA; *Skate*, TV, 87, CDN, Story Ed; "The Campbells" (10 eps)(Wr 1 eps), TV, 85, CDN/USA, GB, Exec Story Ed; *Michael and Kitty/In This Corner*, TV, 85, CDN, Story Ed; "Some Honourable Gentlemen" (9 eps), TV, 81-85, CDN, Story Ed; *Claus Mission '84*, TV, 84, CDN, Wr; *Where the Heart Is/Hide and Seek*, "For the Record", TV, 83-84, CDN, Story Ed; *Case of Libel*, TV, 83, USA, Story Ed; "Home Fires" (16 eps), TV, 79-81, CDN, Story Ed.

MACNEE, Rupert
- see PRODUCERS

MANGAARD, Annette
- see DIRECTORS

MANN, Danny◊
ACTRA, AFTRA, DGA, WGAw. (213)208-7550.
Type of Production and Credits: TV Film-Dir/Act/Wr; TV Video-Dir/Act/Wr.
Genres: Comedy-TV; Variety-TV; Documentary-TV; Animation-TV.
Biography: Born 1948, Toronto, Ontario; resident of Canada and the US. B.F.A., Television, Film, UCLA; two years Journalism, California State University. More than fifteen years in the entertainment business.
Selected Filmography: *New Lang Syne*, TV, 85-86, CDN, Head Wr; *The NHL Awards Special*, TV, 85, CDN, Wr; *Genie Awards*, TV, 85, CDN, Head Wr; *Anything for Money*, TV, 84, USA, Prod/Dir/Act; "Thicke of the Night" (several seg), TV, 83, USA, Prod/Dir/Wr/Act; *The Lost Satellite Network* (2 spec), TV, 83, CDN/USA, Dir/Wr/Act; "An Evening at the Improv" (2 eps), TVV, 81-82, USA, Co-Wr/Act; *The 3rd Annual American Importance Awards*, TV, 82, USA, Dir; *The 1st Annual Hockey Shtick*, TV, 81, CDN, Prod/Dir/Wr/Act; *Miss World Canada*, TV, 80, CDN, Prod/Dir; *Whatta Buncha Bananas!*, TV, 80, CDN, Dir; *Boo!*, TV, 80, CDN/USA, Dir; *Loto Canada*, TV, 80, CDN, Dir; "The Réné Simard Show" (26 eps), TV, 79, CDN, Co-Prod/Dir/Wr/Act; "The Réné Simard Show" (26 eps), TV, 78, CDN, Wr/Act/P Pro Spv.

MANN, Ron
- see DIRECTORS

MARKIW, Gabriel
- see PRODUCERS

MARKIW, Jancarlo
- see DIRECTORS

MARR, Alan
- see DIRECTORS

MARR, Leon
- see DIRECTORS

MARTIN, Bruce
ACTRA. 45 Boswell Ave., Toronto, ON M5R 1M5 (416)964-7490. MGA Agency Inc., 10 St. Mary St., Suite 510, Toronto, ON M4X 1P9 (416)964-3302.
Type of Production and Credits: TV Film-Wr; TV Video-Wr; Th Film-Wr.
Genres: Drama-TV; Action-TV; Documentary-TV; Children's-TV.
Biography: British born; Canadian and British citizenship. Has written many drama and documentary scripts for CBC, CTV, TVO, NFB, independent producers and clients. Awards include Bronze Medal, New York Film Festival and Chris Award, Columbus International Film Festival.
Selected Filmography: "The Nature of Things" (several eps), TV, 75-91, CDN, Wr; "Street Legal" (1 eps), TV, 91, CDN, Wr; "E.N.G." (2 eps), TV, 90-91, CDN, Wr; "Friday the 13th, The Series" (4 eps), TV, 88, CDN/USA, Wr; "Danger Bay" (1 eps), TV, 87, CDN, Wr; "Hot Shots" (1 eps), TV, 86, CDN, Wr; "Night Heat" (6 eps), TV, 86-87, CDN, Wr; "The Edison Twins" (6 eps), TV, 84, CDN, Wr.

MARTIN, Donald
ACTRA. 195 Church Street, Suite 2, Toronto, ON M5B 1Y7 (416)864-9697. FAX: (416) 864-0795. Lynn Kinney, Credentials, 387 Bloor St. E., Suite 500, Toronto, ON M4W 1H7 (416)926-1507. FAX: 926-0372.
Type of Production and Credits: Th Film-Wr; TV Film-Wr.
Genres: Drama-Th&TV; Action-Th&TV.
Biography: Born 1958, Montreal, Quebec. Languages: English, French, Spanish. B.A., English/Drama, New York Univ-ersity. Author of novel, *One Out of Four*; Screenwriter, 89. Author of stage play, *Matrimonium*, produced in New York, London, England and Toronto.
Selected Filmography: *This Time...Last*

Year, TV, 91, CDN/F, Wr; *Berlin Lady/La Dame de Berlin*, TV, 90, CDN/F, Adapt; *Condition Critical*, TV, 90, I, Wr; *The Phone Call*, TV, 89, CDN/F, Wr; *The Thriller*, TV, 89, CDN/F, Wr; *To Touch A Star*, TV, 89, I, Wr; *The Secret of Nandy*, TV, 89, CDN/F, Wr; *Sometimes a Lie/Le Lien du Sang*, TV, 89, CDN/F, Adapt; *No Blame*, TV, 88, CDN/F, Wr.

MARTIN, Susan
- see DIRECTORS

MAYEROVITCH, David
ACTRA. 288 Rushton Rd., Toronto, ON M6C 2X5 (416)651-6744. McKnight Gosewich Associates (MGA), 10 St. Mary St, Suite 510, Toronto, ON M4Y 1P9 (416)964-3302.
Type of Production and Credits: TV Video-Wr.
Genres: Drama-TV; Comedy-TV; Variety-TV; Musical-TV.
Biography: Born 1941, Montreal, Quebec. B.A., McGill University, 64. Playwright: *The Maltese Blue Jay*, *Programmed for Passion* (6-part soap opera stage serial). Writer of songs, sketches for revues; script consultant.
Selected Filmography: "Hangin' In" (4 eps), TV, 83-85, CDN, Wr; "King of Kensington" (12 eps), TV, 78-80, CDN, Wr; "Flappers" (3 eps), TV, 79-80, CDN, Wr; "Wayne & Shuster" (25 eps), TV, 71-77, CDN, Contr Wr; "Famous Jury Trials" (17 eps), TV, 71, CDN/USA, Wr; "Ed Sullivan Show" (12 eps), TV, 70, USA, Co-Wr; "Golddiggers in London" (10 eps), TV, 70, USA/GB, Contr Wr.

McANDREW, Jack
ACTRA. Box 2703, Charlottetown, PE C1A 8C3 (902)892-4173.
Type of Production and Credits: TV Video-Wr/Dir/Prod.
Genres: Drama-TV; Variety-TV; Musical-TV; Documentary-TV.
Biography: Born 1933, New Brunswick. Producer, Charlottetown Festival; head of CBC Variety, 75-80; independent, 80-86. Extensive work as trainer and communications consultant, CBC Radio and TV; artistic director, Canadian Heritage Festival, 85.
Selected Filmography: *One Week in Summer*, TV, 85, CDN, Prod/Dir/Wr; *Rockin' the Blues*, TV, 85, CDN, Prod/Dir/Wr; "Gzowski & Co." (1 eps), TV, 85, CDN, Wr; *Coast of Dreams*, TV, 84, CDN, Wr; "First Choice Rocks" (10 eps), TV, 83, CDN, Prod/Dir; "Romance" (5 eps), TV, 82, CDN, Co-Prod/Co-Wr; *Christmas Fantasy*, TV, 82, CDN/D, Prod/Wr; *Liona Boyd*, TV, 82, CDN, Prod/Dir/Wr.

McCANN, Jerome
ACTRA. 4204 Shalebank Court, Mississauga, ON L5L 3H2 (416)820-3840.
Type of Production and Credits: TV Film-Wr.
Genres: Drama-TV; Comedy-TV; Horror-TV; Children's-TV.
Biography: Born in Belfast, Ireland, in the boring fifties; survived the crazy sixties. Came to Canada in the seventies. Fruit picker, then economist. Now writer; most work in drama, with an affinity for comedy.
Selected Filmography: *Do the Right Thing*, "Katts and Dog", TV, 90, CDN/F, Wr; *The Brother Who Failed*, "Road to Avonlea", TV, 90, CDN, Wr; *Nightmare*, "T and T", TV, 89, CDN, Wr; *Guardian Angel*, "Neon Rider", TV, 89, CDN, Wr; *Horse Cents*, "Adderly", TV, 87, CDN/USA, Wr; *Judgement*, "The Campbells", TV, 86, CDN, Co-Wr; *Perfect Pupils*, "Seeing Things", TV, 86, CDN, Wr; *Lost and Lonely Hearts*, "Street Legal", TV, 86, CDN, Wr; *Here's Looking at You*, "Seeing Things", TV, 85, CDN, Wr; *The Walls Have Eyes*, "Seeing Things", TV, 85, CDN, Wr.

McCURDY, Mark
- see DIRECTORS

McEWEN, Mary Anne
BCMPA, VWFV, ACCT. Forward Focus Productions Ltd., Box 33954, Stn. D, Vancouver, BC V6J 4L7 (604)681-4677.
Type of Production and Credits: TV Film-Wr; TV Video-Wr/Prod/Dir/Ed.
Genres: Documentary-TV; Educational-TV; Commercials-TV; Industrial-TV; Drama-TV; Variety-TV.
Biography: Born 1945, Toronto, Ontario. B.A., University of British Columbia, 67; Film workshop, Simon Fraser University, 70-72. Academy of Canadian Cinema winner, Directors Observers Program, 90. Started as advertising writer, worked as Creative Director at Creative House (AV production) 72-77; opened Forward Focus, 77; originated "Gayblevision" (80-86), 1/2 hr. Gay/Lesbian TV variety program cablecast in Vancouver and San Francisco; now works on TV documentary, educational, industrial TV promos and commercials.
Selected Filmography: *Celebration 90: Opening & Closing Ceremonies*, TV, 90, CDN, Prod/Ed; *NGV: Driving Force of the Future*, ED, 90, CDN, Wr/Prod/Dir/Ed; *Gateway*, ED, 89, CDN, Wr; *Cheer on Canada*, Cm, 88, CDN, Wr/Prod/Dir;

Chemical Sciences at BCIT, ED, 87, CDN, Wr/Prod/Dir; *Dealing With Dobis*, ED, 87, CDN, Wr/Prod/Dir; *It Feels Great!*, ED, 86, CDN, Wr/Prod/Ed; *Summer*, ED, 86, CDN, Wr/Prod/Dir/Ed; *The Goal is a Cure*, TV, 85, CDN, Wr/Prod/Dir/Ed; *God, Gays and the Gospel*, TV, 84, USA, Wr/Prod/Dir/Ed; "Gayblevision" (13 eps), TV, 80-81, CDN, Prod/Dir/Ed; *Burnout*, TV, 79, CDN, Wr; *An Inheritance from Salt*, In, 79, CDN, Wr/Prod/Dir; *Paving for People*, ED, 78, CDN, Wr/Prod/Dir; *Sounds of Silence*, ED, 70, CDN, Wr.

McGREEVY, John
- see PRODUCERS

McHUGH, Fiona
ACTRA. 766 Markham St., Toronto, ON M6G 2M5 (416)531-6149. Krisztina Bevilacqua, 85 Roosevelt Rd., Toronto, ON M4J 4TB (416)463-7009. FAX: 463-2206.
Type of Production and Credits: TV Film-Wr; TV Video-Wr.
Genres: Drama-TV; Documentary-TV; Educational-TV; Children's-TV.
Biography: Born Dublin, Ireland; Canadian citizenship, 81. Languages: English, French and German. B.A., University of Dublin; Master of Letters, Trinity College, Dublin. Extensive writing and research background, TV and radio; has also written for advertising agencies in field-education campaigns, both print and media. Has won 2 Canadian Marketing Awards, 85, 86; the Larry Heywood Award, Canadian Commerical Awards, 84; Gold Medal, Ohio State Award; Gold Medal and Special Jury Gold Medal, Atlanta International Film Festival; Gold Plaque, Chicago.
Selected Filmography: *Waiting for You: Christiane Pflug 1936-1972*, TV, 90-91, CDN, Wr/Dir; *Rap-a-matics*, ED, 90, CDN, Wr; *Lantern Hill*, "Magic Hour", TV, 89-90, USA/CDN, Co-Wr; *A Haunting Harmony*, TV, 89-90, GB/CDN, Wr; *Old Lady Lloyd*, "Road to Avonlea", TV, 89, USA/CDN, Wr; *Spirit of St. Nicholas*, "Man Alive", TV, 89, CDN, Wr; *Ending the Nightmare (I &II)/Children of St. Nicholas*, TV, 85-86, CDN, Wr; *Shroud of Turin*, "Man Alive", TV, 84, CDN, Wr; *The Inside Story*, ED, 84, CDN, Wr; *High Flight*, "Nature of Things", TV, 83, CDN, Wr; *Veronica Tennant: A Dancer of Distinction*, TV, 82, CDN, Wr; "Mr. Dressup" (10 eps), TV, 81-82, CDN, Wr; *The Race/Born to Love*, "The Winners", TV, 80, CDN, Wr; *Joyce's "Portrait of the Artist As a Young Man"*, "Explorations in the Novel", TV, 75, CDN, Wr; "Write On!" (sev eps), TV, 75, CDN, Wr.

McILVRIDE, David
- see DIRECTORS

McINTYRE, JoAnn
- see DIRECTORS

McKEOWN, Bob
- see PRODUCERS

McKEOWN, Brian
- see PRODUCERS

McKNIGHT, Bruce E.
- see PRODUCERS

McLAREN, David◇
ACTRA. (416)469-2027.
Type of Production and Credits: TV Film-Wr.
Genres: Drama-TV; Industrial-TV.
Biography: Born Toronto, Ontario. B.A., Queen's and York Universities; several courses in English towards M.A., University of Toronto. Taught screenwriting, Summer Institute of Film, Ottawa, 84-86. Honourable mention in Citytv's "Toronto Trilogy" Drama Competition. Also has writing credits for radio and the stage. Has written for commercials and industrials, 83-88.
Selected Filmography: "Vanderberg" (eps #6), TV, 83, CDN, Wr; *By Reason of Insanity*, "For the Record", TV, 81, CDN, Wr.

McMANUS, Mike
- see PRODUCERS

MEILEN, Bill◇
ACTRA, WGAw, WGGB, BAE, ACCT. (403)465-4511.
Type of Production and Credits: Th Film-Wr/Act; Th Short-Act; TV Film-Wr/Act; TV Video-Wr/Act.
Genres: Drama-Th&TV; Action-Th&TV; Horror-TV.
Biography: Born in 1932 in Cardiff, Wales; British and Canadian citizenship. Languages: English, Welsh, German, French, Spanish. Actor since 46; writer since 1963. Professor of Dialects and Accents for the Performer, University of Alberta, character actor. Military service Indo-China, 1950, Korea, 1951-53, Africa, 1954. Specialist on military matters, drill etc.; dialect coaching. Best Television Special, *Song for the Eyes of Tovah*; Andrew Allan Award (ACTRA), Best Male Radio Actor, 1986; finalist, Andrew Allan Award, 1988.
Selected Filmography: "The Gunfighters", TV, 87, CDN, Act; *Golden Harvest*, TV, 87, USA, Act; *Western Canada Lottery*, Cm, 87, CDN, Act; *Expo 86 Vancouver Alberta Pavilion*, Th, 86,

CDN, Act; *In the Spirit of Excellence*, TV, 86, CDN, Narr; *Three Minutes to Live*, Ed, 85, CDN, Act; Superchannel, Cm, 84, CDN, Act; *Chautauqua Girl*, TV, 82, CDN, Act; "Stony Plain" (1 eps), TV, 81, CDN, Act; *The Grey Fox*, Th, 80, CDN, Act; *Songs for the Eyes of the Tovah*, TV, 78, CDN, Act; "Front Desk", TV, 78, CDN, Act; *Teach Me to Dance*, Th, 78, CDN, Act; "What If?" (8 eps), TV, 78, CDN, Act; *Marie-Anne*, Th, 77, CDN, Act.

MELLANBY, Ralph
- see PRODUCERS

MENARD, Robert
- voir REALISATEURS

MENDELUK, George
- see DIRECTORS

MERCER, Michael◊
ACTRA, ACCT. (604)684-9781.
Type of Production and Credits: Th Film-Wr; Th Short-Wr; TV Film-Wr; TV Video-Wr.
Genres: Drama-Th&TV; Comedy-Th&TV; Action-Th&TV; Documentary-TV.
Biography: Born 1943, Liverpool, England; Canadian citizenship. Languages: English and French. B.A., Honours English, Sir George Williams (Concordia) University, 67; M.A., University of British Columbia, 72. Served 2 years as National Chairman, ACTRA Writers' Guild; full-time freelance writer since 72. Won ACTRA Award, Best Dramatic Writer (Radio) for *Freydis*, 77; Chalmers Award for theatre for *Goodnight Disgrace*, 86.
Selected Filmography: "The Campbells" (5 eps), TV, 85-86, CDN/USA/GB, Wr; "The Beachcombers" (12 eps), TV, 82-86, CDN, Wr; *Discovery B.C.*, Th, 86, CDN, Wr; *Hail Alley*, Th, 86, CDN, Wr; *The Exile*, TV, 85, CDN, Co-Wr; "Danger Bay" (1 eps), TV, 84, CDN, Wr; "Constable, Constable" (2 eps), TV, 83, CDN, Wr; *Sajo*, Th, 81, CDN, Wr; *Whale*, TV, 81, CDN, Wr; "Ritter's Cove" (4 eps), TV, 80, CDN/D, Wr; *The Little Businessman*, "Magic Lie", TV, 79, CDN, Wr.

MERCIER, Serge
SARDEC. 531, du Palais #2, St-Jérôme, PQ J7G 1Y3 (514)436-3404.
Types de production et générique: TV film-Sc.
Types d'oeuvres: Drame-TV; Documentaire-TV; Education-TV.
Curriculum vitae: Né en 1944, Sherbrooke, Québec. Langues: français, anglais, italien. Formation universitaire en lettres, linguistique. *Dancing Eros* représente le Canada pour le Prix Louis Philippe Kammans, 79; *Encore un peu* est la première pièce canadienne invitée dans la selection officielle du XXXe Festival d'Avignon, France, 76.
Filmographie sélective: "La Photographie: noir et blanc" (6 eps), ED, 86, CDN, Cons scén; *Encore un peu*, "Les Beaux Dimanches", TV, 80, CDN, Aut; *Dancing Eros*, "Les Beaux Dimanches", TV, 79, CDN, Sc/Dial; *XL - 11484*, "La Maisonnée" (2 eps), TV, 76, CDN, Textes.

MESSIER, H. Monique
- voir PRODUCTEURS

METTLER, Peter
- see DIRECTORS

MICAY, Jack
- see DIRECTORS

MICHAELS, Lorne
- see PRODUCERS

MICHEL, Pauline
SARDEC, SOCAN, UDA. 4411 rue St-Denis, app. 403, Montréal, PQ H2J 2L2 (514)288-4467. (819)826-5086.
Types de production et générique: TV film-Sc.
Types d'oeuvres: Variété-TV; Education-TV; Enfants-TV; Drame-TV.
Curriculum vitae: Née en 1949, Asbestos, Québec. Bac. en pédagogie, Université de Sherbrooke, 65; Licence ès Lettres, Université Laval, 69. Expérience: enseignement - Cégep et université; publications - romans, poèmes, livres de chansons, livres scolaires; scénariste - émissions de TV, vidéo-clips, film; parolière - pour séries télévisées; comédienne et chanteuse - tournées en France, au Canada, en Afrique; auteure/compositeur/interprète.
Filmographie sélective: "A la Claire Fontaine" (13 eps), TV, 91, CDN, Sc/Parol; Série de vidéos scolaires, ED, 88-90, CDN, Sc; *Les Héritières D'Esther Blondin*, ED, 89, CDN, Sc/Parol/Com/Chant; *La Poupée abandonnée*, MV, 89, CDN, Sc; "Hello Moineau" (26 eps), TV, 83-86, CDN/F/CH, Parol; "Télé-Ressources" (5 eps), TV, 77-78, CDN, Co sc; "Animagerie" (15 eps), TV, 76-77, CDN, Sc; "You-hou" (10 eps), TV, 76, CDN, Co sc.

MILLAR, Susan
- see PRODUCERS

MINNIS, Jon
- see PRODUCERS

MITCHELL, Ken
ACTRA. 209 Angus Cres., Regina, SK S4T 6N3 (306)757-3820. Bella Pomer Agency, 22 Shallmar Blvd., PH2, Toronto,

ON M5N 2Z8 (416)782-2577.
Type of Production and Credits: Th Film-Wr; Th Short-Wr/Dir; TV Film-Wr; TV Video-Wr.
Genres: Drama-Th; Comedy-Th&TV; Documentary-Th&TV; Educational-Th&TV.
Biography: Born 1940, Moose Jaw, Saskatchewan. Languages: English, French and Chinese. M.A., University of Saskatchewan. Professor of English, University of Regina since 67; Scottish-Canadian exchange writer, 79-80; visiting professor, University of China, 80-81, 86-87. Canadian Authors' Association, Best Canadian Play Award, 85; Genie nomination, Best Original Screenplay, 81. Strong international interest and experience; now working on film/theatre projects in Finland, UK, Korea and Germany.
Selected Filmography: "Through the Eyes of a Writer" (6 eps), TV, 91, CDN, Narr; "The Dream Seekers" (4 eps), TV, 90, CDN, Host; *The Great Electrical Revolution,* Th, 89, CDN, Wr/Narr; "The New Immigrants" (3 eps), TV, 89, CDN, Wr/Host; *The Medicine Line,* Th, 88, CDN, Dir/Wr; *The Giant,* Th, 88, CDN, Dir/Wr; *The Front Line,* "For the Record", TV, 85, CDN, Wr; *Ken Mitchell's Moose Jaw,* "Cityscapes", TV, 85, CDN, Wr/Host; *The Shipbuilder,* Th, 85, CDN, Wr; *St. Laurent,* Th, 85, CDN, Wr; *The Hounds of Notre Dame,* Th, 80, CDN, Wr.

MITCHELL, Nick◊
ACTRA. (204)632-7776.
Type of Production and Credits: TV Film-Wr; TV Video-Wr.
Genres: Drama-TV; Comedy-TV.
Biography: Born in 1949 in Winnipeg, Manitoba. Languages: English, French, Ukrainian. B.A., University of Manitoba; attended the Summer Institute of Film, Ottawa. Particular interest in live theatre; vice-chairman of the Manitoba Association of Playwrights; drama editor of *Prairie Fire* for a number of years; *House* produced by Agassiz Theatre Company, 84; *Mum* produced by Agassiz Theatre Company, 87.
Selected Filmography: *House,* TV, 86, CDN, Wr.

MOHAN, Peter
ACTRA, ACCT. 112 Pinewood Ave., Toronto, ON M6C 2V3 (416)654-3440.
Type of Production and Credits: Th Film-Wr; TV Film-Wr.
Genres: Drama-TV; Comedy-TV; Action-TV.
Biography: Born 1955.
Selected Filmography: "Sweating Bullets" (22 eps)(Wr 4 eps), TV, 90-91, CDN/MEX, Prod/Exec Story Ed/Wr; "Counterstrike" (13 eps)(Wr 2 eps), TV, 89-90, CDN/USA/F, Exec Story Ed/Wr; "E.N.G." (1 eps), TV, 89, CDN, Wr; "Diamonds" (14 eps)(Wr 5 eps), TV, 88-89, CDN/USA/F, Exec Story Ed/Wr; "Friday the 13th: The Series" (2 eps), TV, 88-89, CDN/USA, Wr; "Bordertown" (1 eps), TV, 88, CDN/USA/F, Wr; "Night Heat" (65 eps)(Wr 20 eps), TV, 85-88, CDN/USA, Exec Story Ed/Wr, (GEMINI 88); *Big Deal,* Th, 85, CDN, Co-Wr.

MOHUN, Bruce
3469 Dundas St., Vancouver, BC V5K 1R9 (604)299-6064.
Type of Production and Credits: TV Film-Wr; TV Video-Wr.
Genres: Drama-Th&TV; Comedy-Th&TV; Variety-TV; Documentary-TV.
Biography: Born 1952. B.A.A., Journalism, Ryerson Polytechnical Institute, 80. Winner, Citytv "Toronto Trilogy" Drama Competition, 83. Also writes for magazines and radio. Frequently co-writes with Bill Murtagh. Has received grants from F.U.N.D. and O.F.D.C. to write 4 screenplays.
Selected Filmography: *Evolution in Action,* ED, 91, CDN, Wr; "Mosquito Lake" (1 eps), TV, 88, CDN, Co-Wr; "Starting From Scratch" (1 eps), TV, 87, CDN, Co-Wr; "Comedy Mills" (26 eps), TV, 86-87, CDN, Co-Wr; *Video Bartender,* In, 85, CDN, Co-Wr; "Laughing Matters" (13 eps), TV, 85, CDN, Co-Wr; "The Edison Twins", TV, 85, CDN, Co-Wr; "Hangin' In" (2 eps), TV, 84, CDN, Co-Wr; *Neighbours,* "Toronto Trilogy", TV, 83, CDN, Wr.

MONTESI, Jorge
- see DIRECTORS

MOORE, Mavor
C.C. ACTRA. 2826 Arbutus Rd., Victoria, BC V8N 5X5 (604)721-1920. Faculty of Fine Arts, University of Victoria, P.O. Box 1700, Victoria, BC V8W 2Y2. Gayle Abrams, Oscars & Abrams, 59 Berkeley St., Toronto, ON M5A 2W5 (416)866-1790.
Type of Production and Credits: Th Film-Act; Th Short-Narr; TV Film-Wr/Act; TV Video-Wr/Act.
Genres: Drama-Th&TV; Documentary-Th&TV; Current Affairs-TV.
Biography: Born 1919, Toronto, Ontario. B.A., University of Toronto; has received 5 honorary doctorates (LL.D., D.Litt.). Playwright, has written over 100 produced plays, musicals and operas; also writes for

radio and print (*The Globe and Mail*). First Chief Producer, CBC (English language), 52; former Chairman, Canada Council, 79-84. Companion of the Order of Canada; Queen's Medal; Centennial Medal; 3 Peabody Awards; John Drainie Award, 82; Diplôme d'Honneur from the Canadian Conference of the Arts; Molson Prize, 86.
Selected Filmography: *And the Sea Will Tell* (3 parts), TV, 90, CDN/USA, Act; *Hippocratic Oath*, "Alfred Hitchcock Presents", TV, 88, CDN/USA, Act; *Spot Marks the X*, Th, 85, USA, Act; *The Killing Fields*, Th, 84, GB, Act; *The Olympics* (4 parts), TV, 78, CDN, Wr; *Belinda* (musical), TV, 76, CDN, Adapt; *The Roncarelli Affair*, "The Play's The Thing", TV, 74, CDN, Co-Wr; "Program X" (6 eps), TV, 71-72, CDN, Wr; *Getting In*, TV, 72, GB, Wr; *The Argument*, TV, 72, GB, Wr; *The Store*, TV, 71, CDN, Wr; *Inside Out*, Th, 70, CDN, Wr; *Louis Riel* (opera), TV, 69, CDN, Wr; *Yesterday the Children Were Dancing/The Puppet Caravan*, TV, 67-69, CDN, Trans; *The Son*, TV, 59, CDN, Wr.

MORENCY, Liz◇
UDA. (514)526-9251.
Types de production et générique: c métrage-Sc/Prod; TV film-Sc/Prod.
Types d'oeuvres: Drame-C&TV; Documentaire-C&TV; Nouvelles-C&TV; Sports-C&TV.
Curriculum vitae: Née à Trois-Pistoles, Québec. Etudes en Sciences sociales, Rimouski; théâtre, Université du Québec à Montréal. Reportages cinématographiques, Radio-Canada, 77; assistante à la production, Justine Héroux, 81-82; attachée de presse, René Malo, 82; publiciste, la Télévision Premier Choix, 83; depuis 4 ans travaille à la pige pour Télé Métropole comme attachée de presse et recherchiste.
Filmographie sélective: L'Espirit d'équipe, TV, 87, CDN, Sc/Prod; *Les Expo de Montréal*, TV, 85, CDN, Prod.

MORENCY, Pierre◇
SARDEC. (418)688-1651.
Types de production et générique: TV film-Sc.
Types d'oeuvres: Drame-TV; Documentaire-TV.
Curriculum vitae: Né en 1942, Lauzon, Québec. Licence ès lettres, Université Laval, 66. Chroniqueur et auteur radiophonique; poète et auteur dramatique; animateur de nombreux récitals de poésie. Fonde et dirige la revue *Inédits*, 70. Publications de poèmes dont *Torrential*, 78, *Lieu de naissance*, 73; théâtre: *Ecoles de mon bazou*, *Les Passeuses*, 76 et *Carbonneau et le chef*, 74.
Filmographie sélective: *La Chose la plus douce au Monde/Les Passeuses*, TV, 83, CDN, Aut; *Visiteurs et résidents de l'Arctique*, TV, 81, CDN, Textes/Narr.

MORTIMER, Peter
- see PRODUCERS

MOSSANEN, Moze
- see DIRECTORS

MOZER, Richard
- see PRODUCERS

MURTAGH, Bill
ACTRA. 44 Pintail Cres., Don Mills, ON M3A 2Y7 (416)446-6950.
Type of Production and Credits: TV Film-Wr; TV Video-Wr.
Genres: Drama-TV; Comedy-TV.
Biography: Born 1952, Toronto, Ontario.
Selected Filmography: "My Secret Identity" (5 eps), TV, 88-90, CDN/USA, Wr; "My Secret Identity" (24 eps), TV, 88-90, CDN/USA, Story Ed; "Comedy Mill" (24 eps), TV, 87-88, CDN, Wr; "Hangin' In" (24 eps), TV, 82-87, CDN, Wr; "The Edison Twins" (1 eps), TV, 85, CDN, Wr.

NANTEL, Louise◇
(514)835-3841.
Types de production et générique: l métrage-Sc/Réal; TV film-Sc/Réal.
Types d'oeuvres: Comédie-TV; Documentaire-C; Nouvelles-TV.
Curriculum vitae: Née en 1938, Montréal, Québec. Langues: français et anglais. Brevet d'enseignement et études en lettres, Univ. de Montréal; traduction, Univ. McGill. Nouvelles et affaires publiques (réseau anglais), superviseure de recherches et documentation visuelle pour le service des nouvelles, Radio-Canada, 65-74.
Filmographie sélective: "L'Héritage" (6 eps), TV, 84, CDN, Sc/Co réal; *On est rendu devant le monde!*, C, 80, CDN, Co-réal; "Format 60", TV, 70-71, CDN, Rech; "Hourglass" (52 eps), TV, 70, CDN.

NASIMOK, Briane
ACTRA, ACCT. 11 Bertmount Ave., Toronto, ON M4M 2X8 (416)465-5609. FAX: 462-1777. Krisztina Bevilacqua, 85 Roosevelt Rd., Toronto, ON M4J 4T8.
Type of Production and Credits: Th Film-Wr; Th Short-Wr/Dir; TV Video-Wr.
Genres: Drama-Th&TV; Comedy-Th&TV; Variety-TV; Children's-TV.
Biography: Born 1949, Toronto, Ontario. B.A., University of Toronto. Writer,

performer, radio and TV comedy.
Selected Filmography: "Fred Penner's Place" (35 eps), TV, 87-91, CDN, Contr Wr; "Test Pattern" (65 eps), TV, 90, CDN, Prod; *1990 Gemini Awards (Night One)*, TV, 90, CDN, TV, Contr Wr; "Test Pattern" (130 eps), TV, 88, CDN, Assoc Prod/Wr; *1988 Genie Awards*, TV, 88, CDN, Head Wr; *Crystal Comedy Pageant* (Variety special), TV, 87, CDN, Wr/Co-Prod; *1987 Genie Awards*, TV, 87, CDN, Contr Wr; *1987 Gemini Awards* (Opening Night), TV, 87, CDN, Head Wr; *1986 Gemini Awards* (Opening Night), TV, 86, CDN, Head Wr; "Downtown Saturday Night" (1 eps), TV, 85, CDN, Contr Wr; "Yan Can Cook" (124 eps), TV, 84, CDN, Co-Wr; "Evening at the Improv" (5 eps), TV, 83, CDN/USA, Contr Wr; "In Toronto" (3 eps), TV, 83, CDN, Contr Wr; "Yuk-Yuk's" (2 eps), TV, 82, CDN, Co-Wr; "Nellie, Daniel, Emma and Ben" (2 eps), TV, 81, CDN, Contr Wr.

NATHAN, Deborah A.
Boffo Entertainment Ltd., 105 Arundel Ave., Toronto, ON M4K 3A3 (416)469-1948. Krisztina Bevilacqua, 85 Roosevelt Rd., Toronto, ON M4J 4T8 (416)463-7009.
Type of Production and Credits: TV Film-Wr.
Genres: Drama-TV.
Biography: Born 1949, Detroit, Michigan; resident of Canada since 74. Worked with playwrights' co-op as assistant dramaturge; NDWT Theatre Company as researcher, reader.
Selected Filmography: *King's Ransom*, "Love & Adventure", TV, 91, CDN/F, Story Ed; "Top Cops" (18 eps), TV, 90, CDN/USA, Story Ed/Wr; *Sanctuary*, "Street Legal", TV, 90, CDN, Wr; *Big Horn*, "Magic Hour", TV, 90, CDN/USA, Wr; "War of the Worlds" (19 eps), TV, 89-90, CDN/USA, Story Ed; "Counterstrike", TV, 90, CDN/USA/F, Story Ed; *Concrete Angels*, Th, 88, CDN, Res; *The Campbells*(Co-T'play/Story 1 eps, Wr 1 eps), TV, 85, CDN/USA/GB, Wr; *The Chimney Sweep*, TV, 85, CDN, Wr; "Home Fires" (19 eps) (Wr 1 eps), TV, 79-81, CDN, Res.

NEILSEN, Katherine
The Alphabet Factory Inc., 305 - 2045 Barclay St., Vancouver, BC V6G 1L6 (604)687-6571. Shain Jaffe, Great North Artists Management, 350 Dupont St., Toronto, ON M5R 1V9 (416)925-2051.
Type of Production and Credits: Th Film-Wr; Th Short-Wr; TV Film-Wr.
Genres: Drama-Th&TV; Comedy-Th&TV.
Biography: Born 1958.
Selected Filmography: *Higher Loyalties*, Th, 91, CDN, Wr; *Fieldwork*, Th, 89, CDN, Wr; *Live*, TV, 89, CDN, Wr; *Sticks & Stones*, "The Beachcombers", TV, 89, CDN, Wr; *Beauties & Beasts*, "Street Legal", TV, 88, CDN, Wr; *Maggie*, Th, 81, CDN, Wr/Prod/Act.

NELSON, Barrie
- see DIRECTORS

NEWMAN, Brenda
7873 Ave. de Chateaubriand, Montreal, PQ H2R 2M5 (514)273-5062.
Type of Production and Credits: Th Film-Wr; TV Film-Wr.
Genres: Drama-Th&TV; Comedy-Th&TV Music-Th&TV.
Biography: Bachelor of Fine Art, University of Windsor, 1982; Master of Fine Art, Sculpture, Concordia University, 1988; Winter Cycle Participant, The Banff Centre School of Fine Art, 1982-83. Was the fine art painter and hand model for the feature, *Vincent and Me*; was fine art painter on Alan Rudolph's, *The Moderns*. Co-wrote *Canvas*, a theatrical feature, scheduled production, summer 1991.
Selected Filmography: *Quick Draw*, TV, 88, CDN, Art Dir/Set Des; *Kitchen Culture*, "With Friends Like These", TV, 88, CDN, Art Dir/Set Des; *Madonna (Sins of Seduction)*, Th, 91, USA, Wr; *Montreal Interdit*, Th, 91, CDN, Wr/Narr; *Roy and Dale and Me and Dale*, Th, 91, CDN, Co-Wr.

NEWTON, John
- see DIRECTORS

NICHOL, Gary
- see PRODUCERS

NICHOLL, Jim
- see PRODUCERS

NICHOLLS, Andrew
ACTRA, WGAw, ACCT. Ted Zeigler, 4040 Shadyglade Ave., Studio City, CA 91604 USA (818)985-7867.
Type of Production and Credits: TV Film-Wr; TV Video-Wr.
Genres: Comedy-TV; Variety-TV.
Biography: Born 1957, England; Canadian citizenship. Professional partner is Darrell Vickers. Three Emmy nominations for "The Tonight Show." Contributing writer for Mickey Rooney's *Sugar Babies*, 83-86.
Selected Filmography: "The Tonight Show" (Head Wr 88-92/Wr 86-88), TV, 86-92, USA, Wr; "Shut Up, Kids", TV, 91, USA, Creator; "My Reel Family" (pilot), TV, 88, USA, Co-Wr; "Check It

Out!" (22 eps)(Co-Wr 11 eps), TV, 85-86, CDN/USA, Co-Story Ed; "Danger Bay" (3 eps), TV, 85, CDN, Co-Wr; *George Carlin '2-c'*, TV, 85, USA, Co-Wr; "Love Boat" (1 eps), TV, 85, USA, Co-Wr; *Bizarre*, TV, 85, CDN/USA, Contr Wr; "Thicke of the Night" (85 eps), TV, 83-84, CDN, Contr Wr; "Fast Company" (22 eps), TV, 83, CDN, Co-Wr; "Evening at the Improv" (3 eps), TV, 82, USA, Contr Wr; "Flappers" (3 eps), TV, 81, CDN, Co-Wr.

NICOL, Eric
ACTRA, PUC. 3993 W. 36th Ave., Vancouver, BC V6N 2S7 (604)261-8070.
Type of Production and Credits: TV Film-Wr/Ed; TV Video-Wr/Ed.
Genres: Drama-TV; Comedy-TV; Variety-TV; Documentary-TV.
Biography: Born 1919, Kingston, Ontario. B.A., University of British Columbia, 41; 3 years service, RCAF (ground crew); M.A., U.B.C., 48; attended la Sorbonne, 1 year. Wrote radio, TV comedy series for BBC, London; first book published, 48. Returned to Vancouver, 51, columnist, *The Province*; freelance TV, radio writer. Has published 6 stage plays; 26 books; has won the Leacock Medal for Humour 3 times, for *The Roving I, Shall We Join the Ladies* and *Girdle Me a Globe*.
Selected Filmography: *Ma!*, TV, 84, CDN, Wr.

NICOLLE, Victor W.
- see CINEMATOGRAPHERS

NIELSEN, Susin
76 Dewson St., Toronto, ON M6H 1G8 (416)536-7403.
Type of Production and Credits: TV Film-Wr; TV Video-Spv Wr/Wr.
Genres: Drama-TV; Documentary-TV; Children's-TV.
Biography: It was a dark and stormy night in 1964 when Susin Nielsen was born in Hamilton, Ontario. At a young age she wanted to be a writer or an actor. Twenty-one years later, she graduated from Radio and TV Arts at Ryerson and worked on BBB movie sets until she landed her first writing job in 1987. Susin has been writing for TV ever since. Her acting career never took off, although she did get to play the janitor in a few "Degrassi" episodes. Her most memorable line was, "Good guess, goof ball." Susin has also published 3 young adult books.
Selected Filmography: "Degrassi Talks" (6 eps), TV, 91, CDN, Spv Wr; *Question of Justice*, ED/TV, 90, CDN, Wr; "Degrassi High" (9 eps), TV, 89-90, CDN, Wr; "Degrassi Junior High" (7 eps), TV, 87-88.

NOEL, Jean-Guy
- voir REALISATEURS

NORMAN, Glenn
ACTRA. R.R. #3, Conn, ON N0G 1N0 (519)323-2713. Charles Northcote, The Core Group Talent Agency, 489 College St., Suite 501, Toronto, ON M6G 1A5 (416)944-0193.
Type of Production and Credits: TV Film-Wr.
Genres: Drama-TV; Comedy-TV; Action-TV; News-TV.
Biography: Born 1948, London, England; Canadian citizenship. Educated at De LaSalle College, Toronto. Worked as film editor; freelance aviation writer for international magazines; licenced private pilot with 2,000 hours experience; amateur astronomer for 30 years. Turned to screenwriting, 81.
Selected Filmography: "My Secret Identity" (1 eps), TV, 90, CDN/USA, Wr; "Danger Bay" (5 eps), TV, 86-89, CDN/USA, Wr; "Adderly" (1 eps), TV, 87, CDN/USA, Wr; "Night Heat" (1 eps), TV, 87, CDN/USA, Wr; "Vulcan" (pilot), TV, 86, CDN, Wr/Creator; "The Campbells" (5 eps), TV, 85-86, CDN/USA/GB, Wr; *Flier Beware*, "W5", TV, 85, CDN, Res; *Nothing By Chance*, Th, 73, USA, Act.

NOVAK, Allan Z.
- see DIRECTORS

NOWLAN, John
- see PRODUCER

NURSALL, Tom
ACTRA. 100 Oriole Pkwy., #303, Toronto, ON M5P 2G8 (416)487-4603.
Type of Production and Credits: TV Film-Wr; TV Video-Wr.
Genres: Drama-TV; Comedy-TV; Action-TV.
Biography: Born 1957, Edinburgh, Scotland. B.A., English, University of Western Ontario. Has written monologues for Joan Rivers.
Selected Filmography: *Devil Stuff*, Th, 91, CDN, Wr; *Going for Broke*, Th, 90, CDN, Wr; *Escape from Wanna-Wanna*, Th, 89, CDN, Wr; *Getting Even*, 89, USA, Wr; Montreal International Comedy Festival, 87, CDN, Co-Wr; "The Botts" (6 eps), TV, 86, CDN/USA/F, Co-Wr; *What the World's Been Waiting For*, TV, 86, CDN, Wr/Act/Co-Prod; "Just for Laughs" (81 eps), TV,, 85, CDN, Co-Wr; "Laughing Matters" (3 eps), TV, 85, CDN, Co-Wr.

O'CONNELL, Maura
- see PRODUCERS

O'DELL, Dean A.
- see ART DIRECTORS

O'DWYER, Michael J.
CFTA. 877 Bough Beeches Blvd., Mississauga, ON L4W 2B4. M.J. O'Dwyer Associates Ltd., 884 Queen St. W., Toronto, ON M6J 1G3 (416)536-4991.
Type of Production and Credits: Th Film-Wr; Th Short-Wr; TV Film-Wr; TV Video-Wr.
Genres: Documentary-Th&TV; Educational-Th&TV; Sports-TV.
Biography: Born 1946, Walkerton, Ontario. Diplomas in English, Creative Writing, Public Relations, Business Administration. Background in newspaper and radio; has worked as a magazine journalist; Managing Editor, Senior Communications Practitioner. Films he has written have won awards internationally; has also won awards for print writing/editing.
Selected Filmography: *Schenley Awards Show*, TV, 85/87, CDN, Wr; "Player's/GM Motorsport Series", TV, 87, CDN, Wr; *Audi Experience/The New Voyageur/Rabbit Rallye*, In, 83-84, CDN, Wr; *Wheels in Motion*, TV, 83, CDN, Wr; *Natural Journey*, ED, 82, CDN, Wr; *On Target*, ED, 81, CDN, Wr; *Going for Gold*, ED, 80, CDN, Wr; *Shotpoint 260*, In, 79, CDN, Wr; *Battleground*, Th, 78, CDN, Wr; *Gilles*, TV, 77, CDN, Wr; *Speed*, Th, 77, CDN, Wr; *The Mythmakers*, Th, 76, CDN, Wr.

O'REGAN, James
- see PRODUCERS

O'ROURKE, Denise
ACTRA. 184 Wright Ave., Toronto, ON M6R 1L2 (416)532-1969.
Type of Production and Credits: Th Short-Wr; TV Film-Wr.
Genres: Drama-Th; Documentary-TV.
Biography: Born in Toronto. M.A. Economics from Queen's University. Attended Upper Canada Writers Workshop for 3 years. Short stories published in "White Wall Review" (Coach House Press) and "Quarry Magazine" (Quarry Press). Assistant picture editor, 1984-85. Music teacher 1990-91.
Selected Filmography: *Norha and the Microbabe*, Th, 91, CDN, Wr; *Florida: State of Caring*, "The Last Frontier", TV, 85, CDN, Wr; *The Last Mermaids*, "The Last Frontier", TV, 85, CDN, Wr; "The Last Frontier" (5 eps), TV, 84-85, CDN, Assist Ed.

OBOMSAWIN, Alanis
- see DIRECTORS

OLIVER, Ron
ACTRA. 335 Lonsdale Rd., #406, Toronto, ON M4P 1R4 (416)484-4673. Lesley Harrison/MGA, 10 St. Mary St., Ste. 510, Toronto, ON M4Y 1P9 (416)964-3302.
Type of Production and Credits: Th Film-Wr/Dir; TV Video-Prod/Dir.
Genres: Drama-Th; Comedy-Th&TV; Horror-Th; Children's-TV.
Biography: Born in 1960 in the backseat of a '58 Chevy at a drive-in showing *Psycho*; a proud Canadian; Speaks English and aboriginal Auckland; learned about life the hard way - the mean streets of cottage country in Ontario; went from a stage career as one of Canada's most promising opera stars to his new love as the only director in Canadian film history to move the camera more than twice in a single scene!
Selected Filmography: *Intimate Delusions*, Th, 91, CDN, Dir/Wr; "The Ron Oliver Show" (26 eps), TV, 90, CDN, Prod/Wr/Host; *The Last Kiss - Prom Night III*, Th, 89, CDN, Wr/Co Dir; "YTV Hits", TV, 88-89, CDN, Assist Prod/Host; *Hello Mary Lou - Prom Night II*, Th, 87, CDN, Wr.

ORD, Cathy
- see DIRECTORS

ORR, James
WGA, DGA. James Orr Productions Inc., 500 S. Buena Vista St., Burbank, CA 91521-1825 USA. Jack Rapke, Creative Artists Agency, 9830 Wilshire Blvd., Beverly Hills, CA 90212 USA. (213)288-4545.
Type of Production and Credits: Th Film-Wr/Dir.
Genres: Drama-Th.
Biography: Born 1953, Noranda, Quebec; US resident alien. B.F.A., Film Production, York University; Directing Fellow, American Film Institute.
Selected Filmography: *Father of the Bride*, Th, 91, USA, Co-Wr/Co-Exec Prod; *Mr. Destiny*, Th, 90, USA, Dir/Co-Wr/Co-Prod; *14 Going On 30*, TV, 88, USA, Co-Exec Prod; *Three Men and a Baby*, Th, 87, USA, Co-Wr; *Young Harry Houdini*, TV, 87, USA, Dir/Co-Wr/Co-Prod; *Tough Guys*, Th, 86, USA, Co-Wr; *Breaking All the Rules*, Th, 84, CDN, Dir.

ORVIETO, Denise Agiman
ACCT. 690 Cardinal, Ville St. Laurent, PQ H4L 3C7 (514)744-4648. 6900 St. Denis, Montreal, PQ (514)279-4536.
Types de production et générique: TV vidéo-Sc.
Types d'oeuvres: Variété-TV; Enfants-TV;

Vidéo-clips-TV; Affaires publiques-TV.
Curriculum vitae: Née a Milan, Italie. 5 ans d'animation à la television pour emissons et rubriques format magazine et reportages socio-culturels. Depuis 3 ans directrice à la programmation et assistante à la production. Conception et script de plusieurs commerciaux a la télé ainsi que de plusieurs émissions de vidéo-clips et entraînement a la télé.
Filmographie sélective: "Teleauguri" (40 eps), TV, 90-91, CDN/I, Sc/An; "Télé Domenica" (200 eps), TV, 86-91, CDN/I, Ass pro/An; "Video Espresso" (40 eps), TV, 90, CDN/I, Sc/An; "Video Take" (8 eps), TV, 90, CDN, Sc/An; *Mosîque Montréal*, TV, 90, CDN, Sc/An; "Telethon Italien" (4 eps), TV, 87/88/89/90, CDN, Ass pro/An.

ORZARI, Lorenzo◇
LCA. (514)933-6999.
Type of Production and Credits: Th Film-Wr; TV Film-Prod/Dir/Wr; TV Video-Prod/Dir/Wr.
Genres: Comedy-Th&TV; Action-Th&TV; Drama-Th&TV; Horror-Th&TV; Science Fiction-Th&TV.
Biography: Born 1955, Rotherham, England; Canadian citizen. Languages: English, French, Italian, some German. Stills photographer, associate editor, script reader, storyboard conceptions, actor, narrator, writer, since 72. Has worked on features, TV series, commercials, script reports, publicity, translations, lyrics, comic strips, experimental film/videos, cable TV scripts. Author of book, *The Fading Flesh & Other Stories*. Attended writing seminars; studied acting and directing at Acting Circle, directing at McGill University. VP, Head Writer and Director of LCA Productions Inc.
Selected Filmography: *Meatballs IV*, Th, 88, CDN, Wr; "Taking Off" (pilot), TV, 87, CDN, Wr/Assoc Prod; *Australia's Heron Island*, "The Secret Paradise" (1 eps), TV, 87, CDN, Co-Prod/Wr/Dir; "Unknown Dimensions" (pilot), TV, 86, CDN, Act/Narr/Wr/Dir; *Love Me and Die*, Th, 84, CDN, Wr; *Montréal - joie de vivre*, Th, 82, CDN, Wr.

OSBORNE, Jim
ACTRA, ACCT. 186 Browning Ave., Toronto, ON M4K 1W2 (416)466-1977.
Type of Production and Credits: Th Film-Wr; TV Film-Wr.
Genres: Drama-Th; Horror-TV; Documentary-TV; Educational-TV.
Biography: Born 1943, Foleyet, Ontario. B.A., University of Ottawa, 64; M.A., Theatre Criticism, University of Alberta, 73. Has had several stage plays produced; story editor, CBC-TV Drama, 73-76; script consultant on numerous TV productions, 82 to date. *First Snowfall* won the Gemini for Best Dramatic program, 1990.
Selected Filmography: *First Snowfall*, TV, 90, CDN, Wr, (GEMINI); *Secrets of the Sun*, "Adderly" (1 eps), TV, 87, CDN, Wr; *You Wouldn't Understand*, "Hooked on Reading", TV, 85, CDN, Wr; *The War Boy/Point of Escape*, Th, 84, CDN, Scr; *Stevie and the Dinosaurs*, ED, 84, CDN, Wr; *A Frontier, a Homeland/Tuktoyaktuk: A Piece of the Action*, "Like No Other Place", ED, 79, CDN, Wr; *Winnipeg: Alive or Dead?/Where Have All the Cowboys Gone*, "Like No Other Place", ED, 79, CDN, Wr; *Without an Industry, without a Highway*, "Like No Other Place", ED, 78, CDN, Wr; *50 Cents of Every Dollar/The Price of Power*, "Like No Other Place", ED, 78, CDN, Wr; *The Colonist*, "In Their Shoes", ED, 78, CDN, Wr; *Eye of the Beholder*, TV, 78, CDN, Wr; *Summer's Children*, Th, 78, CDN, Wr.

OUELLET, Yves
164, Marco, Chicoutimi, PQ G7G 4T2 (418)545-6952. CBJ Radio Canada, 500, des Saguenéens, Chicoutimi, PQ (418)696-6600.
Types de production et générique: l métrage-Sc; TV vidéo-Sc/Narr.
Types d'oeuvres: Documentaire-C&TV; Annonces-TV; Affaires publiques-TV.
Curriculum vitae: Né en 1954, Montréal, Québec. Langues: français et anglais. Art et technologie des médias, option radio, Cégep de Jonquière. Recherchiste, interviewer, journaliste, Radio-Canada (radio); recherchiste, scénariste, animateur, interviewer, TV, Radio-Québec, TQS, depuis 85; collaborateur pigiste pour plusieurs magazines; fonde sa propre compagnie, Relations Publiques Yves Ouellet Communications inc., 86. *A la quête du Narval* a gagné 1er Prix, Festival Internationaux du film chasse-Nature de Lamotte-Beauvron, France; Prix du Jury, Festival Internationale du Film d'Autrans, France; 1er Prix, Cat. Interprétation Historique Water, Waker Festival, Ottawa, Canada.
Filmographie sélective: *A la quête du Narval*, TV, 89, CDN, Rech/Sc; *L'Affaire Marie-Andrée Leclerc*, TV, 88, CDN, Sc/Rech; *Loisir Equestre*, TV, 87, CDN, Rech; *Vivre à Peribonka*, TV, 87, CDN, Interv/Anim; *Vivre à l'anse St-Jean*, TV, 87, CDN, Narr; *O rage électrique*, C, 84, CDN, Sc.

OWEN, Don
- see DIRECTORS

PAABO, Iris
- see DIRECTORS

PACHECO, Bruno Lazaro
- see DIRECTORS

PARENT, Gilles
SARDEC. C.P. 154, Val-David, PQ J0T 2N0 (819)322-7015. Suzanne Vachon (SVP), 305 Ave. Elm, Westmount, PQ H3Z 1Z4 (514)937-1057.
Types de production et générique: TV film-Sc.
Types d'oeuvres: Drame-TV; Documentaire-TV; Enfants-TV.
Curriculum vitae: Né en 1942, Montréal, Québec. Langues: français, anglais. Formation académique en architecture et modèle à l'Ecole des Beaux-Arts de Montréal. Scénariste et recherchiste pour télévision et cinéma en drame, documentaire dont 3 épisodes de la série "Les Intrépides", 90-91; 5 épisodes de la série "Les Traquenards," 86-87, du pilote de la série "Légendes de l'ouest." Recherchiste et scénariste pour *La Guerre de la Fourrure*, 88-89 et *The Sacred Pipe*, 84.
Filmographie sélective: *Le Dragon d'Or*, "Les Intrépides", TV, 90-91, CDN, Sc; *Le Faux Numéro*, "Les Intrépides", TV, 90-91, CDN, Sc; *Cargo et beaux plumages*, "Les Intrépides, TV, 90-91, CDN, Sc; *La Guerre de la Fourrure*, TV, 88-89, CDN, Sc/Rech; "Traquenards" (5 eps), TV, 86-87, CDN, Sc/Rég; "Légendes de l'ouest", TV, 86, CDN, Rech; "From the Sky's Rim", TV, 84, USA, Rech/Sc; *La Terrible Conquête de Mrs. Hubbard/Labrador 1905"*, TV, 83, CDN, Sc.

PARTINGTON, Lawrence
- see PRODUCERS

PAYETTE, Lise◊
SARDEC, SACD, UDA. (514)458-7181.
Types de production et générique: TV film-Sc; TV vidéo-Sc.
Types d'oeuvres: Drame-TV.
Curriculum vitae: Née en 1931, Montréal, Québec. Animatrice, radio, télévision, "Appelez-moi Lise", 72-76. Ministre au gouvernement du Québec 76-81; Ministère des Consommateurs, Coopératives et Institutions financières, 76-79; Ministre responsable, Conseil du statut de la femme, 76-81. Auteur, scènarios et dialogues. "La Bonne Aventure" remporte le Prix de l'Association des téléspectateurs.
Filmographie sélective: "La Bonne Aventure" (143 eps), TV, 82-86, CDN, Sc/Dial; "Des dames de coeur" (82 eps), TV, 86, CDN, Sc/Dial; "Bonjour Docteur" (10 eps), TV, 86, CDN, Aut cons; "L'Or et le Papier" (26 eps), TV, 86, CDN/F, Sc/Dial; *La Démesure/Spécial Ginette Reno*, TV, 85, CDN, Aut.

PEARSON, Barry
- see PRODUCERS

PEARSON, Peter
- see DIRECTORS

PEDERSON, Larry V.
WGAw. Dew Line Filmworks, P.O. Box 2716, Beverly Hills, CA 90213 USA. (213)476-0851. Nina Shaw/ Del, Rubel, Shaw, Mason & Derin, 1801 Century Park E., #2500, Los Angeles, CA 90067 USA. (213)286-7100.
Type of Production and Credits: Th Short-Dir/Wr/Ed; TV Film-Wr.
Genres: Drama-Th&TV.
Biography: Born 1957, Medicine Hat, Alberta; US resident alien. B.A., Philosophy, University of Alberta; B.A., Film and TV Production, University of Southern California. Film censor, Alberta government, 78-80.
Selected Filmography: *Money* (miniseries), TV, 90, CDN/F/I, Co-Wr; *Juxtaposition*, Th, 82, USA, Wr/Dir/Ed.

PELLETIER, Maryse
SARDEC, UDA. 4279, Garnier, Montréal, PQ H2J 3R7 (514)526-8447.
Types de production et générique: TV film-Sc; TV vidéo-Sc.
Types d'oeuvres: Comédie-TV.
Curriculum vitae: Née en 1946, Québec. Langues: français et anglais. Etudes en lettres à l'Université Laval; Conservatoire d'art dramatique. Dramaturge; adapte aussi ses pièces pour la télévision. Prix Gemeaux, meilleure émission jeunesse, pour "Traboulidon," 86, et "Iniminimagimo," 87; Grand Prix du Journal de Montréal et Prix du Gouverneur Général, 85 pour *Duo Pour Voix Obstinées*, théâtre.
Filmographie sélective: "Traboulidon" (84 eps) (aut 20 eps), TV, 86-88, CDN, Scripte éd; "Iniminimagimo", TV, 87-88, CDN, Sc; *L'Expérience*, TV, 87, CDN, Adapt; *Du poil aux pattes comme les Cwacs*, TV, 85, CDN, Adapt.

PERRIS, Anthony
- see DIRECTORS

PERRON, Clément
SARDEC. Cinescript inc., 40, Anselme Lavigne, Dollard-des-Ormeaux, PQ H9A 1N6 (514)684-6037.
Types de production et générique: l métrage-Sc/Réal; c métrage-Sc/Réal.
Types d'oeuvres: Drame-C&TV; Documentaire-C&TV.
Curriculum vitae: Né en 1929 dans la Beauce, Québec. Licencié ès lettres,

Université Laval; études en linguistique et cinéma, Académie de Poitière et Institut de Filmologie, Sorbonne, Paris, 55-57. A l'emploi de l'ONF pendant 28 ans comme scénariste, réalisateur, producteur et directeur des programmes français; scénariste pigiste depuis 86. Gagnant de nombreux prix: festivals de Toronto, Chicago, Venise, etc.
Filmographie sélective: *Le Marchand de jouets*, TV, 88, CDN, Sc; *Caroline*, C, 74, CDN, Co réal; *Partis pour la gloire*, C, 74, CDN, Sc/Réal; *Taureau*, C, 72, CDN, Sc/Réal; *Mon oncle Antoine*, C, 70, CDN, Sc, (CFA); *Jour après jour*, C, 63, CDN, Réal.

PETERSEN, Karen
ACTRA. Freelance Rules OK, RR #1, J-9, Bowen, BC V0N 1G0 (604)947-0517. FAX: 947-0519. Jennifer Hollyer, 112 Westmount Ave., Ste. 4, Toronto, ON M6H 3K6 (416)651-8246.
Type of Production and Credits: TV Film-Wr/Story Ed; TV Video-Wr/Story Ed.
Genres: Drama-TV; Comedy-TV; Action-TV; Animation-TV.
Biography: Born in 1953 in Whitehorse, Yukon Territories. Master of Fine Arts in Creative Writing. Taught script editing courses in Vancouver, Calgary, Regina and Toronto. Taught short fiction at University of British Columbia. Published poet who has been anthologized five times.
Selected Filmography: "Northwood" (2 eps), TV, 90, CDN, Story Ed; *Insecurity System*, "Babar", TV, 90, CDN/F, Co Wr; "Inside Stories" (3 eps), TV, 89-90, CDN, Story Ed; "The Beachcombers" (77 eps), TV, 87-90, CDN, Story Ed; "Lies From Lotus Land" (9 eps), TV, 88, CDN, Story Ed.

PETRYSHEN, Eva
- see PRODUCERS
PICK, Anne
- see PRODUCERS
PINSENT, Gordon
- see DIRECTORS
PLAMONDON, Louis
- voir REALISATEURS
PODESWA, Jeremy
- see DIRECTORS
POIRIER, Anne Claire
- voir REALISATEURS
POLLOCK, Sharon
ACTRA. 319 Manora Dr. N.E., Calgary, AB T2A 4R2 (403)235-1945.
Type of Production and Credits: TV Film-Wr.
Genres: Drama-TV; Documentary-TV.
Biography: Born 1936, Fredericton, New Brunswick. Writer, stage plays and radio; won the Governor General's Award, drama, for *Blood Relations* and for *Doc*; ACTRA Award for *Sweet Land of Liberty* (radio); Chalmers Award for *Doc*; *The Persons Case* won a Golden Sheaf, Yorkton Short Film and Televison Festival.
Selected Filmography: *Walsh*, TV, 86, CDN, Wr; *The Komogata Maru Incident*, TV, 84, CDN, Wr; *The Persons Case*, TV, 80, CDN, Wr.

POTTERTON, Gerald
- see DIRECTORS
PRESTON, David
ACTRA. 63 Marie-Anne West, Montreal, PQ H2W 1B7 (514)849-9884. (514)495-3197. Jennifer Hollyer Agency, 4 -112 Westmount Ave., Toronto, ON M6H 3K4 (416)651-8246. FAX: 651-0707.
Type of Production and Credits: Th Film-Wr.
Genres: Drama-Th; Comedy-Th; Action-Th; Science Fiction-Th.
Biography: Born 1951, Windsor, Ontario. B.F.A., Nova Scotia College of Art and Design; M.A., Phil., Dalhousie Univ.
Selected Filmography: *Picture Perfect*, TV, 91, CDN/F, Co-Wr; *Twin Sisters*, Th, 91, CDN, Wr; *Splash '91*, TV, 91, CDN, Wr/2nd U Dir; *Shadows of the Past*, TV, 90, CDN/F, Wr; *Scanners III - The Takeover*, Th, 90, CDN, Co-Wr; *Breaking All the Rules*, Th, 84, CDN, Co-Wr; *The Vindicator*, Th, 84, CDN, Co-Wr; *Spacehunter*, Th, 83, CDN, Co-Wr.

PRICE, Roger Damon
ACTRA, ACTT. 652 Trelawny Priv., Ottawa, ON K2C 3M7 (613)226-4171.
Type of Production and Credits: TV Film-Wr/Prod/Dir; TV Video-Wr/Prod/Dir.
Genres: Drama-TV; Comedy-TV; Science Fiction-TV; Children's-TV.
Biography: Born 1941, U.K. Canadian and British citizenship. Languages: English and good working knowledge of German. Specializes in network television for children: comedy, drama and science-fiction; also adult shows about issues relevant to family and children.
Selected Filmography: *Real Mature*, TV, 91, USA, Creator; "You Can't Do That On Television" (130 eps), TV, 79-90, CDN, Creator/Wr/Prod; "Morningstar, Eveningstar" (6 eps), TV, 86, USA, Creator; "Turkey Television" (65 eps), TV, 85-86, CDN/USA, Creator/Prod; "Don't Look Now" (5 eps), TV, 83, USA, Creator/Prod; "Whatever Turns You On" (14 eps), TV, 79-80, CDN, Creator/Prod; "You Must Be Joking" (13 eps), TV, 75,

GB, Wr/Dir/Prod; "Tomorrow People" (78 eps), TV, 73-79, GB, Wr/Creator/Prod/Dir.

PROCOPIO, Frank
- see PRODUCERS

PURDY, Jim
- see DIRECTORS

PYKE, Roger
- see DIRECTORS

RABINOVITCH, David
- see PRODUCERS

RAKOFF, Alvin
- see DIRECTORS

RANSEN, Mort
- see DIRECTORS

RASKY, Harry
- see DIRECTORS

RAYMOND, Marie-José
- voir PRODUCTEURS

RAYMONT, Peter
- see DIRECTORS

READ, Merilyn
- see PRODUCERS

REDICAN, Dan
ACTRA. The Talent Group, 387 Bloor St. E., 3rd Floor, Toronto, ON M4W 1H7 (416)961-3304.
Type of Production and Credits: TV Film-Wr; TV Video-Wr.
Genres: Comedy-TV; Variety-TV.
Biography: Born 1956, Etobicoke, Ontario. Has worked as standup and sketch comic, puppeteer. Co-writer, "Frantic Times", which won second prize, radio variety, American Major Armstrong Awards. Won Best Variety Writer and Best Variety Performer, Canadian National Radio awards for *The Frantics Look at History*. Gemini award nominee, Best Comedy Writer for "4 on the Floor".
Selected Filmography: "Kids in the Hall" (20 eps), TV, 90-91, CDN/USA, Story Ed; "Mosquito Lake" (18 eps), TV, 90-91, CDN, Act; "The Jim Henson Hour" (12 eps), TV, 88, CDN/USA, Act/Puppeteer; "4 on the Floor" (13 eps), TV, 85, CDN, Co-Wr/Act.

REISLER, Susan
ATPD. 48 Austin Terrace, Toronto, ON M5R 1Y6 (416)536-4636. CBC The Journal, 100 Carlton St., Toronto, ON (416)975-7924.
Type of Production and Credits: TV Video-Report/Prod.
Genres: Documentary-TV; Current Affairs-TV; News-TV.
Biography: Born 1947, Port Hope, Ontario, Languages: English and French, some Spanist; studied Russian and German. Honours B.A., Modern Languages, University of Toronto. Has worked in news and current affairs since 70; 4 years with UPI, the rest with CBC: news, "Sunday Morning," Washington radio correspondent, "The Journal"; has also hosted "As It Happens" and "Sunday Morning".
Selected Filmography: *A Palestinian Conversation: Palestinians During the Gulf War*, TV, 91, CDN, Report/Wr; *Down and Dirty...U.S. Campaigns*, TV, 90, CDN, Report/Wr; *Protest and Prophecy: The Reform Policy*, TV, 90, CDN, Report/Wr; *Panama: Noriega*, "The Journal", TV, 88, CDN, Wr/Report; *The Americans and Gorbachev*, "The Journal", TV, 87, CDN, Wr/Report; *Democrats and Primaries*, "The Journal", TV, 87, CDN, Wr/Report; *Who's Minding the River*, "The Journal", TV, 87, CDN, Wr/Report; *Philippines - Cory's Future*, "The Journal", TV, 87, CDN, Wr/Report; *CF-18: Delivering the Contract*, TV, 87, CDN, Wr/Report; *Mary McCarthy: Profile-Interview*, "The Journal", TV, 87, CDN, Wr/Report; *Stephen Lewis*, "The Journal", TV, 87, CDN, Wr/Report; *Oliver North: Profile*, "The Journal", TV, 87, CDN, Wr/Report; *Groundwater: Documentary*, "The Journal", TV, 87, CDN, Wr/Report; *America's Cup - Canada's Race*, "The Journal", TV, 86, CDN, Wr/Report; *Berlin Game: Tamils in Berlin*, "The Journal", TV, 86, CDN, Wr/Report.

REMEROWSKI, Ted
- see PRODUCERS

RENAUD, Bernadette
CAPAC, SARDEC. 6208, Marie-Victoriny, C.P. 1103, Contrecoeur, PQ J0L 1C0 (514)587-5547. (514)587-2245.
Types de production et générique: l métrage-Sc; TV film-Sc.
Types d'oeuvres: Enfants-C&TV.
Curriculum vitae: Née en 1945, Ascot Corner, Québec. Brevet d'enseignement; 3 ans d'enseignement; 4 ans de secrétariat; écrivaine professionnelle pour jeunes depuis 76; 21 albums; 9 livres dont 3 en anglais, 2 en braille; conférences auprès de plus de 150,000 jeunes à travers tout le Canada; scénarisation d'un pilote pour une série d'émissions destinées au jeune public; créations en cours: scénarios télévision pour la série "WATATATOW," Productions Publivision (pour jeune public). A gagné 2 prix pour son livre *Emilie la baignoire à pattes*; plusieurs prix internationaux ont été attribués à *Bach et Bottine*, France, Alger, Moscou, Martinique, Chicago, etc.
Filmographie sélective: "Franc Ouest" (1 eps), ED, 89, CDN, Sc; *Bach et Bottine*, C, 86, CDN, Sc; "Michou et Pilo" (8 eps),

TV, 84-85, CDN, Sc; "Klimbo" (4 eps), TV, 82-84, CDN, Sc.

REPKE, Ron
- see PRODUCERS

REY, Edith Dora
ACTRA. 63 Marie-Anne W., Montreal, PQ H2W 1B7 (514)849-9884. The Jennifer Hollyer Agency, 4 - 112 Westmount Ave., Toronto, ON M6H 3K4 (416)651-8246. FAX: 651-0707.
Type of Production and Credits: Th Film-Wr.
Genres: Drama-Th; Comedy-Th; Science Fiction-Th; Horror-Th.
Biography: Born 1951, Luzern, Switzerland; Swiss and Canadian citizenship. Graduate of Vancouver School of Art and Nova Scotia College of Art and Design.
Selected Filmography: *The Vindicator*, Th, 84, CDN, Co-Wr; *Breaking All the Rules*, Th, 84, CDN, Co-Wr; *Spacehunter*, Th, 83, CDN, Co-Wr; *Hey Babe!*, Th, 79, CDN, Wr; *Michel Pellus*, ED, 78, CDN, Wr.

REYNOLDS, Gene
- see DIRECTORS

RIIS, Sharon
ACTRA, ACCT, SMPIA. 705 Dufferin Ave., Saskatoon, SK S1N 1C5 (306)665-6194. Van Redler, 3474 Laurelvale Dr., Studio City, CA 91604 (818)985-8590 FAX 985-2577.
Type of Production and Credits: Th Film-Wr; TV Film-Wr.
Genres: Drama-Th&TV.
Biography: Born 1947, High River, Alberta. B.A., History, Simon Fraser University, 69. AMPIA awards for *A Change of Heart*, 85, *Loyalties*, 87; *The Wake* won Yorkton Script Award, 88 and a Gemini award, 88. Novelist: *The True Story of Ida Johnson*, 1976, 1989; *Midnight Twilight Tourist Zone*, 1989.
Selected Filmography: *Daughters of the Country*, TV, 86, CDN, Wr, (GEMINI 87); *Loyalties*, Th, 85, CDN/GB, Scr/Co-Story; *A Change of Heart*, TV, 83, CDN, Wr; *Latitude 55*, Th, 80, CDN, Co-Wr.

RINFERT, Louise
SARDEC, ACCT, UDA. 4458, av. de Lorimier, Montréal, PQ H2H 2B2 (514)598-5766.
Types de production et générique: l métrage-Sc/Com; TV film-Com.
Types d'oeuvres: Drame-C&TV.
Curriculum vitae: Né en Montréal, Québec. Langues: français et anglais. Comédienne au théâtre, au cinéma et à la télévision; a écrit le roman *La Dance en couleurs* d'après le scénario du même nom.
Filmographie sélective: "Le Club Desd 100 Watts", TV, 89-91, CDN, Com; "Il était une fois...dans un piano", TV, 90, CDN, Com; *La Châine*, TV, 88, F, Com; *Onzième Spécial*, C, 88, CDN, Com; *Le Coeur découvert*, TV, 86, CDN, Com; *L'Object*, C, 83, CDN, Com; *La Dance en couleurs*, C, 83, CDN, Co sc; "Sesame Street" (pl seg), TV, 79, USA, Com; *Nest of Shadows*, TV, 76, CDN, Com; "La Petite Patrie" (70 eps), TV, 73-74, CDN, Com; *On n'engraisse pas les cochons à l'eau claire*, C, 73, CDN, Com; *The Pyx*, C, 72, CDN, Com.

RITCHIE, Dawn
ACTRA, EQUITY, AFTRA, SAG. The Coppage Company, 11501 Chandler Blvd., N. Hollywood, CA 91601 USA. (818)980-1106. The Jennifer Hollyer Agency, 4-112 Westmount Ave., Toronto, ON M6H 3K4 (416)651-8246.
Type of Production and Credits: Th Film-Wr; TV Film-Wr; TV Video-Wr.
Genres: Drama-Th&TV; Comedy-Th&TV.
Biography: Born in Toronto, Ontario. Educated at the University of Toronto and the Banff Centre School of Fine Arts. Staff positions at ABC and NBC; worked on "Golden Girls" and various pilots from 86-89. Previously produced theatre: *Islands* and *Alli Alli Oh* which garnered multiple Dora Mavor Moore Award nominations. Screenwriting grants and awards - OAC & F.U.N.D.; Producing grants - Canada Council and Toronto Arts Council.
Selected Filmography: "The Adventures of the Black Stallion" (26 eps), TV, 91, USA/CDN/F, Exec Story Consult; "My Secret Identity" (26 eps), TV, 90, USA/CDN, Story Ed; "Fly By Night", TV, 90, USA, Wr; "Chestnut Avenue", TV, 90, CDN, Wr; "E.N.G.", TV, 89, CDN/USA, Wr; "The Hitchhiker", TV, 89, USA, Wr; *In Opposition*, TV, 89, CDN, Wr.

ROBBINS, Karen
- see PRODUCERS

ROBERT, Michel
SARDEC. 5920, Monkland, #3, Montréal, PQ H4A 1G1 (514)481-2567.
Types de production et générique: TV vidéo-Sc.
Types d'oeuvres: Comédie-TV; Variété-TV.
Curriculum vitae: Né en 1943, Montréal, Québec. Langues: français et anglais. Auteur de textes humouristiques, textes de présentation et d'enchaînement pour radio, télévision et scène.

Filmographie sélective: "Fais-moi un dessin" (608 eps), TV, 87-91, CDN, Rech/Aut; "Québec à la carte" (350 eps), TV, 85-89, CDN, Rech/Aut; "Galaxie" (400 eps), TV, 85-87, CDN, Rech/Aut; "Club Sandwich" (8 eps), TV, 86-87, CDN, Aut; "Gala Artis" (2 eps), TV, 86-87, CDN, Aut; "A la bonne heure" (390 eps), TV, 77-79, CDN, Aut; *Bye Bye 76*, TV, 76, CDN, Aut; "Parlez-moi d'humour" (26 eps), TV, 76, CDN, Aut.

ROBERT, Vincent
1913 de Tripoli, Laval, PQ H7M 3H1 (514)663-1146. Sudden Light Productions, 322 South Westminster Ave., Los Angeles, CA 90020 USA (213)931-0730. John Samsel/Media Artists Group, 6255 Sunset Blvd., #627, Los Angeles, CA 90028 USA (213)463-5610.
Type of Production and Credits: Th Film-Wr; Th Short-Wr/Dir; TV Film-Wr.
Genres: Drama-Th&TV; Comedy-Th; Action-Th; Horror-Th.
Biography: Born in 1958 in Montreal, Quebec. Canadian citizenship and U.S. Green Card; dual residency. Has worked extensively in both countries. Languages; English and French. Bachelor of Arts, Communications, Concordia University, Montreal; Master of Fine Arts, Film Production, University of Southern California School of Cinema & Television, U.S.C. Presently teaches screenwriting. *The Celebration*, received a Gold Medal at the International Film and Television Festival of New York as well as the Youth in Film and Superfest awards. *Red Surf*, a feature he scripted, opened to rave reviews in prestigious first-run theatres.
Selected Filmography: *Second Chance*, Th, 91, USA, Wr/Dir; *The Homeless Cheetah*, "Okavango", TV, 91, USA, Wr; *Kindergarden Cop*, Th, 90, USA, 2nd Unit Dir; *Red Surf*, Th, 90, USA, Wr; *Seeds*, ED/TV, 90, USA, Wr; *The Celebration*, Th, 89, USA, Dir; *La face cachée de Paul Tessier*, TV, 89, CDN, Wr; *Beyond the Line*, Th, 88, GB, Wr; *The Ghouls*, Th, 87, USA, Wr; *Intervention*, Th, 85, USA, Wr/Dir.

ROBERTSON, George
ACTRA. 158 Glen Rd., Toronto, ON M4W 2W6 (416)928-0073.
Type of Production and Credits: Th Film-Wr; TV Film-Wr; TV Video-Wr.
Genres: Drama-Th&TV; Documentary-Th&TV; Children's-TV.
Biography: Born 1922, Regina, Saskatchewan. RCAF, 42-44. Attended Wesley University College, Winnipeg, 44-45. Announcer, CJRM, Regina, 39-40; announcer, actor, CBC Winnipeg, 40-42, 44-45; producer, CBC International Service, 45-46; freelance writer, broadcaster, Montreal, 46-49, Toronto since 49; first radio drama, 43; first TV drama, 52; writing includes commentary and criticism, CBC's "Critically Speaking" and *Canadian Art*; narrator, NFB films; co-founder, Jupiter Theatre, 51; novel, *Face-Off*, 71.
Selected Filmography: "Backstretch" (1 eps), TV, 85, CDN, Wr; "Judge" (4 eps), TV, 83-84, CDN, Wr; "The Law and You" (26 eps), TV, 81-82, CDN, Wr/Assoc Prod; "Snelgrove Snail" (65 eps), TV, 78-80, CDN, Co-Wr/Assoc Prod; *Materials Handling*, In, 78, CDN, Wr; "The Winners" (10 eps) (Wr 2 eps), TV, 77, CDN, Story Ed/Co-Creator; "Sidestreet" (2 eps), TV, 76, CDN, Wr; "House of Pride" (52 eps), TV, 74-75, CDN, Head Wr/Story Ed; *On Site Safety*, In, 74, CDN, Wr; "The Collaborators" (1 eps), TV, 74, CDN, Wr; *Face-Off*, Th, 71, CDN, Scr; "Quentin Durgens, M.P." (26 eps), TV, 67-70, CDN, Creator/Wr; *The Road to Chaldaea*, TV, 68, CDN, Wr; *Mr. Member of Parliament*, "The Serial", TV, 66, CDN, Wr; "Moment of Truth" (52 eps), TV, 65, CDN, Wr.

ROBERTSON, George R.
ACTRA, SAG, AFTRA, AEA, CAEA. 1473 Elite Rd., Mississauga, ON L5J 3B3 (416)823-2133.
Type of Production and Credits: TV Film-W; TV Video-Wr.
Genres: Drama-TV; Comedy-TV; Documentary-TV; Industrial-TV.
Biography: Born 1933, Brampton, Ontario. B.S., Columbia Univesity, 58; M.S., Graduate School of Business, Columbia University, 59. Professional actor since 60; New York 60-67, Los Angeles 67-72, Toronto 72-88; began writing for radio in 74, for TV in 75; stage play *Two Below* produced in 78; translated and produced in French in Quebec, 84. CBC-TV film *The Dawson Patrol* sold to over 40 countries. Has written 33 radio shows for CBC.
Selected Filmography: "The Art of Good Merchandising" (8 eps), In, 88, CDN, Wr/Host; "Store Security" (2 eps), In, 87, CDN, Wr; "Uniform Code Council" (3 eps), In, 86-87, CDN, Wr/Host; *The Dawson Patrol*, TV, 76, CDN, Wr/Act; *Fort Whoop-Up* (True North Special), TV, 75, CDN, Wr.

ROBINSON, John Mark
- see DIRECTORS

RODGERS, Bob
- see PRODUCERS

ROGAN, N. (Bert)
1330 Hornby St., #305, Vancouver, BC V6Z 1W5 (604)688-6500.
Type of Production and Credits: Th Film-Wr; Th Short-Wr/Prod/Dir.
Genres: Drama-Th&TV; Documentary-TV; Industrial-Th&TV.
Biography: Born in 1942 in Bucharest, Romania; Canadian citizenship. Bachelor of Arts, Journalism, Ryerson Polytechnical Institute, Toronto. President of Bert Rogan Associates Inc.; specializing in high-end corporate projects. Has written three theatrical screenplays: *Albatross*, *Yellowhead*, and *Phoenix*; TV series, "Waterfront." Recipient of two US film festival awards and three IABC Awards for corporate film projects. Former reporter with CBC-TV and *Vancouver Sun*.
Selected Filmography: *A Question of Practice*, In, 88, CDN, Wr/Dir/Prod; *Wilderness Photographer*, In, 87, CDN, Wr; *A Bridge to Tomorrow*, In, 86, CDN, Wr; "BCTel News Magazines" (7 eps), In, 85-86, CDN, Wr/Dir/Prod; *DMS: It's Magic*, In, 86, CDN, Wr/Dir/Prod.

ROGERS, Al◇
WGAw. (818)762-9161.
Type of Production and Credits: TV Film-Wr/Prod; TV Video-Wr/Prod.
Genres: Comedy-TV; Variety-TV; Action-TV; Children's-Th&TV.
Biography: Born 1936, North Sydney, Nova Scotia. Has worked on development projects, 87-88.
Selected Filmography: "The Comedy Factory" (8 eps), TV, 85, USA, Prod/Wr; "After School Special", TV, 84, USA, Prod/Wr; "Stockard Channing Show"/ "Just Friends" (26 eps), TV, 83, USA, Prod/Co-Wr; *Superstunt*, TV, 82, USA, Prod/Wr; "John Denver Special" (6 eps), TV, 80-82, USA, Prod/Wr (EMMY); *Frank Sinatra Special*, TV, 80, USA, Wr; *Adventures of a Young Magician in China*, TV, 80, USA, Prod/Wr; "Father O'Father" (2 eps), TV, 79, USA, Prod/Wr.

ROMANOFF, Sergei
Hollywood North Productions, 151 Cypress Crt., Saskatoon, SK S7K 5C3 (306)934-1958. Marion Mills Casting, 1406 Acadia Dr., Saskatoon, SK (306)955-2558.
Type of Production and Credits: TV Video-Dir/Prod.
Genres: Documentary-TV; Educational-TV; Commercials-TV; Music Video-TV.
Biography: Born 1953, Toronto, Ontario. Languages: English, French, Ukrainian, Russian. Has directed more than 1,000 TV commercials; musician.
Selected Filmography: "Every Child a Star" (6 eps), TV, 91, CDN, Prod/Dir; *GST YUK*, "The Licence Plate They Wouldn't Allow", Cm, 91, CDN, Wr/Prod/Dir; *Frontier Mike's Boomtown Christmas*, TV, 90, CDN, Prod/Dir; *Peek-A-Boo Glasses*, International, Cm, 89, CDN, Wr/Prod/Dir; *Henry & Henry*, Fuddruckers (3 cm), Cm, 89, CDN, Wr/Prod/Dir; *U.F.O.s: Facing the Contradictions*, ED, 88, CDN, Prod/Dir/Narr; *Be Fit, Be Fun* Learning Disabilities Assoc. of Canada, ED, 88, CDN, Dir/Prod/Narr; *AIDS: It's Your Choice*, Saskatchewan Catholic Board of Ed, ED, 88, CDN, Prod/Dir; *Ship's Comin' In*, Trevor Dandy, MV, 87, CDN/USA, Prod/Dir.

ROONEY, Edward
- see PRODUCERS

ROSE, Hubert-Yves
- voir REALISATEURS

ROSEMOND, Perry
- see DIRECTORS

ROTHBERG, David◇
(416)536-2874.
Type of Production and Credits: Th Film-Wr; Th Short-Act; TV Film-Wr.
Genres: Drama-Th; Documentary-Th&TV.
Biography: Born 1950, Montreal, Quebec. Worked at CityTV, CBC; performed on the stage. *My Friend Vince* won Best Picture, University of Knoxville Film Festival and was shown at Museum of Modern Art.
Selected Filmography: *Best Revenge*, Th, 80, CDN, Story/Co-Wr; *My Friend Vince*, Th, 75, CDN, Wr/Prod/Dir.

ROWE, Peter
- see DIRECTORS

ROY, Robert L.M.
- see DIRECTORS

ROZEMA, Patricia
- see DIRECTORS

RUBBO, Michael
ACTRA. 719 de l'Epée, Outremont, PQ H2V 3V1 (514)276-1190.
Type of Production and Credits: Th Film-Wr/Dir.
Genres: Drama-Th; Documentary-TV.
Biography: Born 1938, Melbourne, Australia. Studied Anthropology, Sydney University; Film, Stanford University (M.A.). Worked at NFB, 65-84; 30 documentaries which won over 60 prizes. Taught at Australian Film and TV School and Harvard University as visiting Professor of Film. Has written and

directed 3 features with Rock Demers: *The Peanut Butter Solution, Tommy Tricker and the Stamp Traveller, Vincent and Me*; these films won 25 awards.
Selected Filmography: *Vincent and Me*, Th, 89, CDN, Wr/Dir; *Tommy Tricker and the Stamp Traveller*, Th, 88, CDN/RC, Wr/Dir; *The Peanut Butter Solution*, Th, 86, CDN, Dir/Wr; *Daisy: Story of a Facelift*, TV, 80, CDN, Wr/Dir/Ed; *Solzhenitsyn's Children..Are Making a Lot of Noise in Paris*, TV, 78, CDN, Dir/Wr/Ed; *Waiting for Fidel*, TV, 73, CDN, Dir/Wr/Ed; *Wet Earth and Warm People*, TV, 71, CDN, Dir/Wr/Ed; *Sad Song of Yellow Skin*, TV, 69, CDN, Wr/Dir.

RUEL, Francine
SARDEC, CAPAC, UDA. 4072, Laval, Montréal, PQ H2W 2J3 (514)845-1000.
Types de production et générique: 1 métrage-Sc; TV film-Sc; TV vidéo-Sc.
Types d'oeuvres: Drame-C&TV; Comédie-C&TV; Variété-C&TV; Enfants-C&TV; Educational-C&TV.
Curriculum vitae: Née en 1948, Québec. Conservatoire d'art dramatique, 66-69; boursière en Europe, 69-70. Comédienne et écrivaine pour le théâtre. *La Dernière y restera* gagne un prix de l'Institut québécois du cinéma et de Radio-Québec, 81.
Filmographie sélective: *Porte de Secours*, TV, 90, CDN, Sc/Dial; "Manon", TV, 85-87, CDN, Sc; *Un chemin perdu d'avance*, TV, 82, CDN, Co sc; *La Dernière y restara*, C, 81, CDN, Sc/Dial; *Fermer l'oeil de la nuit*, TV, 81, CDN, Sc; *De l'autre côté du miroir*, TV, 77, CDN, Sc.

RUSSELL, Paul
ACTRA, ACCT. 460 Palmerston Blvd., Toronto, ON M6G 2P1 (416)534-8115.
Type of Production and Credits: TV Film-Wr/Prod; TV Video-Wr/Prod.
Genres: Documentary-TV; Educational-TV; Children's-TV.
Biography: Born 1945, Toronto, Ontario. B.A., M.A., University of Toronto. Following art studies in England, held administrative and curatorial positions at Hart House and the Art Gallery of Ontario; critic, journalist: *Maclean's, Toronto Life, Toronto Star, Time*; has published several books on Canada, including *Queen on Moose Handbook*, 85; national adjudicator, "Reach for the Top," 82-91. New York Film & Television Festival award for *Stress*, 81; Emmy nomination for "Untamed World," 76.
Selected Filmography: "Reach for the Top", TV, 85-91, CDN, Wr/Assoc Prod; "Medical Malpractice II" (4 eps), In, 82-83, CDN/USA, Wr/Dir; "Primary Nursing" (12 eps), In, 82-83, CDN, Wr/Dir; *Stress* (10 films), In, 81, CDN/USA, Prod/Dir; *Fitness and Lifestyle* (6 films), In, 81, CDN/USA, Prod/Dir; "Medical Malpractice" (6 eps), In, 80, CDN, Dir/Wr; *The Maya, Children of Time*, TV, 80, CDN/MEX, Wr/Dir; "Dentistry" (6 eps), In, 79, CDN, Wr/Prod; "Trivia" (52 eps), TV, 77, CDN, Assoc Prod; "Lorne Greene's Last of the Wild" (16 eps), TV, 76, CDN/USA, Wr; "Untamed Frontier" (13 eps), TV, 76, CDN, Wr; "Untamed World" (78 eps), TV, 74-76, CDN/USA, Prod/Wr; "Behind the Scenes" (26 eps), TV, 75, CDN, Story Ed; *Elements of the Unknown: The Sea*, TV, 74, CDN, Wr; "Images of Canada" (6 eps), TV, 72-74, CDN, Wr/Story Ed.

RUTHERFORD, John T.
140 Stibbard Ave., Toronto, ON M4P 2C3 (416)488-3028.
Type of Production and Credits: TV Film-Wr/Dir/Prod; TV Video-Wr/Dir/Prod.
Genres: Documentary-TV; Current Affairs-TV; News-TV.
Biography: Born 1930, Chatham, Ontario. Television and radio producer in CBC Washington, D.C., bureau for 6 years; writer, researcher, director for CBC-TV news specials and series; currently on contract as director of patient education videos for the Faculty of Medicine, University of Toronto.
Selected Filmography: "Patient Education Videos", U. of T. (15 eps), TV, 89-90, CDN, Dir; "The Journal" (1 eps), TV, 82, CDN, Dir; *Tito Obituary, Jules Leger Obituary*, "CBC News, TV, 80, CDN, Prod; *Canals and Tunnels, Central Power*, "The Nature of, TV, 68, CDN, Wr; "Man at the Centre" (1 eps), TV, 68, CDN, Dir; "Man at the Centre" (1 eps), TV, 67, CDN, Wr.

RUVINSKY, Morrie
WGA. 520 Strand, Santa Monica, CA (213)392-2726. Quintillion Productions, P.O. Box 5075, Santa Monica, CA 90409-5079 (213)339-5678. Stu Robinson/Robinson, Weintraub, 8428 Melrose Place, Los Angeles, CA 90024 (213)653-5802.
Type of Production and Credits: Th Film-Wr/Prod/Dir; Th Short-Wr/Dir; TV Film-Wr/Prod; TV Video-Wr/Prod.
Genres: Drama-Th&TV; Comedy-Th&TV; Action-Th&TV; Science Fiction-Th&TV.
Biography: Born in Montreal, Quebec.

Canadian citizen. Undergraduate studies at McGill University. Graduate studies at the University of British Columbia and McGill. Taught English and Film at McGill and Concordia. Awards include the Berlin Film Festival, Edinburgh Film Festival, Canada Council and the Shaar Gold Medal in Photography.
Selected Filmography: "The Dick Van Dyke Show" (1 eps), TV, 89, USA, Wr; "Misfits of Science" (17 eps), TV, 86, USA, Wr/Prod; *Rainy Days, Rainy Nights*, Th, 83, USA, Wr; *Improper Channels*, Th, 80, CDN, Wr/Prod; *The Finishing Touch*, Th, 72, CDN, Wr/Dir; *T Women in Film*, TV, 72, CDN, Dir;*he Plastic Mile*, Th, 71, CDN, Wr/Dir; *What If You Threw A War*, Th, 70, CDN, Wr/Dir.

RYAN, Keith
WGC (ACTRA). P.O. Box 3369, Salmon Arm, BC V1E 4S2 (604)832-3418. Gail E. Ross, 1666 Connecticut Ave. N.W., Ste. 501, Washington, DC 20009 (202)328-1666 (U.S. only).
Type of Production and Credits: Th Film-Wr; TV Video-Wr.
Genres: Drama-Th&TV; Comedy-Th&TV.
Biography: Canadian citizen who has lived and worked in the U.S. for far too long.
Selected Filmography: "21 Jump Street" (1 eps), TV, 89, USA, Wr; "The Medical Man" (3 eps), TV, 88, USA, Wr/Creat; "Against the Wind" (3 eps), TV, 88, USA, Wr/Creat; "Magnum P.I." (1 eps), TV, 86, USA, Wr; "Cheers" (1 eps), TV, 83, USA, Wr; *Brothers*, Th, 82, USA, Wr; *Wonder Where the Lions Are*, Th, 81, USA, Wr.

RYLSKI, Nika◆
ACTRA. (416)699-4209.
Type of Production and Credits: Th Film-Wr; Th Short-Wr; TV Film-Wr; TV Video-Wr.
Genres: Drama-Th&TV; Comedy-TV; Documentary-TV; Children's-TV.
Biography: Born in Buenos Aires, Argentina; Canadian citizenship. Languages: English, French, Spanish, Polish. Honours B.A., Political Science, Carleton University. Has written more than 25 radio, TV and film scripts; has also written stage plays. Winner, Eric Harvey Award for Best New Canadian Musical, 82; *Honor Thy Father* won Best TV Drama Award, Yorkton.
Selected Filmography: *Be My Guest*, TV, 87, CDN, Wr; "Prescriptions for Health" (6 eps), TV, 87, CDN, Wr; *Man of Iron*, TV, 83, CDN, Wr; "Nuggets" (3 eps) (pilot), TV, 80, CDN, Wr; *Strangers*, Th, 77, CDN, Wr; *Honor Thy Father*, TV, 76, CDN, Wr; *Summers' Mournings*, TV, 75, CDN, T'play; *Thanks for the Ride*, TV, 75, CDN, T'play; *Last of the Four-Letter Words*, TV, 74, CDN, Wr; *When the Bough Breaks*, TV, 70, CDN, Wr; *The Fastest Wordslinger in the East*, TV, 69, CDN, Wr.

SABOURIN, Marcel
ACTRA, SARDEC, UDA. 224, Richelieu, Beloeil, PQ J3G 4P1 (514)467-3009. FAX: 464-3879.
Types de production et générique: l métrage-Sc/Com; TV film-Com; TV vidéo-Sc/Com.
Types d'oeuvres: Drame-C&TV; Comédie-C&TV; Enfants-C&TV; Animation-C&TV.
Curriculum vitae: Né en 1935, Montréal, Québec. Etudes au Collège Ste-Marie; au Théâtre du Nouveau Monde avec Bill Greaves; à Paris avec Jacques Lecoq. Fait beaucoup de théâtre comme comédien et comme auteur. Professeur d'improvisation pendant 12 ans à l'Ecole Nationale de Théâtre du Canada. Coach à la Ligue Nationale d'Improvisation pour l'équipe des jeunes, 86-91. Donne des cours de scénarisation, a L'Université du Québec à Chicoutimi, à Parlimage, et à Main Films. Parolier d'une trentaine de chansons de Robert Charlebois et Louise Forestier. Gagne le Prix Chalmers pour sa pièce *Pleurer Pour Rire*. *J.A. Martin Photographe* gagne 7 prix aux Palmarès du Film Canadien, dont le meilleur film, et 2 prix à Cannes, dont le prestigieux Prix Oecuménique.
Filmographie sélective: *Le Fabuleux Voyage de l'Ange*, C, 90, CDN, Com; *The Peggy*, TV, 90, CDN, Com; *Il était une fois*, *Les Filles de Caleb*", TV, 90, CDN, Sc/Anim; "C'est la vie" (45 eps), TV, 88-90, CDN, Co sc/Anim; "L'Amour avec un Grand A", TV, 85-88, CDN, Com, (GEMEAUX); *Bach et Bottine*, C, 85, CDN, Cons sc; "Duplessis" (5 eps), TV, 77, CDN, Com; *J.A. Martin Photographe*, C, 76, CDN, Co sc/Com; *Des Armes et Les Hommes*, C, 73, CDN, Com; *Les Cuisines*, TV, 71, CDN, Sc/Com; *La Maudite Galette*, C, 71, CDN, Com; *Le Temps d'une Chasse*, C, 71, CDN, Com; *Eliza's Horoscope*, TV, 70, CDN, Com; "La Ribouldingue" (75 eps), TV, 67, CDN, Sc/Com; *Il ne faut pas mourir pour ça*, C, 66, CDN, Co sc/Com.

SADLER, Richard
- see PRODUCERS

ST-PIERRE, Leopold
72, Somerville, Westmount, PQ H3Z 1J5

(514)482-8891. Les Productions Prisma Inc., 5253, ave. du Parc, #330, Montréal, PQ H2V 4P2 (514)277-6686.
Types de production et générique: 1 métrage-Sc/Prod; TV vidéo-Sc/Prod.
Types d'oeuvres: Drame-TV; Comédie-C&TV; Action-TV; Enfants-TV.
Curriculum vitae: Né à Montréal, Québec. Citoyenneté canadienne. Langues: anglais, français. M.A. (maîtrise) en Film et Communications, Université McGill. Scénariste (3 ans) "All My Children", ABC-TV; "General Hospital", ABC-TV/Scénariste/Producteur Créatif (4 1/2 ans), "La Maison Dechenes", TQS, 1500 épisodes en télévision et plus que j'ai écrits ont été produits. Scénariste, Producteur et Réalisateur *The Modern Man*.
Filmographie sélective: "La Maison Deschenes" (400 eps), TV, 87-90, CDN, Sc/Prod créatif; "General Hospital" (25 eps), TV, 82-83, USA, Sc; "All My Children" (120 eps), TV, 81-82, USA, Sc; *The Modern Man*, Th, 76, CDN, Sc/Prod/Réal.

SALEM, Rob
ACTRA. 59 Beech Ave., Toronto, ON M4E 3H3 (416)699-0393. Toronto Star, 1 Yonge St., Toronto, ON M5E 1E6 (416)869-4195. Four Horsemen Productions, 82 Albany Ave., Toronto, ON M5R 3C3 (416)539-9311.
Type of Production and Credits: Th Film-Wr; TV Video-Wr.
Genres: Comedy-TV; Science Fiction-Th; Horror-Th; Current Affairs-TV.
Biography: Born 1958, Toronto, Ontario. Stand-up comic, Second City workshops, "SCTV" extra, 76-81. Started at *Toronto Star*, 77, writing for entertainment dept.: movie reviews, feature interviews, video columnist, co-editor "What's On" section; Writer/host, "Captain Video Show" (pilot, 85); reporter/writing consultant for CBC's "The Revue," 86; TV critic, CBC Radio, "Prime Time," 88-89; Editor, video & home entertainment magazine, 89; Co-Host/Writer, "Video Preview" (syndicated radio show), 90; movie/video specialist, Citytv, "Breakfast Television," 90-91; movie/gossip specialist, Citytv, "Cityline," 90-91; host/writer, "Please Stand By" (pilot), 91.
Selected Filmography: *Hellvis*, Th, 91, CDN, Wr; "Please Stand By" (pilot), TV, 91, CDN, Head Wr/Host.

SALTSMAN, Terry
ACTRA. 35 Elderwood Dr., Toronto, ON M5P 1W8 (416)484-6127. Lynn Kinney, Credentials, 387 Bloor St. E., Toronto, ON M4Y 1H7 (416)926-1507.
Type of Production and Credits: TV Video-Wr/Prod/Story Ed; TV Film-Wr/Prod/Story Ed.
Genres: Comedy-TV; Variety-TV; Action-TV.
Biography: Born 1951, Toronto, Ontario. B.A., English, York University, 72; LL.B., Osgoode Hall Law School, 75. Has written humour column for *Ontario Lawyers Weekly*; worked as advertising copy writer, legal editor; writer/producer, comedy, industrial videos.
Selected Filmography: "Dog House" (1 eps), TV, 90-91, CDN/USA, Wr; "My Secret Identity" (1 eps), TV, 90-91, CDN/USA, Wr; *1990 Gemini Awards*, TV, 90, CDN, Wr; "Spatz" (13 eps), TV, 89-90, CDN/GB, Exec Story Ed; "Spatz" (3 eps), TV, 89-90, CDN/GB, Wr; *Micki Bear Christmas Show*, TV, 89, CDN, Wr; "In Opposition" (3 eps), TV, 89, CDN, Wr; "Mosquito Lake" (1 eps), TV, 89, CDN, Wr; "Starting from Scratch" (5 eps), TV, 88-89, CDN/USA, Wr/Story Ed; "Learning the Ropes" (6 eps)(Story Ed 18 eps), TV, 88-89, CDN/USA, Wr; "Check It Out!" (3 eps), TV, 87-88, CDN/USA, Wr; "Hangin' In" (21 eps), TV, 84-87, CDN, Wr; "Thrill of a Lifetime" (20 eps), TV, 84, CDN, Story Ed.

SALTZMAN, Deepa Mehta
- see DIRECTORS

SALUTIN, Rick
ACTRA. 350 Markham St., Toronto, ON M6G 2K9
Type of Production and Credits: TV Film-Wr; TV Video-Wr.
Genres: Drama-TV.
Biography: Born 1942, Toronto, Ontario. B.A., Brandeis University; M.A., Columbia University. Chalmers Award (Theatre) for *Les Canadiens*; former chairman, Guild of Canadian Playwrights; novel, *A Man of Little Faith* published by McClelland & Stewart, 88.
Selected Filmography: *Grierson and Gouzenko*, "Some Honourable Gentlemen", TV, 85, CDN, Wr; *Maria*, "Here to Stay", TV, 75, CDN, Wr; "Festival", TV, 74, CDN, Wr.

SAMUELS, Barbara
ACTRA. RR #2, Uxbridge, ON L0C 1K0 (416)852-4030.
Type of Production and Credits: TV Film-Wr/Exec Story Ed.
Genres: Drama-TV; Commercials-TV.
Biography: Montreal native. Began work in feature film and commercial production in 1979, first as a technician and later as a writer and director. Brief experience as an

industry journalist, and several years spent as co-creator and co-director of "Convergence; An International Forum on the Moving Image", a biennial conference that examined the impact of new visual technologies on the motion picture and television industry. Currently involved, with partner Wayne Grigsby, in an exclusive development deal with Alliance Communications to write and produce series, mini-series, features and MOWs.
Selected Filmography: "E.N.G" (44 eps), TV, 89-91, CDN/USA, Exec Story Ed; "ENG" (10 eps), TV, 89-91, CDN/USA, Wr; "The Jim Henson Hour" (9 eps), TV, 88-89, USA, Wr; "Diamonds" (1 ep), TV, 89, USA/CDN/F, Wr; "Mont Royal" (4 eps), TV, 87-88, CDN/F, Wr; *La Rivière*, TV, 87, CDN, Wr/Dir.

SANDOR, Anna
WGA, WGC, ATAS. Steve Weiss, William Morris Agency, 151 El Camino Dr., Beverly Hills, CA 90212 USA (213)859-4423. Adam Berkowitz, William Morris Agency, 1350 Ave. of the Americas, New York, NY 10019 USA (212)903-1153.
Type of Production and Credits: Th Film-Wr; TV Film-Wr/Prod; TV Video-Wr.
Genres: Drama-Th&TV; Comedy-Th&TV; Children's-TV.
Biography: Born Budapest, Hungary; came to Canada, 57; Canadian citizenship. Languages: English, Hungarian, some French and German. B.A., Theatre and English, University of Windsor. Began career as stage and TV actress; started writing, 75; over 50 produced TV scripts; lectures on television and screenwriting; co-chairperson, Crime Writers of Canada, 85-86. Winner of numerous international awards. Has lived in Los Angeles since 89.
Selected Filmography: *Miss Rose White*, "Hallmark Hall of Fame", TV, 91, USA, Wr; *Stolen, One Husband*, TV, 90, USA, Wr; *Tarzan in Manhattan*, TV, 89, USA, Wr; *Two Men*, TV, 88, CDN, Wr; *Mama's Going to Buy You a Mockingbird*, TV, 88, CDN, Wr; "Danger Bay" (4 eps), TV, 86-87, CDN, Wr; *Martha, Ruth & Edie*, Th, 87, CDN, Co-Wr; *The Marriage Bed*, TV, 86, CDN, Wr; "Seeing Things" (9 eps), TV, 83-86, CDN, Co-Wr; "Hangin' In", TV, 80-86, CDN, Co-Creator; *Charlie Grant's War*, TV, 85, CDN, Wr, (ACTRA); *Running Man/High Card*, "For the Record", TV, 81-82, CDN, Wr; "King of Kensington" (30 eps), TV, 75-80, CDN, Head Wr; *A Population of One*, TV, 79, CDN, Wr.

SAPERGIA, Barbara
ACTRA. 48 Moxon Cres., Saskatoon, SK S7H 3B9 (306)955-1912.
Type of Production and Credits: TV Video-Wr.
Genres: Drama-TV; Comedy-TV; Variety-TV.
Biography: Born in 1943, Moose Jaw, Saskatchewan. B.A., History, University of Saskatchewan; M.A., English Literature, University of Manitoba. Writes drama for stage, radio, television and film; 7 professional stage productions - 4 adult shows and 3 for children; has published a novel, *The Foreigners*.
Selected Filmography: *Midnight in Moose Jaw*, TV, 88, CDN, Co-Wr; *Any Farmers Left?*, "The Way We Are", TV, 84, CDN, Wr.

SARNER, Arlene
WGAw. 429 S. Linden Dr., Beverly Hills, CA 90212 (213)286-7200. Pedevex Productions, 9171 Wilshire Blvd., Ste. 500, Beverly Hills, CA 90210. CAA, 9830 Wilshire Blvd., Beverly Hills, CA 90212 (213)288-4545.
Type of Production and Credits: Th Film-Wr; TV Film-Wr; TV Video-Wr.
Genres: Drama-Th&TV; Comedy-Th&TV; Variety-TV.
Biography: Born in Winnipeg, Manitoba. Canadian citizen. Won the Writers' Guild award for Best Variety Special for *Warner Bros. Presents The Earth Day Special*.
Selected Filmography: *Warner Bros. Presents The Earth Day Special*, TV, 90, USA, Co-Wr; *Blue Sky*, Th, 90, USA, Co-Wr; *Peggy Sue Got Married*, Th, 86, USA, Co-Wr.

SAUL, Donaleen
WGC (ACTRA). 563 Kildonan Rd., West Vancouver, BC V7S 1X4 (604)925-9083. Charles Northcote, The Core Group, 501 - 489 College St., Toronto, ON M6G 1A5 (416)944-0193.
Type of Production and Credits: Th Short-Wr; TV Film-Wr; TV Video-Wr.
Genres: Drama-Th&TV; Documentary-Th&TV; Educational-Th&TV; Children's-Th&TV.
Biography: Born in 1947. Works freelance. Has written for film, video, radio, print and audio/visual. Story editor for "Danger Bay", season 5. Has been awarded AMPIA award for writing.
Selected Filmography: "Kidzone" (13 eps), TV, 90, CDN, Wr; *Baby Pinsky*, "Inside Stories", TV, 90, CDN, Story Ed; *AIDS - It's Time To Talk*, Th/TV, 89, CDN, Wr; "Danger Bay" (26 eps), TV, 88, CDN, Story Ed.

SAURIOL, Brigitte
- voir REALISATEURS

SAUVE, Alain
- voir MONTEURS SON

SAVATH, Philip
ACTRA, WGAw, ACCT. 2525 W. 13 Ave., Vancouver, BC V6K 2S9 (604)734-2935. FAX: 732-6001. Suzanne Depoe, Creative Technique, (416)466-4173.
Type of Production and Credits: Th Film-Wr; TV Film-Wr; TV Video-Wr/Prod.
Genres: Drama-Th&TV; Comedy-Th&TV; Variety-TV; Children's-TV.
Biography: Born 1946, Brooklyn, New York; immigrated to Canada, 69. Honours B.A., Theatre, State University of New York, 68. Broadway debut at age 15; founding Director of Homemade Theatre, Toronto; co-creator, Improvisation Olympics; member, Caravan Stage Co.; A&M recording artist with Homemade Theatre; director, Snack Bar Film Corporation, Vancouver; story consultant, guest professional, Praxis Film Development Workshop.
Selected Filmography: "Freedom Ranch" (pilot), TV, 91, CDN/USA/F, Wr/Co-Creator; "Max Glick" (26 eps), TV, 90, CDN, Wr/Prod/Co-Creator; "Comedy Collge" (16 eps), TV, 87-88, CDN, Wr/Prod; *The Outside Chance of Maximilian Glick*, Th, 87, CDN, Scr; "Switchback" (56 eps), TV, 83-86, CDN, Prod/Wr; *Bailey's Law*, TV, 85, CDN, Wr; *Samuel Lount*, Th, 84, CDN, Co-Wr; "Vancouver" (15 wk), TV, 83-84, CDN, Prod; *Sleepless Nights*, TV, 84, CDN, Wr/Prod; *Summer Madness*, TV, 84, CDN, Prod; *Holocaust Remembered*, TV, 84, CDN/Wr/Prod; *High School Confidential*, TV, 84, CDN, Prod; *Wanna Have Fun*, TV, 84, CDN, Prod; "Carroll Baker's Jamboree" (6 eps), TV, 82-83, CDN, Co-Wr; "Paul Anka Show" (24 eps), TV, 82-83, CDN, Co-Wr.

SCAINI, Stefan
- see DIRECTORS

SCANLON, Kevin◊
(416)535-3708.
Type of Production and Credits: TV Film-Wr.
Genres: Drama-TV.
Biography: Born 1949, Cork, Ireland; Canadian citizenship. Has worked as journalist for 20 years.
Selected Filmography: *Midnight in Morocco*, "Adderly" (1 eps), TV, 87, CDN, Co-Wr.

SCARFF, Clive
- see DIRECTORS

SCHADT, Christa
ACFC, LIFT. 39 Sullivan St., Toronto, ON M5T 1B8 (416)597-8619.
Type of Production and Credits: Th Short-Wr/Dir/Prod/Ed.
Genres: Documentary-Th; Experimental-Th.
Biography: Born,1957, Toronto, Ontario. Graduated from the Ontario College of Art in 1981, majored in film, video and sound. Member, Charles Street Video and Trinity Square Video. Has worked in the feature film industry since 1984.
Selected Filmography: *What Television Teaches*, Th, 89, CDN, Wr/Dir/Prod/Ed; *One Man's Illusion is Another Man's Truth*, Th, 86, CDN, Wr/Dir/Prod/Ed; *Thoughts that Breathe Through Birds of Passage*, Th, 84, CDN, Wr/Dir/Prod/Ed; *Perceptual Defence*, Th, 82, CDN, Wr/Dir/Prod/Ed; *Rites of Love*, Th, 82, CDN, Wr/Dir/Prod/Ed; *And Now This...*, Th, 82, CDN, Wr/Dir/Prod/Ed; *Appropriated Love*, Th, 82, CDN, Wr/Dir/Prod/Ed; *Constancy Phenomenon*, Th, 81, CDN, Wr/Dir/Prod/Ed; *Stand By Your Man*, Th, 81, CDN, Wr/Dir/Prod/Ed; *Just Push a Button*, Th, 81, CDN, Wr/Dir/Prod/Ed; *Purple*, Th, 80, CDN, Wr/Dir/Prod/Ed.

SCHECHTER, Rebecca
ACTRA, ACCT. 11 Ashby Place, Toronto, ON M5A 3E3 (416)368-3829. Krisztina Bevilacqua, 85 Roosevelt Rd., Toronto, ON M4J 4T8 (416)463-7009.
Type of Production and Credits: TV Film-Wr.
Genres: Drama-Th&TV; Documentary-TV; Educational-TV.
Biography: Born 1951, Newark, New Jersey; Canadian citizenship, 75. Attended University of Chicago, 68-69; B.A., Social Sciences, York University, 75.
Selected Filmography: "Street Legal" (7 eps), TV, 88-91, CDN, Wr; *Traitors All*, "E.N.G.", TV, 90, CDN, Wr; *Bodyguard*, TV, 89, CDN, Wr; *Taking Care*, Th, 86, CDN, Wr; *Pulling Flowers*, TV, 85, CDN, Co-Wr; *Never Too Young*, "Everybody's Children", ED, 83, CDN, Wr; *Signals, Sounds and Making Sense*, "Everybody's Children", ED, 80, CDN, Wr; *Changing Limits*, "Everybody's Children", ED, 80, CDN, Wr.

SCHERBERGER, Aiken M.
- see DIRECTORS

SCHUURMAN, Hubert
- see DIRECTORS

SCOTT, Desmond
ACTRA. 32 Belcourt Rd., Toronto, ON M4S 2T9 (416)448-9408. Premier Artists Management, 232-C Gerrard St. E.,

Toronto, ON M5A 2E8 (416)929-9922.
Type of Production and Credits: TV Film-Wr; TV Video-Wr.
Genres: Drama-TV; Documentary-TV; Educational-TV.
Biography: Born 1926, London, England; Canadian citizenship. Languages: English, French, some German. M.A., Cambridge University; attended Old Vic Theatre School, London. Director, Manitoba Theatre Centre, 59-63; writer, director, actor. Teacher, National Theatre School, many universities in Canada and USA. Sculptor, several one-man shows.
Selected Filmography: "Ancient Civilizations" (2 eps), TV, 90, CDN, Wr; *Like No Other Place*, TV, 78, CDN, Wr; *Everybody's Children*, TV, 78, CDN, Wr; "Police Surgeon" (1 eps), TV, 71, CDN/USA, Wr; *Three Sisters*, TV, 59, CDN, T'play; *A Cure for the Doctor*, TV, 58, CDN, Wr; *The Cocktail Party*, TV, 58, CDN, Wr.

SCOTT, Munroe
ACTRA. R.R. #1, Fenelon Falls, ON K0M 1N0 (705)454-8773.
Type of Production and Credits: Th Film-Wr; TV Film-Wr/Dir; TV Video-Wr.
Genres: Drama-TV; Documentary-Th&TV.
Biography: Born 1927, Owen Sound, Ontario. B.A., Queen's University; M.A., Cornell University (playwriting major). Has written 2 books and a stage play about Dr. Robert McClure; worte *The Sound and Light Show* (Ottawa parliament); has worked on many educational films and documentaries. Written films that have won more than 20 national and international awards, including a Special Jury Award, Canadian Film Awards; 3 Blue Ribbons, American Film Festival; Gold Medal, Sport Film Festival, Cortina, Italy.
Selected Filmography: "The Killing Zone", TV, 88, CDN, Wr; *The Spirit People*, TV, 86, CDN, Wr; *Land of the Mountain Elephant*, TV, 84, CDN, Wr; *Sixteen Days to Timbuktu*, TV, 83, CDN, Wr; *My People Are Dying*, TV, 80, CDN, Wr; "One Canadian" (The Diefenbaker Memoirs) (13 eps), TV, 75, CDN, Dir/Wr; "First Person Singular" (The Pearson Memoirs) (13 eps), TV, 73, CDN, Dir/Wr; "The Tenth Decade" (The Diefenbaker-Pearson Years) (5 eps), TV, 71, CDN, Dir/Wr; *Inside Out*, Th, 70, CDN, Wr.

SCOTT, T.J.
- see DIRECTORS

SECRETAN-COX, Michael
- see DIRECTORS

SEDAWIE, Gayle Gibson
- see PRODUCERS

SEDAWIE, Norman
- see PRODUCERS

SEGAL, Matthew◊
ACTRA, ACCT. (416)536-2000.
Type of Production and Credits: Th Film-Wr; Th Short-Wr; TV Film-Wr; TV Video-Wr.
Genres: Drama-Th&TV; Comedy-TV; Action-TV; Science Fiction-TV.
Biography: Born 1943, Welland, Ontario. Studied Architecture, UBC. Actor, Assistant set designer at the original Theatre Passe Muraille. Story and script editor, CBC-TV drama, CTV, Twentieth Century Fox program development; co-wrote several specials, CBC Variety, 76. Teaches scriptwriting at Sheridan College.
Selected Filmography: *Forgiving Harry*, "Inside Stories" (1 eps), TV, 88, CDN, Wr; "The Campbells" (1 eps), TV, 86, CDN/USA/GB, Wr; "The Phoenix Team" (1 eps), TV, 80, CDN, Story; "The Collaborators" (1 eps), TV, 77, CDN, Wr; "The Starlost" (1 eps), TV, 74, CDN/USA, Story; *Foxy Lady*, Th, 70, CDN, Co-Wr; *Dulcima*, Th, 70, CDN, Wr.

SENECAL, Marguerite
- see PRODUCERS

SHAPIRO, Paul
- see DIRECTORS

SHEER, Tony
ACTRA. 151 Waverley Rd., Toronto, ON M4L 3T4 (416)690-0935. Troutcake Films Inc., 67 Lee Ave., 3rd Flr., Toronto, ON (416)699-0600. William Bateman, Nobbs, Woods & Clarke, 70 University Ave., Ste. 250, Toronto, ON M5J 2M4 (416)977-1000.
Type of Production and Credits: Th Film-Wr; TV Film-Wr.
Genres: Drama-Th&TV; Comedy-Th&TV; Action-Th&TV; Documentary-TV.
Biography: Born 1937, London, England; Canadian citizenship. Educated at Arnold School, England; trained as actor at London's E 15 Acting School. Worked as an actor in film, TV, stage in England for 3 years. Came to Canada, 71. Has written more than 60 dramas and documentaries.
Selected Filmography: *Life Lines*, Th, CDN, Wr; *Adderly with Eggroll*, "Adderly" (1 eps), TV, 87, CDN, Wr; "Race for the Bomb" (mini-series), TV, 86, CDN/F, Co-Wr; *Chinatown Underground*, TV, 86, USA, Co-Wr; *For Those I Loved* (also 6 eps, TV), Th, 83, CDN/F, Scr; *Final Edition*, "For the Record", TV, 82, CDN,

Wr, (ACTRA); *Maintain the Right*, "For the Record", TV, 80, CDN, Wr; "Fishtales" (13 eps), TV, 79, CDN, Wr; *The Fighting Men*, TV, 78, CDN, Wr, (ACTRA); *The October Crisis*, TV, 76, CDN, Wr; "Sidestreet" (6 eps), TV, 74-75, CDN, Wr; *The Man Inside*, TV, 75, CDN/USA, Wr; "Anthology" (8 eps), TV, 72-74, CDN, Wr; "The Collaborators" (5 eps), TV, 73-74, CDN, Wr.

SHEPPARD, John◊
ACTRA. (213)392-5902.
Type of Production and Credits: Th Film-Wr/Dir; TV Film-Wr/Dir.
Genres: Drama-Th&TV; Comedy-Th; Action-Th; Horror-Th.
Biography: Born 1956, Toronto, Ontario. B.A.A., Journalism, Ryerson Polytechnical Institute.
Selected Filmography: *Higher Education*, Th, 86, CDN, Scr/Dir; *Bullies*, Th, 85, CDN, Co-Wr; *High Stakes*, Th, 85, CDN, Co-Wr; "Mania" (4 eps) (Dir, 1 eps), TV, 85, CDN, Wr; *Flying*, Th, 84, CDN, Wr; *American Nightmare*, Th, 82, CDN, Wr.

SHULMAN, Guy
WGAw. 9948 Robbins Dr., Beverly Hills, CA 90212 (213)282-8120. Robinson, Weintraub & Gross, 8428 Melrose Place, Los Angeles, CA 90069 USA (213)653-5802.
Type of Production and Credits: Th Film-Wr; TV Film-Wr.
Genres: Drama-Th&TV; Comedy-Th&TV; Action-Th&TV; Horror-Th&TV.
Biography: Born in 1945 in Canada. Canadian citizen with U.S. green card. Former psychologist.
Selected Filmography: *Jailbirds*, TV, 91, USA, Wr; "Full House" (12 eps), TV, 90-91, USA, Story Ed; *Return to Green Acres*, TV, 90, USA, Wr; "The Tracy Ullman Show" (3 eps), TV, 89, USA, Wr; "The Hitchhiker" (2 eps), TV, 89, CDN/USA/F, Wr; *All Dogs Go To Heaven*, Th, 88, IRL/USA, Story/Wr; *Separate Ways*, Th, 88, USA, Wr; *Ready-or-Not*, Th, 88, USA, Wr; *Driven*, TV, 88, USA, Wr; "Momma's Nuts" (pilot), TV, 88, USA, Wr/Creator; "The Bots" (30 eps), TV, 87, CDN/F, Wr; "Lady Loveylocks" (pilot), TV, 87, USA/F, Wr.

SIEGEL, Lionel E.
ACTRA, DGA, WGAw. Marty Shapiro, Shapiro-Lichtman, 8827 Beverly Blvd., Los Angeles, CA 90048 (213)859-8877.
Type of Production and Credits: Th Film-Wr; TV Film-Wr/Prod.
Genres: Drama-Th&TV.
Biography: Born 1927, Chicago, Illinois; Canadian citizenship, 85. B.Journalism, University of Missouri. Has won 2 Western Heritage Awards, Best Western TV Scripts for episodes of *Simon* and *Rawhide*. Wrote bible for "Bordertown" series. Executive in charge of Project Development, Simcom, 87-88; Creative consultant, Astral Film Enterprises, Inc., 90-91.
Selected Filmography: "Counterstrike" (7 eps), TV, 90, CDN/USA/F, Spv Prod; "E.N.G." (1 eps), TV, 89, CDN/USA, Wr; "Bordertown" (26 eps)(Wr 2 eps), TV, 88-89, CDN, Prod; *Cold Comfort*, Th, 87-88, CDN, Adapt; *Hoover vs the Kennedys: The Second Civil War* (mini-series), TV, 87, CDN, Wr; "Night Heat" (1 eps), TV, 85, CDN/USA, Wr; "From Here to Eternity"(13 eps)(Wr 2 eps/Story Ed 3 eps), TV, 79, USA, Spv Prod; "Spiderman" (22 eps), TV, 78, USA, Prod; "The Bionic Woman" (22 eps)(Wr 2 eps), TV, 76-77, USA, Exec Prod; "The 6 Million Dollar Man"(57 eps)(Wr 4 eps/Story Ed 13 eps), TV, 75-77, USA, Prod; "The Ultimate Imposter" (1 eps), TV, 76, USA, Wr/Prod; "Exo-Man" (1 eps), TV, 76, USA, Wr/Prod; "Simon" (1 eps), TV, 75, USA, Wr; "Deadly Weekend" (1 eps), TV, 74, USA, Wr; "Kung Fu" (1 eps), TV, 70, USA, Wr.

SILVER, Jonny
- see DIRECTORS
SIMANDL, Lloyd
- see PRODUCERS
SIMONEAU, Guy
- voir REALISATEURS
SIMONEAU, Yves
- voir REALISATEURS
SINGER, Gail
- see DIRECTORS
SKERRETT, Bill
- see PRODUCERS
SKOGLAND, Kari
- see DIRECTORS
SKY, Laura
- see DIRECTORS
SLACK, Lyle
ACTRA. 2085 Gerrard St. E., Toronto, ON M4E 2B6 (416)693-1940. Charles Northcote, The Core Group, 489 College St., Toronto, ON M6G 1A5 (416)944-0193. Michael Van Dyck, The Agency, 10351 Santa Monica Blvd., Los Angeles, CA 90025 USA (213)551-3000.
Type of Production and Credits: TV Film-Wr.
Genres: Drama-TV; Comedy-TV; Action-TV.
Biography: Born in 1946 in Buffalo, NY. B.A. English Lit, Bloomsburg State College

(Pa.); M.A.T. Political Science, Allegheny College. High school teacher, 1968-72; advertising copywriter, 1972-75; drama and film critic, *The Hamilton Spectator*, 1975-85; freelance magazine writer (*Saturday Night, Chatelaine, TV Guide* etc.).
Selected Filmography: "The Adventures of the Black Stallion", TV, 91, CDN/USA/F, Wr; "Dog House", TV, 90, CDA/USA, Wr; "Danger Bay", TV, 89, CDN/USA, Wr; "Emergency Room", TV, 88, CDN, Wr; "T and T", TV, 87, CDN/USA, Wr; "Adderly", TV, 87, CDN/USA, Wr.

SLADE, Bernard◊
WGAw, ACCT. (213)274-7271.
Type of Production and Credits: Th Film-Wr; TV Film-Wr; TV Video-Wr.
Genres: Drama-Th&TV; Comedy-Th&TV.
Biography: Born 1930, Canada. Wrote 20 live and taped TV plays; moved to Los Angeles, 64; worked under contract at Columbia Pictures for 12 years; created 7 TV series, wrote over 100 episodes. Four plays produced on Broadway, *Same Time Next Year, Tribute, Romantic Comedy, Special Occasion*; in West End, London, including *Fatal Attraction; An Act of the Imagination* produced in 87, British tour; *Return Engagements* produced in 88, Westport Playhouse and tour. Has won Drama Desk Award; Tony, Oscar and WGA nominations.
Selected Filmography: *Moving Day*, "Trying Times" (1 eps), TV, 87, USA, Wr; *Romantic Comedy*, Th, 82, USA, Wr; *Tribute*, Th, 80, CDN, Scr; *Same Time Next Year*, Th, 78, USA, Wr; "Everything Money Can't Buy" (pilot), TV, 74, USA, Wr/Creator; "Bobby Sherman Show" (2 eps) (pilot), TV, 73, USA, Wr; "The Girl with Something Extra" (7 eps), TV, 72, USA, Creator/Wr; "Bridget Loves Bernie" (6 eps), TV, 71, USA, Creator/Wr; "Mr Deeds Goes to Town" (3 eps) (pilot), TV, 70, USA, Wr/Adapt; *Stand Up and Be Counted*, Th, 68, USA, Wr; "The Partridge Family" (14 eps), TV, 67, USA, Creator/Wr; "The Flying Nun" (12 eps), TV, 66, USA, Wr/Adapt; "Love on a Rooftop" (18 eps), TV, 65, USA, Creator/Story Ed/Wr; "Bewitched" (18 eps), TV, 64-65, USA, Wr/Story Ed.

SLIPP, Marke
- see EDITORS

SMILSKY, Peter
- see DIRECTORS

SMITH, Arthur
- see PRODUCERS

SMITH, Douglas G.
WGC (ACTRA). P.O. Box 187, St. Andrews West, ON K0C 2A0 (613)936-2734. Charles Northcote, The Core Group, 489 College St., Ste. 501, Toronto, ON M6G 1A5 (416)944-0193.
Type of Production and Credits: Th Film-Wr; TV Film-Wr; TV Video-Wr.
Genres: Drama-Th&TV; Action-Th&TV; Science Fiction-Th&TV; Horror-Th&TV.
Biography: Born in 1958 in Montreal, Quebec. Canadian citizenship. Education: Humber College, Rexdale; Graduated with honours from three year program in film and television production; received the Academic Award of Excellence for graduating with the highest overall average.
Selected Filmography: *Officer Richard Smith*, "Top Cops", TV, 91, USA/CDN, Wr; *The Devil's Music*, "Scene of the Crime", TV, 91,USA/CDN/F. Wr .

SMITH, John N.
- see DIRECTORS

SMITH, Morag
- see PRODUCERS

SMITH, Steve
- see PRODUCERS

SNOOKS, Susan
WGC (ACTRA). 31 Northcliffe Blvd., Toronto, ON M6H 3G9 (416)652-2232.
Type of Production and Credits: Th Film-Wr; TV Film-Exec Story Ed/Wr.
Genres: Drama-TV; Educational-TV; Children's-TV; Animation-Th&TV.
Selected Filmography: *Two For Joy*, TV, 91, CDN, Co-Wr/Exec Story Ed; *David's Dream*, "My Secret Identity", TV, 90, CDN/USA, Wr; *Invisible Dr. J.*, "My Secret Identity", TV 90, CDN/USA, Co-Wr; "My Secret Identity" (29 eps), TV, 89-90, CDN/USA, Exec Story Ed; *Tales of the Canadas*, "The Campbells", TV, 88, CDN/USA/GB, Co-Wr/Exec Story Ed; "The Campbells" (48 eps), TV, 87-88, CDN/USA/GB, Exec Story Ed; *River of Distant Thunder*, "Blizzard Island", TV, 88, CDN/GB, Co-Wr; "Clifford" (3 eps), ED, 88, CDN/USA, Co-Wr; *The Care Bears Adventure in Wonderland*, Th, 86, CDN/USA, Co-Wr; "The Edison Twins" (30 eps), TV, 84-86, CDN/USA, Story Ed; "The Edison Twins" (6 eps), TV, 83-85, CDN/USA, Wr; "The Edison Twins" (22 eps), TV, 83-84, CDN/USA, Assist Story Ed; "20-Minute Workout" (35 eps), TV, 83, CDN/USA, Wr; *The Making of Rock and Rule*, TV, 82, CDN, Wr.

SNOWDEN, Alison
- see DIRECTORS

SOBELMAN, David
ACCT. 77 Huntley St., #812, Toronto, ON M4Y 2P3 (416)925-6258.
Type of Production and Credits: Th Film-Wr; TV Video-Wr/Dir/Prod.
Genres: Drama-Th&TV; Action-Th&TV; Documentary-Th&TV; Science Fiction-Th&TV.
Biography: Born 1950, Haifa, Israel. Educated in Europe; moved to Canada, 72; Canadian citizenship, 77; speaks 4 languages. Hons. B.F.A., York University, 76. Story editor, feature screenplays, *Proteus, Grass Widows, Just a Little Foreplay*, 88; co-writer, *Dangerous Times*, feature film treatment, 84; co-writer, *Home of the Dreamer*, feature film screenplay, 1990.
Selected Filmography: *Journey to Mars*, "The Spacewatch Club", TV, 91, CDN/USA, Wr/Dir; *E.T. Phone Home*, "The Spacewatch Club", TV, 91, CDN/USA, Co-Wr/Dir; *Emily's Dilemma*, "The Spacewatch Club", TV, 90, CDN/USA, Co-Wr/Dir; *W.A.L.T.E.R.'S Mystery*, "The Spacewatch Club", TV, 89, CDN/USA, Co-Wr/Dir; *Runaways: 24 Hours on the Street*, TV, 87, CDN, Wr/Prod, (ANIK/GEMINI 88); *Space Pioneers*, TV, 86, CDN, Wr; "The Space Experience" (6 eps), TV, 86, CDN, Co-Wr; "Enterprise" (22 eps), TV, 83-84, CDN, Co-Prod, (ACTRA); *RCMP on Trial*, TV, 83, CDN, Wr/Dir; *End of Toronto*, TV, 83, CDN, Dir/Wr; "Toronto Trilogy" (3 shows), TV, 83, CDN, Story Ed; "The Shulman Film" (22 eps), TV, 82-83, CDN, Assoc Prod; *Inward Passage/The St. Lawrence Seaway*, Th, 82, CDN, Wr; "Canada AM" (5/week), TV, 79-81, CDN, Story Ed; "CTV News", TV, 81, CDN, News Ed.

SOBOL, Ken
ACTRA, SOCAN. R.R. #5, Alexandria, ON K0C 1A0 (613)525-4338. Philip Spitzer Literary Agency, 788 Ninth Ave., New York, NY 10019 USA (212)628-0352.
Type of Production and Credits: TV Film-Wr; TV Video-Wr.
Genres: Drama-TV; Documentary-TV; Children's-TV; Animation-TV.
Biography: Born 1938, Cleveland, Ohio; Canadian citizenship. Writer for many magazines including *The Village Voice, McCall's, New York, This Magazine, Canadian Geographic*; author of *Babe Ruth and the American Dream* and several children's books, including *The Clock Museum, The Devil and Daniel Mouse, Stories from Inside Out*.
Selected Filmography: "Rigolécole" (20 eps), TV, 91, CDN, Wr; "Reading Rap" (10 eps), TV, 90, CDN, Wr; *Under the Umbrella Tree*, TV, 87-88, CDN, Co-Creator/Head Wr; *Magic Library*, TV, 88, CDN, Wr; "Dear Aunt Agnes" (3 eps), TV, 86, CDN, Wr; "Readalong" (90 eps), TV, 75-86, CDN, Wr; "Téléfrançais" (30 eps), TV, 79-85, CDN, Wr; "Les Grands Moments de l'Histoire" (3 eps), TV, 83, CDN, Wr; *Chairman of the Board*, TV, 82, CDN, Wr; *The Devil and Daniel Mouse*, TV, 78, CDN, T'play; *Cosmic Christmas*, TV, 76-77, CDN, Wr; "Inside Out" (7 eps), TV, 74-75, CDN/USA, Wr, (EMMY).

SOLOMON, Aubrey
WGAw, ACTRA. 12758 La. Maida St., N. Hollywood, CA 91607. Lynn Kinney, 387 Bloor St. E., 5th Floor, Toronto, ON M4W 1H7 (416)926-1507.
Type of Production and Credits: Th Film-Wr; TV Film-Prod/Wr.
Genres: Drama-TV; Action-Th&TV; Science Fiction-TV; Documentary-TV.
Biography: Born in 1949. Canadian citizen. Author of *The Films of 20th Century-Fox*, (Citadel Press) and *20th Century-Fox: A Corporate and Financial History*, (Scarecrow Press). Won the Mystery Writers of America Golden Scroll Award for an episode of "Quincy, M.E.".
Selected Filmography: "Neon Rider" (24 eps), TV, 89-90, CDN, Exec Story Ed/Wr; "Danger Bay" (7 eps), TV, 85-89, CDN, Wr; *Defense Play*, Th, 87, USA, Wr; *It's Howdy Doody Time: A 40 Year Celebration*, TV, 87, USA, Prod/Wr; "Blacke's Magic" (1 eps), TV, 86, USA, Wr; "Adderly" (1 eps), TV, 86, CDN, Wr; "Crazy Life a Fox" (1 eps), TV, 85, USA, Wr; "The Fall Guy" (4 eps), TV, 84-85, USA, Wr; "Half Nelson" (2 eps), TV, 84, USA, Wr; "The Mississippi" (1 eps), TV, 82, USA, Wr; "Cagney & Lacey" (1 eps), TV, 82, USA, Wr; "Chips" (2 eps), TV, 81, USA, Wr; "That's Hollywood" (74 eps), TV, 77-81, USA, Prod/Wr; "Buck Rogers" (1 eps), TV, 79, USA, Wr; "Quincy, M.E." (25 eps), TV, 78-80, USA, Story Ed/Wr.

SOMCYNSKY, Jean-Francois
SARDEC. 5, av. Putnam, Ottawa, ON K1M 1Y8.
Types de production et générique: TV film-Sc.
Types d'oeuvres: Drame-TV.
Curriculum vitae: Né en 1943, Paris, France; citoyenneté canadienne. Economiste de formation; maîtrise, Université d'Ottawa, 70. Diplomate de

carrière depuis 72; a publié 18 ouvrages de fiction (roman, nouvelles, poésie); 7 nouvelles et 9 pièces radiophoniques. Prix Solaris, 81; 2 Prix Boréal, 82; Prix Esso du Cercle du Livre de France, 83; Prix Louis-Hémon de l'Académie du Languedoc, 87. Pseudonyme: Jean-François Somain.
Filmographie sélective: *Un héritage inespéré,* TV, 78, CDN, Aut; *Ton regard dans le miroir,* TV, 73, CDN, Aut.

SPRY, Robin
- see PRODUCERS

STANKE, Alain
- voir PRODUCTEURS

STANSFIELD, David
ACTRA, WGA. 7105 Fernhill Dr., Malibu, CA 90265 (213)457-7500. Glenhill Productions Ltd., 41 Peter St., Toronto, ON M5V 2C2 (416)971-6667.
Type of Production and Credits: Th Film-Wr; TV Film-Wr/Prod.
Genres: Documentary-Th&TV; Educational-Th&TV; Children's-Th&TV; Animation-Th&TV.
Biography: Has won over 40 international film and television awards. Canadian citizen.
Selected Filmography: "The Earth Revealed" (26 eps), ED/TV, 91, USA, Wr; "The Power of Algebra" (10 eps), ED/TV, 90, USA, Wr; "How Do You Do?" (24 eps), ED/TV, 90, CDN, Wr/Prod; "Straight Up" (3 eps), ED/TV, 89, USA, Wr/Prod; "Origins: A History of Canada" (16 eps), ED/TV, 89, CDN, Wr/Prod; "The Middle East" (14 eps), ED/TV, 87, CDN/USA, Wr/Prod; "Bits and Bytes" (12 eps), ED/TV, 83, CDN/USA, Wr/Prod; "It Figures" (25 eps), ED/TV, 80, USA, Wr/Prod; "Eureka!" (30 eps), ED/TV, 78, CDN, Wr/Prod; "Parlez-Moi" (90 eps), ED/TV, 77, CDN, Wr/Prod; "Mathworks" (25 eps), ED/TV, 77, USA, Wr/Prod; "Report French" (25 eps), ED/TV, 75, CDN, Wr/Prod; "The French Show" (13 eps), ED/TV, 75, CDN, Wr/Prod.

STAVRIDES, Stavros
- see DIRECTORS

STEELE, Fraser
- see DIRECTORS

STEELE, Michael
- see PRODUCERS

STEIN, Allan◊
ACCT. (403)424-2519.
Type of Production and Credits: Th Film-Wr/Prod; TV Film-Prod/Wr/Dir; TV Video-Prod/Wr/Dir.
Genres: Drama-Th&TV; Musical-TV; Documentary-Th&TV; Music Video-TV.
Biography: Born 1948, Windsor, Ontario.
Languages: English, French, some Yiddish. M.A., Political Science, University of Calgary. Background in music as performer (instrumental and vocal), arranger, composer. Has written for and performed on national radio and television; has taught university film courses at undergraduate and graduate levels. Founding member/current president AMPIA. Winner of many film awards, including Yorkton, AMPIA, American Film Festival, New York, Chicago.
Selected Filmography: "The Gunfighters" (pilot), TV, 87, CDN, Co-Prod; *Shooting Stars,* TV, 87, CDN, Prod/Dir/Co-Wr; *Get Back the Night,* MV, 87, CDN, Prod/Dir/Co-Wr; *Turn It Off?,* MV, 85, CDN, Prod/Dir/Do-Wr; *The Entrepreneur,* TV, 85, CDN, Dir; *Kaleidoscope,* TV, 83, CDN, Wr; "The Bush Pilots" (1 eps), TV, 83, CDN, Ed; *A Cue for Tomorrow,* Ed, 82, CDN, Wr; *Wide World of Records,* Ed, 81, CDN, Dir; *Old as the Hills,* Ed, 79, CDN, Comp; *Daycare: The Newest Tradition,* Ed, 78, CDN, Ed; *Wide World of Rescue,* Ed, 77, CDN, Prod/Dir; *Supervisor,* Ed, 76, CDN, DOP; *Green Man,* ED, 76, CDN, Prod/Dir; *Boom Town, Boon Town,* Th, 75, CDN, Prod/Dir/Ed.

STERN, Sandor
- see DIRECTORS

STEWART, Barbara J.
National Film Board of Canada, 2001 Cornwall St., Suite 111, Regina, SK S4P 2K6 (306)780-5014.
Type of Production and Credits: TV Film-Wr/Dir/Prod.
Genres: Drama-TV.
Biography: Born 1952, Cambridge, Ontario. Has had one book published, *The Maple Leaf Journal: A Settlement History of Wellesley Township.* Project Coordinator, Saskatchewan Film Development Project, a co-operative project between the National Film Board and the Province of Saskatchewan for the production of 7 original half-hour television dramas.
Selected Filmography: *The Chimney Sweep,* TV, 85, CDN, Wr/Dir/Prod.

STEWART, Gordon
- see PRODUCERS

STIRLING, Michelle G.
- see PRODUCERS

STOCKTON, Brian
- see DIRECTORS

STOLLER, Bryan M.
- see DIRECTORS

STONEMAN, John
- see CINEMATOGRAPHERS

STRANGE, Marc◊
ACTRA, ACCT. (705)277-1072.
Type of Production and Credits: Th Film-Act; TV Film-Wr/Act; TV Video-Wr/Act.
Genres: Drama-TV; Children's-TV.
Biography: Born Kitchener, Ontario. Thirty years in the entertainment business as writer/actor/director.
Selected Filmography: "The Beachcombers" (50 eps), TV, 72-86, CDN, Creator/Wr; "Street Legal" (2 eps), TV, 86, CDN, Wr; *The Morning Man*, Th, 85, CDN, Act; *Act of Vengeance*, TV, 85, USA, Act; "The Campbells" (Co-T'play, 1eps/ Wr-1 eps), TV, 85, CDN/USA/GB, Wr; "Danger Bay" (1 eps), TV, 85, CDN, Wr; *Valentine's Revenge*, TV, 84, USA, Act.

STRATYCHUK, Perry Mark
- see DIRECTORS

STRAYER, Colin J.
- see PRODUCERS

SUCH, Peter◊
ACTRA. (416)534-1398.
Type of Production and Credits: Th Short-Wr; TV Film-Wr; TV Video-Wr.
Genres: Drama-Th&TV; Documentary-Th&TV; Educational-Th&TV; Children's-TV.
Biography: Born 1939, London, England; Canadian citizenship, 53. Began career as a singer, then actor, writer of stage plays, opera; novelist, 5 books; founder, Canadian Studies programs; professor at York University. Has received Canada Council Awards, Chalmers Award. *Free Dive* won First Prize, New York Film Festival (Special UN category)
Selected Filmography: "The Campbells" (1 eps), TV, 85, CDN/USA/GB, Wr; "Home Fires" (24 eps) (Co-Wr 8 eps/Co-Story 16 eps), TV, 81-82, CDN, Co-Creator; *Free Dive*, TV, 82, CDN, Wr.

SUISSA, Danièle J.
- see DIRECTORS

SULLIVAN, Kevin R.
- see PRODUCERS

SUMMERS, Jaron
Doug Brodex/David Shapira and Associates, (818)906-0322.
Type of Production and Credits: Th Film-Wr; TV Film-Wr; TV Video-Wr.
Genres: Drama-Th&TV; Action-Th&TV; Science Fiction-TV.
Biography: Writes for screen and has also written several hundred magazine and newspaper articles. Has published the following books: *The Soda Cracker, Below The Line, Safety Catch, Mall* (hard cover); *Mall/The Duncan Legacy* (paperback).
Selected Filmography: *Killer Image*, Th, 91, CDN, Wr; *The Kill Reflex*, Th, 90, USA, Wr; "Star Trek: The Next Generation" (opening eps), TV, 88, USA, Wr; "Diamonds" (4 eps), TV, 88, CDN/USA/F, Story Ed; "Miami Vice", TV, 88, USA, Wr; *Red Wind*, an adaptation of a Raymond Chandler short story, TV, 85, USA/CDN, Wr; "Hart To Hart", TV, 84, USA, Wr; *Fast Eddie*, Th, 84, USA, Wr; "Adderly", TV, 83, CDN/USA, Wr; "Buck Rogers in the 21st Century", TV, 82, USA, Wr; "The Incredible Hulk", TV, 81, USA, Wr; *Parallels*, Th, 81, CDN, Wr; "Search and Rescue", TV, 80, CDN, Wr.

SUTHERLAND, Ian◊
ACTRA. (416)964-3302.
Type of Production and Credits: Th Film-Wr; TV Film-Wr.
Genres: Drama-Th&TV; Comedy-Th& TV; Action-Th&TV.
Biography: Born 1945, Scotland; landed immigrant Canada. Attended McGill University. *Certain Practices* won a Genie, 80.
Selected Filmography: "Night Heat" (7 eps), TV, 85-86, CDN, Wr; *Certain Practices/Blind Faith/Moving Targets*, TV, 79-82, CDN, Wr; *Improper Channels*, Th, 79, CDN, Co-Wr; *Sunspots*, TV, 79, CDN, Wr; *Rituals*, Th, 76, CDN, Wr.

SUTHERLAND, Neil
- see PRODUCERS

SUTHERLAND, Paul
- see DIRECTORS

SUTTOR, Carmel
ACTRA, TWIFT. 550 Ontario Street, Apt. 420, Toronto, ON M4X 1X3 (416)925-7200.
Type of Production and Credits: TV Film-Wr; TV Video-Wr.
Genres: Drama-TV; Children's-TV.
Biography: Born in 1956 in Australia. Canadian citizen. B.A. English & Drama; Theatre Studies in France. Languages: English and French. Has a radio drama and some feature films in development.
Selected Filmography: "Join In!" (5 eps), TV, 90-91, CDN, Wr; "Polka Dot Door" (7 eps), TV, 90-91, CDN, Wr.

TADMAN, Aubrey
ACTRA, WGA. 5255 Zelzan Ave., #107, Encino, CA 91316 (818)708-3487. Preferred Artists, (818)990-0305.
Type of Production and Credits: TV Film-Wr/Prod; TV Video-Wr/Prod.
Genres: Comedy-Th&TV; Variety-Th& TV; Musical-Th&TV.
Biography: Born in Winnipeg, Manitoba. Canadian citizen. English speaking. 2nd

year, Fine Arts, University of Manitoba. Musician - drummer, singer.
Selected Filmography: "My Secret Identity" (22 eps), TV, 90, CDN/USA, Exec Script Cons; "City" (22 eps), TV, 89-90, USA, Exec Story Cons; "Mama's Family" (3 eps), TV, 88-89, USA, Wr; *Billy Martin Roast*, TV, 88, USA, Spv Prod/Wr; *Elizabeth Manley Special*, TV, 88, CDN, Prod/Wr; "New Love American Style" (30 eps), TV, 87, USA, Exec Story Cons; "Check It Out!" (24 eps), TV, 86, CDN/USA, Prod/Wr; "9 to 5" (5 eps), TV, 86, USA, Wr; "Silver Spoons" (3 eps), TV, 86, USA, Wr; "Snow Job" (60 eps), TV, 82-84, CDN, Prod; "Rhoda" (36 eps), TV, 81-82, USA, Exec Script Cons; "Welcome Back Kotter" (52 eps), TV, 80, USA, Exec Story Ed; "The Tim Conway Show" (35 eps), TV, 77-78, USA, Head Wr; "The Dick Van Dyke Show" (20 eps), TV, 76, USA, Wr Staff; "King of Kensington" (26 eps), TV, 73-74, CDN, Head Wr/Exec Story Ed.

TERRY, Christopher
- see DIRECTORS

TESTAR, Coralee Elliott
WGC (ACTRA), WGA. 643 Plymouth Dr., North Vancouver, BC V7H 2H5 (604)929-7769. FAX: 929-6987.
Type of Production and Credits: Th Film-Wr; TV Film-Wr/Prod.
Genres: Drama-Th&TV; Comedy-Th&TV; Children's-Th&TV.
Biography: Born in Prince Edward Island. Member of the first graduating class of the National Theatre School of Canada. Co-Manager of Testar Productions of Vancouver. *The Little Kidnappers* won a Rockie award, Banff Fest 91.
Selected Filmography: *The Little Kidnappers*, TV, 90, USA, Wr.

THICKE, Alan
- see PRODUCERS

THOMAS, Dave
- see DIRECTORS

THOMAS, R.L.
- see DIRECTORS

THOMAS, William J.
ACTRA. Lakeshore Rd., R.R. #2, Port Colborne, ON L3K 5V4 (416)834-6098. FAX: 835-2717.
Type of Production and Credits: Th Film-Wr.
Genres: Drama-TV; Comedy-TV; Industrial-Th.
Biography: Born 1946, Welland, Ontario. B.A., Wilfrid Laurier University. Writer of weekly humour column syndicated in 30 papers; writes industrial scripts/videos/films; nominated for Gemini Award for writing *Breaking all the Rules - The Story of Trivial Pursuit*. Has written 30 industrials/corporates for various companies including Bell, Canadian Tire and Esso.
Selected Filmography: *Breaking All the Rules*, TV, 87, CDN, Wr.

THOMPSON, Judith
ACTRA. Great North Artists Management, 350 Dupont St., Toronto, ON M5R 1V9 (416)925-2051.
Type of Production and Credits: TV Film-Wr; TV Video-Wr.
Genres: Drama-TV; Comedy-TV.
Biography: Born 1954, Montreal, Quebec. Attended Queen's University; National Theatre School. Playwright; won Governor General's Award for Drama, 84. Wrote 3 feature films, including adaptation of her play, *I Am Yours*; produced for theatre, 87.
Selected Filmography: *Going Crazy*, TV, CDN, Wr; *Don't Talk*, Th, CDN, Wr; *I Am Yours*, Th, CDN, Wr; *The Risk of It*, TV, CDN, Wr; "Adderly" (1 eps), TV, CDN/USA, Wr; *Adolescent Sexuality*, "Life Studies", Th, CDN, Wr; *Turning to Stone*, TV, 85, CDN, Wr; "Airwaves" (2 eps), TV, 85, CDN, Wr.

THOMPSON, Peggy
784 Thurlow, Suite 44, Vancouver, BC V6E 1V9 (604)683-5250.
Type of Production and Credits: Th Film-Wr; Th Short-Wr.
Genres: Drama-Th&TV.
Biography: Born 1953, Vancouver, BC. Partner The Two Pegs Film Company; President, Day for Night Motion Pictures.
Selected Filmography: *In Search of the Last Good Man*, Th, 88, CDN, Wr, (GENIE 90); *It's a Party*, Th, 86, CDN, Wr; "The Beachcombers" (3 eps), TV, 80-81, CDN, Wr.

THURLING, Peter
- see DIRECTORS

TOUGAS, Francine
SOCAN, SARDEC, UDA. 5081, rue Fabre, Montréal, PQ H2J 3W3 (514)525-2787. (514)525-6461.
Types de production et générique: TV film-Sc; TV vidéo-Sc.
Types d'oeuvres: Drame-TV; Documentaire-C&TV; Education-TV; Enfants-TV.
Curriculum vitae: Née en 1952, Dorion, Québec. Langues: français et anglais. Conservatoire d'art dramatique, 69-73. Comédienne, 73-84; auteur et interprète de 3 spectacles solos joués à Montréal et à Québec. Prix Adate, 89, pour "L'Emprise"; Prix CBI, 89 pour version anglaise de "Bibi et Geneviève" ("B.B. and

Jennifer").
Filmographie sélective: "Bibi et Geneviève", Series 1,2,3 (390 eps), TV, 88-91, CDN, Aut/Aut-Coord; "A plein temps" (16 eps), TV, 84-88, CDN, Sc; "Les Enfants de la rue" (1 eps), TV, 88, CDN, Co sc/Dial; "L'Emprise", TV, 88, CDN, Co sc/Dial; *Méno-Tango*, C, 86, CDN, Ass Réal/Cons scén; *Nuageux avec éclaircies*, C, 86, CDN, Ass réal/Cons scén; "Les Enfants mal-aimés" (3 eps), TV, 84, CDN, Co sc/Dial.

TREMBLAY, Jean-Joseph◊
ACCT. (514)521-4370.
Types de production et générique: l métrage-Sc; TV film-Sc; TV vidéo-Sc.
Types d'oeuvres: Drame-C&TV; Comédie-C&TV; Science-fiction-C&TV.
Curriculum vitae: Né en 1950, Saint-Jean-Vianey, Québec. Etudes au Conservatoire d'art dramatique, 72.
Filmographie sélective: *Le Sourd dans la ville*, C, 86, CDN, Co sc.

TREMBLAY, Michel
ACCT. 294 Carré St-Louis, 5e, Montréal, PQ H2X 1A4 (514)281-5044. L'Agence artistique et littéraire, 839 est, rue Sherbrooke, Montréal, PQ H2L 1K6 (514)598-5252.
Types de production et générique: l métrage-Sc; c métrage-Sc; TV film-Sc.
Types d'oeuvres: Drame-C&TV; Comédie-C&TV.
Curriculum vitae: Né en 1942, Montréal, Québec. Langues: français et anglais. Figure dominante du théâtre québécois depuis la fin des années 60, s'est aussi imposé comme romancier, traducteur, adapteur et scénariste. Plusieurs de ses pièces ont été acclamées a l'étranger, notamment *Bonjour, là Bonjour* et *Les Belles-Soeurs*. Auteur, *Les Chroniques du Plateau Mont-Royal*, dont un tôme est publié à tous les 2 ans. Son oeuvre comprend 18 pièces de théâtre, 2 comédies musicales, 8 romans, un recueuil de contes, 7 scénarios de films, 11 traductions ou adaptations d'auteurs étrangers. *Le coeur découvert* a gagné Prix Gémeau, 88 (meilleure dramatique TV), Prix Anik, 88 (meilleure dramatique TV), Prix du public au San Francisco Lesbian & Gay Festival (meilleur long métrage), Prix du public, Festival de Bruxelles, 90; *Françoise Durocher, waitress* a gagné ETROG, 71 (meilleur scénario/court métrage, ETROG, 71 (meilleure oeuvre TV).
Filmographie sélective: *Le Grand Jour*, TV, 88, CDN, Sc; *Six heures au plus tard*, TV, 88, CDN, Sc; *Le coeur découvert*, TV, 87, CDN, Sc; *Parlez-nous d'amour*, C, 76, CDN, Co sc; *Le soleil se lève en retard*, C, 75, CDN, Co sc; *Il était une fois dans l'Est*, C, 74, CDN, Co sc; *Françoise Durocher, waitress*, TV, 70, CDN, Sc, (CFA).

TROFYMOW, L.A.
IATSE 345, NWMNG. 1207 Stafford Dr. N., Lethbridge, AB T1H 2B9 (403)327-7090. The Film & Video Arts Society of Alberta (FAVA), 9722 - 102 St., Edmonton, AB T5K 0X4 (403)429-1671.
Type of Production and Credits: Th Short-Wr/Dir/Prod.
Genres: Experimental-Th.
Biography: Born in 1963 in Lethbridge, Alberta. English with some French. Canadian citizen. BA with Distinction, The University of Alberta, 1985. Film Production Workshop, New York University, New York, 1988. Entering MFA Times Arts Programme, SAIC, Fall 91. Professional writer and film/video artist. First film made in 1986. Special skills: experimental film/video techniques, photography, painting, performing poet and musician, vocalist, actor for film, television and theatre, historical interpretation and roleplaying. Awards: AMPIA Awards, Honorable Mention, Experimental (1990/91) for *Tenochtitlan* and *Uno Animo*. *Tenochtitlan* purchased for the National Gallery of Canada permanent collection.
Selected Filmography: *Paddock Pass*, 91, CDN, Dir/Prod/DOP/Wr; *Uno Animo*, ED, 90, CDN, Dir/Prod/DOP/Wr; *Tenochtitlan*, ED, 89, CDN, Dir/Prod/DOP/Wr; *A Capriccio*, ED, 88, CDN, Dir/Prod/Wr; *Corona Radiata*, ED, 86, CDN, Co-Dir/Co-Prod; *My Favorite Bath*, ED, 86, CDN, Dir/Prod/Wr.

TURL, Jeff
- see PRODUCERS

URSELL, Geoffrey
ACTRA. 48 Moxon Cres., Saskatoon, SK S7H 3B9 (306)955-1912.
Type of Production and Credits: TV Film-Wr/Comp; TV Video-Wr.
Genres: Drama-TV; Comedy-TV; Variety-TV; Documentary-TV.
Biography: Born 1943, Moose Jaw, Saskatchewan. M.A., University of Manitoba; Ph.D., University of London. Award-winning writer of drama (for stage, radio and television), fiction, poetry and songs; his plays have won 3 national awards, including the Clifford E. Lee Award, 77; his novel *Perdue* won *Books in Canada* First Novel Award, 84. Playwright-in-residence at Twenty-fifth Street Theatre, Saskatoon; currently at work on a new play, *Deer Bring the Sun*,

and a novel.
Selected Filmography: *Midnight in Moose Jaw*, TV, 88, CDN, Co-Wr; *Distant Battles*, TV, 85, CDN, Wr; *Words and Music*, TV, 84, CDN, Wr; *The Meewasin Authority*, In, 78, CDN, Comp; *We're Here to Stay*, Th, 74, CDN, Comp; *Prairie Shutdown?*, TV, 74, CDN, Wr.

VAITIEKUNAS, Vincent
- see DIRECTORS

VAN DE WATER, Anton
- see PRODUCERS

VANDERBURGH, Clive
- see PRODUCERS

VARUGHESE, Sugith
- see DIRECTORS

VEVERKA, Jana
- see PRODUCERS

VIALLON, Claudine
3657 W. 1 Ave., Vancouver, BC V6R 1H1 (604)733-6101.
Type of Production and Credits: TV Film-Wr/Dir; TV Video-Wr/Dir.
Genres: Drama-TV; Documentary-TV; Educational-TV; Children's-TV.
Biography: Born in 1948 in France; Canadian citizenship. Languages: French, English, Spanish. Simon Fraser University; University of Paris; art school, France. Film Festival Awards at New York and Montreal. Journalist for CBC/Radio-Canada since 87.
Selected Filmography: *Vancouver on the Move*, TV, 86, CDN, Wr/Co-Dir; *Pitou, Pionnier*, TV, 85, CDN, Wr/Dir; *Pandosy, Okanagan*, TV, 85, CDN, Wr/Dir; *The Voyagers*, TV, 85, CDN, Wr/Dir; *Si on faisait des faces*, TV, 83, CDN, Wr/Dir; *Evolution at Brackendale*, TV, 80, CDN, Wr/Dir; *Brujo*, TV, 79, CDN, Co-Wr/Co-Dir; *Via Dolorosa*, TV, 79, CDN, Co-Wr/Co-Dir; *Tajimultik*, TV, 79, CDN, Co-Wr/Co-Dir; *The Thread*, Th, 75, CDN, Set Des.

VICKERS, Darrell◇
ACTRA, WGAw, ACCT. (818)985-7867.
Type of Production and Credits: TV Film-Wr; TV Video-Wr.
Genres: Comedy-TV; Variety-TV; Children's-TV.
Biography: Born in 1957 in England; Canadian citizenship. Professional partner is Andrew Nicholls, with whom he writes for stage, radio, print and cartoons— "Frank and Ernest", "Ben Wicks"— industrials, special musical and personal appearance material (Alan Thicke, Mickey Rooney), 20 plays, gags for comedians including Joan Rivers aand Rodney Dangerfield. Two Emmy nominations, 86-87, for "The Tonight Show", sketch, monologue and guest-host monologues. Co-writer for stage show, "Sugar Babies", 83-86.
Selected Filmography: "The Tonight Show Starring Johnny Carson", TV, 86-88, USA, Staff Wr; "My Reel Family" (pilot), TV, 88, USA, Co-Wr; "Check It Out!" (22 eps)(Co-Wr 11 eps), TV, 85-86, CDN/USA, Co-Story Ed; "Danger Bay" (3 eps), TV, 85, CDN, Co-Wr; *George Carlin '2-c'*, TV, 85, CDN, Co-Wr; "Love Boat" (1 eps), TV, 85, USA, Co-Wr; "Bizarre" (1 eps), TV, 85, CDN/USA, Contr Wr; "Thicke of the Night" (85 eps), TV, 83-84, USA, Contr Wr; "Fast Company" (22 eps), TV, 83, CDN, Co-Wr; "Evening at the Improv" (3 eps), TV, 82, USA, Contr Wr; "Flappers" (3 eps), TV, 81, CDN, Co-Wr.

VOLKMER, Werner
AQRRCT, CCCVI. Aquilon Film Inc., C.P. 370, Succ. Victoria, Westmount, PQ H3Z 2V8 (514)484-8213. FAX: 484-2856.
Type of Production and Credits: c métrage-Sc/Prod/Cam; TV film-Sc/Prod/Cam; TV vidéo-Sc/Prod/Cam.
Genres: Documentaire-C&TV; Education-C&TV; Industriel-C&TV.
Biography: Né 1944 à Haan, Allemagne; citoyenneté canadien depuis 75. Langues: allemand, français et anglais. Diplômé de la Hochschule fur Gestaltung de Kassel (Allemagne) ou il a étudié en publicité et communications. Travaille comme directeur artistique pour les agences des publicité McCann Erickson et Masius International de Hambourg, puis, après son arrivée à Montréal en 70, pour BPC Publicité. Co-fonde Aquilon Film Inc. en 75. Depuis la création d'Aquilon Film, il a travaillé en tant que réalisateur et caméraman pour sa propre compagnie comme pour d'autres producteurs. Il a gagné de nombreuses récompenses internationales et ses films sont diffusés à travers toute l'Europe et l'Amérique du Nord. *Batiya Bak!* - Gemini 90; *Cirque au ciel* - People's Choice Award, 90, Blue Ribbon, NY, 88; *En bonne compagnie* - Premier prix, Houston 83, Prix Silver Screen, Chicago 83, Bronze, NY 83; *Spirit of the Land* - Premier prix, CFTA, Toronto 83, Premier Prix, Chicago 83, 80; Chris Statuette, Columbus 80; *Moteur* - Pris Sci. et Technologie, Tokyo 79, Deuxième prix, Houston 79; *Cocologie* - Prix, Croix-Rouge, Varna 76, Prix, Tampere 76.
Selected Filmography: *Batiya Bak!*, TV, 90, CDN, Sc/Réal/Cam/Prod, (GEMINI);

L'idée est dans l'air/From Thin Air, ED, 89, CDN, Sc/Réal/Cam/Prod; *Cole Palen's Flying Circus/Cirque au ciel*, TV, 87, CDN, Réal/Cam/Mont; *Yesterday's Hero*, TV, 86, CDN, Cam; *The Owl and the Pussycat*, C, 84, CDN, Cam; *En bonne compagnie*, In, 83, CDN, Prod/Réal/Mont; *Spirit of the Land*, In, 79, CDN, Prod/Cam; *Moteur!/Power Behind the Wings*, ED, 79, CDN, Réal/Cam; *Cocologie*, ED, 76, CDN, Réal/Cam.

WAISGLASS, Elaine
ACTRA, WGAw, ACCT, TWIFT. 6-B Wychwood Park, Toronto, ON M6G 2V5 (416)652-1140.
Type of Production and Credits: Th Film-Wr; TV Film-Wr.
Genres: Drama-Th&TV; Documentary-Th&TV.
Biography: Canadian citizen with employment and residential papers for Great Britain. Has won awards for documentaries and children's television. Has written documentaries for CBC and TVO including "Man Alive" and "Marketplace". Is currently on sabbatical being a mom.
Selected Filmography: "Babar" (4 eps), TV, 88, CDN, Wr; *A Judgement in Stone*, Th, 86, CDN, Wr; "The Edison Twins" (6 eps), TV, 83-84, CDN, Wr.

WALKER, Giles
- see DIRECTORS

WALLACE, Clarke
ACTRA. RR #3, Woodbridge, ON L4L 1A7 (416)964-3302. The Colbert Agency, 303 Davenport Rd., Toronto, ON M5R 1K5 (416)964-3302.
Type of Production and Credits: Th Film-Wr; TV Film-Wr; TV Video-Wr.
Genres: Drama-Th; Variety-TV; Documentary-TV; Children's-TV.
Biography: Born Toronto, Ontario. B.A., Journalism, University of Western Ontario, 62. Author of 5 published books including: *Empire Inc.*, 83; *Hercules Trust*, 82; *Wanted: Donald Morrison*, 77.
Selected Filmography: "Street Legal" (1 eps), TV, 86, CDN, Wr; *The Morning Man*, Th, 85, CDN, Wr; *South Korea*, TV, 80, CDN, Wr; *Sri Lanka*, TV, 80, CDN, Wr; "This Land" (10 eps), TV, 74-78, CDN, Wr; "The Fit Shop" (26 eps), TV, 77-78, CDN, Wr/Co-Host; "The Human Journey" (4 eps), TV, 74-77, CDN, Wr; "The Tommy Hunter Show" (26 eps), TV, 76, CDN, Wr; "Drop In" (60 eps), TV, 69-74, CDN, Wr; "This Land Is People" (52 eps), TV, 68-69, CDN, Wr.

WALLACE, Ratch
- see PRODUCERS

WATSON, John
- see PRODUCERS

WATSON, Patrick
- see PRODUCERS

WAXMAN, Martin
WGC (ACTRA), LIFT. 1472 King St. W., #2, Toronto, ON M6K 1J1 (416)534-5077.
Types of production and Credits: TV Film-Wr/Prod.
Genres: Drama-TV; Comedy-TV.
Biography: Toronto writer and producer; first novel, *The Promised Land* published by Black Moss Press, 87. With his partner, Maureen Judge, he has co-written and produced several comedic films including *Family Business*, 84 and *A Venerable Occasion*, 86. Both were broadcast on CBC TV and screened at numerous festivals. Recently produced and co-wrote (with Maureen Judge) *Altered Ego*, an hour-long 'featurette' (mini-feature); aired on CBC in prime time, 91. Originally from Winnipeg, he has been a stand-up comedy emcee at Yuk Yuk's, has written a humour column for *Metropolis* magazine, contributes book reviews to the *Toronto Star* and was a book and film publicist. Currently completing his second novel and developing several film and TV projects through his company, Makin' Movies Inc.
Selected Filmography: *Altered Ego*, TV, 90, CDN, Co-Wr/Prod; *A Venerable Occasion*, TV, 86, CDN, Co-Wr/Prod; *Family Business*, TV, 84, CDN, Co-Wr/Prod.

WAYNE, Paul
ACTRA, WGAw. 5201 Topeka Dr., Tarzana, CA 91356 (818)344-1070. FAX: 344-1073. Shapiro-Lichtman, (213)859-8877. FAX: 859-7153.
Type of Production and Credits: Th Film-Wr; TV Video-Wr/Prod.
Genres: Comedy-Th&TV; Variety-TV.
Biography: Born 1932, Toronto, Ontario; US resident alien.
Selected Filmography: "Check It Out!" (13 eps), TV, 85, CDN/USA, Head Wr; "Three's Company" (65 eps), TV, 76-78, USA, Head Wr; "Excuse My French" (35 eps), TV, 74-75, CDN, Prod, (ACTRA); "Sonny and Cher" (65 eps), TV, 71, USA, Co-Wr; *Only God Knows*, Th, 69, CDN, Wr; "Smothers Brothers" (26 eps), TV, 69, USA, Co-Wr, (EMMY); *The King's Pirate*, Th, 65, USA, Wr.

WEINTHAL, Eric
DGC, ACTRA, CAPAC. Hania Productions Inc., 523 Manning Ave., Toronto, ON M6G 2V8 (416)533-9803. Gerald Adler, The Adler Agency, 12725 Ventura

Blvd., Suite B, Studio City, CA 91604 (818)761-9850.
Type of Production and Credits: Th Film-Dir/Wr.
Genres: Drama-Th; Comedy-TV; Variety-TV; Action-TV.
Biography: Born 1958, Montreal, Quebec. B.A., Cinema, University of Toronto, 79. After making short films and working as a musician, singer, actor and editor, produced, wrote and directed first feature film independently, co-composing the music score; film invited to festivals in Canada and Colombia and seen in theatres and on TV in Canada and Malaysia; has written 4 screenplays; currently in development on 2 features as writer, director and occasional live singer/performer.
Selected Filmography: "Katts & Dog" (2 eps), TV, 88-91, CDN/F, Wr; "Top Cops" (8 eps), TV, 90-91, CDN/USA, Wr; "My Secret Identity" (Wr 16 eps/Story Ed 69 eps/Dir 1 eps), TV, 87-90, CDN/USA, Wr/Story Ed/Dir; *Our Secret*, TV, 90, CDN/F/GB, Wr; "Time of Your Life", TV, 88, CDN, Dir; "True Confessions" (1 eps), TV, 87, CDN/USA, Dir; "Airwolf" (24 eps)(Ed 2 eps), TV, 86-87, USA, P Pro Spv; *Hoover vs the Kennedys: The Second Civil War* (mini-series), TV, 87, CDN, P Pro Spv; *Martha, Ruth & Edie*, Th, 87, CDN, P Pro Spv/Add'l Dial/Looping Dir; *Way Down Inside*, MV, 86, CDN, Dir/Ed/Comp/Sing; "Family Matters" (5 eps), TV, 86, CDN, Assist Dir/Script Spv; *Timing*, Th, 85, CDN, Dir/Wr/Co-Prod/Ed; "Check It Out!" (2 eps), TV, 85, CDN/USA, Assoc Dir; "Comedy Factory" (8 eps), TV, 85, CDN, P Pro Spv; "Snow Job" (54 eps), TV, 82-85, CDN, P Pro Spv.

WEINTRAUB, William
ACTRA. 433 Wood Ave., Westmount, PQ H3Y 3J4 (514)935-2733.
Type of Production and Credits: Th Film-Wr/Prod; Th Short-Wr/Prod; TV Film-Wr/Dir/Prod.
Genres: Drama-Th&TV; Documentary-Th&TV; Educational-Th&TV.
Biography: Started career as journalist at the *Montreal Gazette*, *Weekend* magazine; joined NFB, 65; has written and/or produced over 100 documentary and dramatic films; author of 2 novels, *The Underdogs* and *Why Rock the Boat?*; lectured on screenwriting at several universities in Canada; worked in Kenya for United Nations, instructing African filmmakers; left the NFB in 86 to do

FUND

The Foundation to Underwrite New Drama for Pay Television

■ FUND offers a programme to assist Canadian Writers and producers in feature-length dramatic script development and an equity investment programme for feature film production.

98 Queen St. E.
Toronto, Ontario
M5C 1S6
(416) 361-1150

Board of Directors
Paul Gratton
Thomas Howe
Peter Mortimer
Marlene Smith
Ian McDougall
Peter Pearson

Stan Thomas
Michael Donovan

Chairperson
Phyllis Yaffe

Corporate sponsor
First Choice Canadian Communications Corporation
An Astral Company
& Viewer's Choice Canada

freelance writing.
Selected Filmography: *Mortimer Griffin and Shalinsky/The Sight/Uncle T/ Connection*, "Bell Canada Playhouse", TV, 85, CDN, Co-Prod; *The Concert Man*, TV, 82, CDN, Wr; *Arthritis: A Dialogue with Pain*, TV, 81, CDN, Prod; *Margaret Laurence: First Lady of Manawaka*, TV, 78, CDN, Prod; *Hold the Ketchup*, Th, 76, CDN, Prod; *Why Rock the Boat?*, Th, 74, CDN, Prod/Scr, (CFA); *Challenge for the Church*, TV, 72, CDN, Wr/Dir; "Struggle for a Border" (9 eps), TV, 69, CDN, Wr; *A Matter of Fat?*, Th, 69, CDN, Wr/Dir, (CFA); *Turn of the Century*, TV, 64, CDN, Wr/Prod; *Anniversary*, Th, 63, CDN, Wr/Prod, (CFA); *Nahanni*, Th, 62, CDN, Wr; "Between Two Wars" (3 eps), TV, 60, CDN, Wr/Prod; "Commonwealth of Nations" (13 eps), TV, 57, CDN, Wr; *Saskatchewan Traveller*, TV, 56, CDN, Wr.

WESTREN, Steven
WGC (ACTRA). 45 Balliol St., Ste. 1010, Toronto, ON M4S 1C3 (416)481-8673. Charles Northcote, The Core Group, 489 College St., Ste. 501, Toronto, ON M5G 1A5 (416)944-0193. FAX: 944-0446.
Type of Production and Credits: TV Film-Wr; TV Video-Wr.
Genres: Comedy-TV; Variety-TV; Children's-TV.
Biography: Born in 1959 in Toronto. Attended the University of Toronto Schools (UTS) and the Ontario College of Art. Editorial cartoon "Steve Westren's Toronto" featured in the *Toronto Star*, 1981-82. Cartoons and illustrations in many more magazines, books and newspapers. Performed throughout North America as half of the comedy juggling team, Circus Shmirkus. Multiple appearances on "The Elephant Show", "Troupers", and "Fred Penner's Place". Guest spots on major network specials such as *Rich Little and Friends at the New Orleans World Fair*. Puppeteer on *Muppets 25th Aniversary Special* and *A Muppet Christmas*.
Selected Filmography: *The Designated Sitter*, "Eric's World", TV, 91, CDN, Wr; *The Trouble with Malcolm*, "Eric's World", TV, 91, CDN, Wr; "Dog House" (6 eps), TV, 90, CDN/USA, Staff Wr; *Rear Window*, "Dog House", TV, 90, CDN/USA, Wr; *Skunk*, "Eric's World", TV, 90, CDN, Wr; *Pumpkinhead*, "Eric's World", TV, 90, CDN, Wr.

WEXLER, Gerald
ACTRA. 5278 Esplanade, Montreal, PQ H2T 2Z7 (514)274-1149.
Type of Production and Credits: Th Film-Wr; Th Short-Wr; TV Film-Wr.
Genres: Drama-Th&TV; Comedy-TV; Educational-TV; Children's-TV.
Biography: Born 1950, Montreal, Quebec. Languages: English and French. B.A., English, McGill University, 71; graduate diploma, Film and TV, Hornsey College of Art, London, England, 73. His television anthology dramas have won awards at the American Film Festival, Columbus Film Festival, Atlantic Film Festival. His movie of the week, *Manuel, Le Fils Emprunté* was selected for competition, Berlin Film Festival, 90. It also won first prize at the Tehran Children's Film Festival, 90 and first prize at Carrousel Rimouski (French language festival for youth films, 90). Script editor on various TV and theatrical projects.
Selected Filmography: *A Feather in Her Cap*, "Smoggies", TV, 90, CDN/F, Wr; *Manuel, Le Fils Emprunté*, Th/TV, 89, CDN, Wr; *I Love You, Cowboy*, "The Way We Are", TV, 86, CDN, Wr; "Sesame Street", TV, 87-88, CDN, Wr; "Emu-TV" (24 eps), TV, 87, CDN, Co-Wr; *Do You Know What You're in For?/Family Matters*, "The Way We Are", TV, 86, CDN, Wr; *Angela's Return*, TV, 85, CDN, Wr; *A Gift for Kate*, TV, 85, CDN, Wr; *Uncle T/Mortimer Griffin and Shalinsky/ Bambinger*, "Bell Canada Playhouse", TV, 84-85, CDN, T'play; *Other Tongues*, Th, 83, CDN, Contr Wr; *A Right to Refuse*, "People at Work", ED, 81, CDN, Wr.

WEYMAN, Peter (Bay)
- see PRODUCERS
WHALEY, Ronald T.
- see PRODUCERS
WHEELER, Anne
- see DIRECTORS
WHITE, Helene B.
- see DIRECTORS
WHITE, Pete◊
ACTRA. (604)733-4432.
Type of Production and Credits: TV Film-Wr.
Genres: Drama-TV; Action-TV; Documentary-TV; Educational-TV.
Biography: Born 1946, Kaslo, BC. Full-time professional writer since 69; former songwriter with 5 albums of produced material for performer Paul Hann; Co-founder, President, Kicking Horse Productions Ltd., 77-82; advisory committee, Alberta Motion Picture Development Corporation, 84-85; Chairman, National Council, ACTRA Writers' Guild, 86.

Selected Filmography: *Striker's Mountain*, TV, 85, CDN, Wr; "The Beachcombers" (6 eps), TV, 82-83, CDN, Wr; "Stony Plain" (1 eps), TV, 81, CDN, Wr; "The Parent Puzzle" (10 eps), TV, 80, CDN, Wr; "Family and the Law" (10 eps), TV, 79, CDN, Co-Wr; "Barry Broadfoot's Pioneer Years" (13 eps), TV, 78, CDN, Co-Wr.

WHITING, Glynis
- see PRODUCERS

WILDEBLOOD, Peter
- see PRODUCERS

WILDMAN, Peter
ACTRA, EQUITY. 1253 Seagull Dr., Mississauga, ON L5J 3T6 (416)855-2828.
Type of Production and Credits: TV Film-Wr; Th Film-Wr.
Genres: Drama-TV; Comedy-TV; Musical-TV.
Biography: Founding member of "The (award-winning) Frantics." Now writing and directing for TV, stage and radio.
Selected Filmography: "Shining Time Station", TV, 91, CDN, Wr; "Maniac Mansion", TV, 90, CDN, Wr; "Mosquito Lake", TV, 90, CDN, Wr/Ed; "Out of the Blue", TV, 89, CDN, Wr/Ed; "Just for Laughs", TV, 87-88, CDN, Wr/Act.

WILKS, Wendell G.
- see PRODUCERS

WILLIAMS, Douglas
- see DIRECTORS

WILSCAM, Linda◇
SARDEC, UDA. (514)861-2227.
Types de production et générique: TV vidéo-Sc/Com.
Types d'oeuvres: Education-TV; Enfants-TV.
Curriculum vitae: Née en 1949. Etudes en journalisme, théâtre, langues et littérature; diplômée de l'Université McGill et du Conservatoire d'Art Dramatique de Montréal. Travaille comme comédienne; enseigne le théâtre; publie des contes pour enfants et des articles sur le théâtre.
Filmographie sélective: "Iniminimagimo", TV, 86-88, CDN, Co aut; "Alexandre et le Roi" (44 eps), TV, 78-80, CDN, Aut; "Picotine" (86 eps), TV, 71-77, CDN, Aut/Com; "Psst Psst, aie-là-clin d'oeil" (13 eps), TV, 74-75, CDN, Aut/Com.

WILSON, Sandra
- see DIRECTORS

WINEMAKER, Mark Joseph
- see PRODUCERS

WINKLER, Donald
- see DIRECTORS

WINKLER, Meita
- see DIRECTORS

WINNING, David
- see DIRECTORS

WODOSLAWSKY, Stefan
- see PRODUCERS

WOLFSON, Steve
- see PRODUCERS

WOODLAND, James◇
(403)249-8006.
Type of Production and Credits: Th Film-Wr; Th Short-Wr/Dir; TV Film-Wr/Dir/Prod.
Genres: Comedy-Th&TV; Science Fiction-Th&TV; Documentary-TV; Educational-TV.
Biography: Born 1960, Trenton, Ontario. Languages: English, German. Diploma, Film Production, Southern Alberta Institute of Technology, 80.
Selected Filmography: *The Ranch*, Th, 88, CDN, 3rd AD; *Personal Exemptions*, Th, 88, CDN, 3rd AD; *Wendy*, TV, 87, CDN, Dir; *My Way Works Best*, TV, 87, CDN, Dir; *Nuclear Freeze/Zero Degrees*, ED, 86, CDN, Wr/Dir; *Nuclear Winter/Death Zone*, ED, 85, CDN, Wr/Dir; *Women's Rights*, ED, 85, CDN, Wr/Dir; *Suzie Reader — A Tribute*, ED, 85, CDN, Prod/Wr/Dir; *Alberta Natural Landscapes*, TV, 85, CDN, Prod/Dir/Wr; *Force Sasquatch Service*, Th, 84, CDN, Co-Wr; *Tour de sasquatch*, Th, 84, CDN, Co-Wr/Dir; *Apartment on the Dark Side of the Moon*, TV, 84, CDN, 2nd AD; *Snowballs*, Th, 84, CDN, Wr; *Sasquatch Summer*, Th, 83, CDN, Co-Wr/Dir; *Death Zone Drug Set/Outside on the Playground* "School Smarts", ED, 82, CDN, Wr/1st AD.

WOODS, Grahame
ACTRA. RR #1, Castleton, ON K0K 1M0 (416)344-7665. Lucinda Vardey, 297 Seaton St., Toronto, ON M5A 2T6 (416)922-0250.
Type of Production and Credits: TV Film-Wr; TV Video-Wr.
Genres: Drama-TV; Comedy-TV.
Biography: Born 1934. Author of over 60 commissioned dramatic productions for Canadian and American networks. Author of the novel *Bloody Harvest* and the book for the musical *A Gift to Last*. Winner of the Margaret Collier Award for major body of work for TV, 1987.
Selected Filmography: *The Courage of the Early Morning*, TV, 91, CDN, Wr; "The Road to Avonlea" (1 eps), TV, 90, CDN, Wr; *Glory Enough for All*, TV, 87, CDN/GB, Wr, (GEMINI); 9B, TV, 86, CDN, Wr; *Anne's Story*, TV, 81, CDN, Wr; *A Question of the Sixth*, "For the Record", TV, 80, CDN, Wr; *War Brides*, TV, 79, CDN, Wr, (ACTRA); "Sidestreet" (1 eps),

TV, 75, CDN, Wr; "The Collaborators" (10 eps), TV, 73-74, CDN, Creator/Wr; "Police Surgeon" (1 eps), TV, 73, CDN/USA, Wr; *Vicky*, TV, 73, CDN, Wr, (ACTRA); *The Disposable Man*, TV, 72, CDN, Wr; *Kalinski's Justice*, TV, 71, CDN, Dir/Wr; *Strike!*, TV, 71, CDN, Wr; *Winter's Discontent*, TV, 71, CDN, Dir/Wr; *12-1/2 Cents*, TV, 70, CDN, Wr; *The Mercenaries*, TV, 70, CDN, Wr/Cin.

WOOLLEY, Stu
34 Lola Rd., Toronto, ON M5P 1E4 (416)483-7068. McCartney Enterprises Ltd., P.O. Box 128, Stn. Z, Toronto, ON M5N 2Z3 (416)250-6541.
Type of Production and Credits: TV Video-Wr.
Genres: Drama-TV; Comedy-TV; Horror-TV; Children's-TV.
Biography: Born in 1950 in London, England. Has both British and Canadian citizenship. Master of Arts in Religion from McGill University, Montreal, 1979. Raised in Montreal. Living in Toronto since 1985. 12 years scriptwriting experience in screenplay and teleplay formats. Has TV credits (episodic) but main commitment to long form projects, i.e. feature-length screenplays. Adaptation from prose is a particular interest. 3-time recipient of screenplay financing from F.U.N.D.
Selected Filmography: *To Make Amends*, "The Scene of the Crime", TV, 91, CDN/USA/F, Wr; *I Love Lucard*, "Dracula: The Series", TV, 91, CDN/USA/L, Wr; *Double Darkness*, "Dracula: The Series", TV, 90, CDN/USA/L, Wr.

WRONSKI, Peter
- see DIRECTORS

YOST, Elwy
- see PRODUCERS

ZALOUM, Alain
7873 Chateaubriand, Montreal, PQ H2R 2M5 (514)273-5062. Les Productions Optima Inc., 1253 McGill College, #452, Montreal, PQ H3B 2Y5 (514)397-9988.
Type of Production and Credits: Th Film-Wr/Dr.
Genres: Drama-Th&TV; Action-Th&TV; Commercials-Th&TV.
Biography: Born in 1961 in Egypt. Canadian citizen. Languages: English and French. Bachelor of Arts degree, majoring in Cinema and TV Production, University of Southern California. Collegial Diploma, majoring in Creative Arts, Vanier College, St-Laurent, Quebec.
Selected Filmography: *The Gypsy Kid*, Th, 91, CDN, Wr; *Canvas*, Th, 91, CDN, Dir/Ed; *Madonna/Sins of Seduction*, Th, 89, CDN, Dir/Ed; *The Classic*, Th, 88, CDN, Wr/Dir; *Quick Draw*, TV, 88, CDN, Dir/Ed; *Dead Man Out*, TV, 88, USA, Prod Assist; *Thirteen*, Th, 88, USA, Prod Assist; *Breakin' All The Rules*, Th, 84, CDN, Wr; *Joshua Then and Now*, Th, 84, USA, Prod Assist; *Habits for Life*, ED, 84, USA, Gaffer/Grip; *Dead Heat*, Th, USA, Prod Assist.

ZARITSKY, John
- see DIRECTORS

ZELDIN, Toby
ACTRA. Laissez-Faire Productions Inc., 5311 St. Urbain, Montreal, PQ H2T 2W8 (514)278-1521. Lesley Harrison, M.G.A. Agency, 10 St. Mary St., Ste. 510, Toronto, ON M4Y 1P9 (416)964-3302.
Type of Production and Credits: Th Film-Wr/Prod; TV Film-Wr.
Genres: Drama-Th&TV; Action-TV; Documentary-Th&TV; Industrial-TV.
Biography: Born in 1960. Bachelor of Applied Arts, Motion Picture Studies & Photographic Arts, Ryerson Polytechnical Institute, Toronto, 1983. Scholarships include: CBC TV Drama Writers' Workshop, Montreal,1991; Banff Screenwriters' Workshop, 1988. Fellowship, Banff Television Festival, 1988 & 1989. Assistant casting director, Toronto, 1982-84. *Max, My Brother*, feature in development, based on *Max, Mein Brüder* (young readers' novel by Sigrid Zeevaert). *Alone Together*, TV movie optioned by Vision 4, Montreal, 1991. Theatre: Cowriter *Exhibiting Disgusting Material*, Nightwood Theatre, Toronto, 1990; writer *Bargirls*, Bathurst St. Theatre premier, Toronto, 1986. Script reader: Telefilm Canada, YTV, Banff Centre for Fine Arts, individual clients. Promotional writer for the National Film Board of Canada. Executive board member, Femmes du cinéma, de la télévision et de la vidéo à Montréal, 1990-91.
Selected Filmography: *Oddy's Moving & Storage*, In, 91, CDN, Prod/Wr/Dir; *The First Step*, ED/TV, 90, CDN, Story Conslt; *Flying High*, "Time to Read", TV, 90, CDN, Wr; *Fire and Ice*, "Urban Angel", TV, 90, CDN, Wr; *Moving Mountains*, TV, 90, CDN, Wr/Res/Assist Prod; *Voices*, ED/TV, 88-90, CDN, Assoc Dir/Assoc Prod; *The Believers*, Th, 86, USA, Assist to Prod; *The Sea In Danger*, "The Last Frontier", TV, 86, CDN, Wr/Assist Ed; "Lifetime", TV, 85-86, CDN, Story Ed; *Head Office*, Th, 84, USA, Assist to Wr/Dir; *Lucian's Conversations in High Society*, ED/TV, CDN, Wr/Dir/Prod.

ZELNIKER, Richard
ACTRA. 21 Tichester Rd., # 1209, Toronto, ON M5P 1P3 (416)654-4691. Ralph Zimmerman, Great North Artists Management, 350 Dupont St., Toronto, ON M5R 1V9 (416)925-2051.
Type of Production and Credits: Th Film-Wr; Th Short-Wr; TV Film-Wr; TV Video-Wr.
Genres: Drama-Th&TV; Comedy-Th&TV; Action-TV; Children's-Th&TV.
Biography: Born 1954, Montreal, Quebec. Has written plays for theatre: *A Test of Will*, 85; *Scorched*, 86. *Destiny's Angel* won an Honourable Mention, American Film Awards, 80.
Selected Filmography: "Check It Out!" (5 eps), TV, 86, CDN/USA, Story Ed/Staff Wr; *Bon Appetit*, Th, 82, USA, Scr; "Littlest Hobo" (1 eps), TV, 81, CDN, Wr; *Destiny's Angel*, Th, 80, CDN, Scr; *Hey Babe!*, Th, 79, CDN, Story Ed; *Pinball Summer*, Th, 79, CDN, Scr; *A Simple Complex*, Th, 78, CDN, Wr.

ZIELIŃSKA, Ida Eva
Spiral Studios Inc., 3170 Place de Ramezay, Montreal, PQ H3Y 2B5 (514)934-3317.
Type of Production and Credits: Th Film-Wr; Th Short-Dir/Prod/Wr/An.
Genres: Drama-Th&TV; Comedy-Th&TV; Action-Th&TV; Science Fiction-Th&TV.
Biography: Born 1957, Warsaw, Poland; resided in India, Egypt, USA, Canada; Canadian citizenship. Languages: English, French, Polish, some Spanish. Bachelor of Fine Arts, Magna Cum Laude, Concordia University, 80; enrolled in Masters of Educational Technology program, Concordia, 86. Background in research, animation, visual arts and music performance. Since 87, specializing in screenwriting (with funding from Telefilm Canada, SOGIC and F.U.N.D.). Founder (81) and President of Spiral Studios Inc., and Ida Vea Publishing (music publishing). *Trespass* won Best Short award at International Film Festival of Ste-Therese. Writer pen-name is Ida Eva Hajmovicz.
Selected Filmography: *Ucopan Barbados Project*, In, 86, CDN, Prod/Wr/Dir; *Trespass*, Th, 85, CDN, Wr/Prod/Dir/Des; *Odd Balls*, Th, 83, CDN, VFX Des; *Screwballs*, Th, 82, CDN, VFX Des; *Agency*, Th, 79, CDN, Co-An/VFX Des; *Old Orchard Beach P.Q.*, Th, 79, CDN, An; Centre du rembourreur, Cm, 79, CDN, Wr/Dir/Des/An; *Heads or Tails*, Th, 78, CDN, Wr/Prod/Dir.

ZOLLER, Stephen◊
(416)366-3966.
Type of Production and Credits: Th Film-Wr/Prod; Th Short-Wr/Prod.
Genres: Drama-Th; Science Fiction-Th; Children's-Th.
Biography: Born in 1952 in Budapest, Hungary. *Snow* received award at Chicago Film Festival and a Genie nomination.
Selected Filmography: *The Office Party*, Th, 88, CDN, Co-Wr; *Snow*, Th, 82, CDN, Co-Prod/Wr; *The Tomorrow Man*, Th, 78, CDN, Wr/Co-Prod, (CFTA); *Metal Messiah*, Th, 76, CDN, Co-Prod/Wr.

ZWICKER, Linda
ACTRA. 30 Hillsboro Ave., #1903, Toronto, ON M5R 1S7 (416)967-4103. Krisztina Bevilacqua, 85 Roosevelt Rd., Toronto, ON M4J 4T8 (416)463-7009.
Type of Production and Credits: TV Film-Wr.
Genres: Drama-TV.
Biography: Born 1944, Saskatchewan. Background in music, arts administration, theatre production. Wrote *The Panther and the Jaguar*, 83, which won an ACTRA Award, Best Radio Program; ACTRA Award, Best Writer, Original Radio Program for *Gray Pearls*, 86.
Selected Filmography: *Easter at Igloolik: Peter's Story*, TV, 87, CDN, Wr; *Tafia's Dream*, "Spirit Bay", TV, 85, CDN, Wr.

Index

A'COURT, Susan ....WR, PR
ABASTADO, Lise ....PD
ABBOTT, Roger ....WR
ABONYI, Susan ....PR
ADAIR, Trayton ....DR
ADAMAKOS, Peter ....PR, WR, DR, ED
ADAMS, Ellen ....SE
ADAMS, G. Chalmers ....PR
ADETUYI, Alfons ....PR, DR
ADETUYI, Robert......................WR, PR
AIKENHEAD, Chris ....PS, WR, DR
AIREY, Paul ....CO
ALEXANDER, Alisa ....CD
ALEXANDER, Andrew ....PR
ALEXANDER, Kelley ....PB
ALEXANDRA, C.P. ....CO, PM, DR, WR
ALIANAK, Hrant ....DR, WR
ALIX, Stephen ....WR, PR
ALLAN, Don ....DR, PR
ALLAN, Sean ....PR, WR
ALLAN, Ted ....WR
ALLEN-WOOLFE, Nicholas CI
ALMOND, Paul ....DR, WR, PR
ALPERT, Herbert CI
ALVAREZ, Paco ....PR, PM
AMES, Paul ....AD
AMINI, Stephen ....DR
AMITAY, Jonathan ....PR, WR, DR
ANDERSON, G. Bruce ....PM
ANDERSON, Jon C. ....PR, DR, WR
ANDERSON, Michael ....DR, PR
ANDREWS, Neil ....PR, WR, DR, PM
ANGELOVICI, Gaston André ....PD, RE
APOR, Gabor ....PR, DR
APPLEBAUM, Louis ....CO
APPLEBY, David ....PE
APPLEBY, George ....ED

AQUILA, James CI
ARBEID, Gerry ....PM
ARCAND, Denys ....RE, SC
ARCAND, Michel ....MO, CM
ARCHER, Tim ....PS
ARCHIBALD, Nancy ....PR, DR
ARMATAGE, Kay ....DR
ARMSTRONG, Antony ....PR, DR
ARMSTRONG, Mary ....PR, DR
ARNOTT, Duane ....WR
ARRON, Wayne ....PR
ARSENAULT, Ray ....DR
ARSENAULT, Yvon ....RE, PD, SC
ARSENEAU, Joanne ....SC
AUCKLAND, Geoff ....ED
AUDY, Michel ....RE, SC, CT, MO
AYLWARD, Alan W. ....DR, WR, PR
AZIZ, Stewart CI
AZZOPARDI, Anthony .....DR, WR, PR
AZZOPARDI, Mario ....DR

B

BACHMAN, Kay ....PR
BACKUS, Barry ....PE, ED, DR, PR
BAILEY, Norma ....DR, PR
BAILIE, Barbara ....PB
BAILIE, Philip ....CD, AD
BAIRD, Douglas CI
BAKER, Bob ....DR, PR, ED
BAKER, Michael Conway ....CO
BALCER, Rene C. ....WR
BALL, Christopher ....DR, PR, CI, SE
BALSER, Dean ....ED
BANNING, Everett ....PR, WR
BARBEAU, Manon ....SC
BARCLAY, John ....DR, ED
BARCLAY, Robert ....DR, PR
BARDE, Barbara ....PR, DR
BARKER, Nicholas ....RG
BARLOW, David ....PR, WR, DR
BARNES, Milton ....CO
BARNEY, Bryan ....WR
BARRA, Gemma ....SC, CM
BARRIE, Scott ....WR, DR, ED
BARRIS, Alex ....WR
BARRIS, Kate ....WR
BARTON, Natalie ....PD, RE
BASARABA, Catherine ....AD
BASEN, Leila ....WR
BATTISON, Jill ....PR, DR
BATTISTA, Franco ....PR, ED
BATTLE, Murray ....DR, WR
BAUMAN, Larry ....DR, WR, PR, ED
BAZAY, David ....PR
BEAIRSTO, Ric ....DR
BEARDE, Chris ....PR, WR
BEAUBIEN, Conrad ....PR, DR, WR
BEAUBIEN, Joseph F. ....PD
BEAUCHEMIN, Claude ....SP
BEAUCHEMIN, François ....DP
BEAUCHEMIN, Guy ....DA

BEAUCHEMIN, Serge ....SP
BEAUCHEMIN, Yves ....SC
BEAUDET, Michel ....RE, PD
BEAUDOIN, Jean ....MO, RE
BEAUDRY, Jean ....RE, SC
BEAUDRY, Michel ....RE, SC
BEDARD, Jean-Thomas ....RE
BEDEL, Jean-Pierre ....DR, PR
BEEFORTH, Doug ....PR
BEETON, William ....AD
BEKKER, Hennie ....CO
BELANGER, André A. ....RE, PD
BELANGER, Jacques ....PD
BELANGER, Raymond ....DR
BELEC, Marilyn A. ....DR, PR
BELEC, Philip ....DR, PR
BELISLE, Pierre ....RE, PD
BELL, Allan Gordon ....CO
BELL, John G. ....DR, PR, WR
BELLEMARE, Rénald ....DP
BELZILE, Jocelyn ....DP
BENISON, Peter CI
BENOIT, Denyse ....RE, SC
BENOIT, Jacques ....SC
BENOIT, Jean-Marie ....CM
BENOIT, Ted ....PR, DR, PM
BENSIMON, Jacques ....RE
BERGERON, Guy ....PD, RE, RG, MO
BERGMAN, Robert ....DR, PR, WR
BERMAN, Brigitte ....DR, PR
BERMAN, Jeffrey ....PM
BERNS, Marvin ....PE
BERRY, Michael J. ....DR, PR
BERTOLINO, Daniel ....PD, RE
BERTON, Pierre ....WR
BESSADA, Milad ....PR, DR, WR
BHATIA, Amin ....CO
BIENSTOCK, Ric Esther ....PR, PM
BINGEMAN, Alison ....WR
BINNINGTON, Andrew CI
BIRD, Christopher ....PM
BISSONNETTE, Sophie ....RE
BITTMAN, Roman ....PR, DR
BJORNSON, Michelle WR, DR, ED, PR
BLACK, Jennifer..................................PR
BLACKIE, John S. ....AD
BLAIS, Micheline ....PD, RE
BLAIS, Pascal ....RE
BLANCHARD, André ....SC, RE, PD
BLICKER, Seymour ....WR
BLOOMFIELD, George ....DR
BLOUIN, C. Denis ....PR
BLOUIN, Paul ....RE
BLOW, Peter ....WR,DR
BLUE, Julie ....CO
BLUM, Jack ....WR, PR
BLUM, Len ....WR
BLYE, Garry ....PR, WR
BOARD, John ....PR
BOBET, Jacques ....PD, SC
BOCKING, Richard C. ......PR, DR, WR

BOCKING, Robert V. ....CI, ED, SE, PR
BODOLAI, Joe ....WR, PR, DR
BOIRE, Roger ....PD
BOISVERT, Dominique ....ED, SE
BOISVERT, Nicole M. ....PD
BOISVERT, Paul CI
BOITEAU, Denise ....WR, PR
BOLAND, Deborah ....PR
BOLEN, Norm ....PR, WR
BOLTON, Michael ....AD
BOMPHRAY, Clinton ....WR
BOND, Richard ....ED, SE
BOND, Timothy ....DR, WR
BONENFANT, Mario ....RE
BONIN, Claude ....PD
BONIN, Jacques ....PD
BONNER, Michael ....DR, WR, CI
BONNIERE, Christophe CI
BONNIERE, Claude ....AD
BONNIERE, René ....DR
BOOK, Don ....PS
BOOTH, Alan ....DR, CI, PR
BORREMANS, Guy ....DP
BORRIS, Clay ....DR, WR
BORSOS, Phillip ....DR
BOUCHARD, Louise ....RE
BOUCHARD, Louise-Anne ....SC
BOUCHARD, Michel ....RE, SC, PD
BOUCHER, Diane ....MP
BOURASSA-DUTTON, John ...DR, ED
BOURDON, Laurent ....PD
BOURGET, Elizabeth ....SC
BOURNE, Lindsay ....WR, PR
BOURQUE, Paul ....PD
BOWIE, Douglas ....WR
BOWLBY, Barbara ....PR
BOYCE, M. Susanne ....PR
BOYDEN, Barbara ....PR, WR, DR
BOYER, Claire ....MO
BRADSHAW, John R. ....DR, WR
BRADSTREET, David ....CO
BRAIDWOOD, Tom ....PM
BRAITHWAITE, Diana ....WR
BRANDES, David ....WR
BRANDT, C.V. (Caryl) ....PR, DR
BRASSARD, André ....RE
BRASSEUR, Raymond ....PD
BRAULT, Michel ....RE, PD, DP
BREDIN, James ....ED
BRENNAN, Fred ....SE
BRESLIN, Mark ....WR
BRINTON, Donald C. ....PR
BROADFOOT, Dave ....WR
BROCHU, Pierre ....SC, RE, PD
BRODIE, Bill ....AD
BROMFIELD, Rex ....WR, DR
BROMLEY, Karen ....AD
BRONFMAN, Paul ....PR
BRONSARD, Louis ....DR, ED
BRONSKILL, Richard ....CO, ME
BROOKS, Nicholas CI

BROOKS, Robert CI
BROUSSEAU, Pierre ....PD
BROWN, Alastair ....DR
BROWN, Alexandra ....PR
BROWN, Barbara ....WR, ED
BROWN, Jamie ....PR, WR
BROWN, Lyal D. ....WR
BROWNE, Christene ....PR, DR
BROWNE, Colin ....DR, WR, ED
BRULOTTE, Gaétan ....SC
BRUNELLE, Wendy A. ......WR, DR, PR
BRUNJES, Ralph ....ED
BRUNTON, John ....PR
BRUYERE, Christian ....WR, DR
BRYANT, Chris ....WR
BRYDON, Loyd ....PR, WR, DR
BUCHAN, Bob ....ED
BUCHANAN, Jack ....PS, PE
BUCHSBAUM, Don ....PM
BUDGELL, Jack ....PR, DR
BUGAJSKI, Richard ....DR, WR
BUJOLD, Paul ....PM
BURKE, Alan ....PR
BURKE, Dennis ....CO, PS, PE
BURKE, Martyn ....DR, WR
BURMAN, Tony ....PR, WR
BURNS, Michael ....PR
BURSTYN, Thomas CI
BURT, Jim ....WR
BURT, Montgomery ....WR
BURTON, Robert H. .PR, PM, WR, DR
BUSATO, Paul ....WR, PR
BUSH, Bert ....ED
BUTLER, Rick ....WR
BUTTIGNOL, Rudy ....PR, WR, DR
BUXTON, Bonnie ....WR

C

CACOPARDO, Max ....RE, SC
CAHILL, T.J. ....WR, PR, DR
CAILHIER, Diane ....DP
CAILLOUX, Michel ....SC
CAINES-FLOYD, Eydi ....CD
CALLAGHAN, Barry ....WR
CAMERON, B.A. ....WR
CAMERON, Silver Donald ....WR
CAMPANELLI, Stephen CI
CAMPBELL, Graeme N. ....DR
CAMPBELL, Harry ....PR
CAMPBELL, Norman ....DR, PR
CAMPBELL, Peg ....DR, WR, PR
CAMPBELL, Robin ....DR, WR
CAMPEAU, Luc ....PM
CANELL, Marrin ....PR, DR
CANNING, Bob ....DR
CAPISTRAN, France ....RE
CAPISTRAN, Michel ....SC
CAPPE, Syd ....PR
CARDINAL, Roger ....RE
CARLE, Gilles ....RE, SC
CARLSON, Elaine ....WR

CARMODY, Don ....PR, WR
CARON, Louis ....SC
CARR, Warren H. ....PR, PM
CARTMER, Debbie ....DR, PR, WR
CARUSO, Elius ....PE
CARWARDINE, D. Bruce ....PS
CASEY, Bill ....CI, PR
CASSAR, Jon CI
CASSON, Barry ....PR, DR
CASTONGUAY, Viateur ....PD
CASTRAVELLI, C. .....DR, PR, WR, ED
CAULFIELD, Paul ....PR, DR
CAVAN, Susan ....PR
CAYWOOD, Bill ....PM
CEREGHETTI, J.-P. ....MO, MS, MM
CHAMBERLAIN, David ....PR
CHAMMAS, Robert ....PR, DR, CI
CHAMPAGNE, Edith ....PR
CHAMPAGNE, François ....PD
CHAMPION, Marc CI
CHAN, David ....PR
CHAPDELAINE, Gérard ....RE
CHAPELLE, Nancy ....PR
CHAPMAN, C. ....DR, PR, ED, CI
CHAPMAN, Dennis ....PM
CHAREST, Gaétan ....PD, RE, SC
CHAREST, Louis ....RE
CHAREST, Micheline ....PR
CHARLES, David Orin ....AD
CHARTRAND, Alain ....RE
CHATO, Paul ....WR
CHAYER, Lise ....RE
CHAYER, Réjean ....RE
CHEIKES, Stephen ....PR
CHENTRIER, Bernard ....DP
CHERCOVER, Murray ....PR, DR, PM
CHERNIACK, David ....DR, WR, PR
CHETWYND, Lionel ....WR, PR, DR
CHETWYND, Robin J. ....PR
CHICK, Russell David ....AD
CHICOINE, Nicole ....RE, DP, MO
CHILCO, Cathy ....PR
CHILCO, Joe ....WR
CHILVERS, Colin ....DR
CHOJNACKI, Julian CI
CHOW, Wang CI
CHRISTIE, Keith ....DR, PR, AD, WR
CHURCH, Babs ....PR
CICCORITTI, Gerard ....DR, WR, PR
CIUP, Charles ....DR
CIUPKA, Richard ....DR, CI
CLACKSON, Brent-Karl ....PM
CLAIROUX, Jacques ....MO, RE
CLARK, Alison ....SE, PS, ED
CLARK, Barry ....PR, WR, DR
CLARK, Bob ....DR, PR
CLARK, Louise ....PR, PM
CLARK, Paulle ....PR, DR
CLARK, Ron ....WR, PR, DR
CLARKSON, Adrienne ....PR, WR
CLEMENTS, Peter ....PS
CLERMONT, Nicolas ....PR
CLYNE, Dale ....PE, SE, ME, PS
COACH, Ken ....PR, WR
COATSWORTH, David ....PM, PR
COCHRAN, Andrew ....PR, WR, DR
COCK, Peter J. B. ....DR, WR, PR, ED
COHEN, Annette ....PR, WR
COHEN, Donald ....PS
COHEN, Jeffrey ....WR
COHEN, Leonard ....CO
COHEN, M. Charles ....WR
COHEN, Ronald I. ....PR
COHEN, Sidney M. ....DR, PR
COLE, Frank ....DR
COLE, Janis ....PR, DR, WR, ED
COLE, Stan ....ED
COLE, Steven ....PE, SE
COLEMAN, Rob ....PM
COLLEY, Peter ....WR, PR
COLLIER, Mike ....PR, DR, ED
COLLIER, Ron ....CO
COLLINS, Alan ....DR, ED, PR
COLLINS, Neil ....WR, PR, DR
COLVIN, Suzanne ....PM
COMEAU, Guy ....RE
COMEAU, Phil ....DR, WR, ED
CONDIE, Richard ....DR
CONNOLLY, Bea Broda ....PR, WR
CONNOLLY, Phillip J. ....DR, WR
CONSTANTINEAU, Daniel ....CM
CONTENT, Phil ....ED
COOK, Heather ....PR, WR, DR
COOK, R. David ....PR, DR
COOKE, Lindsay Ann ....PR, WR
COOPER, Richard .....WR, PR, DR, CO
COOPER, Robert ....PR
COPELAND, Greg ....PR, PM
COPEMAN, Bruce ....ED
CORDER, Sharon ....WR, PR
CORNFORD, Darryl ....ED, SE, ME, PE
CORRIVEAU, André ....MO
CORRIVEAU, Jean ....CM, MP
COSMATOS, George P ....DR
COTE, François J. ....RE
COUELLE, Marcia ....PR
COUSINEAU, Gaston ....PD
COUTURE, Bernard CI
COUTURE, Jacques ....SC
COUTURE, Suzette ....WR, PR
COWLING, Barry ....PR, WR
COX, Kirwan ....PR
CRAIGEN, Geoff ....ED
CRESSEY, John ....CI, DR
CRONE, David CI
CRONE, Robert C. CI
CRONENBERG, David ....DR, WR
CRONENBERG, Denise ....CD
CROSLEY, Lawrence (Larry) ......CO, PR
CROSSLAND, H. ....DR, WR, PR, ED
CSABA, Kertész A. ....AD
CUDDY, Janet ....PM

CULBERT, Bob ....PR
CULLEN, Patricia ....CO
CURNICK, David ....DR
CURRIE, Anthony ....SE, WR, DR
CURTIS, Dan ....DR, WR, PR
CUTAJAR, Susan ....PB
CUTHAND, Doug ....PR, DR, WR
CUTLER, Keith ....PR, WR, DR, ED
CYNAMON, Helena ..PR, DR, WR, ED

D

D'AGOSTINO, Len ....PM, PR
D'AIX, Alain ....RE, SC
DAFOE, Francis ....CD
DAGENAIS, Bernard ....PD
DAIGLE, Marc ....PD
DALE, Holly ....DR, PR
DALE, James ....CO
DALE, Miles ....PR
DALEN, Laara ....PR, PM
DALEN, Zale ....DR, WR
DALTON, Chris .... PR
DALTON, Ninkey ....AD
DAMBERGER, Francis ......WR, DR, PR
DAMUDE, D. Brian ...WR, PR, DR, ED
DANDY, Michael ....SE, ED
DANE, Lawrence ....PR, DR
DANIELS, David J. ....PR
DANIS, Aimée ....PD, RE
DANNA, Mychael ....CO
DANSEREAU, Fernand ....RE
DANSEREAU, Jean ....PD, RE
DANSEREAU, Mireille ....RE, SC
DANYLKIW, John ....PR, PM
DARCUS, Jack ....DR, WR, PR
DARK, Randall Paris ....PR, DR, WR
DARLING, Gillian .....PR, WR, DR, PM
DAVID, Pierre ....PR
DAVIES, Victor ....CO
DAVIS, Bill ....DR
DAVIS, David ....AD
DAVIS, Richard ....PR, DR, PM
DAVIDSON, Tom ....DR
DAY, Deborah ....PR, WR, PM
DE BAYSER, Eric ....MO
DE CARUFEL, René ....DP, PD, RE
de COTIIS, Franco ....AD
DE GRANDPRE, Sylvie ....RG
de LUCY, François ....DA
DE ROCHEMONT, Nicole ....PD, SC
DE SILVA, Paul ....PR, DR
DE VOLPI, David CI
DEL ROSARIO, Linda ....AD
DEFELICE, James ....WR, DR
DELACROIX, Yves ....DP
DELEUZE, Marc ....ED
DELMAGE, John A. ....PR
DELOREY, Walter J. .....PR, DR, CI, ED
DEMERS, Rock ....PD
DEMEULE, Nadine .....RE, PD, MO, SC
DENIKE, Brian ....PR, DR, WR

DENSHAM, Pen ....PR, WR, DR
DEROME, Gilles ....RE
DESBIENS, Francine ....RE
DESCHAMPS, Yvon ....PD, SC
DESCHENES, Clément ....SC, RE
DESCOMBES, J. Michel ....MP
DESHARNAIS, Jacques ....DP, MO
DESJARDINS, Claude ....PD, RE
DESJARDINS, Jacques ....SC, MO, RE
DESJARDINS, Normand ....SC
DESKIN, Andrew ....AD
DEVEAU, Marie-Sylvie ....CD
DEVERELL, Rex ....WR
DEVERELL, William H. ....WR
DEVINE, David ....PR, DR, WR
DEW, Simon Christopher ....PR, DR
DEWALT, Kevin ....PR, DR
DEWAR, David ....PR, DR
DEWAR, Stephen W. ....PR, WR
DEY, Wendy E. ....PR, WR
DI CIAULA, Pia ....ED
DIBAI, Nastaran ....CI, PR
DICK, Jacques ....PD
DIEHL, Barrie ....PR, PM
DIMARCO, Steve ....DR, WR, PR
DIMITROV, Olga ....CD
DINEL, Pierre ....SC, RE, PD
DION, Jean-Yves ....DP, MO, PD, RE
DION, Yves ....RE, MO, SC
DIONNE, Francine ....PD
DIXON, Will ....DR, WR
DOBBIE, Scott ....AD
DODD, Marian ....PR, DR, WR, PB
DOHERTY, Tom ....AD
DOLGAY, Marvin Ian ....CO
DONLON, Denise ....PR, DR, WR
DONOVAN, Michael ....PR
DONOVAN, Michael Leo ....WR
DONOVAN, Paul ....DR, WR
DORN, Rudi ....AD, DR, WR
DORRIS, Jocelyne ....RE
DOSTIE, Alain ....DP
DOUGHTY, Robert ....ED
DOUGLAS, Michael ....DR, WR
DOYLE, Patrick ....PR
DRAKE, Christopher ....CD
DRAKE, Sally ....WR
DRAKE, Tom ....WR, DR, PR
DREW, Rick ....WR
DROT, Jean-Marie ....MO
DROUIN, Dominique ....SC
DRYSDALE, Alyson ....PR, WR
DUBHE, Thérèse ....RE
DUBRO, James R. ....WR, PR, DR
DUFRESNE, Héléne ....PD, RG
DUCHESNE, Christiane ....SC
DUCKWORTH, Martin .....DR, CI, ED
DUDINSKY, Donna ....PR
DUFAUX, Georges ....DP
DUFAUX, Guy ....DP
DUFFELL, Greg ....DR

DUKE, Daryl ....DR
DUMOULIN-TESSIER, Françoise ....SC
DUNBAR, George CI
DUNCAN, Bob ....WR, PR, DR
DUNDAS, Sally ....PR
DUNK, Albert CI
DUNLOP, Charles L. ....AD
DUNNING, John ....PR, WR
DUNPHY, Barbara ....AD
DUNPHY, Timothy ....WR
DUPUIS, François ....MO
DUPUIS, Raymond ....DA, MO
DURBAN, Jan ....PM
DYS, Hans J. ....WR, PR

E

EAMES, David ....WR
EARL, Morgan ....PR, WR
EARNSHAW, Philip CI
EASTMAN, Allan ....DR
EASTWOOD, Janet ....PB
ECKERT, John M. ....PR, DR
EDMONDS, Alan ....PR, WR
EDWARDS, Cash ....WR, PR, DR
EGARHOS, Spyro ....DR
EGOYAN, Atom ....DR, WR, PR
EIGENMANN, Jean-Daniel ....PD
EKMAN, Brian ....PB
EL-SISSI, Azza ....PR, WR, DR, PM
ELDER, Bruce ....DR
ELDRIDGE, Scott ....DR, ED
ELLIOTT, Keith ....PE, CO
ELLIOTT, William G. ....DR
ELLIS, Kathryn ....PB, WR
ELLIS, R. Stephen ....PR
ELLIS, Ralph C. ....PR
ELLIS, Rick ....PE
ELSON, Richard ....PD
EMERSON, Peter ....DI
EMERY, Prudence ....PB
EMPRY, Gino ....PB
ENDERSBY, Clive ....WR
ENGEL, Howard ....WR
ENGEL, Paul David ....PR
ENNIS, Bob ....CI, PR
ERBE, Micky ....CO
ERICKSON, Jim ....DR, PR, ED
ERLICH, Alan ....DR, PR
ERNE, Andreas ....PR, WR, DR
ESSIAMBRE, Gaetan ....CM
ETHIER, Martial ....MO, RE, DP
EVANS, David ....SE
EVANS, Janet ....PR
EVANS, Margaret ....WR, PR
EVDEMON, Nikos CI

F

FAIRE, Sandra ....PR, WR, DR
FALZON, Charles ....PR
FANFARA, Stephan ....ED, PR
FARB, Robin ....PB

FARR, Gordon ....PR, WR, DR
FAUCHER, Jean ....RE
FAUCHER, Nicole ....RE
FAVREAU, Robert ....RE, SC, MO
FEARNLEY, Neill ....DR
FEDORENKO, Eugene ....DR
FEINGOLD, Stan ....WR, PR, DR, CO
FENSKE, Wayne ....PR
FERGUSON, Don ....WR
FERGUSON, Graeme ....DR, PR, CI
FERNANDES, Eliza ....PB
FERNANDES, Gavin ....PE
FERNS, W. Paterson ....PR, WR, DR
FERRAGNE, Marielle ....SC
FERRETTI, Nina ....PR, WR
FERRON, René ....PD, RE
FERSTMAN, Brian ....PM, PR
FICHMAN, Ina ....PR
FICHMAN, Niv ....PR, DR
FIELDING, Joy ....WR
FIKS, Henri CI
FILLINGHAM, Tom C
FILTHAUT, Fred ....PR
FINDLEY, Timothy ....WR
FINE, David ....DR, WR
FINNIGAN, Joan ....WR
FIRUS, Karen ....DR, WR, AD
FISCHER, David ....AD
FLAHERTY, David ....WR
FLAHIVE, Gerry ....PB
FLAK, George ....PR
FLANNERY, Seamus ....AD
FLEMING, Susan K. ....PM
FLOQUET, Franççois ....PD, RE
FLOREN, Russell ....PR
FODOR, Thomas C. ....PR
FOLDY, Peter ....WR, PR
FOLLOWS, E.J.(Ted) ....DR
FORD-BARKER, Heather ....PM
FOREST, Claude ....PR
FOREST, José ....RE
FORMAN, Howard ....CO, ME
FORTIER, Bob ....DR, PR
FORTIER, Josée ....SC
FORTIN, Armand ....RE, MO
FORTIN, Dominique ....MO, SC
FORTIN, Richard ....CO
FOSTER, Christine ....WR
FOSTER, John C. ....PR, DR, WR
FOSTER, Stephen ....PR
FOURNIER, Claude ....RE, SC
FOURNIER, Eric ....PD
FOURNIER, Jacques ....RE
FOURNIER, Lili ....PR
FOURNIER, Robert ....RE
FOURNIER, Roger ....SC, RE
FOX, Beryl ....PR, DR
FOX, Liz ....PR, DR
FOX, Lloyd M. CI
FRANCON, Georges ....RE
FRANK, Anne ....PR

FRANK, Ilana ....PR
FRANK, Jim ....PE
FRANKLIN, Elsa ....PR
FRAPPIER, Roger ....PD
FRASER, Eric ....AD
FRASER, Fil ....WR, PR
FRASER, Louis ....RE
FRECHETTE, Michel ....RE
FREED, Reuben ....AD
FREEDMAN, Harry ....CO
FREEMAN, Jean ....WR
FRENCH, Stuart ....PS
FREWER, Terry ....CO, WR, PR
FRICKER, Brock ....PS, CO, SE
FRITZ, Sherilyn ....CO
FRIZZELL, John ....WR
FROST, F. Harvey ....DR, WR
FRUET, William ....DR, WR, PR
FRUND, Jean-Louis ....RE
FULLER, Michael ....ED
FUREY, Lewis ....CO, DR
FURIE, Sidney J. ....DR, WR
FUSCA, Martha ....PR, DR, WR

G

GABRIELE, Vincent........................PD
GABOURIE, Richard ....PR, WR
GAD, Ezz E. ....PR
GAGLIARDI, Laurent ....RE, SC
GAGNE, Pier ....RE
GAGNON, André ....CM
GAGNON, Claude ....RE, SC, PD
GAGNON, Pierre ....RE
GALLO, Carmi ....AD
GALLUS, Maya ....DR
GAMBLE, Victor ....PS
GANDER, Mogens ....PR, CI
GANDOL, Pedro B. ....DR, PS
GANTON, Douglas ....PS
GAREAU, John ....PR, DR, ED
GAUTHIER, Fred ....ED, DR
GAUTHIER, Vianney ....DA
GAUVIN, Paul ....PD, RE
GAUVREAU, Gil .... PR, WR, CI
GEDDES, David CI
GELDART, Alan ....SE, PS, PE
GELINAS, Gratien ....SC
GELINAS, Josée P. ....SC
GELINAS, Marc ....SC
GELINAS, Marc F. ....CM, SC
GÉLINAS, Michel ....PD, RD, MO, DP
GÉLINAS, Michel F. ....RE
GELLMAN-FRIEDMAN, J. ....CD
GENDRON, Pierre ....PD
GEOFFRION, Robert ....SC
GEORGE, Laszlo CI
GERBER, Sig ....PR, DR, WR
GEROFSKY, Susan ....SE, ED
GERRETSEN, Patricia ....PR, PM
GERRETSEN, Peter ....DR, WR
GERVAIS, Suzanne ....RE

GIBB, Alan D. ....ED, PR
GIBBONS, Bob ....DR, PR
GILBERT, Tony ....PR, DR, WR
GILDAY, Katherine ....WR, DR, PR
GILDAY, Leonard ....CI, DR, PR
GILL, Shirley J. ....PM
GILLARD, Stuart ....DR, WR, PR
GILLIS, Kevin ....PR, WR, DR, CO
GILLSON, Malca ....DR, ED, SE, ME
GILROY, Grace ....PM
GINSBERG, Donald ....PR, DR, ED
GIRALDEAU, Jacques ....RE, SC, PD
GIRARD, Hélène ....MO, RE
GIRARD, Simon ....RE
GIROTTI, Ken ....DR
GJERSTAD, Ole ....PR, WR, DR
GLASSBOURG, Michael ....WR, PR
GLAWSON, Bruce ....PR
GODBOUT, Claude ....PD
GODDARD, Bill ....ED
GODDARD, Eric ....ED
GOETZ, Ron ....PR, DR
GOLD, Howard ....PR
GOLDBERG, Howard ....DR, ED
GOLDMAN, Alvin ....WR
GOLDSTEIN, Allan ....DR
GOLDSTEIN, Roushell ....ED, DR
GOLICK, Jill ....WR
GOODMAN, Paul W. ....PR, DR, WR
GOODWILL, Jonathan ....PR
GOODWIN, Michael ....AD
GOOREVITCH, David S. ....ED, WR
GORBACHOW, Yuri ....PS, ME
GORD, Eva ....CD
GORD, Ken ....PR, PM
GORDICA, Terry ....PE, PS, SE
GORDON, Ben ....WR, PR
GORDON, Lee ....DR
GORRARA, Perri ....AD
GOTTLIEB, Paul ....WR
GOUDSOUZIAN, Hajop ....PR, DR
GOUGH, William ....PR, WR, DR
GOULD, Derek ....PE
GOULET, Stella ....RE, SC
GRACE, Alison ....SE
GRADIDGE, Havelock ....ED
GRANT, Trudy ....PR
GRAVELLE, Raymond ....PD, DP, RE
GRAY, John H. ....WR, CO
GRAY, Nicholas J. ....PM
GRAY, William ....WR, PR
GREAN, Wendy ....PR, PM
GREEN, Cari ....PR
GREEN, Howard ....PR, DR, WR
GREEN, Joseph G. ....PR
GREENBERG, Brenda M. ....PR
GREENBERG, Harold ....PR
GREENE, Charles J. ....PR, WR
GREENLAW, Terry ....PR, PM
GREENWALD, Barry .DR, PR, ED, WR
GREGG, Kenneth W. CI

GREGOIRE, Richard ....CM
GREGORY, Colin CI
GRENIER, Henriette ....RE
GRIFFIN, Wayne ....SE
GRIGSBY, Wayne ....WR
GRIMALDI, Austin ....PE
GRIMALDI, Joseph P. ....PE
GRIMALDI, Sal ....PE
GRIPPO, Michael CI
GRITTANI, Ronald S. ....PR
GROBERMAN, Jeffrey ....WR, PR
GROSS, Bonnie ....PR
GROULX, Sylvie ....RE
GRUBEN, Patricia ....DR, WR, ED
GUENETTE, Pierre ....SC
GUERTIN, Micheline ....RE
GUILBEAULT, Luce ....RE
GULKIN, Cathy ....ED
GULKIN, Harry ....PR
GUNN, John ....DR, WR, PR
GUNNARSSON, Sturla ....DR, PR

H

HAALMEYER, Juul ....CD
HACKBORN, Robert ....AD
HACKETT, Jonathan ....PR, PM
HAIG, Don ....PR
HAIGHT, Adam ....PM
HALDANE, Don ....DR
HALINSKI, Andrzej ....AD
HALISKIE, Brent ....PS
HALL, Grant ....PE, SE, ME
HALL, Mark ....DR, WR
HALL, Ray ....ED
HALLÉ, Roland ....DR, PR, WR
HALLEE, Céline ....RE
HALLER, Ty ....WR
HALLIS, Ophera ....ED, PR, SE
HALLIS, Ron ....DR, CI, WR, PR
HAMELIN, Christiane ....PD
HAMILTON, Elizabeth ....PM
HAMILTON BROWN, Alex ......PR, DR
HAMON-HILL, Cindy ....PR
HAMORI, Andras ....PR, WR
HANDEL, Alan ....DR, PR, WR
HANNIGAN, Teresa......ED, SE, ME, PE
HANUS, Otta ....DR
HARBURY, Martin ....PR, WR, DR
HARDIMAN, Alan ....SE
HARDING, John ....ED, PR
HARDING, Stewart ....PR
HARDY, Hagood ....CO
HAREL, David ....DR, PR
HARRIS, Alfred ....WR
HARRIS, Jane ....PR
HARRIS, Les ....DR, PR
HARRIS SCHIPPER, Jayne ....DR
HARRISON, Jane ....PM
HARRISON, Jim ....DR
HARRON, Don ....WR

HARTMANN, Peter CI
HARVEY, Daniel ....PD
HARVEY, Rolf ....AD
HASIAK, Steve S. ....CO
HASSEN, Christopher CI
HAUKA, David ....DR, PM, PR
HAWKES, Kirk ....ED, SE, ME
HAWKINS, Crawford W. ....PR, DR
HAWLEY, Gay ....WR, PR, DR
HAY, John M. ....CD
HAZZAN, Ray ....PR, DR, WR
HEATON, Pauline CI
HEBB, Brian R.R. ....CI, DR
HEBERT, Bernar ....RE
HECTOR, Nick ....ED, SE
HEINEMANN, Michelle ....WR, PR, DR
HELLIKER, John ....DR, PR, WR
HELWIG, David ....WR
HENAUT, Dorothy Todd ....DR, PR
HÉNAUT, Suzanne ....PD
HENDERS, Karen P. ....PM
HENDERSON, Clark ....DR, CI
HENDERSON, Judy ....CO
HENLEY, Gail ....WR, DR
HENSHAW, Helen ....PR, DR, PM
HENSHAW, Jim ....WR
HERBERMAN, Lee ....PR
HERMANT, Andrew S. ....PS
HÉROUX, Claude ....PD
HÉROUX, Denis ....PD, RE
HÉROUX, Justine ....PD
HÉROUX, Roger ....PD, RG
HERRINGTON, David CI
HERRON, J. Barry ....CI, DR
HERTZOG, Larry ....PR
HESLIP, Dale ....DR, AD
HEYDON, Michael ....PR, ED
HIDDERLEY, Tom ....PS
HILL, Don ....WR, PR
HILL, J. Clark ....SE
HILLER, Arthur ....DR
HILLOCK, Graydon ....CO
HIRSH, Michael ....PR
HODGINS, Barbara L. ....PR, WR
HOEDEMAN, Co ....RE
HOFFERT, Brenda ....CO
HOFFERT, Paul ....CO
HOFFMAN, Kitty ....PR, WR
HOFFMAN, Philip ....DR, CI
HOLE, Jeremy ....WR, ED
HOLENDER, Jacques ....PR, DR
HOLM, Judy ....PB
HOLMES, Gerald ....AD
HOLMES, Robert CI
HOLOSKO, John CI
HOMBERT, Madeline ....PR, WR
HONE, Louis ....MP, MS
HOOD, David ....PM
HOPE, Kathryn Ruth ..PR, DR, WR, ED
HORNBECK, Gordon CI
HORNE, Jerry ....PR, WR, DR

HORNE, Tina .... DR, WR, PR
HORVATH, Stefan CI
HOSEK, George CI
HOUDE, Jean-Claude .... RE
HOUSE, Bill .... PR
HOWARD, Chris .... PR, DR, WR, ED
HOWARD, Dan .... R, PM
HOWARD, Jeff .... PR
HUCULAK, William .... ED, DR, CI
HUDOLIN, Richard .... AD
HUG-VALERIOTE, Joan F. ..... WR, DR
HUNT, Bill .... PR, DR
HUNT, Catherine .... PE, SE
HUNT, Graham .... DR, PR, WR
HUNT, Krystyna .... WR
HUNTER, John .... WR, PR, DR
HURST, Bill .... WR
HUTTON, Douglas .... PR, DR
HUTTON, Howard .... PM
HUTTON, Joan CI
HYDE, Steve .... WR, DR

IANZELO, Tony .... DR, CI
IRISH, William A. .... DR
IRVINE, Frank .... ED
IRVING, Todd CI
IRWIN, Mark CI
ISACSSON, Magnus .... DR
ISRAEL, Charles E. .... WR
IVESON, Gwen .... PM
IVESON, Rob .... PR, WR, DR, PM
IZZARD, Dan .... DR

JACKSON, Doug .... DR, WR
JACKSON, G. Philip .... DR, PR
JACKSON, Joanne P. .... PR
JACOBOVICI, Simcha .... DR, PR, WR
JACOBS, Ronald CI
JACOBSON, Avrum .... WR
JACQUES, Alain .... RE
JACQUES, Blain .... PD
JAMISON, Lorraine .... PB
JAN, Miume .... ED, ME
JANSONS, Maris H. CI
JARROTT, Charles .... DR
JAVAUX, Pierre................................RE
JAY, Paul .... DR, WR, PR, ED
JEAN, Jacques .... DR, ED, PR
JEFFREY, Robert .... PR, WR
JENNINGS, Christina .... PR
JEPHCOTT, Samuel C. .... PR, PM
JESPERSEN, Rik .... PR
JEWISON, Norman .... DR, PR
JOBIN, Daniel .... DP
JOBIN, Louise .... CT, DA
JOBIN, Peter .... WR
JOHNSON, Andrew .... PR, DR
JOHNSON, Dan .... PR
JOHNSON, John A. .... DR, WR, PR
JOHNSON, Nancy .... PR, WR

JOHNSON, Richard .... PR, DR
JOHNSTON, William .... PR, DR
JOLY, Jocelyn .... DA
JONAS, George .... PR
JONES, Barry P. .... PE
JONES, Cliff .... PR, WR, CO
JONES, Dennis .... PR, PM
JORDAN, Eric .... PR
JOUTEL, Jean-Pierre .... MS, MS
JOY, Michael .... AD, CD
JUBENVILL, Ken .... DR, PR
JUDGE, Maureen .... DR, WR, ED

KABELIK, Vladimir ....PR, DR, WR, ED
KACZENDER, George .... DR
KAHN, Mary .... PR, PM
KAIN, Robert .... PR
KANDALAFT, Cécile Gédéon .... SC
KANDALAFT, Pierre .... RE
KARDASH, Virlana .... WR, DR, ED
KAREN, Debra .... ED
KARMAZYN, John .... PR
KATZ, Jeremy .... PB
KATZ, John Stuart .... WR
KAUFMAN, David .... PR, DR, WR
KAUFMAN, James T. .... DR, WR
KAVANAGH, Gregory .... CO
KAYE, Janice .... PB
KEATING, Lulu .... DR, WR, PR, ED
KEATLEY, Philip .... PR, DR
KEELAN, Matt .... DR, PR
KELLNER, Lynne .... PR, DR
KELLY, Barbara .... PM
KELLY, Peter .... PR, DR
KELLY, Peter .... PE
KEMENY, John .... PR
KEMP, Laurie Roy .... DR
KEMP, Lynda .... CD
KENDALL, Nicholas ....DR, PR, CI, WR
KENNEDY, Michael .... DR, WR, PR
KENT, Vincent .... ED
KERRIGAN, Bill .... DR
KEUSCH, Michael .... DR, WR, ED
KEYES, Sonny .... CO
KEYWAN, Alicia .... AD
KIEFER, Douglas .... CI, DR
KIELLERMAN, Gina .... CD
KIERANS, Genevieve .... PB
KIMBER, Les .... PM, PR
KING, Allan .... DR, PR
KING, Durnford .... WR, DR
KING, Jeff .... PR, PM
KING, Robert .... WR, DR
KINSEY, Nicholas .... RE, DP, PD
KISH, Albert .... DR, ED
KLEIN, Bonnie .... DR, PR
KLEIN, Monika .... PR
KLENMAN, Norman .... WR
KLINCK, Elizabeth .... PR, PM
KLIS, Danuta .... SE, ME

KOBYLANSKY, Karl ....CO
KOLBER, Sandra ....WR
KONOWAL, Charles ....CI, PR, DR
KONYVES, Tom ....PR
KOOL, Allen ....PR, DR, WR
KONOPACKI, Margaret ....PB
KORNYLO, Lacia ....PM
KOTCHEFF, Ted ....DR, PR
KOTTLER, Les ....PR, DR, WR
KOYAMA, Andrew ....PE
KOZAK, Sherry ....PR, DR
KRAMREITHER, Anthony ....PR
KRAVSHIK, Marty ....ED
KREPAKEVICH, Jerry PR, DR, WR, ED
KRIZSAN, Les ....CI, DR
KROEGER, Wolf ....AD
KROEKER, Allan ....DR, WR
KROITOR, Roman ....PR, DR
KROONENBURG, Pieter ....PR
KROST, Roy ....PR
KUCHMIJ, Halya ....PR, DR
KUPER, Jack ....DR, PR, WR, AD

L'HERBIER, Benoit ....SC
LABERGE, Pierre ....PD, RG, RE
LABREQUE, Jean-Claude ....RE, DP
LABROSSE, Sylvain ......DP, SC, RE, PD
LACKIE, Sharon ....SE
LADOUCEUR, Serge ....DP
LAFERRIERE, Richard ....PD
LAFFEY, Barbara Joy ....PR
LAFOND, Jean-Daniel ....RE, SC
LAFONTAINE, Lyse ....RG
LAFORÊT, Megan ....PR, DR, WR
LAGER, Martin ....WR, PR
LAHTI, James ....ED
LAING, Alan R ....CO
LALONDE, Richard ....RG
LAMARRE, Louise ....RE
LAMB, Duncan ....PR
LAMBERT, Andrée ....SC
LAMBIN, Diane ....PD
LAMOTHE, Arthur ....RE, SC, PD
LAMY, André ....PD
LAMY, Pierre ....PD
LANCETT, Anthony J. R. ....E, CO
LANCTÔT, François ....CM
LANCTÔT, Micheline ....RE, SC
LANDERS, Ivan ....PR, DR
LANDIS, Evan ....ED
LANG, Robert ....PR, DR
LANGE, Bruce ....ED
LANGEVIN, Andrew A. G. CI
LANGLOIS, Jérôme ....CM
LANGLOIS, Yves ....RE
LANK, Barry ....DR, CI, ED
LANSING, Floyd ....DR, PR, WR, PM
LANTHIER, Stephen ....PR, DR
LANTOS, Robert ....PR
LAPOINTE, Yves ....RE, SC, PD

LARIVIÈRE, Jean Marc ....DR
LAROCHELLE, André ....PD, RE
LARRY, Sheldon ....DR, PR
LARTIGAU, Yvonne ....RE
LARUE, Claude ....DP
LATOUR, Daniel ....PS
LATRAVERSE, Guy ....PD
LAUBER, Anne ....CM
LAURENDEAU, Jean Pierre ....RG, RE
LAURIER, Nicole ....PD, SC
LAVALETTE, Philippe ....DP
LAVERDIERE, Jim CI
LAVOIE, Michel C. ....DR, PR
LAVOIE, Patricia ....PR, DR
LAVUT, Martin ....DR
LAWRENCE, Pierre ....DR
LAWRENCE, Stephen ....ED, SE
LAZER, Charles ....WR
LAZURE, Jacques ....SC
LE BOURHIS, Dominique ....SC, RE
LE BOUTILLIER, Geoff ....WR, PR, PD
LE GRAND, Eva ....SC
LEACH, David ....ED, DR, WR
LEANEY, Cindy ....PR, DR, WR
LeBLANC, Lloyd CI
LEBOWITZ, Michael ....PR
LEBRUN, Luc ....AD
LECKIE, Keith Ross ....WR, DR
LECLERC, Catherine ....DA
LECLERC, Jean ....RE, MO
LECLERC, Martin ....DP
LEDOUX, Paul ....WR
LEDUC, Lucile ....RE
LEDUC, Yves ....PD, RE, MO
LEE, Judith ....AD
LEE, Mike ....ED
LEE, Patrick ....PR
LEE, Terrye ....PR
LEEBOSH, Vivienne .... PR
LEFEBVRE, Jean Pierre ....RE, SC
LEGER, Claude ....PD
LEGRADY, Thomas ....CO
LEHMAN, Douglas E. CI
LEIS, Hank ....PR, WR
LEITERMAN, Douglas ....PR, DI
LEITERMAN, Richard ....CI, DR
LEMAY-ROUSSEAU, Lise ....SC
LENNICK, Michael ....WR, DR
LENNON, Randy ....PR, WR
LENNON, Rob ....WR
LENTE, Miklos ....CI, DR
LEPAGE, Marquise ....RE, SC
LÉPORÉ, Marcella ....CT
LEROUX, Yvon ....SC
LESEWICK, Robert ....PR, DR, ED
LESS, Henry ....DR
LETOURNEAU, Diane ....RE, SC
LEVENE, Sam ....PR
LEVESQUE, Gaétanne ....CT
LEVIN, Victor ....PR
LEVINE, Allan ....PM

LEVITAN, Steven ....PR
LEVY, Joanne T. ....WR, PR, DR
LEWIS, Jefferson ....WR, DR
LHOTSKY, Antonin ....CI, DR
LICCIONI, Jean-Pierre ....SC, RE
LIGHT, Peter F. ....ED
LIGHTSTONE, Richard ....PS, SE
LIIMATAINEN, Arvi ....PR, DR
LILLIE, Ronald ....PR
LINDO, Eleanore ....DR, PR
LINDSAY, Gillian ....PR, PM
LINK, André ....PR
LIOTTA, Michael ....PE
LIPSEY, Stan ....PR, DR
LISHMAN, Eda Lever ....PR, DR, WR
LITINSKY, Irene ....PM
LIU, Harrison ....DR, WR
LIVESLEY, Jack ....WR
LIVINGSTON, Neal ......DR, PR, CI, PS
LLOYD-DAVIES, Scott R. CI
LOBLAW, D. Bob ....WR
LOCK, Keith ....DR, WR, PR
LOCKE, Jeannine ....PR, WR
LOMAGA, Ihor George CI
LONGLEY, Richard ....PR, DR
LONGMIRE, Susan ....AD
LOO, Ao ....PS
LORD, Jean-Claude ....RE, SC
LORD, Roger ....RE, PD
LORTI, Claude ....RE, PD
LOSIER, Aurel ....RG, RE
LOUBERT, Patrick ....PR
LOWER, Peter ....PR, WR
LOWER, Robert ....ED, WR, DR
LOWRY, Christopher ....PR
LUCA, Claudio ....PD, DP
LUCAS, Steve ....WR
LUHOVY, Yurij ....ED, DR, PR
LUKE, Corby ....PE
LUNNY, Shane ....PR, DR
LUPTON, Doug CI
LUSSIER, Jo ....MO, RE
LYNCH, Paul ....DR
LYNN, William ....WR

M
MACADAM, William I. ...PR, DR, WR
MacANDREW, Heather ....PR
MACDONALD, Aleida ....CD
MacDONALD, Brad ....CO
MacDONALD, Michael ....PM
MacDONALD, R. ....DR, WR, PR, ED
MacDONALD, Robert CI
MACFARLANE, Douglas ....PM, PR
MacFARLANE, Duncan CI
MacGILLIVRAY, W....DR, WR, ED, ME
MacGREGOR, Roy ....WR
MacINTYRE, Rod ....WR, ED
MacKAY, Bruce ....DR, WR, ED, PR
MACKAY, David ....PR, DR, AD
MacKAY, Jed ....WR

MacKAY, Lynne ....CD
MACKAY, Margaux ....PM, PR
MACKENZIE, Scott ....PR, PM
MACKEY, Clarke ....DR, WR, PR, ED
MacLAVERTY, Michael ....ED, SE, PE
MacLEAN, Janet ....WR
MACLEAR, Michael ....PR, WR
MACLEOD, Douglas J. ....PR
MACMILLAN, Michael ....WR
MacNAUGHTON, Ann M. ....WR
MACNEE, Rupert ....PR, WR, DR, PM
MacPHERSON, Glen CI
MAGDER, Zale ....CI, PR
MAGUIRE, Rick CI
MAITLAND, Scott ....PM
MAJOR, Pierre ....DA
MALLEN, Bruce ....PR
MALLEN, Carol ....PR
MALLET, Marilu ....RE
MALO, René ....PD
MALTBY, David ....DR
MANATIS, Janine ....DR
MANDALIAN, Joseph ....DA
MANGAARD, Annette ....DR, WR, PR
MANGONE, Rose ....PB
MANKIEWICZ, Francis ....RE
MANN, Danny ....WR, DR
MANN, Ron ....DR, WR, PR
MANNE, Lewis ....CO
MANNE, M.C. ....ED
MARCIL, Michelle ....RG
MARCOUX, Royal ....RE
MARGELLOS, James ....PR, PM
MARGINSON, Karen ....PB
MARION, Jean-Claude ....RE
MARK, Gordon ....PR, PM
MARKIW, Gabriel ....PR, DR, WR, ED
MARKIW, Jancarlo ....DR, WR, PR
MARKS, Julian ....PR
MARKSON, Morley ....DR, PR
MARKWART, Glenn CI
MARR, Alan ....DR, WR
MARR, Leon G. ....DR, WR
MARSHALL, Bill ....PR
MARSHALL, Heather A. ....PR
MARSHALL, Peter D. ....DR
MARSOLAIS, Michel ....DA
MARTIN, Bruce ....WR
MARTIN, Donald ....WR
MARTIN, James G. ....PM
MARTIN, John ....PS
MARTIN, Marcia ....PR
MARTIN, Maude ....RE
MARTIN, Susan ....DR, WR, ED
MARTINELLI, Gabriella ....PR
MATHER, Tom ....PS
MATHESON, Linda F. ....CD
MATHUR, Vishnu ....PR, DR
MATIS, Barbra ....AD
MATTER, Armin CI
MATTHEWS, Bill ....DR

MATTIUSSI, Roger .... ED
MAYEROVITCH, David .... WR
MAZUR, Lara .... ED
McANDREW, Jack .... WR, PR, DR
McBREARTY, Don .... DR
McCANN, Jerome .... WR
McCARTHY, John .... CO
McCARTY, Mary Jane .... CD
McCLELLAN, Gordon .... ED
McCLEMENT, Doug .... PS, PE
McCOWAN, George .... DR
McCROW, William .... AD
McCURDY, Mark .... DR, PR, WR
McDOUGALL, Ian .... PR
McEWAN, Duncan .... PR
McEWAN, Maryke .... PR
McEWEN, Mary Anne WR, PR, DR, ED
McGAW, Jack .... PR
McGILLIVRAY, Derek .... PR
McGLYNN, Gordon Paul ....DR, CI, ED
McGREEVY, John .... PR, WR, DR
McHUGH, Fiona .... WR
McILVRIDE, David .... DR, WR, ED
McINTYRE, JoAnn .... DR, WR
McKAY, Arthur C. .... PS
McKEOWN, Bob .... PR, WR, DR
McKEOWN, Brian .... PR, DR, WR
McKEOWN, Terence .... CO, PS
McKNIGHT, Bruce E. .... PR
McLACHLAN, Robert B. .... CI, DR
McLAREN, David .... WR
McLAREN, Ian .... PR, DR
McLEAN, Andrew R. .... PM
McLEAN, Seaton .... PR
McLELLAN, Doug .... CI, DR
McLENNAN, Peter CI
McLEOD, Ian .... PR
McLEOD, Mary E. .... CD
McMANUS, Mike .... PR, WR
MEARS, Graeme CI
MEDAK, Peter .... DR
MEDINA, Ann .... PR
MEDJUCK, Joe .... PR
MEGILL, John Peter .... PS
MEILEN, Bill .... WR
MELCHIOR, Klaus .... PR, DR
MELLANBY, Ralph .... PR,WR, DR
MENARD, Robert .... RE, SC, PD
MENDELUK, George .... DR, WR, PR
MERCEL, Edward L. .... PR, DR
MERCER, Jim CI
MERCER, Michael .... WR
MERCIER, Serge .... SC
MERRITT, Judith .... ED
MESSIER, H. Monique .... PD, SC
MESTEL, Stanley CI
METCALFE, Bill .... DR, CI
METTLER, Peter .... DR, CI, WR, PR
MICAY, Jack .... DR, WR, PR
MICHAELS, Joel B. .... PR
MICHAELS, Lorne .... PR, WR

MICHEL, Pauline .... SC
MIGNEAULT, Hughes .... RE, PD
MIGNOT, Pierre .... DP
MILINKOVIC, Gerry .DR, PR, ED, PM
MILLAR, Susan .... PR, WR
MILLER, Bob .... PR, DR
MILLS, Michael .... DR, PR
MILLS-COCKELL, John .... CO
MINNIS, Jon .... PR, DR, WR
MIRKIN, Lawrence S. .... PR
MITCHELL, Brian .... PE, PS
MITCHELL, Gavin .... AD
MITCHELL, Ken .... WR, DR
MITCHELL, Nick .... WR
MITCHELL, Steven R. .... SE
MITTON, Susan Young .... PR, DR
MOHAN, Peter .... WR
MOHR, Margaret M. .... CD
MOHUN, Bruce .... WR
MOLLIN, Fred .... CO
MONDION, Denis .... MO
MONK, Roger J .... SE, PS, PE
MONTESI, Jorge .... DR, PR, WR, CI
MONTPETIT, Jean-Guy .... MO
MOORE, James .... ED, CO, SE
MOORE, Mavor .... WR
MOORE-EDE, Carol .... DR
MORAIS, Robert D. .... PM, PR
MOREAU, Michel .... RE
MORENCY, Liz .... SC
MORENCY, Pierre .... SC
MORETTI, Pierre .... RE
MORGAN, June .... PM
MORIDE, Roger .... DP
MORIN, Bertrand .... RE, MO, PD
MORIN, Francyne .... PD
MORIN, Pierre .... RE, PD
MORITA, George CI
MORLEY, Glenn .... CO
MORNINGSTAR, Michael .... ED
MORRIS, Reginald H. CI
MORRONE, Frank .... PS, ME, PE
MORRONE, Tony .... PR, DR, CI, ED
MORTIMER, Peter .... PR, WR
MOSSANEN, Moze ....DR, WR, PR, ED
MOZER, Richard .... PR, WR, DR
MUIR, Linda .... CD
MULLER, Helmfried .... CI, DR, ED
MULLER, Henia .... PR
MULLER, John .... DR, PR
MULLINS, Ronald G. .... DR
MULLER, Helmfried CI
MUNN, Michael .... ED
MUNRO, Douglas CI
MURDOCH, Susan .... PM
MURPHY, Gaye .... PB
MURPHY, Jack F. .... PR, DI
MURPHY, Michael D. .... PR, DR
MURRAY, James .... PR, DR
MURTAGH, Bill .... WR
MYERS, Toni .... ED, WR

N

NADEAU, Jacques ....PD
NADEAU, Pierre ....PD
NANTEL, Louise ....SC, RE
NASIMOK, Briane ....WR
NASON, Kent ....CI, DR
NATALE, Louis ....CO
NATHAN, Deborah A. ....WR
NAYLOR, Steven J. ....CO
NEILSEN, Katherine ....WR
NELSON, Barrie ....DR, WR
NELSON, Dale C. ....PR, DR
NELSON, Keri ....PM
NEMTIN, Bill ....PR
NEUBACHER, Roman M. ...PR, CI, DR
NEW, David ....ED, DR
NEWELL, Jacqueline ....SE
NEWLAND, Marv ....DR, PR
NEWMAN, Brenda ....WR
NEWTON, John ....DR, WR, PR, ED
NICHOL, Gary ....PR, DR, WR, ED
NICHOLLS, Andrew ....WR
NICOL, Eric ....WR, ED
NICHOL, Gary ....PR, DR, WR, ED
NICHOLL, Jim ....PR, WR
NICOLLE, Douglas ....DR
NICOLLE, Victor W. ....CI, WR
NICOLOV, Yordan ....MP
NIELSEN, Susin ....WR
NIMMONS, Phil ....CO
NIRENBERG, Les ....PR, DR
NOEL, Jean-Guy ....RE, SC
NOONAN, Donna ....AD
NORMAN, Glenn ....WR
NOVAK, Allan Z. ....DR, WR
NOWAK, Danny CI
NOWLAN, John ....PR, DR, WR
NURSALL, Tom ....WR
NYSTEDT, Colleen ....PR, PM
NYZNIK, Bruce ....PE, SE, ME

O

O'BRIEN, Ann ....PR
O'CONNELL, Maura ....PR, WR, DR
O'CONNOR, Matthew ....PR
O'DELL, Dean A. ....AD, WR
O'DWYER, Michael ....WR, DR
O'FARRELL, Marc ....CO
O'FARRELL, Michael..........................SE
O'REGAN, James ....PR, WR
O'ROURKE, Denise ....WR
OBOMSAWIN, Alanis ....DR, WR
ODDIE, Jan ....PB
OHASHI, Rene....................................CI
OLDENBURG, Gunther ....ED
OLIVER, Ron ....WR, DR, PR
OLIVERIO, Edmund A. ....PB
OLSEN, Stan ....PR, DR
ONDA, Stephen ....PR, DR
ORD, Cathy ....DR, WR, PR, ED

ORIEUX, Ron CI
ORMEROD, Allen ....PE
ORR, James.................................WR, DR
ORVIETO, Denise Agiman ....SC
ORWIN, J. Graham ....DR
ORZARI, Lorenzo.......................WR, DR
OSBORNE, Jim ....WR
OSTRIKER, David M. ....PR, CI
OUELLET, Gilles ....CM
OUELLET, Yves ....WR
OUELLETTE, Michel L. ....CI, PR
OUELLETTE, Réal.............................AD
OUHILAL, Iskra D. ....DR
OWEN, Don ....DR, WR

P

PAABO, Iris ....DR, CO, PR, WR
PAAKSPUU, Kalli ....DR
PACHECO, Bruno ......DR, WR, ED, PR
PALL, Larry ....DR
PALMER, John ....DR
PAPILLON, Denis ....MO
PAQUET, Denis ....RE
PARCHER, Milton ....AD
PARE, Constance ....RE
PARÉ, Rénald ....PD
PARENT, Gilles ....SC
PARENT, Karl ....RE
PARIS, Richard ....AD
PARISEAU, Marcel ....RE, MO
PARK, Alex ....PR
PARKER, Fred ....DR
PARRELL, Barry CI
PARTINGTON, Joseph ....PR
PARTINGTON, Lawrence ....PR
PARTRIDGE, Wendy ....CD
PATE, Brent ....ED
PATEL, Ishu ....DR, PR
PATERSON, Iain ....PR
PATERSON, Sally ....ED
PATTERSON, Carol ....CI, DR
PATTERSON, David J. ....PR
PAYETTE, Jacques ....PD, RE
PAYETTE, Lise ....SC
PAYRASTRE, Georges ....CI, PR
PEARCE, Adrian Mike CI
PEARCE, Gwyneth ....PR
PEARSON, Barry ....PR, WR
PEARSON, Peter ....DR, WR, PR
PECKAN, Sophia ....PR, PM
PEDERSON, Larry V. ....WR, DR
PELLERIN, Daniel ....PE, PS
PELLETIER, Maryse ....SC
PELLETIER, Vic ....RE
PENDRY, Phillip C. CI
PERAK, Branko CI
PERKINS, Kenneth G. ....DR
PERLMUTTER, David M. ....PR
PERLMUTTER, Renée ....PR
PERRIS, Anthony ....DR, PR, WR
PERRON, Clément ....SC, RE

PERRY, Howard ....PM, PR
PERZEL, Anthony ....PR, DR, CI, ED
PETERSEN, Curtis ....CI, PR, DR
PETERSEN, Karen ....WR
PETKOVSEK, Danny S. ....PR, DR
PETRIE, Daniel M. ....DR
PETRIE, Robert J. ....PR, CI, DR
PETRYSHEN, Eva ....PR, WR
PHILLIPS, Jim ....AD, PM
PICK, Anne ....PR, DR, WR
PIDGURSKI, Karen ....PB
PIGOTT, Susan ....PR
PILON, France ....MO
PINDER, Chris ....ED, SE
PINSENT, Gordon ....DR, WR
PIRKER, Roland K. ....CI, PR, DR, ED
PITTMAN, Bruce ....DR
PLAMONDON, Louis ....RE, SC
PLOUFFE, Jean-Paul ....RE
PODESWA, Jeremy .....DR, PR, WR, PB
POIRIER, Anne Claire ....RE, SC, PD
POLGAR, Tibor ....CO
POLLOCK, Sharon ....WR
POOL, Léa ....RE
POSTER, Steven CI
POTHIER, Marcel ....MO, MS
POTTERTON, Gerald ....DR, WR
POULSSON, Andreas CI
PREDOVICH, Robert ....PE
PRESANT, Donald A. ....ED
PRESTON, David ....WR, DR
PRESTON, Earl ....AD
PRICE, Roger Damon ....WR, PR, DR
PRIETO, Claire ....PR, DR
PRINGLE, Douglas ....PR
PRITCHARD, Anne ....AD, CD
PROCOPIO, Frank ....PR, WR, DR
PROTAT, François ....DP
PROULX, Daniel ....PD
PURDY, Brian E. ....PR, DR
PURDY, Jim ....DR, WR
PURDY, Scott ....PE
PYKE, Roger ....DR, PR, WR, ED

QUAN, Donald ....CO, ME

RABINOVITCH, David ....PR, DR, WR
RACINE, Pierre ....DP, RG, MO, RE
RADFORD, Tom ....PR, DR
RAFFE, Alexandra ....PR, PM
RAINE-REUSCH, Randy ....CO
RAINSBERRY, Linda ....PR
RAKOFF, Alvin ....DR, WR, PR
RANSEN, Mort ....DR, WR, PR
RASKY, Harry ....DR, WR, PR
RASTELLI, Maryse ....PD, RE
RATE, Michèle ....CT
RATHBURN, Eldon ....CO
RATTAN, Amarjeet S. ....PR, DR

RAVOK, Brian ....ED, SE, PE, ME
RAWI, Ousama ....DR
RAYMOND, Bruce ....PR
RAYMOND, Marie-José ....PD, SC
RAYMONT, Peter ....DR, PR, WR
READ, Merilyn ....PR
REDICAN, Dan ....WR
REED, Tony ....ED, SE
REED-OLSEN, Joan ....DR, PR
REGAN, Ted ....PR, DR
REHAK, Peter ....PR
REIART, Arvo ....ED, SE, PE
REICHEL, Stéphane ....PD, RG
REID, Brian ....ED
REID, François ....RG, PD
REID, William ....PR, DR
REISENAUER, George ....DR
REISLER, Susan .... WR, PR
REITMAN, Ivan ....DR, PR
REITMAN, Joel ....PR
REMEROWSKI, Ted ....PR, WR, DR
RENAUD, Bernadette ....SC
REPKE, Ron ....PR, DR, WR, PM
REUSCH, Peter ....DR, PR, CI
REY, Edith Dora ....WR
REYNOLDS, Gene ....DR, PR, WR
REYNOLDS, Stephen P. .....PR, PM, DR
RICH, Ron ....DR
RICHARDSON, Gillian ....PR, PM
RICHER, Simon ....RE, PD
RIDOLFI, Paola ....AD
RIIS, Sharon ....WR
RINFRET, Louise ....SC
RITCHIE, Dawn ....WR
ROBBINS, Karen ....PR, WR, DR
ROBERGE, Hélène ....RE, PD
ROBERT, Michel ....SC
ROBERT, Nicole ....PD
ROBERT, Vincent ....WR, DR
ROBERTS, Rick ....AD
ROBERTS, Tim N. ....SE
ROBERTSON, David M. ....DR
ROBERTSON, Eric N. ....CO
ROBERTSON, George ....WR
ROBERTSON, George R. ....WR
ROBINSON, Gord ....PM
ROBINSON, John Mark ....DR, WR
ROBISON, Michael ....DR
ROCHON, Gerard O. ....PR, DR
RODECK, Ken ....PR, ED
RODGERS, Bob ....PR, DR, PM, WR
RODRIGUE, Michel ....PD
ROGAN, N. (Bert) ....WR, PR, DR
ROGERS, Al ....WR, PR
ROGERS, Allen ....PR, DR
ROLAND, Herb ....PR, DR
ROLLASON, Steve ....DR
ROLOFF, Stephen ....AD
ROMANOFF, Sergei ..WR, PR, DR, PM
ROMANOVICH, Cindy ....SE
ROONEY, Edward ....PR, WR

ROSCOE, Stephen G. ....DR, PR
ROSE, Hubert-Yves ....RE, SC
ROSEMARIN, Hilton ....AD
ROSEMOND, Perry ....DR, PR, WR
ROSEN, S. Howard ....PR
ROSIN, Urmas John ....PE
ROSS, Brian ....PM
ROSS, Gerald ....PD
ROSS, John T. ....PR
ROSS, Rodger W. ....PR, DR, ED
ROSSNER, Danny ....PM
ROTH, Stephen J ....PR
ROTHBERG, David ....WR
ROTSTEIN CHEIKES, Sarina ....AD
ROTUNDO, Nick ....ED, ME, SE
ROUARD, Jean-Michel ....MS
ROULEAU, Mario ....RE
ROULSTON, George P. ....ED
ROUSE, Ted ....PM
ROWAN, Monty CI
ROWAN, Patrick ....AD, PS
ROWE, Peter ....DR, WR, PR
ROWLAND, Wade ....PR
ROY, Maurice ....DP
ROY, Rita ....ED
ROY, Robert L.M. ....DR, WR, PR
ROY-DECARIE, M. ...MS, RE, RG, MO
ROZEMA, Patricia ......DR, WR, ED, PR
ROZON, Gilbert ....DA
RUBBO, Michael ....WR, DR, ED
RUCK, Wolf CI
RUEL, Francine ....SC
RUIMY, Allan ....PR
RUSSELL, Paul ....WR, DR, PR
RUSSELL, Robin ....ED
RUTHERFORD, John T. ..WR, PR, DR
RUVINSKY, Morrie ....WR, DR, PR
RYAN, John ....PR, PM
RYAN, Keith ....WR
RYLSKI, Nika ....WR

SAAD, Robert CI
SABOURIN, Marcel ....SC
SADLER, Richard ....PD, SC
SADR, Seyyed ....DR, PR
SAGER, Ray ....RE
SAHASRABUDHE, Deepak ....PR, DR
ST-ARNAUD, Michèle ....RG
SAINT-LAURENT, Francine ....RE
ST-LAURENT, François ....PD
ST-PIERRE, Leopold ....SC, PD
STE-MARIE, Pierre ....RE
SALEM, Rob ....WR
SALTSMAN, Terry ....WR, PR
SALTZMAN, Deepa Mehta DR, WR, PR
SALTZMAN, Paul ....PR, DR
SALUTIN, Rick ....WR
SALZMAN, Glen ....DR
SAMUELS, Barbara ....WR
SANCHEZ-ARIZA, José ....RE

SANDERS, Ed ....PR, ED, DR
SANDERS, Ronald ....ED, SE, ME
SANDERSON, Deborah ....PR
SANDOR, Anna ....WR, PR
SAPERGIA, Barbara ....WR
SARAFINCHAN, Lillian ....AD
SARIN, Victor ....DR, CI
SARNER, Arlene ....WR
SAROSSY, Ivan ....CI, PR
SAROSSY, Paul ....CI, DR
SARRAZIN, Pierre ....PR, DR
SAUL, Donaleen ....WR
SAUNDERS, Peter ....ED, SE
SAURIOL, Brigitte ....RE, SC
SAURIOL, Gaudeline ....DA
SAUVE, Alain ....MS, MO, RE, SC
SAVATH, Philip ....WR, PR
SAVOIE, Elie ....PR, DR
SAVOIE, Michael Patrick CI
SAVOPOL, Adrian ....MO
SAWCHYN, Norm ....ED
SCAINI, Stefan ....DR, PR, WR
SCANLAN, Joseph L. ....DR
SCANLON, Kevin ....WR
SCARFF, Clive ....DR, WR
SCHADT, Christa ....WR, DR, PR, ED
SCHAEFFER, Shelley ....PB
SCHAFER, Joan ....PR
SCHECHTER, Rebecca ....WR
SCHECTER, Brian ....PR
SCHERBERGER, Aiken .....DR, WR, PR
SCHERER, Karl ....CI, PR, DR, PS
SCHILT, Sara ....CD
SCHMIDT, Phil ....AD
SCHONBERG, Pasia ....PR, DR
SCHULZ, Bob ....DR
SCHUURMAN, H. .....DR, WR, CI, ED
SCHWARTZ, Nadine ....DR, PR
SCHWARZ, Alan J. ....PB
SCOTT, Cynthia ....DR, PR
SCOTT, Desmond ....WR
SCOTT, Michael J.F. ....DR, PR
SCOTT, Munroe ....WR
SCOTT, T.J. ....DR, WR
SEALE, Neil CI
SECORD, Ruth ....CD
SECRETAN-COX, M. ....DR, WR, CI
SEDAWIE, Gayle Gibson ...PR, WR, DR
SEDAWIE, Norman ....PR, WR, DR
SEGAL, Matthew ....WR
SEGUIN, François ....DA
SEGUIN, Jean-Gaétan ....RE
SEGUIN, Roger J. ....AD
SELZNICK, Arna ....DR
SENECAL, Gilles ....RE
SENECAL, Marguerite ....PR, WR, DR
SENGMUELLER, Fred ....PS
SENKYIRE, Opong ....PR, DR
SENS, Al ....PR, DR
SEREDA, John ....CO, PS, SE, ME
SERENY, Julia ....PR, PM

SHAFFER, Beverly ....DR
SHAPIRO, Paul ....DR, WR
SHATALOW, Peter ....DR
SHAVICK, James ....PR
SHAW, Andrea ....PR
SHEBIB, Don ....DR
SHEER, Tony ....WR
SHEKTER, Louise ....DR
SHENKEN, Lionel ....PR, DR
SHEPPARD, John ....WR
SHERRIN, Robert ....PR, DR
SHEWCHUK, Peter ....PS
SHILTON, Gilbert ....DR
SHINER, Judy ....AD
SHORE, Howard ....CO
SHOSTAK, Murray ....PR
SHRAGGE, Lawrence ....CO
SHRAGGE, Sherv ....PR, DR
SHRIER, Barbara ....PM, PR
SHULMAN, Guy ....WR
SHUMAN, Risa ....PR
SHUMIATCHER, Cal ....PR, SE
SIEGEL, Bonita ....PR
SIEGEL, Lionel E. ....WR, PR
SIEGEL, Lois ....DR
SILVER, Jonny ....DR, ED, WR, PR
SILVER, Malcolm ....PR
SIMANDL, Lloyd ....PR, WR, DR
SIMARD, Alain ....PD
SIMARD, Cheryl ....DR
SIMMONDS, Alan Francis ....DR, PR
SIMOENS, Richard ....PR, DR
SIMON, Marty ....CO
SIMONEAU, Guy ....RE, SC, MO
SIMONEAU, Yves ....RE, SC
SIMPSON, Dee E. ....PR, DR, PM
SIMPSON, Peter R. ....PR
SINGER, Gail ....DR, WR, PR
SINGER, Sharon ....PB, PR
SIRETEANU, Ion-Dragos ....PR, DR, CI
SKERRETT, Bill ....PR, DR, WR
SKOGLAND, Kari ....DR, WR, ED
SKOLNIK, Bill ....CO
SKY, Laura ....DR, WR, PR
SLACK, Lyle ....WR
SLADE, Bernard ....WR
SLAN, Jon ....PR
SLIPP, Marke ....ED, PR, DR, WR
SLOAN, Anthony ....ED
SMALE, Joanne Muroff ....PB, PR
SMALLEY, Katherine ....DR, PR
SMILSKY, Peter ....DR, PR, WR, ED
SMITH, Arthur ....PR, DR, WR
SMITH, Derek ....ED
SMITH, Douglas G. ....WR
SMITH, John N. ....DR, WR, PR
SMITH, Morag ....PR, WR
SMITH, Robert F. ....PR, DR
SMITH, Steve ....PR, WR
SMOFSKY, Lenny ....DR, CI
SNETSINGER, Martha ....CD

SNOOKS, Susan ....WR
SNOW, Michael ....DR
SNOWDEN, Alison ....DR, WR
SOBEL, Mark ....DR
SOBELMAN, David ...WR, DR, PR, ED
SOBOL, Ken ....WR
SOLNICKI, Victor ....PR
SOLOMON, Aubrey ....WR
SOLOMON, Maribeth ....CO
SOMCYNSKY, Jean-Francois ....SC
SOMMERS, Frank G. ....PR
SORA, Bob ....PM
SPENCER, Michael ....PR
SPICKLER, Bernard ....PD, RG
SPIER, Carol ....AD
SPIESS, Fritz ....CI, DR
SPRINGBETT, David ....DR, PR
SPRINGGAY, Barry E. CI
SPRY, Robin ....PR, WR, DR
STAMPE, Bill ....DR, PR
STANKE, Alain ....PD, SC
STANKOVA, Maruska ....PR
STANNETT, Ronald Edward CI
STANSFIELD, David ....WR, PR
STANTON, Greg CI
STAROWICZ, Mark ....PR
STARR, Peter G. ....PR
START, Wally ....PR
STAVRIDES, Stavros ....DR, WR, PR
STEELE, Fraser ....DR, WR, PR
STEELE, Michael ....PR, WR, DR
STEER, Kim ....PR, AD
STEIN, Allan ....WR, PR, DR
STEINMETZ, Peter E ....PR
STEPHENS, Paul ....PR
STERN, Sandor ....DR, WR
STERN, Steven ....DR, PR
STEWART, Barbara J ....WR
STEWART, Barney...............................CI
STEWART, Douglas Thane ....PS
STEWART, Gordon ....PR, DR, WR
STEWART, Sandy ....PR
STILIADIS, Nicolas ....PR
STILMAN, Philip S. ......ED, PR, DR, SE
STINSON, Fred T. ....PR, DR
STIRLING, Michelle G. .....PR, WR, DR
STOCKTON, Brian ....DR, WR, ED
STODDARD, Gordon ....ED
STOHN, J. Stephen ....PR
STOLLER, Bryan M. ...DR, WR, PR, ED
STONE, Barry CI
STONEHOUSE, Marilyn ....PM
STONEMAN, John ......CI, PR, DR, WR
STOREY, Michael CI
STORRING, Virginia ....PR
STRANGE, Marc ....WR
STRATYCHUK, P. .....DR, CI, ED, WR
STRAUGHAN, Brent ....CO, ED
STRAYER, Colin J ....PR, WR, DR
STREET, Bill ....DR, ED
STRINGER, Richard A. ....CI, PR

STROMBERG, Jeanne ....PR
STRONG, Philip ....CO
STUNDEN, William J.........................CI
SUCH, Peter ....WR
SUISSA, Danièle J. ....DR, PR, WR
SULLIVAN, Kevin R. ....PR, WR, DR
SULYMA, Michael H. ....PR, DR, PM
SUMMERS, Jaron ....WR
SURJIK, Stephen ....DR
SUSSMAN, Peter ....PR
SUTHERLAND, Ian ....WR
SUTHERLAND, Neil ....PR, WR, DR
SUTHERLAND, Paul ....DR, PR, WR
SUTTOR, Carmel ....WR
SVAB, Lenka ....ED
SVAB, Peter ....ED, PS
SWAN, James ....DR, PR
SWEENEY, Irene M. ....PR
SWEETMAN, Bill ....PR, DR, ED
SWERHONE, Elise ....DR, PR
SWICA, Adam CI
SYMANSKY, Adam ....PR
SZALAY, Attila CI

TABORSKY, Vaclav ....DR
TADMAN, Aubrey ....WR, PR
TAKACS, Tibor ....DR, PR
TAMMARO, Christopher CI
TARKO, Mihai Gabor CI
TASSÉ, Richard ....DA
TATE, Brian ....CO
TATE, Christopher ....ED, PE
TATTERSALL, Jane ....SE
TAYLOR, Rick ....DR, ED, PR
TAYLOR, Robin ....PR
TERRY, Christopher ......DR, CI, PR, WR
TESTAR, Coralee Elliott ....WR, PR
TESTAR, Gerald ....PR
TETRAULT, Cameron ....CI, ED
TÉTREAULT, Louis-Georges ....PD
TETREAULT, Roger ....RE
THATCHER, Tony ....PM
THEBERGE, André ....RE, MO
THEOBALD, Geoff ....DR
THIBAULT, Gilles ....RE
THICKE, Alan ....PR, WR
THILLAYE, Peter ....SE
THOMAS, Dave ....DR, WR, PR
THOMAS, R.L. ....DR, WR
THOMAS, Stan ....PR
THOMAS, William J. ....WR
THOMAS-d'HOSTE, Michel ....DP
THOMPSON, David ....ED
THOMPSON, Don ....ED
THOMPSON, Jane ....DR, ED
THOMPSON, Judith ....WR
THOMPSON, Peggy ....WR, PR
THOMSON, Andy ....PR, DR
THOMSON, Brian ....CI, DR
THOMSON, John J. ....PS

THOMSON, Lorraine ....PR
THORNE, Gordon ....ED
THORNE, John ....DR
THRASHER, Harold E. ....AD
THURLING, Peter ....DR, WR
TICHENOR, Harold ....PR, DR
TILDEN, Annette ....ED
TILL, Eric ....DR
TINGLEY, Cameron ....ED, SE, ME
TKACH, Alex ....PR, DR, ED
TODD, Kim ....PR
TODD, Michael ....ED, DR
TODD, Richard ....ED
TOSONI, Joan ....DR
TOUGAS, Francine ....SC
TOUGAS, Kirk ....CI, DR
TOUSSAINT, Jurgen ....ED
TOVELL, Vincent ....DR, PR
TOWSTEGO, Tony ....PR
TRAEGER, Tracy ....PR, PM, ED
TRANTER, Barbara ....PR, AD
TREMBLAY, Jean-Joseph ....SC
TREMBLAY, Michel ....SC
TREMBLAY, Robert ...RE, PD, MO, MS
TROFYMOW, L.A. ....WR, DR, PR
TROIANO, Domenic ....CO
TROSTER, David ....DR, PR
TROW, Susan CI
TRUDEL, Yvon ....RE
TUNNICLIFFE, Jack ....DR, PR
TURL, Jeff ....PR, WR
TURNER, Brad ....DR
TURNER, Robert ....DR
TURNER, Timothy ....PR
TUSTIAN, Jim ....PR, CI, ED, DR

URSELL, Geoffrey ....CO

VADNAIS, Yvon G. ....PD
VADNAY, Gabor ....PS
VAITIEKUNAS, V. ....DR, ED, WR, PR
VALCOUR, Nicolas M. PD, RG, DT, PL
VALCOUR, Pierre ....PD, RE
VALLÉE, Jacques ....PD
VALLÉE, Jean-Marc ....RE, MO, DP
VAMOS, Thomas ....DP
van den WATER, Anton .....PR, WR, DR
VAN DEN AKKER, Tony ....PE
VAN DER HEYDEN, Jan ....RE
VAN DER KOLK, Henk ....PR
VAN DER LINDEN, Paul CI
VAN DER VEEN, Milton ....DR, PR
VAN EERDEWIJK, Margaret ....ED
VAN LAMBALGEN, Monzine ....PM
VAN VELSEN, Hans ....ED
VANDERBURGH, C. PR, DR, WR, CO
VANHERWEGHEM, Robert ....DP
VARUGHESE, Sugith ....DR, WR
VEILLEUX, Lucille ....PD

VERDY, Paul ....DR
VERGE, Robert ....RE
VERMETTE, Robert..........................SP
VERRIER, Hélène ....PD
VEVERKA, Jana ....PR, WR
VIALLON, Claudine ....WR, DR
VIAU, Catherine ....PD
VICKERS, Darrell ....WR
VICKERY, Dorothy ....PR
VIEIRA, Kathy ....CD
VILLENEUVE, Suzanne ....PL
VINET, Paul ....PR
VOLKMER, Werner ....WR, CI, PR
VON HELMOLT, V. ....PM, PR, AD
VON PUTTKAMER, Peter ....DR

W
ACHNIUC, Michel ....DR, PR
WAISGLASS, Elaine ....WR
WALKER, Giles ....DR, WR, PR
WALKER, Joel ....PR
WALKER, John ....DR, CI, PR
WALKER, Russell ....CO
WALLACE, Clarke ....WR
WALLACE, Ratch ....PR, WR
WALTON, Lloyd ....PR, DR, CI
WANNAMAKER, Tony CI
WARREN, Jeff ....ED
WARREN, Mark ....DR
WATSON, John ....PR, WR, DR
WATSON, Patrick ....PR, WR
WATSON, Wendy ....CO
WATT, Michael ....DR
WAXMAN, Al ....DR
WAXMAN, Martin ....WR, PR
WAYNE, Paul ....WR
WEBB, Dan CI
WEBSTER, Ion ....ED
WEGODA, Ron CI
WEINBERG, Ronald A. ....PR
WEINSTEIN, Larry ....DR, PR
WEINSTEIN, Les ....PR, DR
WEINTHAL, Eric ....WR, DR, ED
WEINTRAUB, William ....WR
WEINZWEIG, Daniel ....PR
WELDON, John ....DR
WELLS, Larry S. ....CD
WELLS, Richard ....ED
WELSMAN, John J. ....CO
WENAUS, Lee ....CD
WERTH, Michael ....SE, ED
WERTHEIMER, Bob ....PR, PM
WESLAK, Steve ....ED
WESTREN, Steven ....WR
WEXLER, Gerald ....WR
WEYMAN, Peter (Bay) PR, DR, WR, ED
WHALEY, Ronald T. ....DR
WHEELER, Anne ....DR, WR, PR
WHITE, Bryon ....ED
WHITE, Don ....PS
WHITE, Helene B. ....DR, PR, WR

WHITE, Nicholas ....AD
WHITE, Pete ....WR
WHITING, Glynis ....PR, WR
WIELAND, Joyce ....DR
WIENER, Martin ....PR
WILCOX, Richard ....AD
WILDEBLOOD, Peter ....PR, WR
WILDMAN, Peter ....WR
WILKINSON, Charles ....DR
WILKINSON, Douglas ....PR
WILKINSON, Mairin ....ED
WILKS, Wendell G. ....PR, WR
WILLIAMS, Don S. ....DR, PR
WILLIAMS, Douglas ....DR, WR, PR
WILLIAMS, Karen ....PB
WILLIAMS, Roger ....CI, PR, DR
WILSCAM, Linda ....SC
WILSON, Sandra ....DR, WR
WILTSHIRE, Peter Wayne CI
WINCENTY, Richard CI
WINEBERG, Tami ....PB
WINEMAKER, Mark ..PR, DR, WR, ED
WINKLER, Donald ....DR, WR
WINKLER, Meita ....DR, PR, WR, PM
WINNING, David ....DR, PR, WR
WINTONICK, Peter ...ED, PR, DR, PM
WISEMAN, Sheldon ....PR
WISMAN, Ron ....ED, ME
WODOSLAWSKY, S..........PR, WR, DR
WOESTE, Peter F CI
WOLFSON, Steve ....PR, WR
WOLINSKY, Sidney ....ED
WOLOSCHUK, Walter ....PR, DR
WOLSZTEJN, Jean-Victor ....PR, CI
WOODLAND, James ....WR, DR
WOODS, Grahame ....WR
WOODWARD, Pamela ....CD
WOOLLEY, Stu ....WR
WRATE, Eric ....ED
WRIGHT, Charles R.D. ....DR
WRIGHT, Paul ....PR
WRIGHT, Richard ....PR
WRONSKI, Peter ....DR, WR, PR
WUNSTORF, Peter CI

X
ALIMAN, Don ....DR, CO

Y
ALDEN-THOMSON, Peter ....DR
YATES, Rebecca ....PR, DR
YOLLES, Edie ....DR, PR
YOSHIHARA, Mark R. G ....PR
YOSHIMURA-GAGNON, Yuri ....PD
YOST, Elwy ....PR, WR
YOUNG, James B. CI
YOUNG, Perci CI
YOUNG, Stephen ....DR
YOUNG LECKIE, Mary ....PR

ZACK, Lawrence ....PR
ZALOUM, Alain ....WR, DR, ED
ZALOUM, Jean ....PR
ZAMARIA, Charles ....PM, PR, ED
ZANDER, Ildy ....ED
ZARITSKY, John ....DR, WR, PR
ZAZA, Paul ....CO
ZBOROWSKY, William ....PM, PR
ZELDIN, Toby....................WR, PR, DR
ZELNIKER, Richard ....WR
ZEMLA, Ed ....DR
ZERAFA, Guy ....CO
ZIELINSKA, Ida Eva ....WR, DR, PR
ZIELINSKI, Rafal ....DR
ZIPURSKY, Arnie ....PR, ED
ZLATARITS, Harvey ....ED, PR
ZNAIMER, Moses ....PR
ZOLF, Janice ....PR
ZOLF, Larry ....PR
ZOLLER, Stephen ....WR, PR
ZWICKER, Linda ....WR

Appendix
Appendice

Employment and Immigration Canada's
CANADIANS FIRST EMPLOYMENT POLICY

Policy

It is the policy of the government of Canada that Canadian citizens and permanent residents be given first opportunity to fill positions in Canada.

Persons who have obtained employment authorizations from the Canada Employment and Immigration Commission are also entitled to work in Canada. These authorizations are issued at a Canadian visa office abroad and, in the case of U.S. residents, at ports of entry.

Procedures for obtaining employment authorization

Film and television producers (employers) who wish to bring foreign workers into Canada, should contact the Canada Employment Centre closest to the location of the production. To ensure expeditious processing of employment authorizations, the employer will be required to provide the following information:

1. Employer name, address, and telephone number;

2. Name, address, and telephone number of employer's representative (if appropriate);

3. A brief description of the film;

4. The approximate number of foreign workers requested and their occupations;

5. The approximate number of Canadians to be hired in each occupation;

6. The duration of stay (dates required);

7. The filming location;

8. The foreign worker's: a) name, b) citizenship and permanent address abroad, c) occupation, d) birthdate, e) entry point into Canada (port of entry), f) date entering Canada.

Generally, a four-week lead time is necessary for consultations between Employment and Immigration, the film and television producers (employers), and the unions and guilds. The purpose of these consultations is to determine the availibility of qualified Canadian workers to fill the jobs for which foreign workers are requested, in order to ensure that job and career opportunities for Canadians will not be adversely affected by the entry of the foreign worker(s). (A list of unions and guild representatives is available from the CEIC offices listed below.)

When a positive decision is made, the responsible Canada Employment Centre will validate the offer of employment. The employer will then advise the foreign worker(s) to contact the appropriate visa office where the foreign worker(s) will be informed of any further steps necessary for the issuance of employment authorization(s). There is a processing fee of $75.00 for an employment authorization. Also, to work in Quebec, it is necessary to obtain a "certificat d'acceptation du Québec" (CAQ) from Quebec Immigration officials.

Those exempted from the employment validation procedures

- Producers who act on their own behalf or represent a company coming into Canada to film should report to an immigration official on initial entry into Canada to clarify their status.

- Some pre-production staff are also allowed to enter temporarily without employment authorization. When they wish to remain or return to Canada for production purposes, they will be required to make an application following the procedures outlined.

- Crews of three or less coming to Canada for a period of less than six weeks to produce travelogues and documentaries for non-North American audiences.
For additional information or assistance depending on location of the production, please consult the following CEIC offices:

BC/Yukon Territory

Labour Market Services
Employment and Immigration Canada
P.O. Box 11145, Royal Centre
1055 West Georgia St.
Vancouver, BC V6E 2P8
Phone: (604) 666-8420
Fax: (604) 666-6308

Alberta/NWT

Employer Services Consultant
Employment and Immigration Canada
1440, 9700 Jasper Ave.
Edmonton, AB T5J 4C1
Phone: (403) 495-5691
Fax: (403) 495-2423

Saskatchewan

Employment Services
Employment and Immigration Canada
800-2101 Scarth St.
Regina, SK S4P 2H9
Phone: (306) 780-6463
Fax: (306) 780-5940

Manitoba

Employment Services Consultant
Employment and Immigration Canada
Room 500, 259 Portage Ave.
Winnipeg, MB R3B 3L4
Phone: (204) 983-0272
Fax: (204) 983-4208

Ontario

Consultant, Human Resources
Employment and Immigration Canada
4900 Yonge St.
Willowdale, ON M2N 6A8
Phone: (416) 224-4751
Fax: (416) 224-4752

Quebec

Consultant, Foreign Worker Recruitment
Employment and Immigration Canada
1441 St. Urbain St., 6th Fl.
C.P. 7500, Succursale A
Montreal, PQ H3C 3L4
Phone: (514) 283-4290
Fax: (514) 283-7273

New Brunswick

Foreign Worker Consultant
Employment and Immigration Canada
615 Prospect St. West
P.O. Box 2600
Fredericton, NB E3B 5V6
Phone: (506) 452-3747
Fax: (506) 452-3145

Prince Edward Island

Chief, Employer Services
Employment and Immigration Canada
85 Fitzroy St.
P.O. Box 8000
Charlottetown, PE C1A 8K1
Phone: (902) 566-7687
Fax: (902) 566-7699

Nova Scotia

Consultant, Employer Services
Employment and Immigration Canada
Metropolitan Place
99 Wyse Rd.
Dartmouth, NS B2Y 4B9
Phone: (902) 426-1534
Fax: (902) 426-8724

Newfoundland/Labrador

Employer Services Consultant
Employment and Immigration Canada
167 Kenmount Rd.
P.O. Box 12051
St. John's, NF A1B 3Z4
Phone: (709) 772-5302
Fax: (709) 772-0816

POLITIQUE FAVORISANT L'EMPLOI DES TRAVAILLEURS CANADIENS

Politique

Le gouvernement du Canada a pour principe de considérer d'abord la candidature des citoyens canadiens et des résidents permanents pour combler les postes vacants au Canada.

Par ailleurs, les personnes qui ont obtenues un permis de travail de la Commission de l'emploi et de l'immigration du Canada ont le droit de travailler au Canada. Cette autorisation est délivrée par les bureaux canadiens des visas à l'étranger et, dans le cas des résidents des Etats-Unis, aux points d'éntrée.

Comment obtenir un permis de travail

Les producteurs de cinéma et de télévision (employeurs) qui souhaitent faire venir des travailleurs étrangers au Canada doivent communiquer avec le Centre d'Emploi du Canada le plus près des lieux de production. Pour assurer le traitement rapide d'une demande de permis de travail, l'employeur devra fournir les renseignements suivants:

1. Nom, adresse et numéro de téléphone de l'employeur;

2. Nom, adresse et numéro de téléphone du représentant de l'employeur (au besoin);

3. Brève description du film;

4. Nombre approximatif de travaillleurs étrangers requis et profession de chacun;

5. Nombre approximatif de canadiens à recruter pour chaque profession;

6. Durée du séjour (les dates sont requises);

7. Lieux de tournage;

8. Travailleurs étrangers: a) Nom et prénom, b) Citoyenneté et adresse permanente à l'étranger, c) Profession, d) Date de naissance, e) Point d'entrée au Canada, f) Date d'éntrée au Canada.

Un délai de quatre semaines est habituellement nécessaire pour les consultations entre Emploi et Immigration Canada, les producteurs de cinéma et de télévision (employeurs) ainsi que les syndicats et les guildes. Ces consultations ont pour objet de déterminer si les postes en question peuvent être comblés par des travailleurs canadiens qualifiés afin que l'autorisation ne nuise pas aux possibilités d'emploi et de carrière des canadiens. (La liste des syndicats et des guildes peut être obtenue d'un agent de la CEIC aux bureaux indiqués ci-après.)

Si la décision est favorable, le Centre d'Emploi du Canada visé validera l'offre d'emploi. L'employeur devra aviser le(s) travailleur(s) étranger(s) de communiquer avec le bureau canadien des visas pour obtenir les renseignements voulus sur la procédure à suivre pour obtenir le permis de travail. Il y a des frais de 75$ pour tout permis de travail. De plus, pour travailler au Québec, il est nécessaire d'obtenir un certificat d'acceptation du Québec (CAQ) des responsables de l'immigration du Québec.

Personnes dispensées de la validation

- Les producteurs indépendants ou à l'emploi des sociétés cinématographiques ou de télévision qui veulent produire un film au Canada doivent se présenter à un agent d'immigration lorsqu'ils entrent pour la première fois au Canada afin de préciser leur statut.

- Certains membres du personnel chargés d'explorer les possibilités de production sont également admis pour un séjour temporaire sans permis de travail. Ils devront toutefois en obtenir un s'ils désirent prolonger leur séjour au Canada ou y revenir pour entreprendre une production.

Les équipes de trois personnes ou moins qui viennent au Canada pour une période de moins de six semaines afin de produire des films de voyage et des documentaires à l'intention d'auditoires non américains.

Pour plus de renseignements concernant les lieux de tournage des productions, prière de contacter l'un des bureaux suivant du CEIC :

Colombie-Britannique/Yukon

Services de marché de travail
Emploi et Immigration Canada
C.P. 11145, Centre Royal
1055, rue Georgia Ouest
Vancouver, BC V6E 2P8
Tel.: (604) 666-8420
Fax: (604) 666-6308

Alberta et Territoires du Nord-Ouest

Conseiller, Services aux employeurs
Emploi et Immigration Canada
1440, 9700, avenue Jasper
Edmonton, AB T5J 4C1
Tel.: (403) 495-5691
Fax: (403) 495-2423

Saskatchewan

Services d'emploi
Emploi et Immigration Canada
800-2101, rue Scarth
Regina, SK S4P 2H9
Tel.: (306) 780-6463
Fax: (306) 780-5940

Manitoba

Conseiller, Services d'emploi
Emploi et Immigration Canada
500, 259, avenue Portage
Winnipeg, MB R3B 3L4
Tel.: (204) 983-0272
Fax: (204) 983-4208

Ontario

Conseiller, Ressources humaines
Emploi et Immigration Canada
4900, rue Yonge
Willowdale, ON M2N 6A8
Tel.: (416) 224-4751
Fax: (416) 224-4752

Québec

Conseiller, Recrutement des travailleurs étrangers
Emploi et Immigration Canada
1441, rue St.-Urbain, 6e étage
C.P. 7500, Succursale A

Montréal, PQ H3C 3L4
Tel.: (514) 283-4290
Fax: (514) 283-7273

Nouveau-Brunswick

Conseiller, Travailleurs étrangers
Emploi et Immigration Canada
615 ouest, rue Prospect
C.P. 2600
Fredericton, NB E3B 5V6
Tel.: (506) 452-3747
Fax: (506) 452-3145

Ile-du-Prince-Edouard

Chef, Services aux employeurs
Emploi et Immigration Canada
85, rue Fitzroy
C.P. 8000
Charlottetown, PE C1A 8K1
Tel.: (902) 566-7687
Fax: (902) 566-7699

Nouvelle-Ecosse

Conseiller, Services aux employeurs
Emploi et Immigration Canada
Place Metropolitan
99, ch. Wyse
Dartmouth, NS B2Y 4B8
Tel.: (902) 426-1534
Fax: (902) 426-8724

Terre-Neuve/Labrador

Conseiller, Services aux employeurs
Emploi et Immigration Canada
167, ch. Kenmount
C.P. 12051
St. John's, NF A1B 3Z4
Tel.: (709) 772-5302
Fax: (709) 772-0816

Advertisers
Commanditaires

Advertisers / Commanditaires

AGFA Canada Inc.	28
Air Canada	290
Film Arts Ltd.	238
FUND	583
MMI Product Placement Inc	421
Numbers	254
Ontario Film Development Corporation	374
Ruben Winkler Entertainment Insurance Limited	440
Sony Canada	1
Telefilm Canada	309
Theatrebooks	449
Thunder Thighs	99
TVOntario	346

Advertising Director/Directrice de la publicité
Marcia Hackborn